The NAFTA Register®

Published by:
Global Contact, Inc.
383 Kings Highway North, Suite 210
Cherry Hill, NJ 08034
Copyright 1999

The NAFTA Register®:   How to use this directory.

A Guide to Helping Buyers Locate Products and Services.

This directory contains an alphabetical listing of U.S. Companies that begins on page number **1**. Immediately following the listing of Companies is a U.S. : Product / Service Index that begins on page number **193**. The Product / Service Index is in alphabetical order by product or service description. Immediately following the description is the company name that provides that product or service. The directory also contains a alphabetical listing of Mexican Companies which begins on page number **279**. Immediately following the listing of Companies is a Mexico : Product / Service Index that begins on page number **311**. Following is a listing of Canadian companies which begins on page number **317** and the Canada : Product / Service index begins on page number **323**.

Further, this directory contains an SIC Code description that begins on page number **325** and a spanish version that begins on page number **331**. Once you have found an SIC code your looking for please refer to the SIC Code Company Index that begins on page number **337**. The SIC Company index lists the SIC Code and immediately following the SIC Code is that name of the company that is listed under that SIC category. If you know the Harmonized System classification number, please refer to page number **355**, where you will find a conversion chart which cross references Harmonized System classifications and SIC Codes.

Table of Contents

U.S. : Company Listings Of Products & Services

"K" Line America, Inc.
301 Concourse Boulevard, Suite 300
Glen Allen, VA 23060
Contact: Y. Iinuma, President/Chief Executive Officer
Telephone: 804-935-3100
Fax: 804-935-3101
Email: book@k-line.com/rates@k-line.com/ docs@k-line.com / URL: http://www.k-line.com
Product Service Description:
Freight & Cargo Transportation
Trucking

3CX
2085 Hamilton Ave., Suite 220
San Jose, CA 95125
Contact: Jack Lii, President & CEO
Telephone: 408-369-8288
Fax: 408-369-8158
Email: jack.lii@3cx.com / URL: http://www.3cx.com
Product Service Description:
Streaming media solutions
Manufactures multimedia streaming engines

3M IBD/Export.
3M Center Bldg., 220-4W-01, P.O. Box 33800
St. Paul, MN 55133
Contact: 3M Products Information Center, *
Telephone: 800-243-3636
Fax: 800-446-4128
Email: ibd_export@mmm.com / URL:
Product Service Description:
Industrial Mineral Products
Marine Trades
Masking & Packaging Systems
Personal Care & Related Products
Safety & Security Systems
Telecom Systems
Traffic Control Materials
Visual Systems
Occupational Health & Environmental Safety Products
Do-It-Yourself & Construction Markets

9TZ Inc
849 S Broadway Ste 201
Los Angeles, CA 90014-3259
Contact: Roland Kosser, Pres.
Telephone: 213-627-3015
Fax: 213-627-3018
Email: ROLAND<rk@9tz.com> / URL: http:/ /www.9tz.com
Product Service Description:
Manufactures men's and women's lingerie
Underwear & nightwear_men's & boys'
Underwear_women's & children's

A & B Aerospace Inc
612 S Ayon Ave
Azusa, CA 91702-5122
Contact: Ken Smith, Pres.
Telephone: 626-334-2976
Fax: 626-334-6539
Email: abaerospace@earthlink.net / URL:
Product Service Description:
Screw machine products, air precision parts
CNC turning & CNC milling
Centerless grinding & thread rolling

A & B Fabrication & Repair, Inc.
PO Box 684
Pooler, GA 31322-0684
Contact: Arthur Edge, Pres., R & D, Sales & Mktg. Mgr.
Telephone: 912-232-1343
Fax: 912-232-5682
Email: / URL:
Product Service Description:
General machining & metal fabrication job shop
Paper handling equipment
Metal products_fabricated

A & J Cheese Company
PO Box 2029
Upland, CA 91785-2029
Contact: Jack G Gaglio, Pres.
Telephone: 909-946-6702
Fax: 909-946-1331
Email: / URL:
Product Service Description:
Produces natural and processed cheeses

A & S Metal Recycling, Inc.
2261 East 15th Street
Los Angeles, CA 90021-2841
Contact: Alexander Scott, Owner
Telephone: 213-623-9443
Fax: 213-488-5854
Email: aseralex@pacbell.net / aserruy@pacbell.net / URL:
Product Service Description:
Scrap Metal Recycler
Hazardous Waste Management
Import/Export Hazardous Waste & Scrap Metal

A & V Refrigeration Corp.
997 S.E. 12th Street
Hialeah, FL 33010
Contact: Servando Cougil,
Telephone: 305-883-0733
Fax: 304-884-2588
Email: @av-refrigeration.com / URL: http://www.av-refrigeration.com
Product Service Description:
Industrial Ice Machines Manufacture

A B C Coke
PO Box 10246
Birmingham, AL 35202-0246
Contact: Ron Daniel, Regional Sales Manager
Telephone: 205-849-1300
Fax: 205-849-1322
Email: / URL:
Product Service Description:
Foundry coke

A B C Sign Design, LLC
117 W Main St
Moore, OK 73160-5105
Contact: Rex Lowell, Owner & GM
Telephone: 405-794-5774
Fax: 405-794-5774
Email: / URL: http://www.abcsigns.com
Product Service Description:
Textile products_fabricated
Interior & exterior signs & fabric banners
Signs & advertising specialties

A B F Industries Inc.
889 Vandalia St
Saint Paul, MN 55114-1304
Contact: Jerol Fleck, Pres., R & D Mgr.
Telephone: 651-647-0598
Fax: 651-647-1008
Email: / URL: http://www.abfdisplay.com
Product Service Description:
Trade show & point-of-purchase displays

A B S Pumps, Inc.
140 Pondview Dr
Meriden, CT 06450-7156
Contact: Gerald Assessor, Pres.
Telephone: 203-238-2700
Fax: 203-238-0738
Email: diane.remetta@abspumps.com / URL: http://www.abspumps.com
Product Service Description:
Submersible industrial pumps, mixers & aerators: Pumps & pumping equipment

A C Products Co., Inc.
390 E Saint Charles Rd
Lombard, IL 60148-2307
Contact: Gerald L. Johnson II, Pres.
Telephone: 630-620-0044
Fax: 630-620-0407
Email: jerryj2@aol.com / URL:
Product Service Description:
General machining job shop, conventional machining : Tappets, mechanical for any size gasoline engines : Vavle lifters, mechanical Honing (Sunnen machines) : Small to large lots, precision machining : Shafts & keyways to 2 inches O.D. (5cm)

A C Welding & Engineering
1075 Morse Ave
Schaumburg, IL 60193-4503
Contact: Otto Jivoin, Owner
Telephone: 847-923-0741
Fax: 847-923-7123
Product Service Description:
General welding job shop
Metal work_miscellaneous

A Fifty Star Flags, Banners & Flagpoles Co.
913 N 31st Ct
Hollywood, FL 33021-5508
Contact: Brad S. Ochs, Pres
Telephone: 954-989-8651 / 1800-486-3524
Fax: 954-983-2787
Email: a50star@aol.com / URL:
Product Service Description:
Pole banners, flags, flagpoles & signs
Full color garphics banners

A H Lundberg Inc
PO Box 1506
Everett, WA 98206-1506
Contact: Brad G Ipsen, V-P.
Telephone: 425-258-4617
Fax: 425-258-4616
Email: ahlundberginc@wiredweb.com / URL: http://www.wiredweb.com
Product Service Description:
Manufactures machinery for the pulp and paper industry— NCG systems, SO2 systems and CLO2
Paper industries machinery
Engineering services

A J Daw Printing Ink Co
3559 Greenwood Ave
Los Angeles, CA 90040-3305
Contact: A. Mark Daw, President
Phone: 323-723-3253 / Fax: 323-725-7885
Email: dawink@earthlink.net / URL:
Product Service Description:
Manufactures printing, lithographic, flexographic and rotogravure inks
Ink_printing

A M Precision Machining, Inc.
170 S. Lively Blvd.
Elk Grove Village, IL 60007
Contact: S. Kozlowski, Pres.
Phone: 847-439-9955 / Fax: 847-439-0483
Email: info@amprecision.com / URL: http://www.amprecision.com
Product Service Description:
Aircraft & weapons components
Aircraft parts & equipment

A P C M Mfg. Llc
PO Box 264
Plainfield, CT 06374-0264
Contact: David Young, Pres.
Phone: 860-564-7817 / Fax: 860-564-1535
Email: dyoung@prepregs.com / URL: http://www.prepregs.com
Product Service Description:
Adhesives: Adhesives & sealants
Epoxy thermoset prepregs

A P T II Products Co.
PO Box 1766
Kerrville, TX 78029-1766
Contact: Jerry O'Brien, Owner
Phone: 830-995-4035 / Fax: 830-995-4036
Email: aptprod@hctc.net / URL:
Product Service Description:
Ceramic Clay & Glaze Additive

A Tail We Could Wag
PO Box 3374
Ketchum, ID 83340-3374
Contact:Steve Frinsko, Sales Mgr.
Telephone: 208-726-1763
Fax: 208-726-4947
Email: sfrinsko@tailwags.com
URL: http://www.taiwags.com
Product Service Description:
Mfrs. dog collars & leashes for pets; belts, t-shirt, winter hats, vest & baseball caps

A Touch Of Country Magic
2836 Skitts Mountain Rd
Cleveland, GA 30528-6420
Contact: Carol Tucker, Ptnr.
Phone: 706-865-1455 / Fax: 706-865-2705
Product Service Description:
"Original" Cinnamon Broom & Potpourri

A'n D Cable Products Inc
1460 Washington Blvd Ste A103
Concord, CA 94521-4047
Contact: Conrad L. Chompff, Pres.
Phone: 925-672-3005 / Fax: 925-672-0317
Email: louisc@andcable.com / URL: http://www.andcable.com
Product Service Description:
Sells communications cable accessories; resells data communications products

A-1 Machining Co.
235 John Downey Dr
New Britain, CT 06051-2905
Contact: Elaine Trerice, Off. Mgr.
Telephone: 860-223-6420
Fax: 860-223-7559
Email: / URL: http://www.a1machining.com
Product Service Description:
Precision machining job shop
See our www.a1machining.com web page.

A-1 Tool
1425 Armitage Ave
Melrose Park, IL 60160-1424
Contact: Geoff Luther, Pres.
Telephone: 708-345-5000
Fax: 708-345-2089
Email: a1toolco@aol.com / URL: http://www.a1tool@a1toolco.com
Product Service Description:
Plastic Molds: Injection & Structural Foam

A-Live Foods
Hc 65 Box 439
Fredonia, AZ 86022-9609
Contact: R Wayne LeBaron, Dir.
Telephone: 520-875-2703
Fax: 520-875-2702
Email: / URL:
Product Service Description:
Creates and sells custom low temperature,
bio-complete, instant-dried foods and juices
Dehydrated fruits, vegetables & soups
Groceries & related products

A-Z Bus Sales, Inc.
1900 S. Riverside Ave.
Colton, CA 92324
Contact: Mike Stich, Used Bus Salesman
Telephone: 909-781-7188
Fax: 909-781-4905
Email: / URL:
Product Service Description:
Buses - Remanufacture & Recondition

A. Berger, Inc.
PO Box 3552
Spartanburg, SC 29304-3552
Contact: Richard J. Hall, General Manager
Telephone: 864-595-1157
Fax: 864-595-0768
Email: jhallabi@aol.com / URL:
Product Service Description:
Precision machine turned parts

A. Daigger & Company, Inc.
675 Heathrow Dr.
Lincolnshire, IL 60069
Contact: Michael Pastrelle, Intj'l Sales
Manager
Telephone: 847-478-9000
Fax: 847-478-9025
Email: daigger@daigger.com / URL:
Product Service Description:
Laboratory Apparatus & Supp., Whsle.
Scientific Instruments, Whsle.
Lab. Glassware & Plasticware, Whsle.

A. I. M. Inc.
19200 Middletown Rd
Parkton, MD 21120-9693
Contact: LeRoy Phillips, V-P., Opers., Sales
& Mktg.
Telephone: 410-329-6801
Fax: 410-357-7016
Email: aimmachining@erols.com / URL:
http://www.aimmachining.com
Product Service Description:
Production & prototype machining job shop

A. J. C. Hatchet Co.
1227 Norton Rd
Hudson, OH 44236-4403
Contact: J. R. Crookston, Pres.
Telephone: 330-655-2851
Fax: 330-650-1000
Email: / URL: http://www.ajctools.com
Product Service Description:
Tools_hand & edge
Roofing hatchets & equipment

A. W. Industries Inc.
6788 Nw 17th Ave
Fort Lauderdale, FL 33309-1522
Contact: Chris Weaver, GM
Telephone: 954-979-5696
Fax: 954-979-5764
Email: awiconnectors@worldnet.att.net /
URL: http://www.awiconnectors.com
Product Service Description:
Electronic connectors
Electronic components

A.C.E. Boiler, Inc.
2701 S. Harbor Blvd.
Santa Ana, CA 92799
Contact: M. Souter, Sales Manager
Telephone: 714-437-9050
Fax: 714-437-9060
Email: aboilerinc.com / URL: http://www.aboilerinc.com
Product Service Description:
Steam boilers
Water Boilers
Water Heaters
Heat exchangers
Storage tanks

A.G. Equipment, Inc.
P.O. Box 16904
Tampa, FL 33687-6904
Contact: George Black,
Telephone: 813-986-2489
Fax: 813-986-3189
Email: / URL:
Product Service Description:
Agricultural Irrigation Equipment Wholesale
Engineering Services, Agricultural
Pre-Engineered Metal Buildings, Wholesale
Used Construction Equipment, Wholesale
Const. Dredges, New & Used, Wholesale

A.J. Buck & Son
11407 Cronhill Drive
Owings Mills, MD 21117
Contact: Al Defontes, Export Admin.
Telephone: 800-638-8672 ext-249
Fax: 410-581-1809
Email: adefontes@mail.ajbuck.com / URL:
Product Service Description:
Veterinary Drugs, Wholesale
Veterinary Equip. & Supp., Wholesale
Medical Instr. & Supplies, Wholesale

A.L.P. Lighting Components, Inc.
6333 Gross Point Rd.
Niles, IL 60714
Contact: Donald L. Michels, International
Sales Manager
Telephone: 773-774-9550
Fax: 773-774-9331
Email: info@alp-ltg.com / URL:
Product Service Description:
Components for Fluorescent Lighting:
Plastic Diffusers, Lenses & Louvers
Enclosed & Gasketed Assembly Units
Aluminum Louvers, Baffles, Reflectors
Emergency Nickel Cadmium Battery Packs

A.N. Deringer, Inc.-Hdqrs.
P.O. Box 1309
St. Albans, VT 05478
Contact: Wayne Burl, *
Telephone: 802/524-8110
Fax: 802-524-5970
Email: / URL:
Product Service Description:
Customhouse Broker
Freight Forwarding, Foreign & Domestic
Freight Consolidation & Deconsolidation
Warehousing & Distribution
Cargo Insurance
U.S.D.A. Meat Inspection
Duty Drawback

A.S. Contin Inc.
714 Spencer Drive
Santa Maria, CA 93455
Contact: Augustin Contin, President
Telephone: 805/934-1300
Fax: 805-937-1519
Email: agustin_contin@msn.com / URL:
Product Service Description:
Translation Svcs., English, Spanish
Translation Svcs., French, Portuguese

A.Y. McDonald Mfg. Co.
P.O. Box 508, 4800 Chavenelle Road
Dubuque, IA 52004
Telephone: 319-583-7311
Fax: 319-588-0702
Email: / URL:
Product Service Description:
Brass Fittings
Pumps
Valves
Gas Valves & Meter Bars
Submersible, Jet, & Solar Pumps
Water Works Brass Goods

AAA International
1340 S. Hill St.
Los Angeles, CA 90015-3040
Contact: Anwar Lalani, Manager
Telephone: 213-747-7544
Fax:
Email: / URL:
Product Service Description:
Watches, Clocks, Calculators, Electronics &
Novelties

AAA Precious Metals Inc
9908 SE Ash St
Portland, OR 97216-2326
Contact: Joe DeCamp, Pres., CEO
Telephone: 503-253-8591
Fax: 503-253-8609
Email: aaapm@teleport.com / URL: http://www.teleport.com/~aaapm/
Product Service Description:
Secondary nonferrous metals
Refines and smelts precious metals

AAA Weigh Inc
415 Park Ave
San Fernando, CA 91340-2525
Contact: Frederick Monsour, Pres.
Telephone: 818-361-6622
Fax: 818-361-0097
Email: aaaweigh@aol.com / URL:
Product Service Description:
Manufactures scales and bar code inventory
control systems; rental services and complete
repair
Scales & balances, except laboratory
Commercial equipment
Computer peripheral equipment
Electrical apparatus & equipment

AATA International Inc.
748 Whalers Way Ste D200
Fort Collins, CO 80525-4872
Contact: John Aronson, President
Telephone: 303-223-1333
Fax: 303-223-9115
Email: / URL:
Product Service Description:
Enviromental Services

ABEL Pumps Corp.
79 N. Industrial Pk.
Sewickley, PA 15143
Contact: Carl Dawson, Sales Manager
Telephone: 412-741-3222
Fax: 412-741-2599
Email: apc.mail@abel.net / URL: http://www.abel.net
Product Service Description:
Industrial pumps
Pumps & pumping equipment

AC Valve Inc.
1335 NW Northrup St.
Portland, OR 97209-2807
Contact: Al F. Laurie, President
Telephone: 503-226-2852
Fax: 503-224-5052
Email: sales@a-cvalve.com / URL: http://www.a-cvalve.com
Product Service Description:
Knife Gate Valves

ACE Printing Company
948 S Vella Rd
Palm Springs, CA 92264-3469
Contact: Mark Lawrence, Ptnr.
Telephone: 760-323-2707
Fax: 760-322-3547
Email: / URL:
Product Service Description:
Commercial printing
Lithographic printing_commercial

ACG Inc.
232 Front Ave
West Haven, CT 06516-2893
Contact: A.C. Grimaldi, *
Telephone: 203-933-8000
Fax: 203-932-5608
Email: / URL:
Product Service Description:
Vibration Test Equipment, Systems, Parts.
Svc.

ACSI Inc.
510 Alder Dr
Milpitas, CA 95035-7443
Contact: Richard Brewer, Pres.
Telephone: 408-321-8900
Fax: 408-321-9321
Email: sales@answerman.com / URL: http://www.answerman.com
Product Service Description:
Manufactures chemicals for the
semiconductor industry

ACZ Laboratories Inc
2773 Downhill Dr
Steamboat Springs, CO 80487-9400
Contact: Russell Vande Velde, Pres.
Telephone: 970-879-6590 / 1800-334-5493
Fax: 970-879-2216
Email: russv@acz.com / URL: http://www.acz.com
Product Service Description:
Analytical environmental laboratory

ACuPowder International, LLC
901 Lehigh Ave.
Union, NJ 07083
Contact: Gail DeSantis,Customer Service Sup
Telephone: 908-851-4500
Fax: 908-851-4597
Product Service Description:
Metal Powders

ADH Health Products Inc.
215 North Route 303
Congers, NY 10920-1726
Contact: Balu Advani, President
Telephone: 914-268-0027
Fax: 914-268-2988
Email: sales@adh-health.com / URL: http://
www.adh-health.com
Product Service Description:
Vitamins Minerals & Herbs
Pharmaceutical Preperations

ADRA International
12501 Old Columbia Pike
Silver Spring, MD 20904-6600
Contact: Ralph Watts, President
Telephone: 301-680-6380
Fax: 301-680-6370
Email: / URL: http://www.adra.org
Product Service Description:
Used Clothing
School Buses
Container Cargo

**AF Industries, Alvey Washing
Equipment Div.**
11337 Williamson Rd.
Cincinnati, OH 45241-2232
Contact: Harley Huddle, Jr., President
Telephone: 513-489-3060
Fax: 513-489-6018
Email: / URL:
Product Service Description:
Industrial Pan Washing Machine
Sanitary Pan Washing Machinery
Sanitary Basket Washing Machine
Industrial Washing Machinery

AG Acid Inc
PO Box 5026
Yuma, AZ 85366-5026
Contact: Mikkel Cavenee, Pres.
Telephone: 520-329-6601
Fax: 520-329-6605
Email: / URL:
Product Service Description:
Wholesales soil amendments for farming
Farm supplies

AG Systems
707 Cesar Chavez (Army) St.
San Francisco, CA 94124
Contact: Alan Grinberg, Pres.
Telephone: 415-821-6300
Fax: 415-821-6332
Email: / URL: http://www.perfectfit.net
Product Service Description:
Computer software to manage an apparel
manufacturing business

AGCO Corporation
4830 River Green Pkwy
Duluth, GA 30096-2568
Contact: Kevin Bien, Natl. Acct.
Telephone: 770-813-6171
Fax: 770-813-6018
Product Service Description:
Agricultural Farm Tractors : Combine
Harvesting Equipment : Haying Equipment
Agricultural Tillage & Planting Equipment

AGE International
P.O. Box 636
Frankfort, KY 40602-0636
Contact: Yutaka Takano,
Telephone: 502-223-9874
Fax: 502-223-9877
Email: blanton@ageintl.com / URL:
Product Service Description:
Distilled Spirits
Balnton's Single Barrel Bourbon

AJ Weller
P.O. Box 17566
Shreveport, LA 71138-0566
Contact: Thomas Edwards, Owner
Telephone: 318-925-1010
Fax: 318-325-8818
Email: sales@ajweller.com / URL: http://
www.ajweller.com
Product Service Description:
Metals Service Centers and Offices
Tubes, pipes & hollow profiles, iron & steel
Cast articles of iron or steel
Wear resistant steel plate
Ceramic panels for wear protection
Parts for cement industry
Wear technology

AJC International Inc.
5188 Roswell Road
Atlanta, GA 30342
Product Service Description:
Meats & Meat Products, Export

ALPNET. INC.
4460 South Highland Drive, Suite 100
Salt Lake City, UT 84124
Contact: John W. Wittwer, *
Telephone: 801-273-6600
Fax: 801-273-6610
Email: / URL:
Product Service Description:
Software Localization & Translation Svcs.,
Technical

**AM Castle Employee Federal Credit
Union**
3400 Wolf Rd.
Franklin Park, IL 60131-1319
Contact: Melody Kusiak, Manager
Telephone: 847-455-7111
Fax: 847-455-7207
Email: / URL:
Product Service Description:
Federal Credit Unions

AMA Plastics
1859 W Grant Rd Ste 101
Tucson, AZ 85745-1214
Contact: Doug Skiles, Plt. Mgr.
Telephone: 520-791-7678
Fax: 520-791-7677
Email: p.crow@amaplastics.com / URL:
Product Service Description:
Manufactures plastic products; plastic
injection molding
Plastic products

AMC Products, Ltd.
663-671 Old Willets Path
Hauppauge, NY 11788
Contact: Joseph R. Accetta, President, Jodi
Cunningham, Secretary-Treasurer
Telephone: 516-234-5468
Fax: 516-234-7290
Email: amcproduct@aol.com / URL:
Product Service Description:
Dance Taps to Specification. London Brand
Proprietary Dance Taps to Order

AMI Trading
1699 Coral Way, Ste. 405
Miami, FL 33145-2860
Contact: Martin Netsky, Owner
Telephone: 305-854-8890
Product Service Description:
Non ferrous scrap metal

AMPAC Seed Company
P.O. Box 318, 32727 Hwy. 99 E.
Tangent, OR 97389
Contact: Jonathan Rupert, Product
Development Manager
Telephone: 800-547-3230
Fax: 541-928-2430
Email: info@ampacseed.com / URL: http://
www.ampacseed.com
Product Service Description:
Turfgrass & Forage Seed , Contract
Production

AMSER Logistics, Inc.
3010 LBJ Freeway, Suite 717
Dallas, TX 75234
Contact: Sales & Marketing,
Telephone: 972-243-4686
Fax: 972-243-4385
Email: amserl@aol.com / URL:
Product Service Description:
Transportation
Warehousing

AP & T Tangent, Inc.
4817 Persimmon Ct.
Monroe, NC 28110
Contact: Ove Moren, President
Telephone: 704-292-2900
Fax: 704-292-2906
Email: info@apt-usa.com / URL: http://
www.apt.se
Product Service Description:
Hydraulic Presses
Automation
Complete Presslines
Hydraulic Transfer Presses

APAC Products
5828 Naylor Ave
Livermore, CA 94550
Contact: John Whitsett, Pres.
Telephone: 925-447-2444
Fax: 925-447-8317
Product Service Description:
Manufactures fittings for water works and
irrigation : Coating & Lining-Epoxy
Drilling Machines-Pipe

APD
5010 S Ash Ave Ste 101
Tempe, AZ 85282-6843
Contact: Dell B Oliver, Pres.
Telephone: 602-345-1987
Fax: 602-345-2153
Email: apdfilms@uswestmail.net / URL:
Product Service Description:
Master distributor for the Ilumar brand of
solar window film for commercial, residential
and vehicle use
Plastic materials & basic shapes

ARA Automated Finishing
1286 Anvilwood Ave
Sunnyvale, CA 94089-2203
Contact: Haig Chakalian, V. Pres.
Telephone: 408-734-8131
Fax: 408-734-8391
Email: Haigc@aol.com / URL:
Product Service Description:
Plating & Anodizing

ARC Industries Inc.
2879 Johnstown Rd.
Columbus, OH 43219
Contact: John S. Siebold,
Telephone: 614-475-7007 / 800-734-7007
Fax: 614-475-3523
Email: arc@arcind.com / URL: http://
www.arcind.com
Product Service Description:
Assembly
Fabrication
Packaging - Shrink, Blister
Salvaging
Wood working
Special Projects

**ASD, Inc. , Architectural Signage &
Design**
3037 Lown St N
Saint Petersburg, FL 33713-2930
Contact: Fred R. Debien, Pres., Mktg. Mgr.
Telephone: 727-323-3553
Fax: 727-321-1910
Email: asdsign@get.net / URL: http://
www.asdsignage.com
Product Service Description:
Architectural signs
Signs, Tenant
Signs, Botanical Garden
Sign Frames
Signs, Braille - American Disability Act
Zoological Signs
Directories
Signs Exterior
Logos, Corporate-Dimensional

ASTI
3610 Birch St.
Newport Beach, CA 92660-2619
Contact: Clifford Crane, Marketing
Consultant
Telephone: 949-852-8008
Fax: 949-852-8484
Email: asti@netbox.com / URL: http://
www.asti-security.com
Product Service Description:
Process Control Equipment, Card Readers
Process Control Equipment, Access Control
Commercial Equipment, Alarm Systems
Software Design, Access/Alarm -Windows 95
Commercial Equipment, Security Equipment,
W/Color Gr.

ASV Wines Inc
1998 Road 152
Delano, CA 93215-9614
Contact: Marko Zaninovich, Pres.
Telephone: 661-792-3159
Fax: 661-792-2875
Email: / URL:
Product Service Description:
Winery
Wines & Juice

ATK North America
3210 S. Croddy Way
Santa Ana, CA 92704-6348
Contact: Steve Resnick, Manager
Telephone: 714-850-1544
Fax: 714-850-9079
Email: sales@atkengines.com / URL: http://
www.atkengines.com
Product Service Description:
General Automotive Repair Shops
Motor vehicle parts and accessories
Parts for use with spark-ignition internal
combustion piston engines
Miscellaneous cargo

ATL Ultrasound, Inc.
P.O. Box 3003
Bothell, WA 98041-3003
Contact: Victor H. Reddick, Sr. VP,
Worldwide Sales
Telephone: 425-487-7076
Fax: 425-485-5656
Email: vreddi@corp.atl.com / URL:
Product Service Description:
Medical Ultrasound Equipment

ATM Exchange, Inc, The
3930 Virginia Ave.
Cincinnati, OH 45227-3412
Contact: Sales & Marketing,
Telephone: 513-272-1081
Fax: 513-272-2076
Email: billm@atmex.com / URL: http://
www.atmex.com
Product Service Description:
Dealer / Remarketer ATM's, Banking
Equipment
Automatic Teller Machine & Equipment
Solutions

ATS Products
1430 Potrero Ave
Richmond, CA 94804-3750
Contact: Doug Williams, V-P., Mktg.
Telephone: 510-234-3173
Fax: 510-234-3185
Email: info@atsduct.com / URL:
Product Service Description:
Manufacturers of fiberglass fume-exhaust
duct work (administration office)
Factory Mutual (FMRC) Approved for use
without
Internal fire suppression devices. FMRC
approved
for smoke removal and for installation inside
Cleanrooms meeting FMRC 4910 protocol.

ATW Manufacturing Company
PO Box 7755
Eugene, OR 97401-0029
Contact: Thomas Drew, Pres.
Telephone: 541-484-2111
Fax: 541-484-1493
Email: info@atwmfg.com / URL: http://
www.atwmfg.com
Product Service Description:
Manufactures packaging machinery— shrink-
wrapping, shrink banding, labeling and heat
seal
Packaging machinery, L sealers, shrink
tunnels, bar sealers

AZ Hydraulic Engineering Inc
PO Box 3615
Kingman, AZ 86402-3615
Contact: Shirley Walton, Pres.
Telephone: 520-757-1400
Fax: 520-757-1004
Email: / URL:
Product Service Description:
Manufactures air operated hydraulic pumps
Fluid power pumps & motors

Aaron-Swiss, Inc.
607 Country Club Dr Ste B
Bensenville, IL 60106-1331
Contact: Roman Vazchur, Owner
Telephone: 630-595-5773
Fax: 630-595-5774
Email: / URL:
Product Service Description:
Automotive & electronic components
Electronic components
Motor vehicle parts & accessories

AbTech Industries Inc.
4110 N Scottsdale Rd Ste 235
Scottsdale, AZ 85251-3999
Contact: Don Thompson,
Telephone: 480-874-4000
Fax: 480-970-1665
Email: info@oars97.com / URL: http://
www.oars97.com
Product Service Description:
Manufactures polymer-based absorbent
products for source pollution control

Abbott Ball Co. (Mfg)
Railroad Place, P.O. Box 330100
West Hartford, CT 06133-0100
Contact: Kelly Parent, Sales Manager
Telephone: 860-236-5901
Fax: 860-233-1069
Email: kelly@abottball.com / URL: http://
www.abbottball.com
Product Service Description:
Mfrs. of Semi Precision Steel Balls
Sizes Range From 1/16" (1.588mm) to 5/8"
(15.875mm) Grades 100, 200, 500, 1000
Available in a variety of Alloys
(Stainless, Carbon, Brass, Aluminum)
And Precious Metals. Burnishing Media
also Available. Product mfg to ABMA STD.

Abco Products
6800 Nw 36th Ave
Miami, FL 33147-6572
Contact: Carlos Albir, Pres.
Telephone: 305-694-2226
Fax: 305-693-4410
Email: / URL:
Product Service Description:
Brooms, mops & lumbar belts
Brooms & brushes
Tray Stand
Banquet Tables
High Chair
Fresh Tilapia Fish Frozen

Ability Engineering Technology, Inc.
16140 Vincennes Ave
South Holland, IL 60473-1256
Contact: Michael Morgan, Pres., Engrg. & R
& D Mgr.
Telephone: 708-331-0025
Fax: 708-331-5090
Email: ability@worldnet.att.net / URL: http://
abilityengineering.com
Product Service Description:
Vacuum, cryogenic, & scientific equipment &
general machining & welding job shop
Plate work_fabricated (boiler shops) ASME
Code (U-Stamp)

Able Builders Export, Inc.
7451 N.W. 63rd St., P.O. Box 660068
Miami, FL 33266-0068
Contact: Stanford W. Freedman, President
Telephone: 305-592-5940
Fax: 305-592-2793
Email: sales@ableexport.com / URL: htp://
www.ableexport.com
Product Service Description:
Scaffold, Steel
Shoring
Toilets, portable
Props and similar equipment for scaffolding,
shuttering or pit-propping, of iron or steel
Casters

Abrasive Distributors Corp.
605 Main St.
Hackensack, NJ 07601
Contact: Jeff Fullam,
Telephone: 201-488-0200
Fax: 201-488-0054
Email: abrasdis@aol.com
URL: http://www.abrasivedist.com
Product Service Description:
Industrial Abrasives : Coated Abrasives,
Belts, Sheets, Discs, Etc. : Abrasives,
Bonded, Coated, Grain, Diamond : Diamond
& CBN Wheels & Tools : Grinding Wheels,
Sticks & Hones : Wire Wheels & Power
Brushes : Blasting Equipment

**Abrasive Service Industries, Century
Hone Div.**
3136 E Columbia St
Tucson, AZ 85714-2001
Contact: Jonathan Morgan, Pres., GM
Telephone: 520-294-3431
Fax: 520-294-3433
Product Service Description:
Manufactures honing machines and portable
hones for polishing cylinders
Machine tools, metal cutting types
Hones form 1/2" to 42"

Absecon Mills, Inc.
P.O. Box 672
Cologne, NJ 08213-0672
Contact: Randolph S. Taylor, President
Telephone: 609-965-5373
Fax: 609-965-7474
Email: exports@abecon.com / URL: http://
www.bpia.org
Product Service Description:
Jaquard Upholstery Fabrics
Polyolefin Upholstery Fabrics
Contract Upholstery & Panel Fabrics
Weaving Mills, Manmade Fiber
Weaving & Finishing Mills

Academic Distributing
PO Box 711
Dewey, AZ 86327-0711
Contact: Shelly Berry, Int'l Sales Mgr.
Telephone: 520-772-7111
Fax: 520-772-8035
Email: sales@academic-wholesale.com /
URL: http://www.academic-wholesale.com
Product Service Description:
Distributes prepackaged academic &
government software & hardware to over
2000 resellers: Computers, peripherals &
software

Academic Press
525 B St Ste 1900
San Diego, CA 92101-4495
Contact: Pieter S H Bolman, Pres.
Telephone: 619-231-0926
Email: / URL: http://www.apnet.com
Product Service Description:
Book publishing : Publishes scientific,
technological, medical books and journals
Periodicals

Accent Windows Inc
1221 E 56th Ave
Denver, CO 80216-1536
Contact: Richard Roeding, VP/GM
Telephone: 303-295-1170 X.21
Fax: 303-295-2088
Email: info@accentwindows.com:
Product Service Description:
Fabricates vinyl replacement & new
construction windows and doors

Accents In Sterling Inc
610 N Alma School Rd Ste 44
Chandler, AZ 85224-3688
Contact: Wayne Helfand, Pres.
Telephone: 602-899-9202
Fax: 602-899-8923
Email: / URL: http://www.aissilver.com
Product Service Description:
Jewelry & precious stones
Wholesales sterling silver with semi-precious
stones
Custom Manufacturing

Accrafect Products Inc.
PO Box 153
Mauston, WI 53948-0153
Contact: Tom Chudy, Pres., Fin. & R & D
Mgr.
Telephone: 608-847-6503
Fax: 608-847-5241
Email: acrafect@mwt.net / URL:
Product Service Description:
Latex glove dispensers
Machinery_special industry

Accu Rest, Inc.
1000 N Rand Rd Ste 120
Wauconda, IL 60084-1199
Contact: Jeff Anderson, Pres., Fin., MIS & R
& D Mgr.
Telephone: 847-487-0636
Fax: 847-487-0642
Email: accurest@accurest.com / URL: http://
www.accurest.com
Product Service Description:
Archery equipment
Sporting & athletic goods

**Accu-Cut Diamond Tool Co., Inc./
Accu-Cut Diamond Bore Sizing Syst**
4238 N Sayre Ave # 40
Norridge, IL 60634-1330
Contact: Stan Domanski, Pres.
Telephone: 708-457-8800
Fax: 708-457-8061
Email: / URL:
Product Service Description:
Diamond bore sizing tools & equipment
systems
Dies, tools, jigs & fixtures_special

Accu-Time Systems
420 Somers Rd
Ellington, CT 06029-2629
Contact: Peter DiMaria, Pres.
Telephone: 860-870-5000
Fax: 860-872-1511
Email: sale@accu-time.com / URL: http://
www.accu-time.com
Product Service Description:
Data collection systems

Accu-Tube Corporation
2960 S Umatilla St
Englewood, CO 80110-1218
Contact: Harold H Lee, Pres.
Telephone: 303-761-2258
Fax: 303-761-2276
Email: accutube@accutibe.com / URL:
www.accutube.com
Product Service Description:
Fabricates stainless steel tubing; bends and
end forms; fabricates other tubular parts of
aluminum, copper & brass

Accurate Circuit Engineering
3019 Kilson Dr
Santa Ana, CA 92707-4202
Contact: George Szell, Chrm.
Telephone: 714-546-2162
Fax: 714-433-7418
Email: sales@ace-pcb.com / URL: http://
www.ace-pcb.com
Product Service Description:
Manufactures printed circuit boards
Printed circuit boards
High tech. circuit boards in one day
Proto types tru production

Accurate Ingredients
160 Eileen Way
Syosset, NY 11791-5301
Contact: Jack Sollazzo, Owner
Telephone: 516-496-2500
Product Service Description:
Fruits and peppers , dried or crushed or
ground : Amino acids - L-cysteine, L-cystine
Seafood extracts - all natural, powder &
pastes : Volatile oil of mustard - natural
Volatile oil of horseradish - natural
Onion oil - natural
Dehyrdrated onion & garlic

Accurate Screening Media, Inc.
560 Chester Ave
Elgin, IL 60120-3032
Contact: Sherman Blair Jr., Pres., R & D Mgr.
Telephone: 847-697-5500
Fax: 847-697-5547
Email: / URL:
Product Service Description:
Security screens
Doors, sash & trim_metal

Accurate Sound Corporation
3475a Edison Way
Menlo Park, CA 94025-1813
Contact: Ronald M Newdoll, Pres.
Telephone: 650-365-2843
Fax: 650-365-3057
Email: ron@accuratesound.com / URL: http://
www.accuratesound.com
Product Service Description:
Manufactures high-speed audio tape
duplicators, instrumentation tape recorders
Radio & TV communications equipment
Digital audio telephone & radio voice loggers

Accurite Development & Mfg
111 Glenn Way Ste 2
San Carlos, CA 94070
Contact: Janos K Istenes, Owner
Telephone: 650-593-5745
Fax: 650-593-3545
Email: / URL:
Product Service Description:
Machine shop
Industrial machinery
Research
Development
Prototype
Tooling
Fixturing
Production
Precision Parts

Accushim Inc. (Mfr)
4633 Lawndale Ave., P.O. Box 65
Lyons, IL 60534
Contact: Roger Braun,
Telephone: 708-442-6448
Fax: 708-442-6918
Email: / URL:
Product Service Description:

Ace-Tek Manufacturing
PO Box 1474
Glendale, AZ 85311-1474
Contact: Mike Anderson, Owner
Telephone: 602-934-6999
Fax:
Email: mikeii@earthlink.net / URL:
Product Service Description:
General machine shop (job work)
Industrial machinery

Ackley Machine Corp.
1273 N Church St
Moorestown, NJ 08057-1115
Contact: Michael Ackley, Pres.
Telephone: 609-234-3626
Fax: 609-234-8657
Email: info@acleymachine.com / URL: http://
www.ackleymachine.com
Product Service Description:
Printing machinery
Printing trades machinery
Tablet Printers
Capsule Printers
Confectionary Printers
Small Product Feeding Systems
Product Orienting Systems

Acme Electric Corp., Power Distribution Products Div.
4815 W 5th St
Lumberton, NC 28358-0425
Contact: Steven Vineis, Sales Mgr.
Telephone: 910-738-4251
Fax: 910-739-0024
Email: svineis@acmepower.com / URL: http:/
/WWW.ACMEELEC.COM
Product Service Description:
Transformers, except electronic
Dry type transformers
DC power supplies

Acme Engineering & Mfg. Corp.
P.O. Box 978
Muskogee, OK 74402
Contact: Larry Cunningham, Export Sales
Mgr.
Telephone: 918/682-7791
Fax: 918-682-0134
Email: acmemkt@acmefan.com / URL: http://
www.acmefan.com
Product Service Description:
Commercial Ventilating Equipment
Industrial Fans & Blowers
Ventilating Equipment, Agricultural

Acme Plastic Products Company
9629 N 22nd Ave
Phoenix, AZ 85021-1806
Contact: Emmett D House, Pres.
Telephone: 602-997-9944
Fax: 602-944-8977
Email: acme_mh@usasn.com / URL:
Product Service Description:
Manufactures plastic products; plastic
injection molding and thermosetting
Plastic products

Acme Wire Products Co., Inc.
PO Box 218
Mystic, CT 06355-0218
Contact: M. Fitzgerals, Mktg. Mgr.
Telephone: 860-572-0511
Fax: 860-572-9456
Email: mfitz@acmewire.com / URL: http://
www.acmewire.com
Product Service Description:
Wire products - Misc. Fabricated

Acorn Industries Inc. (Mfr)
#1 Acorn Lane, P.O. Box 788
Morehead, KY 40351
Telephone: 606-784-9003
Fax: 606-783-1587
Product Service Description:
Hardwood Lumber

Acorn Manufacturing Co., Inc.
457 School Street, P.O. Box 31
Mansfield, MA 02048
Contact: E.L. Delong, President
Telephone: 508/339-4500
Fax: 508-339-0104
Email: info@acornmfg.com / URL: http://
www.acornmfg.com
Product Service Description:
Builders Hardware - Forged Iron
Decorative Colonial & Southwest Designs
Hardware for Full Size Doors & Cabinets

Acra-Ball & Manufacturing Co
2860 E Gretta Ln Ste F
Anaheim, CA 92806-2529
Contact: Dolly R Deneau, Pres.
Telephone: 714-632-3801
Fax: 714-632-9066
Email: www.acraball@aol.com / URL:
Product Service Description:
Manufactures standard and non-standard size
balls

Action International
P.O. Box 1294
Huntington Beach, CA 92647-1294
Contact: Jerry W. Crossett, President
Telephone: 714-968-3993
Fax: 714-968-6585
Email: jcr0518609@aol.com / URL:
Product Service Description:
Artificial Insemination Equipment
Shooting Sports Equipment

Action Media Technologies Inc
9400 Lurline Ave
Chatsworth, CA 91311-6038
Contact: Wil Lang, President, Brent
Lancaster, Mktg. Dir.
Telephone: 818-709-5792 / 18888-AMT-
4LED
Fax: 818-700-7988
Email: amt@amt-inc.com / URL: http://
www.amt-inc.com
Product Service Description:
Manufactures LED signs
Signs & advertising specialties

Action Tool Co., Inc.
1959 Tigertail Blvd.
Dania, FL 33004-2104
Contact: Joel Lazar, President
Telephone: 954-920-2700
Fax: 954-920-8780
Email: / URL: http://www.acttool.com
Product Service Description:
Hand Tools, Wholesale
Hardware, Wholesale

Acu-Gage Systems
175 Ammon Dr
Manchester, NH 03103-3308
Contact: John Kane, Pres.
Telephone: 603-622-2481
Fax: 603-626-1277
Email: info@acu-gage.com / URL: http://
www.acu-gage.com
Product Service Description:
Video based measuring instruments
Process control instruments

Ad-Vance Magnetics, Inc.
625 Monroe St
Rochester, IN 46975-1426
Contact: Richard D. Vance, President
Telephone: 219-223-3158
Fax: 219-223-2524
Email: sales@advancemag.com / URL: http://
www.advancemag.com
Product Service Description:
Magnetic shields
Metal products, fabricated

Adams & Brooks Inc
PO Box 77303
Los Angeles, CA 90007-0303
Contact: John E Brooks, Pres.
Telephone: 213-749-3226
Fax: 213-746-7614
Email: info@adams-brooks.com / URL: http:/
/www.adams-brooks.com
Product Service Description:
Candy & other confectionery products
Specialty confectionery
Internet Sales

Adams Bakery Corp.
PO Box 528
Milford, NJ 08848-0528
Contact: Christine Adams, Pres.
Telephone: 908-995-4040
Fax: 908-995-9669
Email: askus@the-baker.com / URL: http://
www.the-baker.com
Product Service Description:
Bread & rolls
Bread, cake & related products

Adams Truss, Inc.
12420 Collins Rd.
Gentry, AR 72734
Contact: Dale Adams, Pres., Sales & Mktg.
Mgr.
Telephone: 501-736-8581
Fax: 501-736-2690
Email: / URL: http://www.adamstruss.com
Product Service Description:
Steel building trusses & rafters
Structural metal_fabricated

Adaptive Micro Systems, Inc.
7840 N 86th St
Milwaukee, WI 53224-3430
Contact: Sheila Zenner, Export Sales Mgr.
Telephone: 414-357-2020
Fax: 414-357-2029
Email: sales@ams-i.com / URL:
Product Service Description:
Signs
Light Elec. Displays, Wholesale

Adhesive Systems, Inc.
PO Box 1085
Auburn, GA 30011-1085
Contact: Steve Wages, Pres.
Telephone: 770-822-0568
Fax: 770-339-1308
Email: / URL:
Product Service Description:
Hot & cold adhesive extrusion & spray
system parts
Adhesives & sealants
Parts for Nordson & Slautterback & ITW/LTI
Nozzles / Hoses / Filters Replacement
Heads, New for Rebuilt Price
Tanks, New for Rebuilt for Noldson 2300 /
3000 series
Special 24 Outlet Heads / Slot Heads
Special Hot / Cold Adhesive Systems

Adhesive Technologies, Inc.
3 Merrill Industrial Dr.
Hampton, NH 03842-1995
Contact: Sales & Marketing,
Telephone: 603-926-1616
Fax: 6039261780
Email: cricker@adhesivetech.com / URL:
http://www.adhesivetech.com
Product Service Description:
Glue Guns
Glue Sticks, Hot Melt

Adhesives Research, Inc.
400 Seaks Run Road, PO Box 100
Glen Rock, PA 17327-0100
Contact: Edward L. Daisey, Pres., CEO
Telephone: 717-235-7979
Fax: 717-235-8320
Email: mhopp@mail.adhesivesresearch.com /
URL: http://www.adhesivesresearch.com
Product Service Description:
Adhesives & Sealants
Pressure - Sensitive Adhesive Materials

Admore Inc.
16 Chocksett Rd.
Sterling, MA 01564
Contact: Karen Griffin, Asst. Controller
Telephone: 978-422-2300
Fax: 978-422-9699
Email: kgriffin@admore.com / URL: http://
www.admore.com
Product Service Description:
Trade show exhibits, show rooms, museums
Exhibit rentals
Signs & advertising specialties
Setup & dismantle of Exhibits

Advance Aluminum & Brass Inc
1001 E Slauson Ave
Los Angeles, CA 90011-5241
Contact: Michael Welther III, Pres., GM
Telephone: 323-231-9301
Fax: 323-235-2929
Product Service Description:
Bronze and aluminum foundry; manufactures
bearings, gear blanks, bar tube and plate
stock: Foundries_aluminum
Copper foundries
Foundries_nonferrous

Advance Paper & Maintenance
33 W Broadway Rd
Mesa, AZ 85210-1505
Contact: Vivian DeRosa, Pres.
Telephone: 602-964-6108
Fax: 602-461-8964
Email: isupplyu@aol.com / URL:
Product Service Description:
Distributes industrial paper products,
janitorial supplies and cleaning chemicals,
abrasives; pneumatic : Industrial supplies &
hardware : Chemicals & allied products
Maintenance equipment & parts
Floor machines : Vacuum cleaners
Carpet cleaning machines
Sweepers

Advance Research Chemicals, Inc.
5005 Skiatook Rd
Catoosa, OK 74015-3050
Contact: Dayal T. Meshri, Pres., CEO
Telephone: 918-266-6789
Fax: 918-266-6796
Email: advresch@ionet.net / URL:
Product Service Description:
Inorganic chemicals & fluorides
Organic & Inorganic Fluor Compounds

Advanced Circuit Enterprises
1501 Main Street
Tewksbury, MA 01876
Contact: Melba Nazzaro, Sales Manager
Telephone: 978-851-2237
Fax: 978-851-0753
Product Service Description:
Semiconductors & Drams, Wholesale

Advanced Graphics & Publishing
731 N Weber St
Colorado Springs, CO 80903-1015
Contact: Leland Bowers, Pres.
Telephone: 719-632-8142
Fax: 719-632-8143
Email: info@agpnet.com / URL:
Product Service Description:
Digital Prepress and Media Services
Typesetting
Commercial Art & Graphic Design
Banners & Signs
Slide Imaging
Presentation Graphics
Document Imaging

Advanced Heat Treat Corp.
3825 Midport Blvd.
Waterloo, IA 50703
Contact: Gary L. Sharp, President / CEO
Telephone: 319-232-5221
Fax: 319-232-4952
Email: mkt@ion-nitriding.com / URL: http://
www.ahtweb.com
Product Service Description:
Vacuum ion nitriding & induction hardening
Heat treating_metal (Oxidizing/Corrosion
Protection)
Surface Coatings, PVD Etc.
Metallurgical Testing & Failure Analysis
MagnaFlux Testing

Advanced Lighting Systems, Inc.
800 Beltline Rd
Sauk Centre, MN 56378-1741
Contact: Paul Streitz, Pres.
Telephone: 320-352-0088
Fax: 320-352-0089
Email: advlight@advancedlighting.com /
URL: http://www.advancedlighting.com
Product Service Description:
Fiber optic lighting equipment
Fiber optic cable (side & end lite)

Advanced Marine Technology Corp.
2003 Western Ave., Suite 725
Seattle, WA 98121
Contact: Art Kuller, Operations VP
Telephone: 206-443-5663
Fax: 206-443-5661
Email: andym@advmarine.com / URL: http://
www.advmarine.com
Product Service Description:
Navigational Marine Electronics

Advanced Package Engineering Inc
5711 W Washington St
Phoenix, AZ 85043-3649
Contact: Mark Wordekemper, Pres.
Telephone: 602-484-9003
Fax: 602-484-0663
Email: sales@apei.com / URL: http://
www.apei.com
Product Service Description:
Manufactures plastic corrugated returnable
containers and wood boxes; provides package
design and consulting services
Plastic products
Containers_wood
Engineering services

Advanced Power Technology Inc
405 SW Columbia St
Bend, OR 97702-1087
Contact: Patrick Sireta, Pres., CEO
Telephone: 541-382-8028
Fax: 541-388-0364
Email: / URL: http://
www.advancedpower.com
Product Service Description:
Power Semiconductors — MOSFETs, IGBTs
& FREDs

Advanced Tech Industries, Inc.
7441 Nw 8th St Ste J
Miami, FL 33126-2940
Contact: Henry Kourany, Pres., CFO
Telephone: 305-265-7751
Fax: 305-265-7184
Email: / URL:
Product Service Description:
Electronic household water heaters
Appliances_household

Advanced Thermal Products Inc
PO Box 15817
Santa Ana, CA 92735-0817
Contact: Sam Lindley, Pres.
Telephone: 714-556-7252
Fax: 714-556-7259
Email: info@atpwrap.com / URL: http://
www.atpwrap.com
Product Service Description:
Manufactures thermal insulation systems for
commercial diesel engines
High temperature exhaust insulation for heavy
duty, mobile equipment

Advanced Thermal Technologies
12900 Automobile Blvd Ste G
Clearwater, FL 33762-4715
Contact: David Eldridge, Pres.
Telephone: 727-571-1888
Fax: 727-571-2442
Email: advancedth@aol.com / URL: http://
www.advancedthermal.com
Product Service Description:
Dehumidifiers & desiccant wheels
Refrigeration & heating equipment

Advanced Vehicle Systems, Inc.
3101 Parker Ln
Chattanooga, TN 37419-1708
Contact: L. Joe Ferguson, Pres.
Telephone: 423-821-3146
Fax: 423-821-0042
Email: avs@vol.com / URL: http://
www.vol.com/~avs
Product Service Description:
Electric & hybrid electric battery powered
transit buses

**Advantage Buildings & Exteriors,
Inc.**
9741 E 56th St N
Tulsa, OK 74117-4008
Contact: Jenifer Fariss, Pres., CFO
Telephone: 918-272-1191
Fax: 918-272-2517
Email: sales@abewal.com / URL: http://
www.abewal.com
Product Service Description:
Exterior Wall Panels
Concrete Products
Small Metal / Wood Packaged Buildings

Advantage Development Corp
749 Lakefield Rd Ste F
Westlake Village, CA 91361-5924
Contact: William Kern, Pres.
Telephone: 805-446-6251
Fax:
Email: advanteq@advanteq.com /
URL: http://www.advanteq.com
Product Service Description:
Manufactures Tens nerve stimulators and
other medical devices
Surgical & medical instruments

AdvantageTransportation Inc.
P.O. Box 27233
Salt Lake City, UT 84127-0233
Contact: Wayne Parker, President
Telephone: 801-487-9650
Fax: 801-461-8801
Email: / URL:
Product Service Description:
Trucking Except Local
Freight Transportation Arrangement

Advantor Corp.
6101 Lake Ellenor Dr
Orlando, FL 32809-4660
Contact: Bruce Winner, Int'l Manager
Telephone: 407-859-3350
Fax: 407-859-5205
Email: winner@advantor.com / URL: http://
www.advantor.com
Product Service Description:
Communication Equipment, NEC
Electrical Equipment & Supplies, Nec
Security System Services
Electronic Parts & Equip. Wholesale

Aearo Company
5457 West 79th Street
Indianapolis, IN 46268
Contact: Michel Douar, Export Director
Telephone: 317-692-6586
Fax: 317-692-6604
Email: / URL:
Product Service Description:
Hearing Protection, EAR, Peltor
Eye & Face Protection, AOSAFETY
Respiratory Protection, AOSAFETY

Aerko International
3410 NE 5th Ave
Fort Lauderdale, FL 33334-2102
Contact: Kevin Dallett, V.P. Sales
Telephone: 954-565-8475
Fax: 954-565-8499
Email: aerko1@shadow.net / URL: http://
www.shadow.net/~aerko1/index.html
Product Service Description:
Organic Chemicals, Non-Lethal Weapons
Organic Chemicals, Riot Control Weapons
Tear Gas
Pepper Gas

Aero Tech Labs, Inc.
728 Nw 7th Ter
Fort Lauderdale, FL 33311-7313
Contact: Scott Hoffman, GM
Telephone: 954-463-4584
Fax: 954-463-3012
Email: aerotech@fau.campus.mci.net / URL:
Product Service Description:
Aerosol packaging
Pepper Gas
Tear Gas
Custom Packaging

Aero-KAP Inc
PO Box 661240
Arcadia, CA 91066-1240
Contact: Robert E Stabler, Pres.
Telephone: 626-574-1704
Fax: 626-446-8630
Product Service Description:
Manufactures electrical and electronic
components— wire, tubing and cable
assemblies : Electronic components
Nonferrous wiredrawing & insulating
Electrical apparatus & equipment

Aero-Mach Labs, Inc.
7707 E Funston St
Wichita, KS 67207-3121
Contact: Donnie Bolain, Pres.
Telephone: 316-682-7707
Fax: 316-682-3418
Email: sales@aeromach.com / URL: http://
www.aeromach.com
Product Service Description:
Aircraft instrument Service
Aircraft parts & equipment

Aero-Tech Light Bulb Co., Inc.
534 Pratt Ave
Schaumburg, IL 60193-4555
Contact: Ray M. Schlosser, Pres.
Telephone: 847-352-4900
Fax: 847-352-4999
Email: info@aerolights.com / URL: http://
www.aerolights.com
Product Service Description:
Light bulbs - long life 20,000 hr - 120V &
17,000 hr - 240v.

Aerofab Inc
3421 E 44th St
Tucson, AZ 85713-5480
Contact: Catherine E Lhost, Pres.
Telephone: 520-623-3961
Fax: 520-623-9241
Product Service Description:
Precision metal fabrication; Slot Machine
manufacture; electronic assembly

Aerofast Ltd
7363 E Tierra Buena Ln
Scottsdale, AZ 85260-2400
Contact: Robert Smith, Pres.
Telephone: 602-483-8942
Fax: 602-483-9493
Product Service Description:
Distributes aerospace hardware
Transportation equipment & supplies

Aerospace Control Products, Inc.
1314 W 76th St
Davenport, IA 52806-1305
Contact: William K. Stout, Pres
Telephone: 319-391-6051
Fax: 319-391-9231
Email: cme-acpi@qconline.com
Product Service Description:
Aircraft liquid level & pressure switches, gas
flow elements & systems
Aircraft parts & equipment

Aerospace Manufacturing Inc
3103 E Chambers St
Phoenix, AZ 85040-3727
Contact: Danny Sarenac, Pres.
Telephone: 602-276-6046
Fax: 602-276-6624
Product Service Description:
Manufactures aerospace electronics &
medical components : Turbine engine
components : Space vehicle components

Aetna Felt Corp.
2401 W Emmaus Ave
Allentown, PA 18103-7234
Contact: Jim Plunkett, Sales & Mktg. Mgr.
Telephone: 610-791-0900
Fax: 610-791-5791
Email: info@aetnafelt.com / URL: http://
www.aetnafelt.com
Product Service Description:
Felt washers, stripping, gaskets & yard goods
& other non-metallic materials
Adhesive Coating Services

Afab Enterprises
2151 W County Road 44
Eustis, FL 32726-2650
Contact: James O. Corbett, Pres., GM
Telephone: 352-483-1222
Fax: 352-483-1255
Email: jcorb88066@aol.com / URL: http://
www.refractometer.com
Product Service Description:
Refractometers (Inline)
Electronic Measurement Instruments

Afassco, Inc.
P.O. Box 1767
Carson City, NV 89702-1767
Contact: Donald Schumaker, Chairman
Telephone: 775-885-2900
Fax: 775-885-2997
Email: afassco@intercomm.com / URL:
Product Service Description:
Antiseptic Sprays
Antibiotics
Non-Prescription Drugs
Bandages
Dressings
First Aid Kits
Ointments
Cream
Burn Treatments & Kits
Wipes & Swabs

Affinity Industries Inc. (Mfr)
P.O. Box 1000
Ossipee, NH 03864
Contact: Robert B. Tozier, Director of Sales
Telephone: 603-539-3600
Fax: 603-539-8484
Email: sales@affii.com / URL: http://
www.affinitychillers.com
Product Service Description:
Welding Equipment Chillers
Laser Metalworking Equip. Chillers
Laser Woodworking Equip. Chillers
Gen. Ind. Mach., Portable Chilllers
Water Chillers
Heat Exchangers & Steam Condensers
Process Liquid Chillers

Aftermarket Parts Inc.
P.O. Box 12644
New Bern, NC 28561
Product Service Description:
Forestry & Logging Mach. Parts, Whsle.
Construction & Mining Mach. Parts, Whsle

Aftermarket Specialties, Inc.
6200 - C Highlands Pkwy., S.E.
Smyrna, GA 30082-5199
Contact: Dallas Rohrer, President
Telephone: 770-431-0525
Fax: 770-431-0131
Email: aftermkt@mindspring.com / URL:
http://www.aftermkt.com
Product Service Description:
Air conditioning & refrigeration compressors

Afton Plastics
PO Box 97
Lakeland, MN 55043-0097
Contact: Darrell D. Anderson, Pres.
Telephone: 651-436-8058 / 800-344-7499
Fax: 651-436-1345
Email: aftonplastics@worldnet.att.net / URL:
http://www.aftonplastics.com
Product Service Description:
Compression & extrusion & injection
moldings & precision plastics machining
Plastic products : Unsupported plastics film &
sheet : Plastic profile shapes_unsupported
Screw machine products

Agamco Inc
8034 Deering Ave
Canoga Park, CA 91304-5010
Contact: Carol Aronson, Pres.
Telephone: 818-340-4150
Fax: 818-340-6650
Email: bulbcpk@pacbell.net / URL:
Product Service Description:
Manufactures commercial and industrial light
bulbs : Lamps_electric

Age Industries, Inc.
PO Box 367
Cibolo, TX 78108-0367
Contact: Royce Drennan, Pres.
Telephone: 210-659-1301
Fax: 210-659-2096
Email: age@htcomp.net / URL: http://
www.htcomp.net/age/
Product Service Description:
Wooden pallets & corrugated boxes
Pallets & skids_wood
Boxes_corrugated & solid fiber

Aggressive Dies & Cutting
2554 W Via Palma
Anaheim, CA 92801-2623
Contact: Gary Sawyer, Pres.
Telephone: 714-527-0707
Fax: 714-229-7336
Email: garysawyer@aol.com / URL:
Product Service Description:
Manufactures of steer rye dies
Die cutting - decals & paper products

Agri Processors
P.O. Box 920
Postville, IA 52162-0759
Contact: Donald S. Hunt,
Telephone: 319-864-7811
Fax: 319-864-7890
Email: / URL:
Product Service Description:
Frozen Kosher Beef : Fresh Cov Boxed Beef
Frozen Poultry - Kosher & Non Kosher
Full Line of Deli Items
Frozen Veal & Lamb Kosher & Non Kosher
Produces from Beef / Poultry
Producer of Glatt & Regular Kosher Products
Also A Producer of Non Kosher Products
Beef, Veal, Lamb & Poultry
Deli Items - Only in Kosher

Agri-Tech, Inc.
Lakeview Dr., P.O. Box 448
Woodstock, VA 22664-0448
Contact: Michael T. Fuller, President & CEO
Telephone: 540-459-2142 :
Fax: 540-459-4731
Email: mfuller@agritech.agri-tech.com
URL: http://www.agri-tech.com
Product Service Description:
Fresh Fruit Equipment
Fresh Vegetable Equipment

Agrimar Corp.
PO Box 1419
Flowery Branch, GA 30542-0024
Contact: Edward K. Hensley, Pres
Telephone: 770-965-0220
Fax: 770-965-9766
Email: goemar@aol.com / URL: http://
www.goemar.com
Product Service Description:
Agricultural fertilizers
Fertilizers, mixing only

Agro Industrial Management
PO Box 5632
Fresno, CA 93755-5632
Contact: Farouk Hassan, President
Telephone: 209-224-1618
Fax: 209-348-0721
Email: Weaim@aol.com / URL:
Product Service Description:
Irrigation Equipment, Wholesale

Agro-Mar Inc Of Nevada
2908 Lake East Dr
Las Vegas, NV 89117-2203
Contact: Linda Fiore, Pres.
Telephone: 702-228-7110
Fax: 702-228-7109
Email: -lindy-jo@lucm.com / URL:
Product Service Description:
Processes raw aloe vera into liquid form for
resale to cosmetics and suntan lotion
companies
Personal care products
Consulting for new products

Agtrol International
7322 Southwest Fwy., Ste. 1400
Houston, TX 77074-2019
Contact: Tom Chavez, Dir. of Sales Americas
Telephone: 713-995-0111
Fax: 713-995-9505
Email:tchavez@agrol.com
URL: http://www.agtrol.com
Product Service Description:
Copper Hydroxide
Basic Copper Sulfate
Champion Tech Agri Fungicide
Gibberellic Acid
TPTH Fungicide
Mocromized Sulfur
Plant Growth Regulator

Aigner Index, Inc.
218 MacArthure Ave.
New Windsor, NY 12553
Contact: Mark Aigner,
Telephone: 914-562-4510
Fax: 914-562-2638
Email: aigner@frontiernet.net / URL: http://
www.holdex.com
Product Service Description:
Insertable Label Holders
Shelf & Rack Label Holders

Air Chem Systems Inc
15222 Connector Ln
Huntington Beach, CA 92649-1118
Contact: Micky Johnson, Pres.
Telephone: 714-897-1017
Fax: 714-897-0639
Email: / URL: http://
www.airchemsys.thomasregister.com
Product Service Description:
Manufactures and installs air pollution control
equipment : Blowers & fans

Air Cleaners, Inc.
805 N Sycamore Ave
Broken Arrow, OK 74012-2350
Contact: Peggy A. Tillotson, Pres., R & D
Mgr.
Telephone: 918-258-1817
Fax: 918-251-3302
Email: ultra@airclean.com / URL: http://
www.airclean.com
Product Service Description:
Electrostatic air filters

Air Dimensions, Inc.
1015 W Newport Center Dr Ste 101
Deerfield Beach, FL 33442-7707
Contact: Tom English, Pres.
Telephone: 954-428-7333
Fax: 954-360-0987
Email: info@airdimensions.com / URL: http://
www.airdimensions.com
Product Service Description:
Air sampling pumps
Pumps & pumping equipment

Air Energy Heat Pumps
1300 Sw 12th Ave
Pompano Beach, FL 33069-4619
Contact: John Zakryk, Owner
Telephone: 954-785-4900
Fax: 954-784-0408
Email: carlosbenadia@msn.com / URL: http://
/www.air-energy.com
Product Service Description:
Swimming pool heat pumps : Refrigeration &
heating equipment : Swimming Pool Heaters
Heat Pumps : Swimming Pool Chillers
Pool Chiller : Swimming Pool Heating
Swimming Pool Cooling : Spa Heating
Swimming Pool Heating & Cooling

**Air Instruments & Measurements
Inc. (Mfr)**
13300 A Brooks Dr.
Baldwin Park, CA 91706
Contact: Harry C. Lord, President
Telephone: 626-813-1460
Fax: 626-338-2585
Email: aimanalysis@earthlink.net / URL:
http://www.aimanalysis.com
Product Service Description:
Continuous Emissions Monitoring Systems
Analyzers, NOx, SOx, NH3, HCl, O2, Dust.
Analyzers, Process Control, Gas & Liquids

Airborne Technologies, Inc.
PO Box 2210
Camarillo, CA 93011-2210
Contact: Peter Wollons, Pres.
Telephone: 805-389-3700
Fax: 805-389-3708
Email: sales@airbornetech.com / URL:
Product Service Description:
Manufactures and supplies spare parts for
military aircraft, specializing in contoured/
formed items : Aircraft parts & equipment,
specializing in the C130, F16, F15, P3, F4, F5

Airflow Systems Inc. (Mfr)
11370 Pagemill Road
Dallas, TX 75243
Contact: Tony Bodmer, President
Telephone: 214-503-8008
Fax: 214-503-9596
Email: airflow@onramp.net / URL: http://
www.airflowsystems.com
Product Service Description:
Air Cleaners
Dust Collection Equipment
Mist Collection Equipment

Airglas Engineering Co., Inc.
PO Box 190107
Anchorage, AK 99519-0107
Contact: Wes K. Landes, Pres
Telephone: 907-344-1450
Fax: 907-349-4938
Product Service Description:
Fiberglass aircraft & helicopter skis
Plastic products

**Airgroup Express/Airgroup
Corporation**
P.O. Box 3627,
Bellevue, WA 98009-3627
Contact: A.E. Daniel, Vice President
Telephone: 425-462-1094
Fax: 425-462-0768
Email: info@airgroup.com / URL: http://
www.airgroup.com
Product Service Description:
Freight Forwarder : Customs Broker
Freight & Cargo Transportation

Airmetrics
225 5th St., Suite 501
Springfield, OR 97477-4695
Contact: K. Gottfried, Sales & Marketings
Telephone: 541-726-0560
Fax: 541-726-1205
Email: sales@airmetrics.com / URL: http://
www.airmetrics.com
Product Service Description:
Ambient Air Sampler-particulates, Gases

Airo Clean, Inc.
212 Philips Road
Exton, PA 19341
Contact: George Mitchell, CEO, President
Telephone: 610-524-8100
Fax: 610-524-8135
Email: sales@airoclean.com / URL: http://
www.airoclean.com
Product Service Description:
Portable clean rooms & components
Ultraground fan filter modules

Airseal Products Company
PO Box 38700
Los Angeles, CA 90038-0700
Contact: Frank Emley, Export Mgr.
Telephone: 323-856-0606
Fax: 323-876-1609
Email: airseal@worldnet.att.com / URL:
http://www.airseal.com
Product Service Description:
Tires Sealant for Sealing Tires

Airtrol, Inc.
3564 Lasalle St
Saint Louis, MO 63104-1024
Contact: Jack Thompson, Pres.
Telephone: 314-776-0189
Fax: 314-776-4792
Email: airtrol@airtrol.com / URL: http://
www.airtrol.com
Product Service Description:
Dust collecting equipment

Ajax Magnethermic Corp.
1745 Overland Avenue
Warren, OH 44483-2860
Contact: Jack M. Bodi, Dir, Int'l Sales
Phone: 330-372-8511 / Fax: 330-372-8644
Email: intlsales@ajaxmag.com / URL: http://
www.ajaxmag.com
Product Service Description:
Heating Equip Line & Motor-Gen Freq
Induction Furnaces Metal Melting
Induction Furnaces & Heat Equip, Other

Ajax Tool Works, Inc.
10801 Franklin Ave
Franklin Park, IL 60131-1407
Contact: Robert J. Benedict, Pres.
Telephone: 847-455-5420
Fax: 847-455-9242
Email: info@ajaxtools.com / URL: http://
www.ajaxtools.com
Product Service Description:
Pneumatic chisels, hammer accessories &
forged hand tools

Akron Tool & Die Co., Inc.
96 E. Miller Ave.
Akron, OH 44301-1325
Contact: Mike Magee, President
Telephone: 330-762-9260
Fax: 330-762-3233
Email: akrontoolz@aol.com / URL: http://
www.akrontool.com
Product Service Description:
Plastic Extrusion Dies

Alabama Plastic Container
PO Box 1728
Calera, AL 35040-1728
Contact: Wallace Watson, Pres., Opers. Mgr.
Telephone: 205-668-0411
Fax: 205-668-0412
Email: / URL:
Product Service Description:
Plastic containers & blow molded products

Alaco Ladder Co.
5167 G Street
Chino, CA 91710-5143
Contact: Jeff Elliot, President
Telephone: 909-591-7561
Fax: 909-591-7565
Email: / URL:
Product Service Description:
Aluminum Ladders
Fiberglass Ladders
Special Design Equipment
Ground Service Equipment
Wood Ladders

Alamia Inc
2212 S. Wabash St.
Denver, CO 80231-3314
Contact: Saad Bulifa, Pres.
Telephone: 303-752-4652
Fax: 303-752-4642
Email: alamia@mindspring.com / URL: http://
www.alamia.com
Product Service Description:
Distributes industrial equipment— pulleys,
gears and boxes
Industrial supplies
Lawn & garden equipment
Portable generators & pumps
Safety equpment & gear
Tires & tubes
Belts

Alan Ross Machinery Corp
3240 Commercial Ave.
Northbrook (Chicago), IL 60062
Contact: Alan Ross & Rustin Ross,
Telephone: 847-480-8900
Fax: 847-480-1830
Email: director@rossmach.com / URL: http://
www.rossmach.com
Product Service Description:
Recycling Machinery - Used
Shredders
Balers
Granulators
Magnetic Separators

Alaska Airboats
PO Box 879030
Wasilla, AK 99687-9030
Contact: Leonard Haire, Pres., Sales Mgr.
Telephone: 907-376-6183
Fax: 907-376-8708
Email: akairboats@alaska.net / URL:
Product Service Description:
Aluminum airboats
Boat building & repairing

Alaska Gift & Gallery
PO Box 356
Kenai, AK 99611-0356
Contact: Robert J. Cutler, Owner, Fin. & R &
D Mgr.
Telephone: 907-283-3655
Fax: 907-283-6250
Email: robertcutler@gci.net / URL: http://
www.rjcutler.com
Product Service Description:
Silver, brass & copper inlayed wooden bowls
Wood products

Alaska Herb & Tea Co.
6710 Weimer Dr
Anchorage, AK 99502-2054
Contact: Sandra Fongemie, Owner
Telephone: 907-245-3499
Fax: 907-245-3499
Email: / URL: http://www.alaska.net/
~herbtea
Product Service Description:
Tea blending & potpourri
Toilet preparations, oils, hand cream, soaps

Alaska Herb Tea Co. (Mfr)
6710 Weimer Drive
Anchorage, AK 99502
Contact: Charles Walsh, Director
Telephone: 907-245-3499
Fax: 907-245-3499
Email: herbtea@alaska.net / URL: http://
www.alaska.net/~herbtea
Product Service Description:
Herbal Tea
Fragrance Items / Potpourri
Dried Florals/Evergreens
Bath & Body Products

Alaskan Dried Foods
PO Box 610
Kake, AK 99830-0610
Contact: Joe Isturis, Plt. Mgr.
Telephone: 907-785-3130
Fax: 907-785-4108
Email: dryfoods@seaknet.alaska.edu / URL:
Product Service Description:
Salmon jerky & seafood snack products
Fish_fresh or frozen prepared
Smoked and jarred salmon
Smoked & jarred Halibut
Smoked Salmon-kipperd
Dried Halibut
Cold smoked - Lox - Salmon, Halibut
Smoked & jarred Alaskan Oysters

Albis
P.O. Box 711
Rosenberg, TX 77471-0711
Contact: Henry Meijer, President
Telephone: 281-342-3311
Fax: 281-342-3058
Email: / URL:
Product Service Description:
Plastics Materials and Resins
Polysulfides, polysulfones, and synthetic
polymers in primary forms, including
polyxlene resins

Albrecht Co, Inc., Peter
6250 Industrial Ct
Greendale, WI 53129-2432
Contact: Tom Ziolkowski, Pres.,
Treas., R & D Mgr.
Telephone: 414-421-6630
Fax: 414-421-9091
Email: albrechtco@compuserve.com / URL:
Product Service Description:
Theater & television studio rigging equipment

Alcar Industries, Inc.
25 Renwick St
Newburgh, NY 12550-6029
Contact: Philip Merlin, Pres.
Telephone: 914-561-8920
Fax: 914-561-8946
Email: spinozza@firststreetinternet.com /
URL: http://www.alcarindustries.com
Product Service Description:
Bag closures, Twist ties
Twist tie ribbon on spools machine
application
Garden hose packaging, twist tie ribbon
Plastic tubing coiling twist tie ribbon
Bakery and food bag closures
Rotogravure printing, autoclavable indicating
inks

Alco Technologies Inc
1815 W 213th St Ste 160
Torrance, CA 90501-2851
Contact: Lawrence R Lopez, Pres.
Telephone: 310-328-4770
Fax: 310-328-1262
Email: alcotech@alcotech.com / URL: http://
www.alcotech.com
Product Service Description:
EMI/RFI shielding products
Shielded gaskets & vents

Aldridge Industries, Inc.
4815 Commercial Dr Nw
Huntsville, AL 35816-2207
Contact: Warren Aldridge, Pres.
Telephone: 256-837-8981
Fax: 256-837-9025
Email: mail@aldridgegrinders.com / URL:
http://www.aldridgegrinders.com
Product Service Description:
CNC Cylindricals, Chuckers, Crankshaft,
Camshaft & Custom PLC Universal
Industrial Grinding Machines & Systems

Alexeff-Synder Enterprises
9621 York Alpha Dr.
Cleveland, OH 44133-3593
Contact: Alex Alexeff, *
Telephone: 440-237-2300
Fax: 440-237-8228
Email: / URL:
Product Service Description:
Tire Processing Machinery & Equipment
Rubber Machinery & Equipment
Guiding Equipment & Controls
Spreading Equipment & Controls

Alfa International Corporation
4 Kaysal Place
Armonk, NY 10504
Contact: Sales & Marketing,
Telephone: 914-273-2222
Fax: (914)273-3666
Email: info@alfaco.com / URL: http://
www.alfaco.com
Product Service Description:
Meat Slicer Blades and Parts
Mixer Bowls and Accessories
Meat Chopper Knives and Plates

Alfa Southwest Maquiladora Svc
1605 Pacific Rim Ct Ste D
San Diego, CA 92173-3517
Contact: Ernesto Bravo, Pres.
Telephone: 619-661-1251
Fax: 619-661-1252
Email: alfsw@worldnet.att.net / URL:
Product Service Description:
Labor & admin. service for U.S. Mfrs. in
Tijuana, B.C., : Saves 50% of payroll

Alfred Publishing Co Inc
PO Box 10003
Van Nuys, CA 91410-0003
Contact: Andrew Surmani, VP Marketing
Telephone: 818-891-5999
Fax: 818-891-2369
Email: customerservice@alfredpub.com /
URL: http://www.alfredpub.com
Product Service Description:
Publishes music books & software

Alfred's Pictures Frames Inc
3520 Medford St
Los Angeles, CA 90063-2532
Contact: Pat Cochrane, Pres.
Telephone: 323-268-2611
Fax: 323-268-0809
Email: alfreds7@aol.com / URL: http://
www.heather-ann.com
Product Service Description:
Manufactures polyurethane picture frames,
plaques and window treatments :
Manufactures decorative polyurethane wall
mirrors : Manufactures decorative
polyurethane wall shelves, corbels & sconces
Manufactures polyurethane reproductions of
stone & wood artifacts

Alga Plastics Co.
21 Amflex Dr
Cranston, RI 02921-2028
Contact: Joan Parks Moran, President
Telephone: 401-946-2699
Fax: 401-946-6860
Email: customerservice@alga.com / URL:
http://www.alga.com
Product Service Description:
Medical & electronics products packaging
Plastic Packaging Products
Thermoforming

Algoma Lumber Co.
1400 Perry St
Algoma, WI 54201-1680
Contact: Lynn Busch, V-P., Pur.
Telephone: 920-487-3511
Fax: 920-487-3694
Email: / URL:
Product Service Description:
Sawmills & planing mills, general
Lumber processing, wood chips & sawdust
Logging

Alicat Scientific Inc
2200 N Wilmot Rd
Tucson, AZ 85712-3016
Contact: John Bowman, Pres.
Telephone: 520-290-6060
Fax: 520-290-0109
Email: alicat@rtd.com / URL: http://
www.alicat.com
Product Service Description:
Manufactures scientific instruments; flow
meters, controllers and calibrators: Analytical
instruments : Fluid meters & counting devices
Measuring & controlling devices Proportional
Control Valves
Pulse Signal Translators

Alkantec, Inc.
12020 Sunrise Valley Drive, Suite 240
Reston, VA 22091
Contact: Raouf Roushdy, President
Telephone: 703-758-0071
Fax: 703-758-0073
Email: sales@alkantec.com / URL: http://
www.alkantec.com
Product Service Description:
Computer Equipment, & Supplies, Export
Lab Equipment, Export
Test & Measuring Instruments, Export
Diamond Cutting (Saw) Blades, Export
Office Furniture, Export

Alkota Cleaning Systems
110 Iowa St., P.O. Box 288
Alcester, SD 57001
Contact: Gene Bowling, *
Telephone: 605-934-2222
Fax: 605-934-1808
Email: alkota@acsnet.com / URL:
Product Service Description:
High Pressure Washers, Water Treatment
Waste Water Recycling Equipment
Industrial Cleaning Chemicals
Industrial Heaters, Portable

Alkota Cleaning Systems
PO Box 288
Alcester, SD 57001-0288
Contact: Sami Boulds, *
Telephone: 605-934-2222
Fax: 605-934-1808
Email: / URL:
Product Service Description:
High Pressure Washers, Water Treatment
Waste Water Recycling Eqipment
Steam Cleaners
Industrial Heaters, Portable

All American Containers, Inc.
11825 N.W. 100th Rd.
Miami, FL 33178-1034
Contact: Remedios Diaz-oliver, Chief
Executive Officer & President
Telephone: 305-887-0797
Fax: 305-888-4133
Email: sales@americancontainers.com / URL:
http://www.americancontainers.com
Product Service Description:
Industrial Supplies
Glass containers for conveying, packing or
preserving goods; Glass stoppers, lids and
other closures
Carboys, bottles, flasks and similar articles,
of plastics
Stoppers, caps, lids and other closures, of
plastics
Glass containers
Metal cans, barrels, drums & pails
Fiber cans, drums & similar products
Plastic bottles
Packaging machinery
Pet bottles

All American Office Products Inc
8301 W Washington St
Peoria, AZ 85345-6511
Contact: Toni Gutierrez, Pres.
Telephone: 602-979-9570
Fax: 602-878-3781
Email: / URL:
Product Service Description:
Sells office furniture and computer supplies,
recharged toner cartridges and imaging
products
Furniture
Stationery & office supplies

**All American Pharmaceutical &
Natural Foods Corp.**
1831 Main St
Billings, MT 59105-4033
Contact: Tim Romero, VP
Telephone: 406-245-5793
Fax: 406-245-6157
Email: app@aol.com / URL:
Product Service Description:
Manufactures vitamin powders, liquids,
capsules and tablets
Medicinals & botanicals

All Craft Fabricators, Inc.
PO Box 267
Copiague, NY 11726-0267
Contact: Robert Schnebly, Pres., Steve
Schnebly, V.P.
Telephone: 516-225-1001
Fax: 516-226-6235
Email: www.acfacinc@aol.com / URL:
Product Service Description:
Wood Office Furniture
Plastic Laminate Office Furniture
Archetechual Wood Working

All Day Used Auto Parts
12710 Cairo Ln.
Opa Locka, FL 33054-4611
Contact: Joe Hidalgo,
Telephone: 305-688-4118
Fax:
Email: / URL:
Product Service Description:
Automobile Parts & Accessories, Used

All Metals Processing Co Inc
264 W Spazier Ave
Burbank, CA 91502-2546
Contact: Tim Roach, Secy-Treas., GM
Telephone: 818-846-8844
Fax: 818-846-4968
Email: / URL:
Product Service Description:
Plating services—black oxide, bronze,
copper, cadmium plate & zinc plate ; dry
blasting; baking (job shop)
Plating & polishing passivate, zinc nickel,
zinc phosphate
Ebonal C, Degreasing

All Metals Processing of OC
8401 Standustrial St
Stanton, CA 90680-2619
Contact: Stephen W Sellwood, V-P., CFO
Telephone: 714-828-8238
Fax: 714-828-4552
Email: / URL:
Product Service Description:
Priming, painting, plating, anodizing and non-
destructive testing
Plating & polishing
Metal coating & allied services
Testing laboratories
Powder Coating
Packaging Subcontractor

All Neon & Signs
3662 N Milwaukee Ave
Chicago, IL 60641-3032
Contact: Nestor Soriano, Owner
Telephone: 773-736-3880
Fax: 773-736-8082
Product Service Description:
Interior & exterior signs
Signs & advertising specialties
Neon & Channel Letters Manufacturing
Neon Technology Eduational Assistance

All Points International Inc.
800 W. Main St., Ste. 107,
Freehold, NJ 07728
Contact: Martin Rosen,
President
Telephone: 732-866-4000
Fax: 732-866-4081
Email: apiship@aol.com / URL:
Product Service Description:
International Freight & Cargo Transportation

All-Flo Pump Co.
9321 Pineneedle Dr.
Mentor, OH 44060
Contact: Valerie Thomas, V.P. Mktg.
Telephone: 440-354-1700
Fax: 440-354-9466
Email: email@all-flo.com / URL: http://
www.all-flo.com
Product Service Description:
Air driven, double diaphragm pumps

All-States Quality Foods L.P.
PO Box 365
Charles City, IA 50616-0365
Contact: Steve Tenney,
Telephone: 515-228-5023
Fax: 515-228-2624
Email: / URL:
Product Service Description:
Poultry Futher Processor
Rendered chicken fat, chicken broth, cooked
chicken skin

Alldos Inc.
2220 Northwest Pkwy Se Ste 180
Marietta, GA 30067-9314
Contact: Dan Keane, Saels Manager
Telephone: 770-956-7996
Fax: 770-956-7836
Email: alldos@mindspring.com / URL: http://
www.alldos.de
Product Service Description:
Metering pumps
Pumps & pumping equipment

Allegra Industries, Inc.
230 5th Ave., Rm. 406
New York, NY 10001-7704
Contact: Allen Dweck,
President
Telephone: 212-725-0510
Fax: 212-779-3192
Email: / URL:
Product Service Description:
Cannon bath rugs & scatter accent rugs
Sheets & pillow cases poly/cotton blend &
100% cotton : Terry & Velour Towels
Comforters : Juvenile bedding & linens

**Allen Aircraft Products, Inc., Metal
Finishing Div.**
PO Box 1211
Ravenna, OH 44266-1211
Contact: Roger Rollyson, GM, Metal Fin.
Telephone: 330-296-1531
Fax: 330-296-7138
Email: alledmf@raex.com / URL:
Product Service Description:
Metal finishing, sulfuric anodizing, coating &
painting
Metal coating & allied services

Allen Osborne Associates Inc
756 Lakefield Rd
Westlake Village, CA 91361-2624
Contact: Allen W Osborne Jr, Pres., CEO
Telephone: 805-495-8420
Fax: 805-373-6067
Email: aoa@aoa-gps.com / URL: http://
www.aoa-gps.com
Product Service Description:
GPS Reference Receivers TurboRogue
GPS Geodetic network Rcvr BenchMark
GPS Survey Equipment, RTK + Postpr.
Rascal
GPS Timing Receivers, E.G. TTR-6

Allen Tool Co
PO Box 747
Hotchkiss, CO 81419-0747
Contact: Paul B Allen, Owner
Telephone: 970-872-3454
Fax: 970-872-3862
Email: allentoolco@tds.net / URL:
Product Service Description:
Manufactures steel post pullers
Agriculture - fencing ect.

Allenwest Inc
8245 Ronson Rd
San Diego, CA 92111-2004
Contact: Albert Allen, Pres.
Telephone: 619-565-8666
Fax: 619-565-8721
Email: / URL: http://www.allenwest.com
Product Service Description:
Multi color labels, plus UV printed labels up
to 7 colors
Barcode distribuotr of printers, scanners,
software
Thermal transfer ribbons & blank labels
Warehouse barcode systems, asset
managment barcode systems

Alliance International
495 E. Mound St.
Columbus, OH 43215
Contact: Sales & Marketing,
Telephone: 614-224-3035
Fax: 614-224-3132
Email: / URL:
Product Service Description:
Freight & Cargo Transportation
Trucking

Alliance Laundry Systems
Shepard St., P.O. Box 990
Ripon, WI 54971
Contact: Stephanie D. Korb,
Telephone: 920-748-1773
Fax: 920-748-4564
Email: stephanie.korb@alliancels.com / URL:
http://www.comlaundry.com
Product Service Description:
Commercial Laundry Equipment
Household Laundry Equipment

Allied Decals Florida, Inc.
5190 Nw 10th Ter
Fort Lauderdale, FL 33309-3155
Contact: David Schroeder, V-P., Sales &
Mktg.
Telephone: 954-776-0500
Fax: 954-776-6520
Email: / URL: http://www.allieddecals.com
Product Service Description:
Adhesive Backs, Decals, Labels & Signs
Viny Looseleaf Binders & other Heat Sealed
Products

Allied Dynamics Corp.
195L Central Ave.
Farmingdale, NY 11735-6904
Contact: Sales & Marketing,
Telephone: 516-293-6188
Fax: 516-293-9419
Email: alldyn@aol.com / URL: http://
www.allied-dynamics.com
Product Service Description:
Gas Turbine Spare Parts, Hardware &
Accessories : Electrical Components
Repair Services

Allied Flare Inc.
PO Box 58294
Houston, TX 77258-8294
Contact: Lee Hurzeler, Sales & Mktg. Mgr.
Telephone: 281-332-1000
Fax: 281-338-2579
Email: hurzeler@alliedflare.com / URL: http:/
/www.alliedflare.com
Product Service Description:
Flares

Allied Industrial Distributors Inc.
1102 East Cherry Street
Vermillion, SD 57069
Contact: Donald A. Clyde, President
Telephone: 605/624-2685
Fax: 605-624-8761
Email: dclyde@dtgnet.com / URL: http://
sdibi.northern.edu/allied/allied3.htm
Product Service Description:
Pressure Washers , Steam Cleaners

Allied Products Int'l, Inc.
1135 Clifton Ave.
Clifton, NJ 07013-3642
Telephone: 973-472-0757
Fax: 973-472-6679
Email: apisec@api-security.com / URL:
Product Service Description:
Security Equipment

Allied Security Equipment
5901 4th Ave. South
Seattle, WA 98108-3209
Contact: Jim Schuler, Export Sales
Telephone: 206-767-2500
Fax: 206-767-9345
Email: safejim@aol.com / URL: http://
www.aol.com
Product Service Description:
Safes, Iron & Steel
Safe Deposit Boxes

Alljuice Food & Beverage
1275 W. Granada Blvd., Suite 3B
Ormond Beach, FL 32174-8200
Contact: Ron Kahrer, President
Telephone: 904-676-2828
Fax: 904-676-2820
Email: alljuice@aol.com / URL:
Product Service Description:
Bottle private label apple juice, cider & other
juices from
concentrate in plastic & glass

Alloy Wire Belt
2318 Tenaya Dr
Modesto, CA 95354-3926
Contact: Dan Blank, Div. Mgr.
Telephone: 209-575-4900
Fax: 209-575-4904
Product Service Description:
Wire products_misc. fabricated
Manufactures woven wire conveyor belts,
round and flat wire; friction and sprocket
drive

Allpress Equipment Inc.
4524 Curry Ford Road, Suite 533
Orlando, FL 32812
Contact: Jennie M. Schofield, President
Telephone: 407-281-0111
Fax: 407-282-2289
Email: apreeg@aol.com / URL:
Product Service Description:
Offset Printing Machinery, Wholesale
Printing Machinery Parts, Wholesale

Allsafe Co., Inc.
1105 Broadway
Buffalo, NY 14212-1511
Contact: James Pokornowski, Pres.
Telephone: 716-896-4515
Fax: 716-896-4241
Email: jpokornowski@allsafe.com / URL:
http://www.allsafe.com
Product Service Description:
Plastic cards for access control, identification,
(employees / student)
Security Concerns, Library Services,
Membership, Parking Control & Government

Allsop, Inc.
PO Box 23
Bellingham, WA 98227-0023
Contact: Graeme Esarey, International Sales
Manager
Telephone: 360-734-9090
Fax: 360-734-9858
Email: graeme.esarey@allsop.com / URL:
http://www.allsop.com
Product Service Description:
Audio & video accessories
Manufactures consumer electronics &
computer accessories
Coputer peripheral equipment & accessories
Desktop accessories
Laptop accessories

Allstates Textile Machinery
P.O. Box 266
Anderson, SC 29622-0266
Contact: Jeff Willis, President
Telephone: 864-226-6195
Fax: 864-226-0968
Email: sales@allstatestextile.com / URL:
http://www.allstatestextile.com
Product Service Description:
Used textile machinery

Allview Services Inc
2215 S Castle Way
Lynnwood, WA 98036-8338
Contact: Walter E Schaplow, Pres.
Telephone: 425-483-6103
Fax: 425-402-8334
Email: eschap@allview.com / URL: http://
www.seanet.com\~-eschap\
Product Service Description:
Manufactures computer systems and
components, servers and storage solutions
Electronic computers
Computer storage devices
Computers, peripherals & software
Computer & software stores

Almix/Asphalt Equipment Co., Inc.
13333 U.S. 24 West
Fort Wayne, IN 46804
Contact: A. Michael Shurtz, President
Telephone: 219-672-3422
Fax: 219-672-3020
Email: mshurtz@aol.com / URL:
Product Service Description:
Asphalt Drum Mixers & Related Equipment

Alpha 1 Studio, Inc.
6 Park Dr
Shamong, NJ 08088-8994
Contact: Ray Witthauer, Pres.
Telephone: 609-268-2111
Fax: 609-268-7111
Email: manager@signstudio.com / URL:
http://www.signstudio.com
Product Service Description:
Signage, Displays & Graphic Design

Alpha Associates, Inc.
2 Amboy Ave., P.O. Box 128
Woodbridge, NJ 07095
Contact: A. Louis Avallone, President
Telephone: 732-634-5700
Fax: 732-634-1430
Email: guest@alphainc.com / URL: http://
www.alphainc.com
Product Service Description:
Fiberglass Fabric
Coated Fiberglass Fabric
Laminated Insulation Materials

Alpha Coatings Inc.
PO Box 131
Washington, MO 63090-0131
Contact: Bud Cortner, Pres.
Telephone: 314-390-3903
Fax: 314-390-3906
Email: alcoat@mail.usmo.com / URL:
Product Service Description:
Industrial & aircraft coatings
Paints & allied products

Alpha Systems Lab Inc
17712 Mitchell N
Irvine, CA 92614-6013
Contact: Rose Hwang, Pres.
Telephone: 949-622-0688
Fax: 949-252-0887 / 949-622-0597
Email: Rwang@aslrwp.com / URL: http://
www.aslrwp.com
Product Service Description:
Manufactures remote video surveillance for
the security industry

Alpha Technology
471 Nelo St Ste H
Santa Clara, CA 95054-2146
Contact: Fred Pollard, Pres.
Telephone: 408-727-9636
Fax: 408-727-9680
Email: R90K@aol.com / URL: http://
www.alphatechnology.com
Product Service Description:
Remanufactures semiconductor equipment
Semiconductor Equipment, New & Used

Alpha Wire Company
711 Lidgerwood Avenue
Elizabeth, NJ 07207
Contact: Sandra Jaouen, Marketing Manager
Telephone: 908-925-8000
Fax: 908-925-6923
Email: info@alphawire.com / URL: http://
www.alphawire.com
Product Service Description:
Wire & Cable, Tubing, Wholesale

AlphaGraphics Printshops
2918 N Central Ave
Phoenix, AZ 85012-2704
Contact: Cindy Jorgensen, Br. Mgr.
Telephone: 602-274-2345
Fax: 602-274-2836
Product Service Description:
Commercial printing, lithographic and offset
Lithographic printing_commercial

AlphaTest Corporation
557 E Juanita Ave Ste 6
Mesa, AZ 85204-6537
Contact: Dan Rodgers, VP
Telephone: 480-545-5518
Fax: 480-545-5521
Email: message@alphatest.com / URL: http://
www.alphatest.com
Product Service Description:
Manufactures test fixtures and test probes for
testing of electronic components

Alpine Armoring Inc.
503 Carlisle Dr., Ste. 250
Herndon, VA 22070
Contact: Fred Khoroushi, General Manager
Telephone: 703-471-0002
Fax: 703-471-0202
Email: armor@alpineco.com / URL: http://
www.alpineco.com
Product Service Description:
Manufacturer of armored products & ballistic
law enforcement products : Motor vehicles
for the transport of goods : Passenger motor
vehicles : Law Enforcement / Police products
Bank vehicles (vans, trucks) - armored
Prison transfer vehicles - armored
VIP Protection vehicles - armored

Alpine Touch Inc
PO Box 864
Choteau, MT 59422-0864
Contact: Mark Southard, Owner
Telephone: 406-466-2063
Fax: 406-466-2076
Email: mrspice@3rivers.net / URL:
Product Service Description:
Manufactures spice and seasoning products
Food preparations
Groceries & related products

**Alps Sportswear Manufacturing Co ,
Inc**
5 Franklin St
Lawrence, MA 01840-1106
Contact: Marvin Axelrod, Pres.
Telephone: 978-683-2438
Fax: 978-686-8051
Product Service Description:
Knit outerwear mills
Men's, Women's and Boys' Sweaters, Sport
Shirts and Knit Outerwear
Clothing, mens & boys
Fleece sportswear

Alstom Automation Systems Corp.
701 Technology Dr
Canonsburg, PA 15317-9587
Contact: Wayne L. Huff, Pres., CEO
Telephone: 724-873-9300
Fax: 724-873-9416
Email: / URL: http://
www.assembly.alstom.com
Product Service Description:
Industrial automation systems & controls
Relays & industrial controls

Alto-Shaam, Inc.
W164 N9221 Water Street
Menomonee Falls, WI 53051-1401
Contact: Patrick Willis, Vice President/Int'l
Telephone: 414-251-3800
Fax: 414-251-7067
Email: / URL:
Product Service Description:
Commercial Cooking & Food Warm Equip.
Commercial Ovens, Electrical
Commercial Food Warming Equipment
Cooking Equipment, Parts & Accessories

Alum-a-pole Corporation
1011 Capouse Avenue
Scranton, PA 18509-2928
Contact: Donna Anderson, Operations
Manager
Telephone: 717-969-2299
Fax: 717-969-2531
Email: /
Product Service Description:
Aluminum Pump Jack Scaffolding
Bendable Vinyl Coil & Extruded Profiles

Alvey, Inc.
9301 Olive Blvd.
St. Louis, MO 63132-3299
Contact: Roger L. Alderink, Vice President
Telephone: 314-995-2331
Fax: 314-872-5700
Email: ralderink@ibs.alvey.com / URL: http://
www.alvey.com
Product Service Description:
Case Conveyors
Pallet Conveyors
Palletizers
Depalletizers

Alvord Systems, Inc.
PO Box 489
Clairton, PA 15025-0489
Contact: Thomas S. Alvord, X-Ray Sales,
Suzanne Natter (Blade Sales)
Telephone: 412-233-3910
Fax: 412-233-4991
Email: info@alvordsystems.com / URL: http:/
/www.alvordsystems.com
Product Service Description:
Slurry saw blades & x-ray diffraction
machines

Ambco Electronics
15052 Red Hill Ave Ste D
Tustin, CA 92780-6525
Contact: George C Koulures, Pres.
Telephone: 714-259-7930
Fax: 714-259-1688
Email: hearambco@earthlink.net / URL:
Product Service Description:
Manufactures audiometers for hearing testing

Ambox Inc.
PO Box 262218
Houston, TX 77207-2218
Contact: James E. Keith, Pres., R & D Mgr.
Telephone: 713-644-1931
Fax: 713-644-7790
Email: ambox@hti.net / URL: http://
www.thomasregister.com/ambox
Product Service Description:
Metal stampings & fabrication & laser &
CNC machining job shop
Metal stampings
Metal products_fabricated

Ameri Housing
1414 N.W. 107th Ave.
Miami, FL 33172-2732
Contact: Gerardo Capo, Manager
Telephone: 305-513-0501
Fax: 305-513-9109
Email: gcapo30360@aol.com / URL:
Product Service Description:
Subdividers and Developers, NEC
Road tractors for semi-trailers
Mechanical shovels, excavators and shovel
loaders, self-propelled
Doors, windows and frames and thresholds
for doors, of iron or steel

AmeriCares Foundations
161 Cherry St.
New Canaan, CT 06840-4834
Contact: Robert C. Macauley, Chief
Executive Officer, Chairman & Founder
Telephone: 203-972-5500
Fax: 203-966-9434
Email: aweirether@americares.org / URL:
http://www.americares.org
Product Service Description:
Business Associations : Miscellaneous cargo
Instruments and appliances for medical,
surgical or veterinary sciences and parts and
accessories thereof : Sugar confectionary , not
containing cocoa

America Excel, Inc.
1201 Oakton St
Elk Grove Village, IL 60007-2019
Contact: Ivan V. Torrez, Ex. V-P.
Telephone: 847-640-3000
Fax: 847-640-3019
Email: excelaei@aol.com / URL: http://
www.excelaei.com
Product Service Description:
Machine tools
Machine tools, metal cutting types

American & Efird, Inc.
12800 Nw 38th Ave
Opa Locka, FL 33054-4525
Contact: Ben Beasley III, Mktg. Mgr.
Telephone: 305-688-8100
Fax: 305-688-1414
Product Service Description:
Sewing Threads : Notions, zippers, fasteners,
buttons, elastic & pins

American & Efird, Inc.
P.O. Box 507
Mount Holly, NC 28120
Contact: Lynda Treadway, Dir. of Sales Supp
Telephone: 704-827-4311
Fax: 704-822-6054
Email: aesales@amefird.com / URL: http://
www.amefird.com
Product Service Description:
Industrial Sewing Thread : Texturized Sewing
Thread : Spun Polyester Sewing Thread
Air Entangled Polyester Sewing Thread
Polyester Core Thread : Polyester Thread
Filament Thread : Bobbins : Notions
Trim

American Augers Inc.
PO Box 814
West Salem, OH 44287-0814
Contact: Roger K. Eve, CEO
Telephone: 419-869-7107
Fax: 419-869-7425
Email: / URL: http://www.american-
augers.com
Product Service Description:
Construction machinery
Horizontal earth boring & directional drills,
mud, fluid systems, auger sections, cutting
Oil & gas field machinery

American Barcode Concepts
4630 E Elwood St Ste 1
Phoenix, AZ 85040-1962
Contact: Michael Stryczek, Pres.
Telephone: 602-894-5564 / 1800-281-3056
Fax: 602-968-3983
Email: barcode@amerbar.com / URL: http://
www.amerbar.com/barcode
Product Service Description:
Distributes and services bar coding equipment
& software : Repair services for bar code
equipment

American Boa, Inc.
PO Box 1301
Cumming, GA 30028-1301
Contact: J. Kelley Tribble,
V-P., Sales & Mktg.
Telephone: 770-889-9400
Fax: 770-889-0661
Email: sales@iwkabi.com / URL: http://
www.americanboa.com
Product Service Description:
Flexible metal hose, assemblies
Metal expansion joints
Automotive exhaust decoupling joints

American Casein Co.
109 Elbow Ln.
Burlington, NJ 08016-4123
Contact: Clifford E. Lang, Jr.,
Telephone: 609-387-3130
Fax: 609-387-7204
Email: sales@109elbow.com / URL: http://
www.americancasein.com
Product Service Description:
Casein
Caseinates
Hydroloyzed dairy proteins

American Cedarworks, Inc.
PO Box 2164
Hagerstown, MD 21742-2164
Contact: Benjamin F. Kunkleman, Pres., CEO
Telephone: 301-733-7000
Fax: 301-791-3732
Email: taci@pdcreative.pair.com / URL: http:/
/www.pdcreative.pair.com
Product Service Description:
Red, Cedar, oak & cherry wood wall
coverings

American Custom Coatings, Inc.
1433 W Fullerton Ave Ste H
Addison, IL 60101-4366
Contact: Jean Winsor, Pres.
Telephone: 630-629-3266
Fax: 630-629-3272
Email: info@americancustomcoat.com /
URL: http://www.americancustomcoat.com
Product Service Description:
Photocopier Fuser Rollers

American Cylinder Co., Inc.
481 Governor's Highway
Peotone, IL 60468
Contact: Joseph White, VP Sales
Telephone: 708-258-3935
Fax: 708-258-3980
Email: amcy@americancylinder.com / URL:
http://www.americancyliner.com
Product Service Description:
Fluid Power Cylinders & Actuators

American Design & Mfg.
310 Prestige Park Rd
East Hartford, CT 06108-1924
Contact: Bob Vyskocil, Owner
Telephone: 860-282-2719
Fax: 860-282-2721
Email: admsys@aol.com / URL: http://
www.americandes-mfg.com
Product Service Description:
Industrial hydraulic & lubrication systems
Measuring & controlling devices
Aerospace test stands

American Die Technology Inc.
3870 Lakefield Dr
Suwanee, GA 30024-1241
Contact: Bill Griffiths, Wayne Stollenwerk
Telephone: 770-623-6111
Fax: 770-623-5999
URL: http://www.amdie.com
Product Service Description:
Rotary cutting dies

**American Distilling &
Manufacturing Co., Inc.**
P.O. Box 319
East Hampton, CT 06424-0319
Contact: Edward C. Jackowitz, President
Telephone: 203-267-4444
Fax: 203-267-1111
Email: whazel1@prodigy.net / URL:
Product Service Description:
Distilled witch hazel extracts : Distilled spirits
flavors : Vanilla extracts

American Equipment Sales Co.
PO Box 21516
Fort Lauderdale, FL 33335-1516
Contact: Emil Pawuk, Owner
Telephone: 954-525-8165
Fax: 954-761-8137
Email: hoses@bellsouth.com / URL: http://
www.americanequipmentsale.com
Product Service Description:
Hydraulic hose assemblies : Fluid power
valves & hose fittings : Fluid transfer pumps

American European Systems
PO Box 7061
Reno, NV 89510-7061
Contact: Robert G Sapeta, Pres.
Telephone: 770-852-1114
Fax: 770-852-1163
Email: info@aesinc-us.com / URL:
Product Service Description:
Distributes industrial food processing and
packaging machinery
Industrial machinery & equipment

American Fiber Industries, Llc
9100 Frazier Pike Rd.
Little Rock, AR 72206
Contact: Ahmad Hbouss, Chrm.
Telephone: 501-490-1577
Fax: 501-490-1639
Email: 105245.3467@compuserve.com /
Product Service Description:
Plastic injection molding
Plastic products
Pet Bottle Preforms

American Fiberglass Products, Inc.
PO Box 778
Double Springs, AL 35553-0778
Contact: Greg Farris, Pres
Telephone: 205-489-3133
Fax: 205-489-2134
Email: / URL:
Product Service Description:
Fiberglass bath tubs & shower units
Mineral products_nonmetallic
Thermoformed Plastic Products

American Fibre Supplies
5720 S.W. Barnes Rd.
Portland, OR 97221-1523
Contact: John Braestrup, Owner
Telephone: 503-292-1908
Fax: 503-292-2106
Email: john@amfibre.com / URL:
Product Service Description:
Paper

American Forms, Inc.
3463 E. Commerce St.
San Antonio, TX 78238
Contact: Enrique P. DeLeon, COO
Telephone: 210-271-7971
Fax: 210-271-0709
Email: amforms@swbell.net / URL:
Product Service Description:
Business forms printing
Manifold business forms

American Hi-Tech Flooring Co.
952 Norfolk Sq
Norfolk, VA 23502-3212
Contact: Wayne S. Pittman, Pres., Pur., Sales
& Mktg. Mgr.
Telephone: 757-466-2900
Fax: 757-466-1219
Email: wpittman@hitechflooring.com / URL:
http://www.hitechflooring.com
Product Service Description:
Epoxy flooring systems
Floor coverings, hard surface

**American High Performance Seals,
Inc.**
403 Parkway View Dr
Pittsburgh, PA 15205-1408
Contact: Harold Kofler, Pres.,
CFO, R & D Mgr.
Telephone: 412-788-8815
Fax: 412-788-8816
Email: amhseals@amhseals.com / URL:
Product Service Description:
Industrial seals & packings
Gaskets, packing & sealing devices

American Hydraulics
5072 W Mission Blvd
Ontario, CA 91762-4539
Contact: F Baratti, Owner
Telephone: 909-464-0454
Fax: 909-464-0492
Email: / URL:
Product Service Description:
Sells and services hydraulics; welds and
fabricates parts; complete machine shop
Industrial machinery
Repair services
Welding repair
Industrial supplies

**American International Marine
Agency**
80 Maiden Lane, 24 Floor
New York, NY 10038
Contact: Charles Capozzoli, *
Telephone: 212/770-6273
Fax: 212-514-7304
Email: charles.capozzoli@alg.com / URL:
http://www.aig.com
Product Service Description:
Insurance, Marine
Marine products

American Laboratories, Inc. (Mfr)
4410 South 102nd Street
Omaha, NE 68127
Contact: J.E. Jackson, President
Telephone: 402/339-2494
Fax: 402-339-0801
Email: ali@americanlaboratories.com / URL:
http://www.americanlaboratories.com
Product Service Description:
Pharmaceutical Preparations
Food Supplements
Diagnostic Substances
Veterinary Biological Products

American MSI Corp
5245 Maureen Ln
Moorpark, CA 93021-7125
Contact: Tim Triplett, Chrm.
Telephone: 805-523-9593
Fax: 805-523-0575
Email: / URL: http://www.americanmsi.com
Product Service Description:
Process control instruments
Manufactures temperature controls for
plastics industry

American Marking, Inc.
2435 Vale Dr
Birmingham, AL 35244-2275
Contact: Gary Wasmer, V-P., Opers., R & D,
Sales & Mktg.
Telephone: 205-987-0151
Fax: 205-733-1720
Email: ami@american-marking.com / URL:
http://www.american-marking.com
Product Service Description:
Industrial marking devices, inks, stenciling
spray adhesives & paint markers

American Miso Co.
4225 Maple Creek Rd
Rutherfordton, NC 28139-7521
Contact: Leila Bakkum, Sales Manager
Telephone: 828-665-7790
Fax: 828-667-8051
Email: sales@great-eastern-sun.com / URL:
http://www.great-eastern-sun.com
Product Service Description:
Miso & soy sauce
Food preparations

American Omni Trading
3200 Wilcrest Dr., Ste. 415
Houston, TX 77042-6019
Contact: Tom Brackin, Owner
Telephone: 713-785-2700
Fax: 713-785-2245
Email: tbrackin@american-omin.com / URL:
http://www.american-omni.com
Product Service Description:
Tires, tubes, batteries

American Optimum
2239 Lobelia Avenue
Upland, CA 91784-7386
Contact: Mike Sharif, President
Telephone: 909-869-2430
Fax: 909-949-1104
Email: / URL:
Product Service Description:
Chemicals, Export
Stainless Steel, Import

American Piezo Ceramics, Inc.
PO Box 180 Duck Run
Mackeyville, PA 17750-0180
Contact: Ian R. Henderson, President
Telephone: 570-726-6961
Fax: 570-726-7466
URL: http://www.americanpiezo.com
Product Service Description:
Piexoceramic Medical Sensors Transducers

American Piping Products, Inc.
PO Box 928
Chesterfield, MO 63006-0928
Contact: Paul E. Axerolo, Sales Mgr.
Telephone: 314-536-1775
Fax: 314-536-1363
Email: appstl@aol.com / URL: http://
www.ameripipe.com
Product Service Description:
Steel Pipe & Fittings, Wholesale

American Pneumatic Tool
14710 S, Maple Ave.
Gardena, CA 90248-1934
Contact: Al Jacobellis, President
Telephone: 310-538-2600
Fax: 310-323-6656
Email: exec@apt-tools.com / URL: http://
www.apt-tools.com
Product Service Description:
Manufactures pneumatic demolition tools for
the construction industry

American Power Products Inc
14040 Central Ave
Chino, CA 91710-5563
Contact: Atzal Hussain, Pres.
Telephone: 909-590-2626
Fax: 909-591-6778
Email: apppower@aol.com / URL: http://
www.applighting.com
Product Service Description:
Manufactures residential and commercial
fluorescent lights :Compact Fluorescent
Lamps : Fluorescent Night Lights
Under Cabinet Lights
Fluorescent & Halogen Shoplights
Commercial Hi-Gay HID Fixtures

**American Precision Machine
Products, Inc.**
1380 Landmeier Rd
Elk Grove Village, IL 60007-2412
Contact: John Groth, Pres., Pur., Sales &
Mktg. Mgr.
Telephone: 847-439-0050
Fax: 847-439-0117
Email: jgapms@aol.cm / URL: http://
www.user/net/americanprecisionmachine
Product Service Description:
Screw machine products
Screw machine CNC machine products

**American Professional Quilting
Systems**
8033 University Ave., Suite F
Des Moines, IA 50325
Contact: Jeff Jochims, Owner
Email: apqs@netins.net / URL: http://
www.apqs.com
Product Service Description:
Quilting Machines

American Scholar Co.
200 Candlewood Rd
Bay Shore, NY 11706-2217
Contact: Barry Rao, Chrm., Secy.
Telephone: 516-273-6550
Fax: 516-273-6019
Email: scholar@vdot.net / URL: http://
www.americanscholar.com
Product Service Description:
Envelopes, writing tablets, construction paper
bookcovers & notebooks : Envelopes
Stationery products : Converted Paper
Products : Filler Paper
Marble Composition Books

American Sewing Dynamics 1
3009 W Lawrence Ave
Chicago, IL 60625-4303
Contact: Olga F. Chtiguel, President
Telephone: 773-267-5050
Fax: 773-267-5292
Email: amsdyna@aol.com / URL: http://
www.amsdyna.com
Product Service Description:
Leather, nylon & polyester computer carrying
cases, tapestry luggage & handbags
OEM, private label & contract available

American Sign Company
7950 Woodley Ave
Van Nuys, CA 91406-1225
Contact: David Capo, Pres.
Telephone: 818-904-3400
Fax: 818-988-4511
Email: mrsign@earthlink.net / URL: http://
www.americansignco.com
Product Service Description:
Manufactures signs and banners
Signs & advertising specialties

American Sleeve Bearing, Llc
1 Spring St
Stafford Springs, CT 06076-1504
Contact: Howard Buckland, Pres.
Telephone: 860-684-8060 / 800-969-2721
Fax: 860-684-8084 / 800-969-5966
Email: amersleeve@aol.com / URL: http://
www.asbbronze.com
Product Service Description:
Bronze bearings
Power transmission equipment

American Tank & Vessel
P.O. Box 910
Mobile, AL 36601-0910
Contact: William Cutts, President
Telephone: 334-432-8265
Fax: 334-433-3661
Email: atvmob@iar.net / URL: http://www.at-
v.com
Product Service Description:
Field erected tanks API-650, API-620
Field erected vessels ASME
Shop fabricated tanks & vessels

American Textile Machinery
2597 S Millege Ave
Athens, GA 30605-1626
Contact: Henry Walczyk,
Telephone: 706-543-6552
Fax: 706-543-6554
Email: impfex@megia.net / URL:
Product Service Description:
Nonwoven Textile Machinery

American Tool & Engrg Corp
7485 Trade St
San Diego, CA 92121-2409
Contact: Kaz Fukukura, GM
Telephone: 619-566-4880
Fax: 619-566-6307
Email: / URL:
Product Service Description:
Electronic enclosures and sheet metal
assemblies
Sheet metal work

American Towers and Structures
P.O. Box 3241
Sioux City, IA 51102
Telephone: 712-252-0240
Fax: 712-252-0371
Email: / URL:
Product Service Description:
Towers, Guyed / Self-Supporting

American Traditional Stencils
442 1st N Tpke
Northwood, NH 03261-3410
Contact: Judith Barker, Pres.
Telephone: 603-942-8100
Fax: 603-942-8919
Email: amtrad@amtrad-stencil.com / URL:
http://www.amtrad-stencil.com
Product Service Description:
Brass & laser cut polyester stencils
Marking devices

American Traffic Systems Inc
15029 N 74th St
Scottsdale, AZ 85260-2406
Contact: Adam E. Tuton, VP
Telephone: 602-922-2100
Fax: 602-994-3648
Email: atuton@traffic.com / URL: http://
www.traffic.com
Product Service Description:
Manufactures photo-radar equipment
Develops transaction processing software for
Traffic Enforcement
Manufactures red light cameras

**American Valve & Pump, Inc., DBA:
A M J Valve & Service Co.**
PO Box 1169
Hilliard, FL 32046-1169
Contact: Scott E. Chism, Fin.,
GM & Opers. Mgr.
Telephone: 904-845-4050
Fax: 904-845-4162
Email: / URL:
Product Service Description:
Industrial valves
Valves_industrial

American Water Heater Co.
PO Box 1378
Johnson City, TN 37605-1378
Contact: Mike Reid, Pur. Agt.
Telephone: 423-434-1500
Fax: 423-434-1632
Email: / URL:
Product Service Description:
Appliances_household
Gas & electric water heaters

American Wood Fibre, Inc.
PO Box 240785
Montgomery, AL 36124-0785
Contact: Tom Adams, Pres.
Telephone: 334-264-1401
Fax: 334-264-1045
Email: / URL:
Product Service Description:
Wood chips
Wood products

American Zettler Inc
75 Columbia
Aliso Viejo, CA 92656-1498
Contact: Rainer Moegling, Pres.
Telephone: 949-831-5000
Fax: 949-831-8548
Email: / URL: http://www.azettler.com
Product Service Description:
Electronic components
Manufactures electronic components
LCD & Transformers

Americlean, Inc.
11 E Ferguson Ave
Wood River, IL 62095-1903
Contact: George Adams, Pres., R & D Mgr.
Telephone: 618-254-6032
Fax: 618-251-7611
Email: americln@cdmnet.com / URL: http://
www.americlean-inc.com
Product Service Description:
Cleaning & drum process systems
"Pinetrator" Drum punch & sampling
systems

Americoat Corp.
PO Box 2228
Eaton Park, FL 33840-2228
Contact: S. V. Desai,
President. CFO
Telephone: 941-667-1035
Fax: 941-667-0289
Email: ameriCoat@aol.com / URL:
Product Service Description:
Powder coating: Baked on
Sandblasting; Pretreatment
Stripping; Burn off old powder coat
Types of coating applied: decorative
Polyester, TGIC, Polyurethane, Epoxy,
Hybrid, PVC
Types of coating applied, functional
Food grade, epoxy, nylon and Teflon
Non-stick, high tmperature Teflon Ceramic
Reinforced
Corrosive resistant Protective coatings;
Dupont Tefzel
KF Polymer, Dykor (Kynar) Ryton, Halar,
Dupont Abcite

Amerikan Dream Inc.
PO Box 13126
Spokane, WA 99213-3126
Contact: Bob Irwin, Pres.
Telephone: 509-489-9484
Fax: 509-838-3154
Email: ddr@pacnw.com / URL:
Product Service Description:
Manufactures Golf Gift Products

Ameritool, Hand Tool Div.
16741 W Park Circle Dr
Chagrin Falls, OH 44023-4549
Contact: James D. Bares, Opers. & R & D
Mgr.
Telephone: 440-543-2600
Fax: 440-543-6624
Email: / URL: http://www.ameritool.com
Product Service Description:
Tools_hand & edge
Hand tools

Amero Foods Mfg. Corp.
9445-l Washington Blvd.
Laurel, MD 20723
Contact: Theodore Pary, Pres.,
R & D, Sales & Mktg. Mgr.
Telephone: 301-498-0912
Fax: 301-498-0913
Email: mira@pastryonline.com / URL: http://
www.pastryonline.com
Product Service Description:
Baking ingredients
Flour mixes & doughs_prepared
Frozen pastries

**Ameron Intl/Protective Coatings
Group**
PO Box 1020
Brea, CA 92822-1020
Contact: Mike Tornberg, Pres.
Telephone: 714-529-1951
Fax: 714-990-0437
Email: dorothy_tripodi@ameron-intl.com /
URL: http://www.ameron-intl.com
Product Service Description:
Manufactures protective coatings (group
headquarters)
High performance protective coatings, paints
Paints, varnishes & supplies

Ametek Rotron TMD - Industrial Products Group
12 North St
Saugerties, NY 12477-1000
Contact: Dan Spencer, Application Engineer
Telephone: 914-246-3401
Fax: 914-246-3802
Email: info@ametek.com / URL: http://www.rotrontmd.com
Product Service Description:
Blowers & fans
Pressure & vacuum blowers

Amkus, Inc.
2700 Wisconsin Avenue
Downers Grove, IL 60515
Contact: Suzanne Wik, Sales Administration
Telephone: 630-515-1800
Fax: 630-515-8866
Email: experts@amkus.com / URL: http://www.amkus.com
Product Service Description:
Hydraulic Extrication Equipment
Emergency Metal Cutters, Hydraulic
Power Hand Tools

Ammermans, The
4902 Charlie Taylor Rd
Plant City, FL 33565-2257
Contact: Don Ammerman, Owner
Telephone: 813-752-2230
Product Service Description:
Bird & rabbit cages
Wire products_misc. fabricated

Amos Import/Export Management Co.
PO Box 649
Palmer Lake, CO 80133-0649
Contact: Sylvia Amos, President
Telephone: 719-338-6382
Fax: 719-481-8310
Product Service Description:
Cosmetics, Export

Ampel Corp.
PO Box 3628
Des Moines, IA 50322-0628
Contact: Bill Oertel, Pres.
Telephone: 515-278-5900
Fax: 515-278-0101
Product Service Description:
Pelletized gypsum (bulk or bagged)
Pelletized limestone (fine-ground) (bulk or bagged) :Pelletized dolomite (fine-ground) (bulk or bagged)

Ampli-Vox Questron
3149 Macarthur Blvd
Northbrook, IL 60062-1903
Contact: Don Roth, Pres.
Telephone: 847-498-9000
Fax: 847-498-6691
Email: info@ampli.com / URL: http://www.ampli.com
Product Service Description:
Sound systems & amplifiers
Audio & video equipment_household

Amtico International Inc.
6480 Roswell Rd.
Atlanta, GA 30328
Contact: Mary Docker, CEO
Telephone: 404-267-1900
Fax: 404-267-1901
Email: / URL: http://www.amtico.com
Product Service Description:
Luxury vinyl flooring
Chlorine- free flooring (Non PVC)

Amtrade International, Inc.
1700 N. Dixie Hwy., Ste. 142
Boca Raton, FL 33432-1850
Contact: Sales & Marketing,
Telephone: 561-367-7966
Fax: 561-367-7891
Email: amtradeusa@aol.com / URL:
Product Service Description:
Milk Products
Milk Processing Machinery
Parts, Milk Processing Machinery

Amtronics, Inc./Teriminal Div.
210 Douglass St
Brooklyn, NY 11217-3025
Contact: Stephen Kuncio,
Marketing Manager
Telephone: 718-625-3000
Fax: 718-625-1411
Email: solutions@amteonics.com / URL:
http://www.amtronics.com
Product Service Description:
Electronic terminals, connectors &
termination equipment

Amy's Kitchen Inc
PO Box 7868
Santa Rosa, CA 95407-0868
Contact: Andy Berliner, Pres.
Telephone: 707-578-7188
Fax: 707-578-7995
Email: / URL:
Product Service Description:
Manufactures organic frozen foods
Frozen specialties
Canned soups (non-frozen)
Bottled pasta sauces (non-frozen)

Anaheim Automation
910 E Orangefair Ln
Anaheim, CA 92801-1103
Contact: William H Reimbold, Owner
Telephone: 714-992-6990
Fax: 714-992-0471
Email: / URL:
Product Service Description:
Relays & industrial controls
Manufactures step motor drivers and
controllers

Anaheim Marketing International
4332 East La Palma Aveune
Anaheim, CA 92807
Contact: Edward E. Chavez, President
Telephone: 714-993-1707
Fax: 714-993-1930
Email: nafta@go-ami.com / URL: http://www.go.ami.com
Product Service Description:
Garbage Disposal Units , Household, Export
Garbage Disposal Units, Commercial , Export
Dishwashers, Household, Export
Hot Water Dispensers, Household, Export
Trash Compactors, Household, Export
Water Filtration (Commercial & Residential)
Commercial Food Waste Reduction Systems

Analogic Corporation
8 Centennial Dr.
Peabody, MA 01960-7987
Contact: Peter Pulsifer, Dir./Sales & Mktg.
Telephone: 978-977-3000
Fax: 781-245-1274
Email: / URL: http://www.analogic.com/petalmonitor
Product Service Description:
Electromedical Equipment, Fetal Monitors

Analtech, Inc.
PO Box 7558
Newark, DE 19714-7558
Contact: Steven C. Miles, Sales & Mktg. Mgr.
Telephone: 302-737-6960
Fax: 302-737-7115
Email: sales@analtech.com / URL: http://www.analtech.com
Product Service Description:
Thin-layer chromatography plates

Analytica Environmental Lab Inc
325 Interlocken Pkwy Ste 200
Broomfield, CO 80021-3437
Contact: Jeff Lyons, Pres.
Telephone: 303-469-8868
Fax: 303-469-5254
Email: marketing@analyticagroup.com / URL: http://www.analyticagroup.com
Product Service Description:
Environmental analytical laboratory
Abestos testing
Lead paint testing
Volatile & semi-volatile organic testing
Metals & chemistry testing

Anamax Corp.
PO Box 10067
Green Bay, WI 54307-0067
Contact: Leon Tolbert, Dir. Mktg, Hides & Skins, Michael Carlson, Dir. of Mktg.
Rendered Products
Telephone: 920-494-5233
Fax: 920-494-9141
Email: mcarlson@anamax.com / URL:
Product Service Description:
Fats & oils_animal & marine
Protein Feeds
Hids & Skins

Anchor Buddy
2979 N Foothill Rd
Medford, OR 97504-9722
Contact: Ronald Kubli, Owner
Telephone: 541-779-1234
Fax: 541-734-9897
Email: anchor-buddy@juno.com / URL:
Product Service Description:
Manufactures Anchor Rope / Dock Line

Anchor Mfg. Co.
2922 W 26th St
Chicago, IL 60623-4127
Contact: Janice Kacena, Pres., Fin., Mktg. & Pur. Mgr.
Telephone: 773-247-2530
Fax: 773-247-4907
Email: anchormxrs@aol.com / URL: http://www.chicago.i-challenge.com/anchormanufacturing
Product Service Description:
Mortar, plaster, refractory & terrazzo mixing machinery
Construction machinery

Anchor Printing & Graphics
4100 S West Temple
Salt Lake City, UT 84107-1428
Contact: Tanya Henrie, Pres.
Telephone: 801-265-1400
Fax: 801-265-1771
Email: anchorapg@worldnet.att.net / URL:
Product Service Description:
Commercial printing, lithographic and offset; prints multicolor brochures, flyers and news
Direct Mail Advertising Services

Anchor Tool & Die Company
13159 Stephens Drive
Warren, MI 48089
Contact: Vincent Swick, President
Telephone: 810-757-8420
Fax: 810-757-4421
Email: anchortool@americtech.net / URL: http://www.anchortool.com
Product Service Description:
Stamping Dies

Ancor Communications
6130 Blue Circle Dr
Minnetonka, MN 55343-9109
Contact: Cal Nelson, Pres.
Telephone: 612-932-4000
Fax: 612-932-4037
Email: info@ancor.com / URL: http://www.ancor.com
Product Service Description:
Electronic Switches
Fibre Channel Switches
Storage Area Networks

Andersen Rack Systems Inc
1821 E Charter Way
Stockton, CA 95205-7013
Contact: Bob Andersen, CEO
Telephone: 209-948-8023
Product Service Description:
Partitions & fixtures, except wood
Manufactures racking for pallets
Cautilever racks

Anderson Bakery Company, Inc.
2060 Old Philadelphia Pike
Lancaster, PA 17602
Contact: Donald J. Long, President
Telephone: 717-299-2321
Fax: 717-393-3511
Product Service Description:
Pretzel Manufacturer

Anderson Seal Co., Inc.
PO Box 351
Rochester, IL 62563-0351
Contact: Sales & Marketing,
Telephone: 217-529-0217
Fax: 217-529-9439
Product Service Description:
Embeded Rubber Seals for Concrete Pipe
Pipe Joint Testers & Plugs for Sewers
Custom Engineered Seals
Consultant Engineering & Production
Plastic Steel Manhole Steps

Anderson-Bell Corporation
PO Box 745160
Arvada, CO 80006-5160
Contact: Edwin R. Anderson, Pres.
Telephone: 303-940-0595
Fax: 303-940-0595
Email: abell@rmi.net / URL: http://www.andersonbell.com
Product Service Description:
Develops prepackaged research software & surveys
Prepackaged software

Andrew M Martin Company Inc
16539 S Main St
Gardena, CA 90248-2720
Contact: Cliff Miller, V-P.
Telephone: 310-323-2000
Fax: 310-323-2265
Product Service Description:
Manufactures sample and single use sized plastic packages for cosmetic and industrial products : Plastic products

Andwin Corporation
6636 Variel Avenue
Canoga Park, CA 91303
Contact: Marla Rosenthal, Pres.
Telephone: 818-999-2828
Fax: 818-999-0111
Email: info@andwin.com / URL: http://
www.andwin.com
Product Service Description:
Manufacturer of medical collection products
Medical & Hospital Equipment

Andwin Corporation
PO Box 151
Canoga Park, CA 91305-0151
Contact: Abner Levy, Pres.
Telephone: 818-999-1888
Fax: 818-999-0111
Email: mrosen0555@aol.com / URL: http://
www.andwin.com
Product Service Description:
Advanced Medical Collection Products
Medical & hospital equipment including kits
& supplies

Angelus Sanitary Can Machine
4900 Pacific Blvd
Los Angeles, CA 90058-2214
Contact: Richard Cabori, VP Marketing
Telephone: 323-583-2171
Fax: 323-587-5607
Email: angelus@angelusmachines.com /
URL: http://www.angelusmachine.com
Product Service Description:
Manufactures can closing machinery
Can Seamers

Angelus Sanitary Can Machine Co.
4900 Pacific Blvd.
Los Angeles, CA 90058
Contact: Maury Koeberle, President & CEO
Telephone: 323-583-2171
Fax: 323-587-5607
Email: angelus@angelusmachine.com / URL:
http://www.angelusmachine.com
Product Service Description:
Can Seamers

Anguil Environmental Systems, Inc.
8855 N 55th St
Milwaukee, WI 53223-2311
Contact: Christopher Anguil, Dir. of Sales
Telephone: 414-365-6400 / 1800-488-0230
Fax: 414-365-6410
Email: sales@anguil.com
URL: http://www.anguil.com
Product Service Description:
Odor & pollution control equipment
Blowers & fans

Ani-Helser
8823 N Harborgate St
Portland, OR 97203-6316
Contact: John J Snyder, Pres.
Telephone: 503-227-6591
Fax: 503-227-5732
Email: johns@anihelser.com / URL:
Product Service Description:
Manufactures crushers and crusher
replacement parts for mines and quarries
Mining machinery
Construction & mining machinery
Industrial machinery
Repair services

Anicom Inc.
6133 N. River Road
Rosemont, IL 60018
Contact: Daryl Spinell, Vice President Sales
Telephone: 800-889-9473
Email: / URL: http://www.anicommm.com
Product Service Description:
Insulated wire, cable; Opt sheath fib cables
Stranded wire, ropes and cables, not
electrically insulated, of iron or steel
Transmission apparatus incorporating
reception apparatus for radiotelephony,
radiotelegraphy

Anillo Industries Inc
PO Box 5586
Orange, CA 92863-5586
Contact: William J Koch, Pres.
Telephone: 714-637-7000
Fax: 714-637-3022
Product Service Description:
Manufactures aircraft washers
Bolts, nuts, rivets & washers

Animal Health Sales, Inc.
PO Box 127
Teachey, NC 28464-0127
Contact: Don Blake,
Telephone: 910-285-2144
Fax: 910-285-3594
Email: ahs@duplin.net / URL: http://
www.animalhealthsales.com
Product Service Description:
Animal Health Supplies
Feeds, Prepared

Animated Mfg. Co.
PO Box 448
South Holland, IL 60473-0448
Contact: A. E. White, Chrm., CEO
Telephone: 708-333-6688
Fax: 708-333-6692
Email: awhite1019@aol.com / URL:
Product Service Description:
Metal stampings & four slide & spot welding

Ann Edgar
414 E. Magnetic St.
Marquette, MI 49855
Contact: Ann Edgar, *
Fax: 906-228-7315
Email: ctcf84c@prodigy.com / URL:
Product Service Description:
Translation Services

**Anniston Plating & Metal Finishing,
Inc.**
PO Box 4279
Anniston, AL 36204-4279
Contact: James G. Grace, Pres., Engrg. Mgr.
Telephone: 256-236-8641
Fax: 256-236-0673
Email: / URL:
Product Service Description:
Heavy industrial chrome & copper plating &
grinding
Plating & polishing

Annual Reviews Inc
PO Box 10139
Palo Alto, CA 94303-0139
Contact: John Harpster, Marketing Manager
Telephone: 650-493-4400
Fax: 650-855-9815
Email: service@annurev.org / URL: http://
www.annualreviews.org
Product Service Description:
Publishes scientific books in the biological,
medical physical & social sciences

Ano-Coil Corp.
PO Box 1318
Vernon Rockville, CT 06066-1318
Contact: Timothy Fromson, VP
Telephone: 860-871-1200
Fax: 860-872-0534
Email: fromson@ibm.net / URL:
Product Service Description:
Lithographic Printing Plates (Offset)
Platemaking Chemicals
Platemaking Machinery

Anthony International
12812 Arroyo St.
San Fernando, CA 91342
Contact: Kim Wheeler,
Telephone: 818-365-9451
Fax: 818-837-4997
Email: kimw@anthonydoors.com / URL:
http://www.anthonydoors.com
Product Service Description:
Manufactures commercial glass refrigerator
and freezer doors
Glass products from purchased glass
Merchandising equipment

Anti Hydro International, Inc.
45 River Rd
Flemington, NJ 08822-6036
Contact: Bruce Kreielsheimer, Opers. Mgr.
Telephone: 908-284-9000
Fax: 908-284-9464
Email: sales@anti-hydro.com / URL: http://
www.anti-hydro.com
Product Service Description:
Waterproffing materials, concrete admixtures,
epoxies : Curing compounds, hardeners,
toppings, underlayments
Abrasion resistant materials, coatings,
urethanes : Chemical resistant materials,
sealers, sealants : Architectural treatments,
patching & repairing material

Apature Products, Inc.
305 W. Lambert St.
Bunnell, FL 32110
Contact: John T. Slaga, Pres.
Telephone: 904-437-5530
Fax: 904-437-5316
Email: jslaga@apature.com / URL: http://
www.apature.com
Product Service Description:
Audio, stereo & video cables
Radio & TV communications equipment

Apax Corporation
380 Cliffwood Park St
Brea, CA 92821-4103
Contact: Hubert Schroeder, Pres.
Telephone: 714-256-6000
Fax: 714-256-6010
Email: hschroeder@versappl.com / URL:
http://www.versapply.com
Product Service Description:
Manufactures labeling machinery for
pressure-sensitive labels
Packaging machinery
Manufacture print & apply labeling machines

Apex Instruments
PO Box 727
Holly Springs, NC 27540-0727
Contact: William Howe, Pres.
Telephone: 919-557-7300
Fax: 919-557-7110
Email: apexinst@mindspring.com / URL:
http://www.apexinst.com
Product Service Description:
Smokestack emission monitoring equipment

Apollo
3610 Birch St, Suite 100
Newport Beach, CA 92660-2619
Contact: Burt Cook, Sales & Marketing
Telephone: 714-852-8178
Fax: 714-852-8172
Email: apollo@netbox.com / URL: http://
www.apollo-security.com
Product Service Description:
Process Control Equipment, Card Readers
Process Control Equipment, Access Control
Commercial Equipment, Alarm Systems
Software Design, Access / Alarm - Windows
95 : Commercial Equipment, Access/Alarm,
W/Colour Graphics

Apollo Energy
6800 Hickman Rd, Suite #5
Windsor Heights, IA 50322
Contact: Bret Roberts, Owner
Telephone: 515-270-5870
Product Service Description:
The Earth Flag
Products / Merchandise with Earth Flag Logo

Apollo Warehouse, Inc.
201 S. Kresson St.,
Baltimore, MD 21224
Contact: Roger Boschert, President
Telephone: 410-563-7400
Fax: 410-563-7476
Email: / URL:
Product Service Description:
Freight & Cargo Transportation
Trucking
Distribution
Packaging & Crating
Container freight station
Intermodal transportation
Import / Export Services

Apothecary Products Inc.
11750 - 12th Ave, South
Burnsville, MN 55337-7253
Contact: Sales & Marketing,
Telephone: 612-890-1940
Fax: 612-890-0418
Email: pillminder@aol.com / URL: http://
www.cornerdrug.com
Product Service Description:
Over the counter medications : Baby care
Patient Compliance Aids : First Aid Products
Eye care products : Medical ID jewelry

Appalachian Log Structures Inc.
P.O. Box 614
Ripley, WV 25271
Contact: Gary W. Jarrell, President
Telephone: 304-372-6410
Fax: 304-372-3154
Email: applog@citynet.net / URL: http://
www.applog.com
Product Service Description:
Precut Log Home Packages
Prefabricated Wood Buildings

Apparel Suppliers CA/Pagano W
687 Anita St
Chula Vista, CA 91911-4619
Contact: Frank Pagano, Pres.
Telephone: 619-423-8585
Fax: 619-423-5316
Email: ascpagano@aol.com /
paganowest@juno.com / URL:
Product Service Description:
Manufactures men's and women's clothing
and tailored western clothing
Clothing_men's & boys'
Outerwear_women's & misses'

Applied Telecomunications Inc.
4750 Bryant Irvin Rd. N., Ste. B
Fort Worth, TX 76107
Contact: Aidan Stack, President
Telephone: 817-763-5992
Fax: 817-763-5980
Email: aidan@earthsta.com / URL: http://www.earthsta.com
Product Service Description:
System Integrators, Satellite Earth Stations

Aqua Blast Corp.
PO Box 547
Decatur, IN 46733-0547
Contact: Robert Heyerly, Pres.,
Telephone: 219-728-4433
Fax: 219-728-4517
Email: iuablast@decaturnet.com / URL: http://www.aquablast.com
Product Service Description:
High-pressure cleaning systems
Service industry machinery

Aqua Jogger
PO Box 1453
Eugene, OR 97440-1453
Contact: Lewis Thorne, Pres.
Telephone: 541-484-2454
Fax: 541-484-0501
Email: Info@aquajogger.com / URL: http://www.aquajogger.com
Product Service Description:
Manufactures aqua jogger with fitness equipment and women's swimwear
Sporting & athletic goods

Aqua Power Co.
9419 E. San Salvador # 105
Scottsdale, AZ 85258
Contact: Gaylen Brotherson, President
Telephone: 602-391-9959
Fax: 602-391-2402
Product Service Description:
Countertop Water Filters
Fire Retardent Kitchen Cloths

Aqua Signal Corp.
1680 E Fabyan Pkwy
Batavia, IL 60510-1492
Contact: Ron Wiggerman, V-P.
Telephone: 630-232-6425
Fax: 630-232-9481
Email: aquasig@aol.com / URL:
Product Service Description:
Navigational boat lights : Search & navigation equipment : Boat Horns : Docking Lights
Portable Navigation Lights

Aqua-Flo, Inc.
6244 Frankford Ave
Baltimore, MD 21206-4994
Contact: Al Coke, President
Phone: 410-485-7600 / Fax: 410-488-2030
Email: aquaflo@erols.com / URL: http://www.thomasregister.com/aquaflo
Product Service Description:
Water Treatment & Air Purification Equipment, Chemical Free

AquaTec, Inc.
1235 Shappert Dr
Rockford, IL 61115-1417
Contact: Richard J. Ryan, Pres
Telephone: 815-654-1500
Fax: 815-654-0038
Email: rjraqua@aol.com
Product Service Description:
Aeration & waste water treatment systems & equipment : Service industry machinery

Aquacare Environment Inc
1155 N State St Ste 303
Bellingham, WA 98225-5024
Contact: Henning Gatz, Pres.
Telephone: 360-734-7964
Fax: 360-734-9407
Email: ecologic@aquacare.com / URL: http://www.aquacare.com
Product Service Description:
Manufactures machines and equipment for the Controlled environment, agriculture and aquaculture

Aquamatch Inc
22732 Granite Way Unit C
Laguna Hills, CA 92653-1202
Contact: Imad Yassine, Pres.
Telephone: 949-472-8166
Fax: 949-472-9315
Email: imad@aquamatch.com / URL: http://www.aquamatch.com
Product Service Description:
Manufactures Reverse osmosis water desalination systems

Aquapower Co.
9420 E. Doubletree Ranch Rd., Ste. C-101
Scottsdale, AZ 85258-5508
Contact: Gaylen Brotherson, President
Telephone: 602-391-9959
Fax: 602-391-2402
Email: / URL:
Product Service Description:
Mist Bottles
Fire Retardent Kitchen Cloths
Countertop Water Filters
Under-The-Counter Water Filter

Aquatic Eco-Sysytems Inc.
1767 Benbow Ct.
Apopka, FL 32703
Contact: Sales Dept.,
Telephone: 407-886-3939
Fax: 407-886-6787
Email: qes@aquaticeco.com / URL: http://www.aquaticeco.com
Product Service Description:
Aquaculture Equipment & Supplies

Aquion Partners, L.P.
2080 Lunt Ave
Elk Grove Village, IL 60007-5633
Contact: Sales & Marketing,
Telephone: 847-437-9400 / 1800-Rainsoft
Fax: 847-437-1594
Email: markserv@rainsoft.com / URL: http://www.rainsoft.com
Product Service Description:
Water Treatment Systems, Manufacturer of Rainsoft
Water Filtration & Purification

Arabel
16301 N.W. 49th Ave.
Hialeah, FL 33014-6316
Contact: Howard Rothman, President
Telephone: 305-623-8302
Fax: 305-624-0714
Email: arabel@iconect.net / URL: http://www.arabel.com
Product Service Description:
Vertical blinds : Wood blinds
Mini blinds
Fabrics / vertical blinds
PVC / Vertical blinds
Romin wood / 2" horizontal blinds
Components / vertical blinds, wood blinds, mini blinds
Foamwood

Arbiter Systems Inc
1324 Vendels Circle, Suite 121
Paso Robles, CA 93446
Contact: Steven L. Myers, North America Mktg. Mgr.
Telephone: 805-237-3831
Fax: 805-238-5717
Email: sales@arbiter.com / URL: http://www.arbiter.com
Product Service Description:
GPS satellite controlled clocks
Calibration Equipment
Power system analyzers
Revenue meter standards

Arbon Steel & Service, Inc.
2355 Bond St
Park Forest, IL 60466-3121
Contact: Daniel R. O'Connor, CEO
Telephone: 708-534-6800
Fax: 708-534-6826
Email: arbon@interaccess.com / URL:
Product Service Description:
Steel Service Center - Tin Mill Products

Arcadia Chair Company
5692 Fresca Dr
La Palma, CA 90623-1048
Contact: Casey Journigan, Pres.
Telephone: 714-562-8200
Fax: 714-562-8202
Email: / URL:
Product Service Description:
Manufactures wood office furniture
Office furniture_wood

Architectural Building Components
11625 N Houston Rosslyn Rd
Houston, TX 77086-3601
Contact: Charles Smith Jr., Pres., MIS, R & D, Sales & Mktg. Mgr.
Telephone: 281-931-3986
Fax: 281-931-3989
Email: archbldn@firstnethou.com / URL:
Product Service Description:
Sheet metal roofing materials

Architectural Windows & Entries, Inc.
2031 5th Ave. S.
Saint Petersburg, FL 33712-1642
Contact: Michael Zajac-Batell, Pres., Opers. Mgr.
Telephone: 727-821-1333
Fax: 727-821-1333
Email: mzb@architecturalwindows.com / URL: http://www.architecturalwindows.com
Product Service Description:
Wooden windows, entry ways & trim profiles
Millwork

Area Detectors Systems Corp
12550 Stowe Dr
Poway, CA 92064-6804
Contact: Ronald C Hamlin, Pres.
Telephone: 619-486-0444
Fax: 619-486-0722
Email: / URL:
Product Service Description:
Manufactures medical research area detectors and CCD equipment (X-ray defraction equipment)
Surgical & medical instruments
X-ray apparatus & tubes

Aresco, Inc.
5650 E. Seltice Way
Post Falls, ID 83854-7715
Contact: Alex Ritter, President
Telephone: 208-664-9291
Fax: 208-664-9475
Email: admin@arescoinc.com / URL:
Product Service Description:
Mining Machinery : Motor vehicles for the transport of goods : Road tractors for semi-trailers : Moving, grading, leveling, excavating, extracting machinery for earth, minerals or ores : Lube trucks fuel trucks, firetrucks : Service & mechanics trucks for mining & construction

Argents Express Group
200 Sam Miller River Rd.,
Hawthorne, NY 10532
Contact: Joe Chiappetta, Station Manager
Telephone: 914-773-0116
Fax:
Email: / URL:
Product Service Description:
Customs Broker
Freight Forwarder
Freight & Cargo Transportation

Argus International, Inc.
11700 Nw 101st Rd Ste 17
Medley, FL 33178-1019
Contact: Roberto Bequillard, Pres.
Telephone: 305-888-4881
Fax: 305-888-0041
Email: argus@worldnet.att.com / URL:
Product Service Description:
Clothing pattern fabric cutting, apparel / manufacturing
Men's & boy's shirts, pants & knit tops.

Ariel Corp.
35 Blackjack Rd.
Mount Vernon, OH 43050
Contact: Philip Noland, V.P. Int'l Sales
Telephone: 740-397-0311
Fax: 740-397-3856
Email: / URL:
Product Service Description:
Reciprocating Natural Gas Compressors

Ariens Company
655 W. Ryan St.
Brillion, WI 54110-1072
Contact: Daniel T. Ariens, President
Telephone: 920-756-2141
Fax: 920-756-2407
Email: info@ariens.com / URL: http://www.ariens.com
Product Service Description:
Snow Throwers, Riding Mowers, Tillers, Garden Tractors, Lawn Mowers, Chippers & Vacuums
Farm Machinery & Equipment

Arista Industries, Inc.
1082 Post Rd.
Darien, CT 06820
Contact: Steve Weitzer, President
Telephone: 203-655-0881
Fax: 203-656-0328
Email: aristaind@aol.com / URL: http://www.members.aol.com/arisind/aristapg.htm
Product Service Description:
Vegetable / Nut Oils
Marine / Fish Oils
Sesame Oil
Frozen Seafood

Aristocrat Industries, Inc.
PO Box 1117
Mount Vernon, OH 43050-8117
Contact: Robert A. Peters, President
Telephone: 740-393-2121
Fax: 740-393-2200
Email: aristocrat@ecr.net / URL: http://
www.aristocrat.com
Product Service Description:
Chalk Bulletin & Marker Boards

Arizona Daily Star
4850 S Park Ave
Tucson, AZ 85714-1637
Contact: Stephen Auslander, Editor
Telephone: 520-573-4400
Product Service Description:
Publishes daily newspaper (editorial
department)
Newspapers

**Arlon Engineered Laminates &
Coatings Division**
199 Amaral Street
East Providence, RI 02915
Contact: Eric Kleinschmidt, Business Mgr.
Telephone: 800-323-0168
Fax: 401-434-2557
Email: ericep@ix.netcom.com / URL: http://
www.arlon.net
Product Service Description:
Paper, Coated & Laminated

**Arlon Materials for Electronics
Division**
1100 Govenor Lea Road
Bear, DE 19701
Contact: Donna J. Weber, Customer Service
Manager
Telephone: 800-635-9333
Fax: 302-834-2574
Email: arloncs@aol.com / URL: http://
www.arlonmed.com
Product Service Description:
Printed Circuit Laminates

Arlon Silicone Technology Division
1100 Govenor Lea Road
Bear, DE 19701
Contact: Taral Shah, Product Manager
Telephone: 800-635-9333
Fax: 302-834-4021
Email: productmgr@arlonstd.com / URL:
http://www.arlonstd.com
Product Service Description:
Fabricated Rubber Products

Armature Coil Equipment Inc.
4725 Manufacturing Ave
Cleveland, OH 44135-2639
Contact: Scott Heran,
Telephone: 216-267-6366
Fax: 216-267-4361
Product Service Description:
Industrial Heat Cleaning Ovens
Elec. Ind. Coil Winding Machinery

Armstrong Teasdale
One Metropolitan Square, #2700
St. Louis, MO 63102
Contact: Thomas H. Bottini, Partner, Lilian
Castellani de Fernandez, Counsel
Telephone: 314-621-5070
Fax: 314-621-5065
Product Service Description:
Legal Services
Business Services
International Consulting Svcs.
Lilian Castellani de Fernandez, Counsel

Arnet Pharmaceutical Corp.
5900 Miami Lakes Drive
Miami Lakes, FL 33014
Contact: Elsa Ospiua, V.P. Int. Sales
Telephone: 305/558-2929
Fax: 305/558-4844
Email: / URL:
Product Service Description:
Natural Vitamins
Pharmaceuticals, Health & Beauty
Medicinal Minerals

Arno International, Inc.
330 S. State road 7 Suite B
Plantation, FL 33317-3737
Contact: Giandomeni Franci, President
Telephone: 959-583-8111
Fax: 959-583-8119
Email: arnoint@gate.net / URL: http://
www.gat.net/~arnoint/
Product Service Description:
Parts & Components for Frames
Accessories
Reading Glasses, Export
Vigor / Grobet Tools
Displays
Sunglasses, Export
Eye Glasses Frames, Export
Optometric Equipment, Export

Aromaland, Inc.
1326 Rufina Cir
Santa Fe, NM 87505-2927
Contact: Ralf Moller, Pres. / CEO
Telephone: 505-438-0402
Fax: 505-438-7223
Email: info@aromaland.com / URL: http://
www.aromaland.com
Product Service Description:
Essential Oils Products
Body Care Products

Arrow Creative International, Ltd.
652 Glenbrook Rd Ste 3
Stamford, CT 06906-1410
Contact: Mack Ghadiyali, Pres., Pur. Agt.
Telephone: 203-323-3790
Fax: 203-353-8282
Email: asp2005@aol.com / URL:
Product Service Description:
Textile screen printing & embroidery
Automotive & apparel trimmings
Pleating & stitching
Custom labels
Digitizing

Arrow Engineering Inc.
PO Box 1795
Dalton, GA 30722-1795
Contact: Robet B. Collier, Pres., CFO
Telephone: 706-226-5054
Fax: 706-226-8233
Email: / URL:
Product Service Description:
Textile chemicals
Chemicals_industrial inorganic

Arrow Truck Saels Inc.
3200 Manchester Trfy
Kansas City, MO 64129-1336
Contact: Jerome Nerman, Chairman
Telephone: 816-923-5000
Fax: 816-923-9000
Email: jnerman@arrowtruck.com / URL:
http://www.arrowtruck.com
Product Service Description:
Used Trucks & Trailers, Wholesale

Arrowhead Athletics
PO BOX 4264, 220 Andover St.
Andover, MA 01810-0814
Contact: Walter Nugent, Marketing Mgr.
Telephone: 978-470-1760
Fax: 978-475-8603
Email: aatape@aol.com / URL:
Product Service Description:
Athletic Tape Adhesive/Moleskin Adhesive
Athletic Foam Pretape Wrap/Felt

Arrowhead Systems LLC
PO Box 2408
Oshkosh, WI 54903-2408
Contact: Nick C. Osterholt, VP Sale & Mktg.
Telephone: 920-235-5562
Fax: 920-235-3638
Email: mail@arrowheadconveyor.com / URL:
Product Service Description:
Conveyors & conveying equipment
Conveyors
Ionized Air & Water Rinsers
Singl Filer
Gripper Elevator / Lowerator
Controls

Art Institute Glitter
720 N Balboa St
Cottonwood, AZ 86326-4016
Contact: Barbara Trombley, Owner
Telephone: 520-639-0805
Fax: 520-639-4699
Email: artinst@sedona.net / URL: http://
www.artglitter.com
Product Service Description:
Manufactures craft supplies
Mfr. Adhesives

Art Leather Manufacturing Co., Inc.
4510 94th St.
Elmhurst, NY 11373-2873
Contact: Mark H. Roberts, President
Telephone: 718-699-6300 / 888-252-5286
Fax: 718-699-9339 / 800-88-ALBUM
Email: / URL: http://www.artleather.com
Product Service Description:
Blankbooks and Looseleaf Binders
Albums of paper or paperboard

Art's Manufacturing & Supply Inc
105 Harrison St
American Falls, ID 83211-1230
Contact: Tom Von Berg, VP Mktg. & Sales
Telephone: 208-226-2017
Fax: 208-226-7280
Email: tvb@ams-samplers.com / URL: http://
www.ams-samplers.com
Product Service Description:
Sampling equipment for soil, soil gas &
groundwater
Direct push soil sampling systems
(PowerProbe)
Cone penetrometer testing (CPT) equipment
& direct push tooling
Groundwater sampling & monitoring
equipment

Art, Inc.
301 N 3rd St
Coeur D Alene, ID 83814-2861
Contact: Nancy Lynne, Pres., CEO
Telephone: 208-664-4204 / 800-482-4433
Fax: 208-664-1316
Email: nancyl@chiefarch.com / URL: http://
www.chiefarch.com
Product Service Description:
Develops prepackaged architectural software

Artco
1 Stationery Pl
Rexburg, ID 83440-3567
Contact: Debbie Rydalch,
Telephone: 208-359-1000
Fax: 208-356-9395
Product Service Description:
Lithographic printing_commercial
Manufactures custom wedding invitations;
commercial and personal stationery for
wholesaler

Artcrete, Inc.
5812 Hwy 494
Natchitoches, LA 71457
Contact: Frank Piccolo, Pres.
Telephone: 318-379-2000
Fax: 318-379-1000
Email: artcrete@cp-tel.net / URL: http://
www.artcrete.com
Product Service Description:
Brick stencils & concrete color hardener
Chemical preparations

Artech Industries Inc
1966 Keats Dr
Riverside, CA 92501-1747
Contact: Joe Juarez,
Telephone: 909-276-3331
Fax: 909-276-4556
Email: artechind@msn.com / URL:
Product Service Description:
Manufactures load cells for scales
Electronic components

Artemis Industries Inc.
2550 Gilchrist Rd
Akron, OH 44305-4405
Contact: Patricia M. Geiger, CEO, Pur. Agt.
Telephone: 330-798-8991
Fax: 330-798-8995
Email: plasticefx@aol.com / URL: http://
www.artemisindustries.com
Product Service Description:
Plastic & Rubber Raw Materials

Artex Aircraft Supplies Inc
PO Box 1270
Canby, OR 97013-1270
Contact: Ken Stucki, Sales Mgr.
Telephone: 503-266-3959
Fax: 503-266-3362
Email: kens@artex.net / URL: http://
www.artex.net
Product Service Description:
Manufactures emergency locator transmitters
for aircraft : Manufactures Emergency
Locator Transmitter for Liferafts

Artis Metals Company Inc
3323 Chinden Blvd
Boise, ID 83714-6638
Contact: John Lilly, Pres., GM
Telephone: 208-336-1560
Fax: 208-343-9679
Product Service Description:
Sheet metal work, HVAC caps and flashings,
reducers and plugs, ventilators (non-powered)

Artisan Controls Corporation (Mfr)
P.O. Box 233
Parsippany, NJ 07054
Contact: Leigh A. Stevens, Director of Sales
Phone: 973-428-1770 / Fax: 973-428-1426
Email: artisanlei@aol.com
Product Service Description:
Solid State Timing Devices
Controllers, Temperature
Timers for Industrial Use

Artisan Golf
1458 Mt Highway 35 # 2
Kalispell, MT 59901-2916
Contact: Dan J. Nynne, Sales
Telephone: 406-257-8080
Fax: 406-257-9099
Email: artisan@bigsky.net / URL: http://
www.kalispell.bigsky.net/artisan
Product Service Description:
Hand-crafted, custom built golf clubs
Sporting & athletic goods

Artistica, Inc.
1313 Kalakaua Ave
Honolulu, HI 96826-1909
Contact: Stephen Kari, Pres.
Telephone: 808-941-1111
Fax: 808-943-0776
Email: sales@artistica.net / URL: http://
www.artistica.net
Product Service Description:
Jewelry, precious metal, manufacturing

Ase Supply Inc
2321 NE Argyle St Ste C
Portland, OR 97211-1962
Contact: Sandy A Ayers Jr, Pres.
Telephone: 503-288-4866
Fax: 503-288-4328
Email: ase@asesupply.com / URL: http://
www.asesupply.com
Product Service Description:
Distributes heavy duty truck, industrial &
marine auto electric products
Small air-cooled engines & parts

Ashland Chemical
1 Drew Plz.
Boonton, NJ 07005-1924
Contact: Sales & Marketing
Telephone: 973-263-7600
Fax: 973-263-4483
Email: kmjohnson@ashland.com
 URL: http://www.ashchem.com
Product Service Description:
Surface active agents : Water Treatment
Chemicals : Additives for Paint, Latex
Mining Antisealants : Waste Water Treatment
Cooling Water Treatment : Boiler Water
Treatment : Fuel Treatment

Ashlock Company
PO Box 1676
San Leandro, CA 94577-0398
Contact: Thomas A Rettagliata, Pres.
Telephone: 510-351-0560
Fax: 510-357-0329
Product Service Description:
Manufactures food processing machinery—
cherry, olive, date and prune pitters and olive
slicers : Food products machinery

**Ashton Food Machinery Co., Inc.,
Neumunz Div.**
1455 McCarter Hwy.
Newark, NJ 07104
Contact: Larry Oberman,
Telephone: 973-483-8518
Fax: 973-483-0200
Email: loberman@ashtonfood.com / URL:
http://www.ashtonfood.com
Product Service Description:
Peanut Plant Design & Machinery Sales
Peanut Blanching Equipment
Peanut Butter Plant Design & Sales
Drying & Cooling Tables
Cashew Can Openers
Volumetric Fillers

Ashwell Die Corp.
6545 44th St Ste 4003
Pinellas Park, FL 33781-0900
Contact: Howard Clark, V-P.
Telephone: 813-527-0098
Fax: 813-527-0991
Email: / URL:
Product Service Description:
Flatbed steel rule label dies
Magnetic flexible label dies

Aspects Inc
PO Box 1799
Redlands, CA 92373-0561
Contact: Ralf G Zacky, Pres., CEO
Telephone: 909-794-7722
Fax: 909-794-6996
Email: rgzacky@aol.com / URL: http://
www.bristolfurniture.com
Product Service Description:
Manufactures office furniture
Office furniture, except wood

**Aspen Foods, a division of Koch
Poultry**
1115 W Fulton Market
Chicago, IL 60607-1213
Contact: Michael Fields, Pres.
Telephone: 312-829-7282
Fax: 312-829-2570
Email: / URL:
Product Service Description:
Frozen chicken products
Poultry slaughtering & processing

Associated Plastics Inc
2626 Kansas Ave
Riverside, CA 92507-2600
Contact: Mike Loran, President & CEO
Telephone: 909-787-0600
Fax: 909-778-3960
Email: / URL: http://www.quikset.com
Product Service Description:
Manufactures composite plastic enclosures
for underground utilities

Astechnologies
950 Sun Valley Dr., P.O. Box 395
Roswell, GA 30076-1418
Contact: Art Simmons, CEO
Telephone: 770-993-5100
Fax: 770-993-8379
Email: @astechnologies.com / URL: http://
www.astechnologies.com
Product Service Description:
Industrial Machinery and Equipment
Parts for sewing machines
Machinery parts, not containing electrical
connectors, insulators, coils, contacts
Machines and mechanical appliances having
individual functions

**Astro Enterprises Int'l., Inc. (Mfr) /
Distributor**
37 Pemberton Drive
Matawan, NJ 07747-9712
Contact: Robert G. Antonelli, *
Telephone: 732-566-2949
Fax: 732-583-7134
Email: salesczar1@aol.com / URL:
Product Service Description:
Synthetic Lubricants & Greases
Super Lube Engine Treatments & Additives
Super Lube Products
Automotive Engine Treatments
Machining & Component Manufacturing
Glues Adhesives

Astro Optics Corp.
156 Williams St
Carpentersville, IL 60110-1839
Contact: Arthur P. Schueler Jr., Pres.
Telephone: 847-428-3181
Fax: 847-428-3979
Email: astroopt@aol.com / URL: http://
www.astrooptics.com
Product Service Description:
Highway reflectors, reflective lenses &
pavement markers

Astrup Co. (Distributor)
2937 W. 25th St.
Cleveland, OH 44113
Contact: G.A. Faubel, Senior V.P.
Telephone: 216-696-2820
Fax: 216-696-0977
Email: / URL: http://www.astrup.com
Product Service Description:
Industrial Fabrics, Hardware & Trimming
Items.

Atco Pallet Co.
PO Box 5105
Delanco, NJ 08075-0505
Contact: David Hajduk, Pres.
Telephone: 609-461-8141
Fax: 609-461-8146
Email: atcopallet@juno.com / URL:
Product Service Description:
Wooden pallets

Athearn Inc
19010 Laurel Park Rd
Compton, CA 90220-6007
Contact: Bob Macias, Chairman of the Board
Telephone: 310-631-3400
Fax: 310-885-5296
Email: athearn@athearn.com / URL: http://
www.athearn.com
Product Service Description:
Manufactures miniature hobby trains

Athens Industries, Inc.
PO Box 487
Southington, CT 06489-0487
Contact: Richard Emmings, Pres.
Telephone: 860-621-8957
Fax: 860-621-2669
Email: jlbrhe@aol.com / URL:
Product Service Description:
Helicopter parts
Aircraft parts & equipment

Atkins Machinery Inc.
PO Box 3487
Spartanburg, SC 29304-3487
Contact: Robert Atkins, Pres.
Telephone: 864-574-8433
Fax: 864-574-1466
Email: robert@atkinsmachinery.com / URL:
http://www.atkinsmachinery.com
Product Service Description:
Used textile machinery

Atlantic Cold Storage Corporation
18770 N.E. 6th Ave.
Miami, FL 33179-3916
Contact: Dave Cochran, Warehouse Manager
Telephone: 305-652-4622, ext. 206
Fax: 305-653-6420
Email: / URL:
Product Service Description:
Freght Forwarder
Freight & Cargo Transportation
Frozen & Refrigerated Storage
Bonded Storage
Freight Consolidation

Atlantic Machine Tools Inc.
11629 N. Houston Rosslyn Rd.
Houston, TX 77086
Telephone: 713/445-3985
Fax: 713/445-3989
Email: / URL:
Product Service Description:
Hydr. Press Brakes & Shears,
Punch Press Machinery, Cold Saws
Ironworking Machinery
Ind. Laser Cutting Equp.

**Atlantic Pacific Automotive
International**
P.O. Box 381900
Germantown, TN 38183-1900
Contact: Don DeBaer, *
Telephone: 901-757-5700
Fax: 901-753-3777
Email: ddebaer@apparts.com / URL: http://
www.apparts.com
Product Service Description:
Aftermarket, Automotive Parts for American
Cars : Automotive Chemical Additives &
Chemical Fillers

**Atlantic Research Corp., Unit of
Sequa Corp.**
5945 Wellington Road
Gainesville, VA 20155
Contact: J.R. Sides, *
Telephone: 703-754-5601
Fax: 703-754-5120
Email: / URL:
Product Service Description:
Rocket Motors
Gas Generators
Automotive Air Bag Inflators
Liquid Propulsion Thruster Systems

Atlantic Wire Co., The
1 Church St
Branford, CT 06405-3839
Contact: J.W. "Bud" Mathews, VP Sales &
Mktg.
Telephone: 203-488-8331
Fax: 203-488-0740
Email: / URL:
Product Service Description:
Steel wire
Steel wire & related products
Steel wire, Cold Heading Quality
Steel wire, copper & liquor coated
Steel wire, Rivet Quality

Atlas Bolt & Screw Company (Mfr)
1628 Troy Road
Ashland, OH 44805
Contact: Hal Nygaard, *
Telephone: 419/289-6171
Fax: 419-289-2564
Email: / URL:
Product Service Description:
Self-Drilling Screws
Thread Forming Screws, Stainless Steel
Thread Forming Screws, Carbon Steel

Atlas Chemical Corporation (MFR)
P.O. Box 504
Marion, IA 52302
Contact: Ward M. Vanderpool, Board
Chairman
Telephone: 319/377-8921
Fax: 319-377-2419
Email: / URL:
Product Service Description:
Rodenticide, Rodent Gassers, "The Giant
Destroyer"

Atlas/Soundolier, Atapco Security & Communcations Group
1859 Intertech Dr.
Fenton, MO 63026-1926
Contact: Sindi Schubert, *
Telephone: 314-349-3110
Fax: 314-349-1251
Email: info@atlas-soundolier.com / URL:
http://www.atlas-soundolier.com
Product Service Description:
Commercial Loudspeakers, Baffles &
Enclosures
Compression Drivers & Horns
Commercial Sound Accessories

Atomco Corporation , Tru-Mark International
20819 S Western Ave
Torrance, CA 90501-1804
Contact: Jeff Adler, Pres, CEO
Telephone: 310-320-5950
Fax: 310-320-5244
Email: / URL:
Product Service Description:
Manufacturer of coding & marking devices
Pneumatic & roll markers

Atwood Richards
99 Park Ave., 15th Fl.
New York, NY 10016-1503
Contact: Moreton Binn, President, Richard
Guarino, Vice President
Telephone: 212-455-1772
Fax: 212-455-1572
Email: rguarino@arintl.com / URL: http://
www.atwoodrichards.com
Product Service Description:
Food all types: candy cookies cereal
condiments canned goods
Apparel: men women children shoes sneakers
tops pants coats : Electronics: radio stereo
television audio video tapes cassettes
Sporting Goods: exercise equipment
Consumer Products: all packaged consumer
goods : Medical supplies : Hardware: Wall &
floor coverings tools building material

Aubrey Organics Inc.
4419 N. Manhattan Ave.
Tampa, FL 33614-7688
Contact: Susan Hussey, VP International
Telephone: 813-877-4186
Fax: 813-876-8166
Email: aubreyorg@aol.com / URL: http://
www.aubrey-organics.com
Product Service Description:
GPB Hair Conditioner & Nutrient
Herbal Facial Astringent
Blue Camomile Shampoo
Rosa Mosqueta Rose Hip Moistuurizing
Cream
Cleanser, Natural & Herbal Facial

Audico Label Corp.
8313 W. Grand Ave.
River Grove, IL 60171-1434
Contact: Barbara Deletzke, Pres., Mktg. &
Pur. Mgr.
Telephone: 708-456-0003
Fax: 708-456-0418
Email: audicolabell@juno.com / URL:
Product Service Description:
Audio, video & compact disc labels & audio
cassette timers & rewinding equipment
Audio, Video, CD Duplication

Audioplex Technology, Inc.
404 Governer Wentworth Hwy.
Melvin Village, NH 03850
Contact: Ronald Ingham, Pres.
Telephone: 603-544-8601
Fax: 603-544-8901
Email: audioplex@conknet.com / URL: http://
www.audioplex.com
Product Service Description:
Office intercom & speaker systems
Audio & video equipment_household
Communications equipment, nec

Audubon Park Co
49 Main Ave.
Akron, CO 80720
Contact: Matt Ashley, Sales
Telephone: 970-345-2063
Fax: 970-345-2067
Email: audubon@audubonpark.com / URL:
http://www.audubonpark.com
Product Service Description:
Manufactures wild bird food

Auger Fabrication
418 Creamery Way
Exton, PA 19341-2500
Contact: Glenn Edginton, Pres.
Telephone: 610-524-3350
Fax: 610-363-2821
Email: info@auger-fab.com / URL: http://
www.augerfab.com
Product Service Description:
Steel fabrication, augers & machine parts

Aunt Rita's, Inc.
2845 W Picacho Ave
Las Cruces, NM 88005-4722
Contact: Rita Dobie, Pres.
Telephone: 505-524-4700
Fax: 505-527-5610
Email: jjernigan@compuserve.com / URL:
Product Service Description:
Dehydrated Mexican food mixes
Dehydrated fruits, vegetables & soups

Aurora Custom Machining
1041 Grace Ave
Aurora, IL 60506-5816
Contact: Jerry G. Calvin, Pres., Pur., R & D,
Sales & Mktg. Mgr.
Telephone: 630-859-2638
Fax: 630-859-0091
Product Service Description:
Precision machining job shop
Industrial machinery

Aurora Systems, Inc.
2117 Old Union Rd
Cheektowaga, NY 14227-2722
Contact: Paul Levesque, Ex. V-P.
Telephone: 716-668-0115
Fax: 716-668-0350
Email: asisales@auroracranes.com / URL:
http://www.auroracranes.com
Product Service Description:
Overhead cranes : Hoists, cranes & monorails
Stacker Cranes

Austin Continental Industries, Inc.
3636 N Talman Ave
Chicago, IL 60618-4711
Contact: Frank Juzwik, Pres.
Phone: 773-528-9200 / Fax: 773-528-9206
Product Service Description:
Aerospace precision & CNC machining,
turning, drilling & grinding job shop
Aircraft, parts. Pistons, Pumps, Etc.
Forward - Auger Extruding Heads, Etc.

Authentic Mexican Imports
5161 W. 167th St.
Oak Forest, IL 60452
Contact: Laura Bratlien, *
Telephone: 708-560-9007
Fax: 708-560-9008
Email: authenticmexicanimports@ibm.net /
URL: http://www.a-mexican-imports.com
Product Service Description:
Dinnerware
Pottery

Auto Crane Co.
PO Box 581510
Tulsa, OK 74158-1510
Contact: Joe E. Henry, Pres.
Telephone: 918-836-0463
Fax: 918-834-5979
Email: / URL: http://www.autocrane.com
Product Service Description:
Hoists, cranes & monorails
Cranes, crane bodies & air compressors

Autogate
PO Box 50
Berlin Heights, OH 44814-0050
Contact: Robert Rodwancy, CEO
Telephone: 419-588-2796
Fax: 419-588-3514
Email: autogate@nwohio.com / URL: http://
www.autogate.com
Product Service Description:
Stand-alone battery-powered security gate
systems
Electrical equipment & supplies

Automated Applications Inc
5212 Kazuko Ct
Moorpark, CA 93021-1789
Contact: William Merritt, Pres.
Telephone: 805-529-2424
Fax: 805-529-8630
Email: / URL:
Product Service Description:
Manufactures automation assembly
equipment

Automatic Transmission Parts, Inc. A.T.P.
5940 Oakton St.
Morton Grove, IL 60053
Contact: S. N. Ortiz, Export Sales Manager
Telephone: 847-967-6790
Fax: 847-967-8686
Email: nortiz@atp-inc.com / URL:
Product Service Description:
Automatic Transmission Parts and Kits
Flywheels
Automatic Transmission Ring Gears
Clutch Forks
Accelerator, Clutch Release, Detent, &
Transhift Cables
Manual Transmission Ring Gears
Speedometer Cables & Gears

Automatics & Machinery Co., Inc.
175 Commerce Street
Broomfield, CO 80020
Contact: Jay Charness, *
Telephone: 303-404-0123
Fax: 303-404-3111
Email: / URL:
Product Service Description:
Metal Working Machinery, Wholesale
Industrial & Commercial Machinery
General Industrial Machinery
Machine Tools & Metal Cutting Types
Screw Machine Products Used

Auton Company
P.O. BOX 801960
Valencia, CA 91380
Contact: Virgil Walker, Sales & Marketing
Telephone: 661-257-9282
Fax: 661-295-5638
Email: virgil@auton.com / URL: http://
www.auton.com
Product Service Description:
Television Lifts
Television Lift Cabinets

Autopoint, Inc.
1310 Plainfield Ave
Janesville, WI 53545-0434
Contact: David Griffiths, Pres.
Telephone: 608-757-0021
Fax: 608-757-0054
Email: autopt@jvlnet.com / URL: http://
www.jvlnet.com/~autopt
Product Service Description:
Writing instruments
Pens & mechanical pencils

Autoprod Inc.
5355 115th Ave. N.
Clearwater, FL 33760-4840
Contact: Paul De Socio, President
Telephone: 727-572-7753
Fax: 727-573-0367
Email: Sales@autoprodinc.com / URL: http://
www.autoprodinc.com
Product Service Description:
Portion Control Dairy & Food Packaging
Machinery

Autoquip Corporation
P.O. BOX 1058
GUTHRIE, OK 73044
Contact: Allen heckert, Director of Sales
Telephone: 405-282-5200
Fax: 405-282-8105
Email: arhaq@flash.net / URL: http://
www.autoquip.com
Product Service Description:
Elevators Elec-Hydraulic Scissor Type
Overhead Cranes
Industrial Stackers

Autosplice, Inc.
10121 Barnes Canyon Rd.
San Diego, CA 92121
Product Service Description:
Electrical / Electronic Assembly Machines

Autotech USA
PO Box 981718
Park City, UT 84098-1718
Contact: Clyde L Simpson, GM
Telephone: 435-647-0380
Fax: 435-647-0381
Email: autotech@parkcityus.com / URL:
http://www.autotechusa.com
Product Service Description:
Manufactures spare tire covers for sport
utility vehicles
Motor vehicle parts & accessories

Autotek Corp
PO Box 4391
Burlingame, CA 94011-4391
Contact: S D Schieber, Pres.
Telephone: 650-692-2444
Fax: 650-692-2448
Email: sales@autotek.net / URL:
Product Service Description:
Manufactures car amplifiers, signal
processors and speakers

Autron Incorporated
5 Appleton Street, P.o. Box 350
Holyoke, MA 01040
Contact: Dennis R. Pocius,
Telephone: 413-535-4200
Fax: 800-200-0838
Email: / URL: http://www.autron.com
Product Service Description:
Misc. Converted Paper Products
Stationery Products
Paper Products
Engineering Supplies

Available Plastics, Inc.
P.O. Box 924
Huntsville, AL 35804
Contact: Steve Brown, President
Telephone: 205/859-4957
Fax: 205-851-7723
Product Service Description:
Plastic Extrusion Injection Molding, Pvc
Plastic Pipe, Irrigation, Pvc
Plastic Pipe, Conduit, Pvc
Plastic Pipe, Water Well, Pvc

Avesta Sheffield Pipe Co.
1101 N Main St
Wildwood, FL 34785-3432
Contact: Jeffrey H. Stam, Pres.
Telephone: 352-748-1313
Fax: 352-748-2751
Email: jstam@asnad.com / URL:
Product Service Description:
Stainless steel pipe & tubing
Steel pipe & tubes

Aviation Technology, Inc.
225 E Industrial Park Dr
Manchester, NH 03109-5311
Contact: Curtis Lloyd, Pres.
Telephone: 603-666-0200
Fax: 603-666-5546
Email: sales@avitechusa.com / URL:
www.avitechusa.com
Product Service Description:
Aircraft ground support test equipment

Avison Forest Products
PO Box 1309
Molalla, OR 97038-1309
Contact: Rick Schaefer,
Telephone: 503-829-3317
Fax: 503-829-3316
Email: molallaforestproducts.com / URL:
http://www.avison.com
Product Service Description:
General sawmill and planing mill
Sawmills & planing mills, general
Glu-Lam plant

Avjet Corporation
4531 Empire Avenue
Burbank, CA 91505
Telephone: 818/841-6190
Fax: 818-841-6209
Email: / URL:
Product Service Description:
Aircraft Charter & Leasing

Avon Mfg., Inc.
PO Box 1217
Avon, CT 06001-1217
Contact: John LaMonica, GM & R & D Mgr.
Telephone: 860-673-3291
Fax: 860-675-4263
Email: / URL:
Product Service Description:
Steel Forms for Concrete
Steel Hatches

Avs Graphics International
3406 S 1400 W
Salt Lake City, UT 84119-4048
Contact: Gavin Hunter, Off. Mgr.
Telephone: 801-975-9799
Fax: 801-975-0970
Email: avsi_usa@omnibus.co.uk / URL: http:
//www.avsg.co.uk
Product Service Description:
Manufactures character generators and
standard converters

Award Maker
800 Ne 125th St
North Miami, FL 33161-5773
Contact: Archie Retchin, Pres.
Telephone: 305-893-8081
Fax: 305-891-6557
Email: / URL:
Product Service Description:
Plaques, signs & advertising specialties

Axel Plastics Research Laboratories
PO Box 770855
Woodside, NY 11377-0855
Contact: F. Axel, President
Telephone: 718-672-8300
Fax: 718-565-7447
Email: info@axelplast.com / URL: http://
www.axelplast.com
Product Service Description:
Mold Release Agents for Rubber & Plastic
Process Aid Additives for Rubber & Plastic
Semi-Permanent Release Coating

Axic Inc
493 Gianni St
Santa Clara, CA 95054-2414
Contact: Frank Bazzarre, Chrm., CEO
Telephone: 408-980-0240
Fax: 408-980-0524
Email: postmaster@axic.com / URL: http://
www.axic.com
Product Service Description:
Manufactures semiconductor processing
equipment : Machinery_special industry
X-Ray Fluorescence Equipment
Thin Film Thickness Measurement Equipment
Plasma Etch Equipment : Reactive Ion Etch
Equipment : Plasma Assisted Chemical Vapor
Deposition Equipment : Ellipsometers for
Measuring Thin Film : Refurbished
Semiconductor Manufacturing Equipment

Axiom Medical Inc
555 W Victoria St
Rancho Dominguez, CA 90220-5513
Contact: J Rae Walker, Pres.
Telephone: 310-898-1779
Fax: 310-632-1326
Email: / URL: http://www.axiom-med.com
Product Service Description:
Silicone & PVC Extrusion, Silicone Molding,
OEM/Custom : Manufactures Surgical Wound
Drains, Catheters, Cannulas, Silicone
extrusion products : ISO 9002 Certified
manufacture & CE Mark for all medical
products

Ayala Luis A. Colon Sucrs. Inc.
P.O. Box 7066
Ponce, PR 00732-7066
Contact: Herman F. Ayala-Parsi, President
Telephone: 787-848-9000
Fax: 787-848-0070
Email: agencypc@ayacol.com / URL:
Product Service Description:
Stevedores
Steamship Agents

Azure Blue Inc
PO Box 6057
Reno, NV 89513-6057
Contact: Herbert Morghen, Pres.
Telephone: 775-356-2709
Fax: 775-356-7795
Email: cannonbore@aol.com / URL:
Product Service Description:
Manufactures and repairs pressure washing
equipment : Service industry machinery
Repair services

B & A Mfg. Co.
3665 E Industrial Way
Riviera Beach, FL 33404-3401
Contact: C. D. Arrington,
Sales & Mktg. Mgr.
Telephone: 561-848-8648
Fax: 561-848-8621
Product Service Description:
Carbide tipped drill bits
Machine tools, metal cutting types

B & B Design Collections
1010 Wall St.
Los Angeles, CA 90015-2306
Contact: Bijan Navabian, Pres
Telephone: 213-746-8507
Fax: 213-746-6314
Product Service Description:
Manufactures of ladies clothing, missy,
juniors, dresses & seperate

B & B Lumber Co., Inc.
Solvay Rd.
Jamesville, NY 13078
Contact: Jeffrey Booher, Pres., CFO
Telephone: 315-492-1786
Fax: 315-469-4946
Email: palletace@aol.com / URL:
Product Service Description:
Wooden pallets, hardwood grade lumber, KD
& green

B & C Mortensen Wood Prods Inc
1238 E Highway 2
Oldtown, ID 83822-9248
Contact: Chris Mortensen, Pres.
Telephone: 208-437-5665
Fax: 208-437-3884
Email: / URL:
Product Service Description:
Manufactures gazebos, portable arches,
displays and props for weddings, parties and
commercial use

B & D Custom Cabinets, Inc.
1000 Morse Ave
Schaumburg, IL 60193-4504
Contact: Darren Nixon, V-P.
Telephone: 847-985-9606
Fax: 847-985-0169
Email: / URL:
Product Service Description:
Laminated cabinets, counters, store fixtures,
shelving units & displays

B & H Manufacturing Co.
3461 Roeding Rd., P.O. Box 247
Ceres, CA 95307
Contact: Patty Mazariegos, Int'l Sales
Coordinator
Telephone: 209-537-5785 X 124
Fax: 209-537-6854
Email: bhcoord@ix.netcom.com / URL: http:
//www.bhlabelingsystems.com
Product Service Description:
Labeling Equipment

B & L Machine & Design
PO Box 743
Effingham, IL 62401-0743
Contact: Larry Hines, Pres.
Phone: 217-342-3918 / Fax: 217-342-2081
Email: blmachin@advancenet.net / URL:
Product Service Description:
Rebuilt printing equipment & machined parts
Printing trades machinery

B & M Wood Products
4137 Manor Millwood Rd S
Manor, GA 31550-9305
Contact: James Stovall, Owner
Phone: 912-283-0353 / Fax: 912-285-2982
Product Service Description:
Wooden fence posts, poles, gates
Wood preserving

B & S Equine / Cannie Skin Lotion
PO Box 387
Mcintosh, FL 32664-0387
Contact: Robert L. Ferguson, Owner
Telephone: 352-591-3471
Product Service Description:
Horse & dog topical lotions

B A F Communications Corp.
316 Northstar Ct
Sanford, FL 32771-6673
Contact: Walter C. Shelmet, Jr., G.M.
Telephone: 407-324-8250
Fax: 407-324-7860
Product Service Description:
Satellite communication trucks
Trucks & tractors_industrial
Radio & TV communications equipment

B C I Burke Co., LLC
PO Box 549
Fond Du Lac, WI 54936-0549
Contact: Timothy Ahern, Pres., CEO
Telephone: 920-921-9220
Fax: 920-921-9566
Email: bciburke@vbe.com / URL: http://
www.bciburke.com
Product Service Description:
Playground & Recreational Equipment
Sporting & athletic goods

B F Mfg., Inc.
116 Bethea Rd Ste 322
Fayetteville, GA 30214-7239
Contact: Max Bowers,
Telephone: 770-719-2051
Fax: 770-719-9899
Product Service Description:
Coaters on paper, film, plastic, vinyl, canvas
& other : Materials for ink jet printing
industry. We also feature Water resistant
products.

B G Imaging Specialties
1125 Close Ave.
Bronx, NY 10472-3103
Email: info@bgimaging.com / URL: http://
www.bgimaging.com
Product Service Description:
Medical Diagnostic Imaging Equipment

B I C O Drilling Tools, Inc.
3040 Greens Rd
Houston, TX 77032-2204
Contact: Heino Rohde, Pres., CFO
Telephone: 281-590-6966
Fax: 281-590-2280
Email: bicosale@neosoft.com / URL:
Product Service Description:
Downhole oil field motors

B Q Products Inc.
PO Box 218, 170 S. 1st Ave.
Beech Grove, IN 46107-0218
Contact: Dennis Laswell, Pres
Telephone: 317-786-5500
Fax: 317-786-0599
Email: bq@bqproducts.com / URL: http://
www.bqproducts.com
Product Service Description:
Contract electronic assembly
Communications equipment, Tone
RF Coaxial Cables

B&G Export Management Associates
300 High St. PO Box 71
Holyoke, MA 01041-0071
Contact: Gerry Grant, President
Telephone: 413-536-4565
Fax: 413-536-5249
Email: / URL:
Product Service Description:
Stationary & Office Supplies, Export
Converted Paper, Export

B-D Chemical Co Inc
701 Denargo Market
Denver, CO 80216-5049
Contact: Richard Nelson, Pres.
Telephone: 303-296-3800
Fax: 303-296-3138
Email: bdchemco@dnvr.uswest.net / URL:
http://www.bdchemco.com
Product Service Description:
Manufactures various chemical preparations,
detergents, cleaners and chemicals
Soap & other detergents
Polishes & sanitation goods

B. T. M. Inc.
1550 Elmwood Rd
Rockford, IL 61103-1217
Contact: Ginette Y. DeRive, Pres.
Telephone: 815-282-3316
Fax: 815-282-4546
Email: btmusa@btm-usa.com / URL: http://
www.btm-usa.com
Product Service Description:
Welding, general machining, metal fabrication
& industrial assembly job shop
Industrial machinery
Metal products_fabricated

BAND-IT-IDEX Inc
PO Box 16307
Denver, CO 80216-0307
Contact: Roger Gibbins, Pres, Ron Angotti,
Nat'l Saels Manager
Telephone: 303-320-4555
Fax: 303-33-6549
Email: info@band-it-idex.com / URL: http://
www.band-it.idex.com
Product Service Description:
Manufactures clamps, sign mountings, hose
fittings, applicator tools,metal bands &
buckles
Hardware

BAS Recycling Inc
1400 N H St
San Bernardino, CA 92405-4316
Contact: Murray Quance,
Telephone: 909-383-7050
Fax: 909-383-7055
Email: cmqbas@aol.com / URL:
Product Service Description:
Recycles tires into rubber granules
Rubber products_fabricated
Scrap & waste materials

BBA Nonwovens Reemay, Inc.
P.O. Box 511
Old Hickory, TN 37138-0511
Contact: Carol Webster, International
Business Unit Manager
Telephone: 615-847-7000
Fax: 615-847-7068
Email: cwebster@reemay.com / URL: http://
www.reemay.com
Product Service Description:
Nonwoven Fabrics

BBC International Inc.
PO Box 297
Hobbs, NM 88241-0297
Contact: Cliff Brunson, President
Telephone: 505-397-6388
Fax: 505-397-0397
Email: bbc@bbcinternational.com / URL:
http://www.bbcinternational.com
Product Service Description:
Bioremediation of Petroleum Contam.

BCI Burke Co., Inc.
P.O. Box 549
Fond Du Lac, WI 54936-0549
Contact: Tom Casey, VP Sales & Mktg.
Telephone: 920-921-9220
Fax: 920-921-9566
Email: / URL: http://www.bciburke.com
Product Service Description:
Playground Equipment

BEI Sensors & Systems/Kimco Magnetics Division
804 Rancheros Dr Ste A
San Marcos, CA 92069-3093
Contact: Riad Abuelafiya, Director of Sales
& Mktg.
Telephone: 760-744-5671
Fax: 760-744-0425
Email: sales@beikimo.com / URL: http://
www.beikimco.com
Product Service Description:
Manufactures brushless DC motors and voice
coil actuators; OEMs
Electronic components
Process control instruments
Motors & generators
Servo Systems

BJB Enterprises Inc
14791 Franklin Ave
Tustin, CA 92780-7215
Contact: Brian Stransky, Pres.
Telephone: 714-734-8450
Fax: 714-734-8929
Email: tlljill@aol.com / URL: http://
www.bjbenterprises.com
Product Service Description:
Manufactures synthetic resins and plastics
materials
Plastic materials & resins
Plastic profile shapes_unsupported
Plastic materials & basic shapes

BMI Automation, Inc.
2580 S Brannon Stand Rd
Dothan, AL 36305-7042
Contact: Henry K. Burns III, Pres.
Telephone: 334-793-7086
Fax: 334-671-0310
Email: bmi@bmiauto.com / URL: http://
www.bmiauto.com
Product Service Description:
Robotic systems & materials handling
systems
Consultants: Automation

BOC Coating Technology
PO Box 2529
Fairfield, CA 94533-0252
Contact: Rod Stradling, Pres.
Telephone: 707-423-2100
Fax: 707-425-2986
Email: / URL:
Product Service Description:
Manufactures vacuum coating equipment

BR Laboratories Inc
PO Box 1249
Huntington Beach, CA 92647-1249
Contact: Bodh R Subherwal, Pres.
Telephone: 714-891-0206
Fax: 714-893-0818
Product Service Description:
R&D for various related energy products;
manufactures low emission natural gas
burners

BW Lighting Corp
PO Box 530010
San Diego, CA 92153-0010
Contact: Beatriz Huber,
Telephone: 619-661-5597
Fax: 619-661-5521
Email: / URL: http://www.bwlighting.com
Product Service Description:
Manufactures residential lighting
Mfg. of residential oak accessories

BYK-Gardner USA
RiversPark II, 9104 Guilford Road
Columbia, MD 21046-2729
Contact: Randy Snavely, Dir. of Marketing
Telephone: 301-483-6500
Fax: 301-483-6555
Email: / URL: http://www.byk-gardner.com
Product Service Description:
Color, Appearance, Physical Test Equipment
Measuring & Controlling Devices
Analytical Devices

Babcock Textile Machinery, Inc.
PO Box 240212
Charlotte, NC 28224-0212
Contact: Craig Newsome, VP & Gen. Mgr.
Telephone: 704-588-2780
Fax: 704-588-2740
Product Service Description:
Textile Machinery

Babel Ltd.
P.O. Box 767998
Roswell, GA 30076
Product Service Description:
Translation/Interrpretation Svcs.

Bacon Veneer Co.
100 S. Mannheim Rd.
Hillside, IL 60162
Contact: James A. McCracken, President
Telephone: 708-547-6673
Fax: 312-547-7943
Email: / URL:
Product Service Description:
Hardwood Veneer & Veneer Faces

Bag-A-Nut, Inc.
10601 Theresa Dr
Jacksonville, FL 32246-8758
Contact: James Dudley, Pres.
Telephone: 904-641-3934
Fax: 904-645-5918
Email: baganut@msn.com / URL: http://
www.baganut.com
Product Service Description:
Nut Harvesting Equipment

Baja Pacific Light Metals No
15300 Valley View Ave
La Mirada, CA 90638-5228
Contact: Ronn Page, Pres.
Telephone: 562-404-7474
Fax: 562-404-8658
Email: ronn@pacificbaja.com / URL: http://
www.pacificbaja.com
Product Service Description:
Manufactures aluminum sand and permanent
mold castings
Foundries_aluminum

BakeMark
7351 Crider Ave
Pico Rivera, CA 90660-3705
Contact: Tim Pisarski,
Telephone: 562-949-1054
Fax: 562-949-1257
Email: / URL: http://www.bakemark.com
Product Service Description:
Manufactures food, bakers equipment and
supplies; ingredients, food service supplies
and paper goods
Food preparations
Food products machinery
Industrial & personal service paper
Industrial machinery & equipment

Baker Div. Sonoco Products Company
PO Box 668
Hartselle, AL 35640-0668
Contact: Sales & Marketing,
Telephone: 205-773-6581
Fax: 205-773-8706
Email: don.foster@sonoco.com / URL: http://
www.bakerreels.com
Product Service Description:
Wooden Reels - Wire & Cable
Plywood Reels
Steel Rods
Poly-Fiber Reels

Baker Hughes Mining Tools, Inc.
PO Box 531226
Grand Prairie, TX 75053-1226
Contact: Alasdair Shiach, Marketing Mgr.
Telephone: 972-337-9793
Fax: 972-602-3135
Email: / URL:
Product Service Description:
Mining machinery
Drill bits & cutters

Baker Safety Equipment, Inc.
One Pyles Ln.
New Castle, DE 19720
Contact: Ralph Baker, CEO, Dawn M.
(Baker) Nutter, Pres.
Telephone: 302-652-7080 / 1888-lifechute
Fax: 302-652-3205
Email: / URL: http://www.lifechute.com
Product Service Description:
Nylon building escape chutes (high rise
structures)

Baking Machines
4577-B Las Positas
Livermore, CA 94550
Contact: Richard J. Sonsteng, Manager, Int'l
Sales
Telephone: 510-449-3369
Fax: 510-449-2144
Email: info@bakingmachines.com / URL:
http://www.baking machines.com
Product Service Description:
Automatic Bagel Production Systems

Balance Specialties Inc. (Mfr)
5030 W. Lake Street
Chicago, IL 60644
Contact: David C. Zimmer, President
Phone: 773-261-5034 / Fax: 773-261-5030
Email: balanceace@aol.com / URL: http://
www.balancespecialties.com
Product Service Description:
Balancing Machines

Baldor Electric Company
PO Box 2400
Fort Smith, AR 72902-2400
Contact: James Campbell, Int'l Sales Mgr.
Phone: 501-646-4711 / Fax: 501-648-5895
Email: / URL:
Product Service Description:
Electric Motors Industrial
Industrial Controls

Baldwin Aluminum Foundry & Machine Co.
PO Box 57
Ashville, AL 35953-0057
Contact: Forrest W. Baldwin, Pres., Fin., MIS
& R & D Mgr.
Telephone: 205-594-5455
Fax: 205-594-2626
Email: / URL:
Product Service Description:
Aluminum castings & machine patterns
Foundries_aluminum

Baldwin Environmental Inc
895 E Patriot Blvd Ste 107
Reno, NV 89511-1245
Contact: Tom A Baldwin, Pres.
Phone: 775-828-1300 / Fax: 775-828-1305
Email: bel.reno@ix.netcom.com / URL: http:/
/www.bei-reno.com
Product Service Description:
Manufactures industrial instruments for the
measurement, display and control
Process control instruments
Air Pollution Monitoring Equipment

Balemaster
980 Crown Court
Crown Point, IN 46307-2732
Contact: Sam Finlay, VP Sales & Marketing
Phone: 219-663-4525 / Fax: 219-663-4591
Email: sales@balemaster.com / URL: http://
www.balemaster.com
Product Service Description:
Shredders - Paper Waste
Balers - Paper Waste

Ballisti-Cast Mfg., Inc.
6345 49th St Nw
Plaza, ND 58771-9415
Contact: Dennis Edwards, Pres.
Phone: 701-497-3333 / Fax: 701-497-3335
Email: ballisti@ndak.net / URL: http://
www.powderandbow.com/ballist
Product Service Description:
Bullet-casting machinery
Machinery_special industry

Baltimore Aircoil Co., Inc.
PO Box 7322
Baltimore, MD 21227-0322
Contact: Frank J. Bowman Jr., VP Mktg- Int'l
Phone: 410-799-6496/ Fax: 410-799-6346
Email: fbowman@baltaircoil.com / URL:
http://www.baltaircoil.com
Product Service Description:
Evaporative cooling & ice thermal storage
systems: Refrigeration & heating equipment
Cooling Towers & Heat Exchangers

Bandiera Winery
155 Cherry Creek Rd.
Cloverdale, CA 95425-3807
Contact: Yvonne Lozinto,
Controller
Telephone: 707-894-4295
Fax:
Email: / URL:
Product Service Description:
Wine, from grapes & grape must with alcohol
Container cargo

Banner American Products, Inc.
42381 Rio Nedo
Temecula, CA 92590
Contact: Alan Parkhill, Vice Pres./Mktg.
Telephone: 909-699-0872
Fax: 909-699-0273
Email: marketing@banam.com / URL: http://
www.banam.com
Product Service Description:
Laminating Machines

Bannerville U. S. A. Inc.
1428 Hillgrove Ave
Western Springs, IL 60558-1339
Contact: Emil Harley, Pres., CFO
Telephone: 708-246-5788
Fax: 708-246-0172
Email: / URL: http://www.bannerville.com
Product Service Description:
Screen printing
Banners

Bar Maid Corp.
2950 Nw 22nd Ter
Pompano Beach, FL 33069-1045
Contact: George E. Shepherd, Pres., Pur.,
Sales & Mktg. Mgr.
Telephone: 954-960-1468
Fax: 954-960-1647
Email: barmaid@msn.com / URL: http://
www.barmaidwashers.com
Product Service Description:
Glass Washing Equipment, Portable

Bar-S Foods Co.
PO Box 29049
Phoenix, AZ 85038-9049
Contact: Warren Panico, VP, International
Telephone: 602-285-5245
Fax: 602-285-2306
Email: wpanico@bar-s.com / URL: http://
www.bar-s.com
Product Service Description:
Sausages & other prepared meat products
Processes & smokes meats; wholesale
nautural & processed cheese

Barber-Nichols Incorporated
6325 W. 55th Avenue
Arvada, CO 80002-2777
Contact: James E. Dillard, Mktg. Dir.
Telephone: 303-421-8111
Fax: 303-420-4679
Email: info@barber-nichols.com / URL: http:/
/www.barber-nichols.com
Product Service Description:
Turbines Steam Hydro Organic Vapors
Geotherm Solar Heat Power Sys., Wholesale
Compressors
Pumps
Cryogenic Pumps

Barclay Maps
2612 Barrington Ct.
Hayward, CA 94545-1100
Contact: David Clausen, Owner
Telephone: 510-732-3700
Fax: 925-372-3701
Email: barclay1@ix.netcom.com / URL:
Product Service Description:
Publishes road maps for the Bay area &
specialty custom maps: digital data sales
Publishing , Miscellaneous :Data Conversion,
cadastrol maps (parcels, etc) for cities &
countries : Map distributor, California & all
U.S.A.: Custom Map Pu blisher : ESRI
software VAR, Business Partner, (GIS
Software) : GDT VAR (Street data for all
U.S.A.) : Water Districts Applications
Developer : Telecom, PCS & Cable Service
Provider Application Developers : Cadastra L
Data Application Developer

Bargetto's Santa Cruz Winery
3535 N Main St
Soquel, CA 95073-2530
Contact: Beverly Bargetto, Pres.
Telephone: 408-475-2258
Fax: 408-475-2664
Email: rbargetto@aol.com / URL: http://
www.bargetto.com
Product Service Description:
Winery and vineyards; produces premium
tables wines: Wines, brandy, & brandy spirits
Wine & distilled beverages

Barkat
261 5th Ave., 19th Fl., Ste. 1901
New York, NY 10016-7701
Contact: Sales & Marketing,
Telephone: 212-951-3100
Fax: 212-951-7106
Product Service Description:
Articles of bedding and similar furnishings ,
fitted or stuffed, including quilts

Barner, Jerry M. & Sons
P.O. Box 5,
Roselle, NJ 07203
Contact: Sales & Marketing,
Telephone: 908-245-7476
Fax: 908-245-3525
Product Service Description:
Freight & Cargo Transportation
Trucking

Barnhardt Manufacturing Co.
PO Box 34276
Charlotte, NC 28234-4276
Contact:George Hargrove, V.P. Sales & Mktg.
Telephone: 704-376-0380
Fax: 704-342-1892
Email: jenniferh@barnhardt.net / URL: http://
www.barnhardt.net
Product Service Description:
Filter Cloth, Cotton: Bleached Cotton Raw
Stock: Dental Disposables
Cotton Pharmaceutical Coil, Packaging
Beauty Disposables

Baroli Engineering Inc
222 N Sepulveda Blvd Ste 1730
El Segundo, CA 90245-4354
Contact: Kristina Baroli, Pres.
Telephone: 310-726-0172
Fax: 310-726-0173
Email: baroli@prodigy.net
Product Service Description:
Metal stampings : Manufactures metal
stampings; tool and die
Dies, tools, jigs & fixtures_special

Barreto Manufacturing
66498 Highway 203
La Grande, OR 97850-5231
Contact: Greg Barreto, Pres.
Telephone: 541-963-7348
Fax: 541-963-6755
Email: info@barretomfg.com / URL: http://
www.barretomfg.com
Product Service Description:
Manufactures rototillers and trenchers
Lawn & garden equipment

Barrett Carpet Mills, Inc.
P.O. Box 2045
Dalton, GA 30722-2045
Contact: Ron Beauford, President
Telephone: 706-277-2114
Fax: 706-277-3250
Email: service@barrett-cpt.com / URL: http://
www.barrett-cpt.com
Product Service Description:
Carpets and Rugs
Carpets and other textile floor coverings

Barron Industries, Inc.
P.O. Box 570
Leeds, AL 35094-0570
Contact: Daniel Wafford, Vice President &
General Mgr.
Telephone: 205-956-3441
Fax: 205-956-2265
Email: sales@barronind.com / URL: http://
www.barronind.com
Product Service Description:
Fans : Dust Collectors : Exhaust Stacks
Ductwork

Barry Pattern & Foundry
3333 35th Ave N
Birmingham, AL 35207-2927
Contact: Jack S. Barry Sr., CEO
Telephone: 205-841-8725
Fax: 205-841-1972
Product Service Description:
Trench grates & frames
Construction Castings
Foundries_gray & ductile iron & alum.
Stair nosings & treads

Barsallo Deburring
12734 Branford St Ste 17
Pacoima, CA 91331-6833
Contact: Rudy Barsallo, Owner
Telephone: 818-899-8706
Product Service Description:
Deburring services : Plating & polishing
Equipment & supply

Bart Trucking
888 Marin St.,
San Francisco, CA 94107
Contact: Sales & Marketing,
Telephone: 415-824-5566
Product Service Description:
Freight & Cargo Transportation
Trucking
Container Freight Station
Warehousing

Barth & Dreyfuss of California
2260 E. 15th St., P.O. Box 21811
Los Angeles, CA 90021-0811
Contact: Tom Healy, President
Telephone: 213-627-6000
Fax: 213-627-8936
Product Service Description:
Homefurnishings : Textile products & articles
Terry towelling and similar woven terry
fabrics, of cotton

Basic Concepts Inc.
PO Box 698
Sandy Springs, SC 29677-0698
Contact: Edward Van Romer, Pres.,
R & D Mgr.
Telephone: 864-224-7227
Fax: 864-224-7063
Email: bci@carol.net / URL:
Product Service Description:
Pollution control equipment
Machinery_special industry

Basic Electronics Inc
11371 Monarch St
Garden Grove, CA 92841-1406
Contact: Al Balzano, GM
Telephone: 714-530-2400
Fax: 714-898-6750
Email: info@basicinc.com / URL: http://
www.basicinc.com
Product Service Description:
Manufactures electronic printed circuit
boards, flexible circuits, turnkey component
assemblies, power supplies
Engineering services

Basic Foods International, Inc.
P.O. Box 22948
Fort Lauderdale, FL 33335-2948
Contact: John P. Bauer, President
Telephone: 954-467-1700
Fax: 954-764-5110
Email: bauer@basicfood.com / URL: http://
www.basicfood.com
Product Service Description:
Frozen Chicken
Frozen Fish
Corn Oil
Frozen Meat
Food Preparations
Grocery Products
Canned Food

Bass Hunter Boats Inc.
1617 James P Rogers Dr.
Valdosta, GA 31601-6517
Contact: Laury L. Davis, *
Telephone: 800-345-4689
Fax: 912-247-2834
Email: basshunter@datasys.net / URL: http://
www.datasys.net/basshunter
Product Service Description:
Sport Fishing Boats

Batchmaster
P.O. Box 1303
Fayetteville, AR 72702
Contact: Paul Reagan, *
Telephone: 501-521-9208
Fax: 501-442-5860
Email: batchmaster@bmaster.com / URL:
http://www.bmaster.com
Product Service Description:
Food Processing Equip. New, Rebuilt, Used
Automated Kabob Equipment

Batts Inc.
200 N. Franklin St.
Zeeland, MI 49464-1000
Contact: Mark Legters, Mgr. S.Amer. Market
Dev. Rep
Telephone: 616-772-4635
Fax: 616-772-1668
Email: / URL:
Product Service Description:
Plastic Garment Hangers
Wooden Garment Hangers

Baumfolder Corp.
1660 Campbell Rd
Sidney, OH 45365-2480
Contact: Carl Fullenkamp, V-P., Fin.
Telephone: 937-492-1281
Fax: 937-492-7280
Email: baum@bright.net / URL: http://
www.baumfolder.com
Product Service Description:
Industrial paper folding, cutting, drilling &
binding equipment

Baut Studios Inc.
1095 Main St
Wilkes Barre, PA 18704-1308
Contact: Conrad D. Baut, Pres., Mktg. Mgr.
Telephone: 717-288-1431
Fax: 717-288-0380
Email: info@baut.com / URL: http://
www.baut.com
Product Service Description:
Stained & etched glass, aluminum sash &
doors & ecclesiastical art products
Glass products from purchased glass

Bay Area Biscotti Co
3125 W Ali Baba Ln Ste 706
Las Vegas, NV 89118-1610
Contact: Arlene Damele, Pres.
Telephone: 702-795-8700 / 800-497-9556
Fax: 702-795-8704
Email: adamele@msn.com / URL:
Product Service Description:
Manufactures biscotti cookies; distributes
baked goods
Cookies & crackers
Groceries & related products
Gourmet Gift Basket Co.

Beall Corp.
P.O. Box 17095
Portland, OR 97203-6502
Contact: J. E. Beall, President
Telephone: 503-735-2110
Fax: 503-735-2601
Email: j.beall@beallcorp.com / URL: http://
www.beallcorp.com
Product Service Description:
Tank Trailers
Aluminum Bottom Dumps
Aluminum End Dumps
Steel Bottom Dumps
Steel End Dumps
Gasoline Truck Tanks
Semi-Trailer Tanks
Metal Products

Beam Industries
PO Box 788
Webster City, IA 50595-0788
Contact: John Coghlan, President
Telephone: 515-832-4620
Fax: 515-832-6659
Email: info@beamvac.com / URL: http://
www.beamvac.com
Product Service Description:
Central Cleaning Systems
Vacuum Cleaners, Household

Bean Machines Inc
PO Box 2122
Mill Valley, CA 94942-2122
Contact: Wally Rogers, Pres.
Telephone: 707-996-0706
Fax: 707-996-0704
Email: / URL:
Product Service Description:
Manufactures tofu and soy milk equipment;
consulting services for product development

Beauty Plus Beauty Supply
4365 W Bell Rd
Glendale, AZ 85308-3531
Contact: Gregory D. Eastman,
Telephone: 602-229-1155
Fax: 602-547-1266
Email: geastman@worldnet.att.com / URL:
Product Service Description:
Wholesales Hair Care Products to
Distributors

Bec Controls Corp.
2510 Northwest Station
Davenport, IA 52809
Contact: Ed Bee, Mktg. Mgr.
Telephone: 319-285-9008
Fax: 319-285-7761
Email: / URL:
Product Service Description:
Ind Instruments, Pressure / Flow Transmitters
Ind Instruments, Temperature Transmitters
Ind. Instruments, Humidity Transmitters
Ind. Instruments, Current/Voltage Transducers
Ind. Analog to Pneumatic Transducers

Becker-Parkin Dental Supply Co., Inc.
450 West 33 Street
New York, NY 10001
Contact: Barry Salzman, Exec. VP
Telephone: 212-216-0700
Fax: 212-631-0566
Email: becker-parkin@mindspring.com /
URL:
Product Service Description:
Dental Supplies
Dental Equipment

Beere Precision Medical Instruments
2503 Lincolnwood Ct
Racine, WI 53403-3869
Contact: Guy Bradshaw, Pres.
Telephone: 414-554-8505
Fax: 414-554-4486
Email: bpmii@execpc.com / URL: http://
www.beeremedical.com
Product Service Description:
Orthopedic medical products
Dental equipment & supplies

Begneaud Mfg. Inc.
306 E Amedee Dr
Scott, LA 70583-5325
Contact: Donald M. Begneaud, Pres., Sales
Mgr.
Telephone: 318-237-5069
Fax: 318-234-3836
Email: bengo@sprintimail.com / URL:
Product Service Description:
CNC laser-cutting, punching & aluminum &
stainless steel fabrication
Industrial machinery
Metal products_fabricated

Behlen MFG. Co.
P.O. Box 569
Columbus, NE 68602
Contact: Russel D. Ferris, Advertising Mgr.
Telephone: 402-564-3111
Fax: 402-563-7405
Email: behlen@megavision.com / URL: http:/
/www.behlenmfg.com
Product Service Description:
Grain Tanks & Accessories
Prefabricated Metal Buildings
Wire Mesh Products
Farm Equip., Grain Dryers
Machine Tools, Hydraulic Presses
Metal Fabrication

Bell Additives, Inc.
1340 Bennett Dr
Longwood, FL 32750-7623
Contact: Charles G. Williams, Pres.
Telephone: 407-831-5021
Fax: 407-331-1125
Email: bai@belladditives.com / URL: http://
www.belladditives.com
Product Service Description:
Petroleum products, fuel additives &
lubricants

Bell Ceramics Inc. (Mfr)
P.O. Box 120127
Clermont, FL 34712
Contact: Richard Bell, President
Telephone: 352-394-2175
Fax: 352-394-1270
Email: info@bellceramics.com / URL: http://
www.bellceramics.com
Product Service Description:
Porcelain Casting Clays & Ceramic Supplies
Plaster of Paris Molds
Doll Accessories

Bell-Mark Corp.
331 Changebridge Road
Pine Brook, NJ 07058-9516
Contact: Thomas Pugh, VP
Telephone: 973-882-0202
Fax: 973-808-4616
Email: belmarkco@aol.com / URL:
Product Service Description:
Packaging Mach. Coding & Printing
Printing Equipment

Bellwether Inc.
PO Box 190
McDonough, GA 30253-0190
Contact: Wayne Boyd, Sales Mgr.
Telephone: 770-957-6651
Fax: 770-957-6666
Email: blwether@aol.com / URL: http://
www.bellwether.com
Product Service Description:
Weaving machinery parts
Textile machinery

Beloit Corp., Fiber Systems Div.
401 South St.
Dalton, MA 01226
Contact: Lawrence K. Swift, *
Telephone: 413-443-5621
Product Service Description:
Pulp Processing Machinery

Benchmark Fixture Corporation
775 Brookside Drive
Richmond, CA 94801
Contact: H J Kelman, Pres.
Telephone: 510-232-3842
Fax: 510-232-7135
Email: peterh@benfix.com / URL:
Product Service Description:
Manufactures custom casework and store
fixtures (commercial only)
Partitions & fixtures_wood
Furniture & fixtures

Bend Door Co
PO Box 5248
Bend, OR 97708-5248
Contact: Don Schneider, GM
Telephone: 541-385-1422
Fax: 541-385-3266
Email: / URL: http://www.jeld-wen.com
Product Service Description:
Millwork : Manufactures doors—Douglas fir
entry, French bifold and interior

Benshaw, Inc.
1659 E Sutter Rd
Glenshaw, PA 15116-1700
Contact: Ed Coholich, National Sales
Manager
Telephone: 412-487-8235
Fax: 412-487-4201
Email: sales@benshaw.com / URL: http://
www.benshaw.com
Product Service Description:
Solid state motor starters
Variable Frequency Drives

Bentley Manufacturing Co Inc
15123 Colorado Ave
Paramount, CA 90723-4204
Contact: Kevin P Crampton, Pres., CEO
Telephone: 562-634-4051
Fax: 562-634-4309
Email: kevin@gasketsonune.com / URL:
http://www.gasketsonline.com
Product Service Description:
Manufactures precision non-metallic gaskets
and washers
Mechanical rubber goods
Gaskets, packing & sealing devices

Benton Foundry, Inc.
RR 2 Box 110
Benton, PA 17814-9550
Contact: Fritz Hall, Pres.
Telephone: 570-925-6711
Fax: 570-925-6711
Email: benton@epix.net / URL: http://
www.bentonfoundry.com
Product Service Description:
Gray & ductile iron castings
Foundries, gray & ductile iron

Benz Research & Development Corp.
PO Box 1839
Sarasota, FL 34230-1839
Contact: Patrick H. Benz, Pres., Fin., MIS &
R & D Mgr.
Telephone: 941-758-8256
Fax: 941-758-1191
Email: benzrd@mindspring.com / URL: http:/
/www.benzlens.com
Product Service Description:
Optical plastics, contact lens raw materials &
industrial monomers
Contact Lenses
IOL's

Berg Co., Div. DC Int'l
PO Box 7065
Madison, WI 53707-7065
Contact: Terry Singer, Vice President
Telephone: 608-221-4281
Fax: 608-221-1416
Email: sales@berg-controls.com / URL: http:/
/www.berg-controls.com
Product Service Description:
Service Industry Equipment, Liquor Control
Systems

Berg, DeMarco, Lewis, Sawatski & Co.
630 Dundee Road, #425
Northbrook, IL 60062
Contact: Steven F. Sawatski, *
Telephone: 847-291-9600
Fax: 847-291-9693
Email: ssawats@notes.bdls-ms4.com / URL:
Product Service Description:
Accounting Services
Management Consulting Services

Berghausen Corp.
4524 Este Ave.
Cincinnati, OH 45232-1763
Contact: Alfred Berghausen, III, President
Telephone: 513-541-5631
Fax: 513-541-1169
Email: / URL:
Product Service Description:
Quillaia Extract & Powder
Bakery & Confectionary (Air Brush & Icing
Colors)

Beringer Wine Estates
600 Air Park Rd.
Napa, CA 94558
Contact: Peter Gower,
Telephone: 707-259-4617
Fax: 707-259-4625
Email: / URL: http://www.beringer.com
Product Service Description:
Wines, brandy, & brandy spirits
Produces wine

Berkebile Oil Co.
P.O. Box 715
Somerset, PA 15501-0715
Contact: Catherine Poorbaugh, President
Telephone: 814-443-1656
Fax: 814-443-2873
Email: / URL: http://www.shol.com/
berkebile2+2/
Product Service Description:
Automotive chemicals

Berner Cheese Corp.
10010 N Rock City Rd
Rock City, IL 61070-9515
Contact: Stephen Kneubnehl, CEO
Telephone: 815-865-5136
Fax: 815-865-5603
Email: / URL:
Product Service Description:
Low fat & low salt cheese & dairy products
Cheese, natural & processed

Berner International Corp.
PO Box 5205
New Castle, PA 16105-0205
Contact: Georgia Berner, Pres.
Telephone: 724-658-3551
Fax: 724-652-0682
Email: airdoors@berner.com / URL: http://
www.berner.com
Product Service Description:
Air curtain & door systems

Best Jig-Grinding Service
1302 Industrial Dr Ste B
Itasca, IL 60143-1876
Contact: Bob O'Connor, Owner, Engrg.,
Hum. Res. & Opers. Mgr.
Telephone: 630-250-8957
Fax: 630-250-9604
Email: bestjiggrd@aol.com / URL:
Product Service Description:
Jig grinding
Industrial machinery

Best Litho, Inc.
6912 Nw 46th St
Miami, FL 33166-5604
Contact: Ed Garcia, Pres.
Telephone: 305-592-7693
Fax: 305-477-4692
Email: ed@bestlitho.com / URL:
Product Service Description:
Commercial web printing

Best Sand Corp.
PO Box 87
Chardon, OH 44024-0087
Contact: Jim Gledhill, General Sales Mgr.
Phone: 440-285-3132 / Fax: 440-285-4109
Email: jim.gledhill@fairmountminerals.com /
URL: http://www.fairmont-minerals.com
Product Service Description:
Cut stone & stone products
Silica sand & gravel processing

Best Sign Systems
1202 N Park Ave
Montrose, CO 81401-3171
Contact: Sandra Whitley, Pres.
Phone: 970-249-2378 / 1800-235-2378
Fax: 970-249-0223
Email: sales@bestsigns.com / URL: http://
www.bestsigns.com
Product Service Description:
Manufactures architectural ADA signage and
specialties

Best Value Textiles
PO Box 2277
Englewood, CO 80150-2277
Contact: William Sandler, Pres.
Phone: 303-761-1415 / Fax: 303-761-1142
Email: bstvlu@earthlink.net / URL: http://
www.bestvalue.thomasregister.com
Product Service Description:
Manufactures gloves, oven mitts, aprons,
towels, chef clothing
Gloves_fabric dress & work
Apparel & accessories
Furnishings_house
Piece goods & notions

Betatronix, Inc.
110 Nicon Ct.
Hauppauge, NY 11788-4212
Contact: Joseph Yanosik, President
Telephone: 516-582-6740
Fax: 516-582-6038
Email: jyanosik@betatronix.com / URL:
http://www.betatronix.com
Product Service Description:
Electricity Measuring Instruments
Potentionmerters & Electronic Devices

Bete Fog Nozzle Inc. (Mfr)
50 Greenfield St.
Greenfield, MA 01301
Contact: Sue Cole, Export Manager
TPhone: 413-772-0846 / Fax: 413-772-6729
Email: / URL:
Product Service Description:
Industrial Spray Nozzles

Beutlich, L.P. Pharmaceuticals
1541 S Shields Dr
Waukegan, IL 60085-8304
Contact: F. J. Beutlich, GM
Phone: 847-473-1100 / Fax: 847-473-1122
Email: fjb1541@worldnet.att.net / URL:
http://www.beutlich.com
Product Service Description:
Pharmaceutical & dental products

Bevles Company Inc
PO Box 965
Chino, CA 91708-0965
Contact: E John Walter, Pres.
Phone: 909-465-6010 / Fax: 909-465-6020
Email: bevlescomp.@aol.com / URL:
Product Service Description:
Manufactures mobile food bakery equipment
Food products machinery

Bevles Company, Inc.
PO Box 965
Chino, CA 91708-0965
Contact: E. John Walter, Pres.
Telephone: 909-465-6010
Fax: 909-465-6020
Email: / URL:
Product Service Description:
Manufacturer of innovative foodservice
heating, holding &
Transporting equipment

Bezjian Dye-Chem, Inc.
1020 Air Way
Glendale, CA 91201-3030
Contact: Vahe Bezjian, President
Telephone: 323-461-6764
Fax: 323-461-4713
Email: / URL:
Product Service Description:
Dyestuff Specialist: one of the largest
independent : Suppliers of Top Quality Dyes
made in the U.S.A. : Greatest Selection of
Disperse Dyes for Polyester : Acetate &
Nylon. Over 45 years of Experience!
Ink Jet Inks for Printers, Pens, Etc.

Bieber Lighting Corp
970 W Manchester Blvd
Inglewood, CA 90301-1527
Contact: Lawrence Bieber, Chrm., GM
Telephone: 310-645-6789
Fax: 310-216-0333
Email: / URL:
Product Service Description:
Outdoor lighting and custom fixtures,
architectural sports lighting, poles, mounting
hardware
Lighting fixtures_commercial
Electrical apparatus & equipment
Cold cathode & neon

Bifrost
1139 Highland Dr.
Novato, CA 94949-5439
Contact: Janet Niemi, Owner
Telephone: 415-883-7119
Fax: 415-883-3671
Email: bifrost@ix.netcom.com / URL: http://
www.bifrost-intl.com
Product Service Description:
Floor Coverings
Mechanical Equipment
Electrical Equipment
Building Materials
Fire detection
Plumbing Materials
Lighting Fixtures (50hz)
Water Purification / Treatment
Airport Lighting
Wire / Cable

Big Abe No.1. Inc. Auto Sales, Export-Import, General Business
9200 N. Western Ave.
Oklahoma City, OK 73114-2624
Contact: Ibrahim K. El-Samad, Pres. & CEO
Telephone: 405-842-8373
Fax: 405-751-4914
Email: bigabeno1@aol.com / URL:
Product Service Description:
Used car dealers, vans, surubans,
ambulances
Buses, schools, tourist, all kind and sizes.

Big Bike Parts
2300 Pioneer Ave
Rice Lake, WI 54868-2416
Contact: John LaBonte, Manager
Telephone: 715-234-3336
Fax: 715-234-6872
Email: export@bigbikeparts.com / URL:
http://www.bigbikeparts.com
Product Service Description:
Motorcycle accessories
Motorcycle Covers

Big D Metalworks Of Texas
2002 Quincy St
Dallas, TX 75212-5533
Contact: Phillip J. Hoppman, Pres.,
Fin. & GM
Telephone: 214-638-8753
Fax: 214-638-2241
Email: adminstrator@bigdmetal.com / URL:
http://www.bigdmetal.com
Product Service Description:
Architectural metal work & industrial
fabrication
Architectural metal work
Structural metal_fabricated
Metal work_miscellaneous

**Big John Tree Transplanter Mfg.,
Inc.**
PO Box 608
Heber Springs, AR 72543-0608
Contact: Charles Blankenship, Pres.
Telephone: 501-362-8161
Fax: 501-362-5407
Email: / URL: http://www.big-john.com
Product Service Description:
Tree transplanters

Big Soo Terminal
P.O. Box 3809
Sioux City, IA 51102
Contact: Kevin Knepper, *
Telephone: (712) 258-0537
Fax: (712) 258-4649
Product Service Description:
Barge Terminal
Terminal

Big Timber Inc. (Mfr)
5837 29th Ave.
Vinton, IA 52349
Contact: Ted E. Mann, Vice President
Telephone: 319-472-5213
Fax: 319-472-4629
Email: / URL:
Product Service Description:
Sawmill & Dry Kiln Operations

Bigge Crane & Rigging Co.
P.O. Box 1657,
San Leandro, CA 94577
Contact: B. R. Settlemier, President
Telephone: 510-638-8100
Fax: 510-639-4053
Email: skenney@bigge.com / URL: http://
www.bigge.com
Product Service Description:
Freight & Cargo Transportation
Trucking
Heaby Rigging
Specialized Heavy Transportation
Nuclear Decommissioning
Nuclear Spent Fuel Handling &
Transportation
Marine roll or roll off operations
Container Crane Movement
Crane Rental

Bijur Lubricating Corporation
50 Kocher Drive
Bennington, VT 05201
Contact: Kevin Ryan, Mgr. Customer Service
Phone: 802-447-2174 / Fax: 802-447-1365
Email: / URL: http://www.bijur.com
Product Service Description:
Lubricating Systems, Centralized
Fluid Power Valves & Hose Fittings

Billups-Rothenberg, Inc.
PO Box 997
Del Mar, CA 92014-0997
Contact: Barry Rothenberg, President
Phone: 877-755-3309 / Fax: 877-755-3455
Email: bri@mill.net / URL: http://
www.brincubator.com
Product Service Description:
Manufactures tissue culture incubator & hot
box systems for gas containment

Biloff Manufacturing Company Inc
PO Box 726
Shafter, CA 93263-0726
Contact: Arlis Biloff, Pres.
Phone: 661-746-3976 / Fax: 661-746-0426
Product Service Description:
Manufactures ice merchandising cabinets

Bingham Roller Co.
4880 Samuel Bingham Ct
College Park, GA 30349-5930
Contact: Mike Hill / Sales Mgr., Betty
Davenport, Cust. Serv.
Phone: 770-997-3246 / Fax: 770-997-4931
Email: binghamatl@juno.com
Product Service Description:
Printing rollers : Rubber products_fabricated

Bio Zone
1126 E. Crestline Cir.
Englewood, CO 80111-3806
Contact: Gunter Moldzio, Pres
Phone: 303-770-2095 / Fax: 303-689-0065
Product Service Description:
Mfrs. ozone-based water treatment & equipt.

Biocare Labs
PO Box 389045
Chicago, IL 60638-9045
Contact: Betzy Martin, Oper. Mgr.
Phone: 708-496-8657 Fax: 708-496-1946
Email: biocare@mcs.net / URL: http://
www.mcs.net/~biocare
Product Service Description:
Shampoos, conditioners & relaxers
Toilet preparations

Bioelements Inc
4955 Northpark Dr
Colorado Springs, CO 80918-3819
Contact: Customer Service,
Phone: 719-260-0297 / Fax: 719-260-7138
Product Service Description:
Toilet preparations : Manufactures cosmetics
and toilet preparations; skin care and
aesthetics education : Drugs, proprietaries &
sundries : Schools & educational services

Biofix Holdings, Inc.
P.O. Box 2820
Denton, TX 76202-2820
Contact: Mary Ruiz, Traffic Manager
Pone: 940-382-2594 / Fax: 940-387-2294
Product Service Description:
Exporting Firms : Animal feed preparations ,
feed ingredients
Fertilizer, (organic), humicacids, biological
catalysts.

Biomarine Inc.
456 Creamery Way
Exton, PA 19341-2541
Contact: Bill Flynn, Product Line Mgr.
Telephone: 610-524-8800
Fax: 610-524-8807
Email: info@neutronicsinc.com / URL: http://
www.neutronicsinc.com
Product Service Description:
Self-contained breathing apparatus
Machinery_general industrial

Biomedical International
4896 S.W. 74th Ct.
Miami, FL 33155-4454
Contact: Juan Borges, Manager
Telephone: 305-669-1010
Fax: 305-669-1011
Email: biomed@bellsouth.net / URL:
Product Service Description:
Hospital equipments
Laboratory equipment
Turnkey hospitals
Sterilization
Incinerators
I.C.U. equipment
Operating room
Medical gases
Financing for medical equipment
Ambulance

Biomin Industries, Inc.
119 S River Dr
Tempe, AZ 85281-3010
Contact: Carl E Staley, Pres.
Telephone: 480-968-5934
Fax: 480-894-5590
Email: biominindustries@worldnet.att.net /
URL:
Product Service Description:
Manufactures nutritional supplements
Medicinals & botanicals

Bioquest Med Prod Dev
2211 W 1st St Ste 106
Tempe, AZ 85281-7251
Contact: Ron Yapp, Pres.
Telephone: 602-350-9944
Fax: 602-350-9966
Email: / URL:
Product Service Description:
Design, development & Manufacture of
orthopedic instruments for joint replacement

Biotics Research Corp.
PO Box 36888
Houston, TX 77477
Contact: Darryl Deluca, V.P. Sales
Telephone: 713-240-8010
Fax: 713-240-2304
Email: / URL:
Product Service Description:
Botanical Food Supplements
Biological Research, Food Supplements
Botanicals, Vegetable Culture Elements
Vitamin/Mineral Pharmaceutical Preps.

Birmingham News Co., The
PO Box 2553
Birmingham, AL 35202-2553
Contact: Victor H. Hanson II, Pres., Publisher
Telephone: 205-325-2222
Fax: 205-325-3268
Email: / URL:
Product Service Description:
Newspaper printing & typesetting
Newspapers

Biscayne Rod Mfg., Inc.
425 E 9th St
Hialeah, FL 33010-4547
Contact: Kenneth S. Carman, Pres., Fin., R &
D, Sales & Mktg. Mgr.
Telephone: 305-884-0808
Fax: 305-884-3017
Email: bidsrod@aol.com / URL: http://
www.biscaynerod.com
Product Service Description:
Fishing rods & component parts
Sporting & athletic goods

Bissell Inc.(Mfr)
P.O. Box 1888
Grand Rapids, MI 49544 USA
Contact: Don Seale, Dir./Intl. Sales
Telephone: 616-453-4451
Fax: 616-453-1383
Email: 110320,1562@compuserve.com /
URL: http://www.bissell.com
Product Service Description:
Home Cleaning Appliances
Home Cleaning Chemicals

Black Box Corporation
1000 Park Drive
Lawrence, PA 15055
Contact: Bill Vodzak,
Telephone: 412-746-5500
Fax: 412-746-0746
Email: info@blackbox.com / URL: http://
www.blackbox.com
Product Service Description:
Data Communication Services
Comm. Equip. Data Communications,
Wholesale

Blackberry Patch, Inc.
5773 Veterans Memorial Drive
Tallahassee, FL 32308-9802
Contact: Geraldine Rudd, Pres., Fin. & R &
D Mgr.
Telephone: 850-893-3163
Fax: 850-668-2855
Email: geraldine@blackberrypatch.com /
URL: http://www.balckberrypatch.com
Product Service Description:
Jams, jellies, syrups, vinegar & honey,
flavored honey
Biscuit & pancake mix
Gift baskets, gift boxes

Blackburn Mfg. Co.
PO Box 86
Neligh, NE 68756-0086
Contact: James Blackburn, Pres.
Telephone: 402-887-4161
Fax: 402-887-5171
Email: sales@blackburnflag.com / URL:
http://www.blackburnflag.com
Product Service Description:
Marking flags & barricade & underground
utility tapes
Textile products_fabricated
Coated fabrics, not rubberized
Plastic products

Blackburne, Inc., Perry
354 Pine St
Pawtucket, RI 02860-1832
Contact: Perry Mermelstein, Pres.
Telephone: 401-725-1400
Fax: 401-725-7611
Email: / URL:
Product Service Description:
Key chains & leather products
Leather goods

Blansett Pharmacal Co.
PO Box 638
North Little Rock, AR 72115-0638
Contact: Larry Blansett, Pres.
Telephone: 501-758-8635
Fax: 501-758-5369
Email: blanpharm@aol.com / URL:
Product Service Description:
Pharmaceuticals
Pharmaceutical preparations

Blasdel Enterprises, Inc.
PO Box 260
Greensburg, IN 47240-0260
Contact: William Blasdel, Pres., R & D Mgr.
Telephone: 812-663-3213
Fax: 812-663-4968
Email: jacqblas@hsoline.net / URL: http://
www.blasdelent.com
Product Service Description:
Furnaces & ovens_industrial
Infrared & convection ovens, conveyors &
control panels

Blue Atlantic, Ltd.
685 W Shore Rd
Warwick, RI 02889-1352
Contact: Gary MacIsaac, Pres.
Telephone: 401-737-4242
Fax: 401-737-8698
Email: blueatl@netscense.com / URL: http://
www.blueatlantic.com
Product Service Description:
Luggage tags, card cases & key rings
Converted paper products
Plastic products
Business Gift Items
Golf Accessories

Blue Feather Products Inc
PO Box 2
Ashland, OR 97520-0001
Contact: Feather W King, Pres.
Telephone: 541-482-5268
Fax: 541-482-2338
Email: info@blue-feather.com / URL: http://
www.blue-feather.com
Product Service Description:
Manufactures magnetic sewing notions

Blue Sheet Inc., The
PO Box 164
Stapleton, AL 36578-0164
Contact: Alice Mosley, Pres., Pur., Sales &
Mktg. Mgr.
Telephone: 334-937-8468
Fax: 334-580-0292
Product Service Description:
Newspaper printing - Public records print out
for Baldwin County, AL.
Newspapers

Blue Water Spa Covers
3413 N. Forsyth Rd., Suite B
Winter Park, FL 32792-7420
Contact: R. T. Panchal, Pres.
Telephone: 407-678-9960
Fax: 407-678-7758
Email: rtpanchal@mindspring.com / URL:
http://www.spacoverusa.com
Product Service Description:
Insulated Spa Covers & Spas

Boasso America Corporation
PO Box 58
Arabi, LA 70032-0058
Contact: Walter J. Boasso, *
Product Service Description:
Transportation Equipment,

Bob Lewis Machine Co., Inc.
1324 W 135th St
Gardena, CA 90247-1909
Contact: Bob Lewis, Pres.
Telephone: 310-538-9406
Fax: 310-538-0017
Email: bob@blmachine.com / URL: http://
www.blmachine.com
Product Service Description:
Precision CNC machine parts

Bodine Assembly & Test Systems
317 Mountain Grove Street
Bridgeport, CT 06605-2133
Contact: William E. Bodine,
Vice Chairman & CEO
Telephone: 203-334-3100
Fax: 203-330-8716
Email: custserv@bodine-assembly.com /
URL: http://www.bodine-machine.com
Product Service Description:
Ind. Mach. Automatic Assembly & Testing

Bogdana Corporation
8929 Wilshire Blvd Fl 3
Beverly Hills, CA 90211-1938
Contact: Joseph Gruber, CEO
Telephone: 310-289-6800
Fax: 310-289-0399
Email: bogdana@earthlink.net / URL: http://
www.bogdana.com
Product Service Description:
Manufactures health and beauty products

Bolsan West Inc
226 N Sherman Ave Ste B
Corona, CA 91720-7122
Contact: Charles Hawkins, Pres.
Telephone: 909-278-8197
Fax: 909-278-0956
Email: bolsanwestinc@compuserve.com /
URL:
Product Service Description:
Manufactures custom shims, stampings and
fillers made from solid and laminated
materials for the commercial and military
Metal stampings
Metal products_fabricated
Edge-bonded shims
Machined laminated shims

Bond Paint & Chemicals, Inc.
118 Nw 5th St
Fort Lauderdale, FL 33301-3212
Contact: Vlagimir Yarosh, GM
Telephone: 954-763-4231
Fax: 954-763-1249
Email: / URL:
Product Service Description:
Acrylic paint & elastomeric coatings
Alkyd - polyurethane paints & supply

Bondtech Corp.
2400 N. Hwy 27
Somerset, KY 42503
Contact: Elsa Brown, President
Telephone: 800-414-4231 / 606-677-2616
Fax: 606-676-9157
Email: bandted@kih.net / URL:
Product Service Description:
Autoclaves & medical waste sterilizers
Service industry machinery
Autoclavable Bags
Reusable bio-medical waste containers

Bonert's Slice Of Pie
2727 Susan Street
Santa Ana, CA 92704-5808
Contact: Michael Bonert, Pres.
Telephone: 714-540-3535
Fax: 714-540-9615
Product Service Description:
Bread, cake & related products
Manufactures pies

Bonito Mfg.
360 Sackett Point Rd
North Haven, CT 06473-3103
Contact: James Bonito, Pres.
Telephone: 203-248-6190
Fax: 203-248-6399
Email: jinleeb@aol.com / URL:
Product Service Description:
Wooden clock frames, cabinets, countertops
& millwork : Furniture_wood household
Kitchen cabinets_wood : Partitions &
fixtures_wood

Book Covers Inc
935 E 59th St
Los Angeles, CA 90001-1007
Contact: David Newman, GM
Telephone: 323-232-1108
Fax: 323-232-7694
Product Service Description:
Manufactures fiber products for the book,
game, looseleaf & printing industries; grape
packaging : Converted paper products

Boon Edam, Inc.
4050 South 500 West
Salt Lake City, UT 84123-1303
Contact: Derek Nilsen, VP
Telephone: 801-261-8980
Fax: 801-261-1612
Email: derek@boonedam.com / URL: http://
www.boonedam.com
Product Service Description:
Revolving Doors - Manufacturer
Security Revolving Doors, Manufacturer
Turnstyles, Manufacturer

Borco Equipment Co.
50 Johns Street
Johnstown, PA 15901-1534
Contact: John Bortoli, *
Telephone: 814-535-1400
Fax: 814-539-6669
Product Service Description:
Dump Trailers, Steel & Aluminum

Borden Foods Corp.
180 E. Broad St.
Columbus, OH 43215-3799
Contact: J.R. Anderson, *
Telephone: 614-225-7480
Fax: 614-225-7602
Email: / URL:
Product Service Description:
Pasta : Spaghetti Sauce: Snack Food

Border Products Corp
1855 W Grant Rd
Tucson, AZ 85745-1203
Contact: Ray Valenzuela,
Telephone: 520-623-4100
Fax: 520-623-9513
Email: / URL: http://www.bordercorp.com
Product Service Description:
Distributes specialty name brand construction
materials and supplies; rental and forming
equipment: Construction materials &
equipment

Border States Electric Supply
PO Box 11430
Tucson, AZ 85734-1430
Contact: Dave Bills, Br. Mgr.
Telephone: 520-294-1414
Fax: 520-295-1515
Email: rmcmenamy@border-states.com
Product Service Description:
Electrical apparatus & equipment
Sells electrical equipment, wiring supplies
and construction materials
Construction materials

Bow Industries, Inc.
10349 Balls Ford Road
Manassas, VA 20109-2603
Contact: Dale Whysong, President
Telephone: 703-361-7704
Fax: 703-361-7369
Email: bow@dgsys.com / URL: http://
www.bowindustries.com
Product Service Description:
Magnetic Tape Winders / Cleaners / Certifiers

Bowsmith Inc
PO Box 428
Exeter, CA 93221-0428
Contact: Allan L Smith, Pres.
Telephone: 559-592-9485
Fax: 559-592-2314
Email: bowsmithz@lightspeed.net / URL:
Product Service Description:
Manufactures drip and low-volume sprinklers
for agriculture and landscaping; polyethylene
irrigation tubing
Farm machinery & equipment
Plastic pipe

Boxes.Com (A N.J. Corporation)
280 Green St
South Hackensack, NJ 07606-1428
Contact: Daniel Kiselik, V-P.
Telephone: 201-646-9050
Fax: 201-646-0990
Email: info@boxes.com / URL: http://
www.boxes.com
Product Service Description:
Folding paperboard boxes & point-of-
purchase displays
Boxes, folding paperboard

Boyntons Botanicals
9281 87th Pl., S.
Boynton Beach, FL 33437
Contact: Kathleen Kastenholz, Owner
Telephone: 561-737-1490
Fax: 561-738-9598
Email: boynbot@aol.com / URL:
Product Service Description:
Flowers and Florists' Supplies
Live plants , trees and shrubs

Bradley Lifting Corp.
1030 Elm St
York, PA 17403-2508
Contact: Harvey Bradley, Pres.
Telephone: 717-848-3121
Fax: 717-843-7102
Email: info@bradleylift.com / URL: http://
www.bradleylift.com
Product Service Description:
Materials handling equipment
Coil & Ingot Tongs

Bradley Pulverizer Company (Mfr)
123 South Third Street, PO Box 1318
Allentown, PA 18105
Contact: James J. Fronheiser, President
Telephone: 610/434-5191
Fax: 610-770-9400
Email: fronheis@fast.net / URL: http://
www.bradleypulv.com
Product Service Description:
Pulverizing Machinery
Mining Crushing & Pulverizing Machinery

Bradleys' Hermetics, Inc.
6501 Robertson Dr
Corpus Christi, TX 78415-9720
Contact: Warrn Spanutius, V.P.
Phone: 361-854-9833 / Fax: 361-854-1440
Email: bradpart@caller.infi.net / URL: http://
www.bradpart.com
Product Service Description:
Refrigeration compressor parts
Compressors_air & gas
Refrigeration & heating equipment

Brady Products Inc.
P.O. Box 5304
Clearwater, FL 34618
Contact: James Sailor, COO
Telephone: 727-443-4508
Fax: 727-447-8416
Product Service Description:
Plastic Foot Valves & Check Valves
Water Well & Pump Accessories
PVC Pipe & Well Screens

Brady Products, Inc.
PO Box 5304
Clearwater, FL 33758-5304
Contact: James Sailor, COO
Telephone: 727-443-4508
Fax: 727-447-8416
 URL: http://www.bradyproducts.com
Product Service Description:
Air volume controls, gauges, foot & check
valves, well points, screens & air releases

Brahmandeva Federation
1965 E 113th St.
Los Angeles, CA 90059-2005
Contact: Melek Amen - RA., Merchant
Phone: 323-513-7718 / Fax: 323-564-5221
Email: m.amen-ra@worldnet.att.net / URL:
http://www.business.fortunecity.com/del/252
Product Service Description:
Rice

Brake Funderburk Enterprises, Inc.
PO Box 16846
Jacksonville, FL 32245-6846
Contact: Robert Calvin, Pres., CEO
Telephone: 904-268-5531
Fax: 904-260-0283
Email: bfeinc@email.msn.com / URL:
Product Service Description:
Airline foodservice equipment & metal
fabrication : Engineering & Assembly
Services : Metal products_fabricated

Branson Ultrasonics Corp.
PO Box 1961
Danbury, CT 06813-1961
Contact: Anthony Pajk, Pres.
Telephone: 203-796-0400
Fax: 203-796-9838
Email: info@bransonultrasonics.com / URL:
http://www.branson-plasticsjoin.com
Product Service Description:
Plastics Joining & Precision Cleaning
Eqipment

Bremer Group, Co.
11243-5 Saint Johns Industrial Pkwy S
Jacksonville, FL 32246-7648
Contact: Ross Bremer, Pres.
Telephone: 904-645-0004
Fax: 904-645-0990
Email: ross@bremer.net / URL:
Product Service Description:
Spinal support systems

Brenneman & Assocs., Inc.
PO Box 679
Marion, IA 52302-0679
Contact: Ralph F. Brenneman, Pres.
Telephone: 319-377-6394
Fax: 319-377-3674
Email: ralphz01@earthlink.net / URL: http://
www.brennemanandassocs.com
Product Service Description:
Wire harnesses & electronic sub-assemblies
Electronic components, distribution

Brenner Tool & Die, Inc.
921 Cedar Ave
Croydon, PA 19021-7501
Contact: Glenn Cressman, Sales Manager
Telephone: 215-785-5241
Fax: 215-788-4485
Email: gscressman@brennertool.com / URL:
http://www.brennertool.com
Product Service Description:
Tool & die job shop
Dies, tools, jigs & fixtures_special
5 Axis Machining
Precision CNC Machining

Brevis Corp
3310 S 2700 E
Salt Lake City, UT 84109-3056
Contact: J Gordon Short, V-P., R & D
Telephone: 801-466-6677
Fax: 801-485-2844
Email: / URL: http://www.brevis.com
Product Service Description:
Signs & advertising specialties
Manufactures infection control signs;
handwashing motivation and training
materials— vide
Printing_commercial
Motion picture & video production
Laboratory apparatus & furniture

Brewmatic Co
PO Box 2959
Torrance, CA 90509
Contact: H. Gruner, General Manager
Telephone: 310-787-5444
Fax: 310-787-5412
Email: brew_equip@brewmatic.com / URL:
Product Service Description:
Manufactures coffee brewing and restaurant
equipment
Service industry machinery
Service establishment equipment

Brewood Engravers Inc.
808 17th St Nw
Washington, DC 20006-3910
Contact: Ernest Atkinson, President
Telephone: 1800-255-5185
Fax: 1800-969-5185
Email: brewoodeng@aol.com / URL:
Product Service Description:
Engraved stationery
Stationery products

Brickle, Hyman & Son, Inc.
PO Box 309
Woonsocket, RI 02895-0309
Contact: Max Brickle, President
Telephone: 401-769-0189
Fax: 401-769-0192
Email: max@hbrickle.com / URL: http://
www.nwblankets.com
Product Service Description:
Wool & synthetic fiber
Broadwoven fabric mills, manmade
Broadwoven fabric mills, wool
Commission weaving, dyeing, finishing
Manufacturer of Relief blankets & military
blankets

Briggs-Shaffner Co.
PO Box 10579, Salem Station
Winston Salem, NC 27108-0579
Contact: Emmitte Winslow, President
Telephone: 336-722-2571
Fax: 336-722-2355
Email: bscbeams@ix.netcom.com / URL:
http://www.briggsbeams.com
Product Service Description:
Textile Machinery Loom Beams
Textile Machinery Section Beams
Textile Machinery Tricot Beams

Brim Electronics Inc.
120 Home Pl
Lodi, NJ 07644-1514
Contact: Barry Danziger, Pres.
Telephone: 201-796-2886
Fax: 973-778-2792
Email: info@brimelectronics.com / URL:
http://www.brimelectronics.com
Product Service Description:
Insulated wire & cable

Bristol Babcock Inc.
1100 Buckingham Street
Watertown, Ct 06795
Contact: John J. Spagnoletti, Dir./Intl. Sales
Telephone: 860-945-2200
Fax: 860-945-2278
Email: / URL: http://
www.bristolbabcock.com
Product Service Description:
Supervisory Controls, Data Acquisition
Digital Flow Controllers
Process Control, Elec. Transmitters
Gas Flow Measurement

Britt Metal Processing, Inc.
15800 Nw 49th Ave
Miami, FL 33014-6300
Contact: Richard T. Britt Jr., Chrm., CEO
Telephone: 305-621-5200
Fax: 305-625-9487
Email: c.e.o.@brittmetal.com / URL: http://
www.britmetal.com
Product Service Description:
Aircraft turbines & rebuilt APU components
Aircraft parts & equipment

Broadway Sheet Metal
133 Starlite St
South San Francisco, CA 94080-6313
Contact: John Fontaine, Pres.
Phone: 650-873-4585 /Fax: 650-873-4582
Email: bsmmfg@pacbell.net / URL: http://
www.broadwaysheetmetal.com
Product Service Description:
Sheet metal work (food service equipment)

Broaster Co., The
2855 Cranston Rd
Beloit, WI 53511-3991
Contact: Gerald E. Mohr, Pres., COO
Telephone: 608-365-0193
Fax: 608-365-5158
Email: broaster@broaster.com / URL: http://
www.broaster.com
Product Service Description:
Cooking Equipment, Electric gas
Pressure Fryers
Rotisseries
Broilers, Electric & Gas
Warmers, Food
Marinade's & Breading

Brodart Co.
100 North Road, PO Box 300, Clinton
County Industrial Park
McElhattan, PA 17748
Contact: Telephone Sales,
Telephone: 570-769-3265
Fax: 570-769-5100
Email: supplies@brodart.com / URL: http://
www.brodart.com
Product Service Description:
Library & AV Supplies
Library Furniture

Bromley Plastics Corp.
PO Box 5129
Asheville, NC 28813-5129
Contact: David Katterman Sr., Chrm., Pres.,
Fin. & Pur. Mgr.
Telephone: 828-274-5254
Fax: 828-274-5542
Email: shadboy@prodigy.net / URL:
Product Service Description:
Plastic Extrusions : Plastic Profile Shapes,
Unsupported : Non Woven Polypropylene
Scrap - Bales / Waste : Non Woven
Polypropylene Densified Nuggets & Pellets
Polypropylene Compounds - Tale /CaCo3

Brooklyn Bow International
PO Box 10085
Riviera Beach, FL 33419-0085
Contact: Richard Hartman, Pres., CEO
Telephone: 561-840-8801
Fax: 561-840-8901
Email: brooklynbow@flinet.com / URL:
Product Service Description:
Ribbons & bows for apparel & retail -
oriented packaging
Contract packaging for labor oriented tasks

Brooks Internet Software Inc
1820 E 17th St Ste 360
Idaho Falls, ID 83404-6497
Contact: Mark Mansell, Sales & Mktg. Dir.
Telephone: 208-523-6970
Fax: 208-523-9482
Email: sales@brooksnet.com / URL: http://
www.brooksnet.com
Product Service Description:
Develops LPO/LPR, TCP/IP network printing
software for various platforms

Brooktronics Engineering Corp
28231 Avenue Crocker Ste 70
Valencia, CA 91355-1276
Contact: Chris Helwig, President
Telephone: 661-294-1195
Fax: 661-294-9032
Email: sales@brooktronics.com / URL: http://
www.brooktronics.com
Product Service Description:
Manufactures brush electroplating equipment;
supplies, chemicals and services (job shop)

Brookville Mining Equipment Corp.
PO Box 130
Brookville, PA 15825-0130
Contact: Dalph S. McNeil, Pres.
Phone: 814-849-2000 / Fax: 814-849-2010
Email: BMEC@bmec.com / URL: http://www.bmec.com
Product Service Description:
Railroad Equipment, Including Locomotives up to 150 Ton Size : Rail or rubber tired haulage equipment for underground mining & tunneling.

Broward & Johnson
2950 N.W. 72nd Ave.
Miami, FL 33132
Contact: Customer Service,
Phone: 305-717-0990 / Fax: 305-717-0995
Email: solardiam@aol.com / URL: http://www.solardiamond.net
Product Service Description:
Unsupported Plastics Film and Sheet
Plates, sheets, film, foil, tape and other flat shapes of plastics, self-adhesive
Waste, parings and scrap, of plastics

Brown Alcantar & Brown Inc.
9630 Plaza Cir.
El Paso, TX 79927-2105
Contact: Joe Alcantar, Jr., Richard Alcantar
Telephone: 915-858-1022
Fax: 915-859-3521
Email: joe@babinc.com / URL: http://www.babinc.com
Product Service Description:
Customs Broker, Freight Forwarding
Freight Forwarder ; Freight & Cargo Transportation : Warehousing

Brown Bear Corp.
PO Box 29
Corning, IA 50841-0029
Contact: Stan Bronw, Chrm. Pres.
Telephone: 515-322-4220
Fax: 515-322-3527
Product Service Description:
Environemental Equipment for composting & bioremediation: Brush Cutting Equipoement
Backfilling Equipment

Brown Cow West Corporation
3810 Delta Fair Blvd
Antioch, CA 94509-4008
Contact: Steve Ford, Pres.
Telephone: 925-757-9209
Fax: 925-757-9160
Product Service Description:
Manufactures yogurt

Brown Mfg.
RR 3 Box 339
Ozark, AL 36360-9443
Contact: Billy Brown, Pres.
Phone: 334-795-6603 / Fax: 334-795-3029
Product Service Description:
Farm, outdoor power & right-of-way maintenance equipment
Machinery_special industry, mini-trenchers

Broyhill Company, The (Mfr)
North Market Square, Box 475
Dakota City, NE 68731
Contact: Craig G. Broyhill, President
Telephone: 402/987-3412
Fax: 402-987-3601
Product Service Description:
Sprayers (All Types)
Refuse Trucks (Parks & Beaches)
Lawn-Garden Equip, Lawn Aerators

Broyhill Furniture Industries, Inc.
1 Broyhill Park
Lenoir, NC 28633-0001
Contact: Mr. Lynn Siemer, VP Int'l Sales
Phone: 828-758-3111 / Fax: 828-758-3709
Product Service Description:
Upholstered Household Furniture
Wood household furniture
Bedroom, Dining Room, Ocasional

Bruning & Federle Mfg. Co.
PO Box 5547
Statesville, NC 28687-5547
Contact: Thomas H. Bass, Pres.
Telephone: 704-873-7237
Fax: 704-878-0647
Email: salesinfo@abts.net / URL: http://www.bruning-federle.com
Product Service Description:
Dust & fume control systems
Blowers & fans

Brush Wellman Inc. Ceramics Div.
6100 S. Tucson Blvd.
Tucson, AZ 85706-4599
Contact: Lisa Valenzuela, Marketing Communications
Telephone: 520-746-0699
Fax: 520-573-9077
Email: valenzuela@brushwellman.com / URL: http://www.burshwellman.com
Product Service Description:
Copper/Tungsten heatsinks: Manufactures beryllium oxide ceramics for the electronics industry : CuPack power RF packages
Integrated thick-film circuitry

Bubbies Homemade Ice Cream & Desserts
99-1267 Waiua Pl Ste B
Aiea, HI 96701-3277
Contact: Keith Robbins,
Owner & R & D Mgr.
Telephone: 808-487-7218
Fax: 808-484-5800
Product Service Description:
Ice cream & frozen desserts

Buckeye Steel Castings Company
2211 Parsons Ave.
Columbus, OH 43207-2448
Contact: Richard M. Seckel,
Manager, Cust. Serv.
Telephone: 614-444-2121
Fax: 614-445-2084
Email: rmseckel@wthg.com / URL: http://www.buckeyesteel.com
Product Service Description:
Steel Castings

Buckley Company
9400 Activity Rd Ste M
San Diego, CA 92126-4414
Contact: Ted Rahn, Owner
Phone: 619-578-6994 / Fax: 619-578-6995
Product Service Description:
Sells computer supplies; sells new and recycled laser and ink jet cartridges

Bucks Fabricating
3547 Perry Hwy
Hadley, PA 16130-2325
Contact: Sales & Marketing,
Telephone: 724-253-3322
Fax: 724-253-3863
Email: bucks@nauticom.net / URL: http://www.nauticom.net/www/bucks
Product Service Description:
Roll-Off Containers - Steel & Poly

Buckstaff Company
1127 S Main St.
Oshkosh, WI 54901-6021
Contact: Tom Mugerauer, Sales Manager
Phone: 920-235-5890 / Fax: 920-235-2018
Email: / URL: http://www.buckstaff.com
Product Service Description:
Wood Library Furniture - TBL, SHLV, Seating

Budge Industries, Inc.
821 Tech Dr
Telford, PA 18969-1183
Contact: Linda Baron, V-P.
Telephone: 215-721-6700
Fax: 215-721-6707
Email: lbaron@budgeinc.com / URL: http://www.budgeinc.com
Product Service Description:
Automotive covers

Buhl Industries, Inc.
14-01 Maple Avenue
Fair Lawn, NJ 07410-1500
Contact: Ellie marrero, Export Coord.
Telephone: 201-423-2800
Fax: 201-423-2854
Email: / URL:
Product Service Description:
Photo Equip. overhead projectors
Phot Equip, opaque projectors
Electric lamp sockets

Bulbtronics, Inc.
45 Banfi Plz.
Farmingdale, NY 11735
Contact: Fran Thaw, President
Telephone: 1-800-654-8542
Fax: 516-249-6066
Email: bulbs@bulbtronics.com / URL: http://www.bulbtronics.com
Product Service Description:
Industrial Specialty Light Bulbs
Medical Specialty Light Bulbs
Scientific Specialty Light Bulbs
Photographic Light Bulbs
Graphic Art Light Bulbs
Stage & Studio Specialty Bulbs
Sockets
Batteries

Bullet Guard Corp
3963 Commerce Dr
West Sacramento, CA 95691-2168
Contact: Sharon Durst, Pres.
Telephone: 916-373-0402
Fax: 916-373-0208
Email: bgc@bulletguard.com / URL: http://www.bulletguard.com
Product Service Description:
Manufactures bullet-resistant architectural armor for doors, windows, drive-up windows, walls and barriers

Bumper Boats, Inc.
PO Box 739
Newport, RI 02840-0007
Contact: Arthur A. Grover, Pres.
Telephone: 401-849-7233
Fax: 401-849-1591
Email: bumperboat@aol.com / URL: http://www.kiddiebumperboats.com
Product Service Description:
Amusement park bumper boats

Burlington Air Express Inc.
Lot 5-A, Sabana Garden,
Carolina, PR 00984
Contact: Sales & Marketing,
Telephone: 787-752-5353
Fax: 787-762-8610
Email: rvidal@boxglobal.com / URL:
Product Service Description:
Customs Broker : Freight Forwarder
Freight & Cargo Transportation
Ocean Shipping & Receiving

Burlington Chemical Co., Inc. (Mfr)
P.O. Box 111
Burlington, NC 27216
Contact: Charles E. Utberg, Vice Pres./Mktg.
Telephone: 336-584-0111
Fax: 336-584-3548
Email: pbowers@burco.com / URL: http://www.burco.com
Product Service Description:
Soap & Other Detergents
Organic Pigments & Dyes
Surface Active Agents
Industrial Organic Chemicals, N.e.c.
Textile Softeners
Defoamers

Burlington Motor Carriers
14611 W. Commerce Rd.
Daleville, IN 47334
Contact: Ralph Arthur, President
Telephone: 765-378-0261
Fax: 765-378-4175
Email: rarthur@bmtr.com / URL: http://www.bmtr.com
Product Service Description:
Freight & Cargo Transportation
Trucking

Burlytic Systems
100-1 Crawford St.
Leominster, MA 01453-2300
Contact: Sales & Marketing,
Telephone: 978-466-9495
Fax: 978-466-9499
Email: jamesk@rclink.com / URL: http://www.burlytic.thomasregister.com
Product Service Description:
Machine Tools

Burns & McDonnell International
9400 Ward Parkway
Kansas City, MO 64114
Contact: J. Patrick Croker, Jr., Vice President
Telephone: 816-822-3047
Fax: 816-822-3173
Email: bmi@burnsmed.com / URL:
Product Service Description:
Engineering Services
Architectural Services

Burns, Morris & Stewart, Ltd.
PO Box 631247
Nacogdoches, TX 75963-1247
Contact: Rick Hagel, Ex. V-P.,
Mktg. & R & D
Telephone: 409-569-8211
Fax: 409-569-1967
Email: sales@bmslp.com / URL: http://www.bmslp.com
Product Service Description:
Door frames, Framesauer
Millwork

Burnshine Products
1100 Lakeside Dr.
Gurnee, IL 60031-2400
Contact: Patty Vick, National Sales Mgr.
Telephone: 800-837-8140
Fax: 847-263-3700
Email: burnshine@aol.com / URL:
Product Service Description:
Pressroom Chemistry: Fountain Solutions
Blanket & Roller Cleaners, Plate
Cleaners & Conditioners: Desensitizers
Environmentally Friendly Products

Burrell Leder Beltech, Inc.
7501 N. St. Louis Ave.
Skokie, IL 60076-4033
Contact: Luis Zunino,
Telephone: 847-673-6720
Fax: 847-673-6373
Email: sales.vds@worldnet.att.net / URL:
http://www.vsdnet.com
Product Service Description:
Conveyors & conveying equipment
Conveyor belts

Burrows Enterprises Inc
2024 E 8th St
Greeley, CO 80631-9786
Contact: Harvey Burrows, Pres.
Telephone: 970-353-3769
Fax: 970-353-0839
Email: rotogrind@ctos.com / URL: http://
www.rotogrind.com
Product Service Description:
Tub grinders, livestock feeding equipment,
dairy equipment

Burton Woodworks Inc.
4290 Alatex Rd
Montgomery, AL 36108-4867
Contact: Mark Silberman, V-P., Sales
Telephone: 334-281-0097
Fax: 334-281-0575
Email: mhjgroup@aol.com / URL: http://
www.mhjgroup.com
Product Service Description:
Deck components, trellis & lawn edging
Millwork

Burton-Rogers Co., Calibron Instruments Div.
220 Grove St.
Waltham, MA 02453-6550
Contact: William Burton, President
Telephone: 781-894-6440
Fax: 781-893-8393
Email: saels@calibroninst.com / URL: http://
www.calibroninst.com
Product Service Description:
Analog panel meters
Digital panel meters

Bush Boake Allen
2051 N. Lane
Jacksonville, FL 32254
Contact: Shawn Blythe, Manufacturing
Manager
Telephone: 904-783-2180
Email: / URL: http://
www.bushboakeallen.com
Product Service Description:
Chemicals and Allied Products, NEC
Unsaturated acyclic terpene alcohols
Concentrates of essential oils; Terpenic by-
products of the deterpenation of essential oils;
Aqueous distillates and solutions of essential
oils : Terpineols

Business Aviation Courier
3501 Aviation Ave.,
Sioux Falls, SD 57104-0197
Contact: Steve Pendegraft,
Telephone: 605-336-7791
Fax: 605-336-6810
Email: busav@busav.com / URL: http://
www.busav.com
Product Service Description:
Freight Forwarder, Freight & Cargo
Transporation

Busse Inc. (Mfr)
124 N. Columbus Street
Randolph, WI 53956
Contact: Thomas Young, President
Telephone: 920-326-3131
Fax: 920-326-3134
Product Service Description:
Palletizers & Depalletizers : Conveyors :
Retort Crate Loaders & Unloaders :
Singlefilers : Magnetic Palletizers &
Depalletizers

C & B Fosters Inc.
200 Norton Rd
Augusta, GA 30906-2129
Contact: Bruce Foster, Pres.
Telephone: 706-798-6914
Fax: 706-793-9373
Product Service Description:
Metal fabrication & welding job shop
Metal products_fabricated : Enviromental
Clean up & Responce Water & Land
Hauling & Transportation : Paint & Body
Repair : Sanblasting

C & G Manufacturing
243 Little Park Rd
Grand Junction, CO 81503-1725
Contact: Gacia G Saenz, Pres.
Telephone: 970-241-9206
Fax: 970-242-7115
Email: / URL:
Product Service Description:
Custom, sundroe, napkin, vending machines
& supplies

C & H Die Casting, Inc.
Ih-35 N., Box 1170
Temple, TX 76503
Contact: Charles E. Hinkle, Pres.
Telephone: 254-938-2541
Fax: 254-938-7117
Email: chdie@wm.com / URL: http://
www.vvm.com/~chdie/
Product Service Description:
Aluminum die castings & CNC machining job
shop

C & L Transportation Inc.
P.O. Box 2698
Cornelius, NC 28031-2698
Contact: Rebecca M. Pressley, *
Telephone: 704-892-4144
Fax: 704-892-6775
Product Service Description:
Transportation Broker- Truckload Serv.

C & M Enterprises
939 Barnum Ave.
Bridgeport, CT 06608
Contact: Sales & Marketing,
Telephone: 203-332-1488
Fax: 203-336-8459
Email: doublemz@aol.com
Product Service Description:
Management Services : Cigarettes containing
tobacco : Perfumes : Accessories

C & R Industries Inc
1801 Broadway Ste 1205
Denver, CO 80202-3840
Contact: Rich Chuickshank, Pres.
Telephone: 303-296-6612
Fax: 303-296-4856
Email: / URL: http://www.CandRind.com
Product Service Description:
Distributes oil well casing and tubing
Line pipe piling & structural steel

C & W Enterprises
10770 Lower Azusa Rd
El Monte, CA 91731-1306
Contact: Don Bangle, Owner
Telephone: 626-448-1825
Fax: 626-448-9628
Email: / URL:
Product Service Description:
Manufactures industrial detergents; sells and
repairs steam cleaners and high-pressure
washers : Soap & other detergents
Service establishment equipment
Repair services : Jenny Machines, Distributor

C G R Products Inc.
PO Box 2110
Greensboro, NC 27402-2110
Contact: L. Kirk Sparks, Vice President
Telephone: 336-621-4568
Fax: 336-375-5324
Email: cgr-products.com / URL:
Product Service Description:
Die cutting & laminating of non-metallic
materials : Gasket, packing & sealing devices
Specializing in all rubber compounds
including silicones & urethanes, felts, foams,
velcro : Molded & extruded parts : Lord,
Atlantic India, 3M, Parco: CGR has been in
business since 1963 & has plants : In
Greensboro, N.C. & Decatur, Ala. . Planning
to : Open a facility on Mexico / Texas border.

C P Industries, Inc., Christy Park Plt.
2214 Walnut St
Mc Keesport, PA 15132-7054
Contact: Jim Cielinski, VP Sales
Telephone: 412-664-6604
Fax: 412-664-6653
Email: cielinskij@christypark.com / URL:
http://www.christypark.com
Product Service Description:
High-pressure gas containment systems

C S S Technology Inc.
PO Box 1355
Weatherford, TX 76086-1355
Contact: Ervin Merritt, Pres., Opers. Mgr.
Telephone: 817-598-0997
Fax: 817-598-0999
Email: csstenl@csstech.com / URL: http://
www.csstech.com
Product Service Description:
Road base stabilizer
Recycling old asphalt roadbase material.
Stabilizing base material.
Stabilizing sub-base material.

C-Thru Industries Inc
2285 Fleetwood Dr
Riverside, CA 92509-2410
Contact: Rachelle Albany, Pres.
Telephone: 909-369-8777
Fax: 909-369-0847
Product Service Description:
Manufactures patio rooms, garden rooms and
solariums : Prefabricated metal buildings

C. H. Hyperbarics, Inc.
7151 W. Hwy. 98, Ste. 224
Panama City, FL 32407
Contact: Claude Herblot, Pres.,
Fin. & R & D Mgr.
Telephone: 850-265-8049
Fax: 850-265-1045
Email: chhyper@aol.com / URL:
Product Service Description:
Clinical & industrial high pressure air, gas &
hyperbaric systems : Precision Cleaning
Machinery, general industrial : Hospital/
Clinical Breathing Air & Vacuum Systems :
Certified Welding - High Pressure Systems
(ASME / MIL STD)

C. Hoelzle Associates Inc.
17321 Eastman
Irvine, CA 92614-5523
Contact: Sales,
Telephone: 949-251-9000
Fax: 949-251-9291
Email: sales@chainc.com / URL: http://
www.chainc.com
Product Service Description:
Computers & Computer Peripheral
Equipment

C. M. I. Enterprises
4380 E 11th Ave
Hialeah, FL 33013-2533
Contact: Michael Novick, Pres.
Telephone: 305-685-9651
Fax: 305-685-9511
Email: info@cmiautomotive.com / URL:
http://www.cmiautomotive.com
Product Service Description:
Foam laminations, automotive fabrics &
computerized cutting
Automotive & apparel trimmings
Leather
Vinyl

C. S. I. Chemical Corp.
PO Box 39
Bondurant, IA 50035-0039
Contact: L. L. Carpenter, Pres.
Telephone: 515-967-4297
Fax: 515-967-4842
Email: llccsi@aol.com / URL: http://
www.nutri-cal.com
Product Service Description:
Chelated liquid calcium

C. S. S. Publishing Co., Inc.
PO Box 4503
Lima, OH 45802-4503
Contact: Wesley T. Runk, Pres.
Telephone: 419-227-1818
Fax: 419-228-9184
Email: info@csspub.com / URL: http://
www.csspub.com
Product Service Description:
Commercial & book printing
Printing_commercial
Book printing

C. W. C. Steel Services, Inc.
PO Box 71690
Chattanooga, TN 37407-6690
Contact: Paul C. Wright Jr., GM
Telephone: 423-867-1760
Fax: 423-867-2682
Email: c-w-c@bellsouth.net / URL:
Product Service Description:
Metal fabrication
Metal products_fabricated

C.E. Niehoff & Co., Inc.
2021 Lee Street
Evanston, IL 60202-1557
Contact: Bahram khazeni, Export Manager
Telephone: 847-866-6030
Fax: 847-492-1242
Email: bkhazeni@ceniehoff.com / URL:
Product Service Description:
Alternators Motor Vehicle

C.M. Graphics
112 Haddontowne Ct., Ste. 204
Cherry Hill, NJ 08034-3667
Contact: Frank R. Matteo, President
Telephone: 609-795-2100
Fax: 609-795-6411
Email: cmgraphics@mindspring.com / URL:
http://www.cm-graphics.com
Product Service Description:
Printing Machinery
Printing Presses

C.M. Offray & Son Inc./Lion Ribbon Co. (Mfr)
Rt. #24, Box 601
Chester, NJ 07930-0601
Contact: Ronald D. Wallace, *
Telephone: 908/879-4700
Product Service Description:
Ribbon

C.P. Environmental Filters Inc.
1336 Enterprise Dr.
Romeoville, IL 60446
Contact: Carol Jones, Director
Telephone: 630-759-8866
Fax: 630-759-7065
Email: cjones@cpef.com / URL:
Product Service Description:
Industrial Dust Collection Equipment

C.P. Hall Company, The (Mfr)
311 S. Wacker Drive, Suite 4700
Chicago, IL 60606
Contact: William A. Werner, Dev. Mgr. Int'l.
Telephone: 312-554-7400
Fax: 312-554-7439
Email: / URL: http://www.cphall.com
Product Service Description:
Rubber Processing Chemicals
Plasticizers, Synthetic Organic

C.R. Laurence Company, Inc.
2503E Vernon Ave
Los Angeles, CA 90058-1826
Contact: Bernard P. Harris, Board Chairman
Telephone: 213-588-1281
Fax: 213-581-6522
Email: / URL:
Product Service Description:
Chemical Sealants, Export
Ind. Abrasive Products, Export
Power & Hand Tools for Glass
All Products for Automotive & Construction Glass
Shower Door Hardware
Transaction Hardware for Money Handling

C.U.E., Inc. (Mfr)
11 Leonberg Road
Cranberry Township, PA 16066
Contact: Andrew Marcocci, Mktg. Rep.
Telephone: 724-772-5225
Fax: 724-772-5280
Email: cue@cue-inc.com / URL: http://www.cue-inc.com
Product Service Description:
Polyurethane Products, Cast, Thermoset
Corrugated- Rotary Die Cutter Blankets

C2F, Inc.
6600 SW 111th Ave.
Beaverton, OR 97008
Contact: J.F. Marasco, Sr., *
Telephone: 503-643-9050
Fax: 503-643-0194
Email: james_marasco@c2f.com / URL:
http://www.c2f.com
Product Service Description:
Art/Craft Brushes & Paints
Modelling Clays & Supplies
Art Papers/Portfolios
Calligraphy Pens/Papers Supplies
Drafting Instruments

CA Signs
10280 Glenoaks Blvd.
Pacoima, CA 91331
Contact: David Rothstein, Pres.
Telephone: 818-899-1888
Fax: 818-899-4499
Email: dave@casigns.com / URL: http://www.casigns.com
Product Service Description:
Manufactures interior architectural signage
Signs & advertising specialties
Design of all sign systems
Manufacture exterior & garage signage

CAE Screenplates Inc. (Mfr)
Pruyn's Island
Glens Falls, NY 12801
Contact: Christopher Jones, *
Telephone: 518-761-2500
Fax: 518-798-0374
Email: / URL:
Product Service Description:
Drilled/slotted/perforated screen plates and cylinders for food processing, pulp & Paper, etc. Chrome plating services
Support/structural rings manufacturing.

CAS Medical Systems, Inc. (Mfr)
21 Business Park Drive
Branford, CT 06405
Contact: Myron L. Cohen, Exec. Vice Pres.
Telephone: 203/488-6056
Fax: 203-488-9438
Email: custsrv@casmed.com / URL: http://www.casmed.com
Product Service Description:
Medical Instruments & Apparatus

CAT PUMPS
1681 94th Ln. N.E.
Minneapolis, MN 55449-4324
Contact: Darla Jean Thompson, Dir. Of Marketing
Telephone: 612-780-5440
Fax: 612-780-2958
Email: sales@catpumps.com / URL: http://www.catpumps.com
Product Service Description:
High pressure fluid pumps & pressure washers
Pumps & pumping equipment

CBC International, Inc.
P.O. Box 646,
Wood Dale, IL 60191
Contact: Ronald J. Bogdanski, President
Telephone: 630-350-7997
Fax: 630-350-7875
Email: / URL:
Product Service Description:
International Freight Forwarder
Customhouse Broker

CBS (Circuit Board Specialist)
925 W Paul Bond Dr
Nogales, AZ 85621
Contact: Gary Clifford, Owner
Telephone: 520-761-3265
Fax: 520-761-3562
Product Service Description:
Manufactures transformers for electronic circuit boards
Electronic coils & transformers

CEECO Communications Equipment & Engineering Co.
1580 Nw 65th Ave
Plantation, FL 33313-4507
Contact: Maureen C. Gilley,
Telephone: 954-587-5430
Fax: 954-587-5440
Email: sales@ceeco.net / URL: http://www.ceeco.net
Product Service Description:
Telephone equipment & systems
Telephone & telegraph apparatus
Communications equipment, nec

CEI "Pacer"
PO Box 8090
Cedar Rapids, IA 52408-8090
Contact: Don Gaddis, Pres.
Telephone: 319-396-7336
Fax: 319-396-2462
Email: info@ceipacer.com / URL: http://www.ceipacer.com
Product Service Description:
Feed Truck Bodies
Feed truck semitrailers
Conveyors & conveying equipment

CLM, Inc.
982 B bourne Blvd.
Garden City, GA 31408
Contact: Paul Kennedy, President
Telephone: 912-964-4256
Fax: 912-964-2329
Email: PaulKen@ix.netcom.com / URL:
Product Service Description:
Warehousing
Distribution
Freight & Cargo Transportation

CMA Incorporated
904 Kohou Street, Suite 308
Honolulu, HI 96817
Contact: Henry J.S. Choi, President
Telephone: 808-841-8011
Fax: 808-845-7277
Email: / URL:
Product Service Description:
Fishing Equipment, Export
Frozen Seafood Products, Export
Toys, Sheepskin Stuffed, Export
Scrap Copper & Aluminum, Export
Const. Matls., Marble & Granite, Export

CMO Enterprises Inc.
285 Parkway 575, Suite 222
Woodstock, GA 30188-6421
Contact: Dean T. Owens, *
Telephone: 770-928-2860
Fax: 770-928-3241
Email: cmoenterprisesinc@worldnet.att.net /
URL:
Product Service Description:
Poly & Steel Intermediate Bulk Containers
Metal & Plastic Pails
Liquid Filtration Systems & Equipment
Granulators & Grinders
Industrial Packaging
Spill Containment Items

CMP Industries, Inc.
413 No. Pearl St.
Albany, NY 12207
Contact: Export Department,
Phone: 518-434-3147 / Fax: 518-434-1288
Email: briggsb@cmpindustries.com / URL:
Product Service Description:
Dental laboratory materials & eqpt.
Base alloys, investments, colloid, alloy grinders, etc.

CNI Manufacturing
15627 Arrow Hwy
Irwindale, CA 91706-2004
Contact: Toby Argandona, Pres.
Phone: 626-962-6646 / Fax: 626-962-4854
Email: info@cni-mfg.com / URL: http://www.cni-mfg.com
Product Service Description:
Manufactures snaptight, containment and utility boxes for gas stations

CPS Communications, Inc.
7200 W. Camino Real
Boca Raton, FL 33433-5597
Contact: Suzane Besses, Manager
Phone: 561-368-9301 / Fax: 561-368-7870
Email: suzanneb@cpsnet.com / URL: http://www.cpsnet.com
Product Service Description:
Magazines : Printed Matter : Brochures

CTL Engineering, Inc.
2860 Fisher Rd., PO Box 44548
Columbus, OH 43204
Contact: Sales & Marketing,
Phone: 614-276-8123 / Fax: 614-276-6377
Email: davew@ctleng.com / URL: http://www.ctleng.com
Product Service Description:
Transp Engine : Laboratory Testing

CWC Inventories, Inc.
2644 Metro Blvd.
Maryland Heights, MO 63043-2412
Contact: Ron Gravemann,
Phone: 314-739-1311 / Fax: 314-739-7073
Email: rong@cwcinventories.com / URL:
http://www.cwcinventories.com
Product Service Description:
Wholesale closeouts

CYRO Industries
100 Enterprise Dr., Ste. 700
Rockaway, NJ 07866-5055
Contact: Nanci Tolk, Sr. Marketing Communication Project Mgr.
Telephone: 973-442-6000 / 800-631-5384
Fax: 973-442-6117
Email: / URL: http://www.cyro.com
Product Service Description:
Plastics Materials and Resins
Acrylic sheet & polycarbonate sheet products
Acrylic based multipolymer compounds
Acrylic polycarbonate alloys

Cable Marine, Inc.
1517 Se 16th St
Fort Lauderdale, FL 33316-1713
Contact: Phil Lanzo, GM
Telephone: 954-462-2822
Fax: 954-523-3686
Email: yachtfix@aol.com / URL:
Product Service Description:
Rebuilt boats & boat engines
Engines _internal combustion
Boat building & repairing
Engine_ diesel rebuilding
Coast Guard & Defence Force Refitting

Cacheaux, Cavazos, Newton, Martin & Cukjati, L.L.P.
1300 N. 10th Street, Ste. 320
McAllen, TX 78501
Contact: Daniel Cavazos, Esquire
Telephone: 956-686-5883
Fax: 956-686-0142
Email: cachcavmca@aol.com / URL:
Product Service Description:
Legal Services / International
Business Services, N.e.c.
Consulting Svcs., Foreign Trade

Cagema Agencies Inc.
3625 NW 82nd Ave., Ste. 204,
Miami, FL 33166
Contact: Frank Wellnitz, President
Phone: 305-477-0216 / Fax: 305-477-5394
Email: mail@cagema.com / URL: http://
www.cagema.com
Product Service Description:
Freight & Cargo Transportation
Stamship line / agent

Cahners business Information
201 King of Prussia Rd.
Radnor, PA 19089-0002
Contact: Scott R. Sward, Group, V.P.
Phone: 610-964-4353 / Fax: 610-964-4947
Product Service Description:
Publishers, Industrial Trade Magazines

Cajun Injector, Inc.
9180 Hwy 67 S., PO Box 97
Clinton, LA 70722-3603
Contact: Chris Roach, V.P.
Telephone: 225-683-3759
Fax: 225-683-4401
Email: croach@cajuninjector.com / URL:
http://www.cajuninjector.com
Product Service Description:
Marinades : Food preparations

Cal-Coat Corp.
426 Fletcher Ave.
Orange, CA 92865-2503
Contact: Kurtis Breeding, Pres.
Telephone: 714-637-4763
Fax: 714-921-8357
Email: / URL:
Product Service Description:
Applicator of fusion bonded
Powder coating for corrosion protection

Caldon, Inc.
1070 Banksville Ave.
Pittsburgh, PA 15216-3006
Contact: Ernest M. Hauser, V.P. Sales & Mktg.
Telephone: 412-341-9920
Fax: 412-341-9951
Email: hauser@caldon.net / URL: http://
www.caldon.net
Product Service Description:
Industrial flow meters
Process control instruments

Calender Textiles Inc
1616 Perrino Pl
Los Angeles, CA 90023-2625
Contact: Thomas Rhee, Pres., Kenneth Yi,
Manager
Telephone: 323-269-1111
Fax: 323-269-1113
Email: kenyi@calendartextile.com / URL:
http://www.calendartextile.com
Product Service Description:
Fabric knitting
Weft knit fabric mills

Calgon Carbon Corporation (Mfr)
P.O. Box 717
Pittsburgh, PA 15230
Contact: Anthony F. Mazzoni, Director of
Marketing
Telephone: 412/787-6785
Fax: 412/787-6713
Email: mazzoni@calgoncarbon.com / URL:
http://www.calgoncarbon.com
Product Service Description:
Activated Carbon Products
Carbon Water Filters
Carbon Air Filters
Carbon Filtering Products, Whsle.
Vapor / Liquid Equipment Packages
Reactivation Services

Calibron Systems Inc
7861 E Gray Rd
Scottsdale, AZ 85260-3461
Contact: Edward E Francisco Jr, Pres.
Telephone: 602-991-3550
Fax: 602-998-5589
Email: calibron@unidial.com / URL:
Product Service Description:
Manufactures Liquid Flow Provers, Liquid
Density Meters

California & Hawaiian Sugar Co
830 Loring Ave
Crockett, CA 94525-1104
Contact: David Koncelik, Pres., CEO
Telephone: 510-787-2121
Fax: 510-787-1791
Email: / URL:
Product Service Description:
Refined cane sugar, household and industrial
Cane sugar refining
Raw cane sugar

California Exotic Novelties
14211 Ramona Ave
Chino, CA 91710-5751
Contact: Susan Colvin, Pres.
Telephone: 909-606-1950
Fax: 909-606-1951
Email: susan@calexotics.com / URL: http://
www.calexotics.com
Product Service Description:
Manufactures adult novelties
Manufacturing industries

California Fruit Packing Company (CAL-FRUIT)
1321 Harter Road
Yuba City, CA 95993-2604
Contact: Kelly Wells,
Telephone: 530-822-0920
Fax: 530-822-0199
Email: kwells@morningstarco.com / URL:
http://www.monringstarco.com
Product Service Description:
Food products manufacturing
Canned peaches, peaches sliced, peaches
halves
Canned Peaches in light and heavy syrup or
fruit juices

California Journal
2101 K St
Sacramento, CA 95816-4920
Contact: A G Black, Editor
Telephone: 916-444-2840
Fax: 916-446-5369
Email: / URL:
Product Service Description:
Nonpartisan political magazine
Periodicals

California Latex Inc
748 E Bonita Ave Ste 205
Pomona, CA 91767-1922
Contact: Peter Coye, Pres.
Telephone: 909-621-5871
Fax: 909-621-3911
Email: callatex@aol.com / URL:
Product Service Description:
Fabricates latex products
Rubber products_fabricated

California Mop Manufacturing
7108 S Central Ave
Los Angeles, CA 90001-1649
Contact: Ean Chong, Pres.
Telephone: 323-581-8991
Fax: 323-581-8394
Email: pechong@lasd.org / URL:
Product Service Description:
Manufactures quality brooms and wet mops;
all made in USA

California Ranchwear Inc
14600 S Main St
Gardena, CA 90248-1917
Contact: Elisabeth Wallenius, Pres, Roger
Cook, Exec. VP
Telephone: 310-532-8980
Fax: 310-327-0342
Email: rogercook@hbarc.com / URL: http://
www.hbarc.com
Product Service Description:
Men's, Ladies, childrens shirts, T-shirts,
Jeans, suits, coats, & outerwear

California Surface Hardening
PO Box 736
Compton, CA 90223-0736
Contact: Peter A Noonan, Pres., Opers. Mgr.
Telephone: 310-608-5576
Fax: 310-608-2072
Email: / URL:
Product Service Description:
Flame hardening of iron & steel products
Heat treating_metal

California Turbo Inc
4205 E Brickell St
Ontario, CA 91761-1512
Contact: Cameron P. Young, Sales Manager
Telephone: 909-390-2280 / 800-448-1446
Fax: 909-390-2285
Email: info@californiaturbo.com / URL:
http://www.californiaturbo.com
Product Service Description:
Mfrs. transformer cooling fans, 950-8600
CFM, above & below ground transformer
vault fans & blowers
Mfrs. heavy duty all metal construction 8" &
12" portable blowers for
confined work space ventilation

California Wire Products Corp
1128 Bradford Cir
Corona, CA 91720-1874
Contact: Sue Moss, Sales & Marketing
Telephone: 909-371-7730
Fax: 909-735-1070
Email: smoss@cawire.com / URL: http://
www.cawire.com
Product Service Description:
Manufactures wire mesh partitions and in-
plant office partitions
Partitions & fixtures, except wood
Wire products_misc. fabricated
Partitions & fixtures_wood
Manufacturing industries

Caltex Plastics Inc
2380 E 51st St
Los Angeles, CA 90058-2813
Contact: Rafael Rosenfeld, Pres.
Telephone: 323-583-4140
Fax: 323-583-1207
Product Service Description:
Manufactures plastic bags
Bags: plastics, laminated & coated
ESD bags
Military spec. pouches
Barrier Bags
Food bags
Pharmaceutical bags
Desiccant & humidity indicator cards
Long term food storage bags
Laminate rollstock & tubing

Calvert Co., Inc.
PO Box 180358
Richland, MS 39218-0358
Contact: Bob Milliet, Gen. Mgr.
Telephone: 601-939-9191
Fax: 601-932-2513
Email: calvert@calvertbus.com / URL: http://
www.calvertbus.com
Product Service Description:
Electrical bus ducts
Electrical equipment & supplies

Calweld, Inc
PO Box 534
Mc Kinney, TX 75070-0534
Contact: Jack Smart, GM
Telephone: 972-548-9211
Fax: 972-548-9956
Email: webmaster@calweld.com / URL:
http://www.calweld.com
Product Service Description:
Earth-drilling equipment

Cambell & Gardiner Inc.
5 Marineview Plz.
Hoboken, NJ 07030-5722
Contact: Breck P. Benja, *
Telephone: 201-798-3111
Fax: 201-659-8569
Email: candgchb@aol.com / URL:
Product Service Description:
Customhouse Broker

Cambria County Assn. For The Blind & Handicapped
211 Central Ave
Johnstown, PA 15902-2406
Contact: Richard C. Bosserman, Pres., CEO
Telephone: 814-536-3531
Fax: 814-539-3270
Email: ccabh@twd.net / URL:
Product Service Description:
Food service kits, sewn items & wire forms
Wire products_misc. fabricated
Textile products_fabricated
Steel wire & related products

Cambridge Manufacturing, Inc.
PO Box 747, 2100 Texas
Blytheville, AR 72316
Contact: Larry Gunnels, Pres.
Telephone: 870-532-6201
Fax: 870-532-6220
Email: larry@missconet.com / URL:
Product Service Description:
Surgical appliances & supplies
Hospital stretchers, stainless steel carts &
materials handling equipment
Machinery_special industry
Hotel & motel carts, bellman, maid carts
Wood carts, dollies, platform trucks

Cambridge Specialty Co., Inc.
PO Box 188
Kensington, CT 06037-0188
Contact: David Brayton, Pres., Sales & Mktg. Mgr.
Telephone: 860-828-3579
Fax: 860-828-5842
Email: / URL: http://
www.cambridgespecialty.com
Product Service Description:
Aerospace tooling & precision machine parts
Pratt & whitney jet engine service tools
Sikorsky helicopter parts & tools

Camcorp Industries
170 Rich Street
Venice, FL 34292-3107
Contact: David Demarest / Dorian Driscoll,
Telephone: 941-493-0622
Fax: 941-412-9320
Email: camcorpi@sprynet.com / URL:
Product Service Description:
Precision sheet metal fabrication

Campbell & Gardiner, Inc.
1050 Wall Street West
Lyndhurst, NJ 07071
Contact: Sales & Marketing,
Telephone: 201-939-4224
Email: / URL: http://
www.cambellandgardiner.com
Product Service Description:
Customs Broker
Freight Forwarder
Freight & Cargo Transportation

Campus Crafts Inc. (Mfr)
P.O. Box 60650
Rochester, NY 14606
Contact: Greg B. Weinrieb, President
Telephone: 716-328-6780
Fax: 716-328-0898
Email: / URL:
Product Service Description:
Mirrors, Convex & Dome Safety / Security

Canal Cartage Company
4509 Oates Rd.
Houston, TX 77013
Contact: Mark J. Scharringhausen, President
Telephone: 713-672-1779
Fax: 713-672-4006
Email: marks@canalcartage.com / URL:
Product Service Description:
Trucking, Transportation
Warehousing & Distribution

Canari Cycle Wear
10025 Huennekens St
San Diego, CA 92121-2967
Contact: Kathy Kass, Pres.
Telephone: 619-455-8245
Fax: 619-455-8292
Email: / URL: http://www.canari.com
Product Service Description:
Clothing_men's & boys'
Manufactures men's and boys' cyclewear
Men's & boys' clothing
Danskin cyclewear / women's cyclewear

Candy Express
10480 Little Patuxent Pkwy.
Columbia, MD 21044
Contact: Sales & Marketing,
Telephone: 410-964-5500
Email: / URL: http://www.candyexpress.com
Product Service Description:
Candy : Confections
Retail Franchise

Cannon Industries
545 Colfax St
Rochester, NY 14606-3111
Contact: Jack Cannon, CEO
Telephone: 716-254-8080
Fax: 716-254-1352
Email: cannon161@aol.com / URL:
Product Service Description:
Precision sheet metal, welding, metal stampings & turnings job shop
Sheet metal work
Industrial machinery
Metal stampings
Toner cartridge remanufacturing

Canton Drop Forge
PO Box 6902
Canton, OH 44706-0902
Contact: J.P. Bressanelli, President
Telephone: 330-477-4511
Fax: 330-477-2046
Email: cdf@cannet.com / URL: http://
www.conner.com/~cdf
Product Service Description:
Closed die forgings & stainless & titanium steel, carbon & nickel-based alloys
Forgings, iron & steel

Cantrell Hay
410 West Rutledge
Yates Center, KS 66783-1417
Contact: Shawn or Phillip Cantrell, Partners
Telephone: 316-625-2558
Fax: 316-625-2417
Email: cantrellhay@sekansas.com / URL:
Product Service Description:
Animal Feed

Cantrell International
1269 Majesty Dr
Dallas, TX 75247-3917
Contact: Mark Singleton, Pres.
Telephone: 214-630-3311
Fax: 214-630-5511
Email: / URL: http://
www.cantrellinternational.com
Product Service Description:
Food products machinery
Food & vegetable oil processing equipment & metal fabrication
Metal products_fabricated

Canvas Specialty
7344 Bandini Blvd
Los Angeles, CA 90040-3323
Contact: Greg Naiman, Pres.
Telephone: 323-723-8311
Fax: 323-724-3848
Email: / URL:
Product Service Description:
Tents, canopies, fabric tension structures, shade structures
Custom canvas work, tarpaulins, truck covers, straps, bags, covers

Canyon State Inspection
3625 E Ajo Way
Tucson, AZ 85713-6819
Contact: Larry Dolan, Pres.
Telephone: 520-745-3672
Fax: 520-745-8608
Email: / URL:
Product Service Description:
Metallurgical testing laboratory and services
Testing laboratories

Cap Gemini America
1500 SW 1st Ave Ste 890
Portland, OR 97201-5824
Contact: Doug Mendenhall, V-P., Sales
Telephone: 503-295-1909
Fax: 503-295-1923
Email: / URL: http://
www.usa.capgemini.com
Product Service Description:
Information technology consultants; custom programming and prepackaged software
Sap, Baan, oracle, Enterprise Effectiveness
Solution : Hi-tech Manufacturing Practice
Customer Information Management
Specialists : Utilities Trading / Deregulation
Practice : Telecommunications Billing & Customer Care Practice

Capital Information Systems
2580 S Tejon St
Englewood, CO 80110-1128
Contact: Andrew Marcopulos, Pres.
Telephone: 303-922-1001
Fax: 303-922-1717
Email: saks@capinfosys.com / URL: http://
www.capinfosys.com
Product Service Description:
Computer system integrators; value-added reseller
Computer integrated systems design

Capitol Products Co., Inc., The
P.O. Box 710
Winsted, CT 06098-0710
Contact: John R. Colavecchio, President
Telephone: 203-379-3393
Fax: 203-738-0283
Email: / URL:
Product Service Description:
Electric Countertop Cooking Range
Electric Broilers
Electric Sandwich Toaster Grill

Cappuccino America Corp.
765 Rte. 83, Suite 119
Bensenville, IL 60106
Contact: Roland Waller, Pres. / CEO
Telephone: 630-238-9488
Fax: 630-238-9513
Email: rwaller@capamer.com / URL: http://
www.capamer.com
Product Service Description:
Powdered cappuccino & hot chocolate
Frozen cappuccino & smoothies

Captek Softgel International
16218 Arthur St
Cerritos, CA 90703-2131
Contact: James Hao, Pres.
Telephone: 562-921-9511
Fax: 562-921-1687
Email: / URL:
Product Service Description:
Manufactures vitamins
Medicinals & botanicals
Cosmetic
O.J.C. drug

Car-Mon Products, Inc.
1225 Davis Rd
Elgin, IL 60123-1317
Contact: Fred L. Imming, Pres., Sales & Mktg. Mgr.
Telephone: 847-695-9000
Fax: 847-695-9078
Email: / URL: http://www.car-mon.com
Product Service Description:
Exhaust vent & air pollution control equipment

Caravan International
210 E. 86th St.
New York, NY 10028-3003
Contact: Dennis Friedman, Manager
Telephone: 212-772-7160
Fax: 212-737-9401
Email: ucernuschi@caravan-ny.com / URL:
http://www.caravan-ny.com
Product Service Description:
Aircraft Engines & Aircraft Airframe Parts
Tank Parts : Navigational & Communication Systems : EW : Satellite systems & payloads
Ground stations : Antennae
Medical equipment & supplies

Carbone Of America Corp.
PO Box M
Farmville, VA 23901-0276
Contact: Snelly Wooldridge, Hum. Res. Mgr.
Telephone: 804-392-4111
Fax: 804-395-8206
Product Service Description:
Carbon & graphite products
Carbon brushes
Fuses & electrical protection
Chemical engineering equipment

Cardinal Industrial Insulation Co., Inc.
1300 W Main St
Louisville, KY 40203-1436
Contact: Mark C. Mueller, President
Telephone: 502-589-5794
Fax: 502-581-9823
Email: butchk@cardinsul.com / URL: http://
www.cardinsul.com
Product Service Description:
Removable insulation blankets
Asbestos Abatement
Lead Paint Removal
Hazardous Waste Removal

Cardkey Systems Inc
1757 Tapo Canyon Rd
Simi Valley, CA 93063-3391
Contact: Mike Wolpert, Pres.
Telephone: 805-522-5555
Fax: 805-582-7888
Email: / URL:
Product Service Description:
Manufactures card access security management systems (corporate office)

Caretree Systems Inc.
160 Outerbelt St
Columbus, OH 43213-1527
Contact: G. W. Keny Jr., Chrm., Pres., Mktg. Mgr.
Telephone: 614-861-7775
Fax: 614-861-7349
Email: sales@caretree.com / URL: http://
www.caretree.com
Product Service Description:
Hydraulic tree-digging machinery

Cargill Salt Co/Dispensing Sys
2016 Clement Ave
Alameda, CA 94501-1318
Contact: Joseph R Esmond, GM / DSD
Telephone: 510-523-6191
Fax: 510-523-7698
Email: jesmond@cargillsalt.com / URL:
Product Service Description:
Tablet dispensing machines, brine makers, container feedscrews, bulk dispensers
Salt tablets, season tablets, salt seasoning blends

Cargille Laboratories, Inc.
55 Commerce Road
Cedar Grove, NJ 07009
Contact: Marlene Farro, Foreign Orders
Telephone: 973-239-6633
Fax: 973-239-6096
Product Service Description:
Refractive Index Matching Liquids
Sample Storage Systems : Density Measuring
Eqpt. : Plastic Beakers : STABILUR / CULT-
UR Urinary Stabilizers

Cargo Systems, Inc.
PO Box 81098
Austin, TX 78708-1098
Contact: C. Harold McElfish Jr., Pres.,
Telephone: 512-837-1300
Fax: 512-837-5320
Email: carsys@flash.net / URL: http://
www.cargosystems.com
Product Service Description:
Cargo restraint systems & devices

Carico Systems
4211 Clubview Dr
Fort Wayne, IN 46804-4402
Contact: Robert Cooley, Pres.
Telephone: 219-432-6738
Fax: 219-432-2461
Email: carico@caricosystems.com / URL:
http://www.caricosystems.com
Product Service Description:
Wire containers : Wire products_misc.
fabricated : Carts

Carla's Pasta
PO Box 787
Manchester, CT 06045-0787
Contact: Sandro Squatrito, Director of Sales
Telephone: 860-647-8647
Fax: 860-647-8572
Product Service Description:
Pasta : Macaroni & Spaghetti
Pesto Sauces

Carlisle FoodService Products
PO Box 53006
Oklahoma City, OK 73152-3006
Contact: Todd Mauer,
Telephone: 405-528-3011
Fax: 405-528-6338
Email: info@carlislefsp.com / URL: http://
www.carlislefsp.com
Product Service Description:
Plastic Products

Carmenco International
Brooklyn Navy Yard, Bldg. 3,
Brooklyn, NY 11205
Contact: Sales & Marketing,
Telephone: 718-643-9655
Fax: 718-855-2003
Email: carmcointl / URL:
Product Service Description:
Freight Forwarder
Customs Broker
Freight & Cargo Transportation

Carole Fabrics
PO Box 1436
Augusta, GA 30903-1436
Contact: Bill Geiger, Chrm., Pres.
Telephone: 706-863-4742
Fax: 706-863-8186
Product Service Description:
Draperies, bedspreads & shades
Broadwoven fabric mills, manmade
Drapery Fabrics : Upholstery Fabrics
Multi Purpose

Carolina Color Corp.
PO Box 486
Salisbury, NC 28145-0486
Contact: John Carter, Chrm.
Telephone: 704-637-7000
Fax: 704-637-7286
Email: carocolor@aol.com / URL: http://
www.carocolor.com
Product Service Description:
Plastic colorants

Carolina Medical, Inc.
P.O. Box 307
King, NC 27021
Contact: C. Roger Jones, *
Telephone: 336-983-5132
Product Service Description:
Electromagnetic Flowmeters & Probes

Carousel Candies
5130 W 26th St
Cicero, IL 60804-2915
Contact: Mary Jane Silvestri, Pres.,Owner
Telephone: 708-656-1552
Fax: 708-656-0010
Email: / URL: http://
www.carouselcandy.com
Product Service Description:
Caramels, Chocolates, & Caramel Apples

Cars & Custom Inc.
370 Macopin Rd.
West Milford, NJ 07480-3719
Contact: Joel Struble, *
Telephone: 800-836-5220
Fax: 973-838-6823
Product Service Description:
Used Car Dealer

Carstens, Inc.
PO Box 99110
Chicago, IL 60693-9110
Contact: George Block, Chrm., Pres.
Telephone: 708-867-5550
Fax: 708-867-1007
Email: carstens@carstens.com / URL: http://
www.carstens.com
Product Service Description:
Patient charting systems
Surgical appliances & supplies
Patient Carting Work Stations

Carter Brothers
R.R. 1, Box 42
Brundidge, AL 36010-9148
Contact: Ryan W. Daugherty, Vice President,
Sales & Mktg.
Telephone: 334-735-2606
Fax: 334-735-3500
Email: Ryand@carterbro.com / URL: http://
www.carterbro.com
Product Service Description:
Gas Powered Recreational Go-karts
Lawn Mowers

Carter Diamond Tool Corp.
4475 Hamann Pkwy.
Willoughby, OH 44094
Contact: John Carter, V-P., Sales
Telephone: 440-946-7800
Fax: 440-946-5671
Email: / URL: http://
www.carterdiamond.com
Product Service Description:
Machine tool accessories
Natural & synthetic diamond tools
Abrasive products
Machine tools, metal cutting types

Carter Grandle Furniture
2150 Whitfield Ave
Sarasota, FL 34243-3925
Contact: Shirley Cunningham,
Phone: 941-751-1000 / Fax: 941-755-0977
Email: shirley.cfi@juno.com / URL:
Product Service Description:
Aluminum outdoor furniture, umbrella,
cushions : Residential & commercial

Carus Chemical Co.
P.O. Box 599
Peru, IL 61354-0599
Contact: Holly Wilcox, Int'l Program Mgr
Telephone: 815-224-6500
Fax: 815-224-6697
Email: salesmkt@caruschem.com / URL:
http://www.caruschem.com
Product Service Description:
Cairox - Potassium Permanganate
Liquox - Sodium Permanganate
Carulite - Air Emission Control Catalysts
Carusmatic - Potassium Permanganate Dosing
Equipment

Carver, Inc.
115 Coleman Blvd
Savannah, GA 31408-9540
Contact: John E. Lee, Pres.
Telephone: 912-748-5000
Fax: 912-748-0500
Email: carver.inc@worldnet.att.net / URL:
http://www.oilseed.com
Product Service Description:
Seed processing machinery : Oilseed
Machinery

Cascade Empire
4900 Meadows Rd., Ste. 400
Lake Oswego, OR 97035-3298
Contact: Daneil Sprouse,
Telephone: 503-636-5666
Fax: 503-635-1155
Email: sprouse_dan@fctg.com / URL: http://
www.cascade-empire.com
Product Service Description:
Lumber, Plywood, and Millwork
Coniferous wood sawn or chipped
lengthwise, sliced or peeled, whether or not
planed

Casey Sales Company Incorporated
P.O. Box 961
San Leandro, CA 94577
Contact: Thomas E. Casey, *
Telephone: 510-632-2357
Product Service Description:
Snack Foods

Castle Inc
PO Box 750236
Petaluma, CA 94975-0236
Contact: Anthony Lynn, Gen Mgr.
Telephone: 707-765-0982
Fax: 707-765-0953
Email: alynn@castleusa.com / URL:
Product Service Description:
Manufactures woodworking machinery for
cabinetmaking industry

Castletech Ltd
956 Mann Creek Rd
Weiser, ID 83672-5522
Contact: Luane Watson Conway, Owner
Phone: 208-549-2706 / Fax: 208-549-0966
Product Service Description:
Manufactures pillows, golf cart seat covers
and pet beds : Furnishings_house : Sporting
& athletic goods : Manufacturing industries

Catalina Food Ingredients
206 Tower Dr.
Oldsmar, FL 34677-2964
Contact: Bert Sookran, President
Telephone: 813-854-5595
Fax: 813-854-3583
Email: bsookran@cfifoods.com / URL: http://
www.cfifoods.com
Product Service Description:
Miscellaneous Food Stores : Bread, pastry,
cakes, biscuits and similar baked products,
and puddings : Spices : Spiceblends for meat,
poultry, processed meats : Breading & batters
Marinades for meat & seafood items

Catalytic Combustion Corp.
709 21st Ave.
Bloomer, WI 54724-1821
Contact: Sales & Marketing,
Telephone: 715-568-2882
Fax: 715-568-2884
Email: sales@catalyticcombustion.com /
Product Service Description:
Catalytic Incinerators : Thermal Incinerators
Catalyst: All-Metal, Ceramic

Catalytic Products International, Inc.
980 Ensell Rd
Lake Zurich, IL 60047-1557
Contact: Scott Shaver, Manager
Telephone: 847-438-0334
Fax: 847-438-0944
Email: cpilink@aol.com / URL: http://
www.cpilink.com
Product Service Description:
Air pollution control system including
catalytic, thermal & regenerative oxidizers
Fume, VOC, ODOR destruction systems to
meet all clean air act requirements

Catania Spagna
P.O. Box J
Ayer, MA 01432
Contact: Anthony Basile, President
Telephone: 978-772-7900
Fax: 978-772-7970
Product Service Description:
Processors & packers of vegetable oils &
shortenings : Olive oils & blended oils
Servicing retail, food service & industrial

Catching Fluidpower, Inc.
501 W. Lake St. Suite 204
Elmhurst, IL 60126
Contact: Richard J. Guminski, Pres.
Telephone: 630-617-5800
Fax: 630-617-5801
Email: rguminski@catching.com / URL: http:/
/www.catching.com
Product Service Description:
Fluid power cylinders & actuators
Hydraulic & pneumatic systems
Fluid power pumps & motors
Hydraulic hose & fittings
Pneumatic hose & fittings

Cattle Kate Inc
PO Box 572
Wilson, WY 83014-0572
Contact: Kathy Bressler, Pres.
Telephone: 307-733-7414
Fax: 307-739-0767
Email: cattlekate@sisna.com / URL: http://
www.cattlekate.com
Product Service Description:
Manufactures men's and women's 1800-style
clothing : Clothing_men's & boys'
Outerwear_women's & misses'

Cedar & Hardwood Mfg. Company
357 Pitchercane Rd.
Hot Springs, AR 71901-8400
Contact: Hai Nguyen, President
Telephone: 501-321-2637
Fax: 501-321-4003
Product Service Description:
Cedar storage & novelty products. Veneer raised panels

Ceeco
1580 NW 65th Ave
Plantation, FL 33313-4588
Contact: Maureen Gilley, Sales & Mktg. Mgr.
Phone: 954-587-5430 / Fax: 954-587-5440
Email: / URL: http://www.ceeco.net
Product Service Description:
Telephones, Coinless Stainless Steel

Ceilings Plus Inc
6711 E Washington Blvd
Los Angeles, CA 90040-1825
Contact: Nancy Mercolino, Pres.
Telephone: 323-724-8166
Fax: 323-724-8249
Email: ceilingsplus@earthlink.net or ceilingsp@aol.com / URL: http://www.ceilingsplus.com
Product Service Description:
Manufactures ceilings : Acoustical metal ceilings : Wood ceilings : Luminous ceilings Curved metal & wood ceilings

Celotex Corporation
4010 Boyscout Blvd.
Tampa, FL 33607-5727
Contact: Carey Caldwell, Gen. Sales Mgr.
Telephone: 813-873-4212
Fax: 813-873-4287
Email: international@celotex.com / URL: http://www.celotex.com
Product Service Description:
Acoustical Ceiling Tile, Export
Residential & Commercial Roofing, Export
Residential & Commercial Insulation, Export

Cenex Harvest States Cooperatives
5500 Cenex Drive
Inver Grove Heights, MN 55077
Contact: Jim Tibbetts, Executive V.P
Telephone: 651-306-3752
URL: http://www.cemexharveststates.com
Product Service Description:
Soybean processing & refining
Wheat milling

Centerline Sports Inc
14274 Mead St
Longmont, CO 80504-9677
Contact: Mike Brown, Pres.
Phone: 970-535-9220 / Fax: 970-535-9224
Email: sales@centerlinesports.com / URL: http://www.centerlinesports.com
Product Service Description:
Manufactures volleyball equipment
Sporting & athletic goods

Centorr Vacuum Industries, Inc.
55 Northeastern Blvd
Nashua, NH 03062-3126
Contact: Lea levesque, Mktg. Admin.
Telephone: 603-595-7233
Fax: 603-595-9220
Email: sales@centorr.com / URL: http://www.centorr.com
Product Service Description:
Vacuum & controlled atmosphere furnaces & industrial machinery : Furnaces, ovens, Thermal Processing Systems

Central Air Freight Inc.
P.O. BOX 2043
Warren, MI 48090-2043
Contact: Sam W. Frank, President
Telephone: 810-755-4555
Fax: 810-755-2036
Email: sfrank@trancom.com / URL: http://www.trancom.com
Product Service Description:
Trucking Except Local
Air Transportation Scheduled
Air Transportation Nonscheduled
Freight Transportation Arrangement
Transportation Services, Nec

Central Illinois Manufacturing Co (Mfr)
201 N. Champaign Street
Bement, IL 61813
Contact: Gene Gall, *
Product Service Description:
Petroleum Fuel Filters

Central Lock & Hardware Supply Co.
95 N.w. 166th St.
Miami, FL 33169-6013
Contact: Shari Glixman, *
Telephone: 305-947-4853
Product Service Description:
Bathroom Accessories, Wholesale

Central Sprinkler
45 N. Cannon Ave.
Lansdale, PA 19446-2116
Contact: Sales & Marketing,
Telephone: 215-362-0700
Product Service Description:
Valves-Alarm-For Fire Protection Service
Fire Protection Products

Central Transportation Systems
6000 South Loop E.,
Houston, TX 77033-1001
Contact: Sales & Marketing,
Telephone: 713-731-6200
Fax: 713-731-6213
Email: centralfwd@centralsystems.com / URL: http://www.centralsystems.com
Product Service Description:
Freight & Cargo Transportation
Trucking
Packing & Crating

Centron International Inc.
600 FM 1195, S.
Mineral Wells, TX 76067-9475
Contact: Conway Beasley, President
Telephone: 940-325-1341
Fax: 940-325-9681
Email: rjohnson@centrongre.com / URL:
Product Service Description:
Plastics Pipe : Tubes, pipes and hoses, rigid, of plastics : Parts for boring or sinking machinery : Casing, tubing and drill pipe for oil and gas drilling, of seamless iron or steel

Centurion International, Inc.
PO Box 82846
Lincoln, NE 68501-2846
Contact: Mike Powell, Sales
Telephone: 402-467-4491
Fax: 402-467-4528
Email: sales@centurion.com / URL: http://www.centurion.com
Product Service Description:
Communications equipment, nec
Antennas & power products for Wireless communication

Century Multech
3370 Prince St.
Flushing, NY 11354-2745
Contact: Randy Y. Chu, President
Telephone: 718-353-9885
Fax: 718-353-9878
Product Service Description:
Sodium Ferrocyanide : Melamine Cyanurate
Iminodiacetic Acid : Calcium Citrate
Sodium Citrate : Adhesive Promoters

Century Spring Co., Inc.
P.O. Box 15287
Los Angeles, CA 90015-0287
Contact: James Paisley, International Export Manager
Telephone: 213-749-1466
Fax: 213-749-3802
Email: / URL:
Product Service Description:
Industrial Supplies
Helical springs of iron or steel
Miscellaneous cargo

Century West Engineering Corp.
825 NW Multnomah S. 425
Portland, OR 97232
Contact: J. Ned Dempsey, President
Telephone: 503-231-6078
Fax: 503-231-6482
Email: jndempsey@centurywest.com / URL: http://www.centruywest.com
Product Service Description:
Engineering Services, Hazardous Waste
Engineering Services, Water Systems
Mgmt Consulting Project Remediation
Engineering Services, Solid Waste
Business Consulting, Air Research Feas. Imp.
Energy Conservation-Air Compressors

Ceotronics Inc.
2340 E Trinity Mills Rd Ste 112
Carrollton, TX 75006-1900
Contact: Bill Johnson, National Sales Mgr.
Telephone: 972-416-9500
Fax: 972-416-9580
Email: headsets@altinet.net / URL: http://www.ceotronics.com
Product Service Description:
Communications systems
Communications equipment, nec

Ceradyne, Inc.
3169 Red Hill Ave., Suite A
Costa Mesa, CA 92626-3417
Contact: Joel P. Moskowitz, President
Telephone: 714-549-0421
Fax: 714-549-5787
Email: sales@ceradyne.com / URL: http://www.ceradyne.com
Product Service Description:
Advanced Technical Ceramics
Silicon Nitride Components
Silicon Carbide Components
Aluminum Nitride Components
Boron Carbide Components
Titanium DiBoride Components
Ballistic Armor

Cermak Peterka Petersen, Inc.
1415 Blue Spruce Dr.
Fort Collins, CO 80524-2003
Contact: Delores J. Wisner, Dir.of Marketing
Telephone: 970-221-3371
Fax: 970-221-3124
Email: windengr@cppwind.com / URL: http://www.cppwind.com
Product Service Description:
Wind Tunnel Modeling

Chad Therapeutics Inc
21622 Plummer St
Chatsworth, CA 91311-4106
Contact: Thomas E. Jones, CEO
Telephone: 818-882-0883
Fax: 818-882-1809
Email: genchad@aol.com / URL: http://www.chadtherapeutics.com
Product Service Description:
Manufactures respiratory care devices for oxygen delivery systems

Chalet Suzanne Foods, Inc.
3800 Chalet Suzanne Dr
Lake Wales, FL 33853-7060
Contact: Vita P. Hinshaw, Pres., R & D, Sales & Mktg. Mgr.
Telephone: 941-676-6011
Fax: 941-676-1814
Email: info@chaletsuzanne.com / URL: http://www.chaletsuzanne.com
Product Service Description:
Canned gourmet soups & sauces
Canned fruits & vegetables

Challenger Industries Inc.
PO Box 2727
Dalton, GA 30722-2727
Contact: Steve White, Pres.
Telephone: 706-278-7707
Fax: 706-278-3432
Email: challengerind@alltel.net / URL: http://www.challengerind.com
Product Service Description:
Indoor & outdoor carpet & artificial turf, sports surfaces

Challinor Wood Products
328 Linden Avenue
Wilmette, IL 60091
Contact: Mark Challinor, *
Telephone: 847-256-8828
Fax: 847-256-0509
Email: challinor@aol.com / URL:
Product Service Description:
Hardwood Dimension Parts / Panels / Strips

Chambersburg Engineering Co.
P.o. Box V
Chambersburg, PA 17201
Contact: Larry a. Forsythe, Sales Mgr.,
Telephone: 717-264-7151
Fax: 717-267-2201
Email: sales@ceco-beche.com / URL: http://www.ceco-beche.com
Product Service Description:
Machine Tools, Metal Forming Type

Chamfer Master Tool Co.
6320 Danner Dr
Sarasota, FL 34240-9399
Contact: Jeff Wilkes, Pres., MIS, Pur., Sales & Mktg. Mgr.
Telephone: 941-377-0020
Fax: 941-378-2739
Product Service Description:
Industrial cutting tools : Saw blades
Dies, tools, jigs & fixtures_special

Champagne Sauces Inc.
8001 E. Fairmount Ave.
Scottsdale, AZ 85251
Contact: Kay Broderick,
Telephone: 480-941-0557
Fax: 480-947-1120 / 800-342-9336
Product Service Description:
Manufactures sauces, salad dressings and pickled vegetables : Pickles, sauces & salad dressings

Chang Food Company
13321 Garden Grove Blvd
Garden Grove, CA 92843-2253
Contact: Van Nguyen, Pres.
Telephone: 714-750-5413
Fax: 714-750-5496
Email: changfood@dataframe.net / URL:
Product Service Description:
Manufactures Oriental frozen food (eggrools,
wontons, springrolls, shu-mai, sha shu bao (
chinese buns) : Frozen specialties

Chantilly Freight Corporation
P.O. Box 16166
Washington, DC 20041
Contact: William Cartwright, President
Telephone: 703-471-9743
Fax: 703-471-7349
Email: / URL:
Product Service Description:
Customs Broker : Freight Forwarder
Freight & Cargo Transportation

Chaos Comics Inc
7655 E. Gelding Rd., Suite B1
Scottsdale, AZ 85260-6959
Contact: Brian Pulido, Pres.
Telephone: 602-991-9080
Fax: 602-991-6005
Email: agoldfine@choosecomics.com / URL:
http://www.chooscomics.com
Product Service Description:
Publishes monthly comic books
Periodicals

Chariot Mfg. Co., Inc.
3912 Tampa Rd
Oldsmar, FL 34677-3118
Contact: Robert D. Hott Jr., Pres.
Telephone: 813-855-5801
Fax: 813-854-5803
Email: chariot@chariot-trailer.com / URL:
http://www.chariot-trailer.com
Product Service Description:
Motorcycle Carrier / Transport Trailers
Truck Trailers
Utility Trailers Open & Enclosed
Concession Trailers
Fiberglass Trailers

Charlatte America
Bluefield Tazewell Rd.
Bluefield, VA 24605
Contact: Bill Biermann, Mgr. Sales /
Marketing
Telephone: 540-326-1510
Fax: 540-326-1602
Email: charlatee@inetone.net / URL: http://
www.charlatte.com
Product Service Description:
Airports, Flying Fields, and Services
Airline servicing equipment, mobile electric
tow tractors & cargo conveyor belt loaders
Airline servicing equipment, mobile gasoline,
LP gas, diesel powered tow tractors & cargo
belt loaders
Vehiclesused in factories, distribution centers,
post offices, & airport passenger terminals

Charles A Starr Company Inc
5401 Longley Lane #45
Reno, NV 89511
Contact: Ronald Starr, Pres.
Telephone: 775-828-1964
Fax: 775-828-1966
Email: rstarrr@efortress.com / URL:
Product Service Description:
Manufactures ashtrays and cupholders for
custom aircraft

Charles E Gillman Company
907 E Frontage Rd
Rio Rico, AZ 85648-6234
Contact: Alan Gillman, President & CEO
Telephone: 520-281-1141
Fax: 520-281-1372
Email: / URL: http://www.gillman.com
Product Service Description:
Tanks & tank components
Manufactures military vehicle components;
wiring devices & radio frequency cable
assembly
Current-carrying wiring devices
Electronic components

Charlie Chemical & Supply, Inc.
PO Box 4639
Greenville, MS 38704-4639
Contact: Connie Burford,
Telephone: 601-332-9262
Fax: 601-332-9263
Email: coopchar@techinfo.com / URL:
Product Service Description:
Industrial degreasers & cleaners

Chase Industries, Inc.
621 SE 202nd Ave.
Portland, OR 97233
Contact: Raymond Draper, V.P., Int'l Sales
Telephone: 503-661-2389
Fax: 503-667-8349
Email: / URL: http://www.chaseind.com
Product Service Description:
Metal Cold Storage Doors, Elec. & Man.
Metal Doors, Double Acting, Plastic Clad
Plastic (PVC) Strip Doors & Curtains
Prefab, Wood Dock Seals & Shelters

Chase Leavitt & Company
10 Dana Street
Portland, ME 04101-4046
Contact: Alison Leavitt, Vice President
Telephone: 207-772-3751
Fax: 207-772-0297
Email: / URL: http://www.chaseleavitt.com
Product Service Description:
Customhouse Broker
Freight Forwarding, International
Freight Transportation, Steamship Agents

Chatsworth Products Inc
31425 Agoura Rd
Westlake Village, CA 91361-4614
Contact: Joseph Cabral, Pres.
Telephone: 818-735-6100
Fax: 818-735-6199
Email: / URL: http://www.chatsworth.com
Product Service Description:
Manufactures racks and shelving for
computer networks
Cabinets for computer networks
Cable management products

**Chef Paul Prudhomme's Magic
Seasoning Blends**
824 Distributors Row
Harahan, LA 70123-3210
Contact: John L. McBride, Director/
Marketing
Telephone: 504-731-3590
Fax: 504-731-3576
Email: info@chefpaul.com / URL: http://
www.chefpaul.com
Product Service Description:
Dried Seasoning Mixes
Seasonings Pizza & Pasta

Chem-Tex Machinery, Inc.
PO Box 2667
Dalton, GA 30722-2667
Contact: H. Eugene Tapley, Pres., Sales &
Mktg. Mgr.
Telephone: 706-278-6300
Fax: 706-226-5249
Email: gtapley@voy.net / URL:
Product Service Description:
Textile machinery
Machinery Consultant

**Chemco Manufacturing
Incorporated**
4530 Andrews # K
Las Vegas, NV 89031
Contact: Julie Spiegel, Export Director
Telephone: 702-651-0500
Fax: 702-651-0502
Email: export@chemcomfg.com / URL: http:/
/www.chemcomfg.com
Product Service Description:
Collector Filters, Spray Booth, Overspray
Peelable Wall Coatings Spray Booth
Removable Floor Coverings Spray Booth
Dust Collector Cartridges
Powder Coating Replacement Cartridges
Absorbent Media

**Chemdesign Corporation, A Bayer
Company**
99 Development Road
Fitchburg, MA 01420
Contact: Bill Scott, VP Marketing
Telephone: 508-345-9999
Fax: 508-342-9620
Email: / URL: http://www.bayerus.com/
organics
Product Service Description:
Industrial Organic Chemicals, Export

Chemetrics, Inc.
Rte. 28
Calverton, VA 20138
Contact: Shirley Ward, Export Manager
Telephone: 540-788-9026
Fax: 540-788-4856
Email: prodinfo@chemetrics.com / URL:
http://www.chemetrics.com
Product Service Description:
Water analysis test kits & equipment

Chemetron Fire Systems
4801 Southwick Dr Fl 3
Matteson, IL 60443-2254
Contact: Steve Dmitrovich, Cont.
Telephone: 708-748-1503
Fax: 708-748-2847
Email: info@chemetron.com / URL: http://
www.chemetron.com
Product Service Description:
Fire systems & detection equipment

Chemglass Inc.
3861 North Mill Rd.
Vineland, NJ 08360-1505
Contact: Michael Elefante, Mrkt. Mg.
Telephone: 609-696-0014
Fax: 609-696-9102
Email: customer-serive@chemglass.com /
URL: http://www.chemglass.com
Product Service Description:
Scientific glassware
Glass_pressed & blown

Chemgrout Inc.
805 E 31st St
La Grange Park, IL 60526-1224
Contact: Ben P. Schatz, Pres.
Telephone: 708-354-7112
Fax: 708-354-3881
Email: info@chemgrout.com / URL: http://
www.chemgrout.com
Product Service Description:
Pressure grouting equipment

Chemical Distributors, Inc.
3911 Monroe Rd
Farmington, NM 87401-2879
Contact: Bill Williamson, Pres.
Telephone: 505-327-0274
Fax: 505-327-6406
Email: farmcd@fisi.net / URL:
Product Service Description:
Industrial chemicals
Chemical preparations

Chemical Packaging Corp.
PO Box 9947
Fort Lauderdale, FL 33310-0947
Contact: Terry M. Colker, Pres.
Telephone: 954-974-5440
Fax: 954-977-7513
Email: aerosol@gate.net / URL: http://
www.cpcaerosols.com
Product Service Description:
Aerosol packaging

Chemicolloid Laboratories, Inc.
55 Herricks Rd
New Hyde Park, NY 11040-5340
Contact: Anthony C. Pepe, Pres.
Telephone: 516-747-2666
Fax: 516-747-4888
Email: chcolmil@aol.com / URL:
Product Service Description:
Colloid milling machinery
Machinery_special industry

Chempet Corp.
2100 Clearwater Dr., Ste. 207
Oak Brook, IL 60523-1927
Contact: Ronald J. Foitl, Pres., CFO
Telephone: 630-628-2444
Fax: 630-665-8652
Email: chempetc@ix.netcom.com / URL:
Product Service Description:
Industrial oils, chemicals & metalworking
lubricants
Lubricating oils & greases

Chemtrac Systems, Inc.
6991 Peachtree Industrial Blvd.
Norcross, GA 30092-3671
Contact: Sales & Marketing, *
Telephone: 770-449-6233
Fax: 770-447-0889
Email: Chemtrac@mindspring.com / URL:
Product Service Description:
Particle Counters
Charge Analyzers

Chemway Systems, Inc.
1605 Cottonwood
Bay City, TX 77414
Contact: David Deerman, Pres.
Telephone: 409-245-8811
Fax: 409-244-2546
Email: / URL:
Product Service Description:
Chemicals_industrial inorganic
Automotive chemicals & contract packaging

Cheraw Yarn Mills Inc.
P.O. Box 807
Cheraw, SC 29520-0807
Contact: Bill Malloy, Sales Manager
Phone: 843-537-7846 / Fax: 843-537-7665
Email: bill@cym.com / URL:
Product Service Description:
Polyester - Cotton Yarns, Open-End
100% Cotton Yarns, Open-End
100% Acrylic Yarns, Ring-Spun

Cherokee Glass & Mirrors
2200 4th Ave., N., Ste. 1
Lake Worth, FL 33461-3897
Contact: Phil Reynolds, Owner
Phone: 561-586-7060 / Fax: 561-586-4009
Email: PhilRey@aol.com / URL:
Product Service Description:
Paint, Glass: Structures and parts of
structures, of iron or steel

Cherokee Industries, Inc.
16N196 Walker Rd
Hampshire, IL 60140-8227
Contact: Stan Hatfield, Plt. Mgr.
Phone: 847-683-2993 / Fax: 847-683-3270
Email: cherokeeindustries@compuserve.com
Product Service Description:
Precision & production machining, metal
fabrication & assembly job shop : Industrial
machinery : Metal products_fabricated

Cherry Corporation, The
3600 Sunset Ave.
Waukegan, IL 60087-3298
Contact: David Hayes, Int'l Sales Manager
Telephone: 414-942-6500
Fax: 414-942-6336
Email: / URL: http://www.cherrycorp.com
Product Service Description:
Switches, Snap Action, Elec. Circuitry
Hall Effect Sensors
Keyboards

Chester Precision Co.
8 Inspiration Ln
Chester, CT 06412-1366
Contact: Karl G. Ohaus, Pres.
Telephone: 860-526-4980
Fax: 860-526-4347
Email: chstrprec@aol.com / URL:
Product Service Description:
Screw machine products

Chestnut Ridge Foam, Inc.
P.O. Box 781
Latrobe, PA 15650
Contact: Carl Ogburn, V.P. / Sales
Telephone: 724-537-9000
Fax: 724-537-9003
Email: crfoam@westol.com / URL:
Product Service Description:
Mattresses, Flame Resistant : Foamed
Cushioning, Flame Resistant : Padding &
Upholstery Filling, Flame Resistant
Pillows, Chair Pads, Cushions, Flame
Resistant

Chicago Conveyor Corp.
330 S La Londe Ave
Addison, IL 60101-3309
Contact: T.H. Hodanovac, VP Sales
Telephone: 630-543-6300
Fax: 630-543-2308
Email: cccsale@aol.com / URL: http://
members.aol.com/ccceng/ccceng.html
Product Service Description:
Pneumatic conveyor systems & components
Conveyors & conveying equipment

Chicago Steel & Pickling Co.
12500 S Stony Island Ave
Chicago, IL 60633-2406
Contact: K. Rajkumar, Pres.
Telephone: 773-646-3600
Fax: 773-646-0528
Email: dpoleski@compuserve.com / URL:
http://www.thesteelcompany.com
Product Service Description:
Steel pickling, slitting & cold rolling
Cold Rolled Steel Stripmill

Chick Master International, Inc.
120 Sylvan Ave. PO Box 1250
Englewood Cliffs, NJ 07632-0250
Contact: Ralph Magrans, VP/Sales & Mktg.
Telephone: 201-947-8810
Fax: 201-947-4608
Email: cmrmagrans@worldnet.att.net / URL:
http://www.chickmaster.com
Product Service Description:
Poultry Incubators : Poultry-keeping
machinery : Parts of poultry-keeping
machinery or poultry incubators & brooders
Hatchery ve ntilation equiopment, automation
& Incubation systems, plus software

Chickawaw Container Services
8700 Chef Mentor,
New Orleans, LA 70127
Contact: Ernie Buisson, Terminal Manager
Telephone: 504-243-1297
Fax: 504-243-1607
Email: cskwq@aol.com
Product Service Description:
Freight & Cargo Transportation : Trucking

Chief Industries, Inc.
PO Box 2078
Grand Island, NE 68802-2078
Contact: Dick Russell, Mktg. Mgr.
Telephone: 308-389-7403
Fax: 308-389-7448
Email: russelld@chiefind.com / URL: http://
www.chiefind.com
Product Service Description:
Wastewater Treatment Equipment

Child Craft Industries, Inc.
P.O. Box 444
Salem, IN 47167-0444
Contact: George Daleo, Sales Manager
Telephone: 812-883-3111
Fax: 812-883-1819
Email: / URL:
Product Service Description:
Wooden Furniture, Infant, Juvenile & Teen

Children's Furniture Co., The
3800 Buena Vista Ave
Baltimore, MD 21211-1799
Contact: Christopher Murray, Pres., Fin., R &
D, Sales & Mktg. Mgr.
Telephone: 410-243-7488
Fax: 410-243-7489
Email: info@childrens-furniture.com / URL:
http://www.childrens-furniture.com
Product Service Description:
Children's furniture

Chilton Company
One Chilton Way
Radnor, PA 19089
Contact: Scott R. Sward, *
Telephone: 610-964-4353
Product Service Description:
Publishers, of Manufactura. Serving 25,000
Plant,engineering and Corporate Management
Professionals

Chipico Pickles
837 N. California Ave.
Chicago, IL 60622-4401
Contact: Jeff Johns, G.M.
Telephone: 773-278-7711
Fax: 773-278-8627
Product Service Description:
Pickles & relish & peppers

**Chiquita Processing Foods, LLC -
Int'l Div. F/K/A Friday Canning
Corporation**
P.O. Box 129
New Richmond, WI 54017
Contact: Tim Riemenschneider, Director, Int'l
Sales & Mktg.
Phone: 715-246-2241 / Fax: 715-243-8350
Email: triemenschneider@chiquita.com /
URL: http://www.chiquita.com
Product Service Description:
Canned Vegetables (Private Labels)
Canned Soups

**Chiquola Industrial Products
Group, LLC**
PO Box 246
Honea Path, SC 29654-0246
Contact: Harold E. McCarty, Pres & C.O.O.
Telephone: 864-369-7311
Fax: 864-369-3028
Email: glo@carol.net / URL:
Product Service Description:
Broadwoven fabric mills, cotton
Industrial cloth

Chlorine & Chemical Supply Co.
P.O. Box 31
Columbus, TX 78934
Contact: Beverly Simpson, *
Telephone: 409-732-6881
Product Service Description:
Women Owned Company

Chromaline Corp.
4832 Grand Ave
Duluth, MN 55807-2743
Contact: Robert Blanks, Dir/Intl Sales
Telephone: 218-628-2217
Fax: 218-628-3245
Product Service Description:
Photo Supplies Photo Sensitive Films
Screen Printing: Photo Supplies Emulsions &
Chemicals

Chrome Crankshaft Co
PO Box 3030
Bell Gardens, CA 90202-3030
Contact: Ray Carel, Plt. Mgr.
Telephone: 562-806-5231
Fax: 562-928-6773
Product Service Description:
Grinding; chrome plating; sales of
locomotives and related parts : Plating &
polishing : Industrial machinery

Chronomite Labs Inc
1420 240th St
Harbor City, CA 90710-1307
Contact: Robert Russell, Pres.
Telephone: 310-534-2300
Fax: 310-530-1381
Email: info@omnidealers.com / URL: http://
www.omnidealers.com
Product Service Description:
Manufactures water conservation products,
Omni flow control devices and instant-flow
tankless hot water heaters
Plumbing fixture fittings & trim

Ciasons Industrial Inc
1615 Boyd St
Santa Ana, CA 92705-5103
Contact: Paul Hsieh, Pres.
Telephone: 714-259-0838
Fax: 714-259-0883
Email: / URL:
Product Service Description:
Manufactures air compressors
Compressors_air & gas

Cincinnati Test Systems, Inc.
5555 Dry Fork Rd
Cleves, OH 45002-9733
Contact: Gary L. Grebe, Mktg. Mgr.
Telephone: 513-367-6699
Fax: 513-367-5426
Email: ctsinc1@aol.com / URL: http://
www.cincinnati-test.com
Product Service Description:
Pneumatic leak testing equipment & metal
fabrication

Cir-Kit Concepts, Inc.
32 Woodlake Dr Se
Rochester, MN 55904-5506
Contact: Corrine M. Skare, Pres., Engrg.,
Hum. Res. & Opers. Mgr.
Telephone: 507-288-0860
Fax: 507-288-9181
Email: cir.kit@cir-kitconcepts.com / URL:
http://www.cir-kitconcepts.com
Product Service Description:
Doll house & model railroad electrical wiring
& lighting components
Lighting equipment

Circle International
260 Townsend St.
San Francisco, CA 94107-0933
Contact: Carma Caughlan, *
Telephone: 415-978-0600
Fax: 415-978-0699
Email: Caughlan@circleintl.com / URL:
Product Service Description:
Air Freight Forwarders
Warehousing & Inventory Management
Customs Broker
Integrated Transportation / Trade Services
Advanced Logistics Information Systems
Marine Insurance Services
NVOCC

Circle International
P.O. Box 22330
Salt Lake City, UT 84122
Contact: Cynthia Coffin, Branch Manager
Telephone: 435-649-6252
Fax: 435-649-6249
Email: circle@utw.com / URL: http://
www.circleintl.com
Product Service Description:
Freight & Cargo Transportation
Trucking

Circle S Trailers Inc.
7435 E. St. Hwy. E
Fair Grove, MO 65648-9215
Contact: J. L. Sharp, Pres., Pur., Sales &
Mktg. Mgr.
Telephone: 417-759-2606
Fax: 417-759-7502
Email: / URL: http://
www.ecodev.state.mo.us/ded
Product Service Description:
Truck trailers
Horse & livestock trailers, cargo vans &
trailer roof bows
Transportation equipment

Circuit Components, Inc.
2400 S. Roosevelt St.
Tempe, AZ 85282-2006
Contact: Antonio F. Valles, Dir. of Mktg.
Telephone: 480-967-0624
Fax: 480-967-9385
Email: info@surgencontrol.com / URL: http://www.surgencontrol.com
Product Service Description:
Manufactures surge protection devices
Board Stiffeners : Decoupling Capacitors

Circuit Manufacturing Technology
7303 Madison St
Paramount, CA 90723-4029
Contact: Edwin Vinas,
Phone: 562-634-9953 / Fax: 562-634-9954
Email: weeeco@aol.com / URL:
Product Service Description:
Manufactures printed circuit boards
Printed circuit boards

Circuit Technology Corp.
1603 NW 2nd St.
Deerfield Beach, FL 33442
Contact: Frank Savin, President
Telephone: 954-420-0345
Email: cirtech@att.net / URL:
Product Service Description:
Printed & Etched Circuit Boards & Electronic Assembly
Printed Circuit Boards
Electronic Components
Elect. Design & Packaging

City Glass Co.
200 N Dixie Hwy
Hollywood, FL 33020-6705
Contact: Stefan Pandos, President
Telephone: 954-923-2428
Fax: 954-925-4700
Email: cityglassofhollywood@yahoo.com / URL:
Product Service Description:
Glass & mirror cutting & picture frames
Glass products from purchased glass
Wood products

City of Cincinnati Dept. Econ Dev.
805 Central Avenue, Suite 710
Cincinnati, OH 45202-1947
Contact: Andi Udris, Director
Telephone: 513-352-3950
Fax: 513-352-6257
Email: andi.udris@cinecon.rcc.org / URL:
http://www.cincinnatigov.com
Product Service Description:
Economic Development Agency

Cla-val Company
P.O. Box 1325
Newport Beach, CA 92663
Contact: Brooks D. Wiles, Export Sales Mgr.
Telephone: 714/548-2201
Fax: 714-548-5441
Email: / URL:
Product Service Description:
Automatic Regulating Valves

Clareblend Inc
3555 Airway Dr Ste 307
Reno, NV 89511-1828
Contact: Margaret Smith, Mgr.
Telephone: 775-332-3850
Fax: 775-332-3852
Email: / URL: http://www.clareblend.com
Product Service Description:
Manufactures electrolysis, skin care & medical equipment

Clarke's Custom Windows, Inc.
900 S Westgate St
Addison, IL 60101-5020
Contact: Emile Clarke, Pres.
Telephone: 630-543-0013
Fax: 630-543-2715
Product Service Description:
Aluminum & wooden windows
Doors, sash & trim_metal
Millwork

Classic Cosmetics Inc
9601 Irondale Ave
Chatsworth, CA 91311-5009
Contact: Ida Csiszar, Pres.
Phone: 818-773-9042 / Fax: 818-773-9029
Product Service Description:
Manufactures cosmetics
Toilet preparations

Classic Lady Packaging, Inc.
5785 Westwood Dr.
Saint Charles, MO 63304
Contact: Lois M. Schaeffer, Pres., Pur. Agt.
Phone: 314-441-8803 / Fax: 314-441-8532
Email: claslady@tetranet.net / URL: http://www.classicladypkg.com
Product Service Description:
Contract Packaging & Manufacturing
Personal Care Products

Classic Medallics, Inc. (Mfr)
2-15 Borden Avenue
Long Island City, NY 11101
Contact: Lucy Walsh, Executive Assistant
Phone: 718/392-5410 / Fax: 718-784-1757
Email: sales@classic-medallics.com / URL:
http://www.classic-Medallics.com
Product Service Description:
Sports & Religious Jewelry
Trophies, Medals, Medallions, Plaques, Cups
Ribbons, Bowls, Desk Accessories,
Commemorative Coins

Clean Air Consultants, Inc.
2519 National Dr Ste B
Garland, TX 75041-2321
Contact: Cliff Watson, Pres
Telephone: 972-278-2664
Fax: 972-278-1810
Email: filter1@airmail.net / URL: http://www.filter1.com
Product Service Description:
Blowers & fans : Air cleaners :
Dust collectors

Clean Air Filter Co.
212 Main Ave.
Defiance, IA 51527
Contact: Michael Schmitz, Pres.
Telephone: 712-748-3642
Fax: 712-748-3643
Email: caf@cleanairfilter.net / URL: http://www.cleanairfilter.net
Product Service Description:
Blowers & fans systems : Respirator filter systems : Filters

Clean Water Systems Intl
PO Box 146
Klamath Falls, OR 97601-0008
Contact: Charles G Romary, Pres.
Phone: 541-882-9993 / Fax: 541-882-9994
Email: cws@cdsnet.com / URL: http://www.cleanwatersysintl.com
Product Service Description:
Manufactures ultra-violet water treatment systems; electronic monitor & control equipment

Clear Creek Courant
PO Box 2020
Idaho Springs, CO 80452-2020
Contact: Carol Wilcox, Ptnr.
Telephone: 303-567-4491
Fax: 303-567-4492
Email: cccourant@bwn.net / URL: http://www.members.aol.com/cccourant
Product Service Description:
Publishes weekly newspaper
Newspapers
Books, periodicals & newspapers

Clearfield Machine Company (Mfr)
P.O. Box 992A
Clearfield, PA 16830
Contact: Pete Vandewater, Sales Engineer
Telephone: 814-765-6544
Fax: 814-765-4581
Email: PVironman@aol.com / URL:
Product Service Description:
Iron Castings, Gray & Ductile

Cleaver-Brooks
P.O. Box 421
Milwaukee, WI 53201
Telephone: 414-359-0600
Fax: 414-577-2715
Email: info@cleaver-brooks.com / URL:
http://www.cleaver-brooks.com
Product Service Description:
Boilers
Boiler Controls

Cleco Manufacturing, Inc.
346 Quinnipiac St., P.O. Box 517
Wallingford, CT 06492
Contact: Ed Sasso,
Telephone: 203-265-2041
Fax: 203-265-9283
Email: / URL:
Product Service Description:
Concrete Molds

Cleveland Mills
PO Box 68
Lawndale, NC 28090-0068
Contact: Watt Jackson, V.-P., Knitting
Telephone: 704-538-8511
Fax: 704-538-4276
Email: / URL:
Product Service Description:
Weft knit fabric mills
Knit fabric dyeing & finishing

Cleveland Motion Controls, Inc.
7550 Hub Pkwy
Valley View, OH 44125-5705
Contact: Tim A. Schultz, Comm. & Mktg. Mgr.
Telephone: 216-524-8800
Fax: 216-642-2100
Email: tschultz@cmccontrols.com / URL:
http://www.cmccontrols.com
Product Service Description:
Relays & industrial controls
Adjustable speed drives, web tension equipment, sensors & CNC controllers

CliniComp International Inc
9655 Towne Centre Dr
San Diego, CA 92121-1965
Contact: Chris Haudenschild, Pres.
Telephone: 619-546-8202 / 800-350-8202
Fax: 619-546-1801
Email: / URL: http://www.clinicomp.com
Product Service Description:
Develops clinical information systems for hospitals

Clinton Hardwood Inc.
PO Box 835
Clinton, SC 29325-0835
Contact: Benton Lawson, Pres.
Telephone: 864-833-3835
Fax: 864-833-6998
Email: / URL:
Product Service Description:
Sawmills & planing mills, general
Lumber processing

cmiSource.com
280 Connecticut Avenue
Norwalk, CT 06854
Contact: Peter F. Hovell,
Telephone: 203-838-1013
Fax: 203-853-3749
Email: info@cmisource.com / URL: http://www.cmisource.com
Product Service Description:
Microfilm - the Internet Directory of Imaging & Micrographics
Imaging - the Internet Directory of Imaging and Micrographics

Cmp Corporation
P.O. Box 15199
Oklahoma City, OK 73155-5199
Contact: Ben Harrison, Vice President
Telephone: 405-672-4544
Fax: 405-672-4547
Email: / URL:
Product Service Description:
Air Conditioning Compressor Repair Parts
Refrigeration Compressor Repair Parts
Refrig. Compressor Crankshafts

Co-Steel Raritan
PO Box 309
Perth Amboy, NJ 08862-0309
Contact: George Mischenko, V-P., GM
Telephone: 732-442-1600
Fax: 732-442-4020
Email: / URL: http://www.costeel.com
Product Service Description:
Blast furnaces & steel mills
Steel wire rods, metal recycling & rolling
Steel wire & related products
Secondary nonferrous metals

Coast Foundry & Mfg Co
PO Box 1788
Pomona, CA 91769-1788
Contact: Armand Antunez, Pres.
Telephone: 909-596-1883
Fax: 909-596-2650
Email: / URL:
Product Service Description:
Metal sanitary ware
Manufactures sanitary ware, water control valves
Ballcocks & Flushvalves, plastic & brass

Coast Publishing
PO Box 223519
Carmel, CA 93922-3519
Contact: Gary Koeppel, Publisher
Telephone: 408-625-4145
Fax: 408-625-3575
Email: gmk@mbay.net / URL: http://www.henrymillerart.com
Product Service Description:
Publishes books, lithographic and poster reproduction
Publishing_miscellaneous

Coastal Industries
PO Box 16091
Jacksonville, FL 32245-6091
Contact: David L. Herbert, VP Mktg. & Sales
Telephone: 904-642-3970
Fax: 904-642-5015
Email: dherbert@coastalmd.com
Product Service Description:
Tub & Shower enclosures & Shower Doors
Glass products from purchased glass

Coastal Printing Co.
PO Box 1340
Ocean View, DE 19970-1340
Contact: Lance Fargo, General Manager
Phone: 302-537-1700 / Fax: 302-537-2050
Email: coastal@beach.net / URL:
Product Service Description:
Commercial printing
Printing_commercial

Coastal Unilube, Inc.
44 N. Second Street, Suite 1200
Mephis, TN 38103
Contact: Kevin Griggs, Dir. Int'l Bus.
Telephone: 901-525-2300
Fax: 901-525-2300
Email: kevin.griggs@coastalcorp.com / URL:
http://www.coastalcorp.com
Product Service Description:
Automotive lubricants : Lubricating oils &
greases : A utomotive chemicals
Brake fluid : Antifreeze / coolant

Coastal Vision Center
113 City Smitty Dr
Saint Marys, GA 31558-8908
Contact: J. McClane, Pres.
Telephone: 912-882-3040
Fax: 912-882-3786
Email: mcclaneiii@aol.com / URL:
Product Service Description:
Plastic optical lenses : Ophthalmic goods

Coates Electrographics Inc.
Country Club Rd.
Dallas, PA 18612
Contact: Larry Berti, Sales Mgr.
Telephone: 570-675-1131
Fax: 570-675-0415
Email: larry.berti@coatescri.com / URL:
http://www.coates.com
Product Service Description:
Jet Inks : Dry Toners

Cobblecrete International Inc
485 W 2000 S
Orem, UT 84058-7525
Contact: Ken Merrell, Pres.
Telephone: 801-224-6662
Fax: 801-225-1690
Email: / URL: http://www.cobblecrete.com
Product Service Description:
Tools_hand & edge : Manufactures concrete
texturing tools and accessories : Form-liners
manufacturer : Flexible trim & moulding
manufacturer

Cobe Bet, Inc.
1201 Oak St
Lakewood, CO 80215-4438
Contact: Ed Wood, Pres.
Telephone: 303-232-6800
Fax: 303-231-4491
Email: / URL: http://www.cobebet.com
Product Service Description:
Medical instruments : Manufactures blood
separation and processing equipment
Medical & hospital equipment

Coburn Company, Inc.
P.O. Box 147
Whitewater, WI 53190-0147
Contact: Jack Kolo, Export Director
Telephone: 414-473-2822
Fax: 414-473-3522
Email: jkolo@idcnet.com / URL: http://
www.coburnco.com
Product Service Description:
Dairy Milling Equipment
Veterinary Supplies
Livestock Identification Equipment
Catalog Sales Gen Farm Supplies
Portable Milking Machines

**Code 3, Inc. Div of Public Safety
Equipment Inc.**
10986 N. Warson Road
St. Louis, MO 63114
Contact: Ginny Herrick, Export Manager
Telephone: 314-426-2700
Fax: 314-426-1337
Email: export@code3pse.com / URL:
Product Service Description:
Emergency Vehicle Light Bars
Comm. Eq., Emer. Veh. Sirens-Speakers

Coding Products
111 W Park Dr.
Kalkaska, MI 49646-9702
Contact: Rodney Peters, Sales Manager
Telephone: 616-258-5521
Fax: 616-258-6120
Email: / URL:
Product Service Description:
Hot Stamp Pipe/Fiber Optic Cablewire
Marking Ribbon
Hot Stamp IV Solution/Blood Bag Printing

Coeur d'alene Fiber... Inc.
3550 W. Seltice Way
Coeur D Alene, ID 83814-8973
Contact: Ron W Green, GM
Telephone: 208-765-0608
Fax: 208-664-9936
Email: cdagary@aol.com / URL:
Product Service Description:
Pellet mill technology, plant design-
construction, marketing
All natural wood cat litter & small animal
bedding... superior odor control

Cofap of America
10388 Airport Pkwy.
Kingsport, TN 37663
Contact: Sales & Marketing,
Telephone: 423-279-6300
Fax: 423-279-7123
Email: jbarry.cofapusa@ibm.net / URL:
Product Service Description:
Suspension shock absorbers for motor
vehicles
Suspension struts for motor
Steering dampers
Gas springs for trunks & hoods
Engine dampers

**Coffey Seed, Coffey Forage Seeds,
Inc.**
RR 1
Plainview, TX 79072-9390
Contact: Karl Wardlow, President
Telephone: 806-293-5304
Fax: 806-293-5305
Email: coffeyseed@texasonline.net / URL:
Product Service Description:
Field Seeds / Summer Annual Forage Seed
Hybrid Sorghum Sudangrass
Hybrid Pearl Millets

Cogsdill Tool Products Inc. (Mfr)
P.O. Box 7007
Camden, SC 29020-7007
Contact: David Lopes,
Telephone: 803-438-4000
Fax: 803-438-5263
Email: cogsdill@cogsdill.com / URL: http://
www.cogsdill.com
Product Service Description:
Roller Burnishing Tools
Deburring Tools, One Pass
Automatic Recessing Tools
Single-Blade Precision Reaming & Boring
Systems

Coherent Medical Group (CMG)
PO Box 10122
Palo Alto, CA 94303-0810
Contact: James L Taylor, V-P., GM
Telephone: 408-764-3955
Fax: 408-764-3970
Email: james_taylor@cohr.com / URL: http://
www.cohr.com
Product Service Description:
Electromedical equipment
Lasers for ocular and general surgery

Cohler Enterprises
101 N Haven St
Baltimore, MD 21224-1620
Contact: Toby Lipsitz, Pres., Sales & Mktg.
Mgr.
Telephone: 410-342-1400
Fax: 410-558-1816
Email: cohlerent@aol.com / URL: http://
www.cohler.com
Product Service Description:
Precious plating solutions

Coil Co., Inc.
125 S Front St
Darby, PA 19023-2932
Contact: H. N. Jacobs, Pres.
Telephone: 610-461-6100
Fax: 610-532-1289
Email: cci@coilcompany.com / URL: http://
www.coilcompany.com
Product Service Description:
Heat transfer coils, air conditioning &
refrigeration equipment
Heating equipment, except electric
Refrigeration & heating equipment

Coil Company Inc.
125 S. Front St.
Darby, PA 19023-2998
Contact: Nelson Jacobs, Owner
Telephone: 610-461-6100
Fax: 610-532-1289
Email: cci@coilcompany.com / URL: http://
www.coilcompany.com
Product Service Description:
Heating Equipment, Except Electric

Coilplus-Alabama, Inc.
PO Box 767
Athens, AL 35612-0767
Contact: Larry A. Doss, Pres.
Telephone: 205-233-3550
Fax: 205-233-3571
Email: coilplus@hiwaay.net. / URL: http://
www.coilplus.com
Product Service Description:
Steel & aluminum precision coil processing &
fabrication
Blast furnaces & steel mills

Cold Extrusion Co. Of America, Inc.
PO Box 279
Jacksonville, AR 72078-0279
Contact: Ted Rohde, Fin., GM,
Telephone: 501-982-9463
Fax: 501-982-9676
Email: trohde4354@aol.com / URL:
Product Service Description:
Oil field equipment
Sucker rod couplings
Fire sprinkler equipment
Adjustable drop nipples
One piece hydroulic hose fittings

Cold Jet, Inc.
455 Wards Corner Rd
Loveland, OH 45140-9027
Contact: Eugene Cooke III, Sales Mgr.
Telephone: 513-831-3211
Fax: 513-831-1209
Email: info@coljet.com / URL: http://
www.coldjet.com
Product Service Description:
Industrial machinery
Carbon dioxide blast cleaning systems
Mold cleaning systems

Cole Enterprises
2644 National Place
Garland, TX 75041-2343
Contact: Sharon Knight, Intl. Sales Director
Telephone: 214-271-0280
Fax: 214-278-4515
Email: sharon@coleenterprises.com / URL:
http://www.coleenterprises.com
Product Service Description:
Aquariums -"Designer Aquarium Furniture"
Water Walls, Bubbling Palm Trees & Lamps

Cole Instrument Corp
2650 S Croddy Way, PO Box 25063
Santa Ana, CA 92799-5063
Contact: R L Garcia, Pres.
Telephone: 714-556-3100
Fax: 714-241-9061
Email: switch@earthlink.net / URL: http://
www.cole-switches.com
Product Service Description:
Design & manufacture precision rotary
switches : Design & manufacture rotary
mechanical & optical encoders
Aerospace, military, commercial rotary
switches

Cole Screw Machine Products, Inc.
PO Box 1007
Naugatuck, CT 06770-1007
Contact: David Calabrese, Pres.
Telephone: 203-723-1418
Fax: 203-723-1252
Email: colenet@concentric.net / URL: http://
www.colescrew.com
Product Service Description:
Screw machine products : Swiss Precision
Products : B & S Screw Machine Products
CNC Precision Bar Products : Thread Rolling
Knurling

Colite International
PO Box 4005
West Columbia, SC 29171-4005
Contact: Martin Brown, Pres.
Telephone: 803-926-7926
Fax: 803-926-8412
Email: colite@msn.com / URL: http://
www.colite.com
Product Service Description:
Interior & exterior signs
Signs & advertising specialties

Colonial Business Forms, Inc.
355 Sackett Point Rd
North Haven, CT 06473-3164
Contact: Richard Onofrio, Pres.
Telephone: 203-281-4440
Fax: 203-281-7165
Email: / URL:
Product Service Description:
Business forms printing
Manifold business forms
Pads-Single
Wrap around cover books
Single sheets

Colonial Coffee Roasters, Inc.
3250 Nw 60th St
Miami, FL 33142-2125
Contact: Rafael Acevedo, Pres.
Telephone: 305-634-1843
Fax: 305-634-2538
Email: info@colonial-coffee.com / URL:
http://www.colonial-coffee.com
Product Service Description:
Coffee roasting & packaging
Coffee_roasted

Colorado Boxed Beef Co., Inc.
PO Box 899
Winter Haven, FL 33882-0899
Contact: Bryan Saterbo, Sr., VP Opers.
Telephone: 941-967-0636
Fax: 941-965-2222
Email: / URL:
Product Service Description:
Meat packing plants
Beef processing

Colorado Bridge & Iron Inc
2175 Railroad Ave
Grand Junction, CO 81505-9412
Contact: Nancy Seeley, Pres.
Telephone: 970-257-1847
Fax: 970-257-1852
Email: / URL:
Product Service Description:
Manufactures commercial and industrial steel
bridges
Structural metal_fabricated
Architectural metal work

Colorado Cereal, Inc. (Mfr)
P.O. Box 272470
Ft Collins, CO 80527
Contact: Bernie Blach, *
Telephone: 970-282-1222
Fax: 970-223-4302
Email: rmpop@webaccess.net / URL: http://
www.rmpopcorn.com
Product Service Description:
Popcorn, Unpopped, Bagged, Wholesale
Popcorn , Unpopped, Microwave Packed
Popcorn-Unpopped Bulk
Popcorn - Private Label, Microwave

Colorado Frame Company
5910 S University Blvd Ste A8
Greenwood Village, CO 80121-2800
Contact: Patricia Johnson, Pres.
Telephone: 303-798-2430
Fax: 303-798-5168
Email: / URL:
Product Service Description:
Manufactures custom wood frames; hand
blown glass; candles
Wood products
Glass_pressed & blown
Manufacturing industries

Colorado Lining International, Inc.
1062 Singing Hills Rd.
Parker, CO 80134
Contact: John Heap, Owner
Telephone: 303-841-2022 / 800-524-8672
Fax: 303-841-5780
Email: jheap@coloradolining.com / URL:
http://www.coloradolining.com
Product Service Description:
Underground Protective Lining Installation
Fabricated Rubber Products

Colorado Rubber & Supply Co
PO Box 16686
Denver, CO 80216-0686
Contact: William Houston, Pres.
Telephone: 303-296-8726
Fax: 303-297-1322
Email: / URL:
Product Service Description:
Distributes industrial rubber; hose and
belting; fabricates belt products
Rubber products_fabricated
Industrial supplies
Hose & belting_rubber & plastic

Colorado Sweet Gold LLC
PO Box 628
Johnstown, CO 80534-0628
Contact: John D. Hamilton, Manager
Telephone: 970-587-5131
Fax: 970-587-6536
Email: / URL:
Product Service Description:
Produces refined corn starch and other food
ingredients
Wet corn milling
By-products for

**Columbia Cosmetics Manufacturing,
Inc.**
1661 Timothy Dr.
San Leandro, CA 94577-2311
Contact: Rachel Rendel, President
Telephone: 510-562-5900
Fax: 510-562-3544
Email: / URL:
Product Service Description:
Contract Packaging, Private Label
Manufacturing
R & D, Volume Filling Or Bulk Supplied

Columbia Logistics, Inc.
175-11 148 Road
Jamaica, NY 11434
Contact: Simon Tung, Owner
Telephone: 718-995-5071
Fax: 718-995-5078
Email: clogistics@aol.com / URL:
Product Service Description:
International Freight Forwarding, Worldwide
Service

Columbia Machine, Inc.
P.O. Box 8950
Vancouver, WA 98668
Contact: Ricardo Birkner, *
Telephone: 360-694-1501
Fax: 360-695-7517
Email: colmac@pacifier.com / URL: http://
www.pacifier.com/~colmac
Product Service Description:
Concrete Products Making Machinery
Concrete Pavers Making Machinery
Mixing & Batching Equipment, Concrete
Concrete Block Making Machinery

Columbia Winery
PO Box 1248
Woodinville, WA 98072-1248
Contact: David Lake, V-P.
Telephone: 425-488-2776
Fax: 425-488-3460
Email: / URL: http://
www.columbiawinery.com
Product Service Description:
Red & White Wines

Columbian Steel Tank Co.
P.O. Box 2907
Kansas City, KS 66110
Contact: Sales & Marketing,
Telephone: 913-621-3700
Fax: 913-621-2145
Email: tanks@columbiantank.com / URL:
http://www.columbiantank.com
Product Service Description:
Hazardous Waste
Water Treatment
Pumps & Pumping

**Columbus Galvanizing Voigt &
Schweitzer, Inc.**
1000 Buckeye Park Rd
Columbus, OH 43207-2509
Contact: Werner Niehaus, President
Telephone: 614-443-4621
Fax: 614-443-6375
Email: / URL: http://
www.hotdipgalvanizing.com
Product Service Description:
Metal coating & allied services
Corrosion-resistant coatings & hot dip
galvanizing
Galvanizing

Columbus Line USA, Inc.
300 Plaza Two, 3rd Floor, Harborside
Financia
Jersey City, NJ 07311
Contact: R. Wild, Regional Sales Manager
Telephone: 201-432-0900
Fax: 201-433-0616
Email: rwild@columbusline.com / URL:
http://www.columbusline.com
Product Service Description:
Ocean Freight & Cargo Transportation

Cominter Corp.
8427 NW 68 St.
Miami, FL 33166 USA
Contact: Pablo Sanchez, Owner
Telephone: 305-591-0899
Fax: 305-591-0896
Email: sales@cominter.net / URL: http://
www.cominter.net
Product Service Description:
Exporting Firms
Articles of paper pulp, paper, paperboard,
cellulose wadding or webs of cellulose fibers
Paper and paperboard, coated, impregnated
or covered with plastics , in rolls or sheets
Electric motors and generators

Command Corporation Intl. (Mfr)
13931 Sunfish lake Blvd.
Ramsey, MN 55303
Contact: Dale Frandsen, *
Telephone: 612-576-6910
Fax: 612-576-6911
Email: command.tooling@industry.net / URL:
Product Service Description:
Rotating Toolholders, Machining Centers

Commercial Enameling Co
PO Box 848
Huntington Park, CA 90255-0848
Contact: Mike E Hurray, V-P.
Telephone: 323-588-8171
Fax: 323-583-3226
Email: / URL: http://www.cecosinks.com
Product Service Description:
Enameling on porcelain and gray iron castings

**Commercial International
Forwarding Inc.**
P.O. Box 1317
Hurst, TX 76053
Contact: Levent M. Bayraktaroglu, President
Telephone: 817-282-1336
Fax: 817-282-9378
Email: levent@commercial-companies.com /
URL: http://www.commercial-companies.com
Product Service Description:
Integrated Global Logistics
Import / Export
Customs Broker
International Freight Forwarder
Intermodal Transportation & Distribution
NVOCC

Commercial Intertech Corp.
PO Box 239
Youngstown, OH 44501-0239
Contact: G.B. Miller, Jr., VP Sales, Domestic
Metals
Telephone: 216-746-8011
Fax: 216-746-1148
Email: / URL:
Product Service Description:
Metal Stampings & Tank Heads

Commercial Pallet Pak Co.
921 Skipper Ave # B
Fort Walton Beach, FL 32547-7316
Contact: Charles G. Bixel, Pres.
Telephone: 850-862-0021
Fax: 850-862-5714
Email: bixel@fwb.gulf.net / URL:
Product Service Description:
Composite wooden pallets & shipping
containers
High speed surface effect craft (Marine)
Ground effect flight cargo craft

Commision Brokers, Inc.
P.O. Box 8456
Cranston, RI 02920-0456
Contact: Martin Kenner, President
Telephone: 401-943-3777
Fax: 401-943-3670
Email: marty137@aol.com / URL: http://
www.commissionbrokers.com
Product Service Description:
Ind. Braiding Machinery, Export
Cordage & Rope Machinery, Export
Hose Machinery, Export
Shoe Lace Machinery, Export
Twine Machinery, Export
Wire & Cable Machinery, Export

Commodore Machine Co.
26 Maple Ave
Bloomfield, NY 14469-9394
Contact: George Bradon, Pres.
Telephone: 716-657-7004
Fax: 716-657-6400
Email: commodor@servtech.com / URL:
Product Service Description:
Plastic foam products : Polystyrene foam
Tooling for plastic products : Thermoformers
Extruders : Grinders

Common Sensing Inc
PO Box 130
Clark Fork, ID 83811-0130
Contact: Brian G D'Aoust, Pres.
Telephone: 208-266-1541
Fax: 208-266-1428
Email: comsen@dmi.net / URL: http://www.dmi.net/comsen.com
Product Service Description:
Manufactures water quality dissolved gas sensor : Process control instruments

Communi-Creations Inc
2130 S Bellaire St
Denver, CO 80222-4910
Contact: Donald Pfau, Pres.
Telephone: 303-759-1155
Fax: 303-757-1832
Product Service Description:
Produces industrial, commercial and documentary videotapes : Motion picture & video production : Internet media production Audio production : Animation

Communication Certification Lab
1940 West Alexander Street
Salt Lake City, UT 84119-2039
Contact: Joseph W. Jackson, Mktg. Mgr.
Telephone: 801-972-6146
Fax: 801-972-8432
Email: info@cclab.com / URL: http://www.cclab.com
Product Service Description:
Testing Laboratory
Management Consulting Services

Communication Concepts Unlimited
927 Main Street
Racine, WI 53403
Contact: Gabriella S. Klein, *
Telephone: 414/633-4500
Fax: 414-633-0249
Email: / URL:
Product Service Description:
Marketing Consulting Svcs.

Communication Techniques, Inc.
9 Whippany Rd
Whippany, NJ 07981-1540
Contact: Ian Crossley, GM
Telephone: 973-884-2580
Fax: 973-887-6245
Email: icrossley@cti-inc.com / URL: http://www.cti-inc.com
Product Service Description:
Oscillators & synthesizers
Electronic components

Component Engineers, Inc.
108 N. Plains Indl. Rd.
Wallingford, CT 06492
Contact: Ronald Hansen, Pres.
Telephone: 203-269-0557
Fax: 203-269-1357
Email: / URL:
Product Service Description:
Metal stampings

Composition Materials Co., Inc.
1375 Kings Hwy East
Fairfield, CT 06430-5318
Contact: Alan K. Nudelman, Pres.
Telephone: 203-384-6111
Fax: 203-335-9728
Email: alan@compomat.com / URL: http://www.compomat.com
Product Service Description:
Grain abrasives & fillers
Abrasive products

Compu Cover
2104 Lewis Turner Blvd
Fort Walton Beach, FL 32547-1349
Contact: Robert Helms, Pres., Mktg. Mgr.
Phone: 850-862-4448 / Fax: 850-863-2200
Email: info@compucover.com / URL: http://www.compucover.com
Product Service Description:
Computer & keyboard dust covers & accessories : Plastic products : Keyskin Keyboard Protectors : CD Carrying Cases Wooden Disk Boxes

Compu-Aire, Inc.
8167 Byron Rd
Whittier, CA 90606-2615
Contact: Ms. Meena Aurora,
Int'l Dir. of Sales
Phone: 562-945-8971 / Fax: 562-696-0724
Email: compuairi@aol.com / URL:
Product Service Description:
Computer Rooms, A/C : A/C for Telecommunication Facilities : Ceiling And Roof Mounted A/C Units : Wall Hung A/C Systems : Portable A/C Systems

Computerline International
2509 Texas Ave
El Paso, TX 79901-2124
Contact: Thomas Varkonyi, Pres.
Phone: 915-544-9890 / Fax: 915-587-4298
Email: thomasv@whc.net / URL:
Product Service Description:
Computers, Manufacturer

Comstock Cards Inc
600 S Rock Blvd Ste 15
Reno, NV 89502-4115
Contact: Patti P Wolf, Pres.
Phone: 702-856-9400 / Fax: 702-856-9406
Email: comstock@intercomm.com / URL: http://www.comstockcards.com
Product Service Description:
Adult & Everyday Greeting Cards

Con-Tech Power Systems, Inc.
P.o. Box 899
Lakeshore, MS 39558
Contact: Raul Milla, Intl. Trade Mgr.
Phone: 228-533-7800 / Fax: 228-533-7135
Email: raul@contechpower.com / URL: http://www.contechpower.com
Product Service Description:
Design, Mfr. & installation of low & medium voltage custom switchgear & control panel Electrical Control Equipment
Generator Power Distribution Equip.
Primary & Secondary Unit Substations
Interface Panel, Plc-Cntl. & Solid State
Industrial Control Panels
Motor Control Center (MCC)

Conbraco Industries
701 Matthews Mint Hill Rd.
Matthews, NC 28105-1727
Contact: Carl Mosack, President
Telephone: 704-847-9191
Product Service Description:
Plumbing Fixture Fittings and Trim
Taps, cocks, valves and similar appliances for pipes, vats or the like, including thermostatically controlled valves
Ball valves; threaded, S.W. , B.W., flanged
Pneumatic & electric actuators
Butterfly valves : Forged steel gate, flobe & check valves : Backflow prevention devices
Plumbing & heating products : Marine vavles & fittings : Top entry ball vavles

Conbraco Industries, Inc.
P.O. Box 247
Matthews, NC 28106-0247
Contact: Carl Mosack, President
Telephone: 704-847-9191
Fax: 704-841-6021
Email: / URL:
Product Service Description:
Steel Boiler Trims
Bronze Boiler Trims
Backflow Preventers
Brass Valves
Bronze Valves
Stainless Steel Valves
Steel Valves
Plumbing & heating products
Pneumatic & electric actuators
Butterfly valves, Forged steel gate, flob & check valves

Concentrated Aloe Corp.
PO Box 721
Ormond Beach, FL 32175-0721
Contact: Ellen Walsh, VP, Rick Knipple, Sales Director
Telephone: 904-673-4247
Fax: 904-676-0055
Email: cacaloe@msn.com / URL: http://www.conaloe.com
Product Service Description:
Aloe Concentrates & Aloe Powders

Concord Environmental Equipment
PO Box 78
Hawley, MN 56549-0078
Contact: Shawn Tangen, Office Manager
Telephone: 218-937-5100
Fax: 218-937-5101
Email: cee@rrnet.com / URL: http://www.ceesoilsample.com
Product Service Description:
Soil sampling equipment & drilling rigs
Measuring & controlling devices

Concorde Tools, Inc.
1620 S Schroeder Ln
Mc Henry, IL 60050-8251
Contact: John C. West, Pres.
Telephone: 815-344-3788
Fax: 815-344-8621
Email: concordezz@aol.com / URL:
Product Service Description:
Dies, tools, jigs & fixtures_special, CNC machining & assemblies

Condar Co.
PO Box 250
Columbus, NC 28722-0250
Contact: Michael McCue, Pres.
Telephone: 828-894-8383
Fax: 828-894-2718
Email: condar@condar.com / URL: http://www.condar.com
Product Service Description:
Wood stove & fireplace temperature control devices

Condor Seed Production Inc. (Mfr)
P.O. Box 6485
Yuma, AZ 85366
Contact: Thomas W. Tolman, *
Telephone: 602-627-8803
Fax: 602-627-2826
Email: / URL:
Product Service Description:
Vegetable Seed
Herb Seed

Conectec R F, Inc.
2155 Stonington Ave
Hoffman Estates, IL 60195-2039
Contact: Bob Curran, Pres., GM
Telephone: 847-519-0100
Fax: 847-519-1515
Email: ctecrf@ix.netcom.com / URL:
Product Service Description:
Electronic components
Cable assemblies
Contract Assembly

Conexpo-Con Agg Exposition
111 E. WISCONSIN AVE., S. 1000
Milwaukee, WI 53202-4806
Contact: Jason McGraw,
Telephone: 414-272-0943
Fax: 414-272-2672
Email: cima@cimanet.com / URL: http://www.conexpoconagg.com
Product Service Description:
Convention Bureau Construction Equip.

Congdon Printing & Imaging
115 East 2nd
Cedar Falls, IA 50613-0485
Contact: Richard J. Congdon, Pres.
Telephone: 319-266-7578
Fax: 319-277-4817
Email: cpiprintbiz@cfu.net / URL: http://www.congdonprinting.com
Product Service Description:
Commercial offset & direct mail
Graphic Design & Desktop Publishing
Catalogs, Product Bulletins, Trade Journals, Operations Manuals
Corporate Identity Packages, Pricelists, Newsletters
Warehousing, Fulfillment

Congoleum Corp.
PO Box 3127
Mercerville, NJ 08619-0127
Contact: Paul Bielinski, Int'l Sales Mgr.
Telephone: 609-584-3681
Fax: 609-584-3596
Email: webmaster@congoleum.com / URL: http://www.congoleum.com
Product Service Description:
Floor Coverings, Hard Surface
Sheet Vinyl Flooring
Vinyl Tile Flooring
Laminate Flooring

Conibear Equipment Co., Inc.
PO Box 90215
Lakeland, FL 33804-0215
Contact: Robert Conibear, Pres.
Telephone: 941-858-4414
Fax: 941-859-5367
Email: / URL:
Product Service Description:
Fertilizer spreading equipment
Farm machinery & equipment

Conitex (USA) Inc. (MFR)
1302 Industrial Park
Gastonia, NC 28052
Contact: David Monteith, *
Telephone: 704-864-5406
Fax: 704-865-7926
Email: dmonteith@conitex.com / URL: http://www.conitex.com
Product Service Description:
Paper Cones for Textiles
Paper Tubes

Connecticut Micrographics, Inc.
280 Connecticut Ave.
Norwalk, CT 06854
Contact: Peter Hovell, Pres.
Telephone: 203-838-1013
Fax: 203-853-3749
Email: info@micrographics.com / URL: http:/
/www.micrographics.com
Product Service Description:
Microfilm equipment

Connor Formed Metal Products
1451 Railroad St
Corona, CA 91720-6944
Contact: David Palombo, VP Sales & Mktg.
Telephone: 909-273-1200
Fax: 909-371-6075
Email: davidpalombo@cfmp.com / URL:
http://www.cfmp.com
Product Service Description:
Springs, Stampings, Wire Forms, Assemblies

Conserve Engineering Company
303 Broadway St., Ste. 212
Laguna Beach, CA 92651-1816
Contact: Sales & Marketing,
Telephone: 714-494-6440
Fax:
Email: / URL:
Product Service Description:
Ventilation & Emissions Control Eng.
Environmental Control Systems

Consilium US, Inc.
59 Porter Rd
Littleton, MA 01460-1431
Contact: Robert H Osmer, CEO
Telephone: 978-486-9800
Fax: 978-486-0170
Email: info@consiliumus.com / URL: http://
www.consiliumus.com
Product Service Description:
Measuring & controlling devices
Level Gauging Equipment for Liquids and
Slurries
Fluid meters & counting devices

Consler Filtrations Products
300 W Main St.
Honeoye Falls, NY 14472-1197
Contact: Leonard L. Orsini, Dir. Sales &
Marketing
Telephone: 716-624-1330
Fax: 716-624-1205
Email: info@consler.com / URL: http://
www.consler.com
Product Service Description:
Air Intake Filters
Compressed Gas Filters
Liquid Filters
Coalescing Filters
Replacement Filter Cartridges

**Consolidated Baling Machine Co.,
Inc.(Mfr)**
5400 Rio Grande Ave., P.O. Box 61025
Jacksonville, FL 32236
Contact: Robert Turner, VP/ Sales/Marketing
Telephone: 904-356-7411
Fax: 904-358-7013
Email: www.ibcsales@waste-tech.com /
URL:
Product Service Description:
Waste Reduction Equipment
Paper Balers : Textile Balers
Drum Crushers : Waste Recycling Equipment
Spec. Machinery, Recycling Equipment
Spec. Machinery, Environ. Disposal

Consolidated Display Co., Inc.
31W630 Schoger Dr
Naperville, IL 60564-5681
Contact: Sebastian J. Puccio, Pres.
Telephone: 630-851-8666
Fax: 630-851-8756
Email: buzzp@aol.com / URL: http://
www.consolidateddisplay.com
Product Service Description:
Seasonal decorations, theatrical & floral
supplies : Signs & advertising specialties

Consolidated Fabricators Corp.
4848 S Santa Fe Ave
Vernon, CA 90058-2119
Contact: Barbara Ross, Marketing Mgr.
Telephone: 323-586-4545
Fax: 323-586-4516
Email: sales@con-fab.com / URL: http://
www.con-fab.com
Product Service Description:
Refuse & storage containers - Mfg.

Consolidated Trading
1600 Route 208 South
Fair Lawn, NJ 07410
Contact: Sales & Marketing
Telephone: 201-794-8000
Product Service Description:
Faw Cotton Fabric
Rags

Construction Design Associates
820 S Monaco Pkwy PMD 292
Denver, CO 80224-1569
Contact: Michelle Weissman, Mng. Ptnr.
Telephone: 303-758-7872
Fax: 303-758-8189
Product Service Description:
Manufactures architectural millwork
Millwork

**Construction Technology, Inc. (DBA,
CTI Products)**
5070 Oakland St
Denver, CO 80239-2724
Contact: Kel Darnell, V.P. Sales
Telephone: 303-371-8097
Fax: 303-371-8096
Email: sales@cti-products.com / URL: http://
www.cti-products.com
Product Service Description:
Manufactures attachments for construction
equipment : Backhoe & Loader Fork Lift
Attachments : Skid Steer Pallet Forks

Container Machinery Corp.
PO Box 780
Kinderhook, NY 12106-0780
Contact: Heinz Grossjohann, *
Telephone: 518-758-6660
Product Service Description:
Business Services, Cannery Quality Control
Computer Programing, Quality Control

Containment Solutions, Inc.
5150 Jefferson Chemical Rd
Conroe, TX 77301-6834
Contact: Joan Carter, Mrtl. Mgr.
Telephone: 409-756-7731
Fax: 409-756-7766
Email: / URL: http://
www.containmentsolutions.com
Product Service Description:
Underground storage tanks

Contemporary, Inc.
PO Box 2110
Manitowoc, WI 54221-2110
Contact: James Peterson, Vice President
Telephone: 920-682-7754
Fax: 920-682-5520
Email: cawley@namebadges.com / URL:
http://www.namebadges.com
Product Service Description:
Name badges, awards, & identification plates
Metal products_fabricated

Continental Cars, Inc.
1023 Laskin Rd., Ste. K-111
Virginia Beach, VA 23451-6314
Contact: Al Lanese, President
Telephone: 757-425-0131
Fax: 757-491-1845
Email: carsvabh@pilot.infi.net / URL:
Product Service Description:
Exporting Firms
Passenger motor vehicles
Motor vehicles for the transport of goods
Motor vehicle parts and accessories

**Continental Conveyor & Equip.
Co.(Mfr)**
P.O. Box 400
Winfield, AL 35594
Contact: James L. Smothers, *
Telephone: 205-487-6492
Fax: 205-487-4233
Email: / URL:
Product Service Description:
Machinery, Conveyors & Components
Machinery, Bulk Material Conveyor Sys.
Conveyor Idlers
High Angle Conveyors HAC

Continental Cutoff Machines
325 S. Fairbank Street
Addison, IL 60101
Contact: C.W. Craychee, Sales Manager
Telephone: 630-543-7170
Fax: 630-543-5953
Email: / URL:
Product Service Description:
Pipe & Tube Cutoff Machines

Continental Disc Corp.
3160 W. Heartland Dr.
Liberty, MO 64068
Contact: Kenneth R. Shaw, Pres.
Telephone: 816-792-1500
Fax: 816-792-5447
Email: pressure@contdisc.com / URL: http://
www.contdisc.com
Product Service Description:
Rupture discs, holders, alarm systems, vent
panels & burst disc indicators
Valves & pipe fittings

Continental Eagle
P.O. Box 1000
Prattville, AL 36067-0900
Contact: David E. Mrozinski, Vice President
International Sales
Telephone: 334-365-8811
Fax: 334-361-7627
Email: international@coneagle.com / URL:
http://www.coneagle.com
Product Service Description:
Cotton Gin Machinery / Systems
Cotton Gin, Replace Parts
Cottonseed Delint / Decorticate
Cottonseed Delinting - Acid

Continental Electronics Corp.
PO Box 270879
Dallas, TX 75227-0879
Contact: D.F. Burkey, President
Telephone: 214-381-7161
Fax: 214-381-4949
Email: / URL: http://www.contelec.com
Product Service Description:
Radio & TV communications equipment
Radio frequency transmitters
Digital Television Transmitters
Digital Radio Transmitters

Continental Enterprises
17941 Brookshire Ln.
Huntington Beach, CA 92647-7132
Contact: Luis M Lopez, *
Telephone: 714-841-1403
Fax: 714-843-2047
Email: / URL:
Product Service Description:
Air Conditioning Parts
Coolers (Evaporative)
Motors
Air Conditioning Motors

Continental Group
11617 N Sundown Dr
Scottsdale, AZ 85260-5541
Contact: Jorge Castro, Pres.
Telephone: 602-922-9427
Fax: 602-922-4943
Email: / URL:
Product Service Description:
Sells beauty aid products, fragrances and
cosmetics

**Continental Sprayers / AFA
Products, Div. of: Indesco
International Inc.**
950 Third Ave.
New York, NY 10022
Contact: Peter Giallorenzo, VP & CFO
Telephone: 212-593-2009
Fax: 212-593-0433
Product Service Description:
Manufacturing Industries, NEC
Pumps for liquids; Liquid elevators; Parts
thereof : Articles of plastics
Household articles and toilet articles, of
plastics

Control Components, Inc.
22591 Avenida Empresa
Rancho Santa Margarita, CA 92688-2012
Contact: Rob Bodine, Marketing
Communications Manager
Telephone: 949-858-1877
Fax: 949-858-1878
Email: info@ccivalve.com / URL: http://
www.ccivalve.com
Product Service Description:
Severe service control valves
Nuclear valves, turbine bypass valves, valve
parts, retrofits
Plant efficiency studies

Contronic Devices
15661 Producer Ln Ste G
Huntington Beach, CA 92649-1342
Contact: Robert Nibbe, GM
Telephone: 714-897-2266
Fax: 714-897-6262
Email: contronicdevices@hotmail.com /
URL: http://www.contronicdevices.com
Product Service Description:
Manufactures and distributes electronic
production assembly aids

Convaid Products Inc
PO Box 4209
Palos Verdes Peninsula, CA 90274-9571
Contact: Mervyn Watkins, Pres., CEO
Telephone: 310-539-6814
Fax: 310-539-3670
Email: convaid@convaid.com / URL: http://
www.convaid.com
Product Service Description:
Manufactures chairs for the handicapped

Convaquip Industries, Inc.
PO Box 3417
Abilene, TX 79604-3417
Contact: Brad Goodman, V-P., Fin., Pur.,
Sales & Mktg.
Telephone: 800-637-8436
Fax: 915-677-7217
Email: info@convaquip.com / URL: http://
www.convaquip.com
Product Service Description:
Obese convalescent supplies

Convenience Products (Mfr)
866 Horan Drive
Fenton, MO 63026 USA
Contact: John Keegan, *
Telephone: 314/349-5333
Fax: 314-349-5335
Email: / URL: http://www.touch-n-foam.com
Product Service Description:
Sealants : Polyurethane Aerosol Foam

Converse
1 Fordham Rd.
North Reading, MA 01864-2619
Contact: Glenn N. Rupp, Chief Executive
Officer
Telephone: 978-664-1100
Fax: 978-664-7529
Product Service Description:
Rubber and Plastics Footwear
Footwear

Converto Mfg. Co. Inc. (Mfr)
P.O. Box 287
Cambridge City, IN 47327
Contact: Gene Hammond, Sales Manager
Telephone: 765-478-3205
Fax: 765-478-1223
Email: / URL:
Product Service Description:
Industrial Trailers, Push out
Industrial Trailers, Roll off
Ind. Trucks, Lugger Skif
Straight Truck Roll off Hoists

Conveyors Solutions, Inc.
PO Box 127
Lake Zurich, IL 60047-0127
Contact: Joseph Tholl, Pres.
Telephone: 847-240-1720
Fax: 847-240-1715
Email: scott@conveyorsolutions.com / URL:
http://www.conveyorsolution.com
Product Service Description:
Conveyors & conveying equipment
Conveyor components

Cookies For You, Inc.
117 Main St S
Minot, ND 58701-3913
Contact: Mary Helen Hasby, Pres
Telephone: 701-839-4975
Fax: 701-838-8874
Email: cookies@minot.com / URL: http://
www.cookiesforyou.com
Product Service Description:
Cookies & crackers

Cooley Sign & Digital Imaging, A
Division of The Cooley Group
50 Esten Ave
Pawtucket, RI 02860-4871
Contact: Edward J. Silva, V-P.
Telephone: 401-728-0910
Fax: 401-728-1910
Email: info@cooleygroup.com / URL: http://
www.cooleygroup.com
Product Service Description:
Vinyl signs : Signs & advertising specialties
Bill boards : Digital Printing : Awnings
Banners

Cooper Coil Coating, Inc.
5110 140th Ave N
Clearwater, FL 33760-3753
Contact: Mr. Mike Keane, Sales Mgr.
Phone: 727-535-6160 / Fax: 727-531-1218
Product Service Description:
Metal coil coating, slitting & embossing
Metal coating & allied services

Cooper Engineered Products, Div.
Of Cooper Tire & Rubber Co.
725 W 11th St
Auburn, IN 46706-2022
Contact: R. F. Millhof, Pres.
Phone: 219-925-0700 / Fax: 219-925-1473
Email: bvonlanker@coopertire.com / URL:
http://www.coopertire.com
Product Service Description:
Rubber products_fabricated
Molded rubber automotive products
Extruded rubber automotive products

Cooper Industries
2300 Badger Dr.
Waukesha, WI 53188-5931
Contact: Patrick Avery, Director, Div. Mktg.
Telephone: 414-896-2311
Fax: 414-896-2313
Email: pavery@cooperpower.com / URL:
http://www.cooperpower.com
Product Service Description:
Distribution Transformers
Reclosers & distribution switchgear
Capacitors & capacitor switches / controls
Relays & substation automation
Hardware, fuses, connectors & porcelain
Systems engineering analysis & training

Cooper Instrument Corporation
(Mfr)
33 Reeds Gap Road
Middlefield, CT 06455
Contact: Sharon LeGault, Marketing Manager
Telephone: 860-347-2256
Fax: 860-347-5135
Email: carolyn@cooperinstrument.com /
URL: http://www.cooperinstrument.com
Product Service Description:
Thermometers : Timers : Humidity
Instruments

Coopers & Clarke, Inc.
Manufacutures of The Key Marine
Branded Marine Products Lines
2655 Lejeune Road, Suite 600
Coral Gables, FL 33134
Contact: Steven Patz, Sales & Mktg. Mgr.
Telephone: 305-438-0076
Fax: 305-443-5096
Email: cyberfit@bellsouth.net / URL:
Product Service Description:
Marine exhaust systems, hardware, machine
job shop & foundry
Hardware : Metal products_fabricated
Foundries_aluminum : Plating & polishing

Coors Ceramics Co-Pittburgh
91 Mayview Rd.
Lawrence, PA 15055
Contact: Paul Yandora, V-P., GM
Telephone: 724-745-9522
Fax: 724-746-4294
Email: pittsales@coorsceramics.comm /
URL: http://www.coorsceramics.comm
Product Service Description:
Industrial ceramics

Copper Coil Coating
5110 140th Ave., N.
Clearwater, FL 33760-3753
Contact: Ron Vaden, Manager
Phone: 727-535-6160 / Fax: 727-531-1218
Email: cccsales1@earthlink.net / URL:
Product Service Description:
PrePaint Coil Coating of Aluminum & Steel
High Temp & Low Temp Coatings for
Bakeware & Architectural Applications

Cor Enterprises
200 S. 24th St.
Billings, MT 59101-4321
Contact: Gail M. Neal, CFO
Phone: 406-248-9115 / Fax: 406-245-0606
Email: cor@wtp.net / URL:
Product Service Description:
Manufactures wood stakes lath wedges &
cedar planters; commercial sewing
Wooden products

Coral Steel Company
7876 Belvedere Rd.
West Palm Beach, FL 33411
Contact: Lee Disbury, Owner
Telephone: 561-798-8822
Fax: 561-798-5640
Email: rebarlee@aol.com
Product Service Description:
Steel rebar & fabrication
Building Materials

Corcoran International Corp.
15 Park Row, Stes. 904-907,
New York, NY 10038
Contact: Ernest Zapata, President
Telephone: 212-571-0765/0766
Fax: 212-233-7806
Email: cicintcorp@aol.com / URL:
Product Service Description:
Customs Broker : Freight Forwarder
Freight & Cargo Transportation

Cordell Manufacturing Inc
668 Arrow Grand Cir
Covina, CA 91722-2145
Contact: William E. Mathews, III, Exec. VP
Telephone: 626-966-4402
Fax: 626-339-2582
Email: we@cordell.net / URL: http://
www.cordell.com
Product Service Description:
Central office alarm monitoring servers (AC/
DC) (Free) : Alarm control centers
Routers (AC or DC powered) : Terminal
servers (AC or DC Powered) : Modems
(Security - AC or DC powered)

Corfu Foods, Inc.
755 Thomas Dr
Bensenville, IL 60106-1624
Contact: Vasilios S. Memmos, Pres.
Telephone: 630-595-2510
Fax: 630-595-3884
Product Service Description:
Gyro meat processing : Sausages & other
prepared meat products : Pita Bread

Coronis Building Sytems Inc.
PO Box 200
Columbus, NJ 08022-0200
Contact: Emanuel A. Coronis, President
Telephone: 609-723-2600
Fax: 609-723-6700
Product Service Description:
Fabricated Structural Steel Frames

Corrigan Corp. America
104 Ambrogio Dr
Gurnee, IL 60031-3373
Contact: J. Michael Corrigan, Pres., Sales &
Mktg. Mgr.
Telephone: 847-263-5955
Fax: 847-263-5944
Email: CCA@LND.Com / URL:
Product Service Description:
Misting & humidity equipment, Water
treatment systems

Corro-Shield International, Inc.
7047 Barry Ave
Rosemont, IL 60018-3401
Contact: Ralph Sacks, Pres., CFO
Telephone: 847-298-7770
Fax: 847-298-7784
Email: / URL: http://www.corroshield.com
Product Service Description:
Epoxy floor coverings & wall coating, epoxy

Cory Components Inc
2201 Rosecrans Ave
El Segundo, CA 90245-4910
Contact: Eddye C. Abbott, Dir. Sales &
Mktg.
Telephone: 310-536-0034
Fax: 310-536-0206
Email: eddye.abbott@cory.com / URL:
Product Service Description:
Manufactures electronic connectors and cable
harnesses for the aircraft industry
Electronic connectors
Electronic components

Cosmetic Specialty Labs, Inc.
PO Box 187
Lawton, OK 73502-0187
Contact: Philip Ferrel, Secy.
Telephone: 580-355-2182
Fax: 580-355-1195
Email: aloeman@ionet.net / URL: http://
www.aloe-vera.com
Product Service Description:
Cosmetics
Toilet preparations

Cosmos Electronic Machine Corp.
(Mfr)
140 Schmitt Boulevard
Farmingdale, NY 11735
Contact: Kenneth Arutt, President
Telephone: 516/249-2535
Fax: 516-694-6846
Email: kabarmfg@aol.com / URL:
Product Service Description:
Welding Machines, High Frequency
R.F. Sealing Equipment

Couch & Philippi Inc
PO Box A
Stanton, CA 90680-0009
Contact: Richard O Steele, V-P.
Telephone: 714-527-2261
Fax: 714-827-2077
Email: / URL:
Product Service Description:
Manufactures signs, displays and fascia
Signs & advertising specialties

Coughlin Logistics
27050 Wick Rd.,
Taylor, MI 48180
Contact: Sales & Marketing,
Telephone: 734-946-2500
Fax: 734-946-6945
Email: info@fxcoughlin.com / URL: http://
www.fxcoughlin.com
Product Service Description:
International Frieght Forwarder
Warehousing Packaging & Distribution
Customs Broker

Count On Tools, Inc.
2481 Hilton Dr Ste 9
Gainesville, GA 30501-6213
Contact: Curt Couch, Pres.
Telephone: 770-538-0411
Fax: 770-538-0417
Email: cotinc@mindspring.com / URL:
Product Service Description:
Electronic components

Country Home Products, Inc.
Meigs Road, PO Box 25
Vergennes, VT 05491
Contact: Priscilla Parsons,
Telephone: 1800-376-9637
Fax: 802-877-1216
Email: / URL:
Product Service Description:
Farm Equipment, Trimmer / Mower
Farm Equipment, Field & Brush Mowers
Farm Equipment, Power Wagons
Farm Rototillers

County of Cattaraugus
303 Court St.
Little Valley, NY 14755-1028
Contact: John J. Sayegh, Director
Telephone: 716-938-9111, Ext. 331
Fax: 716-938-9431
Email: johnsa@lv.co.cattaraugus.ny.us / URL:
Product Service Description:
Admin of General Economic Development
Programs
Industrial Development Services

Cove Shoe Co., Matterhorn-Corcoran Bts.
107 Highland Street
Martinsburg, PA 16662-1498
Contact: mark Dellinger, Sales & Mktg. Mgr.
Telephone: 814-793-9532
Fax: 814-793-9272
Email: dellingerm@hhbrow.com / URL: http://
www.coveshoe.com
Product Service Description:
Mens & Womens Military Footwear
Mens & Womens Safety Footwear

Cover-It Shelters, Inc.
PO Box 26037
West Haven, CT 06516-8037
Contact: Brian Goldwitz, Pres., R & D Mgr.
Telephone: 203-931-4747
Fax: 203-931-4754
Email: info@coveritshelters.com / URL:
Product Service Description:
Prefabricated portable shelters, instant
garages & greenhouses
Prefabricated metal buildings
Galvanized steel tubing for structures &
fencing
Umbrellas
Canopies
Roll-out Awnings

Covers Unlimited, Inc.
2205 Dutch Ln.
Jeffersonville, IN 47130-6313
Contact: Mark A. Sunderman, President
Telephone: 812-284-5050
Fax: 812-288-8168
Email: info@coversunlimited.com / URL:
http://www.coversunlimited.com
Product Service Description:
Contract Manufacturing & Sewing
Canvas & Related Products
Fulfillment Services & Storage

Covington Aircraft Engine
Hwy. 75 N., Airport Rd.
Okmulgee, OK 74447
Contact: Paul Abbott, Pres., CFO
Telephone: 918-756-8320
Fax: 918-756-0923
Email: david@covingtonaircraft.com / URL:
http://www.covingtonaircraft.com
Product Service Description:
Pratt & Whitney Canada Aircraft Engines &
Parts (R-985, R-1340, & PT6A)

Cox Recorders
1470 W Ninth Street, Suite C
Upland, CA 91786-5634
Contact: Nancy Jensen, *
Telephone: 909-946-4441
Fax: 909-946-0909
Product Service Description:
Temperature Recorders

Cox, Buchanan, Padmore & Shakarchy
630 3rd Avenue
New York, NY 10017-6705
Contact: Steven D. Skolnik, Partner
Telephone: 212-953-6633
Fax: 212-949-6943
Email: cbps@aol.com / URL:
Product Service Description:
Legal Services

Coxwells, Inc., dba CoxReels
6720 S. Clementine Ct.
Tempe, AZ 85283-4323
Contact: Donald Cox, President
Telephone: 480-820-6396
Fax: 480-820-5132
Email: info@coxreels.com / URL: http://
www.coxreels.com
Product Service Description:
Petroleum Hose Reels
Industrial Hose Reels
Automotive Hose Reels

Cozy Inc
PO Box 1020
Fairfield, ID 83327
Contact: Jack Frostenson, Pres.
Telephone: 208-764-2591
Product Service Description:
Manufactures cloth baby carriers
Textile products_fabricated

Craftsman Tool & Mold Co.
2750 Church Rd
Aurora, IL 60504-8733
Contact: Anton G. Sikorcin, Pres.
Telephone: 630-851-8700
Fax: 630-851-3864
Email: info@craftsmanmold.com / URL:
http://www.craftsmanmold.com
Product Service Description:
Mold & die cast bases & frames
Gundrilling & special machining

Cragin Metals, L.L.C.
2900 N Kearsarge Ave
Chicago, IL 60641-5497
Contact: Thomas H. Weber, Pres.
Telephone: 773-283-2201
Fax: 773-283-5699
Email: tweber@craginmetals.com / URL:
http://www.craginmetals.com
Product Service Description:
Steel shearing
Steel distributors & warehouses

Craig Indsutries
325 Payson Ave
Quincy, IL 62301-4849
Contact: Nancy Barry, General Manager
Telephone: 217-228-2421
Fax: 217-228-2424
Email: admin@craigindustries.com / URL:
http://www.craigindustries.com
Product Service Description:
Walk-in & cooler & freezers
Communication Buildings & Shelters

Craig M. Ferguson & Co. Inc.
1281 Main Street
Stamford, CT 06902
Contact: Ronald L. Schumitz, Insurance
Broker, Vice President
Telephone: 203-351-8600
Fax: 203-351-8601
Email: rschumitz@cmferguson.com
Product Service Description:
Insurance Broker, Marine & Casualty

Crane Cams, Inc.
530 Fentress Blvd.
Daytona Beach, Fl 32114
Contact: Eugene E. Ezzell, President
Telephone: 904-252-1151
Fax: 904-258-6167
Email: gezzell@cranemail.com / URL: http://
www.cranecams.com
Product Service Description:
Motor Vehicle Camshafts
Motor Vehicle Valve Train Components
Mot. Veh. Electronic Ignition Systems
Mot. Vehicle Engine Controls

Cranston Apparel Fabrics
469 7th Ave.
New York, NY 10018-7605
Contact: Anthony Palazzo,
Telephone: 212-279-1824
Product Service Description:
Printed & solid textile piece goods

Creations Aromatiques, Inc.
400 Sylvan Avenue
Englewood Cliffs, NJ 07632
Contact: John H. Simpson, *
Telephone: 201-568-4900
Fax: 201-816-4985
Email: / URL:
Product Service Description:
Perfume Bases
Perfume Compounds

Creative Arts
3730 70th Ave
Pinellas Park, FL 33781-4605
Contact: C. Stanmore, CEO
Telephone: 813-525-2060
Fax: 813-525-8689
Email: creative_arts@msn.com / URL: http://
www.creativeartsinc.com
Product Service Description:
Merchandising props & displays
Themed fixtures

Creative Plastics Printing Die
6365 Nancy Ridge Dr
San Diego, CA 92121-2247
Contact: Gerald R McDevitt, Pres.
Telephone: 619-458-1965
Fax: 619-458-9024
Email: creative@sandiego.com / URL: http://
www.creativeplastic.com
Product Service Description:
Prints membership and credit cards; custom
offset printing and die cutting
Printing_commercial
Lithographic printing_commercial
Plastic products

Creative Science & Technolgoy
3180 De La Cruz Blvd., Ste. 102
Santa Clara, CA 95054-2434
Contact: Ted unarce, Principal
Telephone: 408-496-0317
Fax: 408-272-8181
Email: / URL:
Product Service Description:
Manufactures Elisa diagnostics; R&D;
initiates joint ventures with US companies &
foreign counterparts
Surgical & medical instruments
Commercial physical research

Crest Foam Industries
100 Carol Pl
Moonachie, NJ 07074-1387
Contact: Tom Myers, Sales
Telephone: 201-807-0809
Fax: 201-807-1113
Email: info@crestfoam.com / URL: http://
www.crestfoam.com
Product Service Description:
Foam-Industrial - pu Reticulated
Foam-Fuel Cell
Foam Felt-Compressed pu

Crestcom International Ltd
6900 E Belleview Ave
Englewood, CO 80111-1619
Contact: Harold Krause, Pres.
Telephone: 303-267-8200
Fax: 303-267-8207
Email: crestcom@ix.netcom.com / URL:
http://www.crestcom.com
Product Service Description:
Video-based, live-facilitated management,
sales and office personnel training; develops
training materials

Creveling Sawmill
245 Millbrook Rd
Washington, NJ 07882-3715
Contact: James R. Brueckner, General
Manager
Telephone: 908-689-6365
Fax: 908-689-6365
Email: ecreel@juno.com / URL:
Product Service Description:
Dimensional lumber
Sawmills & planing mills, general

Cris-P Produce Co Inc
PO Box 7348
Nogales, AZ 85628-7348
Contact: Theojary Crisantes, Pres.
Telephone: 520-281-9233
Fax: 520-281-4366
Email: crisp2@dakotacom.net / URL: http://
www.cris-p.com
Product Service Description:
Distributer of fresh greenhouse & organic
vegetables

Crosby Group, Inc.
P.O. Box 3128
Tulsa, OK 74101-3128
Contact: Larry Postelwait, President
Telephone: 918-834-4611
Fax: 918-832-0940
Email: / URL: http://
www.thecrosbygroup.com
Product Service Description:
Chains
Sheaves
Shackles
Turnbuckles
Swaging Sleeves
Tackle Blocks
Wire Rope Fitting Hook Hardwar
Chain Fitting Hardware

Cross Mfg. Inc.
100 Factory Street
Lewis, KS 67552
Contact: Linda Baker, Mgr/Mktg. Svc.
Telephone: 316-324-5525
Fax: 315-324-5737
Email: sales@crossmfg / URL: http://
www.crossmfg.com
Product Service Description:
Hydraulic Cylinders Tie Rod
Fluid Power Valves Direct Cntl Manual
Hydraulic Fluid Pumps
Hydraulic Fluid Power Motors
Hydraulic Cylinders Welded

Crossfield Products Corp
3000 E Harcourt St
Compton, CA 90221-5504
Contact: Brad Watt, Vice President, Export Sales
Telephone: 310-886-9100
Fax: 310-886-9119
Email: / URL: http://
www.crossfieldproducts.com
Product Service Description:
Manufactures industrial floor coverings and protective coatings; promenade roof decks,
Floor coverings_hard surface, decorative finishes,
Adhesives & sealants, joint fillers
Waterproofing
Concrete repair

Crown Cork & Seal /Americas Div
669 W Quinn Rd Ste 10
Pocatello, ID 83202-1938
Contact: Brent Holbrook, Mgr.
Telephone: 208-237-0570
Fax: 208-237-3823
Email: dwhaley@crown.com / URL: http://
www.crowncork.com
Product Service Description:
Manufactures metal 3-piece containers
Cans_metal

Crown Divisions Of Trans Pro, Inc., The
1654 Old Mansfield Rd
Wooster, OH 44691-7211
Contact: Mike Hooper, Pres.
Telephone: 330-262-6010
Fax: 330-262-4095
Email: info@crowndivisions.com / URL:
http://www.crowndivisions.com
Product Service Description:
Commercial Van Conversions & Equipment
Fabricated Steel Cabinets & Enclosures
Steel Racks, Bins, Shelves, Partitions for Utility Vehicles

Crown Gym Mats, Inc.
27W929 Industrial Ave
Barrington, IL 60010-2363
Contact: Judy L. Eckert, Pres.,
Telephone: 847-381-8282
Fax: 847-381-8297
Email: mats@crowngymmats.com / URL:
http://www.crowngymmats.com
Product Service Description:
Gymnasium mats
Tactical Training Aids

Crown Hollander Inc.
311 Enford Rd
Richmond Hill, ON L4C3E9
Contact: Harold Hollander, *
Telephone: 905-884-1263
Product Service Description:
Metal Working Machinery

Crown Roll Leaf, Inc.
91 Illinois Ave
Paterson, NJ 07503-1722
Contact: James Waitts, Dev. Mgr.
Telephone: 973-742-4000
Fax: 973-742-0219
Email: / URL: http://www.crownrollleaf.com
Product Service Description:
Hot Stamping Foils
Diffraction patterns, holograms
Heat transfer foils

Crown Truck Sales
220 W. 14th St.
National City, CA 91950
Contact: Tim Flagstad, Owner
Telephone: 619-477-2515
Product Service Description:
Road tractors for semi-trailers
Trucks, Tractors, used & new
Construction Equipment, used
Dump Trucks, Dirt Hauling Equipment & Trailers

Cruising Equipment Company
5245 Shilshole Ave Nw
Seattle, WA 98107-4833
Contact: Bill Merkes, President
Telephone: 206-782-8100
Fax: 206-782-4336
Email: sales@cruisingequip.com / URL: http:/
/www.cruisingequip.com
Product Service Description:
Manufactures battery monitoring charge controls, electronic instrumentation, amps per hour

Cucker Feather
320 Driggs Ave.
Brooklyn, NY 11222-3904
Contact: E Cucker, Owner
Telephone: 718-389-1940
Product Service Description:
Goose & Duck Feathers & Down

Cuda Products Corp.
6000 Powers Ave
Jacksonville, FL 32217-2279
Contact: Joseph Cuda, Pres.
Telephone: 904-737-7611
Fax: 904-733-4832
Email: cudahitec@aol.com / URL: http://
www.cuda.com
Product Service Description:
Medical, surgical & dental fiber optic light guides & accessories : Optical instruments & lenses : Surgical & medical instruments
Dental equipment & supplies
Measuring & controlling devices

Cui Stack Inc
9615 SW Allen Blvd, Ste.103
Beaverton, OR 97005
Contact: James M McKenzie, Pres.
Telephone: 503-643-4899
Fax: 503-643-6129
Email: / URL: http://www.cuistack.com
Product Service Description:
Electronic components
Wholesales electronic components, speakers and connectors; manufactures power supplies
Electronic parts & equipment

Culligan Wate Conditioning, Inc.
3510 S. Dixie Highway., P.O. Box 410
Miami, FL 33133-4342
Contact: Robert D. McDougal, III, President
Telephone: 305-445-3568
Fax: 305-443-8280
Email: rob@culliganmiami.com / URL: http://
www.culliganmiami.com
Product Service Description:
Water Filters
Water Conditioning Equipment
Water Purification Equipment
Sea Water Converters
Small Community Systems
Ultra Violet Lights

Culver Duck Farms
P.O. Box 910
Middlebury, IN 46540-0910
Contact: Herbert R. Culver, President
Telephone: 219-825-9537
Fax: 219-825-2613
Email: / URL: http://www.culverduck.com
Product Service Description:
Poultry Slaughtering and Processing
Parts of birds, with their feathers or down

Cummins SW/Power Systems
2222 N 23rd Dr
Phoenix, AZ 85009-2705
Contact: Greg Czaplewski, VP/GM Onan Power Generation
Telephone: 602-252-8021
Fax: 602-258-1010
Email:
gczaplewski@notesbridge.commins.com /
URL:
Product Service Description:
Sells Onan generators, natural gas engines and chillers; HVAC equipment
Electrical apparatus & equipment
Warm air heating & air conditioning

Cummins-Allison Corp.
9514-A Lee Hwy.
Fairfax, VA 22031-2303
Contact: Lyle Berlin, Government Mgr.
Telephone: 703-385-1700
Fax: 703-385-9422
Email: caberlin@erols.com / URL: http://
www.cumminsallison.com
Product Service Description:
Check signing & endorsing machinery, paper shredders, perforators & coin & currency equip

Curecrete Distribution
1201 Spring Creek Pl.
Springville, UT 84663-3042
Contact: Dal Hills, International Sales
Telephone: 801-489-5663
Fax: 801-489-3258
Email: dal@ashfordformula.com / URL: http:/
/www.ashfordformula.com
Product Service Description:
Concrete hardener / sealer

Curran Coil Spring Inc
9265 SW 5th St
Wilsonville, OR 97070-9744
Contact: John Bachofner, GM
Telephone: 503-682-9003
Fax: 503-682-2825
Email: curransp@aol.com / URL:
Product Service Description:
Manufactures coil springs
Wire forms
Light metal stampings

Current, Inc.
30 Tyler Street
East Haven, CT 06512-3033
Contact: Steven R. Prinz,
Telephone: 203-469-1337
Fax: 203-467-8435
Email: current@ ct 1.nai.net / URL: http://
www.currentcomposites.com
Product Service Description:
Laminated Fabrics
Laminated Plastics Plate Rods & Tubes
Fabric Impregnating & Coating
Coating & Wrapping Svcs. Steel Pipe

Custom Accessories Inc
6440 West Howard St
Niles, IL 60714
Contact: Sales & Marketing,
Telephone: 708-966-6900
Fax: 708-966-9650
Email: / URL:
Product Service Description:
Automotive Accessories

Custom Alloy Corporation (Mfr)
3 Washington Ave.
High Bridge, NJ 08829
Contact: Frank Di Folco, Dir. Marketing
Telephone: 908-638-6200
Fax: 908-638-4499
Email: / URL:
Product Service Description:
Butt Weld Pipe Fittings

Custom Assembly
555 Pond Dr
Wood Dale, IL 60191-1192
Contact: Terry Rizzo,
Telephone: 630-595-4855
Fax: 630-595-6579
Email: / URL: http://
www.phoenixofchicago.com
Product Service Description:
Contract Manufacturing

Custom Bedding Co. & Orange Mattresses
1677 Springfield Ave
Maplewood, NJ 07040-2924
Contact: Marcel Segal, Pres.
Telephone: 973-761-1100
Fax: 973-378-3464
Email: / URL: http://www.waisite.com/
custombedding
Product Service Description:
Mattresses & bedsprings
Mattresses & box springs

Custom Building Products
13001 Seal Beach Blvd
Seal Beach, CA 90740-2753
Contact: Dina Ketcham, *
Telephone: 562-598-8808
Fax: 562-598-3218
Product Service Description:
Concrete, Interior Patching & Repair
Concrete Building Materials

Custom Cable Industries Inc.
3221 Cherry Palm Dr
Tampa, FL 33619-8334
Contact: Earla Turcich, AD Sales Supervisor
Telephone: 813-623-2232
Fax: 813-626-9630
Email: ad_sales@customcable.com / URL:
http://www.customcable.com
Product Service Description:
Network cable assemblies & wiring harnesses

Custom Engraving
1700 W. New Haven Ave
Melbourne, FL 32904-3916
Contact: Peter DeLagaza, Owner
Telephone: 407-676-9885
Fax: 407-676-9920
Email: orders@autoplates.com / URL: http://
www.autoplates.com
Product Service Description:
License plate & key chain engraving
Metal coating & allied services

Custom Extrusions & Molding Inc
211 S 49th Ave Ste 2
Phoenix, AZ 85043-3806
Contact: Janice Bates, Pres.
Telephone: 602-233-1153
Fax: 602-233-9725
Product Service Description:
Manufactures plastic extruded tubing &
profiles : Manufactures plastic injection
molded products

Custom Glass Corp.
PO Box 944
Kittanning, PA 16201-0944
Contact: John Rice, Pres., R & D Mgr.
Telephone: 724-543-6013
Fax: 724-543-6041
Email: sales@customglass.com / URL: http://
www.customglass.com
Product Service Description:
Bent, laminated & flat glass : Glass_flat
Bullet Resistant Glass : Security Glass
Blast Resistant Glass : Insulated Glass

Custom Machine Works, Inc.
301 New Natchitoches Rd., P.O. Box 245
West Monroe, LA 71294
Contact: Ralph E. Magouirk, Chairman of the
Board
Telephone: 318-325-6844
Fax: 318-387-4013
Product Service Description:
Paper Converting Machinery

Custom Modular Solutions
PO Box 347
Baxley, GA 31515-0347
Contact: Jack Morris, Owner
Telephone: 912-367-9089
Fax: 912-367-9426
Product Service Description:
Modular buildings
Prefabricated metal buildings
Prefabricated wood buildings

Custom Screens, Inc.
PO Box 352
Madison, NC 27025-0352
Contact: John P. McMichael, Pres., Opers.
Mgr.
Telephone: 336-427-0265
Fax: 336-427-5348
Email: csi3@ix.netcom.com / URL:
Product Service Description:
Screen printing
Fabric Welding

Custom Trailer
362 Aerodrome Way
Griffin, GA 30224-5401
Contact: Dan Schmit, International Sales
Telephone: 770-228-6091
Fax: 770-229-9265
Email: custrl@bellsouth.com / URL: http:/
www.custom-trailer.com
Product Service Description:
Flatbed equipment trailers

Customcraft Fixtures
4914 Pan American East Fwy. NE
Albuquerque, NM 87109-2207
Contact: Reinhard J. Heidfeld, President
Telephone: 505-881-9200
Fax: 505-881-9204
Email: ccfixtures@aol.com / URL: http://
www.ccfixtures.com
Product Service Description:
Store Fixtures
Partitions & Fixtures, Wood

Cutco Cutlery Corp.
1116 E. State Street
Olaan, NY 14760-3814
Contact: Brent A. Driscoll, President
Telephone: 716-372-3111
Fax: 716-373-6155
Product Service Description:
Kitchen Cutlery
Hunting & Folding Knives
Butchers & Meatpacking Cutlery

Cutting Edge Tool Supply Inc
1715 Monterey Rd Ste 10
Colorado Springs, CO 80910-1877
Contact: Kevin Gardner, Pres.
Telephone: 719-575-0033 / 800-769-3343
Fax: 800-697-3343 / 719-575-0035
Email: cets1@msn.com or cets3@msn.com /
Product Service Description:
Distributes industrial machinery and
equipment : Cutting tools, inserts & safety
equipment : Carbide, abrasives, hand tools &
endmills

Cybertec, Inc.
153 W. Westfield Avenue
Roselle Park, NJ 07204
Contact: Joseph Nunes, *
Telephone: 908-245-3305
Fax: 908-245-5434
Product Service Description:
Translation Services:
All Languages,
Technical & Business

Cypress Systems, Inc.
P.O. BOX 3931
Lawrence, KS 66046-0931
Contact: A.R. El-Koubysi,
Telephone: 785-842-2511
Fax: 785-832-0406
Email: information@cypresshome.com /
URL: http://www.cypresshome.com
Product Service Description:
Laboratory Analytical Instruments

D & D Machine & Hydraulics
10945 Metro Pkwy
Fort Myers, FL 33912-1202
Contact: Tom Akeley, Sales Manager
Telephone: 941-275-7177
Fax: 941-275-5350
Email: ddpumps@earthlink.com / URL: http:/
/www.ddpumps.com
Product Service Description:
Hydraulic dewatering pumps

D & D Products, Inc.
PO Box 215
North Prairie, WI 53153-0215
Contact: J. M. Dauffenbach, V-P., Hum. Res.,
Opers. & Pur.
Telephone: 414-392-2162
Fax: 414-392-2984
Email: sales@aquarius-systems.com / URL:
http://www.aquarius-systems.com
Product Service Description:
Aquatic weed harvesters, metal fabrication &
material handling equipment
Farm machinery & equipment

D & H Enterprises
207 Old Daytona Road
DeLand, FL 32724-1913
Contact: Howard Mark, Owner
Telephone: 904-734-4556
Fax: 904-734-4466
Email: / URL:
Product Service Description:
Automotive machining job shop
Motor vehicle parts & accessories

D & L Thomas Equipment
Route 9
Spofford, NH 03462
Contact: David Thomas, President
Telephone: 603-363-4706
Email: thomas@driller.com / URL: http://
www.driller.com
Product Service Description:
Rock drilling equipment for mining
construction : Blasting accessories and
supplies : Waterwell drilling equipment &
supplies

D & S Exports
24 Broad St.
Norwalk, CT 06851-6114
Contact: Steven Straut, Executive Director
Telephone: 203-847-6446
Fax: 203-849-9526
Email: dsexports@mindspring.com / URL:
Product Service Description:
Management Services - export
Machinery for the industrial preparation or
manufacture of food or drink
Machinery, parts & supplies for commercial
laundries

D C Thermal, Inc.
12430 Hwy. 3, Ste. E-20
Webster, TX 77598
Contact: Mike Pollard, V-P., Fin., GM &
Opers.
Telephone: 281-486-0507 / 800-590-7500
Fax: 281-486-0531
Email: mango-@msn.com / URL: http://
www.dcthermal.qpg.com
Product Service Description:
Direct current heaters

D G P Inc.
PO Box 155
Marlette, MI 48453-0155
Contact: Chris Clark, Pres.
Telephone: 517-635-7531
Fax: 517-635-7136
Email: / URL:
Product Service Description:
Plastic Products : Fiberglass Reinforced
Plastic Parts

D H Satellite
600 N Marquette Rd
Prairie Du Chien, WI 53821-0239
Contact: Michael Doll, GM, Sales & Mktg.
Mgr.
Telephone: 608-326-8406
Fax: 608-326-4233
Email: mdoll@mhtc.net / URL: http://
www.designhomes.com/dhsat.html
Product Service Description:
Television antennas
Radio & TV communications equipment

D R Technology, Inc.
73 South St
Freehold, NJ 07728-2317
Contact: Richard Schwartz, Pres.
Telephone: 732-780-4664
Fax: 732-780-1545
Email: drtchnj@aol.com / URL:
Product Service Description:
Air Pollution control scrubbers

D W C Assocs., Inc.
40 Longmeadow Rd
Portsmouth, NH 03801-6010
Contact: Dennis Chalmers, Pres.
Telephone: 603-431-1906
Fax: 603-431-2143
Email: dwcsales@nh.ultranet.com / URL:
Product Service Description:
Prototype equipment
Manufacturing Facilities Design

D.B.C. Enterprises, Inc.
7135 W. Tidwell, Ste. M-111
Houston, TX 77092
Contact: David B. Clarke, President
Telephone: 713-939-9009
Fax: 713-460-1222
Email: dclarke@accesscomm.net / URL:
Product Service Description:
Pipes : Valves : Fittings : Steel Products

DAC International, Inc.
6390 Rose Ln
Carpinteria, CA 93013-2922
Contact: James W. Drain, President
Telephone: 805-684-8307
Fax: 805-566-2196
Email: jdrain@dac-intl.com / URL: http://
www.dac-intl.com
Product Service Description:
Manufactures contact and intraocular lens
lathes, drills and mills
Machinery_special industry
DAC surfacing system for spectacle lens

DANZAS Corporation
3650 131st Avenue S.E.
Bellevue, WA 98006
Contact: Lesley A. Rollo,
Telephone: 425-649-9339
Fax: 425-649-4914
Email: / URL: http://www.us.danzas.com
Product Service Description:
Customs Broker : Freight Forwarder

**DCR / Diversified Communications
ReMarketing**
4256 Madison Ave
Culver City, CA 90232-3224
Contact: Ben Youngblood, Pres.
Telephone: 310-280-0333
Fax: 310-280-0133
Product Service Description:
Used & refurbed telecommunications, data
communications & networking hardware

DELTA H. SYSTEMS, INC.
1223 Barnett Rd
Columbus, OH 43227-1185
Contact: Richard Conway, Pres., Opers. & R & D Mgr.
Telephone: 614-235-1830, 888-868-2457
Fax: 614-235-8652
Email: solution@delta-h.com / URL: http://www.delta-h.com
Product Service Description:
Industrial Furnaces & Ovens

DFP International Inc
331 Corporate Cir Unit F
Golden, CO 80401-5607
Contact: Michael Nelson, Pres.
Telephone: 303-278-8299
Fax: 303-278-8244
Email: pizzelle@earthlink.com / URL: http://www.d.f.p.-intl.com
Product Service Description:
Manufactures Italian pizzelle cookies
Cookies & crackers

DNE Technologies Inc.
50 Barnes Pk. North, P.O. Box 30
Wallingford, CT 06492-0030
Contact: Margaret Cooley, Mkt Comm Mgr.
Telephone: 203-265-7151
Fax: 203-284-8414
Email: dnesales@aol.com / URL: http://www.dnetech.com
Product Service Description:
Datacomm Equipment - Multiplexers
Aerospace - Ice Detectors, Light Controllers

DRS Precision Echo
3105 Patrick Henry Dr
Santa Clara, CA 95054-1815
Contact: James J. Murphy, Pres.
Telephone: 408-988-0516
Fax: 408-727-7491
Email: / URL: http://www.drs.com
Product Service Description:
Manufactures military tactical data systems, airborne shipboard and land-based recording systems : Search & navigation equipment
Audio & video equipment_household

DSM Melamine Americas, Inc.
P.O. Box 327
Addis, LA 70710-0327
Contact: Will Williams, President
Telephone: 225-685-3030
Fax: 225-685-3003
Email: will.williams@dsm-group.com / URL: http://www.dsmmelamine.com
Product Service Description:
Melamine crystal

DV Industries Inc
2605 Industry Way
Lynwood, CA 90262-4007
Contact: Carl LaBarbera, Ex. V-P.
Telephone: 323-563-1338
Fax: 323-567-7130
Email: clabarbera@dvindustries.com / URL: http://www.dvindustries.com
Product Service Description:
Metal finishing; anodizing, painting, polishing, titanium processing, shot peening, testing : Plating & polishing
Metal coating & allied services

DWIN Electronics Inc
5838 San Fernando Rd Ste D
Glendale, CA 91202-2768
Contact: Edward Bagjian, Pres.
Telephone: 818-956-1608
Fax: 818-956-0721
Email: info@dwin.com / URL: http://www.dwin.com
Product Service Description:
Manufactures television projectors and line doublers : Radio & TV communications equipment

Daburn Electronics & Cable Corp.
225 G. Pegasus Ave.
Northvale, NJ 07647
Contact: Howard Danziger, President
Telephone: 201-768-5400
Fax: 201-768-9642
Email: daburn@daburn.com / URL: http://www.daburn.com/~daburn/
Product Service Description:
Electronic Wire #36awg to #0000. Insulated with PVC, Tefelon. : Electronic Cable - Sheilded & Unsheilded Multi Conductor & Paired : Insulated Hardware Banana plugs,Jacks. Binding Posts : Fastening Devices : Flexible Non-Metallic Tubing & Sleeving, Shrinkable Tubing

Daco Enterprises Inc
178 E 8720 S
Sandy, UT 84070
Contact: Dave Carter, Pres.
Telephone: 801-255-6011
Fax: 801-561-4916
Email: daco@xmission.com / URL: http://www.dacoprecision.com
Product Service Description:
Precision machining & assembly for medical, electronic & aerospace : Engineering, laser/CMM digitizing & inspection services

Dade Behring Inc.
3403 Yerba Buena Road
San Jose, CA 95135
Contact: Dan Roth, Director, Marketing
Telephone: 408-239-2000
Product Service Description:
Researches, develops & manufactures diagnostic test kits

Daetwyler Corp., Max
13420 Reese Blvd W
Huntersville, NC 28078-7922
Contact: Peter Daetwyler, Pres.
Telephone: 704-875-1200
Fax: 704-875-0781
Email: / URL: http://www.daetwyler.com
Product Service Description:
Photographic equipment & supplies
Printing blades, plating & washing equipment
Ultrasonic cleaners, cleaning chemistry
Pre-press equipment : Gravure cylinder engraving equipment : Gravure cylinder plating & polishing equipment
Cylinder handling equipment

Dahmes Stainless, Inc.
6300 County Rd. 40 NE
New London, MN 56273-0506
Contact: Forrest Dahmes, Pres.
Telephone: 320-354-5711
Fax: 320-354-5712
Email: dahmes@dahmes.com / URL:
Product Service Description:
Stainless steel dryers, food processing equipment & cip systems
Industrial Machinery

Daiber Co., Inc., E. J.
36400 Biltmore Pl
Willoughby, OH 44094-8221
Contact: E. J. Daiber, Pres., Engrg., R & D, Sales & Mktg. Mgr.
Telephone: 440-953-1175
Fax: 440-953-9336
Email: kdaiber@mindspring.com / URL: http://www.daiber.com
Product Service Description:
Tools_hand & edge : Torque tools

Daiei Papers U.S.A. Corp.
5757 W. Century Blvd. Ste. 865
Los Angeles, CA 90045-6456
Contact: Chris Burns, Manager
Telephone: 310-641-5092
Fax: 310-641-5096
Email: ckb@usa.daieipapers.com / URL: http://www.daieipapers.com
Product Service Description:
Bleached Hardwood : Plates, sheets, film, foil & strip of plastic, not self adhesive, non cellular

Dakota Granite Company
P.O. Box 1351
Milbank, SD 57252
Contact: Susan Stengel, Tile Coordinator
Telephone: 605-432-5580
Fax: 605-432-6155
Email: dakota@dakgran.com / URL: http://www.dakgran.com
Product Service Description:
Granite Tile, Slabs, Blocks

Daktronics, Inc.
331 32nd Ave.
Brookings, SD 57006
Contact: Sales & Marketing,
Telephone: 605-697-4300
Fax: (605)697-4700
Email: / URL:
Product Service Description:
Electronic Score Boards
Electronic Voting Systems
Electronic Advertising Displays

Dale Medical Products, Inc.(Mfr)
P.O. Box 1556
Plainville, MA 02762
Contact: John C. Brezack, *
Telephone: 508/695-9316
Product Service Description:
Orthopedic & Surgical Supplies

Dale's Wild West Products
PO Box 368
Brighton, CO 80601-0368
Contact: Dale Beier, Owner
Telephone: 303-659-8796
Fax: 303-659-0255
Email: dalesmeats@aol.com / URL:
Product Service Description:
Buffalo, Venison (Jerky, Sausages, Canned Products) : Custom canning available

Dalhart R & R Machine Works, Inc.
PO Box 1330
Dalhart, TX 79022-1330
Contact: Wes Wood, Pres., GM & Pers. Mgr.
Telephone: 806-244-5686
Fax: 806-244-6096
Email: rrmacwor@xit.net / URL: http://www.r-rmachine.com
Product Service Description:
Feed roll grinding & corrugation & roll changes : Grain Roller / Flaker Mills & Stam Chests

Dalloz Safety
PO Box 622
Reading, PA 19603-0622
Contact: Jason Leniski, VP Americas
Telephone: 610-371-7925
Fax: 610-371-7740
Email: jwomer@ix.netcom.com / URL: http://www.cdalloz.com
Product Service Description:
Safety personal protection equipment - eye, face, hearing, head
Manufacturing industries

Dalloz Safety, Inc.
5300 Region Ct
Lakeland, FL 33815-3121
Contact: Richard Pellegrini, V-P., GM
Telephone: 941-687-7266
Fax: 941-687-0431
Email: rpellegr@gte.net / URL:
Product Service Description:
Industrial safety eye & head protection equipment : Measuring & controlling devices

Dalton Enterprises, Inc.
131 Willow St
Cheshire, CT 06410-2732
Contact: Peter F. Dalton, Pres.
Telephone: 203-272-3221
Fax: 203-271-3396
Product Service Description:
Driveway sealants, pavement crack repair products & athletic surface acrylic coatings
Adhesives & sealants

Damar Machine Co
PO Box 9
Monroe, WA 98272-0009
Contact: Thom Kroon, CEO
Telephone: 425-646-9288
Fax: 360-794-8144
Email: tkroon@damarmachine.com / URL: http://www.damarmachine.com
Product Service Description:
Industrial machinery
General machine shop (job work); manufactures aircraft parts for airlines
Aircraft parts & equipment

Damascus Peanut Co.
PO Box 526
Arlington, GA 31713
Contact: Bryan WIllis, Pres.
Telephone: 912-725-4236
Fax: 912-725-4350
Email: gwillis@surfsouth.com / URL:
Product Service Description:
Raw & Blanched Shelled & Inshell Peanuts
Processed Peanut Products

Dan Transport Corporation
1404 E. North Belt, Ste. 110,
Houston, TX 77032
Contact: Henrik F. Mikuta, Branch Manager
Telephone: 281-590-5590
Fax: 281-590-5511
Email: dl_houston@dantran.com / URL: http://www.dantran.com
Product Service Description:
Freight Forwarder
Customs Broker
Freight & Cargo Transportation
IATA Licenced Agent
NVOCC Bonded
Project cargo handling
Track & trace
"Just in Time" Concept
AOG Handling
Worldwide network

Dana Corp./Wichita Clutch Co.
2800 Fisher Rd
Wichita Falls, TX 76302-5917
Contact: Lonnie Wilkerson, Materials Manager
Telephone: 940-723-3405
Fax: 940-723-3436
Email: lonnie.wilkerson@dana.com / URL:
http://www.warnernet.com
Product Service Description:
Power transmission equipment
Industrial clutches & brakes

Daniel Woodhead Company
3411 Woodhead Dr.
Northbrook, IL 60062-1812
Contact: Patrick Stearns, *
Telephone: 708-272-7990
Fax: 708-272-8133
Email: / URL:
Product Service Description:
Wiring Device, Caps & Plugs Attachment

Darigold Inc.
635 Elliott Ave W.
Seattle, WA 98119-3983
Contact: Roger Miller, *
Telephone: 206-284-7220
Fax: 206-298-6894
Email: cromill@darigold.com / URL:
Product Service Description:
Creamery Butter
Cheese
Dry Whey & Dry Yogurt
Dry Buttermilk & Dry Whole Milk
Nonfat Dry Milk

Darley & Co., W. S.
2000 Anson Dr
Melrose Park, IL 60160-1019
Contact: W. J. Darley, Chrm., CEO
Telephone: 708-345-8050
Fax: 708-345-8993
Email: darley@wsdarley.com / URL: http://
www.wsdarley.com
Product Service Description:
Fire fighting equipment, pumps, & apparatus
Law enforcement equipment

Darling International Inc.
251 O'Connor Ridge Blvd., Suite 300
Irving, TX 75038
Contact: Mitch Kilanowski, Executive Vice
President, Mktg.
Telephone: 972-717-0300
Fax: 972-717-1588
Email: sales@darlingii.com / URL: http://
www.darlingii.com
Product Service Description:
Meat By Products / Co-Products
Feather Meal
Poultry By-Product Meal
Tallow
Yellow Grease
C-Meal / fish analog

Dartrans, Inc.
6610 Tributary St., Ste. 201,
Baltimore, MD 21224
Contact: David A. Rice, President
Telephone: 410-633-4450
Fax: 410-633-5351
Email: dartrans@dartrans.com / URL: http://
www.dartrans.com
Product Service Description:
Customs Broker & Freight Forwarder
International Logistics & Transportation
Sea & Air Freight : Trucking, Warehousing &
Distribution

Dasco Pro Inc (Mfr)
2215 Kishwaukee Streeet
Rockford, IL 61104
Contact: Tedd Lamprecht, *
Telephone: 815-962-3727
Fax: 815-962-4972
Product Service Description:
Chisels : Punches : Levels : Handles

Datacom Textron
11001 31st Pl W.
Everett, WA 98204-1301
Contact: Beth Cote, Marketing
Communications Manager
Telephone: 425-355-0590
Fax: 425-290-1600
Email: info@datacom.textron.com / URL:
http://www.datacom.textron.com
Product Service Description:
Network Analyzers, LAN Cable Tester

Datamarine International Inc
7030 220th St Sw
Mountlake Terrace, WA 98043-2125
Contact: David C Thompson, CEO
Telephone: 425-771-2182
Fax: 425-771-2650
Email: salesmktg@sea-dmi.com / URL: http:/
/www.sea-dmi.com
Product Service Description:
Manufactures marine and land mobile
communications equipment (holding
company)

David Adam Promotions Inc
10105 E Via Linda Ste 103-387
Scottsdale, AZ 85258-5311
Contact: Cynthia S Keller, Pres.
Telephone: 602-391-1056
Fax: 602-314-5660
Product Service Description:
Distributes advertising specialties,
promotions, caps, jackets, T-shirts, water
bottles, mugs, pens and calendars
Nondurable goods
Advertising

Davidson International Inc.
11465 Melrose Ave
Franklin Park, IL 60131-1324
Contact: Ron Basick, Owner
Telephone: 847-455-2929
Fax: 847-455-0953
Product Service Description:
Printing equipment manufacturer
Printing_commercial

Davis Bynum Winery
8075 Westside Rd
Healdsburg, CA 95448-9463
Contact: Davis Bynum, Pres.
Telephone: 707-433-5852
Fax: 707-433-4309
Email: / URL:
Product Service Description:
Family wine business, limited production of
premium varietals from the Russian River
Valley : Wines, brandy, & brandy spirits
Wine & distilled beverages

Davis Co., E. J.
PO Box 326
North Haven, CT 06473-0326
Contact: Gregory Godbout, Owner
Telephone: 203-239-5391
Fax: 203-234-7724
Product Service Description:
Industrial insulation die-cutting & processing
Plastic foam products : Polyimide Foam

Davis Colors
3700 E. Olympic Blvd.
Los Angeles, CA 90023
Contact: Nick Paris, Export Manager
Telephone: 213-269-7311
Fax: 213-269-1053
Email: sales_service@daviscolors.com /
URL: http://www.daviscolors.com
Product Service Description:
Inorganic Pigments & Dry Colors
Inorg. Pigments, Concrete Mix-In Color
Chem. Paint Additives, Corrosion Inhib.

Davis Colors
PO Box 23100
Los Angeles, CA 90023-0100
Contact: Nick L Paris, Pres.
Telephone: 323-269-7311
Fax: 323-269-1053
Email: / URL: http://www.daviscolors.com
Product Service Description:
Manufacturer, color additives for concrete

Davis Liquid Crystals
15021 Wicks Blvd
San Leandro, CA 94577-6621
Contact: Frederick Davis, Pres.
Telephone: 510-351-2295
Fax: 510-351-2328
Email: dle@jps.net / URL:
Product Service Description:
Color Changing (Thermochronic) Pigments /
Inks
Color Changing Toy, Gift & Novelty Items
Interactive, Color Changing Promotional
Items
Liquid Crystals & Thermometers & Films

De Francesco & Sons Inc
PO Box 605
Firebaugh, CA 93622-0605
Contact: Mario De Francesco Jr, Pres.
Telephone: 209-364-7000
Fax: 209-364-7001
Email: / URL:
Product Service Description:
Manufactures dehydrated vegetables
Dehydrated garlic, onion, parsley, red beet
powder &
other vegetable products

De La Rue Cash Systems
PO Box 200
Watertown, WI 53094-0200
Contact: Edward Opperud, President
Telephone: 920-261-1780
Fax: 920-261-1783
Email: edward.opperud@us.delarue.com /
URL:
Product Service Description:
Calculating & accounting equipment
Currency & coin counting, wrapping, sorting
& dispensing machines
Vending machines_automatic
Packaging machinery

De Marco MAX VAC Corporation
1412 Ridgeview Dr
Mc Henry, IL 60050-7022
Contact: Thomas M. DeMarco, Pres.
Telephone: 815-344-2222
Fax: 815-344-2223
Email: maxvac@maxvac.com / URL: http://
www.maxvac.com
Product Service Description:
Industrial vacuum cleaners & loaders &
exhaust mufflers

DeFinco Ltd.
25 Midwood Drive
Greenwich, CT 06831-4412
Contact: Nicholas B. Tournillon, President
Telephone: 203-661-0808
Fax: 203-661-2055
Email: / URL:
Product Service Description:
Management consulting services, trade
finance
Trade financing
Direct foreign investment

Dean Foods (Mfr)
3600 River Road
Franklin Park, IL 60131
Contact: Kevin Nemepz, General Manager
Telephone: 708-678-1680
Fax: 708-678-2779
Email: / URL:
Product Service Description:
Non-Dairy Creamers
Nutritional Beverage Drinks
Cheese Sauce
Puddings
Pickles, Relish, Olives
Syrup
Specialty Sauces

Debbeler Co.
1309 N 38th St
Milwaukee, WI 53208-2839
Contact: Guenther Block, Owner
Telephone: 414-344-4474
Fax: 414-344-7938
Email: ghblock@debbeler.com / URL: http://
www.debbeler.com/badges
Product Service Description:
Button Machinery & Supplies, Badge &
Button Machines & Supplies
Machinery, Special Industry - Badge &
Button Machines

Dec-E-Tech
10 Lomar Park Drive
Pepperell, MA 01463
Contact: William Mortimer, *
Telephone: 508-433-6440
Fax: 508-433-6443
Email: decetech@empire.net / URL:
Product Service Description:
Industrial Drying Systems
Industrial Process Heating Systems
Pollution Control: Oxidizers

Decor Guild Mfg., Co.
1052 W Florence Ave
Los Angeles, CA 90044-2442
Contact: Salvador R Hernandez, Pres.
Telephone: 323-751-1888 / 888-670-5047
Fax: 323-751-0900
Email: dguild@ix.netcom.com / URL: http://
www.decorlamps.com
Product Service Description:
Electric lamps (Incandescent), Manufactures
Resident Light Fixtures; Table, Floor & Wall
Lamps

Dedert Corp.
20000 Governors Dr
Olympia Fields, IL 60461-1034
Contact: Thomas W. Dedert, Pres.
Telephone: 708-747-7000
Fax: 708-755-8815
Email: dedert@dedert.com / URL: http://
www.dedert.com
Product Service Description:
Evaporators : Crystallizers
Steam Tube Dryers

Dedouch Co. Studios, J. A.
608 Harrison St
Oak Park, IL 60304-1329
Contact: Richard Stannard, President
Telephone: 708-386-1130
Fax: 708-386-2671
Email: / URL:
Product Service Description:
Porcelain monument portraits

Deep Ocean Engineering Inc
1431 Doolittle Dr
San Leandro, CA 94577-2225
Contact: Dirk Rosen, Pres.
Telephone: 510-562-9300
Fax: 510-430-8249
Email: deepoceans@aol.com / URL: http://
www.deepocean.com
Product Service Description:
Underwater vehicles, manufacturer

Deer-Off, Inc.
1492 High Ridge Rd Ste
Stamford, CT 06903-4124
Contact: Athena Loucas, Pres.
Telephone: 203-968-8485
Fax: 203-968-2882
Email: deeroff@deer-off.com / URL: http://
www.deer-off.com
Product Service Description:
Deer repellent : Organic gardening
Garden supplies

Deerfield Specialty Papers, Inc.
PO Box 5437
Augusta, GA 30916-5437
Contact: Ronald J. Hermus, General Sales
Mgr.
Telephone: 706-798-1861
Fax: 706-798-2270
Product Service Description:
Glassine & grease proof paper
Specialty papers

Deering Fabricators
196 Asa Cash Rd
Bremen, GA 30110-3751
Contact: Howard Deering, Owner
Telephone: 770-574-2013
Fax: 770-574-8018
Product Service Description:
Stainless steel food equipment legs
Heat treating_metal

Deeter Foundry Inc.
PO Box 29708
Lincoln, NE 68529-0708
Contact: Deb Bitzer, Pur. Agt.
Telephone: 402-464-7466
Fax: 402-464-8533
Email: sales@deeter.com / URL: http://
www.deeter.com
Product Service Description:
Gray iron castings
Foundries, gray & ductile iron

Defco, Inc.
PO Box 1209
Decatur, AL 35602-1209
Contact: J. O. Sims, Pres., Engrg. Mgr.
Telephone: 205-353-7697
Fax: 205-350-6540
Email: / URL: http://www.defco.com
Product Service Description:
Fluid power cylinders & actuators
Air & hydraulic centrifugal & submersible
pumps, cylinders, valves & metering devices
Fluid power pumps & motors
Pumps & pumping equipment

Degen Pipe & Supply Co.
5000 Southwest Blvd.
Tulsa, OK 74107
Contact: Joe I. Degen, *
Telephone: 918-446-6152
Fax: 918-446-6156
Product Service Description:
Water Well Drilling Equipment

**Del's Lemonade & Refreshments,
Inc.**
1260 Oaklawn Ave
Cranston, RI 02920-2640
Contact: Bruce Delucia, Pres.
Telephone: 401-463-6190
Fax: 401-463-7931
Email: / URL: http://www.dels.com
Product Service Description:
Lemon, cherry, watermelon syrup
or powder for granitas

Delaire U. S. A., Inc.
1553 Sterling Dr
Manasquan, NJ 08736-2511
Contact: Lori Hallock, Pres.
Telephone: 732-528-4520
Fax: 732-528-4521
Email: sales@delaireusa.com / URL: http://
www.delaireusa.com
Product Service Description:
RF Cable Assemblies : Electronic & RF
Components : RF Contract Manufacturer

Delgado R. E. Inc.
P.O. Box 9024136
San Juan, PR 00902-4136
Contact: Paulette Diaz, Administrative
Assistant
Telephone: 809-722-6750
Fax: 809-723-1506
Email: / URL:
Product Service Description:
Air Freight Forwarders
Customhouse Broker

Delicato Vineyards
12001 S. Highway 99
Manteca, CA 95336-9209
Contact: Vincent Indelicato, President
Telephone: 209-824-3600
Fax: 209-824-3510
Email: wine@delicato.com / URL: http://
www.delicato.com
Product Service Description:
Bottled & Bulk Wines

**Delo Screw Products, A Park-Ohio
Co.**
PO Box 1203
Delaware, OH 43015
Contact: Mike Green, Pres.
Telephone: 740-363-1971
Fax: 740-363-0042
Email: deloscrew@aol.com / URL:
Product Service Description:
Screw machine products

**Delta Communications &
Electronics**
2162 South Jupiter Rd.
Garland, TX 75041-6004
Contact: Wayne Lott, Owner
Telephone: 214-278-0202
Fax: 214-278-5085
Email: export@delta2000.com / URL: http://
www.delta2000.com
Product Service Description:
2-Way Radios, Wholesale
Electronic Repair svcs , 2-Way Radios

Delta Faucet
55 E. 111th St.
Indianapolis, IN 46280
Contact: Brad Hillam, Director, International
Telephone: 317-574-5562
Fax: 317-573-3499
Email: bkh@deltafaucet.com / URL: http://
www.deltafaucet.com
Product Service Description:
Plumbing Fixture Fittings and Trim
Taps, cocks, valves and similar appliances for
pipes, vats or the like, including
thermostatically controlled valves
Table, kitchen or other household articles and
parts thereof, of stainless steel

Delta International
PO Box 188
Fairfield, CT 06430-1088
Contact: Gerald L. Berk,
Telephone: 203-255-1969
Fax: 203-254-2906
Email: berkseek@iconn.net / URL: http://
www.delta-trade-intl.com
Product Service Description:
Wheat
Corn
Soybeans
Turkey & Eggs
Food Products Machinery

Delta Machine & Tool, Inc.
1501 Lexington Ave
Deland, FL 32724-2117
Contact: Norbert Ruppert, Pres., CFO
Telephone: 904-738-2204
Fax: 904-738-9674
Email: / URL:
Product Service Description:
Plastic insert molding & general machining
job shop
Industrial machinery
Plastic products

Delta Precision Alloys
121 Domorah Dr
Montgomeryville, PA 18936-9635
Contact: Ted Davis Sr., Pres.
Telephone: 215-540-9797
Fax: 215-628-4576
Email: deltadpa@aol.com / URL:
Product Service Description:
Round & Shaped & Electroplated Wire
Ferrous & non ferrous drawing, stranding &
insulating
Reel to reel continuous plating of Gold,
Silver, Nickel
Copper, Tin & Tin Alloys

Delta Products Corporation
4405 Cushing Pkwy
Fremont, CA 94538-6475
Contact: Frank Hsiung, VP
Telephone: 510-668-5100
Fax: 510-668-0680
Email: / URL: http://www.deltaca.com
Product Service Description:
Manufactures standard/custom computer
power supplies, power adapters, telecom
power system, UPS, : LCD/CRT monitors,
LCD projectors, EMI/RFI filters, brushless
DC-fans/spindle motor, networking
Components/products, RF/microwave
components, fiber optic transceiver, AC
motor drive, Electronic
Ballast, CD-ROM, NiMH rechargeable
battery pack, thin film components, voltage
controlled oscillator, Window-based terminals
& motherboard.

Delta Products Group
P.O. Box 6466
Aurora, IL 60598-0466
Contact: Mark Ostermeier,
Telephone: 1-888-337-2253
Fax: 1-630-717-5973
Email: solutions@deltaproducts.com / URL:
Product Service Description:
Liquid Chemical Descalers

Deltrol Controls
2740 S 20th St
Milwaukee, WI 53215-3708
Contact: Robert Oster, Pres.
Telephone: 414-671-6800
Fax: 414-671-6809
Email: info@deltrol.com / URL: http://
www.deltrol.com
Product Service Description:
Electrical controls, relays, solenoids & valves
Relays & industrial controls

Delvest, Inc.
PO Box 747
West Chester, PA 19381-0747
Contact: Anthony R. Micola, Chrm., R & D
Mgr.
Telephone: 610-436-6380
Fax: 610-430-1534
Email: delvest@aol.com / URL: http://
www.delvest.com
Product Service Description:
Investment castings
Foundries_steel investment
Nonferrous Foundries

Delyse Inc
505 Reactor Way
Reno, NV 89502-4108
Contact: Elisabeth Galvin, Pres.
Telephone: 775-857-1811
Fax: 775-857-4722
Email: / URL: http://www.delyse.com
Product Service Description:
Manufacturer of Snacks

Demco Electronics
10516 S Grevillea Ave
Inglewood, CA 90304-1819
Contact: Darrell Hoblack, Owner
Telephone: 310-677-0801
Fax: 310-674-5445
Email: / URL:
Product Service Description:
Manufactures security products for the self-
storage industry
Communications equipment, nec

Dempster Industries, Inc.
711 S 6th St.
Beatrice, NE 68310-4606
Contact: David P Suey, President
Telephone: 402-223-4026
Fax: 402-228-4389
Email: dempsterinc@beatricene.com / URL:
Product Service Description:
Submersible Pumps, IOHP & Under for
Water Wells: Vertical Turbine Pumps,
Linshaft & Submersible :Hand & Windmill
Pumps, Jacks & Cylinders for Pumping Water
Farm Windmill Heads & Towers for Pumping
Water : Fertilizer Distributors, Drygravity &
Liquid Sprayers : Trailers for
ollecting,Sorting & Hauling Recyc.Solid
Waste

Denice & Filice Packing
10001 Fairview Rd.
Hollister, CA 95023-9426
Contact: Charles Filice, Owner
Telephone: 408-637-7491
Product Service Description:
Puple Table Onions : Fresh Garlic
Yellow Onions : Cherries

Dennis Aluminum Products
6611 Bon Secour Hwy
Bon Secour, AL 36511-3212
Contact: Gary Dennis, Owner
Telephone: 334-943-6496
Fax: 334-943-1544
Product Service Description:
Aluminum tanks, grills, picnic tables &
fishing accessories
Products for commercial fisherman

Dent Tools, Inc.
PO Box 26742
Olathe, KS 66225
Contact: Scott Clifton, Pres.
Telephone: 913-397-8005
Fax: 913-397-9092
Email: / URL: http://www.usdent.com
Product Service Description:
Paintless dent repair tools, body shop
equipment

Dentech Corporation
529 Front St
Sumas, WA 98295-9604
Contact: Kent Fletcher, President
Telephone: 360-988-7911
Fax: 360-988-7906
Email: fletcher@dentechcorp.com / URL:
http://www.dentechcorp.com
Product Service Description:
Manufactures dental instruments, equipment
and supplies, dental chairs and stools

Dentsply International Inc.
PO Box 872
York, PA 17405-0872
Contact: George Rhodes, V-P., Comm.
Telephone: 717-845-7511
Fax: 717-854-2343
Email: / URL: http://www.dentsply.com
Product Service Description:
Dental equipment & supplies
Dental prosthetics, laboratory products &
equipment

Denver Seating Inc
4701 National Western Dr
Denver, CO 80216-2124
Contact: Leroy Gurule, Pres.
Telephone: 303-294-0147
Fax: 303-297-8170
Product Service Description:
Manufactures custom upholstered furniture
for restaurants, public buildings and hotels
Furniture_public building & related

Dependable/Redford-Carver
PO Box 3210
Tualatin, OR 97062-3210
Contact: Debra Groves, Assoc/Intl Sales
Telephone: 503-692-5526 Ext.332
Fax: 503-692-4477
Email: sales@dfrc.com / URL: http://
www.dfrc.com
Product Service Description:
Ind. Core/Mold Blowing Equipment
Ind. Batch/Cont. Sand Prep. Equip.
Ind. Sand Reclamation Equip.

**Des Champs Laboratories
Incorporated**
Route 130 Douglas Way
Natural Bridge Station, VA 24579
Contact: Vicki Layne,
Telephone: 540-291-1111
Fax: 540-291-2222
Email: / URL: http://www.deschamps.com
Product Service Description:
Industrial Energy Recovery Systems
Commercial Energy Recovery-HVAC

Desert Laboratories Inc
3136 E Columbia St
Tucson, AZ 85714-2001
Contact: Jonathan Morgan, Pres.
Telephone: 520-294-3431
Fax: 520-294-3433
Product Service Description:
Machine job shop; manufactures honing tools
and machines, two wheel dollies
Machine tools, metal cutting types
Hones from 1/2" to 42"

Design Display, Inc.
PO Box 19458
Birmingham, AL 35219-9458
Contact: Eric Colee, Pres.
Telephone: 205-945-8130
Fax: 205-945-8227
Email: ddd@traveller.com / URL: http://
www.designdisplay.com
Product Service Description:
Trade show displays
Signs & advertising specialties

**Designers Resource, DBA Country
& Casual**
1855 Griffin Rd., Ste. B272
Dania, FL 33004-2241
Contact: Barry & Beverly Clarke, Owners
Telephone: 954-921-4696
Fax: 954-921-4705
Email: bbclarke97@aol.com / URL:
Product Service Description:
Bernhardt Furniture & Upholstery
Ficks Reed Wicker & Rattan Furniture
Elden Country Furniture
Sligh Home Office Furniture
Lexington Furniture & Upholstery

Desmark Industries, Inc.
10 Industrial Dr
Smithfield, RI 02917-1502
Contact: Robert McClintock, Pres.
Telephone: 401-232-0803
Fax: 401-231-8111
Product Service Description:
Metal products_fabricated
Metal Christmas ornaments & gift items

Desmoines Truck Brokers Inc.
PO Box 337 / 1505 North Avenue
Norwalk, IA 50211
Contact: James Dematteis, *
Product Service Description:
Trucking, Local, U.S., Canada, Mexico

Detex International
302 Detex Dr.
New Braunfels, TX 78130-3099
Contact: Anthony Mudford, VP
Telephone: 830-629-2900
Fax: 830-620-6711
Email: detex@detex.com / URL: http://
www.detex.com
Product Service Description:
Security & Alarm Systems & Equipment
Communication Equipment, Nec

Dewald Northwest Co
33710 Oakville Rd SW
Albany, OR 97321-9479
Contact: Roger Oukrop, Pres., GM
Telephone: 541-926-5578
Fax: 541-926-7558
Email: sales@dewaldnw-crw.com / URL:
http://www.dewaldnw-crw.com
Product Service Description:
Manufactures & distributes commercial metal
containers & plastic lids for refuse, recyling

Dews Research
PO Box 637
Mineral Wells, TX 76068-0637
Contact: Jim Dews, Pres., Fin., R & D, Sales
& Mktg. Mgr.
Telephone: 940-325-0208
Fax: 940-328-1439
Email: dewsres@wf.net / URL:
Product Service Description:
Toilet preparations
Health & beauty products
Food preparations
Dry, condensed, evaporated products
Medicinals & botanicals

Dezign Sewing Inc.
4001 N Ravenswood Ave
Chicago, IL 60613-2434
Contact: Barbara Vincent, Pres.
Telephone: 773-549-4336
Fax: 773-549-7085
Email: / URL:
Product Service Description:
Draperies & bedding : Curtains & draperies

Dezion Signs
46-020 Alaloa St M5
Kaneohe, HI 96744-3815
Contact: Glenn Racoma, Owner
Telephone: 808-247-7450
Fax: 808-247-7450
Product Service Description:
Metal, wooden & painted signs : Signs &
advertising specialties : Vinyl Signs &
graphics : Vehical Signage : Vinyl Letters &
Graphics to order : Lighted signs - banners

Dharma Publishing
2910 San Pablo Ave
Berkeley, CA 94702-2426
Contact: Rima Tamar, Sales Mgr.
Telephone: 510-548-5407
Fax: 510-548-2230
Email: dharma-publishing@nyingma.org /
URL: http://www.nyingma.org
Product Service Description:
Publishes books on Eastern philosophy
Book publishing
Multi-Cultural Children's Books
Asian Art Prints
Buddhist Philosphy History, Culture & Art
Books in Meditation, Relaxation, Healing

Diablo Industries
2245 Meridian Blvd
Minden, NV 89423-8614
Contact: James Dishon, Pres.
Telephone: 702-782-1041
Fax: 702-782-1044
Email: sales@ditf.com / URL: http://
www.ditf.com
Product Service Description:
Manufactures thin film microwave integrated
circuits, chip resistors and capacitors
Semiconductors & related devices
Electronic capacitors: Electronic resistors
Custom Microwave Circuit Devices

Dial Manufacturing Inc
25 S 51st Ave
Phoenix, AZ 85043-3711
Contact: Duane Johnston, Pres.
Telephone: 602-278-1100
Fax: 602-278-1991
Email: duanejohnston@dialmfg.com / URL:
http://www.dialmfg.com
Product Service Description:
Manufactures evaporative air cooler parts and
accessories; outdoor mist cooling systems
Refrigeration & heating equipment
Motors & generators
Warm air heating & air conditioning
Industrial machinery & equipment

Diamond Electronics Inc.
PO Box 200
Lancaster, OH 43130-0200
Contact: Richard Tompkins III, Sales
Manager
Telephone: 740-756-9222
Fax: 740-756-4237
Email: rick.tompkins@ultrak.com / URL:
http://www.diamondelectronics.com
Product Service Description:
Closed Circuit Television/Surveillance

Diamond Head Golf Club Mfg Co
11351 Trade Center Dr Ste 350
Rancho Cordova, CA 95742-6235
Contact: Alan R Wagner, Owner
Telephone: 916-638-7220
Fax: 916-638-2024
Email: / URL:
Product Service Description:
Manufactures golf clubs; irons woods
Sporting & athletic goods

Diamond Rubber Products Co., Inc.
4000 50th St Sw
Birmingham, AL 35221-1848
Contact: Dan Blumenthal,
Telephone: 205-925-3791
Fax: 205-925-3793
Email: diamonddann@diamondrubber.com /
URL: http://www.diamondrubber.com
Product Service Description:
Industrial rubber products
Wheel chocks
Moded rubber products
Extruded rubber products
Rubber rollers; bonds rubber to metal
Airline & ground support rubber products

Diamond Turf Equipment Inc.
1911 Nw 32nd St
Pompano Beach, FL 33064-1303
Contact: Brian Utley, Pres.
Telephone: 954-984-9111
Fax: 954-984-9630
Email: / URL:
Product Service Description:
Golf course maintenance equipment
Greens Mowers
Gang Mowers
Trap Rakes
Sprayers
Greens Maintenance Systems
Sweeper Vacuums
Verticutters
Sports field mowing
Sports field finishing

Diamond V Mills, Inc.
PO Box 74570
Cedar Rapids, IA 52407-4570
Contact: Jerry Chaffee, Dir, Intl Sales
Telephone: 319-366-0745
Fax: 319-366-6333
Email: jchaffee@diamondv.com / URL: http://
www.diamondv.com
Product Service Description:
Prepared Animal Feeds

Diamond Z Manufacturing
1102 Franklin Blvd
Nampa, ID 83687-6754
Contact: Sam Ozuna, Senior Mtg. Rep.
Phone: 208-467-6229 / Fax: 208-467-6390
Email: diamondz@diamondz.com / URL:
http://www.diamondz.com
Product Service Description:
Manufactures industrial tub grinders and
trommel screens

Dicey Fabrics
Neisler St. & Highway 74, W.
Shelby, NC 28150
Contact: Henry P. Neisler, Owner
Telephone: 704-487-6324
Product Service Description:
Wholesale residental upholstery fabric made
with both cotton & manmade fibers

Diego & Son Printing
2104 National Ave
San Diego, CA 92113-2209
Contact: Nicholas Aguilera, Pres.
Phone: 619-233-5373 / Fax: 619-233-4937
Email: diegoandsonprinting / URL: http://
www.diegoandsonprinting.com
Product Service Description:
Lithographic printing_commercial
Commercial printing

Diehl, Inc.
24 N. Clinton St.
Defiance, OH 43512
Contact: John F. Diehl, V.P. Sales & Mktg.
Telephone: 419-782-5010
Fax: 419-784-5924
Email: diehl@bright.net / URL:
Product Service Description:
Non Dairy Creamer : Powdered Vegetable
Shortening : Whip Toppings : Emulsifiers
(Baking) : Specialty Dairy , Powders
Evaporated Milk : Non-Dairy Milk
Substitute: Vanilla, Chocolate

Dielectric Polymers, Inc.
218 Race St.
Holyoke, MA 01040-5710
Contact: Lawrence G. Kuntz, President
Telephone: 413-532-3288
Fax: 413-533-9316
Email: info@dipoly.cm / URL:
Product Service Description:
Industrial Adhesive Film : Pressure Sensitive
Adhesive : Laminating Adhesives

Diemasters, Inc.
1627 W. 31st St.
Kansas City, MO 64108-3641
Contact: Robert Gallagher, Pres.
Telephone: 816-753-3466 / 800-525-4036
Fax: 816-561-1280
Email: sales@die-masters.com / URL: http://
www.diemasters.com
Product Service Description:
Steel Rule Cutting Dies : Scrapping Tools
Blanking Tools : Custom Die Cutting
Clicker Dies

Diesel Parts of America
13150 Leadwell Street
N. Hollywood, CA 91605
Contact: Ara Mansourian, President
Telephone: 818-765-3344
Fax: 818-765-1412
Email: dpausa@pacificnet.net / URL: http://
www.dpausa.com
Product Service Description:
Diesel Fuel Injector & Engine Parts
Diesel Engine Parts

Dieterich & Ball Incorporated
1021 Commerce Dr
Prescott, AZ 86301-3701
Contact: Wolfgang Dieterich, Pres.
Telephone: 520-776-8773
Fax: 520-776-1966
Product Service Description:
Designs and manufactures trade show
exhibits and commercial interiors
Show services & warehousing

Dietrich & Son, Inc.
128 Flushing St., P.O. Drawer 318
Burlington, NC 27216-0318
Contact: Helmut Dietrich, *
Telephone: 336-226-5844
Product Service Description:
Textile Machinery / Export

Digilube Systems, Inc.
545 S Main St
Springboro, OH 45066-1419
Contact: Dave Hamilton, Pres.
Telephone: 513-748-2209
Fax: 513-748-0597
Email: / URL: http://www.digilube.com
Product Service Description:
Lubricating oils & greases
Industrial conveyor lubrication equipment,
lubricants & pneumatic equipment

Digital Interface Systems Inc.
241 W. Federal Plz.
Youngstown, OH 44502
Contact: Lee Kareem, Pres., R & D Mgr.
Telephone: 330-743-1987
Fax: 330-743-1966
Email: disystem@ix.netcom.com / URL:
http://www.digitalinterfacesystems.com
Product Service Description:
Data acquisition systems & signal detectors
Electronic computers : Computer peripheral
equipment : Network Systems Integration
Electronic Schematic Archiving

Digital Link Corp
217 Humboldt Ct
Sunnyvale, CA 94089-1300
Contact: Murray Wicks,
Telephone: 408-745-4230
Fax: 408-745-6250
Email: inh-info@dl.com / URL: http://
www.dl.com
Product Service Description:
Data Communication Products for Internet,
Frames Relay, SMDS, Acces

Digital Nation
150 Varick St
New York, NY 10013-1218
Contact: William Prusack, Pres., CFO
Telephone: 212-633-8800
Fax: 212-633-8900
Product Service Description:
Typesetting : Electronic pre-press
Desktop publishing : Drum scanning
Hi end retouching : Printing - b/c & coating

**Digital Telephone Sys., Harris Corp.
(Mfr)**
300 Bel Marin Keys Blvd.
Novato, CA 94949
Contact: Julie Carlson,
Telephone: 415-382-5268
Fax: 415-382-5222
Email: Info@dts.harris.com / URL:
Product Service Description:
Elec. Private Branch Exchange (Pbx) Eq.

Dimco-Gray Co.
8200 S Suburban Rd
Centerville, OH 45458-2710
Contact: David W. Scott, Pres., CEO
Telephone: 937-433-7600
Fax: 937-433-0520
Email: sales@dimco-gray.com / URL: http://
www.dimco-gray.com
Product Service Description:
Thermoset knobs & handles,
electromechanical & electronic timers,
fasteners, thermoplastic : Plastic products,
Screw Machine Parts, Cold Headed Parts

Dippin Dots, Inc.
5101 Charter Oak Dr
Paducah, KY 42001-5209
Contact: Curt Jones, Pres.
Telephone: 502-443-8994
Fax: 502-443-8997
Email: email@dippindots.com / URL: http://
www.dippindots.com
Product Service Description:
Ice cream, yogurt & flavored ices
Ice cream & frozen desserts

Dipwell Co., Inc., The
PO Box 3228
Erie, PA 16508-0228
Contact: Lynn Perry Alstadt, Pres., Mktg. &
Pur. Mgr.
Telephone: 814-454-4641
Fax: 814-455-9641
Email: rinse@dipwell.com / URL: http://
www.dipwell.com/
Product Service Description:
Food Service Cleaning Equipment

Discovery Toys
6400 Brisa St.
Livermore, CA 94550-9763
Contact: Rich Newton, V.P. of Operations
Telephone: 925-606-2600
Fax: 925-606-2687
Email: rich.newton@cwix.com / URL: http://
www.discoverytoysinc.com
Product Service Description:
Toys, books, games & software

Disposable Products Company Inc.
313 W. 4th St.
Bridgeport, PA 19405
Contact: Mr. Jack Berk,
Telephone: 610-277-3000
Fax: 610-277-1264
Product Service Description:
Paper & Non Woven Wiping Materials

Distinctive Foods, Inc.
654 Wheeling Rd
Wheeling, IL 60090-5707
Contact: Mark Lepp,
Telephone: 847-459-3600
Fax: 847-459-3660
Email: distfoods@starnetusa.com / URL:
Product Service Description:
Flat bread
Bread, cake & related products

Distribution Services of America
208 North St.,
Foxboro, MA 02035-1099
Contact: Mark Slattery,
Telephone: 508-543-9700
Fax: 508-543-7406
Email: mslattery@dsa-inc.com / URL:
Product Service Description:
Full service transportation capabilities
Warehousing & distribution
Supply chain managment / logistics

Distributors Processing Inc
17656 Avenue 168
Porterville, CA 93257-9263
Contact: Judy Meadows, V.-P., GM
Telephone: 209-781-0297
Fax: 209-781-4632
Email: dpiyucca@lightspeed.net / URL: http:/
/www.micro-aid.com
Product Service Description:
Produces yucca juice feed additives
Feeds_prepared
Farm supplies

Diversified Coatings, Inc.
4580 Mack Ave Ste C
Frederick, MD 21703-7158
Contact: David Lagarde, V.-P., Sales & Mktg.
Telephone: 301-293-0223
Fax: 301-631-9093
Email: dcoats@xecu.net / URL: http://
www.dcoats.com
Product Service Description:
Industrial finishing, powder coating & screen
printing
Plating & polishing
Metal coating & allied services
Printing_commercial

Diversified Fastener & Tool Co.
PO Box 308
Elk Grove Village, IL 60009-0308
Contact: Mark Kramer, Pres.
Telephone: 847-593-8114
Fax: 847-228-1051
Email: divfasttl@aol.com / URL:
Product Service Description:
Standard & industrial fasteners
Bolts, nuts, rivets & washers

Divine Brothers Company (Mfr)
200 Seward Avenue, P.O. Box 438
Utica, NY 13503
Contact: B.L. Divine, *
Telephone: 315-797-0470
Fax: 315-797-0058
Email: / URL:
Product Service Description:
Buffing, Polishing & Contact Wheels
Industrial Casters & Caster Wheels
Lift & Pallet Truck Wheels
Buffing & Abrasive Belt Machinery
Industrial Mixing & Size Reduction
Machinery

Dixie Chemical Co., Inc.
PO Box 130410
Houston, TX 77219-0410
Contact: Malcolm Johnson, Mktg. Mgr.
Telephone: 281-474-3271
Fax: 281-474-9251
Email: dcc1@accesscomm.net / URL:
Product Service Description:
Chemical processing
Chemical preparations

Dixie Electro Plating Co., Inc.
3001 Engelke St
Houston, TX 77003-1293
Contact: Jim Hollingsworth, Facility Mgr.
Telephone: 713-224-1826
Fax: 713-225-0799
Email: / URL:
Product Service Description:
Plating & Polishing, Grinding I.D. & O.D.
Chrome, Anodizing & Metal Finishing,
Sulfamate Nickel
Industrial Zinc, Rack & Barrel
Gold & Silver

Dixie Machine Shop
PO Box 680962
Fort Payne, AL 35968-1610
Contact: Charles Stephens, Pres., Fin., Pur.,
Sales & Mktg. Mgr.
Telephone: 256-845-4752
Fax: 256-845-7673
Email: / URL:
Product Service Description:
General machining & metal fabrication job
shop
Industrial machinery
Metal products_fabricated

Dixie Seal & Stamp Co., Inc. (Mfr)
P.O. Drawer 54616
Atlanta, GA 30308
Contact: E.B. Scot Roehm, *
Telephone: 404-875-8883
Fax: 404-872-3504
Email: dixie@sd-software.com / URL:
Product Service Description:
Embossed Alum. Automobile License Plates
Embossed Aluminum Signs up to 14"x 24"

Dixie Yarns, Inc.
1100 S. Watkins St., P.O. Box 751
Chattanooga, TN 37401
Contact: Tom Sutter, *
Telephone: 423-698-2501
Fax: 423-493-7488
Email: mwrich@dxyn.com / URL:
Product Service Description:
Mercerized Cotton Yarns - Dyed & Natural
Manmade Spun Yarns - Ring & Air Jet Spun
Lycra Corespun (Cotton or Pima Sheath)
Lycra Corespun (Synthetic Sheath)
Combed Cotton Ring & Open End Spun
Yarns
Pima Ring Spun Yarns
Synthetic Performance Yarns

Dixie-Pacific Mfg. Co., Inc.
1700 W Grand Ave
Gadsden, AL 35901-8202
Contact: Karen Phillips,
Telephone: 256-442-4513
Fax: 256-442-4794
Email: karen_phillips@ingerrand.com / URL:
Product Service Description:
Wooden Columns, Posts
Fiberglass Columns

Dixon Mfg., Inc.
701 Clinton St
Arkadelphia, AR 71923-5921
Contact: Martha Dixon, Pres., R & D Mgr.
Telephone: 870-246-6645 / 800-256-8505
Fax: 870-246-3165
Email: sales@marthaskids.com / URL: http://
www.marthaskids.com
Product Service Description:
Nursing & food processing uniforms &
children's school uniforms

Dixon Southwestern Graphite Inc.
2444 Ridgeway Blvd
Lakehurst, NJ 08733-1903
Contact: Maryann Cattonar, Off. Mgr.
Telephone: 732-657-2255
Fax: 732-657-2323
Email: / URL: http://www.asbury.com
Product Service Description:
Minerals, ground or treated
Graphite lubricants

Doane Co., Inc., L. C.
PO Box 975
Essex, CT 06426-0975
Contact: Margaret Egan, Pres., CFO
Telephone: 860-767-8295
Fax: 860-767-1397
Email: sales@lcdoane.com / URL: http://
www.lcdoane.com
Product Service Description:
Fluorescent lighting fixtures
Lighting fixtures_commercial

Dodson Steel Products, Inc.
PO Box 279
Ellenwood, GA 30294-0279
Contact: Stephen Letko, Pres.
Telephone: 404-363-8900
Fax: 404-363-4954
Email: www.dspi_a@email.com / URL: http:/
/www.dodsonsteel.com
Product Service Description:
Valves & pipe fittings
Steel pipe fittings
High-Yield Pipeline Fittings
Flanges - 96" & 2500#

Doemelt Racing, G. L.
PO Box 157
Arcola, IL 61910-0157
Contact: Gary Doemelt, Pres., GM
Telephone: 217-268-4243
Fax: 217-268-3615
Email: / URL:
Product Service Description:
CNC machining job shop

Doerksen Precision Products
2725 Chanticleer Ave
Santa Cruz, CA 95065-1841
Contact: Robert Doerksen, Pres.
Telephone: 408-476-1843
Fax: 408-476-4783
Email: dan@doerksenpp.com / URL: http://
www.doerksenpp.com
Product Service Description:
Manufactures metal, plastic and steel machine
parts
Industrial machinery

Dolphin Mfg. Inc.
2929 E Apache St Bldg 2
Tulsa, OK 74110-2245
Contact: Edward Kurtz, Pres.
Telephone: 918-838-3920
Fax: 918-838-8561
Email: fixture@ionet.net / URL: http://
www.dolphinmfg.com
Product Service Description:
Wooden Store Fixtures
Showcases
Fixtures: Free Standing
Islands & Back Islands
Kiosks
Rollout Programs
Fixtures; Loose

Don Hurst Enterprises
4573 N Hansa Dr
Tucson, AZ 85705-2119
Contact: Don Hurst, Pres.
Telephone: 520-888-9105
Fax: 520-888-3831
Email: / URL:
Product Service Description:
Manufactures pre-engineered steel buildings
Prefabricated metal buildings

Donlee Technologies, Inc.
693 N. Hills Rd.
York, PA 17402-2212
Contact: Charles Alcorn, *
Telephone: 717-755-1081
Fax: 717-755-0020
Email: dontech@cyberia.com / URL: http://
www.donleetech.com
Product Service Description:
Heating Equipment
Process Steam Equipment
Boiler Shop Fabricated Plate Work
Boiler Service Operation & Training
HVAC Equipment
Airconditioning & Refrigeration Training
EPA Refrigerant Certification

Donmar Enterprises, Inc.
7980 Bayberry Road
Jacksonville, FL 32256-4408
Contact: Marc Levinson, VP/Mktg. & Sales
Telephone: 904-731-3393
Fax: 904-731-0004
Email: info@donmar.com / URL: http://
www.donmar.com
Product Service Description:
Sunroofs Pop-Up Sliding & Electric
Sport Truck Accessories
Luggage Racks Roof & Deck Permanent
Aerodynamic Styling Access Wings
Sunroof Wind Deflectors

Dorado Seafood Inc
211 W Orange Grove Ave
Burbank, CA 91502-1830
Contact: Andre J Alba, Pres.
Telephone: 818-843-6100
Fax: 818-843-6107
Email: dor8436100@aol.com / URL:
Product Service Description:
Manufactures cooked shrimp

Doral Publishing Inc
8560 SW Salish Ln Ste 300
Wilsonville, OR 97070-9625
Contact: Alvin Grossman, Publisher
Telephone: 503-682-3307
Fax: 503-682-2648
Email: doralpub@easystreet.com / URL:
http://www.doralpub.com
Product Service Description:
Book publishing (dog books)

Dorissa Of Miami, Inc.
2751 N Miami Ave
Miami, FL 33127-4439
Contact: Doree Selevan Bloom, Pres.
Telephone: 305-573-3600
Fax: 305-573-4602
Email: dorissa97@aol.com / URL:
Product Service Description:
Girls' dresses
Dresses & blouses_girl's & children's

Dorma Mills(Mfr)
184-10 Jamaica Avenue
Hollis, NY 11423
Contact: Howard Franco, V.P.
Telephone: 718-264-7150
Fax: 718-264-7300
Email: tricoman@aol.com / URL: http://
www.dormamills.com
Product Service Description:
Warp Knit Textiles, Nylon Tricots
Knit Outerwear, Nylon Tricot
Knitted Curtains
Knitted Bedding Fabrics
Linings, Dress & Bathing Suits
Mesh For Athletic Wear

Dorrough Electronics
20434 Corisco St
Chatsworth, CA 91311-6121
Contact: Kay Dorrough, Ptnr.
Telephone: 818-998-2824
Fax: 818-998-1507
Email: dorroughe1@aol.com / URL: http://
www.dorrough.com
Product Service Description:
Manufactures audio loudness meters
Electricity measuring instruments

Doskocil Industries Inc
1324 W Rialto Ave
San Bernardino, CA 92410-1611
Contact: David Doskocil, Pres.
Telephone: 909-885-0988
Fax: 909-381-4743
Email: / URL:
Product Service Description:
Manufactures stump grinders and chippers,
root cutters, trenchers and chipper mulchers
Lawn & garden equipment

Double-T Mfg. Corp.
PO Box 1371
Elkhart, IN 46515-1371
Contact: Howard Carpenter, Pres. & CEO
Telephone: 219-262-1340
Fax: 219-262-2066
Email: garytaska@double-t-usa.com / URL:
Product Service Description:
High pressure laminated products, medicine
cabinets, flat stock laminate

Douglas Engineering
1015 Shary Circle
Concord, CA 94518-2420
Contact: Douglas J. Gore, General Manager
Telephone: 925-827-4100
Fax: 925-827-4999
Email: dgore@douglaseng.com / URL: http://
www.douglaseng.com
Product Service Description:
Ind. Oil Skimmers & Decanters

**Dover Chemical Corp., Sub. of ICC
Industries, Inc.**
460 Park Ave.
New York, NY 10022
Contact: John J. Farber, Chairman of the
Board
Telephone: 212-521-1700
Fax: 212-521-1794
Email: / URL:
Product Service Description:
Flame Retardants
Chlorinated Paraffins
Organo Phosphites

Dowels, Pins & Shafts, Inc.
PO Box 1135
Dunedin, FL 34697-1135
Contact: Thomas Mickelson, Pres
Telephone: 813-461-1255
Fax: 813-441-8341
Product Service Description:
Screw machine products, shafts, dowels &
taper pins

Doyle & Roth Mfg. Co., Inc.
26 Broadway Ste 911
New York, NY 10004-1701
Contact: Rohit patel, Vice President
Telephone: 212-269-7840
Fax: 212-248-4780
Email: doyleroth@aol.com / URL:
Product Service Description:
Heat exchangers & pressure vessels

Dr. Saul Cano
PO Box 34697
Louisville, KY 40232-4697
Contact: Dr. Saul Cano,
Telephone: +52 (29) 32-06-52
Fax: +52 (29) 32-17-95
Email: scano@infosel.net.mx / URL: http://
aquarius.net/saul_cano
Product Service Description:
Translation Services: English>Spanish

Dr. T's Nature Products Inc.
U.s. Hwy. 19 N.e., Box 682
Pelham, GA 31779
Contact: James B. Tennyson, Pres., Pers., Pur.
& R & D Mgr.
Telephone: 912-294-9742
Fax: 912-294-3027
Email: drts@rose.net / URL: http://
www.animalrepellents.com
Product Service Description:
Pest control chemicals
Agricultural chemicals
Janitorial Chemicals
Lawn & Garden Chemicals

Dragoco Inc.
10 Gordon Dr
Totowa, NJ 07512-2204
Contact: Raymond J. Hughes, Pres. & CEO
Telephone: 973-256-3850
Fax: 973-256-6420
Email: / URL: http://www.dragoco.com
Product Service Description:
Flavoring extracts & syrups
Fragrances & flavors
Chemicals_industrial organic

Dragon Enterprises
PO Box 200
Genoa, NV 89411-0200
Contact: Nancy Miluck, Ptnr.
Telephone: 702-782-2486
Product Service Description:
Publishes history coloring books and books
on Nevada
Book publishing

Drapes 4 Show Inc.
5171 N. Douglas Fir Road, #2
Calabasas, CA 91302
Contact: Karen Honigberg, Pres.
Telephone: 818-591-1777
Fax: 818-222-7469
Email: staff@drapes.com / URL: http://
www.drapesforshow.com
Product Service Description:
Manufactures table skirting, linens, place
mats; pipe & drape & specialty items.

Dresser Instrument Div.
250 E. Main St.
Stratford, CT 06497-5145
Contact: J. W. Caldwell, President
Telephone: 203-378-8281
Fax: 203-385-0357
Email: bvarga@dresser.com / URL: http://
www.dresser.com/instruments
Product Service Description:
Industrial Machinery and Equipment
Parts and accessories for measuring or
checking instruments, appliances and
machines
Electrical switches
Pressure & temperature Instruments
Transducers / Transmitters

Drever Company
300 Red Lion Road , PO Box 98
Huntingdon Valley, PA 19006-0098
Contact: David S. Rohrbaugh, V.P. Sales
Telephone: 215-947-3400
Fax: 215-947-7934
Email: rohrbaugh@drever.com / URL: http://
www.drever.com
Product Service Description:
Industrial Furnaces

Drexelbrook International, Inc.
205 Keith Valley Rd.
Horsham, PA 19044-1408
Contact: Teresa Parris, Mktg. Comm. Mgr.
Telephone: 215-674-1234
Fax: 215-674-2731
Email: deinfo@drexelbrook / URL: http://
www.drexelbrook.com
Product Service Description:
Level Controls Instr. Electrical

Dri Steem Humidifier
14949 Technology Dr
Eden Prairie, MN 55344-2269
Contact: Lori Pomroy, Marketing Manager
Telephone: 612-949-2415
Fax: 612-949-2933
Email: sales@dristeem.com / URL: http://
www.dristeem.com
Product Service Description:
Industrial humidifiers
Refrigeration & heating equipment

Dri-Rite Co.
4711 Midlothian Tpke Ste 15
Crestwood, IL 60445-4900
Contact: Patrick W. Perry, Pres.
Telephone: 708-385-7556
Fax: 708-389-8716
Email: info@dririte.com / URL: http://
www.dririte.com
Product Service Description:
Contract Packaging

DriWater Inc
715 Southpoint Blvd Ste P
Petaluma, CA 94954-6836
Contact: Harold W Jensen, GM
Telephone: 707-769-5345
Fax: 707-769-0335
Email: driwater@driwater.com / URL: http://
www.driwater.com
Product Service Description:
Manufactures time-released gel for watering
plants over 30 to 90 days
Chemical preparations
Hydro Mix for tackifier / water retention in
hydro mulch

Drillunit
11450 Stephens Drive
Warren, MI 48089-3861
Contact: John barla, Dir/Sales & Mktg.
Telephone: 313-756-3730
Fax: 313-756-5832
Product Service Description:
Machine Tool Drill Units : Machine Tools
Multiple Spindle Heads : Machine Tools
Slides : Machine Tools Index Tables
Machine Tools Tap Units

**Drum-Mates, Inc, Drum Mixer &
Pump Div.**
PO Box 636
Lumberton, NJ 08048-0636
Contact: David Marcmann, Intl Sales Dir.
Telephone: 609-261-1033
Fax: 609-261-1034
Product Service Description:
Drum Mixers Bung Entering & Open Drum
Drum & Tote/Tank Pumps, Bung Mounting
Nozzles, Liquid, Hand Dispensing

Dual-Tech, Inc.
715 Orange St
Auburndale, FL 33823-4436
Contact: Donald Roberts, Pres., R & D Mgr.
Telephone: 941-967-0011
Fax: 941-965-1169
Product Service Description:
Two car carrier beds

Duenner Supply Co. Of Texas
6610 Rupley Cir.
Houston, TX 77087-3444
Contact: Sales & Marketing,
Telephone: 713-649-5342
Fax: 713-649-5320
Product Service Description:
Stainless Steel Plaste Rod Pipe Grating
Aluminum Plate Bar Pipe Tubing
Nickel Plate, Bar Pipe Tube

Duer/Carolina Coil Inc.
PO Box 730
Reidville, SC 29375-0730
Contact: Richard Bates, Mgr, Outside Sales
Telephone: 864-989-4141
Fax: 864-989-4144
Email: dickb@dccoil.com / URL: http://
www.dccoil.com
Product Service Description:
Springs_steel, except wire : Coil springs

Duffy Golf, Inc.
3013 30th Street Dr Se
Cedar Rapids, IA 52403-1550
Contact: Rocklin Duffy, Pres.
Telephone: 319-366-2500
Fax: 319-366-3000
Email: info@dreamgreen.com / URL: http://
www.dreamgreen.com
Product Service Description:
Contourable indoor putting greens
Sporting & athletic goods

Duke Scientific Corporation
PO Box 50005
Palo Alto, CA 94303-0005
Contact: Heather Vail,
Telephone: 650-424-1177
Fax: 650-424-1158
Email: info@dukesci.com / URL: http://
www.dukescientific.com
Product Service Description:
Manufactures particle size standards for
calibration of scientific instruments
Components for analytical instruments

Dulin Date Gardens
5635 Gila Ridge Rd.
Yuma, AZ 85365-7630
Contact: Arlin Dulin, Owner
Telephone: 520-344-2685
Fax: 520-305-6257
Email: sdulin@primenet.com / URL: http://
www.medjooldate.com
Product Service Description:
Dates Medjool Variety

Dulmison Incorporated
1725 Purcell Road
Lawrenceville, GA 30043-5748
Contact: John Whitehair, Export Manager
Telephone: 770-339-3350
Fax: 770-339-3770
Email: johnw@dulmison-us.com / URL: http:/
/www.dulmison-us.com
Product Service Description:
Dist & Trans Line Vibration Controls
Misc. Wireformed Products
Fiber Optic Cable , Hardware

**Dunbarton Corp. /Rediframe/
Slimfold**
PO Box 6416
Dothan, AL 36302-6416
Contact: Robert Theune, Vice President Sales
& Marketing
Phone: 334-794-0661 / Fax: 334-794-9184
Email: sales@dunbarton.com / URL: http://
www.dunbarton.com
Product Service Description:
Steel Bifold Doors for Closet Openings
Mirror Doors for Closet Openings
Steel Door Frames (Prefinished)

**Duncan Industries Parking Control
Systems**
PO Box 849
Harrison, AR 72602-0849
Contact: Dick Farrell, Pres.
Telephone: 870-741-5481
Fax: 870-741-2868
URL: http://www.duncanparking.com
Product Service Description:
Parking meters & integrated parking control
systems

Duncan-Leigh-Schiffer
8512 White Horse Road
Greenville, SC 29617-1423
Contact: Art Schiffer, President
Phone: 803-246-2886 / Fax: 803-246-8820
Product Service Description:
Brake Lathe Automobile Disc Stabilizer

**Dura Automotive: Stockton Seat
Group**
301 S Simmons St
Stockton, IL 61085-1513
Contact: Richard Fetzer, Director
Telephone: 815-947-3333
Fax: 815-947-3010
Product Service Description:
Automotive hardware

Dura Temp Corp.
PO Box 368
Holland, OH 43528-0368
Contact: Brian T. Summerson, Pres., Hum.
Res. & Opers. Mgr.
TPhone: 419-866-4348 / Fax: 419-866-4656
Email: sales@duratemp.com / URL: http://
www.duratemp.com
Product Service Description:
Hot glass handling plastic materials & resins
Plastic materials & resins

Duracote Corp.
PO Box 1209
Ravenna, OH 44266-1209
Contact: William R. Truog, Pres.
Telephone: 330-296-9600
Fax: 330-296-5102
Email: / URL: http://www.duracote.com
Product Service Description:
Vinyl laminated & coated non-textile
Products for aircraft, marine, automotive,
tents, : Awnings, shades, medical & industrial

Duracote Corporation
350 N Diamond St.
Ravenna, OH 44266-2155
Contact: Cally Rose, *
Telephone: 330-296-9600
Fax: 330-296-5102
Email: custserv@duracote.com / URL: http://
www.duracote.com
Product Service Description:
Vinyl Laminated & Coated Fabrics

Durafiber Corp.
112 W. Rte. 120
Mc Henry, IL 60050
Contact: Greg Schams, Pres.
Telephone: 815-344-5566
Fax: 815-344-5588
Email: valis2000@msn.com / URL: http://
www.durafiber.com
Product Service Description:
Concrete & mortar fiber reinforcements
Concrete products
Cellulosic manmade fibers

Duraform
1435 S. Santa Fe Ave.
Compton, CA 90221
Contact: Joe Bonadona, *
Telephone: 310-761-1640
Fax: 310-761-1646
Email: / URL:
Product Service Description:
Fiberglass Seating
Fiberglass Planters
Fiberglass Household Furniture
Fiberglass Trash Receptacles
Recycle Containers

Durham Mfg. Co.
PO Box 230
Durham, CT 06422
Contact: Richard Patterson, President
Telephone: 860-349-3427
Fax: 860-349-8572
Email: rpatterson@durhammfg.com / URL:
http://www.durhammfg.com
Product Service Description:
Metal & Plastic Storage Conatiners,
Fabricated
Metal Bins, Plastic, Boxes & Storage
Cabinets
Metal & Plastic First Aid Kits & Cabinets
Metal Literature Racks

Duro Bag Mfg. Co.
1 Duro Way
Walton, KY 41094-9325
Contact: Ed Gallop, V-P., Sales
Telephone: 606-485-6660
Fax: 606-485-4641
Email: / URL: http://www.durobag.com
Product Service Description:
Paper Handled Shopping Bag
All Subtrates Including Laminated
Flex & Offset Printing
Paper Grocery & Sacks
Gift Bags

Duron Neckwear Inc
1633 Washington Blvd
Montebello, CA 90640-5423
Contact: Ron Dutchen, Pres.
Telephone: 323-720-4001
Fax: 323-720-4004
Email: rondutchen@wilshire.iccas.com
Product Service Description:
Manufactures men's and boys' neckwear
Neckwear_men's & boys' : Pleated ties
Formal wear : Bow ties & cummerbunds
Corporate design neckwear

Dustvent, Inc.
100 West Fay Street
Addison, IL 60101-5180
Contact: A. Neil Rosenquest, President
Telephone: 630-543-9007
Fax: 630-543-1407
Email: / URL:
Product Service Description:
Dust Collection Equipment

Dutchess Bakers' Machinery Co., Inc.
1101 John Ave
Superior, WI 54880-1640
Contact: Jim McCusker, VP/Mktg. Dir.
Telephone: 715-394-2396
Fax: 715-394-2406
Email: dutchess@lidgerwood.com / URL:
http://www.lidgerwood.com/dutchess
Product Service Description:
Bakery Machinery
Dough Dividers, Manually Operated
Dough Dividers, Semi-Automatic

Dvorak Automatic & Machine
11109 Ne Us Highway 301
Waldo, FL 32694-4327
Contact: Daniel Dvorak, Owner
Telephone: 352-468-1353
Fax: 352-468-1050
Email: / URL: http://www.dvorakmachine.com
Product Service Description:
High performance engines
Machine shop
High performance parts & accessories

Dvorak International Linguistics
HC 01 Box 4250
Oracle, AZ 85623
Contact: Claudia Dvorak, *
Telephone: 888-4-dilinc
Fax: 520-896-9224
Product Service Description:
Translation Services, Multi - Lingual

Dyadic International, Inc.
140 Intercoastral Point Dr.
Jupiter, FL 33477-5092
Contact: Thomas Bailey, V.P. Sales
Telephone: 561-743-1081
Fax: 461-743-8343
Email: / URL: http://www.dyadic-group.com
Product Service Description:
Enzyme

Dyer Tool & Die, Inc.
379 S Long Hollow Rd
Maryville, TN 37801-8381
Contact: Mark Dyer, Pres.,
Telephone: 423-983-7593
Fax: 423-983-0736
Email: dtd001@icx.net / URL:
Product Service Description:
Jigs & Fixtures, Special
Design & Bld. Automated Equipment

Dylon Industries, Inc.
7700 Clinton Rd.
Cleveland, OH 44144
Contact: W.C. Bachman, Bus. Manager
Telephone: 216-651-1300
Fax: 216-651-1777
Email: dylon@postoffice.worldnet.att.net
Product Service Description:
High Temperature Metal Working Lubricants,
Ceramic Cements, Greases, Oils & Release
Agents

Dyna-Tech Adhesives, Inc.
PO Box 628
Grafton, WV 26354-0628
Contact: Dvid Allen, Manager, Sales & Mktg.
Phone: 304-265-5200 / Fax: 304-265-5202
Email: widebdy747@aol.com / URL:
Product Service Description:
Water Based Adhesives, Pressure Sensitive
(Acrylic & Rubberbase)

Dynalock Corp.
PO Box 9470
Bristol, CT 06011-9470
Contact: Ralph A. Sittnick, Pres.
Telephone: 860-582-4761
Fax: 860-585-0338
Email: dynalock.corp@snet.net / URL: http://
www.dynalock.com
Product Service Description:
Electro-magnetic locks
Hardware

Dynametal Technologies
400 Dupree Ave.
Brownsville, TN 38012
Contact: Bob Nolan, Pres.
Telephone: 901-772-3780
Fax: 901-772-3784
Email: dynamet@ibm.net / URL:
Product Service Description:
Powdered metal bearings & structural parts

Dynamic Air Inc.
1125 Willow Lake
St. Paul, MN 55110-5193
Contact: Bob Adamzak, Marketing Manager
Telephone: 651-484-2900
Fax: 651-484-7015
Email: / URL: http://www.dynamicair.com
Product Service Description:
Industrial Machinery and Equipment
Pneumatic elevators and conveyors

Dynamic Language Center, Ltd
5200 South Center Blvd. 5
Seattle, WA 98188-2383
Contact: Maria Tere Antezana, Director
Telephone: 206-244-6709
Fax: 206-243-3795
Email: dynamic@d-l-c.com / URL: http://
www.d-l-c.com
Product Service Description:
Translation Services, All Languages, All
Fields : Interpreting Services, Major
Languages

Dynamic Packing & Logistics
13795 Rider Tr. N.
St. Louis, MO 63045-1216
Contact: Joe Noernberg, Pres.
Telephone: 314-298-7999
Fax: 314-298-1110
Email: dynamic@i1.net / URL: http://
www.dynamicpacking.com
Product Service Description:
Complete Worldwide Logistics Services
Packing, Crating, Rigging, Shipping

Dynamic Research Co Inc
6950 SW Hampton St Ste 100
Portland, OR 97223-8330
Contact: Dale Burson, Pres.
Telephone: 503-684-3923
Fax: 503-684-6030
Email: dburson@saf-t-step.com / URL: http://
www.saf-t-step.com
Product Service Description:
Polishes & sanitation goods
Manufactures cleaning, polishing, sanitation
preparations, safety products and anti-slip

Dynamic Sciences Int'l Inc
6130 Variel Ave
Woodland Hills, CA 91367-3721
Contact: Eli Shiri, Chrm., CEO
Telephone: 818-226-6262
Fax: 818-226-6247
Email: / URL:
Product Service Description:
Manufactures RF emission measuring &
control systems & products;
Tempest Security / Surveillance MIL STD &
Commerical EMC Systems
and products

Dynaoptic-Motion Corporation
23561 Ridge Route Dr Ste U
Laguna Hills, CA 92653-1521
Contact: Hans Bannies, Pres.
Telephone: 949-770-9911
Fax: 949-770-2492
Email: dynaoptic@aol.com / URL: http://
www.dynaoptics.com
Product Service Description:
Manufactures micro positioning tables for
science labs
Laboratory apparatus &
Piezo Electric Actuators & Power Supplies
Precision Positioners

Dynapower Corporation
P.O. Box 9210
South Burlington, VT 05407-9210
Contact: Laura Williams, Marketing
Telephone: 802-860-7200
Fax: 802-864-3782
Email: info@dynapower.com / URL: http://
www.dynapower.com
Product Service Description:
Rectifiers
Transformers

Dynasonics
2200 South Street
Racine, WI 53404
Contact: William Roeber, GM
Telephone: 414-639-6770
Fax: 414-639-2267
Email: / URL: http://www.dynasonics.com
Product Service Description:
Process control instruments
Industrial instruments & flow meters

Dynasonics-Divison of Racine Federated, Inc.
2200 South Street
Racine, WI 53404
Contact: Sales & Marketing,
Telephone: 414-639-6770
Fax: 414-639-2267
Email: info@dynasonics.com / URL: http://
www.dynasonics.com
Product Service Description:
Liquid Level Monitors

Dynatest Consulting, Inc.
RR 6 Box 1510
Starke, FL 32091-9443
Contact: William Beck II, V-P., Prodn.
Telephone: 904-964-3777
Fax: 904-964-3749
Email: psc@dynatest.com / URL: http://
www.dynatest.com
Product Service Description:
Highway testing equipment
Measuring & controlling devices

Dynetcom, Inc.
12620 Darby Brooke Ct
Woodbridge, VA 22192-2457
Contact: Russell Phipps, VP, David
VanDerveer, Sales/Mktg.
Telephone: 703-490-7320
Fax: 703-490-4398
Email: sales@dynetcom.com / URL: http://
www.dynetcom.com
Product Service Description:
Telephone & telegraph apparatus
Telecommunication & data systems
Matrix & Data Switching

E & M Intl.
2840 Vassar Dr Ne
Albuquerque, NM 87107-1804
Contact: Ed Vaillancourt, Owner
Telephone: 505-883-8955
Fax: 505-883-7133
Email: emigroup@aol.com / URL:
Product Service Description:
Fire Detection & Suppression Systems
Communications equipment

E B I/R J Trausch Industries
720 Northwestern Ave
Audubon, IA 50025-1610
Contact: Robert J. Trausch, Pres., CEO
Telephone: 712-563-4623
Fax: 712-563-2000
Email: refurb@netins.net / URL: http://
www.ebi.idsite.com Or Http://
www.rjtrausch.com
Product Service Description:
Remanufactured Supermarket Equipment

E C M Motor Co.
1099 Proctor Dr
Elkhorn, WI 53121-2027
Contact: Kraig Tabor, General Manager
Telephone: 414-723-6400
Fax: 414-723-7373
Email: ecm@elknet.net / URL: http://
www.fasco.com
Product Service Description:
AC & DC & fractional gear motors
Motors & generators

E F C O Corp.
1000 County Rd.
Monett, MO 65708
Contact: Chris Fuldner, Pres., CEO
Telephone: 417-235-3193
Fax: 417-235-7313
Email: / URL: http://www.efcocorp.com
Product Service Description:
Doors, sash & trim_metal
Architectural windows, doors, storefront &
curtain wall systems
Aluminum extruded products
Architectural metal work

E F T Systems, Inc.
709 Bradfield Rd
Houston, TX 77060-3108
Contact: Michael G. Colescott, Pres.
Telephone: 281-445-4196
Fax: 281-445-1462
Email: eft@wt.net
Product Service Description:
Electrical connectors

E L X Group,Washex Machinery Co.
5000 Central Freeway
Wichita Falls, TX 76306-1599
Contact: Sales & Marketing,
Telephone: 940-855-3990
Fax: 940-855-9349
Email: mktgserv@elxgroup.com / URL: http:/
/www.elxgroup.com
Product Service Description:
Industrial Laundry Equipment
Industrial Dryers, Folders, Etc.

E M I S, Inc.
PO Box 1607
Durant, OK 74702-1607
Contact: Lynda Blake, Chrm., Pres.
Phone: 580-924-0643 / Fax: 580-924-9414
Email: emis@redriverok.com / URL: http://
www.emispub.com
Product Service Description:
Medical textbook printing & typesetting
Book publishing : Typesetting

E-FAB Inc
PO Box 239
Santa Clara, CA 95052-0239
Contact: J William Scales Jr, Pres.
Telephone: 408-727-5218
Fax: 408-988-3342
Email: eng@e-fab.com
 URL: http://www.e-fab.com
Product Service Description:
Photochemical machining

E-Tec Marine Products Inc.
7555 Garden Rd
Riviera Beach, FL 33404-3411
Contact: Robert Jordan, Pres.
Telephone: 561-848-8351
Fax: 561-848-8354
Email: sales@e-tec.com / URL: http://
www.etecmarine.com
Product Service Description:
Anodized aluminum extrusions & fittings
Aluminum extruded products
Aluminum pipe & tubes

E-Tech Products Inc
4975 Paris St
Denver, CO 80239-2805
Contact: Thomas Warda, Pres.
Telephone: 303-373-0100
Fax: 303-373-0200
Email: kris@e-techproducts.com / URL:
http://www.e-techproducts.com
Product Service Description:
Manufactures packaging material made of
recycled paper

E-Z Lift Ltd International
PO Box 1499
Estes Park, CO 80517-1499
Contact: Genevieve Shanks, Pres.
Phone: 970-586-5195 / Fax: 970-586-5195
Email: sales@e-zlift.com
URL: http://www.e-zlift.com
Product Service Description:
Manufactures kits that convert standard U.S.
1/2 & 3/4 ton pick-up trucks to dump trucks

E-Z-Em, Inc.
717 Main St
Westbury, NY 11590-5021
Contact: Joseph Palma, V-P., Sales
Telephone: 516-333-8230
Fax: 516-333-8278
Email: jpalma@ezem.com / URL: http://
www.ezem.com
Product Service Description:
Barium & Radiology Chemicals

E-Z-Go Textron
PO Box 388
Augusta, GA 30903-0388
Contact: David L. Davis, Director of Int'l
Sales
Telephone: 706-798-4311
Fax: 706-796-4540
Email: / URL: http://www.ezgo.textron.com
Product Service Description:
Transportation equipment
Golf & utility vehicles

E. Fougera & Co.
60 Baylis Road
Melville, NY 11747
Contact: Charles Moore, *
Telephone: 516/454-7677
Product Service Description:
Topical Pharmaceuticals, Preparations

E/M Corporation (Mfr)
P.O. Box 3969
Peachtree City, GA 30269-7969
Contact: William J. Megofna, Sr., *
Telephone: 770-631-6694
Fax: 770-631-0833
Email: / URL:
Product Service Description:
Lubricating Oils & Greases
Misc. Chemicals, Dry Lubricants
Ind. Prod. Finishes, Protective Coatings
Metal Coatings Services

EBM Imports
2 Lancewood Lane
Baltimore, MD 21234
Contact: Concepcion C. Muneses,
Telephone: 410-665-0432
Fax: 410-661-8407
Email: EBMImports@hotmail.com / URL:
Product Service Description:
Tires - used / new

EBway Corporation
6750 N.W. 21 Avenue
Ft. Lauderdale, FL 33309
Contact: Terry Walker, *
Telephone: 954-971-4911
Fax: 954-971-5516
Email: ebway@worldnet.att.net / URL: http://
www.ebway.com
Product Service Description:
GRIPflow Metal Stampings - An Alternative
to Fineblanking

ECS Refining
705 Reed St
Santa Clara, CA 95050-3942
Contact: Cliff Wells, VP Sales & Mktg.
Telephone: 408-988-4386
Fax: 408-988-5154
Email: cwells@ecsrefining.com / URL: http://
www.ecsrefining.com
Product Service Description:
Certified destruction of electronic scrap
Gold, silver, tin, lead refiners
Component recovery from electronics
Recycling of hazardous tin & tin/lead material

EEI / Mod-Tech Industries
1166 Kapp Drive
Clearwater, FL 33765
Contact: Sue Englander, Pres., GM
Telephone: 727-461-4755
Fax: 727-442-5855
Email: eeiint@mindspring.com / URL:
Product Service Description:
Printed circuit board assembly

EFCO
1000 County Rd.
Monett, MO 65708-9214
Contact: Chris Fuldner, President
Telephone: 417-235-3193
Fax: 417-235-7313
Email: / URL:
Product Service Description:
Aluminum Extruded Products
Aluminum doors, windows and their frames
and thresholds for doors

ELF
2000 Market St.
Philadelphia, PA 19103-3231
Contact: Bernard Azoulay, Chief Executive
Officer
Telephone: 215-419-7000
Fax: 215-418-7930
Email: Identino@ato.com / URL: http://
www.elf-atochem.com
Product Service Description:
Chemical Preparations, NEC
Polysulfides, polysulfones, and synthetic
polymers in primary forms, including
polyxlene resins

ELS Language Centers
5761 Buckingham Pkwy, Suite 85
Culver City, CA 90230-6515
Contact: Faith Stanis, *
Telephone: 310-342-4100
Fax: 310-342-4104
Email: info@els.com / URL: http://
www.els.com
Product Service Description:
Educational Services, English Language
Instruction
Customized English Lessons for Executives
English Study - Vacation Programs
University Placement Services

EMC Technologies
4150 S. 87th E. Ave.
Tulsa, OK 74145
Contact: Sales & Marketing,
Telephone: 918-660-7000
Fax: 918-627-5449
Email: emc@galaxy.galstar.com / URL:
Product Service Description:
Electric Motors
Electronic Products

EPM Environmental, Inc.
834 E Rand Rd.
Mount Prospect, IL 60056-2569
Contact: Hans J. Brouwers, Sales
Telephone: 847-255-4494
Fax: 847-255-1959
Email: epmusa@epmenvironmental.com /
URL: http://www.epmenvironmental.com
Product Service Description:
Sampling Equipment for Smoke Stacks &
Process Sources
Mercury Monitors

ERICA and ERICA INTERNATIONAL CORP.
7349 Via Paseo Del Sur
Scottsdale, AZ 85258-3700
Contact: Leonard Manson Chrm. ERICA,,
Leonard Manson II, Pres, ERICA Int'l Corp.
Telephone: 602-951-1560
Fax: 602-951-1601
Email: ercainc@aol.com / URL:
Product Service Description:
Manufacatures & distributes all types of
water bottling & purification equipment
Designs & installs turn key, State-of-the-Art
water bottling & purification plants
Bottles purified potable water under the
trademarked names of "RAINBOW" &
"RAINBOW SPRINGS" in Puerto Rico
Utilizes water purification & bottling facility
in Puerto Rico as training center for
personnel of companies that purchase
equipment form the company
Manufactures & distributes down hole
electronic oil recovery tool for increasing
Production in oil wells with declining
production (patent pending)
Exports disposable paper diapers

ESCO Services Inc
3250 Quentin St Ste 100
Aurora, CO 80011-1841
Contact: Johnna Meysman, Ops Manager
Telephone: 303-360-8008 / 800-824-5579
Fax: 303-360-8044
Email: escoco@aol.com / URL: http://
www.escoservices.com
Product Service Description:
Service station equipment repair, electronic
compoenet parts sales
Printers, Intercoms, Laser Scanners, Cash
Drawers Sales & Service
Lock out / tag out, emergency stop &
isolation equipment sales

ETC de Las Americas, Inc.
751 East Brookhaven Cl.
Memphis, TN 38117
Contact: Michael Cimbalo, Dir. of Operations
Telephone: 901/685-2077
Fax: 901-685-2261
Email: mikeetc@aol.com / URL:
Product Service Description:
Mgmt. Consulting Svcs., Environ. Eng.
Commercial Testing Lab., Environmental
Mgmt. Consulting, Remediation Projects
Comm. Research, Feasibility Studies

ETS Research & Development Inc
PO Box 3164
Palos Verdes Peninsula, CA 90274-9164
Contact: Erica Tonello-Stuart, Pres.
Telephone: 310-377-7608
Fax: 310-377-2178
Email: / URL:
Product Service Description:
Business consulting services, international
trade and investments; political risk
management, trade missions
Travel agencies - trade & business missions,
inbound - out bound tours

Eagle Circuits, Inc.
10820 Sanden Dr
Dallas, TX 75238-5325
Contact: H. Savalia, Pres.
Phone: 214-349-0288 / Fax: 214-349-1210
Email: sales@eagle-circuits.com / URL: http:/
/www.eagle-circuits.com
Product Service Description:
Printed circuit boards

Eagle Metalizing Coatings Co
PO Box 1169
Eagle, CO 81631-1169
Contact: Stephen Isom, Pres.
Telephone: 970-328-6265
Fax: 970-328-6266
Email: isoma@vail.net / URL:
Product Service Description:
Manufactures metalizing equipment & wire
for coating large objects
Machinery_special industry

Eagle Star Electronics LLC
PO Box 7296
Loveland, CO 80537-0296
Contact: Marilyn Valdez-Campbell, Owner
Telephone: 970-669-7210
Fax: 970-669-0907
Email: / URL:
Product Service Description:
Assembles printed circuit boards and cable
harnesses on a subcontract basis

Eagle Technology, Inc.
10500 N Port Washington Rd.
Mequon, WI 53092-5539
Contact: Harshad Shah, President
Telephone: 414-241-3845
Fax: 414-241-5248
Email: eagle@execpc.com / URL: http://
www.eaglecmms.com
Product Service Description:
Computerized Maintenance Managment
Systems

Earnest Machine Products Co.
7310 Vine Street Ct
Davenport, IA 52806-1354
Contact: Paul Snell, GM
Telephone: 319-386-3382
Fax: 319-386-3386
Email: earnest-davenport@worldnet.att.net /
URL: http://www.earnestmachine.com
Product Service Description:
Nuts, bolts, screws, & washers
Bolts, nuts, screws & washers

Easley Co., Jeff
215 8th Avenue South, PO Box 502
Willman, IA 52356 USA
Contact: Jeff Easley, Owner
Telephone: 319-646-2521
Fax: 319-628-4766
Email: jeasley811@aol.com / URL:
Product Service Description:
Abstract wall sculptures (wood)

East Coast Induction, Inc.
P.O. Box 2039
Brockton, MA 02405-2039
Contact: Gene Tosti, General Manager
Telephone: 508-587-2800
Fax: 508-587-9079
Email: ann@eastcoastind.com / URL:
Product Service Description:
Induction Heating Equipment

East Iowa Plastics, Inc.
PO Box 350
Independence, IA 50644-0350
Contact: Bret Kivell, Pres.
Telephone: 319-334-2552
Fax: 319-334-2555
Email: eip@sbtek.net / URL:
Product Service Description:
Plastic products

East Park Research Inc
PO Box 530099
Henderson, NV 89053-0099
Contact: Gordon Melcher, Pres.
Telephone: 702-837-1111
Fax: 702-837-1110
Email: epri@eastparkresearch.com / URL:
http://www.eastparkresearch.com
Product Service Description:
East Park TM Olive Leaf Extract, the
broadest spectrum natural anit-biotic you can
buy without prescription : East Park TM Flu-
Ban for relief of colds or flu. "Beyond
Sympton Relief" : East Park TM Topical Gel,
a solution for skin disorders : East Park TM
Cleansing Bar, preparation for the application
of topical gel.

East-west Publishing Company
563 Shoreham Rd
Grosse Pointe, MI 48236-2469
Contact: Dona De Santis-Reynolds, Pres.
Telephone: 313-885-7308
Fax:
Email: / URL:
Product Service Description:
Publishing_miscellaneous

Eastern Carbide Tool Co. Llc.
130 Freight St
Waterbury, CT 06702-1804
Contact: Ronald DePinho, Pres.
Telephone: 203-754-8585
Fax: 203-596-0505
Email: eastern.carbide.tool / URL: http://
www.easterndeepdraw.com
Product Service Description:
Carbide tool & die job shop
Deep draw stamping products

Eastern Color & Chemical Co.
P.O. Box 6161
Providence, RI 02940-6161
Contact: Fred B. Savell III, Technical
Manager
Telephone: 401-331-9000
Fax: 401-331-2155
Email: tech@ecco-lenox.com / URL: http://
www.ecco-lenox.com
Product Service Description:
Metallic Print Binders
Pigments & Dyes
Dye Carriers & Fixatives
Textile Dye & Print Auxiliaries
Resin Binders
Flame Retarders
Fibre Processing Chemicals
Textile Yarn Lubricants Antistats & Cohesive
Agents

Eastern Europe Inc.
460 W. 34th St.
New York, NY 10001 USA
Contact: Robert Ross, President
Telephone: 212-947-8585
Fax: 212-629-3147
Email: info@easteurinc.com / URL: http://
www.easteurinc.com
Product Service Description:
Chemicals
Fertilizers
Grains
Steel
A;i,omi,
Coal
Chemicals

Eastern Smelting & Refining
37 39 Bubier St.
Lynn, MA 01901
Contact: Customer Service,
Telephone: 781-599-9000
Fax: 781-598-4880
Email: inquiry@eastern-smelting.com / URL:
http://www.eastern-smelting.com
Product Service Description:
Refines & Smelts Prescious Metals

Eaton Corp., Engineered Fasteners Div.
P.O. Box 6688
Cleveland, OH 44101
Contact: Lori Kapp, *
Telephone: 330-220-5121
Fax: 330-220-5797
Email: / URL:
Product Service Description:
Industrial Fasteners
Metal Stampings, N.E.C.
Metal Plastic Fasteners
Wire Formed Retaining Rings

Eby Co.
4300 N. H Street
Philadelphia, PA 19124
Contact: Maurice Sterling, Sales Manager
Telephone: 215-537-4700
Fax: 215-537-4780
Email: sales@ebyco.com / URL: http://
www.cdcom.com/eby
Product Service Description:
Connectors
Sockets
Binding Posts
Test Jacks
Cable & Harness Assemblies

Echo International
313 Sixth Ave.
Pittsburgh, PA 15222-2509
Contact: Sales & Marketing,
Telephone: 412-261-1101
Fax: 412-261-1159
Email: email@echotrans.com / URL: http://
www.echotrans.com
Product Service Description:
Transl Svcs Tech, Legal, Finance, Software
Localization, Web Site

Eckstein Bros Inc
4807 W 118th Pl
Hawthorne, CA 90250-2702
Contact: Leo H Eckstein, Pres.
Telephone: 323-772-6113
Fax: 310-644-3869
Email: ebinc@jps.net / URL:
Product Service Description:
Audiometers and auditory trainers
Electromedical equipment
Medical & hospital equipment

Eclectic Products Inc.
4507 Willamette Blvd
Pineville, LA 71360-3993
Contact: Robert Bright, Plt. Mgr.
Telephone: 318-640-5828
Fax: 318-640-3225
Email: / URL:
Product Service Description:
Adhesives & sealants
Adhesives
Wood fillers

Eclipse Mfg. Co.
115 Oakwood Rd
Lake Zurich, IL 60047-1501
Contact: Robert T. Hinman, Pres., Treas.
Telephone: 847-438-2137
Fax: 847-438-2672
Email: eclipse@foxvalley.net / URL: http://
www.foxvalley.net/~eclipse
Product Service Description:
Plastic injection molding
Plastic products

Eco Environmental Filtration, Inc.
11300 Electron Dr
Louisville, KY 40299-3830
Contact: Keith Blair, Pres.
Telephone: 502-267-1807
Fax: 502-267-3045
Email: ecoenvironmental@mindspring.com /
URL: http://www.ecoenvironmental.com
Product Service Description:
Industrial filter dust collectors

Eco Vacuum Mfg. Corp.
3231 Commander Dr
Carrollton, TX 75006-2506
Contact: Doug Swift, Pres.
Telephone: 972-733-3061
Fax: 972-733-3861
Email: vacland@aol.com / URL:
Product Service Description:
Vacuum cleaners, Household
Vacuum cleaners

Economy Optical, Inc.
2901 Mall Dr
Florence, AL 35630-1582
Contact: Alvin McLendon, Pres.
Telephone: 205-764-3937
Fax: 205-760-8649
Email: / URL: http://www.id52.com/
mclendon
Product Service Description:
Ophthalmic goods : Eyeglasses

Ecosystem Inc.
PO Box 1893
Thomasville, GA 31799-1893
Contact: Graham Bell, Pres., Plt. Opers. Mgr.
Telephone: 912-228-6888
Fax: 912-228-9728
Email: / URL: http://
www.ecosystemsave.com
Product Service Description:
Recycling machinery
Antifreeze recycling machinery

Ecrevisse Acadienne (Mfr)
PO Box 429
Belhaven, NC 27810
Contact: Frances Williams, Christine Costley
Telephone: 800-688-6174
Fax: 252-943-3083
Email: crawfish@microweb.com / URL:
Product Service Description:
Prepared Seafood, Crawfish, Crabmeat,
Calamari : Frozen Seafood & Seafood
Sauces, Clams, Crabcakes : Seafood
Appetizers, Boneless Stuffed Chickens

Edgewood Fine Log Structures Ltd
PO Box 1030
Coeur D Alene, ID 83816-1030
Contact: Brian L Schafer, Owner
Phone: 208-762-8181 / Fax: 208-762-1270
Product Service Description:
Prefabricated wood buildings, log homes &
award winning designs

Edina Mfg. Co., Inc.
PO Box 130
Edina, MO 63537-0130
Contact: Jerry Novak, Pres., Fin., Pur., R & D
& Sales Mgr.
Telephone: 660-397-3337
Fax: 660-397-2291
Email: edinamfg@marktwain.net / URL:
Product Service Description:
Gloves & mittens_leather
Driving gloves, welders gloves, leather-cotton
combination & medical exam gloves

Edwards Mfg. Inc. (Mfr)
2441 SE Stubb Street
Milwaukie, OR 97222
Contact: Tom Reser, Sales Manager
TPhone: 503-659-4198 / Fax: 503-654-3110
Email: sales@edwardsmfg.com / URL:
Product Service Description:
Rotary Gear Pumps / For all Processing
Industries : AFFF Foam Pumps For Fire
Protection Systems

Eemus Manufacturing Corp
11111 Rush St
South El Monte, CA 91733-3548
Contact: Gitte Simonian, CEO
Telephone: 626-443-8841
Fax: 626-443-3518
Email: eemusmfg@aol.com / URL:
Product Service Description:
Electronic components
Manufactures electronic parts for the
electronics and computer industry

Egla International
1323 S.E. 17th St., Ste. 471
Fort Lauderdale, FL 33316-1707
Contact: Jaime Constain, President
Telephone: 954-463-0880
Fax: 954-463-9485
Email: eglacol@norma.net / URL:
Product Service Description:
Synthetic Resins : Injection Machinery
Traffic Engineering Products

El Camino Printers
6074 Corte Del Cedro
Carlsbad, CA 92009-1514
Contact: Arlene D Betti, Owner
Telephone: 760-931-6828
Fax: 760-931-2527
Product Service Description:
Commercial printing
Lithographic printing_commercial

El Dorado National Co.
PO Box 6260
Salina, KS 67401-0260
Contact: Sheldon Walle, Sr. V-P., GM
Telephone: 785-827-1033
Fax: 785-827-0965
Email: eldorado@midkan.com / URL:
Product Service Description:
Transit, tour & shuttle buses
Truck & bus bodies

El Hispanic News
PO Box 306
Portland, OR 97207-0306
Contact: Clara Padilla Andrews, President
Telephone: 503-228-3139
Fax: 503-228-3384
Email: hispnews@hispnews.com / URL:
http://www.hispnews.com
Product Service Description:
Publishes weekly Hispanic bilingual
newspaper

El Semanario
1675 Broadway Ste 1800
Denver, CO 80202-4682
Contact: Christophe Fresquez, CEO
Telephone: 303-575-9180
Fax: 303-575-9197
Email: semanario@aol.com / URL: http://
www.elsemanario.com
Product Service Description:
Publishes weekly newspaper
Newspapers

El Toro Food Products Inc
109 Lee Rd # B
Watsonville, CA 95076-9422
Contact: Richard Thomas, Pres.
Telephone: 831-728-92669
Fax: 831-786-1662
Product Service Description:
Manufactures fresh salsa, sauces and
vegetables : Canned & bottled Salsa, Hot
Suaces : Bottled Salad Dressings, Sauces

Elcon Products International
PO Box 1885
Fremont, CA 94538-0188
Contact: Robert G Foley, Pres.
Telephone: 510-490-4200
Fax: 510-490-3740
Email: sales@elcon-products.com / URL:
http://www.elcon-products.com
Product Service Description:
Electronic connectors : Manufactures and
packages electronic and electrical connectors
Current-carrying wiring devices

Eldorado Chemical Co., Inc.
PO Box 34837
San Antonio, TX 78265-4837
Contact: J. R. Fredricksen, Pres.
Telephone: 210-653-2060
Fax: 210-653-0825
Email: ecci-tx@juno.com / URL: http://
www.members.gnn.com/jmjasper/index.htm
Product Service Description:
Specialized cleaning compounds for the
aircraft industry. : Cleaners for the pulp paper
industry. : Cleaners/phosphatizers for metal
finishing : Lubricants for stamping in the
metal-finishing. : Water treatment

Electralloy
175 Main St
Oil City, PA 16301-1038
Contact: Tracy T. Rudolph, Pres.
Telephone: 814-678-4100
Fax: 814-678-4172
Email: sales@electralloy.com / URL: http://
www.electralloy.com
Product Service Description:
Stainless steel & alloy ingots, bars & billets
Blast furnaces & steel mills

Electric City Corp.
1280 Landmeier Rd
Elk Grove Village, IL 60007-2410
Contact: Stephanie Cox, Director of Mktg. &
Public Relations
Telephone: 847-437-1666
Fax: 847-437-4969
Email: emss1@poweruser.com / URL: http://
www.electriccityeccc.com
Product Service Description:
Energy Saver: State of the art lighting control
technology
Reducing lighting costs 20-50%
Custom manufacturer of switchgear, panels,
pull boxes & trough : Distibutor of Siemens
& Cutler - Hammer products: UL Listed

Electric Motors & Drives, Inc.
PO Box 2565
Anderson, SC 29622-2565
Contact: David Cothran, Pres.
Telephone: 864-224-6623
Fax: 864-225-5936
Email: emd@carol.net / URL: http://
www.emd-inc.com
Product Service Description:
Motors & generators
Rebuilt electric motors

Electro Abrasives Corp.
701 Willet Road
Buffalo, NY 14218
Contact: Allan D. Ramming, President
Telephone: 716/822-2500
Fax: 716-822-2858
Email: info@electroabrasives.com / URL:
http://www.electroabrasives.com
Product Service Description:
Abrasive Prod., Black Silicon Carbide
Refrac. Grains/Powder, Silicon Carbide
Boron Carbide Powder

Electro Cam Corp.
13647 Metric Rd
Roscoe, IL 61073-7637
Contact: Donald L. Davis, Pres.
Telephone: 815-389-2620
Fax: 815-389-3304
Email: ecam@electrocam.com / URL: http://
www.electrocam.com
Product Service Description:
Electronic rotary cam & programmable limit
switches

Electro Stylus
31 Cheyenne Blvd.
Colorado Springs, CO 80906-2225
Contact: Lucille Murray, Owner
Telephone: 719-633-5969
Fax: 719-633-3344
Product Service Description:
Manufactures vibrating, marking & etching
Instruments, : Marking Devices
Industrial Machinery & Equipment

Electro-Numerics, Incorporated (Mfr)
42213 Sarah Way
Temecula, CA 92590
Contact: John A. Wills, President
Telephone: 909/699-2437
Fax: 909-695-7246
Email: sales@electronumerics.com / URL:
http://www.electronumerics.com
Product Service Description:
Digital Panel Meters

Electro-Science Labs Inc.
416 E Church Rd
King Of Prussia, PA 19406-2625
Contact: Dr. Richard S. Webb, Director /
Sales & Mktg.
Phone: 610-272-8000 / Fax: 610-272-6759
Email: sales@electroscience.com / URL:
http://www.electroscience.com
Product Service Description:
Electrical paste

Electrochem
25020 Viking St
Hayward, CA 94545-2704
Contact: Fred Koelling, Pres.
Phone: 510-887-5559 / Fax: 510-887-7394
Product Service Description:
Metal plating : Plating & polishing
Anodizing

Electronic Manufacturing Svc
PO Box 4117
Santa Clara, CA 95056-4117
Contact: Matt Tan, President
Telephone: 408-727-3085
Fax: 408-727-5674
Email: ems-matt@email.msn.com / URL:
http://www.emssiliconvalley.com
Product Service Description:
Printed circuit board assembly
Through - hole & surface mount printed
circuit board assembly
Electro mechanical assembly
Ribbon & Transmission Cable Asemblies
Wire Wrapping
Power & Signal Card Assemblies
Custom Harness Assemblies
Complete Functional Testing of Finished
Products
Functionality Testing
Complete Electro Mechanical Test System
Assembly

Electronic Materials Inc
1814 Airport Rd.
Breckenridge, CO 80424-4599
Contact: Edward Salmon, Pres.
Telephone: 970-547-0807
Fax: 970-547-0817
Email: emi@colorado.net / URL: http://
www.electronicmaterialsinc.com
Product Service Description:
Electroinc adhesives & sealants
Adhesives & sealants - UV cure epoxies
UV and/or heat cured optical epoxies
UV and/or heat cure epoxy chip glop tops
UV and/or heat cure epoxy B.G.A. underfills
UV cure encapsulants : Heat cure
I comp heat cure S.M.T. adhesives
Electrically conductive epoxies
Thermally conductive epoxies

Electronic Packaging Co., Inc.
2209 Wisconsin St Ste 101
Dallas, TX 75229-2060
Contact: Cynthia Jane Whitehead, Pres.
Telephone: 972-484-7671
Fax: 972-484-0550
Email: elecpack@gte.net / URL: http://
www.electronicpackaging.com
Product Service Description:
Computer-aided repair work stations

Electronic Packaging Systems
PO Box 679
Marion, IA 52302-0679
Contact: Ralph Brenneman, Pres
Telephone: 319-377-3423
Fax: 319-377-3674
Email: Ralphz01@earthlink.net / URL: http://
www.brennemanandassoc.com
Product Service Description:
Electronics racks & enclosures
Card cages

Electronic Tele-Communications Inc
1915 Mac Arthur Road
Waukesha, WI 53188
Contact: Frank Kurka, Int'l Sales Mgr.
Telephone: 414-542-5600 ext. 284
Fax: 414-542-1524
Email: kurka@etcia.com / URL: http://
www.etcia.com
Product Service Description:
Voice Processing Equipment :
Telecommunication Equipment, Voice
Response : Telecommunication Equipment -
Time & Temperature Announcers
Telecomm Equipment, Digital Announcers

Electronic Weighing Systems, Inc.
664 Fisherman St
Opa Locka, FL 33054-3810
Contact: Victor Perez, Pres.,
Telephone: 305-685-8067
Fax: 305-685-2440
Email: scales@electronicweighing.com
Product Service Description:
Electronic scales
Scales & balances, except laboratory

Elementis Performance Polymers
600 Cortlandt St.
Belleville, NJ 07109-3328
Contact: Jeff Tyrell, Mktg. Manager
Telephone: 973-751-3000
Fax: 973-751-8407
Email: / URL: http://www.elementis.com
Product Service Description:
Epoxy & polyurethane for electrical potting &
encapsulating : Structural adhesive
Filter adhesive : Sound damping for
automotive : Depolymerized natural, synthetic
& butyl rubber

Elevator Industries Inc.
P.O. Box 2713
Waterloo, IA 50704
Contact: Larry Brooks, *
Telephone: 319-277-7952
Fax: 319-277-7952
Email: / URL:
Product Service Description:
Incline Elevators, Residential & Commercial
Elevators, Personnel (Manlifts)
Elevators, Explosion Proof, Corros. Res.

Elevator World
PO Box 6507
Mobile, AL 36660-0507
Contact: Robert Caporale, Editor
Telephone: 334-479-4514
Fax: 334-479-7043
Email: editorial@elevator-world.com / URL:
http://www.elevator-world.com
Product Service Description:
Magazine typesetting
Periodicals
Typesetting

Elf Atochem North America Inc.
Wire Mill Product Dept.
PO Box 350
Homer, NY 13077-0350
Contact: James L. Marr, G.M.
Telephone: 604-749-2652
Fax: 604-749-4804
Email: / URL:
Product Service Description:
Chemical Preparations
Metal processing chemicals, soap powders &
lubricating greases & oils
Lubricating oils & greases

Elge Precision Machining, Inc.
360 Blair Ave
Reading, PA 19601-1908
Contact: Hermann R. Pfisterer, Pres & GM
Telephone: 610-376-5458
Fax: 610-376-6143
Email: elge@early.com / URL:
Product Service Description:
Automatic screw machine products
Spark Wheels
Sparking files & spark lighters

Elgee Mfg. Co.
107 Trumbull St Bldg J-1
Elizabeth, NJ 07206-2165
Contact: S. Heinle, President
Telephone: 908-527-8277
Fax: 908-527-8155
Email: sales@elgee.com / URL: http://
www.elgee.com
Product Service Description:
Walk Behind Industrial Commercial Vacuum
Sweepers

Elias Diamond Cutting
36 Ne 1st St Ste 915
Miami, FL 33132-2414
Contact: Sol Wigutow, Owner
Telephone: 305-374-5585
Fax: 305-374-5574
Email: eliasdiam@aol.com / URL: http://
www.worldbiz.net/diamond
Product Service Description:
Diamond cutting
Find Diamond Sales & Lapidary Work

Elite Mfg. Corp.
6063 NW 31st Ave. Ste. B
Fort Lauderdale, FL 33309-2209
Contact: Peter Samai Sr., Pres.
Telephone: 954-975-4077
Fax: 954-975-3648
Email: emimfg@bellsouth.net / URL: http://
www.thomasregional.com/fgl/elitemfg
Product Service Description:
Precision Machining Job Shop
Industrial Machinery

Elixir Industries, Inc.
17925 S. Broadway, P.O. Box 470
Gardena, CA 90248
Contact: Julie Cameron, International Sales
Manager
Telephone: 310-767-3409
Fax: 310-767-3411
Email: Elixir1001@aol.com / URL: http://
www.Elixirind.com
Product Service Description:
Doors
Extrusions
Aluminum & Steel Siding / Roofing
Vinyl Siding
Vacuum Formed / Injection Molded Plastics

Elizabeth Carbide Components
200 Monastery Dr
Latrobe, PA 15650-2656
Contact: Kenneth J. Plunko, Sales
Telephone: 724-539-3574
Fax: 724-537-4732
Email: ecc@westol.com / URL: http://
www.eliz.com
Product Service Description:
Tungsten Carbide, Tool Steel & Ceramic -
Tooling, Wear Parts &
Specialty Components (Grinding, Machining
& EDM)

Elk Run Vineyards Inc.
15113 Liberty Rd
Mount Airy, MD 21771-9502
Contact: Fred Wilson, Pres., CFO, R & D
Mgr.
Telephone: 410-775-2513
Fax: 410-875-2009
Email: elk_run@msn.com / URL: http://
www.elkrun.com
Product Service Description:
Wines

Elliot Tool Technologies, LTD.
1760 Tuttle Avenue
Dayton, OH 45403-3428
Contact: Pedro Prada,
Telephone: 937-253-6133
Fax: 937-253-9189
Email: pedrop@elliottool.com / URL: http://
www.elliotttool.com
Product Service Description:
Power Handtools Tube Expanders
Ind. Equip. Tube Cleaners
Hand Tools Tube Testing Equipment
Power Handtools Retubing Tools
Burnishing Tools

Elliott Bay Industries
470 S. Kenyon St.
Seattle, WA 98108-4324
Contact: Joe Agbalog,
Telephone: 206-762-6560
Fax: 206-762-9272
Product Service Description:
Veneer Clippers
Moisture Detectors

Ellis Corporation
1400 West Bryn Mawr Avenue
Itasca, IL 60143-1384
Contact: Robert Fesmire Jr., Director / Sales
Telephone: 630-250-9222
Fax: 630-250-9222
Email: / URL: http://www.elliscorp.com
Product Service Description:
Wastewater Treatment Equipment
Commercial Laundry Equipment

Ellis Enterprises, T. J.
18264 S. Road 189
Columbus Grove, OH 45830-9207
Contact: Sales & Marketing,
Telephone: 419-642-2261
Fax: 419-642-7105
Email: tjellis@worcnet.gen.oh.us / URL:
Product Service Description:
Veneer Logs : LBR Logs : Veneer
Lumber

Ellis Hosiery Mills, Inc.
PO Box 1088
Hickory, NC 28603-1088
Contact: Dick Stober, Pres.
Telephone: 828-322-1010
Fax: 828-328-5618
Email: terrik@ellishosiery.com / URL:
Product Service Description:
Hosiery
Men's & women's socks

Ellis Popcorn Co., Inc.
101 Poplar St
Murray, KY 42071-2533
Contact: Dave Roberts,
Telephone: 502-753-5451
Fax: 502-753-7002
Email: epcmurray@ldd.net / URL: http://
www.ellispopcorn.com
Product Service Description:
Blue Ribbon Popcorn

Elmagco Corp
PO Box 1615
Bisbee, AZ 85603-2615
Contact: George Pittenger, Pres.
Telephone: 520-432-2380
Fax: 520-432-1409
Product Service Description:
Manufactures DC drives; wholesales
electronic parts : Motors & generators
Electronic parts & equipment

Elmco, Inc.
P.O. Box 176
Cooksville, IL 61730
Contact: Bob Furgeson, President / CEO
Telephone: 309-725-3533
Fax: 309-725-3556
Email: bob_furgeson@elmcoinc.com / URL:
http://www.elmcoinc.com
Product Service Description:
Custom Neighborhood Electric Vehicles &
Luxury Golf Cars. Cadillacs, Rolls Royce &
Others

Elsner Engineering Works Inc.
P.O. Box 66
Hanover, PA 17331-0066
Contact: Bertram F. Elsner, President
Telephone: 717-637-5991
Fax: 717-633-7100
Email: een@mail.cvn.net / URL: http://
www.elsnereng.com
Product Service Description:
Paper Industry Machinery
Rewinders for consumer products
Folders for baby wipes

Ely Energy, Inc.
11385 E 60th Pl
Tulsa, OK 74146-6828
Contact: Gary Eaton, Managing Director
Telephone: 918-250-6601
Fax: 918-254-5412
Email: inquiries@elyenergy.com / URL: http:/
/www.elyenergy.com
Product Service Description:
LPG/Air Blending Systems
LPG Vaporization Equipment

Embee Corp.
552 W State St
Springfield, OH 45506-2533
Contact: James Gartland, Pres.
Telephone: 800-228-9245
Fax: 800-320-0733
Email: jgartland@erinet.com / URL:
Product Service Description:
Tools_hand & edge

Emblem & Badge Inc.
PO Box 6226
Providence, RI 02940-6226
Contact: David Resnik, Pres.
Telephone: 401-331-5444 / 800-875-5444
Fax: 401-421-7941
Email: sales@recognition.com / URL: http://
www.recognition.com
Product Service Description:
Trophies, plaques & awards

Embroidertex West Ltd
435 E 16th St
Los Angeles, CA 90015-3726
Contact: Leonard Kleiderman, Pres.
Telephone: 213-749-4319
Fax: 213-749-9430
Product Service Description:
Pleating & stitching
Embroiders on fabrics

Embry Engineering & Mfg
740 Metcalf St Ste 22
Escondido, CA 92025-1671
Contact: William Ray Embry, Owner
Telephone: 760-741-9073
Fax: 760-741-9319
Product Service Description:
Manufactures molded seals; injection molding
of plastics ; Gaskets, packing & sealing
devices : Plastic products

Emerson Radio Corp.
P.O. Box 430
Parsippany, NJ 07054-0430
Contact: Michael Finley, International
Director
Telephone: 973-428-2038
Fax: 973-428-2039
Email: / URL:
Product Service Description:
Household Audio & Video Equipment
Microwave ovens

Emi-Tech Inc.
RR 1 Box 133
Timpson, TX 75975-9718
Contact: Mary Lola Gouge, Pres., Hum. Res.
& MIS Mgr.
Telephone: 409-254-3451
Fax: 409-254-3049
Email: vacutec@aol.com / URL: http://
www.vacutec.com &
www.flattoptoolbox.com
Product Service Description:
Automotive vacuum leak detection systems &
fuel system analyzers: Metal Fabrication &
Trusses

Empire Electronics Corp.
1629 Litton Dr
Stone Mountain, GA 30083-1116
Contact: Pravin Kakadiya, Sales Mgr.
Telephone: 770-934-1500
Fax: 770-934-8177
Email: eecpcb@aol.com / URL: http://
www.empire-elec.com
Product Service Description:
Printed circuit boards

Empire State Leather Corp.
400 Gotham Pkwy
Carlstadt, NJ 07072-2410
Contact: Lewis Green, Dir. Sales & Mktg.
Telephone: 201-896-8100
Fax: 201-896-9061
Email: salesempireleather.com / URL: http://
www.empireleather.com
Product Service Description:
Leather goods : Bonded Leather

Emx Inc.
P.O. Box 195039
Winter Springs, FL 32719
Contact: Tim Arion, *
Telephone: 407/366-7443
Fax: 407-366-7444
Email: emx@gate.net / URL:
Product Service Description:
Rear Vision Video Systems, RV's, Truck, Bus

Encore Paper Co.
1 River St
South Glens Falls, NY 12803-4718
Contact: Joseph F. Raccuia, Pres., CEO
Telephone: 518-793-5684
Fax: 518-745-1091
Email: / URL:
Product Service Description:
Paper mills
Folded & roll towels, toilet tissue & napkins

Enderes Tool Company Inc
14925 Energy Way
Apple Valley, MN 55124
Contact: Mark Bothum, President
Telephone: 612-891-1200
Fax: 612-891-1202
Product Service Description:
Screw Drivers,punches,chisels
Construction Bars

Endress & Hauser, Inc.
PO Box 246
Greenwood, IN 46142-0246
Contact: Kathy Kieffer, Mktg.
Communications Coordinator
Telephone: 317-535-7138
Fax: 317-535-8498
Email: info@endress.com / URL: http://
www.endress.com
Product Service Description:
Process level, flow, pressure, liquid analysis
& moisture measurement instruments & syst.

Ener-G Foods Inc
PO Box 84487
Seattle, WA 98124-5787
Contact: Sam Wylde Sr, Chrm.
Telephone: 206-767-6660
Fax: 206-764-3398
Email: / URL: http://www.ener-g.com
Product Service Description:
Wheat Free & Gluten Free Foods
Allergy Free Foods
Low Protein, Sodium, Potasium Phophorus
Foods

Enercept, Inc.
3100 9th Ave Se
Watertown, SD 57201-9170
Contact: John Devine, Pres.
Telephone: 605-882-2222
Fax: 605-882-2753
Email: enercept@icontrol.net / URL: http://
www.enercept.com
Product Service Description:
Structural insulated building panels

Enerfab
4955 Spring Grove Ave
Cincinnati, OH 45232-1925
Contact: Jeff Raasch, Executive V.P.
Telephone: 513-641-0500
Fax: 513-241-6833
Email: jeff_raasch@enerfab.com / URL: http:/
/www.enerfab.com
Product Service Description:
Tank Lining
Fabricated Metal Products

Energy Economics, Inc.
PO Box 220
Dodge Center, MN 55927-0220
Contact: Jeffrey Spencer, VP Sales
Telephone: 507-374-2557
Fax: 507-374-2646
Email: eeimarketing@eei.com / URL: http://
www.eei.com
Product Service Description:
Gas meters, repair & remanufacturing
New gas meters & regulators
High potential anodes
Cathodic protection service
Sonic nozzle provers for gas meters

Energy Machinery Inc
10 Reservoir Park Dr
Rockland, MA 02370-1092
Contact: Richard Wheeling Sr, Pres.
Telephone: 781-871-6220
Fax: 781-878-7085
Email: energymch@aol.com / URL:
Product Service Description:
Compressors_air & gas
Stationary Diesel Engines and Components
Chicago Pneumatic Compressor Parts

Energy Sales
355 E Middlefield Rd
Mountain View, CA 94043-4003
Contact: Robert R Wilke, Pres., CEO
Telephone: 650-969-0800
Fax: 650-961-2000
Email: info@energy-sales.com / URL: http://
www.energy-sales.com
Product Service Description:
Distributes port, dry cell, rechargable and
disposable batteries and related products;
value-added assembly
Batteries_storage
Electrical apparatus & equipment

Energy Suspension
1131 Via Callejon
San Clemente, CA 92673-6211
Contact: Mike Papazian, Sales Manager
Telephone: 949-361-3935
Fax: 949-361-3940
Email: hyperfx@ibm.net / URL: http://
www.energysuspension.com
Product Service Description:
Auto. Polyurethane Suspension Component

Enflo Corp.
PO Box 490
Bristol, CT 06011-0490
Contact: Janice Champa, Sales & Mktg. Mgr.
Telephone: 860-589-0014
Fax: 860-589-7179
Email: ptfe.enflo@snet.net / URL: http://
www.enflo.com
Product Service Description:
Plastic sheet, rod & tube
Unsupported plastics film & sheet

Enform-Aeon Inc
PO Box L
Jerome, AZ 86331-0337
Contact: Paul Nonnast, Pres.
Telephone: 520-634-2846
Fax: 520-634-2846
Email: / URL:
Product Service Description:
Commercial industrial design; industrial
design prototyping; products, packaging
Commercial physical research

Engine Systems
6 Norway Ln.
Latham, NY 12110
Contact: Robert Singleton, VP, Mktg. & Sales
Telephone: 518-783-0545
Fax: 518-783-0496
Email: / URL: http://www.motivepower.com
Product Service Description:
Turbines & turbine generator sets
Locomotive engine turbo chargers
Diesel Engine Cmponents

Engineered Lighting Products
10768 Lower Azusa Rd
El Monte, CA 91731-1306
Contact: R Swarens, Pres.
Telephone: 626-579-0943
Fax: 626-579-6803
Email: elp2@aol.com / URL: http://
www.elplighting.com
Product Service Description:
Manufactures lighting fixtures
Lighting equipment

Engineered Lubricants Co.
11525 Rock Island Ct.
Maryland Heights, MO 63043
Contact: Don Wachter, Pres.
Telephone: 314-872-9540
Fax: 314-872-9544
Email: / URL:
Product Service Description:
Lubricating oils & greases
Greases, oils & lubricants
Petroleum products & lab testing
Metalworking fluids of all types

Engineered Plastics, Inc.
211 Chase St.
Gibsonville, NC 27249
Contact: Pete Mottinger, *
Telephone: 336-449-4121
Fax: 336-449-6352
Product Service Description:
Food Service Equipment

Engineered Products Co.
PO Box 598
Waterloo, IA 50704-0598
Contact: Ron Kelderman, Sales Manager
Telephone: 319-234-0231
Fax: 319-234-8922
Email: engpro@forbin.com / URL: http://
www.filterminder.com
Product Service Description:
Motor vehicle parts & accessories

Enjoy Foods International
10601 Beech Ave
Fontana, CA 92337-7204
Contact: Loretta Heyne, Chrm.
Telephone: 909-823-2228
Fax: 909-355-1573
Email: / URL:
Product Service Description:
Beef jerky, and turkey jerkys

Enkotec Co., Inc.
31200 Solon Rd Ste 16
Solon, OH 44139-3556
Contact: Jan Sorige, Pres.
Telephone: 440-349-2800
Fax: 440-349-3575
Email: enkotec@nls.net / URL:
Product Service Description:
Cold forming metal machinery
Rolling mill machinery

Entenmann-Rovin Company
2425 Garfield Ave
City Of Commerce, CA 90040-1811
Contact: Mildred Tanaka, GM
Telephone: 323-278-1999
Fax: 323-278-1980
Email: / URL: http://www.entenmann-
rovin.com
Product Service Description:
Manufactures service pin jewelry, official
police and fire badges
Jewelry_custom
Manufacturing industries

Enterprise Electronics Corp.
128 Industrial Blvd S
Enterprise, AL 36330-3168
Contact: Larry Collins, Pres.
Telephone: 334-347-3478
Fax: 334-393-4556
Email: eecsales@eecrader.com / URL: http://
www.eecradar.com
Product Service Description:
Meteorological radar equipment
Search & navigation equipment

Enterprising Kitchen
4545 N Broadway St
Chicago, IL 60640-5601
Contact: Joan Pikas, Dir.
Telephone: 773-506-3880
Fax: 773-506-3881
Email: tekitchen@aol.com / URL: http://
www.concentric.net/~flieb/
Product Service Description:
Soap - natural / no animal products
Gourmet grains - tabooli, black beans,
polenta couscous

Enting Water Conditioning Inc.
PO Box 546
Dayton, OH 45449-0546
Contact: Mel Entingh, President
Telephone: 937-294-5100 / 800-735-5100
Fax: 937-294-5485
Email: / URL: http://www.enting.com
Product Service Description:
Service Industry Machinery
Water Softeners, Deionizers, Reverse
Osmosis, Filters & Solution Pumps

Entrac, Inc.
47 Van Nostrand Ave
Englewood, NJ 07631-4309
Contact: Naren Doshi / Amit Parekh,
Telephone: 201-894-0616
Email: entracinc@aol.com / URL: http://
www.entracinc.com
Product Service Description:
Diesel Engine Parts

Envirobate Inc.
3301 E. 26th St.
Mpls, MN 55406
Contact: Scott Larson / Steve Wallingua, *
Telephone: 612-729-1080
Product Service Description:
Franchises, Environmental Services

Environmental Compliance Systems, Inc.
30 Martin St
Cumberland, RI 02864-5321
Contact: Michael Devine, Pres., CFO
Telephone: 800-368-4762
Fax: 401-334-2757
Email: ecs_inc@edgenet.net / URL: http://
www3.edgenet.net/ecs.html
Product Service Description:
Silver recovery equipment & penetrating oil
destruct systems

Environmental Dynamics, Inc.(Mfr)
5601 Paris Road
Columbia, MO 65202-9399
Contact: Charles E. Tharp, President
Telephone: 573-474-9456
Fax: 573-474-6988
Email: edi@wastewater.com / URL: http://
www.wastewater.com
Product Service Description:
Aeration Mixers, Wastewater Treatment

Environmental Protective Coatings, Inc.
2035 Regency Rd Ste 5
Lexington, KY 40503-2333
Contact: Homer Hart, President
Telephone: 606-277-0014
Fax: 606-278-4973
Email: envirocoat@aol.com / URL:
Product Service Description:
Industrial structural steel coatings & ceramic
insulating : Paints & moisture cure polyethane
primers

Environmental Services & Technology
15510 Montanus Drive
Culpeper, VA 22701
Contact: Mike Slivinski, President
Telephone: 540-825-9083
Fax: 540-825-9087
Email: ensat@citizen.infi.net / URL: http://
www.ensatcorp.com
Product Service Description:
Emergency Spill Response Operations
Underground Storage Tank Design /
Construction : Groundwater Remediation
Water Supply : Water Well Location &
Design : Fuel Storage Design / Construction
Wastewater Treatment : Hazardous Waste
Management : Geological Consulting
Facility Construction

Environmental Soil Systems Inc
13234 Whistler Ave
Granada Hills, CA 91344-1141
Contact: Rick Granard, Pres.
Telephone: 818-368-4115
Fax: 818-368-9393
Email: rgranard@soilmasterwr.com / URL:
http://www.soilmasterwr.com
Product Service Description:
Plastic materials & resins : Manufactures
liquid copolymers, erosion and dust control
products : Agricultural chemicals

Environmental Solutions, Inc.
PO Box 1064
Yazoo City, MS 39194-1064
Contact: Alan Ramsay, Pres.
Telephone: 601-746-7470
Fax: 601-746-7474
Email: envsol@dixienet.com / URL: http://
www.environmentalsolution.com
Product Service Description:
Silver recovery equipment

Environmental Technologies, Inc.
PO Box 4489
Clearwater, FL 33758-4489
Contact: Kent Rawson, Pres, Dvid Geldbart,
Intl Sls. Mgr.
Telephone: 813-541-3531
Fax: 813-545-1028
Email: tpeeples@environmental-tec.com /
URL: http://www.environmental-tec.com
Product Service Description:
HVAC equipment, electric heating, pneumatic
& electronic controls : Terminal Units
Air Handling Units : Air Diffusers & Grilles
Fire Dampers

Envirozone Systems Corp.
PO Box 371
Monett, MO 65708-0371
Contact: R. Scott Decker, Pres.
Telephone: 417-235-5318
Fax: 417-235-8817
Email: sdecker@mo-net.com / URL:
Product Service Description:
Ozone generators

Epsilon Industrial, Inc.
2215 Grand Avenue Pkwy
Austin, TX 78728-3812
Contact: Tom Prud'Homme, GM
Telephone: 512-251-1500
Fax: 512-251-1593
Email: info@epsilon-gms.com / URL: http://
www.epsilon-gms.com
Product Service Description:
Spectrometers
Analytical instruments

Equipment & Systems Engineering
14260 S.W. 136th St., Unit #4
Miami, FL 33186-6718
Contact: Jose Masis, President
Telephone: 305-378-4101
Fax: 305-378-4121
Email: jotoma1@shadow.net / URL: http://
www.aquachlorese.com
Product Service Description:
Sodium Hypochlorite on-site Generators
Marine Waste Water Treatment Plants
Packaging Equipment
Gaseous Fuels Carburetion Equipment
Water Treatment Plants

Equipment Development Co., Inc.
100 Thomas Johnson Dr
Frederick, MD 21702-4600
Contact: Paul J. Gorgol, Pres.
Telephone: 301-663-1600
Fax: 301-663-1607
Email: sales@edcoinc.com / URL: http://
www.edcoinc.com
Product Service Description:
Construction machinery
Concrete resurfacing equipment, sheet metal
fabricaton & precision machining job shop

Equipsa, Inc.
P.O. Box 521043,
Miami, FL 33152
Contact: Elsie U. Aviles, Vice President
Traffic
Telephone: 305-592-7610
Fax: 305-591-9709
Email: equipsa@equipsa.com / URL: http://
www.equipsa.com
Product Service Description:
Freight Forwarder
Freight & Cargo Transportation
NVOCC / Ocean & Air Consolidators

Equity Industries
5721 Bayside Rd.
Virginia Beach, VA 23455-3092
Contact: Bruce Thomas, President
Telephone: 804-460-2483
Product Service Description:
Alarm clock quartz
Electronic Digital Alarm Clock
Quartz wall clocks
Mechanical alarm clocks
Spalding massagers

Era Aviation Inc.
6160 Carl Brady Dr.
Anchorage, AK 99502
Contact: Bryan Blixhavn, Sr. V.P. Mktg.
Telephone: 907-248-4422
Fax: 907-266-8383
Email: info@eraaviation.com / URL: http://
www.eraaviation.com
Product Service Description:
Helicopter / Fixed Wing Charter Service
Helicopter / Fixed Wing Contract Service
Fixed Wing Scheduled Service

Eraser Co., Inc.
PO Box 4961
Syracuse, NY 13221-4961
Contact: Linda Cahill, Sales & Mktg. Mgr.
Telephone: 315-454-3237
Fax: 315-454-3090
Email: info@eraser.com / URL: http://
www.eraser.com
Product Service Description:
Lead forming & wire stripping machines &
fiberglass erasers & brushes
Wire, Cable & Tubing Cutters

Ericson Manufacturing, Inc.
4215 Hamann Pkwy.
Willoughby, OH 44094-0890
Contact: Joseph A. Tarulli,
Mgr.- Mktg. & Sales
Telephone: 216-951-8000
Fax: 216-951-1867
Email: info@ericson.com / URL: http://
www.ericson.com
Product Service Description:
Portable Hand Lamps : Wiring Devices: Plugs
& Connectors : Low Voltage Safety Lights
Temporary Lighting : Ground Fault Circuit
Interrupters : Electrical Cable Reels
Flexible Power Cords

Ericyan II
499 Broadway
New York, NY 10012-4401
Contact: Daniel Gabay, Manager
Telephone: 212-226-5446
Fax: 212-334-8039
Email: danielg@ericyan.com / URL: http://
www.sohomenyc.com
Product Service Description:
Wholesale, Export & Domestic
Major brands, bed & bath linens
Close outs & regular line

Erin's Original Horseplay Rugs
5090 W Horseshoe Ln
Mc Neal, AZ 85617-9654
Contact: Judith McGraw-Sperling, Owner
Telephone: 520-364-7764 / 1800-323-9665
Fax: 520-364-7764
Product Service Description:
Manufactures play rugs for use with toy
horses and toy cars
Games, toys & children's vehicles
Carpets & rugs

Ernest F Mariani Co.
614 West 600 South
Salt Lake City, UT 84104
Contact: Wil Fiedler, President & CEO
Telephone: 801-359-3744
Fax: 801-531-9615
Email: wil@efmco.com or clay@efmco.com
/ URL: http://www.efmco.com
Product Service Description:
Suppliers of equipment services, &
ingredients to the food, beverage &
pharmceutical industries

Esco International
2050 W Balmoral Ave
Chicago, IL 60625-1002
Contact: Tom Franklin, Pres.
Telephone: 773-271-2002
Fax: 773-271-3836
Email: www.tomfranklin@escolighting.com /
URL: http://www.escolighting.com
Product Service Description:
Industrial, commercial & institutional high
intensity lighting fixtures
Lighting fixtures_commercial
Back Light Display Signs

Esco Rubber Products Inc
PO Box 849
Brea, CA 92822-0849
Contact: Patrick Sullivan, Pres.
Telephone: 714-529-3049
Fax: 714-529-3380
Email: rubberdude@msn.com / URL:
Product Service Description:
Rubber plumbing items
Mechanical rubber goods

Esico-Triton
112 W Elm St.
Deep River, CT 06417-1687
Contact: Dennis Kosky, Customer Service
Telephone: 860-526-9524
Fax: 860-526-9524
Email: triton.industries@snet.net / URL: http:/
/www.esico-triton.thomasregister.com
Product Service Description:
Soldering Equipment

Eskra Inc. (Mfr)
2510 Harrison Street
Evanston, IL 60201
Contact: Dale Eskra, *
Telephone: 847-475-1267
Product Service Description:
Prepackaged Software

Essen Nutrition Corp.
1414 Sherman Rd
Romeoville, IL 60446-4046
Contact: M. Anirudhan, Pres.
Telephone: 630-739-6700
Fax: 630-739-6464
Email: ani@essen-nutrition.com / URL:
Product Service Description:
Dietetic foods, sports drinks & vege burgers

Essential Products Co., Inc.
90 Water St.
New York, NY 10005-3587
Contact: Barry Striem, *
Telephone: 212-344-4288
Fax:
Email: / URL:
Product Service Description:
Fragrances - Bargain Priced Versions
Liquor, Wine Agers - Mellow Blenders

Essex Cryogenics Of Missouri, Inc.
8007 Chivvis Dr.
Saint Louis, MO 63123-2395
Contact: Roy Spaulding, V-P., GM
Telephone: 314-832-8077
Fax: 314-832-8208
Email: cryo@essexind.com / URL: http://
www.essexind.com
Product Service Description:
Fixed & portable liquid oxygen life support
breathing systems & components
Surgical & medical instruments
Sheet metal work

Essex Group Inc. (Mfr)
1710 Wall Street, P.O. Box 1750
Ft. Wayne, IN 46801
Contact: Joseph B. Millay, Mgr./ Intl. Mktg.
Telephone: 219-461-5626
Fax: 219-461-5660
Email: millay_berk@essexgroup.com / URL:
Product Service Description:
Telephone Wire & Cable
Computer Cable (Lan)
Telephone Inside Wiring Cable

Estad Stamping & Mfg. Co.
1005 Griggs St
Danville, IL 61832-4116
Contact: Paul Skinner, Pres., Engrg. & Fin.
Mgr.
Telephone: 217-442-4600
Fax: 217-442-4632
Email: estadstp@aol.com / URL: http://
www.estadstamping.com
Product Service Description:
Wardrobe hanger bars, metal products, drum
accessories & joint nails
Metal stampings & tool & die

Estee Bedding Co., Inc.
945 E 93rd St
Chicago, IL 60619-7813
Contact: Tim Enright, Pres., CFO
Telephone: 773-374-4714
Fax: 773-374-4034
Email: esteebed@msn.com / URL:
Product Service Description:
Institutional & contract mattresses
Mattresses & bedsprings

Etalon Inc.
PO Box 127, 1600 W. Main St.
Lebanon, IN 46052-0127
Contact: Adam Morris, VP Operations
Telephone: 765-483-2550
Fax: 765-483-2560
Email: etalon@in-motion.net / URL: http://
www.etaloninc.com
Product Service Description:
Piezoelectric & ultrasonic transducers

Etcon Corp.
7750 S Grant St
Burr Ridge, IL 60521-5945
Contact: Joe Rocci, Pres., Engrg. & R & D
Mgr.
Telephone: 630-325-6100
Fax: 630-325-6838
Email: info@etcon.com / URL: http://
www.etcon.com
Product Service Description:
Electrical testing equipment
Measuring & controlling devices

Ethylene Control Inc
PO Box 571
Selma, CA 93662-0571
Contact: David Biswell, Pres.
Telephone: 209-896-1909
Fax: 209-896-3232
Email: / URL:
Product Service Description:
Manufactures ethylene filters
Machinery_general industrial
Ethylene removal equipment
Mold & rot removal

Euclid Hitachi Heavy Equipment
22221 St. Clair Ave.
Cleveland, OH 44117
Contact: Keith Richardson, President
Telephone: 216-383-3499
Fax: 216-383-3423
Email: / URL: http://www.euclid.hitachi.com
Product Service Description:
Construction Machinery
Chassis fitted with engines for tractors, motor
vehicles for passengers, goods transport
Motor vehicles for the transport of goods
Bodies for road tractors for semi-trailers,
motor vehicles for public-transport of
passengers

Eureka Welding Alloys
5225 E Davidson
Detroit, MI 48212
Contact: Glenn E. Stempowski, General Mgr.
Telephone: 313-366-5757
Fax: 313-369-1344
Email: eurekagm@compuserve.com / URL:
http://www.eurekaweldingalloys.com
Product Service Description:
Tool & Die Maintenance Welding Electrodes,
Alloy Core Wire &
Solid Wire for Mig & Tig Welding

**Euro-American Air Frt. Fwdg Co.,
Inc.**
375 Airport Drive
Worcester, MA 01602-2294
Contact: David D. Busenburg, Vice President
Telephone: 508-755-5050
Fax: 508-752-6020
Email: / URL:
Product Service Description:
Freight Forwarding
Public Warehouse
Bonded Container
Custom Brokerage
Common Carrier
Bonded Carrier

Euro-Tech Corporation
14823 E Hinsdale Ave
Englewood, CO 80112-4243
Contact: Dolf Schroeder, Pres.
Telephone: 303-690-9000
Fax: 303-690-9010
Email: dolf@europlotter.com / URL: http://
www.europlotter.com
Product Service Description:
Distributes computer equipment, electronic
parts and industrial machinery and equipment

Europawatch.Com
6733 S. Sepulveda Blvd. 115
Los Angeles, CA 90045-1562
Contact: Stephen Soffa, VP
Telephone: 310-417-8409
Fax: 310-417-3883
Email: steve@europawatch.com / URL: http:/
/www.europawatch.com
Product Service Description:
Watches Customized

Evans Components Inc
2004 N Vancouver Ave
Portland, OR 97227-1917
Contact: Robert Evans, CEO
Telephone: 503-282-1584
Fax: 503-282-1484
Email: bobe@evanscomponents.com / URL:
Product Service Description:
Manufactures component parts— tubing,
fittings, valves, electro polished tubing
Valves & pipe fittings
Electronic components

Evans Cushing, Inc.
PO Box 1608
Cushing, OK 74023-1608
Contact: Robert Evans, Pres.
Telephone: 918-225-0095
Fax: 918-225-0100
Email: / URL:
Product Service Description:
Barrels, drums & pails_metal
Steel drums

Evans Mfg. Co., John Evans Trailers
PO Box 669
Sumter, SC 29151-0669
Contact: Thomas R. Spencer, CEO
Telephone: 803-773-7329
Fax: 803-778-1256
Email: evanstrailer@ftc-i.net / URL:
Product Service Description:
Utility trailers & lowbeds
Transportation equipment
Loggin trailers
Gas cylinder trailers
Portable bridges

Everett J. Prescott
PO Box 600
Gardiner, ME 04345-0600
Contact: David G. Gardner, Sr., Vice President
Telephone: 207-582-1851
Fax: 207-582-5637
Email: ejp@evprescott.com / URL: http://www.ejprescott.com
Product Service Description:
Industrial Supplies, Water, Sewer & Drain, Wholesale
Construction Services, Utility Lines
Trucking, Except Local

Everybody's Bagel Co Inc
PO Box 29352
Oakland, CA 94604-9352
Contact: Marshall Goldberg, Pres.
Telephone: 510-553-8980
Fax: 510-553-8988
Email: bagel@netwizards.net / URL:
Product Service Description:
Manufactures bagels
Bread, cake & related products

Evey Engineering Co., Inc.
730 S West Blvd
Vineland, NJ 08360-5510
Contact: Gaylord Evey, Pres.
Telephone: 609-692-2610
Fax: 609-692-6554
Email: john@evey.com / URL: http://www.evey.com
Product Service Description:
Vacuum Pumps New & Rebuilt
Vacuum Metalizers, New & Rebuilt
Rebuilding Service & Vacuum Pumps, Blower Systems

Evtec Corp.
1414 Brook Dr
Downers Grove, IL 60515-1025
Contact: Robert P. Allison, Pres.
Telephone: 630-916-0342
Fax: 630-916-0575
Email: rpas@aol.com / URL:
Product Service Description:
Printing trades machinery
Printing press sheeting & stacking equipment

Ewald Instrument Corp.
28 Maple Street
Kent, CT 06757
Contact: Richard S. Vreeland II, *
Telephone: 860-927-3278
Fax: 860-927-3031
Email: rsv2@aol.com / URL:
Product Service Description:
Cable Cutting Machinery
Fusing Machinery
Flash Strippers For Shielding Braid
Small Resistance Welders

Excel Design Inc.
267 Commonwealth Dr
Carol Stream, IL 60188-2450
Contact: Mel Thomas, Pres.
Telephone: 630-681-1122
Fax: 630-681-0066
Email: exceldsign@aol.com / URL:
Product Service Description:
Wood products
Framed artwork
Printing_commercial

Excel Industries, Inc.
PO Box 7000 200 S. Ridge Rd.
Hesston, KS 67062-2097
Contact: Doug Stutzman, Export Manager
Telephone: 316-327-4911
Fax: 316-327-3123
Email: jsiebert@southwind.net / URL: http://www.excelhustler.com
Product Service Description:
Professional Lawn Mowers Ride-On

Excel Of Stockton
301 S Simmons St
Stockton, IL 61085-1513
Contact: Richard Fetzer, Plt. Mgr.
Telephone: 815-947-3333
Fax: 815-947-3010
Product Service Description:
Motor vehicle parts & accessories
Seat Systems Hardware
Seat Track Mechanisms
Seat Recliner Mechanisms

Excel Spring & Stamping Co.
1080 Industrial Dr
Bensenville, IL 60106-1215
Contact: Phillip B. Matthaei, Pres.,
Telephone: 630-595-8585
Fax: 630-595-0029
Product Service Description:
Wire springs & forms, precision
Metal stampings & flat springs

Excelta Corp
60 Easy St
Buellton, CA 93427-9560
Contact: Greg Johnson, VP Marketing
Telephone: 805-686-4686
Fax: 805-686-9005
Email: sales@excelta.com / URL: http://www.excelta.com
Product Service Description:
Manufactures hand tools and tweezers
Clean room production tools

Exclusive Findings
812 Branch Ave.
Providence, RI 02904-1707
Contact: Kathy McCoy, Div. Manager
Telephone: 401-331-8199
Fax: 401-273-2940
Product Service Description:
Brass Engraveable Plates
Nickel Silver Engraveable Plates
Engraveable Bookmarks, Keytags, Pet Tags
Engraveable Luggage Tags

Executive Door Company
3939 W Clarendon Ave
Phoenix, AZ 85019-3607
Contact: Jerry Crittenden, Pres.
Telephone: 602-272-8076
Fax: 602-272-9460
Email: / URL:
Product Service Description:
Manufactures custom wood doors
Environmental Doors

Exelint International, Inc.
PO Box 3194
Culver City, CA 90231-3194
Contact: Armand Hamid, Director
Telephone: 310-649-0707
Fax: 310-649-1178
Email: exelmed@exelmed.com / URL: http://www.exelint.com
Product Service Description:
Disposable Medical Products, Wholesale
Hypodermic Syringes / Needles, Wholesale

Exeltech
2225 E Loop 820 N
Fort Worth, TX 76118-7101
Contact: Gary Chemelewski, Pres., CEO, Opers. Mgr.
Telephone: 817-595-4969
Fax: 817-595-1290
Email: info@exeltech.com / URL: http://www.exeltech.com
Product Service Description:
Power inverters
Electrical industrial apparatus

Exergetic Systems Inc
12 San Marino Dr
San Rafael, CA 94901-1536
Contact: Fred Lang, Pres.
Telephone: 415-455-0100
Fax: 415-455-0215
Email: / URL: http://www.exergeticsystems.com
Product Service Description:
Computer related services
Engineering services
Power plant thermal performance

Exeter Engineering Inc
PO Box 457
Exeter, CA 93221-0457
Contact: Jeff Batchman, Pres.
Telephone: 209-592-3161
Fax: 209-592-3223
Product Service Description:
Manufactures equipment for processing fresh fruits and vegetables including citrus
Potatoes, avocados, kiwi, tree fruit
Manufacture of electronic sizing and
Grading machines primarily for citrus & potatoes

Exide Corporation
4512 Andrews St
North Las Vegas, NV 89031-2712
Contact: Art Newman, Br. Mgr.
Telephone: 702-643-4720
Fax: 702-643-4868
Product Service Description:
Batteries_storage
Manufactures automotive and marine storage batteries; distributes starters and alternators
Motor vehicle supplies & new parts
Electrical apparatus & equipment

Exothermics, Inc.
5040 Enterprise Blvd
Toledo, OH 43612-3840
Contact: Bruce A. McKenna, Pres., GM & Sales Mgr.
Telephone: 419-729-9726
Fax: 419-729-9705
Email: sales@exothermics.com / URL: http://www.exothermics.com
Product Service Description:
Industrial waste heat recovery & heat exchangers : Air to Air Heat Exchangers
Stainless Steel Plate & Tubular Exchangers
Air Preheaters

Expanded Technologies Inc.
3075 Jonquil Dr Se
Smyrna, GA 30080-3719
Contact: John Liverato, Pres. / Greg Guy, Sales & Mktg. Mgr, Walt Minor, R&D / Yolande Liverato,Finance & Acctg
Telephone: 770-333-6116
Fax: 770-438-7804
Product Service Description:
Expanded metals for filtration & other applications

Expo Displays
3203 Queen Palm Drive
Tampa, FL 33619
Contact: Tim Packrall, Pres.
Telephone: 813-623-2402
Fax: 813-621-7904
Email: webuildimages@expodisplays.com / URL: http://www.expodisplays.com
Product Service Description:
Portable & modular displays, exhibits, & trade show booths

Export FSC International LTD
11200 Montgomery Blvd, NE Ste 8
Albuquerque, NM 87111-2679
Contact: Robert J. Thornton, *
Telephone: 800-243-1372
Product Service Description:
Business Services, Foreign Sales Corporation

Export Parts Center
719 Old Highway 90
Mabank, TX 75147-7964
Contact: Lynette Ortiz, Owner
Telephone: 903-887-6999
Fax:
Email: / URL:
Product Service Description:
Used Diesel Motor & Parts
Buy - Sell - Trade Used Trucks

Export Procedures Co.
109 South High St., Suite 200
Zelienople, PA 16063-1318
Contact: Catherine Thornberry, President
Telephone: 724-452-6816
Fax: 724-452-0486
Email: exptproc@fyi.net / URL: http://www.exportproco.com
Product Service Description:
Management Consulting Service, Export Operation Systems

Expressway USA Freightlines Inc.
1000 Port Carteret Dr.,
Port Carteret, NJ 07008
Contact: Steve Fleischer, President
Telephone: 732-541-3372
Fax: 732-541-1275
Email: / URL: http://www.expresswayusa.com
Product Service Description:
Freight & Cargo Transportation
Trucking & Warehousing
U.S. Customs Control Exam Site

Extru-Tech, Inc.
P.O. Box 8, 100 Airport Rd.
Sabetha, KS 66534
Contact: Ken Matsony, President / CEO
Telephone: 785-284-2153
Fax: 785-284-3143
Email: extru-techinc@extru-techinc.com / URL: http://www.extru-techinc.com
Product Service Description:
Food processing machinery
Human foods, pet foods, aquaculture foods

Eye Lighting International Of North America, Inc.
9150 Hendricks Rd
Mentor, OH 44060-2146
Contact: Bill Jenkins, Pres.
Telephone: 440-350-7000
Fax: 440-350-7001
Email: / URL: http://www.eyelighting.com
Product Service Description:
Lighting equipment
Industrial & commercial high intensity lamps

F & G Multi-Slide, Inc.
130 Industrial Dr
Franklin, OH 45005-4428
Contact: Gene Benninger, Sales Rep
Telephone: 513-746-3658
Fax: 513-746-1885
Email: fgmultislide@erinet / URL:
Product Service Description:
Electronic, appliance & automotive stampings

F S P Machinery
201 15th St Unit 2
Walhalla, ND 58282-4208
Contact: Peter Friesen, Pres.
Telephone: 877-552-5200
Fax:
Email: info@fspmachinery.com / URL: http://
www.fspmachinery.com
Product Service Description:
Plastic molding machinery
Industrial machinery
Material Handling Systems
Powder Coating Ovens
Industrial Paint Lines

F W Tool & Die Works, Inc.
205 Beechtree Blvd
Greenville, SC 29605-5100
Contact: Jerry Pentaleri, Pres.
Telephone: 864-422-1020
Fax: 864-422-9905
Email: ftoolmaker@aol.com / URL:
Product Service Description:
Packaging & automated machinery
Industrial machinery

F&J Specialty Products, Inc.
404 Cypress Road
Ocala, FL 34472
Contact: Frank M. Gavila, President
Telephone: 352-680-1177
Fax: 352-680-1454
Email: fandj@atlantic.net / URL: http://
www.fjspecialty.com
Product Service Description:
Lab Equipment & Apparatus

FET Test Inc
15920 Concord Cir
Morgan Hill, CA 95037-5451
Contact: George Kurtz, Pres.
Telephone: 408-778-0234
Fax: 408-778-0822
Email: facts@facts-inc.com / URL: http://
www.fettest.com
Product Service Description:
Electricity measuring instruments
Automatic transistor testers
Process Control Systems for Rubber &
Plastics Industries

FICI Export
8550 W. Flagler St., Ste. 101
Miami, FL 33144-2037
Contact: Louis Andrews, President
Telephone: 305-554-6046
Fax: 305-554-7013
Email: sales@ficimiami.com / URL:
Product Service Description:
Plastics Materials and Resins
Polysulfides, polysulfones, and synthetic
polymers in primary forms, including
polyxlene resins
Synthetic staple fibers, carded, combed or
otherwise processed for spinning
Gelatin and gelatin derivatives; Isinglass;
Other glue of animal origin

FPA Customs Brokers, Inc.
152-31 134th Ave.,
Jamaica, NY 11434
Contact: Stan Wawrzonek, CEO
Telephone: 718-527-2280
Fax: 718-276-3345
Email: www.fpajfk@aol.com / URL: http://
www.fpajfk.com
Product Service Description:
Customs Broker
Freight & Cargo Transportation

FTC
1165 Walnut Ave
Chula Vista, CA 91911-2621
Contact: Max Friedheim, Mktg. Mgr.
Telephone: 619-575-7155
Fax: 619-575-4067
Email: ftcn1@aol.com / URL:
Product Service Description:
Manufactures steamers for cleaning and
degreasing small parts; sells tools, supplies
and equipment : Service industry machinery
Industrial machinery & equipment

Fab Industries Inc
2401 S 49th Ave
Phoenix, AZ 85043-8107
Contact: Lewis Weaver, Pres.
Telephone: 602-352-0644
Fax: 602-352-0500
Email: info@enviro-cool.com / URL: http://
www.enviro-cool.com
Product Service Description:
Manufactures restaurant equipment— sinks,
tables, shelves and hoods; enviro-cool;
evaporative cooling
Precision sheet metal & enclosures

Fab-Tech Industries Of Brevard Inc.
435 Gus Hipp Blvd
Rockledge, FL 32955-4810
Contact: Seth Updegraff III,
Pres., Secy-Treas.
Telephone: 407-633-6040
Fax: 407-636-9073
Product Service Description:
Sheet metal fabrication & precision
machining job shop
Sheet metal work
Industrial machinery

Fabor Fourslide, Inc.
PO Box 2420
Waterbury, CT 06722-2420
Contact: George Strobel, Jr., Pres., Dave
Bartolmeo, Engineer
Telephone: 203-753-4380
Fax: 203-755-9263
Email: dave@faborfourslideinc.com / URL:
http://www.fourslideinc.com
Product Service Description:
Four slide parts
Metal stampings
Wire forming

Fabreeka International Inc
696 W Amity Rd
Boise, ID 83705-5401
Contact: Toby Grindstaff, Br. Mgr.
Telephone: 208-342-4681
Fax: 208-343-8043
Email: fabboi@babreeke.com / URL: http://
www.fabreeka.com
Product Service Description:
Manufacturer & Fabricator of
Rubber, Plastic, PVC, & Urethane
Flat, Cleated & Special Profile
Conveyor Belting

Fabrication Specialties
108 E Jackson St
Joliet, IL 60432-1723
Contact: Bob Okroi, Sales Mgr.
Telephone: 815-726-2322
Fax: 815-726-7070
Email: fsi@fabricationspecialties.com / URL:
http://www.fabricationspecialties.com
Product Service Description:
Thermal & Acoustical Insulation

Fabtron Corp.
1820 Sprott St
Auburn, IN 46706-3429
Contact: Kevin Marquardt, Pres.
Telephone: 219-925-5770
Fax: 219-925-9553
Email: fabtron@fabtroncorp.com / URL:
http://www.fabtroncorp.com
Product Service Description:
Engine oil tank reservoirs & metal fabrication
Screens - Hammers (Agricultural
Replacement Parts)

Facemakers Inc.
140 5th St.
Savanna, IL 61074
Contact: Alan St. George, Pres.
Telephone: 815-273-3944
Fax: 815-273-3966
Email: facemakers@aol.com / URL: http://
members.aol.com/facemakers/f.html
Product Service Description:
Costumes & mascots
Videos for Children

Facemate Corporation
880 Johnnie Dodds Blvd., Suite 4
Mt. Pleasant, SC 29464
Contact: Robert Mcadam, Sr., V.P. Global
Markets
Telephone: 843-884-6061
Fax: 843-884-6042
Email: rcmhc57@aol.com / URL: http://
www.facematecorp.com
Product Service Description:
Textile Manufacturer, Weave, Finish, Diecut,
Dye, Nap, Etc.
Interlining Fabrics

Facial Concepts Inc.
PO Box 99
Blue Bell, PA 19422-0099
Contact: William F. Hellings, Pres.
Telephone: 610-539-5869
Fax: 610-539-9430
Email: facialflex@aol.com / URL: http://
www.facialconcepts.com
Product Service Description:
Facial exercise equipment

Factory Automation Systems, Inc.
1902 Providence Ct
College Park, GA 30337-6611
Contact: Ross Pryor, Pres.
Telephone: 770-996-6955
Fax: 770-996-7186
Email: carlosr@csi.com / URL: http://
www.factoryautomation.com
Product Service Description:
Electrical control panels
Switchgear & switchboard apparatus
Software development & integration
Control systems integration

Facts, Inc.
2737 Front St
Cuyahoga Falls, OH 44221-1904
Contact: Thomas W. Fisher III, Pres.
Telephone: 330-928-2332
Fax: 330-928-3018
Email: gkurtz@fettest.com / URL: http://
www.facts-inc.com
Product Service Description:
Relays & industrial controls
Industrial automation control systems

Fagen's Building Center
9824 Ideal Ln
Hudson, FL 34667-4913
Contact: David Simon, GM
Telephone: 727-868-1874
Fax: 727-862-5887
Product Service Description:
Wooden trusses & doors : Structural wood
members : Millwork

Faip North America Inc.
560 S Vermont St
Palatine, IL 60067-6948
Contact: Gus Alexander, Pres.
Telephone: 847-882-6601
Fax: 847-882-7229
Email: faip@ix.netcom / URL: http://
www.faipnorthamerican.com
Product Service Description:
Pressure washers & pumps
Fluid power valves & hose fittings
High pressure hose & air compressor hose

Fair Manufacturings, Inc.(Mfr)
P.O. Box 306
Menno, SD 57045 Usa
Contact: Norma Fair, Vice President
Telephone: 605/387-2389
Fax: 605-387-2436
Email: wilddog@fairmfg.com / URL: http://
www.fairmfg.com
Product Service Description:
Snowblowers, Commercial
Snow Body Insert

Fair-Rite Products Corp.
1 Commercial Rd.
Wallkill, NY 12589
Contact: Carol Rapp, Int'l Sales
Telephone: 914-895-2055
Fax: 914-895-2629
Email: ferrites@fair-rite.com / URL: http://
www.fair-rite.com
Product Service Description:
Ferrite cores

Fairbanks Morse Pump Corp.
PO Box 6999
Kansas City, KS 66106-0999
Contact: Mike Medhurst, Hum. Res. Mgr.
Telephone: 913-371-5000
Fax: 913-371-2272
Email: / URL: http://www.pentair.com
Product Service Description:
Pumps & pumping equipment
Industrial & municipal pumps

Fairey Arlon Inc.
PO Box 807
Sturtevant, WI 53177-0807
Contact: William S. Dawson, Pres.
Telephone: 414-886-0888
Fax: 414-886-6099
Email: webmaster@faireyarlon.com / URL:
http://www.faireyarlon.com
Product Service Description:
Hydraulic filters

FalconRoc Management Services, Inc.
645 Chatham Rd.,
Somerdale, NJ 08083
Contact: Rodney W. Falkenstein, President
Telephone: 800-320-3656
Fax: 609-346-2445
Email: general@falconroc.com / URL: http://www.falconroc.com
Product Service Description:
Transporation for cargo

Famarco Ltd. Inc./B & K International
PO Box 5152
Virginia Beach, VA 23471-0152
Contact: Bruce Martin, Pres.,
Telephone: 757-460-3573
Fax: 757-460-2621
Product Service Description:
Food preparations
Spices & botanicals
Carob powder & products

Fancort Industries, Inc.
31 Fairfield Ave
West Caldwell, NJ 07006-7603
Contact: Ron Corey, Pres.
Telephone: 973-575-0610
Fax: 973-575-9234
Email: fancort@worldnet.att.net / URL: http://www.fancort.com
Product Service Description:
Form & trim tooling
Dies, tools, jigs & fixtures_special
PCB Storage & Transport Racks
Solder Recovery System
PCB Assembly Fixtures
PCB Depaneling Machines

Far West Tech Health Physics
330 S Kellogg Ave Ste D
Goleta, CA 93117-3814
Contact: Waldo O Wilde, Pres.
Telephone: 805-964-3615
Fax: 805-964-3162
Email: wilde@fwt.com / URL: http://www.fwt.com
Product Service Description:
Manufactures instrumentation for detection of ionizing radiation

Farbest Foods, Inc.
PO Box 240
Huntingburg, IN 47542-0240
Contact: Greg Meyer, GM
Telephone: 812-683-4200
Fax: 812-683-4226
Email: gmeyer@psci.net / URL:
Product Service Description:
Turkey slaughtering & processing
Fresh / Frozen Meats - Parts

Faria Corp.
385 Norwich-New London Tpke.
Uncasville, CT 06382-0983
Contact: D. BlackburnCEO
Telephone: 860-848-9271
Fax: 860-848-2704
Email: / URL:
Product Service Description:
Instruments to Measure Electricity
Motor vehicle parts and accessories
Electronic Programmable Speedometers
Tachmoteters : Tach/hourmeters
Mechanical Pressure Gages : Temperature
Gages : Warning Light Clusters :Voltmeters
Ammeters

Farm & Ranch Systems South, Llc.
PO Box 847
Moultrie, GA 31776-0847
Contact: Dick Friedlander, Ptnr. & GM
Telephone: 912-985-9188
Fax: 912-890-2155
Product Service Description:
Irrigation & livestock equipment

Farmers Rice Cooperative
PO Box 15223
Sacramento, CA 95851-1223
Contact: Kirk Messick, V.P. - Marketing
Telephone: 916-923-5100
Fax: 916-920-3321
Email: messick@farmersrice.com / URL:
Product Service Description:
Milled Rice, Export
Rice Byproducts, Export

Farmland Transportation Inc.
P.O. Box 7305, Dept. 173
Kansas City, MO 64116
Contact: Mike Davis, General Manager
Telephone: 800/356-7284
Fax: 816-891-7473
Product Service Description:
Freight Transportation Broker, Us/Canada, International

Farrel Corp.
25 Main St
Ansonia, CT 06401-1605
Contact: Alberto Shaio, Sr. V-P., GM
Telephone: 203-736-5500
Fax: 203-735-6267
Email: ashaio@farrel.com / URL: http://www.farrel.com
Product Service Description:
Industrial machinery : Rubber & plastics compounding equipment, batch & continuous mixers, pelletizers, extruders

Fast Air Carrier S.A.
P.O. Box 520846 AMF
Miami, FL 33152
Contact: Evelyn Alfonso, Sales Manager
Telephone: 1-800-327-2578
Fax: 305-870-0429
Email: ealfons@fast-air.com / URL:
Product Service Description:
Air Freight Forwarders

Fata Hunter, Inc.
6147 Rivercrest Dr.
Riverside, CA 92507
Contact: A. Tropeano, President / CEO
Telephone: 909-653-1440
Fax: 909-653-5260
Email: fatahunker@compuserve.com / URL: http://www.fatagroup.it
Product Service Description:
Secondary Aluminum
Process lines - steel

Fathoms Plus
P.O. Box 6307
San Diego, CA 92166-0307
Contact: John Tarantino, Owner
Telephone: 619-222-8385
Fax: 619-222-8247
Email: fathoms@pacbell.net / URL: web.home.pacbell.net/fathoms
Product Service Description:
Shellfish Traps, lobster, shrimp, crab, prawns
Line fishing tackle, nets , decoy birds and similar hunting equipment; Parts and accessories : Crab Traps : Shrimp Traps
Prawn Traps : Lobster Traps

Faultless Caster Division
1421 N. Garvin St.
Evansville, IN 47711-4687
Contact: Scott Love, V.P. Sales & Mktg.
Telephone: 812-425-1011
Fax: 800-322-9329
Email: fcaster@faultlesscaster.com / URL: http://www.faultlesscaster.com
Product Service Description:
Caster & Wheels
Furniture Hardware, Office Chair Mech.
Materials Handling Equipment

Fay & Quartermaine Machining
2745 Seaman Ave
El Monte, CA 91733-1935
Contact: David A. Cary, V.President
Telephone: 626-579-3829
Fax: 626-579-3007
Email: planemaker@earthlink.net / URL:
Product Service Description:
Precision CNC machining of aircraft, missile and commercial parts; short- to long-run production; castings : Guided missile & space vechicle parts & equipment

Fedco Electronics Inc.
PO Box 1403
Fond Du Lac, WI 54936-1403
Contact: Stephen P. Victor Jr., Pres.
Telephone: 920-922-6490
Fax: 920-922-6750
Email: sales@fedcoelectronics.com / URL: http://www.fedcoelectronics.com
Product Service Description:
Battery packs & batteries
Batteries_storage
Batteries & Battery Packs for Computers

Feeley Company, Inc.
232 Water St
Quincy, MA 02169-6534
Contact: J Feeley, Pres, Stephen Feely, VP
Telephone: 617-773-1711
Fax: 617-479-0492
Email: / URL:
Product Service Description:
Metal coating & allied services
Coating, Engraving, Enameling, Powder Coating

Fermented Products
P.O. Box 1483
Mason City, IA 50402
Contact: Stan Zinnel, President
Telephone: 515/423-1460
Fax: 515-423-0832
Email: intlwhey@fermented-products.com
Product Service Description:
Animal Feed
Feeds, Prepared

Ferrer Brokers, Inc.
9840 Via De La Amistad, Ste. A
San Ysidro, CA 92173-3226
Contact: Leonor Ferrer, President
Telephone: 619-661-6755
Fax: 619-661-6758
Email: ferrerbrokers.com / URL:
Product Service Description:
Customs Broker

Ferry Roberts Nut
20493 Yosemite Blvd.
Waterford, CA 95386-9506
Contact: Dan Mallory, Jr, Owner
Telephone: 209-874-3247
Product Service Description:
Edible Nuts

Fiber Mark Inc.
161 Wellington Rd
Brattleboro, VT 05302 USA
Contact: John Field, Latin Amreica Saels Manager
Telephone: 802-257-5987
Fax: 802-257-5912
Email: jfield@www.fibermark.com / URL: http://www.fibermark.com
Product Service Description:
Premium Cover Materials & Binding Products : For Offic e, School & Industrial Applications : Fitter Media for Automotive & Industrial Applications : Saturated & Coated Substrates for Tape Applications

Fiber Master Inc./Thermocon Inc.
PO Box 1712
Monroe, LA 71210-1712
Contact: Max Meinel, Pres.
Telephone: 318-323-1337
Fax: 318-323-1338
Email: fmtcom@iamerica.net / URL: http://www.thermocon.com
Product Service Description:
Cellulose insulation
Cellulose Spray Acoustic Insulation

Fiberesin Industries, Inc.
PO Box 88, 37031 E. Wisconsin Ave
Oconomowoc, WI 53066-0088
Contact: Todd Schwaba, VP Sales & Mktg.
Telephone: 414-567-4427
Fax: 414-567-4814
Email: / URL:
Product Service Description:
Wood Lockers Plastic Laminate
Racquetball Court Wall & Ceiling Panels
Squash Court Wall Panels

Fibrotek Industries Inc
1840 Boston Ave
Longmont, CO 80501-7930
Contact: Susan Routt, Pres.
Telephone: 303-772-0352
Fax: 303-772-4250
Email: / URL:
Product Service Description:
Manufactures cleanroom & ESD (anti-static) garmetns including
Coveralls, lab coats, frocks & hoods for the pharmaceutical, medical,
Aerospace, semiconductor & automotive industries.

Field Equipment & Service Co.
701 Sampson St
Houston, TX 77003-3397
Contact: R. C. Howard, V-P., Opers., Sales & Mktg.
Telephone: 713-227-3280
Fax: 713-247-9619
Email: dickhl@flash.net / URL: http://www.field-equipment-svc-co.com
Product Service Description:
Portable Inplace Machining
General Machining & Fabrication
Welding

Fiero Enterprises, Inc.
201 Nw 5th Ave # 205
Hallandale, FL 33009-4019
Contact: J. Fiero, Pres.
Telephone: 954-454-5004
Fax: 954-454-5007
Email: / URL:
Product Service Description:
Water Walls / Columns made into store fixtures

Filenco Div.
65 Industrial Park Cir
Rochester, NY 14624-2403
Contact: Basil J. Michel, Pres.
Telephone: 716-426-1310, 800-333-7937
Fax: 716-426-2164
Email: jsjfil@frontiernet.net / URL: http://
www.filenco.com
Product Service Description:
Compressed air filters & dryers

Filler Specialties, Inc.
440 100th Ave
Zeeland, MI 49464-2061
Contact: Jim Geib, Sales & Marketing
Telephone: 616-772-9235
Fax: 616-772-4544
Email: rslagh@filler-specialties.com / URL:
Product Service Description:
Capping Equipment
Liquid Filling Systems

Fillette Green Shipping Services (USA) Corp.
3333 W. Kennedy Blvd, Ste 207
Tampa, FL 33609-2953
Contact: Dennis M. Martin, Assistant Vice
President
Telephone: 813-348-1481
Fax: 813-348-1400
Email: dmm@fillettegreen.com / URL: http://
www.fillettegreen.com
Product Service Description:
Freight Transportation Arrangement

Filpro Corporation
P.O. Box 374
West Point, PA 19486
Contact: Sales, *
Telephone: 215-646-5800
Fax: 215-641-5817
Email: filpro1@djs.com / URL: http://
www.filpro.com
Product Service Description:
Filtration Products, Air & Gas
Filtration Products, Liquid
Air Intake Filters
Air Brakes, Railroad
Vacuum Pumps
Filters, Air

Filtrine Manufacturing Company
15 Kit Street
Kaene, NH 03431
Contact: Phillip Tussing, Intl. Sales
Telephone: 603-352-5500
Fax: 603-352-0330
Email: filtrine@top.monad.net / URL: http://
www.filtrine.com
Product Service Description:
Process Liquid Chillers
Drinking Fountains
Ultraviolet Water Sterilizers
Water Purification Equipment

Fine Craft Unlimited
60933 Joes Rd.
Hatley, WI 54440
Contact: Michael Hemauer, Owner
Telephone: 715-446-2301
Fax: 715-446-2305
Email: hemauer@dwave.net / URL: http://
www.finecraftunlitmited.com
Product Service Description:
Commercial & residential wooden furniture &
fixtures
Furniture_wood household
Office furniture_wood
Partitions & fixtures_wood

Fine Line Interiors
311 E 77th Ave
Anchorage, AK 99518-3020
Contact: James Dixon, Owner
Telephone: 907-349-4442
Fax: 907-349-4426
Email: / URL:
Product Service Description:
Upholstered aircraft furniture & wing covers
Furniture & fixtures, upholstered boat &
interiors

Fingers Inc
853 Via Alondra
Camarillo, CA 93012-8046
Contact: Len Indelicato, Pres, Emile
Lemoime, VP Int'l
Telephone: 805-987-7771
Fax: 805-987-7775
Email: / URL:
Product Service Description:
Manufactures nail care products,
artificial nails
Nail polish, bear shape bottles
Nail polish, cat shpe bottles

Finish Thompson Inc.
921 Greengarden Rd
Erie, PA 16501-1525
Contact: H. David Bowes, Pres., CEO
Telephone: 814-455-4478
Fax: 814-455-8518
Email: finish@erie.net / URL: http://
www.finishthompson.com
Product Service Description:
Solvent & coolant distillation equipment
Industrial Pumps

Finish Thompson, Inc.
921 Greengarden Rd.
Erie, PA 16501-1525
Contact: H. David Bowes, Chief Executive
Officer
Telephone: 814-455-4478
Fax: 814-455-8518
Email: / URL:
Product Service Description:
Dram / Barre Pumps
Plastic Centrifugal Pumps
Stainless Steel Centrifugal Pumps
Solvent Recovery Equipment
Magnetic Drive Sealless Pumps

Finishes Unlimited
PO Box 69
Sugar Grove, IL 60554-0069
Contact: Henry W. Godshalk, Pres.
Telephone: 630-466-4881
Fax: 630-466-1064
Email: / URL: http://
www.finishsunlimited.com
Product Service Description:
Paints
Paints & allied products

Finley & Associates P.A.
1645 Palm Beach Lakes Blvd. S. 520
West Palm Beach, FL 33401-2216
Contact: Chandler R. Finley,
Telephone: 407-478-9930
Fax: 407-478-9945
Email: cfinley2@bellsouth.com / URL:
Product Service Description:
Legal Services International
Legal Services, Immigration & Natural.
Legal Services, Import & Export

Finn Tool & Instruments Inc
8758 Remmet Ave
Canoga Park, CA 91304-1518
Contact: Hans Jucker, Pres.
Telephone: 818-341-4485
Fax: 818-341-6220
Email: / URL:
Product Service Description:
Precision machining (Job-Shop) Prototypes &
Experimental Parts for the Aerospace
Manufacturer of precision shop accessories

Fire Equipment, Inc
88 Hicks Ave
Medford, MA 02155-6319
Contact: R. William Murphy, Pres.
Telephone: 781-391-8050
Fax: 781-391-8835
Email: billmurphy@firefire.com / URL: http://
www.firefire.com
Product Service Description:
Clean agent fire suppression systems

Fireboy - Xintex
P.O. Box 152
Grand Rapids, MI 49501-0152
Contact: Larry Akins, President
Telephone: 616-454-8337
Fax: 616-454-8256
Email: fireboy@fireboy-Xintex.com / URL:
http://www.Fireboy-Xintex.com
Product Service Description:
Automatic Fire Extinguisher Systems
Vapor Detection Equipment - Gasoline, Co,
Propane

Firefreeze Worldwide, Inc.
270 Rte. 46
Rockaway, NJ 07866
Contact: Stephanie Giessler,
Vice President
Telephone: 973-627-0722
Fax: 973-627-2982
Email: info@firefreeze.com / URL: http://
www.firefreezeww.com
Product Service Description:
Fire suppressing & retarding agents & odor
eliminators

Firman Pinkerton
P.O. Box 2216
Wenatchee, WA 98807
Contact: Bob Rogers, President
Telephone: 509-662-6055
Fax: 509-663-4387
Email: produce@produceusa.com / URL:
http://www.produceusa.com
Product Service Description:
Fresh Fruits and Vegetables
Onions and shallots, fresh or chilled
Apples & pears, fresh or chilled

First Card Co.
79 Commercial Way
East Providence, RI 02914-1019
Contact: Ron Marks,
Telephone: 401-434-6140
Fax: 401-434-9031
Email: firstcard@ids.net / URL:
Product Service Description:
Plastic jewelry cards
Paperboard Cards
Labels

First Security Bank
41 East 100 South
Salt Lake City, UT 84111-1912
Contact: Ranoy Roberts, VP & Mgr. Int'l
Telephone: 801-246-5604
Fax: 801-246-5992
Email: rroberts@fscnet.com / URL: http://
www.firstsecuritybank.com
Product Service Description:
Natl Commercial Bank Intl Banking
Foreign Currency Exchange
Depository Banking, Letters of Credit
Collection Services

First State Map & Globe Co., Inc.
12 Mary Ella Dr
Wilmington, DE 19805-1548
Contact: Patrick Keane, Pres., Pur. Agt.
Phone: 302-998-6009 / Fax: 302-998-6009
Email: / URL: http://www.globeworld.com
Product Service Description:
Map laminating & wooden plaques
Plastic products : Wood products

First Weigh
210 Tech Dr.
Sanford, FL 32771-6662
Contact: David Lucas, Sales Manager
Phone: 407-330-5000 / Fax: 407-323-5402
Email: firstweigh@aol.com / URL:
Product Service Description:
Measuring Equipment

Fiscal Systems, Inc.
102 Commerce Circle
Madison, AL 35758-1864
Contact: Tom Mitchell, Vice President, Sales
Telephone: 256-772-8920
Fax: 256-772-8590
Email: prmoore@hiwaay.net / URL: http://
www.fis-cal.com
Product Service Description:
Prepackaged Software Design Financial
Prepack Software Design Point of Sale

Fischbach U S A, Inc.
900 Peterson Dr
Elizabethtown, KY 42701-9365
Contact: Reinhard P. Rieder, V-P
Telephone: 502-769-9333
Fax: 502-769-9623
Email: fischbachusa@uky.campus.mci.net
Product Service Description:
Plastic caulking cartridges & accessories

Fish Processors Inc
PO Box 479
Hagerman, ID 83332-0479
Contact: Leo E Ray, Pres.
Telephone: 208-837-6114
Fax: 208-837-6254
Email: fpi@cyberhighway.com
Product Service Description:
Processes rainbow trout, channel catfish,
tilapia, sturgeon and alligator
Fish, fresh or frozen prepared, Alligator hides

Fisher Pumps Inc
2024 E 8th St
Greeley, CO 80631-9786
Contact: Harvey Burrows, Pres.
Telephone: 970-353-6962
Fax: 970-353-0839
Email: rotogrind@ctos.com / URL: http://
www.fisherpumps.com
Product Service Description:
Pumps-irrigation, oilfield, flood, dewater,
industrial : Electric, hyrdaulic, PTO -
stationary, floeting, trailer

Fisher Research Laboratory
200 W Willmott Ave
Los Banos, CA 93635-5501
Contact: Roger Cimino, Pres., GM
Telephone: 209-826-3292
Fax: 209-826-0416
Email: info@fisherlab.com / URL: http://www.fisherlab.com
Product Service Description:
Manufactures metal, leak and voltage detectors; pipe and cable finders; rebar locators

Fisher Space Pen Co
711 Yucca St
Boulder City, NV 89005-1912
Contact: Paul Fisher, Pres.
Telephone: 702-293-3011
Fax: 702-293-6616
Email: fisher@spacepen.com / URL: http://www.spacepen.com
Product Service Description:
Pressurized ball point pens & refills

Fisherman's Wharf Food Product
1401 Elwood St
Los Angeles, CA 90021-2812
Contact: Nick Abood, Pres.
Telephone: 213-746-1541
Fax: 213-746-1542
Product Service Description:
Refrigerated salad dressings, seafood sauces, honey, stuffed baked potatoes

Fishery Products International Inc.
18 Electronics Ave
Danvers, MA 01923-1011
Contact: John D Cummings, Pres.
Telephone: 978-777-2660
Fax: 978-720-5271
Email: jcummings@fpil.com / URL: http://www.fpil.com
Product Service Description:
Fish_fresh or frozen prepared : Fresh and Frozen Packaged Fish : Shrimp frozen, prepared : Shellfish frozen, prepared

Fisk Alloy Wire, Inc.
PO Box 26
Hawthorne, NJ 07507-0026
Contact: Eric Fisk, Pres.
Telephone: 973-427-7550
Fax: 973-427-4585
Email: faw@fiskalloy.com / URL: http://www.fiskalloy.com
Product Service Description:
Bare & electroplated wire
Rolling & drawing, copper alloy

Fitel Lucent Technologies
One Lucent Dr
Carrollton, GA 30117-5261
Contact: John Ervin, Pres. & CEO
Phone: 770-836-0877 / Fax: 770-836-8820
Email: fitelinfo@fitel.com / URL: http://www.fitel.com
Product Service Description:
Fiberoptic cable
Nonferrous wiredrawing & insulating

Fitting House Inc
PO Box 486
Fort Morgan, CO 80701-0486
Contact: Floyd Deal, Pres.
Phone: 970-867-8288 / Fax: 970-867-8280
Product Service Description:
Sells hydraulic hose and fittings; army surplus equipment and forklifts : Rubber Hose
Industrial Hose & Couplings

Five Rivers Electronic Innovations, LLC
PO Box 1830
Greeneville, TN 37744-1830
Contact: Tom Hopson, V-P., Opers.
Telephone: 423-636-5100
Fax: 423-636-5501
Email: tom_hopson@taygrwhite.com / URL: http://www.taylorwhite.com
Product Service Description:
Color televisions & electronic products
Contract manufacturing, electronics; plastic; wood products
Distribution services

Flaghouse, Inc.
601 Flaghouse Drive
Hasbrouck Heights, NJ 07604
Contact: Ms. Leslie Geist, *
Telephone: 201-288-7600
Fax: 201-288-3897
Email: info@flaghouse.com / URL: http://www.flaghouse.com
Product Service Description:
Sports & Recreation Equipment
Rehabilitation Equipment & Orthopedic Equipment

Flagman Of America
PO Box 440
Avon, CT 06001-0440
Contact: Dave Dimesky, Pres.
Telephone: 860-678-0275
Fax: 860-678-8812
Email: ddimesky@aol.com / URL: http://www.flagman.com
Product Service Description:
Flags & banners
Textile products_fabricated
Advertising Specialties (Importing)

Flagship Converters, Inc.
205 Shelter Rock Rd
Danbury, CT 06810-7049
Contact: Michael Davies, Pres.
Telephone: 203-792-0034
Fax: 203-797-0410
Email: / URL:
Product Service Description:
Plastic film
Unsupported plastics film & sheet

Flavor Dynamics, Inc.
400 Apgar Dr Ste L
Somerset, NJ 08873-1154
Contact: Dolf DeRovira, Pres.
Telephone: 732-271-7773
Fax: 732-271-5927
Email: thenose@ix.netcom.com / URL: www.//flavdyn.com
Product Service Description:
Flavoring extracts
Flavoring extracts & syrups
Coffee Flavors
Powdered Beverage Mixes, Cappuccino - Cocoa

Fleck Controls, Inc.
PO Box 730
Brookfield, WI 53008-0730
Contact: Jorge Fernadez, Pres.
Telephone: 414-784-4490
Fax: 414-784-7794
Email: ffernandez@fleckcontrols.com / URL: http://www.fleckcontrols.com
Product Service Description:
Valves & pipe fittings
Water softener control valves
Filter control valves

Fleet Air Industries
PO Box 4836
Oneida, TN 37841-4836
Contact: W. Dale Gordon, Pres., R & D Mgr.
Telephone: 423-569-6965
Fax: 423-569-8009
Email: fleetairceo@highland.net / URL:
Product Service Description:
Automotive & jeep hard tops
Motor vehicle parts & accessories

Fleetwood Enterprises Inc
PO Box 7638
Riverside, CA 92513-7638
Contact: Glenn Kummer, Chrm., CEO
Telephone: 909-351-3500
Fax: 909-351-3690
Email: / URL: http://www.fleetwood.com
Product Service Description:
Manufactured Housing : Motor Homes
Travel Trailers & Slide-In Truck Campers
Folding trailers

Fleming Steel Co.
P.O. Box 1487
New Castle, PA 16103-1487
Contact: Seth Kohn, President
Telephone: 412-658-1511
Fax: 412-658-7018
Email: fleming@ccia.com / URL:
Product Service Description:
Industrial Metal Doors
Airplane Hangar Doors
Craneway doors
Blast doors
Vertical lift doors
Siwng doors
Paint booth doors

Flex-Pak Manufacturing Inc
4540 S Navajo St Unit 4
Englewood, CO 80110-8211
Contact: Allen Irsik, Pres.
Telephone: 303-789-1445
Fax: 303-789-1535
Email: flexpak@msn.com / URL:
Product Service Description:
Manufactures OEM machinery for manufacturing medical gloves, peel pouches & bag-in-box

Flexicell, Inc.
4329 November Ave
Richmond, VA 23231-4309
Contact: Hans Schouten, V.P. of Sales
Telephone: 804-222-1400
Fax: 804-222-1496
Email: flexicell@erols.com / URL: http://www.flexicell.com
Product Service Description:
Robotic packaging equipment
Packaging machinery

Flexicon Corporation
P.O. Box 5269
Phillipsburg, NJ 08865
Contact: David R. Gill,
Telephone: 908-859-4700
Fax: 908-859-4820
Email: sales@flexicon.com / URL: http://www.flexicon.com
Product Service Description:
Dry Bulk Material Conveyors & Systems
Bulk Bag Filling Stations : Weigh Batching Systems : Conveyors & Conveying Equipment : Screw Conveyors : Integrated Process Systems : Drum Dumpers : Dust Collectors : Bulk Bag Unloading Stations
Blending Systems

Flexmaster U S A Inc.
PO Box 40727
Houston, TX 77240-0727
Contact: John R. Weyker, V-P.
Telephone: 713-462-7694
Fax: 713-939-8441
Email: info@flexmasterusa.com / URL: http://www.flexmasterusa.com
Product Service Description:
Sheet metal work
Flexible air conditioning ducts & fittings
Metal work_miscellaneous
Access Doors
Industrial Hose & Duct

Flight Tech, Inc
PO Box 3205
Grand Junction, CO 81502
Contact: Eileen Lassiter, Pres.
Telephone: 1800-221-0348
Email: / URL: http://www.flight-tech.com
Product Service Description:
Records & tapes_prerecorded
Produces home course audio cassettes designed to help applicants pass FAA knowledge test

Flinchbaugh Co., Inc.
390 Eberts Ln
York, PA 17403-1139
Contact: Harry F. Miller, Pres., Fin. & R & D Mgr.
Telephone: 717-848-2418
Fax: 717-843-7385
Email: flinchbaug@aol.com / URL:
Product Service Description:
Wheelchair lifts, chair stair climbs, automatic dumbwaiters & contract machining

Flip Chip Technologies LLC
3701 E University Dr
Phoenix, AZ 85034-7284
Contact: Harry Hollack, Pres.
Telephone: 602-431-6020
Fax: 602-431-6021
Email: / URL:
Product Service Description:
Wafer bumping services
Semiconductors & related devices

Flir Systems Inc
16505 SW 72nd Ave
Portland, OR 97224-7705
Contact: J.Kenneth Stringer, President & CEO
Telephone: 503-684-3731
Fax: 503-684-5452
Email: marketing@flir.com / URL: http://www.flir.com
Product Service Description:
Designs and manufactures thermal imaging systems for search, detection, navigation
Search & navigation equipment
Computer programming services

Flite Technology, Inc.
411 Shearer Blvd
Cocoa, FL 32922-7249
Contact: Ronald Anderson, Pres.,
Telephone: 407-631-2050
Fax: 407-632-1401
Email: feedscrews@flitetech.com / URL: http://www.flitetech.com
Product Service Description:
Extrusion & injection molding equipment, feed screws & barrels
Machinery_general industrial
Machinery_special industry
Metal work_miscellaneous

Flo's Wreaths
RR 1 Box 487
Machias, ME 04654-9764
Contact: Flora Hanscom, Ptnr.
Telephone: 207-255-3094
Fax: 207-255-6059
Email: / URL:
Product Service Description:
Manufacturing Industries : Christmas Wreaths
& Other Holiday Balsalm Products

Flo-Tork Inc. (Mfr)
P.O. Box 68
Orrville, OH 44667-0068
Contact: Thomas M. Leaver, V.P. -Sales
Telephone: 330-682-0100
Fax: 330-683-6857
Email: tmleaver@flo-tork.com / URL: http://
www.flo-tork.com
Product Service Description:
Butterfly Valve Actuators
Power Actuators, Pneumatic
Plug Valve Actuators
Gate & Globe Valve Actuators
Ball Valves Alloy Steel & Other Metals

Flojet Corp
12 Morgan
Irvine, CA 92618-2003
Contact: Chris Pribus, Export Manager
Telephone: 949-859-4945
Fax: 949-859-1153
Email: / URL: http://www.flojet.com
Product Service Description:
Fluid power pumps & motors
Manufactures diaphragm motor pump units,
air-driven pumps and perm magnet motors
Refrigeration & heating equipment

Flomed Corporation
8355 NW 54th Street
Miami, FL 33166
Contact: Fabio Lisboa, V.P./Intl.
Telephone: 305/477-5352
Fax: 305/477-2296
Email: flomed@icanect.net / URL:
Product Service Description:
Medical & Surgical Supplies & Equip.,
Wholesale
Pharmaceutical Products, Wholesale

Flora Distributors, Inc.
1400 S.W. 1st Ct.
Pompano Beach, FL 33069-3206
Contact: John Flora, Owner
Telephone: 954-785-3100
Fax: 954-785-2353
Email: flora@florafoods.com / URL: http://
www.florafoods.com
Product Service Description:
Gourmet - Imported Dry
Cheese - Imported & Domestic

Florida Bolt & Nut Co.
3875 Fiscal Ct Ste 300
Riviera Beach, FL 33404-1707
Contact: Cheryl A. Warner, Pres., Fin. &
Pers. Mgr.
Telephone: 561-842-2658
Fax: 561-540-2658
Email: flabolt@worldnet.att.net / URL:
Product Service Description:
Bolts, Nuts & Screws

Florida Candy Factory, Inc.
721 Lakeview Rd
Clearwater, FL 33756-3422
Contact: Gerald S. Rehm, Pres.,
Scott Rehm, V.P.
Telephone: 727-446-0024
Fax: 727-446-7346
Product Service Description:
Heavenly Delicious Peppermint "Angel Mint"
Chocolate Angel Mint

Florida Food Products, Inc.
PO Box 1300
Eustis, FL 32727-1300
Contact: Jerry P. Brown, Pres.
Telephone: 352-357-4141
Fax: 352-483-3192
Email: flafood@magicnet.net / URL: http://
www.floridafood.com
Product Service Description:
Freeze-dried & concentrated vegetable juices
& aloe vera : Fruits & vegetables, frozen

Florida Wire & Cable Inc.
825 N. Lane Ave.
Jacksonville, FL 32254-2893
Contact: Sam Lande, Sr. VP Sales
Telephone: 904-781-9224
Email: fwcsales@fwcable.com / URL: http://
www.fwcable.com
Product Service Description:
Steel Wire and Related Products: Stranded
wire, ropes and cables, not electrically
insulated, of iron or steel

Flow Boy Manufacturing Co.
P.O. Box 720660
Norman, OK 73070-4500
Contact: Scott Smith, Int'l Div. Mgr.
Telephone: 405-329-3765
Fax: 405-329-8588
Email: flowboy@ionet.net / URL: http://
www.flowboy.com
Product Service Description:
Semi - Trailers

Flower Products Company
PO Box 80268
Athens, GA 30608-0268
Contact: Graham Selick, *
Telephone: 706-549-3300
Fax: 706-548-1278
Product Service Description:
Filling Machine, Post Mix Syrup

Flowery Beauty Products, Inc.
PO Box 4008
Greenwich, CT 06831-0401
Contact: Geoffrey Geils, Pres., Sales & Mktg.
Mgr.
Telephone: 203-661-0995
Fax: 203-661-5630
Email: flowery-info@flowery.com / URL:
Product Service Description:
Fingernail Files
Beauty Products
Pumice Stones
Manicure Products

Floyd's Awning & Canvas Shop
7344 Bandini Blvd
Los Angeles, CA 90040-3323
Contact: Gregory Naiman, Pres.
Telephone: 323-722-1156
Fax: 323-724-3848
Product Service Description:
Canvas & related products
Tents & Canapys

Fluid Dynamics Inc
6595 Odell Pl Ste E
Boulder, CO 80301-3316
Contact: Kurt O Plache, Pres.
Telephone: 303-530-7300
Fax: 303-530-7754
Email: bstone@dynablend.com / URL: http://
www.dynablend.com
Product Service Description:
Manufactures measuring and dispensing
pumps and polymer blending equipment
Measuring & dispensing pumps

Fluid Metering, Inc.
5 Aerial Way, Suite 500
Syosset, NY 11791
Contact: Herb Werner, Marketing Manager
Telephone: 516-922-6050
Fax: 516-624-8261
Product Service Description:
Metering Pumps

Foam Supplies, Inc.
4387 Rider Tr. N.
Earth City, MO 63045
Contact: David G. Keske, Pres, Tim Kirby,
Sales Manager
Telephone: 314-344-3330
Fax: 314-344-3331
Email: fsifoam@aol.com / URL:
Product Service Description:
Urethane foam chemicals, dispensing
equipment & industrial packaging

Focus Electronic Corporation
21078 Commerce Point Dr
Walnut, CA 91789-3051
Contact: Mandy Chen, Mgr.
Telephone: 909-468-5533
Fax: 909-468-5525
Email: sales@focus-usa.com / URL: http://
www.focus-usa.com
Product Service Description:
Manufactures computer keyboards
(distribution office)

Fogg Filler Co.
3455 John F. Donnelly Dr.
Holland, MI 49424-9207
Contact: Chip Mazurek, President
Telephone: 616-786-3644
Fax: 616-786-0350
Email: info@foggfiller.com / URL: http://
www.foggfiller.com
Product Service Description:
Machinery for filling, closing, sealing, bottles

Foil Graphics, Inc.
2600 S 7th St
Keokuk, IA 52632-3532
Contact: George White, President
Telephone: 319-524-3364
Fax: 319-524-3655
Email: gwhite@foilgraphicsinc.com / URL:
Product Service Description:
Metal foil & leaf : Die-cut paper & board

Folding Bleacher Company
PO Box 320
Altamont, IL 62411-0320
Contact: Sales & Marketing,
Telephone: 618-483-6157
Fax: 618-483-5539
Email: fbc@altomont.net / URL: http://
www.foldingbleacher.simple.net.com
Product Service Description:
Gymnasium Bleacher Seating
Wood & Plastic Bleacher Seating
Telescopic Platform Seating

Fonar Corp.
110 Marcus Dr
Melville, NY 11747-4228
Contact: Raymond Damadian, Chrm.
Telephone: 516-694-2929
Fax: 516-249-3734
Email: info@fonar.com / URL: http://
www.fonar.com
Product Service Description:
X-ray apparatus & tubes
Magnetic resonance imaging (MRI) Scanners

Fontana Wholesale Lumber
PO Box 1070
Fontana, CA 92334-1070
Contact: Harold W Logsdon, Pres.
Telephone: 909-350-1214
Fax: 909-350-9623
Email: / URL:
Product Service Description:
Wood preserving

Food Engineering Corporation
2765 Niagara Lane
Plymouth, MN 55447
Contact: Donald Lyman, Dir/Saels Tech
Telephone: 612-559-5200
Fax: 612-559-4657
Email: / URL:
Product Service Description:
Industrial Process Dryers, Conveyor Type
Vibratory Conveyors, Screeners, distrib.

Food Science Laboratories
20 New England Drive, C-1504
Essex Junction, VT 05453-1504
Contact: Carl Bryce, Sales Manager
Telephone: 802/878-5508
Fax: 802-878-0549
Email: / URL:
Product Service Description:
Vitamins, Immune Response / Arthritis

Food Technology Service, Inc.
502 Prairie Mine Rd
Mulberry, FL 33860-9167
Contact: Harley Everett, Ex. V-P., Opers.
Telephone: 941-425-0039
Fax: 941-425-5526
Email: danac69@aol.com / URL:
Product Service Description:
Food irradiation processing
Food products machinery

Foote Axle & Forge Company LLC
3954 Whiteside St
Los Angeles, CA 90063-1615
Contact: Michael F Denton, Jr. VP
Telephone: 323-268-4151
Fax: 323-268-9085
Email: mikesr@footeaxle.com / URL: http://
www.footeaxle.com
Product Service Description:
Manufactures replacement axle shafts
Motor vehicle parts & accessories

Ford Tool & Machining Inc.
2205 Range Rd
Rockford, IL 61111-2761
Contact: David Beto, President
Telephone: 815-633-5727
Fax: 815-633-0380
Email: / URL:
Product Service Description:
Fastener Tooling, Cold Header
Dies, Carbide Header

Foreign Trade Marketing
1279 Starboard Lane
Sarasota, FL 34242
Contact: Karen Bello, Purchasing Director
Telephone: 914-346-9900
Fax: 914-349-8181
Product Service Description:
Groceries, Diapers, General Line: Cosmetics,
Health & Beauty : General Merchandise
Full USA Sourcing

Foreign Trade Zone 42
Orlando Int'l Airport 4101 Lindy Circle
Orlando, FL 32827
Contact: Linda Smith, Cargo Dev Mgr.
Telephone: 407-825-2213
Fax: 407-857-0683
Product Service Description:
Freight & Cargo: Transportation & Insurance

Foreign Trade Zone 72
P.O. Box 51681,
Indianapolis, IN 48251
Contact: Kent R. Ebbing,
Telephone: 317-487-7200
Fax: 317-487-7203
Email: kebbing@baai.com / URL: http://
www.indianapolisairport.com
Product Service Description:
Freight & Cargo Transportation

Forest Packaging Corp
1955 Estes Ave
Elk Grove Village, IL 60007-5415
Contact: Greg Kula, Pres.
Telephone: 847-981-7000
Fax: 847-981-7233
Product Service Description:
Corrugated Cartons
Boxex_Corrugated & Solid Fiber

Forester Rollers
PO Box 2067
Lawrenceville, GA 30046-2067
Contact: Tim Forester, Pres.
Telephone: 770-822-9299
Fax: 770-822-9360
Email: / URL:
Product Service Description:
Fabricated Rubber Products not elsewhere
classified
Printing Trades Machinery & Equipt.
Coated & Laminated Paper , not elsewhere
classified

Forkner Farms / Truline Genetics
Route 1, Box 19
Richards, MO 64778
Contact: Everett Forkner, Owner
Telephone: 417/484-3306
Fax: 417-484-3317
Email: / URL:
Product Service Description:
Livestock Svcs., Swine Breeding Stock

Form Cut Industries, Inc.
197 Mount Pleasant Ave
Newark, NJ 07104-3814
Contact: Ken De Graaf, Adv., PR, Sales &
Mktg. Mgr.
Telephone: 973-483-5154
Fax: 973-483-4512
Email: sales@formcut.com / URL: http://
www.formcut.com
Product Service Description:
Precision wire forms, leads, pins, Swiss
screw machine & cold headed products

Formworks Building Inc
PO Box 1509
Durango, CO 81302-1509
Contact: Dale Pearcey, Pres.
Telephone: 970-247-2100
Fax: 970-247-9190
Email: formworks@rmi.net / URL: http://
www.formworksbuilding.com
Product Service Description:
Manufactures concrete forming systems
Structural Systems for Shelters
Structural Systems for Earth Sheltered
Storage

Forney
3405 Wiley Post Rd.
Carrollton, TX 75006
Contact: Jan Kreminski, President
Telephone: 972-458-6100
Fax: 972-458-6195
Email: / URL: http://www.forneycorp.com
Product Service Description:
Duct burners
Environmental systems & analyzers
Low nox burners
BMS, flame scanners & igniters for all types
of boilers

Forster-Long Inc.
3280 Ramos Cir.
Sacramento, CA 95827-2513
Contact: Peter Quinones, Client Relations
Manager
Telephone: 916-362-3276
Fax: 916-362-5643
Email: clientrelations@forster-long.com /
URL:
Product Service Description:
Publishes legal & judicial direcotories
The American Bar - Canadian Bar - Mexican
Bar - Int'l Bar
The American Bench , Judges of the Nation

Fort Pitt Acquisition
400 Chess Street
Coraopolis, PA 15108
Contact: Dennis Katawczik, *
Telephone: 412/269-2950
Fax: 412-264-5696
Email: / URL:
Product Service Description:
Shampoos
Hair Conditioners
Hair Sprays
Hair Coloring Preparations

Fortress Mfg. Inc.
2225 S. 170th Street
New Berlin, WI 53151-2289
Contact: Richard Clemins, President
Telephone: 414-797-7520
Fax: 414-797-0882
Email: / URL:
Product Service Description:
Wire Formed Products
Screw Machine Products
Fabricated Metal Prod, Cold Headed

Fortress Mfg., Inc. (Mfr)
2225 S. 170th Street
New Berlin, WI 53151
Contact: Richard Clemins, President
Telephone: 414-797-7520
Fax: 414-797-0882
Email: / URL:
Product Service Description:
Wire Formed Products
Screw Machine Products
Fabricated Metal Prod., Cold Headed

Forum Communications Systems, Inc.
1223 N Glenville Dr
Richardson, TX 75081-2412
Contact: Gayne Ek, Pres., Fin. & Opers. Mgr.
Telephone: 972-680-0700
Fax: 972-680-2700
Email: info@forum-com.com / URL: http://
www.forum-com.com
Product Service Description:
Teleconferencing peripherals
Telephone & telegraph apparatus

Foster Co., L. B.
6500 Langfield Rd
Houston, TX 77092-1099
Contact: Robert Young, GM
Telephone: 713-466-2745
Fax: 713-466-2736
Email: / URL: http://www.foster.com
Product Service Description:
Pipe & fittings_fabricated
Pump columns
Couplings
Inner column

Foster Corp.
PO Box 997
Dayville, CT 06241-0997
Contact: Larry Acquarulo, Pres.
Telephone: 860-774-3964
Fax: 860-779-0805
Email: l.acqua@snet.net / URL: http://
www.fostercomp.com
Product Service Description:
Custom compound purchased resins
Thermoplastic resin compounding
Critical medical compounds
Specialty wire & cable compounds

Fostoria Industries Inc. (Mfr)
1200 N. Main Street
Fostoria, OH 44830
Contact: Steve Fruth, *
Telephone: 419-435-9201
Fax: 419-435-0842
Email: gpfostor@bright.net / URL: http://
www.fostoriaindustries.com
Product Service Description:
Machine Tool Lighting
Lighting Fixtures, Industrial
Electric Infrared Heating Equipment
Electric Infrared Ovens, Industrial Process

Fourjay Industries, Inc.
3400 Stop Eight Rd.
Dayton, OH 45414
Contact: M.W. Frawley, Director/Sales
Telephone: 937-890-6444
Fax: 937-890-1692
Email: 4j@fourjay.com / URL: http://
www.fourjay.com
Product Service Description:
Loudspeakers & Enclosures
Speaker Baffles & Mounting Dev., Metal
Speaker Enclosures

Fowler Cabinet & Hardware Co
5433 S Clovis Ave
Fresno, CA 93725-9794
Contact: Dorothy Tharp, Pres.
Telephone: 209-834-2569
Fax:
Email: / URL:
Product Service Description:
Manufactures custom kitchen cabinets and
bathroom vanities
Kitchen cabinets_wood

Fox Laminating Co., Inc.
84 Custer St
W Hartford, CT 06110-1909
Contact: Joe Fox, Pres., Sales & Mktg. Mgr.
Telephone: 860-953-4884
Fax: 860-953-1277
Email: foxlam@erols.com / URL:
Product Service Description:
Laminators, Cameras & ID Supplies

Francis Torque Tools
735 Peters Road
Harvey, LA 70058
Contact: Dale L. Francis, Pres.
Telephone: 504-368-7153
Fax: 504-368-7178
Email: info@francistorque.com / URL: http://
www.francistorque.com
Product Service Description:
Hydraulic torque wrenches

Frank B. Ross Co., Inc. (Mfr)
22 Halladay Street
Jersey City, NJ 07304
Contact: Donald Ayerlee, Vice President
Telephone: 201/433-4512
Fax: 201-332-3555
Email: / URL:
Product Service Description:
Chemical Waxes (Natural)

Franklin Brass Manufacturing
PO Box 4887
Carson, CA 90749-4887
Contact: Howard Levy, Pres., COO
Telephone: 310-885-3200
Fax: 310-885-5739
Email: floriaq@franklinbrass.com / URL:
http://www.franklinbrass.com
Product Service Description:
Metal sanitary ware
Manufactures bathroom accessories and
bathroom safety products
Plumbing fixture fittings & trim

Franklin Hardwoods, Inc.
PO Box 134
Abbeville, AL 36310-0134
Contact: Tommie Parker, Plt. Mgr.
Telephone: 334-585-5059
Fax: 334-585-6393
Email: / URL:
Product Service Description:
Veneer board
Wood products

Franklin Industrial Minerals
612 10th Ave. N.
Nachville, TN 37203
Contact: VP Sales,
Telephone: 615-259-4222
Fax: 615-726-2693
Email: acaulkins@frankmin.com / URL: http:/
/www.frankmin.com
Product Service Description:
Crushed stone
Cut stone & stone products
Alumina Trihydrate

Frasca International, Inc.
906 Airport Rd
Urbana, IL 61802-7375
Contact: Rudy Frasca, Pres.
Telephone: 217-344-9200
Fax: 217-344-9207
Email: postmaster@frasca.com / URL: http://
www.frasca.com
Product Service Description:
Pilot ground instrument trainers

Frazier Industries Inc.
5204 Mills Indl. Pkwy.
North Ridgeville, OH 44039
Contact: George Frazier Sr., Pres., Fin., MIS
& R & D Mgr.
Telephone: 440-327-4830
Fax: 440-327-2245
Email: frazier@ohio.net / URL:
Product Service Description:
General machining job shop
Fabricating / Welding

Free Choice Enterprises
10055 County K
Lancaster, WI 53813
Contact: Mark Bader, Pres.
Telephone: 608-723-7977
Fax: 608-723-2035
Email: fcepcii.net
Product Service Description:
Livestock feed: Feeds_prepared

Freedom Driving Aids
23855 W Andrew Rd
Plainfield, IL 60544-9588
Contact: Richard Rosebush, Owner
Telephone: 815-254-2000
Fax: 815-254-2001
URL: http://www.freedomdrivingaids.com
Product Service Description:
Disabled drivers wheelchair lifts accessible
vans & hand controls

Freezing System Inc.
17625 130th Ave. NE, Suite 101
Woodinville, WA 98072
Contact: S.A Sterling, Vice Pres./Sales
Telephone: 425-486-8852
Fax: 425-483-0759
Email: fsi@freezingsystems.com / URL: http:/
/www.freezingsystems.com
Product Service Description:
Manufactures Iqf Tunnel & Spiral Freezers
Refrigeration & Heating Equipment

French Connection, The
101 Judith Lane
Media, PA 19063-4924
Contact: Carol C. Macomber, Owner
Telephone: 610/891-1983
Fax: 610-891-7870
Email: macuse@aol.com / URL: http://
www..bestofpa.com/frenchconnection/
index.htm
Product Service Description:
Translation Services French <—> English
Commercial Research Via Minitel

Fresca Mexican Foods Inc.
11193 Emerald St.
Boise, ID 83713
Contact: Rick Kay, Marketing
Telephone: 208-376-6922
Fax: 208-375-2330
Product Service Description:
Corn Tortillas & Corn Tortilla Chips
Flour Tortillas, Homestyle, Die Cut, Hand
Stretched

**Friendly Appropriate Solar
Technologies**
800 Loyola Dr.
Los Altos, CA 94024
Contact: Sales & Marketing,
Phone: 650-948-8294 / Fax: 650-948-8294
Email: aligtenber@aol.com
URL: http://www.bali-i.com/fast-solar
Product Service Description:
Solar cookers / dryers / water pasteurizers

Friendly Public Warehouses Inc.
5992 Griggs Rd.,
Houston, TX 77023
Contact: Sales & Marketing,
Telephone: 713-242-0594
Fax: 713-242-0604
Email: hve@sprynet.com / URL:
Product Service Description:
Warehouse Storage, Long & Short Term /
Food & Hazmat Certified
Freight & Container Transportation &
Transloading
Trucking Statewide to any point in lower 48 /
Hazmat & T.A.B.C. Licensed
Four locations w / 24 hour electronic security

Fritz Companies
4980 Amelia Earhart Drive
Salt Lake City, UT 84116-2861
Contact: Ross Kirkley, District Manager
Telephone: 801-531-0369
Fax: 801-531-0462
Email: ross.kirkley@frtiz.com / URL: http://
www.fritz.com
Product Service Description:
Freight Forwarder
Customs Brokers

Fritz Maritime Agencies
111 Pine St., Ste. 1605,
San Francisco, CA 94111
Contact: Gregory Canonica, President
Telephone: 415-362-6266
Fax: 415-986-4491
Email: info@fritzmaritimeagencies.com /
URL: http://www.fritzmaritimeagencies.com
Product Service Description:
Freight & Cargo Transportation
Steamship Agent

Frontier Soups
970 N Shore Dr
Lake Bluff, IL 60044-2202
Contact: Trisha Anderson, Pres.
Telephone: 847-615-0551
Fax: 847-615-0561
Email: info@frontiersoups.com / URL: http://
www.frontiersoups.com
Product Service Description:
Dehydrated soups
Dehydrated fruits, vegetables & soups
Pasta Salad Mixes

Frontier Trophy Buckles
PO Box 58
Aztec, NM 87410-0058
Contact: Vicki Felder, Ptnr.
Telephone: 505-334-7136
Fax: 505-334-2923
Email: frontierbuckels@acrnet.com / URL:
http://www.frontierbuckles.com
Product Service Description:
Custom hand-crafted buckles

Frontline Systems
20817 N 19th Ave Ste 5
Phoenix, AZ 85027-3560
Contact: Anne Heady, Pres.
Telephone: 602-581-5188
Fax: 602-581-5285
Email: frontline@forntlinesystems.com /
URL:
Product Service Description:
Manufactures point-of-sale equipment for the
fast food industry
Color LCD Displays

Frugal Water Corporation
1130 E Missouri Ave Ste 202
Phoenix, AZ 85014-2714
Contact: Richard L Schnakenberg, Pres.
Telephone: 602-264-3211
Fax: 602-230-2557
Email: FrugalTTF@aol.com / URL:
Product Service Description:
Manufactures plumbing fixture fittings and
plastic plumbing fixtures

Fruit-A-Freeze Inc
12919 Leyva St
Norwalk, CA 90650-6855
Contact: David MacDonald, VP Sales
Telephone: 562-407-2881
Fax: 562-407-2889
Email: fafdavemac@fruitafreeze.com / URL:
Product Service Description:
Fruit Bars & Chocolate Dipped Fruit Bars

Frye Tech, Inc.
10550 New York Ave
Urbandale, IA 50322
Contact: Russ Dohrmann, President
Telephone: 515-331-6100
Fax: 515-331-6106
Email: / URL:
Product Service Description:
Carbon Paper
Carbon Paper Ink
MICR Ribbons

Fujipoly America Corp.
PO Box 679
Kenilworth, NJ 07033-0679
Contact: Robert Bjornsen Jr., Marketing Mgr.
Telephone: 908-298-3850
Fax: 908-298-1232
Email: fujipoly@aol.com / URL: http://
www.fujipoly.com
Product Service Description:
Silicone rubber electronic components
Electronic components
Thermal insulators
Elastomeric connectors

Fuller & Son Co., George H.
PO Box 620
Pawtucket, RI 02862-0620
Contact: F. Paul Mooney, Pres.
Telephone: 401-722-6530
Fax: 401-723-1720
Email: GHF1858@aol.com / URL: http://
www.fullerfindings.com
Product Service Description:
Jewelry findings
Jewelers' materials & lapidary work
Coin Jewelry

Fusion Coatings Inc.
PO Box 143
Winona, MN 55987-0143
Contact: Dick Whitaker, Sales Manager
Telephone: 507-452-1112
Fax: 507-452-9099
Email: wn5052@softshare.com / URL: http://
www.fusioncoatings.com
Product Service Description:
PVC coated metal outdoor residential &
commercial furniture & hog containment
flooring : Plastic materials & resins
Furniture & fixtures

**Future Automation Inc - A Technic
Division**
5400 N Commerce Ave
Moorpark, CA 93021-1762
Contact: Heinz Schlenker, Pres.
Telephone: 805-378-0030
Fax: 805-532-1344
Email: heinzs@futureautomation.com / URL:
http://www.technic.com
Product Service Description:
Automated & manual wafer plating systems
Manufactures automated & manual I.C. strip
plating systems for the semi conductor
industry

Future Packaging Inc
1500 Duane Ave
Santa Clara, CA 95054-3413
Contact: R A Vega, Pres.
Telephone: 408-988-5444
Fax: 408-986-8682
Email: / URL:
Product Service Description:
Builds crates; packaging service
Nailed wood boxes & shook
Packing & crating service
Industrial wood products
Hazardous material packing
Corrugated & foam packs
Packaging material

Future Primitive Designs Ltd
2219 S 48th St
Tempe, AZ 85282-1010
Contact: Susan Michelson, Pres.
Telephone: 602-431-2100
Fax: 602-431-6800
Email: kl@futureprimitive.com / URL: http://
www.futureprimitive.com
Product Service Description:
Jewelry_costume
Manufactures costume jewelry, novelties and
ornaments
Manufacturing industries

G & H Diversified Mfg. Inc.
11660 Brittmoore Park Dr
Houston, TX 77041-6917
Contact: Hal Pastner, VP Sales & Mktg.
Telephone: 713-849-2111
Fax: 713-849-2430
Email: hpastner@ghdiversi.com / URL: http://
www.ghdiversi.com
Product Service Description:
Laser Cutting of Flat & Tubular Metals

G D Branch Corp
92 Argonaut
Aliso Viejo, CA 92656-4116
Contact: Gary D Branch, Pres.
Telephone: 949-588-6399
Fax: 949-699-1331
Email: gary@gdbranch.com / URL:
Product Service Description:
Manufactures electronic test equipment
Electricity measuring instruments

G E I Mateer-Burt Co., Inc.
700 Pennsylvania Dr
Exton, PA 19341-1129
Contact: Stephen Murphy, V-P., Sales
Telephone: 610-321-1100
Fax: 610-321-1199
Email: 110146.1321@compuserve.com /
URL: http://www.gei-int.com
Product Service Description:
Automatic & semi-automatic powder & liquid
filling equipment & roll-through & pressure
sen: Packaging machinery

G K N Sinter Metals Emporium
RR 2 Box 47
Emporium, PA 15834-9797
Contact: Fred Simons, Cost Mgr.
Telephone: 814-486-9233
Fax: 814-486-9273
Email: / URL:
Product Service Description:
Bearings_ball & roller
Bearings, gears, sprockets, levers & bushings
Speed changers, drives & gears
Speed changers, drives & gears

G M M Van Dock Distributors
484 Main Street
West Chicago, IL 60185-2864
Contact: Lloyd J. Gorence, Sales Manager
Telephone: 630-231-5770
Fax: 630-231-5779
Email: / URL:
Product Service Description:
Van, pick-up, recreational vehicle &
automobile parts, accessories & conversions

G-Wood Finishing Co. Inc.
5680 N Northwest Hwy
Chicago, IL 60646-6136
Contact: Anthony Bnomo, Pres.
Telephone: 773-631-9201
Fax: 773-631-9203
Email: / URL:
Product Service Description:
Wood finishing

GDC Casino Tokens
2912 N Commerce St
North Las Vegas, NV 89030-3945
Contact: J C Buffington, Sales Mgr., Natl.
Telephone: 702-642-2404
Fax: 702-642-0474
Email: / URL:
Product Service Description:
Manufacturing industries
Manufactures casino coins

GNLD International
PO Box 5012
Fremont, CA 94537-5012
Contact: James Arnott, Pres., John Ziegler,
VP Operations
Telephone: 510-651-0405
Fax: 510-657-7563
Email: / URL:
Product Service Description:
Food supplements & botanicals
Personal care & toilet preparations
Water filtration units
Home care / cleaning

GNY Equipment LLC
71 E. Industry Ct., P.O. Box 9013
Deer Park, NY 11729
Contact: Herman Kornahrens, *
Telephone: 516-667-1010
Fax: 516-242-3444
Product Service Description:
Aircraft Refueling Equipment

GS Sportwear / Golden Squeegee
900 Santa Fe Dr
Denver, CO 80204-3937
Contact: Larry Meer, General Manager
Telephone: 303-572-1164
Fax: 303-572-1190
Product Service Description:
Automotive & apparel trimmings
Textile screen printers : Embroidery
Advertising Specialties

GSE Lining Technology, Inc.
19103 Gundle Rd.
Houston, TX 77073-3515
Contact: Joe Young, VP Sales, Mike
Mathieson, VP Mktg & Bus Dev.
Telephone: 713-443-8564
Fax: 713-875-6010
Email: / URL: http://www.gseworld.com
Product Service Description:
Plastic Liners

GSIGLOBAL , INC.
3020 Bridgway # 555
Sausalito, CA 94965
Contact: Johnathan Edwards, Pres.
Telephone: 415-331-1434
Fax: 415-331-5134
Email: jse@gsiglobal.com / URL: http://
www.gsiglobal.com
Product Service Description:
Designs interactive television & Internet
systems for hotels & cable networks

GSO: Grapeseed Oil Corporation
701 Ivy Street
Glendale, CA 91204
Contact: Souren Pirjanian, Pres.
Telephone: 818-546-6973
Fax: 818-546-6969
Email: grapeseedoilcorp.com / URL:
Product Service Description:
Grapeseed Oil (special 100 % Natural)
cooking & salad dressing oil which lowers
colesterol

GTI Industries, Inc.
3303 N.W. 112th St.
Miami, FL 33167-3312
Contact: Stephen Zuckerman, President
Telephone: 305-681-5000
Fax: 305-688-3204
Email: gtiinc@gate.net / URL: http://
www.gtiinc.com
Product Service Description:
Adhesives and Sealants
Plates, sheets, film, foil, tape and other flat
shapes of plastics, self-adhesive, in rolls
Plates, sheets, film, foil and strip of plastics,
not self-adhesive, non-cellular
Binders, folders and file covers, of paper or
paperboard

Gabrielle, Inc.
PO Box 63
Alma, AR 72921-0063
Contact: Larry Hood, Pres., GM
Telephone: 501-632-2226
Fax: 501-632-3143
Email: / URL:
Product Service Description:
Skin care products
Toilet preparations

**Gainesville Welding & Rendering
Equipment, Inc.**
37 Henry Grady Hwy
Dawsonville, GA 30534-5717
Contact: Terry Stephens, Pres.
Telephone: 706-216-2666
Fax: 706-216-4282
Email: gwrender@stc.net / URL: http://
www.gwrendering.com
Product Service Description
Rendering feed mill heavy equipment &
quarry equipoment.

Galaxy Foods, Inc.
2441 Viscount Row
Orlando, FL 32809-6217
Contact: Angelo Morini, Pres.
Telephone: 407-855-5500
Fax: 407-855-7485
Email: galxsales@galaxyfoods.com / URL:
http://www.galaxyfoods.com
Product Service Description:
Dairy products : Cheese, natural & processed
Milk_fluid : Dairy - Related Products

**Galloway Office Supplies &
Equipment**
6802 S.W. 81st St.
Miami, FL 33143-7708
Contact: Jim Toural, Owner
Telephone: 305-665-2116
Product Service Description:
Office Supplies & Equipment
Office Furniture : Toners & Ribbons

Galow Trading
6995 N.W. 82nd Ave. Bay# 42
Miami, FL 33166-4691
Contact: Alfredo Gargaglione, President
Telephone: 305-593-0406
Fax: 305-593-7419
Email: galowtv@mail.icanet.net / URL:
Product Service Description:
Cable TV Equipment : Passives, linegear,
headed & cable & transmission

Gamma Products, Inc.
PO Box 190
Palos Park, IL 60464-0190
Contact: Walter Meier, Pres.,
Telephone: 708-974-4100
Fax: 708-974-0071
Email: 103106.65@compuserve.com / URL:
http://www.gammrproducts.com
Product Service Description:
Scientific instruments, radiation shielding,
sample changers, low-level alpha-beta
counter

Garbel Products Company
240 Michigan Street
Lockport, NY 14094-1797
Contact: James M. Carbone, President
Telephone: 716-434-6010
Fax: 716-434-9148
Product Service Description:
Garbage Disposers, Commercial

Gardner Denver, Inc. (Mfr)
1800 Gardner Expressway
Quincy, IL 62305
Contact: Kent W. Mason, Director, Sales
Telephone: 217-222-5400
Fax: 217-228-8247
Email: mktg@gardnerdenver.com / URL:
http://www.gardenerdenver.com
Product Service Description:
Compressors & Vacuum Pumps : Industrial
Blowers : Pumps

Gared Sports
1107 Mullanphy St.
St. Louis, MO 63106-4334
Contact: C. J. Engle, President
Telephone: 314-421-0044
Fax: 314-421-6014
Email: info@garedsports.com / URL:
Product Service Description:
Sporting and Recreational Goods
Articles and equipment for sports or outdoor
games; Swimming pools and wading pools;
Parts

Garnac Grain
7101 College Blvd., Ste. 800
Overland Park, KS 66210-4031
Contact: Jeff Brandon, Vice President
Telephone: 913-661-6100
Fax: 913-661-6159
Email: garnac@aol.com / URL:
Product Service Description:
Durable Goods, NEC
Corn , other than seed corn
Soybeans, whether or not broken
Flour and meal of soybean
Cocoa & cocoa products
Rice

Garrett Metal Detectors
1881 W State St.
Garland, TX 75042-6761
Contact: Henry Tellez, *
Telephone: 214-494-6151
Fax: 214-494-1881
Email: / URL: http://www.garrett.com
Product Service Description:
Metal Detector Walk Through, Handheld

Garrett Sound & Lighting
2780 N.W. 55th Ct.
Fort Lauderdale, FL 33309-2543
Contact: Kenneth Watkivs, President
Telephone: 954-777-3277
Fax: 954-777-3284
Email: gslinc@bellsouth.net / URL: http://
www.garrettsound.com
Product Service Description:
Staging
Sound Systems
Lighting Systems
Video Production

Garrison's Prosthetic Service
17184 Ne 19th Ave
North Miami Beach, FL 33162-3102
Contact: Kevin Garrison, Owner
Telephone: 305-949-1888
Fax: 305-949-5546
Email: lobo2@ix.netcom.com / URL: http://
www.oandp.com/garrison's
Product Service Description:
Artificial limbs
Surgical appliances & supplies

Gary Stull Goldsmith
231 Milwaukee St
Denver, CO 80206-5000
Contact: Gary Stull, Owner
Telephone: 303-333-4068
Product Service Description:
Custom goldsmith services
Jewelry, precious metal. gem stones
Vintage men & ladies pocket watches

Gas Corp. Of America
PO Box 5183
Wichita Falls, TX 76307-5183
Contact: Ben Wilson, Pres.
Telephone: 940-723-6015
Fax: 940-767-5737
Email: gascorp@wf.net / URL: http://
www.wf.net/~gascorp.com
Product Service Description:
Natural gas processing equipment & high
pressure storage tanks
Oil & gas field machinery

Gas Liquids Recovery Corp.
PO Box 5183
Wichita Falls, TX 76307-5183
Contact: Ben Wilson, Pres.
Telephone: 940-723-6015
Fax: 940-767-5737
Email: gascorp@wf.net / URL: http://
www.gascorp.com
Product Service Description:
Propane tanks & gas plant equipment
Plate work_fabricated (boiler shops)

GasTech, Inc.
8407 Central Ave.
Newark, CA 94560
Contact: Stephaie Kubina,
Maketing. Manager.
Telephone: 510-794-6200
Fax: 510-794-6210
Email: sales@gastech-inc.com URl: http://
www.gastech-inc.com
Product Service Description:
Manufactures Gas & Vapor Detectors
Process control instruments

Gasboy International, Inc.
707 North Valley Forge Road, PO Box 309
Lansdale, PA 19446
Contact: Product Specialist,
Telephone: 800-444-5529
Fax: 215-855-0341
Email: helpdesk@gasboy.com / URL:
Product Service Description:
Custom computer system integration;
manufactures fuel pumps and equipment
Gasoline pumps & dispensers
Fleet management systems & equipment

**Gaslamp Quarter Investigations /
Investigaciones De Mexico**
425 F. St.
San Diego, CA 92101-6117
Contact: Ben Harroll, CFE, CIP, CPI, CII
Telephone: 619-239-6991
Fax: 619-239-0545
Email: gq-eye@home.com / URL: http://
www.gqi.net
Product Service Description:
Private Investigations - Worldwide

Gator Pump, Inc.
PO Box 57
Brownwood, TX 76804-0057
Contact: Carol W. Lemmons, Chrm., Pres.
Telephone: 915-643-3502
Fax: 915-643-5760
Email: gator@gator-pump.com / URL: http://
www.gator-pump.com.
Product Service Description:
Centrifugal pumps & pumping equipment
Pumps & pumping equipment

Gaylord Industries, Inc.
10900 S.W. Avery St., P.O. Box 1149
Tualatin, OR 97062
Contact: Edson C. Gaylord, President
Telephone: 503-691-2010
Fax: 503-692-6048
Email: edsong@gaylordusa.com / URL:
Product Service Description:
Commercial Kitchen Hoods
Heat Reclaiming Units
Rooftop Exhaust Packages

Geier & Bluhm, Inc.
594 River St.
Troy, NY 12180-1599
Contact: David B. Oster, Vice President
Telephone: 518-272-6951
Fax: 518-272-0533
Email: levels@geier-bluhm.com / URL: http://
www.geier-bluhm.com
Product Service Description:
Engineering Instr., Spirit Levels
Handtools Spirit Level Assemblies
Machinists Levels
Handtools Levels Plate & Precision

Gel-Tec Co.
PO Box 4133
Norwalk, CT 06855-0133
Contact: David Luty, Owner,
Telephone: 203-331-1133
Fax: 203-331-1133
Product Service Description:
Reel sharpening compounds
Abrasive products

Geltman Industries
1901 Sacramento St.
Los Angeles, CA 90021-1608
Contact: Shari Rezai, Pres.
Phone: 213-622-2015 / Fax: 213-622-4572
Email: geltmanind@aol.com
URL: Http://www.geltman.com
Product Service Description:
Fabric finishing, laundry & bonding
Finishing Plants, Cotton

Gem Engineering Co., Inc.
10970 Stancliff Rd
Houston, TX 77099-4206
Contact: Todd McCombs, Pres.
Telephone: 281-561-9225
Fax: 281-561-9399
Email: tmccombs@gemengr.com / URL:
http://www.gemengr.com
Product Service Description:
Communication towers, monopoles, lattice,
guyed : Site acquisition - zoning
Engineering services
Construction of communication sites

Gem Industries, Inc.
PO Box 450061
Fort Lauderdale, FL 33345-0061
Contact: Steve Gaynor, Pres.
Telephone: 954-749-1228
Fax: 954-749-3564
Email: gem@gem-industries.com / URL:
http://www.gem-industries.com
Product Service Description:
Automotive, marine & aircraft orbital
polishing equipment & supplies

Gem State Manufacturing Inc
PO Box 987
Caldwell, ID 83606-0987
Contact: Mike Lemrick, Pres.
Telephone: 208-455-7551
Fax: 208-455-7554
Product Service Description:
Manufactures heavy truck trailers
Truck trailers

Gemco
1019 Griggs St
Danville, IL 61832-4116
Contact: Greg Rew, Pres., Secy., Pur. Agt.
Telephone: 217-446-7900
Fax: 217-443-2582
Product Service Description:
Insulation Pins, Hanger & Washers

Gemini Aluminum Corp
3255 Pomona Blvd
Pomona, CA 91768-3291
Contact: Jackie Neag, G.M.
Telephone: 909-595-7403
Product Service Description:
Extrudes aluminum : Aluminum extrusions
AA 6063, AA 6005

Genca Corp.
13805 58th St N
Clearwater, FL 33760-3733
Contact: Geoff Apthorp, Pres., GM
Telephone: 727-524-3622
Fax: 727-531-5700
Email: genca@gate.net / URL: http://
www.genca.com
Product Service Description:
Extrusion tooling & crossheads for plastics
Dies, tools, jigs & fixtures_special

General Air Corporation
9252 Deering Ave
Chatsworth, CA 91311-6957
Contact: David Sagi, Pres.
Telephone: 818-718-8955
Fax: 818-718-0359
Email: genair@gte.net / URL: http://
home1.gte.net/genair/
Product Service Description:
Manufactures environmental chambers, wet
bench process equipment, gas panels,
stainless steel gas lines
Machinery_special industry
Analytical instruments
Laboratory apparatus & furniture
Machinery_general industrial

**General Business International
Trade**
16 Herbert St.
Newark, NJ 07105
Contact: Hussein Hakim, Vice President
Telephone: 973-817-9700
Fax: 973-817-9104
Email: gbcexport@aol.com / URL: http://
www.generalbusinesscorp.com
Product Service Description:
Used clothing & usedshoes
Fabrics & textiles

General Carbon Corp.
33 Paterson St
Paterson, NJ 07501-1015
Contact: Robert Muller, Pres.
Telephone: 973-523-2223
Fax: 973-523-1494
Email: sales@generalcarbon.com / URL:
http://www.generalcarbon.com
Product Service Description:
Activated carbon & air & water filtering
equipment
Carbon activation/reactivation furnaces

General Drapery Services, Inc.
135 E. 144th St.
Bronx, NY 10451-5435
Contact: Paula Belmont, President
Telephone: 718-665-9200
Fax: 718-665-9672
Email: / URL:
Product Service Description:
Sun Shades
Drapery
Sound Proof Upholstered Walls
Counter Weight Systems
Cinematographic Equipment
Theatrical Hardware

General Econopak, Inc.
1725 N 6th St
Philadelphia, PA 19122-2912
Contact: Margaret Gerhard, Pres., Pers.
Telephone: 215-763-8200
Fax: 215-763-8118
Email: info@GeneralEconopak.com / URL:
http://www.generaleconopak.com
Product Service Description:
Surgical "Disposable" & protective apparel
Disposable medical,veterinary,safety &
coveralls,lab coats,body bags,linen
packs,gowns

General Electrodynamics Corp.
PO Box 150089
Arlington, TX 76015-6089
Contact: Tom Smith, Pres., CEO
Telephone: 817-572-0366
Fax: 817-572-0373
Email: gec@digitex.net / URL: http://
www.gecscales.com
Product Service Description:
Portable truck & aircraft weigh scales, test
equipment & instrumentation
Scales & balances, except laboratory
Aircraft parts & equipment
Electronic assembly

General Fabrics
45 Washington St.
Pawtucket, RI 02860-3615
Contact: Edward Odessa, President, David
Odessa, Exec. VP
Telephone: 401-728-4200
Fax: 401-728-2580
Email: genfabco@aol.com / URL:
Product Service Description:
Cotton Fabric : 100% cotton printed fabric for
the quilter & crafter : Novelty fabric
Home decorator fabric

**General Machinery Corporation
(Mfr)**
1831 N 18th St., P.O. Box 717
Sheboygan, WI 53082
Contact: Michael Horwitz, Sec. / Treas.
Telephone: 920-458-2189
Fax: 920-458-8316
Email: sales@genmac.com / URL: http://
www.genmac.com
Product Service Description:
Food Processing Machinery, Frozen Block
Flakers : Food Prod. Mach., Fresh Meat
Dicers : Food Prod., Mach. Frozen Meat
Dicers : Food Prod. Mach., Meat Tenderizers
Food Prod., Mach. Frozen Meat Grinder

General Manufactured Housing, Inc.
PO Box 1449
Waycross, GA 31502-1449
Contact: Glendale Sullivan, Pres., CEO
Telephone: 912-285-5068
Fax: 912-285-1397
Email: / URL:
Product Service Description:
Mobile homes

General Pencil Co.
67 Fleet St
Jersey City, NJ 07306-2213
Contact: Oscar Weissenborn, Pres.
Telephone: 201-653-5351
Fax: 201-653-2298
Product Service Description:
Wooden-cased lead pencils
Lead pencils & art products
Cosmetic pencils
Erasers

General Precision Tool & Die Inc.
2721 E Avalon Ave
Muscle Shoals, AL 35661-2705
Contact: James Martin, Pres., Pers. Mgr.
Telephone: 256-383-7300
Fax: 256-383-7340
Email: martinja@mangastool.com / URL:
Product Service Description:
Die cast dies
Dies, tools, jigs & fixtures_special

General Robotics Corporation
1978 S Garrison St Ste 6
Lakewood, CO 80227-2243
Contact: Constant Brown, Pres.
Telephone: 303-988-5636
Fax: 303-988-5303
Email: rb5x@edurobot.com / URL: http://
www.edurobot.com
Product Service Description:
Manufactures educational personal computer
robots for all grade levels

General Safety Equipment
25900 Fallbrook Ave N
Wyoming, MN 55092-9078
Contact: Kevin Kirvida, Pres.
Telephone: 651-462-1000
Fax: 651-462-1700
Email: info@general-safety.com / URL: http:/
/www.general-safety.com
Product Service Description:
Fire fighting equipment
Machinery_general industrial

General Sealants Inc
PO Box 3855
City Of Industry, CA 91744-0855
Contact: Clyde Boyle, Pres.
Telephone: 626-961-0211
Fax: 626-968-5140
Email: sticktoquality@generalsealants.com /
URL: http://www.generalsealants.com
Product Service Description:
Manufactures extruded sealants

General Tool & Supply Co
2705 NW Nicolai St
Portland, OR 97210-1818
Contact: Bill Derville, Pres.
Telephone: 503-226-3411
Fax: 503-778-5518
Email: / URL: http://www.generaltool.com
Product Service Description:
Distributes MRO, Industrial & Electronic
Tools

General Waste Trading Company
1920 N. Broadway
St. Louis, MO 63102-1302
Contact: Jeffrey Hochman, President
Telephone: 314-231-7966
Fax: 314-231-9616
Email: gwtrading@msn.com / URL: http://
www.gwtrade.com
Product Service Description:
Apparel Used, Wholesale : Textile Waste,
Wholesale : Wiping Cloths, Wholesale

Genevieve Tournebize - Iliev
5710 Wood Ridge Drive
Shreveport, LA 71119
Contact: Genevieve Alba, Translator /
Interpreter
Telephone: 318-631-9360
Fax: 318-635-0865
Email: genevie141@aol.com / URL:
Product Service Description:
Translation & Interpreting Services, Travel

Genie Co., The
22790 Lake Park Blvd
Alliance, OH 44601-3456
Contact: Lisa Cathey, Export Coordinator
Telephone: 330-821-5360
Fax: 330-821-4702
Email: genie_company@overheaddors.com /
URL: http://www.geniecompany.com
Product Service Description:
Relays & industrial controls
Garage door opener systems, remote control
switches & utility vacuum cleaners
Vacuum cleaners_household

Gentek Building Products
11 Cragwood Road
Woodbridge, NJ 07095
Contact: Leonard Sprinkle, Export Manager
Telephone: 732-827-2355
Fax: 732-381-1162
Email: exportsales@gentekinc.com / URL:
Product Service Description:
Aluminum siding, Residential
Steel Siding, Residential
Vinyl Siding, Residential

Genzyme Corp
1 Kendall Sq
Cambridge, MA 02139-1562
Contact: Henri A Termeer, Chrm., CEO
Telephone: 617-252-7500
Fax: 617-252-7600
Email: / URL:
Product Service Description:
Diagnostic substances
Diagnostic Enzymes and Biotherapeutic
Products
Biological products, except diagnostic

Geo E. Alexander & Son, Inc.
45 Lower Main Street
Sunapee, NH 03782-2912
Contact: Guy E. Alexander, President
Telephone: 603-763-2221
Fax: 603-763-2221
Email: / URL:
Product Service Description:
Wooden Crutches

Geo Specialty Chemicals, Inc.
PO Box 190467
Little Rock, AR 72219-0467
Contact: Peter Bertasi,
Telephone: 501-888-1211
Fax: 501-888-1148
Email: nascarn986@aol.com / URL:
Product Service Description:
Water Treatment Pulp & Paper Chemicals &
Clay Products
Stuctural Clay Products
Polyaluminum Chloride
Aluminum Chlorohydrate
Coagulant Products NSF Aproved
Coagulant Blends
Disperesants
Defoamers

Geochem International
137 Rowayton Ave., Bldg. 330
Norwalk, CT 06853-1413
Contact: David Castagna, President
Telephone: 203-854-9979
Fax: 203-855-0570
Product Service Description:
Thermoplastic Resins
Plastic Extrusion Equipment & Printers
Polystyrene : High Density Polyethylene Resi
Kraft Paper

Geophysical Survey Systems, Inc.
13 Klein Drive, PO Box 97
North Salem, NH 03073
Contact: Paul Hague, Dir. Int. Sales
Telephone: 603-893-1109
Fax: 603-889-3984
Email: paul@geophysical.com / URL: http://
www.geophysical.com
Product Service Description:
Geophysical Electronic Equipment
Radar Equipment, Ground Penetrating
Graphic Recording Meters
Computer Color Graphic Displays

**George F. Cram Company Inc., The
(Mfr)**
301 South Lasalle Street
Indianapolis, IN 46201
Contact: Sarah E. Scott, Export Manager
Telephone: 317/635-5564
Fax: 317/635-2720
Email: sscott@georgefcram.com / URL:
Product Service Description:
Globes, Geographical

Georgetown Wire Co. K-Lath Div
PO Box 489
Fontana, CA 92334-0489
Contact: Frank H Hoang, V-P., GM
Telephone: 909-360-8288
Fax: 909-360-6663
Email: / URL: http://www.k-lath.com
Product Service Description:
Wire products_misc. fabricated
Welded and woven wire products
Plastering, drywall & insulation
Terrazzo, tile, marble, mosaic work

Georgia Ports Authority
PO Box 2406
Savannah, GA 31402-2406
Contact: Brian X. Hock, *
Telephone: 912-964-3880
Fax: 912-966-3615
Email: / URL:
Product Service Description:
Marine Cargo Handling
Port Authority

Geotech Environmental Equipment
8035 East 40th Avenue
Denver, CO 80207
Contact: Candice B. Popiel, International
Sales
Telephone: 303-320-4764
Fax: 303-322-7242
Email: geotech@ix.netcom.com / URL: http://
www.geotechenv.com
Product Service Description:
Manufactures groundwater sampling,
filtration, analytical & remediation equipment
Pumps, bailers, filters, meters, product
recovery systems, air strippers, others.

Geothermal Power Company Inc.
1460 W Water St.
Elmira, NY 14905-1923
Contact: Gary Shulman,
Telephone: 607-733-1027
Fax: 607-734-2709
Email: agetraer-gpc@erols.com / URL: http://
www.expresspages.com/glgeothermalpower
Product Service Description:
Skid Mounted Steam Turbine Generator
Modules

Germfree Laboratories, Inc.
7435 Nw 41st St
Miami, FL 33166-6715
Contact: Katharine Lo,
Telephone: 305-592-1780
Fax: 305-591-7280
Email: info@germfree.com / URL: http://
www.germfree.com
Product Service Description:
Biological safety equipment, glove boxes,
laminar flow, fume, lab & pharmacy hoods
Laboratory apparatus & furniture

Getz Recycle Inc
PO Box 6249
Phoenix, AZ 85005-6249
Contact: Roland A Getz, Pres.
Telephone: 602-278-7600
Fax: 602-272-5668
Email: / URL:
Product Service Description:
Manufactures construction machinery and
equipment
Construction machinery
Construction & mining machinery
Recycle crushers for concrete
Recycle crushers for asphalt
Recycle crushers for wood

Giancola Exports, Inc., D. J.
4317 E. Genesee St., P.O. Box 4
Syracuse, NY 13214-0004
Contact: Charles C. Giancola, President
Telephone: 315-446-1002
Fax: 315-446-2431
Email: sales@djgexports.com / URL: http://
www.djgexports.com
Product Service Description:
Commercial Laundry Equipment
Dry Cleaning Equipment

Giant Horse Printing Inc
1336 San Mateo Ave
South San Francisco, CA 94080-6501
Contact: Steve Ma, Pres.
Telephone: 650-875-7137
Fax: 650-875-7194
Email: / URL:
Product Service Description:
Commercial printing and offset
Lithographic printing_commercial
Short to medium run book printer

Gibbs Die Casting Corp.
369 Community Dr
Henderson, KY 42420-4336
Contact: Nick Gibbs, Pres.
Telephone: 502-827-1801
Fax: 502-827-7840
Email: nfedie@gibbsdc.com / URL: http://
www.gibbsdc.com
Product Service Description:
Aluminum & magnesium die-castings
Aluminum die-castings
Nonferrous die-casting, except aluminum

Gibbs Products Inc
2608 E 3820 S
Salt Lake City, UT 84109
Contact: Peter Gibbs, Pres.
Telephone: 801-272-8354
Fax: 801-277-6564
Email: pgibbs@aol.com / URL: http://
members.aol.com/pgibbs
Product Service Description:
Manufacture Climbing, Caving, Rescue
Equipment

Gilbert Industries Inc.
5611 Krueger Drive
Jonesboro, AR 72401
Contact: David Gilbert, President
Telephone: 870-932-6070
Fax: 870-932-5609
Email: / URL: http://www.gilbertinc.com
Product Service Description:
Elec. Equip., Insect Light Traps

Gilbert Mfg. Co.
PO Box 309
South Hill, VA 23970-0309
Contact: Donna Simpson, Plt. Mgr.
Telephone: 804-447-8223
Fax: 804-447-7434
Email: / URL:
Product Service Description:
Wire products_misc. fabricated
Wire harnesses
Mini strip lights UL Listed

Gilbert Paper
PO Box 260
Menasha, WI 54952-0260
Contact: Robert Feeser, Pres.
Telephone: 920-729-7605
Fax: 920-729-7716
Email: raf@mead.com / URL: http://www.gilbertpaper.com
Product Service Description:
Stationery, technical & security paper, test & cover papers

Giles Chemical Corp.
PO Box 370
Waynesville, NC 28786-0370
Contact: Richard N. Wrenn Jr., Pres.
Telephone: 828-452-4784
Fax: 828-452-4786
Email: rwrenn@gileschemical.com / URL: http://www.gileschemical.com
Product Service Description:
Chemicals_industrial inorganic
Magnesium sulfate & sodium sulfate

Gilman Brothers
P.O. Box 38
Gilman, CT 00636
Contact: Evan Gilman, President
Telephone: 860-889-8444
Fax: 860-889-5226
Email: / URL: http://www.gilmanbrothers.com
Product Service Description:
Plastics Products, NEC
Plates, sheets, film, foil and strip of plastics or cellular plastics
Containers specially designed and equipped for carriage by one or more modes of transport
Miscellaneous cargo

Gilroy Foods, Inc. (Mfr)
1350 Pacheco Pass Hwy.
Gilroy, CA 95020
Contact: G.M. Booth, General Manager, Intl
Telephone: 408-846-3401
Fax: 408-846-3523
Email: / URL: http://www.gilroyfoods.com
Product Service Description:
Dried Onions & Garlic
Gardenfrost
Citrus Peel
Capsicums
Oleoresins

Gilson, Inc.
PO Box 620027
Middleton, WI 53562-0027
Contact: Dan Maffet, V-P., COO
Telephone: 608-836-1551
Fax: 608-831-4451
Email: sales@gilson.com / URL: http://www.gilson.com
Product Service Description:
Laboratory instruments
Analytical instruments

Gimbal Brothers Inc
PO Box 876
South San Francisco, CA 94083-0876
Contact: Rochard Butler, Pres.
Telephone: 650-588-4844
Fax: 650-588-0150
Email: gimbalbro@aol.com / URL: http://www.gimbalcandy.com
Product Service Description:
Candy & other confectionery products
Manufactures candies

Gingerich Draperies Inc
8913 National Blvd
Los Angeles, CA 90034-3307
Contact: Carter Aljadar, Pres.
Telephone: 310-836-2527
Fax: 310-559-7090
Email: / URL:
Product Service Description:
Manufactures and installs draperies, curtains, bedspreads, drapery hardware and blinds

Giovanna Cavagna
12911 Buccaneer Road
Silver Spring, MD 20904
Contact: Giovanna Cavagna, *
Telephone: 301-384-9243
Product Service Description:
Italian, Translation, Interpreting Svcs.
ATA Certified Eng to Ital. Ital / Eng

Gise Inc
295 Distribution St
San Marcos, CA 92069-4359
Contact: Bob Anderson, Pres.
Telephone: 760-752-5230
Fax: 760-752-1322
Email: / URL:
Product Service Description:
Manufactures ice cream and frozen dessert powders
Ice cream & frozen desserts

Giuliano-Pagano Corp
1117 E Walnut St
Carson, CA 90746-1317
Contact: Nancy Giuliano, Pres.
Telephone: 310-537-7700
Fax: 310-537-7981
Email: delibakery@aol.com / URL: http://www.giulianos.com
Product Service Description:
Manufactures bread and bakery products
Bread, cake & related products
Manufactures of Delicatessen & deli products

Glas-Col Apparatus Company (Mfr)
711 Hulman Street, P.O. Box 2128
Terre Haute, IN 47802-0128
Contact: Karen Elliott, Int'l Acct. Mgr.
Telephone: 812-235-6167
Fax: 812-234-3121
Email: pinnacle@glascol.com / URL: http://www.glascol.com
Product Service Description:
Laboratory Equipment

Glas-Master / Wehr Engineering
8192 W 700 N
Fairland, IN 46126-9507
Contact: Tom Wehr, Owner,
Telephone: 317-835-7824 / 800-457-4527
Fax: 317-835-2992
Email: wehrresqn@aol.com / URL: http://www.glasmaster.com
Product Service Description:
Rescue & fire fighting equipment & tools

Glasscraft Inc
626 Moss St
Golden, CO 80401-4047
Contact: Homer Hoyt, Pres.
Telephone: 303-278-4670
Fax: 303-278-4672
Email: glacraft1@aol.com / URL: http://www.glasscraftinc.com
Product Service Description:
Distributes glass blowing tools, equipment and supplies : Industrial machinery & equipment

Glassmaster
P.O. Box 826
Lexington, SC 29071-0826
Contact: Melvin Chavis, Vice President
Telephone: 803-359-0706
Product Service Description:
Plastics Products, NEC
Twine, cordage, rope and cable, whether or not plaited or braided or coated with rubber
Cotton yarn nu85%cot no retail
Woven cotton fabrics
Monofilament fibers

Glen Ullin Times
PO Box 668
Glen Ullin, ND 58631-0489
Contact: Nancy Bittner, Owner
Telephone: 701-348-3325
Fax: 701-348-3325
Email: gutime@westriv.com / URL: http://www.gutimes@westrio.com
Product Service Description:
Newspapers
Newspaper printing

Glenayre Western Multiplex
1196 Borregas Ave
Sunnyvale, CA 94089-1302
Contact: Amir Zoufonoun, Pres., GM
Telephone: 408-542-5231
Fax: 408-542-5300
Email: / URL: http://www.wirelessinterconnect.com
Product Service Description:
Wireless communications equipment
Manufactures microwave communications equipment
Communications equipment, nec
Wireless data communications equipment
Wireless ethernet bridges
Digital microwave radios

Glenmarc Mfg. Inc.
25661 Hillview Ct
Mundelein, IL 60060-9436
Contact: David Greenwood, Pres., R & D, Sales & Mktg. Mgr.
Telephone: 847-540-0100
Fax: 847-540-0193
Email: glenmarc@aol.com / URL: http://www.glenmarc.com
Product Service Description:
Epoxy metering & dispensing machines, adhesive dispensers, automation equipment
Machinery_special industry

Glentek Inc
208 Standard St
El Segundo, CA 90245-3834
Contact: Milt Vasak, GM
Telephone: 310-322-3026
Fax: 310-332-7709
Email: sales@glentek.com / URL: http://www.glentek.com
Product Service Description:
Designing and manufacturing both custom and standard, brushless, high performance, analog and digital servo amplifiers, servo motors and motion controllers for over 35 years

Glideway Bed Carriage Mfg. Co.
8226 Lackland Rd.
St. Louis, MS 63114
Contact: Ron Fredman,
Telephone: 800-428-5222 / 314-426-3999
Fax: 314-426-4676
Email: rfredman@glideway.com / URL:
Product Service Description:
Slatless bed firming rails, frames & components : Mattresses & bedsprings

Global Architectural Models
3863 S Valley View Blvd Ste 10
Las Vegas, NV 89103-2944
Contact: Todd Throgmorton, Owner
Telephone: 702-220-7879
Fax: 702-220-7880
Email: gamlvnv@aol.com / URL: http://www.globalarchitectmodels.com
Product Service Description:
Builds scale models for architectural firms & developers : for presentation & study

Global Associates, LLC
210 East Capitol St., Suite 2130
Jackson, MS 39201
Contact: William Lilly, *
Telephone: 601-352-7464
Fax: 601-353-1459
Email: global@intop.net / URL:
Product Service Description:
Business Consulting, International

Global Electric Products
3105 Avenue E
Arlington, TX 76011-5228
Contact: Eric Lee, President
Telephone: 817-633-3544
Product Service Description:
Residential Lighting Fixtures
Fans, table, floor, wall, window, ceiling or roof, with self-contained electric motor

Global Kitting
PO Box 1757
Roseburg, OR 97470-0466
Contact: Ulrich Wettstein, Owner
Telephone: 541-672-5332
Fax: 541-672-8737
Email: global@sorcom.com / URL: http://www.globalkitting.com
Product Service Description:
Electronic Parts Organizers, Plastic
ESD Static Safe Devices

Global Leasing & Sales, Inc.
650 N.W. 123rd St.
Miami, FL 33168
Contact: Casey Raja, President
Telephone: 305-688-8700
Fax: 305-688-9455
Product Service Description:
Complete line of restaurant equipment
Manufactures of cracked tube ice-machines

Global Market Partners, Inc.
PO Box 38957
Germantown, TN 38183-0957
Contact: R. Lanny Trottman, President
Telephone: 901-755-6758
Fax: 901-753-7966
Email: / URL:
Product Service Description:
Wood Flooring, Export
Protective Knee Pads, Export
Flooring Finishes, Export

Global Material Supply
1205 Temple Ave. # C
Long Beach, CA 90804
Contact: Sales & Marketing,
Telephone: 562-438-1870
Fax: 562-438-1870
Email: / URL:
Product Service Description:
Mixed Building Material & Hardware

Global Parts & Equipment
514 N. Laurel Rd.
London, KY 40741-6024
Contact: Jeff Price, Owner
Telephone: 606-878-5535
Fax: 606-878-5542
Email: global@global-parts.com / URL: http:/
/www.global-parts.com
Product Service Description:
Construction and Mining Machinery

Global Solutions Insurance Services, Inc.
880 Apollo St., Ste. 200,
El Segundo, CA 90245
Contact: Glenn A. Stebbings,
Chief Executive Officer
Telephone: 310-414-4114
Fax: 310-414-4177
Email: gstebbings@gsis.com / URL: http://
www.gsis.com
Product Service Description:
Cargo Insurance : U.S. Customs Bonds

Global Specialties
70 Fulton Ter
New Haven, CT 06512-1817
Contact: Eric Blauvelt, Pres., CFO
Telephone: 203-466-6103
Fax: 203-468-0060
Email: / URL:
Product Service Description:
Electricity measuring instruments
Electronic testing & measuring equipment
Electronic Curcuit Simulation Software
Electronic Prototyping Products
Electronic Training Products

Global Vision
5053 Ocean Blvd., Suite 1
Sarasota, FL 34242
Contact: Susan Khrystal, *
Product Service Description:
Promotions of Exporters, Catalog Expos

Globe Fire Sprinkler Corp.
4077 Air Park Dr.
Standish, MI 48658
Contact: Robert C. Worthington, Jr.,
Executive Vice President
Telephone: 517-846-4583
Fax: 517-846-9231
Email: globe_man@msn.com / URL: http://
www.globesprinkler.com
Product Service Description:
Alarm Valves, Dry Valves, Deluge Valves
Commercial & Residential Fire Sprinkler

Globe Shipping, Globe Ship Managment, Inc.
999 Brickell Bay Dr., Suite 1405
Miami, FL 33131-2934
Contact: Helmut Heinrich, Owner
Telephone: 305-374-7988
Fax: 305-374-4523
Email: gsmmiami@aol.com / URL:
Product Service Description:
Ship Management
Ship Owners Representative
Crew Agency Representative

Go Industries, Inc.
420 Grove St.
Richardson, TX 75081
Contact: Bob Orth Sr., Pres., Engrg. & R & D Mgr.
Telephone: 972-783-7444
Fax: 972-437-3425
Email: goindustries@topher.net / URL: http://
www.goindustries.com
Product Service Description:
Pick-up Truck Accessories

Goal Oriented Inc
1360 Bellaire St
Denver, CO 80220-2424
Contact: Dan Grunfeld, Pres.
Telephone: 303-393-6040
Fax:
Email: goals@ix.netcom.com / URL: http://
www.soccergoals.com/soccer
Product Service Description:
Sporting & athletic goods
Manufactures portable soccer goals

Goex International, Inc.
423 W Vaughn Rd
Cleburne, TX 76031-1368
Contact: Kenny Jordan, Director of Sales & Mktg.
Telephone: 817-641-2261
Fax: 817-556-0657
Email: goex@htcomp.net / URL:
Product Service Description:
Oil well perforating & pipe recovery
equipment & military & defensive explosive
components
Oil & gas field machinery

Goff's Curtain Walls/Goff's Enterprises Inc.
1228 Hickory St
Pewaukee, WI 53072-3955
Contact: Tony Goff, General Manager
Telephone: 414-691-4998
Fax: 414-691-3255
Email: goffs@execpc.com / URL: http://
www.goffscurtainwalls.com
Product Service Description:
Curtains; Industrial
Track & Roller Hardware

Golden Bear Oil Specialties
10100 Santa Monica Blvd Ste 1470
Los Angeles, CA 90067-4105
Contact: Rachel L Cohen, Executive Vice
President, Mktg. & Sales
Telephone: 310-277-4511
Fax: 310-201-0383
Email: cohenra@lacorp.goldenbearoil.com
Product Service Description:
Naphtheme base & process oils
Asphalt & road repair agents

Golden Circle Air, Inc.
PO Box 676
De Soto, IA 50069-0676
Contact: Robert J. Ellefson, Pres., Opers.,
Sales & Mktg. Mgr.
Telephone: 515-834-2225
Fax: 515-834-2152
Email: bobdorly@netins.net / URL: http://
www.aircraftsuper-market.com
Product Service Description:
Aircraft components & supplies
Aircraft parts & equipment
Ultralight plane kits, manufacturer
Aircraft kit manufacturer

Golden Fleece Designs Inc
441 S Victory Blvd
Burbank, CA 91502-2353
Contact: Symeon Argyropoulos, Pres.
Phone: 818-848-7724 / Fax: 818-566-7100
Product Service Description:
Manufactures awnings, tents and related
canvas products— flags, boat covers and
bags : Canvas & related products

Golden State Bulb Growers
P.O. Box 1120
Watsonville, CA 95077-1120
Contact: Tom Lukens, President
Telephone: 831-728-0500
Product Service Description:
Ornamental Nursery Products
Bulbs, tubers, tuberous roots, corms, crowns
and rhizomes, dormant

Golten Service
2323 N.E. Miami Ct.
Miami, FL 33137-4844
Contact: Steinar Danielsen, President
Phone: 305-576-4410 / Fax: 305-576-3827
Email: miami@goltens.com / URL: http://
www.goltens.com
Product Service Description:
Diesel engine service & spare parts.
Turbo charger service & spare parts
Diesel engine part overhaul & reconditioning
Crankshaft grinding in-situ and in bench.
Line boring of engine blocks & in-situ
machining. : Repair & reconditioning of
reduction gears Clutches & Dampers
Repair & reconditioning of Thrusters,
Stabilizer Fins, Propellers, Rudders &
Auctions. Service & repair of Waste
Handling Equipment.: Repair of Deck
Equipment, Winches & Cranes
Certified Welding & Steel Construction.

Gonzalez Integrated Marketing
2863 E Grand Blvd
Detroit, MI 48202-3150
Contact: Tony Hernandez, Pres.
Telephone: 313-871-1535
Fax: 313-871-4462
Product Service Description:
Lithographic printing_commercial
Platemaking Services: Publsihing
miscellaneous : Graphic Design
Pre-Press : Color separations

Gonzalez T.H. Inc
4116 Trade Center
Laredo, TX 78045
Contact: Keith Ayers, President
Telephone: 210-717-3750
Fax: 210-717-8389
Email: keithayers@aol.com / URL:
Product Service Description:
U.S. Customs Broker, Freight Forwarding
Mexican Customs Broker

Goodtrade Corporation
8139 N.W. 66th St.
Miami, FL 33166
Contact: Ray N. Soares, *
Telephone: 305-593-2663
Fax: 305-593-6997
Email: goodtrad@icanect.net / URL: http://
www.goodtradeusa.com
Product Service Description:
Equipment, Accessories & Parts For Mining
Construction, Quarrying, Water-Well Drilling
Utilities Applications, Cement Conveying
Mineral Separation & General Industrial
Purposes.

Goodyear International Corporation
1144 East Market Street
Akron, OH 44316
Contact: Keith Collett, *
Telephone: 330-796-3400
Fax: 330-796-7178
Email: usgtr682@ibmmail / URL:
Product Service Description:
Rubber & Plastics Belts, Flat
Rubber & Plastics Belts, Transmission
Rubber Hose & Hydraulic Hose
Industrial Hose, Long Length

Gorman Rupp Co., The
305 Bowman St.
Mansfield, OH 44901-1217
Contact: Randy Crawford, Director of
International Sales
Telephone: 419-755-1011
Fax: 419-755-1266
Email: intsales@gormanrupp.com / URL:
http://www.gormanrupp.com
Product Service Description:
Pumps & Related Pump Systems

Gothic Arch Greenhouses, Inc.
PO Box 1564
Mobile, AL 36633-1564
Contact: William Sierke Jr., Pres.
Telephone: 334-432-7529
Fax: 334-432-7972
Email: gothic@zebra.net / URL: http://
www.zebra.net/~gothic
Product Service Description:
Prefabricated greenhouses & horticultural
supplies

Gould & Goodrich
709 East Mcneil St.
Lillington, NC 27546
Contact: P. Gould, Marketing Manager
Telephone: 910-893-2071
Fax: 910-893-4742
Email: service@gouldusa.com / URL: http://
www.gouldusa.com
Product Service Description:
Holsters Leather
Holsters, Nylon
Belts, Leather
Leather Gun Accessories
Leather Goods, Nec.

Gould Plastics, Inc.
1600 Distribution Drive, Suite D.
Duluth, GA 30097
Contact: Nicole P. Norris,
Telephone: 678-475-1647
Fax: 678-475-1747
Email: nicolepn@mindspring.com / URL:
http://www.gouldplastics.com
Product Service Description:
Plastic Literature Shelves for Floor & Wall
Wooden literature Shelves for Floor & Wall
Plastic Storage Bins

Gould Shawmut
374 Merrimac St
Newburyport, MA 01950-1930
Contact: William A Trotman, Pres.
Telephone: 978-462-6662
Fax: 978-465-6790
Email: info@gouldshawmut.com / URL: http://www.gouldshawmut.com
Product Service Description:
Switchgear & switchboard apparatus
Fuses, Fuse and Power Distribution Blocks
Current-carrying wiring devices

Grace Mfg. Co., Inc.
19 Superior Blvd Se
Rome, GA 30161-9571
Contact: Lindsay Mastro, Pres.
Telephone: 706-234-4470
Fax: 706-234-3378
Product Service Description:
Wrought iron furniture
Cast Table Bases
Swords & medieval armor

Graham Paint & Varnish Co., Inc.
4800 S Richmond St
Chicago, IL 60632-2022
Contact: Harry True, Pres.
Telephone: 773-376-7676
Fax: 773-376-9449
Email: grahampt@aol.com / URL:
Product Service Description:
Paints & varnishes
Paints & allied products

Grain Processing Corporation (Mfr)
1600 Oregon Street
Muscatine, IA 52761
Contact: Dan Lawhorn, Export Mgr.
Telephone: 319-264-4265
Fax: 319-264-4289
Email: / URL: http://www.grainprocessing.com
Product Service Description:
Maltodextrins : Corn Syrup Solids
Corn Starch : Ethyl Alcohol
Fermentation Alcohol : Corn Gluten Meal
Distillers Grains with Solubles

Granco Pump, Div. Challenge Mfg.
1308 67th St.
Oakland, CA 94608-1121
Contact: Ivan Dimcheff, General Manager
Telephone: 510-652-8847
Fax: 510-652-1565
Product Service Description:
Pumps, Rotary Displacement

Grand Silver Co., Inc.
289 Morris Ave
Bronx, NY 10451-6101
Contact: Barry Kostrinsky, Pres.
Telephone: 718-585-1930
Fax: 718-412-4724
Email: grandsilve@aol.com / URL:
Product Service Description:
Institutional silver-plated holloware

Grande Ronde Sign Co
PO Box 1429
La Grande, OR 97850-6429
Contact: Mat Barber, Pres.
Telephone: 541-963-5841
Email: grsign@oregontrail.net / URL:
Product Service Description:
Manufactures all types of signs
Signs & advertising specialties

Granlunds Sweet Temptations
12164 California St
Yucaipa, CA 92399-4333
Contact: Scott Burkle, CEO
Telephone: 909-790-1876
Fax: 909-790-2383
Product Service Description:
Candy and confectionery products

Granutec Inc
100 Davis St # 537
East Douglas, MA 01516-2310
Contact: Merritt Tetreault, Pres.
Telephone: 508-476-3801
Fax: 508-476-3179
Email: / URL:
Product Service Description:
Granulators for recycling plastics

Graphic Ways Inc
8332 Commonwealth Ave
Buena Park, CA 90621-2526
Contact: Lloyd T Crelia, Pres.
Telephone: 714-739-4224
Fax: 714-228-0403
Email: / URL:
Product Service Description:
Commercial printing
Lithographic printing_commercial

Graphics Plus Printing, Inc.
3736 Kellogg Rd # 709
Cortland, NY 13045-8818
Contact: Robert C. Eckard, Pres
Telephone: 607-753-9815
Fax: 607-753-0115
Email: info@gpprinting.com / URL: http://www.gpprinting.com
Product Service Description:
Offset printing
Lithographic printing_commercial
3D Animation Production
Computer Graphic Design
Interactive CD Rom Design

Graphite Products Inc
761 N Monterey St Ste 106
Gilbert, AZ 85233-3820
Contact: Greg Holtz, Pres.
Telephone: 480-926-0601
Fax: 480-926-0670
Email: gregandshariholtz@worldnet.att.net / URL:
Product Service Description:
Manufactures graphite products
Carbon & graphite products

Graphite Sales, Inc.
16715 W. Park Circle Dr., P.O. Box 185
Chagrin Falls, OH 44023-4549
Contact: George Hanna, President
Telephone: 216-543-8221
Fax: 216-543-5183
Email: / URL:
Product Service Description:
Graphite Powder
Electrical Grounding Systems
Machined graphite products
Graphite Electrodes

Grayson Mountain Water Co.
1120-B Sparkleberry Lane
Columbia, SC 29223
Contact: Roger J. Catarino, Pres., CEO
Telephone: 803-788-8067
Fax: 803-788-8748
Email: astraridge@aol.com / URL:
Product Service Description:
Bottled water & sparkling water

Great Dane Terminal, The
PO Box 188
Audubon, IA 50025-0188
Contact: Richard Parkhurst, Plt. Mgr.
Telephone: 712-563-4251
Fax: 712-563-4340
Email: / URL:
Product Service Description:
Fertilizers, mixing only

Great Northern Coffee Co Inc
PO Box 1643
Jackson, WY 83001-1643
Contact: Diane Wolfe, Pres.
Telephone: 307-733-5323 / 800-216-5323
Fax: 307-733-4152
Email: gncoffee@wyoming.com / URL: http://www.greatnortherncoffee.com
Product Service Description:
Roasted Coffee
Espresso

Great Northern Lumber, Inc.
2200 W. 127th St.
Blue Island, IL 60406
Contact: Jeff Currier, Pres.
Telephone: 708-388-1818
Fax: 708-388-9235
Email: jcurrier@greatnorthernlumber.com / URL: http://www.greatnorthernlumber.com
Product Service Description:
Sawmills & planing mills, general
Lumber processing & wooden products
Wood products

Great Southern Insulation Corp.
PO Box 22337
Fort Lauderdale, FL 33335
Contact: Don Barnett, Pres., GM
Telephone: 954-763-1844
Fax: 954-763-1873
Email: barnettgsi@earthlink.net / URL:
Product Service Description:
Sound & heat insulation blankets & covers
Custom Sound Shields for Generators
Sound Deapening Carpet Underlayment
Acoustical Materials for Industrial,
Automotive & Marine Applications

Great Western Tortilla Company, The
P.O. Box 16346
Denver, CO 80216
Contact: William A. Ralston, President
Telephone: 303/298-0705
Fax: 303-298-0216
Email: rally@tortilla-chips.com / URL: http://www.tortilla-chips.com
Product Service Description:
Tortilla Chips, Baked, Reduced Fat & Fried
Organic Tortilla Chips

Greco Homes
11403 58th Ave E
Puyallup, WA 98373-4351
Contact: Daniel Greco, Pres.
Telephone: 253-848-5537
Fax: 253-848-7847
Email: grecohomes@msn.com / URL: http://www.grecohomes.com
Product Service Description:
Manufactures custom homes & sunrooms
Prefabricated wood buildings
Manufactures log sunrooms

Green Bay Packaging, Inc./ Coated Products Operations
PO Box 19017
Green Bay, WI 54307-9017
Contact: Franklin Arias, International Sales Mgr.
Telephone: 920-337-1830
Fax: 920-337-1797
Email: farias@gbp.com / URL: http://www.gbp.com
Product Service Description:
Paper coated & laminated
Pressure-sensitive roll labels

Green Valley Pecan Company
PO Box 7
Sahuarita, AZ 85629-0007
Contact: Tim Minnehan, V.P. Sales & Marketing
Telephone: 520-791-2852
Fax: 520-791-2853
Email: timm@zapecans.com / URL: http://www.azpecans.com
Product Service Description:
Shelled Pecans

GreenDisk Inc
16398 Ne 85th St Ste 100
Redmond, WA 98052-3527
Contact: David Beschen, Pres., CEO
Telephone: 425-883-9165
Fax: 425-883-0425
Email: / URL: http://www.greendisk.com
Product Service Description:
Manufactures recycled computer supplies
Manufactures recycled magnetic diskettes

Greendale Nursery
28300 S.W. 177th Ave.
Homestead, FL 33030-1911
Contact: Mark Wilson, President
Telephone: 305-248-7070
Fax: 305-947-4558
Email: sales@greendalenursery.com / URL: http://www.greendalenursery.com
Product Service Description:
Plants

Greene Poultry, Don
12701 N.W. 38th Ave.
Opa Locka, FL 33054
Contact: Sales & Marketing, *
Telephone: 305-687-0000
Product Service Description:
Frozen French Fries

Greener Corp.
1110 Beach Ave
Beachwood, NJ 08722-2202
Contact: M. Wojtech, GM
Telephone: 732-341-3880
Fax: 732-286-7842
Email: mikew@greenercorp.com / URL: http://www.greenercorp.com
Product Service Description:
Packaging machinery

Greenfield Industries
PO Box 2587
Augusta, GA 30903-2587
Contact: John Woodbridge, Dir/Int'l Sales
Telephone: 706-650-4253
Fax: 706-860-6021
Email: / URL: http://www.GFII.com/it
Product Service Description:
Cutting Tools Twist Drills Reamers
Metalworking Taps Dies & Gauges
Metalworking End Mills
Geometric Die Heads & Chasers

Greenleaf Wholesale Florist Inc
909 E Indian School Rd
Phoenix, AZ 85014-4745
Contact: Vincent C. Tromatore, Mgr.
Telephone: 602-264-3781
Fax: 602-230-0922
Email: / URL:
Product Service Description:
Wholesales flowers, nursery stock and
florists' supplies

Greenmont Lumber Corp. (Mfr)
P.O. Box 25
Underhill, VT 05489
Contact: Ron Villeneuve, President
Telephone: 802-899-2311
Fax: 802-899-4498
Email: / URL:
Product Service Description:
Hardwood Lumber

Gregory Truck Body & Fire Apparatus, Inc.
711 Kevin Ct
Oakland, CA 94621-4039
Contact: Jesse Jones, GM
Telephone: 510-635-7171
Product Service Description:
Manufactures beverage truck bodies and fire
apparatus : Truck & bus bodies & emergency
vehicles : Motor vehicle supplies & new parts

Gribetz International, Inc.
13800 Nw 4th St
Sunrise, FL 33325-6221
Contact: John Garrett, Pres.
Telephone: 954-846-0300
Fax: 954-846-0381
Email: / URL: http://www.gribetz.com
Product Service Description:
Textile machinery : Quilting & other machines
for the mattress industry

Griffin Food Company
111 South Cherokee, PO Box 1928
Muskogee, OK 74402-1928
Contact: Mike Miller, Dir/Sales & Mktg.
Telephone: 918-687-6311
Fax: 918-687-3579
Product Service Description:
Jelly / Preserves
Syrups
Mustards
Dressings
Coconut

Griffin Pipe Products Co.
PO Box 740
Lynchburg, VA 24505-0740
Contact: Lewis H. Higginbotham, Export
Manager
Telephone: 804-522-4738
Fax: 804-522-4739
Email: griffin@griffinpipe.com / URL: http://
www.griffinpipe.com
Product Service Description:
Ductile Iron Press. Pipe, 3-48 D.
Ductile Iron Compact Fittings 3-48 D
Ductile Iron Sewer Pipe 4-48 D.

Griffith Shade Co.
308 Washington Ave
Nutley, NJ 07110-1926
Contact: John K. Griffith, Pres.
Telephone: 973-667-1474
Fax: 973-667-0469
Product Service Description:
Vertical blinds & shades
Drapery hardware & blinds & shades

Groom Industries, Inc.
PO Box 5723
Rockford, IL 61125-0723
Contact: Franklin C. Beach, Pres.
Telephone: 815-874-7212
Fax: 815-874-1616
Email: xhmw70a@prodigy.com / URL: http://
www.perkycarpetcare.com
Product Service Description:
Carpet grooming tools, chemicals & brushes
Tools_hand & edge
Chemical preparations
Brooms & brushes

Grote Industries, Inc.
PO Box 1550
Madison, IN 47250-0550
Contact: Dominic Grote, Marketing Manager
Telephone: 812-273-1296
Fax: 812-265-8440
Email: safety@grote.com / URL: http://
www.grote.com
Product Service Description:
Truck Safety Equipment
Lighting Equipment, Vehicular
Wiring Harnesses
Reflective Devices
Mirrors

Grover Manufacturing Corp.
P.O. Box 986
Montebello, CA 90640-0986
Contact: Arlene D. Meeker, President
Telephone: 213-724-3444
Fax: 213-724-3596
Email: / URL:
Product Service Description:
Hose Reels
Air Operated Pumps
Industrial Pumping Systems
Vehicle Lubrication Equipment
Industrial Lubrication Equipment

Guard Lee, Inc.
1723 Benbow Ct
Apopka, FL 32703-7730
Contact: Edward Guard, Pres.
Telephone: 407-886-7112
Fax: 407-886-3819
Email: shuttlesrus@earthlink.net / URL:
Product Service Description:
Space vehicle and aircraft replicas (full scale)
Space theme park design and construction
Robots and electro/mechanical exhibits
Training devices, military and aerospace
Large custom fiberglass and steel/aluminum
structures : Museum artifact repair and space
suit fabrication : Film industry props (ref.
"From the Earth to the Moon")

Guardian Metal Sales, Inc.
6132 Oakton St.
Morton Grove, IL 60053-2735
Contact: Joe Yereb, Vice Pres,. Sales
Telephone: 708-967-7400
Fax: 708-967-0879
Product Service Description:
Metal Slitting Warehouse

Guava Beach
20807 Belshaw Ave
Carson, CA 90746-3511
Contact: Michael Biscotto, Ptnr.
Telephone: 310-537-5858
Fax: 310-537-1249
Email: guavabch@aol.com / URL:
Product Service Description:
Manufactures resort wear for men, women
and children

Guide Corporation
2915 Pendleton Ave
Anderson, IN 46016-4848
Contact: John Underwood,
Sales & Mktg. Mgr.
Telephone: 765-641-6439
Fax: 765-641-5066
Email: lnusguid.wz0hq9@eds.com / URL:
Product Service Description:
Lighting equipment_vehicular
Automotive lighting equipment, automotive
components : Engineering automotive lighting
optics : Manufacturing automotive lighting

Gulf Coast Seal, Inc.
9119 Monroe Rd
Houston, TX 77061-5232
Contact: Steve Leatherwood, President
Telephone: 713-910-7700
Fax: 713-910-6600
Email: seals@gulfcoastseal.com / URL: http:/
/www.gulfcoastseal.com
Product Service Description:
Parker Seals, O-rings, Polypaks, Rubber
Moldings : Oilpatch Seals, Valve Stem
Packing, Wellhead Packoffs
Teflon, PEEK, Ryton (PPS), Nylon
Machining

Gulf Valve Company
6511 Winfree Dr.
Houston, TX 77087-2217
Contact: Jim Phillips, Mktg. Mgr.
Telephone: 713-644-7333
Fax: 713-644-0047
Email: wcheck@juno.com / URL: http://
www.gulfvalve.com
Product Service Description:
Check Valves

Gulfstream Aerospace Corp.
PO Box 2206
Savannah, GA 31402-2206
Contact: Christian H. Flathman
Telephone: 912-965-5951
Fax: 912-965-4333
Email: christian.flathman@gulfaero.com /
URL: http://www.gulfstreamaircraft.com
Product Service Description:
Corporate jet aircraft
Gulfstream V
Gulfstream IV-SP
Gulfstream Aircraft Services
Gulfstream Financial Services Corp.
Gulfstream Lease
Gulfstream Charter Services
Gulfstream Management Services
Gulfstream Shazes

Gum Tech International(Mfr)
P.O. Box 36195
Phoenix, AZ 85067-6195
Contact: Jerry Kern, *
Telephone: 602-277-0606
Fax: 602-277-1765
Product Service Description:
Nutrient Chewing Gum

Gunnell Inc.
8440 State Rd.
Millington, MI 48746
Contact: Dwight Gay, Pres.
Telephone: 517-871-4529
Fax: 517-871-4563
Email: info@gunnell-inc.com / URL: http://
www.gunnell-inc.com
Product Service Description:
Surgical appliances & supplies
Wheelchairs

H & H Seed Company Inc
PO Box 1688
Yuma, AZ 85366-1688
Contact: Patrick K Hodges Jr, Pres.
Telephone: 520-783-7821
Fax: 520-343-0156
Email: h1835@aol.com / URL: http://
www.hhseed-swt.com
Product Service Description:
Wholesales seed and grain
Farm supplies
Grain & field beans
Seed production
Sudan
Alfalfa
Vegetable seed

H & K Equipment Inc.
Arch St. Ext.
Carnegie, PA 15106
Contact: George Koch, Pres., Sales Mgr.
Telephone: 412-279-9953
Fax: 412-279-7415
Email: hkequip@hkequipment.com / URL:
http://www.hkequipment.com
Product Service Description:
Industrial forklift trucks
Trucks & tractors_industrial

H & R Industries, Inc.
PO Box 1191
Beecher, IL 60401-1191
Contact: Renee Normoyle, Customer Service
Telephone: 708-946-3244
Fax: 708-946-3251
Email: / URL: http://www.hrind.com
Product Service Description:
Insulated shipping & storage equipment

H & R Mfg. & Supply, Inc.
PO Box 3183
Conroe, TX 77305-3183
Contact: Harvey Hivnor, Pres., Fin. & R & D
Mgr.
Telephone: 409-856-5529
Fax: 409-856-8550
Email: hrm@lcc.net / URL:
Product Service Description:
Chuck & machine tool parts
Machine tool accessories

H & S Tool & Die Co.
PO Box 260
Warrensburg, IL 62573-0260
Contact: L. L. Smith, Pres.
Telephone: 217-672-3622
Fax: 217-672-8313
Email: hstool@hstool.com / URL:
Product Service Description:
General machining & tool & die job shop,
metal stampings & plastic injection molding
Dies, tools, jigs & fixtures_special

H P J, Inc.
3290 Overland Rd
Apopka, FL 32703-9473
Contact: Arturo Gonzales, V-P., GM
Telephone: 407-292-7557
Fax: 407-292-7676
Email: / URL:
Product Service Description:
Automotive air conditioning condensers &
evaporators

H.A. Stiles
170 Forest St.
Westbrook, ME 04092
Contact: Ambrose Berry, President
Telephone: 207-854-8458
Fax: 207-854-3863
Email: info@hastiles.com / URL: http://
www.hastiles.com
Product Service Description:
Hardwood Dimension and Flooring Mills
Oak wood in the rough, whether or not
stripped of bark or sapwood or roughly
squared, not treated
Hardwood Dowels
Hardwood Turnings
Moulded & Shaped Wood Products
Hardwood Furniture Panels
Hardwood Lumber
Wooden Handles
Hardwood Furniture Blanks
Hardwood Squares & Rounds

H.K. Systems, Von Gal Palletizers
P.O. Drawer 177
Montgomery, AL 36101-0177
Contact: M.G. Smith, *
Telephone: 334-261-2818
Fax: 334-261-2800
Email: jack.smith@hksystems.com / URL:
Product Service Description:
Conveying Equipment: Process, Carton,
Palletizers: Low, Medium, High Speed
Depalletizers: Bulk, Carton

H.M. Electronics, Inc.
6675 Mesa Ridge Rd.
San Diego, CA 92121-3996
Contact: Sales & Marketing,
Telephone: 619-535-6000 / 800-848-4468
Fax: 619-552-0139
Email: jramirez@hme.com / URL: http://
www.hme.com
Product Service Description:
Wireless drive-thru intercoms

H2O, Inc.
110 Row 1
Lafayette, LA 70508
Contact: Jesse Fike, Pres.
Telephone: 318-234-8017
Fax: 318-233-3919
Email: h2oinc@worldnet.att.net / URL: http://
www.watermaker.com
Product Service Description:
Reverse osmosis equipment
Machinery, special industry

H2oil Corporation
2509 Technology Dr.
Hayward, CA 94545-4869
Contact: Kevin Johnson, Manager
Telephone: 510-785-8833
Fax: 510-786-8778
Email: bcsong@aol.com / URL: http://
www.h2oil.com
Product Service Description:
Microemulsion fuel additive to produce 21st
century clean gasoline & diesel fuel

HASP Inc
2707 W Eisenhower Blvd Ste 8
Loveland, CO 80537-3141
Contact: Ronnie Hogan, Pres.
Telephone: 970-669-6900
Fax: 970-669-7901
Email: shirley@hasp.com / URL:
Product Service Description:
Computers, peripherals & software Hewlett
Packard

HB Environmental Engineers Inc
3000 Honolulu Ave Apt 4
Glendale, CA 91214-3767
Contact: Harry Bronozian, Pres.
Telephone: 818-248-3529
Fax: 818-248-6343
Email: hbenviro@ix.netcom.com / URL:
http://www.hbenvironmental.com
Product Service Description:
Industrial wastewater treatment & recycling
systems

HBS Equipment Corp
14700 Alondra Blvd
La Mirada, CA 90638-5616
Contact: Don LeBaron, Pres.
Telephone: 714-522-4100
Fax: 714-521-4488
Email: / URL:
Product Service Description:
Manufactures electroplating and plating
equipment
Rectifiers and DC power supplies
Anodizing systems

HH ele Corporation
10891 Business Dr
Fontana, CA 92337-8235
Contact: Mike Khavarinejad, Dir. of
Operations
Telephone: 909-355-4200
Fax: 909-355-2700
Email: mkhavar@hhele.com / URL:
Product Service Description:
Custom plastic injection molding
Plastic products

HK Systems, Inc.
2100 Litton Ln
Hebron, KY 41048-9508
Contact: Sales & Marketing,
Telephone: 606-334-2400
Fax: 606-334-2689
Product Service Description:
Auto Pallet Loaders / Unloaders
Case & Pallet Conveying Systems & Controls
Distribution Centers, Auto Storage/Retrg.
High Speed Sortation Systems

HMW Enterprises, Inc.
P.O. Box 309
Waynesboro, PA 17268-0309
Contact: H. M. Wutz, President
Telephone: 717-765-4690
Fax: 717-765-4660
Email: hmwent@planetcable.net / URL: http:/
/www.hmwent.com
Product Service Description:
Industrial Computers
Motion Control Systems & PLC

HTA
9 Hero Ct.
Pleasant Hill, CA 97523
Contact: William B. Hawe, Owner
Telephone: 925-938-9011
Fax: 925-939-9013
Email: htabillhawe@home.com / URL:
Product Service Description:
Customized Scientific High Vacuum
Equipment : Remanufactured Scientific High
Vacuum Equipment : Used Scientific High
Vacuum Equipment : New Scientific High
Vacuum Equipment : Remanufactured
Scientific Ultra High Vac. Equipment
Customized Scientific Ultra High Vac.
Equipment : Used Scientific Ultra High
Vacuum Equipment : New Scientific Ultra
High Vac. Equipment

Haber Co., D. W.
825 E 140th St
Bronx, NY 10454-1903
Contact: Robert Haber, CEO
Telephone: 718-993-6405
Fax: 718-585-0726
Email: sales@habersilver.com / URL: http://
www.habersilver.com
Product Service Description:
Silverware & plated ware
Silverware

Habitat Softwear
PO Box 2086
Montrose, CO 81402-2086
Contact: Drew Farnese, Pres.
Telephone: 970-249-3333
Fax: 970-249-0328
Email: / URL: http://www.habitatonline.com
Product Service Description:
Prints on T-shirts, sweatshirts and mugs;
embroidered garments

Hach Company
P.O. BOX 389
Loveland, CO 80529-0389
Contact: Sales & Marketing,
Telephone: 970-669-3050
Fax:
Email: / URL:
Product Service Description:
Chemicals & Allied Products
Proces Control Instruments
Analytical Instruments

Hagadone Directories Inc
PO Box 1266
Coeur D Alene, ID 83816-1266
Contact: James Hail, Pres.
Telephone: 208-667-8744
Fax: 208-765-2616
Email: / URL:
Product Service Description:
Publishes telephone directories— North
Idaho Regional Directory, Paradise Valley
Regional Directory
North Central Washington Directory
Columbia Gorge Directory, Northwest
Montana Directory

Hale Co., F. E.
650 W German St
Herkimer, NY 13350-2134
Contact: James Benson, Pres.
Telephone: 315-866-4250
Fax: 315-866-6417
Email: hale@ntcnet.com / URL: http://
www.woodbookcases.com
Product Service Description:
Wooden bookcases
Office furniture_wood

Hale Engineering Co.
100 Gordon St
Elk Grove Village, IL 60007-1120
Contact: Curtis B. Hale, Pres., Pur. & Sales
Mgr.
Telephone: 847-956-1600
Fax: 847-956-0595
Email: halco4@juno.com / URL: http://
www.halco-products.com
Product Service Description:
Clean room systems, heating & air
conditioning equipment, chillers,heat pumps
water source

Hale Products, Inc.
700 Spring Mill Ave
Conshohocken, PA 19428-1996
Contact: Bob Talladay, V-P., CEO
Telephone: 610-825-6300
Fax: 610-825-3555
Email: / URL: http://www.haleproducts.com
Product Service Description:
Pumps & pumping equipment
Pumps & rescue tools

Hall Co., The
PO Box 38158N
Urbana, OH 43078-2176
Contact: Rick Hunt, Sls. Mgr.
Telephone: 800-441-4255 or 937-652-1376
Fax: 937-653-7447
Email: hallco@foryou.net / URL: http://
www.hallco.com
Product Service Description:
membrane Switches, Metal & Plastic Panel
Fronts, Nameplates & Screen Printing
Surfact Mount Components
Large Surface Switches

Hall Industrial Services
PO Box 9544
Wichita, KS 67277-0544
Contact: Scott Hall,
Vice President
Telephone: 316-945-4255
Fax: 316-945-4494
Email: hallindsvc@aol.com / URL: http://
www.hallservices.com
Product Service Description:
Rebuilt industrial machinery
Industrial machinery, movers, rigging

Hall-Welter Co.
485 Hague St.
Rochester, NY 14606-1209
Contact: Philip A. Collins,
President
Telephone: 716-235-8240
Fax: 716-235-8807
Email: / URL:
Product Service Description:
Check-Writing Machinery
Check-Signing Machinery

Halm Industries Company Inc.
180 Glen Head Rd.
Glen Head, NY 11545-1995
Contact: Ralph Thomas, Vice President /
Sales & Marketing
Telephone: 516-676-6700
Fax: 516-676-6751
Email: halm@panix.com / URL: http://
www.halm.com
Product Service Description:
Envelope Printing Machinery

Halton Co.
101 Industrial Dr
Scottsville, KY 42164-7932
Contact: Rick Bagwell,
President
Telephone: 502-237-5600
Fax: 502-237-5700
Email: rickbagwell@haltroncompany.com /
URL: http://www.haltroncompany.com
Product Service Description:
Commercial Kitchen Ventilation Systems

Hamer, Jim C.
P.O. Box 480
Kenova, WV 25530
Contact: Jim C Hamer, President
Telephone: 304-453-6381
Fax: 304-453-6587
Email: hamerjh@zoonet.com / URL: http://
www.jimchamer.com
Product Service Description:
Sawmills; timberlands; kiln drying facilities;
veneer mill; pellet mill
Green & kiln dried, rough or planed, random
& sorted for width hardwood grade lumber
Green, rough & sized heart-centered cants
Logs : Basswood veneer for plywood
Densified hardwood pellet fuel
Hardwood chips & unprocessed bark
Hardwood mulch

Hamilton Beach/Proctor Silex, Inc.
4421 Waterfront Dr.
Glen Allen, VA 23060-3375
Contact: Brent Gilchrist, International
Financial Planning Supervisor
Telephone: 804-527-7270
Fax: 804-527-7196
Email: / URL:
Product Service Description:
Irons
Blenders
Toasters
Toaster Ovens
Food Processors
Mixers
Drink Mixers
Juicers / Extractors
Coffeemakers
Electric Knives

Hamilton Bell Co., Inc.
30 Craig Rd
Montvale, NJ 07645-1709
Contact: Jim Sanvito, Pres.
Telephone: 201-391-4100
Fax: 201-391-5994
Email: hamiltonbell@mindspring.com / URL:
http://www.hamiltonbell.com
Product Service Description:
Laboratory centrifuges
Laboratory apparatus & furniture

Hamilton Embroidery Co., Inc.
907 21st St
Union City, NJ 07087-2104
Contact: Frank Blaso, Pres.
Telephone: 201-867-4084
Fax: 201-867-2066
Email:
hamiltonembroidery@compuserve.com /
URL: http://www.expresspages.com/h/
hamiltonembroidery.com
Product Service Description:
Embroidered Schiffli Laces & Fabrics

Hammett Co., Inc., J. L.
Hammett Pl., P.O. Box 9057
Braintree, MA 02184
Contact: David H. Shepard, Director
Telephone: 781-848-1000
Fax: 781-843-4901
Email: dave.shepard@hammett.com / URL:
http://www.hammett.com
Product Service Description:
School supplies instructional materials
Stationary & office supplies
Art materials
School furniture & equipment
Early childhood ed materials

Hampshire Pewter Co.
43 Mill St
Wolfeboro, NH 03894-4328
Contact: R. Steele, Pres.
Telephone: 603-569-4944
Fax: 603-569-4524
Email: hpewter@worldpath.net / URL: http://
www.hampshirepewter.com
Product Service Description:
Hand-cast pewter tableware & Christmas
ornaments

Hampton Lumber Sales Co
9400 SW Barnes Rd Ste 400
Portland, OR 97225-6660
Contact: Mike Phillips, Pres.
Telephone: 503-297-7691
Fax: 503-203-6604
Email: / URL: http://www.hamptn.com
Product Service Description:
Sawmills & planing mills, general
General sawmill (wholesale distribution
center)
Lumber, plywood & millwork

Hamre Equipment
3930 Esplanade
Chico, CA 95973-0200
Contact: Lee Hamre, Owner
Telephone: 530-895-8955
Fax: 530-895-8959
Email: lilenus@hamrenet.com / URL: http://
www.hamrenet.com
Product Service Description:
Heavy construction equipment - reconditioned
& new
Industrial machinery & equipment
Logging & sawmill equipment
Complete sawmills re-conditioned

**Handy Geotechnical Instruments,
Inc.**
1502 270th St
Madrid, IA 50156-7522
Contact: Richard Handy, Chrm., R & D Mgr.
Telephone: 515-795-3355
Fax: 515-795-3998
Email: rlhandy@picnet.net / URL:
Product Service Description:
Geotechnical testing equipment

Hanjin Shipping Co. Ltd.
1521 Pier C St.
Long Beach, CA 90813
Contact: Christian Sur, *
Telephone: 310-499-4600
Product Service Description:
Freight & Cargo Transportation

Hankison International
1000 Philadelphia St
Canonsburg, PA 15317-1777
Contact: Robert D. Marshall,
Telephone: 724-746-4240 X. 216
Fax: 724-745-6040
Email: bmarshall@hankisonintl.com / URL:
http://www.hankisonintl.com
Product Service Description:
Compressed air dryers & filters

Hanlon International
145th Ave. & Hook Creek Blvd.,
Valley Stream, NY 11581
Contact: Raymond Mojica, President
Telephone: 516-568-0880
Fax: 516-568-0883
Email: hanlonintl@aol.com / URL:
Product Service Description:
Customs Broker

Hannah Katherine Fashions Corp.
419 B 35th St # B
Union City, NJ 07087
Contact: Cesar Fonseca,
Telephone: 201-866-9000
Fax: 201-866-1616
Email: hkfashns@bellatlantic.net / URL:
http://www.hannahkatherine.com
Product Service Description:
Bikinis
Outerwear_women's & misses'
Dresses
Dance Wear

Hanover Clocks & Banners
5316 Us Highway 421 N
Wilmington, NC 28401-2254
Contact: Ken Woodcock, Pres.
Telephone: 910-343-0400
Fax: 910-343-0101
Email: hanoverclo@aol.com / URL: http://
www.hanover.com
Product Service Description:
Wooden & Plastic Clocks & Banners
(Custom)

Hanover Wire Cloth
500 East Middle St., P.O. Box 473
Hanover, PA 17331
Contact: Darrell Raubenstine, Dir. / Int'l
Sales
Telephone: 717-637-3795
Fax: 717-637-5949
Email: hwcexport@cvn.net / URL: http://
www.hanoverwire.com
Product Service Description:
Woven Wire Products, Insect Screening
Aluminum Drawn Wire
Plastic Window Screen
Fiberglass Yarn PVC Coated

Hans Rudolph, Inc. (Mfr)
7200 Wyandotte Street
Kansas City, MO 64114
Contact: John Rudolph, President
Telephone: 816-363-5522
Fax: 816-822-1414
Email: hri@rudolphkc.com / URL:
Product Service Description:
Medical Respiratory Instruments

Hansen Machine & Tool Co., N. M.
PO Box 6938
Toledo, OH 43612-0938
Contact: Ron W. Clark, Chrm Engrg Mgr.,
Roger Burditt, VP GM
Telephone: 419-476-5500
Fax: 419-476-8169
Email: kcimt@netscape.net / URL:
Product Service Description:
Aerospace CNC & general machining job
shop
Machine build & rebuild
Glass delivery equipment
Tooling rework programs

Hanson Welding Machines, Inc.
PO Box 710
Fletcher, NC 28732-0710
Contact: Charles R. Miller, Pres.
Telephone: 828-687-3701
Fax: 828-687-1712
Email: hanson@ioa.com / URL:
Product Service Description:
Welding machinery
Industrial machinery

Hapco Aluminum Poles
P.O. Box 547
Abingdon, VA 24212-0547
Contact: David Oakley, Marketing & Bus.
Dev. Mgr.
Telephone: 540-628-7171
Fax: 540-628-7707
Email: info@hapco.com / URL: http://
www.hapco.com
Product Service Description:
Light Poles & Brackets & Flagpole Shafts

Harbingers Of a New Age
717 E Missoula Ave
Troy, MT 59935-9609
Contact: James A Peden, Owner
Telephone: 406-295-4944
Fax: 406-295-7603
Email: vegepet@aol.com / URL: http://
www.montanasky.net/vegepet
Product Service Description:
Manufactures vegetarian pet food
supplements; publishes book referring to
products
Feeds_prepared
Book publishing

Harco Manufacturing Co.
7700 S.W. 69th Ave.
Portland, OR 97223
Contact: R. L. Harris, President
Telephone: 503-244-7571
Fax: 503-244-7589
Email: / URL:
Product Service Description:
Tractor Cab Air Pressurizers
Oily Water Separators
Engine Exhaust Spark Arrestors

Hardwood Veneer
3700 Blackhawk Rd., PO Box 78
Sherrard, IL 61281
Contact: Sales & Marketing,
Telephone: 309-793-1188
Fax: 309-787-2843
Email: hvc94@aol.com / URL:
Product Service Description:
Lumber
Container Cargo
Hardwood Logs

Harken International, Ltd.
1251 E. Wisconsin Ave.
Pewaukee, WI 53072-3755
Contact: Olaf Harken, VP
Telephone: 414-691-3320
Fax: 414-691-3008
Email: harken@harken.com / URL: http://
www.harken.com
Product Service Description:
Sailboat Equipment
Marine Hardware
Boat Shoes
Sunglasses
Sailing Watches

Harley-Davidson, Inc.
1425 Eden Rd.
York, PA 17402-1507
Contact: Dave Alamshah, Director of
Transportation
Telephone: 717-848-1177
Product Service Description:
Motorcycles, Bicycles, and Parts
Motorcycles and cycles fitted with an
auxiliary motors; Side-cars
Parts and accessories of motorcycles
Road wheels and parts and accessories
thereof for vehicles

Harmon Industries, Inc.
1600 NE Cornado Drive
Blue Springs, MO 64014
Contact: Lloyd T. Kaiser, EX.VP Sales &
Service, William P. Marberg, EX. VP Sys.
Telephone: 816-229-3345
Fax: 816-229-0556
Email: Sbrumbac@harmonind.com / URL:
http://www.harmonind.com
Product Service Description:
Railroad crossing signal & communication
equipment & systems
Communications equipment, nec

Harmon Technological
3746 Johnson Ave.
Gowrie, IA 50543-9317
Contact: Doug Harmon, V-P., Pur.
Telephone: 515-352-3574
Fax: 515-879-2780
Product Service Description:
Medicinals & biological serum production
Anitibody negative (IBR-BVD)

Harmony Enterprises, Inc. G P I
PO Box 479
Harmony, MN 55939-0479
Contact: Steve Cremer, Pres.
Phone: 507-886-6666 / Fax: 507-886-6706
Email: harmony1@harmony1.com / URL:
http://www.harmony1.com
Product Service Description:
Paper baling equipment & stationary
compactors: Recycling & Waste Handling
Equipment

Harmony Laboratories, Inc.
PO Box 39
Landis, NC 28088-0039
Contact: J. Michael Gorman,
Telephone: 704-857-0707
Fax: 704-855-1090
Email: harlab@comcentric.net / URL: http://
www.harmonylabs.com
Product Service Description:
Cosmetics & pharmaceuticals

Harrington & King South, Inc.
PO Box 2248
Cleveland, TN 37320-2248
Contact: Jimmy Thurman, GM
Phone: 423-479-8691 / Fax: 423-479-8694
Email: sales@hkperf.com / URL: http://
www.hkperf.com
Product Service Description:
Metal perforating: Metal stampings

Harris Moran Seed Co.
P.O. Box 4938
Modesto, CA 95352
Contact: Jean - Charles Ganas, COO
Phone: 209-549-5271 / Fax: 209-548-9973
Email: jc.ganas@harrismoran.com / URL:
http://www.harrismoran.com
Product Service Description:
Vegetable Seeds

Harris-Welco Co.
PO Box 69
Kings Mountain, NC 28086-0069
Contact: Bill Roland, Pres.
Phone: 704-739-6421 / Fax: 704-739-2801
Email: broland@jwharris.com / URL: http://
www.j.w.harris.com
Product Service Description:
Aluminum, Stainless, Copper Base Alloy,
Mild Steel for MIG & TIG Welding
Brazing & Soldering Alloys
Welding Accessories

Harriss & Covington Hosiery Mills, Inc.
PO Box 1909
High Point, NC 27261-1909
Contact: John Boylan, Sales Mgr.
Telephone: 336-882-6811
Fax: 336-889-2412
Email: jboylan@harrissandcov.com / URL:
Product Service Description:
Men's, women's & children's casual athletic
socks with logos

Hart Design & Mfg, Inc.
1940 Radisson St.
Green Bay, WI 54302-2037
Contact: Dennis Adelmeyer I nt'll Sales
Telephone: 414-468-5927
Fax: 414-468-5888
Email: hartdesn@netnet.net / URL: http://
www.hartdesign.com
Product Service Description:
Food Products Machinery
Packaging Machinery

Hartel Systems Division, Advanced Separations & Process Systems, Inc.
201 N. Main Street
Fort Atkinson, WI 53538-0369
Contact: Chet Luch, VP Marketing & Sales
Telephone: 920-563-8461
Fax: 920-563-7417
Email: hartel@intaccess.com / URL: http://
www.hartelcorp.com
Product Service Description:
Food, dairy, cosmetic, chemical &
pharmaceutical biotechnology processing
systems : Food products machinery

Hartland Sales
7381 E 6th Ave # 4
Scottsdale, AZ 85251-3401
Contact: Ken Simpson, Owner
Telephone: 602-874-3908
Fax: 602-874-3968
Email: sales@hartlandsales.com / URL: http:
//www.hartlandsales.com
Product Service Description:
Manufacturers' rep for electronic parts
Electronic Components

Hartlee System Inc
1695 W Sheri Ln
Littleton, CO 80120-1018
Contact: Lee Milligan, CEO
Telephone: 303-794-3250
Fax: 303-797-4807
Product Service Description:
Manufactures thermoset plastic products to
help people breathe easier or stop snoring

Hartley Gove Sons
PO Box 909
Brookhaven, MS 39602-0909
Contact: Ed Gove Jr., Pres.
Telephone: 601-833-2911
Fax: 601-833-2913
Product Service Description:
Thermometer Tubes (Glass Liquid Filled)

Hartson Kennedy Cabinet Top Co.
PO Box 6569
Gulfport, MS 39506-6569
Contact: Chris Kennedy, V-P., GM
Phone: 228-896-1548 / Fax: 228-896-3903
Email: info@hartsonkennedy.com / URL:
http://www.hartsonkennedy.com
Product Service Description:
Plastic laminated countertops &
Solid surface countertops & products

Hartz Mountain
400 Plaza Dr., Ste. 400
Secaucus, NJ 07094-3688
Contact: Edward Stern, President
Telephone: 201-271-4800
Fax: 201-271-0134
Email: ejstern@hartz.com / URL: http://
www.hartz.com
Product Service Description:
Dog and Cat Food
Saddlery and harness for any animal ,
of any material
Flea & Tick Powders
Pet toys
Bird & small animal edibles
Fish food
Rawhide bones & natural treats
Cat litter

Hartzell Hardwoods Inc.
P.O. Box 919
Piqua, OH 45356
Contact: John Owsiany, General Manager
Telephone: 937-773-7054
Fax: 937-773-6160
Email: sales@hartzellhardwoods.com / URL:
Product Service Description:
Hardwood Lumber, Rough, Sawed

Harva Co., Inc., The
100 Fair St.
Schoharie, NY 12157
Contact: S. McGiver, President
Telephone: 518-295-8101
Fax: 518-295-7827
Email: harva@harva.com / URL: http://
www.harva.com
Product Service Description:
Fabricated Plastic Parts

Hastings Industries
Hastings Ind. Pk., P.O. Box 548
Hastings, NE 68901
Contact: Ronald L. Hartzell, *
Telephone: 402-463-9821
Fax: 402-462-8006
Email: / URL:
Product Service Description:
Refrigeration & Heating Equipment
Direct Gas & Indirect Gas Fired Make-Up
Air
Air Handling Units
Gas Fired Unit Heaters
Direct & Indirect Evaporative Cooling
Oil Fired Heating Units

Hatch & Kirk
5111 Leary Ave., N.W.
Seattle, WA 98107-4888
Contact: Jim Griffiths, VP Sales & Mktg.
Telephone: 1-800-426-2818
Fax: 206-782-6482
Email: jgriffiths@hatchkirk.com / URL: http:/
/www.hatchkirk.com
Product Service Description:
Parts of railway or tramway locomotives

Hatfield, Inc.
PO Box 902
Hatfield, PA 19440-0902
Contact: David Budnick, CFO
Telephone: 215-368-2500
Fax: 215-362-1750
Email: daveb@hqm.com / URL: http://
www.hqm.com
Product Service Description:
Meat processing
Meat packing plants

Hatzlachh Supply Inc.
935 Broadway, 6th Fl.
New York, NY 10010
Contact: Jesse Broker, *
Telephone: 212-254-9012
Fax: 212-529-0620
Product Service Description:
Television Set & Radio combination

Havetronix, Inc.
2507 W. Schneidman Ave.
Quincy, IL 62301
Contact: Robert Havermale, Pres.
Telephone: 217-222-2186
Fax: 217-222-2263
Email: / URL: http://www.havetronix.com
Product Service Description:
Electronic assembly

Hawaii Pacific Associates
3095 Crocker Rd.
Eugene, OR 97404-1874
Contact: Edmond D. Baekus,
Telephone: 503-689-9611
Fax:
Email: / URL:
Product Service Description:
Water Treatment Purification Commercial
Switchgear & Switchgear Apparatus

Hawaiian Eateries, Inc.
46-168 Malina Pl
Kaneohe, HI 96744-3803
Contact: Frank Baker, Pres.
Telephone: 808-247-1223
Fax: 808-247-2228
Email: / URL:
Product Service Description:
Refrigerated Hawaiian Food, Salads
Vacuum Packed Vegetables, Shredded
Cabbage

Hawaiian Host, Inc.
500 Alakawa St Rm 111
Honolulu, HI 96817-4576
Contact: Dennis Teranishi, Pres.
Telephone: 808-848-0500
Fax: 808-848-0055
Email: dteranishi@hawaiianhost.com / URL:
http://www.hawaiianhost.com
Product Service Description:
Chocolate-covered macadamia nuts
Candy & other confectionery products
Canned Macadamia Nuts & Almonds

Hawaiian King Candies
P.O. Box 29500
Honolulu, HI 96820
Contact: J. Marvin Fialco, President
Telephone: 808-833-0041 Ext. 104
Fax: 808-839-7141
Email: / URL:
Product Service Description:
Chocolate Covered Macadamia Nuts
Chocolate Covered Almonds
Macadamia Nuts
Macadamia Nut Cookies

Hawaiian Vintage
4614 Kilauea Ave Ste 435
Honolulu, HI 96816-5309
Contact: Jim Walsh, Pres., Fin. & R & D
Mgr.
Telephone: 808-735-8494
Fax: 808-735-9640
Email: hwvi@hwvi.com / URL: http://
www.hawaiia@choclate.com
Product Service Description:
Chocolate & cocoa products

Hawe Technical Associates (HTA)
9 Hero Ct.
Pleasent Hill, CA 94523
Contact: William B. Hawe, Owner
Telephone: 925-938-9011
Fax: 925-938-9013
Email: htabillhawe@home.com / URL:
Product Service Description:
Customized Scientific High Vacuum
Equipment : Remanufactured Scientific High
Vacuum Equipment : Used Scientific High
Vacuum Equipment : New Scientific High
Vacuum Equipment : Remanufactured
Scientific Ultra High Vacuum
New Scientific Ultra High Vacuum

Hawker Pacific, Inc.
11310 Sherman Way
Sun Valley, CA 91352
Contact: John V. Shade, *
Telephone: 818-765-6201
Fax: 818-765-2065
Product Service Description:
Aircraft & Equipment, Export

Hawkeye Forest Products Inc
305 W Bannock St
Boise, ID 83702-6033
Contact: John J Hawkinson, Pres.
Telephone: 208-344-8865
Fax: 208-344-8801
Email: jgeiger@micron.net / URL: http://
www.hawkeyeforest.com
Product Service Description:
Produces Kiln-dried Hardwood Lumber

Hawkeye Steel Products, Inc.
PO Box 2000
Houghton, IA 52631-2000
Contact: Cindy Wellman, Sales & Mktg. Mgr.
Telephone: 319-469-4141
Fax: 319-469-4402
Email: broweriowa@aol.com / URL: http://
www.hawkeyesteel.com
Product Service Description:
Livestock & grain handling equipment

Hawks Express Inc.
32 Jacobus Ave.,
Kearny, NJ 07032
Contact: Sales & Marketing,
Telephone: 973-344-5400
Fax: 973-344-2525
Product Service Description:
Freight & Cargo Transportation
Trucking
Warehousing & Distribution

Haworth Press, Inc., The
10 Alice Street
Binghamton, NY 13904
Contact: William Cohen, Pres.
Telephone: 607-775-3385
Fax: 607-722-1424
Product Service Description:
Publisher
"Latin American Business Review"

Hawthorne Paint Co., Inc.
PO Box 157
Hawthorne, NJ 07507-0157
Contact: Murray Greene, Pres.
Telephone: 973-423-2335
Fax: 973-423-9363
Email: / URL:
Product Service Description:
Commercial, residential, industrial &
automotive paint
Paints & allied products

Hawthorne Power Systems
16945 Camino San Bernardo
San Diego, CA 92127
Contact: Bob Price, Exec. Vp, Div. Mgr.
Telephone: 619-974-6800
Fax: 619-974-6819
Email: / URL: http://www.hawthorne-
hps.com
Product Service Description:
Engines_internal combustion
Internal combustion engines, generator sets,
cogeneration systems and parts
Motors & generators
Industrial machinery & equipment

Hayes Lemmerz International, Inc.
14500 Firestone Blvd
La Mirada, CA 90638-5913
Contact: Jesus Bonilla, Plt. Mgr.
Telephone: 714-994-0150
Fax: 714-670-1227
Email: jbonilla@hayes-lemmerz.com / URL:
Product Service Description:
Manufactures aluminum wheels for cars

Hayes Tool Inc.(Mfr)
P.O. Box 4582
Martinsville, VA 24115
Contact: David Hayes, President
Telephone: 540-627-8665
Fax: 540-627-8000
Email: hayes@digdat.com / URL: http://
www.hayestool.com
Product Service Description:
Solid Carbide Router Bits

Health Impact Inc
130 Nickerson St Ste 212
Seattle, WA 98109-1658
Contact: Madeline Beery, Pres.
Telephone: 206-284-3865
Fax: 206-284-3879
Email: ai@nwlink.com / URL:
Product Service Description:
Retails educational video and audio tapes;
manufactures educational books for health
Publishing, miscellaneous
Record & prerecorded tape stores

Health Valley Foods
16100 Foothill Blvd
Irwindale, CA 91706
Contact: Ron Rash, VP
Telephone: 626-334-3241 X. 212
Fax: 626-969-9176
Email: rdrash@earthlink.net / URL:
Product Service Description:
Food products
Manufactures natural & organic foods
Private label & contract manufacturing

Heartland Communications Group Inc.
PO Box 1052
Fort Dodge, IA 50501-1052
Contact: James B. kersten, Sr. V.P. & C.O.O.
Telephone: 800-247-2000
Fax: 515-955-1600
Email: jbkathlipublishing.com
URL: http://hlipublishing.com
Product Service Description:
Info. Retrieval, Used & New Const. Eq.
Database/Magazine : Info. Retrieval, Used &
New Agri. Eq. Database/Magazine
Info. Retrieval, Used & New Plane/Jet Eq.
Database/Magazine : Used & New Industrial
Machinery / Magazine :Used & New Plastic
Equipment Magazine

Heartland Flagpoles, Inc.
PO Box 526
Brooklyn, IA 52211-0526
Contact: Alexander Wehrle, Pres., Fin.,
Opers. & R & D Mgr.
Telephone: 515-522-7060
Fax: 515-522-7162
Email: / URL:
Product Service Description:
Aluminum & fiberglass flagpoles, flags,
banners & accessories

Heartland Mill, Inc.
RR 1 Box 2
Marienthal, KS 67863-9557
Contact: Mark Nightingale, GM
Telephone: 316-379-4472
Fax: 316-379-4459
Email: hartland@pta6000.pld.com / URL:
Product Service Description:
Organic grain & flour processing
Flour & other grain mill products
Organic Oat Products
Organic Beans
Organic Sunflower Nutrients

Heavy Duty Hydro Blasting, Inc.
1360 53rd St
West Palm Beach, FL 33407-2207
Contact: Ali Sader, GM, Sales & Mktg. Mgr.
Telephone: 561-842-2338
Fax: 561-842-2811
Email: / URL:
Product Service Description:
Hydroblasting surface preparation equipment
Pumps & pumping equipment
Fluid power pumps & motors
40,000 PSI Waterblasting services

Heavy Equipment Parts Co., Div. of Paul E. Volpp Tractor Par
9240 Pizototype Dr.
Reno, NV 89511
Contact: Paul A. Volpp, President
Telephone: 702-851-6510
Fax: 702-851-6518
Email: sales@hepco.com / URL: http://
www.hepco.com
Product Service Description:
Hydraulic Cylinder Seals
Mobile Equipment Seals
Engine Gaskets
Tractor Parts

Hebco Products, Inc.
PO Box 46
Bucyrus, OH 44820-0046
Contact: Kevin Hessey, Pres.
Telephone: 419-562-7987
Fax: 419-562-8577
Email: hebco@hebco-products.com / URL:
http://www.hebco-products.com
Product Service Description:
Automotive & heavy duty brake parts & air
brake hose assemblies
Motor vehicle parts & accessories

Hecla Industries, LLP
PO Box 128
Hecla, SD 57446-0128
Contact: Corwin Osterloh, CFO
Telephone: 605-994-2171
Fax: 605-994-2645
Email: joco@uslink.net / URL: http://
www.uslink.net/~joco/hi
Product Service Description:
Skid Steer Loaders & Hay Moving
Equipment

Hector Turf
1301 N.W. 3rd St.
Deerfield Beach, FL 33442-1697
Contact: James R. Mantey, President
Telephone: 954-429-3200
Fax: 954-360-7657
Email: execoffc@hectorturf.com / URL: http:/
/www.hectorturf.com
Product Service Description:
Lawn & golf course equipment
Irrigation equipment

Hedges & Bros., L.P.
115 S Lincoln Ave
Washington, NJ 07882-2175
Contact: John Walsh, Owner
Telephone: 908-689-6440
Fax: 908-689-6390
Email: hedges@enter.net / URL: http://
www.hedgesandbrother.com
Product Service Description:
General machining job shop
Industrial machinery
"Pilot" Flush Valves & Strainers

Heil Trading Co. Inc.
3808 Bells Lane
Louisville, KY 40211
Contact: Larry Stivers, President
Telephone: 502-772-7200
Fax: 502-778-5400
Email: larrystivers@paragon-trailer.com /
URL: http://www.paragon-trailer.com
Product Service Description:
Truck Tanker Trailers, Wholesale
Truck Trailers, Wholesale
Tank Trailer Parts

Heinzen Manufacturing Inc
405 Mayock Rd
Gilroy, CA 95020-7040
Contact: Alan Heinzen, Pres.
Telephone: 408-842-7233
Fax: 408-842-6678
Email: hmisales@heinzen.com / URL: http://
www.heinzen.com
Product Service Description:
Food products machinery
Manufactures food processing equipment

Helander Products, Inc.
PO Box 247
Clinton, CT 06413-0247
Contact: Gordon Helander, Pres., R & D
Mgr.
Telephone: 860-669-7953
Fax: 860-669-6756
Email: / URL:
Product Service Description:
Miniature clutches

Held & Associates, Inc.
P.O. Box 34470,
Kansas City, MO 64116-0870
Contact: Richard L. Held, President
Telephone: 816-842-6701
Fax: 816-842-6724
Email: info@held-assoc.com / URL: http://
www.held-assoc.com
Product Service Description:
Customs Broker
Freight Forwarder
Freight & Cargo Transportation

Heldenfels Enterprises, Inc.
PO Box 4828
Corpus Christi, TX 78469-4828
Contact: Fred W. Heldenfels IV, Pres.
Telephone: 361-883-9334
Fax: 361-883-8914
Email: fred.heldenfels@heldenfels.com
Product Service Description:
Prestressed & precast concrete products
Concrete products

Helical Wire Inc
PO Box 6630
Incline Village, NV 89450-6630
Contact: Jack Staten, Pres.
Telephone: 775-832-7444
Fax: 775-832-7454
Email: helicalwir@aol.com / URL:
Product Service Description:
Manufactures screw thread inserts and related
tooling

Helicoid Div., Bristol Babcock Inc.
1100 Buckingham St.
Watertown, CT 06795-1631
Contact: Joe McGrail, Marketing
Telephone: 860-945-2218
Fax: 860-945-2220
Email: 110362.1534@compuserve.com /
URL: http://www.bristolbabcock.com/
helicoid.htm
Product Service Description:
Pressure Gauges - Cam & Roller Design
Pressure Indicating Switches
Diaphragm Seals
Bimetalic Thermometers
Exclusive Cam & Roller Movement Means
Lowest Life Cycle Cost To You

Heliodyne, Inc. (Mfr)
4910 Seaport Avenue
Richmond, CA 94804
Contact: Christel D. Bieri, Vice President
Telephone: 510-237-9614
Fax: 510-237-7018
Email: / URL:
Product Service Description:
Solar Energy Collectors
Solar Hot Water

Heller Industries
4 Vreeland Rd.
Florham Park, NJ 07932-1593
Contact: Marc Peo, President
Telephone: 973-377-6800
Fax: 973-377-3862
Email: hellerind@aol.com / URL: http://
www.hellerindustries.com
Product Service Description:
Ovens

Helsel Lumber Mill, Inc.
3446 Johnstown Rd
Duncansville, PA 16635-3308
Contact: Charles Salyards Jr.,
Telephone: 814-696-0869
Fax: 814-696-3857
Email: info@helsellumber.com / URL: http://
www.helsellumber.com
Product Service Description:
Sawmills & planing mills, general
Kiln dried lumber & mouldings

Hemisphere Enterprises
4100 N.W. 72nd Ave.
Miami, FL 33166-6840
Contact: Raphael Restrepo, Owner
Telephone: 305-477-8899
Product Service Description:
Packing Materials
Metal Scrap & Strapping Equipment
Corrugated Boxes
Carton Sealing Tape
Strech Systems & Supplies
Shrink Systems & Supplies
Stapling Systems
Warehouse Equipment
Automatic Tape Systems
Automatic Strapping Systems

Henderson Mills Inc.
48100 E. 160th Avenue
Keenesburg, CO 80701
Contact: Gerald Dalke, President,
Telephone: 303-644-4384
Fax: 303-644-3132
Email: / URL:
Product Service Description:
Corn, Blue Yellow & White - Organic

Hendrix Manufacturing Co., Inc.
P.O. Box 919
Mansfield, LA 71052-0919
Contact: G. B. Hall, III, President
Telephone: 318-872-1660
Fax: 318-872-1508
Email: / URL: http://www.hendrixmfg.com
Product Service Description:
Dragline buckets, excavator buckets,
hydraulic
Couplers, compaction wheels, rippers, wear
Parts for construction & mining industry.

Hendrix, Miles, Hendrix Company
P.O. Box 2047
Presidio, TX 79845
Contact: Sales & Marketing,
Telephone: 915-229-3208
Fax: 915-229-3660
Email: hendrix.miles@internetmci.com /
URL:
Product Service Description:
Customs Broker
Freight Forwarder
Freight & Cargo Transportation

Henny Penny Corp.
PO Box 60
Eaton, OH 45320-0060
Contact: John S. Carver, Marketing Manager
Telephone: 937-456-8400
Fax: 937-456-8956
Email: sales@hennypenny.com / URL: http://
www.hennypenny.com
Product Service Description:
Pressure fryers, display & holding cabinets,
breading machines & rotisseries
Service industry machinery

Henri Studio Inc.
1250 Henri Dr
Wauconda, IL 60084-1000
Contact: Robert J. Borta, VP Sales & Mktg.
Telephone: 847-526-5200
Fax: 847-526-6782
Email: / URL: http://www.henristudio.com
Product Service Description:
Concrete Fountians & Statuary
Pond & Water Garden Products
Resin Fountains & Garden Gift Products
Rotational - Molded Poly Planters

Henry Company International
2900 Bristol St. # A-101
Costa Mesa, CA 92626
Contact:Richard Adamson, Marina Cammero
Telephone: 714-557-8133
Fax: 714-557-9361
Email: / URL: http://www.henry.com
Product Service Description:
Roof coatings & cements
Elastomeric roof coatings
SBS membranes
Auto undercoatngs & sound deadeners
Wax emulsions for gypsum industry
Polyurethane foam
Sealants for ships
Air barriers
Roof Underlayments
Waterproofing

Herba Aromatica Inc
23785 Cabot Blvd., Suite 318
Hayward, CA 94545
Contact: Galina Lisin, Pres.
Telephone: 510-266-0850
Fax: 510-266-0825
Email: aromaplant@aol.com / URL:
Product Service Description:
Custom formulation & manufacturers of
Phyto-Aromatherapy products
Importers of High Quality Essential Oils

Herbco International Inc.
11016 152nd Ave.
Kenosha, WI 53142-7999
Contact: Taras Remeniuk,
Telephone: 414-857-2373 - 414-857-3555
Fax: 414-857-9501
Product Service Description:
Botanicals - roots, barks, herbs
Plants and parts of plants , used primarily in
perfumery, pharmacy or for insecticides
Vegetables, dried and vegetable mixtures,
dried , but not further prepared

Herburger Publications Inc
PO Box 307
Galt, CA 95632-0307
Contact: Roy Herburger, Chrm.
Telephone: 916-685-5533
Fax: 209-745-4492
Email: / URL: http://www.gultherald.com
Product Service Description:
Publishes newspapers and other publications
Newspapers

Hercules Hydraulics Inc.
1016 N. Belcher Rd.
Clearwater, FL 33765
Contact: John Hoopes, Marketing Manager
Telephone: 727-796-1300
Fax: 727-797-8849
Email: jhoopes@herchyd.com / URL: http://
www.herculeshydraulics.com
Product Service Description:
Seals & Seal Kits, Mob. Hydraul.
Pumps, Cylinders, Valves, Wholesale
Hydraulic Parts, Wholesale
Seals & Seal Kits, Industrial, Wholesale

Herlocher Foods, Inc.
415 E Calder Way
State College, PA 16801-5663
Contact: Neil Herlocher, Vice President
Telephone: 814-237-0134
Fax: 814-237-1893
Email: herlochern@aol.com / URL: http://
www.iul.com/herlochr/
Product Service Description:
Mustard: Pickles, sauces & salad dressings

Hermetic Machines Inc.
3613 Pine St
New Orleans, LA 70125-1017
Contact: S. J. Deleon, Pres.
Telephone: 504-486-5471
Fax: 504-488-3939
Email: deleon@gs.verio.net / URL: http://
www.hemetic-machines.com
Product Service Description:
Compressors_air & gas
Rebuilt air conditioning & refrigeration
compressors

Hermle Black Forest Clocks
PO Box 670
Amherst, VA 24521
Contact: Helmut Mangold, General Manager
Telephone: 804-946-7751
Fax: 804-946-7747
Email: / URL:
Product Service Description:
Mechanical & Quartz Clocks Movements
Wall & Mantle Clocks

Hernandez Mattress, Inc.
2324 Port St
New Orleans, LA 70117-7416
Contact: Gloria S. Hernandez, Pres., Pur. Agt.
Telephone: 504-944-5571
Fax: 504-944-9648
Email: / URL: http://www.mypid.com/
hernandez
Product Service Description:
Mattresses, boxsprings, antiques
Government, maritime & coast guard
mattresses, sleepers & bedding
Offshore living quarters, any size or shape

Hernon Manufacturing Inc.
121 Tech Drive
Sanford, FL 32771-6663
Contact: Harry Arnon, President
Telephone: 407-322-4000
Fax: 407-321-9700
Email: hernon@totcon.com / URL: http://
www.hernomfg.com
Product Service Description:
Adhesives & Sealants & Dispensing
Equipment

Hershey Industries, Inc.
1209 Central Ave
Hillside, NJ 07205-2613
Contact: Henry Herbst, Pres.
Telephone: 908-353-3344
Fax: 908-351-4411
Email: / URL: http://www.lallypak.com
Product Service Description:
Bags; plastics, laminated & printed up to 8
colors

Hess Machine International
1054 S State St, PO Box 788
Ephrata, PA 17522-0788
Contact: E. Austin Hess, President
Telephone: 717-733-0005
Fax: 717-733-2255
Email: ozone@hessmachine.com / URL:
http://www.hessmachine.com
Product Service Description:
Special Industrial Machinery, Ozone
Machines

Hess Pumice Products Inc
PO Box 209
Malad City, ID 83252-0209
Contact: Marvin Hess, Pres.
Telephone: 208-766-4777
Fax: 208-766-4776
Email: salesmgr@hesspumice.com / URL:
http://www.hesspumice.com
Product Service Description:
Mines and manufactures pumice
Minerals, ground or treated
Miscellaneous nonmetallic minerals

Hess Pumice Products, Inc.
P.O. Box 209
Malad, ID 83252-0209
Contact: J. Marvin Hess, President
Telephone: 208-766-4777
Fax: 208-766-4776
Email: custserv@hesspumice.com / URL:
http://www.hesspumice.com
Product Service Description:
Abrasive Products
Mineral fillers & extenders
Pumice, other than crude or in irregular pieces
or crushed

Hexaport International, Ltd.
10 N Riverdale Rd
Weare, NH 03281-5545
Contact: Anthony Attalla, Pres., Scott M.
Coulombe, VP
Telephone: 603-529-1000
Fax: 603-529-0400
Email: sales@hexaport.com / URL: http://
www.hexaport.com
Product Service Description:
Commercial & residential steel building
frames
Prefabricated metal buildings
Social Housing
Light Gauge Metal Trusses

HeyMac Publishing, Inc.
3098 Piedmont Rd Ne Ste 150
Atlanta, GA 30305-2600
Contact: Robin Heyden, Ptnr.
Telephone: 404-816-4242
Fax: 404-816-3737
Email: heymac@mindspring.com / URL:
http://www.atlaptbook.com
Product Service Description:
Publish Free "Atlanta Apartment Book"

Heyden Mold & Bench Co.
PO Box 441
Tallmadge, OH 44278-0441
Contact: Gene Heyden, Pres., Sales Mgr.
Telephone: 330-630-2504
Fax: 330-630-3984
Email: / URL:
Product Service Description:
Dies, tools, jigs & fixtures_special
Rebuilt plastic injection molds
Specializing in welding & Diamond Finishing

Hi-Pro Industries, Inc.
11-D Empire Blvd.
South Hackensack, NJ 07606-1805
Contact: David Mike, Owner, Agnes
Nasinska
Telephone: 201-440-2838
Fax: 201-440-2753
Email: hipro@idt.net / URL:
Product Service Description:
AC Delco, GM, Chrysler, Motorcraft, Ford
Auto Parts

Hi-Tech Electronic Displays
13900 Us Highway 19 N
Clearwater, FL 33764-7238
Contact: Ralph J. Paonessa III, Pres.
Telephone: 727-531-4800
Fax: 727-524-6655
Email: sales@hitechled.com / URL: http://
www.hitechleo.com
Product Service Description:
Electronic moving message signs
Signs & advertising specialties

Hibel Corp., Edna
P.O. Box 9967
Riviera Beach, FL 33419
Contact: Andy Plotkin, President
Telephone: 561-848-9633
Fax: 561-848-9640
Email: hibel@worldnet.att.net / URL: http://
www.hibel.com
Product Service Description:
Collectable Art Gifts

Hick International Fastener Div
PO Box 5268
Carson, CA 90749-5268
Contact: Jim Dauw, V-P., GM
Telephone: 310-830-8200
Fax: 310-830-1436
Email: / URL: http://www.huck.com
Product Service Description:
Manufactures aerospace fasteners and
aerospace bolts
Bolts, nuts, rivets & washers

Hickory Specialties
P.O. Box 1669
Bremwood, TN 37027
Contact: D. Lindrum, *
Telephone: 615-373-2581
Fax: 615-371-1780
Product Service Description:
Liquid Smoke

High Country Plastics Inc
5118 N Sawyer Ave
Boise, ID 83714-1489
Contact: Tony Stevenson, Pres.
Telephone: 208-373-0957
Fax: 208-373-0965
Email: / URL:
Product Service Description:
Sells rotational, agricultural plastic water
tanks and feeders and other equine equipment

High Country Proco
PO Box 779
Berthoud, CO 80513-0779
Contact: John B. Hawley, Pres.
Telephone: 970-532-3711
Fax: 970-532-2107
Email: / URL:
Product Service Description:
Assembles propane trucks
Truck & bus bodies
Automobiles & other motor vehicles
Decals & lettering

High Steel Structures
PO Box 10008
Lancaster, PA 17605-0008
Contact: Steven Bussanmas, Sr, VP Sales &
Mktg.
Telephone: 717-299-5211
Fax: 717-399-4102
Email: / URL:
Product Service Description:
Blast furnaces & steel mills
Steel fabrication

High-Tech Conversions, Inc.
7 Taylor Rd
Enfield, CT 06082-4001
Contact: Caludio Orefice, Pres., GM
Telephone: 860-749-1622
Fax: 860-749-0747
Email: hitekcon@aol.com / URL: http://
www.high-techconversions.com
Product Service Description:
Clean room wiping cloths

Highland Laboratories
PO Box 199
Mount Angel, OR 97362-0199
Contact: Kenneth D Scott, Pres.
Telephone: 503-845-9223
Fax: 503-845-6364
Product Service Description:
Manufactures vitamins and health food
supplements; beauty creams and beauty aids

**Hill Country Newspapers Inc. / The
Boerne Star**
PO Box 820
Boerne, TX 78006-0820
Contact: Edna Keasling, Publisher
Telephone: 830-249-2441
Fax: 830-249-4607
Email: boerstar@aol.com / URL: http://
www.texhillcountrymall.com/boerstar.htl
Product Service Description:
Newspaper typesetting : Newspapers
Typesetting

Hilltop Ranch
13890 Looney Rd.
Ballico, CA 95303-9710
Contact: David H Long, Owner
Telephone: 209-874-1875
Fax: 209-874-1877
Email: hilltopdl@aol.com / URL: http://
www.hilltopranch.com
Product Service Description:
Crop Preparation Services for Market
Almonds, fresh or dried, shelled

Himmelstein & Co., S.
2490 Pembroke Ave
Hoffman Estates, IL 60195-2011
Contact: Sydney Himmelstein, Pres.
Telephone: 847-843-3300
Fax: 847-843-8488
Email: himmeltorq@aol.com / URL: http://
www.himmelstein.com
Product Service Description:
Precision instruments, rotary transformers,
torque meters, temperature monitor
equipment

Hispanic Books Distributors Inc
1328 W Prince Rd
Tucson, AZ 85705-3115
Contact: Arnulfo D Trejo, Pres.
Phone: 520-690-0643 / Fax: 520-690-6574
Email: hbdus@azstarnet.com / URL: http://
www.agstarnet.com/commrece/hbdusa
Product Service Description:
Distributes books and periodicals
Books, periodicals

Hitachi Maxco, Inc.
1630 Albritton Dr.
Kennewaw, GA 30152-4353
Contact: Kary Sugiyama, President
Phone: 770-424-9350 / Fax: 770-424-9145
Product Service Description:
Chains for Conveyors
Chain Tensioner
Free Access Floor Panels

Hitech Polymers, Inc.
1151 Aviation Blvd
Hebron, KY 41048-9333
Contact: M. McKinney, Opers. Mgr.
Telephone: 606-334-4500
Fax: 606-334-4501
Email: info@hitechpolymers.com / URL:
http://www.hitechpolymers.com
Product Service Description:
Compounded Thermoplastic Resins

Hobart Laboratories, Inc.
350 N Ogden Ave
Chicago, IL 60607-1135
Contact: Ramon Badillo, Pur. Agt.
Telephone: 312-432-1009
Fax: 312-432-1087
Email: kkostecka@aol.com / URL: http://
www.numotizine.simplenet.com
Product Service Description:
Pharmaceutical preparations
Medicines & pharmaceuticals

Hobi International, Inc.
1185 W Hawthorne Ln
West Chicago, IL 60185-1913
Contact: Cathy Hill, Pres.
Telephone: 630-231-6540
Fax: 630-231-6641
Email: cboswell@hobi.com / URL: http://
www.hobi.com
Product Service Description:
Recycling electronic equipment
Electronic components

Hodge Manufacturing Company
55 E Fisk Ave
Springfield, MA 01107-1056
Contact: Edwin L Kossoy, Pres., Treas.
Telephone: 413-781-6800
Fax: 413-733-6573
Email: hodgemfg@javanet.com / URL: http://
www.hodgemfg.com
Product Service Description:
Material Handling Equipment and Metal
Waste Receptacles
Metal Stampings
Metal Cabinets, Carts, Benches & Tucks

Hoffman Tool & Die Inc.
PO Box 257
Fairbury, IL 61739-0257
Contact: Ron Hoffman, Pres.
Telephone: 815-692-2628
Fax: 815-692-3840
Email: htdinc@hoffmantool.com / URL: http:/
/www.hoffmantool.com
Product Service Description:
Tool & die job shop
Dies, tools, jigs & fixtures_special
Machine tools, metal forming types
Rolling mill machinery
Industrial machinery

**Hoffmann Pulications DBA:
Blacksmith's Journal**
PO Box 193
Washington, MO 63090-0193
Contact: Jerry Hoffmann, President
Telephone: 314-239-7049
Fax:
Email: journal@mail.usmo.com / URL: http://
www.blacksmithsjournal.com
Product Service Description:
Periodicals
Blacksmithing publication

Holbrooks
5111 Grumman Dr
Carson City, NV 89706-0436
Contact: Ray Holbrooks, Pres.
Telephone: 702-883-5556
Fax: 702-883-6616
Email: / URL:
Product Service Description:
Edge grip, wafer handler (silicon wafers)
Electronic design
Mechanical Design
Mechanical & electronic packaging

Holcroft
12068 Market Street
Livonia, MI 48150
Contact: Timothy J. McMann,
V.P Mktg. & Sales
Telephone: 734-591-1000
Fax: 734-591-6443
Email: / URL: http://www.holcroft.com
Product Service Description:
Heat Treating Furnaces, Electrical
Steel Reheating Furnaces, Fuel Fired

Holland House Moving Inc., Ron
35545 Hwy. 69
Forest City, IA 50436
Contact: Ron Holland, Pres., Engrg., Hum.
Res. & Opers. Mgr.
Telephone: 515-585-3630
Fax: 515-585-2525
Email: rholland@netins.net / URL:
Product Service Description:
House moving dollies & pneumatic tire
machinery
Trucks & tractors_industrial

Hollingsworth & Vose Co.
112 Washington St.
East Walpole, MA 02032
Contact: Dianne Newman,
Telephone: 508-668-0295
Fax: 508-668-6526
Email: info@hollingsworth-vose.com / URL:
http://www.hollingsworth-vose.com
Product Service Description:
Automotive Gasket Composite Materials
Automotive Filter Papers : High Efficiency
Filter Papers : Computer Disk Liners
Apparel, Interlining : Battery Separator,
Storage Batteries & Primary Batteries
Filtration Media : Electrical Insulation
Materials

Hollow Metal Specialists, Inc.
740 Apex Rd
Sarasota, FL 34240-8759
Contact: Don Hilliard, Pres.
Telephone: 941-379-1970
Fax: 941-371-4026
URL: http://www.hollowmetalspecialists.com
Product Service Description:
Hollow Metal Doors & Frames : Hollow
Metal Windows : Wood Doors
Door Hardware

Hollymatic Corporation (Mfr)
600 E. Plainfield Road
Countryside, IL 60525
Contact: Don Berkey, Corporate Director /
Sales & Marketing
Telephone: 708-579-3700
Fax: 708-579-1057
Email: hollyinfo.com / URL: http://
www.hollymatic.com
Product Service Description:
Food Products Machinery

Hollywood
P.O. Box 7201
Hackettstown, NJ 07840-1114
Contact: Kasim Hadzozic, Owner
Telephone: 908-813-9600
Fax: 908-813-0219
Email: rocky@goes.com / URL: http://
www.hollywood-usa.net
Product Service Description:
Drugs, Proprietaries, and Sundries
Depilatories and other perfumery, cosmetic or
toilet preparations : Beauty or make-up
preparations and preparations for care of the
skin including sunscreens and suntan
preparations : Preparations for use on the hair

Holman Label Company
PO Box 198, 60 E. Hanover Ave.
Morris Plains, NJ 07950-0198
Contact: George W. Mueller, Office Coord.
Telephone: 201-267-5400
Fax: 201-267-3713
Email: / URL: http://www.holmanlabel.com
Product Service Description:
Custom printed pressure sensitive labels
Coating & engraving, Nameplates

Holmes Ice & Cold Storage Co
340 N I St
San Bernardino, CA 92410-1814
Contact: Harry Holmes, Pres.
Telephone: 909-884-2151
Fax:
Email: / URL:
Product Service Description:
Manufactures ice; public cold storage
Ice_manufactured
Refrigerated warehousing & storage
Manufactures bottled water
Dry ice & propane

Home Dynamix
17 Empire Blvd
South Hackensack, NJ 07606
Contact: Sales & Marketing,
Telephone: 201-807-0111
Fax: 201-329-7491
Email: / URL:
Product Service Description:
Vinyl Tile
Rugs
Mats

Home Safeguard Industries Inc.
P.O. Box 6030
Malibu, CA 90264-6030
Contact: Leon Cooper, President
Telephone: 310/457-5813
Fax: 310-457-4862
Email: export@homesafeguard.com / URL:
http://www.homesafeguard.com
Product Service Description:
Smoke Detector Tester & Accessories
Heat Detector Testers
Carbon Monoxide Detector Tester ("Co
Check")
Dustair (Clean Smoke Detectors on Site)

**Home With Homeland News &
Printing Services**
PO Box 454
Forrest City, AR 72336-0454
Contact: Henerine Hunter, Owner
Telephone: 870-630-6450
Fax: 870-630-9072
Email: / URL:
Product Service Description:
Newspaper typesetting
Typesetting

**Homer Laughlin China Company,
The**
Harrison Street
Newell, WV 26050
Contact: Richard Blatchford,
Telephone: 304-387-1300
Fax: 304-387-0593
Product Service Description:
Commercial China

Hoodsport Winery Inc.
N. 23501, Hwy. 101
Hoodsport, WA 98548
Contact: Peggy J. Patterson, President
Telephone: 206-877-9760
Fax: 206-877-9508
Email: hoodsport@hotc.com / URL: http://
www.hoodsport.com
Product Service Description:
Wine, Brandy, & Brandy Spirits
Chocolate, Truffles
Canned & Smoke Fish; Smoked Trout

Hoover Machine Co., Inc.
624 Pinellas St # C
Clearwater, FL 33756-3368
Contact: Scott Hoover, Pres.
Telephone: 813-446-6338
Fax: 813-446-2839
Email: hoover@vwc.net / URL: http://
vwc.net/hoover/
Product Service Description:
Packaging & die cutting machinery
Packaging machinery
Paper industries machinery

Hope Industries
3206 N Central Ave
Rockford, IL 61101-1756
Contact: Linda tuttle, Production Mgr.
Telephone: 815-964-9275
Fax: 815-964-9607
Product Service Description:
Contract packaging : Plastic products

**Hopeman Brothers Marine
Interiors, LLC**
PO Box 820
Waynesboro, VA 22980-0606
Contact: David Rathburn, Pres.
Telephone: 540-949-9200
Fax: 540-949-9259
Email: hopeman@hopemanbrothers.com
Product Service Description:
Marine interior products
Furniture & fixtures

Hoppmann Corporation
14560 Lee Road, PO Box 601
Chantilly, VA 20153-0601
Contact: Tome Egan, Vp / Sales & Mktg.
Telephone: 703-631-2700
Fax: 703-631-9824
Email: feeder@hoppmann.com / URL: http://
www.hoppmann.com
Product Service Description:
Packaging Machinery

Horizon Forwarders Inc.
One Edgewater Plz.
Staten Island, NY 10305
Contact: Philip S. Rosso Jr., Chairman
Phone: (718) 727-3600 / Fax: (718) 442-7147
Email: grosso@horizonfwd.com / URL: http:/
/www.horizonfwd.com
Product Service Description:
Freight Forwarding : Freight Consolidation
Specializing in Prime & Waste Paper
Worldwide: Reefer Service Worldwide

Horizon Technology Group
1988 S County Road 593
Tiffin, OH 44883-9275
Contact: Gary Smith, Hum. Res. & Opers.
Mgr.
Telephone: 419-447-2221
Fax: 419-447-2842
Email: / URL: http://www.horizonet.com
Product Service Description:
Motor vehicle parts & accessories
Automotive wheel nuts & fasteners

Horner Discus International
5755 Powerline Road
Ft. Lauderdale, FL 33309-2001
Contact: Gera Kent, *
Telephone: 954-938-5355
Fax: 954-938-5244
Email: gkent@horner.mhs.compuserve.com /
URL:
Product Service Description:
Swimming Pool Parts & Access., Export
Spa Parts & Accessories, Export
Water Treatment Equipment
Swimming Pool Equipment & Spa Equipment
Chemicals
Water Purification / Water Treatment

Horsburgh & Scott Co., The
5114 Hamilton Ave
Cleveland, OH 44114-3908
Contact: J. J. Echko, Pres., D.J. Kraninger,
Sr. Vice Pres.
Telephone: 216-431-3900
Fax: 216-432-5850
Email: / URL: http://www.horsburgh-
scott.com
Product Service Description:
Speed changers, drives & gears
Industrial drive gears

Horton Homes, Inc.
PO Box 4410
Eatonton, GA 31024-4410
Contact: William I. Weeks, Ex. V-P.
Telephone: 706-485-8506
Fax: 706-485-4446
Email: / URL: http://www.hortonhomes.com
Product Service Description:
Modular / Manufactured Homes
Building Supplies

Hosokawa Micron Powder Systems
10 Chatham Rd.
Summit, NJ 07901
Contact: F. Sawamura, President
Telephone: 908-273-6360
Fax: 908-273-6364
Email: / URL:
Product Service Description:
Particle Size Reduction Equipment
Particle Size Classification Equipment
Industrial Mixing & Drying Equipment
Laboratory Analytical Devices

Hospi-Tel Manufacturing Co.
545 N. Arlington Ave., P.O. Box 4209
East Orange, NJ 07017
Contact: David Freedland, President
Telephone: 201-678-7100
Fax: 201-678-1482
Email: davidfr@aol.com / URL: http://
www.hospi-tel.com
Product Service Description:
Polyester Cubicle Curtains
Plastic Shower Curtains
Fabric Shower Curtains

Hoss Equipment
3131 N. Highway
Irving, TX 75062
Contact: Gregg Hoss, Owner
Telephone: 972-257-1244
Fax: 972-594-0622
Email: ghoss@dozernet.com / URL:
Product Service Description:
Construction and Mining Machinery
Dump trucks designed for off-highway use
Crawler tractors : Mechanical shovels,
excavators and shovel loaders, self-propelled
Wheel loaders : Motor scrapers : Water
trucks & tanks : Combination end dump,
bottom dump trailers, on-highway use

Hot Cell Services Corporation
22626 85th Place South
Kent, WA 98031
Contact: Mike Kalkwarf, *
Telephone: 253-854-4945
Fax: 253-854-4947
Email: hotcell@hotcell.com / URL: http://
www.hotcell.com
Product Service Description:
Window frames, Steel Radiation Shield

Hotsy Corporation, The
21 Inverness Way East
Englewood, CO 80112-5796
Contact: Carol Nazarenus, Mktg. / Export
Mgr.
Telephone: 303-792-5200
Fax: 303-792-0547
Email: / URL: http://www.hotsy.com
Product Service Description:
Steam Cleaning Equipment
Washer Pressure
Water Purification & Filtration Equipment
Pumps
Soap & Other Detergents

Houghton International, Inc.
PO Box 930
Valley Forge, PA 19482-0930
Contact: William F. MacDonald Jr., Chrm.,
Pres.
Telephone: 610-666-4000
Fax: 610-666-1376
Email: / URL: http://www.houghtonint2.com
Product Service Description:
Chemicals_industrial inorganic
Industrial chemicals

House Of Fashion Jewelry
14743 Lull St
Van Nuys, CA 91405-1211
Contact: George Antounian, Owner
Telephone: 818-902-1236
Fax: 818-902-9353
Email: / URL:
Product Service Description:
Jewelry_costume
Manufactures custom jewelry

House of Spices
12740 Willets Point Blvd.
Flushing, NY 11368-1506
Contact: G. L. Soni, Owner
Telephone: 718-507-4600
Fax: 718-507-4798
Email: hosindia@aol.com / URL: http://
www.hosindia.com
Product Service Description:
Durable Goods, NEC - Indian, Pakistani
Food & Groceries : Spices : Indian Style
Pickles, Chutneys, Pastes, & Condiments
Indian Style Snack Foods & Sweets
Fruit Drinks - Mazza Brand - Syrups

Houston Fearless 76
203 W Artesia Blvd
Compton, CA 90220-5550
Contact: Sales & Marketing Dept.,
Telephone: 310-605-0755 / 800-421-5000
Fax: 310-608-1556
Email: sales@houstonfearless.com / URL:
http://www.houstonfearless.com
Product Service Description:
Manufactures photographic and Microgarphic
equipment & supplies : Scanners: Fiche /
Jackets & 16/35mm Roll Film : Pollution
Control "True Zero Discharge" Systems

Houston Mfg. & Specialty Co., Inc.
PO Box 24339
Houston, TX 77229-4339
Contact: Morris Goolsby, Pres.
Telephone: 713-675-7400
Fax: 713-672-6613
Email: hms@houmfg.com / URL: http://
www.houmfg.com
Product Service Description:
Oil field gaskets
Gaskets, packing & sealing devices
Flange Insulation Sets
Teflon Gaskets & Packing
Fluid power cylinders & actuators

Houston Transfer & Storage Co.
6666 Mykawa Rd.
Houston, TX 77033
Contact: James Walt, President
Telephone: 713-645-4080
Fax: 713-649-0164
Email: / URL:
Product Service Description:
Trucking, Transportation
Warehousing & Distribution

Howard Industries
P.O. Box 1588
Laurel, MS 39441-1588
Contact: Billy W. Howard, CEO
Telephone: 601-425-3151
Fax: 601-422-1195
Email: bwhoward@howard.ind.com / URL:
http://www.howardcomputers.com
Product Service Description:
Transformers, Pole Pds, U/G
Electronic Fluorescent Ballast
Magnetic Fluorescent Ballast
HID Ballast
Computers, Desk Top (Personal)
Personal Computer Towers
Computer Servers
Notebook Personal Computers

Howard Leight Industries
7828 Waterville Rd
San Diego, CA 92173-4205
Contact: Thomas W. Klein, President
Telephone: 619-661-8383
Fax: 619-661-8393
Email: / URL: http://www.howardleight.com
Product Service Description:
Manufactures ear plugs and ear muffs

Howard, Bill
2266 Sylvan Rd.
East Point, GA 30344
Contact: Bill Howard,
Telephone: 404-669-8327
Fax: 404-669-8327
Email: / URL:
Product Service Description:
Service Establishment Equipment
Merry-go-rounds, boat-swings, shooting
galleries and other fairground amusements

**Howard-McCray Refrigerator Co.
Inc. (Mfr)**
Grant Ave. & Bluegrass Rd.
Philadelphia, PA 19114
Contact: Jeffrey Fogel, President
Telephone: 215-464-6800
Fax: 215-969-4890
Email: how-mcra@netreach.net
URL: http://www.howardmccray.com
Product Service Description:
Commercial Refrigerators

Howe & Howe Lexis Sales Corp
PO Box 10497
Phoenix, AZ 85064-0497
Contact: Roger Hilderbrand, Pres.
Telephone: 602-264-7971
Fax: 602-263-8914
Email: howehowe@aol.com / URL:
Product Service Description:
Manufacturers' rep for electromechanical
products & passive electronic components
Distributor for packaging products used in
Industry including plastic cases

Hoyin Industries
1815 Arnold Dr Ste 24
Martinez, CA 94553-6815
Contact: John Voorhees, Pres.
Telephone: 925-228-1240
Fax: 925-228-1241
Email: / URL:
Product Service Description:
Manufactures back-up monitor systems for
RV's and buses : Video inspection cameras
for engines : Video inspection systems for
pipe - sewers - tanks

Hoyle Products
345 E. Plato Blvd.
St. Paul, MN 55107
Contact: Jon Wiebusch, Vice President, Sales
& Marketing
Telephone: 651-293-7521
Fax: 651-293-7511
Email: wiebuschohoyleproducts.com
Product Service Description:
Playing Cards
Puzzles

Hsu's Ginseng Enterprises, Inc.
T6819 County Hwy. W., P.o. Box 509
Wausau, WI 54402
Contact: Paul Hsu, President
Telephone: 715/675-2325
Fax: 715-675-3175
Email: info@hsuginseng.com / URL: http://
www.hsuginseng.com
Product Service Description:
Ginseng Roots,capsules & Extracts,tea,seeds

Hubbell / The Ohio Brass Co. (Mfr)
P.O. Box 1001
Wadsworth, OH 44281
Contact: John S. Rumble, *
Telephone: 216-335-2361
Fax: 216-336-9252
URL: http://www.hubbellpowersystems.com
Product Service Description:
Electrical Composite Insulators

Huck Store Fixture Co.
PO Box 3007
Quincy, IL 62305-3007
Contact: Ron Hamann, Plt. Mgr.
Telephone: 217-222-0713
Fax: 217-222-0751
Product Service Description:
Wooden store fixtures

Hudnut Industries Inc
1720 SE Poplar Ave Ste B
Portland, OR 97214-4829
Contact: Ken Goehner, Pres.
Telephone: 503-293-7474
Fax: 503-239-5973
Email: hi@hudnut.com / URL: http://
www.hudnut.com
Product Service Description:
Makes cyclonic thermoplastic foam & film
recycling densifier & dryer systems
Builds related burners & cyclonic systems for
organic & inorganic particle mixing &
heat processing.

Hudson Products Corp.
PO Box 36100
Houston, TX 77236-6100
Contact: Fred Russell, V-P., GM
Telephone: 713-914-5700
Fax: 713-914-5990
Email: hudson.products@mcdermott.com /
URL: http://www.hudsonsprducts.com
Product Service Description:
Air-Cooled Heat Exchangers
Air-Cooled Steam Condensers
Axial Flow Fans
Heat Pipe Heat Exchangers

Hughes Compaction Equipment, Inc.
355 Mitchell Rd
Norcross, GA 30071-4239
Contact: Brett Hughes, Pres.
Telephone: 770-448-0224
Fax: 770-448-0866
Email: hughescompaction@netcom.com /
URL: http://www.hughescompaction.com
Product Service Description:
Industrial machinery

Hughes Electron Dynamics
PO Box 2999
Torrance, CA 90509-2999
Contact: Levon Thorose, Mktg. Manager
Telephone: 310-517-6196
Fax: 310-517-6301
Email: / URL: http://www.hughes.com
Product Service Description:
Communications equipment
Manufactures microwave electron tubes and
communications equipment
Microwave traveling wave tube amplifiers
(TWTAs)

Hull Forest Products, Inc.
101 Hampton Rd.
Pomfret Center, CT 06259
Contact: Duncan Mackintoch, V.P. Sales
Telephone: 860-974-0127
Fax: 860-974-2963
Email: / URL:
Product Service Description:
Hardwood Lumber & Dimension Mfg.

Hull Speed Data Products, Inc.
1800 Penn St Ste 8
Melbourne, FL 32901-2625
Contact: Donn Estus, Pres.
Telephone: 407-768-0063
Fax: 407-768-6730
Email: hsd@hullspeed.com / URL: http://
www.hullspeed.com
Product Service Description:
Interface converters, digital bridges & data
communication accessories

8 4

tact's

Humboldt Mfg. Co., Inc.
7300 W Agatite Ave
Norridge, IL 60656-4704
Contact: Dennis Burgess, Pres.
Telephone: 708-456-6300
Fax: 708-456-0137
Email: isabelle_hmc@msn.com / URL: http://www.hmc-hsi.com
Product Service Description:
Chemical laboratory, scientific & civil engineering testing equipment
Measuring & controlling devices

Hunt-Wilde Corp.
2835 Overpass Rd
Tampa, FL 33619-1315
Contact: Doug Hunt, Pres.
Telephone: 813-623-2461
Fax: 813-621-0664
Email: sales@huntwilde.com / URL: http://huntwilde.com
Product Service Description:
Injection molded handlebar grips, bicycle accessories & vinyl extrusions
Plastic products
Plastic foam products
Plastic profile shapes_unsupported

Hunte, Andrew
121 N. Royhill Blvd.
Goodman, MO 64843
Contact: Andrew Hunte, President
Telephone: 417-364-8597
Fax: 417-364-7700
Email: hunte@netins.net / URL: http://www.thehuntecorporation.com
Product Service Description:
The worlds leading supplier of quality puppies
Household goods, we are experienced in export
Over 50 breeds weekly to choose from.

Hunter, Anne M.
24200 Wildbrook Ct., Apt. 208
Southfield, MI 48034
Contact: Anne M. Hunter, Translator
Telephone: 248-357-4209
Fax: 248-357-4209
Email: / URL:
Product Service Description:
Translation Svcs., French, German, Spanish

Hunting Industrial Coatings
10448 Chester Rd
Cincinnati, OH 45215-1202
Contact: Ivan Banks, Sr. V-P., GM
Telephone: 513-771-6870
Fax: 513-771-2308
Email: jmthic@aol.com / URL:
Product Service Description:
Paints & Allied Products
Industrial, OEM & Maintenance Coatings

Huntington Mechanical Labs Inc
1040 Lavenida St
Mountain View, CA 94043-1422
Contact: Gerald H Hooper, Chrm.
Telephone: 650-964-3323
Fax: 650-964-6153
Email: vacman@huntvac.com / URL: http://www.huntvac.com
Product Service Description:
Stainless steel fabrication : design, machine weld, electropolish, leak chk
High vacuum & UHV components for research, aerospace, Semi. OEM's, etc.
Vacuum valves, motion feed throughs, positioning devices, chambers

Hurd Millwork Company, Inc.
575 South Whelen Ave.
Medford, WI 54451
Contact: Robert Reimann, Int'l Sales Mgr.
Telephone: 715-748-2011
Fax: 715-748-6043
Email: hurdint@midway.tds.net / URL: http://www.hurd.com
Product Service Description:
Windows & Patio Doors
Aluminum Clad Wood Windows & Patio Drs.
PVC Windows & Patio Doors

Hurdt & Associates Machinery
10260 S.W. 122nd St.
Miami, FL 33176-4816
Contact: Jack Hurdt, Owner
Telephone: 305-252-2247
Fax:
Email: / URL:
Product Service Description:
Industrial Machinery and Equipment - bakery products
Bakery machinery and machinery for the manufacture
Material handling machinery & equipment

Hutchens Bit Service, Inc.
11898 Commerce Ln.
Benton, IL 62812
Contact: Danny Robey, Oper. Pres.
Telephone: 618-439-9485
Fax: 618-439-9487
Email: HBSINC@Midwest.net / URL:
Product Service Description:
Rotary & percussion rebuilt drill bits.

Hutchison & Co.
6000 S Oak Park Ave
Chicago, IL 60638-4012
Contact: Charles L. Hutchison, Pres., Plt. & Sales Mgr.
Telephone: 708-594-2277
Fax: 708-594-8472
Email: / URL:
Product Service Description:
Unsupported plastics film & sheet
Plastic film converting & sausage casing aluminum tab assembly
Metal products_fabricated
Tubing, Mylar & Plastic films
Shirring of tubed product from 1" to 11" lay flat tube width
Plastic clipping
cook-in-bags from -75 deg. to 490 deg.

Hutzler Mfg. Co., Inc.
PO Box 969
Canaan, CT 06018-0969
Contact: Lawrence R. Hutzler, Pres.
Telephone: 860-824-5117
Fax: 860-824-5116
Email: hutzler@snet.net / URL:
Product Service Description:
Plastic housewares
Plastic products

Hybrid Semiconductors/Electronics Inc.
3194 Lawson Blvd
Oceanside, NY 11572-3716
Contact: Irv Gips, Pres.
Telephone: 516-763-6262
Fax: 516-763-2207
Email: igips@aol.com / URL:
Product Service Description:
Transistors & Diodes
Capacitors, Resistors
Connectors

Hyde Manufacturing Co.
54 Eastford Rd.
Southbridge, MA 01550-3604
Contact: Ralph Lawrence, President
Telephone: 508-764-4344
Fax: 508-765-9929
Email: custrelations@hydetools.com / URL: http://www.hydetools.com
Product Service Description:
Putty knives, paint scrappers & joint knives
Wall covering tools & hand knives

Hydra Management Inc.
10500 Richmond Ste., 228
Houston, TX 77042
Contact: James A. Swann, *
Telephone: 713-785-1451
Product Service Description:
Freight Forwarding

Hydra-Tech Systems Inc.
2416 Jonesboro Rd
West Monroe, LA 71292-6824
Contact: Tim Olson, Pres., Plt., Sales & Mktg. Mgr.
Telephone: 318-323-8289
Fax: 318-323-8544
URL: http://www.hydratechsystems.com
Product Service Description:
Fluid power pumps & motors, cylinders & valves

Hydratecs Injection Equipment, Inc.
430 Morgan Ave.
Akron, OH 44311
Contact: Carl A. Chiofolo, President
Telephone: 216-773-0491
Fax: 216-773-3800
Email: chiofolo@ix.netcom.com / URL: http://www.rubberword.com/hie
Product Service Description:
New Rubber Injection Equipment
Used Rubber Injection Equipment

Hydraulic Industrial Resources
PO Box 705
Hope Mills, NC 28348-0705
Contact: Marian Inman, Owner
Telephone: 910-426-0491
Fax: 910-424-4477
Email: hirs@fayettevillenc.com / URL: http://www.fayettevillenc.com/hirs
Product Service Description:
Hydraulic trailer & automotive hoses
Hose & belting_rubber & plastic
Motor vehicle parts & accessories

Hydro Engineering, Inc.
PO Box 300
Young America, MN 55368
Contact: Thomas Huffman, Vice President
Telephone: 612-467-3100
Fax: 612-467-4000
Email: hydro@hydro-eng.com / URL: http://www.hydro-eng.com
Product Service Description:
Farm Irrigation Equipment : Bio Sludge & Manure Injection Systems By Pumping

Hydro-Line Inc. Div. of IMC, Inc.
4950 Marlin Dr.
Rockford, IL 61108
Contact: Mike Peters, President
Telephone: 815-654-9050
Fax: 815-654-3393
Product Service Description:
Hydraulic Cylinders
Pneumatic Cylinders
Electric, Linear Positioning Cylinders

Hydroform USA Inc
2848 E 208th St
Carson, CA 90810-1101
Contact: Chet Jablonski, Pres.
Telephone: 310-632-6353
Fax: 310-632-0932
Email: hydroform@aol.com / URL:
Product Service Description:
Aircraft detail parts fabrication, specializing in forming sheet metal; hydroforming

Hygienic Products Laboratories
21-23 Industrial Park
Waldwick, NJ 07463-1540
Contact: Ernest Pedicano, Pres.
Telephone: 201-444-5140
Fax: 201-444-7112
Email: hygienic@bellatlantic.net / URL: http://www.hygienicproducts.com
Product Service Description:
Cleaning compounds, air fresheners & deodorizers
Urinal Screens & Bowl Cleaners

Hypro Corp.
375 5th Ave Nw
New Brighton, MN 55112-3239
Contact: Don Jorgensen, Pres.
Telephone: 651-766-6300
Fax: 651-766-6600
Email: / URL: http://www.hypropumps.com
Product Service Description:
Pumps & pumping equipment
Roller, centrifugal, diaphragm, pistons, plunger, turbine pumps, gears & impellers
Fluid meters & counting devices

Hyundai Precision & Industry
475 Sansome St Ste 1730
San Francisco, CA 94111-3103
Contact: Yong W. Lee, GM
Telephone: 415-788-5336
Fax: 415-788-1724
Email: ywlee96@aol.com / URL:
Product Service Description:
Manufactures transportation equipment
Transportation equipment

I P I International
1151 Atlantic Dr Unit 5
West Chicago, IL 60185-5104
Contact: Steven A. Wernicke, V-P.
Telephone: 630-293-7135
Fax: 630-293-9363
Email: wernicke@isoform.com / URL: http://www.isofoam.com
Product Service Description:
Plastic foam products
Urethane foam chemicals & dispensing equipment

I P S C O Steel Inc.
1770 Bill Sharp Blvd
Muscatine, IA 52761-9419
Contact: Joe Russo, Pres.
Telephone: 319-381-5300
Fax: 319-381-5329
Email: aparker@ipsco.com / URL: http://www.ipsco.com
Product Service Description:
Steel mills
Electric arc furnaces
Hot rolled coil
Hot rolled heavy plate
Discrete plate

To order copies of or advertise in The NAFTA Register®, call Global Contact at 856-642-9045 or fax 856-642-9056

I V Phoenix Group, Inc.
123 Marcus Blvd
Hauppauge, NY 11788-3702
Contact: Richard Pandolfi, Pres.
Telephone: 516-951-2700
Fax: 516-951-4290
Email: ivpgi@ix.netcom.com / URL: http://www.ivpgi.com
Product Service Description:
Electronic computers
Computers

I.C.E. (International Carbide & Engineering, Inc.)
5000 Main St.
Drakes Branch, VA 23937-0216
Contact: R.S. Ponton, President
Telephone: 804/568-3311
Fax: 804-568-3421
Email: iceva@npwt.net / URL: http://www.ice-va.com
Product Service Description:
Diamond Grinding Wheels
Saw Sharpening Supplies

IC Medical Inc
5170 W Phelps Rd
Glendale, AZ 85306-1309
Contact: Ioan Cosmescu, Pres.
Telephone: 602-547-9200
Fax: 602-547-0750
Product Service Description:
Manufactures surgical and medical equipment
Surgical & medical instruments
Medical & hospital equipment
Surgical smoke evacuation

ICA International Inc
2055 Anglo Dr Ste 200
Colorado Springs, CO 80918-3694
Contact: Phillip Fox, Pres.
Telephone: 719-533-0704
Fax: 719-528-1564
Email: service@icaeztoolcom / URL: http://www.eztool.com
Product Service Description:
Manufactures holding fixtures for inspecting machined parts

ICI Paints International - Export - Licensing
801 Canterbury Road
Westlake, OH 44145
Contact: G.M. Amato, Director - International
Telephone: 440-892-2916
Fax: 440-892-2970
Email: jerry_amato@ici.com / URL: http://www.icipaintexportusa.com
Product Service Description:
Acrylic Latex Coatings
Latex & Alkyd. Architectural Finishes
Acrylic Water Base Ind. Enamel
Paints, Wholesale : Paints, Protective
Coatings & Linings : Caulks, Sealants,
Adhesives : Aerosol Paints

ICS Electronics
473 Los Coches St
Milpitas, CA 95035-5422
Contact: Gerald K Mercola, Pres.
Telephone: 408-263-5500
Fax: 408-263-5896
Email: custsvc@icsselect.com / URL: http://www.icsselect.com
Product Service Description:
Manufactures and sells GPIB and VXI
interface products : Manufactures & sells
GPIB - Modbus controllers

ICS Penetron International
11 Seacliff Ln.
Miller Place, NY 11764-1529
Contact: Robert Revera, President
Telephone: 516-928-8282
Fax:
Email: / URL:
Product Service Description:
Waterproofing Compounds
Concrete protection

ICS Penetron International Ltd.
45 Research Way, Suite, 203
East Setauket, NY 11733
Contact: Robert G. Revera, Managing director
Telephone: 516-941-9700
Fax: 516-941-9777
Email: info@penetron.com / URL: http://www.penetron.com
Product Service Description:
Waterproofing Compounds
Concrete Protection

IDQ Books Worldwide Inc
919 E Hillsdale Blvd
San Mateo, CA 94404-4247
Contact: Stuart Crumbaugh, Director, Investor Reporting
Telephone: 415-655-3000
Fax: 415-655-3299
Email: ir@idqbooks.com / URL: http://www.idqbooks.com
Product Service Description:
Book publishing
Prepackaged software
Information: Knowledge products & content

IM & M Exercise Equipment Inc
0155 Shoop Dr
Penrose, CO 81240-9502
Contact: Frank Huerta, Pres.
Telephone: 719-784-4088
Fax: 719-784-3788
Email: extreme@ris.net / URL:
Product Service Description:
Manufactures exercise equipment

IMC Chemical, Inc.
8300 College Blvd.
Shawnee Mission, KS 66210-1841
Contact: Avinash Puri, VP
Telephone: 913-344-9200
Fax: 913-338-7926
Email: / URL:
Product Service Description:
Chemicals and Allied Products, NEC
Anhydrous disodium tetraborate, Sodium
Borates (Borax), Boric Acid, Specialty borates
Disodium carbonate
Sodium sulfates

INTERDEVCO & Associates
32960 Stagecoach Road
Nuevo, CA 92567-USA
Contact: Captain Ted Fekula, Chairman & CEO
Telephone: 909-928-3165
Fax: 909-928-3165
Email: Interdevco@aol.com / URL: http://home.earthlink.net/~interdevco
Product Service Description:
200 + Knot + Patrol Craft, Passenger Ferries,
Conatiner Ships, Yachts
Oil Refineries, (Refurbished & Modernized)
Turnkey Installation

IRA Levy & Associates
P.O. Box 1188
Rome, GA 30162-1188
Contact: Ira Levy, *
Telephone: 706-291-2944
Product Service Description:
Secondary Fibers
Linerboard
Kraft Paper
Printing & Writing

ITT Flygt Corp
35 Nutmeg Dr.
Trumbull, CT 06611-5448
Contact: Edward Pirro, Mgr./ Intl. Sales
Telephone: 203-380-4700
Fax: 203-380-4705
Email: / URL:
Product Service Description:
Electric Pumps, Submersible
Industrial Electric Mixers, Submersible
Hydroturbines, Submersible
Engineering Services
Electric Industrial Controls

IXMICRO
2085 Hamilton Ave Ste 300
San Jose, CA 95125-5924
Contact: Jack Lii, Pres.
Telephone: 408-369-8282
Fax: 408-369-0128
Email: jack.lii@ixmicro.com / URL: http://www.ixmicro.com
Product Service Description:
Computer peripheral equipment
Manufactures computer graphics boards &
ATM / ADSL communication hardware products

Icor International Inc.
2351 Kentucky Ave
Indianapolis, IN 46221-5008
Contact: Dick Perk, National Sales Mgr.
Telephone: 317-486-1851
Fax: 317-486-1853
Email: icorinfo@icorinternational.com / URL:
http://www.icorinternational.com
Product Service Description:
Refrigerant recovery equipment assembly
Alternate refrigerant R-414B, replacment for
R-12, R-134a, R-500

Idaho Frank Association
2175 N. California Blvd.
Walnut Creek, CA 94596
Contact: Sales & Marketing,
Telephone: 925-937-0240
Fax: 925-937-0129
Email: texp@mindspring.com / URL:
Product Service Description:
Potatoes, Dehyrdrated (Flakes, Granules, Slices)

Idaho Sewing For Sports
RR 2 Box 245
Grangeville, ID 83530-9615
Contact: Gail Williams, Pres.
Telephone: 208-983-0988
Fax: 208-983-1390
Email: / URL:
Product Service Description:
Manufactures protective padding for skiing area's
Sporting & athletic padding
Tubing hill supplies
Mfg. Ski area supplies
Mfg. Racing & athletic padding

Idea Engineering Company (Mfr)
1115 Race Street
Plattsmouth, NE 68048
Contact: Don R. Simms, *
Telephone: 402/296-3915
Fax: 402-298-8573
Email: / URL:
Product Service Description:
Printing Presses, Hot Stamp
Photoengraving Machines
Automatic Tag Stringing Machines

Ideal Stitcher Company(Mfr)
2323 N. Knox Avenue
Chicago, IL 60639
Contact: James Sullivan, General Mgr.
Telephone: 773-486-4141
Fax: 773-486-4812
Email: / URL:
Product Service Description:
Wire Stitchers & Staplers, Industrial
Wire & Stitching Wire

Ideal Transportation Co. Inc.
19 LeBlanc Dr.,
Peabody, MA 01960
Contact: Nadine DiGuilio, President
Telephone: 978-531-3161, 24 H
Fax: 978-532-0489
Email: idealtruck@aol.com / URL:
Product Service Description:
Freight & Cargo Transportation
Trucking

Identatronics, Inc.
425 Lively Blvd
Elk Grove Village, IL 60007-2011
Contact: GerardoTalavera, International Sales
Telephone: 847-437-2654
Fax: 847-437-2660
Email: / URL: http://www.indentatronics.com
Product Service Description:
ID Badges & Tags
Video Imaging Systems & Supplies

Identicator Inc.
4051 Glencoe Ave.
Naruba del Rey, CA 90292
Contact: John H. Martin, Director, Int'l Sales
Telephone: 310-305-8181
Fax: 310-578-1910
Email: info@indenticatorinc.com / URL:
http://www.identicatorinc.com
Product Service Description:
Manufactures fingerprinting devices (factory office)

Ikela Co.
4405 Independence Ct., Northgate Bus Ctr
Sarasota, FL 34234
Contact: Inge Kuschnitzky, Pres., CFO
Telephone: 941-355-6498
Fax: 941-355-1391
Email: sales@ikela.com / URL:
Product Service Description:
Hot foil stamping systems for label printing industry
Foil stamping dies & materials

Illinois Tool Works, Inc.
200 Chaffee Rd
Oconomowoc, WI 53066-2671
Contact: Rocky Turner, Plt. Mgr.
Telephone: 414-567-3760
Fax: 414-567-4562
Email: / URL:
Product Service Description:
Bolts, nuts, rivets & washers
Automotive screws

Image Maker Enterprises
PO Box 44498
Boise, ID 83711-0498
Contact: Bud Katich, Pres.
Telephone: 208-378-4417
Fax: 208-323-6130
Email: info@artofcom.com / URL:
artofcom.com
Product Service Description:
Art prints & greeting cards of scenic / wildlife
images

Image Printing
3913 Todd Ln Ste 507
Austin, TX 78744-1060
Contact: Joel Terrazas, V.-P., Sales & Mktg.
Telephone: 512-445-2202
Fax: 512-445-4565
Email: adame@texas.net / URL: http://
www.cycorp.com/imp/imphp.htm
Product Service Description:
Commercial printing

Image Processor Inc. (Mfr)
1744 Portland Ave. / P.O. Box 606
Walla Walla, WA 99362
Contact: Max Rutzer, *
Telephone: 509-522-2471
Fax: 509-529-8149
Email: sales@imageprocessor.com / URL:
http://www.imageprocessor.com
Product Service Description:
Microfilm & Microfiche Printing Machines,

Imaging Technologies, Inc.
445 Universal Dr
Cookeville, TN 38506-4603
Contact: Loyd E. Tarver, Pres.
Telephone: 931-432-4191
Fax: 931-432-4199
Email: ITI@iti-inkjet.com / URL: http://
www.iti-inkjet.com
Product Service Description:
Ink jet printers
Bar Code Printing Machinery

Imco Inc
6212 E 18th St
Vancouver, WA 98661-6840
Contact: Todd B. Purnick, Sales Supervisor
Telephone: 800-804-4626
Fax: 360-694-7144
Email: imcomail@imcomfg.com / URL: http:/
/www.imcomfg.com
Product Service Description:
Prepaid Phone Card Vending Equipment

Immix Telecom Inc.
1948 Mears Pkwy
Margate, FL 33063-3701
Contact: Claude Simpson, Pres.
Telephone: 954-968-5725
Fax: 954-968-6527
Email: sales@immixtel.com / URL: http://
www.immixtel.com
Product Service Description:
Automatic telephone dialing equipment

Imperial Electric Co.
1533 Commerce Dr
Stow, OH 44224-1711
Contact: Randy Bays, Pres.
Telephone: 330-686-4500
Fax: 330-686-4499
Email: sales@imperialelectric.com / URL:
Product Service Description:
Motors & generators
Electrical equipment & motors
Permanent Magnet Motors

Imperial Electronic Assembly
28 Commerce Dr
Danbury, CT 06810-4131
Contact: Ed O'Donnell, Ptnr. & Plt. Mgr.
Telephone: 203-792-7418
Fax: 203-792-1804
Email: ed@impea.com / URL: http://
www.impea.com
Product Service Description:
Printed Circuit BD Assemblies
Electro/Mechanical Assembly
Cable/Harness Assemblies

Imperial Pools Inc.
33 Wade Road
Latham, NY 12110
Contact: Charlie Vennard, Vice President
Telephone: 518/786-1200
Fax: 518/786-0954
Email: info@www.imperialpools.com / URL:
http://www.imperialpools.com
Product Service Description:
Inground Steel Wall Swimming Pool Kits
Swimming Pool Steps, One-Piece
Vinyl Liners, Swimming Pools
Spas, Acrylic

Impol Aluminum
481 Main St., Ste. 509
New Rochelle, NY 10801
Contact: Miro Skrlj, President
Telephone: 914-636-2606

Product Service Description:
Importing Firms
Aluminum, not alloyed, unwrought
Aluminum plates, sheets & strip
over .2mm thick
Aluminum bars, rods and profiles, not alloyed
Aluminum Bars, Rods & Profiles, Alloyed
Aluminum Foil

Improved Construction Methods
PO Box 5798
Jacksonville, AR 72078-5798
Contact: Chuck Fisher, Pres.
Telephone: 501-982-2945 / 1800-877-2945
Fax: 501-985-3280
Email: califark@msn.com / URL: http://
www.improvedcontruction.com
Product Service Description:
Plastic Manhole Forms & Plastic Products /
Forms
Truck Tarps, Canvas & Related Products

Impulse Wear
225 Business Center Dr N
Blacklick, OH 43004-9452
Contact: Larry Levine, Pres.
Telephone: 614-575-1157
Fax: 614-575-1163
Email: info@impulsewear.com / URL:
Product Service Description:
T-shirt, sweatshirt, & tote bag heat transfers
Lithographic printing_commercial

Imtec Inc.
1 Imtec Lane
Bellows Falls, VT 05101-3120
Contact: Mark Brooke, Director of Sales &
Mktg.
Telephone: 802-463-9502
Fax: 802-463-4334
Email: imtec@sover.net / URL:
Product Service Description:
Labels
Label Printing Supplies
Printer Laminators
Label Printer Applicators

Inca Paint & Print
11680 Quay St
Broomfield, CO 80020-2921
Contact: James Thompson, Pres.
Telephone: 303-460-9950
Fax: 303-460-7527
Email: / URL:
Product Service Description:
Industrial paint shop for metal and plastic
surfaces
Pad Printing
Conductive coatings

Inca Plastics Molding Co Inc
948 E Belmont St
Ontario, CA 91761-4549
Contact: Howard Haigh, Pres.
Telephone: 909-923-3235
Fax: 909-923-3018
Email: / URL:
Product Service Description:
Rotational molding, injection molding, R.V.
tanks

Incare Cargo Services
8402 Osage Ave.,
Los Angeles, CA 90045
Contact: Sales & Marketing,
Telephone: 310-670-9360
Fax: 310-670-5004
Email: incarela@worldnet.att.net / URL:
Product Service Description:
Customs Broker
Freight Forwarder
Freight & Cargo Transportation

Incinerator International Inc.
P.O. Box 8617
Houston, TX 77249
Contact: Mike Morgan, President
Telephone: 713-227-1466
Fax: 713-227-0884
Email: sales@incinerators.com / URL: http://
www.incinerators.com
Product Service Description:
Incinerators, Air, Solid & Liquid Waste

Incon Overseas Marketing, Inc.
P.O. Box 376, 12 East 41st St.
New York, NY 10163-0376
Contact: David Miller, Director / Intl.
Telephone: 212-371-0868
Fax: 212-750-3693
Email: rmsincon@msn.com / URL: http://
www.kreativekabinetry.com
Product Service Description:
Petroleum Crude Export
Semifinished Metal Products, Export
Chemicals & Allied Products, Export
Furniture, Export
Case Good Manufacturer & Exporter
Laminates & Architectural Woodwork
Healthcare Cabinets & Counters, Etc.

Independent Ink Inc
14705 S Avalon Blvd
Gardena, CA 90248-2009
Contact: Barry Brucker, GM
Telephone: 310-523-4657
Fax: 310-329-0943
Email: barry@independentink.com / URL:
http://www.independentink.com
Product Service Description:
Marking inks, marking devices, pads, ink
stamping, inkjet ink
Marking devices
Ink_printing
Chemical preparations

Independent Mfg. Co., Inc.
2656 St. Hwy. 38
Cabot, AR 72023
Contact: Phillip Montague, Pres.
Telephone: 501-843-5358
Fax: 501-605-0177
Product Service Description:
Foundation ventilators

**Independent Restaurant & Bakery
Equipment**
2320 N Atlantic St
Spokane, WA 99205-4811
Contact: Steven Croonquist, Pres.
Telephone: 509-327-8855
Fax: 509-327-8356
Email: independent@eznet.com / URL: http://
www.eznet.com\foodequipment
Product Service Description:
Manufactures obsolete mixer parts for
bakeries; custom rebuilds food equipment
Food products machinery

Independent Trailer & Equip Co
1602 Rudkin Rd
Yakima, WA 98901-4030
Contact: Michael Nash, Pres.
Telephone: 509-452-3672
Fax: 509-452-3721
Email: / URL: http://www.itec.inc.com
Product Service Description:
Transportation equipment
Manufactures C-dollies and hitches

Independent Welding Co.
321 Richard Mine Rd
Wharton, NJ 07885-1801
Contact: Guy Dellatore, Pres.
Telephone: 973-361-9731
Fax: 973-361-3817
Product Service Description:
Telephone enclosures
Metal products_fabricated
Distributor of payphone related items

Indiana Tube
P.O. Box 3005
Evansville, IN 47730-3005
Contact: Marc R. Choate, Customer Service
Manager
Telephone: 812-424-9028
Fax: 812-424-0340
Email: / URL:
Product Service Description:
Small Diameter Low Carbon Steel Tubing
Refrigeration Condensers

Induction Technology Corp
9924 Rancho Rd
Adelanto, CA 92301-2235
Contact: Michael Dicken, Pres.
Telephone: 760-246-7333
Fax: 760-246-4366
Email: itcorp@earthlink.net / URL: http://
www.inductiontech.com
Product Service Description:
Manufactures induction heating and melting
equipment

Inductoheat Inc.
32251 N. Avis Drive
Madision Heights, MI 48071
Contact: Walter B. Albert, Dir./Intl. Sales
Telephone: 248-585-9393
Fax: 248-589-1062
Email: / URL: http://www.inductoheat.com
Product Service Description:
Industrial Furnaces & Ovens
Induction & Electric Heating

Industrial Acoustics Co. Inc.
1160 Commerce Ave.
Bronx, NY 10462
Contact: Robert A. Schmidt, *
Telephone: 718/931-8000
Fax: 718-863-1138
Email: info@industrialacoustics.com / URL: http://www.industrialacoustics.com
Product Service Description:
HVAC / Power Plant Silencers
Audiometric / Medical Test Rooms
Acoustical Doors / Operable Walls
Anechoic Chambers / Reverb Rms /
Acoustical Ceilings

Industrial Crane & Equipment Co., Inc.
4701 W Iowa St
Chicago, IL 60651-3324
Contact: Gerald S. Cole, Pres.
Telephone: 773-378-0100
Fax: 773-378-7273
Email: / URL:
Product Service Description:
Hoists, Cranes, Monorails & JibCranes
Humphrey Belt Manlifts

Industrial Crating, Inc.
851 Expressway Dr
Itasca, IL 60143-1323
Contact: Mark Pflanz, Pres.
Telephone: 630-595-1230
Fax: 630-595-7230
Email: mail@industrialcrating.com / URL:
http://www.industrialcrating.com
Product Service Description:
Wooden crates
Nailed wood boxes & shook

Industrial Design Fabrication
350 Fortner Rd
Mc Ewen, TN 37101-5430
Contact: Charles Phy, Pres.
Telephone: 931-582-8844
Fax: 931-582-7818
Email: idf@waverly.net / URL:
Product Service Description:
Custom Designed Industrial Machines
Automation & Integration
International Sales Base

Industrial Diamond Labs
528 Tiffany Street
Bronx, NY 10474
Contact: Vincent Lisanti, President
Telephone: 718-991-7200
Fax: 718-617-3632
Email: / URL:
Product Service Description:
Industrial Diamonds
Diamond Reclamation
Diamond Powders & Compounds, Micron & Mesh

Industrial Fiber Optics
627 S 48th St Ste 100
Tempe, AZ 85281-2326
Contact: Randy Dahl, Pres.
Telephone: 602-804-1227
Fax: 602-804-1229
Email: / URL: http://www.I-fiberoptics.com
Product Service Description:
Manufactures fiber optic and laser systems
for industry and education
Glass_pressed & blown
Electrical equipment & supplies
Fiber optics LEDs
Fiber optics photodetectors
Fiber optics cable

Industrial Gastruck, Inc.
1301 N Old Rand Rd
Wauconda, IL 60084-9764
Contact: Todd Hendrix, Pres., Fin., Pur., Sales & Mktg. Mgr.
Telephone: 847-526-1700
Fax: 847-526-1705
Email: igimail@aol.com / URL: http://www.hendrixsystems.com
Product Service Description:
Carburetor units & truck engine conversions, propane, natural gas & exhaust purifiers
Motor vehicle parts & accessories

Industrial Opportunities, Inc., Elastic Produc, Div.
PO Box 39
Marble, NC 28905-0039
Contact: Harry Baughn,
Telephone: 828-837-9047
Fax: 828-837-4074
Email: ioi@grove.net / URL:
Product Service Description:
Suspenders, contract sewing & packaging

Industrial Process Equipment
1061 Leslie St
La Habra, CA 90631-6843
Contact: Michael J Waggoner, Pres.
Telephone: 714-447-0171 ext. 313
Fax: 714-447-1312
Email: mail@ipeontime.com / URL:
Product Service Description:
Manufactures & installs turnkey powder
coating systems
Industrial ovens
Conveyorized spray washers
Overhead conveyor systems

Industrial Specialty Chemicals, Inc.
16880 S. Lathrop
Harvey, IL 60426
Contact: Jose Jacob, Pres.
Telephone: 708-339-1313
Fax: 708-339-6430
Email: isc@orbitel.com / URL:
Product Service Description:
Water treatment compounds, corrosion
inhibitors & pollution prevention chemicals
Chemical preparations

Indy Honeycomb
82 Campbell Dr
Highland Heights, KY 41076-9794
Contact: Steven E. Barnett, Pres.
Telephone: 606-572-4357
Fax: 606-572-4359
Email: indyhcomb@aol.com / URL: http://www.indyhoneycomb.com
Product Service Description:
Metal honeycomb

Information Specialist Inc
141 Union Blvd Ste 120
Lakewood, CO 80228-1838
Contact: John Scott, Pres.
Telephone: 303-969-0195
Fax: 303-969-0197
Email: jscott.isi@ibm.net / URL:
Product Service Description:
IBM authorized industry re-marketer, retailing
mid-range computer products
Computers, peripherals & software
Computer programming services
Prepackaged software - job shop custom
order mfg.
Computer integrated systems design

Ingredient Resources, Inc.
160 Eileen Way
Syosset, NY 11791-5301
Contact: Jack Sollazzo, President
Telephone: 516-496-2500
Fax: 516-496-2516
Product Service Description:
Onion Oil
Dehydrated Onion
Mustard Oil
Horse radish oil
Amino acids, L-Cysteine, L-Cystine

Inline Plastics Corp.
PO Box 713
Shelton, CT 06484-0713
Contact: Dick Daniels, Dir.-Food Service Packaging
Telephone: 518-743-1280
Fax: 518-743-1255
Email: inline@capital.net / URL: http://www.inlineplastics.com
Product Service Description:
Clear plastic disposable containersfor bakery
& food

Innerpac Southwest, Inc.
5 Founders Blvd # A
El Paso, TX 79906-4905
Contact: Karl Hall, GM
Telephone: 915-771-0500
Fax: 915-771-0515
Email: inrpacsw@whc.net / URL: http://www.innerpac.com
Product Service Description:
Corrugated & chipboard partitions & pads

Innovair Corporation
10880 NW 27th Street (bay 100)
Miami, FL 33172
Contact: Julio Gomez, President
Telephone: 305-463-9998
Fax: 305-463-9161
Email: sales@innovairmiami.com / URL: http://www.innovairmiami.com
Product Service Description:
Air conditioning units & parts

Innovasive Devices Company
734 Forest St
Marlborough, MA 01752-3032
Contact: Richard Randall, Pres.
Telephone: 508-460-8229
Fax: 508-460-6661
Email: / URL:
Product Service Description:
Surgical & medical instruments
Medical Instruments

Innovative Organics Inc
4905 E Hunter Ave
Anaheim, CA 92807-2058
Contact: Robert Lopez, Sales Manager
Telephone: 714-701-3900
Fax: 714-701-3912
Email: rlopez@innovativeorganics.com /
Product Service Description:
Manufactures specialty chemicals for the
computer disk drive and micro-electronics
industries: Chemical preparations
Chemicals_industrial organic

Innovative Sensors, Incorporated
4745 E. Bryson St.
Anaheim, CA 92807-1993
Contact: Stev Ruff, *
Telephone: 714-779-8781
Product Service Description:
Electrodes

Innovative Stamping Corp
PO Box 5327
Compton, CA 90224-5327
Contact: Gerald Czaban, President
Telephone: 310-537-6996
Fax: 310-537-0312
Email: info@innovative-sys.com / URL: http://www.innovative-sys.com
Product Service Description:
Metal stampings, fabrication & machining of
metal parts, display materials
Convention & trade show equipment

Innoventions Inc
5921 S Middlefield Rd
Littleton, CO 80123-2877
Contact: Edward Bettinardi, Pres.
Telephone: 303-797-6554
Fax: 303-727-4940
Email: magnicam@magnicam.com / URL:
http://www.magnicam.com/magnicam/
Product Service Description:
Optical instruments & lenses
Manufactures electronic magnifying
instruments for people with low vision
Electronic parts & equipment

Instant Copy, Inc.
131 W Marion St
Elkhart, IN 46516-3206
Contact: Bill Robinson, Opers. Mgr.
Telephone: 219-295-0024
Fax: 219-293-8261
Email: / URL: http://www.xyan.com
Product Service Description:
Lithographic printing_commercial
Instant printing

Instrumentation & Control Systems, Inc.
520 W Interstate Rd
Addison, IL 60101-4415
Contact: Marion Servos, Pres., Sales Mgr.
Telephone: 630-543-6200
Fax: 630-543-6244
Email: / URL: http://www.eemonline.com/instrumentation
Product Service Description:
Infrared sensing controls, timer modules &
uninterruptible power, inverters
TD relays & custom industrial electronic
controls

Insul-Vest, Inc.
6417 S. 39th West Avenue
Tulsa, OK 74132
Contact: Bob Anderson, Gen. Mgr.
Telephone: 918-445-2279
Fax: 918-445-2330
Email: ivsales@insul-vest.com / URL: http://www.insul-vest.com
Product Service Description:
Plastics Injection & Extruder Barrel
Insulation

Insulgard Corporation
PO Box 278
Hyattsville, MD 20781-0278
Contact: Mardy Tranby, VP Operations
Telephone: 301-927-8855
Fax: 301-927-4531
Email: Insulgard@aol.com / URL: http://www.insulgard.com
Product Service Description:
Bullet Resistant Doors, Windows & Walls
Blast-Resistant Doors, Windows, Walls
Security Doors, Windows, Walls

Int'l Equipment Distributors
2561 S 1560 W
Woods Cross, UT 84087-2327
Contact: Robert Burton, CEO
Telephone: 801-295-3835
Fax: 801-296-6442
Email: iedi@mail.vii.com / URL: http://
www.vii.com/~iedi
Product Service Description:
Manufactures seismic equipment for the oil
field industry
Measuring & controlling devices

Int'l Fabricators & Engineers
1126 Rockwood Ave
Heber, CA 92249-9754
Contact: Marcio Botta-Sills, Pres.
Telephone: 760-352-1101
Fax: 760-352-1104
Product Service Description:
Fabricates pipes and fittings cement lined &
coated : Pipe & fittings_fabricated fusion
epoxy, lined & coated : Flanges to AWWA
Spec. : Steel pipe cement lined, tape coated
Pipe supports : Misc. metal fabricators
Trench boxes : Galvanized fittings

Integra Window & Door Inc
2002 N Stone Ave
Tucson, AZ 85705-5645
Contact: Bambi L Corso, Pres.
Telephone: 520-622-9396
Fax: 520-622-3662
Email: / URL: http://www.integrawd.com
Product Service Description:
Distributes wood, clad and aluminum doors;
vinyl, aluminum and clad windows; skylights;
door hardware

Integrity Manufacturing Co
50 Mount View Ln Ste B
Colorado Springs, CO 80907-4362
Contact: Gary L Allen, Pres.
Telephone: 719-531-7676
Fax: 719-531-9574
Email: / URL:
Product Service Description:
Precision machining for the aerospace,
medical and electronics industries
Industrial machinery

Intek Plastics, Inc.
800 E. 10th St.
Hastings, MN 55033-2217
Contact: Craig Wallin, VP Of Fianance
Telephone: 651-437-7700
Fax: 651-437-3805
Email: / URL: http://www.intekplastics.com
Product Service Description:
Plastic extrusion manufacturer specializing in
custom co-extruded profiles
Common materials include thermoplastics,
reinforced composites, thermoset foams
Plastic weathersealing products for windows
& doors

Intelligent Peripheral Devices
20380 Town Center Ln Ste 270
Cupertino, CA 95014-3292
Contact: Ketan Kothari, Pres.
Telephone: 408-252-9400
Fax: 408-252-9409
Email: info@alphasmart.com / URL: http://
www.alphasmart.com
Product Service Description:
Manufactures computer keyboards used for
writing/keyboarding in education.
Computer peripheral equipment used for
writing/keyboarding in education

Inter-Jet Systems, Inc.
151-04 132nd Ave.,
Jamaica, NY 11434-3507
Contact: Jerome C. Trimboli, Chairman of the
Board/Chief Executive Officer
Telephone: 718-276-8500
Fax: 718-276-4250
Email: sales@interjet.com / URL: http://
www.interjet.com
Product Service Description:
Customs Broker : Freight Forwarder (NYC,
ATL, MIA, LAX, CHI) : Freight & Cargo
Transportation : NVOCC

Inter-Technical Export Corporatioin
P.O. Box 535, 175 Clearbrook Road
Elmsford, NY 10523
Contact: Judith Ellis, President
Telephone: 914-347-2474
Fax: 914-347-7230
Email: itec@inter-technical.com
Product Service Description:
Electronic Components

Inter-World Customs Broker Inc.
PO Box 9023568
San Juan, PR 00902-3568
Contact: Larry Colon, President
Telephone: 787-793-4280
Fax: 787-793-4282
Email: / URL:
Product Service Description:
Customs Broker

Inter-World Customs Broker, Inc.
Marketing Building, Lobby, J. F. Kennedy
Aven
Puerto Nuevo, PR 00920
Contact: Larry Colon, President
Telephone: 787-793-4280
Fax: 787-793-6801
Email: / URL:
Product Service Description:
Customs Broker
Freight Forwarder
Freight & Cargo Transportation
Local Tax Clearence

InterFET Corporation
1000 N Shiloh Rd
Garland, TX 75042-5720
Contact: Daniel E. Roberts, CEO
Telephone: 972-487-1287
Fax: 972-276-3375
Email: / URL: http://www.interfet.com
Product Service Description:
Semiconductors & related devices
Transistor semiconductors & field effect
transistors
Electronic components
Mulit-chip module hybrid circuits

Interbath, Inc
665 Baldwin Park Blvd
City Of Industry, CA 91746-1502
Contact: Claus D Zieger, Pres.
Telephone: 626-369-1841
Fax: 626-961-3534
Email: / URL: http://www.interbath.com
Product Service Description:
Plumbing fixture fittings & trim
Manufactures showerheads, handheld
showers and accessories
Shower Organization
Valves
Spouts

Interbulk Shipping, Inc.
803 Queens Rd.,
Pasadena, TX 77502
Contact: Sales & Marketing,
Telephone: 713-946-3433
Fax: 713-943-1299
Email: mailinbulk@aol.com / URL: http://
www.interbulkshipping.com
Product Service Description:
Steamship agents

Inter cultural Development
755 San Mario Dr.
Solana Beach, CA 92075-1605
Contact: Selma Myers, Pres.
Telephone: 619-755-3160
Fax: 619-755-8637
Email: selma@coyote.csusm.edu
URL: http://www.interworld.net/smyers
Product Service Description:
Consulting service for managing cultural
diversity in industrial Settings: Publisher of
10 " Diversity at Work" trainer's guides
Pre-departure training for business people
going overseas: Workshops for understanding
impact of culture or International business
comuunications: English for Business
Purposes: Adjusting to U.S. Culture (for
International living & working in the U.S.)

Interdevelopment Inc.
515 -B East Braddock Road
Alexandria, VA 22314
Contact: Margareta K. Luddemann, CEO
Telephone: 703-548-1909
Fax: 703-548-2029
Email: 2598217@mcimail.com / URL: http://
www.interdevelopment.com
Product Service Description:
Business Research Svcs., Exp. / Imp Asst.
Bus. Svcs., Technology Transfer
Marketing Consulting Services

Interdynamics, Inc.
80 39TH ST.
Brooklyn, NY 11232-2692
Contact: Eric Trachtenberg, Export Manager
Telephone: 718-499-0608
Fax: 718-789-0914
Product Service Description:
Automotive Chemicals : Parts & Accessories
for Motor Vehicles : Lubricants
12 Volt Portable Air Compressors
Refrigerant - Automotive

Interface Design Inc.
6116 Skyline Dr Ste 106
Houston, TX 77057-7019
Contact: Alan Gow, Pres.
Telephone: 713-783-3607
Fax: 713-783-4971
Email: adam@interfacedesigninc.com / URL:
http://www.interfacedesigninc.com
Product Service Description:
Analytical instruments
Scientific spectrometer instrumentation &
industrial nameplates
Emission spectrometer service & parts

Interfreight Inc.
1480 Elmhurst Road
Elk Grove Village, IL 60007
Contact: Kurt Konodi-Floch, CEO
Telephone: 847-981-1999
Fax: 847-981-0566
Email: / URL:
Product Service Description:
Customs Broker : Freight Forwarding
Freight & Cargo: Transportation & Insurance

Interior Products Inc.
2630 Sidney Lanier Dr
Brunswick, GA 31525-6811
Contact: J. Edward Peede, CEO, Opers. Mgr.
Telephone: 912-264-6496
Fax: 912-262-9763
Email: ipi@technonet.com / URL:
Product Service Description:
Architectural wall panels : Architectural wood
ceilings : Radius furniture components
Radius store fixtures : Tambour Panels
Laminated panels

Intermountain Canola Cargill
2300 N Yellowstone Hwy Ste 122
Idaho Falls, ID 83401-1665
Contact: Ernie H Unger, Br. Mgr.
Telephone: 208-522-4113
Fax: 208-522-0794
Product Service Description:
Fats & oils_edible
Producers of canola specialty oil

International Air Filtration
413 University Dr.
Arlington Heights, IL 60004
Contact: John M. Rammel, Chairman & CEO
Telephone: 847-797-1000
Fax: 847-797-1001
Email: e:cleanairiaf@worldnet.att.net / URL:
http://www.iafcleanair.com
Product Service Description:
Gas filtration equipment

International Baler Corp.
5400 Rio Grande Ave., P.O. Box 6922
Jacksonville, FL 32236-6922
Contact: Robert C. Turner, VP/ Sales/Mktg.
Telephone: 904-358-3812
Fax: 904-358-7013
Email: ibc@intl-baler.com / URL: http://
www.intl-baler.com
Product Service Description:
Commercial Baling Systems : Industrial
Baling Systems : Conveyors

International Beauty Design
15010 S Main St
Gardena, CA 90248-1945
Contact: Lee Tomlinson, Pres.
Telephone: 310-324-6680
Fax: 310-217-1497
Product Service Description:
Nail care products for salons
Nail care products for retail consumers

International Bioflavors Inc.
PO Box 1021
Oconomowoc, WI 53066-6021
Contact: Scott Olstad, VP, Sales & Mktg.
Telephone: 414-569-6200
Fax: 414-569-6202
Email: solstad@bioflavors.com / URL: http://
www.bioflavors.com
Product Service Description:
Food flavorings: Flavoring extracts & syrups

International Components Plus, Inc.
1427 Boulder Ct # A
Greensboro, NC 27409-8906
Contact: Mike Longoni, Pres.
Telephone: 336-294-9072
Fax: 336-294-9496
Email: icp@worldnet.att.net / URL: http://
www.icplus.com
Product Service Description:
WoodVneer, Melamine, Polyester, Metallic
Edgebanding : DecoPaper & Vaneer for
Profile Wrapping & Sheets

International Consultants of Del.
109 Barksdale Professional Ctr.
Newark, DE 19711-3258
Contact: Louis Arena, Vice President
Telephone: 302-737-8715
Fax: 302-737-8756
Email: icd@icdel.com / URL:
Product Service Description:
Education: Foreign Credentials Evaluations

International Custom Products
302 W. Washington Ave.
Du Bois, PA 15801
Contact: Dennis Raybuck, President
Telephone: 814-375-9600
Fax: 814-375-0718
Email: dairyex@penn.com / URL:
Product Service Description:
Dairy Products, Except Canned : Cheese,
including cheddar and colby : Food
preparations : Whey, whether or not
concentrated or containing added sweeteners
Soup base mixes : Edible fat preparations

International Cybernetics Corp.
PO Box 17246
Clearwater, FL 33762-0246
Contact: Robert E. Olenoski, President
Telephone: 727-547-0696
Fax: 727-547-0251
Product Service Description:
Profilers : Profilographs

International Dairy Equipment Associates, Inc.
P.O. Box 271
Nazareth, PA 18064-0271
Contact: Gregory D. Prendes, President
Telephone: 610-759-1228
Fax: 610-759-3195
Product Service Description:
Dairy & Food Processing Equipment
Complete Ingredient & Supply Lines for
Dairy Operations

International Dehydrated Foods Inc.
P.O. Box 10347
Springfield, MO 65808
Contact: Ann Hollis, *
Telephone: 417-881-7820
Fax: 417-881-7274
Email: customerservice@idf.com / URL:
Product Service Description:
Powdered Chicken Meat, Fat & Broth
Frozen & Shelf Stable Chicken Broth,
and Liquid Chicken Fat

International Enviromental Corp.
5000 I-40 W
Oklahoma City, OK 73128
Contact: Larry Jewell, Pres.
Telephone: 405-605-5000
Fax: 405-605-5001
Email: Marketing@iec-okc.com / URL: http://
www.iec-okc.com
Product Service Description:
Fan coil units
Air filtration units

International Hobbycraft Co., Inc.
3340 Dundee Rd., Suite 2c-4
Northbrook, IL 60062-2331
Contact: Joel Davis, *
Telephone: 847-564-9945
Fax: 847-564-9951
Product Service Description:
Model Construction Kits/ Hobby Kits

International Homes Of Cedar (Mfr)
P.O. Box 886
Woodinville, WA 98072
Contact: Pete Geffe, President
Telephone: 425-481-9393
Fax: 360-668-5562
Email: ihc@ihoc.com / URL: http://
www.ihoc.com
Product Service Description:
Resid / Comm, Building, Pre-Cut Cedar

International Lubricants, Inc.
7930 Occidental South
Seattle, WA 98108
Contact: Frank Erickson, *
Telephone: 206-762-5343
Fax: 206-762-7989
Email: lubegard@concentric.net / URL: http:/
/www.lubegard.com
Product Service Description:
Lubegard Automotive & Industrial Lubricants
Worker, Environment Safe Lubricant
Additives
Seed Oil Based Functional Specialty
Chemicals

International Machinery Exchange
214 N. Main St.
Deerfield, WI 53531-9644
Contact: Sales & Marketing,
Telephone: 608-764-5481
Fax: 608-764-8240
Email: saledesk@imexchange.com / URL:
http://www.imexchange.com
Product Service Description:
S/S Storage & Process Tanks
Cheese Processing Equipment

International Multifoods Corp.
PO Box 59062
Minneapolis, MN 55459-0062
Contact: Rose M. Heruth, Int'l Bus. Dev.
Manager
Telephone: 612-404-7500
Fax: 612-404-7670
Email: rheruth@multifoodsbakery.com /
URL: http://www.multifoods.com
Product Service Description:
Bakery Mixes, Frozen Bakery Products,
Fillings For
Cakes, Muffins, Donuts, Danish

International Nutrition, Inc.
PO Box 27540
Omaha, NE 68127-0540
Contact: Reid S. Adkins, V-P.
Telephone: 402-331-0123
Fax: 402-331-0169
Email: ini@agworld.com / URL:
Product Service Description:
Manufacturers of Quality Nutritional &
Health Products for Livestock & Poultry
Throughout the World

International Paint Inc.
PO Box 4806
Houston, TX 77210-4806
Contact: Jon Bradley, V-P., GM
Telephone: 713-682-1711
Fax: 713-684-1327
Email: / URL: http://www.international-
pc.com
Product Service Description:
Floor coatings
Industrial, oil, gas, marine coatings & tank
linings
Paints & allied products

International Paper Co., Texarkana Mill
PO Box 870
Texarkana, TX 75504-0870
Contact: Greg Wanta, Mill Manager
Telephone: 903-796-7101
Fax: 903-796-1440
Product Service Description:
Paperboard mills
Paperboard & pulp processing
Pulp mills

International Peripheral Systems
530 S Juniata St
Lewistown, PA 17044-2323
Contact: James H. Jiranck, Chrm., Pres.
Telephone: 717-248-9665
Fax: 717-248-4241
Email: ipsus.net / URL:
Product Service Description:
Stamp Cancelling Machines, Post Office

International Plastic Cards
366 Coral Cir
El Segundo, CA 90245-4619
Contact: John A Rosso, Pres.
Telephone: 310-322-4472
Fax: 310-322-3489
Email: staff@ipccards.com / URL: http://
www.ipccards.com
Product Service Description:
Manufactures, embosses, encodes and direct
mails plastic cards

International Relations-Advanced Bio Institute, Inc.
1530 Baker Street, Suite J
Costa Mesa, CA 92626
Contact: Aramand Wijckmans, Consultants
Telephone: 714-540-0727
Fax: 714-540-0873
Email: abil@earthlink.net / URL: http://
www.nos.net/abi
Product Service Description:
Management Consulting Services
Manufacturer Nutritional Supplements

International Reserve Equip.
P.O. Box 198
Clarendon Hills, IL 60514
Product Service Description:
Industrial Centrifuges, Separators

International Shoe Machine Corporation
165 Ledge St.
Nashua, NH 03060-3014
Contact: Michael Taricano, President & CEO
Telephone: 603-883-5500
Fax: 603-882-7560
Product Service Description:
Machinery, Special Industry
Shoe Machinery

International Soc For Technology In Education (ISTE)
1787 Agate St
Eugene, OR 97403-1923
Contact: Maria Howes, Exec. Secty
Telephone: 541-346-4414
Fax: 541-346-5890
Email: iste@oregon.uoregon.edu / URL:
http://www.iste.org
Product Service Description:
Publishes educational books & courseware;
organization dedicated to education
improvement : Book publishing
Publishing_miscellaneous

International Tool Boxes
1280 Frontenac Raod
Naperville, IL 60563
Contact: Brian Ericson, *
Telephone: 708/778-8934
Fax: 708/778-8846
Email: / URL:
Product Service Description:
Plastic, Metal Tool Boxes,

International Translating Br., Inc.
16125 W. Twelve Mile
Southfield, MI 48076-2912
Contact: Mariano Pallares, President
Telephone: 248-559-1677
Fax: 248-559-1679
Email: itbinc@itbtranslations.com / URL:
http://www.ltbtranslations.com
Product Service Description:
Translation & Interpreting Services, All
Languages
Technical, Legal, Medical
Typesetting & Voice Overs

International Turbine Systems
99 Main St., Warehouse Pt.
East Windsor, CT 06088
Contact: Steven Lamond, Pres.
Telephone: 860-623-1058
Fax: 860-623-9028
Email: itsi2@aol.com / URL:
Product Service Description:
Turbine engine components

International Vitamin Corporation
500 Halls Mill Rd.
Freehold, NJ 07728
Contact: Rick Scrocca, Vice President
Telephone: 732-308-3000
Fax: 732-308-3398
Email: / URL: http://www.ivcinc.com
Product Service Description:
Vitamins
Herbal Supplements
Soft Gels

Interpax
1117 Upland Dr.
Houston, TX 77043-4798
Contact: Steve Schneider, Owner
Telephone: 713-973-9730
Fax: 713-973-0887
Email: interpax@interpax.com / URL: http://
www.interpax.com
Product Service Description:
Exporting Firms
Motor vehicle parts and accessories
Parts for fork-lift trucks and other works
trucks fitted with lifting or handling
equipment
Construction machinery & parts

Interpretive Marketing Products
PO Box 21697
Billings, MT 59104
Contact: William Gibson Jr, Pres.
Telephone: 406-248-3555
Fax: 406-248-9998
Email: gibco@imt.net / URL:
Product Service Description:
Manufactures games and custom specialty
promotional products
Puff Stickers
Inflatables
Plush / Berme Dolls
Magnets

Interroll Corp.
3000 Corporate Dr
Wilmington, NC 28405-7422
Contact: Ken Cowlin, VP Sales
Telephone: 910-799-1100
Fax: 910-799-9626
Email: info@interroll.com / URL: http://
www.interroll.com
Product Service Description:
Conveyors & conveying equipment
Materials handling systems & components

Interstate Steel Inc.
925 W. Hatcher Rd.
Phoenix, AZ 85021-3138
Contact: Gary Knudsen, Pres.
Telephone: 602-944-7905
Fax: 602-678-1477
Email: gknudsen@za.rmci.net / URL:
Product Service Description:
Buys & sells steel, aluminum, stainless steel,
brass, copper and remnants

Intersystems, Inc.
13330 1 St.
Omaha, NE 68137-1191
Contact: Bob Moser, Exec. VP Mktg.
Telephone: 402-330-1500
Fax: 402-330-3350
Email: bulkmatl@intersystems-inc.com /
URL: http://www.intersystems-inc.com
Product Service Description:
Bulk Materials Handling Equipment
Machinery, Special Industry

Intertape Polymer
PO Box 1880
Evans, GA 30809-1880
Contact: Hugh Hamilton,
Operations. Manager.
Telephone: 706-860-3499
Fax: 706-860-3798
Email: / URL: http://
www.intertapepolymer.com
Product Service Description:
Bags: plastics, laminated & coated
Polypropylene semi-bulk bags

Intimate Touch, Inc.
38 East 32nd St. 10th floor
New York, NY 10016
Contact: Stacey Christakos,
Senior Vice President
Telephone: 212-447-7222
Fax: 212-447-5998
Email: staceychristakos@intimatetouch.com
Product Service Description:
Lace manufacturer

Intraco Corp.
530 Stephenson Hwy.
Troy, MI 48083
Contact: Nicola M. Antakli,
Chief Executive Officer
Telephone: 248-585-6900
Fax: 248-585-6920
Email: intraco@IntracoUSA.com / URL:
http://www.IntracoUSA.com
Product Service Description:
Automotive & Heavy Duty Engine Parts
Automotive Fluids & Lubricants
Automotive & Architectural Glass

Intracor-Familian International
15500 S.W. 72nd Ave., Ste. 200
Portland, Oregon (USA), 97224-7971
Contact: Scott Havens, President
Telephone: 503-603-0800
Fax: 503-603-0505
Email: scott@intracor.com / URL: http://
www.familiannw.com
Product Service Description:
Products for plumbing, industrial & piping
installations , Sewer, Water: Gas, Mining,
Valves, Piping, Fittings : Steel Structures,
prefabricated, build to suit for the client:
Sports products: Tennis, running tracks,
gymnasium flooring & finish products from
USA. Architectural products for high quality
buildings; doors, windows, specialties.

Intramar, Inc.
10497 Town & Country Way, Ste. 225
Houston, TX 77024-1118
Contact: Willard Renshaw, President
Telephone: 713-984-2791
Fax: 713-984-2379
Email: export@intramarinc.com / URL: http://
www.intramarinc.com
Product Service Description:
Exporting Firms : Electrical parts & lighting
fixture : Construction material, doors,
windows : Spare parts, consumables & tools
Hotel & commercial furniture : Automotive
parts for trucks & special vehicles : Refinery
& chemical plant equipment & spare parts :
Oil field equipment & spare parts

Invacare Corporation
2101 E Lake Mary Blvd
Sanford, FL 32773-6099
Contact: James Hadland, Director of Mktg.
Telephone: 407-321-5630
Fax: 407-321-4288
Email: jhadland@invacare.com / URL: http://
www.invacare.com
Product Service Description:
Therapeutic Support Surfaces / Low Air Loss
Systems : Homecare & Nursing Home Beds

Inweld Corp.
PO Box 40
Coplay, PA 18037-0040
Contact: Jerome L. Robinson, Pres.
Telephone: 610-261-1900
Fax: 610-261-0744
Email: sales@inweldcorporation.com / URL:
http://www.inweldcorporation.com
Product Service Description:
Welding Alloys : Welding Accessories

Inx International Ink Co.
3100 W Wisconsin Ave
Appleton, WI 54914-1705
Contact: Edward Fischer, GM
Telephone: 920-739-4446
Fax: 920-739-8115
Product Service Description:
Ink_printing : Printing inks

Iridio
509 Fairview Ave N
Seattle, WA 98109-5507
Contact: Robert Michels, Pres.
Phone: 206-587-0278 / Fax: 206-625-9315
Email: / URL: http://www.iridio.com
Product Service Description:
Platemaking services : Lithographic printing
film and pre-press services ; Typesetting
Digital Printing: Film & Digital Photography
Online Communications : Website
Development: Digital Asset Managment

Iron Mountain Trap Rock Co.
325 Highway W.
Iron Mountain, MO 63650-9137
Contact: Jerry Stewart, GM
Telephone: 573-734-6106
Fax: 573-734-2521
Email: / URL: http://www.fredweberinc.com
Product Service Description:
Cut stone & stone products
Crushed stone

Irrometer Co. Inc. (Mfr)
P.O. Box 2424
Riverside, CA 92516
Contact: William R. Pogue, President
Telephone: 909-689-1701
Fax: 909-689-3706
Email: irrometer@aol.com / URL: http://
www.irrometer.com
Product Service Description:
Soil Moisture Measuring & Sampling
Instrumentation

Irwin Naturals / 4 Health Inc
10549 West Jefferson Blvd.
Culver City, CA 90232
Contact: R Lindsey Duncan, Chairman
Telephone: 310-253-5305
Fax: 310-253-9715
Email: lindsey@irwinnaturals.com / URL:
http://www.irwinnaturals.com
Product Service Description :
Medicinals & botanicals : Manufactures
vitamins, herbs & all high quality nutritional
supplements

**Isco Incorporated, Environ.
Div.(Mfr)**
531 Westgate Blvd.
Lincoln, NE 68528
Contact: Marty Thomas, *
Telephone: 402/474-2233
Product Service Description:
Open Channel Water Flow Meters

Ismay International L.L.C.
1169 Chain Bridge Rd.
Mc Lean, VA 22101-2215
Contact: Arthur P. Ismay, President
Telephone: 703-790-7805
Fax: 703-790-8890
Email: artismay@aol.com / URL:
Product Service Description:
Develops Markets in the U.S. for Overseas
Products & Services

Isom Brothers Inc
PO Box 1243
Caldwell, ID 83606-1243
Contact: Dallas Isom, Pres.
Telephone: 208-459-6077
Fax: 208-459-9320
Email: ibisteve@micron.net / URL: http://
www.isombros.com
Product Service Description:
Manufactures steel tanks
Plate work_fabricated (boiler shops)

Iss Inc.
2604 N. Mattis Ave.
Champaign, IL 61821
Contact: Beniamino Barberi, President
Telephone: 217-359-8681
Fax: 217-359-7879
Email: iss@iss.com
 URL: http://www.iss.com
Product Service Description:
Photon Counting Spectrofluorometers
Multi-Frequency Phase Fluorometers

Items Products Inc.
6703 Theall Rd
Houston, TX 77066-1215
Contact: Paul Schnizler, Pres.
Telephone: 281-893-0100
Fax: 281-893-4836
Email: sales@item-products.com / URL:
http://www.item-products.com
Product Service Description:
Modular aluminum construction systems for
machine building
Aluminum modular T-Slot extrusions

J & B Services: Import / Export
33661 Calle Miramar
San Juan Capistrano, CA 92625
Contact: Bessie Blazejewski,
Telephone: 714-240-2560
Fax: 714-240-3856
Email: bessie@bessieblaze.com / URL: http://
www.bessieblaze.com
Product Service Description:
Import / Export Broker
Real-Estate
Finance

J & H Deburring Inc
307 N Euclid Way Ste H-2
Anaheim, CA 92801-6741
Contact: Harold Thurber, Pres.
Telephone: 714-635-3251
Fax: 714-635-1168
Email: jhdeburr@aol.com / URL: http://
www.members.aol.com/jhdeburr/index.html
Product Service Description:
Mass metal finishing— tumbling, sand
blasting, shot peening, burnishing and plastic
blasting

J & J Wall Baking Company Inc
8806 Fruitridge Rd
Sacramento, CA 95826-9708
Contact: John Wall, Chrm.
Telephone: 916-381-1410
Fax: 916-381-6008
Email: jwall@ns.net / URL: http://
www.jjwallbaking.com
Product Service Description:
Bread, cake & related products
Frozen unbaked bread, rolls, and sweet goods

J D B Dense Flow, Inc.
PO Box 38
Palm Harbor, FL 34682-0038
Contact: Cam Boothe, Pres.
Telephone: 727-785-8500
Fax: 727-785-8506
Email: sales@jdbdenseflow.com / URL: http:/
/www.jdbdenseflow.com
Product Service Description:
Pneumatic conveying systems
Conveyors & conveying equipment

J G B Enterprises, Inc.
115 Metropolitan Dr.
Liverpool, NY 13088
Contact: J. Bernhardt, Pres., CFO
Telephone: 315-451-2770
Fax: 315-451-8503
Email: jgb2@ix.netcom.com / URL: http://
www.solcity.comjgb.htm
Product Service Description:
Rubber & metal coupled hoses
Hose , Military Spec.

J Hewitt Inc
6 Faraday Ste B
Irvine, CA 92618-2770
Contact: James D Hewitt, Pres.
Phone: 949-855-8104 / Fax: 949-855-8233
Email: / URL: http://www.jhewitt.com
Product Service Description:
Surgical & medical instruments:Manufactures surgical and medical instruments : Medical & hospital equipment : Antiseptics, medicinal Cosmetics : Costume Jewelry, exc. Prec. metal or stones : Antiseptics, Wholesale Cosmetics, Wholesale : Medical Rubber goods, wholesale

J I M Mfg., Inc.
1638 Hwy 62/412 Bldg. 3
Hardy, AR 72542
Contact: James D. Hill, Pres.
Telephone: 870-856-4788
Fax: 870-856-4627
Email: vader@mobilwash.com.uri / URL: http://www.mobilwash.com
Product Service Description:
Mobile truck & bus washers

J K Label Co.
2364 Houston St Ste 102
Grand Prairie, TX 75050-4933
Contact: James Sizemore, Owner
Telephone: 972-623-1400
Fax: 972-623-1415
Email: jklabel1@compuserve.com / URL:
Product Service Description:
Label printing
Printing, commercial

J R C Web Accessories, Inc.
46 Passaic Ave
Fairfield, NJ 07004-3510
Contact: Virginia L. Ryan, V-P., Treas., Off.
Telephone: 973-625-3888
Fax: 973-226-4249
Email: / URL:
Product Service Description:
Pneumatic & mechanical chucks & shafts
Hardware : Printing trades machinery
Packaging machinery

J W Mfg. Co.
PO Box 216
Mineral Springs, AR 71851-0216
Contact: Glen Winchester, Pres.
Telephone: 870-287-4716
Fax: 870-287-5316
Product Service Description:
Mops

J-Mac Plastics Inc.
40 Lafayette Pl
Kenilworth, NJ 07033-1105
Contact: John McNamara, Pres.
Telephone: 908-709-1111
Fax: 908-709-0153
Product Service Description:
Plastic injection molding : Plastic products

J-Pac Corp.
PO Box 854
Dover, NH 03821-0854
Contact: Andrew Janetos, Pres.
Phone: 603-749-5019 / Fax: 603-749-0082
Email: ae.janetos@j-pac.com / URL: http://www.j-pac.com
Product Service Description:
Custom Manufacturing of Plastic Products
Contract packaging, plastic thermoforming & medical products : Contract Packaging of Surgical & Medical Instruments

J-Star Industries Inc.
801 Janesville Ave.
Fort Atkinson, WI 53538-2496
Contact: Bill Dzienkowski, *
Telephone: 920-563-5521
Fax: 920-563-2089
Email: / URL:
Product Service Description:
Dairy Feed Handling & Process. Equipment
Agricultural Feed Mixers
Alley Scrapeis & Gutter Cleaners
Manure Slurry Pumping Equipment
Farm & Agricultural Electronic Scales

J. C. Marine Diesel, Inc.
277 Howard Ave
Biloxi, MS 39530-4513
Contact: Keith Covacevich, Pres.
Telephone: 228-436-3316
Fax: 228-435-5939
Email: jcmar39530@aol.com / URL:
Product Service Description:
Generator sets
Motors & generators

J. D American Workwear, Inc.
46 Olf Flat River Rd.
Coventry, RI 02816-5121
Contact: David De Baene, Pres., CEO
Telephone: 401-397-6800
Fax: 401-397-6804
Email: jdsafety@aol.com / URL:
Product Service Description:
Safety Work Clothing
Clothing, Men's & Boys' Work

J. H. World Express, Inc.
110 Standard St.,
El Segundo, CA 90245
Contact: James Hsu, President
Telephone: 310-364-0000
Fax: 310-364-0066
Email: / URL:
Product Service Description:
Freight Forwarder

J. J. Precast
8 Amlajack Blvd
Newnan, GA 30265-1010
Contact: Jim Johnson, Owner
Telephone: 770-254-0378
Fax: 770-251-2681
Email: / URL:
Product Service Description:
Concrete septic tanks & manholes
Concrete products

J. Line Pump Company
185 Progress Drive
Collierville, TN 38017
Contact: Mohan Chand, Dir. of Export
Telephone: 901-860-2300
Fax: 901-860-2333
Email: exportjl@aol.com / URL:
Product Service Description:
Turbine Water Pumps, J Line Vertical
Turbine Pumps, J Line Submersible

J.D. International Used Auto Parts
630 NW 7th Terrace
Ft. Lauderdale, FL 33311-7311
Contact: James Derosa, President
Telephone: 305-767-8888
Fax: 305-767-0242
Email: sales@partspro.com / URL: http://www.partspro.com
Product Service Description:
Used Auto Parts Foreign & Domestic Whsle.

J.J. Trucking Services of Jacksonville, Inc.
2445 Dunn Ave., Ste. 516
Jacksonville, FL 32218
Contact: Jose B. Rodriguez,
Telephone: 904-714-1417
Fax: 904-696-9651
Email: jjtrucking@worldnet.att.net / URL: http://www.jjtrucki.qpg.com
Product Service Description:
Freight & Cargo Transportation

J.L. Darling Corporation
2614 Pacific Highway East
Tacoma, WA 98424-1017
Contact: Todd Silver,
Telephone: 253-922-5000
Fax: 253-922-5300
Email: sales@riteintherain.com / URL: http://www.riteintherain.com
Product Service Description:
Weatherproof writing & copier paper
Weatherproof field books

J.M.S. Ltd
P.O. Box 11525
Norfolk, VA 23517
Contact: James Stewart,
Telephone: 757-627-2997
Fax: 757-627-3213
Email: / URL:
Product Service Description:
Police & Military Equipment
Chemical Weapons & Training

J.R. McDade Marble & Granite
1101 N 21st Ave
Phoenix, AZ 85009-3722
Contact: Troy Jensen, Manager
Telephone: 602-254-8162
Fax: 602-254-8314
Product Service Description:
Fabricates and installs marble and granite
Cut stone & stone products

J.Ray McDemott, Inc.
801 North Eldridge Street
Houston, TX 77079-2701
Contact: Robert H. Rawle, Pres., COO
Telephone: 281-870-5000
Fax: 281-870-5152
Email: bobby.rawle@mcdermott.com / URL: http://www.jraymcdermott.com
Product Service Description:
Worldwide offshore oil & gas construction
Engineering design & project managment
Platform fabrication & installation
Subsea system design & pipelay

J.V. Thecno Surgical, Inc.
4700 140th Ave N, Ste 111
Clearwater, FL 33762
Contact: Julio Vallette, *
Telephone: 813-726-4896
Fax: 813-726-6226
Product Service Description:
Orthopedic & Med. Trauma Equip., Export

JASA Publications
PO Box 55276
Sherman Oaks, CA 91413-0276
Contact: Joel Kaye, Pres.
Telephone: 818-988-9044
Fax: 818-785-2334
Email: jasaguide@worldnet.att.net / URL:
Product Service Description:
Publishes apparel manufacturers' and contractors' directories for Los Angeles area
Publishing_miscellaneous

JB Research Inc
9062 Rosecrans Ave
Bellflower, CA 90706-2038
Contact: Gayle Gerth, Pres., Claudio Palladini, Int'l Sales Mgr.
Telephone: 562-790-2400
Fax: 562-790-8355
Email: / URL: http://www.relaxor.com
Product Service Description:
Manufactures electrical massage equipment

JBR Inc
1933 Davis St Ste 308
San Leandro, CA 94577-1259
Contact: Jin Rogers, VP
Telephone: 510-638-1300
Fax: 510-638-0760
Email: / URL: http://www.gourmet-coffee.com
Product Service Description:
Coffee_roasted
Manufactures roasted coffee

JD Tool & Machine Co Inc
12321 Sampson St Unit Defg
Riverside, CA 92503-4837
Contact: Donna Coulter, Pres.
Telephone: 909-371-6653
Fax: 909-371-6652
Email: martycoulter@jdtool.com / URL: http://www.jdtool.com
Product Service Description:
Precision Machine Shop, Rubber molds, machined parts
CNC milling, tools, dies, jigs & fixtures, Prototype parts

JDC (Hawaii) Inc., Advance Foods Div., Oligopower Div.
76-787 Hualalai Rd.
Kailua Kona, HI 96740
Contact: Allen I. Konno, Pres.
Telephone: 808-329-0100
Fax: 808-329-0073
Email: / URL:
Product Service Description:
Food plant engineering
Health consulting
Musical Magic Show for Non Profit Organization

JH Design Group
931 E Pico Blvd Ste 401
Los Angeles, CA 90021-2200
Contact: Albert Elkouby, Pres.
Telephone: 213-747-5700
Fax: 213-747-3648
Email: / URL:
Product Service Description:
Manufactures men's and women's leather jackets
Leather & sheep-lined clothing
Women's & children's clothing
Wool & leather outerwear jackets
All twill nasear uniform jackets

JHB International, Inc.
1955 S. Quince St.
Denver, CO 80231-3206
Contact: Jean H. Barr, *
Telephone: 303-751-8100
Fax: 303-752-0608
Email: / URL:
Product Service Description:
Buttons

JL Tool & Machine
930 W 23rd St Ste 7
Tempe, AZ 85282-1820
Contact: Jack Leckington, Owner
Telephone: 602-966-5067
Fax: 602-966-0902
Product Service Description:
Tool racks for end mills & collets, metric &
american ; Industrial machinery

JLG Industries, Inc.
1 JLG Dr.
McConnellsburg, PA 17233
Contact: Thomas Mrozinski, Mgr.
Telephone: 717-485-5161
Fax: 717-485-6416
Email: comments@jlg.com
URL: http://www.jlg.com
Product Service Description:
Aerial Work Platforms: Boomlift, Scissor Lift

JPS Communications Inc
5720 M Capital Blvd.
Raleigh, NC 27616
Contact: Sales & Marketing,
Telephone: 919-790-1011
Fax: 919-790-1456
Email: jps@jps.com / URL: http://
www.jps.com
Product Service Description:
Telephone & Telephone Apparatus
Radio & Tv Broadcasting Comm Equip
Comm Equip Not Elsewhere Classified

JSAM
377 Fisher Rd., Ste. F
Grosse Pointe, MI 48230-1600
Contact: Thomas C. White, III, Owner
Telephone: 313-885-4848
Product Service Description:
Premium Soft Packaging
Embroidery : Woven cotton fabrics & knits

JSJ Corp/Sparks Belting Div
16000 Phoenix Dr
City Of Industry, CA 91745-1623
Contact: Cal Tenharmsel, GM
Telephone: 626-333-2249
Fax: 626-333-0311
Email: ctensbc@msn.com / URL: http://
www.sparksbelting.com
Product Service Description:
Manufactures rubber and thermoplastic
conveyor belting and motorized conveyor
pulleys : Hose & belting_rubber & plastic

JSP International
4062 Georgia Blvd
San Bernardino, CA 92407-1847
Contact: Lewis Bowman, Opers. Mgr.
Telephone: 909-880-1855
Fax: 909-887-1309
Email: / URL:
Product Service Description:
Rubber products_fabricated
Expanded foam products

Jabitex Corporation
313 High Crest Dr.
West Milford, NJ 07480
Contact: Sales & Marketing,
Telephone: 973-838-7007
Fax: 973-492-2790
Email: jabitex1@aol.com / URL: http://
www.jabitex.com
Product Service Description:
All type of yarn in seconds & close-out
All type of fabrics, seconds & close-out
Limestone all type of cuts & colors

Jaccard Corporation
3421 North Benzing Road
Orchard Park, NY 14127
Contact: Andre Jaccard, President
Telephone: 716/825-3814
Fax: 716/825-5319
Email: / URL:
Product Service Description:
Auto. Food Slicing/Dicing Mach., Whsle
Vacuum Packaging Machines, Whsle
Meat Cutlet Flattening Device., Whsle
Pickling Injector/Machines, Whsle
Mechanical Meat Tenderizing Machines,
Whsle

Jackson Transformer Co.
4709 W Cayuga St
Tampa, FL 33614-6948
Contact: William E. Terlop, Pres.
Telephone: 813-879-5811
Fax: 813-870-6405
Email: JACTRANS@ix.netcom.com / URL:
Product Service Description:
Transformers & magnetic products
Transformers, except electronic

Jacksonlea
7020 Vine St
Cincinnati, OH 45216-2032
Contact: Craig Hoffheimer, Sales Mgr.
Telephone: 513-761-7100
Fax: 513-761-7842
Email: jacksonlea@aol.com / URL: http://
www.jacksonlea.com
Product Service Description:
Metal finishing & buffing compounds
Abrasive products

Jade Food Products, Inc.
401 N Cane St Ste A15
Wahiawa, HI 96786-2170
Contact: Hollis Ho, Pres.
Telephone: 808-621-5566
Fax: 808-621-8226
Email: / URL:
Product Service Description:
Nuts & seeds_salted & roasted

Jaeckle Fleischmann & Mugel, LLP
Fleet Bank Bldg. 12 Fountain Plaza
Buffalo, NY 14202-2292
Contact: Renee A. Filip, *
Telephone: (716) 856-0600
Fax: (716) 856-0432
Product Service Description:
Attorneys, Legal Services

Jaffrey Fire Protection Co., Inc.
PO Box 490
Jaffrey, NH 03452-0490
Contact: Charles H. Krause, *
Telephone: 605-532-7746
Fax: 605-532-7745
Email: / URL:
Product Service Description:
Fire Fighting Equipment

James Heavy Equipment Specialist
2150 S Valentia St
Denver, CO 80231-3325
Contact: Fred M James, Pres.
Telephone: 303-695-4739
Fax: 303-695-1647
Email: djames@jamesheavyequip.com / URL:
Product Service Description:
Sales, service and parts for engines, forklifts
and cranes
Industrial machinery & equipment
Repair services

James Instruments, Inc.
3727 N Kedzie Ave
Chicago, IL 60618-4503
Contact: William Hogg, Pres., Fin., Hum.
Res. & MIS Mgr.
Telephone: 773-463-6565
Fax: 773-463-0009
Email: custserv@dtjames.com / URL: http://
www.ndtjames.com
Product Service Description:
Concrete testing equipment
Machinery, Special Industry

Jamison Bedding Co.
PO Box 3126
Albany, GA 31706-3126
Contact: Bill Jones, Dist. Mgr.
Telephone: 912-436-6318
Fax: 912-434-0441
Email: / URL:
Product Service Description:
Mattresses & box springs
Mattresses & bedsprings

Jan Packaging, Inc.
P.O. Box 448
Dover, NJ 07801
Contact: Diane Smilari, Sales Manager
Telephone: 973-361-7200
Fax: 973-361-3835
Email: janpkg@aol.com / URL:
Product Service Description:
Packing & Crating, Industrial Machinery
Packing & Crating, Military Specs.
Trans. Svcs. Truck/Rig. Oversized Units
Freight Forwarding, International
General Warehousing

Jason Industrial, Inc.
PO Box 10004
Fairfield, NJ 07004-6004
Contact: Phillip Cohenca, Pres.
Telephone: 973-227-4904
Fax: 973-227-1651
Email: jasonpc@planet.net / URL: http://
www.jasonindustrial.com
Product Service Description:
Rubber timing belts
Hose & belting_rubber & plastic

Jason International, Inc.
8328 Macarthur Dr
North Little Rock, AR 72118-2029
Contact: Remo Jacuzzi, Pres.
Telephone: 501-771-4477
Fax: 501-771-2333
Email: sales@jasonint.com / URL: http://
www.jasonint.com
Product Service Description:
Whirlpool baths

Jaw Manufacturing Co.
P.O. Box 213
Reading, PA 19603-0213
Contact: James A. Williamson, Sr., Chairman
of the Board
Telephone: 610-376-2019
Fax: 610-378-1022
Email: jawco@jawco.com / URL: http://
www.jawco.com
Product Service Description:
Hand Tools
Flexible Shaft Tools
Hex Rethreader Dies
Thread Restoring Files
Impact Drivers
Screw Extractors

Jay R. Smith Mfg. Co.
2781 Gunter Dr. E., P.o. Box 3237
Montgomery, AL 36109
Contact: Michael Maddox, Export Manager
Telephone: 334-277-8520
Fax: 334-272-7396
Email: michael.maddox@jrsmith.com / URL:
http://www.jrsmith.com
Product Service Description:
Plumbing Products

Jayline International Corp.
1301 W Elizabeth Ave Ste E-1
Linden, NJ 07036-6389
Contact: Jay Weinstock, Pres.
Telephone: 908-474-1040
Fax: 908-474-1044
Email: jaylinenj@aol.com / URL: http://
www.jaylineworld.com
Product Service Description:
Plastic promotional products

Jaypro Corporation
976 Hartford Tpke
Waterford, CT 06385
Contact: Mark Ferrara,
Telephone: 203-447-3001
Fax: 203-444-1779
Email: / URL:
Product Service Description:
Sporting Goods

Jeb Lighting Co., Llc
2705 Ginkgo Ave
Washington, IA 52353-9425
Contact: Larry J. Harris, Pres., Fin. & R & D
Mgr.
Telephone: 319-653-6832
Fax: 319-653-9602
Email: kaylee@lisco.net / URL:
Product Service Description:
Lighting fixtures_commercial
5", 6" & 7 1/2 " Orbit (Ball) Lights

Jeco Plastic Products, Inc.
PO Box 26
Plainfield, IN 46168-0026
Contact: Craig S. Carson, CEO
Telephone: 317-839-4943
Fax: 317-839-1209
Email: jeco@iquest.net / URL: http://
www.jecoplastics.com
Product Service Description:
Rotationally Molded Plastic Products
Pallets & Material Handling Containers

Jefferson Mills, Inc.
Valley & Commerce Sts., P.O. Box 698
Pulaski, VA 24301
Contact: David B. Spangler, President &
CEO
Telephone: 540-980-1530
Fax: 540-980-6388
Email: dspang@jeffersonmills.com / URL:
Product Service Description:
Textured Nylon & Polyester Yarns
Textured & Twisted Synthetic Fiber Yarns

Jell Chemicals, Inc.
1281 Arthur Ave
Elk Grove Village, IL 60007-5705
Contact: Joseph Gayton Sr., Pres.
Telephone: 847-952-1081 / 800-747-5355
Fax: 847-952-1068
Email: info@jellchemicals.com / URL: http://
www.jellchemicals.com
Product Service Description:
Pressroom chemicals blending
Chemical preparations

Jennings Technology Company
970 McLaughlin Ave.
San Jose, CA 95122
Contact: Kurt Gallo, Export Sales Manager
Telephone: 408-292-4025
Fax: 408-286-1789
Email: kgallo@jenningstech.com / URL:
http://www.jenningstech.com
Product Service Description:
Electric Welding Contactors : Vacuum Relays
Electron Tubes Vacuum Capacitors :
Switchgear Vacuum Interrupters : Coaxial RF
Vacuum Switches : High Voltage Test
Instruments

Jensen Tools, Inc.
7815 S. 46th St.
Phoenix, AZ 85044-5313
Contact: Gary Treiber, President
Telephone: 602-453-3169
Fax: 602-438-1690
Email: jensen@stanleyworks.com / URL:
http://www.jensentools.com
Product Service Description:
Hardware

Jensen, Norman G., Inc.
3050 Metro Dr., Ste. 300,
Minneapolis, MN 55425
Contact: Dennis Jensen, Vice President
Telephone: 612-854-7363
Fax: 612-854-8302
Email: dfj@njjensen.com / URL: http://
www.ngjensen.com
Product Service Description:
Customs Broker
Freight Forwarder
Freight & Cargo Transportation

Jerryco Machine & Boilerworks
PO Box 11908
Houston, TX 77293-1908
Contact: Jerry Campbell, Pres.
Telephone: 713-224-7900
Fax: 713-224-4311
Email: jerryco1@juno.com / URL:
Product Service Description:
Rebuilt boilers : Plate work_fabricated (boiler
shops) : Sell Boilers : Repair Boilers
Rent Boilers : Machine Shop

Jessup Manufacturing Co.
PO Box 366
Mc Henry, IL 60051-0366
Contact: Alan M. Carlson, Int'l Sales
Manager
Telephone: 815-385-6650
Fax: 815-385-0079
Email: / URL:
Product Service Description:
Abrasive Products, Anti-Slip Tapes
Specialty tapes, Pressure Sensitive
Adhesive Coating & Laminating
Glow-in-the-dark- Tapes

Jet Air Service, Inc.
JFK Int'l Airport, Cargo Bldg. 80,
Jamaica, NY 11430
Contact: Joseph W. Podbela, President
Telephone: 718-656-7430
Fax: 718-244-0942
Email: jetairsvc@aol.com / URL:
Product Service Description:
Customs Broker
Freight Forwarder
Freight & Cargo Transportation
Warehousing & distribution

Jet Import Brokers
650 N. Sam Houston Pkwy., Ste. 329,
Houston, TX 77060
Contact: Jim Towsend, Contact
Telephone: 281-448-5253
Fax: 281-447-6440
Email: eibrokers@aol.com / URL:
Product Service Description:
Customs Broker

Jet, Inc.
750 Alpha Dr.
Cleveland, OH 44143
Contact: Tom WIlliams, Dir. of Engineering
Phone: 216-461-2000 / Fax: 216-442-9008
Product Service Description:
Wastewater Treatment Equipment

Jg Creations Inc
7665 Mossy Cup St
Boise, ID 83709-2844
Contact: Juanita Grimes, Pres.
Phone: 208-362-0188 / Fax: 208-362-0272
Email: / URL: http://www.jgcreations.com
Product Service Description:
Textile products_fabricated
Manufactures sewn products

Jianlibao America, Ltd.
420 5th Ave., 26th Floor
New York, NY 10018
Contact: Sales & Marketing,
Telephone: 212-354-8898
Fax: 212-354-8838
Email: ganlibo@tdt.net / URL: http://
www.janlibo.com
Product Service Description:
Importing Firms Oriental Food Stuff
Tea & Beverages

Jiffy Tite Co., Inc.
PO Box 570
Lancaster, NY 14086-0570
Contact: Steven Zillig, Pres.
Telephone: 716-681-7200
Fax: 716-681-7788
Email: jiffy@jiffy-tite.com / URL:
Product Service Description:
Fluid couplings & hose fittings for automotive
OEM & after market : Quick connect
coupling for cooling systems : Quick
disconnect fluid coupling for high flow
industrial applications : Fluid coupling
solutions to improve your system reliability
Over 50 million fluid connectors in use on
passenger cars : Connectors for your injection
mold cooling system

Jim C. Hamer Co.
PO Box 418
Kenova, WV 25530-0418
Contact: Steve Hamer, Export Sls Mgr.
Telephone: 304-453-3274
Fax: 304-453-6587
Email: jchamer@zoomnet.net / URL: http://
www.jimchamer.com
Product Service Description:
Appalachian hardwood lumber, logs & veneer

Jim C. Lane Inc.
607 S Evers St
Plant City, FL 33566-5421
Contact: Jim Lane, Pres.
Telephone: 813-754-5779 / 800-736-0291
Fax: 813-754-5779
Product Service Description:
Hardwood circular stairs : Stair parts
Production stairs : Architectural millwork
Millwork

Jim O'Neil Environmental Consultant
PO Box 55591
North Pole, AK 99705-0591
Contact: Jim O'Neil, *
Telephone: 907-488-6661
Fax: 907-488-6661
Product Service Description:
Management Consulting Services,

Jim Teeny, Inc.
2750 SW Butler Rd
Gresham, OR 97080-5495
Contact: Jim Teeny, Pres.
Telephone: 503-667-6602
Fax: 503-667-2917
Email: tnymph@transport.com / URL: http://
www.teeny-nymph.com
Product Service Description:
Manufactures fly fishing tackle

Joaquin Manufacturing Corp
6900 Elm Dr
Commerce City, CO 80022-1844
Contact: D X Bargas, CEO, Mark Bargas
Telephone: 303-286-7060
Fax: 303-286-7067
Email: / URL:
Product Service Description:
Concrete products
Manufactures concrete products; integrated
portable shelters and enclosures; above-
ground
Prefabricated metal buildings
Prefabricated wood buildings
Structural metal_fabricated
Tanks, AST, Custom, Fuel
Has-mat-flamable material storage bldg's
EMI/RFI Shielded enclosures / shelters

Jobe Industries Inc.
1600 W. Elizabeth, P.O. Box 1367
Linden, NJ 07036
Contact: Joe Beer, President
Telephone: 908/862-0400
Fax: 908-862-1039
Email: jobeind@ix.netcom.com / URL: http://
www.jobe-industries.com
Product Service Description:
Cleaning Compounds, Vehicle (Cars, Buses,
Trucks)
Cleaning Compounds, Janitorial

Jobquest
1522 N Washington St Ste 200
Spokane, WA 99201-2454
Contact: Drew M Brooks, Pres., CEO
Telephone: 509-535-5000
Fax: 509-535-1011
Email: jobquest@jobquest.com / URL: http://
www.jobquest.com
Product Service Description:
Designs, develops & distributes jobs
exploration software;
Career software products & services for
career planning
Prepackaged Software

Jogler, Inc.
9715 Derrington Rd
Houston, TX 77064-5807
Contact: William A. Jackson, Pres.
Telephone: 281-469-6969
Fax: 281-469-0422
Email: jskinner@jogler.com / URL: http://
www.jogler.com
Product Service Description:
Liquid level gauges & site flow indicators
Magnetic Level Gauges & Controls

John Amann Sons Co.
10435 Argonne Woods Drive
Woodridge, IL 60517-4927
Contact: Robert A. Amann, V.P.
Telephone: 630-972-9473
Fax: 630-972-1717
Email: sales@jamann.com / URL: http://
www.jamann.com
Product Service Description:
Fourslide Wire Forms
Fourslide Metal Stampings
Fabricated Wire Products

John Blue Co.
PO Box 1607
Huntsville, AL 35807-0607
Contact: Michael A. Poland, President
Telephone: 205-721-9090
Fax: 205-721-9091
Email: info@johnblue.com / URL: http://
www.johnblue.com
Product Service Description:
Pumps, Meters
Irrigation Injection Pumps

John Crane Inc.
6400 Oakton St
Morton Grove, IL 60053-2725
Contact: Bob Wasson, Pres.
Telephone: 847-967-2400
Fax: 847-967-3915
Email: inet@johncrane.com / URL: http://
www.johncrane.com
Product Service Description:
Gaskets, packing & sealing devices
Mechanical seals, packings & lapping
machines & oil seals

John Deere Harvester Works, Cylinder Div.
909 River Dr
Moline, IL 61265-1202
Contact: Lee Fluck, Sales Mgr.
Telephone: 309-765-7596
Fax: 309-765-7379
Email: ax@00318.deere.com / URL: http://
www.deere.com/oem_harvester/
Product Service Description:
Construction & agricultural hydraulic
cylinders
Bore sizes 50 - 200 mm

John N Hansen Co Inc
369 Adrian Rd
Millbrae, CA 94030-3104
Contact: Mary J. Hansen,
Telephone: 650-697-7353
Fax: 650-697-1748
Email: / URL:
Product Service Description:
Manufactures and imports games and toys
Games, toys & children's vehicles
Toys & hobby goods & supplies
Plastic products

John Zink Company
PO Box 21220
Tulsa, OK 74121-1220
Contact: Sales & Marketing,
Telephone: 918-234-1800
Fax: 918-234-2700
Email: / URL: http://www.johnzink.com
Product Service Description:
Burner Systems
Flare Systems
Incineration Systems

Johnny Gibson Gym Equipment Co
11 S 6th Ave
Tucson, AZ 85701-1805
Contact: Steve Gibson, V-P.
Telephone: 520-622-1275
Fax: 520-622-1505
Email: johnnygibson@earthlink.net / URL:
http://www.johnnygibson.com
Product Service Description:
Manufactures gym equipment
Sporting & athletic goods

Johnson Lumber Co., Llc.
Rte. 26 box 111-A
Carthage, NY 13619
Contact: Robert Johnson, VP
Telephone: 315-493-1774
Fax: 315-493-9663
Email: rrlumber@gisco.net / URL:
Product Service Description:
Sawmills & planing Mills, General
Kiln-Dried & Paned Lumber
12 Million WhitePine

Johnston Pumps
800 Koomey Rd.
Brookshire, TX 77423
Contact: Cheryl Parker-Reznicek,
Telephone: 281-934-6009
Fax: 281-934-6090
Email: cparker@flow-products.com / URL:
Product Service Description:
Pumps
Agricultural Machine
Oil Field Equipment

Jonal Laboratories, Inc.
PO Box 743
Meriden, CT 06450-0743
Contact: Marc Nemeth, Pres.
Telephone: 203-634-4444
Fax: 203-634-4448
Email: jonal@jonal.com / URL: http://
www.jonal.com
Product Service Description:
Aircraft engine parts, plastic seals & gaskets
Aircraft engines & engine parts
Aircraft parts & equipment

Jonathan Virginia, Inc.
PO Box 652
Charlottesville, VA 22902-0652
Contact: Jon Fink, Pres., R & D, Sales &
Mktg. Mgr.
Telephone: 804-979-0585
Fax: 804-977-4356
Email: sales@jvi.com / URL: http://
www.jvi.com
Product Service Description:
Wood products, stone products, marble
products
Wooden display cases, humidifiers, funeral
urns, speakers & flat component parts
Millwork

Jones Companies LTD. (Mfr)
P.O. Box 367
Humboldt, TN 38343USA
Contact: J. Andrew Dailey, *
Telephone: 901-784-2832
Fax: 901-784-7131
Email: / URL:
Product Service Description:
Apparel Yarn, Conveyor Belt Yarn
Rug Yarns
Mop Yarns
Weaving Yarns
Upholstery Yarns

Jones Dairy Farm
PO Box 808
Fort Atkinson, WI 53538-0808
Contact: Mark Spengler,
Telephone: 920-563-2431
Fax: 920-563-6801
Email: / URL: http://www.jonessausage.com
Product Service Description:
Further Processed Pork & Beef

Jones Lumber Co., Inc., J. M.
PO Box 1368
Natchez, MS 39121-1368
Contact: L. Kenneth Jones, Pres
Telephone: 601-442-7471
Fax: 601-446-7448
Email: hjones@bkbank.com / URL: http://
www.jolumco.com
Product Service Description:
Lumber processing
Sawmills & planing mills, general

Jonti-Craft, Inc.
PO Box 30
Wabasso, MN 56293-0030
Contact: John N. Franta, *
Telephone: 507-342-5169
Fax: 507-642-5617
Product Service Description:
Wood Play Equipment, Childrens Educational

Joplin Printing Co.
PO Box 25
Joplin, MO 64802-0025
Contact: Stephen L. Barnett, Pres.
Telephone: 417-623-4460
Fax: 417-623-7570
Email: / URL: http://www.joplinprint.com
Product Service Description:
Printing_commercial
Commercial printing & rubber stamps
Marking devices

Joseph Industries, Inc.
10039 Aurora Hudson Rd
Streetsboro, OH 44241-1622
Contact: Sales & Marketing,
Telephone: 216-528-0091
Fax: 216-342-3896
Email: joseph@en.com / URL: http://
www.joseph.com
Product Service Description:
Driveline Repair Parts - Lift Trucks
Service Repair Parts - Backhoe Loaders
Rebuilt Transmission Components Lift Trk.
Engine Parts - Lift Truck

Julia P. Poger Associates
2701 Connecticut Ave., NW, #502
Washington, DC 20008
Contact: Julia Poger, *
Telephone: 202-332-8592
Fax: 202-667-8892
Email: 102753.3476@compuserve.com /
URL:
Product Service Description:
English, Russian, French, Interpreting

Jun-Air USA, Inc.
1350 Abbott Ct
Buffalo Grove, IL 60089-2378
Contact: Jesper Torp, Pres.
Telephone: 847-215-9444
Fax: 847-215-9449
Email: info@jun-air.com / URL: http://
www.jun-air.com
Product Service Description:
Compressors_air & gas
Air compressors

Juno International
135 W. 29th St., 8th Fl.
New York, NY 10001-5104
Contact: Sales & Marketing,
Telephone: 212-967-8770
Fax: 212-714-1902
Email: buy1@juno.com / URL: http://
www.junointl.com
Product Service Description:
Casio & Sharp Digital Diaries
Casio Watches : G-Shock Watches
Casio Calculators : Sharp Calculators
Mont Blanc Pens

Jupiter Chemicals, Inc.
PO Box 789
Westlake, LA 70669-0789
Contact: Ed Aucoin, Plt. Mgr.
Telephone: 318-882-0401
Fax: 318-882-1305
Email: eaucoin@tkinet.com / URL:
Product Service Description:
Chemicals_industrial inorganic
Sodium sulfide

Just A Stretch
P.O. Box 189
Hope, RI 02831
Contact: Robert Laferriere, President
Telephone: 401-822-0730
Fax: 401-826-2318
Email: / URL:
Product Service Description:
Narrow Fabric Mills : Elastic Trim
Knitted Elastic : Woven Elastic
Manufacturing Facility in Dominican
Republic : Intimate Apparel
Printing, All Types

Just Merino Sheepskin Products
5090 W Horseshoe Ln
Mc Neal, AZ 85617-9654
Contact: Judith McGraw-Sperling, Pres.
Telephone: 520-364-7764/1800-323-9665
Fax: 520-364-7764
Email: / URL:
Product Service Description:
Manufactures saddlery and consumer
products for retail and catalog sales; imports
Australian Merino wool skin
Sheepskins: Manufacturing industries to pet
stores & catalogs : Farm supplies for animal
care : Catalog & mail-order houses &
retailers for travel & comfort products

Just Truffles
350 Market St
Saint Paul, MN 55102-1430
Contact: Kathleen O'Hehir Johnson, Pres.
Telephone: 651-222-6922
Fax: 651-228-3810
Email: justruffle@aol.com / URL: http://
www.justruffles.com
Product Service Description:
Handmade chocolate truffles
Chocolate & cocoa products

Justice Brothers, Inc.
2734 E. Huntington Drive
Duarte, CA 91010-2301
Contact: Edward Justice, President
Telephone: 818-359-9174
Fax: 818-357-2550
Email: @justicebrothers.com / URL: http://
www.justicebrothers.com
Product Service Description:
Automotive Cleaners
Automobile Parts & Supplies - Wholesale &
Manufacturers

K & B Machine Works Inc.
3238 Grand Caillou Rd
Houma, LA 70363-7148
Contact: Kenneth Wood, Pres., R & D Mgr.
Telephone: 504-868-6730
Fax: 504-868-6036
Email: kwood@db-machine.com / URL:
http://www.kb-machine.com
Product Service Description:
General machining job shop
CNC production machining & milling
Oilfield manufacturing & repair

K & K Express
144-24 156th St.
Jamaica, NY 11434
Contact: Frank Slaughter, Regional Vice
President
Telephone: 718-527-6002
Fax: 718-527-5011
Email: newyork@kkexpress.com / URL:
http://www.globalcontact.com/market/
kkair.htm
Product Service Description:
Customs Broker
Freight Forwarding
Air Freight Cargo: Transportation &
Insurance

K & W Popcorn Inc. (Mfr)
P.O. Box 275
Trenton, MO 64683
Contact: Bill Kennebeck, President
Telephone: 660-359-2030
Fax: 660-359-3026
Email: kenebeck@lyn.net / URL:
Product Service Description:
Popcorn, Raw Unpopped, Commercial

K & W Products
239 W. Grimes Ln.
Bloomington, IN 47403
Contact: John Goode, Jr., *
Telephone: 812-336-3083
Fax: 213-722-0678
Email: / URL:
Product Service Description:
Radiator Block Sealers
Engine Block Sealers
Gasket Compounds
Automotive Cleaners
Oil Additives

K F Industries, Inc.
1500 Se 89th St
Oklahoma City, OK 73149-4607
Contact: Maury J. Mills, V-P., Sales & Mktg.
Telephone: 405-631-1533
Fax: 405-631-8978
Email: kfinfo@kfvalves.com / URL: http://
www.kfvalves.com
Product Service Description:
Valves

K W Products, Inc.
500 57th St
Marion, IA 52302-3801
Contact: David J. Parks, Pres.
Telephone: 319-377-9421
Fax: 319-377-9101
Email: kwikway@mcleod.net / URL: http://
www.kwik-way.comm
Product Service Description:
Boring equipment, automotive valve grinders,
engine reconditioning equipment
Metalworking machinery

K-D Lamp Company (Mfr)
1910 Elm Street
Cincinnati, OH 45210
Contact: Bill Mosey, *
Telephone: 513-621-4211
Product Service Description:
Truck Vehicle Lighting
(Airblade) Mirror Cleaning System

K. G. Fiber, Inc.
701 W 5th St
Palmyra, NJ 08065-2493
Contact: Kirit Patel, Pres.
Telephone: 609-786-6800
Fax: 609-786-1331
Email: kgfibers@erols.com / URL:
Product Service Description:
Cotton batting : Textile goods

KBS Exports
110 State St., E., Ste. 3
Oldsmar, FL 34677-3651
Contact: Muriel Yantiss, Owner
Telephone: 727-786-9400
Product Service Description:
Engineering Services
Motor vehicle parts and accessories

KD Water Sports
PO Box 2131
Auburn, WA 98071-2131
Contact: Matt Kaplan, Vice President
Telephone: 253-735-9226
Fax: 253-735-9319
Email: / URL: http://www.kdskis.com
Product Service Description:
Sporting & athletic goods
Manufactures water skis, wakeboards and
accessories : Brand names: KD Waterskis,
Kidder Waterskis, Blindside Wakeboards

KLD Associates Inc.
300 Broadway
Huntington Station, NY 11746
Contact: Edward Lieberman, President
Telephone: 516-549-9803
Fax: 516-351-7190
Email: kldhunt@aol.com / URL: http://
www.kldassociates.com
Product Service Description:
Traffic Engineering Studies & Visualization
Simulation, Animation & Visualization of
Traffic Flow : Transportation Safety Analyses
Evaluation of ITS Applications
Toll Plaza Simulation & Evaluation
Transit Priority Simulation & Evaluation

KLM International
7203 Belgold # 4
Houston, TX 77066
Contact: Lois Maier, Owner
Telephone: 281-586-4000
Fax: 281-586-4040
Email: klmint@worldnet.att.com / URL:
Product Service Description:
Valves, Crane, Balon, Cooper & Kinka, Etc.
Pipe, Carbon Steel, Fabricated Etc.
Fittings, Carbon Steel, Etc.

KNI Incorporated
1261 S State College Pkwy
Anaheim, CA 92806-5240
Contact: Jerry R Bernstein, Pres.
Telephone: 714-956-7300
Fax: 714-635-1744
Email: knimb@aol.com / URL:
www.kninc.com
Product Service Description:
Prints books (soft & hard cover)

KOA Speer Electronics, Inc.
P.O. Box 547
Bradford, PA 16701-0547
Contact: Jeffrey Rice,
Telephone: 814-362-5536
Fax: 814-362-8883
Email: / URL:
Product Service Description:
Carbon Film Resistors
Fixed Radio Frequency Inductors
Metalfilm Resistors
Metal Oxide Resistors
Network Resistors
Thick Film Flat Chip Resistors
Thin Film Flat Chip Resistors
Integrated Passive Components
(Resistor, Resostro Capacitors, Resistor,
Capacitor, Diodes)
Tontalum Capacitors

KSA Engineers, Inc.
P.O. Box 1552
Longview, TX 75606
Contact: Walter T. Winn Jr., Vice President
Telephone: 903/236-7700
Fax: 903/236-7779
Email: wwinn@ksaeng.com / URL: http://
www.ksaeng.com
Product Service Description:
Engineering Services
Surveying Services

KSC Industries Inc
8653 Avenida Costa Norte
San Diego, CA 92173-2218
Contact: Richard Eilenberg, GM
Telephone: 619-671-0110
Fax: 619-671-0330
Email: kscind@kscind.com / URL: http://
www.kscind.com
Product Service Description:
Manufactures speakers
Audio & video equipment_household
Electrical appliances, TV & radios

Ka-Bar Knives, Inc.
1125 E State St
Olean, NY 14760-3813
Contact: Peter Laine, Pres.
Telephone: 716-372-5952
Fax: 716-373-6245
Email: info@ka-bar.com / URL: http://
www.ka-bar.com
Product Service Description:
Sporting & hunting knives

Kalman Electronics Of Arizona
12648 N 57th St
Scottsdale, AZ 85254-4334
Contact: Yadi Rezvani, Pres.
Telephone: 602-998-5300
Fax: 602-998-0212
Email: nhcp@msn.com / URL:
Product Service Description:
Refurbishes & overstock telephones

Kamen Wiping Materials Co., Inc.
PO Box 2077
Wichita, KS 67201-2077
Contact: Len Goldstein, President
Telephone: 316-265-8615
Fax: 316-267-1957
Email: kamen@southwind.net / URL: http://
www.kamenwipers.com
Product Service Description:
Textile wiping cloths

Kanawha Scales & Systems, Inc.
PO Box 569
Poca, WV 25159-0569
Contact: James A. Bradbury, Chrm., Pres.
Telephone: 304-755-8321
Fax: 304-755-3327
Email: sales@kanawhascales.com / URL:
http://www.kanawhascales.com
Product Service Description:
Weighing, control & data collection systems
& control panels
Switchgear & switchboard apparatus
High Speed Coal Loading System for Trains
Truck Scale Data Collection Systems

Kann Mfg. Corp.
PO Box 400
Guttenberg, IA 52052-0400
Contact: Dirk Kann, Pres.
Telephone: 319-252-2035
Fax: 319-252-3069
Email: kannman@netins.net / URL:
Product Service Description:
Recycling & solid waste trucks

Karavan Trailers, Inc.
PO Box 27
Fox Lake, WI 53933-0027
Contact: Scott Boyd, Pres., Cont.
Telephone: 920-928-6200
Fax: 920-928-6201
Email: karavan@powerweb.net / URL: http://
www.powerweb.net/karavan
Product Service Description:
Boat, snow, watercraft & utility trailers
Transportation equipment

**Karlan Research Products
Corporation**
3343 Industrial Dr Ste 9
Santa Rosa, CA 95403-2060
Contact: Stuart Lancaster, Managing Director
Telephone: 707-576-1225
Fax: 707-576-1349
Email: info@karlan.com / URL: http://
www.karlan.com
Product Service Description:
Areas of activity include enzyme production,
antibodies,
Molecular biology reagents & selected
consumable items for
Clinical, diagnostic and research use.

Karp Associates, Inc.
54-54 43rd St.
Maspeth, NY 11378-1028
Contact: Burton Gold, President
Telephone: 718-784-2105
Fax: 718-784-9169
Email: info@karpinc.com / URL: http://
www.karpinc.com
Product Service Description:
Metal Access Doors
Miscellaneous Building Materia

Kasko Enterprises Inc.
PO Box 411205
Charlotte, NC 28241-1205
Contact: Dick Tomlinson, V-P., GM & Opers.
Telephone: 704-583-1499
Fax: 704-583-1430
Email: kasko@bellsouth.net / URL: http://
www.kasko.com
Product Service Description:
Fiberglass insulation mats
Bulk Processed Fiberglass Products

Kason Corporation (Mfr)
67-71 East Willow Street
Millburn, NJ 07041
Contact: Lawrence Stone, President
Telephone: 201-467-8140
Fax: 201-258-9533
Email: kason@mail.idt.net / URL: http://
www.kason.com
Product Service Description:
Circular Vibratory Screen Separators
Centrifugal Sifters
Static Dewatering Sleeves
Vibrating Fluid Bed Dryers / Coolers
Agglomerators

Katolight Corp.
PO Box 3229
Mankato, MN 56002-3229
Contact: Al Prosser, Industrial Sales Mgr.
Telephone: 507-625-7973
Fax: 507-625-2968
Email: ki@katolight.com / URL: http://
www.katolight.com
Product Service Description:
Engine generator sets & controls
Engine electrical equipment

Kauai Coffee Company
PO Box 8
Eleele, HI 96705
Contact: Annette Burton,
Telephone: 808-335-5497
Fax: 808-335-0036
Email: greensales@kauaicoffee.com / URL:
http://www.kauaicoffee.com
Product Service Description:
Coffee, Roasted
Coffee not roasted

Kay & L Draperies, Inc.
602 Industrial Rd
Waverly, IA 50677-1810
Contact: Jeffrey Ferguson, GM, Engrg.
Telephone: 319-352-1934
Fax: 319-352-6482
Email: kandl@forbin.com / URL: http://
www.ferg.forbin.com
Product Service Description:
Curtains & draperies
Draperies, bedspreads & decorative fabrics

Kay-Ray/Sensall, Inc.
1400 E Business Center Dr Ste 100
Mount Prospect, IL 60056-6074
Contact: Michael L. Ortengren, Mktg. Mgr.
Telephone: 847-803-5100
Fax: 847-803-5466
Email: info@kayray-sensall.com / URL: http:/
/www.kayray-sensall.com
Product Service Description:
Level, density, weigh scale & flow process
control instrumentation
Relays & industrial controls

Kaydon Corp.
1571 Lukken Industrial Dr.
Lagrange, GA 30240
Contact: Patti Woitena, Inside Sales
Supervisor
Telephone: 706-884-3041
Fax: 706-883-6199
Email: kaydonsales@mindspring.com / URL:
http://www.kaydoncorp.com
Product Service Description:
Oil filtration systems, flow sights & indicator
& liquid metering devices

Kae Co., Inc.
1500 S, Western Ave.
Chicago, IL 60608-1828
Contact:Dawn Koehlinger, Pres., G.M.
Telephone: 312-738-3202
Fax: 630-968-6362
Email: kae@mcs.com
URL: http://www.mcs.com/~kae
Product Service Description:
Manufactures pet and personal care
shampoos and conditioners; detergents and
cleaning agents

Kaygeeco Inc
786 California St
Rathdrum, ID 83858-9251
Contact: Mike Hill, General Manager
Telephone: 208-687-5127
Fax: 208-687-9477
Email: info@kaygeeco.com / URL: http://
www.kaygeeco.com
Product Service Description:
Manufactures pet and personal care
shampoos and conditioners; detergents and
cleaning agents

Keating Fibre Inc
501 Office Center Dr.
Fort Washington, PA 19034
Contact: Frank J. Keating, *
Telephone: 215-628-3000
Product Service Description:
Kraft Linerboard

Keen, R. H. & Co., Inc.
3801 N.Causeway Blvd., Ste. 310,
Metairie, LA 70002
Contact: Sales & Marketing,
Telephone: 504-834-8080
Fax: 504-834-9599
Email: / URL:
Product Service Description:
Freight Forwarder
Customs Broker
Freight & Cargo Transportation
Warehousing

Keeper Thermal Bag Co. Inc.
93 E. Berkshire Dr. #E
Crystal Lake, IL 60014
Contact: Eleanor Workman, *
Telephone: 1-800-765-9244
Fax: 815-479-0225
Email: keeper@wwa.com / URL:
Product Service Description:
Thermal Insulated Food Bags For
Pizza, Catering, Vending, Etc.

Keiko Hirokawa
2715 Windwood Drive, #59
Ann Arbor, MI 48105
Contact: Keiko Hirokawa, *
Telephone: 313-663-5645
Fax: 313-761-6421
Email: / URL:
Product Service Description:
Translation & Interpretation Services,

Kel-Glo Corp.
54 Ne 73rd St
Miami, FL 33138-5397
Contact: Ron Smalzer, Pres., Fin. & R & D
Mgr.
Telephone: 305-751-5641
Fax: 305-756-6481
Email: ron@kelglo.com / URL: http://
www.@kelglo.com
Product Service Description:
Industrial coatings & paint

Kellett Enterprises Inc.(Mfr)
P.O.Box 2265
Greenville, SC 29602
Contact: Lois W. Foster, VP Sales & Mktg.
Telephone: 864-244-7248
Fax: 864-292-8612
Email: lois@kellettent.com / URL: http://
www.kellettent.com
Product Service Description:
Vibration Machinery Mounting Pads / LP-13
Shake Absorber®

Kelley Mfg. Co.
PO Box 1467
Tifton, GA 31793-1467
Contact: Maylon Nicholson, Export
Coordinator
Phone: 912-382-9393 / Fax: 912-382-5259
Email: info@kelleymfg.com / URL: http://
www.kelleymfg.com
Product Service Description:
Agricultural equipment: Farm machinery &
equipment : Poultry house clean-out
equipment

Kemco Tool & Machine Co., Inc.
615 Rudder Rd.
Fenton, MO 63026-2071
Contact: Rafath Ali, Chairman
Phone: 314-343-1168 / Fax: 314-343-1677
Email: / URL: http://www.kemco1.com
Product Service Description:
Industrial machinery
General machining job shop

Kemet Electronics Corp.
PO Box 5928
Greenville, SC 29606-5928
Contact: David Maguire, Chrm., Pres., CEO
Telephone: 864-963-6300
Fax: 864-963-6322
Email: / URL: http://www.kemet.com
Product Service Description:
Electronic capacitors, Tantalum
Electronic capacitors, Ceramic

Kemlite
PO Box 2429
Joliet, IL 60434-2429
Contact: Barbara Beaubien, Ex. Dir, Intl
Telephone: 815-467-8600
Fax: 815-467-8666
Email: kemlite@pop.wwa.com / URL: http://
www.kemlite.com
Product Service Description:
Fiberglass Reinoforced Panels : Plastic
Products : Sanitary Wall Coverings & Ceiling
Panels

Kemper International
500 W. Madison Ave., Suite 1100
Chicago, IL 60661-2555
Contact: Tarja Bentgarde-Childers, CEO
Phone: 312-559-2103 / Fax: 312-559-2131
Email: tbentgar@kemperinsurance.com
Product Service Description:
Insurance, Property & Casualty

Ken McRight Supplies, Inc.
7456 South Oswego
Tulsa, OK 74136-5903
Contact: Ken McRight, President
Phone: 918-492-9657 / Fax: 918-492-9694
Email: bbd4@juno.com
URL: ID: MCRIGHT99
Product Service Description:
Inflatable Wheel Chair Cushions, Rubber
Inflatable Mattress Overlay, Rubber
Inflatable Back Support, Rubber

Ken-A-Vision Mfg. Co., Inc.
5615 Raytown Rd.
Kansas City, MO 64133-3318
Contact: Thomas M. Dunn, Pres.
Phone: 816-353-4787 / Fax: 816-358-5072
Email: info@ken-a-vision.com / URL:
Product Service Description:
Microscopes, micro-projectors & video
imaging devices
Surgical & medical instruments

Ken-Lab, Llc
29 Plains Rd
Essex, CT 06426-1503
Contact: Ron Denman, Pres., Pur. Agt.
Phone: 860-767-3235 / Fax: 860-767-7843
Product Service Description:
Gyroscope stabilizers & precision instruments
Optical instruments & lenses

Kenalex Printing Forms, Inc.,
Kenalex Prints & Design
PO Box 980113
Houston, TX 77098-0113
Contact: Kenneth Finch, Pres.
Phone: 713-529-3559 / Fax: 713-529-3291
Email: info@kenalex.com
Product Service Description:
Business forms printing & commercial
printing & graphic design : Manifold business
forms

Kendon Industries Inc
3711 E La Palma Ave
Anaheim, CA 92806-2121
Contact: Tony Risberg, Sales Mgr.
Phone: 714-630-7144 / Fax: 714-630-7132
Email: ktkendon@aol.com / URL: http://
www.kendontrailers.com
Product Service Description:
Manufactures stand-up trailers to haul
motorcycles; suspension systems for Harley
Davidson motorcycles: Truck trailers
Motorcycles, bicycles & parts

Kent Corp.
PO Box 170399
Birmingham, AL 35217-0399
Contact: M. Oztekin, CEO
Phone: 205-853-3420 / Fax: 205-856-3622
Email: sales@kentcorp.com / URL: http://
www.kentcorp.com
Product Service Description:
Steel Gondola Display Shelving For
Supermarkets, Drug, Discount, AutoParts &
Other self service / retail industries.

Kent Oil Company Inc.
P.O. Box 2211
Lakeland, FL 33806
Contact: Jerard A. Kent, President
Telephone: 941-665-0070
Fax: 941-665-8242
Product Service Description:
Specialty Lubricating Oils, Treatments &
Greases, Wholesale
Lubrication Equipment, Wholesale

Kenyon & Sons, Inc., William
90 Ethel Rd W
Piscataway, NJ 08854-5929
Contact: Dewitt Oliver, Sales Mgr.
Telephone: 732-985-8980
Fax: 732-985-8984
Email: diane@williamkenyon.com / URL:
http://www.williamkenyon.com
Product Service Description:
Carrier Rope : Carrier Rope Eqipment

Keri Systems Inc
1530 Oakland Rd Ste 100
San Jose, CA 95112-1241
Contact: Dennis Geiszler, VP Sales
Telephone: 408-451-2520 / 800-260-5265
Fax: 408-441-0309
Email: sales@kerisys.com / URL: http://
www.kerisys.com
Product Service Description:
Manufactures proximity access control
products

Kessler International Corp.
15946 Derwood Rd.
Rockville, MD 20855-2123
Contact: Mohan Wadhwani, President
Telephone: 301-519-3429
Fax: 301-975-0712
Email: / URL:
Product Service Description:
Exporting Firms: Parts of railway or tramway
locomotives: Moving, grading, leveling,
excavating, extracting machinery for earth,
minerals or ores; Parts of airplanes, aircrafts
and helicopters

Kester Solder, Div. Litton Industries
515 E. Touhy Ave
Des Plaines, IL 60018
Contact: Dennis Gulino, *
Telephone: 847-297-1600
Fax: 847-390-9338
Email: / URL: http://www.kester.com
Product Service Description:
Electronic Solders
Electronic Chemicals
Bar Solders

Kevlin Corporation(Mfr)
5 Cornell Place
Wilmington, MA 01887
Contact: Mark C. Federico, Dir. of Sales &
Mktg.
Telephone: 508/657-3900
Fax: 508-658-5170
Email: / URL:
Product Service Description:
Microwave Rotary Couplers
Slip Rings

Kevry Corporation
16133 W 45th Dr
Golden, CO 80403-1791
Contact: Michael Ackerman, Chrm.
Telephone: 303-271-9300
Fax: 303-271-3645
Email: / URL:
Product Service Description:
Fabricates food service equipment, Sneeze
guards & display units

Keyper Systems, Inc.
6636 E Wt Harris Blvd Ste D
Charlotte, NC 28215-5125
Contact: Bob Conder, President
Telephone: 800-399-7888
Fax: 704-566-9114
Email: info@keypersystems.com / URL:
http://www.keypersystems.com
Product Service Description:
Key management systems
Padlock management systems

Kex Power
36 E Main St.
Charleston, NC 28215-5125
Contact: Joe Smith
Product Service Description:
Transportation Service

Keystone Electronics Corp.
31-07 20th Rd.
Astoria, NY 11105
Contact: R. David, President
Telephone: 718-956-8900
Fax: 718-956-9040
Email: troy@keyelco.com / URL: http://
www.keyelco.com
Product Service Description:
Electronic Hardware
Electronic Components
Battery Clips, Contacts & Holders
Insulating Hardware
Interconnect Hardware & Terminals
Mounting Hardware & Handles

Keystone Food Products Inc.
PO Box 326
Easton, PA 18044-0326
Contact: David L. Bowman, President &
CEO
Telephone: 610-258-0888 X 219
Fax: 610-250-0721
Email: ddave@keystonesnacks.com / URL:
http://www.keystonesnacks.com
Product Service Description:
Corn-based & extruded snack foods,
popcorn, party mix, onion rings,
Corn chips, Cheese Curls, Tortila Chips

Keystone Vanessa, Inc.
9700 W. Gulf Bank Rd.
Houston, TX 77040
Contact: Paul Woodward, *
Telephone: 713-937-5396
Fax: 713-895-4080
Email: / URL:
Product Service Description:
Butterfly Valves

Keystone Veneers, Inc.
PO Box 3455
Williamsport, PA 17701-0455
Contact: Vijay S. Reddy, Dir of Marketing
Telephone: 570-322-4400
Fax: 570-322-0333
Email: vijayreddy@worldnet.att.net / URL:
http://www.keystoneveneers.com
Product Service Description:
Decorative Hardwood veneers

Kichler Lighting Group
7711 E Pleasant Valley Rd
Cleveland, OH 44131-5532
Contact: Steven Firstenberg, Director, Int'l
Sales
Telephone: 216-573-1000
Fax: 216-573-1003
Email: sfirstenberg@kichler.com / URL:
kichler@kichler.com
Product Service Description:
Lighting fixtures_residential
Indoor & outdoor, incandescent & fluorescent
decorative lighting fixtures & portable lamps

Kidde Aerospace, Walter
4200 Airport Dr Nw
Wilson, NC 27896-8630
Contact: Charles B. Backus, CFO
Telephone: 252-237-3787
Fax: 252-237-9407
Email: chuck.backus@wkakti.com / URL:
http://www.kiddle.co.uk
Product Service Description:
Measuring & controlling devices
Fire detection & suppression systems
Communications equipment, nec

KieTek International, Inc.
4673 Aircenter Cir.
Reno, NV 89502-5948
Contact: David Brierton, Sales & Engineering
Phone: 775-827-1660 / Fax: 775-827-1677
Email: kietek@kietekint.com / URL: http://
www.kietekint.com
Product Service Description:
Air Cargo Ground Support Equipment /
Systems : Ball Transfers/Rollers/Casters
Mezzanine Systems - Wire / Steel / Fiberglass
Scales ULD Air Cargo
Metal Fabrication / Engineering

Kimball Sign & Woodcarving Co.
4201 Bull St
Savannah, GA 31405-4010
Contact: Kenny H. Kimball, Pur., Sales &
Mktg. Mgr.
Phone: 912-232-6561 / Fax: 912-232-6561
Product Service Description:
Wooden sign carving equipment, sandblasted,
carved & painted wooden signs, magnetic,
engraved brass

Kinamed
2192 Anchor Ct
Newbury Park, CA 91320-1605
Contact: Clyde Pratt, Pres.
Telephone: 805-499-5999
Fax: 805-498-8684
Email: / URL: http://www.kinamed.com
Product Service Description:
Manufactures orthopedic prosthetic &
neurosurgical surgical appliances and supplies
Surgical appliances & supplies

Kind & Knox Gelatine, Inc.
PO Box 927
Sioux City, IA 51102-0927
Contact: Charles P. Markham, V-P., GM
Telephone: 712-943-5516
Fax: 712-943-3372
Email: kindknox@kkgel.com / URL: http://
www.kindknox.com
Product Service Description:
Gelatine manufacturer

Kinedyne Corp.
1104 Washington Ferry Rd
Prattville, AL 36067-4898
Contact: Jamie Klausmann,
GM & Opers. Mgr.
Telephone: 334-365-2919
Fax: 334-361-1665
Email: / URL: http://www.kinedyne.com
Product Service Description:
Cargo control equipment

Kinetic Ceramics Inc
26242 Industrial Blvd
Hayward, CA 94545-2922
Contact: James Banister, Pres.
Phone: 510-264-2140 / Fax: 510-264-2159
Product Service Description:
Manufactures electromechanical sensors and
actuators : Semiconductors & related devices

King Buck Technology
2356 Moore St Ste 102
San Diego, CA 92110-3018
Contact: F A M Buck, Principal
Phone: 619-299-8431 / Fax: 619-299-8437
Email: kingbuck@worldnet.att.net / URL:
http://www.kingbuck.com
Product Service Description:
Emission control systems for air, soil and
water remediation
Measuring & controlling devices

King Design International
3850 W 1st Ave
Eugene, OR 97402-5367
Contact: Bill Volm, Pres.
Telephone: 541-686-2848
Fax: 541-686-8418
Email: / URL: http://www.kingdesign.com
Product Service Description:
Designs, manufactures & installation of
interior decor
Manufactures signs and advertising displays
for grocery store, restaurant and retail

King International Inc.
P.O. Box 337
Mauldin, SC 29662
Contact: Bennie Langley, VP Sales
Telephone: 864-963-2819
Fax: 864-963-7018
Email: kingintl@usit.net / URL:
Product Service Description:
Textile Machinery / ovens / dryers

King J.A. & Company
2620 High Point Road, PO Box 21225
Greensboro, NC 27420-1225
Contact: Riley Azbell, Director of Sales &
Mktg.
Telephone: 336-292-0511
Fax: 336-294-9664
Email: info@jaking.com / URL: http://
www.jaking.com
Product Service Description:
Scales & Balances

King Metal Products, Inc.
2151 Opa Locka Blvd
Opa Locka, FL 33054-4229
Contact: Carlos Garcia, Pres., Jose R.
Rodriguez, Sales Mgr.
Telephone: 305-685-9144
Fax: 305-685-9314
Email: kingmet@aol.com / URL: http://
www.barbecuen.com/king-q/
Product Service Description:
O.E.M. food service equipment
Stainless barbecue grills king "Q"

Kingsdown, Inc.
3rd & Holt St. PO Box 388
Mebane, NC 27302-0388
Contact: Lee W. Hinshaw,
Director. - Int'l Sales
Telephone: 919-563-3531
Fax: 919-563-0405
Email: / URL: http://www.kingsdown.com
Product Service Description:
Innerspring Mattress
Other Mattresses
Bedsprings
Convertible Sofas

Kintronic Laboratories, Inc.
PO Box 845
Bristol, TN 37621-0845
Contact: Tom King, Pres., R & D Mgr.
Telephone: 423-878-3141
Fax: 423-878-4224
Email: ktl@kintronic.com / URL: http://
www.kintronic.com
Product Service Description:
Radio antenna & broadcasting equipment
Radio & TV communications equipment

Kirby Risk Service Center
PO Box 6089
Lafayette, IN 47903-6089
Contact: Curt Jenkins, Plt. Mgr.
Telephone: 765-448-4748
Fax: 765-449-7557
Email: cjenkins@kirbyrisk.com / URL:
Product Service Description:
Electronic components
Wire harness
Custom Control Panels
Transformers
Electric Motors
Machined Castings

Kirkhill Rubber Co
PO Box 1270
Brea, CA 92822-1270
Contact: Steve barton, President / CEO
Telephone: 714-529-4901
Fax: 714-529-6783
Email: / URL: http://www.kirkhill.com
Product Service Description:
Mechanical rubber goods
Manufactures custom molded, extruded,
calendared and fabricated rubber and plastic
product
Plastic products

Kirkland's Custom Meats
1101 Bulls Bay Hwy
Jacksonville, FL 32220-2500
Contact: Evelyn Kirkland, Owner & GM
Telephone: 904-783-6868
Fax: 904-783-8508
Email: / URL:
Product Service Description:
Meat processing
Meat packing plants

Kirkpatrick Shipping Inc.
P.O. Box 50
Mobile, AL 36601
Contact: John F. Kirkpatrick, *
Telephone: 205-438-9741
Fax: 205-438-9743
Email: / URL:
Product Service Description:
Freight & Cargo Transportation
Steamship Agents

Kiteguild International Inc.
4816 N 13th St.
Philadelphia, PA 19141-3427
Contact: Claudia Gale, *
Telephone: 215-324-8390
Fax: 215-324-0985
Email: kiteguild-international-inc@msn.com /
URL:
Product Service Description:
Pumps
Valves
Compressors
Mining Equipment & Parts
Construction Equipment & Parts
Refining, Spare Parts
Mining Equipment & Parts

Klein Pickle Company
4118 W Whitton Ave
Phoenix, AZ 85019-3625
Contact: Byron Arnold, Pres.
Telephone: 602-269-2072
Product Service Description:
Grows, packs and distributes pickled
products
Pickles, sauces & salad dressings
Groceries, general line

Klose Fabrication, Inc.
2214 1/2 W 34th St
Houston, TX 77018-6005
Contact: David Klose, Pres., MIS, Pur., Sales
& Mktg. Mgr.
Telephone: 713-686-8720
Fax: 713-686-8793
Email: bbqpits@mns.com / URL: http://
www.bbqpits.com
Product Service Description:
Metal fabrication, industrial steel ladders,
platforms, scaffold braces, soldier dollies
Metal products_fabricated : Pipe &
fittings_fabricated : Structural
metal_fabricated

Knaack Mfg. Co.
420 E Terra Cotta Ave
Crystal Lake, IL 60014-3611
Contact: Bob Ripley, Pres.
Telephone: 815-459-6020
Fax: 815-459-9097
Product Service Description:
Steel chests, boxes, work benches, cabinets,
tool chests, pickup truck tool boxes &
accessories & van equipment

Knozall Systems
375 E Elliot Rd Ste 10
Chandler, AZ 85225-1130
Contact: Don R Lundell, Pres.
Telephone: 602-545-0006
Fax: 602-545-0008
Email: / URL: http://www.knozall.com
Product Service Description:
Network managment software

Knud Nielsen Company, Inc.
217 Park St.
Evergreen, AL 36401-0746
Contact: Ruth Leonard, Export Sales
Coordinator
Telephone: 334-578-2900
Fax: 334-578-1887
Email: ruth@knudnielsen.com / URL:
Product Service Description:
Floral Industries
Dried Flowers, Pods, Foliages, Cones

Kompan Inc
7717 New Market St Sw
Olympia, WA 98501-7228
Contact: David Morgan, Pres.
Telephone: 360-943-6374
Fax: 360-943-6254
Email: judy.ratlif@kompan.com / URL: http://
www.kompan.com
Product Service Description:
Manufactures playground equipment

Kona Paradise Candies Corp.
128 S School St
Honolulu, HI 96813-1609
Contact: Wendy Loh, Pres., Fin. & GM
Phone: 808-599-8777 / Fax: 808-599-8777
Email: kpcandi@gte.net / URL:
Product Service Description:
Chocolate & cocoa products

Konecrane Landel Inc
7300 Chippewa Boulevard
Houston, TX 77086-3231
Contact: Doug Maclam, VP Mktg. & Sales
Phone: 281-445-2225/ Fax: 281-445-9355
Email: doug.maclam@kcinet.com / URL:
Product Service Description:
Manufactures, distributes and sells hoists,
cranes, monorails, and overhead crane
equipment: Hoists, cranes & monorails

Kool Star
15001 S Broadway St
Gardena, CA 90248-1819
Contact: James Pak, Pres.
Telephone: 310-851-6060
Fax: 310-715-1110
Email: / URL: http://www.koolstar.com
Product Service Description:
Refrigeration & heating equipment
Manufactures walk-in coolers and freezers

Kop-Coat Inc
PO Box 911207
City Of Commerce, CA 90091-1207
Contact: Ray A DiMaio, V-P., GM
Telephone: 323-560-5700
Fax: 323-560-5734
Email: vkopcoat@aol.com / URL: http://
www.kop-coatla.com
Product Service Description:
Paints & allied products
Manufactures marine coatings— synthetic
enamels, paints, varnishes and lacquers

Kornfections & Treasures
14516c Lee Rd
Chantilly, VA 20151-1638
Contact: Gerald Lerner, Pres.
Telephone: 703-378-0009
Fax: 703-817-9560
Email: krnfection@aol.com / URL: http://
members.aol.com/krnfection/home.htm
Product Service Description:
Popcorn, Confections & Fudge

Kovil Manufacturing LLC
925 Sherman Ave
Hamden, CT 06514-1150
Contact: Vilmos Kovacs, Pres., GM
Telephone: 203-230-8464
Fax: 203-288-2621
Email: kovil@snet.net / URL: http://
www.kovil.com
Product Service Description:
Precision machining
Industrial machinery
Create your own Tool Rack on-line;

Kowa California Inc.
20001 S. Vermont Ave.
Torrance, CA 90502-1326
Contact: Tae Nemoto, V.P.
Telephone: 310-515-0438
Fax: 310-217-0586
Email: tae@kowa.com / URL:
Product Service Description:
Imitation Brick
Optical Equipment
Fishing Tackle
Footwear
Latan Furniture
Fabric
Apparel

Kraft Masters Cabinets
1215 Oliver Drive
Gadsden, AL 35904
Contact: Doyce Gargus, Owner
Telephone: 256-547-7408
Fax:
Email: / URL:
Product Service Description:
Wooden cabinets
Kitchen cabinets_wood
Counter Tops
Vanities

Kraissl Co., Inc., The
299 Williams Ave.
Hackensack, NJ 07606
Contact: Richard C. Michel, President
Telephone: 201-342-0008
Fax: 201-342-0025
Email: kraissl@aol.com / URL: http://
www.strainers.com
Product Service Description:
Strainers and Filters
Pumps
Valves

Krieger, Norman, Inc.
P.O. Box 92599,
Los Angeles, CA 90009
Contact: Sales & Marketing,
Telephone: 310-215-0071
Fax: 310-215-9823
Email: nki@nkinc.com / URL: http://
www.nkinc.com
Product Service Description:
Customs Broker
Freight Forwarder

Kromer Co.
2365 Commerce Blvd
Mound, MN 55364-1447
Contact: O. W. Kromer, Owner
Telephone: 612-472-4167
Fax: 612-472-4371
Email: kromer@kromer-afm.com / URL:
http://www.kromer-afm.com
Product Service Description:
Athletic field maintenance equipment

Krooked Kreek Logging Co.
Hc 73 Box 80
Dogpatch, AR 72648-9720
Contact: Darryl Cold, Pres.
Telephone: 870-743-9036
Product Service Description:
Lumber processing
Sawmills & planing mills, general
Timber marking
Timber harvesting
Road building

Kurt Manufacturing Co.
5280 Main St Ne
Minneapolis, MN 55421-1544
Contact: Brad Ross, Corporate Mktg. Mgr.
Telephone: 612-572-1500
Fax: 612-571-8466
Email: bradleyr@kurt.com / URL: http://
www.kurt.com
Product Service Description:
Metal products_fabricated
Assembly
Precision Machining
Screw Machining
Die Casting
Workholdings
SPC Gaging Systems
Durable Medical Equipment
Powder Coat Painting
Hydraulic Couplings

Kyle Marine Products Llc
685 Glenairy Dr Ne
Atlanta, GA 30328-4214
Contact: Donald Sanford, Pres.
Telephone: 404-257-0031
Fax: 404-257-0031
Email: / URL:
Product Service Description:
Underwater television cameras
Photographic equipment & supplies

Kyzen Corp.
430 Harding Industrial Dr
Nashville, TN 37211-3106
Contact: Tom Herrmann, Vice President
Telephone: 615-831-0888
Fax: 615-831-0889
Email: kyzen@kyzen.com / URL: http://
www.Kyzen.com
Product Service Description:
Cleaning fluids & solutions

L & E International Service
380 West 78th Rd.
Hialeath, FL 33014
Contact: Lorena Gomez, *
Telephone: 305-827-2487
Fax:
Email: / URL:
Product Service Description:
Groceries
Tea
Pork Tails
Cereal
Spices
Canned Butter

L & M Machining Corporation
4421 E La Palma Ave
Anaheim, CA 92807-1803
Contact: Mike Mai, Pres.
Telephone: 714-701-1620
Fax: 714-701-1624
Email: mikemai@lmcnc.com / URL:
Product Service Description:
Industrial machinery
General machine shop (job work)

L C R Electronics, Inc.
9 S Forrest Ave
Norristown, PA 19401-5217
Contact: Nissen Isakov, Pres.
Telephone: 610-278-0840
Fax: 610-278-0935
Email: lcrmail@lcr-inc.com / URL: http://
www.lcr-inc.com
Product Service Description:
EMI filters, RFI Filters, X & Y Capacitors
Inductors, Coils, Chokes
EMC Testing, CE Marking
Suppression Filters, Surge Suppression

L H B Industries
10616 Trenton Ave.
Saint Louis, MO 63132-1209
Contact: Robert Snell,
Telephone: 314-423-7955
Fax: 314-423-6918
Email: ssres@aol.com / URL: http://
www.lhb.thomasregister.com
Product Service Description:
Soap & other detergents
Cleaning chemicals, aerosol paints, lubricants,
paper conversions & contract packaging
Paints & allied products
Lubricating oils & greases
Converted paper products

L M K Enterprises, Inc.
1779 Chessie Ln
Ottawa, IL 61350-9687
Contact: Larry Kiest, Pres.
Telephone: 815-433-1275
Fax: 815-433-0107
Email: / URL: http://
www.performanceliner.com
Product Service Description:
Cured in place pipelining kits

L M N Printing Co., Inc.
118 N Ridgewood Ave
Edgewater, FL 32132-1721
Contact: Nanette Amalfitano, Pres., CFO, R
& D Mgr.
Telephone: 904-428-9928
Fax: 904-428-9907
Email: lmnprint@aol.com / URL: http://
www.lmn-printing.com
Product Service Description:
Raffle & coupon book & ticket printing &
typesetting: Commercial Web Printing,
Numbering , Cross Perfs

L N P Engineering Plastics, Inc.
475 Creamery Way
Exton, PA 19341-2546
Contact: R. Schulz, Pres., CEO
Telephone: 610-363-4500
Fax: 610-363-4749
Email: inp@lnp.com / URL: http://
www.lnp.com
Product Service Description:
Custom compound thermoplastics

L P I, Inc.
800 Wisconsin St, Mail Box 10
Eau Claire, WI 54703-3607
Contact: Mike Singer, Sales & Mktg. Mgr.
Telephone: 800-657-6956
Fax: 715-839-8647
Email: sales@lpi-inc.com / URL: http://
www.lpi-inc.com
Product Service Description:
Pneumatic personnel lifts & hazardous
location lighting

L S M Labs, Inc.
99 Central Ave
Ravena, NY 12143-1331
Contact: Adrien Larrivee, President
Telephone: 518-756-3164
Fax: 518-756-6922
Email: info@lsmlabs.com / URL: http;//
www.lsmlabs.com
Product Service Description:
Silicone rubber products
Rubber, synthetic
Medical, Health & Safety
Electronics, Automotive
Industrial

L W T Pit Hog Dredge
PO Box 250
Somerset, WI 54025-0250
Contact: Peter Bowe, Pres.
Telephone: 715-247-5464
Fax: 715-247-3934
Email: info@lwtpithog.com / URL: http://
www.lwtpithog.com
Product Service Description:
Liquid waste handling equipment
Dredge Equipment

L. D. Tonsager & Sons, Inc.
P.O. Box 55517,
Portland, OR 97238-5517
Contact: Eric R. Tonsager, President
Telephone: 503-284-6307, 24 Hr
Fax: 503-284-6452
Email: eric@tonsager.com / URL: http://
www.tonsager.com
Product Service Description:
Customs Broker
Freight Forwarder
Freight & Cargo Transportation

L.A. MarKom de Mexico, S.A. de C.V.
Descartes 51/102
Col. Anzures, Mexico, DF 11590
Contact: Eric Lund,
Telephone: 520-624-4877
Fax: 520-624-4868
Email: lam@lamarkom.com / URL: http://
www.lamarkom.com
Product Service Description:
L.A. MarKom de Mexico is an American
owned & managed crossborder marketing
services company experienced in guiding
foreign based companies inot the Mexican &
USA Markets, building their sales &
safeguarding their investments. Our
specialties include facilitating all
incorporations & legal requirments for
product & service companies entering either
market, strategic/marketing planning
distribution searches / partnering, developing
sales channels, promotions advertising,
business to business marketing,direct
marketing merchandising/point-of-sale pieces
& design. We have offices in Mexico City,
Mexico & Tucson, Arizona. For more
information visit our web site at
www.lamarkom.com.

L.A.C. Leather Abrasive Co.
PO Box 950958
Mission Hills, CA 91395-0958
Contact: George Kohl,
Telephone: 818-546-6972
Fax: 818-546-6968
Email: leatherabrasive@usa.net / URL:
Product Service Description:
Abrasives (buffing & polishing papers) for
leather

L.B.I.
20801 Nordhoff Street
Chatsworth, CA 91313
Contact: Keith M. Lehrer, President
Telephone: 818-407-1890
Fax: 818-407-1895
Email: KeithL@LBIOPTICALGROUP.COM
/ URL: http://www.libopticalgroup.com
Product Service Description:
Eyeglass Spectacle Frames : Sunglasses
Ophthalmic Lenses : Eyeglass Cases
Sunglass Cases : Finished Single Vision CR-
39 Lenses : Optical Lenses : Eyeglass Lenses
Eyeglass Frames : Sunglass Frames

LA Machine Shop
12563 Venice Blvd
Los Angeles, CA 90066-3712
Contact: Herzel Ben Marome, Pres.
Telephone: 310-390-7507
Fax: 310-391-1631
Email: hbmarom@earthlink.net / URL:
Product Service Description:
Automotive machine shop
Industrial Machinery

LEMCO
1933 W 11th St Ste L
Upland, CA 91786-3562
Contact: Gene Logan, Ptnr.
Phone: 909-949-1181 / Fax: 909-949-9862
Product Service Description:
Manufactures and assembles parts for the
printing industry; outside diameter and inside
diameter grinding : Printing trades machinery
Industrial machinery : Welding repair
Tooling & Jig Fixture Work : Aerospace
Machining : Spurgears : Faburication : CAD/
CAM Machining : Designing

LRF Business Solutions
412 Ne 16th Ave
Gainesville, FL 32601-3701
Contact: Clarence E. Polke,
Phone: 352-371-3570 / Fax: 352-371-0330
Email: lrfbus01@bellsouth.net / URL:
Product Service Description:
Rebuilt laser toner cartridges
Photographic equipment & supplies

LRH Enterprises Inc
6961 Valjean Ave.
Van Nuys, CA 91406
Contact: Norm Hubert, V.P. Sales & Mktg.
Telephone: 818-782-0226
Fax: 818-909-7602
Email: sales@lrhent.com / URL: http://
www.lrhent.com
Product Service Description:
Manufactures cutting tools for the
woodworking industry; specifically shaper
cutters : Woodworking machinery

La Crosse Milling Co.
PO Box 86
Cochrane, WI 54622-0086
Contact: Rick L. Schwein, Pres., Pur. Agt.
Telephone: 608-248-2222
Fax: 608-248-2221
Email: lmc@mwt.net / URL: http://
www.lacrossemilling.com
Product Service Description:
Oat processing : Feeds_prepared

La Machine Shop Inc.
15740 Lincoln St Ne
Ham Lake, MN 55304-5535
Contact: Ben Mark, Sales Mgr.
Telephone: 612-434-6108
Fax: 612-434-6188
Email: lamach2@juno.com / URL:
Product Service Description:
General Machining job shop
Certified Supplier for United Defense L.P.

La Mar Mfg. Co.
202 W College St
Bowdon, GA 30108-1308
Contact: Elizabeth A. Plunkett Buttimer,
Chrm., CEO
Telephone: 770-258-7201
Fax: 770-258-7098
Product Service Description:
Men's & women's tailored clothing
Clothing_men's & boys'
Outerwear_women's & misses'

La Marche Mfg. Company (Mfr)
106 Bradrock Drive
Des Plaines, IL 60018
Contact: John S. Pawula, Nat'l. Sales Mgr.
Telephone: 847-299-1188
Fax: 847-299-3061
Email: lamarche@mcs.net / URL: http://
www.lamarche-power.com
Product Service Description:
Industrial Battery Chargers

La Perla Ice Cream Co.
1406 Mercantile Ct
Plant City, FL 33567-1151
Contact: Margarita Sanchez, Owner
Telephone: 813-754-7901
Fax: 813-707-0376
Email: laperla@eni.net / URL: http://
www.naturesfruit.com
Product Service Description:
Ice cream & frozen desserts
Gourmet frozen fruit bars

LaBelle Rothery Movers, Inc.
80 Genesee St.
Lake Zurich, IL 60047
Contact: Sales & Marketing,
Telephone: 847-726-8850
Fax: 847-726-9035
Email: LaBelle_Movers@Compuserve.com /
URL:
Product Service Description:
Freight Forwarder
Customs Broker
Freight & Cargo Transportation
Storage

Laboratory Testing Supply Inc.
PO Box 6366
Arlington, TX 76005-6366
Contact: Thomas K. Lane, Pres., Sales Mgr.
Telephone: 817-261-9121
Fax: 817-860-3175
Email: www.ltsupply.com / URL: http://
www.ltsupply.com
Product Service Description:
Soil, concrete & asphalt testing equipment
Measuring & controlling devices

Ladson Noodle Company
3334 W Wilshire Dr Ste 33
Phoenix, AZ 85009-1455
Contact: Gary Capra, Pres.
Telephone: 602-353-0874
Fax:
Email: / URL:
Product Service Description:
Manufactures macaroni, spaghetti, vermicelli
and noodles
Macaroni & spaghetti

Laidig Industrial System
14535 Dragoon Tr.
Mishawaka, IN 46544-6814
Contact: Jon J. Laidig, President
Telephone: 219-256-0204
Fax: 219-256-5575
Email: sales@laidig.com / URL: http://
www.laidig.com
Product Service Description:
Agricultural Machine
Hoists
Cranes
Silos
Silo bottom Unloaders
Bins
Bin Dischargers
Bolted Silos
Welded Silos

Lake County Leader
229 Main St Sw
Ronan, MT 59864-2706
Contact: John Schnase, Publisher
Telephone: 406-676-3800
Fax: 406-676-3801
Email: leader@cyberport.net / URL: http://
www.leaderadvertiser.com
Product Service Description:
Publishes weekly newspaper and shopper
Newspapers
Publishing_miscellaneous

Lake Park Tool & Machine, Inc.
1221 Velma Ct.
Youngstown, OH 44512-1829
Contact: James F. Cain, President
Telephone: 330-788-2437
Fax: 330-788-4946
Product Service Description:
Heavy Extrusion Press Tools

Lake Shore Electric Corp.
205 Willis St
Bedford, OH 44146-3505
Contact: Paul E. Shane, Chrm., Pres.
Telephone: 440-232-0200
Fax: 440-232-5644
Product Service Description:
Switchgear & switchboard apparatus
Automatic transfer & bypass-isolation
switches & generator control switchgear
Electrical industrial apparatus
Engine electrical equipment

Lakin Tire East, Inc.
240 Frontage Rd.
West Haven, CT 06516
Contact: Sales & Marketing,
Telephone: 203-932-5801
Product Service Description:
Automobile Tires
Rubber Products
Truck Tires

Lamaur
5601 E River Rd
Fridley, MN 55432-6134
Contact: Robert Eriksson, V-P., Opers.
Telephone: 612-571-1234
Fax: 612-572-2781
Email: / URL:
Product Service Description:
Toilet preparations
Personal grooming products
Household Products
Contract Manufacturing

Lamb, Inc., J.
50 S Van Brunt St
Englewood, NJ 07631-3419
Contact: William Sarina, National Sales Mgr.
Telephone: 201-569-0001
Fax: 201-569-3426
Email: bills@jlamb / URL: http://
www.philmontmfg.com
Product Service Description:
Protective bedding; waterproof,
Allegy relief & anit-microbial

Lamb-Weston Inc
PO Box 1900
Pasco, WA 99302-1900
Contact: Bobby Horowitz, President
Telephone: 509-735-4651
Fax: 509-736-0386
Email: info@lambweston.com / URL: http://
www.lamb-weston.com
Product Service Description:
Fruits & vegetables, frozen
Processes frozen potatoes (corporate office)
Frozen specialties

Laminated Glass
P.O. Box 1003
Telford, PA 18969-1778
Contact: Michael Lerner, Owner
Telephone: 215-721-0400
Fax: 215-721-0402
Email: lgcsales@laminatedglass.com / URL:
http://www.laminatedglass.com
Product Service Description:
Flat Glass
Laminated safety glass, not suitable for
incorporation in vehicles, aircraft, spacecraft
or vessels
Security glass
Bullet resistant glass
Insulating glass units
Glass clad poly carbonates
Laminated polycarbonates

Laminations Inc.
1300 Meylert Avenue.
Scranton, PA 18501
Contact: Gary C. Borgia, Sales Mgr.
Telephone: 717/348-2956
Fax: 717/348-2963
Email: / URL:
Product Service Description:
Plastics, Polyethylene Sheet

Lamkin Corp.
6530 Gateway Park Dr.
San Diego, CA 92173-3510
Contact: R. E. Lamkin, President
Telephone: 619-661-7090
Fax: 619-661-7098
Product Service Description:
Sporting and Recreational Goods
Articles and equipment for sports or outdoor
games; Swimming pools and wading pools;
Parts

Lamons Power Engineering
189 Arthur Rd
Martinez, CA 94553-2205
Contact: Bill Hinderman, GM
Telephone: 925-313-9080
Fax: 925-313-9348
Email: billh@lamonsgasket.com / URL: http:/
/www.lamonsgasket.com
Product Service Description:
Mechanical Packing
Mechanical rubber goods
Plastics
Hose-Rubber & Metal
Expansion Joints

Lampi, LLC
PO Box 1769
Huntsville, AL 35807-0769
Contact: Steve Lake, National Sales Mgr.
Telephone: 256-837-3110
Fax: 256-830-9518
Email: lake@lampi.com / URL: http://
www.lampi.com
Product Service Description:
Residential & commercial fluorescent
lighting fixtures

Lanca Sales, Inc.
16 South St.
Morristown, NJ 07960-4136
Contact: Thomas Haralmpoudis, Vice
President
Telephone: 973-326-8000
Fax: 973-326-8008
Email: sales@lancasales.com / URL: http://
www.lancasales.com
Product Service Description:
Exporting Firms : Tableware and kitchenware
of plastics : Ceramic tableware, kitchenware,
other household and toilet articles, other than
of porcelain or china : Trays, dishes, plates,
cups and the like, of paper or paperboard
Foodservice Disposables : Restaurant Support
Disposable Dinnerware : Retail Packaging
Closeout & Obsolete Merchandise

Lance Metal Arts
2183 Parkway Dr. S.E.
Leeds, AL 35094
Contact: Ralph Lance, Owner, Opers., Pers.,
Sales & Mktg. Mgr.
Telephone: 205-699-3040
Fax: 205-699-2127
Product Service Description:
Steel stairs / Steel Railings & fencing

Land & Water Consulting, Inc.
PO Box 8254
Missoula, MT 59807-8254
Contact: Sales & Marketing,
Telephone: 406-721-0354
Fax: 406-721-0355
Email: info@landandwater.com / URL:
Product Service Description:
Vegetation Stud
Hydrogeological

Land And Sky Mfg., Inc.
5410 Nw 44th St
Lincoln, NE 68524-2365
Contact: Deb Yeutter, Director
Telephone: 402-470-2468
Fax: 402-470-3135
Email: dyeutter@landandsky.com / URL:
http://www.landandsky.com
Product Service Description:
Plastic products
Flotation mattresses
Air Mattresses
Innerspring Mattresses

Landmark Tower Corp.
PO Box 7497
Fort Worth, TX 76111-0497
Contact: H. J. McGinnis, Pres., Engrg. Mgr.
Telephone: 817-335-8666
Fax: 817-335-2171
Email: hmcginnis@worldnet.att.net / URL:
http://www.landmarktower.com
Product Service Description:
Metal communication towers, non-cable
elevators & structures
Erect in ONE day a self support Landmark
Dart.

Landstar Ranger, Inc.
P.O. Box 19060,
Jacksonville, FL 32245
Contact: Bill A. Yost,
Telephone: 904-398-9400 ext. 1145
Fax: 800-872-9521
Email: byost@landstar.com / URL: http://
www.landstar.com
Product Service Description:
Freight & Cargo Transportation
Trucking

Lane Co., Inc., The
P.O. Box 151
Altavista, VA 24517-0151
Contact: Ed Fritz, VP International
Telephone: 804-369-3793
Fax: 804-369-3629
Email: efritz@laneglobal.com / URL: http://
www.laneglobal.com
Product Service Description:
Wood Household Furniture
Furniture and parts thereof
Tobacco, not stemmed/stripped

Lane-Merritt Float Co
1488 Pioneer Way Ste 17
El Cajon, CA 92020-1633
Contact: Richard Merritt, Off. Mgr.
Telephone: 619-444-9988
Fax: 619-444-9996
Email: / URL:
Product Service Description:
Manufactures deepwater floats & marker
buoys
Plastic injection products

Language Express
60 1/2 Rogers Rd.
Los Gatos, CA 95030-7031
Contact: Elena Vialo, President
Telephone: 408-395-5917
Fax: 408-395-3457
Email: evialo@compuserve.com / URL:
Product Service Description:
Translation Services, SP / ENG Transl. /
Interp. - Business, Legal, Technical

Language Interface, Ltd.
2899 S. Rochester Rd., Suite 462
Rochester Hills, MI 48307-4585
Contact: Janice L. Israel,
Telephone: 800-745-7178
Fax: 888-745-7178
Email: Mail@interfacefamily.com / URL:
Product Service Description:
Translation Services
Software Localization

Language Masters, Inc.
29777 Telegraph Rd., Suite 1670
Southfield, MI 48034-7663
Contact: Carole Starcher, President
Telephone: 248-350-2444 / 888-679-9170
Fax: 248-350-1629 / 888-679-9175
Email: / URL:
Product Service Description:
Educational Svcs. Corp Language Training
Translation Services, Technical, Legal,
Medical
Educational Services, Business Culture &
Etiquette Seminars

Language Plus
4110 Rio Bravo, Suite 202
El Paso, TX 79902
Contact: Cheryl B. Gordon,
Telephone: 915-544-8600
Fax: 915-544-8640
Email: langplus@aol.com / URL:
Product Service Description:
Spanish Course on Video
Customized Language Courses
Executive Spanish Camp
Cross Cultural Management Seminar
Language Proficiency Testing

Language Services Associates
607 N. Easton Rd., Suite D2
Willow Grove, PA 19090-2538
Contact: Laura Schriver, Coordinator
Telephone: 800-305-9673 / 215-657-6571
Fax: 215-659-7210
Email: lsa@call-lsa.com / URL: http://
www.call-lsa.com
Product Service Description:
Interpreters & translators
InterpreTalk, over-the-telephone interpreter
services

Lanman & Kemp-Barclay & Co.
25 Woodland Ave
Westwood, NJ 07675-3113
Contact: Stephen Cooper, Pres.
Telephone: 201-666-4990
Fax: 201-666-5836
Email: scoop@carroll.com / URL:
Product Service Description:
Murray & Lanman's FLORIDA WATER
Cologne
Air Freshener, Soap, Hair & Toilet Preps

Larco, Div. Of Acrometal Companies, Inc.
PO Box 547
Brainerd, MN 56401-0547
Contact: Craig Kochsiek, VP, Joe Schultz, Sales Mgr.
Telephone: 218-829-9797
Fax: 218-829-0139
Email: sales@larcomfg.com / URL: http://www.larcomfg.com
Product Service Description:
Industrial Safety Mat Systems
Automatic Door Mats & Wallswitches

Larcom & Mitchell
1320 Route 37, W.
Delaware, OH 43015-1446
Contact: Charles Mitchell, President
Telephone: 740-363-6691
Fax:
Email: / URL:
Product Service Description:
Manufacture Horse & Dog Race Track Equipment

Laren Industries
54 W. 39th Street
New York, NY 10018
Contact: Steve Horowitz, Owner
Telephone: 212-382-0800
Fax: 212-382-1097
Email: / URL:
Product Service Description:
Woven fabrics - cottons & blends
Yarn dyed fabrics & printed fabrics
Top weight & bottom weight
Flannel plaids
Seersuckers

Larson & Associates Inc
PO Box 1101
Pocatello, ID 83204-1101
Contact: Virginia Larson, Pres.
Telephone: 208-232-2034
Fax: 208-234-1741
Email: filters@stellarcom.com / URL:
Product Service Description:
Wholesales filtration for hazardous waste, mining, water treatment, food processing
Industrial machinery & equipment

Las Dos Victorias Candies
9606 Valley Blvd
Rosemead, CA 91770-1510
Contact: Willy or Marta Valenzuela,
Telephone: 626-448-4611
Fax: 626-448-7172
Email: L K R I M.@aol.com / URL:
Product Service Description:
Manufactures Mexican candy
Camete - Calabaza-Cocada-Alfastor - Jamoncillo

Lasag
601 W Campus Dr Ste B5
Arlington Heights, IL 60004-7800
Contact: Fritz Muller, V.-P.
Telephone: 847-593-3021
Fax: 847-593-5062
Email: lasers@lasag.com / URL: http://www.lasag.com
Product Service Description:
Pulsed laser sources & laser cutting, welding & drilling job shop
Electrical equipment & supplies
Industrial machinery

Laser Armor Tech Corporation
10575 Roselle St
San Diego, CA 92121-1505
Contact: Herbert Karlinski, Pres.
Telephone: 619-453-0670
Fax: 619-453-2638
Email: theo@latco.com / URL:
Product Service Description:
Manufactures laser-welded stainless steel tubing incorporating optical fibers in long lengths for communications

Laser Creations Inc.
946 Century Ln
Apopka, FL 32703-3709
Contact: Phil Kimmel, Pres., R & D Mgr.
Telephone: 407-880-7151
Fax: 407-880-7150
Email: info@lasermagic.net / URL: http://www.lasermagic.net
Product Service Description:
Laser cutting & engraving
Plastic products for cars & office

Laser Imaging International
7920 Deering Ave.
Canoga Park CA 91304-5007
Contact: Eyal Alkoby, Pres
Telephone:818-587-9700
Fax: 818-587-6775
Product Service Description:
Photographic Equipment & Supplies
Laser printer cartridges / fax cartridges

Lasertechnics Marking Corp.
5500 Wilshire Ave Ne
Albuquerque, NM 87113-1960
Contact: Rich Bronge, Sr VP Sales & Mktg.
Telephone: 505-822-1123
Fax: 505-821-2213
Email: info@lasertechnics.com / URL: http://www.lasertechnics.com
Product Service Description:
Laser marking & coating equipment

Lasting Impressions Soaps
6405 Congress Ave Ste 160
Boca Raton, FL 33487-2861
Contact: Joanne Stoll, Pres.
Telephone: 561-995-0395
Fax: 561-995-0795
Email: soapart@flinet.com / URL: http://www.soapart.com
Product Service Description:
Decorative soap & candles

Latimer County News-Trib
PO Box 10
Wilburton, OK 74578-0010
Contact: Russ Mabry, Publisher
Telephone: 918-465-2321
Fax: 918-465-3011
Email: lcnt@cwis.net / URL:
Product Service Description:
Newspaper & commercial printing
Newspapers
Printing_commercial

Lauren Mfg. Co.
2228 Reiser Ave Se
New Philadelphia, OH 44663-3334
Contact: Karen thompson, Field Sales Mgr.
Telephone: 330-339-3373
Fax: 330-339-1515
Email: sales@lauren.com / URL: http://www.lauren.com
Product Service Description:
Extruded & molded rubber products
Rubber products_fabricated

Lays Mining Service, Inc.
1121 S 10th St
Mount Vernon, IL 62864-5401
Contact: Herald Mallott, Pres.
Telephone: 618-244-6570
Fax: 618-244-6830
Email: lmsinc@midwest.net / URL: http://www.scribers.midwest.net/lmsinc
Product Service Description:
Coal mine equipment
Industrial machinery

Lazar Research Laboratories
731 N La Brea Ave Ste 5
Los Angeles, CA 90038-3324
Contact: Dan Altura, Pres.
Telephone: 323-931-1433
Fax: 323-931-1434
Email: service@lazar.com / URL: http://www.lazarlab.com
Product Service Description:
Manufactures pH electrodes, meters and controllers
Redox, dissolved oxygen, conductivity, and ion electrodes
HPLC, protein, chromatography, and ion chromatography equipment

Lazer Transportation Services
1254 Mark St.
Bensenville, IL 60106
Contact: Kathleen Royal, Branch Manager
Telephone: 630-860-0220
Fax: 630-860-7012
Email: kroyal@lazertrans.com / URL: http://www.lazertrans.com
Product Service Description:
Customs Broker
Freight Forwarder

Lazer Transportation Services
27050 Wick Rd.,
Taylor, MI 48180
Contact: Samuel C. DeCarlo, Sr. Director of Operations
Telephone: 734-946-2500
Fax: 734-946-6945
Email: sdecarlo@lazertrans.com / URL: http://www.lazertrans.com
Product Service Description:
Customs Broker
Freight Forwarder
Freight & Cargo Transportation

Le Claire Mfg. Co.
PO Box 1344
Bettendorf, IA 52722-0023
Contact: Robert Zimmerman Sr., CEO
Telephone: 319-332-6550
Fax: 319-332-9868
Email: LeClaire@LeClairemfg.com / URL: http://www.leclairemfg.com
Product Service Description:
Foundries_aluminum
Aluminum castings, sand & perminent mold

Le Fiell Company
5601 Echo Ave.
Reno, NV 89506
Contact: Baldwin Schmidt, Pres.
Telephone: 775-677-5300
Fax: 775-677-5319
Email: meatsys@lefiellco.com / URL: http://www.lefiellco.com
Product Service Description:
Manufactures trolleys & kill floor equipment for red meat processing companies
Conveyors & conveying equipment
Engineering services

Le Parisien Vinaigrette
PO Box 1735
Salt Lake City, UT 84110-1735
Contact: Max Mercier, Pres.
Telephone: 801-521-5200
Fax: 801-532-2332
Email: / URL: http://www.webdirelle.com/vinaigrette
Product Service Description:
Pickles, sauces & salad dressings
Manufactures vinaigrette salad dressings and dressing bases

Le Sueur Mfg. Co.
3220 Lorna Rd
Birmingham, AL 35216-5404
Contact: Janett LeSueur, V.-P., Hum. Res.
Telephone: 205-822-0720
Fax: 205-822-0749
Email: lesmfg@bellsouth.net / URL:
Product Service Description:
Electronic moisture controls for the concrete block, pipe, and Precast Industries
Monitoring & detection equipment for the concrete industry

Le Truss Co., Tien
PO Box 1091
Tavares, FL 32778-1091
Contact: Tien Le, Pres.
Telephone: 352-343-7477
Fax: 352-343-4969
Product Service Description:
Wooden trusses
Structural wood members

Leavitt Communications, Inc.
600 Knightsbridge Parkway, PO Box 1492
Lincolnshire, IL 60069-1492
Contact: Philip Leavitt, President
Telephone: 847-676-8282
Fax: 847-676-8744
Email: pcleavitt@leavittcom.com / URL: http://www.leavittcom.com
Product Service Description:
Motorola pagers, accessories & parts

Lectralite Corporation
494 Sheridan Blvd Ste C200
Lakewood, CO 80226-8106
Contact: Ron Freemond, Pres.
Telephone: 303-936-9505
Fax: 303-936-9507
Email: @lectralite.com / URL: http://www.lectralite.com
Product Service Description:
Manufactures electric cigarette lighters
Manufacturing industries

Leemark, Inc.
920 Hillview Court 135
Milpitas, CA 93035-4558
Contact: Sales & Marketing,
Telephone: 408-945-8666
Product Service Description:
Mgmt. Connsulting : Business Consulting

Legal Plus Software Group Inc
PO Box 9759
Seattle, WA 98109-0759
Contact: Timothy Sooter, CEO
Telephone: 206-286-3600
Fax: 206-283-8445
Email: pres@legalplus.com / URL: http://www.legalplus.com
Product Service Description:
Prepackaged software
Develops prepackaged family law software
For child support determination

Legg, Inc., A. C.
PO Box 10283
Birmingham, AL 35202-0283
Contact: Sandra K. Purvis, Exec. Vice
President
Telephone: 205-324-3451
Fax: 205-324-5971
Email: spurvis@www.aclegg.com / URL:
http://www.aclegg.com
Product Service Description:
Blended food seasonings
Food preparations

Legge Co., Inc., Walter G.
444 Central Ave.
Peekskill, NY 10566-2003
Contact: Walter Wowtschuk, President
Telephone: 914-737-5040
Fax: 914-737-2636
Email: wlegge1@aol.com / URL: http://
www.leggesystems.com
Product Service Description:
Modern environmental maitenance product
for Health care industries. Conductive
Coatings: Anti-Static Devices : Germicidal
Cleaners : Natural stone & tile maintenance
products

Lehigh Coal & Navigation Co.
Rte. 209, Box 311
Tamaqua, PA 18252
Contact: Erwin O. Beck, V-P., Sales & Mktg.
Telephone: 717-645-2141
Fax: 717-645-4430
 URL: http://www.underbridge.com/lcn
Product Service Description:
Petroleum & coal products
Coal processing

Lemhi Post & Poles Inc
RR 1 Box 49
Salmon, ID 83467-9701
Contact: Quinton A Snook, Pres.
Telephone: 208-756-2787
Product Service Description:
Manufactures wooden fence posts and poles
Wood products
Logging
Rough cut lumber

Lenape Forge, Inc.
1280 Lenape Rd
West Chester, PA 19382-2096
Contact: Frank Krempa, Pres.
Telephone: 610-793-1500
Fax: 610-793-3240
Email: lenape@cccbi.chester.pa.us / URL:
http://www.lenapeforge/lenforge
Product Service Description:
Ferrous & non-ferrous forgings & elliptical &
quick-opening manways
Forgings, nonferrous

Lenox Chemical Company
PO Box 6422
Providence, RI 02940 USA
Contact: Fred B. Savell III, Technical
Manager
Telephone: 401-521-7474
Fax: 401-331-2155
Email: tech@ecco-lenox.com / URL: http://
www.ecco-lenox.com
Product Service Description:
Textile Yarn Lubricants, Antistats & Cohesive
Agents
Fibre Spin Finishes
Metal Working Fluids
Wire Lubricants & Drawing Oils

Leo A. Daly Company
8600 Indian Hills Dr.
Omaha, NE 68114-4039
Contact: M.J. Riordan, Associate
Telephone: 402-391-8111
Fax: 402-391-1418
Email: mjriordan@leoadaly.com / URL: http:/
/www.leoadaly.com
Product Service Description:
Engineering Services
Business Services, Interior Design
Architectural Services
Surveying Services

Leo's Dancewear Inc.
1900 N. Narragansett Ave.
Chicago, IL 60639
Contact: Barbara Kanies, Dir. Int'l Sales
Telephone: 773-889-7700
Fax: 773-889-7593
Email: leos@ais.com / URL:
Product Service Description:
Women's Athletic Wear
Women's Dance Apparel
Footwear, Dance & Gymnastics

Leonard Automatics, Inc.
PO Box 501
Denver, NC 28037-0501
Contact: Len Frushtick, President
Telephone: 704-483-9316
Fax: 704-483-4538
Email: lafinisher@aol.com / URL: http://
www.leonard-automatics.com
Product Service Description:
Ind. Laundry Tunnel Finishing Equip.
Ind. Laundry Garment Finishing Equip.
Garment Tunnel Finishing Equip
Garment Manf. Automated Pressing Equip.
Dry Cleaning Tunnel Finishing Equip.

Leonard Valve Co.
1360 Elmwood Ave
Cranston, RI 02910-3817
Contact: Roger Hicks, Int'l Sales Mgr.
Telephone: 401-461-1200
Fax: 401-941-5310
Email: lvalve@ail.com / URL: http://
www.leonardvalve.com
Product Service Description:
Water temperature control valves
Valves & pipe fittings

Leschen Wire Rope Co.
609 N. 2nd St.
Saint Joseph, MO 64501-1136
Contact: C.W. Salanski, Pres.
Telephone: 816-233-2563
Fax: 816-236-5000
Email: leschen@srca.com / URL: http://
www.wrca.com
Product Service Description:
Wire products, misc. fabricated
Industrial wire rope

Lessco
PO Box 1971
Dalton, GA 30722-1971
Contact: Herman L. Caldwell, VP, Intl Mktg.
Telephone: 706-278-0272
Fax: 706-275-6222
Email: hcaldwell@lessco.com / URL: http://
www.lessco.com
Product Service Description:
Textile curing ovens, dryers, laminators, foam
machines & industrial machinery

Lester Electrical Of Nebraska, Inc.
625 West A Street
Lincoln, NE 68522
Contact: Paul Schmidt, Sales
Telephone: 402-477-8988
Fax: 402-474-1769
Email: pauls@lesterelectrical.com / URL:
http://www.lesterelectrical.com
Product Service Description:
Deep Cycle Battery Chargers

Letro Products
1497 George Dr.
Redding, CA 96003-1461
Contact: Jeri Campbell, Owner
Telephone: 530-247-8181
Fax:
Email: / URL: http://
www.letrotechnologies.com
Product Service Description:
Manufacturing. design — mold & tooling
capabilities

Lewcott
86 Providence Rd.
Millbury, MA 01527
Contact: Thomas Ronay, President
Telephone: 508-865-1791
Fax: 508-865-0302
Email: / URL: http://www.lewcott.com
Product Service Description:
Blowers and Fans
Glass fibers and articles thereof
Glass slivers, rovings, yarn and chopped
strands
Miscellaneous cargo

Lewgust Co., Inc.
4001 Dell Ave # 15
North Bergen, NJ 07047-2496
Contact: Rosetta Standig, Pres.
Telephone: 201-864-5330
Fax: 201-864-1266
Email: lewisohn@aol.com / URL: http://
www.lewisohn.com
Product Service Description:
Sheet metal fabrication, metal fabrication
Sheet metal work, truck & trailer parts
Butcher - block
Aluminum extrusions & castings
Hardware for emergency & service vehicles

Lexard Corporation
5601 South Boyle Avenue
Los Angeles, CA 90058
Contact: Brian Lundstram, Dir./intl.
Telephone: 213-583-1054
Fax: 213-583-5244
Email: lexard@worldnet.att.net / URL:
Product Service Description:
Soap Active Products
Organic Surface Active Agents
Lubricating Oils & Greases
Household Cleaners
Cosmetic & Personal Care Products

Lexington Cutter, Inc.
2951 63rd Ave E
Bradenton, FL 34203-5308
Contact: Paul Enander, Pres.
Telephone: 941-739-2726
Fax: 800-882-3637
Email: lexcut@packet.net / URL: http://
www.lexcut.com
Product Service Description:
Carbide tipped cutting tools
Machine tools, metal cutting types

Liberty Fastener Co.
2950 W Chicago Ave
Chicago, IL 60622-4307
Contact: Larry Scharringhausen, Pres.
Telephone: 773-489-1499
Fax: 773-489-5250
Email: mn1005@aol.com / URL:
Product Service Description:
Industrial fasteners
Bolts, nuts, rivets & washers

Liberty Industries, Inc.
133 Commerce St.
East Berlin, CT 06023-1106
Contact: Robert C. Kaiser, General Manager
Telephone: 860-828-6361
Fax: 860-828-8879
Email: 73662.1460@compuserve.com / URL:
Product Service Description:
Clean Rooms Laminar Flow Equipment
Clean Room Contaminating Control Products
Tracky Mats

Liberty Mfg., Inc.
PO Box 2114
Mission, TX 78573-2114
Contact: Mike Bravo, V-P., Opers. & Plt.
Telephone: 956-580-1144
Fax: 956-580-2919
Email: libertymfg1002.com / URL: http://
www.liberty-mfg.wi.com
Product Service Description:
Drinking water filters & 3 wheel electric
scooters
Refrigerant recovery recycling / recharging
machines
Sheet metal Mfg., carbon steel, stainless steel,
aluminum

Liebel-Flarsheim
211 E. Galbraith Rd.
Cincinnati, OH 45237-1640
Contact: Ramon L. Vega,
Telephone: 513-761-2700
Fax: 513-761-2388
Email: / URL: http://www.liebel.com
Product Service Description:
Urological Imaging & Procedural Systems
Power Contrast Injectors for CT,
Angiography & MR

Liebert Corporation
PO Box 19576
Irvine, CA 92623-9576
Contact: Robert J. Miller,
Telephone: 949-457-3600
Fax: 949-457-3677
Email: / URL: http://www.liebert.com
Product Service Description:
Three-phase uninterruptible power systems,
10-4000 KVA
Single-phase power systems, all sizes
Precision air conditioning & environmental
control products
Power conditioning & distribution equipment

LifeSource Engineering Inc.
PO Box 3153
Seminole, FL 33775-3153
Contact: Preston S. Baggerly, President
Telephone: 727-393-5886
Fax: 727-391-7093
Email: lifesorce@aol.com / URL: http://
www.LifeSourceEngineering.com
Product Service Description:
Water Purification & Wastewater Treatment
Systems : Resorts / Hotels / Small
Municipalities : Sales / Service / O&M

Lifestream Watersystems Inc
PO Box 634
Huntington Beach, CA 92648-0634
Contact: Edward Kimmel, Pres.
Telephone: 714-375-6583
Fax: 714-375-6586
Email: lifstream@aol.com / URL: http://
www.lifestreamwater.com
Product Service Description:
Manufactures water purification equipment

Lifetime Products Inc
PO Box 160010
Clearfield, UT 84016-0010
Contact: Aaron Hill, Export Director
Telephone: 801-776-1532
Fax: 801-776-4397
Email: / URL: http://www.lifetime.com
Product Service Description:
Sporting & athletic goods & outdoor furniture
Manufactures basketball equipment—
portable basketball sets and pro-style acrylic
backboar : Folding banquet & utility tables &
chairs, folding picnic tables

Liftmasters, Inc.
12875 58th St N
Clearwater, FL 33760-3966
Contact: Ha Nguyen, Pres., Treas.
Telephone: 813-535-2174
Fax: 813-531-4733
Product Service Description:
Boat davits / cradle lifts / hoists

Light Solutions
82 Coit Street
Irvington, NJ 07111-4206
Contact: M. Scariati, Bookkeeper
Telephone: 973-399-7300
Fax: 973-399-0075
Email: light12v@eclipse.net / URL: http://
www.lightsolutions.com
Product Service Description:
Lighting equipment 12v / 24v

Light Sources, Inc.
37 Robinson Blvd
Orange, CT 06477-3623
Contact: David Myers, Dir. of Sales & Mktg.
Telephone: 203-799-7877
Fax: 203-795-5267
Product Service Description:
Ultraviolet Tanning Lamps
Ultraviolet Germicidal Lamps
Specialty Fluorescent Lamps

Lighting Metal Specialties
123 Scott St.
Elk Grove Village, IL 60007-1210
Contact: Frank Dotzler, Ron Arder, Jr.
Telephone: 847-956-6700
Fax: 847-956-6899
Email: / URL: http://www.lightingmetal.com
Product Service Description:
Fabricated metal products, integrated
assemblies : and services from "concept to
grave"

Lighting Resources, Inc.
1522 E. Victory
Phoenix, AZ 85040-1306
Contact: Sales & Marketing,
Telephone: 602-276-4278
Product Service Description:
Ballast Recycling
Flourescent Lamps
Mercury Devices
CRTs CPUs
Batteries

Lightware Inc
1329 W Byers Pl
Denver, CO 80223-1723
Contact: Paul Peregrine, Pres.
Telephone: 303-744-0202
Fax: 303-722-4545
Email: / URL: http://www.lightwareinc.com
Product Service Description:
Luggage : Manufactures lightweight, airline
shippable cases for Photographic equipment,
supplies, also computer & electronic
Equipment

Lil Orbits, Inc.
2850 Vicksburg Ln.
Minneapolis, MN 55447-1899
Contact: Ed Anderson, President
Telephone: 612-559-7505
Fax: 612-559-7545
Email: contact@lilorbits.com / URL: http://
www.lilorbits.com
Product Service Description:
Donut or Doughnut Machines

Lilly Industries, Inc.
PO Box 2358
High Point, NC 27261-2358
Contact: Hugh Cates, V-P., GM
Telephone: 336-889-2157
Fax: 336-802-4709
Email: / URL: http://www.lillyindustries.com
Product Service Description:
Furniture Finishes

Lily Of Colorado
PO Box 12471
Denver, CO 80212-0471
Contact: Lily Morgan, Pres.
Telephone: 303-455-4194
Fax: 303-455-2613
Email: / URL: http://www.lilyofcolorado.com
Product Service Description:
Manufactures skin care products
Toilet preparations

**Lin Container Freight Station &
Distribution Center**
1000 Port Carteret Dr.,
Port Carteret, NJ 07008
Contact: Steve Fleischer, President
Telephone: 732-541-3372
Fax: 732-541-1275
URL: http://www.expresswayusa.com
Product Service Description:
Freight & Cargo Transportation: Trucking
U.S. Customs Central Exam Site

Lincoln Manufacturing Co.
P.O. Box 30303
Lincoln, NE 68503-0303
Contact: David Hubertus, Vice President
Telephone: 402-464-7418
Fax: 402-464-8469
Email: dhubertus@lincoln-mfg.com / URL:
http://www.lincoln-mfg.com
Product Service Description: :
Tire Vulcanizers : Ductwork : Stacks

Lindal Cedar Homes
PO Box 24426
Seattle, WA 98124-0426
Contact: Sir Walter Lindal, Chrm. Emeritus
Telephone: 206-725-0900
Fax: 206-725-1615
Email: / URL: http://www.lindal.com
Product Service Description:
Manufactures custom cedar homes, solid
cedar homes, commercial buildings

Lindgren Pitman
2615 N.E. 5th Ave.
Pompano Beach, FL 33064-5415
Contact: Peter Lindgren, President
Telephone: 954-943-4243
Fax: 954-943-7877
Email: logline@gate.net / URL:
Product Service Description:
Monofilaments Over 1.5mm
Long Line Fishing Gear Equipment
Chemical Light Sticks
Monofilaments & Chemical Light Sticks

Lindgren R F Enclosures Inc.
400 High Grove Blvd
Glendale Heights, IL 60139-4019
Contact: William E. Curran Sr., Chrm., Pres.
Telephone: 630-307-7200
Fax: 630-307-7571
Email: lrfe@interserv.com / URL: http://
www.lindgrenrf.com
Product Service Description:
Radio frequency interference shielded
enclosures : MRI shielded enclosures
Anchor chambers

Linemaster Switch Corp.
29 Plaine Hill Rd., P.O. Box 238
Woodstock, CT 06281
Contact: Donald Goodwin, *
Telephone: 860-974-1000
Fax: 860-974-0691
Product Service Description:
Electric Foot& Air Operated Switches

Lingo Systems
One SW Columbia,Suite 300
Portland, OR 97258
Telephone: 503-224-2256
Fax: 503-224-3663
Email: / URL: http://www.lingosys.com
Product Service Description:
Translation & Localization Services

Lingo, Inc., Acme Flagpole Div.
PO Box 1237
Camden, NJ 08105-0237
Contact: John Lingo Jr., Pres.
Telephone: 609-964-0487
Fax: 609-342-7653
Email: poler@lingoinc.com / URL: http://
www.lingoinc.com
Product Service Description:
Flag poles & lightning protection masts
Architectural metal work

Linguistic Systems
130 Bishop Allen Drive
Cambridge, MA 0213-2497
Contact: Martin Roberts, President
Telephone: 617-864-3900
Fax: 617-864-5186
Email: / URL:
Product Service Description:
Translation Services

Link Snacks, Inc.
PO Box 397
Minong, WI 54859-0397
Contact: Jay Link, V-P., Sales
Telephone: 715-466-2234
Fax: 715-466-5151
Email: jlsfood@centuryinter.net / URL: http://
www.linksnacks.com
Product Service Description:
Snack foods : Beef Jerky : Meat Snacks
Salty Snacks : Cheese Snacks

Linker Machines
20 Pine St.
Rockaway, NJ 07866-3130
Contact: Jean Hebrank, Pres.
Telephone: 973-983-0001
Fax: 973-983-0011
Email: sales@linkermachines.com / URL:
http://www.linkermachines.com
Product Service Description:
Meat processing equipment
Sausage linking & peeling, Machinery

Lins Trading
355 W. Lake Sammamish Pkwy., N.E.
Bellevue, WA 98008
Contact: Sales & Marketing,
Telephone: 206-746-1199
Fax: 206-746-5599
Email: markymlin@aol.com / URL:
Product Service Description:
Non-Alcoholic Beverages
Organic foods, organic wine, coffee
Healthcare herbal & vitamins
Frozen Seafood

Liquinox Co
221 W Meats Ave
Orange, CA 92865-2621
Contact: Hap Garner, Pres.
Telephone: 714-637-6300
Fax: 714-637-6302
Email: liquinox1@aol.com &
polyfabric@aol.com / URL: http://
www.liquinox.com & polyfabrics.com
Product Service Description:
Manufactures liquid fertilizer; tank and pond
liners

Litco, Inc.
PO Box 399
Carpentersville, IL 60110-0399
Contact: Robert Litschewski, Pres.
Telephone: 847-428-3641
Fax: 847-428-4202
Email: / URL:
Product Service Description:
Metal fabrication
Machinery & Coupling Guards
Oil Tight Chain Guards

Litec Inc.
8652 Thornton Ave
Newark, CA 94560-3330
Contact: E.H. Fontane, VP
Telephone: 510-608-8960
Fax: 510-608-8969
Email: techsales@litecinc.com / URL: http://
www.litecinc.com
Product Service Description:
Contract Manufacturing
Machine & Sheet Metal Shop
PC Board Assembly
Electro-Mechanical Assembly
ISO 9002 Certified
Rapid Prototypes to Volume Mfg.
Metallic / Non-Metallic Components
Full Turnkey Manufacturing

Lithotype Co Inc
PO Box 2885
San Francisco, CA 94126-2885
Contact: Chris Sewell, CEO
Telephone: 650-871-1750
Fax: 650-871-0714
Email: csewell@lithotype.com / URL:
Product Service Description:
Printing on flexible packaging material

Little Lift Inc.
604 Washington St.
Woodstock, IL 60098
Contact: Tim Porter, *
Telephone: 815/338-3553
Fax: 815-338-3556
Product Service Description:
Boat Lift, Personal Watercraft

Littleford Day., Inc. (Mfr)
7451 Empire Drive
Florence, KY 41042
Contact: Robert Blank, Vice Pres./Sales
Telephone: 606/525-7600
Fax: 606-525-1446
Email: littlefd@iac.net / URL: http://
www.iac.net/~littlefd
Product Service Description:
Ind. Mixing, Drying & Reacting Mach.

Litton Data Systems, Division
6608 Sunscope Dr
Ocean Springs, MS 39564-8608
Contact: David Johnson, VP & GM
Telephone: 228-872-7525
Fax: 228-872-7325
Email: infodsdms@littondsd.com / URL:
http://www.littondsdms.com
Product Service Description:
Shipboard electronics & communications
equip.

Litton Industries Inc
21240 Burbank Blvd
Woodland Hills, CA 91367-6675
Contact: Michael R. Brown, Chrm.
Telephone: 818-598-5000
Fax: 818-598-5940
Email: / URL: http://www.litton.com
Product Service Description:
Search & navigation equipment
Manufactures guidance, navigation and
control equipment; electronic warfare
Electronic components
Communications equipment, nec

Litton Systems, Inc. Laser Sys, Inc.
2787 S. Orange Blossom Trail
Apopka, FL 32703-2010
Contact: Sales & Mktg.,
Telephone: 407-297-4552
Fax: 407-297-4640
Email: rraulerson@littonlaser.com / URL:
Product Service Description:
Laser Range Finder
Target Designators

Live Earth Products
PO Box 76
Emery, UT 84522-0076
Contact: David Taylor, Manager
Telephone: 801-286-2222
Fax:
Email: / URL:
Product Service Description:
Soil Conditioners
Humates & Humic Acids

Living Earth Crafts
600 E Todd Rd
Santa Rosa, CA 95407-5508
Contact: Don Payne, Pres.
Telephone: 707-584-4443
Fax: 707-585-6167
Email: info@livingearthcrafts.com / URL:
http://www.livingearthcrafts.com
Product Service Description:
Manufactures massage, chiropractic, salon,
spa tables; sells massage & spa accessories

Liway International, Inc.
41 N. Garfield Ave., Suite 203
Alhambra, CA 91801-3556
Contact: Larry Y. Lee, President
Telephone: 626-289-6060
Fax: 626-289-3339
Email: yninglee@worldnet.att.net / URL:
Product Service Description:
Flavors, Extracts & Syrups (Natural or
Artificial) : Oriental Flavors / Custom
Formulations : Food Additives, Emulsifiers /
Gums, Vitamin Premixes : Food
Manufacturing & Laboratory Equipments

Load Llama Products
PO Box 2177
Vail, CO 81658-2177
Contact: Ted Simonett, Pres.
Telephone: 970-476-5511
Fax: 970-476-5551
Email: nett@csn.net / URL: http://
www.loadllama.com
Product Service Description:
Manufactures expandable racks for bicycles
Sporting & athletic goods

Lobo Machinery Corp.
9034 Bermudez St.
Pico Rivera, CA 90660-4520
Contact: Robin Yuan, Owner
Telephone: 562-949-3747
Fax: 562-948-4171
Email: info@lobomachine.com / URL: http://
www.lobomachine.com
Product Service Description:
Woodworking Machine

Lochinvar Water Heater
2005 Elm Hill Pike
Nashville, TN 37210-3810
Contact: Mike Lahti,
Telephone: 615-889-8900
Fax: 615-885-4403
Email: lahtivar@aol.com / URL:
Product Service Description:
Heating Boilers Copper Tube
Elec. Water Heaters, Household
Elec Water Heaters Commercial
Gas Water Heaters, Household, to 100 gal.
Plate Work Insulated Storage Tanks

**Lockheed Martin Launching
Systems**
PO Box 4931
Baltimore, MD 21220-0931
Contact: Michael Hughes, V-P.
Telephone: 410-682-1000
Fax: 410-682-3694
Email: / URL: http://www.lmco.com
Product Service Description:
Ocean Research Vessel
Missile launching systems
Commercial - Fast Ferry

Lockwood Industries Inc
21054 Osborne St
Canoga Park, CA 91304-1744
Contact: James F Hoffman, GM
Telephone: 818-709-1288
Fax: 818-709-1738
Email: / URL:
Product Service Description:
Conversion, lamination and close tolerance
die cutting; EMI/RFI shielding; electrical
insulation; custom laminates : Rubber
products_fabricated : Plastic products
Industrial machinery : Secondary nonferrous
metals :Cirlex : Kapton

Lois Yee Cosmetics Inc
PO Box 6188
Stockton, CA 95206-0188
Contact: Lois K. Yee, President
Telephone: 209-466-3337
Fax: 209-463-8658
Email: lyc@cwws.net / URL:
Product Service Description:
Manufactures skin care and hair care
products, lotions, fragrances and skin care
equipment

Loose Ends
PO Box 20310
Keizer, OR 97307-0310
Contact: Art Reinke, Owner
Telephone: 503-390-7457
Fax: 503-390-4724
Email: info@4loosends.com / URL: http://
www.4loosends.com
Product Service Description:
Designs journals and stationery paper
products; sells earth-safe products—
Handmade papers

Loranger International Corp.
817 4th Ave
Warren, PA 16365-1801
Contact: J. Albert Loranger II, Pres., CEO
Telephone: 814-723-2250
Fax: 814-723-5391
Email: licsales@loranger.com / URL: http://
www.loranger.com
Product Service Description:
Automatic test equipment, printed circuit
boards, sockets, connectors
Measuring & controlling devices
Electricity measuring instruments

Lorcin Engineering
3830 Wacker Dr
Mira Loma, CA 91752-1147
Contact: James Waldorf, Pres.
Telephone: 909-360-1406
Fax: 909-360-0623
Email: / URL:
Product Service Description:
Small arms
Manufactures hand guns

**Lord Corporation, Mechanical
Products, Division**
111 Lord Drive, PO Box 8012
Cary, NC 27512-8012
Contact: Lawrence J. Bindseil, P.E. , Director,
Int'l Business
Telephone: 919-468-5981, Ext. 6412
Fax: 919-469-5811
Email: larry_bindseil@lord.com / URL: http://
www.lordcorp.com
Product Service Description:
Bonded rubber & metal aerospace parts
Mechanical rubber goods

Los Angeles Scrap Iron & Metal
1910 E. Olympic Blvd.
Los Angeles, CA 90021-2422
Contact: Sales & Marketing,
Telephone: 213-622-5744
Fax: 213-622-8501
Email: sales@lascrap.com / URL: http://
www.lascrap.com
Product Service Description:
Stainless Steel Scrap
Brass Scrap
Copper Scrap
Aluminum Scrap

Lotus Exim International
359 Alfred Ave.
Teaneck, NJ 07666
Contact: Rajendra Kankariya, Owner
Telephone: 201-837-8089
Fax: 201-837-8099
Email: lotusexim@hotmail.com / URL: http://
www.lotusexim.com
Product Service Description:
Brick, Stone, and Related Materials
Kraftliner, uncoated, unbleached, in rolls or
sheets : Waste and scrap of paper or
paperboard, including unsorted waste and
scrap : Waste and scrap of unbleached kraft
paper or paperboard or of corrugated paper or
paperboard

Louis M Martini Winery
PO Box 112
Saint Helena, CA 94574-0112
Contact: Carolyn Martini, Pres., CEO
Telephone: 707-963-2736
Fax: 707-963-8750
Email: / URL: http://www.louismartini.com
Product Service Description:
Produces wine
Wines, brandy, & brandy spirits

Louisiana Gourmet Enterprises
PO Box 97
Hahnville, LA 70057-0097
Contact: Charles C. Wilson, Chrm.
Telephone: 504-783-2446
Fax: 504-783-6079
Email: / URL: http://
www.diamondbullet.com/mampapaul
Product Service Description:
Cajun Dinner Mixes & Specialty Cakes

Love's Bakery, Inc.
PO Box 294
Honolulu, HI 96809-0294
Contact: Mickey W. Coffman, Pres.
Telephone: 808-841-2088
Fax: 808-841-2646
Email: / URL:
Product Service Description:
Bread, cake & related products
Bread, rolls, doughnuts & pies

Low Humidity Systems, Inc.
10117 Industrial Dr Ne
Covington, GA 30014-1494
Contact: Jerry Orr, Pres., R & D Mgr.
Telephone: 770-385-8690
Fax: 770-385-8783
Email: dehumidifiers@mindspring.com /
URL:
Product Service Description:
Industrial dehumidifiers
Refrigeration & heating equipment

Lucas Products Corp.
PO Box 6570
Toledo, OH 43612-0570
Contact: David H. Orwick, Sls. Mgr.
Telephone: 419-476-5992
Fax: 419-476-0144
Email: lucasproducts@glasscity.net / URL:
http://www.lucasproducts.com
Product Service Description:
Textile heat seal mending products & plastic
eyeshields
Deodorizing, Disinfecting Cleaner

Luckicup Company
1850 Garden Tract Rd.
Richmond, CA 94801-1217
Contact: John G. MacPherson, Owner
Telephone: 510-237-9420
Fax: 510-237-7560
Email: luckicup@pacbell.net / URL: http://
www.luckicup.com
Product Service Description:
Manufactures dice cups & games

Lucks Food Decorating Co.
3003 South Pine St.
Tacoma, WA 98409-4713
Contact: John Lantz, President
Telephone: 253-383-4815
Fax: 253-502-4592
Email: john@lucks.com / URL: http://
www.lucks.com
Product Service Description:
Manufactures decorations, flavors, edible
image base &
Licensed & custom edible images

Lucky Seven Food Inc
1214 S Weller St
Seattle, WA 98144-2049
Contact: Yann Tseng, Pres.
Telephone: 206-324-2822
Fax: 206-230-0751
Email: spaceneedle@wa.freei.net / URL:
http://welcome.to/lucky7food
Product Service Description:
Food wholesale
Chinese Dim-Sum & bakery products
Humbows, eggroll, sliced roll, steamed bun,
etc.

Lufthansa Cargo AG
3400 Peachtree Rd. NE, Ste. 1225,
Atlanta, GA 30326
Contact: Michael Vorwerk,
Vice President, Cargo (USA/CAN./Mex.)
Telephone: 404-814-5311
Fax: 404-814-5300
Email: lhcargo.usa.can.mex@dlh.de / URL:
http://www.lufthansa-cargo.com
Product Service Description:
Air Cargo Carrier

**Lufthansa Cargo, Executive Offices
Cargo USA**
3400 Peachtree Rd., N.E., Lenox Towers,
Suite 1225
Atlanta, GA 30326
Contact: Judit E. Wells,
Manager Marketing USA
Telephone: 404-814-5313
Fax: 404-814-5330
Email: judit.welss@dlh.de / URL: http://
www.lhcargo.com
Product Service Description:
Air Cargo
Air Freight Forwarder

Luke Tool & Engineering Co.
PO Box 528
Hammonton, NJ 08037-0528
Contact: Dimenic Lucca, Owner
Telephone: 609-561-4048
Fax: 609-561-3765
Email: lukela@erols.com / URL:
Product Service Description:
Machine tools
Machine tools, metal cutting types

Luke's Ice Cream
5604 Georgia Ave
West Palm Beach, FL 33405-3710
Contact: Kevin Luke, Pres.
Telephone: 561-588-5853
Fax: 561-586-8937
Product Service Description:
Ice cream tubs & ice cream mixes
Yogurt & sugar free tubs & mixes
Pints & cups

Lumber Tag Specialties
PO Box 903
Cypress, TX 77410-0903
Contact: Victoria McCord, Pres., CEO
Telephone: 281-304-0771
Fax: 281-256-2712
Email: / URL: http://www.lumbertag.com
Product Service Description:
Printing_commercial
Bar coded labels / tags

Lumenite Control Technology Inc.
2331 N. 17th Ave.
Franklin Park, IL 60131
Contact: Ronald V. Calabrese, Pres., Engrg.,
Sales & Mktg. Mgr.
Telephone: 847-455-1450
Fax: 847-455-0127
Email: lct@interaccess.com / URL: http://
www.lumenite.com
Product Service Description:
Electronic time switches, liquid level controls,
programmable timing controls & milk paste
Process control instruments
Fluid meters & counting devices

Lumitron Corp.
P.o. Box 267
Summit, NJ 07902
Contact: Gil Chassie, President
Telephone: 908-273-8998
Fax: 908-273-0853
Email: info@lumitroncorp.com / URL: http://
www.lumitroncorp.com
Product Service Description:
Subminiature Incandescent Lamps

Lumlog, Inc.
PO Box 883
Kilgore, TX 75663-0883
Contact: Harry Rawls, Plt. Mgr.
Telephone: 903-984-0493
Fax: 903-984-3773
Product Service Description:
Hardwood Sawmill & Chipmill

Luna Defense Systems Inc
5040 Calmview Ave
Baldwin Park, CA 91706-1895
Contact: Albert Luna, Pres.
Telephone: 626-960-5147
Fax: 626-337-7853
Email: lunadsys@aol.com / URL:
Product Service Description:
Manufactures precision machined parts

Lutron Electronics Co., Inc.
7200 Suter Rd
Coopersburg, PA 18036-1299
Contact: Joel Spira, Chrm., CEO
Telephone: 610-282-3800
Fax: 610-282-3090
Email: / URL: http://www.lutron.com
Product Service Description:
Relays & industrial controls
Light dimmers & electric fluorescent dimming
ballasts & light, fan speed & motor speed
con.

Lynare Scientific, Inc.
4990 SW 72 Ave. Unit 107
Miami, FL 33155
Contact: Armando B. Arrue, *
Telephone: 305-668-0023
Fax: 305-668-0026
Email: / URL:
Product Service Description:
Medical Equipment
Laboratory Equipment

Lyncole XIT Grounding
3547 Voyager St Ste 104
Torrance, CA 90503-1673
Contact: Betty Robertson, ISO 9000 Certified
Telephone: 310-214-4000
Fax: 310-214-1114
Email: president@lyncole.com / URL: http://
www.lyncole.com
Product Service Description:
Manufactures electrical grounding rods;
distributes ground resistance test meters
Current-carrying wiring devices
Electrical apparatus & equipment
Engineering services

Lynne Signs, Lori
1201 W Parker St
Baxley, GA 31513-0621
Contact: Lori Lynne, Pres., GM & Sales Mgr.
Telephone: 912-366-0526
Fax: 912-366-0906
Email: / URL: http://
www.godswordworks.com
Product Service Description:
Interior & exterior signs
Signs & advertising specialties

Lyon Metal Products LLC
PO Box 671
Aurora, IL 60507-0671
Contact: J.L. Wiebusch, International Sales &
Mktg
Telephone: 630-892-8941
Fax: 800-367-6681 / 630-892-8966
Email: lyon@lyon-metal.com / URL: http://
www.lyon-metal.com
Product Service Description:
Steel Shop Equipment & Shelving
Steel Racks, Lockers & Tool Storage
Ergonomic Seating & Work Stations
Modular Drawer Cabinets

**M & C Enterprises, div of Accent
Enterprizes, Inc.**
PO Box 53
Woodhull, IL 61490-0053
Contact: Connie Landuyt, Pres.
Telephone: 1-800-639-3185
Fax: 309-334-3485
Email: mcland@geneseo.net / URL: not
available yet
Product Service Description:
Dinner ware ceramics
Semivitreous table & kitchenware

M & E Components, Inc.
20654 Amherst Ct
Joliet, IL 60433-9716
Contact: Bill Reilly, Pres., CFO
Telephone: 815-723-0400
Fax: 815-723-0404
Email: / URL:
Product Service Description:
Truck Trailer Airline Components
Electrical & mechanical components &
injection molding
Specialty Products ABS Systems

M & E Mfg. Co.
266 Union Ave Ste 1
Laconia, NH 03246-3139
Contact: Bill Veith,
General Manager
Telephone: 603-528-1217
Fax: 602-528-6306
Email: / URL: http://www.plastekgroup.com
Product Service Description:
Brooms & brushes
Cosmetic & medical brushes, plastic injection
& blow molding
Plastic products

M & J Valve Services, Inc.
110 Gill Dr
Lafayette, LA 70507-5402
Contact: Dick James,
Vice. President
Telephone: 318-264-9319
Fax: 318-233-7603
Email: / URL:
Product Service Description:
Valves_industrial
Compressor valves

M & M Corporation
6725 Somerset Blvd
Paramount, CA 90723-3706
Contact: Mario Montenegro,
President
Telephone: 562-531-8955
Fax: 562-531-2989
Email: / URL:
Product Service Description:
Machining parts for aircraft and commercial;
lathe and mill CNC
Industrial machinery
Industrial machinery & equipment

M C Davis Company
PO Box 2266
Arizona City, AZ 85223-2266
Contact: Jerry Tooley,
President
Telephone: 520-466-5151
Fax: 520-466-5152
Email: jwtmco@aol.com / URL:
Product Service Description:
Manufactures electronic coils, transformers,
inductors and assemblies; sells to OEM's

M C E Systems Corp.
PO Box 40466
Houston, TX 77040
Contact: Jim C. Epps,
President
Telephone: 713-462-6231
Fax: 713-462-1936
Email: sales@quikserv.com / URL: http://
www.quikserv.com
Product Service Description:
Drive-through windows & transaction
drawers

M F Automation Inc.
335 Wyoming St
Pittsburgh, PA 15211-1739
Contact: Mario Huser,
President
Telephone: 412-488-3488 or 1-888-638-6337
Fax: 412-488-3498
Email: info@meto-fer-usa.com / URL: http://
www.meto-fer-usa.com
Product Service Description:
Automation components
Industrial machinery
Aluminum Structural Extrusions.

M M I Display Group, Inc.
960 Dieckman St
Woodstock, IL 60098-9287
Contact: Craig W. Timpe, Pres.
Telephone: 815-334-8200
Fax: 815-3334-8213
Email: mmi8200@aol.com / URL:
Product Service Description:
Point-of-purchase displays
Signs & advertising specialties

M P I International Inc.
2129 Austin Ave
Rochester Hills, MI 48309-3668
Contact: Karl Pfister, Pres.
Telephone: 248-853-9010
Fax: 248-853-5107
Email: MPIsales@mpi-int.com / URL: http://
www.mpi-int.com
Product Service Description:
Automotive stampings

M-B Cos., Inc. Of Wisconsin
1615 Wisconsin Ave.
New Holstein, WI 53061
Contact: Steve Karlin, Pres.
Telephone: 920-849-2313
Fax: 920-898-4588
Email: sales@m-bco.com / URL: http://
www.m-bco.com
Product Service Description:
Machinery_special industry
Pavement marking equipment & power
broom attachments

M. A. Hanna Rubber Compounding
100 No. Main St., Ste. 220
Chagrin Falls, OH 44022
Contact: John E. Quinn, Pres.
Telephone: 440-247-2364
Fax: 440-247-9305
Email: john.quinn@hannarubber.com / URL:
http://www.hannarubber.com
Product Service Description:
Rubber & plastic compounds
Custom rubber and plastics mixing

M. Brown & Sons, Inc.
118 S. Center St., P.O. Box 188
Bremen, IN 46506
Contact: Rob Brown, *
Telephone: 219-259-7000
Fax: 219-258-7464
Product Service Description:
Essential Oils, Mints, Whsle.

M. C. Marble Co., Inc.
316 S 16th St
Lafayette, IN 47905-1128
Contact: Mike Bryan, Pres.
Telephone: 765-742-2919
Fax: 765-742-2919
Email: beaches@pop.nlci / URL: http://
www.nlci.com/mcmarlbe
Product Service Description:
Chemist & Perfumers
Pheromone Based Cosmetics

M.D. International Co.
6735 E. Greenway Pkwy, Suite 2005
Scottsdale, AZ 85254
Contact: Dr. Martin Miller, President
Telephone: 602-951-2350
Fax: 602-609-7418
Email: millermd3@aol.com / URL: http://
www.americanbusiness.com/cust/mdintl
Product Service Description:
Medical equipment new & recond, wholesale

M.M. Electric Products Ltd.
7 Corporate Dr Ste 117
North Haven, CT 06473-3258
Contact: Frank Manzi, Pres., R & D Mgr.
Telephone: 203-239-7099
Fax: 203-239-9343
Email: m.m.electronics@snet.net / URL:
Product Service Description:
Alligator clips
Binding posts, etc.

M.Putterman & Company Inc.
4834 S Oakley Ave
Chicago, IL 60609-4036
Contact: Tom Byrne, Director of Sales
Telephone: 773-927-4120
Fax: 773-650-6046
Email: ereic@aol.com / URL:
Product Service Description:
Gym Floor Covers
Athletic Field Covers
Indoor Tennis Curtains
Gym Equipment, Vinyl Divider Curtains

M2 Limited
9210 Wightman Road, #300
Montgomery Village, MD 20886
Contact: Mercedes Pellet, Michael R. Pellet
Telephone: 301-977-4281
Fax: 301-926-5046
Email: Marketing@m2ltd.com / URL: http://
www.m2ltd.com
Product Service Description:
Localization / Translation / Publishing /
Globalization

MBS Industrial Service Inc
2243 Cerritos Ave
Long Beach, CA 90806-3411
Contact: Eric Letson, General Manager
Telephone: 562-424-4481
Fax: 562-490-0642
Email: mbsindustrial@compuserve.com
Product Service Description:
Babbitt bearing repair, manufacturing and
grinding
Manufacturing of bus bars & heatsinks

MCP Metalspecialties, Inc.
515 Commerce Dr
Fairfield, CT 06432-5541
Contact: Michael Ian, Pres.
Telephone: 203-384-0335
Fax: 203-368-4082
Email: mcp-metspec@juno.com / URL: http://
www.mcp-group.com
Product Service Description:
Metal fabrication
Metal products_fabricated
Low temperature alloys

MG Electronics
32 Ronick Rd.
Hauppauge, NY 11788
Contact: Stan Grey,
Telephone: 516-582-3400
Fax: 516-582-3229
Email: mgelec@spec.net / URL: http://
www.mgelectronics.com
Product Service Description:
Television and Radio
and parts and accessories thereof
Loudspeaker products (CEM)
Loudspeaker products (commercial sound)
Loudspeaker products (security)
Power supplies : Cooling fans : Switches
Buzzers & Transducers

MIA Express Inc.
6417 S.W. 96th Ave.
Miami, FL 33173-2253
Contact: Mario Pensel,
Telephone: 305-595-0142
Fax: 305-596-1884
Email: mia.express@cwixmail.com / URL:
Product Service Description:
Lighting - Sylvania / OSRAM distributor,
lamps, Exporting firms

MIO Corp.
27237 Piles Lane
Albuquerque, NM 87109-5800
Contact: Sales & Mktg. *
Product / Service Description:
Boats

MIOX Corp.
5500 Midway Park Pl Ne
Albuquerque, NM 87109-5800
Contact: Jacqueline E. Barnett, VP Marketing
& Intl. Mkt. Dev.
Telephone: 505-343-0090
Fax: 505-343-0093
Email: info@miox.com / URL: http://
www.miox.com
Product Service Description:
Water treatment units

MITEQ, Inc.
100 Davids Dr
Hauppauge, NY 11788-2043
Contact: Arthur Faverio, Pres., CEO
Telephone: 516-436-7400
Fax: 516-436-7430
Email: sales@miteq.com / URL: http://
www.miteq.com
Product Service Description:
Electronic components
Solid state microwave components & satellite
communication subsystems
Radio & TV communications equipment

MK Distributors Inc
278 Berland Rd
Conrad, MT 59425-9204
Contact: Marvin Kaptein, Pres.
Telephone: 406-278-7665
Fax: 406-278-3221
Email: / URL: http://www.hoppercone.com
Product Service Description:
Farm machinery & equipment
Manufactures farm machinery and equipment

MKS Instruments, Inc.
6 Shattuck Rd.
Andover, MA 01810-2495
Contact: Lisa Robillard, Manager of Corp.
Comm.
Telephone: 978-975-2350
Fax: 978-975-0093
Email: mks@mksinst.com / URL: http://
www.mksinst.com
Product Service Description:
Pressure & Flow Meas. / Control Instruments
Process Control Instruments

MMC International Corp.
60 Inip Dr.
Inwood, NY 11696-1011
Contact: Chuck Elder, Sales Manager
Telephone: 516-239-7339
Fax: 516-371-3134
Email: mmcinwd@aol.com / URL: http://
www.mmcintl.com
Product Service Description:
Commercial Marine Equipment

MPC International LLC
1984 E Gladwick St
Rancho Dominguez, CA 90220-6201
Contact: C Brian Musick, Sales & Mktg.
Mgr.
Telephone: 323-583-4727
Fax: 323-583-4728
Email: mpcintl@msn.com /
hippocoat@mpcintl.cc / URL: http://
www.mpcintl.cc
Product Service Description:
PVC coating & epoxy coating for electrical
supplies and other metal products
Distributor of PVC coated electrical products
Powder coatings, electrostatic fushion bonded

MPI Products Div. of Miro Precision
7546 W Mcnab Rd
Pompano Beach, FL 33068-5484
Contact: Ed Miro, Owner
Telephone: 954-726-1633
Fax: 954-720-9812
Email: / URL:
Product Service Description:
Wire crimping tools

MSI International
10700 North Freeway, Suite 100
Houston, TX 77037
Contact: Doyle W. Brewington, CEO
Telephone: 281-820-6622
Fax: 281-820-8979
Email: msiintl@flash.net / URL:
Product Service Description:
Aircraft, Rotor Win, Commercial
Motor Boats, Patrol & Offshore
Engineering Svcs, Railroads
Railroad Equipment Rail Cars & Kits
Engineering Services, Incinerator Plants,
Waste to Energy
Civil Engineering, (Complete Development
Infra-Structure)
Water Treatment & Sewage Treatment Plants
Power Generating Plants
Topographic 3D Surveys
Aquaculture Farming Design & Implement

MTH Tool Co. Inc.
401 W. Main St.
Plano, Il 60545-1436
Contact: G.E. Martens, Marketing Manager
Telephone: 630-552-4115
Fax: 630-552-3688
Email: sales@mthpumps.com / URL: http://
www.mthpumps.com
Product Service Description:
Pumps & Pumping Equipment

Maac Machinery Co., Inc.
801 Hilltop Dr
Itasca, IL 60143-1327
Contact: Paul V. Alongi, CEO
Telephone: 630-285-1500
Fax: 630-285-1506
Email: maacsales@aol.com / URL: http://
www.maacmachinery.com
Product Service Description:
Industrial thermoforming machinery

Maasdam Pow'r-Pull Inc.
PO Box 6130
Burbank, CA 91510-6130
Contact: Brad Tukey, V.P.
Telephone: 818-845-8769
Fax: 818-846-6058
Email: / URL: http://www.maasdam.com
Product Service Description:
Hand Hoists
Construction Winches

Mac Company
300 Lehi Ln
Newcastle, CA 95658-9609
Contact: John McAulay, Owner
Telephone: 530-823-6484
Fax: 530-823-6482
Email: macco@foothill.net
Product Service Description:
Manufactures bottling machinery for the
bottled water industry
Ozonation / Equipment

Mac Farms of Hawaii, Inc.
89-406 Mamalahoa Hwy.
Captain Cook, HI 96704
Contact: Brian Loader, VP Sales
Telephone: 916-446-7600
Fax: 916-444-9832
Email: / URL: http://www.macfarms.com
Product Service Description:
Nuts & Seeds, Salted & Roasted
Macadamia nut products
Branded cosumer packages of macadamia
Bulk supply for macadamia grades

Mac-Lyn Industries Inc
1918 E Occidental St
Santa Ana, CA 92705-5116
Contact: Gary McAllister, Pres.
Telephone: 714-258-7606
Fax: 714-258-1259
Product Service Description:
Machine shop-manufacturer of aircraft
components

Machine Tech, Inc.
2988 E 24th Rd
Marseilles, IL 61341-9619
Contact: George Sandora, Pres.
Telephone: 815-795-6818
Fax: 815-795-6535
URL: http://www.mtco.com/~machtech
Product Service Description:
Portable Pipe Cutting Equip.
Pipe cutting equipment

Machinery Dealers Natl. Assn.
315 S. Patrick St.
Alexandria, VA 22314
Contact: Darryl D. McEwen, Exec. V.P.
Telephone: 703-836-9300
Fax: 703-836-9303
Email: office@mdna.org
URL: http://www.mdna.org
Product Service Description:
Trade Association, Machinery Dealers
Metal Working Machinery, Used & New
Complete

Macro Plastics Inc
2250 Huntington Dr
Fairfield, CA 94533-9732
Contact: C Heywood, Pres.
Telephone: 707-437-1200
Fax: 707-437-1201
Email: info@macroplastics.com / URL: http://www.macroplastics.com
Product Service Description:
Manufactures plastic macrobins
Plastic products

Made In Maui Neon
PO Box 959
Kihei, HI 96753-0959
Contact: Eric Seibert, Owner
Phone: 808-879-6366 / Fax: 808-874-5599
Product Service Description:
Lighting equipment : Signs & advertising
specialties : Worldwide Neon Service

Madison Co.
27 Business Park Dr
Branford, CT 06405-2925
Contact: Steven E. Schickler, Pres.
Telephone: 203-488-4477
Fax: 203-481-5036
Email: sales@madisonco.com / URL: http://www.madisonco.com
Product Service Description:
Process control instruments
Liquid level indicators & switches

Madison Company
27 Business Park Drive
Branford, CT 06405
Contact: Catherine Hartmann, Marketing
Telephone: 203-488-4477
Fax: 203-481-5036
Email: sales@madisonco.com / URL: http://www.madisonco.com
Product Service Description:
Liquid Level Instruments, Switches &
Controls

Madys Company
1555 Yosemite Ave Ste 46
San Francisco, CA 94124-3268
Contact: Christopher Lee, Pres.
Telephone: 415-822-5656
Fax: 415-822-3673
Email: madystea@aol.com / URL:
Product Service Description:
Manufactures natural herb and health
products
Medicinals & botanicals

Mag-Tran Equipment Corp
14700 Alondra Blvd
La Mirada, CA 90638-5616
Contact: Don Lebaron, Pres.
Telephone: 714-522-4100
Fax: 714-521-4488
Product Service Description:
Manufactures and repairs transformers
Reactors
Inductors
Chokes

MagicBox Inc
850 SW 15th St Ste 128
Corvallis, OR 97333-4858
Contact: Tom Searcy, Pres.
Telephone: 541-752-5654
Fax: 541-752-5614
Email: / URL: http://www.magicboxinc.com
Product Service Description:
CD Rom based character generators for cable
or CC TV

Magna Industries, Inc.
1825 Swarthmore Ave
Lakewood, NJ 08701-4540
Contact: Jerry Kazeminski, Pres.
Telephone: 732-905-0957
Fax: 732-367-2989
Email: / URL:
Product Service Description:
Food products machinery
Bakery equipment

Magna Interior Systems
19700 Haggerty Road
Livonia, MI 48152
Contact: Scott E. Paradise, *
Telephone: 313-591-4440
Fax: 313-591-1146
Email: / URL:
Product Service Description:
Automotive Seats

Magnaflux
3624 W Lake Ave
Glenview, IL 60025-1215
Contact: Bob Evans, Cont.
Telephone: 847-657-5300
Fax: 847-657-5388
Email: / URL: http://www.magnaflux.com
Product Service Description:
Machinery_general industrial
Non-destructive testing materials &
equipment

Magnaray International
PO Box 990
Bradenton, FL 34206-0990
Contact: Lorence E. Leetzow, Chrm., Pres.,
Opers. Mgr.
Telephone: 941-755-2111
Fax: 941-751-5483
Email: sales@magnaray.com / URL: http://www.magnaray.com
Product Service Description:
Outdoor fluorescent lighting fixtures
Lighting fixtures_commercial : Tennis Court
Lighting : Security Lighting : Emergency
Lighting : Solar Lighting : Energy Efficient
Flourescent Lighting : Energy Efficient Solar
Lighting

Magnesia Products Inc.
265 Pioneer Blvd.
Springboro, OH 45066
Contact: Robert Mastandrea, Pres.
Telephone: 513-746-5509
Fax: 513-743-7786
Email: sales@chew-rite.com / URL: http://www.chew-rite.com
Product Service Description:
Chew-Rite Cushion Dentrue Retainer
Toilet preparations

Magness Land & Cattle
P.o. Box 190
Platteville, CO 80651
Contact: Wendell Geeslin, Manager
Telephone: 970-785-6170
Fax: 303-659-3822
Email: wendell@magnesscattle.com / URL:
Product Service Description:
Beef Cattle, Limousin Breeding Stock

Magnetic Metals Corp.
21 Hayes Ave.
Camden, NJ 08101
Contact: Frank A. Raneiro,
Telephone: 609-964-7842
Fax: 609-963-8569
Email: chavous1@bellatlantic.com / URL: http://www.magnet.com
Product Service Description:
Metal stampings

Magnetic Radiation Laboratories Inc.
690 Hilltop Dr
Itasca, IL 60143-1326
Contact: Alan J. Barone, Ex. V-P., Sales &
Mktg.
Telephone: 630-285-0800
Fax: 630-285-0807
Email: sales@magrad.com / URL: http://www.magrad.com
Product Service Description:
Magnetic shielding
Metal products_fabricated
Metal, Deep Drawn
Metal, Hydroformed
Machine NC & CNC

Magnolia, Div. Sanderson Plmbg.
P.O. Box 1367
Columbus, MS 39703
Contact: Jackie DiGiglia, Intl. Sales Mgr.
Telephone: 601/328-4000
Fax: 601-329-4362
Email: sales@sppi.com / URL: http://www.sppi.com
Product Service Description:
Toilet Seats, Plastic
Toilet Seats, Wood
Toilet Seats, Soft Vinyl

**Magnum Group, Inc. Translation &
Related Svcs.**
610 South 2nd Street
Philadelphia, PA 19147
Contact: Vivian Isaak, President
Telephone: 215-413-1614
Fax: 215-413-1615
Email: translations@magnumgroupinc.com / URL: http://www.magnumgroupinc.com
Product Service Description:
Technical Translations, Typesetting
Spanish & From/Into Most Languages
Foreign Language Voice Over
Advertising Medical Cosmetics
Marketing, Financial

Magnum Machinery Services Inc
7626 79th Ave Se
Mercer Island, WA 98040-5523
Contact: Luis F Antezana, Pres.
Telephone: 206-236-2628
Fax: 206-232-4598
Email: lfantezana@aol.com / URL: http://www.magnummach.com
Product Service Description:
Manufactures woodworking machinery &
designer
Woodworking machinery
Log handling systems
Chip screening
Log feeder singulators

Mahar
3812 Wheeler Ave
Fort Smith, AR 72901-6647
Contact: James Mahar, Pres.
Telephone: 501-646-4499
Fax: 501-646-9101
Email: ctmtspec@mahar.net / URL: http://www.mahar.net
Product Service Description:
Cots
Mats
Preschool furniture

Maine Plastics Inc.
1550 24th Street
North Chicago, IL 60064-0939
Contact: Henry Render, Pres., R & D Mgr.
Telephone: 847-473-3553
Fax: 847-473-3611
Email: mainepls@interaccess.com / URL: http://www.maineplastics.com
Product Service Description:
Plastic recycling
Plastic products

Maine Poly Inc
Route 202
Greene, ME 04236
Contact: Stephen D. Spencer, Pres.
Telephone: 207-946-7440
Fax: 207-946-5492
Product Service Description:
Flexible Printed Packaging & Bags

Mainley Flags, Inc.
990 Lafayette Rd
Portsmouth, NH 03801-5480
Contact: Richard LaFrance,
Telephone: 603-430-7887
Fax: 603-430-7901
Email: info@flagstore.com / URL: http://
www.flagstore.com
Product Service Description:
Flags, banners & pennants

Mainstreet Menu Systems
P.O. Box 0748
Brookfield, WI 53008
Contact: Bruce Johnson, Natl. Sales Mgr
Telephone: 414/782-6000
Fax: 414-782-6515
Email: / URL:
Product Service Description:
Illum. Menu Systems

Major Industries, Inc.
7120 Stewart Ave
Wausau, WI 54401-8410
Contact: Wayne A. Toenjes, Pres., Treas.
Telephone: 715-842-4616
Fax: 715-848-3336
Email: wtoenjes@majorskylights.com / URL:
http://www.majorskylights.com
Product Service Description:
Skylights

Major Metalfab Co.
370 Alice St
Wheeling, IL 60090-5806
Contact: Val Burlini, Pres.
Telephone: 847-537-7890
Fax: 847-537-1120
Email: mmfind@wwa.com / URL:
Product Service Description:
Bank & cashier supplies
Machinery_special industry

Malbert Mitchell Grinding Corp
901 S Cypress St
La Habra, CA 90631-6833
Contact: Larry Plank, Pres.
Telephone: 714-525-9009
Fax: 714-525-9010
Email: ILWP@worldnet.att.net / URL: http://
www.malbertmitchellgrind.com
Product Service Description:
General machine shop (job work); precision
grinding
Aero space Mfg.

Mallinckrodt Inc.
2703 Wagner Pl.
Maryland Heights, MO 63043-3421
Contact: Les Sabo, Plt. Mgr.
Telephone: 314-654-7800
Fax: 314-654-7998
Email: nlmktjke@ibmmail.com / URL: http://
www.mkg.com
Product Service Description:
Radioactive diagnostic pharmaceuticals
Medicinals & botanicals

Malo & Weste Corp.
809 3rd Ave
Asbury Park, NJ 07712-5934
Contact: Ted Block, Pres.
Telephone: 732-774-7070
Fax: 732-774-2012
Product Service Description:
Contract Plastic Sealing Services

Maloney Technical Product, Inc.
1300 E Berry St
Fort Worth, TX 76119-3003
Contact: Pamela Murrin, Pres.
Telephone: 817-923-3344
Fax: 817-923-1549
Email: sbtech@gte.net / URL: http://
www.maloneytech.com
Product Service Description:
Rubber & Plastic Pipeline Products
Custom Rubber Molding

Management Engineering Associates
3709 NW 16th Ave
Camas, WA 98607-9050
Contact: William S. Ward, Managing
Principal
Telephone: 360-834-3004
Fax: 360-834-0107
Email: mea@pacifier.com / URL:
Product Service Description:
Engineering Services

Manic Impressions
1533 Monrovia Ave # C
Newport Beach, CA 92663-2869
Contact: Jennifer Irani, Owner
Telephone: 949-650-0520
Email: manic-mouse@att.net / URL: http://
www.manicimpressions.com
Product Service Description:
Furnishings_house
Shirts_men's & boys'
Blouses & shirts_women's & misses'
Bags_textile
Pillows
Tote bags
Art
Paintings

Manrob Sales
1001 Avenue of the Americas
New York, NY 10018-5411
Contact: Bob Ficarra, Manager
Telephone: 212-221-7525
Product Service Description:
Textiles

**Mansfield Plumbing Products, Inc.,
Corporate Headquarters**
1070 Polaris Parkway, Suite 200
Columbus, OH 43240
Contact: David M. "Pete" Kirkpatrick,
Director of Wholesale Sales
Telephone: 614-825-0960
Fax: 614-825-0989
Email: custserv@mansfieldplumbing.com /
URL: http://www.mansfieldplumbing.com
Product Service Description:
Plumbing fixtures, vitreous
Vitreous china & enameled steel plumbing
fixtures
Metal sanitary ware
Acrylic whirlpools & bathware

**Manufacturers Equipment
Company-Meco**
35 Enterprise Dr.
Middletown, OH 45044-8928
Contact: Sales & Marketing,
Telephone: 513-424-3573
Fax: 513-424-3576
Email: / URL: http://www.meco-wires.com
Product Service Description:
Brick / Clay Cutting Wires

Maple Valley Hardwoods
10660 Maple Grove Rd.
Freedom, NY 14065
Contact: Don Wagner,
Telephone: 716-492-4800
Fax: 716-496-5222
Email: mapleval@buffnet.net / URL:
Product Service Description:
Lumber
Dimension

Maplehurst Genetics Intl. Inc.
32323 190th St.
Keota, IA 52248
Contact: R.A. Carmichael, General Manager
Telephone: 515/636-3811
Fax: 515-636-3838
Email: mapgen@se-iowa.net / URL: http://
www.maplehurstgenetics.com
Product Service Description:
Semen, Embryos
Veterinary Diagnostic Substances, Drugs,
Vaccines

Mapletex
PO Box 771
Tacoma, WA 98401-0771
Contact: Steven Geffre, Pres.
Telephone: 253-572-3608
Fax: 253-627-5452
Email: mapletex@aol.com / URL:
Product Service Description:
Manufactures resin impregnated paper
products into food grade cutting boards,
steamboards
Bakery Tables.
Industrial Phenolic Laminates

Mapmakers Alaska
259 S Alaska St
Palmer, AK 99645-6335
Contact: Brit Lively, Owner, Fin., MIS & R
& D Mgr.
Telephone: 907-745-3398
Fax: 907-745-6733
Email: mapalaska@micronet.net / URL: http://
/www.mapalaska.com
Product Service Description:
Oil & gas maps for Alaska

Maratech International
7111 Stewart Ave.
Wausau, WI 54401-9339
Contact: Calvin S. Frost, President
Telephone: 715-842-8232
Fax: 715-848-2159
Email: maratech@gza.net / URL: http://
www.members.aol.com/chresovr/cri.htm &
www.channeldresources.com
Product Service Description:
Die-Cut Paper and Board
Electrical parts of machinery or apparatus
Articles of paper pulp, paper, paperboard,
cellulose wadding or webs of cellulose fibers
Miscellaneous cargo
Silicne release papers & film
Pressure sensitive roll label stocks - paper &
film

Marathon Corp.
PO Box 509
Childersburg, AL 35044-5509
Contact: Mike Roberts, V-P.
Telephone: 205-378-8060
Fax: 205-378-3418
Email: marappz@aol.com / URL:
Product Service Description:
Men's clothing : Clothing, men's & boys'
Embellished T's & Fleece

Marbledge, Inc.
1800 4th Ave N
Lake Worth, FL 33461-3895
Contact: Hank Venter, Pres.
Telephone: 561-582-0304
Fax: 561-585-0191
Email: jf2388@aol.com / URL:
Product Service Description:
Marble & Granite
Cut & Installation of Stone Products
Granite Mining

Marcal Paper Mills
1 Market St.
Elmwood Park, NJ 07407-1401
Contact: John Engel, Export Dept.
Telephone: 201-796-4000
Fax: 201-796-0470
Email: / URL: http://www.marcalpaper.com
Product Service Description:
Waxed Paper : Toilet Paper : Paper Towels
Facial Tissues : Paper Napkins

Marcotex International
27 8th St.
Passaic, NJ 07055-7903
Contact: Marc Moyal, President
Telephone: 201-471-0500
Fax: 201-471-3380
Email: marcotex@compuserve.com / URL:
Product Service Description:
Textile Seconds
Bedsheets / Towels

Marcus Brothers
1755 McDonald Ave.
Brooklyn, NY 11230-6906
Contact: S. Marcus, President
Telephone: 718-645-4565
Fax: 718-376-0385
Email: marcusbros@att.net / URL: http://
www.marcusbros.com
Product Service Description:
Baby Bedding

Mardan Fabricators
222 Sw 33rd Ct
Fort Lauderdale, FL 33315-3306
Contact: Daniel R. Foldy, Pres.
Telephone: 954-463-5820
Fax: 954-763-6829
Product Service Description:
Cashier & toll booths, walkway covers &
canopies

**Margaret Cullen Expert
Translations**
41 Linda Avenue
Framingham, MA 01701
Contact: Margaret Cullen, Translator
Telephone: 508/877-4490
Fax: 508-788-1522
Email: 104141.2500@compuserve.com
Product Service Description:
Translation Svcs., French to English
Translation Svcs., Spanish to English
Transl. Svcs., Medical, Business Spec.
Transl. Svcs, Computer Science Specialty

Mariah Boats Inc.
10231 Sugar Creek Rd
Benton, IL 62812-4332
Contact: J. Rance Fulks, Exec. V.P. Ops. Mgr.
Telephone: 618-435-5300
Fax: 618-435-3500
Email: mariah@midwest.net / URL: http://
www.mariahboatsinc.com
Product Service Description:
Fiberglass boats : Boat Building

Marianna Importers, Exporters & Manufacturers, Inc.
11222 I Street
Omaha, NE 68137-1237
Contact: Mike Cosentino, Sr., President
Phone: 402-593-0211 / Fax: 402-593-0614
Email: / URL: http://www.marianna-inc.com
Product Service Description:
Manufacturing Industries, NEC
Shampoo for hair

Marjan, Inc.
PO Box 2420
Waterbury, CT 06722-2420
Contact: Marcel Brouillard, GM
Telephone: 203-573-1742
Fax: 203-757-0369
Email: edw@marjaninc.com / URL: http://www.marjaninc.com
Product Service Description:
Hot tin dipping plating : Metal coating & allied services : 100% pure tin, 90/10 and 60/40 tin lead coatings : Connectors : Electronics

Mark VII International
12707 North Frwy., Ste. 442,
Houston, TX 77060
Contact: Howard Leff, Vice President
Telephone: 281-873-0250
Fax: 281-873-6801
Email: mviintlhou@aol.com / URL: http://www.markvII.com
Product Service Description:
Freight & Cargo Transportation
Trucking : IMC : Logistics
Domestic & International

Marketing Concepts
1420 E State St
Sharon, PA 16146-3232
Contact: James Thomas, Pres.
Telephone: 724-983-1066
Fax: 724-983-1905
Email: info@mccprint.com / URL: http://www.mccprint.com
Product Service Description:
Scratch-off tickets & promotional items
Lithographic printing_commercial
Fund Raising : Lottery Tickets

Marley Mouldings Inc.(Mfr)
P.O. Box 610
Marion, VA 24354
Contact: Marshall Quina / Derrick Johnson,
Phone: 540-783-8161 / Fax: 540-782-3292
Email: marley@netva.com / URL: http://www.marleymouldings.com
Product Service Description:
Interior Embossed Polymer Moldings, Prefinished : Interior Polymer Moldings, Primed & Prefinished : Polymer Window & Door Components & Systems : Exterior Polymer Moldings : Polymer Picture Frame Moldings, Hot Stamped, Mylared, Painted, Glazed : Window Treatment Polymer Components : No Rot Polymer Garage Door Trim System : Polymer Cabinet & Furniture Components : Polymer Drywall Accessories Polymer Siding & Panel Accessories

Marmara, Inc.
6-10 Self Boulevard
Carteret, NJ 07008-1005
Contact: F. J. Fassbender, Vice President
Phone: 732-750-8900
Fax: 732-750-4666 ; 732-750-5884
Email: marmarainc@aol.com
Product Service Description:
International Freight Forwarder

Marport Smelting Co., Llc
4323 Kennedy Ave
East Chicago, IN 46312-2723
Contact: Arthur Mendoza, Pres.
Telephone: 219-397-0562
Fax: 219-392-0517
Email: marport@/congrp.com / URL:
Product Service Description:
Aluminum dross processing
Secondary nonferrous metals
Rotary furnace manufacturer design & installation

Marquis Distributing Co
PO Box 606
Page, AZ 86040-0606
Contact: Jerry Marquis, Owner
Telephone: 520-645-5378
Product Service Description:
Wholesales dairy and bakery products
Dairy products, except dried or canned
Groceries & related products

Mars Air Doors
14716 S. Broadway
Gardena, CA 90248
Contact: Martin Smilo, President
Telephone: 213-770-1555
Fax: 310-324-3030
Product Service Description:
Heated & Unheated Air Curtains
Packaged Make-up Air Systems, Heating, Cooling & Ventilating.

Marshall Miller & Associates
P.O. Box 848
Bluefield, VA 24605
Contact: Tracy Paine, Dir./ Mktg., Marshall S. Miller, President
Telephone: 540-322-5467
Fax: 540-322-5460
Email: mmablfd@aol.com / URL:
Product Service Description:
Geologists
Geophysicists
Engineering Services, General
Air & Water Resource & Solid Waste Management
Drilling Oil & Gas Wells
Oil & Gas Field Exploration
Oil & Gas Field Services
Surveying Services
Geophysical Services

Marshall Thomas Co. Inc.
1621 Kensington Way
Lexington, KY 40513-9407
Contact: Colonel M.H. Thomas, *
Telephone: 606-254-0703
Fax: 606-255-9104
Email: / URL:
Product Service Description:
Agricultural Chemicals - All Crops

Marsulex Environmental Technologies LLC
200 N 7th St
Lebanon, PA 17046-5054
Contact: M. Ruth Miller,
Telephone: 717-274-7288
Fax: 717-274-7103
Email: rmiller@marsulex.com / URL: http://www.met.marsulex.com
Product Service Description:
Air pollution control equipment
Cyclone Collectors
FCC Cyclones

Mart Corporation
PO Box 969
Sanford, NC 27331-0969
Contact: Kay Brown Faucette,
Phone: 919-776-7648 / Fax: 919-774-7131
Email: kay@interpath.com / URL: http://www.martcorp.com
Product Service Description:
Textile Machinery - Air Filters
Industrial Air Filters

Mart Corporation
PO Box 969
Sanford, NC 27331-0969
Contact: Kay Brown Faucette, *
Telephone: 919-776-7648
Product Service Description:
Air filters

Martin Marietta Magnesia Specialties
P.O. Box 15470
Baltimore, MD 21220-0470
Contact: Sales & Marketing,
Telephone: 410-780-5500
Fax: 410-780-5777
Email: magchem@martinmarietta.com / URL: http://www.magspecialties.com
Product Service Description:
Wastewater Equip/Systems
Dust Suppression Chemicals

Martindale Electric Company
PO Box 430
Cleveland, OH 44107-0430
Contact: Jeffrey Snyder, Int'l Sales Mgr.
Telephone: 216-521-8567
Fax: 216-521-9476
Product Service Description:
Saws, Circular, High Speed, Steel & Carbide
Electric Motor Parts & Supplies

Marty Wolf Game Co
2120 S Highland Dr Ste G
Las Vegas, NV 89102-4622
Contact: Marty Wolf, Owner
Telephone: 702-385-2963
Fax: 702-385-6963
Email: gameco@vegas.quik.com / URL: http://www.galaxymall.com/products/gamblingsupplies
Product Service Description:
Manufactures Home & Party Casino Tables & Equipment

Mary K Active Wear Inc
M K Active / Solar Eclipse / 8240 E Gelding Dr Ste 102
Scottsdale, AZ 85260-3618
Contact: Mary K McCormick, Pres.
Telephone: 480-991-0911
Fax: 480-991-1036
Product Service Description:
Manufactures women's & misses clothing
Outerwear_women's, misses', and men's
Sun protective active wear-men, women & children

Mas-Hamilton Group
805 Newtown Cir Ste D
Lexington, KY 40511-1240
Contact: J. D. Hamilton, Pres.
Telephone: 606-253-4744
Fax: 606-253-4748
Email: mhgmktg@mas-hamilton.com / URL: http://www.mas-hamilton.com
Product Service Description:
Electronic components
Electronic access control systems

Mason Corp.
PO Box 59226
Birmingham, AL 35259-9226
Contact: Tim S. Tennyson, VP of Sales
Telephone: 205-942-4100
Fax: 205-945-7393
Email: webmaster@masoncorp.com / URL: http://www.masoncorp.com
Product Service Description:
Metal building products
Screen Frame & Accessories

Mass Medical Equipment
1 A Melvin Street
Wakefield, MA 01880
Contact: Thomas Taranto, President
Telephone: 781-246-3368
Fax: 781-246-5351
Email: www.mmeci@aol.com / URL:
Product Service Description:
Medical Diagnostic Equip., Used, Whsle.

Master Craft Plaque Co.
4810 Fulton Indl. Blvd.
Atlanta, GA 30336
Contact: Ruben Estes, Pres.
Telephone: 404-691-0000
Fax: 404-691-0000
Product Service Description:
Wooden plaques

Master Line U S A
13459 Lake Butler Blvd
Winter Garden, FL 34787-5450
Contact: Russell Gay, Pres.
Telephone: 407-656-1133
Fax: 407-656-6486
Email: mlusa@masterlineusa.com / URL: http://www.masterlineusa.com
Product Service Description:
Ski equipment
Sporting & athletic goods

Master Marine, Inc.
PO Box 665
Bayou La Batre, AL 36509-0665
Contact: Steven Roppoli, V-P., Sales
Telephone: 334-824-4151
Fax: 334-824-7050
Email: maf00039@maf.mobile.al.us / URL:
Product Service Description:
Boats & commercial, industrial & marine metal fabrication

Master Motor Rebuilders
1204 W National Ave
Addison, IL 60101-3131
Contact: Chuck Hanson, Pres.
Telephone: 630-628-7940
Fax: 630-628-7946
Email: mmrmotors@aol.com / URL: http://www.mmr-motors.com
Product Service Description:
Rebuilt forklift motors
Lift Truck Parts

Mastercraft Companies
3301 W Vernon Ave
Phoenix, AZ 85009-1495
Contact: Dave Larson, VP/COO
Telephone: 602-484-4520
Fax: 602-484-4525
Email: webmaster@mastercraft-companies.com / URL: http://www.mastercraft-companies.com
Product Service Description:
Full service custom injection molding and manufactures injection and die cast molds

Masterpiece Accessories Inc
1201 Francisco St
Torrance, CA 90502-1207
Contact: Tom Koch, Pres.
Telephone: 310-660-0470
Fax: 310-660-0477
Email: info@masterpieceaccessories.com /
http://www.masterpieceaccessories.com
Product Service Description:
Accessories & lamps manufacturer
Lamps & Accessories, Manufacturer

Masterpiece Prdctns Nevada
PO Box 44304
Las Vegas, NV 89116-2304
Contact: Sharon Hulihan, Pres.
Telephone: 702-438-7005
Product Service Description:
Film and video tape production
Motion picture & video production
Television Service : Producers : Writers
Directors

Mastin Motors
5520 Old Winter Garden Rd.
Orlando, FL 32811-1525
Contact: Sales & Marketing,
Telephone: 407-295-2789
Fax: 407-295-2528
Email: busboybob@mpinet.net / URL: http://
www.mastinmotors.com
Product Service Description:
Used School Buses

Mat, Inc.
12402 Hwy. 2
Floodwood, MN 55736
Contact: Joseph T. Karpik, Pres., Secy.
Telephone: 218-476-2033
Fax: 218-476-2039
Email: matinc@soilguard.com / URL: http://
www.soilguard.com
Product Service Description:
Mulch processing : Wood Mulch Products
(Soil Guard, Mat-Fiber) : Wood Fiber
Blankets

Matador Processors, Inc.
PO Box 2200
Blanchard, OK 73010-2200
Contact: Betty Wood, Pres., Keith Bolding,
Telephone: 405-485-3567
Fax: 405-485-2597
Email: matador@matadorprocessors.com /
URL: http://www.matadorprocessors.com
Product Service Description:
Ethnic foods
Frozen specialties

Match Maker, The
P.O. Box 13259
Florence, SC 29504
Contact: Bert Belk, President
Telephone: 843-665-4968
Fax: 843-665-5073
Email: bertbsc@aol.com / URL: http://
www.matchmaker-sc.com
Product Service Description:
Freight & Cargo Transportation
Trucking

Matel Bank and Desk Accessories
12811 S. Figueroa
Los Angeles, CA 90061
Contact: Paul Whitehead, V.P. Sales &
Marketing
Phone: 1-800-217-7606 / Fax: 310-538-8949
Email: info@matelinc.com
URL: http://www.matelinc.com

Product Service Description:
Leather & Metal Desk Accessories
Ash / Trash Receptacles : Office/Hotel
Equip., Stanchions : Bank Furniture,
Checkstands & Accessories : Security Pen
Sets : Occasional Tables / Benches

Material Testing Technology Co.
400 W Palatine Rd
Arlington Heights, IL 60004-3844
Contact: Walter Scott Thielman, Pres.
Phone: 847-255-8378 / Fax: 847-253-5873
Email: mttusa.hotmail.com / URL: http://
www.mttusa.net
Product Service Description:
Testing equipment
Material Testing Equipment

Materials Research Group, Inc.
12441 W 49th Ave Ste 3
Wheat Ridge, CO 80033-1927
Contact: Dr. Pawan Bhat, President
Phone: 303-425-6688 / Fax: 303-425-6562
Email: salesmrg@aol.com / URL: http://
www.matresgrp.com
Product Service Description:
Thin Film Deposition Equipment, Process
Controls & Instrumentation

Mathers Controls, Inc.
675 Pease Rd.
Burlington, WA 98233-3103
Contact: Tammy Cannon, Marketing Manager
Telephone: 206-757-6265
Fax: 206-757-2500
Email: tammyc@matherscontrols.com / URL:
http://www.matherscontrols.com
Product Service Description:
Motor Parts, marine Propeller Cntl. Comp
Electronic Equipment

Mathews Assocs, Inc.
645 Hickman Cir.
Sanford, FL 32771-6920
Contact: Daniel Perreault, Pres.
Telephone: 407-323-3390
Fax: 407-323-3115
Email:Maifl @worldnet.att.net
 URL: http://wwwmaifl.com
Product Service Description:
Electronic Products : Electronic Compoenents
Batteries_Storage: Battery Pack & Batteries
Primary

Matrix Controls Co., Inc.
330 Elizabeth Ave
Somerset, NJ 08873-7009
Contact: Robert Lindemann, Pres.
Telephone: 732-469-5551
Fax: 732-469-7299
Product Service Description:
Fabric defect scanners & thread counters
Measuring & controlling devices
Fluid meters & counting devices

Matrix Imaging Solution
2221 Niagara Falls Blvd Ste 14
Niagara Falls, NY 14304-1696
Contact: Alan Olivero, Pres.
Telephone: 716-731-7830
Fax: 716-731-1306
Email: sales@matriximaging.com / URL:
http://www.matriximaging.com
Product Service Description:
Printing_commercial
Commercial & label printing
Bar coding & supplies
Packaging equipment
Laser printing : Mailing

Maui Divers Of Hawaii, Ltd.
1520 Liona St.
Honolulu, HI 96814-2441
Contact: Robert M.. Taylor
Telephone: 808-946-7979
Fax: 808-946-0406
Product Service Description:
Gold Jewelry
Jewelry, Precious Metal

Mawson & Mawson Inc.
1800 Old Lincoln Hwy
Langhorne, PA 19047
Contact: Gregory Mann, Vice President
Telephone: 215-750-1100
Product Service Description:
Trucking, Transportation, Warehousing &
Distribution

Maxi-Vac, Inc.
367 S Rohlwing Rd Ste F
Addison, IL 60101-3064
Contact: James R. Nolan, Pres.
Telephone: 630-620-6669
Fax: 630-620-6683
Email: maxivac@starnetinc.com / URL: http:/
/www.maxi-vac.com
Product Service Description:
Pressure washers, tube cleaners & steam
cleaners

Maxport International
9457 E. Rush St.
South El Monte, CA 81733
Contact: Sales & Marketing,
Telephone: 818-443-8377
Product Service Description:
Automobiles
Construction Equipment
Korfe paper
Packaging materials
Stereo speakers
Electronic devices
Fish
Sporting shoes

Maxtek Inc
2908 Oregon Ct Ste G3
Torrance, CA 90503-2683
Contact: Valli K. Febbraro, Marketing
Telephone: 310-320-6604
Fax: 310-320-6609
Email: sales@maxtekinc.com / URL: http://
www.maxtekinc.com
Product Service Description:
Thin film deposition equipment

Maxton Security Systems
5961 Topeka Dr
Tarzana, CA 91356-1319
Contact: Anthony B Bennett, Pres.
Telephone: 818-776-8557
Fax:
Email: / URL:
Product Service Description:
Manufactures lock-down devices and security
products for PC's and other business
machines
Computer peripheral equipment

Mayacamas Vineyards
1155 Lokoya Rd
Napa, CA 94558-9566
Contact: Robert B Travers, Pres.
Telephone: 707-224-4030
Fax: 707-224-3979
Product Service Description:
Grows grapes and produces wine
Wines

Mayfair Mills, Inc.
P.O. Box 850
Arcadia, SC 29320
Contact: Frederick Dent Jr,
President
Telephone: 864-576-2610
Fax: 864-576-0454
Email: www.brilyfabric.com / URL: http://
www.brilyfabric.com
Product Service Description:
Broadwoven Fabric Mills, Manmade
Woven cotton fabrics

Mayhew Tools
2 Sears Street Ext., P.O. Box 68
Shelburne Falls, MA 01370-0068
Contact: John C. Lawless, President
Telephone: 413-625-6351
Fax: 413-625-6395
Email: sales@mayhew.com / URL: http://
www.mayhew.com
Product Service Description:
Punches, chisels, pry bars

Maytag International
8700 W. Bryn Mawr Ave.
Chicago, IL 60631-3507
Contact: Sales & Marketing,
Telephone: 773-714-0100
Fax: 773-714-8180
Email: / URL: http://www.maytag.com
Product Service Description:
Appliances
Refrigeration Equipment
Laundry Machinery
Cooking Products
Floorcare Products
Commercial Laundry

Mc Clarin Plastics, Inc.
PO Box 486
Hanover, PA 17331-0486
Contact: Todd R. Kennedy, President , CEO,
Roger Kipp, V.P. / Sales
Telephone: 717-637-2241
Fax: 717-637-2091
Email: mcclarin@cyberia.com / URL:
Product Service Description:
Thermoforming & fiber reinforced
composites
Contract Manufacturing
Engineering & Design Solutions for FRP &
Thermoforming Production

Mc Kee Button Co.
PO Box 239
Muscatine, IA 52761-0239
Contact: Marco A. Adasme
Telephone: 319-263-2421
Fax: 319-264-5365
Email: madasme@mckee.com / URL: http://
www.mckeebutton.com
Product Service Description:
Plastic buttons & button feeding equipment
Plastic products (Rings)
Belts for disposables undergarments (adults)

Mc Kee Carbide Tool Co.
RR 1 Box 490
Olanta, PA 16863-9209
Contact: Ed Fogg,
Vice President Operations
Telephone: 814-236-3108
Fax: 814-236-3651
Email: / URL:
Product Service Description:
Dies, tools, jigs & fixtures_special
Precision tooling & dies

Mc Kinley Leather Of Hickory
PO Box 1030
Claremont, NC 28610-1030
Contact: Lewis Mitchell, Pres.
Telephone: 828-459-2884
Fax: 828-459-9738
Product Service Description:
Furniture_upholstered household
Leather furniture

Mc Millan Co., Inc., R. D.
PO Box 1340
Georgetown, TX 78627-1340
Contact: John mcMillan, Sales Manager
Telephone: 512-863-0231
Fax: 512-863-0671
Email: john@mcmilloncompany.com / URL:
http://www.mcmillancompany.com
Product Service Description:
Process control instruments : Gas & liquid
flow sensors, meters & controllers, lowflow

Mc Neil & N R M, Inc.
96 E Crosier St
Akron, OH 44311-2342
Contact: David Caniglia, Sales Mgr.
Telephone: 330-252-0688
Fax: 330-252-0361
Email: titantmg@aol.com / URL: http://
www.titan-tmg.com
Product Service Description:
VBM, HBM, Gantry Mills

McAlpine & Salyer Construction
PO Box 649
Paramount, CA 90723-0649
Contact: Jack G Salyer, Pres.
Telephone: 562-634-1161
Fax: 562-634-3611
Email: mscibutler@aol.com / URL:
Product Service Description:
General contractors; commercial and
industrial; Butler pre-engineered buildings
design and build contractor : Prefabricated
metal buildings : Nonresidential construction,
nec : Industrial buildings & warehouses

McBride Shopa & Co
270 Presidential Drive
Wilmington, DE 19807-3353
Contact: Thomas Shopa, Managing Director
Telephone: 302-656-5500
Fax: 302-656-8024
Email: consulting@McBrideshopa.com /
URL: http://www.McBrideShopa.com
Product Service Description:
Accounting Auditing & Bookkeeping Svcs.
U.S. & International Taxes

McCain Citrus Inc
11020 Poplar Ave
Fontana, CA 92337-7344
Contact: Bill Eakle, GM & Plt. Mgr.
Telephone: 909-355-4888
Fax: 909-823-0415
Product Service Description:
Manufactures citrus juices
Canned fruits & vegetables

McCammisn Mfg. Co., Inc.
148 Winn Ave
Winchester, KY 40391-1554
Contact: Jim Flowers, General Manager
Phone: 606-744-8292 / Fax: 606-744-4573
Email: rmoberly@mccammisn.com / URL:
http://www.mccammish.com
Product Service Description:
Wooden & plastic motel & hotel furniture
Furniture_public building & related

**McCann's Engineering &
Manufacturing Co.**
4570 W. Colorado Blvd.
Los Angeles, CA 90039
Contact: Ivan D. Abernathy, *
Telephone: 818-240-9990
Fax: 818-240-9956
Email: ivan@mccannseng.com / URL:
Product Service Description:
Post Mix Beverage Dispensing Systems
Beverage Fittings : Bar Hose Faucets
Automatic Ice Transporting Systems
Carbonators : Electric Beverage Faucets

McClary, Swift & Co., Inc.
360 Swift Avenue
South San Francisco, CA 94080
Contact: James W. Swift, President
Telephone: 650-872-2121
Fax: 650-872-3465
Product Service Description:
Customs Broker
Freight Forwarder
Freight & Cargo Transportation

McCook Metals, LLC
4900 1st Ave.
McCook, IL 60525
Contact: Keith Heston,
Telephone: 708-387-8395
Fax: 708-387-8905
Email: / URL: http://
www.McCookmetals.com
Product Service Description:
Aluminum plate & sheet
Aircraft, aerospace & distribution

McCord Consulting Group, Inc.
PO Bo x11024
Cedar Rapids, IA 52410-1024
Contact: Sam McCord, President & CEO
Telephone: 319-378-0077
Fax: 319-378-1577
Email: sam.mccord@usa.net / URL: http://
www.mccordgroup.com
Product Service Description:
Business Consulting, Site Selection Svcs.
Business Consulting, Industrial Recruitment

McGough Industries Inc
2634 S Cherry Ave
Fresno, CA 93706-5420
Contact: James G. Dailey, Pres.
Telephone: 559-266-1960
Fax: 559-266-1938
Email: / URL:
Product Service Description:
Gloves & mittens, leather
Winter Ski Gloves
Dog Treats, Flavored
Cotton Work Gloves
Garden Gloves

**McGovern G. T. Trucking &
Warehouse Co., Inc.**
55 Hook Rd.
Bayonne, NJ 07002-5006
Contact: Jack McGovern, *
Telephone: 201-437-4347
Fax: 201-437-5455
Email: mcgoverntrucking@worldnet.att.net /
URL:
Product Service Description:
Comprehensive Warehouse Service
Local Trucking & Pier Work
U.S. Customs Bonded Space Available
Secure Yard For Trailer Drop & Pick
Fully Alarmed & Insured
Cross Dock & Consolidation for Export

McKee - Addison Tube Forming
2695 State Route 73 South
Wilmington, OH 45177
Contact: Wayne D. Long, General Manager
Telephone: 937-382-4490
Fax: 937-382-4963
Email: mckee@erinet.com / URL:
Product Service Description:
Tube/Pipe Bending Tools
Tube/Pipe Bending Machines
Tube/Pipe Sizing & Endforming Tools
Tube/Pipe Sizing & Endforming Machines

McLarens Toplis North America
5670 Wilshire Blvd. 20th Fl.
Los Angeles, CA 90036
Contact: Bill J. Stewart, *
Telephone: (213) 964-8500
Product Service Description:
Marine Surveyors / Adjusters , Loss

McMurray Co
702 N Mariposa St
Burbank, CA 91506-1629
Contact: Robert McMurray, Pres.
Telephone: 818-841-1970
Fax: 818-841-5378
Email: / URL:
Product Service Description:
Manufactures drapery hardware
Drapery hardware & blinds & shades

McPherson Inc.
7A Stuart Road
Chelmsford, MA 01824
Contact: D.m. Schoeffel, C.O.O.
Telephone: 978-256-4512
Fax: 978-250-8625
Email: mcp@mcphersoninc.com / URL: http:/
/www.mcphersoninc.com
Product Service Description:
Scientific Instruments
Spectrometers
Monochromators

Mectra Labs, Inc.
PO Box 350
Bloomfield, IN 47424-0351
Contact: Thomas P. Clement, Pres., Mktg.,
Opers. & R & D Mgr.
Telephone: 812-384-3521
Fax: 812-384-8518
Email: mectralabs@mectralabs.com / URL:
http://www.mectralabs.com
Product Service Description:
Laparoscopic surgical devices
Surgical & medical instruments

Med-Ipet U S A, Inc.
420 W Frontage Rd Ste 102
Northfield, IL 60093-3046
Contact: Carol Shah-Mirany, Pres.
Telephone: 847-724-4300
Fax: 847-724-1831
Email: medipet@medipet.com / URL: http://
www.medipet.com
Product Service Description:
Pet first aid kits

Medal Textiles, Inc.
270 W. 39th St.
New York, NY 10018-4409
Contact: Aaron Lieberman, Owner
Telephone: 212-921-2662
Fax: 212-575-3082
Email: faust@medaltextiles.com / URL: http:/
/www.medaltextiles.com
Product Service Description:
Textiles, wholesale & converting

**Medical Device Resource Corp.
(M.D. Resource Corporation)**
23392 Connecticut St
Hayward, CA 94545-1607
Contact: Melbourne Kimsey II, Pres., CEO
Telephone: 510-732-9950
Fax: 510-785-8182
Email: / URL: http://
www.mdengineering.com
Product Service Description:
Manufactures plastic / general surgery equip:
Aspirators, Insulflatores, etc.

Medical Gas Services Inc
2020 W Melinda Ln
Phoenix, AZ 85027-2622
Contact: Gary Vaughn, Pres.
Telephone: 602-581-3200
Fax: 602-581-0727
Email: / URL:
Product Service Description:
Sells and services nitrous oxide gases and
sedation equipment; installs medical gas
systems
Chemicals & allied products
Medical & hospital equipment
Business services

Medical Indicators, L.P.
1589 Reed Rd
Trenton, NJ 08628-1409
Contact: Robert Witonsky, Cheif Operating
Officer
Telephone: 609-737-1600
Fax: 609-737-0588
Email: / URL:
Product Service Description:
Clinical thermometers
Measuring & controlling devices

Medical Specifics, Inc.
3306 Wiley Post Rd Ste 106
Carrollton, TX 75006-5127
Contact: Howard G. Chilton Jr., Secy-Treas.
Telephone: 972-980-6870
Fax:
Email: sales@medicalspecifics.com / URL:
http://www.medicalspecifics.com
Product Service Description:
Medical aspirators & compressor assembly
Surgical & medical instruments

Medical Technology Products Inc.
405 Oakwood Rd Ste A
Huntington Station, NY 11746-7207
Contact: T. J. Hartnett Jr., Chrm., Pres.
Telephone: 516-549-4350
Fax: 516-549-0247
Email: gy@medtechprodts.com / URL: http://
www.medtechproducts.com
Product Service Description:
Intravenous infusion pumps

Medicore Inc.
2337 W 76th St
Hialeah, FL 33016-1842
Contact: Bonnie Kaplan, V-P., Opers., Sales
& Mktg.
Telephone: 305-556-5084
Fax: 305-825-0961
Email: / URL:
Product Service Description:
Disposable medical products
Surgical & medical instruments
Diabetic medical products

Medipoint, Inc.
72 E 2nd St
Mineola, NY 11501-3505
Contact: Peter Gollobin, Pres.
Phone: 516-294-8822 / Fax: 516-746-6693
Email: medipoint1@aol.com / URL: http://
www.medipoint.com
Product Service Description:
Disposable blood lancets & splinter removers

Mediterranean Shipping Company (USA) Inc.
330 Shipyard Blvd.,
Wilmington, NC 28412
Contact: W. L. Montgomery, Equipt Control
Phone: 910-392-8200 / Fax: 910-392-8247
Product Service Description:
Freight & Cargo Transportation : Trucking

Medstone International Inc
100 Columbia Ste 100
Aliso Viejo, CA 92656-4114
Contact: David Radlinski, Chrm., CFO
Telephone: 949-448-7700
Fax: 949-448-7880
Email: eva@medstone.com / URL: http://
www.medstone.com
Product Service Description:
Manufactures medical equipment
Urology equipment

Mega Plastics, Inc.
111 Industrial Park Dr.
Clinton, MS 39056
Contact: Wayne Davis, Vice President
Phone: 601-924-1712 / Fax: 601-924-1719
Email: megaplasti@aol.com / URL:
Product Service Description:
Plastic bags & film

Meilink Safe Co., A Fireking International Co.
111 Security Pkwy.
New Albany, IN 47150
Contact: Van G. Carlisle, President
Telephone: 812-941-0024 / 800-634-5465
Fax: 800-896-6606
Email: VanC@fireking.com
Product Service Description:
Fire Resistant Filing Cabinets : Fire Resistant
Safes : Burgular Resistant Safes ; Gun Safes
Electronic Locks : Fire Resistant Data Safes

Melmat Inc
5333 Industrial Dr
Huntington Beach, CA 92649-1516
Contact: John A Mellott, Pres.
Telephone: 714-379-4553
Fax: 714-379-4554
Email: cases@melmat.com / URL: http://
www.melmat.com
Product Service Description:
Molds and fabricates plastic carring cases;
protective containers

Melotte-Morse-Leonatti Stained Glass, Inc.
213 1/2 S 6th St
Springfield, IL 62701-1502
Contact: Richard Morse,
GM, Sales & Mktg. Mgr.
Telephone: 217-789-9523
Fax: 217-789-6582
Email: mmlltd-adg@fgi.net / URL: http://
www.mml-adg.com
Product Service Description:
Stained glass architectural windows, storm
glazing & etching
Glass products from purchased glass

Mendoza Textiles Manufacturing
2515 N 34th Dr
Phoenix, AZ 85009-1422
Contact: Adrian Mendoza, Pres, Anna
Mendoza, Nat'l Sales Mgr.
Phone: 602-269-7482 / Fax: 602-269-9418
Email: anna@extremezone.com
mendoza@extremezone.com / URL:
Product Service Description:
Manufactures nylon tool bags and belts for
the construction industry

Mensor Corporation
2230 I H 35 S.
San Marcos, TX 78666-5917
Contact: Sales,
Telephone: 512-396-4200
Fax: 512-396-1820
Email: sales@mensor.com / URL: http://
www.mensor.com
Product Service Description:
Pressure Gauges (Digital)
Pressure Controllers / Calibrators

Meridian Data Inc
5615 Scotts Valley Dr.
Scotts Valley, CA 95066
Contact: Sales & Marketing,
Telephone: 831-438-3100
Fax: 831-438-6816
Email: mjacobs@meridian-data.com / URL:
http://www.meridian-data.com
Product Service Description:
Network Attach Storage Servers
CD-Rom Network Servers

Meridian Products Corp.
14005 N Stemmons Fwy
Dallas, TX 75234-3460
Contact: Jim Foxx, Pres.
Telephone: 972-484-7300
Fax: 972-484-7302
Email: meridian@cyberramp.net / URL: http:/
/www.meridianproductscorp.com
Product Service Description:
Plastic products : Plastic injection molding

Merrill Mfg. Co., Inc.
PO Box 392
Storm Lake, IA 50588-0392
Contact: Stephen Anderson, Pres.
Telephone: 712-732-2760
Fax: 712-732-4401
Email: anyflow@ncn.net / URL: http://
www.merrillmfg.com
Product Service Description:
Frost-proof yard hydrants, well adapters, pipe
fittings & air volume controls

Messina Metal Mfg
5050 Hillsdale Cir
El Dorado Hills, CA 95762-5706
Contact: Sal Messina, Ptnr.
Telephone: 916-933-1966
Fax: 916-933-1810
Product Service Description:
Sheet metal fabrication : Sheet metal work

Metacrylics
142 N 27th St
San Jose, CA 95116-1118
Contact: Mark C Anthenien, Pres.
Telephone: 408-280-7733
Fax: 408-280-6329
Email: sales@metacrylics.com / URL: http://
www.metacrylics.com
Product Service Description:
Manufactures, distributes and sells
elastomeric roofing and deck materials

Metal Cutting Corporation (Mfr)
89 Village Park Road
Cedar Grove, NJ 07009
Contact: Fran Mongioi, Director of Sales
Telephone: 973-239-1100
Fax: 973-239-6651
Email: sales@metalcutting.com / URL:
Product Service Description:
Burr-Free Cut-Off Metal Parts

Metal Finishing Technologies, Inc.
PO Box 9098
Bristol, CT 06011-9098
Contact: Frank Brindisi Jr., V.-P., Sales &
Mktg.
Telephone: 860-582-9517
Fax: 860-584-8472
Email: mft@megahits.com / URL: http://
www.mftech.com
Product Service Description:
Zinc, nickel, electroless nickel, copper,
cadmium, silver, gold & die-cast components
Plating & polishing
Metal coating & allied services

Metal Finishing, Inc.
PO Box 441
Trussville, AL 35173-0441
Contact: James R. Thompson, Pres.
Telephone: 205-655-5375
Fax: 205-655-5391
Email: mfi@worldnet.att.net / URL:
Product Service Description:
Metal fabrication & general machining job
shop : Metal products_fabricated
Industrial machinery

Metal Master
1440 S Alvernon Way
Tucson, AZ 85711-5604
Contact: John Richards, Pres.
Telephone: 520-325-3059
Fax: 520-325-6776
Email: / URL:
Product Service Description:
Stainless steel products for industry, medical,
lab & foodservice
Cabinets, workstations, tables and custom
Office furniture, except wood
Sheet metal work
Furniture

Metal Master Inc
7320 Convoy Ct
San Diego, CA 92111-1110
Contact: Ben Garrido, Pres.
Telephone: 619-292-8880
Fax: 619-292-0739
Email: / URL:
Product Service Description:
Metal products_fabricated
Fabricates metal products
Sheet metal work
Assembly
CNC Milling

Metal Rubber Corporation
1225 S Shamrock Ave
Monrovia, CA 91016-4244
Contact: Fernando Alvarez, Pres.
Telephone: 626-358-3274
Fax: 626-303-5978
Email: metalrubber@metalrubber.com / URL:
http://www.metalrubber.com
Product Service Description:
Manufactues rubber rollers; bonds
rubber to metal
Rubber products_fabricated

Metal-Matic Inc.
629 2nd St Se
Minneapolis, MN 55414-2106
Contact: G. J. Bliss Sr., Pres.
Telephone: 612-378-0411
Fax: 612-378-0012
Product Service Description:
Steel pipe & tubes
Steel tubing

Metallic Ceramic Coating Inc.
55 E Front St Ste A200
Bridgeport, PA 19405-1482
Contact: Mike Novakovic, Pres.
Telephone: 610-277-2444
Fax: 610-277-0135
Email: jethot@aol.com / URL:
Product Service Description:
Metallic ceramic, wire spray & header
coatings
Metal coating & allied services

Metalsoft, Inc.
2130 S. Yale St.
Santa Ana, CA 92704
Contact: Jeff Harig,
Telephone: 714-549-0112
Fax: 714-549-3949
Email: jeff@metalsoft.com / URL: http://
www.metalsoft.com
Product Service Description:
Sheetmetal fabrication software
Flat part, digitizing scanner

Metcoe Specialty Co Inc
PO Box 1011
Gardena, CA 90249-0011
Contact: Andre Sarai, Pres.
Telephone: 310-354-0030
Fax: 310-523-5805
Email: andre@metcoe.com / URL: http://
www.metcoe.com
Product Service Description:
Metal framed skylights, & specialty aluminum
products

Methods West Machine Tools
4645 S 36th Street
Phoenix, AZ 85040-2903
Contact: William E Ankrom, V-P.
Telephone: 602-437-2220
Fax: 602-437-2362
Email: crmmw@aol.com / URL: http://
www.methodswest.com
Product Service Description:
CNC machine tool sales, service and parts
stock
Engineering services and turnkey machining
systems
High-speed machining systems and
engineering
CNC wire and die-sinking EDM
Classroom and on-site operations training

Metrix Instrument Co.
1711 Townhurst Dr
Houston, TX 77043-2810
Contact: Steve Suarez, Sales Manager
Telephone: 713-461-2131
Fax: 713-461-8223
Email: ssuarez@metrix1.com / URL: http://
www.metrix1.com
Product Service Description:
Vibration analyzers, switches, monitors &
transducers
Relays & industrial controls
Electrical industrial apparatus
Electronic components
Measuring & controlling devices

Metron Solutions Inc
PO Box 1491
San Clemente, CA 92674-1491
Contact: John Giangardella, Pres.
Telephone: 949-366-0912
Fax: 949-492-8346
Email: metron@aol.com / URL:
Product Service Description:
Manufactures consumer electronic stop light
that signals where to park in the garage
Personal Security Devices

Metropolitan Graphics
4001 E Bell Rd # 114-497
Phoenix, AZ 85032-2242
Contact: Jennifer Patterson, Pres.
Telephone: 602-788-7332
Fax: 602-788-7325
URL: http://www.relocationinformation.net
Product Service Description:
Publishes yearly metropolitan relocation
guides for realtors / General public
Publishing_miscellaneous : Publishes
relocation guides for 20 major U.S. metro
areas

Mexpo International Inc
2671 Mccone Ave
Hayward, CA 94545-1603
Contact: Tim Thai, V-P., GM & Mktg.
Telephone: 510-293-6800
Fax: 510-293-9056
Email: mexpoglove@aol.com / URL: http://
www.mexpo-glove.com
Product Service Description:
Examination Gloves

Mexxon International
14781 Carmenita Rd.
Norwalk, CA 90650-5230
Contact: Mohammad Anwar, Owner
Telephone: 562-802-1533
Fax: 562-802-0753
Email: manwar487 / URL:
Product Service Description:
Wearing Apparel (used)

Mfm Sensors Inc
PO Box 88607
Steilacoom, WA 98388-0607
Contact: Gregory Baxter, Pres.
Telephone: 253-589-1912
Fax: 253-589-1340
Email: mfmsensorsinc@juno.com / URL:
Product Service Description:
Manufactures vehicle sensor systems

Micco Aircraft Co.
3100 Airmans Dr
Fort Pierce, FL 34946-9131
Contact: F.DeWitt Beckett,
Telephone: 561-465-9996
Fax: 561-465-9997
Product Service Description:
Aircraft

Michaels Of Oregon Co
PO Box 1690
Oregon City, OR 97045-0690
Contact: Dennis Pixton, CEO
Telephone: 503-557-0536
Fax: 503-655-7546
Email: info@uncle-mikes.com / URL: http://
www.uncle-mikes.com/
Product Service Description:
Manufactures hunting, shooting and law
enforcement accessories
Sporting & athletic goods
Manufacturing industries

Michels Machinery Co
1973 N Nellis Blvd. PMB 320
Las Vegas, NV 89115-3647
Contact: Jim Michels, Owner
Telephone: 702-459-9311
Fax: 702-459-9351
Email: jmichels@2kweb.net / URL: http://
www.michelsmachinery.com
Product Service Description:
Distributes construction and mining
machinery and equipment; cranes
Construction & mining machinery

Michigan Wheel Corporation
1501 Buchanan Ave., S.W.
Grand Rapids, MI 49507
Contact: Martin Ronis, V.P. Marketing &
Sales
Telephone: 616-452-6941
Fax: 616-247-0227
Email: info@miwheel.com / URL: http://
www.miwheel.com
Product Service Description:
Marine Propellers

**Michigan Wholesalers Automotive
Supply Co.**
100 N. Rose St., Suite 101
Mount Clemens, MI 48043-5405
Contact: John Busch,
Telephone: 810-469-9029
Fax: 810-469-9166
Email: j.busch5730@aol.com / URL:
Product Service Description:
Auto Parts Surplus

Micon Telecommunications Inc
142 N Milpitas Blvd Ste 309
Milpitas, CA 95035-4401
Contact: Evangelina Calderon, Pres.
Telephone: 510-661-0141
Fax: 510-661-0140
Email: pics@micon1.com / URL: http://
www.micontelecommunication.com
Product Service Description:
Manufactures telephone, telegraph and
interface equipment
Telephone & telegraph apparatus
Radio & TC Communications Equipment
Communications Equipment Installation
Removals
Toll Transmission
Communications Equipment
Telephone Communications Exc. Radio
Computer Programming Service
Computer Maintenance & Repair

Micro 100, Inc.
875 N. Virgil Ave.
Los Angeles, CA 90029
Contact: Remo Buhlmann, General Manager
Telephone: 213-668-0491
Fax: 213-668-0183
Email: / URL:
Product Service Description:
Carbide Cutting Tools

Micro Audiometrics Corp.
2200 S. Ridgewood Ave.
South Daytona, FL 32119
Contact: Jason Keller, President
Telephone: 904-788-9331
Fax: 904-788-9332
Email: Sales@microaud.com / URL: http://
www.microaud.com
Product Service Description:
Audiometers

Micro Carbide Corp
3169 E 36th St
Tucson, AZ 85713-5202
Contact: Bob Kaplan, President
Telephone: 520-624-4600
Fax: 520-624-0494
Product Service Description:
Manufactures solid carbide & PCD tipped
rotary cutting tools

Micro Communications, Inc.
P.O. Box 4365
Manchester, NH 03108
Contact: Dennis Heymans, Mamager
Broadcast Sales
Phone: 603-624-4351 / Fax: 603-624-4822
Email: dheymans@sprynet.com / URL: http://
www.mcibroadcast.com
Product Service Description:
Passive RF Components DTV, FM

Micro-Med, Inc.
4400 Breckenridge Ln Ste 413
Louisville, KY 40218-4082
Contact: Patrick D. Harris, Pres.
Telephone: 502-491-3880
Fax: 502-491-1259
Email: micromed@iglou.com / URL:
Product Service Description:
Pre-clinical, medical research & physiological
data acquisition equipment

Microcosm
1699 S 55th Ave
Chicago, IL 60804-1817
Contact: John Justice, Owner
Telephone: 708-656-3250
Fax: 708-656-6049
Email: amazinchem@aol.com / URL:
Product Service Description:
Pressure sensitive coatings
Paper coated & laminated

Microcurrent Research Inc
3810 E Desert Cove Ave
Phoenix, AZ 85028-3430
Contact: Darren Starwynn, President
Telephone: 602-494-5626
Fax: 602-953-0544
Email: info@eastwestmed.com / URL: http://
www.eastwestmed.com
Product Service Description:
Wholesales pain management devices and
medical equipment

Microflex, Inc.
PO Box 730068
Ormond Beach, FL 32173
Contact: Joseph Rushton,
Phone: 904-677-8100 / Fax: 904-672-7623
Email: info@microflexinc.com / URL: http://
www.microflexinc.com
Product Service Description:
Flexible metal hose, bellows & expansion
joint : Metal products_fabricated

Micromeritics Instrument Corp.
1 Micromeritics Dr
Norcross, GA 30093-1877
Contact: Dale Hiler, Ex. V-P., COO
Phone: 770-662-3633 / Fax: 770-662-3696
URL: http://www.micromeritics.com
Product Service Description:
Analytical instruments : Surface analysis
instruments & equipment & particle size &
density analyzers : Solid & envelope density
Electrozone sensing particle size counting &
sizing : On-line particle size analysis &
monitoring

Micronics, Inc.
200 West Rd
Portsmouth, NH 03801-5637
Contact: Barry Hibble, Pres.
Telephone: 603-433-1299
Fax: 603-433-6673
Email: info@micronicsinc.com / URL:
Product Service Description:
Filter media (CWTH)
Filter presses
Filter press plates
Industrial filtration service

Micropure Filtration, Inc.
1100 Game Farm Cir.
Mound, MN 55364-7900
Contact: Robert A. Pollmann, President
Telephone: 800-654-7873
Fax: 815-654-4194
Email: rap@micropure.com / URL:
Product Service Description:
Food Proc. Mach., Air Filters, Wholesale
Food Proc. Mach., Gas Filters, Wholesale
Auto. Sanitary Liq. Sampling Eq., Whsle.

Mid-Mountain Materials Inc
PO Box 80966, 7600 5th Avenue South
Seattle, WA 98108-0966
Contact: Jay R. Engelbrecht, VP
Telephone: 206-762-7600
Fax: 206-762-7694
Email: info@mid-mountain.com / jre@mid-
mountain.com / URL: http://www.mid-
mountain.com
Product Service Description:
Manufacturer of high-temperature-resistant
textiles; Coated textile products;
Fabricated or sewn, gasketing, seals, blankets
& curtains; High-temperature-resistant
insulations; Refractory specialties.

**Mid-South Electronics-Alabama,
Inc.**
PO Box 1308
Gadsden, AL 35902-1308
Contact: Jerry Sheldon, V-P., GM
Telephone: 256-492-8997
Fax: 256-492-0625
Email: jsheldon@mseal.com / URL: http://
www.midsouthindustries.com
Product Service Description:
Household appliances : Electronics
Contract Manufacturing
Plastic Injection Molding

Mid-West Instrument
6500 Dobry Dr.
Sterling Heights, MI 48314
Contact: Glenn Durrant, Sr. Sales Coordinator
Telephone: 810-254-6500
Fax: 810-254-6509
Email: sales@midwestinstrument.com / URL:
http://www.midwestinstrument.com
Product Service Description:
Indicating Pressure Switched
Switches : Averaging Pitot Tubes
Differential Pressure Gages
Instrument Valves / Manifolds

Midlab, Inc.
PO Box 720
Sweetwater, TN 37874-0720
Contact: Kevin Kirkland, Pres.
Telephone: 423-337-3180
Fax: 423-337-3369
Email: chrisg@midlab.com / URL: http://
www.midlab.com
Product Service Description:
Janitorial Cleaning Chemicals

Midland Bioproducts Corp.
PO Box 309
Boone, IA 50036-0309
Contact: Richard Harrington, Manager, Sales & Mktg.
Telephone: 515-432-7799
Fax: 515-432-7790
Email: midlandbio@opencominc.com / sales@midlandbioproducts.com / URL: http://www.midlandbioproducts.com
Product Service Description:
Immunodiagnostic products : Diagnostic substances: Polyclonal antibodies
Human serum calibrators : Contract manufacturing : Animal diagnostic products
Dairy calf diagnostic kits : Horse foal diagnostic kits : Bulk antiserum

Midland Machinery Co., Inc.
101 Cranbrook Ext.
Tonawanda, NY 14150
Contact: B.W. Blanks, Exec. V.P.
Telephone: 716-692-1200
Fax: 716-692-1206
Email: mmccoinc@aol.com / URL: http://www.midlandmachinery.com
Product Service Description:
Road construction & asphalt mixing equipment

Midland Steel Products Co.
PO Box 6386
Cleveland, OH 44101-1386
Contact: Bernard Baka, VP. Sales & Mktg.
Telephone: 216-281-3323
Fax: 216-651-7817
Email: bbaka@immsp.com / URL: http://www.immsp.com
Product Service Description:
Transportation equipment
Truck & bus chassis frames & components & heavy metal stampings

Midori America Corp
2555 E Chapman Ave Ste 40
Fullerton, CA 92831-3639
Contact: Terry Tsugawa, Pres.
Telephone: 714-449-0997
Fax: 714-449-0139
Product Service Description:
Manufactures sensors to measure rotary or linear position

Midwest Art Metal
PO Box 277
Edinburgh, IN 46124-0277
Contact: Fred Stadler, CEO
Telephone: 812-526-2666
Fax: 812-526-2695
Email: fstadler@mametal.com / URL: http://www.mametal.com
Product Service Description:
Metal Stamping, Nec Contract
Welded Steel Tubes
Fabricated Metal Products, Nec.

Midwest Builders Supply, Inc.
3430 W. Henderson Street
Chicago, IL 60618-5405
Contact: Lester Gizynski, Owner
Telephone: 773-279-9200
Fax: 773-478-9601
Product Service Description:
Ganite, Marble, Ceramic Tile, Vinyl Tile, hardwood flooring : Cut stone & stone products, stucco materials : Windows, glass blocks, highest noise reduction windows
Kitchen cabinets, countertops, bathrooms
Structural steel & color metal fabrication

Midwest Industries Inc.
701 W. Main St.
Meeker, OK 74855
Contact: Ross Coleman, GM,
Telephone: 405-279-2706
Fax: 405-279-2771
Email: okmagnet@aol.com / URL: http://www.magnets101.com
Product Service Description:
Magnets

Midwest International Standard Prod, Inc
105 Stover Rd
Charlevoix, MI 49720-1756
Contact: Ron Pair, Owner
Telephone: 616-547-4000
Fax: 616-547-9453
Email: midwest@freeway.net / URL: http://www.midwestmagic.com
Product Service Description:
Loading Spouts (for dust free loading)
Dust Collectors, Bin Vents : Gate Valves

Midwest Ohio Tool Company
P.O. Box 269 , 215 Tarhe Trail
Upper Sandusky, OH 43351-0269
Contact: F. David Gibson, Vice Pres. &GM
Telephone: 419/294-1987
Fax: 419-294-5433
Email: fdgibson@udata.com / URL:
Product Service Description:
Special Precision Metal Cutting Tools
Cutting Tools - Special
Boring Bars - Special
Tools - Special Cutting

Midwest Truck & Auto
4200 S. Morgan St.
Chicago, IL 60609-2517
Contact: Mark Chudacoff, President
Telephone: 312-225-1550
Fax: 312-225-1615
Product Service Description:
Automobile Gears
Steel Truck Parts
Automobile Related Parts

Mifran Boman Corp
8015 S Alameda St
Los Angeles, CA 90001-4107
Contact: Stanley J Grinstein, Pres.
Telephone: 323-587-5241
Fax: 323-587-4279
Email: bforklift / URL: http://www.bomanforklift.com
Product Service Description:
Trucks & tractors_industrial : Manufactures and distributes industrial forklifts

Migar Enterprises, Inc.
PO Box 315
Bloomingdale, IL 60108-0315
Contact: Michael garcia, President
Telephone: 630-980-3961
Fax: 630-980-4033
Product Service Description:
Freight Forwarding Intl Air/Ocean

Mil Bar Plastics Co
PO Box 51
Dana Point, CA 92629-0051
Contact: John A Murphy, Pres.
Telephone: 714-540-0366
Fax: 714-557-7680
Product Service Description:
Manufactures all types of plastic products and plastic military items
Plastic products, tool & die, metal stamping

Milco Industries, Inc.
PO Box 568
Bloomsburg, PA 17815-0568
Contact: Norman Belmonte, Pres.
Telephone: 570-784-0400
Fax: 570-387-8433
Email: / URL:
Product Service Description:
Ladies Sleepwear / Lingerie
Warp Knit Textile Products

Milcon, Inc.
555 Pond Dr
Wood Dale, IL 60191-1192
Contact: Terry Rizzo,
Telephone: 630-595-2366
Fax: 630-595-6579
Email: / URL: http://www.phoenixofchicago.com
Product Service Description:
Electronic connectors

Miles Label Company Inc
PO Box 36690
Tucson, AZ 85740-6690
Contact: Paul W Miles, Pres.
Telephone: 520-744-0696
Fax: 520-744-0262
Email: / URL: http://www.mileslabel.com
Product Service Description:
Paper coating and laminating; label manufacturing; business forms
Paper coated & laminated
Manifold business forms
Paper coated & laminated, packaging

Milford Stitching Co., Inc.
PO Box 353
Milford, DE 19963-0353
Contact: Herbert Konowitz, Pres., Fin., R & D, Sales & Mktg. Mgr.
Telephone: 302-422-8021
Fax: 302-422-7858
Email: ckonowitz@aol.com / URL:
Product Service Description:
Bedspreads & shower & window curtains - hotel - motel
Furnishings_house
Curtains & draperies

Milgard Manufacturing Co
PO box 11368
Tacoma, WA 98411-0368
Contact: Erik Barrett, Export Manager
Telephone: 253-922-6030
Fax: 253-922-2983
Email: exporters@milgard.com / URL: http://www.milgard.com
Product Service Description:
Residential & light commercial: Aluminum, vinyl & wood windows
Patio doors & skylights
Available in standard U.S. Sizes, custom or metric sizes.

Miller Ag-Renewal, Inc.
1710 N Airport Rd
Weatherford, OK 73096-3321
Contact: Weldon Miller, Pres.
Telephone: 580-772-7059
Fax: 580-772-6887
Email: ag-renewal@itlnet.net / URL: http://www.ag-renewal.com
Product Service Description:
Wildflower seed & grass seed harvester

Miller Corp., Harry
4th & Bristol Sts.
Philadelphia, PA 19140
Contact: Bruce Entwisle, President
Telephone: 215-324-4000
Fax: 215-324-1258
Email: harrymiller@nni.com / URL: http://www.harrymillercorp.com
Product Service Description:
Corrosion Inhibitors : Cleaners
Grinding Machine Lubricants
Pickling Inhibitors

Miller Design & Equipment
2231 Fortune Dr # C
San Jose, CA 95131-1806
Contact: Robert L Haapoja, Pres.
Telephone: 408-434-9544
Fax: 408-943-1491
Email: / URL:
Product Service Description:
Repairs & Remanufactures Silicon Wafer Probers , Manual - Automatic : Manufactures Manual Silicon Wafer Probe Stations & Probe Positioners : Manufactures Wafer Prober Controller Hardware & Software
Designs Parts & Associated Assemblies for Wafer Probers

Miller Machine
18171 Territorial Rd
Osseo, MN 55369-9293
Contact: Steven Miller, Pres., R & D Mgr.
Telephone: 612-428-2499
Fax: 612-428-4234
Email: millermachine@msn.com / URL:
Product Service Description:
General machining job shop

Miller Mill Co., Inc., T.R.
P.O. Box 708
Brewton, AL 36427-0708
Contact: Gordon W. Ahrens, *
Telephone: 205-867-4331
Product Service Description:
Utility Line Poles Wood

Milwaukee Electronics Corp.
PO Box 090920
Milwaukee, WI 53209
Contact: P. Michael Stoehr, Pres.
Telephone: 414-228-5000
Fax: 414-228-5501
Email: jscholler@mec-net.mhs.compuserve.com / URL:
Product Service Description:
Industrial electronic control modules
Test equipment & power supplies
Electronic automated conveyor controls

Minco Sales Corp.
1001 Franklin Ave.
Garden City, NY 11530
Contact: Joseph La Rocco, President
Telephone: 516-741-8755
Fax: 516-741-8764
Email: minco@mincosales.com / URL:
Product Service Description:
Mining Truck Parts
Drilling Steel & Accessories
Steel Plate, Channels & Bars
Oil Field Equipment
Pumps, Mining & Oilfeild
Pump and Compression Parts
Compression: Stationary & Portable
Trolley Mine Hardware
Bearings, Seals & Speed Reducers
Tools, Hardware, McMaster Care, Grainger

Minco Technology Labs, Inc.
1805 Rutherford Ln
Austin, TX 78754-5101
Contact: Susan Goodrich,
Telephone: 512-834-2022
Fax: 512-837-6285
Email: donp@mincotech.com / URL: http://
www.mincotech.com
Product Service Description:
Microchip packaging & opto products

Mini Golf, Inc.
202 Bridge Street
Jessup, PA 18434
Contact: Joseph J. Rogari, *
Telephone: 717/489-8623
Fax: 717-383-9970
Email: jrogari@epix.net / URL: http://
www.minigolfinc.com
Product Service Description:
Gen. Contractors, Miniature Golf Courses

Mini-Lace, Inc.
345 W 74th Pl
Hialeah, FL 33014-5024
Contact: Louis Sarmiento, Pres.
Telephone: 305-821-3300
Fax: 305-823-1021
Email: louisla@aol.com / URL: http://
www.minilace.com
Product Service Description:
Lace trimmings
Raschel Lace Allover, Nylon /Lycra

Minolta Corporation
101 Williams Dr.
Ramsey, NJ 07446-1293
Contact: Hiro Fujii, President & CEO
Telephone: 201-825-4000
Fax: 201-825-0870
Email: / URL:
Product Service Description:
Copiers
Cameras

Miracles Amusement
355 Kingsland Ave.
Brooklyn, NY 11222-1907
Contact: Nissim Amar, President
Telephone: 718-383-3939
Fax: 718-383-7899
Email: nissim@mindspring.com / URL: http://
www.miraclesamusements.com
Product Service Description:
Video games sales

Miss Scarlett Inc
PO Box 1488
Burlingame, CA 94011-1488
Contact: Peggy Luper, Pres.
Telephone: 650-340-9600
Fax: 650-340-9680
Email: / URL:
Product Service Description:
Manufactures fruits, vegetables and olives
Fruits & vegetables in glass jars
Salads, savorys, spreads
Fruits, Brandied

Mistco, Inc.
PO Box 694854
Miami, FL 33269-1854
Contact: Stuart Freides, Pres., Sales Mgr.
Telephone: 305-653-2003
Fax: 305-653-0733
Email: mistco@worldnet.att.net / URL: http://
www.mistco.com
Product Service Description:
Gift items & jewelry

Mitchell Daily Republic
PO Box 1288
Mitchell, SD 57301-7288
Contact: Noel Hamiel, Publisher
Telephone: 605-996-5514
Fax: 605-996-5020
Email: daily@mitchell.net / URL: http://
www.mitchellrepublic.com
Product Service Description:
Commercial printing
Printing_commercial

Mitronic Trading Corp
242 Route 109
Farmingdale, NY 11735
Contact: Robert J. Calzola, *
Telephone: 516-753-1670
Fax: 516-753-1676
Email: / URL:
Product Service Description:
Electronic Parts & Equipment
Hardware
Electrical Apparatus & Eq.,

Mitsubishi Electric Power Products, Inc.
512 Keystone Dr
Warrendale, PA 15086-7537
Contact: Jack Greaf, VP Marketing
Telephone: 724-772-2120
Fax: 724-772-2146
Email: Jack.Greaf@meppi.mea.com / URL:
http://www.meppi.com
Product Service Description:
Power circuit breakers- SF6
Gas Insulated Substations

Mity Lite
1301 W. 400, N.
Orem, UT 84057-4442
Contact: Greg Wilson, President
Telephone: 801-224-0589
Fax: 801-224-6191
Email: / URL: http://www.mitylite.com
Product Service Description:
Folding Tables

Mize & Co., Inc.
2020 N. Koch Indl. Ave.
Kingman, KS 67068
Contact: Max Mize, Pres.
Telephone: 316-532-3191
Fax: 316-532-2459
Email: / URL:
Product Service Description:
Motor vehicle parts & accessories
Automotive wire connectors

Mizell Brothers Company
99 Armour Dr. N.E.
Atlanta, GA 30324
Contact: Lonnie McCarron, President
Telephone: 404-875-9361
Fax: 404-607-8408
Email: mizellsales@mizellbros.com / URL:
Product Service Description:
Manufactures insulation for metal buildings
Plastic foam products

Mod-Tech, Inc.
PO Box 1220
Elm City, NC 27822-1220
Contact: Tony Inscore, Pres., CFO
Telephone: 252-236-3500
Fax: 252-236-3700
Email: tonyin@costalnet.com / URL:
Product Service Description:
Commercial household cabinets
Partitions & fixtures, wood

Modern Art Foundry, Inc.
1870 41st St
Long Island City, NY 11105-1025
Contact: Robert Spring, Pres.
Telephone: 718-728-2030
Fax: 718-267-0819
Email: info@modernartfoundry.com / URL:
http://www.modernartfoundry.com
Product Service Description:
Metal art castings & sculptures
Foundries_nonferrous

Modern Woodcrafts, Inc.
PO Box 464
Farmington, CT 06034-0464
Contact: Donald Ramsay, Pres.
Telephone: 860-677-7371
Fax: 860-676-8381
Email: pgs@modernwoodcrafts.com / URL:
http://www.modernwoodcraftsinc.com
Product Service Description:
Architectural millwork & wooden store
fixtures : Store & Office Interiors Decor
Showcases / Cashwraps / Gondolas
Louvered Doors Solid Woods
Restaurant Interiors / Fixtures
Hotels / Custom Furniture

Modified Polymer Components
1030 E Duane Ave Ste D
Sunnyvale, CA 94086-2624
Contact: James M Taylor, Pres.
Telephone: 408-733-8900
Fax: 408-733-8905
Email: modified@modifiedpolymer.com /
URL: http://www.modifiedpolymer.com
Product Service Description:
Manufactures custom components for medical
device and diagnostic industry
Surgical & medical instruments

Modular Components National, Inc.
PO Box 453
Forest Hill, MD 21050-0453
Contact: Irka Zazuliak, Pres.
Telephone: 410-879-6189
Fax: 410-838-7629
Email: modular@ari.net / URL: http://
www2.ari.net/modular
Product Service Description:
Printed circuit boards, soft substrates
(Tefelon)

Moeller Manufacturing Supply
805 E Cerritos Ave
Anaheim, CA 92805-6328
Contact: Ron H Moeller, Pres.
Telephone: 714-999-5551
Fax: 714-999-5970
Email: info@moellermfg.com / URL: http://
www.mollermfg.com
Product Service Description:
Metal stampings
Washers - shims - spacers
Fasteners

Mohawk International
P.O. Box 800, Industrial Blvd.
Chatsworth, GA 30705
Contact: Richard J. Burkemper,
Telephone: 706-695-9611, Ext. 1
Fax: 706-695-0507
Email: burkemr@alltel.net / URL: http://
www.mohawkind.com
Product Service Description:
Carpets

Mohawk Mfg. Corp.
25 Ridge Rd
Whitehouse Station, NJ 08889-3641
Contact: Bob O'Conner, GM
Telephone: 908-534-2148
Fax: 908-534-5045
Email: p.fitzgerald@mohawkmfg.net / URL:
http://www.mohawkmfg.net
Product Service Description:
Pressure Vessels
ASME Fabrication
Vessels: Stainless Steel
Piping: Pressure
Piping: Assembly

Mohnton Knitting Mills, Inc.
Front & Main Sts, PO Box 99
Mohnton, PA 19540-0099
Contact: Gary W. Pleam, President
Telephone: 215-777-7676
Fax: 215-777-0690
Email: mkm@talon.net / URL:
Product Service Description:
Mens & Boys Thermal Underwear
Mens & Boys T-Shirts

Mojave Granite Co Inc
1651 Miller Ave
Los Angeles, CA 90063-1612
Contact: Wayne Sangren, Pres.
Telephone: 323-268-3164
Fax: 323-268-1831
Email: / URL:
Product Service Description:
Manufactures granite surface plates, machine
bases and accessories; calibration service

Moldowan Lab Inc
PO Box 788
Philomath, OR 97370-0788
Contact: Merv Moldowan, Pres.
Telephone: 541-929-2455
Fax: 541-929-3473
Email: mlincorp@aol.com / URL:
Product Service Description:
Manufactures alcohol oxibase & alco-level - a
disposable test strip for alcohol detection

Molecu Wire Corporation
P.O. Box 495
Farmingdale, NJ 07727
Contact: Jack Stein, Vice Pres./Sales
Telephone: 732-938-9473
Fax: 732-938-3189
Email: infosales@molecu.com / URL:
Product Service Description:
Wire Products, Fine Diameter

Moli-Tron Company Inc.
85 South Union Blvd., #202
Lakewood, CO 80228
Contact: Arlen Gallagher, President
Telephone: 303/969-8888
Fax: 303-969-8110
Email: moli-tron@ix.netcom.com / URL:
http://www.molitron.com
Product Service Description:
Air Washers / Scrubbers / Grease & Particle
Extract
Air Pollution Control Equipment
Kitchen Exhaust Hoods, (Commercial)
Emission Control Wet Scrubbers

Molinos de Puerto Rico, Inc., A ConAgra Company
P.O. Box 364948
San Juan, PR 00936-4948
Contact: Manuel Orlando Herrera, President
Telephone: 787-793-1111
Fax: 787-781-7650
Email: info@molinospr.com / URL: http://www.molinospr.com
Product Service Description:
Bakery Flour
Cornmeal
Brewer's Grits
Snack Grits
Milled Corn
Commodities

Monahan Co., The Thomas
PO Box 250
Arcola, IL 61910-0250
Contact: Thomas F. Monahan Jr., Chrm., Pres., Mktg. Mgr.
Telephone: 217-268-4955
Fax: 217-268-3113
Email: / URL:
Product Service Description:
Broom, brush & mop handles, fibers & parts
Brooms & brushes

Monarch International Inc. Monarch Instrument Div.
15 Columbia Drive
Amherst, NH 03031-2334
Contact: Martin T. Morrissey, Sales Manager
Telephone: 603/883-3390
Fax: 603/886-3300
Email: sales@monarchinstrument.com / URL: http://www.monarchinstrument.com
Product Service Description:
Tachometers
Stroboscopes
Paperless Recorders
Vibration Meters

Monarchy International
PO Box 5517
South San Francisco, CA 94083-5517
Contact: C.C. Poon, Pres.
Telephone: 650-873-3055
Fax: 650-588-0335
Email: monarchy@earthlink.net / URL: http://www.monarchyaudio.com
Product Service Description:
Manufacturer of High-End Audio Amplifiers

Mondics/Greenhaw Insurance Agency
8235 Douglas Ave., #828
Dallas, TX 75225
Contact: Larry D. Greenhaw, Partner
Telephone: 214/739-4800
Fax: 214/987-1955
Email: larry@mondics-greenhaw.iix.com / URL: http://www2.iix.com/tx/mondics-greenhaw
Product Service Description:
Insurance Agent, Exim Bank Broker

Monin, Inc.
2100 Range Rd
Clearwater, FL 33765-2125
Contact: Olivier Monin, Pres.
Telephone: 727-461-3033
Fax: 727-441-3191
Email: monin-usa@monin.com / URL: http://www.monin.com
Product Service Description:
Fruit syrups
Tea Concentrates

Monroe Fluid Technology, Inc.
36 Draffin Rd
Hilton, NY 14468-9708
Contact: James E. Silloway, Chrm.
Telephone: 716-392-3434
Fax: 716-392-2691
Email: mksmft@ix.netcom.com / URL: http://www.monroefluid.com
Product Service Description:
Water-soluble metal working fluids, coolants & rust preventatives
Lubricating oils & greases

Montana Aromatics
3481 Balsam Root Dr
Stevensville, MT 59870-6749
Contact: Lori Johnson, Owner
Telephone: 406-777-3493
Email: aromatic@montana.com / URL:
Product Service Description:
Cultivates, dries and packages dried herbs and smudge sticks

Montana Essence Company
PO Box 1425
Hamilton, MT 59840-1425
Contact: John L Boland, Ptnr.
Telephone: 406-363-6957
Fax: 406-363-0441
Email: mtessenc@montana.com / URL: http://www.incensestore.com
Product Service Description:
Manufactures incense : Chemical preparations
Native American Goods : Aromatherapy
Fragrances

Monteverdi-Young Inc
12155 Mora Dr # 9
Santa Fe Springs, CA 90670-6040
Contact: Margaret Clarke, Mgr.
Telephone: 562-903-5678
Fax: 562-903-8436
Product Service Description:
Manufactures leather office and club chairs, love seats and sofas; cabinet work, executive wood desks

Montgomery Cabinetry Co., Inc.
2191 Dixie Ln
Alva, FL 33920-3611
Contact: Paul R. Montgomery, V.Pres., Fin., MIS, Opers. & R & D Mgr.
Telephone: 941-728-3320
Fax: 941-728-3517
Product Service Description:
Laminated & wooden cabinets
Kitchen cabinets_wood

Mooney Farms
1220 Fortress St
Chico, CA 95973-9029
Contact: MaryEllen Mooney,
Telephone: 530-899-2661
Fax: 530-899-7746
Email: www.mooneyfarm@aol.com / URL:
Product Service Description:
Manufactures sun-dried tomato products, sun-dried tomatoes in olive oil and sun dried tomato pesto

Moos Machine Works
685 Mapunapuna
Honolulu, HI 96819-2032
Contact: Moo Y Sung,
Telephone: 808-839-5633
Fax: 808-833-3542
Product Service Description:
Ind Hydraulic Equipment, Export
Industrial Valves, Export

Moran, J. F. Co., Inc.
P.O. Box 17070,
Smithfield, RI 02917
Contact: Philip A. Boscalia, Senior Vice President, Marketing
Telephone: 401-941-2670
Fax: 401-467-6280
Email: / URL:
Product Service Description:
Customs Broker, Freight Forwarder
Agents Worldwide, Air & Ocean
Boston, Jacksonville, Charleston, New York
Los Angeles, Houston, Chicago, Providence

Morgan Denver Sales Co
2045 W 8th Ave
Denver, CO 80204-3803
Contact: Russell Overgard, Pres.
Telephone: 303-623-3141
Fax: 303-623-5304
Email: rdhouse3@aol.com / URL:
Product Service Description:
Distributes industrial machinery and equipment
Tool & cutter grinders, manual, new & rebuild
Water tank manufacturing equipment, for 500-10,000 liter sizes, turnkey supplier

Morning Sun
PO Box 3488
Albuquerque, NM 87190-3488
Contact: Joseph Giorgi, Owner
Telephone: 505-884-3484
Fax: 505-883-6613
Email: / URL:
Product Service Description:
Sterling silver jewelry

Morrison Co., The D. C.
201 Johnson St., P.O. Box 586
Covington, KY 41011-1437
Contact: Henry E. Reder, President
Telephone: 606-581-7511
Fax: 606-581-9642
Email: rvbbs@juno.com / URL: http://www.dcmorrison.com
Product Service Description:
Milling Machinery
Machine Tools
Speed Lathes
Key Seaters

Morrison Construction Service
1990 Saint St.
Richland, WA 99352-2102
Contact: Paul Miles, President/CEO
Telephone: 509-375-1818
Fax: 509-375-1708
Email: paul@morrisoninc.com / URL: http://www.morrisoninc.com
Product Service Description:
Plumbing, Heating, Air-Conditioning
Structures and parts of structures, of iron or steel

Morrow Tech Industries
2150 W 6th Ave Ste B
Broomfield, CO 80020-7116
Contact: Collin Eidsness, Pres.
Telephone: 303-404-9353
Fax: 303-404-0385
Email: eidsness@morrowtech.com / URL: http://www.morrowtech.com
Product Service Description:
Manufactures robotic welding equipment for electronic packaging
Resistance Welding Equipment
Vacuum Ovens

Morse Starrett Products Company
184 Northwest 10th Street
Meridian, ID 83642
Contact: Sue Paul, Vice Pres./ Sales
Telephone: 208-888-7571
Fax: 208-888-2092
Email: sales@morse-starrett.com / URL: http://www.morse-starrett.com
Product Service Description:
Wire Rope Cutters

Morton International, Inc.
1500 Lathem St.
Batavia, IL 60510-1449
Contact: Gerald W. Kelly, VP, GM
Telephone: 630-879-6800
Fax: 630-761-0560
Email: / URL: http://www.morton.com
Product Service Description:
Paints & allied products
Industrial coatings

Morton Manufacturing
17341 Sierra Hwy
Canyon Country, CA 91351-1625
Contact: Yolanda Morton, CEO
Telephone: 805-298-0895
Fax: 805-298-1162
Email: / URL:
Product Service Description:
Aircraft Engine Bolts

Moser & Co. Neon Specialists
1940 Nw Miami Ct
Miami, FL 33136-1316
Contact: Steve Moser, Ptnr.
Telephone: 305-576-2990
Fax: 305-576-2991
Email: moserandco@aol.com / URL: http://www.neonspecialties.com
Product Service Description:
Neon signs & gift items
Signs & advertising specialties

Motoman, Inc (Mfr)
805 Liberty Lane
West Carrollton, OH 45449
Contact: Sally Fairchild, *
Telephone: 937-847-3300
Fax: 937-847-3288
Email: / URL: http://www.motoman.com
Product Service Description:
Special Industrial Machinery

Motorkote Inc
1386 E Clinton Trl
Charlotte, MI 48813-9387
Contact: David Persell, Pres.
Telephone: 517-543-3552
Fax: 517-543-3178
Email: / URL:
Product Service Description:
Chemical preparations / engine wear protector
Chemical preparations / fuel treatment
Petroleum products

Motorola Integrated Electronic Systems Sector
4000 Commercial Ave
Northbrook, IL 60062-1829
Contact: Joe Guglielmi, Ex. V-P & President
Telephone: 847-480-8000
Fax: 847-480-5486
Email: / URL: http://www.mot.com
Product Service Description:
Electronic modules & systems
Automotive computer, telecommunications, imaging & Mnaufacturing system electronics

Motortronics, Inc.
P.O. Box 17159
Clearwater, FL 34622-4268
Contact: Jim Mitchell, President
Telephone: 717-573-1900
Fax: 717-573-1803
Email: motroctrl@aol.com / URL: http://
www.motortronics.com
Product Service Description:
Solid State Motor Starters
SCR Power Controllers
Electronic Brakes
AC Drives
Medium Voltage Soft Starter

Mott Corp.
84 Spring Ln
Farmington, CT 06032-3142
Contact: Customer Service / Sales,
Telephone: 860-747-6333
Fax: 860-747-6739
Email: csc@mottcorp.com / URL: http://
www.mottcorp.com
Product Service Description:
Primary metal products
Industrial filters

Mouldings Unlimited, Inc.
PO Box 595
Cartersville, GA 30120-0595
Contact: Reid Dunn, Pres., Pur., Sales &
Mktg. Mgr.
Telephone: 770-383-8100
Fax: 770-383-8070
Email: / URL:
Product Service Description:
Wooden household furniture mouldings
Furniture_wood household

Moultrie Post Form, Inc.
PO Box 459
Moultrie, GA 31776-0459
Contact: Dale Wynn, Pres.
Telephone: 912-985-6655
Fax: 912-985-0693
Email: / URL:
Product Service Description:
Partitions & fixtures_wood
Countertops, furniture & cabinet doors
Upholstered parson chairs
Millwork

Mount Hope Machinery Co.
15 Fifth Street
Taunton, MA 02780
Contact: Carl V. Wertz, *
Telephone: 508/824-6994
Fax: 508-822-3962
Email: / URL:
Product Service Description:
Textile Machinery, Finishing
Rolls: Expander or Spreader Rolls
Chucks; Safety Chucks

Mount Olive Pickle Co., Inc.
Corner of Cucumber & Vine, PO Box 609
Mount Olive, NC 28365-0609
Contact: Larry H. Graham, Ex. V-P.
Telephone: 919-658-2535
Fax: 919-658-6296
Email: lgraham@mtolivepickles.com / URL:
http://www.mtolivepickles.com
Product Service Description:
Pickles
Peppers
Relish

Mount Sopris Instrument Co Inc
17301 W Colfax Ave Ste 255
Golden, CO 80401-4800
Contact: James L. LoCoco, Global Business
Development
Telephone: 303-279-3211
Fax: 303-279-2730
Email: sopris@rmii.com / URL: http://
www.mountsopris.com
Product Service Description:
Manufactures geophysical logging equipment;
data acquisition hardware and software

Mountain Meadows Pet Products
PO Box 778
Lewistown, MT 59457-0778
Contact: Lynda Turco, VP Sales
Telephone: 406-538-2544
Fax: 406-538-2545
Email: mmeadows@tein.net / URL: http://
www.mtnmeadowspet.com
Product Service Description:
Pet Products, Manufactures pellet grass fiber
animal litter and bedding

Mounting Systems Inc
11520 E Germann Rd
Chandler, AZ 85249-1305
Contact: Phil Tancredi, Ptnr.
Telephone: 602-917-9043
Fax: 602-917-9045
Email: / URL:
Product Service Description:
Manufactures steel TV and security camera
mounts
Hardware

Movement Control, Inc.
2900 Bristol Street, Suite B-104
Costa Mesa, CA 92626 USA
Contact: J. Peter Cunliffe, *
Telephone: 714-557-9980
Product Service Description:
Transport Systems Engineering & Forensics

Mowrey Elevator Company Inc
3300 Sw 50th Avenue
Davie, FL 33314
Contact: Victor m. Taveras, Int'l, Sales
Manager
Telephone: 954-581-8900
Fax: 954-583-1119
Email: mowrey@gate.net / URL: http://
www.mowreyelevator.com
Product Service Description:
Hydraulic & Traction Elevators
Residential Elevators

Mr. V's, Inc.
6109 Wheatland Rd
Catonsville, MD 21228-2763
Contact: F. Viscardi, Pres.
Telephone: 410-747-5886
Fax:
Email: mail@indestructablehose.com / URL:
http://www.indestructablehose.com
Product Service Description:
Fishing lures

Mrs. Cubbison's Foods
1325 Peerless Way
Montebello, CA 90640-6725
Contact: Woody Coale
Telephone: 213-727-9363
Fax: 213-727-0257
Email: / URL:
Product Service Description:
Poultry Stuffing Mix
Salad Croutons

**Mueller Steam Specialty Co., A
United Dominion Co., Fluid Central
Div.**
1491 NC Hwy 20 West
St. Pauls, NC 28384
Contact: Paul Bowler, President, *
Telephone: 910-865-8241
Fax: 910-865-8245
Email: mueller.steam.specialty@industry.net /
URL:
Product Service Description:
Pipeline Strainers
Check Valves
Butterfly Valves
Duplex Strainers
Gas Separators
Liquid Separator

Mullen Circle Brand, Inc.
3514 W Touhy Ave
Chicago, IL 60645-2718
Contact: Shirley R. Reed, Pres.
Telephone: 847-676-1880
Fax: 847-676-3748
Email: mullenoil@aol.com / URL:
Product Service Description:
Industrial lubricants
Lubricating oils & greases

Muller Studios
59 Rindge Rd
Stafford Springs, CT 06076-4820
Contact: Clyde Muller, Pres., GM
Telephone: 860-974-2161
Fax: 860-974-1396
Email: / URL:
Product Service Description:
Interior & exterior signs
Signs & advertising specialties
Pneumatic Hand Tools

**MultiSpiro, Inc. / Creative
Biomedics**
934 Calle Negocio, Suite E
San Clemente, CA 92673-6210
Contact: Daniel Brown, Pres.
Telephone: 949-366-0110 / 949-366-2300
Fax: 949-366-0115 / 949-366-2400
Email: admin-co@multispiro.com / URL:
http://www.multispiro.com
Product Service Description:
Medical equipment, pulmonary testing
devices
Spirometers & related accessories

Multimedia, Inc.
7061 Grand National Dr. Ste 127
Orlando, FL 32819-8377
Contact: Fernando Mariano, President
Telephone: 407-903-5000
Fax: 407-363-9809
Email: adsales@multimediausa.com / URL:
http://www.multimediausa.com
Product Service Description:
Newspaper Advertising Representative

Multiplex Technology Inc
3001 Enterprise St
Brea, CA 92821-6213
Contact: Peter Schwartz, Marketing
Telephone: 714-996-4100
Fax: 714-996-4900
Email: inquirys@channelplus.com / URL:
http://www.channelplus.com
Product Service Description:
Manufactures communications equipment &
video distribution systems

Multiquip
18910 S. Wilmington Ave.
Carson, CA 90746-2820
Contact: Irving M Levine,
President
Telephone: 310-537-3700
Fax: 310-537-3927
Email: mq@multiquip.com / URL: http://
www.multiquip.com
Product Service Description:
Construction and Mining Machinery
Spark-ignition reciprocating or rotary internal
combustion piston engines

Municipal Equipment Exports
11580 Seaboard Cir.
Stanton, CA 90680-3407
Contact: Neil McDowell, President
Telephone: 714-898-4830
Fax: 714-897-2810
Email: tools@flexmax.com / URL: http://
www.flexmax.com
Product Service Description:
Sewer & drain cleaning & maintenance
equipment

Murray, Thomas W.
309 Lotus St.
Dover, DE 19901-4461
Contact: Thomas W. Murray, Jr., Owner
Telephone: 302-736-1790
Fax: 302-974-8230
Email: murco@dmv.com / URL:
Product Service Description:
Trucks & Parts

Music Unlimited Inc
PO Box 68
Hot Sulphur Springs, CO 80451-0068
Contact: Joyce Ackerson, Pres.
Telephone: 970-725-3392
Fax: 970-725-3392 *51
Email: organmusic@rkymtnhi.com / URL:
http://www.rkymtnhi.com
Product Service Description:
Produces and markets CDs of traditional and
classical wedding music

Mustang Auto Sales
727 El Cajon Blvd.
El Cajon, CA 92020-4905
Contact: Gary Gunter, Owner
Telephone: 619-440-3673 / 800-44mustang
Fax: 619-440-1969
Email: sales@mustangauto.com / URL:
Product Service Description:
Used and Antique Car Dealers
Passenger motor vehicles
Mustang Parts - New & Used
Mustang Restoration
Mustang Auto Sales
Mustang Service

Mustang Industrial Equipment
7607 Wallisville Rd.
Houston, TX 77020-3699
Contact: Mark Slator, Vice President
Telephone: 713-675-1552
Fax:
Email: / URL: http://www.mustangcat.com
Product Service Description:
Special Trade Contractors, NEC
Fork-lift trucks; Other works trucks with lifts

My Bed, Inc.
1527 Mound Rd
Rockdale, IL 60436-2841
Contact: Frank G. Cavazos, Pres.
Telephone: 815-744-0190
Fax: 815-744-0192
Email: / URL: http://www.mybed.com
Product Service Description:
Mattresses & bedsprings
Furnishings_house

My-Tana Mfg. Co., Inc.
534 Selby Ave
Saint Paul, MN 55102-1729
Contact: J. Donaidson, Pres.
Telephone: 651-222-1738
Fax: 651-222-1739
Email: mytana@skypoint.com / URL:
Product Service Description:
Sewer & sink cleaning machines

Myers Engineering Inc. (Mfr)
8376 Salt Lake Avenue
Bell, CA 90201
Contact: Ron Tymins, Sales Manager
Telephone: 323-560-4723
Fax: 323-771-7789
Email: sales@myersmixer.com / URL:
Product Service Description:
Industrial Mixers & Dispersers

Myers Industries, Inc., Myers Tire Supply Div.
P.O. Box 1029
Akron, OH 44309-1029
Contact: Stephen E. Myers, President
Telephone: 330-253-5592
Fax: 330-761-6226
Email: sales@myersinternational.com / URL:
http://www.myerstiresupply.com
Product Service Description:
Adhesives : Tire Repair Materials
Curing Tubes: Tools : Tire Making Machinery
Parts : Machinery Parts : Automobile Parts

Myricom Inc
325 N Santa Anita Ave
Arcadia, CA 91006-2870
Contact: Charles Seitz, President & CEO
Telephone: 626-821-5555
Fax: 626-821-5316
Email: / URL: http://www.myri.com
Product Service Description:
Computer peripheral equipment
Manufactures computer networking hardware

Myro, Inc.
8440 N. 87th St.
Milwaukee, WI 53224
Contact: Dennis Jacobson, Int'l Sales Mgr.
Telephone: 414-354-3678
Fax: 414-354-3618
Email: myroinc@mixcom.com / URL:
Product Service Description:
Adhesives & Sealants

Myron L Company
6115 Corte Del Cedro
Carlsbad, CA 92009-1516
Contact: Carol S. Solinger, Dir. of Marketing
Telephone: 760-438-2021
Fax: 760-931-9189
Email: / URL: http://www.myronl.com
Product Service Description:
Manufactures conductivity monitors and
conductivity meters: Process control
instruments : Measuring instruments ph, orp,
temperature, resistivity : Manufactures
resistivity monitors

N G K Metals Corp.
Tuckerton Road, PO Box 13367
Reading, PA 19612-3367
Contact: Y. Josh Niwa, Pres.
Phone: 610-921-5000 / Fax: 610-921-5358
Email: marketing@ngkmetals.com / URL:
Product Service Description:
Beryllium alloys
Nonferrous rolling & drawing

N W L Capacitors
PO Box 97
Snow Hill, NC 28580-0097
Contact: Robert Seitz, Pres.
Phone: 252-747-5943 / Fax: 252-747-8979
Email: flcaps@nwl.com / URL:
Product Service Description:
Capacitors : Electronic Capacitors
High Voltage Capacitors
Water Cooled Capacitors

N-Con Systems Co., Inc.
PO Box 809
Crawford, GA 30630-0809
Contact: Martha I. Beach, Pres.
Phone: 706-743-8110 / Fax: 706-743-8114
Email: nconsys@n-con.com / URL: http://
www.n-con.com
Product Service Description:
Water quality monitoring & control systems
Process control instruments

N. E. W. Plastics Corp.
PO Box 480
Luxemburg, WI 54217-0220
Contact: Irvin G. Vincent, Pres., CEO, CFO
Phone: 920-845-2326 / Fax: 920-845-2439
Email: renew@dct.com / URL: http://
www.renewplastics.com
Product Service Description:
Plastic containers, blow molded parts &
extrusion, recycled plastic lumber & sheeting
Plastic products

N. Wood Counter Laboratory, Inc.
P.O. Box 2509
Chesterton, IN 46304
Contact: Marjory Wood Crawford, Director
Telephone: 219-926-3571
Fax: 219-926-3571
Email: marge@nwooddetectors.com / URL:
http://www.nwooddetectors.com
Product Service Description:
Nuclear Radiation Detection Instruments

NAPA Pipe Corporation
1025 Kaiser Rd
Napa, CA 94558-6257
Contact: Larry Lawrence, V-P.
Phone: 707-257-5000 / Fax: 707-257-5137
Email: / URL: http://www.napapipe.com
Product Service Description:
Blast furnaces & steel mills
Steel pipe & tubes

NAPP Systems Inc
260 S Pacific
San Marcos, CA 92069-2430
Contact: Kai Wenk-Wolff, Pres.& COO
Phone: 760-510-6277 / Fax: 760-489-1853
Email: info@nappsystems.com / URL: http://
www.nappsystems.com
Product Service Description:
Manufactures & distributes photopolymer
printing plates: Platemaking services
Industrial machinery & equipment
Manufacture metal decorating plate
Manufacture coating plate & equipment

NJM/CLI Packaging Systems International
56 Etna Rd
Lebanon, NH 03766-1446
Contact: Robert Van Rootselaar, Dir. Int'l
Sales
Telephone: 603-448-0300
Fax: 603-448-4810
Email: rvrbc@compuserve.com / URL: http://
www.njmcli.com
Product Service Description:
Pressure Sensitive Labeling Machinery
Cold Glue, Labeling Equipment
Thermo-Sensitive Labeling Equipment
Tablet Counters : Cappers (Inline)
Cottoners : Complete Packaging Lines
Unscramblers : Neck Banders

NSI Communications Inc.
30915 18th Ave S # C
Federal Way, WA 98003-4907
Contact: Yuri Sushkin, Pres.
Telephone: 253-946-2426
Fax: 253-946-8311
Email: info@nsiradio.com / URL: http://
www.nsiradio.com
Product Service Description:
Export agent and distributor for ICOM,
Kenwood, Vaesu and Motorola

NVF Company (Mfr)
P.O. Box 68 / 1166 Yorklyn Rd.
Yorklyn, DE 19736
Contact: Edward Slavin, V.P. Sales & Mktg.
Telephone: 302-239-5281
Fax: 302-239-4323
Email: nvf@nvf.com / URL: http://
www.nvf.com
Product Service Description:
Thermoset composite laminates
Fiber Glass Reinforced Polyester
Vulcanized Fibre Sheets & Rods

Nabi
5800 Park of Commerce Boulevard NW
Boca Raton, FL 33487
Contact: David Muth, Senior Vice President,
Business Operations
Telephone: 561-989-5800
Fax: 561-989-5899
Web site: URL: http://www.nabi.com
Product Service Description:
Antibody Products - Non Specific Antibodies;
Specialty Antibodies : Pharmaceuticals
WinRho SDF™ Autoplex ® T, Nabi-HB™

Nabolom Bakery
2708 Russell St
Berkeley, CA 94705-2318
Contact: Elise Lee, CEO
Telephone: 510-845-2253
Product Service Description:
Manufactures bread and bakery products,
specializing in cheese danish and danish
pastries : Bread, cake & related products

Nacco Grow More
15600 New Century Dr
Gardena, CA 90248-2129
Contact: John F Atwill, Pres., CEO
Telephone: 310-515-1700
Fax: 310-515-4937
Product Service Description:
Manufactures photographic specialties, foliar
fertilizers, chelated micronutrients,
combustion catalysts : Photographic
equipment & supplies : Agricultural chemicals
Cyclic crudes & intermediates : Fertilizers,
mixing only

Nameplates, Inc.
PO Box 4608
Tulsa, OK 74159-0608
Contact: Claudia C. Hamilton, Pres.
Telephone: 918-584-2651
Fax: 918-561-8711
Email: claudia@name-plates.com / URL:
http://www.name-plates.com
Product Service Description:
Metal name plates & decals
Signs & advertising specialties

Napp Technologies
P.O. Box 893
Saddle Brook, NJ 07663-5312
Contact: Thomas A. Smith, Director
Telephone: 201-843-4664
Fax: 201-843-4737
Email: / URL: http://www.napptech.com
Product Service Description:
Active Pharmaceutical Ingredients
Pharmaceuticals

Nasco, Inc.
PO Box 2420
Waterbury, CT 06722-2420
Contact: George Strobel, Pres., Mark
Southland, GM / Richard Strobel, Sales
Telephone: 203-574-1998
Fax: 203-757-0369
Email: mark@nascoslitting.com / URL: http://
www.nascoslitting.com
Product Service Description:
Toll slitting services
All alloys & plastic in the form of strip

Nassau Tape & Webbing Mills, Inc.
P.O. Box 39
Alamance, NC 27201-0039
Contact: Alan Thoenen, President
Telephone: 910-570-0091
Fax: 910-570-0680
Product Service Description:
Mattress Tape
High Quality Mattress Ticking

National Alum Corp.
PO Box 2529
Kingsland, GA 31548-2529
Contact: Robert Garza, Plt. Mgr.
Telephone: 912-729-6524
Fax: 912-729-6524
Product Service Description:
Aluminum sulfate : Chemicals_industrial
inorganic : Polymers

National Art Publishing Corp.
11000 Metro Pkwy Ste 32
Fort Myers, FL 33912-1244
Contact: David H. Boshart, Pres
Telephone: 941-939-7518
Fax: 941-936-2788
Email: art@artlithos.com / URL: http://
www.artlithos.com
Product Service Description:
Wildlife lithographic prints, stamps,
medallions & sculptures : Lithographic
printing_commercial : Posters

National Can Manufacturing Inc
535 W Walnut Ave
Orange, CA 92868-2232
Contact: Rande Hirschfield, Pres.
Telephone: 714-288-8410
Fax: 714-288-8415
Product Service Description:
Manufactures hats, caps and millinery
Hats, caps & millinery
Wallets & accessories

National Commercial Envelope Co.
US Route 30 Stewart Road
Chester, WV 26034
Contact: William A. Gray, Sales
Representative
Telephone: 800-627-9900
Fax: 304-387-5266
Email: / URL:
Product Service Description:
Microfiche Envelopes

National Compressor Exchange, Inc.
1856 Troutman St.
Ridgewood, NY 11385-1061
Contact: Richard Staiano, President
Telephone: 718-417-9100
Fax: 718-821-7032
Email: / URL:
Product Service Description:
Air Conditioner & Refrigeration Compressors
& Parts

National Contract Furnishings
3034 S 38th St
Phoenix, AZ 85040-1613
Contact: Robert Nudel, Pres.
Telephone: 602-470-0770
Fax: 602-470-0435
Email: / URL:
Product Service Description:
Manufactures upholstered wood furniture for
the home, office, motel and health care
Furniture_upholstered household
Furniture

National Copper Products
415 E. Prairie Ronde St.
Dowagiac, MI 49047-1348
Contact: Ken Harrington, Manager
Telephone: 616-782-2141
Fax:
Email: / URL:
Product Service Description:
Copper Rolling and Drawing
Tubes and pipes of refined copper
Parts of refrigeration or freezing equipment
and heat pumps
Articles of copper

**National Customs Brokers &
Forwarders Association of America**
1200 18th Street NW, SUite 901
Washington, NY DC
Contact: Eric Scharf, *
Telephone: 202-466-0222
Fax: 202-466-0226
Email: Staff@ncbfaa.org/ncbfaa / URL: http://
www.ncbfaa.org/ncbfaa
Product Service Description:
Online membership Directory

National Electric Gate Co.
PO Box 706
Pooler, GA 31322-0706
Contact: Ron Sass, Pres.
Telephone: 912-748-5090
Fax: 912-748-7542
Email: negate1@worldnet.att.net / URL:
Product Service Description:
Railroad crossing gate arms
Railroad equipment
Communications equipment, nec
Bondstrand / trackwire
Articulated gate arms
Conversion brakets - breakaway
LED Lights
New gate / saver breakaways
New easy gate light assembly's
Insulated tools - osha approved

National Embroidery Services
3390 E Main Rd
Portsmouth, RI 02871-4240
Contact: Dale Wood, Pres.
Phone: 401-683-4724 / Fax: 401-683-0012
Email: dwood243@aol.com / URL:
Product Service Description:
Sportwear, Embroidery
Advertising Specialties

National Flight Sales Corporation
402 Reo Street, Suite 201
Tampa, Fl 33609
Contact: Donald Snow, Vice President
Telephone: 813-282-8180
Fax: 813-282-8366
Email: nfsc123@aol.com / URL:
Product Service Description:
Aviation - Gas Turbine Engine Overhaul;
Garrett TPE331, T-76 ; Aviation - Turbine
Engine Components; Garrett TPE331
Aviation - Fuel Nozzles; TFE331, PW100,
LTS101 : Aviation - Engine Lube/Scav
Pumps; TFE731, ALF502, CF34, LTS101
Aviation - Engine Lube/Scav Pumps; CT-7,
AE3007, ALF502/LF507 : Helicopter - Main
Rotor Transmission Pumps; B205, B214,
B222, B205 : Helicopter - Main Rotor
Transmission Pumps; B212, B412, B230
Aircraft - Hydraulic Pumps; Lear, Westwind,
Hawker, Citation, Falcon : Aircraft -
Hydraulic Pumps; Canadair Challenger,
Gulfstream, Bell, Sikorsky

National Health Care, Inc.
12648 N 57th St
Scottsdale, AZ 85254-4334
Contact: Yadi Rezvani, Pres.
Telephone: 602-998-2659
Fax: 602-998-0212
Email: nhcp@msn.com / URL:
Product Service Description:
Wholesale gauze sponges, bandages & other
surgical dressings
Medical & hospital equipment & supplies

National Ink
10870 Hartley Rd, Suite A
Santee, CA 92071-2802
Contact: Saul Heiman, Pres.
Phone: 619-449-1035 / Fax: 619-449-7528
Email: natinkinc@aol.com / URL: http://
www.national-ink.com
Product Service Description:
Produces inks for writing and marking
instruments : Chemical preparations

National Pen Corp.
342 Shelbyville Mills Rd
Shelbyville, TN 37161-0001
Contact: Mary Hart, Sales Mgr.
Phone: 931-684-6677 / Fax: 931-684-8325
Email: mhart@pens.com / URL: http://
www.pens.com
Product Service Description:
Lead pencils & art goods
Markers, ball point pens & imprinted pencils

National Pen Corporation
16885 Via Del Campo Ct Ste 100
San Diego, CA 92127-1700
Contact: Bill Hanna, V-P.
Phone: 619-675-3000 / Fax: 619-675-0890
URL: http://www.pens.com
Product Service Description:
Signs & advertising specialties
Manufactures advertising, specialty products
and plastic molding : Plastic products
Pens & mechanical pencils

National Plastic Printing, Inc.
130 Furler St
Totowa, NJ 07512-1825
Contact: Kenneth D. Ullman, Pres.
Telephone: 973-785-0828
Fax: 973-785-1710
Email: npp@pop.cybernex.net / URL: http://
www.npp-inc.com
Product Service Description:
Printing_commercial
Printed plastic cards
Plastic Printing

National Pump
7600 W. Olive Ave.
Peoria, AZ 83543
Contact: Brian Sullivan, Sales Mgr.
Telephone: 623-979-3560
Fax: 623-979-2177
Email: npcaz@worldnet.att.net / URL:
Product Service Description:
Vertical turbine, lineshaft & submersible
pumps

National Research & Chemical Co.
15600 New Century Dr.
Gardena, CA 90248-2140
Contact: Stephanie Atwill, President
Telephone: 310-515-1700
Fax: 310-527-4963
Email: nacco2@aol.com / URL: http://
www.earthsafe.net
Product Service Description:
Photographic Equipment and Supplies
Coatings, Protective
Chemicals, Cleaners (non-toxic,
biodegradable)

National Seal Co.
1245 Corporate Blvd Ste
Aurora, IL 60504-6407
Contact: Larry Lydick,
Telephone: 630-898-1161
Fax: 630-898-6556
Email: ncs@nationalseal.com / URL: http://
www.nationalseal.com
Product Service Description:
Plastic landfill lining materials

National Stabilizers Inc
1846 Business Center Dr
Duarte, CA 91010-2901
Contact: Robert C Burger, Pres.
Telephone: 626-359-4584
Product Service Description:
Manufactures, distributes and sells stabilizers
for ice cream manufacturers

National Standard Parts Assocs. Inc.
4400 Mobile Hwy
Pensacola, FL 32506-4210
Contact: Albert Graf, Chrm., Pres.
Telephone: 850-456-5771
Fax: 850-456-5376
Email: nspa@nationalstandardparts.com /
URL: http://www.nationalstandardparts.com
Product Service Description:
Electrical terminals
Current-carrying wiring devices

National Wire & Cable Corp
136 N San Fernando Rd
Los Angeles, CA 90031-1726
Contact: A.J. Evangelista, President & CEO
Telephone: 323-225-5611
Fax: 323-225-4630
Email: / URL: http://www.nationalwire.com
Product Service Description:
Manufacturers of Electronic Wire & Cable

Nationwide Equipment
11950 New Kings Rd.
Jacksonville, FL 32219
Contact: Ed Kostenski, Owner
Telephone: 904-924-2500
Fax: 904-924-2525
Email: sales@nwe-usa.com / URL: http://
www.nationwideequipment.com
Product Service Description:
Construction and Mining Machinery
Mechanical shovels, excavators and shovel
loaders, self-propelled : Bulldozers and
angledozers, self-propelled, other than track
laying

Nationwide Graphics, Inc.
6930 W 62nd St
Chicago, IL 60638-3934
Contact: Bruce Matuszak, Secy.
Telephone: 773-586-4858
Fax: 773-586-4921
Product Service Description:
Auxiliary printing equipment & rebuilt
printing presses : Printing trades machinery

Nationwide Retail Interiors Inc
2155 E Jones Ave
Phoenix, AZ 85040-1482
Contact: Charles Shaughnessy, Pres.
Telephone: 602-268-2810
Fax: 602-268-2576
Email: / URL: http://www.natwide.com
Product Service Description:
Manufactures slatwall, knockdown store
fixtures & shelving

Natra US Inc.
2801 Ponce de Leon Blvd., Ste. 1070
Coral Gables, FL 33134
Contact: Elpido De La Teja, Tech.1 Sales Mgr
Telephone: 305-447-8999
Fax: 305-447-0885
Email: natraus@msn.com / URL:
Product Service Description:
Cocoa Powder & Cocoa Butter,
Caffeine, Tolopheroe, Color Extract

Natural Choice Foods
PO Box 1029
Denver, CO 80237-0122
Contact: Jeffrey J Diehl, Pres.
Telephone: 303-750-2600
Fax: 303-750-0207
Email: / URL: http://www.ncfinc.com
Product Service Description:
Organic sorbets, soups & finished food
products

Natural Life Pet Products
PO Box 943
Frontenac, KS 66763-0943
Contact: Patrick Mendicki, Brand Manager
Telephone: 316-231-7711
Fax: 316-231-0071
Email: natlife@mail.fament.com / URL: http:/
/www.fament.com/natlife
Product Service Description:
Pet food : Dog & cat food

Natural Line
PO Box 3508
Montgomery, AL 36109-0508
Contact: Deland Wylie, GM
Telephone: 334-272-2140
Fax: 334-272-0299
Email: deland@caffco.com / URL:
Product Service Description:
Polyurethane statues, urns & pots
Misc. Dried products & fall oak leaves

Natural Line - Div of CCC
PO Box 3508
Montgomery, AL 36109-0508
Contact: Deland Wylie, GM
Telephone: 334-272-2140
Fax: 334-277-6023
Email: / URL:
Product Service Description:
Polyurethane indoor/outdoor containers

Nature Plus, Inc.
555 Lordship Blvd
Stratford, CT 06497-7156
Contact: Sheldon Murphy, Pres.
Telephone: 203-380-0316
Fax: 203-380-0358
Email: info@nature-plus.com / URL: http://
www.nature-plus.com
Product Service Description:
Soil Stabilization
Enzyme Cleaners
Odor Eliminators

Naugatuck Glass Company, The
P.O. Box 71
Naugatuck, CT 06770
Contact: Peter T. Racevicius, *
Telephone: 203/729-5227
Fax: 203/729-8781
Email: p.racevicius@naugatuckglass.com /
URL: http://www.naugatuckglass.com
Product Service Description:
Glass, Flat

Nauticon, Inc.
PO Box 389
Cibolo, TX 78108-0389
Contact: George C. Briley, Pres.
Telephone: 210-658-5602
Fax: 210-658-5675
Email: nauticon@powercold.com / URL:
http://www.powercold.com
Product Service Description:
Evaporative condensers & fluid coolers
Refrigeration equipment

Nav-X Corp.
1386 W Mcnab Rd
Fort Lauderdale, FL 33309-1120
Contact: Brian Sheehan, Sales & Mktg. Mgr.
Telephone: 954-978-9988
Fax: 954-974-5378
Email: info@fortressanchors.com / URL:
http://www.fortressanchors.com
Product Service Description:
Aluminum boat anchors

Nedco Conveyor Technology Corp.
967 Lehigh Ave
Union, NJ 07083-7632
Contact: Curtis Tarlton, Pres.
Telephone: 908-964-9600
Fax: 908-964-9411
Email: nedconvey@aol.com / URL: http://
www.nedcoconveyor.com
Product Service Description:
Conveyors & bucket elevators

Neighborhood Electric Vehicle Co
PO Box 11319
Eugene, OR 97440-3519
Contact: Carl Watkins, Sales & Mktg. Mgr.
Telephone: 541-687-5939
Fax: 541-343-6610
Email: gizmo@nevco.com / URL: http://
www.nevco.com
Product Service Description:
Manufactures electric vehicles
Transportation equipment

Neil Laboratories, Inc.
PO Box 1088
Hightstown, NJ 08520-1088
Contact: Bharat Patel, Chrm., Pres.
Telephone: 609-448-5500
Fax: 609-443-9316
Email: neillabs@aol.com / URL:
Product Service Description:
Pharmaceuticals
Pharmaceutical preparations

Neil Langdon Inglis
4998 Battery Lane, #502
Bethesda, MD 20814
Contact: Neil Langdon Inglis, *
Telephone: 301-718-9326
Product Service Description:
Translation Service:

Nell Joy Industries, Inc.
8 Reith St
Copiague, NY 11726-1414
Contact: Benenati Emilio, CEO
Telephone: 516-842-8989
Fax: 516-842-8040
Email: info@nelljoy.com / URL: http://
www.nelljoy.com
Product Service Description:
Aircraft parts & equipment

Nellie & Joe's, Inc.
PO Box 2368
Key West, FL 33045-2368
Contact: Rod Millar, Pres.
Telephone: 305-296-5566
Fax: 305-293-8838
Email: limepie@mindspring.com / URL:
http://www.keylimejuice.com
Product Service Description:
Salad dressings & lime juice & lemon juice

Nelson Aircraft Corp.
420 Harbour Drive
Naples, FL 34103-4010
Contact: Charles Rhoades, President
Telephone: 941-263-1670
Fax: 941-261-8345
Email: / URL:
Product Service Description:
Aircraft Engines & Engine Parts, FAA
Certified Small HP (48-60 HP)

Nelson Products Co.
PO Box 390
Sioux Rapids, IA 50585-0390
Contact: Alan Hulsebus, Fin., GM, Mktg. &
Pur. Mgr.
Telephone: 712-283-2562
Fax: 712-283-2950
Email: / URL:
Product Service Description:
Farm machinery & equipment
Sheet metal work
Plastic bottles
Lawn & garden equipment

Neogen Corp.
620 Lester Place
Lansing, MI 48912
Contact: ,
Telephone: 517-372-9200
Fax: 517-372-0108
Email: neogen-info@neogen.com / URL:
http://www.neogen.com
Product Service Description:
Measuring Devices, Test Kits
Chemical Reagents
Equine/Vetrinary Instr. & Apparatus
Chemicals, Nec., Seafood Testing

Neon Fx Sign & Display
203 S 24th St
Tacoma, WA 98402-2901
Contact: Kevin Russell, Pres.
Telephone: 253-272-6366
Fax: 253-272-3034
Email: / URL: http://www.neonfx.com
Product Service Description:
Signs & advertising specialties
Manufactures neon tubes, signs, transformers,
custom displays, acrylics, vinyl signs
Commercial art & graphic design
Neon specializing sign company

Neoperl, Inc.
PO Box 1862
Waterbury, CT 60705-1862
Contact: Fred Luedke, Pres.
Telephone: 203-756-8891
Fax: 203-755-5717
Email: neousa@neoperl.com / URL: http://
www.neoperl.com
Product Service Description:
Faucet aerators, check valves & flow
controllers

Net Power Solutions
1440 N. Lake Shore Drive, Suite 8A
Chicago, IL 60610
Contact: Mary O'Keefe, President
Telephone: 312-482-9701
Fax: 312-482-9703
Email: meokeefe@klx.com / URL:
Product Service Description:
Neural Network Coal Combustion
Optimization

Netafim Irrigation Inc
5470 E Home Ave
Fresno, CA 93727-2107
Contact: Zvi Sella, Pres.
Telephone: 559-453-6800
Fax: 559-453-6803
Email: / URL: http://www.netfim-usa.com
Product Service Description:
Manufactures & distributes precision micro-
irrigation products
Farm machinery & equipment
Agricultural equipment
Landscaping equipment
Greenhouse & nursury equipment
Mining equipment
Wastewater equipment
Forestry equipment

Neuero Corp.
1201 W Hawthorne Ln
West Chicago, IL 60185-1815
Contact: Scott Neidigh, Pres.
Telephone: 630-231-9020
Fax: 630-231-6120
Email: neuero@neuero.com / URL:
Product Service Description:
Pneumatic grain conveyors
Ship Unloaders: Ship Loaders

Neuman Bakery Specialties, Inc.
1405 Jeffrey Dr
Addison, IL 60101-4331
Contact: George G. Neuman Jr., Pres., CFO
Telephone: 630-916-8909
Fax: 630-916-8919
Email: neuman546@aol.com / URL:
Product Service Description:
Fruit breads : Bread, cake & related products
Muffins : Kolackys : Rugelach : Stollen
Pound Cake

Neurocom International Inc.
9570 SE Lawnfield Rd.
Clackamas, OR 97015-9611
Contact: Jon F. Peters, Mktg. Mgr.
Telephone: 503-653-2144
Fax: 503-653-1991
Email: Jon_F_Peters@compuserve.com /
URL: http://www.onbalance.com
Product Service Description:
Medical Rehabilitation Balance Equipment
Electromedical Posturography Equipment
Medical Apparatus, Balance Equipment

Nevada Automotive Test Center
PO Box 234
Carson City, NV 89702-0234
Contact: Henry C. Hodges, Jr., President
Telephone: 775-629-2000
Fax: 775-629-2029
Email: hhodgesjr@natc-ht.com / URL: http://
www.natc-ht.com
Product Service Description:
Engineering Services, Automotive
Testing Laboratories, Automotive
Business Consulting Services, Automotive

Nevco Scoreboard Co.
301 E. Harris Ave.
Greenville, IL 62246-2151
Contact: M. G. Nevinger, President
Telephone: 618-664-0360
Fax: 618-664-0398
Email: nevco@nevcoscoreboards.com / URL:
http://www.nevcoscoreboards.com
Product Service Description:
Electronic Scoreboards for Sports Events

Never Boring Design Associates
1016 14th St
Modesto, CA 95354-1002
Contact: David Boring, Owner
Telephone: 209-526-9136
Fax: 209-526-1485
Email: / URL: http://www.neverboring.com
Product Service Description:
Graphic designers; sign manufacturers and
advertising : Signs & advertising specialties
Commercial art & graphic design

New American Industries Inc
5475 E Hedges Ave # 101
Fresno, CA 93727-2252
Contact: Nanci Mathers, General Manager
Telephone: 559-251-1581
Fax: 559-251-1479
Email: golfgal@pacbell.net / URL:
Product Service Description:
Sewing Manufacturer, by contract
Golf & Gift products

New Era Cap Co., Inc.
8061 Erie Rd.
Derby, NY 14047-9503
Contact: Christopher H. Koch, *
Telephone: 716-549-0445
Product Service Description:
Baseball Caps

**New Jersey Semicondutor Products,
Inc.**
20 Stern Ave
Springfield, NJ 07081-2905
Contact: Robert Hildebrandt, President
Phone: 973-376-2922 / Fax: 973-376-8960
Email: njs@njsemi.com / URL: http://
www.njsemi.com
Product Service Description:
Semiconductors : Semiconductors & related
devices

New Orleans International Airport/
C/O New Orleans Aviation Board
P.O. Box 20007
New Orleans, LA 70141
Contact: Larry Johnson, Mgr. Air Cargo
Development
Telephone: 504-464-2673
Fax: 504-463-1086
Email: / URL: http://www.gnofn.org/~airport
Product Service Description:
Airport

New River Building Supply &
Lumber Co.
PO Box 2960
Boone, NC 28607-2960
Contact: Perry Yates, Pres., GM
Telephone: 828-264-5650
Fax: 828-265-2226
Email: / URL: http://
www.newriverbuilding.com
Product Service Description:
Sawmills & planing mills, general
Lumber processing

New Tech Machinery Inc
1300 40th St
Denver, CO 80205-3311
Contact: Ronald W. Schell, Plant Mgr.
Telephone: 303-294-0538
Fax: 303-294-9407
Email: / URL:
Product Service Description:
Seamless Gutter Machine, Mfg.
Manufactures metal roll forming equipment
Roof panel machine, Mfg.

New West Business Forms
PO Box 24110
San Francisco, CA 94124-0110
Contact: James E Armstead, Owner
Telephone: 415-822-6225
Fax: 415-822-6255
Email: nwbf@eclipsetel.com / URL: http://
www.newestforms.qpg.com
Product Service Description:
Prints business forms
Manifold business forms
Labels
Business Check (both laser & continuous)
Medical form
Restaurant form

New York Blower Co.
7660 S Quincy St
Hinsdale, IL 60521-5530
Contact: Gary P. Benson, V.-P., Mktg.
Telephone: 630-794-5700
Fax: 630-794-5776
Email: nyb@nyb.com / URL: http://
www.nyb.com
Product Service Description:
Industrial fans
Blowers & fans

New York Wire Co.
152 N. Main Street
Mt. Wolf, PA 17347
Contact: Edme'e O'Farrill, Director of Int'l
Sales
Telephone: 717-266-5626
Fax: 717-266-5871
Email: info@ny-wire.com / URL: http://
www.ny-wire.com
Product Service Description:
Insect Wire Screening, Aluminum
Aluminum Wire
Solar Protection Screening
Insect Screening-Fiberglass

Newark Caplan Sewing Machine,inc
858 Summer Ave.
Newark, NJ 07104
Contact: Mel Maher, *
Telephone: 973-481-4400
Fax: 973-481-0839
Email: / URL: http://www.n-ccarpet.com
Product Service Description:
New & Rebuilt Industrial Sewing Machines
Full Line of Replacement Parts for Ind. Mach.
Full Line of Trimmaster Thread, Trimmers &
Parts : Full Line of New & Rebuilt Cutting
Machines

Newark Group, Inc.
PO Box 970
Atlanta, TX 75551-0970
Contact: Carl DePalma, GM
Telephone: 903-799-5100
Fax: 903-799-5101
Product Service Description:
Fibre Tubes & Cores : Die Cut Paper &
Board : Converted Paper Products - Slitting &
Rewinding

Newell Porcelain Company, Inc.
Fifth & Harrison Sts., P.O. Box 309
Newell, WV 26050
Contact: Rick Stanley, V.P. International Sales
Telephone: 304/387-2700
Fax: 304-387-2792
Email: insulators@compuserve.com / URL:
Product Service Description:
Porcelain Insulators, High Voltage
Porcelain Pin Type Insulator & Line Posts
Switch & Bus Insulators Cap Pin & Post

Newood Display Fixture Mfg Co
PO Box 21808
Eugene, OR 97402-0412
Contact: Gerry Moshofsky, Pres.
Telephone: 541-688-0907
Fax: 541-688-5868
Email: newoodsales@newood.com / URL:
http://www.newood.com
Product Service Description:
Manufactures wood shelving and store
fixtures : Partitions & fixtures_wood

Newport Biosystems, Inc.
1860 Trainor St
Red Bluff, CA 96080-4545
Contact: Jerry Case, Marketing & Sales
Telephone: 530-529-2448
Fax: 530-529-2648
Email: biobags@hotmail.com / URL: http://
www.bioweb.net/users/biotech
Product Service Description:
Sterilized Plastic bags for Biotech Fluids
Bags, Plastic Sterilized for Bioprocessing
Fluids
Biological products, Bioprocess Containers &
Bags

Ney Dental, Inc.
13553 Calimesa Blvd
Yucaipa, CA 92399-2303
Contact: Vern Goodwalt, V-P., GM
Telephone: 909-795-2461
Fax: 909-795-5268
Email: neyinfo@neydental.com / URL: http://
www.neydental.com
Product Service Description:
Manufactures bench top furnaces and
ultrasonic cleaners; small hi-speed hand
grinders : Dental lab, scientific lab & jewelry
Mfg. equipment
Laboratory apparatus

Nielsen-Massey Vanillas(Mfr)
1550 Shields Drive
Waukegan, IL 60085
Contact: Craig Nielsen, Vice President
Telephone: 847-578-1550
Fax: 847-578-1570
Product Service Description:
Pure Vanilla Extract

Nilfisk-Advance America, Inc.
300 Technology Dr
Malvern, PA 19355-1345
Contact: Robert S. Magdelain, Pres.
Telephone: 610-647-6420
Fax: 610-647-6427
Email: questions@nilfisk-advance.com /
URL: http://www.nilfisk-advance.com
Product Service Description:
Industrial Vacuum Cleaners
Industrial machinery

Nippert Co., The
801 Pittsburgh Dr
Delaware, OH 43015-2860
Contact: R. A. Nippert, Pres., GM
Telephone: 740-363-1981
Fax: 740-363-3847
Email: / URL: http://
www.nippertcompany.com
Product Service Description:
Copper rolling & drawing - strip, profiles
shapes : Copper rod & wire : Manufactures
Resistance Welding Electrodes

Nippon Express USA, Inc.
15402 E. Vantage Pkwy., Ste. 316,
Houston, TX 77032
Contact: Sales & Marketing,
Telephone: 281-987-2300
Fax: 281-987-1150
URL: http://www.nipponexpressusa.com
Product Service Description:
Freight & Cargo Transportation
Trucking

Nippon Express USA, Inc.
8065 Tristar,
Irving, TX 75063
Contact: Masaru Yokoyama, Branch Manager
Telephone: 972-621-1911
Fax: 972-929-0881
Email: cowboy15@ix.netcom.com / URL:
Product Service Description:
Air & Ocean Freight Forwarding
Custom Brokerage
Warehouse & Distribution

Nishizawa
19301 Pacific Gateway Dr.
Torrance, CA 90502-1017
Contact: H. Mabuchi, President
Telephone: 310-532-7407
Fax: 310-532-7408
Product Service Description:
Textile Goods : Men's Under Garments
Menswear : Leather Shoes : General
Merchandise : Swimwear : Automobiles

Nitta Gelatin
201 W. Passaic St.
Rochelle Park, NJ 07662-3100
Contact: Juergen Gallert, Mgr. Sales & Mktg.
Telephone: 201-368-0071
Fax: 201-368-0282
Email: / URL: http://www.nitta-gelatin.com
Product Service Description:
Edible Gelatin : Photographic Gelatin
Pharmaceutical gelatin

Noamex
625 Wortman Ave.
Brooklyn, NY 11208-5438
Contact: Harvey Schefren, President
Telephone: 718-342-2278
Fax: 718-342-2278
Email: noamex@msn.com / URL: http://
www.noamex.com
Product Service Description:
Used clothing
Second hand clothing

Noble Popcorn Farms
PO Box 157
Sac City, IA 50583-0157
Contact: Dan Martin, Manager
Telephone: 712-662-4728
Fax: 712-662-4797
Email: noblepop@pionet.net / URL: http://
www.pionet.net/~noblepop
Product Service Description:
Popcorn; Raw, Microwave & Pre-popped

Noble Systems Corp.
4151 Ashford Dunwoody
Atlanta, GA 30319
Contact: Jim Noble, Pres.
Telephone: 404-851-1331
Fax: 404-851-1421
Email: info@noblesys.com / URL:
Product Service Description:
Automatic telephone dialers / ACD
Telephony Servers / CTI

Nofire Technologies Inc.
21 Industrial Ave
Upper Saddle River, NJ 07458-2301
Contact: Sam Oolie, Chrm., CEO
Telephone: 201-818-1616
Fax: 201-818-8775
Email: nofire@aol.com / URL: http://
www.nofiretechnologies.com
Product Service Description:
Fire retardant coatings

Noga Commodities
1 World Trade Ctr., Ste. 8041
New York, NY 10048-0157
Contact: Keith Weithorn, Executive V.P.
Telephone: 212-938-8800
Product Service Description:
Commodity trading of all grains, oilseeds,
wheat flours, as exporters / principals
Waste and scrap of paper or paperboard,
including unsorted waste and scrap /
Exporters of kraft liner board

Noland
8901 N.W. 20th St., Ste. A
Miami, FL 33172-2617
Contact: Lazaro R. Figueroa, International
Sales Manager
Telephone: 305-471-0031
Fax: 305-471-0696
Email: lazarofigueroa@noland.com / URL:
http://www.noland.com
Product Service Description:
Air Conditioning Wholesaler
Air Conditioning Distributor
Air conditioning machines incorporating a
refrigerating unit
Air Conditioning Equipment
Air Conditioning Units
RVVD Air Conditioning Equipment
Air Conditioning Residential
Air Conditioning Commercial
Air Conditioning International
Air Conditioning Export

Nor-Lake, Inc. (Mfr)
727 Second Street, PO Box 248
Hudson, WI 54016
Contact: Barbara Belongia, ,
Phone: 715-386-2323 / 800-955-5253
Fax: 715-386-6149
Email: sales@norlake.com / URL: http://
www.norlake.com
Product Service Description:
Refrigeration & Heating Equipment
Commercial Refrigeration Units
Laboratory Equipment

Norac Co., Inc., The
405 S. Motor Ave.
Azusa, CA 91702-3232
Contact: Wally McCloskey, President
hone: 626-334-2908 / Fax: 626-334-3512
Email: noracca@earthlink.net / URL:
Product Service Description:
Industrial Organic Chemicals, NEC
Organic peroxides, ether peroxides, ketone
peroxides : Hydroxides and peroxides
Benzoyl peroxide : Organic Peroxides
Metallic Stearates : Fine Chemicals
Pharmaceutical

Noraxon USA Inc
13430 N Scottsdale Rd Ste 104
Scottsdale, AZ 85254-4059
Contact: Frank Hosnor,
Phone: 602-443-3413 / Fax: 602-443-4327
Email: noraxon@aol.com / URL: http://
www.noraxon.com
Product Service Description:
Manufactures and distributes EMG
instruments and medical electronics
Medical instruments
Electromedical equipment
Medical & hospital equipment

Norco Products
PO Box 4227
Missoula, MT 59806-4227
Contact: Mary L Sneddon, Sales Mgr.
Telephone: 406-251-3800
Fax: 406-251-3824
Email: mary@norcoproducts.com / URL:
http://www.norcoproducts.com
Product Service Description:
Manufactures school furniture & equipment;
institutional & commercial storage cabinets
Furniture_public building & related
Partitions & fixtures_wood
Furniture

**Nordam Group Inc., Tranparencies
Div. The**
7018 N. Lakewood Ave
Tulsa, OK 74117-1814
Contact: Phil Bashaw, Director of Marketing
Telephone: 918-274-2700
Fax: 918-274-2777
Email: ntd@nordam.com / URL: http://
www.nordam.com
Product Service Description:
Aircraft Acrylic Cabin Windows
Aircraft Cockpit Windows
Aircraft Wing Tip Lenses

Nordic Boats, Inc.
770 Lake Havasu Ave N
Lake Havasu City, AZ 86403-2965
Contact: Orval R Sommerstedt, Pres.
Telephone: 520-855-7420
Fax: 520-855-0332
Email: nordicbt@ctaz.com / URL:
Product Service Description:
Manufactures Performance Boats & Trailers

Nordic Saw & Tool Manufacturer
PO Box 1128
Turlock, CA 95381-1128
Contact: Dewey Larson, Pres., GM
Telephone: 209-634-9015
Fax: 209-634-9010
Email: / URL:
Product Service Description:
Manufactures new carbide-tipped cutting
tools for wood, plastics, & non-ferrous
industries. : Carbide - tipped router bits,
standard, custom & CNC : Carbide - tipped
shaper cutters, standard & custom

Nordstrom Valves, Inc.
PO Box 501
Sulphur Springs, TX 75483-0501
Contact: Benny E. Boss,
Telephone: 903-439-3446
Fax: 903-439-3411
Email: nvi.mkt@btrinc.com / URL:
Product Service Description:
Iron & Steel Lubricated Tapered Plug Vavles
Polyethylne Ball Valves
Metal Ball Valves
Valve Remanufacture

Nordyne Inc.
1801 Park 270 Drive
St. Louis, MO 63146
Contact: Aldo J. Magnani, Dir / Prod Plan
Telephone: 314-878-6200
Fax: 314-878-4815
Email: / URL:
Product Service Description:
Unitary Air Conditioners
Warm Air Furnaces

Norman G. Jensen, Inc.
3050 Metro Drive, Suite 300
Minneapolis, MN 55425
Contact: Dennis Jensen, Vice Pres./Sales
Telephone: 612/854-7363
Fax: 612-854-8302
Email: sales@ngjensen.com / URL: http://
www.ngjensen.com
Product Service Description:
Customs Broker
Freight Forwarder

Norman Levy Associates
21415 Civic Center Dr., Suite 306
Southfield, MI 48076
Contact: Robert Levy,
Telephone: 248-353-8640
Fax: 248-353-1442
Email: headquarters@nlainc.com / URL:
http://www.nlainc.com
Product Service Description:
Auctioneers,Appraisers &
Liquidators,Primarily of Industrial Machinery

Norman Tool, Inc.
15415 Old St. Rd.
Evansville, IN 47711
Contact: John Norman, Fin., Pur., Sales &
Mktg. Mgr.
Telephone: 812-867-3496
Fax: 812-867-6790
Email: normtool@evansville.net / URL:
Product Service Description:
Abrasion wear testers
Measuring & controlling devices
Machinery_special industry
Key Pad Testing
Inked Surface Testers
Tester, Abrasion
Wear Testers
Testers, Key Pad

Norman, Fox & Co
PO Box 58727
Vernon, CA 90058-0727
Contact: James E. Morgan, Director of
Marketing
Telephone: 323-583-0016
Fax: 323-583-9769
Email: norfox@worldnet.att.net / URL: http://
www.norfoxx.com
Product Service Description:
Manufactures soaps, detergents, amides and
esters; custom synthesis
Soap & other detergents
Chemicals_industrial inorganic
Surface active agents

Norotos Inc
201 E Alton Ave
Santa Ana, CA 92707-4416
Contact: Ronald Soto, Pres.
Telephone: 714-662-3113
Fax: 714-662-7950
Email: norotosl@earthlink.net / URL: http://
www.norotos.com
Product Service Description:
Precision machined night vision
Components & helmet mounts

Norpac Foods Inc
PO Box 458, 930 West Washington
Stayton, OR 97383-5000
Contact: Rick Jacobson, Pres., CEO
Telephone: 503-769-2101
Fax: 503-769-1274
Email: / URL: http://www.norpac.com
Product Service Description:
Fruits & vegetables, frozen
Soups, Frozen
Canned fruits & vegetables

Norren Manufacturing Inc
440 E Bonita Ave
Pomona, CA 91767-1928
Contact: Torben Zangenberg, Pres.
Telephone: 909-482-4649
Fax: 909-482-4651
Email: norren@gte.net / URL:
Product Service Description:
Manufactures steel storage cabinets—
flammable, modular instrument and office
form

Norse, Inc.
100 Franklin Dr
Torrington, CT 06790-6501
Contact: Alfred C. Langer, Pres., R & D Mgr.
Telephone: 860-482-1532
Fax: 860-482-5059
Email: norse@snet.net / URL: http://
www.norse-inc.com
Product Service Description:
Fasteners - Latches
Sealed Latches
Multilatches
Remotely Operated Latches

Norstan Electronics Inc
1911 E, Carnegie Ave
Santa Ana, CA 92705
Contact: Bonnie Peteson, Sales Mgr.
Telephone: 949-250-4903
Fax: 949-250-0135
Email: sales@norstan.net / URL: http://
www.norstan.net
Product Service Description:
Distributes electronic parts and equipment;
relay specialty house
Electronic parts & equipment

North American Export Company
P.O. BOX 164
Harwinton, CT 06791-0164
Contact: Ronald Cassidento, President
Telephone: 860-496-9350
Fax: 860-496-1369
Email: naexco@pobox.com / URL: http://
www.naexco.com
Product Service Description:
Certified Organic Fertilizer
Geno's Ice Cream Mix (www.genos.net)
Roots Organic Biostimulant

North American Green
14649 Highway 41 North
Evansville, IN 47711
Contact: Jim Niemeier, President
Telephone: 800-772-2040
Fax: 812-867-0247
Email: niemeir@nagreen.com / URL: http://
www.nagreen.com
Product Service Description:
Textile Goods, Erosion Control Blanket

North American Wood Products Inc.
8255 S.W. Hunziker Rd.
Portland, OR 97223-2318
Contact: Cliff Chulos, President
Telephone: 503-620-6655
Fax: 503-598-7959
Email: nawp@pcez.com / URL:
Product Service Description:
Lumber, Plywood, and Millwork
Builders' joinery and carpentry of wood
Coniferous wood sawn or chipped
lengthwise, sliced or peeled, whether or not
planed : Nonconiferous wood, sawn or
chipped lengthwise, sliced or peeled, whether
or not planed

North Atlantic Fish Co , Inc
88 Commercial St
Gloucester, MA 01930-5025
Contact: Frank Cefalo, Pres., Treas.
Phone: 978-283-4121 / Fax: 978-283-5948
Email: nafish@aol.com / URL:
Product Service Description:
Fish_fresh or frozen prepared
Fresh and Frozen Packaged Fish

North West Labs Inc
901 N Lincoln Ave
Jerome, ID 83338-1814
Contact: Dr. Rob E. Whitchurch, Pres.
Phone: 208-324-7511 / Fax: 208-324-2936
Email: nwlabs@northrim.net / URL:
Product Service Description:
Testing laboratory and services for agriculture

Northeast Fabricators, L.L.C.
30-35 Williams St.
Walton, NY 13856
Contact: John Phraner, Plt. Mgr.
Telephone: 607-865-4031
Fax: 607-865-8306
Email: nfllc@catskill.net / URL:
Product Service Description:
Sheet Metal Work
Conveyors & Equipment

Northerm Windows Corp.
4970 Fairbanks St
Anchorage, AK 99503-7440
Contact: Walt Murphy, Fin., GM & Pur. Mgr.
Phone: 907-563-0091 / Fax: 907-563-2028
Email: northerm@alaska.net / URL: http://
www.northerm.com
Product Service Description:
Vinyl windows

Northern Pump & Irrigation
P.O. Box 576
Henderson, NE 68371-0576
Contact: Randy Ratzlaff, Manager
Phone: 402-723-4501 / Fax: 402-723-4523
Email: northernpump@telcoweb.net / URL:
http://www.telcoweb.net/northern
Product Service Description:
Agricultural Machine
Irrigation equipment

Northern Star Co., Inc.
3171 5th St Se
Minneapolis, MN 55414-3305
Contact: J. D. Clarkson, Pres.
Telephone: 612-339-8981
Fax: 612-331-3434
Email: nstar@minn.net / URL: http://
www.michaelfoods.com
Product Service Description:
Potato Products , Refrigerated Potato
Products : Diced, Sliced, Shredded, Redskin
& Mashed Potatoes : 30 Day Shelf-Life,
Sulfite Free : Foodservice & Retail Packaging
Available

**Northland Organic Foods /
Northland Seed & Grain**
462 Holly Avenue
St. Paul, MN 55101 USA
Contact: Sales & Marketing,
Telephone: 651-221-0855
Fax: 651-221-0856
Email: soybean@northlandorganicfoods.com /
URL: http://www.northlandorganicfoods.com
Product Service Description:
Certified organic & conventional non-gmo
soybeans, corn, cerial grains
Oils, meals, other value added products
Certified organic & non-gmo identity
preserved seeds : Non-gmo certification
program (US patent pending)

Northridge Laboratories Inc
20832 Dearborn St
Chatsworth, CA 91311-5915
Contact: Brett Richman, President
Telephone: 818-882-5622
Fax: 818-998-2815
Product Service Description:
Manufacturer of cutting private label
vitamins, herbs & nutritional
supplements in tablet, powder & 2-piece hard
shell capsule form.

Northwest Cedar Inc
8765 Pueblo Ave NE
Salem, OR 97305-9727
Contact: Mike Cooke, Pres.
Telephone: 503-390-3433
Fax: 503-304-1062
Email: nwcedar@teleport.com / URL: http://
www.teleport.com/~nwcedar
Product Service Description:
Manufactures cedar prefabricated gazebos,
saunas and accessories; sauna cabinets
Prefabricated wood buildings
Wood products

Northwest Coatings Corp.
7221 S 10th St
Oak Creek, WI 53154-1903
Contact: Dennis J. Gaber, President
Telephone: 414-762-3330
Fax: 414-762-9132
Email: nwc@northwestcoatings.com / URL:
http://www.northwestcoatings.com
Product Service Description:
UV-cured adhesives & coatings

Northwest Paper Box Mfrs Inc
400 N Thompson St
Portland, OR 97227-1819
Contact: Rod Van Allen, V-P., GM & Opers.
Telephone: 503-249-1028
Fax: 503-249-2060
Product Service Description:
Boxes_corrugated & solid fiber
Manufactures boxes, corrugated items, pads,
die cuts, setup boxes, retail packaging
Boxes_setup paperboard
Fiber cans, drums & similar products
Boxes_folding paperboard

Northwest Pipe Company
12005 N Burgard
Portland, OR 97203-6432
Contact: Gary A. Stokes, Vice President
Telephone: 503-285-1400
Fax: 503-285-2913
Email: / URL: http://www.nwpipe.com
Product Service Description:
Steel pipe & tubes
Manufactures large diameter, high-pressure
steel pipes for water transmission

**Northwest Regulator Supply Inc.
(Mfr)**
4444 S.E. 27th Ave
Portland, OR 97202
Contact: Alan Melton, *
Telephone: 503-235-1038
Fax: 503-239-9996
Email: alan@nwreg.com / URL:
Product Service Description:
Elec. Testing Equip., Alternators

Northwestern Tools, Inc.
3130 Valleywood Drive
Dayton, OH 45429-3900
Contact: JamesThomeczek, Sales Manager
Telephone: 513-298-9994
Fax: 513-298-3715
Product Service Description:
Metalworking Machine Tool Holders
Bolts, Nuts, Studs & Washers

Norton Industries
1833 Stearman Avenue
Hayward, CA 94545
Contact: Ted Bulotti, Sales Manager
Telephone: 510-786-3638
Fax: 510-782-5329
Product Service Description:
Hose Clamps, Stainless Steel, Worm Drive

Nova Grass
P.O. Box 21764
Chattanooga, TN 37424-0764
Contact: Rick Burke, President
Telephone: 423-499-5546
Fax: 423-499-8882
Email: nova@vol.com / URL:
Product Service Description:
Heavy Construction, NEC
Articles and equipment for sports or outdoor/
indoor games; Swimming pools and wading
pools; Parts : Container cargo

Nova Products
4861 Old Sparta Rd
Cookeville, TN 38506-5959
Contact: John McDermit, Pres.
Telephone: 931-528-3828
Fax: 931-526-3535
Email: nova@midtenn.net / URL: http://
www.nova-usa.com
Product Service Description:
Nonlethal law enforcement weapons

Nova Science Inc
9101 E Gelding Dr
Scottsdale, AZ 85260-7048
Contact: Vern Griffin, Pres.
Telephone: 480-860-4447
Fax: 480-860-1376
Email: verngriffin@earthlink.com / URL:
Product Service Description:
Manufactures test burn-in sockets for
semiconductors
Electronic parts & equipment

NovaWeb Technologies Inc
48511 Warm Springs Blvd Ste 208
Fremont, CA 94539-7746
Contact: Baldev Krishan, Pres., CEO
Telephone: 510-249-9500
Fax: 510-249-9380
Email: balden@novweb.com / URL: http://
www.novaweb.com
Product Service Description:
Home networking & internet sharing
apparatus
Manufactures products which are PC
compatible

Novatrix Inc
6078 Corte Del Cedro
Carlsbad, CA 92009-1514
Contact: John Kasper, VP Bus. Dev.
Telephone: 760-431-0013
Fax: 760-431-0018
Email: / URL:
Product Service Description:
Manufactures Labor Assister, an Obstetric
device designed to reduce
the duration of second stage labor and the
need for operative deliveries

Novo Industries Inc.
11801 Nw 100th Rd
Miami, FL 33178-1040
Contact: Pelayo Mazorra, GM
Telephone: 305-885-8855
Fax: 305-885-7600
Email: mazorrp@royal-novo.com / URL:
Product Service Description:
Vertical blinds
Drapery hardware & blinds & shades

Now Structures, Inc.
Rte. 2, Box 126-b, Hwy. 71
Nevada, MO 64772
Contact: Tom M. Nowak, Pres., Secy-Treas.,
Pur. Agt.
Telephone: 417-667-3022
Fax: 417-667-5823
Email: tnowak@trussnow.com / URL: http://
www.trussnow.com
Product Service Description:
Structural wood members
Wooden roof & floor trusses

Nu Arc Co., Inc.
6200 W Howard St
Niles, IL 60714-3404
Contact: Don Cims, Pres, Carlos G. Acosta,
Int'l Sales Mgr.
Telephone: 847-967-4400
Fax: 847-967-9664
Email: nuarc@ccm.net / URL: http://
www.nuarcco.com
Product Service Description:
Printing equipment
Printing trades machinery
Pre-press equipment offset applications
Pre-press equipment screen printing
applications

Nu-Metal Finishing Inc
2262 Calle Del Mundo
Santa Clara, CA 95054-1005
Contact: Mark Danitschek, GM
Telephone: 408-727-1050
Fax: 408-727-7231
Email: mark@nu-metal.com / URL: http://
www.nu-metal.com
Product Service Description:
Plating & polishing
Provides plating, electronic component
plating & UHV spec cleaning services

Nutech Environmental Corp.(Mfr)
5350 N. Washington St.
Denver, CO 80216
Contact: Ken Heller, Sales Manager
Telephone: 303-295-3702
Fax: 303-295-6145
Email: necdenver@aol.com / URL:
nutechenvironmental.com
Product Service Description:
Odor Control Solutions

Nutro Products, Inc.
3710 NW 221st Street
Ridgefield, WA 98642
Contact: Matt DeFreitas, VP, Export
Telephone: 360-887-0926
Fax: 360-887-0933
Email: nutromat@pacifier.com / URL:
Product Service Description:
Manufactures Nutro max & Nutro's Choice
Pet Food for Specialty Pet Outlets
Dog & Cat Food

Nutter Machine Inc.
3356 National Rd.
Hebron, OH 43025
Contact: Mark Nutter, Pres.,
Opers. & R & D Mgr.
Telephone: 740-928-6025
Fax: 740-928-6464
Email: mnutter@nutter11.com / URL: http://
www.nutter11.com
Product Service Description:
Industrial machinery
General machining job shop
Auxiliary Plastics Machinery
Tube bending machinery

Nylacarb Corp.
1725 98th Ave
Vero Beach, FL 32966-3032
Contact: Frank Cooley, Pres., Engrg., Fin. &
Pur. Mgr.
Telephone: 561-569-5999
Fax: 561-569-5922
Email: nylacarb@metrolink.net / URL: http://
www.spacecst.nylacarb
Product Service Description:
Plastic products
Thermoplastics injection molding

O C V Control Valves
7400 E 42nd Pl
Tulsa, OK 74145-4702
Contact: Chuck Whisenhunt, Sales Mgr.
Telephone: 918-627-1942
Fax: 918-622-8916
Email: sales@controlvalves.com / URL: http:/
/www.controlvalves.com
Product Service Description:
Automatic control valves & general
machining job shop
Fluid power valves & hose fittings
Industrial machinery

O S F Flavors, Inc.
PO Box 591
Windsor, CT 06095-0591
Contact: Eduardo DeBotao, Pres.
Telephone: 860-298-8350
Fax: 860-298-8363
Email: osfflavors@earthlink.net / URL:
Product Service Description:
Food flavorings
Flavoring extracts & syrups
Masking Agents
Vanilla Extracts

O'Brien International
PO Box 97020
Redmond, WA 98073-9720
Contact: Jon A. Gluydon, Pres.
Telephone: 425-202-2100
Fax: 425-202-2195
Email: / URL: http://www.obrien.com
Product Service Description:
Sporting & athletic goods
Manufactures water skis, kneeboards and
wakeboards

O'Hara Metal Products Co
PO Box 960
Brisbane, CA 94005-0960
Contact: John F. Avery, CEO
Telephone: 415-468-3350
Fax: 415-468-5464
Email: omp@oharamfg.com / URL:
Product Service Description:
Manufactures coil springs, four-slide
products, stampings and assemblies
Springs_steel, except wire
Metal stampings

O. Berk Company
3 Milltown Court
Union, NJ 07083-8108
Contact: Marketing,
Telephone: 908-851-9500
Fax: 908-851-9367
Email: obc@oberk.com / URL: http://
www.OBerk.com
Product Service Description:
Bottles Wholes

OSI Security Devices
1580 Jayken Way
Chula Vista, CA 91911-4644
Contact: Ron Perkins, VP Sales & Marketing
Telephone: 619-628-1000
Fax: 619-628-1001
Email: osirep@aol.com / URL: http://
www.osisecurity.com
Product Service Description:
Manufactures electronic access control
devices

OTM Engineering, Inc.
7035 Bee Caves Road
Austin, TX 78746-500
Contact: Jim Sinopoli, President
Telephone: 512-328-8801
Fax: 512-328-2725
Email: jms@otm-eng.com / URL: http://
www.otm-eng.com
Product Service Description:
Business Consulting, Voice Communications
Business Consulting, Data Communications
Business Consulting, Video
Training Seminars Communications
Engineering Services
Telephone Communication- Except Radio

Oak Grigsby, Inc.
84 N Dugan Rd
Sugar Grove, IL 60554-9417
Contact: C. Rodriguez, Pres.
Telephone: 630-556-4200
Fax: 630-556-4216
Email: info@oakgrigsby.com / URL: http://
www.oakgrigsby.com
Product Service Description:
Electronic switches
Current-carrying wiring devices
Electronic components
Solenoids

Oakwood Interiors
1333 S Bon View Ave
Ontario, CA 91761-4404
Contact: Larry Parnell, President
Telephone: 909-930-3500
Fax: 909-930-3501
Email: / URL: http://www.fineoak.com
Product Service Description:
Manufactures oak bedroom furniture
Furniture_wood household
Manufactures oak home office

Oasis Corporation
265 N. Hamilton Road
Columbus, OH 43213-0150
Contact: Bobo Hanby, Reg. Saels Mgr.
Telephone: 614-861-1350
Fax: 614-861-6783
Email: 110257.157@compuserve.com / URL:
Product Service Description:
Dehumidifiers
Water Coolers
Portable Dehumidifiers

Oberg Mfg. Co.
PO Box 368, Silverville Road
Freeport, PA 16229-0315
Contact: John Maholtz, VP of Mktg.
Telephone: 724-295-2121
Fax: 724-295-2588
Email: john.maholtz@oberg.com / URL:
http://www.oberg.com
Product Service Description:
Precision carbide & steel stamping dies
Metal Stampings
Injection molded plastic parts
Automated assembly services

Ocalas Corporation
1471 SW 124th Ct.# F
Miami, FL 33184-2372
Contact: William Lopez, President
Telephone: 305-220-9384
Fax: 305-220-9396
Email: ocalas@bellsouth.net / URL:
Product Service Description:
Electronic Equipment & Parts, Export
Cables, T.V.

Ocean Design Inc.
9 Aviator Way
Ormond Beach, FL 32174-2983
Contact: Mike Vollmar, Pres.
Telephone: 904-673-3575
Fax: 904-673-3671
Email: sthumbeck@oceandesigninc.com /
URL: http://www.oceandesigninc.com
Product Service Description:
Electrical & Electro-optic Connectors for
Deepwater Applications
Subsea Connection Systems
Electrical & Optic Penetrators
Junction boxes

Oceanogaphic Industries, Inc.
547 West Ave
Miami Beach, FL 33139-6306
Contact: Carlos L. Perez, Pres.
Telephone: 305-673-8600
Fax: 305-531-9691
Product Service Description:
Scientific underwater sensor anti-fouling
devices: Search & navigation equipoment

Oceanside Engineering & Mfg
490 Via Del Norte
Oceanside, CA 92054-1233
Contact: Nancy Kjorlien, Owner
Telephone: 760-722-6599
Fax: 760-967-9218
Email: denox@pacbell.net / URL:
Product Service Description:
Pollution Control Equipment
Pump Skids; SNCR/SCR

Oceco, Inc.
PO Box 159
Tiffin, OH 44883-0159
Contact: Richard Borer, Pres., Opers. Mgr.
Telephone: 419-447-0916
Fax: 419-447-5514
Email: oceco@bright.net / URL:
Product Service Description:
Petroleum & liquid, vapor conservation, fire
prevention & digest gas control equipment

Ochman Systems, Edward
P.O. Box 339
Fairfield, CT 06430-0339
Contact: Edward Ochman, Sr., *
Telephone: 203-259-1927
Fax: 203-259-1927
Email: eosi@juno.com / URL:
Product Service Description:
Magnetic Dry Erase White Boards W/
Accessories
Computer Supplies
Electronic Copy Boards
Cork Bulletin Boards
Directory Letter Boards W/Accessories
Conference Cabinets
Magnetic Visual Planning Systems (1000
Models)
Communication Boards
Magnetic Flow Charting & Pert Kits

Ocularvision Inc
360 S Fairview Ave Ste D
Santa Barbara, CA 93117-3630
Contact: Richard Ingram, Pres., Jerry Wilson,
VP
Telephone: 805-964-4523
Fax: 805-964-0199
Email: ocular@silcom.com / URL:
Product Service Description:
Manufactures intraocular lenses, viscoelastic
surgical fluid and technology

Odor Control Co., Inc.
PO Box 5740
Scottsdale, AZ 85261-5740
Contact: Barbara Lang,
Telephone: 602-488-2126
Fax: 602-488-9439
Email: noodors@msn.com / URL: http://
www.odorcontrolco.com
Product Service Description:
Odor Control Systems

Ogden Engineering Corp.
PO Box 148
Schererville, IN 46375-0148
Contact: Ralph Ogden Sr., Pres.
Telephone: 219-322-5252
Fax: 219-865-1825
Email: ogden@jorsm.com / URL: http://
www.ogdeneng.com
Product Service Description:
Automatic welding equipment
Welding apparatus
Stiffener fitting gantries
Weld gantries
Seam weld gantries
Tractor welders
Tank welders
Flux recycling systems
Material handling

Ohio Blenders
2404 N. Summit St.
Toledo, OH 43611-3599
Contact: Rolland Turnow, President
Telephone: 419-726-2655
Fax: 419-726-6629
Email: www.ohioblen@glasscity.net / URL:
http://members.tripod.com/~ohioblenders/
main.html
Product Service Description:
Dehydrated Alfalfa Products

Ohio Moulding Corp., The
30396 Lakeland Blvd
Wickliffe, OH 44092-1748
Contact: Edward F. Gleason, Pres.
Telephone: 440-944-2100
Fax: 440-944-8309
Email: tcarleton@omcoform.com / URL:
http://www.omcoform.com
Product Service Description:
Steel roll forming

Ohio Pipe & Steel Corp.
PO Box 091213
Columbus, OH 43209-7213
Contact: Marvin Silberstein, President
Telephone: 614-899-1770
Fax: 614-899-1771
Email: / URL:
Product Service Description:
Steel Pipe , Wholesale

Ohio Willow Wood Co.
PO Box 130
Mount Sterling, OH 43143-0137
Contact: Robert Arbogast, Pres.
Telephone: 740-869-3377
Fax: 740-869-4374
Email: / URL: http://www.owwco.com
Product Service Description:
Surgical appliances & supplies
Orthopedic & prosthetic supplies

Oilpure Refiner Co
1001 E Slauson Ave
Los Angeles, CA 90011-5241
Contact: John Morse, Pres.
Telephone: 323-231-9301
Fax: 323-235-2929
Email: / URL:
Product Service Description:
Manufactures oil refiners, diesel dialyser,
engineering products; fire hydrant caps-nylon
pipe bushings
Oil & gas field machinery
Power transmission equipment
Foundries_nonferrous
Hardware

Old Fashioned Kitchen Inc
160 Newport Center Dr Ste 210
Newport Beach, CA 92660-6912
Contact: Albert L Bonugli, Chrm., CEO
Telephone: 949-720-7060
Fax: 949-720-1439
Email: ofknb@aol.com / URL:
Product Service Description:
Manufactures frozen kosher food
Frozen specialties
Refrigerated deli products

Old World Cone
12602 1st Ave S
Seattle, WA 98168-2617
Contact: Ray Elkins, Pres.
Telephone: 206-241-0333
Fax: 206-248-4922
Email: Oworldcone@aol.com / URL: http://
www.oldworldcone.com
Product Service Description:
Manufactures waffle cone and Belgian waffle
equipment; cone and Belgian mixes
Food products machinery
Flour mixes & doughs_prepared

Old World Spices & Seasonings, Inc.
PO Box 300409
Kansas City, MO 64130
Contact: John Jungk, Pres.
Telephone: 816-861-0400
Fax: 816-861-7073
Email: / URL:
Product Service Description:
Food Seasonings
Bakery Seasonings
Dairy Seasonings
Soup & Pasta Seasonings
Meat Rub & Marinade Seasonings

Olivine Corporation
928 Thomas Rd.
Bellingham, WA 98226
Contact: Corky Smith, Jr., Chief Executive
Telephone: 360-733-3332
Fax: 360-671-9462
Email: / URL:
Product Service Description:
Wood Waste Incinerators
Municipal Solid Waste Incinerators
Medical Waste Incinerators

Olson Industries, Inc.
PO Box 880
Atkinson, NE 68713-0880
Contact: Ted Olson Jr., Pres., Fin. & R & D
Mgr.
Telephone: 402-925-5090
Fax: 402-925-5717
Email: / URL:
Product Service Description:
Airport Canisters

Olson Irrigation Systems
PO Box 711570
Santee, CA 92072-1570
Contact: Donald O Olson, Pres.
Telephone: 619-562-3100
Fax: 619-562-2724
Email: bldwin@aol.com / URL: http://
www.olsonirrigation.com
Product Service Description:
Manufactures low volume drip and micro
irrigation systems for farming and landscaping
Farm machinery & equipment
Lawn & garden equipment
Irrigation systems

Olympia Gold Inc.
11540 Wiles Rd Ste 2
Coral Springs, FL 33076-2119
Contact: Skip Wilson, Pres., R & D Mgr.
Telephone: 954-345-6991
Fax: 954-344-4360
Email: permagold@aol.com / URL: http://
www.olympiagold.com
Product Service Description:
Precious metal & costume jewelry
Jewelry, precious metal
Jewelry_costume

Olympia International, Div. of Olympic Steel
600 Grant St., Ste. 3246
Pittsburgh, PA 15219-2702
Contact: Clayton Treska, Director
Telephone: 412-391-4777
Fax: 412-391-4810
Email: ctreska@olysteel.com / URL: http://
www.olysteel.com
Product Service Description:
Metals Service Centers and Offices
Articles of iron or steel

Olympic Aviation
612 E Franklin Ave.
El Segundo, CA 90245-4111
Contact: Joe Ouchida, President
Telephone: 310-640-8444
Fax: 310-640-2247
Email: / URL:
Product Service Description:
Aviation Products Export - Metals, Parts,
Chemicals
Electrical Electronic Parts, Aircraft

Olympic Foundry Inc
5200 Airport Way S
Seattle, WA 98108-1725
Contact: Scott McLaughlin, GM
Telephone: 206-764-6200
Fax: 206-764-1170
Email: ofco@olympicfoundry.com / URL:
http://www.olympicfoundry.com
Product Service Description:
Manufactures cast iron, ductile, and steel
castings—municipal and waterworks;
winches
Foundries_malleable iron
Foundries_gray & ductile iron
Foundries_steel
Construction machinery, counterweights

Omaha Standard, Inc.
2401 W Broadway
Council Bluffs, IA 51501-3675
Contact: Tom Maser, Co-Pres.
Telephone: 712-328-7444
Fax: 712-328-8383
Email: os@omahastd.com / URL: http://
www.omahastd.com
Product Service Description:
Stake, grain & livestock bodies & hydraulic
hoists & lift gates
Farm Machinery & Equipment
All Types of Truck Bodies

Omega Flex, Inc.
451 Creamery Way
Exton, PA 19341-2508
Contact: Kevin R. Hoben, Pres.
Telephone: 610-524-7272
Fax: 610-524-7282
Email: jirvine@erols.com / URL: http://
www.omegaflex.com
Product Service Description:
Metal flexible hose products

Omega Graphics, Inc.
1028 Rte. 23
Wayne, NJ 07470
Contact: Brian Madigan, Pres.
Telephone: 973-628-1996
Fax: 973-628-7012
Email: omega@warwick.net / URL: http://
www.omegagraphics.com
Product Service Description:
Fine art Iris Giclee Reproductions

Omega Heater Co., Inc.
2059 9th Ave
Ronkonkoma, NY 11779-6254
Contact: A. Gaudio, Pres., Enrique Hernan
Telephone: 516-588-8820
Fax: 516-588-8953
Email: omegaheat@earthlink.net / URL: http:/
/www.omegaheater.com
Product Service Description:
Electrical industrial heaters
Furnaces & ovens_industrial
Temperature Controls

Omega Plastics, Inc.
P O Box 46997
Clinton Twp, MI 48036
Contact: Jeff Kaczperski,
Telephone: 810-954-2100
Fax: 810-954-2126
Email: / URL: http://www.opinc.com
Product Service Description:
Fabricated Plastic Products
Plastic Injection molds

Omega Products, Inc.
PO Box 122
Waterloo, IL 62298-0122
Contact: Scott Hovis, General Mgr.
Telephone: 618-939-3445
Fax: 618-939-3299
Email: / URL:
Product Service Description:
Stainless steel, showers & boat doors
Metal work_miscellaneous

Omega Shielding Products Inc.
1384 Pompton Avenue
Cedar Grove, NJ 07009
Contact: Ken Taylor, Sales Co-Ordinator
Telephone: 973-890-7455
Fax: 973-890-9714
Email: sales@omegashielding.com / URL:
http://www.omegashielding.com
Product Service Description:
Electronic Shielding Strips & Gaskets
Electromagnetic Interference Shields
EMI / RFI Shielding
Electronic Components

Omex Technologies
3673 Woodhead Dr
Northbrook, IL 60062-1816
Contact: Alexander Zaltz, Pres.
Telephone: 847-564-0206
Fax: 847-564-0306
Email: omex1@aol.com / URL: http://
www.omextech.com
Product Service Description:
Inspection & quality control optical
instruments
Optical instruments & lenses
Medical Video Couplers for Endoscopes

Omicron Video
21828 Lassen St. # K
Chatsworth, CA 91311-3693
Contact: Kimi Akiyama, President
Telephone: 818-700-0742
Fax: 818-700-0313
Email: kimi@omicronvideo.com / URL: http:
//www.omicronvideo.com
Product Service Description:
Manufactures television broadcast studio
equipment; custom industrial control systems
Radio & TV communications equipment
Relays & industrial controls
Electronic parts & equipment
Industrial machinery & equipment

Omni Controls, Inc.
13540 N Florida Ave Ste 105
Tampa, FL 33613-3209
Contact: Bob Lamb, Pres.
Telephone: 813-960-3445
Fax: 813-960-4779
Email: sales@omnicontrols.com / URL: http:/
/www.omnicontrols.com
Product Service Description:
Environmental control gages
Measuring & controlling devices

Omnimark Instrument Corp
1320 S Priest Dr Ste 104
Tempe, AZ 85281-6959
Contact: Charlene Byers, Pres.
Telephone: 602-784-2200
Fax: 602-784-4738
Email: inf@omniwww.com / URL: http://
www.omniwww.com
Product Service Description:
Consulting, sales, service and support of
moisture analysis instrumentation

Omnimount Systems
PO Box 60695
Phoenix, AZ 85082-0695
Contact: Garret E Weyand, Chrm., CEO
Telephone: 602-829-8000
Fax: 602-756-9000
Email: / URL: http://www.omnimount.com
Product Service Description:
Manufactures mounting hardware for
speakers and televisions

Onodi Tool & Engineering Co.
19150 Meginnity St
Melvindale, MI 48122-1934
Contact: John Onodi, Pres.
Telephone: 313-386-6682
Fax: 313-386-8696
Email: ote@a1access.net / URL:
Product Service Description:
Complete CNC machining & manufacturing

Onsrud Machine Corporation
110 W. Carpenter Ave
Wheeling, IL 60090
Contact: Lawrence D. Levine, President
Telephone: 847-520-5300
Fax: 847-520-5423
Email: onsrdmch@mcs.net / URL: http://
www.onsrudmachine.com
Product Service Description:
Milling Machines, Routers & Woodworking
Machines
Woodworking Machinery
Machine Tools Metal Cutting Types
Machiner Tool Accessories

OpenDisc Systems Inc
4940 Pearl East Cir Ste 104
Boulder, CO 80301-2442
Contact: Chuck Schmidt, President
Telephone: 303-546-0460
Fax: 303-546-0459
Email: / URL:
Product Service Description:
Computer programming services
Develops custom software for optical storage
on CD/ROM

Opti-Forms Inc
42310 Winchester Rd
Temecula, CA 92590-4810
Contact: Clint Tinker, President
Telephone: 909-676-4724
Fax: 909-676-1178
Email: info@optiforms.com / URL: http://
www.optiforms.com
Product Service Description:
Optical instruments & lenses
Precision Metal Reflectors
Thin film optical coatings
Electrodepistied metal coatings
Electroformed reflectors & products
Mirrors, parabolic & elliptical

Optical Polymer Research, Inc.
5921 Ne 38th Street
Gainesville, FL 32609
Contact: Paul D. Schuman, Ph.D., President
Telephone: 352-378-1027
Fax: 352-373-7712
Email: info@opri.net / URL: http://
www.opri.net/
Product Service Description:
Oxygen Permeable & Soft Contact Lens
Buttons / Blanks
Plastic products related to fiberoptic cladding
polymers

Opticomm Corp
6046 Cornerstone Ct W Ste 209
San Diego, CA 92121-4734
Contact: Ezzy Weisman, Pres.
Telephone: 619-450-0143
Fax: 619-450-0155
Email: info@opticomm.com / URL: http://
www.opticomm.com
Product Service Description:
Manufactures fiber optic communication
cable for video, RGB, data, voice and audio
systems

Optimation, Inc.
300 N. Osage
Independence, MO 64050-2705
Contact: Beth Foulk, Marketing Director
Telephone: 816-836-2000
Fax: 816-836-8589
Email: bfoulk@optinest.com / URL: http://
www.optimation.com
Product Service Description:
Prepack Software, Auto Part Program
Prepack Software, Sheet Metal Fab.

OraLabs Holding Corp
2901 S Tejon St
Englewood, CO 80110-1314
Contact: Gary Schlatter, Chrm., CEO
Telephone: 303-783-9499
Fax: 303-783-5759
Product Service Description:
Toilet preparations
Manufactures lip balm, cough and cold
products, vitamins and breath fresheners
Pharmaceutical preparations
Medicinals & botanicals

Oregon Analytical Laboratory
14855 SW Scholls Ferry Rd.
Beaverton, OR 97007-8482
Contact: Kim Hughes, Lab Mgr.
Telephone: 503-590-5300 / 800-644-0967
Fax: 503-590-1404
Email: / URL: http://www.oalab.com/oal
Product Service Description:
Testing Laboratories
Testing Lab & Services

Oregon Freeze Dry Inc
PO Box 1048
Albany, OR 97321-0407
Contact: Herb Aschkenasy, Pres.
Telephone: 541-812-6605
Fax: 541-967-6527
Email: linda_b@ofd.com / URL: http://
www.ofd.com
Product Service Description:
Freeze dried fruits, vegetables, soups,
complete meals in cups, meats, poultry

Oregon Log Home Co Inc
PO Box 1377
Sisters, OR 97759-1377
Contact: Mike Neary, Pres.
Telephone: 541-549-9354
Fax: 541-549-1135
Email: business@oregonloghomes.com
Product Service Description:
Manufactures prefabricated log buildings
Prefabricated wood buildings
Single-family housing construction

Oregon Micro Systems
1800 NW 169th Pl Ste 100C
Beaverton, OR 97006-7362
Contact: Gary Garleb, GM
Telephone: 503-629-8081
Fax: 503-629-0688
Email: sales@omsmotion.com / URL: http://
www.omsmotion.com
Product Service Description:
Manufactures intelligent motion controllers
Markets step motors & drivers

Oregon Potato
P.O. Box 169
Boardman, OR 97818-0169
Contact: Barry Stice, Director of Sales
Telephone: 541-481-2715
Fax: 541-481-3443
Product Service Description:
Dehydrated Potato Flakes & Flour
Dehydrofrozen Diced Potatoes

Orfila Vineyards Inc
13455 San Pasqual Rd
Escondido, CA 92025-7833
Contact: Alejandro Orfila, Pres.
Telephone: 760-738-6500
Fax: 760-745-3773
Email: orfilavine@aol.com / URL: http://
www.orfila.com
Product Service Description:
Wines, brandy, & brandy spirits
Winery and vineyards

Organic Dyestuffs Corporation
74-84 Valley St.
East Providence, RI 02914-4451
Contact: Sales & Marketing,
Phone: 401-434-3300 / Fax: 401-438-8136
Email: orco@organicdye.com / URL: http://
www.organicdye.com
Product Service Description:
Textile Auxiliaries : Pigments
Dyes & Dyestuffs : Ink Dyes

Organic Milling Inc
505 W Allen Ave
San Dimas, CA 91773-1445
Contact: Vincent Dachary, Pres.
Telephone: 909-599-0961
Fax: 909-599-5180
Email: / URL:
Product Service Description:
Manufactures granola and cereals
Cereal breakfast foods

Organic Valley / Cropp Cooperative
507 W. Main St. - PO Box 159
La Farge, WI 54639
Contact: Sales & Marketing,
Telephone: 608-625-2602
Fax: 608-625-2600
Email: organic@organicvalley.com / URL:
http://www.organicvalley.com
Product Service Description:
Certified Organic Milk & Cheese / Eggs /
Meats / Bulk Ingredients

Organomation Associates, Inc.
266 River Road West
Berlin, MA 01503-1699
Contact: Andrew McNiven, Export Manager
Telephone: 978-838-7300
Fax: 978-838-2786
Email: organomation@worldnet.att.net /
URL: http://www.organomation.com
Product Service Description:
Analytical Lab Evaporators & Extractors

Orgill Inc.
P.O. Box 140
Memphis, TN 38101-0140
Contact: Pritpal S. Bansel, Int'l Sales Mgr.
Telephone: 901-948-3381 Ext. 554
Fax: 901-942-6174
Email: pritpal@orgill.com / URL: http://
www.orgill.com
Product Service Description:
Hardware Wholesale
Plumbing & Heating Equip. Wholesale
Farm & Garden Machinery, Wholesale
Dry Products, Housewares, & Toys

Original Bradford Soap Works, Inc.
200 Providence St., P.O. Box CS1007
West Warwick, RI 02893
Contact: Stephen Svehlik, Sr. Vice President
Telephone: 401-821-2141
Fax: 401-821-5960
Product Service Description:
Bar Soap : Toilet preparations
Industrial Soaps, Flake & Powder
Soap Base, Milled, Translucent, Vegetable

Original Design Silkscreen Co.
Rte. 3, R.f.d. 1, Box 89
North Woodstock, NH 03262
Contact: Jeff Martel, Ptnr.
Telephone: 603-745-6277
Fax: 603-745-8053
Email: odsilk@together.net / URL: http://
www.odimprinteowear.com
Product Service Description:
Textile screen printing & embroidery

Original Impressions, Inc.
12900 Sw 89th Ct
Miami, FL 33176-5876
Contact: Roland Garcia Sr., Pres
Phone: 305-233-1322 / Fax: 305-251-1190
Email: info@originalimpressions.com / URL:
http://www.originalimpressions.com
Product Service Description:
Printing, Commercial

Original Mink Oil Co.
10652 N.E. Holman St.
Portland, OR 97220-1202
Contact: N. P. Wood, President
Telephone: 503-255-2814
Fax: 503-255-2487
Email: / URL:
Product Service Description:
Animal fats and oils and their fractions,
whether or not refined
Leather waterproofer & conditioners

Ortek Data Systems Inc
10445 SW Canyon Rd # S115
Beaverton, OR 97005-1916
Contact: James Strelchun, Pres.
Telephone: 503-626-0475
Fax: 503-644-0171
Email: express@ortekdata.com / URL: http://
www.ortekdata.com
Product Service Description:
Interactive audience,group reponse systems
for : Research, Meetings, Training,
Voting,Surveys

Ortiz Villafane, Rene, Inc.
P.O. Box 9022562
Old San Juan, PR 00902-2562
Contact: Sales & Marketing,
Telephone: 787-793-7141, 24 H
Fax: 787-782-9542
Email: rov_inc@msn.com / URL: http://
www.rovinc.com
Product Service Description:
Customs Broker
Freight Forwarder
Freight & Cargo Transportation

Oryan Industries Inc
PO Box 8978
Vancouver, WA 98668-8978
Contact: Rick Grant, Pres.
Telephone: 360-892-0447
Fax: 360-892-6742
Email: oryan@pacifier.com / URL:
Product Service Description:
Manufactures low-voltage lighting for spas;
fiber optic lighting equipment for the medical
Dental & Industrial

Osmonics, Inc.
5951 Clearwater Dr.
Minnetonka, MN 55343
Contact: D Dean Spatz, CEO
Telephone: 612-933-277
Fax: 612-933-0141
Email: / URL: http://www.osmonics.com
Product Service Description:
Service industry machinery
Water Purification Equipment
Filters, Depth
Filters, Pleated
Membrane Elements & Housings
PVM PS, Centrifugal

Osmose Wood Preserving, Inc.
PO Box O
Griffin, GA 30224
Contact: Paul Goydan, Ex. V-P., GM
Telephone: 800-241-0240
Fax: 770-229-5225
Email: / URL:
Product Service Description:
Wood preservatives
Stains & coatings
Utility pole maintenance
Railway & bridge maintenance

Ossid Corp.
P.o. Drawer 1968
Rocky Mount, NC 27802
Contact: Sidney Tolson, Pres.
Telephone: 252-446-6177
Fax: 252-442-7694
Email: sales@ossid.com / URL: http://
www.ossid.com
Product Service Description:
Packaging equipment

Otec, Inc.
5612 Lafayette Pl
Hyattsville, MD 20781-2351
Contact: John Sullivan, Pres.
Telephone: 301-864-2461
Fax: 301-864-2163
Email: otecinc@erols.com / URL: http://
www.candysnacks.com
Product Service Description:
Candy & other confectionery products
Cotton candy, chocolate items, snacks

Outdoor Cap
P.O. Box 210
Bentonville, AR 72712-0210
Contact: Paul Mahan,
Telephone: 501-273-5870
Fax: 501-273-2144
Email: / URL: http://www.outdoorcap.com
Product Service Description:
Durable Goods, NEC
Woven cotton fabrics

Outdoor Environments, LLC.
2787 R.F.D. Old Rte. 53
Long Grove, IL 60047
Contact: Micheal Pastenak, Pres.
Telephone: 847-358-3558
Fax: 847-537-6768
Product Service Description:
Analog Weather Instruments
Commercial / Marine Applications

Outlook Graphics
PO Box 748
Neenah, WI 54957-0748
Contact: Joseph Baksha, Pres.
Telephone: 920-722-2333
Fax: 920-727-8529
Email: / URL: http://www.outlookgroup.com
Product Service Description:
Printing_commercial
Folding cartons, contract packaging &
commercial printing
Converted paper products
Boxes_folding paperboard

Overland Express Company Inc.
P.O. Box 262322
Houston, TX 77207-2322
Contact: Cecil Simmons, President
Telephone: 713-672-6161
Fax: 713-672-5040
Product Service Description:
Trucking, Transportation
Warehousing & Distribution
Packing & Crating

Overnite Transportation Co.
6150 S. Inkster Rd.,
Romulus, MI 48174
Contact: Sales & Marketing,
Telephone: 313-295-1300
Fax: 313-295-4140
Email: / URL: http://www.overnite.com
Product Service Description:
Freight & Cargo Transportation
Trucking

Owen Mfg. Co., Charles D.
PO Box 457
Swannanoa, NC 28778-0457
Contact: Charles D. Owen III, Pres.
Telephone: 828-298-6802
Fax: 828-299-0901
Email: / URL:
Product Service Description:
Furnishings_house
Blankets & crib sets

Owen Tool & Mfg. Co., Inc.
PO Box 8
Plainville, CT 06062-0008
Contact: Frank Orlando, Gen. Mgr.
Telephone: 860-628-6540
Fax: 860-621-0911
Email: / URL:
Product Service Description:
Tool & die & metal stampings job shop
Metal stampings
Dies, tools, jigs & fixtures_special
Screw Machine Products
Drilling, tapping, milling, spot welding

Ozotech Inc
2401 E Oberlin Rd
Yreka, CA 96097-9577
Contact: Kenneth Mouw, Pres.
Telephone: 530-842-4189
Fax: 530-842-3238
Email: ozotech@ozotech.com / URL: http://
www.ozotech.com
Product Service Description:
Manufactures ozone generators for use in
bottled water systems; water treatment
systems: Manufactures Oxygen Generators

P & D Polygraphics, Inc.
823 Manatee Ave W
Bradenton, FL 34205-8646
Contact: John C. Bigham, Pres., Engrg.,
Opers. & R & D Mgr.
Telephone: 941-748-5510
Fax: 941-747-8188
Email: fauxbronze@earthlink.net / URL:
http://www.albany.net/~fey/fauxbronze.htm
Product Service Description:
Signs, displays & architectural scale models
Signs & advertising specialties
Simulated cast metal signs & plaques

P & J Oyster Co., Inc.
1039 Toulouse St
New Orleans, LA 70112-3425
Contact: Alfred R. Sunseri, Pres., Fin., Pur. &
R & D Mgr.
Telephone: 504-523-2651
Fax: 504-522-4960
Email: pjoyster@iamerica.net / URL:
Product Service Description:
Fish_fresh or frozen prepared
Oyster processing

P & M Sign, Inc.
PO Box 567
Mountainair, NM 87036-0567
Contact: Phil Archuletta, Pres.
Telephone: 505-847-2850
Fax: 505-847-0007
Email: pmsigns@highfiber.com / URL: http://
www.pmsignsinc.com
Product Service Description:
Aluminum & plywood decals & traffic signs
Signs & advertising specialties
Metal products_fabricated
Wood products

P C & E, Fabcon Div.
2280 Schuetz Rd.
Saint Louis, MO 63146
Contact: James I Johnson, GM
Telephone: 314-872-8623
Fax: 314-872-8617
Email: john2@pceinc.com / URL: http://
www.fabcon.com
Product Service Description:
Custom control panels & buildings
Skid mounted process & control equipment
Analyzer system packages

P E I Electronics Inc.
PO Box 1929, 110 Wynn Drive
Huntsville, AL 35807-0929
Contact: Don L. Bullock, VP Marketing &
Bus. Dev.
Telephone: 256-895-2025
Fax: 256-895-2453
Email: info@fury.chry-pei.com / URL: http://
www.pei-electronics.com
Product Service Description:
Electronic Components
Automatic Test Equipment
Electronic Measuring Instruments

P G I International
16101 Vallen Dr
Houston, TX 77041-4030
Contact: Spencer Nimberger, Pres.
Telephone: 713-466-0056
Fax: 713-744-9892
Email: webmaster@pgiint.com / URL: http://
www.pgiint.com
Product Service Description:
Valves_industrial
Industrial valves, manifolds & sample
cylinders & systems

P G Molinari & Sons Inc
1401 Yosemite Ave
San Francisco, CA 94124-3321
Contact: Frank Giorgi, Pres.
Telephone: 415-822-5555
Fax: 415-822-5834
Email: / URL:
Product Service Description:
Prepares Italian dry salami
Sausages & other prepared meat products

P H B Inc.
N48862 Us Highway 53
Osseo, WI 54758-9116
Contact: Marion B. Phillips, Pres.
Telephone: 715-597-3935
Fax: 715-597-3802
Email: info@phbinc.com / URL: http://
www.phbinc.com
Product Service Description:
Tooth Brushes, Floss, Probes, Pediatric &
Geriatric Supplies
RX Ultra Suave, Chemo therapy brushes
Peridontal Health Brush

P R I D E Enterprises, Inc., Baker Paint Industry
PO Box 500
Sanderson, FL 32087-0500
Contact: Don Bryant, Prod. Mgr., Indl.
Telephone: 904-758-0666
Fax: 904-431-1681
Email: / URL: http://www.pridefl.com
Product Service Description:
Traffic paint
Paints & allied products

P T L Equipment Mfg. Co., Inc.
4136 W. Currahee St.
Toccoa, GA 30577
Contact: Robert M. Coronato, VP R&D,
Irene Coronato, Pres, Jon Mata, GM / Jon
Helffer, Sales & Mktg.
Telephone: 706-886-2121
Fax: 706-886-1351
Email: sales@ptlequipment.com / URL: http:/
/www.ptlequipment.com
Product Service Description:
Elevators & moving stairways
Metal elevators & escalator parts
Accessories
NEMA
Car Stations
Elevator Panels
Esculator Safety Switches

P T R-Precision Technologies, Inc.
120 Post Rd
Enfield, CT 06082-5625
Contact: Don Powers, Sales Mgr.
Telephone: 860-741-2281
Fax: 860-745-7932
Email: dpowers@ptreb.com / URL:
Product Service Description:
Electron beam & laser beam systems & job
shops

P.D.I. INC.
PO Box 130
Circle Pines, MN 55014-0130
Contact: Daniel D. Ruege, Director /
Marketing
Telephone: 612-785-2156
Fax: 612-785-2058
Email: pdi@plastidip.com / URL: http://
www.plastidip.com
Product Service Description:
Adhesives

PAI Industries Inc. (Mfr)
950 Northbrook Parkway
Suwanee, GA 30174
Contact: Kin Baker, Mgr. / Intl. Sales
Telephone: 770-822-1000
Fax: 770-822-1421
Email: / URL:
Product Service Description:
Truck Replacement Parts (Mack)
Transmission Replacement Parts (Fuller)
Truck Axle Replacement Parts (Rockwell /
Eaton) : Cummins 855 Replacement Parts
Air Valve Replacement Parts (Bendix/
Midland) : U-Joints (Spicer-type)

PAM International Co., Inc.
45 Mayhill St
Saddle Brook, NJ 07663-5301
Contact: Don Kreiter, Chrm.
Telephone: 201-291-1200
Fax: 201-291-0021
Email: www.sales@pamint.com / URL: http://
www.pamint.com
Product Service Description:
Display fixtures

PC Services
235 Montgomery St Ste 643
San Francisco, CA 94104-2909
Contact: Philip Casey, Owner
Telephone: 415-398-2599
Fax: 415-398-1135
Email: pcasey@slip.net / URL:
Product Service Description:
Word processing; typesetting service
Secretarial & Legal Secretarial

PCIE DBA; The France Group
1511 S Grant St
Goldendale, WA 98620-4019
Contact: Jim Fraser, GM
Telephone: 509-773-4400
Fax: 509-773-6972
Email: info@247snow.com / URL: http://
www.247snow.com
Product Service Description:
Snowboards, Wakeboards, Skateboards,
Fiberglass Lay Ups, (Manufacturer)
Sporting & athletic goods
Plastic products
Dies, tools, jigs & fixtures_special

PDG Associates, Inc.
1903 U.S. 50
Batavia, OH 45103-8604
Contact: Perry Gerome, President
Telephone: 513-732-3344
Fax: 513-732-3363
Email: pdg@one.net / URL: http://
www.pdgassociates.com
Product Service Description:
Bus. Svcs, Manufacturers Agents & Reps
Marketing Consulting Services
Wood Paneling, Wholesale

PDP Systems
2140 Bering Dr
San Jose, CA 95131-2013
Contact: Paul Jones, Pres., CEO
Telephone: 408-944-0301
Fax: 408-944-0811
Email: pdpsys@ix.netcom.com / URL: http://
www.pdpsys.com
Product Service Description:
Distributes peripherals; manufactures memory
upgrades for the PC industry
Semiconductors & related devices
Computers, peripherals & software
Distributor of computer peripherals &
manufacturer of
Memory modules.

PFS Corporation
2402 Daniels St.
Madison, WI 53718-6708
Contact: Michael J. Slifka, President
Telephone: 608-221-3361
Fax: 608-221-0180
Email: pfsteco@pfs-teco.com / URL: http://
www.pfs-teco.com
Product Service Description:
Business Services, Building Products
Inspection

PHD Manufacturing, Inc.
44018 Col-Waterford Rd.
Columbiana, OH 44408-0278
Contact: Dave Neal, Sales
Telephone: 330-482-9256
Fax: 330-482-2763
Email: hammer@theonramp.net / URL:
Product Service Description:
Pipe Hangers & Supports
Metal Struts & Accessories

PMC Electronics
PO Box 11148
Marina Del Rey, CA 90295-7148
Contact: Paul Perelman, Pres.
Telephone: 310-822-5050
Fax: 310-827-1852
Product Service Description:
Manufactures video phones and integrated
circuits : Semiconductors & related devices
for video : Short range video transmitters &
receivers

PPG Industries Inc.
PO Box 1000
Lake Charles, LA 70602-1000
Contact: R.E. Eakin, Wks. Mgr.
Telephone: 318-491-4500
Fax: 318-491-4083
Email: reeakin@ppg.com / URL: http://
www.ppg.com
Product Service Description:
Industrial chemicals
Chemicals_industrial inorganic

PS International
2605 Meridian Pkwy., Ste. 215
Durham, NC 27713-2294
Contact: Mike Fields, President
Telephone: 919-544-9199
Fax: 919-544-4065
Email: psintl@mindspring.com / URL:
Product Service Description:
Milk and cream, concentrated, whether or not
sweetened, in powder, granules or other solid
forms
Rice, semi-milled or wholly milled, whether
or not polished or glazed
Sugar, all grades
Pulses, all types

PSI Inc
13910 Oaks Ave
Chino, CA 91710-7010
Contact: Kim Liberato, Vice President
Telephone: 909-590-8822
Fax: 909-627-2926
Email: / URL:
Product Service Description:
Rubber_synthetic
Design, development & production of
customized silicone

PTX Food Corp.
2269 Sawmill River Rd, Bldg.# 2
Elmsford, NY 10523
Contact: Amy Buteau,
Telephone: 914-941-5635
Fax: 914-592-2408
Email: / URL: http://www.members.aol.com/
ptxl/homepage.html
Product Service Description:
Natural mold inhibitors, flavor enhancers,
baking & dairy ingredients
Food preparations
Flavoring extracts & syrups

PVI International
P.o. Box 7124, 3209 Galvez
Fort Worth, TX 76111
Contact: Gene Ward,
Telephone: 817-335-9531
Fax: 817-332-6742
Email: intsales@pvi.com / URL: http://
www.pvi.com
Product Service Description:
Commercial Water Heater
Steam Hot Water Boilers
Hot Water Storage Tanks

Pace Manufacturing, Inc.
P.O. Box 288
Sagle, ID 83860
Contact: Brenda Griffin, *
Telephone: 208-263-9411
Fax: 208-263-8192
Email: / URL:
Product Service Description:
Hardware, Telescopic Extension Handles
Industrial Molds, Plastic Injection Molded
Parts : Ringdome, Plastic Jewelry Storage
Container

Pace Motor Lines Inc.
P.O. Box 87
Bridgeport, CT 06601
Contact: William T. Pacelli, Vice President
Telephone: 203-366-3881
Fax: 203-381-9062
Email: pacemotor.com / URL: http://
www.pacemotor.com
Product Service Description:
Trucking, Transportation
Warehousing & Distribution

Pace Transducer Co
PO Box 570430
Tarzana, CA 91357-0430
Contact: C J Tucker, Pres.
Telephone: 818-996-4131
Fax: 818-700-8272
Email: / URL:
Product Service Description:
Manufactures measuring and controlling
devices : Measuring & controlling devices
Pressure transducers : Accelerometers
Force Transducers (Load Cells)
Displacement transducers
Oxide insulated aluminum wire

Pacer Pumps
41 Industrial Cir
Lancaster, PA 17601-5927
Contact: Glenn Geist, Export Sls Mgr.
Telephone: 717-656-2161
Fax: 717-656-0477
Email: pacer@success.net / URL: http://
www.industry.net/pacer.pumps
Product Service Description:
Self-priming centrifugal pumps & hand
pumps : Pumps & pumping equipment

Pacific Consolidated Indus
3430 W Carriage Dr
Santa Ana, CA 92704-6412
Contact: Martin Self,
Telephone: 714-979-9200 X203
Fax: 714-436-9150
Email: talkall@pci-intl.com / URL:
Product Service Description:
Manufactures portable air separation
equipment : Electronic components
Nitrogen Generating Equipment
Oxygen Generating Equipment

Pacific Cranes & Equipment Sales
12751 Willard St.
North Hollywood, CA 91605-1149
Contact: Tony Thomas, Owner
Telephone: 818-982-8141
Fax: 818-982-8240
Email: tonythomas@pacificcranes.com /
URL: http://www.pacificcranes.com
Product Service Description:
Cranes : Heavy Equipment : Construction
Equipment & Machinery : Drilling Machinery
Container Handeler Machines & Forklift

Pacific Crest Manufacturing Inc
1130 NW 5th Pl
Canby, OR 97013-3410
Contact: Phyllis Morris, CEO
Telephone: 503-263-6198
Fax: 503-266-5078
Email: pcm@spiritone.com / URL:
Product Service Description:
Manufactures restaurant furniture, table tops,
signage and granitic wood floor inlays
Furniture & fixtures : Hardwood dimension &
flooring mills : Signs & advertising specialties
Parts for furniture & sign industry
CNC parts

Pacific Electricord Company
747 W Redondo Beach Blvd
Gardena, CA 90247-4203
Contact: Jeff Miller-Sax, Director of Mktg.
Telephone: 310-532-6600
Fax: 310-532-5044
Email: jmillarsax@leviton.com / URL:
Product Service Description:
Nonferrous wiredrawing & insulating
Manufactures cord sets, cord assemblies, wire
harnesses, line cords, rubber molding,
Surge Protectors: Telephone & telegraph
apparatus: Current-carrying wiring devices

Pacific Fabric Reels Inc
3401 Etiwanda Ave Ste 811c
Mira Loma, CA 91752-1132
Contact: Remy O'Neill, Pres.
Telephone: 909-681-2993
Fax: 909-681-8065
Product Service Description:
Spiral Tubes; small convolute tubes
Fabric winding boards & spools

Pacific Harvest Products Inc.
P.O. Box 52666
Bellevue, WA 98015-266
Contact: Peggy Bukota, President
Telephone: 425-401-7990 1-888-8premit
Fax: 425-401-7996
Email: pacharv@nwlink.com / URL: http://
www.harvestfoods.net
Product Service Description:
Food - Spices & Soup Bases

Pacific Pac International Inc
2340 Bert Dr
Hollister, CA 95023-2510
Contact: Leif Syrstad, Pres.
Telephone: 831-636-5151
Fax: 831-636-5157
Email: / URL: http://www.pacificpac.com
Product Service Description:
Chemical Preparations

Pacific Phoinix Inc.
2588 Progress St., Unit 28
Vista, CA 92083
Contact: Sales & Marketing,
Telephone: 760-598-7255
Fax: 760-598-7257
Product Service Description:
Telephone & Telegraph Apparatus

Pacific Plastics
111 S. Berry St.
Brea, CA 92821-4827
Contact: Anayat Raminfar, President
Telephone: 714-990-9050
Fax: 714-990-9070
Email: rahim.arian@internetmci.com / URL:
Product Service Description:
PVC & CPVC Plastic Pipes
PVC & CPVC Plastic Fittings, Unions,
Flanges, etc.
Corrosion resist thermoplastic valves
Cements, cleaners & primers for PVC, CPVC
& ABS plastic pipes

Pacific Poultry Co. Ltd.
1818 Kanakanui Street
Honolulu, HI 96819
Contact: E.f. Morgado, *
Telephone: 808/841-2828
Fax: 808-842-0872
Email: hulix2@aol.com / URL:
Product Service Description:
Food Specialties, Sauces
Hawaii's Famous Huli Huli Sauce

Pacific Roller Die Co., Inc.
1321 W. Winton Ave.
Hayward, CA 94540-3398
Contact: Sales & Marketing,
Telephone: 510-782-7242
Fax: 510-887-5639
Product Service Description:
Spiral Weldseam Pipe Making Equipment

Pacific States Felt & Mfg Co
PO Box 5024
Hayward, CA 94540-5024
Contact: Walter Perscheid Jr, Pres.
Telephone: 510-783-0277
Fax: 510-783-4725
Product Service Description:
Gaskets, packing & sealing devices
Manufactures gaskets & parts— cork, plastic,
rubber, : Sponge, foam & felt

Pacific Sun Casual Furniture
340 E Menlo Ave
Hemet, CA 92543-1424
Contact: Larry Snell, Pres.
Telephone: 909-658-3156
Fax: 909-658-0254
Product Service Description:
Manufactures Faux Stone Table Tops
Manufactures aluminum outdoor furniture

Pacific Sun Industries Inc
710 Sandoval Way
Hayward, CA 94544-7111
Contact: Doug Moore, Pres.
Telephone: 510-489-7405
Fax: 510-489-4494
Email: info@pacificsuninc.com / URL:
Product Service Description:
Manufactures beef jerky

Pacific Utility Equipment Co
PO Box 24387
Seattle, WA 98124-0387
Contact: Jim Young, Br. Mgr.
Telephone: 206-764-5025
Fax: 206-762-4973
Email: jsturmer@pacutil.com / URL:
Product Service Description:
Industrial machinery & equipment
Wholesales aerial manlifts and truck-mounted
equipment to utilities and municipalities
Mobile 120 volt AC inverters & generators
Van interiors - sales & installation
Service bodies & ladder racks

Pacific Western Container
1535 E Edinger Ave
Santa Ana, CA 92705-4907
Contact: Tim Bynon, Mgr.
Telephone: 714-547-9266
Fax: 714-953-9270
Email: pwc@pacificwestern.com / URL:
http://www.pacificwetern.com
Product Service Description:
Boxes_corrugated & solid fiber

Packaging Center, Inc.
7330 N.W. 79th Terr.
Miami, FL 33166-2212
Contact: Dick Siu, Owner
Phone: 305-884-1572 / Fax: 305-883-7605
Email: packctr@icanect.net / URL: http://
www.packagingcenter.com
Product Service Description:
Bags: Plastics, Laminated, and Coated
Articles for the conveyance or packing of
goods, of plastics: Containers specially
designed and equipped for carriage by one or
more modes of transport : Articles of plastics

Packaging Systems International, Inc.
4990 Acoma St.
Denver, CO 80216
Contact: Alan Guyton, V.P. Sales & Mktg.
Telephone: 303-296-4445
Fax: 303-298-1016
Email: sales@pkgsys.com / URL:
Product Service Description:
Bag Packers : Bag Palletizers

Pacway Food International Corp
23840 Foley St
Hayward, CA 94545-1619
Contact: Anthony Ang, Pres.
Telephone: 510-786-3885
Fax: 510-786-1323
Email: tamcormex@aol.com / URL:
Product Service Description:
Manufactures and distributes frozen Oriental
products : Frozen specialties / eggrolls
Packaged frozen foods

Pafco Importing Co.
1601 Bayshore Hwy., Ste. 346
Burlingame, CA 94010-1514
Contact: Terence S. Fitzgerald, President
Telephone: 650-692-6161
Fax: 650-692-8950
Product Service Description:
Fish and Seafoods
Almonds, fresh or dried, shelled
Almonds, fresh or dried, in shell
Salmon, prepared or preserved, whole or in
pieces, but not minced
Condensed Sweetened milk

Page Seed Co., Inc.
P.O. Box 158
Greene, NY 13778-1108
Contact: William E. Page, President
Telephone: 607-656-4107
Fax: 607-656-8558
Email: pageseed@aol.com / URL:
Product Service Description:
Garden Seed Packets
Potpourri (Scent Filled Packets)
Packets Filled with Bath Salts
All custom packets (seed, potpourri & bath
salts) have custom imprint
Area available for personalized message on
all custom packets
Minums vary, please inquire

Pagotto Industries
6350 N.E. 4th Ave.
Miami, FL 33138-6101
Contact: Frank Bagottu, Owner
Telephone: 305-758-1575
Fax: 305-758-1653
Email: pagotto@gate.net / URL: http://
www.pagottoindustries.com
Product Service Description:
Washing, bleaching or dyeing machines for
textiles yarns, fabrics or made up textiles
articles : Refurbishing of used industrial
laundry equipment, for exportation

Painted Bird
770 Rte. 47
Woodbury, CT 06798
Contact: Sandy Morgan, Pres.
Telephone: 203-263-4601
Fax: 203-263-0024
Email: berdcarve@aol.com / URL: http://
www.thepaintedbird.com
Product Service Description:
Decorative Hand Carved Birds
Bird Carvings in Wood

Palco Connector
555 Pond Dr
Wood Dale, IL 60191-1192
Contact: Terry Rizzo,
Phone: 630-595-2300 / Fax: 630-595-6579
URL: http://www.phoenixofchicago.com
Product Service Description:
Electronic connectors

Palco Telecom Service Inc
2914 Green Cove Road
Huntsville, AL 35803
Contact: Joe Vaughn, Vice President / Sales
& Marketing
Telephone: 205/883-3400
Fax: 205-883-3499
Email: sales@palco-telecom.com / URL:
http://www.palco-telecom.com
Product Service Description:
Elec Telecom Equipment Repair Shop
Elec Telecom Equip Refurbishment

Palisade Corporation
31 Decker Road
Newfield, NY 14867
Contact: Vera Gilliland, Director / Mktg.
Telephone: 607-277-8000
Fax: 607-277-8001
Email: sales@palisade.com / URL: http://
www.palisade.com
Product Service Description:
Prepack. Software Design, Risk Analysis
Decision Analysis

Palm Peterbilt - GMC Trucks, Inc.
2441 S. State Road 7
Fort Lauderdale, FL 33317-6910
Contact: Victor Weiger, Owner
Telephone: 954-584-3200
Fax: 954-584-3228
Email: email@palmtruckrv.com / URL: http://
www.palmtruckrv.com
Product Service Description:
Automobile & RV Parts, RV Rentals
New & Used Trucks,Trailers and RV'S

Palnut Co., The
152 Glen Rd
Mountainside, NJ 07092-2915
Contact: Stan Erman, President
Telephone: 908-233-3300 Ext. 734
Fax: 908-654-0243
Email: Stan_Erman@palnut.com / URL: http:/
/www.palnut.com
Product Service Description:
Fasteners

Palone & Associates
6452 Fig St Ste A
Arvada, CO 80004-1041
Contact: Tony Palone, Pres.
Phone: 303-424-2755 / Fax: 303-420-0961
Email: palonea@aol.com / URL: http://
www.proforma.com/palone
Product Service Description:
Screen printing, flexographic, offset,
letterpress, photo composition; photocopying
Printing_commercial
Lithographic printing_commercial
Photocopying & duplicating services

Pan Abode Cedar Homes, Inc.
4350 Lake Washington Blvd., N.
Renton, WA 98056-1545
Contact: John L. Hubbard, President
Phone: 245-255-8260 / Fax: 245-255-8630
URL: http://www.panabodehomes.com
Product Service Description:
Custom Designed Cedar Home Kits

Pan American Plastics Co., Div. of Hunt-Wilde Corp.
2835 Overpass Rd.
Tampa, FL 33619
Contact: Doug Hunt, President
Telephone: 813-623-2461
Fax: 813-621-0664
Email: / URL:
Product Service Description:
Rigid Vinyl Extrusions
Flexible Vinyl Extrusions

Panametrics, Inc
221 Crescent St.
Waltham, MA 02154-3418
Contact: Risa Chleck,
Telephone: 781-899-2719
Fax: 781-894-8582
Email: pci@panametrics.com / URL: http://
www.panametrics.com
Product Service Description:
Flow Instruments/Industrial Process Type
Humidity Instruments/Industrial Process

Pandrol Jackson Inc.
200 S Jackson Rd
Ludington, MI 49431-2473
Contact: Johnathan Reilly, VP Sales
Telephone: 616-843-7429
Fax: 616-843-6507
Email: sales@pandroljackson.com / URL:
http://www.pandroljackson.com
Product Service Description:
Railroad maintenance equipment,
Manufacturer
Rail grinding & rail flaw detection services

Panel Built, Inc.
PO Box 2658
Blairsville, GA 30514-2658
Contact: Mike Kiernan, Pres.
Telephone: 706-745-0622
Fax: 706-745-1450
Email: info@panel-built.com & sales@panel-
built.com / URL: http://www.panel-built.com
Product Service Description:
Panelized metal building systems
Metal products_fabricated

Pantos Corp
74 Rumford Ave # 585
Waltham, MA 02154-3845
Contact: D Pantos, Chrm., Treas.
Telephone: 781-891-4930
Fax: 781-891-4931
Email: / URL:
Product Service Description:
Luggage : Soft Side Luggage, Sporting
Goods, Coolers and Insulating Bags
Sporting & athletic goods
Plastic products
Plastic foam products

Pantropic Power Products, Inc.
8205 N.W. 58th St.
Miami, FL 33166-3406
Contact: Luis Botas, President
Telephone: 305-592-4944
Fax: 305-477-1943
Email: lbotas@pantropic.com / URL: http://
www.pantropic.com
Product Service Description:
Pumps and Pumping Equipment
Generating sets with spark-ignition internal
combustion piston engines
Generating sets, electric, parts & accessories
Agricultural, horticultural, forestry, bee-
keeping machinery, including germination
plant

Paper Pak Products Inc
PO Box 1060
La Verne, CA 91750-0960
Contact: James Bogner,
Telephone: 909-392-1200
Fax: 909-392-1237
Product Service Description:
Paper mills : Manufactures tissue paper,
hospital underpads, OB pads and adult briefs
Sanitary paper products : Meat, Poultry &
Fish Soaker Pads : Manufactures Non-
Wovens

Par Products
902 W Kirby St
Wylie, TX 75098-3917
Contact: Linda Coker, Sales Dept.
Telephone: 972-442-9000
Fax: 972-429-0350
Email: parproducts@worldnet.att.net / URL:
Product Service Description:
Tire repair plugs : Self-Vulcanizing Repairs

Par Vision Systems Corporation
220 Seneca Turnpike
New Hartford, NY 13413
Contact: John Kiehm, President
Telephone: 315-738-0600
Fax: 315-738-0562
Email: john_kiehm@partech.com / URL:
Product Service Description:
Food Inspection Equipment
X-Ray Food Inspection Equipment

Paradise Sportswear, Inc.
PO box 1027
Kalaheo, HI 96741-1027
Contact: Erica Franklin, Marketing Mgr.
Telephone: 808-335-5670
Fax: 808-335-3478
Email: reddirt@aoloha.net / URL: http://
www.dirtshirt.com
Product Service Description:
Naturlly Dyred Red Dirt Shirts
Tees, Polos, Sweatshirts
Sized Infant to 4XL

Paradise Textiles Co
14207 Monte Vista Ave
Chino, CA 91710-5724
Contact: Chul Kang, Pres.
Telephone: 909-591-8202
Fax: 909-591-6722
Product Service Description:
Finishing plants, cotton

Paraflex Industries, Inc.
PO Box 920
Beacon, NY 12508-0920
Contact: Michael A. James, Pres.
Telephone: 914-831-9000
Fax: 914-831-6763
Email: salesinfo@paraflex.com / URL: http://
www.paraflex.com
Product Service Description:
Lighting fixtures & plastic products
Lighting equipment : Plastic products
Lighting Components

Paragon Industries, Inc.
2011 S Town East Blvd
Mesquite, TX 75149-1122
Contact: John R. Hohenshelt, Pres.
Phone: 972-288-7557 / Fax: 972-222-0646
Email: paragonind@worldnet.att.net / URL:
http://www.paragonweb.com
Product Service Description:
Electric kilns & furnaces
Furnaces & ovens_industrial

Paragon Water Systems
14001 63rd Way N
Clearwater, FL 33760-3619
Contact: John H. Douglas, Pres.,
Phone: 727-538-4704 / Fax: 727-536-8368
Email: paragonsys@earthlink.net / URL:
http://www.paragonwater.com
Product Service Description:
Water filtration equipment
Process control instruments

Paramount Truck Body & Equip
6901 Cherry Ave
Long Beach, CA 90805-1720
Contact: Raymond D Anderson, Pres.
Telephone: 562-634-2010
Fax: 562-531-4218
URL: http://www.paramounttruckbody.com
Product Service Description:
Dump truck bodies & heavy duty flat bed
bodies

Parisi-Virana Co., Inc.
545 Broadway, 3rd Fl.
New York, NY 10012-3921
Contact: R. Parisi, President
Telephone: 212-966-6405
Product Service Description:
Textile Products : Sugar : Rice
Trucks & Parts

Park Metal Products Co.
19197 Sherwood St
Detroit, MI 48234-2818
Contact: Rand Overdorf, Pres.
Telephone: 313-366-2200
Fax: 313-366-1540
Email: parkdetroit@msn.com / URL: http://
www.parkdetroit.com
Product Service Description:
Switchgear & switchboard apparatus

Parking Products, Inc.
PO Box S
Willow Grove, PA 19090-0921
Contact: Dieter E. Niebisch, Pres., Mktg.,
Opers., Pur. & R & D Mgr.
Telephone: 215-657-7500
Fax: 215-657-4321
URL: http://www.parkingproducts.com
Product Service Description:
Machinery_special industry
Parking gates, ticket, coin & token machines,
directional enforcers, proximity, bar code

Parkwest Industries Inc
4143 E Quartz Cir
Mesa, AZ 85215-9116
Contact: Richard L Porter, GM
Telephone: 602-396-1100
Fax: 602-396-1145
Email: parkwestaz@worldnet.att.net / URL:
http://www.parkwesthomes.com
Product Service Description:
Manufactures mobile homes : Mobile homes
Travel trailers & campers

Parpro, Inc.
11315 Rancho Bernardo Rd Ste 148
San Diego, CA 92127-1464
Contact: Kevin D. Atkins, V.P.Sales & Mktg.
Phone: 619-673-7127 / Fax: 619-673-8108
Email: katkins@parpro.com / URL: http://
www.parpro.com
Product Service Description:
Manufactures electromechanical assemblies-
harnesses & cables : Electrical equipment &
chassis : Thru-hole PCB's : Kitting bulk
components

Parris Mfg. Co.
PO Box 338
Savannah, TN 38372-0338
Contact: Craig Phillips, Pres.
Telephone: 901-925-3918
Fax: 901-925-1139
Email: parrismfg@centuryinter.net / URL:
http://www.parrismfg.com
Product Service Description:
Wooden & steel toy guns & archery sets
Bunk Beds, bedroom furniture

Pars Manufacturing Co.
PO Box 149
Ambler, PA 19002-0149
Contact: Stanley Solnick, Dir. Intl. Sales
Telephone: 215-646-1300
Fax: 215-646-1368
Email: pars@parsmfg.com / URL: http://
www.parsmfg.com
Product Service Description:
Gaskets, rubber/Fiberglass/Ceramic
Packing Devices : Expansion Joints,
Removable Pipe Covers : High-Temp.
Refractories

Parsons Behle & Latimer
201 S. Main Street, Suite 1800,
P.O. Box 45898
Salt Lake City, UT 84145-0898
Contact: Raymond J. Etcheverry, President
Telephone: 801-532-1234
Fax: 801-536-6111
Product Service Description:
Legal Services

Partnership Press, Inc.
PO Box 380
Ames, IA 50010-0380
Contact: Gary Gerlach, Publisher
Telephone: 515-232-2160
Fax: 515-232-2364
Product Service Description:
Newspapers

Parts Services International LLC
P.O. Box 845
Westfield, MA 01086-0845
Contact: Jon Hilberg, President
Telephone: 413-562-2324
Fax: 413-562-7234
Email: psi@psiparts.com / URL: http://
www.psiparts.com
Product Service Description:
Compressor Replacement Parts
Lubricants - Compressor
Air Filtration Equipment
Compressor Valves
Desiccants

Parts Tires Imports
2137 Flinstone Dr. #J
Tucker, GA 30084-5022
Contact: Wadie Ibrahim, *
Telephone: 404-934-8987
Fax: 404-934-9004
Product Service Description:
Spare Parts For Heavy Equipment

Paschall Export-Import Co., Inc.
PO Box 2100
Peachtree City, GA 30269-0100
Contact: Norman Paschall, Pres., Sales Mgr.
Telephone: 770-487-7945
Fax: 770-487-0840
Email: fibers@paschall.com / URL:
Product Service Description:
Textile waste processing
Textile goods

Pasco Tool & Die
140 Baldwin St. Ext.
Meadville, PA 16335
Contact: Anthony Passilla, Pres., CFO
Telephone: 814-724-7760
Fax: 814-333-1249
Email: tony@pascotool.com / URL:
Product Service Description:
Molds & dies
Dies, tools, jigs & fixtures_special

Pass Distributing Corporation
18021 Sky Park Cir Ste E
Irvine, CA 92614-6523
Contact: Joan I Davis-Pass, V-P.
Telephone: 949-261-2040
Fax: 949-833-0807
Email: kisolthr@pacbell.net / URL: http://
www.passcastle.com
Product Service Description:
Designs & manufactures men's & women's
lingerie in lace, leather, latex & patent leather
Furniture, Fetish : Fetish Accessories & Toys
Books, Video & CD's : Sexy lingerie &
hosiery & stockings

Patchkraft Inc.
70 Outwater Ln
Garfield, NJ 07026-3854
Contact: Paula Markowitz, Pres.
Telephone: 973-340-3300
Fax: 973-340-7278
Email: patchkraft@aol.com / URL:
Product Service Description:
Infant bedding & accessories

Patterson Avenue Tool Co.
6515 Rfd
Long Grove, IL 60047-2020
Contact: Jim Clark, V-P., Prodn.
Telephone: 847-949-8100
Fax: 847-949-8149
Email: sales@tjak.com / URL: http://
www.tjak.com
Product Service Description:
Carpenters' hand tools
Tools_hand & edge

Patterson Equipment
PO Box T
Bastrop, TX 78602-1993
Contact: Robert Patterson, Owner
Telephone: 512-321-4114
Fax: 512-321-5959
Email: / URL:
Product Service Description:
Construction Equipment

Paul Marsh, LLC
654 Madison Ave., 20th Fl.
New York, NY 10021-8404
Contact: Paul Marsh, Owner
Telephone: 212-759-9060
Fax: 212-319-6214
Email: pmarsh@dti.net
Product Service Description:
Purchasing agent & consolidations
Export agent for U.S. Manufacturers
China bristles, fine hair, horse hair, synthetics
Machine & tools (new & used)
Brushes - hair, makeup, paint, paint roller,
fabric, etc. : Chemicals - Pharmaceutical,
cosmetic, paint & asphalt : Laboratory
products & equipment : Computer hardware,
software & accessories : Raw materials &
machinery for the textile industry
Packaging, sorting & labeling equipment
Dry spices, nuts, oak barrels, bottling
machinery

Paul's Cabinets Co.
2416 Hwy. 35
Manasquan, NJ 08736
Contact: Paul Waltsak, Pres.
Phone: 732-528-9427 / Fax: 732-528-6131
Email: pwaltsak@aol.com / URL:
Product Service Description:
Wooden cabinets : Kitchen cabinets_wood

Paulik International Co.
17552 -12 Vanderberg Ln.
Tustin, CA 92780
Contact: John Paulik, President
Telephone: 714-832-1989
Fax: 714-669-9063
Email: paulikexport@juno.com / URL: http://
www.paulik.com
Product Service Description:
General U.S. Made Products, Vehicles

Pauwels Transformers Inc.
#1 Pauwels Drive
Washington, MO 63090-0189
Contact: Francis Robberechts, Pres.
Telephone: 314-239-6783
Fax: 314-239-1926
Email: francis.robberechts@pauwels.com /
URL: http://www.pauwels.com
Product Service Description:
Transformers, except electronic up to 500
MVA (Pauwels Group)
Pad & pole mounted three-phase transformers
45 kva - 5000 kva

Paxar Iimak
310 Commerce Dr
Amherst, NY 14228-2303
Contact: Nicholas Mandrycky, Sr. V-P., Sales
Telephone: 716-691-6333
Fax: 716-691-3395
Email: nick_mandrycky@iimak.com / URL:
http://www.iimak.com
Product Service Description:
Carbon paper & inked ribbons
Printer & fax machine thermal transfer
ribbons

Payton Granite & Monument Co.
2254 Harmony Rd
Elberton, GA 30635-3741
Contact: Roger Payton, Owner
Telephone: 706-283-3070
Fax: 706-283-0401
Email: bpayton@elbertonga.com / URL:
Product Service Description:
Burial monuments & granite processing
Cut stone & stone products
Pet monuments

Pearpoint Inc
72055 Corporate Way
Thousand Palms, CA 92276-3334
Contact: Alan Sefton, Pres.
Phone: 760-343-7350 / Fax: 760-343-7351
Email: / URL: http://www.pearpoint.com
Product Service Description:
Manufactures camera inspection equipment
for pipelines : Manufactures license plate
capture cameras

Pearson Southwest Marketing
2432 W Peoria Ave Ste 1043
Phoenix, AZ 85029-4729
Contact: Jim Kelly,
Phone: 602-944-7474 / Fax: 602-997-8773
Email: candjkelly@msn.com:
Product Service Description:
Manufacturers' rep for electrical industrial
apparatus

Pecard Leather Care Products
1836 Industrial Dr
Green Bay, WI 54302-2108
Contact: Steven W. Wadzinski, President
Telephone: 920-468-5056
Fax: 920-468-1399
Email: pecard@dct.com / URL: http://
www.pecard.com
Product Service Description:
Leather care products & preservatives
Polishes & sanitation goods

Pedigree Cats Inc
1835 Ocean Ave
Raymond, WA 98577-2818
Contact: Kelly Habersetzer, Pres.
Telephone: 360-942-2810
Fax: 360-942-2936
Email: info@pedigreecats.com / URL: http://
www.PedigreeCats.com
Product Service Description:
Builds custom power and sailing catamarans

Pedrizzetti Winery
1645 San Pedro Ave
Morgan Hill, CA 95037-9667
Contact: Ed Pedrizzetti, Ptnr.
Telephone: 408-779-7389
Fax: 408-779-9083
Email: / URL:
Product Service Description:
Produces and bottles wines; crushing and
producing services for vineyard owners or
other wineries

Peerless Industries, Inc.
P.O. Box 272
Burlington, MA 01803-0472
Contact: Frank C. Caliri, President
Telephone: 781-273-2168
Fax: 781-273-2208
Email: / URL:
Product Service Description:
Model Railroad Electronic Cont

Peking Noodle Co Inc
1514 N San Fernando Rd
Los Angeles, CA 90065-1225
Contact: Frank Tong, Pres.
Telephone: 323-223-2023
Fax: 323-223-3211
Email: ftong@pekingnoodle.com / URL:
http://www.pekingnoodle.com
Product Service Description:
Food preparations
Manufactures, distributes and sells oriental
noodles

Pel Assocs., Inc.
PO Box 5298
North Branch, NJ 08876-1303
Contact: Joseph Ringwood, VP
Telephone: 908-725-6060
Fax: 908-725-1932
Email: / URL:
Product Service Description:
Chemical preparations
Aerosol container filling

Pelican Co
1914 B St
Marysville, CA 95901-3732
Contact: Lulu Z Korshak, Pres.
Telephone: 530-741-2317
Fax: 530-741-2317
Email: / URL:
Product Service Description:
Patinted baby plastic products
Baby feeding accessories

Pelican Rope Works
4001 W Carriage Dr
Santa Ana, CA 92704-6301
Contact: Gaylord C Whipple, Pres.
Telephone: 714-545-0116
Fax: 714-545-3311
Email: sales@pilicanrope.com / URL: http://
www.pelicanrope.com
Product Service Description:
Cordage & twine
Manufactures braided ropes (nylon, polyester,
spectra and Kevlar) for marine & Industrial

Pellerin Milnor Corp.
PO Box 400
Kenner, LA 70063-0400
Contact: James W. Pellerin, Pres.
Telephone: 504-467-9591
Fax: 504-468-9307
Email: mktg@milnor.com / URL: http://
www.milnor.com
Product Service Description:
Commercial laundry machinery
Laundry equipment_commercial

Pelmor Labs, Inc.
401 Lafayette St
Newtown, PA 18940-0309
Contact: E. William Ross Sr., Pres.
Telephone: 215-968-3334
Fax: 215-968-6415
Email: pelmor@voicenet.com / URL: http://
www.pelmor.com
Product Service Description:
Rubber Molding & Extrusions

Pelouze/Health-O-Meter, Inc.
7400 W 100th Pl
Bridgeview, IL 60455-2406
Contact: Mary Beth Shay, Pur. Agt.
Telephone: 708-430-8330
Fax: 800-654-7330
Email: / URL: http://www.sigbrands.com
Product Service Description:
Scales & balances, except laboratory
Mechanical & electronic scales

Pelseal Technologies, LLC
401 Lafayette St.
Newtown, PA 18940-0309
Contact: E. William Ross, Jr., President
Telephone: 215-497-1088
Fax: 215-245-7606
Email: sales@pelseal.com / URL: http://
www.pelseal.com
Product Service Description:
Fluoroelastomer Based Adhesives & Sealants

Peltier Glass Co., The
518 DeLeon St., P.O. Box 490
Ottawa, IL 61350-0490
Contact: J. L. Jankowski, President
Telephone: 815-433-0026
Fax: 815-433-5787
Email: / URL:
Product Service Description:
Glass Marbles
Votive Candle Holders
Automotive Carburetor Bowls
Automotive Lenses

Penates General Welding
11200 Nw South River Dr
Miami, FL 33178-1137
Contact: Rolando Penates, Pres.
Telephone: 305-863-6398
Product Service Description:
Dump bodies, truck & trailer manuf.

Pendl Co., Inc.
1825 Dolphin Dr # B
Waukesha, WI 53186-1430
Contact: Randy Pendl, Pres.
Telephone: 414-896-8888
Fax: 414-896-8899
Email: pendl@pendl.com / URL:
Product Service Description:
Rebuilt laser printer toner cartridges
Tektronix color printers

Penichet Carpet
4208 Laguna St.
Coral Gables, FL 33146-1801
Contact: Felipe Penichet, Owner
Telephone: 305-445-0575
Fax: 305-446-4675
Email: penichetfl@aol.com / URL:
Product Service Description:
Floor Covering Stores
Carpets and other textile floor coverings

Penn Big Bed Slate Co., Inc.
PO Box 184
Slatington, PA 18080-0184
Contact: Peter Papay, Pres., Fin., Pur., R & D
& Sales Mgr.
Telephone: 610-767-4601
Fax: 610-767-9252
Email: / URL:
Product Service Description:
Cut stone & stone products
Roofing slate, structural slate, floor tile, slate
fireplace facings, chimney tops, turkey
Mineral products_nonmetallic

Penn Terminals Inc.
One Saville Avenue
Eddystone, PA 19022-1583
Contact: G.A. Hopper, President
Telephone: 610-499-3000
Fax: 610-499-3014
Email: / URL: http://www.pennterminals.com
Product Service Description:
Container Freight Station
Container Repairs
Distribution
Heavy Lifts
Terminal Operators
Warehouse Services

Penn Yan Marine Mfg. Corp.
Waddell Ave.
Penn Yan, NY 14527
Contact: Camille J. Amato, Pres., Pur. Agt.
Telephone: 315-536-7755
Fax: 315-536-0107
Email: pennyan@eznet.net / URL: http://
www.pennyanboats.com
Product Service Description:
Fiberglass pleasure, patrol & fishing boats
Law Enforcement Boats

Pennsylvania Machine Works, Inc.
100 Bethel Rd
Aston, PA 19014-3407
Contact: John P. Lafferty, Marketing Manager
Telephone: 610-497-3300
Fax: 610-497-3325
Email: johnp@pennusa.com / URL: http://
www.pennusa.com
Product Service Description:
Forged steel high pressure pipe fittings &
piping outlets
Valves & pipe fittings

Pennsylvania Scale Co.
PO Box 566
Leola, PA 17540-0566
Contact: Marge Maccubbin, Dir., Int'l Sales
Telephone: 717-656-2653
Fax: 717-656-3216
Email: / URL: http://www.pascale.com
Product Service Description:
Scales & balances, except laboratory
Laboratory & industrial electronic weighing
& counting scale systems

Pennsylvania Sewing Machine Co.
215 Vandale Dr
Houston, PA 15342-1250
Contact: Robert Matusic, Pres.
Telephone: 724-746-8800
Fax: 724-746-3122
Email: pennsewl@pulsnet.com / URL: http://
www.pennsew.com
Product Service Description:
Sewing machines : Appliances_household

Pennsylvania Tool & Gages, Inc.
PO Box 534
Meadville, PA 16335-0534
Contact: Irene Burns, Pres.
Telephone: 814-336-3136
Fax: 814-333-9131
Email: pennsylvaniatool-gages.com / URL:
http://www.pennsylvaniatool-gages.com
Product Service Description:
Precision Tool & Die Shop

Penny Newman Milling LLC
619 S Williams St
Hanford, CA 93230-5344
Contact: James Netto, Br. Mgr.
Telephone: 209-582-0399
Fax: 209-582-5782
Email: / URL:
Product Service Description:
Produces feed grain
Feeds_prepared
Flour & other grain mill products

Penray Companies Inc.(Mfr)
1801 Estes Avenue
Elk Grove Village, IL 60007
Contact: John W. Brown, *
Telephone: 847-981-2105
Fax: 847-439-7997
Email: penexport@aol.com / URL:
Product Service Description:
Automotive Fuel Additives, Oil Additives

Pepperell Paper Co., Inc.
128 Main Street
Pepperell, MA 01463-1563
Contact: Stephen Ulicny, Sales Manager
Telephone: 978-433-6951
Fax: 978-433-6427
Email: SULicny@merrimacpaper.com / URL:
http://www.merrimacpaper.com
Product Service Description:
Specialty Papers

Perdue Farms Inc. Grain & Oilseed Div.
PO Box 1537
Salisbury, MD 21802-1537
Contact: Richard Willey, V-P G.M.
Telephone: 410-543-3847
Fax: 410-860-4421
Email: dick.willey@perdue.com / URL: http:/
/www.perdue.com
Product Service Description:
Fats & oils_edible
Edible oils & protein blending

Peregrine Marine, Inc.
3020 Rampart Dr
Anchorage, AK 99501-3131
Contact: Jeff Johnson, Pres
Telephone: 907-243-6448
Fax: 907-243-4654
Product Service Description:
Aluminum boats & yachts
Boat building & repairing

Perfection Machinery
2550 Arthur Ave.
Elk Grove Village, IL 60007
Contact: Patrick Angus, President
Telephone: 847-427-3333
Fax: 847-427-3333
Email: sales@perfectionmachinery.com /
URL: http://www.perfectionmachinery.com
Product Service Description:
Fabricating Machinery
Power presses & related equipment
Machine tools, CNC & non CNC

Perfection Machinery Sales, Inc.
2550 Arthur Ave.
Elk Grove Village, IL 60007
Contact: Nicolette Grieco, *
Telephone: 708-427-3333
Fax: 708-427-8884
Product Service Description:
Metal Working Machinery

Performahome (Mfr)
317 Highway 620 South, Suite 200
Austin, TX 78734
Contact: Keven Clark, *
Telephone: 512-263-5199
Fax: 512-263-5499
Product Service Description:
Voice Activated Home Automation Equip.

Perimeter Products, Inc.
1130 Terra Bella Avenue
Mountain View, CA 94043-1832
Contact: Martha A. Lee, President
Telephone: 650-966-8550
Fax: 650-966-8517
Email: mkt@perimeterproducts.com / URL:
http://www.perimeterproducts.com
Product Service Description:
Alarms Intrusion Detection Fence Mount
Alarms, Personal Duress
Comm. Eq. Outdoor Microwave Sensors

Peripherals Manufacturing Inc
4775 Paris St
Denver, CO 80239-2803
Contact: Ronald Carboy, Pres.
Telephone: 303-371-8651
Fax: 303-371-8643
Email: periphman@periphman.com / URL:
http://www.periphman.com
Product Service Description:
Manufactures computer media backup
products; computer tape, cartridges, diskettes
&
Disk packs, Computer storage devices
Duplication / Replication / in all computer
media; diskettes & CDR

Perma-Cal Industries Inc
1742 Orbit Way
Minden, NV 89423-4114
Contact: David Myers, Sales Mgr.
Telephone: 775-782-1026
Fax: 775-782-1056
Email: / URL: http://www.perma-cal.com
Product Service Description:
Manufactures pressure instrumentation

Perma-Pipe Ricwil, Industrial
7720 N. Lehigh Ave.
Niles, IL 60714-3416
Contact: Sales & Marketing,
Telephone: 847-966-2235
Fax: 847-470-1204
Email: marketing@permapipe.com / URL:
http://www.permapipe.com
Product Service Description:
Leak Detection / Location Equipment
Leak Detection, Fuel Oil
Leak Detection, Piping
Conduit Underground Piping
Pip, Jacketed
Pipe, Preinsulated
Pipe, Steam Traced

Permaluster Company
1844 N Keystone St
Burbank, CA 91504-3417
Contact: Henry D Walker, Owner & GM
Telephone: 818-566-4231
Fax: 818-566-4232
Email: / URL:
Product Service Description:
Manufactures electronic wire, cable and
molded cables
Nonferrous wiredrawing & insulating -
anodizing - flatten
Electronic components
Coil & winding
Responding
Specialty wires
Flat wire
Strip
Bare wire
Insulated

Permatron Corporation
11400 Melrose Ave.
Franklin Park, IL 60131-1325
Contact: Todd K. Oberg, Director Sales &
Marketing
Telephone: 847-451-0999
Fax: 847-451-1811
Email: obergtko@aol.com / URL:
Product Service Description:
Odor / Fume Removal Filters Carbon-Zeolite
Filtration Equipment - Air Filters

Perrone Leathers, Inc.
48 S Main St # 50
Gloversville, NY 12078-3810
Contact: William P. Perrone Sr., Pres., CFO
Telephone: 518-725-9144
Fax: 518-725-7044
Email: interior@perroneleather.com/ / URL:
http://www.perroneleather.com/
Product Service Description:
Leather jackets
Leather & sheep-lined clothing
Leather tanning & finishing

Perry Co., The
P.O. Box 7187
Waco, TX 76714
Contact: C. Ray Perry, President
Telephone: 254-756-2139
Fax: 254-756-2166
Email: perryco@perry-co.com / URL: http://
www.perry-co.com
Product Service Description:
Farm Machinery & Equipment, Tractor
Canopies

Perry Equipment Corp.
P.O. Box 640
Mineral Wells, TX 76067
Contact: Dunman Perry, Jr., Chairman of the
Board
Telephone: 940-325-2575
Fax: 940-325-4622
Email: corp@pecousa.com / URL: http://
www.pecousa.com
Product Service Description:
Filtration/Separation Equipment
Filter Cartridge Elements
Flow Measurement Systems
Pipeline Equipment
Filters, Air
Filters, Chemical
Filters, Collant
Filters, Fuel
Filters, Liquid
Filters, Paint

Petersen Products Co.
421 Wheeler Ave.
Fredonia, WI 53021-9306
Contact: Philip L. Lundman, President
Telephone: 414-692-2416
Fax:
Email: / URL:
Product Service Description:
Pipe Plug
Pipeline Relining Packers
Drain Cleaning Tools
Sewer Cleaning Tools

Petrified Wood Co
PO Box 239
Holbrook, AZ 86025-0239
Contact: Jim Gray, Owner
Telephone: 520-524-1842
Fax: 520-524-6866
Email: cgpetwood@aol.com / URL:
Product Service Description:
Manufactures rough and finished petrified
wood products
Cut stone & stone products
Durable goods

Petro Chemical Products Inc.
PO Box 41585
Jacksonville, FL 32203-1585
Contact: Gary Galligar, V-P., Mktg. & Sales
Telephone: 904-388-5732
Fax: 904-389-5752
Email: gary.galligar@petro-chemical.com /
URL:
Product Service Description:
Car care chemicals
Lubricating oils & greases

Petroferm Inc.
5415 First Coast Hwy
Fernandina Beach, FL 32034-5427
Contact: Craig Hood, Director of Mktg.
Telephone: 904-261-8286
Fax: 904-261-6994
Email: / URL: http://www.petroferm.com
Product Service Description:
Chemical preparations
Electronic & industrial chemicals
Cleaning solvents
Fuel Emulsions
Surfactants
Silicone specialties
Vegatable oils
Custom / Toll Blending
Waxes

Petroleum Helicopters
118 Shepard Dr.
Lafayette, LA 70509-0808
Contact: Ben Schrick, Manager
Telephone: 318-235-0303
Product Service Description:
Helicopter & airplane transportation service
Helicopter parts

Petron Industries Inc.
PO Box 41166
Houston, TX 77241-1166
Contact: Peter Buckley, V-P.
Telephone: 713-693-8700
Fax: 713-722-9459
Email: petron@petronworld.com / URL:
http://www.petronworld.com
Product Service Description:
Oil field monitoring equipment / drilling
instrumentation
Mud logging instrumentation

Petroplast Chemical Corp.
700 White Plains Rd., Ste. 354
Scarsdale, NY 10583
Contact: Isaac Nidam, President
Telephone: 914-725-3700
Product Service Description:
Urea Resins
Polyvinyl Chloride Resins
Alcohols
Butanols
Chlorine
Petrochemicals

Petrotech Inc.
3520 General De Gaulle, Suite 5055
New Orleans, LA 70114
Contact: George Trautman, V-P., Sales &
Mktg.
Telephone: 504-361-1142
Fax: 504-361-4246
Email: ptmrkting@aol.com / URL:
Product Service Description:
Oil & gas safety & production control
systems, turbo machinery & generator
controls, gas
Engineering Studies
Process control instruments
Systems Integration
Instrument & Electrical Services

Pettit Paint Co., Inc.
36 Pine St., P.O. Box 278
Rockaway, NJ 07866
Contact: Cameron Metz, *
Telephone: 201-625-3100
Fax: 201-625-8303
Email: / URL:
Product Service Description:
Yacht Coatings, Anti Fouling, Topside
Enamel

Pexim International
884 Baldwin Rd.
Woodbridge, CT 06525
Contact: Sales & Marketing,
Telephone: 203-389-1314
Fax: 203-389-6767
Email: pexim@worldnet.att.net / URL:
Product Service Description:
Exporting Firms
Machines and mechanical appliances having
individual functions
Synthetic polymers in primary forms,
including polyxlene
Plates, sheets, film, foil and strip of plastics,
not self-adhesive, non-cellular
Polyethylene scrap

Pharr Brand Name Apparel, LLC
1300 Maco Dr.
Pharr, TX 78577
Contact: Mike Coggins, Pres.
Telephone: 956-702-4100
Fax: 956-781-8909
Email: mfc@pbna.vt.com / URL: http://
www.pbna.vt.com
Product Service Description:
Men's & women's leather outerwear
Leather & sheep-lined clothing

Philadelphia Resins
130 Commerce Dr.
Montgomeryville, PA 18936-9624
Contact: Sales & Marketing,
Telephone: 215-855-8450
Fax:
Email: / URL:
Product Service Description:
Plastics Materials and Resins
Container cargo
Sands, natural, except metal bearing or silica
or quartz sands
Epoxide resins, in primary forms

Philippine News Inc
PO Box 2767
South San Francisco, CA 94083-2767
Contact: Cherie Querol Moreno, Publisher
Telephone: 650-872-3000
Fax: 650-872-0217
Email: / URL:
Product Service Description:
Publishes weekly newspaper

Phillips Industries
5701 S Eastern Ave Ste 650
Commerce, CA 90040-2927
Contact: Willaim A. Phillips, Director of Int'l
Sales
Telephone: 323-721-2323
Fax: 323-721-4923
Email: bphil2323@aol.com / URL: http://
www.phillipsind.com
Product Service Description:
Manufactures truck parts
Motor vehicle parts & accessories
Coiled electrical & air assemblies
7-Pin connectors & coupling valves
Trailer wire harness

Phillips Motors, Larry
1502 Carter St., Ste. 100
Gainesville, GA 30501-6168
Contact: Larry W. Phillips, Jr., Owner
Telephone: 706-535-2739
Fax: 404-503-9204
Email: / URL:
Product Service Description:
Automobiles sales & used auto parts &
exporter
Trucks sales & exports
Federal construction & development
Federal feed & seed exporter

Phoenix Barge Corporation
PO Box 834
Middletown, CT 06457-0384
Contact: Malcom Chapman, *
Telephone: 203-347-8453
Fax: 203-347-8453
Email: / URL:
Product Service Description:
Draft River Barges, Extremely Shallow
Paint, Debris, Dredge Barges, Push Boats

Phoenix Gear Inc
2002 E. Watkins
Phoenix, AZ 85034
Contact: Jay Donkersloot, President
Telephone: 602-712-9000
Fax: 602-712-9001
Email: eda@phoenixgear.com / URL:
Product Service Description:
Manufactures, hardens and grinds gears,
splines and shafts
Speed changers, drives & gears
Industrial machinery

Phoenix Manufacturing Inc
PO Box 20663
Phoenix, AZ 85036-0663
Contact: Scott W. Robins, Dir. Int'l Sales
Telephone: 602-437-1034
Fax: 602-437-4833
Email: scott_robins@phxmfg.com / URL:
http://www.evapcool.com
Product Service Description:
Manufactures evaporative air coolers
Refrigeration & heating equipment
Warm air heating & air conditioning
Manufactures desert coolers

Photon Technologies, Inc.
1960 E. I-30
Rockwall, TX 75087
Contact: Michael R. Brown, Chrm., Pres.
Telephone: 972-722-2522
Fax: 972-722-2422
Email: photon@photontechnologies.com /
URL: http://www.photontechnologies.com
Product Service Description:
Glass coating (optical interference)
Glass products from purchased glass

Physical Acoustics
195 Clarksville Rd, Princeton Jct.
Trenton, NJ 08550
Contact: Terry Tamutus, Inside Sales
Manager
Telephone: 609-716-4000
Fax: 609-716-0706
Email: sales@pacndt.com / URL: http://
www.pacndt.com
Product Service Description:
Non-destructive ultrasonic & acoustic testing
equipment
Measuring & controlling devices

Pic Corp.
23 S Essex Ave
Orange, NJ 07050-0543
Contact: Eric Rubel, Director, Global Sales
Telephone: 973-678-7300
Fax: 973-678-1583
Email: info@pic-corp.com / URL: http://
www.pic-corp.com
Product Service Description:
Insect & Rodent Control

Picard Inc., C. A.
103 S 11th St
West Des Moines, IA 50265-4410
Contact: Lon Smallridge, GM
Telephone: 515-222-1855
Fax: 515-222-1856
Email: / URL:
Product Service Description:
Rendering & vegetable oil equipment & parts

Piccone Apparel Corp
3740 Motor Ave
Los Angeles, CA 90034-6404
Contact: Robin Piccone, Pres.
Telephone: 310-559-6702
Fax: 310-559-2361
Email: rpicc4@aol.com / URL:
Product Service Description:
Manufactures women's, misses' and juniors'
outerwear— pants, tops and swimwear
Outerwear_women's & misses'
Blouses & shirts_women's & misses'

Pick Heaters, Inc.
730 S Indiana Ave
West Bend, WI 53095-4050
Contact: Prudence Pick Hway,
Telephone: 414-338-1191
Fax: 414-338-8489
Email: info@pickheaters.com / URL: http://
www.pickheaters.com
Product Service Description:
Direct Steam Injection Liquid Heaters
Direct Steam Injection Sanitary Heaters

Picture Woods Ltd
5060 Chaparral Ct
Boulder, CO 80301-3351
Contact: Mark Thorpe, Pres.
Telephone: 303-530-4848
Fax: 303-530-4040
Email: picwoods@indra.com / URL:
Product Service Description:
Manufactures hardwood frame moldings
Wood mouldings

Pierburg Instruments, Inc.
1797 Atlantic Boulevard
Auburn Hills, MI 48326
Contact: Wei Wu,
Telephone: 248-391-3311
Fax: 248-391-3771
Email: sales@pierburginstruments.com /
URL: http://www.pierburginstruments.com
Product Service Description:
Flow Meters
Pressure Regulators
Calibrators
Mass Flow Indicators
Exhaust Emission Analyzers
Emissions Testing Equipment

Pierce Corporation
P.O. Box 528
Eugene, OR 97440
Contact: Ed Brockett, *
Telephone: 503-485-3111
Fax: 503-345-8799
Product Service Description:
Irrigation Equipment

Pierce Packaging Company
PO Box 15600
Loves Park, IL 6112-5600
Contact: Kevin Hogan, President, Richard
McEllen, Logistics
Telephone: 815-636-5656
Fax: 815-636-5660
Email: pdscrich@aol.com / URL: http://
www.piercedistribution.com
Product Service Description:
Packing & Crating, Export : Worldwide
Distribution : Int'l Import-Export Forwarder
Operator Foreign Trade Zone for Mexico
Operator Foreign Trade Zone for Canada
Warehousing : Site Development
WMS/MIS : Inventory Procurement
Mexico / Canada Dist / Whse

Piggott Wire & Cable Company
308 Providence St
Rehoboth, MA 02769-1005
Contact: Burton K Piggott, Pres.
Phone: 508-336-6240 / Fax: 508-336-3032
Email: / URL: http://www.piggottwire.com
Product Service Description:
Wire products_misc. fabricated
Wire and Cable

Pike Lumber Company, Inc.
Pine & Front Streets
Akron, IN 46910
Contact: John R. Brown, Sales Manager
Phone: 219-893-4512 / Fax: 219-893-7400
Email: pikelumber@hoosierlink.net / URL:
http://www.pikelumber.com
Product Service Description:
Hardwood Lumber : Hardwood Logs

Pikes Peak Lithographing Co
PO Box 7122
Colorado Springs, CO 80933-7122
Contact: Scott L. McLeod, Vice President
Phone: 719-632-7276 / Fax: 719-632-0585
Email: pplitho@ix.netcom.com / URL: http://
www.netcom.com/~pplitho
Product Service Description:
Oversize sheet printers of fine art posters and
maps; sublimation printing
Lithographic printing_commercial
Printing_commercial

Pincock Allen & Holt
274 Union Blvd., Ste. 200
Lakewood, CO 80228-1835
Contact: Toni L. Wallis, Marketing &
Information Service
Telephone: 303-986-6950
Fax: 303-987-8907
Email: pah@hartcrowser.com / URL: http://
www.hartcrowser.com/pincode
Product Service Description:
International Mineral Industry Consultants

Pine Bluff Cutting Tools, Inc.
1805 W 5th Ave
Pine Bluff, AR 71601-3875
Contact: Martin L. Yun, President
Telephone: 870-535-4000
Fax: 870-534-8665
Email: amerimill@earhtlink.net :
Product Service Description:
End Mills

Pine Grove Group
PO Box 131
Pine Grove, CA 95665-0131
Contact: Dan Nolting, President
Telephone: 209-295-5505
Fax: 209-295-3185
Email: dan@pingrovegroup.com / URL: http:/
/www.pinegrovegroup.com
Product Service Description:
Manufactures printed circuit and turnkey
electronic boards : Printed circuit boards,
cable & harness manufacture

Pinnacle Research Institute
141 Albright Way
Los Gatos, CA 95032-1801
Contact: K Tsai, Pres.
Phone: 408-379-1900 / Fax: 408-379-1974
Email: pricap@pacbell.net / URL: http://
www.home.pacbell.net/pricap
Product Service Description:
R&D of batteries and capacitors
Batteries_storage: Commercial physical
research : Electronic capacitors

Pioneer Conveyors Inc
8941 Murray Ave
Gilroy, CA 95020-3633
Contact: John W Briggs, Pres.
Telephone: 408-842-1212
Fax: 408-842-1210
Email: briggswill@aol.com / URL: http://
pioneerconveyors.com
Product Service Description:
Manufactures conveyors
Conveyors & conveying equipment

Pioneer Mat Co., Inc.
PO Box 5757, 2000 Stuart St.
Chattanooga, TN 37406
Contact: Mack Hedges, Pres.
Telephone: 423-622-4272
Fax: 423-622-7787
Email: customer.serice@pioneermat.com
Product Service Description:
Logo Entrance Way Matting
Commercial Floor Matting

Pioneer Plastics Corporation
One Pionite Road
Auburn, ME 04211
Contact: Virginia Archambault, Project
Manager
Telephone: 207/784-9111
Fax: 207/784-0392
Email: info@pionitelaminates.com / URL:
http://www.pionitelaminates.com
Product Service Description:
Decorative Laminates ,Industrial Laminates,
Sold Surface

Pipefine Furniture, Inc.
3485 Nw 19th St
Fort Lauderdale, FL 33311-4224
Contact: Shlomo Nir, Pres.
Telephone: 954-486-3388
Fax: 954-486-3433
Email: pipefine@aol.com / URL: http://
www.enterit.com/pipefine3388.htm
Product Service Description:
Patio furniture
Furniture_household

Piping Technology & Products, Inc.
3701 Holmes Road
Houston, TX 77051-1545
Contact: Randy Bailey, Vice President
Telephone: 713-731-0030
Fax: 713-731-8640
Email: info@pipingtech.com / URL: http://
www.pipingtech.com
Product Service Description:
Pipe Hangers Supports & Fittings

Pitco Frialator, Inc. (Mfr)
P.O. Box 501
Concord, NH 03302
Contact: Philip Dei Dolori, V.P., Sales.
Telephone: 603/225-6684
Fax: 603-224-6930
Email: / URL:
Product Service Description:
Fryers, Deep Fat Filtration Systems

Pittsburg Tank & Tower Co., Inc.
PO Box 913
Henderson, KY 42419-0913
Contact: Bob Green, International Sales
Telephone: 502-826-9000
Fax: 502-827-4417
Email: watertank@dynasty.net / URL: http://
www.watertank.com
Product Service Description:
Welded / Bolted Steel Storage Tanks

Pittsburgh Flatroll Co.
31st St. & A.v.r.r.
Pittsburgh, PA 15201
Contact: Jeffrey L. McKee, G.M.
Telephone: 412-765-3322
Fax: 412-765-3430
Email: sales@flatroll.com / URL: http://
www.flatroll.com
Product Service Description:
Flat-rolled steel
Super Alloy Plate & Sheet

Planet Machinery Company
451 E. Wilson
Pontiac, MI 48341
Contact: Jack Ruth,
Telephone: 248-335-8330
Fax: 248-335-3680
Email: pmcsales@planetmachinery.com /
URL:
Product Service Description:
Used Metalforming Machinery, Export
Used Tube Manufacturing Equip., Export

Plasco, Inc.
16151 N.W. 57th Ave.
Miami Lakes, FL 33014-6707
Contact: George R. Mendelson, President
Telephone: 305-625-4222
Fax: 305-620-0647
Email: sales@plascoID.com / URL: http://
www.plascoID.com
Product Service Description:
Printed Plastic Cards
Dye Sublimation Thermal Transf
Embossers
Encoders
Imprinters
Phot ID Sytems
Photo ID Software

Plasmatic Systems, Inc.
1327 Aaron Rd
North Brunswick, NJ 08902-1032
Contact: Aaron Ribner, Pres.
Telephone: 732-297-9107
Fax: 732-297-3306
Email: aribner@idt.net / URL:
Product Service Description:
Electronics plasma cleaning equipment
Electrical industrial apparatus

**Plastic Development
Company(MFR)**
P.O. Box 4007, West Fourth St.
Williamsport, PA 17701
Contact: Ross Whitesell, Director / Marketing
Telephone: 1800-451-1420
Fax: 717-323-8485
Email: pdcspas@pldevco.com / URL: http://
www.pldevco.com
Product Service Description:
Spas
Whirlpool Baths
Plastics, Vacuum Forming

Plastic Extruded Parts Inc.(Mfr)
P.O. Box 540
Nassau, NY 12123
Contact: Alan Hart, President
Telephone: 518/766-9878
Fax: 518-766-3229
Email: ahart@pepico.com / URL: http://
www.pepico.com
Product Service Description:
Wire Markers

Plastic Injection Molders Inc.
PO Box 167
Fertile, IA 50434-0167
Contact: Greg Knopf, Pres., Engrg., Opers. &
Pur. Mgr.
Telephone: 515-797-2265
Fax: 515-797-2800
Email: tomd@netins.net / URL:
Product Service Description:
Plastic injection molding, hot stamping,
welding & assembly
Plastic products
Industrial machinery

Plastic Packaging Corp.
750 S 65th St
Kansas City, KS 66111-2301
Contact: Brook Maese, Pres.
Telephone: 913-287-3383 x 3024
Fax: 913-287-2402
Email: bmaese@plaspack.com / URL: http://
www.plaspack.com
Product Service Description:
Flexible packaging: plastics, laminated &
coated
Plastic bags

Plastic Techniques, Inc.
PO Box 250
Goffstown, NH 03045-0250
Contact: Chris McRae,
Telephone: 603-645-6800
Fax: 603-623-0918
Email: / URL:
Product Service Description:
Plastic products, insulating basket liners,
lineman's tools & safety lighting

Plastic Works Inc
1038 Ashby Ave
Berkeley, CA 94710-2808
Contact: Jeffrey D Weinstein, Pres.
Telephone: 510-841-1001
Fax: 510-841-6116
Email: / URL:
Product Service Description:
Manufactures acrylic store display fixtures for
videos and stationery; custom thermoforming;
mammographic paddles
Partitions & fixtures, except wood
Plastic products
CD, CD-ROM, DVD display fixtuers
Mammography paddles & bushings

Plastic-View ATC
4585 Runway St.
Simi Valley, CA 93063-3479
Contact: Sonny Voges, Owner
Telephone: 805-520-9390
Fax: 805-520-6301
Email: / URL:
Product Service Description:
Window Shades For Airport Control Towers
Films-To-Glass for Glare Heat Shatter

Plastics Design & Manufacturing
6284 S Nome Ct
Englewood, CO 80111
Contact: Jon Giacchino, Pres.
Telephone: 303-768-8380
Fax: 303-768-8350
Email: / URL:
Product Service Description:
Vacuum forming; pressure forming; acrylic
fabricating; profile extrusion of plastics
Plastic products

Plastinetics, Inc.
439 Main Rd.
Towaco, NJ 07082-1201
Contact: Richard Zaleski, President
Telephone: 973-316-6600
Fax: 973-316-0300
Email: / URL: http://www.plastinetics.com
Product Service Description:
Plastic Pipe Fittings & Valves
Plastic Pipe (PVC)
Laboratoryware, Plastics

Plato Trading
2001 Holcombe Blvd. # 3501
Houston, TX 77030-4222
Contact: T.A. Plato,
Telephone: 713-797-0406
Fax: 713-795-4665
Email: plato@nol.net / URL:
Product Service Description:
Peanuts , not roasted or otherwise cooked,
shelled, whether or not broken
Insecticides : Peanuts , not roasted or
otherwise cooked, in shell

Platoon Uniform & Sportswear
PO Box 156
Comer, GA 30629-0156
Contact: Thomas Kontonickas, Pres.
Telephone: 706-783-5112
Fax: 706-783-3524
Product Service Description:
Trousers & slacks_men's & boys'

Platt Electric Supply
10605 Sw Allen Blvd.
Beaverton, Or 97005
Contact: David Currier, Director / Globex
Int'l Div.
Telephone: 503-641-6121
Fax: 503-643-5862
Product Service Description:
Relays & Ind. Controls
Elec. Appar., Whsle.
Elec. Switches
Power-Driven Handtools
Business Services Nec.

Platt Luggage, Inc.
4051 W 51st St
Chicago, IL 60632-4211
Contact: Allan Evavold, Executive V.P.
Telephone: 773-838-2000
Fax: 773-838-2010
Email: allan@plattcases.com / URL: http://
www.plattcases.com
Product Service Description:
Tool, sample, circuit board & industrial cases
& attaches

Pleko Southwest Inc
1824 E 6th St
Tempe, AZ 85281-2950
Contact: Larry C Fischer, Pres.
Telephone: 602-968-0113
Fax: 602-968-2816
Product Service Description:
Manufactures synthetic coatings for EIFS,
glitter coatings, flakes and chips for use in
seamless flooring

Plumb Shop
39600 Orchard Hill Pl
Novi, MI 48375-5331
Contact: James Whiteherse, Sr. V.-P., Sales
Telephone: 248-305-6000
Fax: 248-305-6007
Product Service Description:
Plumbing fixture fittings & trim

Plymouth Industries, Inc.
607 Bell St
Plymouth, OH 44865-1000
Contact: Carl Ganzhorn, Sales Mgr.
Telephone: 419-687-4641
Fax: 419-687-8112
Email: plymouth@willard-oh.com / URL:
http://www.plymouthindustries.com/
Product Service Description:
Locomotives, Lift Trucks, Die Handlers,
Railroad Equipment, & Extrusion Equipment

Pocatello Precast Inc
3650 Highway 30 W
Pocatello, ID 83201-6075
Contact: Wayne Smith, Pres.
Telephone: 208-233-1095
Fax:
Email: / URL:
Product Service Description:
Manufactures concrete precast products,
septic tanks and manhole materials
Concrete products

Pochet Of America, Inc.
415 Hamburg Tpk.
Wayne, NJ 07470
Contact: Jerry Tirico, CFO
Telephone: 973-942-4923
Fax: 973-942-5364
Email: gerrytirico@worldnet.att.net / URL:
Product Service Description:
Perfume bottle screen printing
Manufacturers of glass cosmetic bottles

Pointblank Body Armor, Inc.
4031 Ne 12th Ter
Oakland Park, FL 33334-4671
Contact: Sandra Hatfield, Pres.
Telephone: 954-630-0900
Fax: 954-630-9225
Email: / URL:
Product Service Description:
Bullet resistant clothing & soft body armor
Surgical appliances & supplies

Pole-Tech Co., Inc.
P.O. Box 715
East Setauket, NY 11733
Contact: Anthony Barbarite, Vice President
Telephone: 516/689-5525
Fax: 516/689-5528
Email: info@poletech.com / URL: http://
www.poletech.com
Product Service Description:
Metal Flag Poles
Metal Light Poles

Policonductos S.A. de C.V.
San Antonio 105 Col. Sta. Maria
Monterry, Nuevo Leon, MX 64650
Contact: Cliff I. Simon,
Telephone: 528-335-7770
Fax: 528-335-7775
Email: camcliff@giga.com / URL:
Product Service Description:
Plastic Pipe HDPE pipe 1/2" to 36" PE 3408 -
Water Pipe
Plastic Pipe Hdpe Pipe 1/2" to 12" PE 2406 -
Gas Pipe
Fusion Eqipment
Electro Fusion Equipment
Valves - Plastic
Risers - Gas
Fittings - Plastic

Poly Conversions Inc.
PO Box 55
Rantoul, IL 61866-0055
Contact: Ronald Smith, V-P., Mktg.
Telephone: 217-893-3330
Fax: 217-893-3003
Email: polycon@cu-online.com / URL:
Product Service Description:
Industrial & disposable plastic & paper
medical gowns & aprons
Plastic products

Poly Masters Industries Inc
2821 Century Blvd
South Gate, CA 90280-5503
Contact: Karnig Oughourlian, VP
Telephone: 323-564-7824
Fax: 323-564-1418
Email: anatech@polymasters.com / URL:
http://www.ana-techshoes.com
Product Service Description:
Footwear_women's, except athletic
Footwear_men's, except athletic

Poly-Flex Inc.
2000 W Marshall Dr.
Grand Prairie, TX 75051
Contact: William C. Neal, Vice President
Telephone: 972-337-7353
Fax: 972-337-7233
Email: billn@poly-flex.com / URL: http://
www.poly-flex.com
Product Service Description:
Polyethylene Geomembrane Liners
Geo Textiles : Geonets : Geocomposites

Polygem
1105 Carolina Drive
West Chicago, IL 60185
Contact: Jay Schmid, GM
Telephone: 630-231-5600
Fax: 630-231-5604
Email: / URL: http://www.polygem.com
Product Service Description:
Epoxy Abrasion Resistant Compounds
Concrete Restoration Epoxies
Construction Epoxies : Chemical Fasteners
Chemical Resistant Epoxies: Polyurethane
Grouts : Hi-Temperature Epoxies
Sculpturing Epoxies : Electrical Potting
Compounds : Epoxy Floor Systems

Polymer Trading Services Limited
2301 Maitland Center Parkway, Suite 240
Maitland, FL 32751
Contact: David Derhagopian, President
Telephone: 407-875-9595
Fax: 407-875-5700
Email: / URL: http://
www.entecpolymers.com
Product Service Description:
Polycarbonate Resins
Polyacetal Synthetic Resins
Polyamid Resins
ABS Resins
Synthetic Resins
Engineering Resins

Polymet Corp.
10073 Commerce Park Dr
Cincinnati, OH 45246-1333
Contact: Joe hirscher, Dir. of Sales & Mktg.
Telephone: 513-874-3586
Fax: 513-874-2880
Email: polymet@cinti.net / URL: http://
www.polymetcorp.com
Product Service Description:
Welding & hard-facing & Thermal Spraywire

Polymetallurgical Corp.
262 Broad Street, PO Box 3249
North Attleboro, MA 02761
Contact: Armen Iskenderian, President
Telephone: 508-695-9312
Fax: 508-695-7512
Email: armen@polymet.com / URL: http://
www.polymet.com
Product Service Description:
Clad Metals Electrical Applications
Precious Metal Inlays

Polyproducts Corp.
PO Box 42
Roseville, MI 48066-0042
Contact: Richard B. Platt, Pres.
Telephone: 810-774-2500
Fax: 810-78-7775
Email: / URL:
Product Service Description:
Scales & balances, except laboratory

Polywood, Inc.
3615 Kennedy Rd
South Plainfield, NJ 07080-1801
Contact: James J. Kerstein, Pres.
Telephone: 908-754-0043
Fax: 908-754-1460
Email: info@polywood.com / URL: http://
www.polywood.com
Product Service Description:
Recycled Plastic Lumber

Porcelain Products Company(Mfr)
225 N. Patterson Street
Carey, OH 43316
Contact: D. Nelson Lester, Senior Vice
President
Telephone: 419/396-7621
Fax: 419-396-7128
Email: / URL:
Product Service Description:
Pintype & Line Post Insulators
Suspension Insulators, 7 1/2in. Disc &
Smaller : Suspension Insulators, Larger than 7
1/2in. Disc : Switch & Bus Insulators
Guy Strain & Spool Insulators
Component Parts of Other Electrical
Equipment : Service Wireholders, cleats
,knob s,tubes : Fuseholders,& Other Dry
Process Electrical Porcelain

Porex Surgical, Inc.
4715 Roosevelt Hwy
College Park, GA 30349-2417
Contact: Franklin Bost, Pres.
Telephone: 770-969-8145
Fax: 770-969-8045
Email: / URL: http://www.porex.com/
surgical
Product Service Description:
Surgical appliances & supplies
Surgical supplies

Port Elizabeth Terminal & Warehouse
201 A Export Street
Port Newark, NJ 07114
Contact: Patrick Wynne, President
Telephone: 973-491-0600
Fax: 973-491-0066
Email: pwynne@judgeorg.com / URL: http://
www.judgeorg.com
Product Service Description:
Warehousing
Trucking

Port of Palm Beach District
4 East Port Road, P.O. Box 9935
Riviera Beach, FL 33419 USA
Contact: Louis J. Perez, *
Telephone: 561-842-4201
Fax: 561-842-4240
Email: / URL: http://
www.portofpalmbeach.com
Product Service Description:
Port Authority

Porta-Fab Corp.
18080 Chesterfield Airport Rd.
Chesterfield, MO 63005
Contact: Wayne R. McGee, *
Telephone: 314-537-5555
Product Service Description:
Prefabricated Buildings & In Plant Offices
Cleanrooms

Portable Energy Products Inc
940 Disc Dr
Scotts Valley, CA 95066-4544
Contact: Ernie Porcelli, Pres.
Telephone: 831-439-5100
Fax: 831-439-5118
Email: sales@portable-energy.com / URL:
http://www.portable-energy.com
Product Service Description:
Batteries_storage
Manufactures rechargeable sealed-lead cells
and batteries

Portadrill Corp.
5970 Marion Drive
Denver, CO 80216
Contact: Josef Obermayr, Parts Manager
Telephone: 303-296-6123
Fax: 303-296-6264
Email: / URL:
Product Service Description:
Portable Parts & Accessories

Portatalk Electronics Inc
947 S 48th St
Tempe, AZ 85281-5122
Contact: Barbara Lockley, Pres.
Telephone: 602-967-9100
Fax: 602-967-2669
Email: portatalk@aol.com / URL: http://
www.portatalk.com
Product Service Description:
Manufactures wireless portable public
address systems

Portec Rail Products Inc.
Box 3825
Pittsburgh, PA 15238
Contact: Rich J. Jarosinski, President & GM
Telephone: 412-782-6000
Fax: 412-782-1037
Email: rmpsales@portecrail.com / URL: http:/
/www.PortecRail.com
Product Service Description:
Railroad maintenance materials
Railroad equipment
Rail lubrication systems
Insulated / non-insulated rail joints

Porter Athletic Equipment (Mfr)
2500 S. 25th Ave., P.O. Box 2500
Broadview, IL 60153-2500
Contact: Carlos Castellon, *
Telephone: 708-338-2000
Fax: 708-338-2060
Email: / URL:
Product Service Description:
Sporting Goods
Basketball Equipment

Porter Instrument Co.
PO Box 907
Hatfield, PA 19440-0907
Contact: Bud Loughery, V-P., Opers.
Telephone: 215-723-4000
Fax: 215-723-2199
Email: / URL: http://www.porterinst.com
Product Service Description:
Process control instruments
Flow control instruments
Dental products, Nitrous Oxide / Oxygen
Sedation Equipment
Dental products, steam sterlizers

Portland Bolt & Mfg Company
PO Box 2866
Portland, OR 97208-2866
Contact: Brian Sonnenberg, Pres.
Telephone: 503-227-5488
Fax: 503-227-4634
Email: / URL: http://www.portland-bolt.com
Product Service Description:
Bolts, nuts, rivets & washers
Manufactures bolts

Power & Industrial Service Corp.
450 Millers Run Rd.
Morgan, PA 15064
Contact: Laurence G. Shekell,
Telephone: 412-221-7116
Fax: 412-221-8656
Email: / URL: http://www.piburners.com
Product Service Description:
Coal fired utility burner replacements - B&W,
F-W, C.E. - A.B.B., R/S
Pendent Tube Alignment Castings
Boiler & Windbox Access Doors
Ash Handling Replacement Parts

Power Vacuum Trailer Co.
PO Box 472
Crystal Lake, IL 60039-0472
Contact: Bob Prentice, Pres.
Phone: 815-455-2672/ Fax: 800-711-4788
Email: pvt-systems@worldnet.att.net / URL:
Product Service Description:
Air duct cleaning equipment
Industrial machinery

Power-Sonic Corp
PO Box 5242
Redwood City, CA 94063-0242
Contact: Bruno A Ender, V-P., Mktg.
Phone: 650-364-5001 / Fax: 650-366-3662
Email: battery@power-sonic.com / URL:
http://www.power-sonic.com
Product Service Description:
Manufactures rechargeable batteries (sales
and marketing office)

Powerline Solar Products, Inc.
32 S Ewing St Ste 331
Helena, MT 59601-5749
Contact: Jerry Spencer, Pres.
Phone: 406-442-3434 / Fax: 406-457-0460
Email: / URL: http://www.powerexperts.com
Product Service Description:
Manufactures solar chargers for portable
devices

Powermaster Pacific
2841 Turnpike Indl. Pk.
Middletown, PA 17057
Contact: Darlene Regal, Pres.
Phone: 717-939-0427 / Fax: 717-939-0756
Email: pppparts@bellatlantic.net
Product Service Description:
Industrial oil & gas burner parts & boilers,
Parts

Powertech! Marine Propellers
8101 Kingston Rd.
Shreveport, LA 71108-5745
Contact: Mary Morris, *
Telephone: 318-688-1970
Fax: 318-686-7082
Product Service Description:
Marine Propellers, Stainless Steel

Powertronix Corporation
1125 E Hillsdale Bldg. 108
San Mateo, CA 94404-1631
Contact: Carl Svensson, Pres.
Telephone: 650-345-6800
Fax: 650-345-7240
Email: info@powertronix.com / URL: http://
www.powertronix.com
Product Service Description:
Transformers
Manufactures transformers

Prada Enterprises, Inc.
PO Box 352587
Palm Coast, FL 32135-2587
Contact: Andy Porada, Pres.
Telephone: 904-445-9627
Fax: 904-445-5515
Product Service Description:
Kitchen cabinets & furniture

Prager Incorporated
PO Box 61670
New Orleans, LA 70161-1670
Contact: Jeanne B. Bertrand, Market
Research Admin.
Telephone: 504-524-2363
Fax: 504-593-9920
Email: prager-custservice@worldnet.att.net
Product Service Description:
Gears & Gear Boxes
Gears & Gear Boxes, Repair

Pragmatic Environmental Solutions Company Inc.
1866 Technical St Se
Roanoke, VA 24013-2940
Contact: Luke Staengl, Pres.
Telephone: 540-427-3588
Fax: 540-427-3590
Email: lukestaengl@mindspring.com / URL:
http://www.pescova.com
Product Service Description:
Solvent & oil recovery equipment
Solvent & Oil Recycling Equipment
Chemical Processing Equipment
Molecular Sieves

Precious Plate Florida
2656 Electronics Way
West Palm Beach, FL 33407-4607
Contact: Dave Hurst, Ptnr.
Telephone: 561-820-8150
Fax: 561-820-9711
Product Service Description:
Batteries_storage
Rechargeable battery electrode substrate

Precise Flight Inc
PO Box 7168
Bend, OR 97708-7168
Contact: Connie LeHuquet, Pres.
Telephone: 541-382-8684
Fax: 541-388-1105
Email: conniel@preciseflight.com / URL:
http://www.preciseflight.com
Product Service Description:
Aircraft parts & equipment
Manufactures aircraft equipment

Precision Art Coordinators, Inc.
22 Alameida Ave.
East Providence, RI 02914
Contact: James Higgins, Pres.
Telephone: 401-438-9800
Fax: 401-434-5360
Email: / URL: http://www.precisionart.com
Product Service Description:
Photochemical etching

Precision Booth Mfg.
2410 W 18th St
Chicago, IL 60608-1724
Contact: Michael J. Slotnick, Chrm., Pres.
Telephone: 312-243-6999
Fax: 312-243-6664
Email: foracowboy@cowboys.com / URL:
http://www.precisionbooth.com
Product Service Description:
Restaurant booths
Furniture_public building & related

Precision Custom Coatings
200 Maltese Dr.
Totowa, NJ 07512
Contact: Sales & Marketing,
Telephone: 973-890-3873
Fax: 973-785-8180
Product Service Description:
Interlining - nonwoven & knit
Fusible interlining - polyester, nylon, rayon
Apparel interlining
Industrial nonwovens

Precision Die & Stamping Inc
1704 W 10th St
Tempe, AZ 85281-5208
Contact: Ben Costabile, Pres.
Telephone: 602-967-2038
Fax: 602-829-0838
Product Service Description:
Metal stampings

Precision Flow, Inc.
PO Box 7137
Odessa, TX 79760-7137
Contact: Clyde Shugart, Pres.
Telephone: 915-381-5131
Fax: 915-381-3537
Email: pfi_clyde@powr.net / URL: http://
www.powr.net/preflow
Product Service Description:
Measuring & controlling devices
Orifice measurement equipment

Precision Hermetic Technology
786 S Gifford Ave
San Bernardino, CA 92408-2449
Contact: Daniel Schachtel, Pres.
Telephone: 909-381-6011
Fax: 909-884-1043
Email: dbs@pht.net / URL: http://
www.pht.net
Product Service Description:
Manufacturer of hermetic connectors
Glass to metal seals
Mil - Spec. connectors

Precision Machine Products
PO Box 1576
Gastonia, NC 28053-1576
Contact: Robert Blalock, *
Telephone: 704-865-8507
Fax: 704-865-7412
Email: premachpro@aol.com / URL: http://
www.members.aol.com/premachpro/pmp.htm
Product Service Description:
Repair Textile Machinery & Parts
Fabricated Metal Products

Precision Measurement Labs
201 W Beach Ave
Inglewood, CA 90302-2902
Contact: David Tolin, Pres.
Telephone: 310-671-4345
Fax: 310-671-0858
Email: info@pmli.com / URL: http://
www.pmli.com
Product Service Description:
Contract inspection services— parts,
machines, castings, forgings :Patterns,
industrial : Engineering Services
Aluminum Foundry : Digitizing & Reverse
Engineering

Precision Motion Controls
160 E Virginia St Ste 264
San Jose, CA 95112-5848
Contact: Jim Siebert, Ptnr.
Telephone: 408-298-0898
Fax: 408-298-0899
Email: / URL: http://www.premotn.com
Product Service Description:
Relays & industrial controls
Manufactures controls for motors

Precision Press
876 Kawaiahao St.
Honolulu, HI 96813-5225
Contact: Maneck B. Minoo, Pres.
Telephone: 808-593-9964
Fax: 808-593-9969
Email: maneck@hawaii.oo.com / URL:
Product Service Description:
Printing_commercial

Precision Products Co
28380 SE Stone Rd
Boring, OR 97009-9415
Contact: LeRoy Cothrell, Pres.
Telephone: 503-663-4811
Fax: 503-663-9555
Product Service Description:
Woodworking machinery
Manufactures manual cut-off saws
Power-driven handtools

Precision/Triumph Twist Drill Co.(Mfr)
One Precision Plaza
Crystal Lake, IL 60014
Contact: Randall J. Beck, *
Telephone: 815/459-6250
Fax: 815/459-2804
Product Service Description:
High Speed Steel Drill Bits & Sets
Cobalt Steel Drill Bits & Sets

Premco Machine Co Inc
PO Box 6806
Ketchem, ID 83340-1029
Contact: Belinda Fergeon,
Telephone: 800-9premco
Fax: 707-542-3217
Email: bforgeon@aol.com / URL:
Product Service Description:
Manufactures commercial refrigeration
hardware walk-in and reach-in
Refrigeration & heating equipment
Refrigeration equipment & supplies

Premier Hardwood Products Inc.
Solvay Road, PO Box 434
Jamesville, NY 13078
Contact: Marcus Welsh,
Telephone: 315-492-4006
Email: premhard@aol.com
Product Service Description:
Wood Product Flooring

Premier Machinery
990 Sunshine Ln
Altamonte Springs, FL 32714-3803
Contact: John Grabenau, Pres.
Telephone: 407-786-2000
Fax: 407-786-2001
URL: http://www.premierequipment.com
Product Service Description:
Machine tools, metal cutting types
Machine tools : Machine tools, metal
forming types

Premier Manufactured Systems, Inc.
17431 N. 25th Ave.
Phoenix, AZ 85023
Contact: Jerry B. Monroe, Vice Pres. / Sales
Telephone: 602-931-1977
Fax: 602-931-0191
Email: mailpremierh20.com / URL: http://
www.premierh20.com
Product Service Description:
Water Purification Equip., Household /
Commercial : Water Conditioning Equip.,
Wholesale

Premier Spring Water Inc
11818 Glenoaks Blvd
San Fernando, CA 91340-1804
Contact: Paul Blum, Pres.
Telephone: 818-838-4800
Fax: 818-838-4808
Email: premierpumps@earthlink.net / URL:
Product Service Description:
Manufactures pumping systems for pools and
spa's : Pumps & pumping equipment

Premier Turbines
3551 Doniphan Dr.
Neosho, MO 64850-9163
Contact: Jim Robertson, V-P., GM
Telephone: 417-451-1810
Fax: 417-451-7245
Email: premierturbines@worldnet.att.net /
URL: http://www.premierturbines.com
Product Service Description:
Overhaul & repair of aircraft gas turbine
engines

Premier Valley Foods, Inc.
1625 Tulare St.
Fresno, CA 93706
Contact: Sales & Marketing,
Telephone: 559-495-4247
Fax: 559-264-1831
Email: burrir@mail.premiervalley.com / URL:
http://www.premiervalley.com
Product Service Description:
Dried Prunes : Dried Fruit

Premium Parasail Boats, Inc.
928 Ne 24th Ln Unit 4
Cape Coral, FL 33909-2926
Contact: Gilbert Gibbs, Pres., CEO
Telephone: 941-458-1858
Fax: 941-458-0574
Email: para1sail@aol.com / URL: http://
www.vistech.net/users/premium
Product Service Description:
Parasailing, Diving & Fishing Custom Boat
Bldr.

Prepared Food Products, Inc.
PO Box 13569
Mobile, AL 36663-0569
Contact: Jack Stallworth, Pres.
Phone: 334-456-4556 / Fax: 334-456-4557
Product Service Description:
Frozen barbecued meat products, gumbo &
shrimp Creole

Presentation South, Inc.
4249 L B Mcleod Rd
Orlando, FL 32811-5616
Contact: Robert Buck, Pres.
Telephone: 407-843-2535
Fax: 407-849-0930
Email: poixpo@nebula.ispace.com / URL:
http://www.exhibitron.com/pai/
Product Service Description:
Trade show exhibits & advertising displays
Signs & advertising specialties
Museum & Attraction Exhibits

Preserved Treescapes Intl
4039 Avenida De La Plata
Oceanside, CA 92056-5802
Contact: Dennis Gabrick, Pres.
Phone: 760-631-6789 / Fax: 760-631-6780
Email: dennis@treescapes.com / URL: http://
www.treescapes.com
Product Service Description:
Manufactures preserved trees
Manufacturing industries

Preso Meters, Corp.
35 Gateway Dr
Plattsburgh, NY 12901
Contact: Jean Pierre Brunet, Pres.
Telephone: 518-562-3182
Fax: 518-562-3227
Email: preso@together.net / URL:
Product Service Description:
Flow meters & equipment
Process control instruments

Presses, LTD
PO Box 2277
Fullerton, CA 92837-0277
Contact: George Skybrock, Sales
Telephone: 714-879-0544
Fax: 714-523-1670
Email: presses-ltd@home.com / URL: http://
www.thomasregister.com/pressesltd
Product Service Description:
Presses; Hydraulic, Pneumatic, & Manual
Presses; Forming, Deep Drawing & Punching

Pressner & Co., Inc., M.
99 Gold St.
Brooklyn, NY 11201
Contact: Jerry S. Pressner, President
Telephone: 718-858-1000
Fax: 718-802-1697
Product Service Description:
Toys : Craft Supplies : Party Favors

Pressure Devices Inc.
PO Box 130
West Union, SC 29696-0130
Contact: Peter LeRoy, Pres.
Telephone: 864-638-5491
Fax: 864-638-7562
Email: pdi@carol.net / URL: http://
www.pressuredevices.thomasregister.com
Product Service Description:
Pressure temperature diferential & vacuum
switches
Pressure, vacuum transducers

Prestige Auto
3366 Pomona Blvd.
Pomona, CA 91768-3234
Contact: Daniel R. Cahill, Export Sales Exec
Phone: 909-595-7221 / Fax: 909-595-7048
Email: pcwusa@pcw.co.id / URL: http://
www.pcw.co.id
Product Service Description:
Panther custom alloy road wheels &
accessories

Preston Cinema Systems Inc
1659 11th St Ste 100
Santa Monica, CA 90404-3707
Contact: Howard Preston, Pres.
Telephone: 310-453-1852
Fax: 310-453-5672
Email: / URL:
Product Service Description:
Manufactures, distributes and sells
photographic equipment and supplies
Photographic equipment & supplies
Photographic equipment & supplies
Camera & photographic supply stores

Pretty Products, Inc. / Rubber Queen
437 Cambridge Rd
Coshocton, OH 43812-2260
Contact: Customer Service,
Telephone: 740-622-3522
Fax: 740-622-4915
Email: info@rubberqueen.com / URL: http://
www.rubberqueen.com
Product Service Description:
Motor vehicle parts & accessories
Automotive floor mats & accessories

Price Products Inc
106 State Pl
Escondido, CA 92029-1323
Contact: John W Price, Pres.
Telephone: 760-745-5602
Fax:
Email: cnc@priceproducts.com / URL: http://
www.priceproducts.com
Product Service Description:
Machine shop for custom plastic and metal
products

Price Transfer, Inc.
2711 E. Dominguez St.,
Long Beach, CA 90810
Contact: Frederick C. Lorenzen, President
Telephone: 310-639-6074
Fax: 310-632-9506
Email: rlorenzn@pricetransfer.com / URL:
http://www.pricetransfer.com
Product Service Description:
U.S. Customs Centralized Examination
Station
Warehousing & Distribution
Local & Domestic Transportation

Pride International
110 W. 40th St., Ste. 2404
New York, NY 10018-3616
Contact: Edward Mahanna, President
Telephone: 212-921-8300
Fax: 212-869-5108
Email: sales@pridefabrics.com / URL: http://
www.pridefabrics.com
Product Service Description:
Cotton Denims all weights
Cotton Twills
Shirting Fabrics

Priefert Mfg. Co. Inc.(Mfr)
P.O. Box 1540
Mt. Pleasant, TX 75456
Contact: David Bynum, Sales Manager
Telephone: 903/572-1741
Fax: 903-572-2798
Email: sales@priefert.com / URL: http://
www.priefert.com
Product Service Description:
Holding Gates, Livestock
Portable Corrals, Squeeze Chute, Calf Tables,
Headgate
Horse Stalls

Prime Screw Machine Products Inc.
PO Box 359
Watertown, CT 06795
Contact: Dennis Izzo, Pres.
Telephone: 860-274-6773
Fax: 860-274-7939
Email: / URL: http://www.primesmp.com
Product Service Description:
Screw machine products

Print Proz, Inc.
205 Kalihi St.
Honolulu, HI 96819
Contact: Jim Beaumont, Pres.,
Telephone: 808-842-1644
Fax: 808-847-4840
Email: jimboaka@aloha.net / URL:
Product Service Description:
T-shirt screen printing
Automotive & apparel trimmings

Printed Circuit Solutions Mfg.
115 Jack Guynn Dr
Galax, VA 24333-2536
Contact: Jack Galyean, Pres, Jenny Buchanan
/ Don Ayers, Sales
Telephone: 540-236-4921
Fax: 540-236-2458
Email: sales@pcsm-pcb.com / URL: http://
www.pcsm-pcb.com
Product Service Description:
Printed circuit boards

Printers Repair Parts, Inc.
2706 Edgington St
Franklin Park, IL 60131-3406
Contact: Nikki Calhoun, Pres., Opers. Mgr.
Telephone: 847-288-9000
Fax: 847-288-9010
Email: prpsales@printersrepairparts.com /
URL: http://www.printersrepairparts.com
Product Service Description:
Printing press components, parts & equipment

Prismflex Inc.
1325 Eddy-scant Rd., PO Box 160
Arab, AL 35016
Contact: J.D. Campbell, V.P. Reg.Affairs
Telephone: 256-586-2490
Fax: 256-586-2497
Email: sales@prismflex.com / URL: http://
www.prismflex.com
Product Service Description:
Commercial & pad printing & pad & screen
printing inks : Printing, commercial
Lithographic printing, commercial
Ink, printing

Pritchard Brown
6501 Erdman Ave
Baltimore, MD 21205-3527
Contact: Charles Gears, V-P.
Telephone: 410-483-5600
Fax: 410-483-5695
Email: info@pritchardbrown.com / URL:
http://www.pritchardbrown.com
Product Service Description:
Aluminum generator enclosures
Steel Generator Enclosures
Custom Shelters for Electro-Mechanical
Systems : Low & Medium Voltage
Switchgear : Custom Controls for Electrical
Systems : Pump & Pump System Controls
Above Ground Rectangular U.L. Listed Fuel
Tanks : Custom Trailers : Electro-Mechanical
System Integration : Switchgear Shelters

Pritchett Technology, Inc.
929 Dalton St.
Ellijay, GA 30540
Contact: Timothy H. Pritchett, President
Telephone: 706-635-7745
Fax: 706-635-7716
Email: pritchetttec@ellijay.com / URL: http://
www.pritchetttech.com
Product Service Description:
Textile machinery: air entanglers & rewinders
Replacement parts for all major twisters

Pro Chem Tech, Internatinal, Inc.
RR 2 Box 282
Brockway, PA 15824
Contact: Tim Keister, Pres.
Telephone: 814-265-0959
Fax: 814-265-1263
Email: prochem@prochemtech.com / URL:
http://www.chemtech.com
Product Service Description:
Water / Wastewater Treatment Systems
Boiler, Cooling, Wastewater Treatment ,
Chemicals & Control Systems

Pro Electric Vehicles, Inc.
2322 S.W. 58th Terrace
Hollywood, FL 33023-4039
Contact: Albert Navarro, Owner
Telephone: 954-983-6003
Fax: 954-983-6088
Email: / URL: http://
www.proelectricvehicles.com
Product Service Description:
Golf car / industrial vehicles / gas & electric

Pro Tool & Design, Inc.
321 Ellis St
New Britain, CT 06051-3504
Contact: Michael Bosse, Pres.
Telephone: 860-826-7658
Fax: 860-225-5110
Email: pro.tool@snet.net / URL:
Product Service Description:
Cutting tools

Pro-Seal Products Inc
13631 Ne 126th Pl Ste 440
Kirkland, WA 98034-8731
Contact: Tal Brammer, Pres., CEO
Telephone: 425-821-0723
Fax: 425-821-1006
Email: prosealproducts@worldnet.att.net /
URL: http://www.prosealproducts.com
Product Service Description:
Adhesives & sealants
Manufactures industrial waterproofing and
roofing sealants, coatings and grouts

Probita Inc
4949 Pearl East Cir Ste 300
Boulder, CO 80301-2477
Contact: Donald Burt, Pres.
Telephone: 303-449-7665
Fax: 303-449-4640
Email: sakes@probita.com / URL: http://
www.probita.com
Product Service Description:
Supplier of Software products & services to
the telecommunications & cable industries

Proceco, Inc.
14790 Saint Augustine Rd
Jacksonville, FL 32258-2464
Contact: Bero Burghard, Pres.
Phone: 904-886-0200 / Fax: 904-886-0232
Product Service Description:
Metal finishing equipment
Railway & industrial cleaning equipment

Process Equipment, Inc.
PO Box 1607
Pelham, AL 35124-5607
Contact: James Woods, Chrm.
Telephone: 205-663-5330
Fax: 205-663-6037
Email: process@traveller.com / URL: http://
www.bhm.tis.net/~process
Product Service Description:
Industrial fans, material handling equipment,
dust collectors & boiler retrofit
Blowers & fans

**Process Filtration Div., Parker
Hannifin**
PO Box 1300
Lebanon, IN 46052-3006
Contact: Dave Perorazio, GM
Telephone: 765-482-3900
Fax: 765-482-8410
Email: / URL: http://www.parker.com
Product Service Description:
Machinery_general industrial
Filters & filtration systems

Process Graphics Corp.
2125 Kishwaukee St
Rockford, IL 61104-7040
Contact: Tim Farrell, Pres., Sales & Mktg.
Mgr.
Telephone: 815-965-1862
Fax: 815-965-6890
Email: us@pgdisplay.com / URL: http://
www.pgdisplay.com
Product Service Description:
Screen printing & point-of-purchase displays
Printing_commercial
Signs & advertising specialties
Trade show exhibits

Process Technologies Inc.
436 W Rawson Ave
Oak Creek, WI 53154-1414
Contact: Manfred K. Stelter, Pres., Fin., GM,
R & D & Sales Mgr.
Telephone: 414-571-9200
Fax: 414-571-9202
Email: pti@execpc.com / URL: http://
www.execpc.com/~pti
Product Service Description:
Microelectronic & liquid crystal display
masks, reticles & prototypes

Proctor & Schwartz
121 Proctor Ln
Lexington, NC 27295-7565
Contact: Mark Wilhelm, Supv.
Telephone: 336-248-5181
Fax: 336-248-5118
Email: / URL:
Product Service Description:
Machinery_special industry
Industrial dryers

Proctor Companies
10497 Centennial Road
Littleton, CO 80127
Contact: Bruce B. Proctor, President
Telephone: 303-973-8989
Fax: 303-973-8884
Email: pdi@proctorco.com / URL: http://
www.proctorco.com
Product Service Description:
Ice Making Machines
Concession Stands
Popcorn Equipment & Machines

Procunier Safety Chuck Co.
304 Winston Creek Pkwy
Lakeland, FL 33810-2866
Contact: R. A. McConnell, Pres.
Telephone: 941-688-0071
Fax: 941-682-6233
Product Service Description:
Machine tools, metal cutting types
High speed tapping machine attachments &
multiple spindle drill heads

Prodelin Corp.
PO Box 368
Conover, NC 28613-0368
Contact: Jim Hartman, VP Sales
Telephone: 828-464-4141
Fax: 828-466-0860
Email: jim.hartman@prodelin.com / URL:
http://www.prodelin.com
Product Service Description:
Satellite Earth Station Antennas
Radio & TV Communications Equipment

Products Techniques Inc
PO Box 760
Bloomington, CA 92316-0760
Contact: Steven Andrews Or Caris Boden,
Telephone: 909-877-3951
Fax: 909-877-6078
Email: / URL: http://www.ptipaint.com
Product Service Description:
Manufactures protective coatings, industrial
and maintenance paints and coatings, dryfilm
lubricants
Paints & allied products; solvents & greases

Professional Discount Supply
1029 S Sierra Madre St, Suite B
Colorado Springs, CO 80903-4234
Contact: Frank Mesce, Ptnr.
Telephone: 719-444-0646
Fax: 719-442-2384
Email: pdsfm@worldnet.att.net / URL: http://
www.radonpds.com
Product Service Description:
Radon Fans & Supplies
Ventilation Fans

**Professional Services International,
Inc.**
2201 Water Ridge Pkwy.
Charlotte, NC 28217
Contact: James D. McClaskey, President
Telephone: 704-357-3311
Fax: 704-357-3318
Email: / URL:
Product Service Description:
Industrial Equipment
Industrial Machinery
Alloy Steel
Catalyst
Reformer Tubes
Heat Recovery Units
Valves
Structural Steel Plates

Progressive Crane, Inc.
13721 Bennington Ave.
Cleveland, OH 44135-4951
Contact: Wayne R. Goforth, President
Telephone: 216-251-6126
Fax: 216-941-3383
Email: / URL:
Product Service Description:
Hoists - shawbox & budgit
Cranes
Crane & hoist parts

Progressive Industries, Inc.
PO Box 1329
Sylacauga, AL 35150-1329
Contact: Don Jones, Pres. / Chris Meadows - Sales Mgr., Andy Jones, Engr Sales
Telephone: 205-249-4965
Fax: 205-245-7506
Email: ajones@progressiveindustries.com / URL: http://www.progressiveindustries.com
Product Service Description:
Air classification & fine particle separation equipment

Progressive Metal Forming Inc.
PO Box 145
Hamburg, MI 48139-0145
Contact: R. G. Owens, Pres.
Telephone: 810-231-1100
Fax: 810-231-1141
Email: pmfinc@ismi.net / URL: http://www.pmfdraw.com
Product Service Description:
Manufacture of deep drawn stampings. Transfer and Progressive Die metal stampings. : Custom Eyelets, drawn metal consulting. : Solenoid and Motor Housing. Plumbing hardware. : Design, tool, build, produce, consult.

Promotional Resources Group
PO Box 19235, University Blvd.@esses Entr., Bldg. 2704 B-1
Topeka, KS 66619-0235
Contact: Jim Oxandale,
Telephone: 785-862-3707
Fax: 785-862-1424
Email: jimo@prgnet.com / URL: http://www.prgnet.com
Product Service Description:
Meal packaging - cartons & snacks
Promotional toys - retailer

Promotional Trim Components
908 Ne 24th Ln
Cape Coral, FL 33909-2915
Contact: Paul Hutchins, Pres.
Telephone: 941-458-1348
Fax: 941-458-4094
Email: / URL: http://www.ptc-auto.com
Product Service Description:
Spoilers & Running Boards
Motor vehicles & car bodies
Plastic Vacumming
Plastic Blow Molding

Prosoco Inc.
755 Minnesota Ave.
Kansas City, KS 66101-2703
Contact: Mike Dickey, *
Telephone: 913-281-2700
Fax: 913-281-4385
Email: / URL:
Product Service Description:
Chemical, Masonry Cleaners, Misc.
Water Repelling Compounds

Prospect Machine Products, Inc.
PO Box 7022
Prospect, CT 06712-0022
Contact: Richard A. Laurenzi, VP Sales & Marketing
Telephone: 203-758-4448
Fax: 203-758-5736
Email: prospectmachine@snet.net / URL: http://www.prospectmachineeyelets.com
Product Service Description:
Eyelet machine products (deep draw)
Specialty eyelets to blueprint

Prospect Steel, Inc.
PO Box 16390
Little Rock, AR 72231-6390
Contact: Eugene Riley Jr., Pres.
Telephone: 501-490-4200
Fax: 501-490-4411
Email: / URL: http://www.schueck.com
Product Service Description:
Blast furnaces & steel mills
Steel fabrication

Prospector & Treasure Hunters Hdqters., Inc.
1503 Us Highway 395 N Ste I
Gardnerville, NV 89410-5227
Contact: Robert Yocum, Pres.
Telephone: 775-782-6664
Fax: 775-782-6650
Email: omni@path-inc.com / URL: http://www.path-inc.com
Product Service Description:
Manufactures precious metal indicators and mining supplies, Mining Machinery
Omni-Range Master & Fort Knox mineral locators

Protect All, Inc.
1910 E. Via Burton
Anaheim, CA 92806-1215
Contact: Al Baudoin, President
Telephone: 714-635-4491
Fax: 714-635-9716
Email: abaudoin@protectall.com / URL: http://www.protectall.com
Product Service Description:
Automotive cleaners, waxes, polishes
Manufactures industrial lubricants
Metal working fluids

Protection Development International
PO Box 2048
Corona, CA 91718-2048
Contact: Norman E Smith, Pres.
Telephone: 909-734-7531
Fax: 909-734-7570
Email: info@armor-pdi.com / URL: http://www.armor-pdi.com
Product Service Description:
Manufactures armet opaque armor; bomb handling systems and equipment; armored vehicles

Protex International Corp.
180 Keyland Ct
Bohemia, NY 11716-2657
Contact: David Wachsman, CEO
Telephone: 516-563-4250
Fax: 516-563-4206
Email: protex@protex-intl.com / URL: http://www.protex-intl.com
Product Service Description:
Safety & detection mirrors, loss prevention
Security Systems
Theft Deterrent Products

Protos Inc.
460 Glenmeade Rd
Greensburg, PA 15601-1138
Contact: W. Logan Dickerson, Pres.
Telephone: 724-836-1802
Fax: 724-836-1895
Email: royalos@westol.com / URL: http://www.protos-inc.com
Product Service Description:
Sports Nutrition Food Products
Ostrim, High-Protein, Low-Fat Meat Snacks

Psychological Corp., The
555 Academic Ct
San Antonio, TX 78204-2455
Contact: Joanne M. Lenke, Pres.
Telephone: 210-299-1061
Fax: 210-270-0327
Email: joanne.lenke@hbtpc.com / URL: http://www.hbem.com
Product Service Description:
Printing_commercial
Test printing

Public Health Equipment Supply Inc.
P.O. Box 10458
San Antonio, TX 78210
Contact: C. Mills Reeves, President
Telephone: 210-532-3846
Fax: 210-532-9703
Email: phesco@world-net.net / URL: http://www.phesco.com
Product Service Description:
Ind. Pest Rodent Control Equip, Wholesale Svc. Ind. Equip., Sprayers/Foggers, Wholesale
Mosquito & Vector Control Equip & Chemicals

Pulizzi Engineering Inc
3200 S Susan St
Santa Ana, CA 92704-6839
Contact: Peter S Pulizzi, Pres.
Telephone: 714-540-4229 ext.36
Fax: 714-641-9062
Email: sales@pulizzi.com / URL: http://www.pulizzi.com
Product Service Description:
Manufactures AC power distribution and control systems for mainframe computers and OEMs

Pupi Enterprises LLC
PO Bo x 20199
Riverside, CA 92516-0199
Contact: Richard N. Essig, Tech Mgr.
Telephone: 909-684-4443
Fax: 909-684-4447
URL: http://www.pupi-enterprises.com
Product Service Description:
Manufactures fiberglass beams (Technical Office) : Plastic Products : Plastic materials & basic shapes

Pulse Medical Products, Inc.
4131 Sw 47th Ave
Davie, FL 33314-4036
Contact: Barbara Boyce, Pres.
Telephone: 954-587-8867
Fax: 954-587-8853
Email: info@rci-pulsemd.com / URL: http://www.rci-pulsemed.com
Product Service Description:
X-Ray Accessories

Purdy Corp.
PO Box 1898
Manchester, CT 06045-1898
Contact: Andrew A. Sadanowicz, Pres.
Telephone: 860-649-0000
Fax: 860-645-6293
Email: sales@purdytransmissions.com / URL: http://www.purdytransmissions.com
Product Service Description:
Helicopter Transmissions & Rotorhead Components
Aircraft Engine Systems & Flight Safety Parts
Spiral Bevel, Spur & Helical Gears, Curvic Couplings & Splines

Pure Water, Inc.
3725 Touzalin Ave., P.O. Box 83226
Lincoln, NE 68501-3226
Contact: A. E. Meder, President
Telephone: 402-467-9300
Fax: 402-467-9393
Email: / URL: http://www.purewaterinc.com
Product Service Description:
Home Water Purification Equipm
Commercial Water Purification

Purepak Inc
PO Box 588
Oxnard, CA 93032-0588
Contact: Dean Walsh, Pres.
Telephone: 805-485-1127
Fax: 805-278-9617
Email: / URL:
Product Service Description:
Grows organic vegetables, melons and citrus fruits; processes strawberries

Purnell Co., R. C.
4 Maynard Cir
Old Saybrook, CT 06475-2210
Contact: Robert Purnell, Owner
Telephone: 860-388-2681
Fax: 860-388-5068
Email: rakmagic@connix.com / URL: http://www.connix.com/~rakmagic
Product Service Description:
Wooden storage products
Wood products (home use)

Purolator Products Air Filtration Co.
P.O. Box 1637 - 880 Facet Road
Henderson, NC 27536
Contact: John Hanna, VP Sales & Marketing
Telephone: 252-492-1141
Fax: 252-492-6157
Email: ppafc@aol.com / URL: http://www.purolatorair.com
Product Service Description:
Heating & Air Conditioning Filters
HVAC Housing & Equipment
Cleanroom Filtration Products

Purr-Fect Growlings
P.O. Box 90275
Los Angeles, CA 90009-0275
Contact: Suzanne Simmons, President
Telephone: 323-751-3613
Fax: 323-751-3693
Email: / URL:
Product Service Description:
Dog Biscuits
Cat Toys
Doggie T-Shirts
Doggie Bandannas
People T-Shirts

Pyott-Boone Electronics
PO Box 809
Tazewell, VA 24651-0809
Contact: Nancye K. Howell, Vice President
Telephone: 540-988-5505
Fax: 540-988-6820
Email: nhowell@netscope.net / URL: http://www.pyottboone.com
Product Service Description:
Loudspeaking Page Telephone: Model 112
Loudspeaking Weatherproof Page Telephone: Model 117 : Loudspeaking Desk Page Telephone: Model 118 : Conveyor Belt Motion Switch, 2 Channel: Model 405 A/II Conveyor Belt Motion Switch, 3 Channel: Model 405A/III : Convyor Blet Motion Switch, 2 Channel, Digital Technology

Pyramid Granite & Metals, Inc.
660 Superior St.
Escondido, CA 92029-1130
Contact: Philip m. Hoadley, Pres.
Telephone: 760-745-6309
Fax: 760-741-6201
Email: sales@pyramidgranite.com / URL:
http://www.pyramidgranite.com
Product Service Description:
Manufactures black granite surface-plates

Pyramid Machine & Tool, Inc.
PO Box 1455
Rowlett, TX 75030-1455
Contact: Chuck McCasland, Pres., Engrg.,
Sales & Mktg. Mgr.
Telephone: 972-412-4661
Fax: 972-475-4074
Email: cam.pyramid@att.worldnet.net / URL:
Product Service Description:
Powder Coating & Precision Machining Job
Shop of Plstic / Metal
Precision Sheet Metal Fabrications

Q C A Pools & Spas
1021 State Street
Bettendorf, IA 52722
Contact: Keith Hall, Pres.
Telephone: 319-359-3558
Fax: 319-359-3018
Email: qcaspas@qcaspas.com / URL: http://
www.qcaspas.com
Product Service Description:
Pools & spas & saunas
Sporting & athletic goods

Q E I, Inc.
60 Fadem Rd
Springfield, NJ 07081-3116
Contact: Stephen Dalyai, President
Telephone: 973-379-7400
Fax: 973-379-2138
Email: sales@qeiinc.com / URL: http://
www.qeiinc.com
Product Service Description:
Computers
Electronic computers

Q. Up Arts
PO Box 979
Grass Valley, CA 95445
Contact: Susan Morton, Ptrn
Telephone: 530-477-8128
Fax: 530-477-5935
Email: info@quparts.com / URL: http://
www.quparts.com
Product Service Description:
Disigns & manufactures CD-Rom sound &
music libraries for the film & computer
industries
Records & tapes, prerecorded

Quad Group
1815 S Lewis St.
Spokane, WA 99224-9789
Contact: Maria Riegert, President
Telephone: 509-458-4558
Fax: 509-458-4555
Email: / URL:
Product Service Description:
Measuring Devices, Adhesion Testers
Measuring Devices, Adhesion & Adherence
Testers : Measuring Devices, Universal
Materials Testers : Adhesion testers, Paints &
Coatings : Measuring Devices, Diamond
Scratch Coat, Tester
Measuring Devices, Materials
Characterization Tester

Quaker Plastic Corp.
P.O. Box 557
Mountville, PA 17554-0557
Contact: Mark Steller, VP Sales & Mktg.
Telephone: 717-285-4571
Fax: 717-285-7740
Email: info@quakerplastic.com / URL: http://
www.quakerplastic.com
Product Service Description:
Plastic Products
Plastic Thermoforming

Qual-Pro Corporation
18101 Savarona Way
Carson, CA 90746-1411
Contact: Gerald Shane, Pres.
Telephone: 310-329-7535
Fax: 310-329-0201
Email: info@qual-pro.com / URL:
Product Service Description:
Turnkey and consignment electronic
manufacturing, assembly and auto-insertion
from : board level to total system electronics.
Also Test trouble shoot, product burning.

Quali-Tech Manufacturing Co
2041 E Del Amo Blvd
Rancho Dominguez, CA 90220-6131
Contact: Song B Kim, Pres.
Telephone: 310-637-8900
Fax: 310-763-2100
Email: sales@quali-techmfg.com / URL:
http://www.quali-techmfg.com
Product Service Description:
Manufactures paint applicators and related
products

Qualitek International, Inc.
315 Fairbank St
Addison, IL 60101-3123
Contact: Charles Han, Dir., Sales & Mktg.
Telephone: 630-628-8083 Ext. 138
Fax: 630-628-6543
Email: qualitek@ix.netcom.com / URL: http:/
/www.qualitek.com
Product Service Description:
Soldering paste, chemicals, solder bar, wire &
BGA

Quality Boat Lifts, Inc.
17030 Alico Center Rd
Fort Myers, FL 33912-6018
Contact: Darrel Reardon, Sales & Mktg. Mgr.
Telephone: 941-432-9110
Fax: 941-432-0019
Product Service Description:
Boat lifts : Hoists, cranes & monorails

Quality Brass & Aluminum Foundry
7531 NE 33rd Dr
Portland, OR 97211-2013
Contact: Ray Ghiselline, Consultant
Telephone: 503-287-8454
Fax: 503-287-1942
Email: qba@web-ster.com / URL:
Product Service Description:
Sand-casts brass and aluminum raw castings
Foundries_aluminum : Copper foundries

Quality Customs Broker, Inc.
4464 S. Whitnall Ave.
Milwaukee, WI 53235
Contact: Jean VanderMeer, V.P. - Freight
Telephone: 414-482-9447
Fax: 414-482-9448
Email: qcb@pitnet.net / URL:
Product Service Description:
U.S. Customs Broker : Int'l Freight
Forwarder

Quality Embroidery
2823 S Olive St
Los Angeles, CA 90007-3339
Contact: Osher Peretz, Owner
Telephone: 213-746-6363
Fax: 213-746-9110
Email: / URL:
Product Service Description:
Embroideries and screen printing on apparel
Hi-frequency & sonic welding

Quality Forest Products
21144 Hwy 301 S.
Enfield, NC 27823-0696
Contact: Rick Phillips, Vice President
Telephone: 252-445-2113
Fax: 252-445-2771
Email: qfp@3rddoor.com / URL: http://
www.3rddoor.com/homepages/QFP
Product Service Description:
ACQ Pressure Treated SYP & D.Blaze Fire
Retardant
Lumber & Plywood

Quality Industries, Inc.
PO Box 406
Thibodaux, LA 70302-0406
Contact: Edward Comeaux, General Manager
Telephone: 504-447-4021
Fax: 504-447-4028
Email: edc@qualityindustries.com / URL:
http://www.qualityindustries.com
Product Service Description:
Construction Equipment, Amphibious
Pumps for Drainage & Irrigation
Trailers & Wagons for Sugarcane

Quality Mold Inc.
99 East Seiberling Street
Akron, OH 44305
Contact: Steve Zoumbezakis, President
Telephone: 330-798-4600
Fax: 330-798-4633
Email: qtech@qualitymold.com / URL: http://
www.qualitymold.com
Product Service Description:
Aluminum & steel tire molds
Automotive stampings
Containers For Molds
Engraved Molds
Foundry Molds & Castings
Engineering & Technical Support

Quality Scientific Plastics
1260 Holm Road
Petaluma, CA 94954-1182
Contact: Patty Doerpinghaus, V.P. Mktg.
Telephone: 707-763-1552
Fax: 707-762-9215
Email: patty-doerpinghaus@porex.com /
URL:
Product Service Description:
Laboratory Plastics, Disposable
Tips / Stnd, Filtered, Robotic, Conductive
Cent. Tubes / Snap, Screw, Tethered, Racks
PCR Tubes, Plates, Racks

Quantic Industries Inc
PO Box 148
Hollister, CA 95024-0148
Contact: Robert Valenti, Pres.
Telephone: 831-637-5851
Fax: 831-637-1013
Email: valenti@ix.netcom.com / URL: http://
www.quanticindustries.com
Product Service Description:
Explosive devices, cartridges; initiators,
igniters
Safe-arm devices, arm-fire devices

Quantum Color Graphics Inc.
6511 Oakton St
Morton Grove, IL 60053-2728
Contact: Al Cudahy, Pres.
Telephone: 847-967-3600
Fax: 847-967-3610
Email: qcolor@aol.com / URL: http://
www.quantumcolor.com
Product Service Description:
Digital Pre-Press /
Commercial Offset Lithography

Quantum Conveyor Systems, LLC
119 Rockland Ave
Northvale, NJ 07647-2144
Contact: Matthew Mulhern, Pres.
Telephone: 201-767-0300
Fax: 201-767-4639
Email: quantco@aol.com / URL: http://
www.quantumconveyor.com
Product Service Description:
Conveyor systems
Conveyors & conveying equipment
Sortation Systems
Accumulation Conveyor
Product Stackers
Dynamic Merging
Transpiration Conveyor
Small parcel Sortation
Carton Sortation
Mail Order Sortation

Quantum Group, Inc.
11211 Sorrento Valley Road
San Diego, CA 92121-1324
Contact: Mark Goldstein, President
Telephone: 619-457-3048
Fax: 619-457-3229
Email: mktsls@qginc.com / URL: http://
www.qginc.com
Product Service Description:
Manufactures carbon monoxide alarms &
detectors
Measuring & controlling devices (ventilation
control)

Quartzdyne Inc.(Mfr)
1020 Atherton Drive, Bldg. C
Salt Lake City, UT 84123
Contact: Roger Ward, *
Telephone: 801/266-6958
Product Service Description:
Quartz Crystal Pressure Transducers

Ques Industries, Inc.
5420 W 140th St
Cleveland, OH 44142-1703
Contact: Quent Meng, Pres.
Telephone: 216-267-8989
Fax: 216-267-8998
Email: quesinc@aol.com / URL:
Product Service Description:
Water treatment chemicals & industrial
cleaning agents - Private label

Quest & Sons, Inc.
222 E 34th St
Lubbock, TX 79404-2212
Contact: Ralph Quest II, Pres., Fin., MIS,
Pur. & R & D Mgr.
Telephone: 806-744-2351
Fax: 806-747-6936
Email: rbquest@hub.ofthe.net / URL: http://
www.quest2.com
Product Service Description:
Tarps, gym mats, boat, pool & truck covers &
foam rubber
Canvas & related products
Bags, Disaster Bag

Quincy Compressor
3501 Wisman Ln.
Quincy, IL 62301-1257
Contact: Ken Rollins, Pres.
Telephone: 217-222-7700
Fax: 217-222-5109
Email: trueblue@quincycompressor.com /
URL: http://www.quincycompressor.com
Product Service Description:
Compressors, air & gas
Air compressors & vacuum pumps

Quinn Process Equipment Co
3400 Brighton Blvd
Denver, CO 80216-5023
Contact: Richard Quinn, Pres.
Telephone: 303-295-2872
Fax: 303-295-2706
Email: quinnproc@aol.com / URL: http://
www.quinnprocess.com
Product Service Description:
Manufactures mineral processing equipment;
conveyors and conveying equipment; pumps
and pumping equipment
Pilot plant equipment
Pumps & pumping equipment
Flotation machines
Solvent extraction mixer-settlers
Grinding mills
Thickeners
Filters
Mineral jigs

Quintus Inc
PO Box 3930
Camp Verde, AZ 86322-3930
Contact: Richard L Cook, Pres.
Telephone: 520-567-3833
Fax: 520-567-3913
Email: / URL:
Product Service Description:
Manufactures composite medical parts;
aircraft components, string instruments

Quirin Machine Shop Inc., E. A.
PO Box 98
Saint Clair, PA 17970-0098
Contact: Edmund Quirin, Pres.
Telephone: 717-429-0590
Fax: 717-429-2793
Email: / URL:
Product Service Description:
Steel grating

Qwikstamp Corporation
PO Box 5433
Los Alamitos, CA 90721-5433
Contact: Susan Pezze, Pres.
Telephone: 562-596-0051
Fax: 562-596-4811
Email: / URL:
Product Service Description:
Manufactures pre-inked stamps
Marking devices
Rubberstamps
Engraving

R & D International Inc.
2151 Le Jeune Road, Suite 306
Coral Gables, FL 33134
Contact: Artur Ferrari, Manager
Telephone: 305-447-0008
Fax: 305-447-6878
Email: ferrari@instantshop.com / URL:
Product Service Description:
Commercial Equipment, NEC - Store Fixtures
Structures and parts of structures, of iron or
steel
Articles of plastics

R & R Insurance Services, Inc.
PO Box 1610
Waukesha, WI 53187-1610
Contact: John D. Buechel,
Telephone: 414-574-7000
Fax: 414-574-7080
Email: buechejo@rrins.iix.com / URL:
Product Service Description:
Insurance Agents & Brokers
Insurance Agent Livestock/Animal Insurance
Insurance Agent, Bull Semen Insurance

R & R Machine Industries, Inc.
1 Tupperware Dr Ste 10
North Smithfield, RI 02896-6815
Contact: Roland Legare, Pres.
Telephone: 401-766-2505
Fax: 401-762-3536
Email: rmachine@tp.net / URL: http://
www.rrmachine.com
Product Service Description:
General machining job shop
Industrial machinery

R & R Rubber Molding Inc
PO Box 3533
South El Monte, CA 91733-0533
Contact: Richard A Norman Sr, Pres.
Telephone: 626-575-8105
Fax: 626-575-3756
Email: rrrubber@aol.com / URL: http://
www.rruber.com
Product Service Description:
Gaskets, packing & sealing devices
Manufactures rubber sealing devices (job
shop)
Mechanical rubber goods

R & S Sportswear Inc; dba FILATI
2640 E 26th St
Vernon, CA 90058-1218
Contact: Edit Mondelo, Pres., Randi
Mondello, VP / Danny Mondello, Sec.
Telephone: 323-585-9945
Fax: 323-585-9275
Email: filatiedi@geis.com / URL:
Product Service Description:
Manufactures women's, misses' and juniors'
sportswear
Outerwear_women's & misses'
Women's & children's clothing

R & T Truck Inc.
P.O. Box 1261,
Lubbock, TX 79408
Contact: Mike McBain,
Telephone: 806-744-1461
Fax: 806-744-3317
Email: rttruck@aol.com / URL:
Product Service Description:
Freight & Cargo Transportation
Trucking

R A M Products
3330 Nw 48th St
Miami, FL 33142-3326
Contact: Jose Andino, Pres.
Telephone: 305-634-0012
Fax: 305-634-6477
Email: ramsale@aol.com / URL:
Product Service Description:
Steel fabrication
Metal forming
Wall framing
Studs & tracks
Roll forming
Steel profiles
Drywall

R L S Lighting, Inc.
2160 Sw 58th Way
Hollywood, FL 33023-3043
Contact: Gordon Holmes, Sales Mgr.
Telephone: 954-983-4340
Fax: 954-983-3691
Email: rlslight@aol.com / URL:
Product Service Description:
Security, sports, landscape, decorative &
parking lot exterior lighting
Lighting equipment

**R O T H B R O S., Inc., A First
Energy Co.**
3847 Crum Rd
Youngstown, OH 44515-1414
Contact: Samuel A. Roth, Pres., CEO
Telephone: 330-793-5571
Fax: 330-799-9005
Email: moreinfo@rothbros.com / URL: http://
www.rothbros.com
Product Service Description:
Industrial Metal Fabrication
Sheet metal fabrication

R W C Inc.
PO Box 920
Bay City, MI 48707-0920
Contact: Aaron Mortin, VP of Sales & Mktg.
Telephone: 517-684-4030
Fax: 517-684-3960
Email: amortin@rwcinc.com / URL: http://
www.rwcinc.com
Product Service Description:
Machinery_special industry

R Wales & Son LLC
2665 N Flowing Wells Rd
Tucson, AZ 85705-4017
Contact: Al Rennie, Ptnr.
Telephone: 520-791-9001
Fax: 520-791-7974
Email: alrennie@aol.com / URL:
Product Service Description:
Fabricates rubber linings for mining industry;
rubber pump parts
Rubber products_fabricated

R&D Enterprises, Inc.
P.O. Box 5380
Northville, MI 48167
Contact: Richard D. Cox, President
Telephone: 248-349-7077
Fax: 248-349-0021
Email: / URL:
Product Service Description:
Heat Exchangers, Tube & Shell

R. B. R. Productions, Inc.
PO Box 3599
Teaneck, NJ 07666-9110
Contact: Richard Rosenberg, Pres.
Telephone: 201-871-3444
Fax: 201-871-9020
Email: / URL:
Product Service Description:
Beauty salon disinfectants & fingernail glue
accelerator & wrap systems

R. F. Technology, Inc.
16 Testa Pl
Norwalk, CT 06854-4638
Contact: M. Wanduragala, Pres.
Telephone: 203-866-4283
Fax: 203-853-3513
Email: / URL: http://www.rftechnology.com
Product Service Description:
Radio & TV communications equipment
Television & satellite equipment

R. P. Creations, Inc.
8 Brown St
Berlin, NH 03570-1901
Contact: Raymond A. Paulin, Pres., GM
Telephone: 603-752-1198
Fax: 603-752-1197
Email: creation@ncia.net / URL: http://
www.rpcreations.com
Product Service Description:
Sporting & amusement fiberglass fabrication
Plastic products
Business Enhancements
Theming Specialist

R.A. Pearson Company
W. 8120 Sunset Highway
Spokane, WA 99204
Contact: John Donovar, Mktg. Manager
Telephone: 509-838-6226
Fax: 509-747-8532
Email: jdonovar@pearsonpkg.com / URL:
http://www.pearsonpkg.com
Product Service Description:
Packaging Machinery, Secondary

R.B. Annis Company, Inc.
1101 N. Delaware St.
Indianapolis, IN 46202-2599
Contact: Robert Annis, President
Telephone: 317-637-9282
Fax: 317-637-9282
Email: / URL:
Product Service Description:
Demagnetizers - Over 100 Models.
Eraser, Bulk Audio & Vedeo Tape Cassette
Magnetic Field Indicators

R.B. Packing, Inc
PO Box 1586
Nogales, AZ 85628-1586
Contact: Francisco obregon, VP/General
Manager
Telephone: 520-281-0821
Fax: 520-281-2614
Email: fobregon@rbpacking.com / URL:
http://www.rbpacking.com
Product Service Description:
Fresh fruits & vegetables

**R.C. Technical Welding &
Fabricating Co., Inc.**
12814 Mula Lane
Stafford, TX 77477-3317
Contact: Raul C. Coardona, President
Telephone: 281-933-6004
Fax: 281-933-1548
Email: rctfab@ix.netcom.com / URL:
Product Service Description:
Alloy pressure vessels, silos, tanks, pipes &
pipe spooling & welding job shop
Pipe & fittings, Fabricated
Overlay 1/2" to large DIA pipe, Vessel or
fitting w/nickel, or stainless

R.D.D. Enterprises
2031 E. 25th St.
Los Angeles, CA 90058
Contact: Edward Diskin, President
Telephone: 323-234-4445
Fax: 323-234-4692
Email: / URL:
Product Service Description:
Exporting Firms
Military tents, clothing, field gear, new &
used
Woven fab of syn fil yn, incl monofil 67 dec
Miscellaneous cargo

R.E. Uptegraff Mfg. Company
PO Box 182, Uptegraff Drive
Scottdale, PA 15683-0182
Contact: Walter Scheller, Sales Manager
Telephone: 724-887-7700
Fax: 724-887-4748
Email: info@uptegraff.com / URL: http://
www.uptegraff.com
Product Service Description:
Transformers
Reactors

R.J. Commodities
4407 N. Division St., Ste. 811
Spokane, WA 99207-1613
Contact: Sales & Marketing,
Telephone: 509-487-0755
Product Service Description:
Commodity Contracts Brokers, Dealers
Animal feed preparations , other than dog or
cat food : Peas , dried shelled, dry beans,
sunflower seed, millets, soybeans
Popcorn, safflower, organics, lentils, flax,
canola : Buckwheat, rolled oats

R.W. Hatfield Co., Pro-Line Div.
12 Rogers Road
Haverhill, MA 01835
Contact: Robert Hatfield, Vice President
Telephone: 978-521-2600
Fax: 978-374-4885
Email: bench@1proline.com / URL: http://
www.1proline.com
Product Service Description:
Industrial Workbenches

RAM Sports Inc
3660 East 40th Ave.
Denver, CO 80205
Contact: Randy Jones, Pres.
Telephone: 303-394-6966
Fax: 303-394-6982
Email: info@classicsport.com / URL:
Product Service Description:
Manufactures all types of sport balls from
composite leather
Sporting & athletic goods
Manufactures lawn games including; croquet,
bocce, volleyball, badminton

RBM Manufacturing Co., Inc.
1570 W Mission Blvd
Pomona, CA 91766-1247
Contact: Roobik Kureghian, Pres.
Telephone: 909-620-1333
Fax: 909-620-6119
Email: rbmmfg@aol.com / URL:
Product Service Description:
Custom design, engineering and fabrication of
bulk, packed material handling equipment
Conveyors & conveying , surge & distribution
systems.
Natural frequency vibrating conveyors.
Belt conveyors & bucket elevators
Complete automated systems design,
fabrication & installation

RDM Multi-Enterprises Inc.
105 N. Silver
Anaconda, MT 59711
Contact: Dominic Difrancesco, *
Telephone: 406/563-3433
Fax: 406-563-3435
Email: / URL:
Product Service Description:
Sandblasting Media

RDO Equipment Co
PO Box 27267
Tucson, AZ 85726-7267
Contact: Tom Smith, Store Manager
Telephone: 520-294-5262
Fax: 520-573-1295
Email: ttsrdosw@primenet.com / URL:
Product Service Description:
Distributes mining and industrial machinery
and equipment; John Deere dealership,
Parts & service

RK Pipe & Supply
4115 S. Lewis St.
New Iberia, LA 70560-8757
Contact: Russell Sandridge, Owner
Telephone: 318-367-9224
Fax: 318-365-7083
Email: sales@rkpipe.com / URL: http://
www.rkpipe.com
Product Service Description:
Tubulars & Drilling Equipment
Oil & Gas Sales

RO Ultratec USA Inc
541 Industrial Way Ste 1
Fallbrook, CA 92028-2257
Contact: Augustin Pavel, Pres.
Telephone: 760-723-5417
Fax: 760-728-5062
Email: apavel@ix.netcom.com / URL: http://
www.roultratec.com
Product Service Description:
Manufactures membranes for reverse osmosis
water treatment - residential & industr. types
Light industrial R.O. machines - up to 10,000
GPD : Stocking distr. for filter hsg's &
cartridges : Stocking distr. for carbon blocks
& KDF cartridges : Stocking distr. for Hi-
pressure pumps & electric motors

ROW, Inc.
729 W Winthrop Ave
Addison, IL 60101-4310
Contact: William Vischer, Pres.,
CFO, Sales Mgr.
Telephone: 630-628-9221
Fax: 630-628-9229
Email: row@inforel.com / URL: http://
www.row-inc.com
Product Service Description:
Encapsulated o-rings, gaskets, & cam lock
coupling gaskets

RS Technical Services Inc
PO Box 750579
Petaluma, CA 94975-0579
Contact: Rod Sutliff, CEO
Telephone: 707-778-1974
Fax: 707-778-1981
Email: mshepard@rstechserv.com / URL:
http://www.rstechserv.com
Product Service Description:
Video Inspection Equipment Design &
Manufacture

RSM Products, Inc.
31943 Amaral St
Hayward, CA 94544-7804
Contact: Hans Schau, President
Telephone: 510-489-3990
Fax: 510-489-2348
Email: rsmproducts@msn.com / URL:
Product Service Description:
Screw machine products, single & multi
spindle : CNC Machining
Wire products, wire forming

Racom Products Inc.
5504 State Rd
Cleveland, OH 44134-2250
Contact: John M. Dukovich, Product
Manager
Telephone: 216-351-1755 / 800-722-6664
Fax: 216-351-0392
Email: sales@racominc.com / URL: http://
www.racominc.com
Product Service Description:
Telphonic Intercom Systems
Teleprinter
Telephone Answering Machine / Digital
Audio Type

Rad-Elec Inc.
5714 Industry Ln Ste C
Frederick, MD 21704-8244
Contact: Paul Kotrappa, President
Telephone: 301-694-0011
Fax: 301-694-0013
Email: pkotrappa@aol.com / URL: http://
www.radelec.com
Product Service Description:
Radon & Radiation Monitorying Instruments

Radial Bearing Corp.
21 Taylor St
Danbury, CT 06810
Contact: S.Papish, President
Telephone: 203-744-0323
Fax: 203-744-1691
Email: / URL:
Product Service Description:
Bearings, Spherical & Rod End, Aircraft

Radiant Communications Corp.
PO Box 867
South Plainfield, NJ 07080-0867
Contact: Mike Thaw, Pres.
Telephone: 908-757-7444
Fax: 908-757-8666
Email: radiant3@ix.netcom.com / URL: http://
/www.rccfiber.com
Product Service Description:
Fiber optic components
Fiber Optic Patch & Splice
Fiber Optic Network Electronics
Fiber Optic video Electronics
Fiber Optic Cable Assemblies

Radiant Communications Corporation
PO Box 867, 5001 Hadley Road
South Plainfield, NJ 07080
Contact: Patricia Traina, Marketing Manager
Telephone: 908-757-7444 / 800-969-3427
Fax: 908-757-8666
Email: radiant3@ix.netcom.com / URL: http:/
/www.rccfiber.com
Product Service Description:
Manufacturer of fiber optic cable plant
products, electronics for distance learning &
LAN/WAN application products.

Radiator Specialty Co.
P.O. Box 34689
Charlotte, NC 28234
Contact: John Gonzalez, Dir. Int'l Saels
Telephone: 704-377-6555
Fax: 704-334-9237
Email: www.export@gunk.com / URL:
Product Service Description:
Automotive Chemical Specialties
Plumbing Chemical Specialties
Rubber Products
Traffic Safety Products

Radio Materials Corp.
PO Box 339
Attica, IN 47918-0339
Contact: Joseph F. Riley III, Director, Sales
& Marketing
Telephone: 765-762-6773
Fax: 765-762-6814
Email: jriley0707@aol.com / URL: http://
www.radiomaterials.com
Product Service Description:
Ceramic capacitors & dielectric ceramic
materials

Radiometer, Inc.
810 Sharon Dr
Westlake, OH 44145-1521
Contact: Customer Service,
Telephone: 440-871-8900 / 800-736-0600
Fax: 440-871-2633
Email: marketing@radiometer.com / URL:
http://www.radiometer.com
Product Service Description:
Electromedical equipment
Arterial blood samplers, medical electronic
components & equipment

Rahco Rubber, Inc.
1633 Birchwood Ave
Des Plaines, IL 60018-3003
Contact: William Anton, Chrm., Pres.
Telephone: 847-298-4200
Fax: 847-298-4201
Email: Rahco@Mcs.net / URL: http://
www.rahco-rubber.com
Product Service Description:
Molded Rubber Products & Molded
Thermoplastics
Rubber Products_fabricated

Rahoy Coccia Gabriella
175-06 Devonshire Road, #2C
Jamaica Estates, NY 11432 USA
Contact: Gabriella Coccia Rahoy, Translator /
Interpreter
Telephone: 718-523-6864
Fax: 718-523-6864
Email: 103667.3620@compuserve.com
Product Service Description:
Translation / Interpreting : English / Italian
ATA Accredited - BA Philosophy - MA
Theology : Law / Business / Banking /
Astronomy

Raibeam
5638 W Alice Ave
Glendale, AZ 85302-4722
Contact: S C Smith, Pres.
Telephone: 602-931-9135
Email: sales@raibeam.com / URL: http://
www.raibeam.com
Product Service Description:
Manufactures communication antennas
Manufactures amateur radio antennas

Railroad Signal, Inc.
15110 E Pine St
Tulsa, OK 74116-2214
Contact: Eddie Burns, Pres.
Phone: 918-234-1522 / Fax: 918-234-1529
Email: info@railroadsignal.com / URL: http://
www.railraodsignal.com
Product Service Description:
Communications equipment, AEI readers,
radios : Railroad crossing signals
Train control - wayside signals
Hot box detectors - drag detectors
Power switches & yard control signals
Rail operation control centers
Engineering Service

Railroad Signal, Inc.
3050 Tamarron Blvd, Suite 1211
Austin, TX 78746
Contact: Alan Barker, VP Marketing
Phone: 512-328-1159 / Fax: 512-328-2478
Email: alan.barker@railroadsignal.com /
URL: http://www.railroadsignal.com
Product Service Description:
Communications equipment, AEI readers,
radios : Railroad crossing signals : Train
control - wayside signals : Hot box detectors -
drag detectors : Power switches & yard
control signals : Rail operation control centers
Engineering Service

Rainbow Crane Corp
12220 Parkway Centre Dr
Poway, CA 92064-6867
Contact: Stann Smith, V/P Sales
Telephone: 619-748-7157
Fax: 619-679-3576
Email: / URL: http://www.rainbowcrane.com
Product Service Description:
Manufactures vending machines (skill crane)
amusement games

Raines Technologies Inc
2410 W 14th St
Tempe, AZ 85281-6920
Contact: Charlie Stamps, Operations Manager
Telephone: 602-966-4040
Fax: 602-966-6758
Email: charlie@rainestech.com / URL: http://
www.rainestech.com
Product Service Description:
Manufactures and services semiconductor
etching equipment and parts
Data gathering & machine control solutions

Rainhandler
2710 North Ave.
Bridgeport, CT 06604-2352
Contact: Frank Natale, Technical Svcs. Mgr.
Telephone: 203-382-2991 / 800-942-3004
Fax: 203-382-2995 / 800-606-2028
Email: rainhandle@aol.com / URL: http://
www.rainhandler.com
Product Service Description:
Aluminum rain handling systems
Roof algae, mold & fungas inhibitors
Rainhandler rain dispersal system - better
than gutters

Ralph Tire & Service, Inc.
5157 N.W. 74th Ave.
Miami, FL 33166-4215
Contact: Margarita G. Rios, President
Telephone: 305-592-8096
Fax: 305-592-5706
Email: ralphstire@shadow.net / URL: http://
www.ralphstireandservice.com
Product Service Description:
Tires and Tubes
Industrial Equipment Parts & Accessories

Ram Forest Products
HCR1 Box 15a
Shinglehouse, PA 16748
Contact: Robert A Mallery, President
Telephone: 814-697-7181
Fax: 814-697-7393
Email: ramsales@netsync.net / URL:
Product Service Description:
Lumber, Plywood, and Millwork
Oak wood, sawn or chipped lenghtwise,
sliced or peeled, whether or not planed
Nonconiferous wood, sawn or chipped
lengthwise, sliced or peeled, whether or not
planed

Rame-Hart, Inc.
8 Morris Avenue
Mountain Lakes, NJ 07046-0098
Contact: K. Christiansen, President
Telephone: 973-335-0560
Fax: 973-335-2920
Email: ramehart@idt.net / URL: http://
www.ramehart.com
Product Service Description:
Syringe Filling Machinery
Pharmaceutical Machinery
Egg-Culture Vaccine Machinery
Interfacial Tension Apparatus
Surface Tension Apparatus
Optical Instrumentation

Ramsey Winch Co.
PO Box 581510
Tulsa, OK 74158-1510
Contact: Joe Henry, Pres.
Telephone: 918-438-2760
Fax: 918-438-6688
Email: / URL: http://www.ramsey.com
Product Service Description:
Construction machinery : Winches

Ranchland News
PO Box 307
Simla, CO 80835-0307
Contact: Susan Lister, Owner
Telephone: 719-541-2288
Fax: 719-541-2289
Product Service Description:
Publishes periodicals : Periodicals
Books, periodicals & newspapers

Rancho Metal Polishing
8434 Rochester Ave
Rancho Cucamonga, CA 91730-3904
Contact: Richard Malnar, Pres.
Telephone: 909-466-1944
Fax: 909-466-0863
Product Service Description:
Manufactures metal polishing machinery;
polishes metal (job shop)
Wheel polishing machines

Rancho Suspension
500 North Field Dr.
Lake Forest, IL 60045
Contact: Mark Boyle, Marketing Manager
Telephone: 847-482-5625
Fax: 847-482-5739
Email: / URL: http://www.gorancho.com
Product Service Description:
Manufactures light truck and automobile four-
wheel drive suspensions : Motor vehicle
parts & accessories : Truck & bus bodies

Ranger Industries
15 Park Road
Tinton Falls, NJ 07724
Contact: Vincent Di Lascia, Director/
Marketing
Telephone: 908-389-3535
Fax: 908-389-1102
Product Service Description:
Specialty Inks, Epoxy, Flexo, Indel, Jet
Stamp Pads, Commercial, Decorative

Rankin Industries Inc
2285 Main St
San Diego, CA 92154-4702
Contact: Lynn Bailey, Pres.
Phone: 619-575-6000 / Fax: 619-575-6003
Email: hardface@rankinind.com / URL:
Product Service Description:
Hardfacing welding electrodes, wire

Rapid Air & Ocean
6974 NW 12th St.,
Miami, FL 33126
Contact: Salvator Arzillo, Jr., President
Telephone: 305-591-7506
Fax: 305-477-4045
Email: / URL:
Product Service Description:
Customs Broker
Freight Forwarder
Freight & Cargo Transportation

Rapid Development Service
18421 Edison Ave.
Chesterfield, MO 63005
Contact: Leon Gurevich, Owner & GM
Telephone: 314-519-1444
Fax: 314-519-0809
Email: lgleon@aol.com / URL: http://
www.rapidds.com
Product Service Description:
Industrial machinery
Industrial machinery
Special Machinery
Robotic System, Integrtor
Testing Equipment
Fixturing & Tooling
Mechanical Design

Rapid Purge Corp.
2285 Reservoir Ave
Trumbull, CT 06611-4743
Contact: Dennis L. Slavin, Pres.
Telephone: 203-372-5677
Fax: 203-371-6253
Email: / URL: http://www.rapidpurge.com
Product Service Description:
Industrial purging compounds for plastic
industry only

Rapid Rack Industries
14421 Bonelli Ave
City Of Industry, CA 91746-3021
Contact: Ken Blankenhorn, Pres.
Telephone: 626-333-7225
Fax: 626-333-5265
Email: / URL:
Product Service Description:
Manufactures storage racks and material
handling equipment
Partitions & fixtures, except wood
Trucks & tractors_industrial

Rapid Reproductions Printing
4836 Stratos Way Ste A
Modesto, CA 95356-9557
Contact: Raheel Oraha, Asst. Mgr.
Telephone: 209-527-6370 / 1888-527-2700
Fax: 209-527-4209
Email: printing@thevision.net / URL: http://
www.thevision.net/rapid
Product Service Description:
Quick printing and copying
Lithographic printing_commercial
Photocopying & duplicating services
Business forms

Rausch, Ted L. Co., The
1300 Rollins Road
Burlingame, CA 94010
Contact: Ted L. Rausch, President
Telephone: 650-348-2211
Fax: 650-348-8811
Email: rauschco@ix.netcom.com / URL:
Product Service Description:
Customs Broker
Freight Forwarder

Rayonier
4470 Savannah Highway, P.O. Box 2070
Jesup, GA 31545
Contact: Pulp Marketing Department,
Telephone: 912-427-5580
Fax: 912-427-5587
Email: julian.allum@rayonier.com / URL:
http://www.rayonier.com
Product Service Description:
Chemical Cellulos/Dissolving Pulp
Dissovling, Fluff & Paper Pulp

Reaction Technology Inc
3400 Bassett St
Santa Clara, CA 95054-2703
Contact: James Jacobson, CEO
Telephone: 408-970-9601
Fax: 408-970-9695
Email: sales@reactiontechnology.com / URL:
http://www.reactiontechnology.com
Product Service Description:
Manufactures epitaxial silicon wafers

Reading Bakery Systems
380 Old West Penn Ave
Robesonia, PA 19551-8903
Contact: E. Terry Groff, Pres.
Telephone: 610-693-5816
Fax: 610-693-5512
Email: info@readingbakery.com / URL: http:/
/www.readingbakery.com
Product Service Description:
Food Products Machinery

Reagan Equipment Co., Inc.
PO Box 1850
Gretna, LA 70054
Contact: Tom DeMoss, Sales Manager
Telephone: 504-367-2401
Fax: 504-367-4044
Email: / URL:
Product Service Description:
Prime power natural gas engine driven
generator sets
Standby diesel generator sets
Remanufactured natural gas engines

Realys Inc
7601 Woodwind Dr
Huntington Beach, CA 92647-7142
Contact: Michael A Falley,
Chairman., CEO
Telephone: 714-842-1702
Fax: 714-848-0946
Email: / URL:
Product Service Description:
Contract manufacturer of abrasive specialties;
imprinting for the trade
Abrasive products
Largest private label manufacturer of
Nail files & nail buffers

Recognition Systems Inc
1520 Dell Ave
Campbell, CA 95008-6918
Contact: Bill Wilson,
President
Telephone: 408-364-6960
Fax: 408-370-3679
Email: / URL: http://www.recogsys.com
Product Service Description:
Manufactures and assembles three-
dimensional hand geometry recognition
security systems

Recycled Business Systems LLC
2631 S Roosevelt St
Tempe, AZ 85282-2017
Contact: Lynne Busby, Off. Mgr.
Telephone: 480-921-8325
Fax: 480-921-3951
Email: / URL:
Product Service Description:
Remanufactures Canon and Sharp copiers

Red Bud Industries
200 B&E Industrial Drive
Red Bud, IL 62278-2198
Contact: Kalin Liefer, Pres.
Telephone: 618-282-3801
Fax: 618-282-6718
Email: rbi@redbudindustries.com / URL:
http://www.redbudindustries.com
Product Service Description:
Steel Coil Handling Equipment
Metalworking Machinery

Red River Instruments Co.
RR 3 Box 148
Fouke, AR 71837-9710
Contact: Sam Kelley, Pres.
Telephone: 870-653-6621
Fax: 870-653-2123
Email: sambo870@aol.com / URL:
Product Service Description:
Natural gas measuring instruments & parts

Red Wing Shoe Co.
314 Main St
Red Wing, MN 55066-2300
Contact: Joseph P. Goggin, Pres.
Telephone: 651-388-8211
Fax: 651-388-7415
Email: redwing@pnms.com / URL: http://
www.redwingshoe.com
Product Service Description:
Sport & leisure shoes & work boots
Footwear, except rubber

Reedco Research
88 Middle Street, PO Box 148
Geneva, NY 14456
Contact: Dan Kelsey,
Telephone: 800-357-3459
Fax: 315-781-3271
Email: ccmi@fltg.net / URL:
Product Service Description:
Body Posture & Range of Motion Instruments

Reemay, Inc.
70 Old Hickory Blvd
Old Hickory, TN 37138-3159
Contact: Carol Webster, Int'l. Business Unit
Manager
Telephone: 615-847-7000
Fax: 615-847-7068
Email: cwebster@reemay.com / URL: http://
www.reemay.com
Product Service Description:
Nonwoven polyester & polypropylene

Reference Recordings
PO Box 77225x
San Francisco, CA 94107-0225
Contact: Marcia Martin, Ptnr.
Telephone: 650-355-1892
Fax: 650-355-1949
Email: rrec@aol.com / URL: http://
www.referencerecordings.com
Product Service Description:
Manufactures phonograph records and
prerecorded audio discs

Reflexite Corp.
315 South St
New Britain, CT 06051-3719
Contact: Matt Guyer, Pres.
Telephone: 860-223-9297
Fax: 860-832-9267
Email: / URL: http://www.reflexite.com
Product Service Description:
Vinyl & polyester reflective tape
Plastic products

Refractory Materials International
267 W Valley Ave Ste 222
Birmingham, AL 35209-4817
Contact: James M. Britt, Pres.
Telephone: 205-942-2564
Fax: 205-942-2643
Email: rmiincorp@aol.com / URL:
Product Service Description:
Refractory materials
Ladle Sand
FCE Sand
Chromite
Zircon
Olivine

Refrigeration Resources Co.
360 Crystal Run Rd.
Middletown, NY 10941
Contact: William Bryant,
Telephone: 914-692-8778
Fax: 914-692-9032
Email: sales@mechres.com / URL: http://
www.mechres.com
Product Service Description:
Industrial refrigeration equipment
Refrigeration & heating equipment

Regal Carpets Inc.
PO Box 1157
Chatsworth, GA 30705-1157
Contact: Dorothy Charles, Pres.
Telephone: 706-695-5797
Fax: 706-695-1218
Email: regalcpts@alltel.net / URL: http://
www.regalcarpets.com
Product Service Description:
Carpet, rugs, area rugs & accessories
Carpets & rugs

Regent Labs Inc.
700 W Hillsboro Blvd Ste 2-206
Deerfield Beach, FL 33441-1616
Contact: Gene Re, Pres.
Telephone: 954-426-4403
Fax: 954-426-8535
Email: / URL:
Product Service Description:
Denture Cleansers & Adhesives
Household Cleaners / Silver Tarnish Remover
Flyswatter / Bugwacker
Perfumes & Colognes

Rejuvi Cosmetic Laboratory
PO Box 24454
San Francisco, CA 94124-0454
Contact: David rosprim, Mktg. Coordinator
Telephone: 650-588-7794
Fax: 650-588-7796
Email: rejuvi@mindspring.com / URL: http://
www.dalnet.se/~rejuvi
Product Service Description:
Skin Lotions Creams & Gels
Skin Bleaching Gel
Sunscreen Spf5-spf20
Hair Restorers & Hair Loss Tonics
Professional Treatment for Problem Skin

Relaxor / JB Research Inc
9062 Rosecrans Ave
Bellflower, CA 90706-2038
Contact: Gayle Gerth, Pres.
Telephone: 562-790-2400
Fax: 562-790-8355
Email: relaxor@relaxor.com / URL: http://
www.relaxor.com
Product Service Description:
Manufactures electrical massage equipment -
oem : Consumer products
Massage pads, portable massage

Reliable Communications Inc
PO Box 816
Angels Camp, CA 95222-0816
Contact: Robert W Henkel, Pres.
Telephone: 209-736-0421
Fax: 209-736-0425
Email: bhenkel@rcisystems.com / URL: http:/
/www.relcomm.com
Product Service Description:
Manufactures & sells peripheral control
devices including Code Operated & Fallback
Switches; Current Loop Conversion Devices;
Data Buffers & Port Sharing Devices
Provides SMT, THT Printed Board Assembly
& Electro-Mechanical Assembly Services

Reliable Plastics Seals, Inc.
620 Fox Run Pkwy
Opelika, AL 36801-5967
Contact: John A. King, GM
Telephone: 334-742-0005
Fax: 334-742-0007
Email: rpsinc@mindspring.com / URL: http://
www.reliableplasticsseals.com
Product Service Description:
Heat shrinkable tubing
Plastic products

Reliance Glass Works, Inc.
220 Gateway Rd., P.O. Box 825
Bensenville, IL 60106
Contact: Lyle D. WInkler, *
Telephone: 708-766-1816
Fax: 312-766-0147
Email: service@relianceglass.com / URL:
http://www.relianceglass.com
Product Service Description:
Laboratory Distillation Apparatus
Laboratory Glassware & Equipment

Remco Products Corp.
4735 W. 106TH ST.
Zionsville, IN 46077
Contact: David Garison, President
Telephone: 317-876-9856
Fax: 317-876-9858
Email: remco@iquest.net / URL: http://
www.remcoproducts.com
Product Service Description:
Polypropylene Retort Divider Sheets
Shovels Polypropylene Food Grade
Tubs Polyethylene Food Grade

Remco Technology, Inc.
4437 N Ravenswood Ave
Chicago, IL 60640-5802
Contact: Zorick Dralyuk, Pres.
Telephone: 773-989-8090
Fax: 773-989-8099
Email: zdrick@remco-tech.com / URL: http://
www.remco-tech.com
Product Service Description:
Removable & Reusable Blankets
Fiberglass & fluoropolymer insulation covers
Acoustical Covers

Remet Corp.
210 Commons Rd
Utica, NY 13502-6300
Contact: Charles H. Matzek, VP
Telephone: 315-797-8700
Fax: 315-797-4848
Email: sales@remet.com / URL: http://
www.remet.com
Product Service Description:
Investment casting supplies - expendables &
consumables : Alumina, silica & zirconia
binder chemicals : Waxes

Renfro Franklin Company
525 Brooks St
Ontario, CA 91762-3702
Contact: Thomas G Turner, Pres.
Telephone: 909-984-5500
Fax: 909-984-2322
Email: rfccompany@aol.com / URL:
Product Service Description:
Fabricates wire products, fan guards, motor
mounts, magazine and newspaper display
racks : Wire products_misc. fabricated

Renite Co., Lubrication Engineers
2500 E. 5th Ave.
Columbus, OH 43230
Contact: Stephen M. Halliday, Chairman of
Board, Dr. John T. Golden, V.P. Technical
Telephone: 614-253-5506
Fax: 614-253-1333
Email: contact@renite.com / URL: http://
www.renite.com
Product Service Description:
Glass Mold Lubricants
Automatic Spray Equipment
Water Based Die Release Agents
Lubricating Oils & Greases
General Industrial Machine & Equipment

Renmark Pacific Corporation
327 E Harry Bridges Blvd
Wilmington, CA 90744-6603
Contact: Thomas Reiner, Marketing
Telephone: 818-981-1819
Fax: 818-981-0812
Email: Renmark-pac@worldnet.att.net / URL:
http://www.cargoequipment.com
Product Service Description:
Manufactures air cargo handling, weighing &
storing systems & equipment
Industrial Scales : conveyors & other material
handling equipment

Renmark-Pacific Inc
14110 Valley Vista Blvd
Sherman Oaks, CA 91423
Contact: Thomas Reiner, Marketing
Telephone: 818-981-1819
Fax: 818-981-0812
Email: renmark-pak@worldnet.att.net / URL:
http://www.cargoequipment.com
Product Service Description:
Manufactures industrial weighing, materials
handling systems; air cargo systems
Conveyors & conveying equipment

Repro-Med Systems, Inc.
24 Carpenter Rd
Chester, NY 10918-1057
Contact: A. Sealfon, President
Phone: 914-469-2042 / Fax: 914-469-2042
Email: info@repreo-med.com / URL: http://
www.repro-med.com
Product Service Description:
Surgical appliances & supplies
Airway hand aspirator & portable nonelectric
home care IV devices

Repro-Products & Services
4479 Atlanta Rd Se
Smyrna, GA 30080-6537
Contact: Bob Feldberg, Owner
Telephone: 770-434-3050
Fax: 770-434-0774
Email: / URL:
Product Service Description:
Lithographic printing_commercial
Autodesk reseller and training center
Xerox wide format reseller
HP plotters reseller
Color / Graphics printing
Compaq reseller

Republic Metals Corp.
12900 Nw 38th Ave
Opa Locka, FL 33054-4527
Contact: Richard Rubin, Pres.
Telephone: 305-685-8505
Fax: 305-685-8506
Email: dcomite@republicmetalscorp.com /
URL: http://www.republicmetalscorp.com
Product Service Description:
Metals refining
Nonferrous metals_primary
Analytical & assay. services
Precious metal consulting

Republic Wire, Inc.
5525 Union Centre Dr
West Chester, OH 45069-4820
Contact: Ron Rosenbeck, Pres., Sales Mgr.
Telephone: 513-860-1800
Fax: 513-860-8817
Email: / URL: http://www.republicwire.com
Product Service Description:
Bare & Tinned Copper
Insulated copper -THHN & THW

Republic-Lagun CNC Corp
PO Box 5328
Carson, CA 90710-1607
Contact: Joseph Bezic,
Telephone: 310-518-1100
Fax: 310-830-0923
Email: info@lagun.com / URL: http://
www.lagun.com
Product Service Description:
Machine tools, metal cutting types (vertical
machining centers & CNC-Turning centers)
Milling machines & turning equipment
Oil & gas field machinery

Research Products Co.
P.O. Box 1460
Salina, KS 67402-1460
Contact: Sales & Marketing,
Telephone: 785-825-2181
Fax: 785-825-8908
Email: rpcsal@aol.com / URL: http://
www.viobinusa.com
Product Service Description:
Vitamin / mineral premixes
Defatted wheat germ
Wheat germ oil

Resonance Instruments Inc.
9054 Terminal Ave
Skokie, IL 60077-1512
Contact: Clarence Arnow, Chrm., Pres., CFO
Telephone: 847-583-1000
Fax: 847-583-1021
Email: rii@wwa.com / URL: http://
www.resonanceinstruments.com
Product Service Description:
Microwave instruments

Resource Recovery Systems Inc. KW
511 Pawnee Dr.
Sterling, CO 80751-8661
Contact: Sales & Marketing,
Telephone: 970-522-0663
Fax: 970-522-3387
Email: rrskw@kci.net / URL: http://
www.rrskw.com
Product Service Description:
Composting Equipment
Waste Reduction & Disposal Equipment, Ind.

Resource Technology
513 Haines St
Boise, ID 83712-8014
Contact: Mark Leister, Owner & MIS Mgr.
Telephone: 208-336-5743
Fax: 208-331-8535
Email: resorcetec@aol.com / URL:
Product Service Description:
Buys and sells surplus technological,
industrial and logistic equipment &
machinery; Also
Certified Appraisals

Respond Cargo Services Corp.
15711 W. Hardy Rd., Ste. 3,
Houston, TX 77060
Contact: Bashir Sarakbi, Vice President
Telephone: 281-445-9494
Fax: 281-447-7124
Email: respond@pdq.net / URL: http://
www.respondgroup.com
Product Service Description:
Freight Forwarder : Customs Broker
Freight & Cargo Transportation
Logistics : Distribution

Respond Group of Companies
P.O. Box 60824
Houston, TX 77205-0824
Contact: Ben Bengert, CEO
Telephone: 281-445-1788
Fax: 281-445-6956
Email: respond.group@pdq.net / URL: http://
www.respondgroup.com
Product Service Description:
Glycols : Alcohol : High Density
Polyethylene : Folding Bottle Carts
Cable : Small Casters : Zeolite Molecular
Sieve Materi : Refractory Bonding Mortars
Industrial Equipment / Spare Parts
Logistics / Transporation Services

Restorative Care Of America, Inc.
11236 47th St N
Clearwater, FL 33762-4952
Contact: Nancy Tiller, International Sales
Telephone: 727-573-1595
Fax: 727-573-1886
Email: info@rcai.com / URL: http://
www.rcai.com
Product Service Description:
Orthopedic devices

Retlaw Tools & Plastics Co., Inc.
520 Industrial Dr.
Hartland, WI 53029
Contact: Walter E. Eberhardt, Pres., Fin.,
Pur., Sales & Mktg. Mgr.
Telephone: 414-367-2230
Fax: 414-367-5162
Email: retlaw@execpc.com / URL: http://
www.execpc.com/~retlaw
Product Service Description:
Plastic injection molding, hot stamping, pad
printing, ultrasonic welding & assembly
Plastic products : Dies, tools, jigs &
fixtures_special : Idler Pulleys

Revere Plastic, Inc.
16 Industrial Ave
Little Ferry, NJ 07643-1913
Contact: Edward Smith, Pres.
Telephone: 201-641-0777
Fax: 201-641-1086
Email: / URL: http://www.revereplastics.com
Product Service Description:
Canvas tarpaulins & protective covers
Canvas & related products

Reynard Corp
1020 Calle Sombra
San Clemente, CA 92673-6227
Contact: Forrest Reynard, Pres.
Telephone: 949-366-8866
Fax: 949-498-9528
Email: sales@reynardcorp.com / URL: http://
www.reynardcorp.com
Product Service Description:
Manufactures optical products and
instruments—lenses, specialty coatings,
filters, interferometers
Optical instruments & lenses, prisms

Rheem Air Conditioning Div.
PO Box 17010
Fort Smith, AR 72917-7010
Contact: Michael Bee, Director, Internatioal
Sales
Telephone: 501-646-4311
Fax: 501-648-4133
Email: dvmab@mail.rheemote.com / URL:
http://www.rheemac.com
Product Service Description:
Refrigeration & heating equipment
Heating & air conditioning equipment

Rhino Linings USA Inc
9151 Rehco Rd
San Diego, CA 92121-2270
Contact: Kirk E. Jeffries, Dir. OEM & Natl
Accts., Intl Sales Mgr.
Telephone: 619-450-0441
Fax: 619-450-6881
Email: / URL: http://www.rhinolinings.com
Product Service Description:
Manufactures polyurethane spray sytems &
spray on polyurethane linings & coatings
Plastic products

Rhino Tool Co.
P.O. Box 111
Kewanee, IL 61443-0111
Contact: Robert Martin, President
Telephone: 309-853-5555
Fax: 309-856-5905
Email: / URL:
Product Service Description:
Air Operated Post Drivers
Air Throttle Valves

Ribbon Division Inc
5720 S Valley View Blvd Ste 103
Las Vegas, NV 89118-3108
Contact: Mark Roggero, Pres.
Telephone: 702-597-5366
Fax: 702-597-1098
Email: / URL: http://
www.imagingtechnologies.com
Product Service Description:
Carbon paper & inked ribbons
Remanufactures computer printer ribbons and
toner cartridges

Riceland Foods Inc.
2120 S. Park Ave
Stuttgart, AR 72160
Contact: Becky Goetz, Rice Export Sales
Telephone: 870-673-5500
Fax: 870-673-3366
Email: riceexport@riceland.com / URL:
Product Service Description:
Milled Rice, Long, Med., Parboiled
Brown Rice, Regular & Parboiled

Richard Boas
7211 S.W. 24th St.
Miami, FL 33155-1401
Contact: Richard Arias, Owner
Telephone: 305-262-2722
Fax: 305-262-3362
Email: acebus@bellsouth.net / URL:
Product Service Description:
Mineral Oil
Chloromethyl Naphthalene
Labels
Steel Articles
Electrical Cables
Electric Motors
Cylinders
Automobile Parts
Copiers
Copier Parts & Supplies

Richard Industries, J.
3934 Concord St
Toledo, OH 43612-1460
Contact: Lawrence J. Weber, Pres.
Telephone: 419-476-4911
Fax: 419-476-2546
Email: sales@jrionline.com / URL: http://
www.jrionline.com
Product Service Description:
Steel Tube & Bar Fabrication
Conveyor Rollers
Rotary Swaging
Steel Tube & Bar Cutting

Richard Sewing Machine
2303 N.W. 2nd Ave.
Miami, FL 33127-4350
Contact: Ricky Miranda, President
Telephone: 305-573-6292
Fax: 305-573-6353
Email: / URL:
Product Service Description:
Industrial Sewing Machines
Large inventory on new & used machinery
Sewing Machine Parts
Faney Stitch machines, specialtys

Richard T. Opie & Company, Inc.
10 State St
Newburyport, MA 01950-6604
Contact: Robert J. Murphy, *
Telephone: 978-463-0047
Fax: 978-462-7136
Email: opie&co@greennet.net / URL: http://
www.opie-credit-insurance.com
Product Service Description:
Export Credit Insurance Agents/Brokers

Richard's Machine Tool Co., Inc.
3753 Walden Ave
Lancaster, NY 14086-1405
Contact: Dennis Richards, Pres.
Telephone: 716-683-3380
Fax: 716-683-3408
Email: rmtcinc@aol.com / URL:
Product Service Description:
Machine tools : Machine tool accessories
Industrial Coolant Recycling Systems

Richards Metal Products, Inc.
PO Box 6290
Wolcott, CT 06716-0290
Contact: C. Cobb,
Phone: 203-879-2555 / Fax: 203-879-0007
Product Service Description:
Metal stampings

Richardson Engineering Svcs Inc
PO Box 9103
Mesa, AZ 85214-9103
Contact: John H Heitkamp, Pres.
Telephone: 480-497-2062
Fax: 480-497-5529
Email: sales@resi.net /
URL: http://www.resi.net
Product Service Description:
Publishes technical estimating manuals;
general construction and processing plant
planning and scheduling : Publishing -
miscellaneous : Business services
Management consulting services
Cost estimating software

Richland Mills
3965 E 10th Ct
Hialeah, FL 33013-2923
Contact: Richard B. Wolf, Pres.
Telephone: 305-836-5826
Fax: 305-836-5864
Email: rmills@gate.net / URL:
Product Service Description:
Knit outerwear mills : Knit piece goods

Richmill USA Inc
9124 Norwalk Blvd
Santa Fe Springs, CA 90670-2534
Contact: Ted Daita, GM
Telephone: 562-699-5008
Email: richmill@angelfire.com / URL: http://
www.angelfire.com/biz2/richmill
Product Service Description:
Manufactures precision machine tools
Machine tool accessories

Riley Equipment Co., Inc.
PO Box 435
Vincennes, IN 47591-0435
Contact: Charles G. Riley, Pres., CEO
Telephone: 812-886-5500
Fax: 812-886-5515
Email: edhagemersales@rileyequipment.com
/ URL: http://www.rileyequipment.com
Product Service Description:
Dry Bulk Material Handling Machinery

Rimoldi of America
400 North Lexington Avenue
Pittsburgh, PA 15208-2521
Contact: Louis Melocchi, President
Telephone: 412-247-3763
Fax: 412-247-3086
Email: rimoldius@aol.com / URL: http://
www.rimoldius.com
Product Service Description:
Industrial Sewing Machines & Attachments
Industrial Boot, Shoe & Leather Working
Machinery

Rineer Hydraulics
331 Breesport St
San Antonio, TX 78216-2602
Contact: Ben B. Wallace, Pres., CEO
Phone: 210-341-6333 / Fax: 210-341-1231
Email: salesteck@rineer.com / URL: http://
www.rineer.com
Product Service Description:
Fluid power pumps & motors
Hydraulic motors

Rio Products International Inc
5050 S Yellowstone Hwy
Idaho Falls, ID 83402-5804
Contact: James Vincent, Pres.
Telephone: 208-524-7760
Fax: 208-524-7763
Email: rio@rioproducts.com / URL: http://
www.rioproducts.com
Product Service Description:
Manufactures fly lines , leaders, tippet

Ripley Co., Inc.
46 Nooks Hill Rd
Cromwell, CT 06416-1533
Contact: Ken MacCormac, Pres.
Telephone: 860-635-2200
Fax: 860-635-3631
Email: info@ripley-tools.com / URL: http://
www.ripley-tools.com
Product Service Description:
Wire strippers & cable preparation tools

Ripon Pickle Co., Inc.
1039 Beier Rd. Indl. Pk.
Ripon, WI 54971
Contact: Sally A. Wiese, Plt., Pur., Sales Mgr.
Telephone: 920-748-7110
Fax: 920-748-6013
Email: rpi@vbe.com / URL:
Product Service Description:
Pickles & pickle relishes, peppers,
cauliflower, celery, carrots & sauerkraut

Risdon-AMS (USA) Inc.
1 Risdon St
Naugatuck, CT 06770-4301
Contact: Tom Dunleavy, President
Telephone: 203-723-6100
Fax: 203-723-6101
Email: / URL: http://www.resdon-ams.com
Product Service Description:
Metal cosmetic boxes : Metal stampings

Rittenhouse Co
75 Arkansas St Ste 1
San Francisco, CA 94107-2434
Contact: Simon J Blattner, Co-Chrm.
Telephone: 415-861-5297
Fax: 415-861-4897
Email: info@rithouse.com / URL: http://
www.rithouse.com
Product Service Description:
Converted paper rools for POS & large
format systems, : Bar code & scale label
media, entertainment tickets, &
Imaging supplies

Rivers Bus & RV Sales
10626 General Ave.
Jacksonville, FL 32220
Contact: Larry Schaffer, Owner
Telephone: 904-783-0313
Fax: 904-783-1067
Email: info@riversbus.com / URL: http://
www.riversbus.com
Product Service Description:
Recreational Vehicle Dealers
Public-transport type passenger motor
vehicles - buses

Rjg, Inc
3111 Park Dr
Traverse City, MI 49686-4713
Contact: Brad Watkins, Pres.
Telephone: 616-947-3111
Fax: 616-947-6403
Email: / URL: http://www.rjgtech.com
Product Service Description:
Electronic devices for injection molding

Ro-Tile
1615 S Stockton St
Lodi, CA 95240-6353
Contact: Dan Roulston, GM
Telephone: 209-334-1380
Fax: 209-334-1384
Email: / URL: http://www.rotile.com
Product Service Description:
Manufactures floor tile; concrete
Ceramic wall & floor tile
Concrete products

Roadway Express, Inc.
1077 Gorge Blvd., PO Box 471
Akron, OH 44310
Contact: Elisa Urquhart, Asst. Mgr. Mktg. &
Prod. Dev.
Telephone: 330-384-1717
Fax: 330-643-6771
Email: eurquhart@roadway.com / URL: http:/
/www.roadway.com
Product Service Description:
Freight & Cargo Transportation
Trucking

Roanoke Brokerage Services, Inc.
1501 E. Woodfield Road, Suite 302N
Schaumburg, IL 60173
Contact: Marketing Department,
Telephone: 800-ROANOKE
Fax: 847-969-8200
Email: / URL:
Product Service Description:
Ocean Marine Insurance
Customs Bonds
Carnets / Carnet Bonds
Freight Insurance, International
Surety Bonds

Robbins Corp. E.S.
2802 E. Avalon Ave.
Muscle Shoals, AL 35661
Contact: Edward Robbins III, President
Telephone: 256-383-0124
Fax: 256-381-0876
Email: esr@hiway.net / URL:
Product Service Description:
Plastic mats & floor Runners beverage
containers & infant nursing products
Wire reinforced plastic fencing
Plastic measuring canisters & plastic
adjustable food storage containers
Plastic sheets & strips

Robbins Industries Inc.
4420 Helton Dr
Florence, AL 35630-6236
Contact: Rodney Robbins, Pres.
Telephone: 205-760-8900
Fax: 205-760-8919
Email: / URL:
Product Service Description:
Plastic products
Kitchen gadgets assembly, pad printing parts
& packaging

Roberson Products
519 N Washington Ave
Prescott, AZ 86301-2643
Contact: Gary Roberson, Pres.
Telephone: 520-445-5333
Fax: 520-445-8702
Email: graitran@robersonproducts.com /
URL: http://www.robersonproducts.com
Product Service Description:
Track & base automatic transmission parts
reman.

Robert Pepi Winery
PO Box 328
Oakville, CA 94562-0328
Contact: Christopher Pappe, Marketing
Telephone: 707-944-2807
Fax: 707-944-5628
Product Service Description:
Wines

Robert Raikes Enterprizes
PO Box 8428
Catalina, AZ 85738-0428
Contact: Robert Raikes, Owner
Telephone: 520-825-5788
Fax: 520-825-5789
Email: raikes4u@azstarnet.com / URL: http://
www.raikes.com
Product Service Description:
Manufactures hand-carved woodfaced and
wooden collectibles

Robert's Honing & Gundrilling Inc.
13546 Pumice St
Norwalk, CA 90650-5249
Contact: Robert Pirillo, Pres.
Telephone: 800-263-7862
Fax: 562-921-1084
Email: rpiri47330@aol.com / URL:
Product Service Description:
Honing from .060 to 18 inches ID, up to 12
feet long; vertical and horizontal hones; long
and short production
Industrial machinery
Gundrilling from 3/16 to 2" ID X 72" long

Roberts Co., The John
9687 E River Rd
Minneapolis, MN 55433-5514
Contact: Michael Keene, Pres.
Telephone: 612-755-5500
Fax: 612-754-4400
Email: / URL: http://www.johnroberts.com
Product Service Description:
Printing_commercial
Commercial printing

Roberts Industries
3158 Des Plaines Ave
Des Plaines, IL 60018
Contact: Thomas I. Rodhouse, CEO &
Chairman
Telephone: 847-699-0080
Fax: 847-699-0082
Product Service Description:
Tubes, pipes & hollow profiles, iron & steel

Roberts Irrigation Products
700 Rancheros Dr
San Marcos, CA 92069-3007
Contact: John Roberts, Pres.
Telephone: 760-744-4511
Fax: 760-744-0914
Email: cust-serv@robertsirrigation.com /
URL: http://www.robertsirrigation.com
Product Service Description:
Manufacturer of premium quality micro &
drip irrigation products for over thirty years.
Patented RO-DRIP ® & RO-DRIP XL ®
drip tape deliver water & nutrients directly to
a plant's root zone via a precision-molded
channel. A vortex action within the channel
creates turbulence, keeping particulate
moving through the tape. RO-DRIP® is used
for row crops, greenhouses / nurseries and
field flowers. SPOT-SPITTER ® , the
original mini-sprayer, offers a variety of
wetting patterns and flow rates making it a
cost-effective versatile solution for mini-spray
nursery & greenhouse applications.

Robett Mfg. Co.
PO Box 3286
Riceville, TN 37370-3286
Contact: Cindy Lovingood, Pres.
Telephone: 423-462-2443
Fax: 423-462-2831
Email: c.louingood@worldnet.att.net / URL:
http://home.att.net/c.lovingood
Product Service Description:
Trousers & slacks_men's & boys' : Men's &
boys' pants & jackets : Clothing_men's &
boys' : Child Saftey Device

Robinair, A Div. of SPX Corporation
Robinair Way
Montpelier, OH 43543
Contact: George Gardner,
Telephone: 419-485-5561
Fax: 419-485-5468
Product Service Description:
Manifold Sets : Vacuum Pumps
Refrigerant Leak Detection Instruments
Refrigerant Charging Equipment
Refrigerant Recovery & Recycling Equipment
Engine Coolant Recycling Equipment
Air Conditioning Flushing Equipment
Fittings & Valves : Refrigerant Identification

Robinson H.W. & Company Inc.
P.O. Box 300962 JFK Int'l Airport
Jamaica, NY 11430
Contact: James Maloney, President
Telephone: 718-656-5685
Fax: 718-917-6382
Email: jim@hwrobinson.com / URL:
Product Service Description:
Customs Broker : Freight Forwarding
Freight & Cargo: Transportation & Insurance

Robison-Anton Textile Company (Mfr)
P.O. Box 159
Fairview, NJ 07022
Contact: Bruce Anton, President
Telephone: 201-941-0500
Fax: 201-941-8994
Email: rathread@halper.com / URL: http://
www.miamigate.com\ergo\ra
Product Service Description:
Thread : Embroidery Yarn , Thread
Metallic Thread : Rayon Thread
Polyester Thread : Schiffli Yarn

Robohand, Inc.
482 Pepper St
Monroe, CT 06468-2653
Contact: Daneil Peretz, National Saels
Manager
Telephone: 203-261-5558
Fax: 203-452-7418
Email: Peretd@robohand / URL: http://
www.robohand.com
Product Service Description:
Automation equipment components

Robus Leather
1100 W. Hutchinson Ln.
Madison, IN 47250-7891
Contact: Garry Barber, President
Telephone: 812-273-4183
Fax: 812-273-6671
Email: robusleath@aol.com / URL: http://
www.robus.com
Product Service Description:
Leather Goods, NEC : Bonded leather in
sheets & rolls for use in shoe Components,
personal leather goods, belts, luggage,
Handbags, automotive interiors, sports balls,
and Much more.

Roc Carbon Co.
1605 Brittmoore Rd.
Houston, TX 77043-3107
Contact: Pamela R. Carlson, President
Phone: 713-468-7743 / Fax: 713-465-2158
Email: sales@roccarbon.com / URL: http://
www.roccarbon.com
Product Service Description:
Rotating equipment carbon /PTFE
replacement parts
Carbon / Graphite raw materials

Rocamar Services, Inc.
12764 NW 9th Terrace
Miami, FL 33182-1841
Contact: Bernardo Cardenal, President
Phone: 305-221-7121 / Fax: 305-221-6385
Product Service Description:
Engineering Consulting, Mechanical &
Electrical

Rochester Corp., The
751 Old Brandy Rd
Culpeper, VA 22701-2866
Contact: Gary C. Hyde, Pres.
Telephone: 540-825-2111
Fax: 540-825-2238
Email: info@rochester-cables.com / URL:
http://www.rochester-cables.com
Product Service Description:
Electrical & Fiber Optic Cable
Wire products_misc. fabricated
Current-carrying wiring devices
Electronic components

Rochester Shoe Tree Company
One Cedar Lane
Ashland, NH 03217
Contact: Jim Fox, President
Telephone: 603/968-3301
Fax: 603/968-3197
Product Service Description:
Shoe Trees / Shoe Care

Rock-Tenn Company
504 Thrasher Street
Norcross, GA 30071
Contact: Ron Hood,
Telephone: 770-448-2193
Fax: 678-291-7382
Email: ppd@rocktenn.com / URL: http://
www.rocktenn.com
Product Service Description:
Paperboard products including furniture board
& cover board products

Rockbestos Surprenant Cable Corp.
172 Sterling St.
Clinton, MA 01510
Contact: Bal Kher, VP Int'l Sales & Mktg.
Telephone: 978-365-1277
Fax: 978-365-4054
Email: balkher@compuserve.com / URL:
Product Service Description:
High Temp Wire & Cable Nonferrouse
Power & Control Cable Nonferrous - For Oil
Rig, Production Platforms : Locomotive &
Transit Cars, Utilities & Other
Industrial Applications

Rockford Systems Inc.(Mfr)
4620 Hydraulic Rd.
Rockford, IL 61109-2695
Contact: Larry Johnson, Director/Sales
Phone: 815/874-7891 / Fax: 815-874-6144
Email: sales@rockfordsystems.com / URL:
http://www.rockfordsystems.com
Product Service Description:
Industrial Machinery Controls & Safeguards

Rockwell Automation
1201 S 2nd St
Milwaukee, WI 53204-2410
Contact: Keith Nosbusch, President Control
Systems COO
Telephone: 414-382-2000
Fax: 414-382-4444
Email: / URL: http://
www.automation.rockwell.com
Product Service Description:
Relays & industrial controls
Industrial automation controls

Rockwell International Corp., Collins Commercial Avionics
1500 State St
Bellevue, IA 52031-9177
Contact: Dave Latting, Plt. Mgr.
Telephone: 319-872-4096
Fax: 319-295-9717
Email: / URL: http://www.rockwell.com
Product Service Description:
Aircraft parts & equipment
Avionics equipment assembly

Rockwood Retaining Walls, Inc.
7200 N. Hwy. 63
Rochester, MN 55906
Contact: Ray Price, President
Telephone: 800-535-2375
Fax: 507-288-3810
Email: rockwood@infonet.is1.net / URL:
http://www.retainingwall.com
Product Service Description:
Manufacturer of concrete retaining wall
products
Franchising of Rockwood Retaining Wall
products
in the United States & Worldwide.

Rocky Mount Cord Co.
381 N. Grace St. / PO Box 4304
Rocky Mount, NC 27803-0304
Contact: Andrew K. Barker, Executive V.p.
Telephone: 800-342-9130
Fax: 252-977-9123
Email: rmcord@earthlink.net / URL: http://
www.rmcord.com
Product Service Description:
Braided Cordage & Twisted Rope

Rocky Mountain Propellers Inc
Tri-county Airport
Erie, CO 80516
Contact: Dave Hampel, Mgr.
Telephone: 303-665-7905
Fax: 303-665-7164
Email: rockyprop@rockyprop.com / URL:
http://www.rockyprop.com
Product Service Description:
Repair / Overhaul Propellers; Hartzell,
mcCauley, Sensenich, Dowty
Repair / Overhaul, Govenors; Hartzell,
McCauley, Woodward
Piston Engine & PT6 Engine Instalations

Rodak Plastics Co., Inc.
31721 Knapp St
Hayward, CA 94544-7827
Contact: Charles Romero, Pres.
Telephone: 510-471-0898
Fax: 510-471-4592
Email: / URL:
Product Service Description:
Plastic injection molding and mold making
Plastic products
Dies, tools, jigs & fixtures_special

Rodix, Inc.
4904 Colt Rd
Rockford, IL 61109-2644
Contact: Jeff Johnson, VP
Telephone: 815-874-6200
Fax: 815-874-6604
Email: custserve@rodix.com / URL: http://
www.rodix.com
Product Service Description:
Industrial Automation Vibration Control
Products

Rofren Disc Brake, Inc.
241 Ledyard St
Hartford, CT 06114-2029
Contact: Nino Cirinno, Pres.
Telephone: 860-296-1524
Fax: 860-296-6272
Email: / URL:
Product Service Description:
Disc brake pads

Rogers & Brown Custom Brokers, Inc.
PO Box 20160
Charleston, SC 29413-0160
Contact: Dan Carroll, Contact
Telephone: 843-577-3630
Fax: 843-722-1839
Email: dan_carroll@rogers-brown.com /
URL: http://www.rogers-brown.com
Product Service Description:
Customs Broker
Freight Forwarder
Freight & Cargo Transportation

Rogers Corporation
One Technology Drive
Rogers, CT 06263-9999
Contact: Debra Granger, Intl. Mktg. Spec.
Telephone: 860-774-9605
Fax: 860-779-5509
Email: ie@rogers-corp.com / URL:
Product Service Description:
Printed Circuit Boards
Plastic Materials
Elec. Comp., Microwave Circuits
Plastic Foam Products
Mechanical Rubber Goods

Roll Master Corporation
PO Box 890
Pomona, CA 91769-0890
Contact: Sandy Tucker, Pres., GM
Telephone: 909-620-8840
Fax: 909-620-7753
Email: rollmaster@earthlink.net / URL: http://
www.roll-master.com
Product Service Description:
Industrial & Institutional casters & wheels

Roll-a-Way Inc.
10601 Oak St Ne
Saint Petersburg, FL 33716-3301
Contact: Moshe Gershuny,
Dir, Commercial Div.
Telephone: 727-576-1143
Fax: 727-579-9410
Email: comm@roll.a.way.comm / URL: http:/
/www.roll-a-way.comm
Product Service Description:
Exterior rolling & Folding Storm & Security
Shutters

Rolled Steel Products Corp
2187 Garfield Ave
Los Angeles, CA 90040-1805
Contact: Steve Alperson, Vice President
Phone: 323-723-8836 / Fax: 323-888-9866
Email: salperson@rolledsteel.com / URL:
http://www.rolledsteel.com
Product Service Description:
Cold rolled, hot rolled, galvanized & stainless
steel : Flat rolled steel, sheet and strip; steel
slitting, leveling, shearing, edging
Metal service centers

Rolling Hills Progress Center Inc.
PO Box 85
Lanark, IL 61046-0085
Contact: Peter Hermes, Ex. Dir.
Phone: 815-493-2321 / Fax: 815-493-2350
Email: rhpc@internetni.com / URL:
Product Service Description:
Industrial assembly & packaging
Imprinted Promotional Products

Rolls-Royce & Bertley Motors Cars Inc.
3800 Hamlin Road
Auburn Hills, MI 48326
Contact: Alasdair Stewart, President & CEO
Telephone: 248-340-6450
Fax: 248-340-6455
Email: alasdair.stewart@rrmci.com / URL:
Product Service Description:
Passenger motor vehicles

Root Co., Inc., A. I., The
PO Box 706
Medina, OH 44258-0706
Contact: John Root, Chrm., Pres.
Telephone: 330-725-6677
Fax: 330-725-5624
Email: / URL: http://www.airoot.com
Product Service Description:
Periodicals : Candles : Manufacturing
industries

Roots Division, Dresser Equipment Group Inc., A Halliburton Company
900 W Mount St
Connersville, IN 47331-1694
Contact: R. P. Morrison, Pres.
Telephone: 765-827-9200
Fax: 765-825-7669
Email: roots@thepoint.net / URL: http://
www.rootsblower.com/
Product Service Description:
Rotary blowers, vacuum pumps & centrifugal
compressors : Blowers & fans

Rosary House, Inc.
PO Box 9668
New Iberia, LA 70562-9668
Contact: Susan Minvielle, Controller
Telephone: 318-364-5401
Fax: 318-364-1503
Email: / URL: http://www.rosaryhouse.com
Product Service Description:
Handmade Sterling Silver rosaries - Our
Speciality : Saints Medals, Religiuos Art &
Jewelry, Holy Cards : Curcifixes, Church
Items, Bibles & Gifts

Roselle Paper Co., Inc.
615 E 1st Ave
Roselle, NJ 07203-1562
Contact: Sam Lefkovits, Pres.
Phone: 908-245-6758 / Fax: 908-245-9434
Email: rosellepap@aol.com / URL:
Product Service Description:
Converted paper products

Roselon Industries, Inc.
18 S. 5th St.
Quakertown, PA 18951-1661
Contact: Robert R. Adams, President
Telephone: 215-536-3275
Fax: 215-536-7284
Email: / URL:
Product Service Description:
Specialty Textured Yarns: Nylon, Poly, Olefin
Knit de Knit, Stuffer Box Crimped, Cilki II
In Stock Dyed Stretch Nylon, Merino Wool

Rosen Product Development Inc
PO Box 21636
Eugene, OR 97402-0410
Contact: Terry Melvin, Pres.
Telephone: 541-342-3802
Fax: 541-485-8791
Email: info@rosenproducts.com / URL: http:/
/www.rosenproducts.com
Product Service Description:
Automotive video entertainment systems
Aircraft parts & equipment
Aircraft sunvisor systems
Video entertainment systems
Flat panel displays
Sunviser Systems
Video electronics
Liquid crystal displays

Roses Southwest Papers
1701 2nd St Sw
Albuquerque, NM 87102-4505
Contact: Roberto E. Espat, Owner
Telephone: 505-842-0134
Fax: 505-242-0342
Email: rswpree@aol.com / URL:
Product Service Description:
Paper bags & tissue, napkins & towels
Bags: uncoated paper & multiwall
Sanitary paper products
Papaya (Fruta Maya)
Oranges: Grapefruit

Ross Engineering Corp
540 Westchester Dr
Campbell, CA 95008-5012
Contact: Hugh C Ross, Pres.
Telephone: 408-377-4621
Fax: 408-377-5182
Email: / URL:
Product Service Description:
Manufactures HV relays, vacuum contactors,
circuit breakers, fiber optics, voltmeters and
HV devices
Switchgear & switchboard apparatus
Electrical industrial apparatus
Electronic components
Electricity measuring instruments

Ross Engineering Corp.
540 Westchester Dr.
Campbell, CA 95008
Contact: Hugh C. Ross, President
Telephone: 408-377-4621
Fax: 408-377-5182
Email: rosseng@earthlink.net / URL: http://
www.rossengineering.com
Product Service Description:
High Voltage Relays
High Voltage Digital Voltmeters
High Voltage Devices
High Voltage Vacuum Contactors
High Voltage Circuit Breakers
High Voltage Wideband Dividers
Fiber Optic Analog Transmission Systems
Power Quality Monitors, HV.

Ross Systems Inc.
Tow Concourse Parkway
Atlanta, GA 30328
Contact: Sales & Marketing,
Telephone: 877-767-7462
Fax: 770-351-0036
Email: / URL: http://www.rossinc.com
Product Service Description:
Prepackaged Software

Rosy Services Forwarders Corp.
7025 NW 52nd St.,
Miami, FL 33166
Contact: Dan Nicholas, Traffic Manager
Telephone: 305-591-4443 (24 Hr)
Fax: 305-591-4163
Email: dnicholas@rfsintl.com / URL:
Product Service Description:
Customs Broker
Freight Forwarder
Freight & Cargo Transportation

Rotary Systems Inc.
1036 Mckinley St
Anoka, MN 55303-1093
Contact: Jeff Meister, Chrm.
Telephone: 612-323-1514
Fax: 612-323-1622
Email: info@rotarysystems.com / URL: http://
www.rotarysystems.com
Product Service Description:
Rotary joints, swivels & couplings

Rothco
25 Ranick Rd, Dept. NR
Smithtown, NY 11788-4208
Contact: John Ottaviano, Sales & Mktg.
Telephone: 516-234-8000
Fax: 516-234-8772
Email: bdus@rothco.com / URL: http://
www.rothco.com
Product Service Description:
Military & Outdoor Clothing & Accessories
Law Enforcement, Survival, Hunting &
Camping Gear

Rotor Tech Inc.
10696 Haddington Dr., Suite 110
Houston, TX 77043-3247
Contact: Richard Garrett, *
Telephone: 713-984-8900
Fax: 713-984-9425
Product Service Description:
Glycol Pumps, Natural Gas Dehydration

Round Hill Winery
1680 Silverado Trl S
Saint Helena, CA 94574-9798
Contact: Virginia VanAsperen, Pres.
Telephone: 707-963-5251
Fax: 707-963-0834
Email: / URL: http://
www.roundhillvineyards.com
Product Service Description:
Wines, brandy, & brandy spirits
Winery

Rover Vinyl Tech Industries
20 Kiji Dava
Prescott, AZ 86301-5613
Contact: Harold Maffet, Ptnr.
Telephone: 520-445-6565
Fax: 520-776-7001
Email: / URL:
Product Service Description:
Manufactures polyvinyl animal cages and
hammocks
Pet products

Rowat Cut Stone & Marble Co.
110 Se 7th St
Des Moines, IA 50309-4906
Contact: Teresa Van Vleet, Pres.
Telephone: 515-244-8604
Fax: 515-244-1634
Email: / URL:
Product Service Description:
Cut stone & stone products
Marble
Granite
Limestone
Landscape Stone
Veneer Stone

Rowtex
3191 Commonwealth
Dallas, TX 75247
Contact: Ray Shewitz, Director of Sales
Telephone: 214-688-0338
Fax: 214-688-4181
Email: rshewitz@rowclothing.com / URL:
Product Service Description:
Wiping Rags: George Cotter
Used Clothing : Contact: Roy Shewitz

Roy E Hanson Jr Manufacturing
1924 Compton Ave
Los Angeles, CA 90011-1325
Contact: Roy E Hanson Jr, Pres.
Telephone: 213-747-7514
Fax: 213-747-7724
Email: / URL: http://www.hansontank.com
Product Service Description:
Manufactures pressure vessels— water
storage tanks, air receivers, propane tanks

Royal Dental Manufacturing Co.
12414 Highway 99, Bay 29
Everett, WA 98204
Contact: Harold Tai, President
Telephone: 425-743-0988
Fax: 425-743-3588
Email: htai@royaldental.com / URL: http://
www.royaldental.com
Product Service Description:
Dental Delivery Units
Dental Chairs
Dental Stools
Dental Lights
Dental cabinets

Royal Enterprises, Inc. (Mfr), Urnex Div.
170 Ludlow Street
Yonkers, NY 10705
Contact: Jason Dick, Export Mgr.
Telephone: 914/963-2042
Fax: 914-963-2145
Email: royalent@juno.com / URL: http://
www.urnex.com
Product Service Description:
Cotton Gauze Lemon Covers, Foodservice
Cleaning Compounds, For Coffee & Tea
Equipment

Royal Oak Industries, Inc.
4800 S Lapeer Rd
Lake Orion, MI 48359-1877
Contact: Patrick Carroll, CEO
Telephone: 248-340-9200
Fax: 248-340-9200
Email: / URL:
Product Service Description:
Engine & Drivetrain Manufacturing
Fuel System Manufacturing

Royal Sales Corp.
Bath Beach Station
Brooklyn, NY 11214
Contact: Bernard Weisman, Pres.
Telephone: 718-946-5947
Fax: 718-996-9726
Email: royal@royalsales.com / URL: http://
www.royalsales.com
Product Service Description:
Wooden Folding Chairs

Rubber City Machinery Corp.
PO Box 2043
Akron, OH 44309-2043
Contact: Robert J. Westfall, Ex. V-P., Sales &
Mktg.
Telephone: 330-434-3500
Fax: 330-434-2244
Email: info@rcmc.com / URL: http://
www.rcmc.com
Product Service Description:
Machinery_special industry
Rebuilt rubber processing machinery

Rubber Engineering
P.O. Box 26188
Salt Lake City, UT 84126-0188
Contact: Ron Wright, Director of Marketing
Telephone: 801-530-7887
Fax: 801-261-5587
Email: wright@envirotechslc.com / URL:
http://www.rubeng.com
Product Service Description:
Fabricated rubber products
Rubber lined pipe
Rubber liners for ball & sag mill grinding
equipment

Rubber Queen
299 Cramer Creek Ct.
Dublin, OH 43017-2586
Contact: Lisa Wiater, Marketing Manager
Telephone: 614-761-1646
Fax: 614-761-0951
Email: info@rubberqueen.com / URL: http://
www.rubberqueen.com
Product Service Description:
Motor Vehicle Parts & Accessories

Rucker Lumber Co., Inc.
1700 22nd Ave N
Birmingham, AL 35204-1797
Contact: Robert N. Newland, General
Manager
Telephone: 205-323-1671
Fax: 205-323-1675
Email: ruckerlbrl@aol.com / URL: http://
www.ruckerlumber.com
Product Service Description:
Pipe Palletizing, Skids & Timbers
Industrial Chocks, Blocks & Wedges
Wooden House & Garden Planters

Rudolph Instruments, Inc.
40 Pier Lane
Fairfield, NJ 07004
Contact: Kumar Utukuri, Sales Manager
Telephone: 973-227-0139
Fax: 973-227-4576
Email: rudinst@aol.com / URL: http://
www.rudolphinst.com
Product Service Description:
Polarimeters, Laboratory Instruments
Saccharimeters, Laboratory Instruments
Polariscopes
Saccharimeters, NIR
Ellipsometers
Light Sources

Ruen Drilling International
P.O. Box 267
Clark Fork, ID 83811-0267
Contact: Arlan Ruen, President
Telephone: 208-266-1151
Fax: 208-266-1379
Email: driller@nidlink.com / URL: http://
www.ruendrilling.com
Product Service Description:
Water Well Drilling
Geotechnical drilling services
Drilling consulting

Rugby Manufacturing Co.
Industrial Park, P.O. Box 229
Rugby, ND 58368
Contact: Gerhard P. Socha, President
Telephone: 701-776-5722
Fax: 701-776-6235
Email: / URL:
Product Service Description:
Truck Bodies : Dump Truck Bodies
Truck Hoists : Truck Platforms

Russ Chemical Co., Inc.
PO Box 2688
Odessa, TX 79760-2688
Contact: G. G. Russell, Pres.
Telephone: 915-366-5911
Fax: 915-367-7159
Email: russchemco@aol.com / URL:
Product Service Description:
Aluminum sulfate & Alum polymer blends
Chemicals_industrial inorganic

Russ Optical, Inc.
320 W Avalon Ave
Muscle Shoals, AL 35661-2806
Contact: Tim Russ, Pres.
Telephone: 205-314-1125
Fax: 205-381-2323
Product Service Description:
Eyeglasses : Ophthalmic goods

Russ Paladino
16 Musconetcong Avenue
Hopatcong, NJ 07843-1610
Contact: Russ Paladino, President
Telephone: 201-398-1568
Fax: 201-398-1945
Email: russpal@aol.com / URL:
Product Service Description:
Translation Svcs.English into Italian & Italian
into English

Russell-Stanley Corp.
685 Route 202/206
Bridgewater, NJ 08807
Contact: Ronald A. Aloisio,
Telephone: 908-203-9500
Fax: 908-203-1944
Email: info@russell-stanley.com / URL: http:/
/www.russell-stanley.com
Product Service Description:
Manufactures Plastic Containers
Plastic Products

Rutledge Books, Inc.
PO Box 315
Bethel, CT 06801-0315
Contact: Arthur Salzfass, Pres.
Telephone: 203-778-5925
Fax: 203-798-7272
Email: info@rutledgebooks.com / URL: http:/
/www.rutledgebooks.com
Product Service Description:
Subsidy Book Publisher : Book Packager
Book Publisher

RxCount Corp
13717 Alma Ave
Gardena, CA 90249-2513
Contact: Patricia Ubank,
Telephone: 310-538-2363
Fax: 310-538-0637
Product Service Description:
Manufactures electronic tablet counters for
pharmacies

Ryan Trading
560 White Plains Rd.
Tarrytown, NY 10591
Contact: John Ryan, Owner
Telephone: 914-631-8023
Fax: 914-631-8339
Email: jgrrtc@aol.com / URL:
Product Service Description:
Apple juice, unfermented and not containing
added spirit, whether or not sweetened
Juice of any other single fruit or vegetable,
unfermented and not containing added spirit

Rychter Trading Corporation
107 Gilette Circle
Springfield, MA 01118-1225
Contact: Victor Rychter, President
Telephone: 413-782-8312
Fax: 413-782-8606
Email: / URL:
Product Service Description:
Air Cond & Heating Equip., Export

Ryder-Heil Bronze Inc.
126 E Irving St
Bucyrus, OH 44820-1409
Contact: Mary Worden, V-P., Fin. & MIS
Telephone: 419-562-2841
Fax: 419-562-8006
URL: http://ry.ryderheil.thomasregister.com
Product Service Description:
Bronze bearings

Ryobi Outdoor Products Inc
550 N 54th St
Chandler, AZ 85226-2434
Contact: Singh Suchdev, Ex. V-P., COO
Telephone: 602-961-1002
Fax: 602-961-1401
Email: / URL:
Product Service Description:
Manufactures hand-held lawn and garden
equipment— weed trimmers, leaf blowers,
vacuums

S & S Dynamic Mfg. Llc
137 Mattatuck Heights Rd
Waterbury, CT 06705-3832
Contact: Peter J. Sandore, Owner, David
Elliott, Sales
Telephone: 203-759-3744
Fax: 203-759-3748
Email: info@ssdynamic.com / URL: http://
www.ssdynamic.com
Product Service Description:
Metal stampings
Tool design & production

S & S Industries, Inc.
385 Gerard Ave
Bronx, NY 10451-5441
Contact: J. Horta, Pres., CEO
Telephone: 718-585-1333
Fax: 718-292-2132
Email: ssisales@ssi-wireforms.com / URL:
http://www.ssi-wireforms.com
Product Service Description:
Brassiere underwire
Wire products_misc. fabricated

S & S Precision Machine Corp.
4 Britton Dr
Bloomfield, CT 06002-3617
Contact: Laura Smith, Pres., CFO
Telephone: 860-286-9382
Fax: 860-286-9532
Email: s-spre@erols.com / URL:
Product Service Description:
Helicopter parts
Aircraft parts

S C I Systems, Inc.
PO Box 1000
Huntsville, AL 35807
Contact: A. E. Sapp Jr., Pres.
Telephone: 256-882-4800
Fax: 256-882-4466
Email: bill.quinn@scismail.sci.com / URL:
http://www.sci.com
Product Service Description:
Electronic Manufacturing Services

S C I-Agra, Inc.
5704 Industrial Rd
Fort Wayne, IN 46825-5128
Contact: G. Irving Latz, Pres., CFO
Telephone: 219-484-1267
Fax: 219-482-3072
Email: info@sciagra.com / URL: http://
www.sciagra.com
Product Service Description:
Electronic sensors

S D Modular Displays, Inc.
1140 W Sunrise Blvd
Fort Lauderdale, FL 33311-7133
Contact: Lou Burruezo, V-P.,
GM, Sales & Mktg.
Telephone: 954-462-1919
Fax: 954-462-1938
Product Service Description:
Trade show displays
Partitions & fixtures_wood

S E R F I L C O, Ltd.
1777 Shermer Rd
Northbrook, IL 60062-5316
Contact: Richard W. Crain, GM
Telephone: 847-559-1777
Fax: 847-559-1995
Email: sales@serfilco.com / URL: http://
www.serfilco.com
Product Service Description:
Pumps & filters : Pumps & pumping
equipment : Machinery_general industrial

S O N Corp.
PO Box 684
Wichita, KS 67201-0684
Contact: Robert E. Penquite, CEO
Telephone: 316-831-9494
Fax: 316-831-9595
Email: builder@soncorp.com / URL:
Product Service Description:
Matric Buildings
Temporary Bank & Office Buildings
Construction Trailers

S O R, Inc.
14685 W 105th St
Lenexa, KS 66215-2003
Contact: Daniel A. Dever,
Telephone: 913-888-2630
Fax: 913-888-0767
Email: sorinc-webmaster@worldnet.att.net /
URL: http://www.sorinc.com
Product Service Description:
Level Controls : Pressure & Temperature
Controls : Flow Switches

S P S Technologies, Inc., Automotive Fasteners Group
4444 Lee Rd
Cleveland, OH 44128-2902
Contact: Ronald Nordstorm, GM
Telephone: 216-581-3000
Fax: 216-581-7642
Email: bwalczak@spstech.com / URL: http://www.spstech.com
Product Service Description:
Bolts, nuts, rivets & washers
Bolts & nuts

S T C Machine Shop
PO Box 1706
Fort Dodge, IA 50501-1706
Contact: Deb Gregerson, Owner
Telephone: 515-955-2725
Fax: 515-573-5331
Product Service Description:
Automotive parts & general machining job shop : Industrial machinery
Motor vehicle parts & accessories

S T I International, Inc.
114 Halmar Cv
Georgetown, TX 78628-2331
Contact: David L. Skinner, Pres.
Telephone: 512-819-0656
Fax: 512-819-0465
Email: sales@sti-guns.com / URL: http://www.sti-guns.com
Product Service Description:
Small arms : Guns

S-Line
11414 Mathis Ave
Dallas, TX 75234-9407
Contact: Jerry Squyres, Pres.
Telephone: 972-402-9000
Fax: 972-402-9020
Email: sales@s-line.com / URL: http://www.s-line.com
Product Service Description:
Nylon cargo control straps
Broadwoven fabric mills, manmade
Cordage & twine

S.G. International
18056 Mallard Bend
Seneca, SC 29672
Contact: Sales & Marketing,
Telephone: 864-882-3204
Fax: (864)882-3129
Email: goodwin-sgi@worldnet.att.net / URL:
Product Service Description:
Lumber Exporters
Aroatic Red Cedar - Logs & Lumber
Cypress Lumber
Hickory Lumber & Dimension
Southern Yellow Pine Lumber
White Ash Lumber
Oak (Red & White) Lumber & Logs
Walnut Lumber & Logs

S.I. Tech, Inc.(Mfr)
901 N. Batavia Avenue
Batavia, IL 60510
Contact: Wendy Wersching, Marketing Executive
Telephone: 630-232-8640
Fax: 630-232-8677
Email: sales@sitech-bitdriver.com / URL: http://www.sitech-bitdriver.com
Product Service Description:
Telecommunication Modems & Multiplexers
Communication Equip., Fiber Optic Cable Systems : Fiber Optic Cable, Devices
Computer Peripherals - Modems, Multiplixers

S.K. Plastics
1040 Metropolitan Ave.
Brooklyn, NY 11211-2711
Contact: Henry Schwalbe, President, Josef Schwalbe, Exec. Vice Pres.
Telephone: 718-782-6095
Fax: 718-387-5494
Email: / URL:
Product Service Description:
Plastics Products, NEC
Articles of plastics
Swimming pool liners
Swimming pool covers
Swimming pool accessories

S.K. Ross & Assoc., P.C.
5777 West Century Blvd., Suite 520
Los Angeles, CA 90045
Contact: Susan Kohn Ross, Attorney
Telephone: 310/410-4414
Fax: 310-410-1017
Email: skross@skralaw.com / URL: http://www.skralaw.com
Product Service Description:
Legal Services, Legislative Consulting
Government Legal Counsel

SANYO Energy (USA) Corp
2055 Sanyo Ave
San Diego, CA 92173-2229
Contact: Sales & Marketing Department,
Telephone: 619-661-4888
Fax: 619-661-6743
Email: / URL: http://www.sanyobatteries.net
Product Service Description:
Manufactures batteries

SARA's Sausage
PO Box 645
Palmer Lake, CO 80133-0645
Contact: Pierre Letellier, Pres.
Telephone: 719-488-0530
Fax:
Email: / URL:
Product Service Description:
Manufactures sausages and prepared meat products; processes meat
Sausages & other prepared meat products

SDC Technologies Inc
1911 E Wright Cir
Anaheim, CA 92806-6028
Contact: Miriam McGorrin, Director of Marketing
Telephone: 714-939-8300
Fax: 714-939-8330
Email: / URL: http://www.sdccoatings.com
Product Service Description:
Abrasion resistant coatings for transparent materials.

SEC Industrial Battery Co., Inc.
768 N Bethlehem Pike, Ste. 105
Lower Gwynedd, PA 19002-2658
Contact: Alden Thorndike, General Manager
Telephone: 215-654-9334
Fax: 215-654-9871
Email: 105533,2403@compuserve.com / URL: http://www.battery-vrla.com
Product Service Description:
Industrial Storage Batteries
Batteries - VRLA
Gel/AGM Batteries
UPS/Telecom Batteries
Lead Acid 12V 3AH-4000AH
Ni-Cad Batteries
Rack Mounted Batteries

SFI Anco Fine Cheese
149 New Dutch Ln.
Fairfield, NJ 07004-2597
Contact: Alvaro ipparraguirre, Mktg. Director
Phone: 973-575-9120 / Fax: 973575-1165
Product Service Description:
Specialty Cheeses - Refrigerated

SKW Biosystems
620 Progress Ave
Waukesha, WI 53187
Contact: Jack O'Niell, Tech. Mktg. Dev. Mgr.
Phone: 414-547-5531 / Fax: 414-549-2577
Email: jack.O'Neill@skwbio.com / URL:
Product Service Description:
Gelatin : Pharmaceutical, edible, photographic : Hydrolyzed gelatin

SME, a division of FAES USA, Inc.
207 Beasley Dr
Franklin, TN 37064-3907
Contact: Marcel Kunz, GM
Telephone: 615-794-6161
Fax: 615-794-8636
Email: mkunz@faesusa.com / URL: http://www.cbr-sme.com
Product Service Description:
Ink Jet Refilling Equipment / Ribbon Production Equipment

SNC Manufacturing Co., Inc.
101 West Waukau Ave.
Oshkosh, WI 54901
Contact: Maria Sturino, Dir. Int'l Sales & Mktg.
Telephone: 920-231-7370
Fax: 920-231-1090
Email: intl@sncmfg.com / URL: http://www.sncmfg.com
Product Service Description:
Transformers
Transformers, Induction Neutralizing

SOQ Environmental Tech Corp
PO Box 28450
Tempe, AZ 85285-8450
Contact: Olabisi Carlton-Carew, Pres.
Telephone: 602-966-2892
Fax: 602-966-2912
Email: bisi@worldnet.att.net / URL:
Product Service Description:
Manufacturers of biodegradable, water-based cleaners, degreasers, & foam reducers
Polishes & sanitation goods

SOS Metal San Diego
635 Anita St.
Chula Vista, CA 91910
Contact: D. Patrick Hubbard , Gen. Manager, Elba Rhoads, Account Manager
Phone: 619-628-1242 / Fax: 619-628-1253
Product Service Description:
Scrap Metal Including Aluminum, Copper Brass, Nickel Alloy, Stainless Steel Titanium, Metal Residue, Also Plastic

SOS Metals, Inc.
5103 Paramount Blvd.
Pico Rivera, CA 90660-2512
Contact: Sanford Shadrow, President, Don Shadrow, V. Pres.
Phone: 562-949-4446 / Fax: 562-942-1365
Email: sosmetal@flash.net / URL: http://www.sosmetals.com
Product Service Description:
Copper & Brass : Titanium : Metal Residue, Metal Grindings : Scrap Metal : Stainless Steel Scrap: Nickel Alloy Scrap Cobalt Alloys : Aluminum Scrap

SP Pharmaceuticals LLC
4272 Balloon Park Rd Ne
Albuquerque, NM 87109-5801
Contact: Arthur C. Solomon, VP Bus. Dev.
Telephone: 505-761-9230
Fax: 505-761-9229
Email: usolomon@sppharma.com / URL: http://www.sppharma.com
Product Service Description:
Contract pharmaceutical manufacturers
Sterile pharmaceutical products

SP3
505 E Evelyn Ave
Mountain View, CA 94041-1613
Contact: James Herlinger, Pres.
Telephone: 650-966-0630
Fax: 650-966-0633
Product Service Description:
Diamond coated cutting tools - inserts & round tools : Diamond coating systems
Diamond coating services

SPM Thermo-Shield, Inc.
Route 2, Box 208
Custer, SD 57730-9507
Contact: Joe Raver, President
Telephone: 605-673-3201
Fax: 605-673-3200
Email: spm@thermoshield.com / URL:
Product Service Description:
Roof Coating Protective Insulating
Wall Coatings Protective Insulating

SVC Labs
245 Santa Ana Ct
Sunnyvale, CA 94086-4511
Contact: Javad Sahbari, Pres.
Telephone: 408-732-4700
Fax: 408-732-0733
Email: sales@svclabs.com / URL: http://www.svclabs.com
Product Service Description:
Manufactures chemicals for the semiconductor industry
Chemicals_industrial organic solvents
Cleaning solvents, paint strippers, wax removers, ink removers, degreasers
Safe replacement solvents for acetone, xylene, I,I,I-TCA, & methylene chloride

SW Sash & Door
17282 Mount Wynne Cir
Fountain Valley, CA 92708-4107
Contact: Carl Hoelscher, Pres.
Telephone: 714-546-1016
Fax: 714-433-2464
Email: / URL:
Product Service Description:
Manufactures wood windows and doors
Millwork

SWD Urethane
222 South Date Street
Mesa, AZ 85211-1422
Contact: Steven J Perkins, Pres.
Telephone: 480-969-8413
Fax: 480-461-6926
Email: whip@swdurethane.com / URL: http://www.swdurethane.com
Product Service Description:
Manufacturers of plastic foam products
Manufacturers of resins, polyols, and coatings
Manfuacturers of two component polyrethane foam systems for multiple mrkts.
Manufacturers of spary, pour & froth, rigid flotation, packaging &
Flexible, self-skinning foams for world wide markets

Sabel Engineering Corp.
P.O. Box 1223
Sonoma, CA 95476-1223
Contact: Herbert J. Sabel, President
Phone: 707-938-4771 / Fax: 707-938-4772
Email: sales@sabelengr.com / URL: http://www.sabelengr.com
Product Service Description:
Automatic Case Packers (Packaging Machinery)

Saber Diamond Tools
101 Saber Pkwy
Villa Rica, GA 30180-1083
Contact: David G. Freund, Pres.
Telephone: 770-456-0101
Fax: 770-456-0102
Product Service Description:
Industrial diamond tools
Machine tools, metal cutting types

Saber Technologies, LLC
301 Commerce Dr
Fairfield, CT 06432-5510
Contact: Dwain Simpson, Pres.
Telephone: 203-335-0205
Fax: 203-335-0228
Email: saberllc@aol.com / URL:
Product Service Description:
Vapor recovery pumps : Pumps & pumping equipment : Fuel dispnsing nozzles
Vapor recovery nozzles
Electronic display nozzles

Saddle Barn Tack Distributors, Inc.
1102 N Garden Ave
Roswell, NM 88201-7422
Contact: Mark Andrus, Pres.
Telephone: 505-622-9344
Fax: 505-622-0663
Email: info@saddlebarn.com / URL: http://www.saddlebarn.com
Product Service Description:
Horse equipment & tack : Leather goods
Rodeo gear

Saegertown Mfg. Corp.
PO Box 828
Saegertown, PA 16433-0828
Contact: Gary Stanton, Sales Manager
Telephone: 814-763-2655
Fax: 814-763-2069
Email: smc@toolcity.net / URL: http://www.smc-coldform.com
Product Service Description:
Steel component parts

Saf-Tee Siping & Grooving Inc
3451 S 40th St
Phoenix, AZ 85040-1905
Contact: Wesley G Sprunk, Pres.
Telephone: 602-437-5020
Fax: 602-437-5025
Email: tsi-ssg@worldnet.att.net / URL: http://www.tsissg.com
Product Service Description:
Manufactures tire siping and grooving machines : Machinery_special industry

Safe Strap Co., Inc.
30 Centre Rd., Unit 1, 2, 3
Somersworth, NH 03878
Contact: Paul Giampavolo, Pres.
Telephone: 603-692-6196
Fax: 603-692-5094
Email: sscoinc@aol.com / URL:
Product Service Description:
Seat belts & safety straps
Textile products_fabricated

Safe T-Tank Corp.
25 Powers Dr
Meriden, CT 06451-5578
Contact: Sheila R. Bartis, Pres., CFO
Telephone: 203-237-6320
Fax: 203-235-2749
Email: safe.t.tank@snet.net / URL:
Product Service Description:
Steel storage tanks

SafeWay Hydraulics, Inc.
4040 Norex Dr.
Chaska, MN 55318-3000
Contact: Steven J. Berkey, President
Telephone: 612-448-2600
Fax: 612-448-3466
Email: mail@safewayhyd.com / URL: http://www.safewayhyd.com
Product Service Description:
Hydraulic Quick Couplers

Safeline Corp
1777 S Bellaire St Ste 330
Denver, CO 80222-4318
Contact: Philip Wyers, Pres.
Telephone: 303-757-2400
Fax: 303-757-1988
Email: service@safelinecorp.com / URL: http://www.safelinecorp.com
Product Service Description:
Manufactures baby car seat that converts into a stroller: Car seats, booster seats & strollers

Safetech International, Inc.
PO Box 14363
Shawnee Mission, KS 66285-4363
Contact: Gaylen Davenport, Pres.
Telephone: 913-894-4855
Fax: 913-894-4899
Email: sales@safetechintl.com / URL: http://www.safetechintl.com
Product Service Description:
Fire alarm control systems & Accessories

Safeway Stores Inc., Export Sales
2800 Ygnacio Valley Rd.
Walnut Creek, CA 94598-3592
Contact: Ron Messner, Export Director
Telephone: 510-944-4192
Fax: 510-944-4133
Email: / URL:
Product Service Description:
Cheese, Processed & Natural
Ice Cream & Novelties
Mayonnaise, Salsas, Jams & Jellies
Dry Pet Food
Carbonated Beverages

Sagaz Industries, Inc.
16241 Nw 48th Ave
Miami, FL 33014-6438
Contact: Sam Dewar,
Telephone: 305-620-1851
Fax: 305-624-2458
Email: sagazmkt@netrox.net / URL: http://www.sagaz.com
Product Service Description:
Automobile seat covers & floor mats
Textile products_fabricated

Sahalee Of Alaska, Inc.
PO Box 104174
Anchorage, AK 99510-4174
Contact: Albin Lind, COO
Telephone: 907-349-4151
Fax: 907-349-4161
Product Service Description:
Fish & seafood processing
Fish_fresh or frozen prepared

Sahar Industries
1628 W 139th St
Gardena, CA 90249-3003
Contact: Simon Khazani,
Telephone: 310-515-1477
Fax: 310-515-3615
URL: http://www.saharindustries.com
Product Service Description:
Refrigeration & heating equipment
Manufactures air conditioning condensers
Manufactures air conditioning & heating coils
Coil

Sahara Springs Cosmetics
PO Box 1740
Hollywood, CA 90078-1740
Contact: Musa Kannike-Martins, Pres.
Telephone: 323-292-0731
Fax: 323-292-4803
Email: / URL: http://www.saharasprings.com
Product Service Description:
Manufactures cosmetics and hair care products

Saint George Crystal Ltd.
PO Box 709
Jeannette, PA 15644-0709
Contact: Ray Balbach, VP Sales
Telephone: 724-523-6501
Fax: 724-523-0707
Email: rb@stgeo.com / URL: http://www.stgeo.com
Product Service Description:
Lead crystal stemware, bar products & accessories : Glass products from purchased glass : Lead Crystal Lighting Components
Lead Crystal Giftware

Salco Circuit
1825 Sampson Ave
Corona, CA 91719-6009
Contact: Dan P Saldana, Ptnr.
Telephone: 909-371-6210
Fax: 909-371-6138
Email: salco@salcocircuits.com / URL: http://www.salcocircuits.com
Product Service Description:
Designs & manufactures & distributes flexible and multilayered printed circuits and assoc
Printed circuit boards
Electronic components
Electrical apparatus & equipment
Assemblies & Turnkey

Salco Products Inc
PO Box 248
Lawndale, CA 90260-0248
Contact: Sam Tobey, Pres.
Telephone: 310-973-2400
Fax: 310-973-4679
Email: salco023@aol.com / URL: http://www.salcodrip.com/salcodrip
Product Service Description:
Manufactures drip irrigation equipment

Sam's Auto Glass & Exports
2099 Opa Locka Blvd.
Opa Locka, FL 33054-4227
Contact: Jutso Gonzalez, Manager
Telephone: 305-681-7035
Fax:
Email: / URL:
Product Service Description:
Motor vehicle parts and accessories
Spark-ignition reciprocating or rotary internal combustion piston engines
Auto glass, all car & truck
Used parts all cars & trucks

Sam's Homemade Cheesecake Inc
PO Box 26850
San Diego, CA 92196-0850
Contact: Elizabeth Terris, Pres.
Telephone: 619-578-3460
Fax: 619-578-3346
Email: etsams@aol.com / URL:
Product Service Description:
Manufactures frozen gourmet desserts
Ice cream & frozen desserts

Samtan Engineering Corp
127 Wyllis Ave
Malden, MA 02148-7525
Contact: Samuel Askenazy, Pres., George Laberis, GM
Telephone: 781-322-7880
Fax: 781-397-7684
Email: samtaneng@erols.com / URL:
Product Service Description:
Marine cable, wireway & pipe hangers & supports : Metal stampings & deep drawn parts

San Juan International, Inc.
27 Industrial Dr
Trenton, NJ 08619-3244
Contact: Roberto Flores, Pres.
Telephone: 609-586-9500
Fax: 609-586-3425
Email: s9ji@aol.com
Product Service Description:
Automotive chemicals
Chemical preparations

Sanda Corp.
4005 Gypsy Ln
Philadelphia, PA 19144-5427
Contact: Traude Sadtler, Pres., Opers., Sales & Mktg. Mgr.
Telephone: 215-849-8100
Fax: 215-849-8102
Email: info@sanda.com / URL: http://www.netaxs.com/~sanda
Product Service Description:
Computerized titration equipment

Sandbagger Corp.
PO Box 626
Wauconda, IL 60084-0626
Contact: Stacey Kanzler, Pres.
Phone: 815-363-1400 / Fax: 815-363-8809
Email: stacey@thesandbagger.com / URL: http://www.thesandbagger.com
Product Service Description:
Bag filling machinery
Sand bag filling machinery

Sanderson Farms Inc.
PO Box 988
Laurel, MS 39441
Contact: Tommy Satterthwaite, Corporate Frozen Sales Representative
Phone: 601-426-1313 / Fax: 601-426-1319
Email: tsatterthwaite@sandersonfarms.com
Product Service Description:
Poultry slaughtering & processing
Chicken processing

Sandler, Travis & Rosenberg, P.A.
5200 Blue Lagoon Dr. Ste. 600
Miami, FL 33126
Contact: Kimberlee A. Mark, Dir.of Mrkt
Phone: 305-267-9200 / Fax: 305-267-5155
Email: info@strtrade.com / URL: http://www.strtrade.com
Product Service Description:
Trade Association: International Trade Law Firm

Sandpiper Publications
1197 W 500 S
Woods Cross, UT 84087-2233
Contact: Jerry Clausing, Owner
Telephone: 801-292-6511
Fax: 801-298-0672
Email: sabre@sanpiperpublications.com /
URL: http://www.sandpiperpublications.com
Product Service Description:
Aircraft Ground Service Guide, Aircraft
Crash Rescue Guide
Military aircraft crash rescue - aviation
consulting

Sandy's Trophies
800 W Lewis St
Pasco, WA 99301-5542
Contact: Mark Howell, Owner
Telephone: 509-547-0007
Fax: 509-545-4034
Email: sandys@3-cities.com / URL: http://
www.busdir.com/sandysinc/index.html
Product Service Description:
Metal coating & allied services
Engraves plaques, labels and trophies
Commercial art & graphic design
Metal products_fabricated
Brail sign
Glass engraving
Name badges
Banners
Full color printing
Mugs

Sandy-Alexander, Inc.
200 Entin Rd
Clifton, NJ 07014-1423
Contact: Roy Grossman, Pres.
Telephone: 973-470-8100
Fax: 973-470-9269
Email: sandy@sandyinc.com / URL: http://
www.sandyinc.com
Product Service Description:
Printing_commercial
Commercial printing

Santa Barbara Control Systems
5375 Overpass Rd
Santa Barbara, CA 93111-2007
Contact: Jacques M Steininger, Pres.
Telephone: 805-683-8833
Fax: 805-683-1893
Email: chemtrol@sbcontrol.com / URL: http:/
/www.sbcontrol.com
Product Service Description:
Manufacturer, automated water treatment
controllers

Santa Cruz Valley Pecan Company
PO Box 7
Sahuarita, AZ 85629-0007
Contact: Tim Minnehan, *
Telephone: 520-791-2852
Fax: 520-791-2853
Email: scvpco@azpecans.com / URL: http://
www.azpecans.com
Product Service Description:
Shelled Pecans

Santa Monica Propeller Inc
3135 Donald Douglas Loop
Santa Monica, CA 90405
Contact: Leonid Polyakov, President
Telephone: 310-390-6233
Fax: 310-398-3471
Email: / URL:
Product Service Description:
Aircraft parts & equipment
Manufactures aircraft propellers

Sara Lee Bakery Co.
PO Box 1009
Traverse City, MI 49685-1009
Contact: George Chivari, Pres.
Telephone: 616-947-2100
Fax: 616-922-3294
Email: / URL:
Product Service Description:
Bakery products_frozen, except bread
Bakery products_frozen, except bread
Bread, cake & related products

Sardelli & Sons, Inc., T.
195 Dupont Dr
Providence, RI 02907-3105
Contact: Paul Sardelli, Pres.
Telephone: 401-944-8510
Fax:
Email: / URL:
Product Service Description:
Jewelry, precious metal
Precious metal earrings

Sargon Digital Inc
8954 Lurline Ave
Chatsworth, CA 91311-6103
Contact: Misha Dooman, Pres.
Telephone: 818-882-6904
Fax: 818-718-8206
Email: rdooman@earthlink.net / URL: http://
www.sargon-dro.com
Product Service Description:
Process control instruments
Manufactures digital read-out systems for
scales

Sashco Sealants Inc
10300 E 107th Pl
Brighton, CO 80601-7176
Contact: Lester Burch, Pres.
Telephone: 303-286-7271
Fax: 303-286-0400
Email: / URL: http://www.sashco.com
Product Service Description:
Adhesives & sealants
Manufactures industrial and household
caulking

Satellite Transmission Systems
125 Kennedy Dr.
Hauppauge, NY 11788-4072
Contact: Oleandro Mancini,
Telephone: 516-272-5660
Fax: 516-272-5517
Email: oleandro.mancini@L-3com.com /
URL: http://www.L-3com.com/sts
Product Service Description:
Integrator of satellite & wireless
communication systems & networks
Network monitor & control Mgmt. systems

Saucony, Inc.
P.O. Box 6046
Peabody, MA 01961
Contact: Charles A. Gottesman, Executive
Vice President
Telephone: 978-532-9000
Fax: 978-532-6105
Email: / URL: http://www.saucony.com
Product Service Description:
Athletic Footwear / Branded by "Saucony"
Saucony Running & Biking Performance
Apparel
Hind Performance Technical Wear
Merlin, Quintana Roo, Real Bicycles &
Components

Sauder Mfg. Co.
PO Box 230
Archbold, OH 43502-0230
Contact: Virgil Miller, Pres., GM
Telephone: 419-445-7670
Fax: 419-446-3697
Email: sales@saudermfg.com / URL: http://
www.saudermanufacturing.com
Product Service Description:
Furniture_public building & related
Church & institutional furniture

Saunders Thread Co., Inc.
PO Box 4016
Gastonia, NC 28054-0020
Contact: Charles Saunders, Pres.
Telephone: 704-866-9156
Fax: 704-861-9293
Email: saunders@saunders-thread.com /
URL: http://www.saunders-thread.com
Product Service Description:
Industrial sewing thread
Nomex-Spun & Filament
Kevlar - Spun & Filament
PTFE Coated Fiberglass
Polypropylene
Vectran

Sauvage Swimwear
3940 Ruffin Rd # A
San Diego, CA 92123-1826
Contact: Simon Southwood, V-P.
Telephone: 619-514-8229
Fax: 619-514-8233
Product Service Description:
Clothing_men's & boys'
Manufactures men's activewear and women's
and men's swimwear
Outerwear_women's & misses'

Sav-On Plating/Powder Coating
15523 Illinois Ave
Paramount, CA 90723-4110
Contact: Carmen Trimino, Pres.
Telephone: 562-634-6189
Fax: 562-602-0690
Email: sales@sav-onplating.com / URL:
Product Service Description:
Plating of zinc, brass, copper, bronze, nickel,
cadmium, passivating, powder coating
Plating & polishing
Metal coating & allied services

Savage Universal Corporation
550 E Elliot Rd
Chandler, AZ 85225-1116
Contact: Sylvester J Hank, V-P., GM
Telephone: 602-632-1320
Fax: 602-632-1322
Email: info@savagepaper.com / URL: http://
www.savagepaper.com
Product Service Description:
Converts paper and paperboard products
Converted paper products
Industrial & personal service paper

Savant Audio & Video
287 Clarksville Rd
Princeton Junction, NJ 08550-1415
Contact: J. Cintron, Pres.
Telephone: 609-799-9664
Fax: 609-739-8480
Email: savant@savantaudio.com / URL: http:/
/www.savantaudio.com
Product Service Description:
Audio & video amplifiers & electronic
circuits : Audio & video equipment ,
household : Printed circuit boards

Scalemen Of Florida, Inc.
2280 Sw 71st Ter
Davie, FL 33317-7136
Contact: James Kirkham, Pres.
Telephone: 954-370-5700
Fax: 954-370-8800
Email: info@scalemen.com / URL: http://
www.scalemen.com
Product Service Description:
Scales : Scales & balances
Force Measurement Testing Equipment
Vehicle Scales : Load Cells - Mechanical,
Hydraulic, Electronic : Speed Measurement,
Tachometer

Scalewatcher North America Inc.
345 Lincoln St
Oxford, PA 19363-1500
Contact: Jan de Baat Doelman, Pres.
Telephone: 610-932-6888
Fax: 610-932-7559
Email: swna@scalewatcher.com / URL: http:/
/www.scalewatcher.com
Product Service Description:
Water treatment electronic descaling
Residential, Commercial, Industrial

**ScanRite Systems, Smith Companies
Dental Products**
4368 Enterprise St
Fremont, CA 94538-6305
Contact: Barry J. Walter, VP
Telephone: 510-490-8999
Fax: 510-659-1855
Email: info@smithdental.com / URL: http://
www.smithdental.com
Product Service Description:
Manufactures medical and dental equipment
and supplies

Scanlan International Inc.
One Scanlan Plaza
St. Paul, MN 55107-1681
Contact: Keth Walli-Ware, Dir/Intl Mktg.
Telephone: 651-298-0997
Fax: 651-298-0018
Email: / URL: http://www.scanlangroup.com
Product Service Description:
Surgical Instruments
Surgical Instruments, Cardiovascular &
Vascular
Surgical Instruments, Disposable Single Use

Scapa Filter Media
4563 Jordan Rd.
Skaneateles Falls, NY 13153
Contact: Paul Wrobleski, General Manager
Telephone: 315-685-3466
Fax: 315-685-5574
Email: scapafiltr@aol.com / URL:
Product Service Description:
Filterbelts & Filtercloth

**Scarsdale Quilting Converting
Corp., Inc.**
PO Box 824
Tupelo, MS 38802-0824
Contact: Gary Kutak, Pres.
Telephone: 601-842-4635
Fax: 601-680-5571
Email: tckus@ebicom.net / URL:
Product Service Description:
Quilted fabrics & bedspreads
Pleating & stitching

Scenario International Co.
4092 Deervale Dr.
Sherman Oaks, CA 91403-4609
Contact: Elke Heitmeyer, *
Telephone: 818-986-3777
Fax: 818-906-7417
Email: / URL:
Product Service Description:
Nail Polish, Export
Bath Products, Export
Hair Tints, Natural Henna, Export

Schenker International, Inc.
7550 22nd Ave. S., Ste. 127,
Minneapolis, MN 55450
Contact: Sales & Marketing,
Telephone: 612-726-5123
Product Service Description:
Customs Broker
Freight Forwarder
Freight & Cargo Transportation

Schenker International, Inc.
West 2 Schenker Dr.,
Kenner, LA 70062
Contact: Christian Finnern,
Telephone: 504-469-8511
Fax: 504-467-7047
Email: cfinnern@schenkerusa.com / URL:
http://www.schenkerusa.com
Product Service Description:
Freight Forwarder & CHB

Scheu Products Co.
P.O. Box 250
Upland, CA 91785-0250
Contact: George Stoneback, Dir. of Sales &
Mktg.
Telephone: 909-982-8933
Fax: 909-982-2851
Email: scheuco@earthlink.net / URL: http://
www.scheuco.com
Product Service Description:
Heating Equipment, Portable, Construction,
Industrial & Agricultural
Concrete Vibrators & Finishing Equipment

Schlage Lock Company (Mfr)
2401 Bayshore Blvd.
San Francisco, CA 94134
Contact: Jeff Shilakis, *
Telephone: 415-468-1942
Fax: 415-468-3523
Email: / URL:
Product Service Description:
Door Locks, Cylindrical
Door Locks, Mortise
Deadlocks, Tubular & Mortise

Schmalz European, Inc.
57 Napoleon St
Newark, NJ 07105-3113
Contact: John Schmalz, V-P.
Telephone: 973-589-3459
Fax: 973-589-0772
Email: schmalz57@aol.com / URL:
Product Service Description:
Meat processing

Schmeltzer: Master Group
400 Greenwood Avenue
Wyncote, PA 19095
Contact: Richard Schmeltzer, *
Telephone: 215/572-7100
Fax: 215-572-5048
Email: smg@smgpc.com / URL:
Product Service Description:
Accounting, Auditing & Consulting Svcs.

Schmidt Printing, Inc.
1101 Frontage Rd Nw
Byron, MN 55920-1386
Contact: Joel Skinner, National Director of
Sales
Telephone: 507-775-6400
Fax: 507-775-6655
Email: jskinner@schmidt.com / URL: http://
www.schmidt.com
Product Service Description:
Printing_commercial
Magazine insert & business reply cards
printing

Schnee-Morehead of California
PO Box 2465
Santa Fe Springs, CA 90670-0465
Contact: Rusty Goger, V-P., Sales
Telephone: 562-698-9735
Fax: 562-698-9730
Email: rustyg@schneemorehead.com / URL:
http://www.trustsm.com
Product Service Description:
Manufactures caulks and sealants for
construction, aircraft, automotive and general
industries
Adhesives & sealants

Schneider Enterprises
1876 Fireside Dr
Cincinnati, OH 45255-2540
Contact: R. L. Schneider, Owner, Fin., MIS
& R & D Mgr.
Telephone: 513-474-0203
Fax: 513-474-6418
Email: eznail@aol.com / URL: http://
www.ea-door-guide.com
Product Service Description:
Sliding closet door guides, a replacement
door guide designed
to replace all other types. Install in 4-5
munites
over carpet & padding, wood floors with only
a hammer.

Schnepper-International, Inc.
3162 Hwy B
Platteville, WI 53818-9653
Contact: Russ Schnepper, President
Telephone: 608-348-6141
Fax: 608-348-6146
Email: rschnep@mhtc.net / URL:
Product Service Description:
Veterinary Medicines & Supp., Wholesale
Veterinary Consulting, Food Animals

Schofield Printing, Inc.
211 Weeden St
Pawtucket, RI 02860-1807
Contact: Bob Chito, Pres.
Telephone: 401-728-6980
Fax: 401-724-0820
Email: screenprint@schofield.com / URL:
http://www.screenprint.schofield.com
Product Service Description:
Screen printing

Schramm, Inc.(Mfr)
800 E. Virginia Ave.
West Chester, PA 19380
Contact: Bob Edwards, *
Telephone: 610-696-2500
Fax: 610-696-6950
Email: schramm@schramminc.com / URL:
Product Service Description:
Mining Equipment, Rotary Drill Rigs
Water Drilling Equipment
Oil & Gas Field Machinery

Schroeder United Van Lines
2720 E. Winslow Ave.
Appleton, WI 54911-8646
Contact: John Schroeder, Trans Consultant
Telephone: 800-242-3577
Fax: 414-739-5324
Email: gsharpe@schroedermoving.com /
URL: http://www.schroedermoving.com
Product Service Description:
Freight Forwarding Ocean & Air
Origin & Destination Services, Storage
Packing, Crating, Rigging, Container
Shipping Documents Preparation

Schroer Manufacturing Co.
2221 Campbell St.
Kansas City, MO 64108
Contact: Richard Donahue, *
Telephone: 816-471-0488
Fax: 816-471-5339
Email: / URL:
Product Service Description:
Veterinarian Equipment

Schueler & Co., Inc.
420 Hempstead Tpke.
West Hempstead, NY 11552
Contact: Robyn A. Burchman, *
Telephone: 516-489-4000
Fax: 516-489-4949
Email: info@schuelerinc.com / URL: http://
www.schuelerinc.com
Product Service Description:
Medical Supplies
Export Distributor of 100 U.S. Medical Mfr.s

Schuff Steel Company
420 S. 19th Ave., PO Box 39670
Phoenix, AZ 85069
Contact: Daniel T Kneifl, V-P.
Telephone: 602-252-7787
Fax: 602-251-0319
Email: dan@schuff.com / URL: http://
www.schuff.com
Product Service Description:
Fabricates structural steel stairs, handrails and
industrial plate products, process bins,
Structural metal_fabricated
Architectural metal work
Plate work_fabricated (boiler shops)

Schulz Electric Co.
30 Gando Dr
New Haven, CT 06513-1049
Contact: Robert Davis, Pres.
Telephone: 203-562-5811
Fax: 203-562-1082
Email: sales-marketing@schulzelectric.com /
URL: http://www.schulzelectric.com
Product Service Description:
Control panels & rebuilt motors
Motors & generators
Armatuer rewinding

Schulze Manufacturing
50 Ingold Rd
Burlingame, CA 94010-2206
Contact: William Sunderland, Manager Sales
& Mktg.
Telephone: 650-692-1944
Fax: 650-692-9350
Email: bills@schulzemfg.com / URL: http://
www.schulzemfg.com
Product Service Description:
Precision stampings and sheet metal
assemblies for the computer industry
Metal stampings
Dies, tools, jigs & fixtures_special

Schweitzer Engineering Labs Inc.
2350 NE Hopkins Ct.
Pullman, WA 99163-5600
Contact: ,
Telephone: 509-332-1890
Fax: 509-334-8280
Email: info@selinc.com / URL: http://
www.selinc.com
Product Service Description:
Power Protection Equipment, Numerical
Relays

Schwerdtle Stamp Co., Inc.
PO Box 14611
Bridgeport, CT 06601
Contact: John Schwerdtle, Pres.
Telephone: 203-330-2750
Fax: 203-330-2760
Email: schwerco@aol.com / URL: http://
www.thomasregister.com/schwerdtle
Product Service Description:
Marking & decorating tools & devices
Marking devices
Hot Stamping Dies
Silicone Rubber Hot Stamps

Schwing America, Inc.
5900 Centerville Rd
Saint Paul, MN 55127-6805
Contact: Thomas M. Anderson, President
Telephone: 651-429-0999
Fax: 651-429-3464
Email: tgooroa@schwing.com / URL: http://
www.schwing.com
Product Service Description:
Construction & mining machinery
Motor vehicles for the transport of goods
Concrete pumps
Road tractors for semi-trailers
Sludge pumps
Concrete pump with placing boom
Trailer mounted concrete pumps

Scientech Inc.
5649 Arapahoe Ave.
Boulder, CO 80303
Contact: Tom Campbell, Vice President
Telephone: 303/444-1361
Fax: 303-444-9229
Email: inst@scientech-inc.com / URL: http://
www.scientech-inc.com
Product Service Description:
Laboratory Balances & Scales
Commercial Scales
Laboratory Analytical Instruments

Scientific Industries, Inc.
70 Orville Dr
Bohemia, NY 11716-2512
Contact: Lowell A. Kleiman, Pres., Treas.
Telephone: 516-567-4700
Fax: 516-567-5896
Email: info@scind.com / URL: http://
www.scind.com
Product Service Description:
Laboratory equipment, vortex mixers,
rotators, shakers, stirrers, peristalic pumps &
timer: Analytical instruments

Sconza Candy Co.
919 81st Ave.
Oakland, CA 94621-2581
Contact: James R. Sconza, President
Telephone: 510-568-8137
Fax: 510-638-5792
Product Service Description:
Candy and Other Confectionery Products
Sugar confectionary , not containing cocoa
Miscellaneous cargo

Scot Forge Co.
PO Box 8
Spring Grove, IL 60081-0008
Contact: Sharon Hauerstock, VP Marketing
Telephone: 847-587-1000
Fax: 847-587-2000
Email: sales@scotforge.com / URL: http://www.scotforge.com
Product Service Description:
Open die forgings & rolled rings
Forgings_iron & steel

Scotchman Industries, Inc.(Mfr)
180 East Highway 14
Philip, SD 57567
Contact: Jerry Carley, President
Telephone: 605/859-2542
Fax: 605-859-2499
Email: scotchman@scothman.com / URL: http://www.scotchman.com
Product Service Description:
Machine Tools, Hydraulic Ironworkers
Circular Cold Saws
Jewelry Boxes (Metal)

Scotia Technology Div., Lakes Region Tubular Products, Inc.
PO Box 1190
Laconia, NH 03247-1190
Contact: Gail Brewer, President, Ms. Katt Stewart, Sales
Telephone: 603-528-2838
Fax: 603-528-4184
Email: scotiatech@cyberportal.net / URL: http://www.scotia-tech.com
Product Service Description:
Tubular aircraft components & engine parts
Aircraft parts & equipment
Engine Parts, ie, Fuel, Hyd. & Air Lines S.S.

Scotsman Industries
775 Corporate Woods Pkwy.
Vernon Hills, IL 60061
Contact: Randy Rossi, President
Telephone: 847-215-4500
Fax: 847-913-9844
Email: customer.service@scotsman-ice.com / URL: http://www.scotsman-ice.com
Product Service Description:
Ice Making Machinery
Ice Storage Bins
Ice Dispensers
Ice / Beverage Dispensers

Scott Electronics, Inc.
33 Northwestern Dr
Salem, NH 03079-4809
Contact: John Metzemaeker, Pres.
Telephone: 603-893-2845
Fax: 603-894-5420
Email: / URL: http://www.scottelec.com
Product Service Description:
Electronic components
Electronic cable & wire harness assemblies

Scott Foresman
1900 E Lake Ave
Glenview, IL 60025-2055
Contact: Paul McFall, Pres.
Telephone: 847-729-3000
Fax: 847-729-8910
Email: / URL: http://www.scottforesman.com
Product Service Description:
Book publishing
Textbook & multimedia educational materials, K-6

Scott Resources, Inc.
P.O. Box 2121
Fort Collins, CO 80522-2121
Contact: Steve Thygesen, Export Manager
Telephone: 303-484-7445
Fax: 303-484-8093
Email: sthygese@amep.com / URL: http://www.amep.com
Product Service Description:
Educational Science Kits, Math
Manipulatives, Astromony

Scott Specialty Gases
6141 Easton Road Box 310
Plumsteadville, PA 18949
Contact: Robert G. Jefferys,
Telephone: 215-766-8861
Fax: 215-766-2476
Email: / URL: http://www.scottgas.com
Product Service Description:
Gases_industrial
Industrial gases

Scott's Of Wisconsin / Mille Lacs M. P. Company
301 Broadway Dr
Sun Prairie, WI 53590-1742
Contact: Amy M. Wollangk, Int'l / Domestic Sales Coordinator
Telephone: 608-837-8535
Fax: 608-825-6463
Email: mlintl@globaldialog.com / URL: http://www.scotts-of-wis.com
Product Service Description:
Chocolate confectionery, cheese, salsa, cookies, jams & jellies; gift baskets

Screw Conveyor Corp. (Mfr)
700 Hoffman Street
Hammond, IN 46327
Contact: Randolph E. Block, *
Telephone: 219-931-1450
Fax: 219-931-0209
Email: / URL: http://www.screwconveyorcorp.com
Product Service Description:
Screw Conveyors
Drag Conveyors
Bucket Elevators
Elevator Buckets
Hydraulic Truck Dump
Belt Conveyor Idlers
Feeders

Se-Kure Controls, Inc.
3714 Runge St
Franklin Park, IL 60131-1112
Contact: Warren Morrison, Dir. Int'l Sales
Telephone: 847-288-1111
Fax: 847-288-9999
Email: sekure@msn.com / URL: http://www.se-kure.com
Product Service Description:
Anti-shoplifting devices
Electrical equipment & supplies
Electronic components

Sea Forest Enterprises Inc
PO Box 2960
Florence, OR 97439-0167
Contact: Gerald Lewis, Pres.
Telephone: 541-997-6442
Fax: 541-997-8421
Email: sea4st@presys.com / URL:
Product Service Description:
Logging
Helicopter Logging Consultant

Seal-Seat Company
1200 Monterey Pass Rd
Monterey Park, CA 91754-3617
Contact: Kathleen Trenschel, Mgr.
Telephone: 323-269-1311
Fax: 323-269-0529
Email: / URL:
Product Service Description:
Manufactures & distributes replacement parts for gas welding torches & regulators & parts for oxygen therapy regulators & flowmeters

Sealing Devices, Inc.
4400 Walden Ave
Lancaster, NY 14086-9716
Contact: Terry S. Galanis Sr., Chrm.
Telephone: 716-684-7600
Fax: 716-684-0760
Email: seals@sealingdevices.com / URL: http://www.sealingdevices.com
Product Service Description:
Gaskets & sealing devices
Gaskets, packing & sealing devices

Seamodal Transport Corp.
P.O. Box 3398
Norfolk, VA 23514-3398
Contact: Clifton N. Byrd, District Manager
Telephone: 757-625-1928
Fax: 757-625-0146
Email: stcnfk@mcimail.com / URL:
Product Service Description:
Freight Forwarding
Customshouse Broker
Insurance / Drawback

Sears Steele, III
4745 Queen Lane
Jacksonville, FL 32210
Contact: Sears Steele, III, Translator / Interpreter
Telephone: 904-388-3251
Fax: 904-387-6570
Product Service Description:
Translation Services
English, Russian
Member, Florida Bar
Technical Translations

Seattle Post/Intelligencer Div
PO Box 1909
Seattle, WA 98111-1909
Contact: J D Alexander, Publisher
Telephone: 206-448-8308
Fax: 206-448-8292
Email: jdalexander@seattle-pi.com / URL: http://www.seattle-pi.com
Product Service Description:
Newspapers
Publishes daily newspaper

Second Chance Body Armor, Inc.
PO Box 578
Central Lake, MI 49622-0578
Contact: Dianne S. Blamer, *
Product Service Description:
Bullet & Slash Resistant Vests

Secura Key
20447 Nordhoff St
Chatsworth, CA 91311-6112
Contact: Ken Cecil, International Director
Telephone: 818-882-0020
Fax: 818-882-7052
Email: mail@securakey.com / URL: http://www.securakey.com
Product Service Description:
Manufactures access control systems

Secure-IT Inc. (Mfr)
18 Maple Court
East Longmeadow, MA 01028
Contact: Bill Brady, President
Telephone: 413-525-7039
Fax: 413-525-8807
Email: secure-it@secure-it.com / URL: http://www.secure-it.com
Product Service Description:
Computer Periph., Security Devices

Security Engineered Machinery Co.
PO Box 1045
Westboro, MA 01581-6045
Contact: Jack McIsaac, International Sales
Telephone: 508-366-1488 Ext.232
Fax: 508-366-6814
Email: www.info@semshred.com / URL: http://www.semshred.com
Product Service Description:
Documentation / Data Waste Disintegrators
Paper Shredders
Briquettors
Banknote Destroyers

Security Equipment Corp.
330 Sun Valley Cir.
Fenton, MO 63026
Contact: Larry Nance, Pres., Pur. Agt.
Telephone: 314-343-0200
Fax: 314-343-1318
Email: sabre@stlnet.com / URL: http://www.sabredefensesprays.com
Product Service Description:
Aerosol tear gas
Chemical preparations

Seedcraft
P.O. Box 1085
Morgan Hill, CA 95038-1085
Contact: Mike Go, President
Telephone: 408-779-6868
Fax: 408-779-6870
Email: seedcrft@aol.com / URL: http://www.seecraftinc.com
Product Service Description:
Vegetable seeds for planting
Broccoli seeds for sprouting (fighting cancer)
Seeds of coriander : Peas, dried shelled, including seed : Seedless watermelon seed
Bacterial wilt resistant tomato seed : Long shelf life tomato seed : Heat resistant cabbage seed : Supersweet (SH2) sweet corn seed

Seeley's Ceramic Service, Inc.
9 River St., P.O. Box 669
Oneonta, NY 13820-0669
Contact: Rolf E. Ericson, President
Telephone: 607-433-1240
Fax: 607-432-2042
Email: seeleys@aol.com / URL: http://www.seeleys.com
Product Service Description:
Glazes: China Paints : Porcelain Doll Making
Books : Porcelain & Stoneware Slips
Doll & Ceramic Molds (Plaster)
Ceramic Tools : Composition Doll Bodies

Seepage Control Inc
PO Box 51177
Phoenix, AZ 85076-1177
Contact: James E Bone, Pres.
Telephone: 602-254-4501
Fax: 602-829-1106
Email: seepcon@aol.com / URL: http://www.seepagecontrol.com
Product Service Description:
Manufactures industrial and soil sealants and enzymes

Segrest International Realtors
PO Box 30563
Charlotte, NC 28230-0563
Contact: Dadvis S. Segrest, President
Telephone: 704-331-0433
Fax: 704-333-5365
Email: david@segrestrealty.com / URL: http:/
/www.segrestrealty.com
Product Service Description:
Real Estate Agents

Seidelhuber Metal Products Inc
PO Box 56688
Hayward, CA 94545-6688
Contact: Michael Seidelhuber, Pres.
Telephone: 510-293-0733 / 888-727-8204
Fax: 510-293-0787
Product Service Description:
Manufactures and distributes all types of
grating : Clean room floor panels

Sem Chi Rice Products
P.O. Box 1097
Loxahatchee, FL 33470-1097
Contact: Klause Sengelmann, Vice President,
General Manager
Telephone: 561-996-6054
Fax: 561-996-9059
Email:
klaus_sengelmann@floridacrystals.com /
URL:
Product Service Description:
Rice Milling
Rice, long grain polished or brown rice
Aromatic jasmin & basuati rice
Organic rice

Semco Inc.
1025 Pole Lane Rd
Marion, OH 43302-8524
Contact: Bob Diersing, President
Telephone: 740-387-2229
Fax: 740-387-6127
Email: / URL:
Product Service Description:
Industrial Machining
Beryllium & copper die castings & general
machining job shop
Shot End Components

Semco Manufacturing
P.O. Box H
Pharr, TX 78577-1208
Contact: James R. Hatton, President
Telephone: 956-787-4203
Fax: 956-781-0620
Email: semco@quik.com / URL:
Product Service Description:
Refrigeration Equipment
Vegetable harvesting equipment
Vegetable washing, grading & packing
equipment
Industrial ice plants

**Semel's Embroidery & Screen
Printing, Inc.**
76 Lexington Ave
Passaic, NJ 07055
Contact: Charlotte Semel, Chrm.
Telephone: 973-473-6868
Fax: 973-473-8895
Email: embroideri@aol.com / URL: http://
www.thenetl.com/semels
Product Service Description:
Pleating & stitching
Textile embroidery & screen printing
Automotive & apparel trimmings
Chenille : Chainstitch : Patches

Semiconductor Technology, Inc.
3131 Se Jay St
Stuart, FL 34997-5964
Contact: Fred G. Seigel, Mktg. Mgr.
Telephone: 561-283-4500
Fax: 561-286-8914
Email: data1@semi-tech-inc.com / URL:
http://www.semi-tech-inc.com
Product Service Description:
High Voltage Low, Medium & High Power
Transistors, Dual Transistors &
General Purpose Transistors

Senderex Cargo Co., Inc.
P.O. Box 90277,
Los Angeles, CA 90009-0277
Contact: R. C. Anderson, President
Telephone: 310-342-2900
Fax: 340-642-0427
Email: intl@senderex.com / URL: http://
www.senderex.com
Product Service Description:
Customs Broker
Freight Forwarder
Freight & Cargo Transportation

Senga Engineering Inc
1525 E Warner Ave
Santa Ana, CA 92705-5419
Contact: Bill Hicks, Vice President
Telephone: 714-549-8011
Fax: 714-549-3940
Email: bhicks@senga-eng.com / URL: http://
www.senga-eng.com
Product Service Description:
Contract machining
Manufactures machined parts for the
electronic connector industry
Aerospace component manufacturing

Senior Flexonics Inc., Hose Div.
815 Forestwood Dr
Romeoville, IL 60446-1167
Contact: Bill Collins, V-P., GM
Telephone: 815-886-1140
Fax: 815-886-4550
Email: flexonic@flexonics-hose.com / URL:
http://www.flexonics-hose.com
Product Service Description:
Composite, metal & teflon hose
Metal products_fabricated

Sense Technology Inc.
3251 Old Frankstown Rd
Pittsburgh, PA 15239-2902
Contact: Joseph M. Evans, Pres.
Telephone: 724-733-2277
Fax: 724-733-1531
Email: sensetec@nb.net / URL: http://
www.nb.net/~sensetec/
Product Service Description:
Physical Medicine - Rehabilitative
Instrumentation

Sensormedics Corporation
22705 Savi Ranch Pkwy
Yorba Linda, CA 92887-4609
Contact: Ed Pulwer, V-P., Sales
Telephone: 714-283-1830
Fax: 714-283-8439
Email: / URL:
Product Service Description:
Manufactures cardiopulmonary, metabolic,
nutritional assessment instrumentation
Sleep diagnostic instrumentation
Critical care ventilators
Medical & hospital equipment

Sentrol Industrial
12345 SW Leveton Dr
Tualatin, OR 97062-6001
Contact: Geraldine F Williams, Mktg. Mgr.
Telephone: 503-691-7331
Fax: 503-691-7563
Email: geraldine.williams@sentrol.com /
URL: http://www.thomasregister.com/sentrol
Product Service Description:
Electronic components
Manufactures safety interlocks and sensors
for OEMs

Sentry Chemical Co.
1481 Rock Mountain Blvd
Stone Mountain, GA 30083-1505
Contact: Charles Reeves, CEO
Telephone: 770-934-4242
Fax: 770-934-0932
Email: info@sentrychem.com / URL: http://
www.sentrychem.com
Product Service Description:
Industrial, agricultural & institutional
maintenance & cleaning chemicals
Sanitation & disinfection products for poultry,
swine & animal health industries.

Sepco (Mfr)
P.O. Box 1599
Pelham, AL 35124
Contact: Norka Gonzalez, *
Telephone: 205/663-2251 Ext.226
Fax: 205-663-4602
Email: sepco@alonline.com / URL:
Product Service Description:
Fluid Sealing Products for Pumps & Valves
Gasket Packing & Sealing Devices
Seals, Industrial Wholesale

Sergeant At Arms Entry Systems
2189 Joy Rd
Occidental, CA 95465-9257
Contact: Bob Morgan,
Telephone: 707-874-2473
Product Service Description:
Manufactures electrical operating system for
gates

Service For Science & Industries
15 E. Ridge Pike, Suite 325
Conshohocken, PA 19428-2116
Contact: Samy F. Faltas, President
Telephone: 610-825-8393
Fax: 610-825-9640
Email: sfsi@earthlink.net / URL:
Product Service Description:
Professional Equipment, NEC
Distibutor of laboratory supplies &
equipment, reagents
Glassware, culture media

Service Hydraulics Inc.
PO Box 4313
Corpus Christi, TX 78469-4313
Contact: H. Falgout, V-P.
Telephone: 512-883-3891
Fax: 512-883-3893
Email: servicehvd@aol.com / URL:
Product Service Description:
Rebuilt hydraulic machinery & parts
Fluid power valves & hose fittings
Engineer, Design, Systems
Hydrostatic System Testing
Pump & Motors Rebuilt
Cylinders Rebuilt & Testing
Winches Rebuilt & Testing
Marine, Offshore, Agriculture
Military, Construction
Automated Systems

Service Ideas, Inc.
2354 Ventura Drive
Woodbury, MN 55125-3929
Contact: Greg A. Loffler, VP / Sales
Telephone: 651-730-8800
Fax: 651-730-8880
Email: siinc@serviceideas.com / URL: http://
www.serviceideas.com
Product Service Description:
Plastic Coffee Carafes

Service International
11617 W. Bluemound Rd., Ste. 3
Wauwatosa, WI 53226-3959
Contact: John W. Eggen, Owner
Telephone: 414-453-2131
Fax: 414-453-2425
Email: / URL: serviceinternational.com
Product Service Description:
Construction Machinery
Parts and attachments, for derricks, cranes,
self-propelled bulldozers, graders and other
grading

Service Quality Institute
9201 E Bloomington Fwy
Minneapolis, MN 55420-3437
Contact: John Tschohl, President
Telephone: 612-884-3311
Fax: 612-884-8901
Email: quality@servicequality.com / URL:
http://www.customer-service.com
Product Service Description:
Customer Service Training
Book publishing
Typesetting

Service Tectonics, Inc.
2827 Treat Street
Adrian, MI 49221
Contact: Joy L. Dalton, *
Telephone: 517/263-0758
Fax: 517-263-4145
Email: sti@tc3net.com / URL: http://
www.sti.thomasregister.com
Product Service Description:
Printing Machines, Pad Transfer
Plas. Work Mach., Hot Air Staking
Plas. Work Mach., Fusion Bonding

Setco Industries
5880 Hillside Ave
Cincinnati, OH 45233-1524
Contact: M. G. Ferguson, V-P., Opers.
Telephone: 513-941-5110
Fax: 513-941-6913
Email: sales@setcousa.com / URL: http://
www.setcousa.com
Product Service Description:
Machine tool components, spindles & slides
Machine tools, metal cutting types
Repair Services - Spindles & Slides
Three Axis Modules

Seton Name Plate Company
20 Thompson Road
Branford, CT 06405-2899
Contact: Richard L. Fisk, President
Telephone: 203-488-8059
Fax: 203-488-4114
Email: dick_fisk@seton.com / URL:
Product Service Description:
Signs
Printed Labels Lithogrphic
Printed Tags, Lithographic
Barricade Signs
Pipe Markers

Sew Feiel
P.O. Box 10
Queenstown, MD 21658-0010
Contact: S E W Friel, Owner
Telephone: 410-827-8841
Fax:
Email: / URL: http://www.friend.ly.net/user-homepages/j/jfriel/
Product Service Description:
Groceries, General Line : Sweet corn, prepared or preserved, not frozen
Corn , other than seed corn
Tomato Juice: Canned Vegetables
Vegetable Juice

Sextet Fabrics, Inc.
21 Ryder Pl
East Rockaway, NY 11518-1215
Contact: Ron Ross, Pres.
Telephone: 516-593-0608
Fax: 516-593-0430
Email: 2119213@mcimail.com / URL:
Product Service Description:
Textile products_fabricated
Fabric converting - specialty circular knits

Shachihata
3305 Kashiwa St.
Torrance, CA 90505-4034
Contact: Sam Asano, President
Telephone: 310-530-4445
Fax: 310-530-2892
Email: sasano@xstamper.com / URL: http://www.xstamper.com
Product Service Description:
Marking Devices : Miscellaneous cargo

Shaffer & Max
9311 Garrison Rd.
Charlotte, NC 28208-9791
Contact: Dick Zelickson, Vice President
Telephone: 704-588-3226
Fax: 704-588-4652
Email: zeeman351@aol.com / URL: http://www.shaffermax.com
Product Service Description:
Textile Machinery

Shallbetter, Inc.
2050 S. Oakwood Rd.
Oshkosh, WI 54904
Contact: Greg Shallbetter, *
Telephone: 920-232-8888
Fax: 920-232-8977
Product Service Description:
Switchgear

Shanklin Corporation
PO box 447
Ayer, MA 01432-0447
Contact: Ed Turlington, VP Sales
Telephone: 508-772-3200
Fax: 508-772-5660
Email: info@shanklincorp.com / URL: http://www.shanklincorp.com
Product Service Description:
Shrink Packaging Machinery

Sharn, Inc.
4801 George Rd Ste 180
Tampa, FL 33634-6200
Contact: Bruce Tomlinson, Pres., CFO
Telephone: 813-889-9614
Fax: 813-886-2701
Email: jtomlinson@sharn.com / URL: http://www.sharn.com
Product Service Description:
Numimed Medication Dispensers
Instrument Cleaning Brushes

Sharp Bros Seed Co.
396 S.W. Davis St. Ladue
Clinton, MO 64735
Contact: Wayne Vassar, General Manager, Judith Rogers, Sales Manager
Telephone: 816-885-7551
Fax: 816-885-8647
Email: sharpbros@sprintmail.com / URL:
Product Service Description:
Wild Flower Seeds : Native Grass Seeds

Shaw-Clayton Corporation
123 Carlos Dr
San Rafael, CA 94903-2005
Contact: Howard G Shaw, Pres., GM
Telephone: 415-472-1522
Fax: 415-472-1599
Email: sccorp@marincounty.net / URL: http://www.shaw-clayton.com
Product Service Description:
Mfr. golf practice equipment; hinged lid containers, molded letters and medication organizers

Shawnee Products, Inc.
PO Box 369
Tecumseh, OK 74873-0369
Contact: Karen Southers, Fin. Mgr.
Telephone: 405-598-6502
Fax: 405-598-6306
Email: shawneepr@aol.com / URL:
Product Service Description:
First aid & survival bandages
Surgical appliances & supplies

Sheepscot Machine Works
1130 US Rt 1
Newcastle, ME 04553
Contact: Todd Williams, Sales Manager
Telephone: 207-563-2299
Fax: 207-563-2619
Email: smw@lincoln.midcoast.com / URL: http://www.lincoln.midcoast.com/~smw
Product Service Description:
Meter Mix & Dispensing Equipment
Industrial Dispensing Valves

Sheepskin Coat Factory
PO Box 838
Ketchum, ID 83340-0838
Contact: David Norton, Pres.
Telephone: 208-726-3588
Fax: 208-726-4063
Product Service Description:
Manufactures men's, women's and children's leather, fur and sheep-lined outerwear
Leather & sheep-lined clothing

Sheftel International
2121 31st St., S.W.
Allentown, PA 18103-7006
Contact: Milton Sheftel, President
Telephone: 610-797-9420
Fax: 610-797-7272
Email: sheftintl@aol.com / URL:
Product Service Description:
Bleached Cotton : Rags
Container Cargo : Industrial Wiping Cloths
Textile Piece Goods & Remnants

Shelby Group International
P.O. Box 171814
Memphis, TN 38187-1814
Contact: Hilliard Crews, President
Telephone: 901-362-1573
Fax: 901-362-0369
Email: rheros@crewsinc.com / URL:
Product Service Description:
Industrial work gloves

Shelton's Sheen Wave Labs Inc
3911 W Jefferson Blvd
Los Angeles, CA 90016-4211
Contact: Billy Jack Shelton, Pres.
Telephone: 323-732-0759
Fax: 323-732-3042
Email: / URL:
Product Service Description:
Manufactures personal care products— hair spray, vitamin E, wheat germ oil, cuticle conditioner, sprays, talcs: Toilet preparations
Drugs, proprietaries & sundries 18 products, shampoos & conditioners : Relaxers - color rinsers. Spray talcum powder : Hair lightener , brightener : Cuticle condition for nails
Spray glitter 3 - colors : Silk press - creme press , scalp conditioner

Shemshad Food Products Inc
PO Box 1413
Glendale, CA 91209-1413
Contact: Hassan Teadolmanesh, Pres.
Telephone: 818-241-2215
Fax: 818-241-2353
Email: / URL:
Product Service Description:
Distributes dairy products; manufactures Persian foods & fruit snacks

Shepher Distribution & Sales
2300 Linden Blvd.
Brooklyn, NY 11208-4899
Contact: Hal Monchik, President
Telephone: 718-649-2525
Fax: 718-649-1068
Email: shephertoy@aol.com / URL:
Product Service Description:
Games, dolls, electronic toys & close outs

Shindaiwa Inc
PO Box 1090
Tualatin, OR 97062-1090
Contact: Jorge Lazo, Vice President
Telephone: 503-692-3070
Fax: 503-692-6696
Email: info@shindaiwa.com / URL: http://www.shindaiwa.com
Product Service Description:
Wholesales outdoor power equipment
Industrial machinery & equipment
Farm & garden machinery

Shine Jewelry
116 E Alameda Ave
Burbank, CA 91502-2003
Contact: Karapet Dedeian, Pres.
Telephone: 818-556-5025
Fax: 818-556-3483
Email: sales@shinejewelry.com / URL: http://www.shinejewelry.com
Product Service Description:
Manufactures 14k gold jewelry
Jewelry, precious metal

Shinwa (USA) Inc.
300 Harmon Meadow Blvd.
Secaucus, NJ 07094
Contact: T. Morishima, President
Telephone: (201) 348-2101
Fax: (201) 319-0305
Email: / URL:
Product Service Description:
Ship Brokers & Agents
Steamship Companies

Ship & Shore a Subsidary of C.D.I.
2474 N Palm Dr
Long Beach, CA 90806-4007
Contact: Anoosheh Mostafaei,
Telephone: 562-595-8889
Fax: 562-595-8990
Email: anoosheh@shipandshore.com / URL:
Product Service Description:
Pollution Control Systems
Custom sheet metal fabrication; heat processing and hydraulics equipment fabrication and overhaul
Blowers & fans, mechanical equipment

Ship Chandler
518 E. Northwest Hwy.
Mount Prospect, IL 60056-3306
Contact: Richard Lund, Pres.
Telephone: 847-577-8044
Fax: 847-577-9355
Email: LNA647A@sprynet.com / URL:
Product Service Description:
Ship & boat models sales, repairs & appraisals

Shock Tech, Inc.
35 Whitney Rd # B
Mahwah, NJ 07430-3129
Contact: Serge Seguin, Pres.
Telephone: 201-848-1000
Fax: 201-848-1355
Email: info@shocktech.com / URL: http://www.shocktech.com
Product Service Description:
Shock & vibration mounts, Shock & Vibration Analysis & Testing
Rugged Enclosures, Cabinets, Racks, Cases
Shipboard Racks, Cabinets, Enclosures
Mechanical Packaging
Electronic Integration

Shotcrete Technologies Inc
PO Box 3274
Idaho Springs, CO 80452-3274
Contact: Kristian Loevlie, Pres.
Telephone: 303-567-4871
Fax: 303-567-4605
Email: shotset250@aol.com / URL:
Product Service Description:
Manufactures equipment for shotcrete work; Robotic arm & nozzle assemblies for mining & tunnel
Construction machinery
Mining machinery
Shotcrete Accelerators, Chemicals

Shred-Tech Chicago
1907 S Busse Rd
Mount Prospect, IL 60056-5506
Contact: Rob Glass, Sales Mgr.
Telephone: 847-593-8100
Fax: 847-593-8102
Email: shred@shred-tech.com / URL: http://www.shred-tech.com
Product Service Description:
Industrial Shreding Equipment

Shrimp World Inc.
417 Eliza St
New Orleans, LA 70114-2335
Contact: William D. Chauvin, Pres.
Telephone: 504-368-1571
Fax: 504-368-1573
Email: chauvin@shrimpcom.com / URL: http://www.shrimpcom.com
Product Service Description:
Publishes shrimp market analysis
Consulting - World shrimp market

Shu-Re-Nu Equipment, Inc.
1730 Cumberland Point Dr Se Ste 5
Marietta, GA 30067-9205
Contact: Raymond J. Margiano, Pres.
Telephone: 770-955-3375
Fax: 770-951-2666
Email: shurenu@bellsouth.net / URL:
Product Service Description:
Shoe repair equipment & supplies
Business Opportunities

Shubb Capos
PO Box 550
Valley Ford, CA 94972-0550
Contact: Rick Shubb, Ptnr.
Telephone: 707-876-3001
Fax: 707-876-3034
Email: shubb@shubb.com / URL: http://
www.shubb.com
Product Service Description:
Manufactures musical instruments,accessories

Shuffle Master, Inc.
10901 Valley View Rd
Eden Prairie, MN 55344-3730
Contact: Joseph Lahti, Pres., CEO
Telephone: 612-943-1951
Fax: 612-943-2090
Email: / URL: http://www.shufflemaster.com
Product Service Description:
Casino Gaming Equipment; Shufflers &
Games

Shur - Co., Inc.
PO Box 713
Yankton, SD 57078-0713
Contact: Kelly Kneifl, Sales Manager
Telephone: 605-665-6000
Fax: 605-665-0501
Email: Shurco@willinet.net / URL: http://
www.shurco.com
Product Service Description:
Truck & Trailer Tarps

Shure Bros. Inc.
222 Hartrey Ave
Evanston, IL 60202-3632
Contact: S. La Mantia, President & CEO
Telephone: 847-866-2200
Fax: 847-866-2279
Email: marcdm@shure.com / URL: http://
www.shure.com
Product Service Description:
Microphones & Audio Electronics
Audio & video equipment_household

Shurfine
2100 N. Mannheim Rd.
Northlake, IL 60164
Contact: James R. Barth, President
Telephone: 708-236-6100
Fax: 708-236-6101
Email: jim_barth@shurfine.com / URL: http://
www.shurfine.com
Product Service Description:
Grocery Stores

Shurflo
12650 Westminster Avenue
Santa Ana, CA 92706
Contact: Herb Soto, Export Manager
Telephone: 714-554-7709
Fax: 714-554-4721
Email: / URL: http://www.shurflo.com
Product Service Description:
Ind. Mach., Pump Spraying Systems
Ind. Mach., Pumps, Beverage Dispensing
Ind. Mach. Pumps Marine & RV
Ind. Mach Pumps Domestic Water Systems

Shurtleff-G A H A R A N, Inc.
RR 4 Box 262
Paris, TX 75462
Contact: George H. Gaharan, CEO
Telephone: 903-785-6844
Fax: 903-785-5139
Email: sginc@1starnet.com / URL:
Product Service Description:
Sheet metal fabrication & ultra seam metal
roofing : Standing seam metal roofing
contractor

Sieflor
11712 Moorpark St., Ste. 101
Studio City, CA 91604-2163
Contact: Rolf Eis, President
Telephone: 818-762-6300
Fax: 818-760-8946
Email: sieflor@greenheart.com / URL:
Product Service Description:
Chemical products and preparations and
residual products of the chemical or allied
industries

Sieling & Jones, Inc.
PO Box 159
New Freedom, PA 17349-0159
Contact: Edward G. Jones III, Pres.
Telephone: 717-235-7931
Fax: 717-235-3233
Email: sjplywood@aol.com / URL:
Product Service Description:
Architectural & hardwood plywood products
Hardwood veneer & plywood

Sierra Electronic Assembly
PO Box 235
Ahwahnee, CA 93601-0235
Contact: Jenene Jones, Pres.
Telephone: 559-683-2234
Fax: 559-658-2210
Email: willbuild@sierratel.com / URL: http://
www.willbuild4u.com
Product Service Description:
Subcontractor for printed circuit boards
Populate printed circuit boards : Turnkey :
Through hole - mixed or smt tec. : Potting

Sifco Selective Plating
5708 Schaaf Rd
Cleveland, OH 44131
Contact: Andrew Garstka, Dir. of sales& Svc.
Telephone: 216-524-0099
Fax: 216-524-6331
Email: info@brushplating.com / URL: http://
www.brushplating.com
Product Service Description:
Plating & polishing : Brush plating

Sign Connection
520 Hartford Tpke
Vernon Rockville, CT 06066-5037
Contact: Bo Muschinsky, Sales Manager
Telephone: 860-870-8855
Fax: 860-870-8865
Email: sign.connection@snet.net / URL:
Product Service Description:
Interior & exterior signs : Decals & Labels
Industrial Marking / Safety Graphics

Sign Products International
13700 58th St N
Clearwater, FL 33760-3757
Contact: Kelly R. Coleman, Pres
Phone: 813-538-3863 / Fax: 813-535-7776
Email: spi@sign-products-intl.com / URL:
http://www.sign-products-int.com
Product Service Description:
Electric signs & aluminum extrusions

Signals & Systems Inc.
333 Park Dr
Troy, MI 48083-2778
Contact: Robert Bloom, Pres.
Telephone: 248-585-0600
Fax: 248-585-5139
Email: / URL:
Product Service Description:
Electronic components
Electronic components
Commercial physical research

Signart, Inc.
9030 Premier Row
Dallas, TX 75247-5406
Contact: Oren Newton, Pres.
Telephone: 214-637-4455
Fax: 214-637-4456
Email: oren@signart.com / URL: http://
www.signart.comm
Product Service Description:
Architectural signs
Signs & advertising specialties
Waterjet cutting

Signs & Signs, Inc.
PO Box 4056
Dalton, GA 30719-1056
Contact: John Boykin, Pres.
Telephone: 706-275-8808
Fax: 706-275-0421
Email: / URL:
Product Service Description:
Signs

Silicon Sensors, LLC
PO Box 10
Dodgeville, WI 53533-0010
Contact: Paul D. Ludwig, VP
Telephone: 608-935-2707
Fax: 608-935-2775
Email: ssi@siliconsensors.com / URL: http://
www.siliconsensors.com
Product Service Description:
Custom Optoelectronic Assemblies
Photodiodes

Silkwood Wholesale, Inc.
321 Mokauea St
Honolulu, HI 96819-3222
Contact: Greg McCaul, Pres., Fin., MIS & R
& D Mgr.
Telephone: 808-845-0655
Fax: 808-841-3564
Email: silkwoodhi@aol.com / URL:
Product Service Description:
Manufacturing industries
Silk flower distributor
Silk folage assembly, distributor
Tropical silk flower arrangements
Retail, wholesail, commercial
Tropical artificial palms
Basket wholesale, detail
Ship worldwide

Silver & Co., Inc., Fred
145 Sussex Ave
Newark, NJ 07103-3220
Contact: David McFadden, GM
Telephone: 973-621-8848
Fax: 973-621-8037
Email: thnkmirror@aol.com / URL:
Product Service Description:
Mirror, Safety & Security

Silver Lite Trailers Inc
1291 S A St
Springfield, OR 97477-5214
Contact: Dave Hyland, Pres.
Telephone: 541-744-1215
Fax: 541-744-9277
Email: silverlite@pacwest.net / URL: http://
www.silverlite.com
Product Service Description:
Manufactures horse, stock and car carrier
trailers
Transportation equipment
Travel trailers & campers

Silver Meadow Honey
PO Box 428
Aguila, AZ 85320-0428
Contact: Charles Robson, Owner
Telephone: 520-685-2439
Fax: 520-685-2343
Email: / URL:
Product Service Description:
Wholesales honey & hive products - pollen,
propolis & royal jelly

Silver Needles
938 Austin Ln Ste 201
Honolulu, HI 96817-4574
Contact: Lee Dunning, Owner & Sales Mgr.
Telephone: 808-841-2231
Fax: 808-842-1182
Email: / URL:
Product Service Description:
Clothing_men's & boys'
Outerwear_women's & misses'
Outerwear_girl's & children's
Swimwear - men's & boys' & women & girls
Aloha fashions - men's & boys' & women &
girls

Silveron Industries Inc
182 S Brent Cir
Walnut, CA 91789-3050
Contact: Steve Lee, Pres.
Telephone: 909-598-4533
Fax: 909-594-9234
Email: silv@worldnet.att.net / URL:
Product Service Description:
Military Contractor
Milspec Electro/Mechanical Components
Mil/Cable Harness Assy.

Simon Candy Co.
31 N Spruce St
Elizabethtown, PA 17022-1936
Contact: Andrew Deck, Project Manager
Telephone: 717-367-2441
Fax: 717-367-4055
Email: andyd@joelinc.com / URL: http://
www.joelinc.com
Product Service Description:
Hard candy

Simonds Mfg. Corp.
304 Progress Rd
Auburndale, FL 33823-2711
Contact: Thomas C. Leavey, Pres., Fin. & R
& D Mgr.
Telephone: 941-967-8566
Fax: 941-967-8538
Email: / URL:
Product Service Description:
Incinerators medical waste
Incinerators - municipal waste
Waste to energy systems
Incinerators - pathological waste
Crematories

Simpson Tool Box Co
2440 W Mcdowell Rd
Phoenix, AZ 85009-2909
Contact: Marc Faigus, Pres.
Telephone: 602-269-5769
Fax: 602-352-0042
Email: mail@stbtrucks.com / URL: http://
www.stbtrucks.com
Product Service Description:
Warehouses and distributes pickup truck
accessories & van equipment
Motor vehicle supplies & new parts
Auto & home supply stores
General warehousing & storage
New & Used Truck Dealerships

Sims Bait Mfg. Co.
20 Commerce Ave
Hueytown, AL 35023-2851
Contact: Steve Sims, Pres.
Telephone: 205-497-1102
Fax: 205-497-1064
Email: s.g.sims@worldnet.att.net / URL:
Product Service Description:
Soft Plastic fishing lures: worms, lizards,
shads, & etc.

Sims Bros., Inc.
RR 3 Box 265
Union Springs, AL 36089-9499
Contact: William R. Sims, Chrm., Pres.
Telephone: 334-738-2619
Fax: 334-738-2620
Email: simsbros@ustconline.net / URL:
Product Service Description:
Harvest seed processing
Seed sales

Sinterite, Furance Div.
310 Ridgway Rd
Saint Marys, PA 15857-2616
Contact: Patrick Bown, Dir. , Mktg & Sales
Telephone: 814-834-2200
Fax: 814-834-9335
Email: furnace_sales@gasbarre.com / URL:
http://www.gasbarre.com
Product Service Description:
Continuous Belt & Industrial Furnace
Thermal Processing Furnaces
Specialty Alloy Fabrication Services

Sioux Chief Manufacturing Co.,Inc.
24110 South Peculiar Drive
Peculiar, MO 64078
Contact: Don A. Gooch, Mgr., Intl. Bus. Dev.
Telephone: 816-779-6104
Fax: 816-758-4071
Email: dgooch@worldnet.att.net / URL: http:/
/www.siouxchief@msn.com
Product Service Description:
Water Hammer Arresters
Brass, Copper, & Plastic Injection Molded
Plumbing Products
Pipe & Fittings-Fabricated

**Sioux City Brick & Tile Co.,
Sergeant Bluff Plt.**
PO Box 763
Sioux City, IA 51102-0763
Contact: Steve Lithe, Customer Service
Telephone: 712-258-6571
Fax: 712-252-3215
URL: http://www.siouxcitybrick.com
Product Service Description:
Brick
Concrete block & brick
Structural Glazed Tile : Clay Roffing Tile
Masonry Products : Cleaning Products

Sipcam Agro USA, Inc.
70 Mansell Ct, Suite 230
Roswell, GA 30076-4807
Contact: Fred Hallemann, Pres.,
Telephone: 770-587-1032
Fax: 770-587-1115
Email: / URL:
Product Service Description:
Agricultural chemicals

Siplast Inc.
1111 Hwy. 67 S.
Arkadelphia, AR 71923
Contact: Greg Faherty, Pres.
Telephone: 870-246-8095
Fax: 870-246-6768
Email: communication@siplast.com / URL:
http://www.siplast.com
Product Service Description:
Roofing & waterproofing materials
Asphalt felts & coatings
Lightweight insulating concrete

Sirex Pulse Hydraulic Systems
PO Box 10127
Prescott, AZ 86304-0127
Contact: Helmut E Sieke, Pres.
Telephone: 520-759-2943
Fax: 520-759-2944
Email: sirex@sieke.de / URL:
Product Service Description:
Manufactures backhoe attachments for the
construction industry : Construction & Mining
Machinery : Test Equipment : Waste - Water
Treatment Systems

Sirex, Ltd.
475 Northern Blvd., Ste.36
Great Neck, NY 11021-4802
Contact: Raymond F. Finel, President
Telephone: 516-829-4444
Fax: 516-829-6352
Email: sirex@idt.net / URL:
Product Service Description:
Construction Equipment & Parts
Oilfield Equipment & Parts

Sitma U S A, Inc.
45 Empire Dr
Saint Paul, MN 55103-1856
Contact: Pete Butikis, Pres.
Telephone: 651-222-2324
Fax: 651-222-4652
Email: sitmausa@worldnet.att.net / URL:
http://www.sitmagroup.com
Product Service Description:
Packaging equipment
Packaging machinery

Six-Eleven Ltd Inc
PO Box 15489
North Hollywood, CA 91615-5489
Contact: George Gruber, Pres.
Telephone: 818-764-5810
Fax: 818-764-3501
Product Service Description:
Manufactures and distributes cast polymer
bath products and tubs (sales support office)
Custom whirlpool bathing tubs & pools

Sixnel Sheet Metal
5415 Nw 15th St Ste 6
Pompano Beach, FL 33063-3712
Contact: Eddy Lanberti, Pres.
Phone: 954-970-0409 / Fax: 954-971-4601
Email: sixnel@ibm.net
Product Service Description:
Sheet metal fabrication : Sheet metal work
Milling Machinery

Skaps Industries, Inc.
571 Industrial Park Way
Commerce, GA 30529-1326
Contact: Perry Vyas, Pres.
Telephone: 706-336-7000
Fax: 706-336-7007
Email: skaps@negia.net / URL: http://
www.skaps.com
Product Service Description:
Geonet & Geo Composite Product

Skatell's Jewelers
743 Congaree Rd.
Greenville, SC 29607-3559
Contact: Anthony Skatell, Owner
Telephone: 864-288-2501
Fax: 864-675-9733
Email: foursees@skatellsjewelers.com / URL:
http://www.skatellsjewelers.com
Product Service Description:
Diamond & Platinum Jewelry, Precious
Gemstones : Black Tahitian Pearl, 18K Gold,
14K Gold Sterling

Skechers USA Inc
228 Manhattan Beach Blvd
Manhattan Beach, CA 90266-5347
Contact: Robert Greenberg, Chrm.
Telephone: 310-318-3100
Fax: 310-318-5019
Email: / URL: http://www.skechers.com
Product Service Description:
Footwear

Ski Co Inc
PO Box 417
Sun Valley, ID 83353-0417
Contact: Bobbie Burns, Pres.
Telephone: 208-622-3200
Fax: 208-622-4488
Email: / URL:
Product Service Description:
Manufactures skis The Ski
Bobbie Burns, Clothing

Sky Mfg. Co.
100 Production Ct
New Britain, CT 06051-2914
Contact: Joseph Tierpack, Pres.
Telephone: 860-229-1312
Fax: 860-224-3585
Email: skymfg1@yahoo.com / URL:
Product Service Description:
Helicopter parts & assemblies

Sloan & Assocs. Inc., Leonard
2720 Manor Way
Dallas, TX 75235-5616
Contact: Leonard Sloan, CEO, Sales Mgr.
Telephone: 214-350-2440
Fax: 214-350-2355
Email: lsainc.onramp.net / URL: http://
www.leonardsloan.com
Product Service Description:
Embroidery & screen printing
Automotive & apparel trimmings
Pleating & stitching

**Slosson Educational Publications,
Inc.**
PO Box 280
East Aurora, NY 14052-0280
Contact: Steven W. Slosson, Pres.
Telephone: 716-652-0930
Fax: 716-655-3840
Email: slosson@slosson.com / URL: http://
www.slosson.com
Product Service Description:
Educational publication printing

Smart Industries
1626 Delaware Avenue
Des Moines, IA 50317
Contact: Jeff Smart, Vice President
Telephone: 515/265-9900
Fax: 515-265-3148
Email: / URL:
Product Service Description:
Auto. Vending Mach., Amusement/Games

Smart Products Inc
1710 Ringwood Ave
San Jose, CA 95131-1711
Contact: Alex Romo, Sales
Telephone: 408-436-0740
Fax: 408-436-0744
Email: sales@smartproducts.com / URL:
http://www.smartproducts.com
Product Service Description:
Check valves for flow control (for low
pressure, low flow gas or liquid applications)
Pressure relief valves
Liquid, air & vacuum diaphragm pumps (for
low pressure, low flow applications)

Smart Sensors Inc.
14803 Park Almeda Dr
Houston, TX 77047-7005
Contact: Buck France, V-P.
Telephone: 713-433-2222
Fax: 713-433-3332
Email: ssijb@aol.com / URL:
Product Service Description:
Temperature sensors

Smarts Broadcast Systems
P.O. BOX 284
Emmetsburg, IA 50536-0284
Contact: David Potratz, Sales Manager
Telephone: 712-852-4047
Fax: 712-852-3061
Email: smarts@ncn.net / URL:
Product Service Description:
Radio Station Automation Equipment

Smiland Paint Company
620 Lamar St.
Los Angeles, CA 90031
Contact: Steve Shelburne, VP Int'l Sales
Telephone: 323-222-7616 X. 231
Fax: 323-222-8606
Email: spcintldiv@aol.com / URL: http://
www.morwear.com
Product Service Description:
Paints and Allied Products

**Smirnoff Communications Group,
Inc.**
3581 Kachemak Circle, Suite B
Anchorage, AK 99515-2337
Contact: Steve R. Smirnoff, Director
Telephone: 907-349-5481
Fax: 907-522-1489
Email: bahamas@alaska.net / URL: http://
www.wwte.com/carib/bahamas4.htm
Product Service Description:
Marketing Consulting Services
Business Brokering Services
Int'l Public Relations

Smith & Loveless, Inc.
14040 Santa Fe Trail Dr.
Lenexa, KS 66215-1234
Contact: Stuart B. Marschall, Int'l Div. Pres.
Phone: 913-888-5201 / Fax: 913-888-2173
Email: answers@smithandloveless.com /
URL: http://www.smithandloveless.com
Product Service Description:
Water & Wastewater Treatment Equipment

Smith & Nephew Inc.
1450 E. Brooks Rd.
Memphis, TN 38116-1804
Contact: Larry W. Papasan, President
Telephone: 901-396-2121
Fax: 901-332-7289
Email: / URL:
Product Service Description:
Surgical Apparatus
Medical Apparatus
Ear Surgical Supplies
Orthopedic Supplies
Orthopedic Instruments

Smith & Nephew United, Inc., Orthopaedic Divsion
1400 E. Brooks Rd.
Memphis, TN 38116-1892
Contact: Larry W. Papasan, Pres.
Telephone: 901-396-2121
Fax: 901-399-6151
Email: ortho@smithnephew.com / URL: http:/
/www.smithnephew.com
Product Service Description:
Orthopedic & Prosthetic Applicances
Surgical Appliances & Supplies

Smith Eng & Environmental Corp
2837 E Cedar St
Ontario, CA 91761-8515
Contact: Sean Gribbon,
Telephone: 909-673-9369
Fax: 909-947-2006
Email: sgribbon@smitheng.com / URL: http://
www.smithenv.com
Product Service Description:
VOC, air toxicity and odor control systems
for industry

Smith Equipment USA Inc
PO Box 3487
Bozeman, MT 59772-3487
Contact: Frank Smith, Pres., Kim Wild, VP
Telephone: 406-388-3424
Fax: 406-388-1925
Email: towhaul@theglobal.net / URL: http://
www.towhaul.com
Product Service Description:
Designs and manufactures heavy equipment
and open pit mining trailers for worldwide use
Mining machinery
Trucks & tractors_industrial

Smith Fiberglass Products Company
2700 W. 65th St.
Little Rock, AR 72209
Contact: S.B. Jones, Manager, Marketing
Services
Telephone: 501-568-4010
Fax: 501-568-4465
Email: sjones@aosmith.com / URL: http://
www.smithfiberglass.com
Product Service Description:
Fiberglass Reinforced Pipe Systems

Smith Systems, Inc.
PO Box 667
Brevard, NC 28712-0667
Contact: Claire Smith, V-P.
Telephone: 828-884-3490
Fax: 828-877-3100
Email: / URL: http://www.smith-systems-
inc.com
Product Service Description:
Speed, temperature & motion sensors

Smoke Guard Corporation
PO Box 2275
Boise, ID 83701-2275
Contact: Frank Hertzog, VP Sales & Mktg.
Telephone: 208-383-3789
Fax: 208-376-1600
Email: fhertzog@smokeguard.com / URL:
http://www.smokeguard.com
Product Service Description:
Manufactures tight fitting smoke - and draft-
control assemblies for elevator hoisway doors
This rolling magnetic gasketing system adapts
well to tight spaces, provides for minimal
disruption of the architects aesthetic design

Smoot Co.
PO Box 3337
Kansas City, KS 66103-0337
Contact: Patty Shroeder, Marketing Director
Telephone: 913-362-1710
Fax: 913-362-7863
Email: mktg@smootco.com / URL: http://
www.smootco.com
Product Service Description:
Pneumatic conveyor systems
Conveyors & conveying equipment

Snyder Equipment Co., Inc.
PO Box 381
Nixa, MO 65714-0381
Contact: Joseph M. Nusbaumer, Chrm.
Telephone: 417-725-4067
Fax: 417-725-4846
Email: info@snyderequip.com / URL: http://
www.snyderequip.com
Product Service Description:
Locomotive Fueling & Servicing Equipment
Automatic Diesel Locomotive Fueling
Fuel Management Control Systems
Fuel & Lube Oil Pumping Systems
Transit Sanitary Water Cabinets
Custom Fabrication

Snyders of Hanover
P.O. Box 917
Hanover, PA 17331-6917
Contact: Sales & Marketing,
Telephone: 717-632-4477
Fax: 717-632-7207
Email: consumeraffairs@snyders-han.com /
URL: http://www.snydersofhanover.com
Product Service Description:
Pretzels, Potato Chips, Tortilla Chips

Software Integrators
51 Evergreen Dr Ste A
Bozeman, MT 59715-2458
Contact: Joseph McCarthy, Pres.
Telephone: 406-586-8866
Fax: 406-586-9145
Email: / URL: http://www.si87.com
Product Service Description:
Computer peripheral equipment
Manufactures computer graphics cards

Soil Purification Inc.
PO Box 72787
Chattanooga, TN 37407
Contact: Wendell Feltman, Vice President,
Shadi Nikfarjam, Applications Engineer
Telephone: 423-867-4210
Fax: 423-867-1550
Email: / URL:
Product Service Description:
Thermal Treatment Equipment
Incineration Equipment
Soil Stabilization Equipment

Soil Technologies Corp.
2103 185th St.
Fairfield, IA 52556-9232
Contact: Sales & Marketing,
Telephone: 515-472-3963
Fax: 515-472-6189
Email: soiltech@lisco.com / URL: http://
www.lisco.com/soiltech
Product Service Description:
Biopesticides
Growth Stimulants

Solar Color Chemical Corp.
180 River Rd
Edgewater, NJ 07020-1003
Contact: Randy Stasi, Pres.
Telephone: 201-945-5775
Fax: 201-945-6778
Email: / URL:
Product Service Description:
Screen printing ink
Ink_printing

Solarex
630 Solarex Ct
Frederick, MD 21703-8624
Contact: Sarah Howell, Media & Govt.
Relations
Telephone: 301-698-4200
Fax: 301-698-4201
Email: info@solarex.com / URL: http://
www.solarex.com
Product Service Description:
Solar panels
Semiconductors & related devices

Solaronics, Inc.
704 Wood Ward, P.o. Box 217
Rochester, MI 48063
Contact: T.D. Lester, Vice President
Telephone: 248-651-5333
Fax: 248-651-0357
Email: sales@solaronicsusa.com / URL: http:/
/www.solaronicsusa.com
Product Service Description:
Infra-Red Space Heaters, Gas Fired
Infra-Red Burners, Gas Fired, N.e.c.

Solbern Div. Howden Food Eqip.
8 Kulick Road
Fairfield, NJ 07004-3308
Contact: Gil Foulon, President
Telephone: 973-227-3030
Fax: 973-227-3069
Email: sales@solbern.com / URL: http://
www.solbern.com
Product Service Description:
Food Products Machinery

Solid State Electronics Corp
18646 Parthenia St
Northridge, CA 91324-4027
Contact: Edward Y Politi, Pres.
Telephone: 818-993-8257
Fax: 818-993-8259
Email: / URL:
Product Service Description:
Manufactures FM telemetering equipment,
FM transceivers, wireless computer
networking and data acquisition
Radio & TV communications equipment
Process control instruments
Telephone & telegraph apparatus
Trasnsistors, diodes, semiconductors
Solid state relays
Frequency - to - voltage converters
Radar FM Discriminators
Solid state & electromechanical choppers
Spread - spectrum radiomodems

Soliman Brothers
3816 Pine Creek Cir.
New Albany, IN 47150-3317
Contact: Wadie Soliman, Owner
Telephone: 812-752-5276
Fax: 812-752-2268
Email: / URL:
Product Service Description:
Lumber
Logs
Veneer

Solo Enterprise Corporation
220 California Ave
City Of Industry, CA 91744-4323
Contact: Richard Mugica, Pres.
Telephone: 626-961-3591
Fax: 626-968-3320
Email: / URL: http://www.sologolf.com
Product Service Description:
Manufactures aircraft and precision machined
aerospace parts; golf products
Aircraft parts & equipment
Sporting & athletic goods

Soluol Chemical Co., Inc.
Green Hill & Market Sts., P.O. Box 112
West Warwick, RI 02893
Contact: Warren J. Simmons, President
Telephone: 401-821-8100
Fax: 401-823-6673
Email: / URL:
Product Service Description:
Polyurethane Coating Compounds

Somat Company (Mfr)
855 Fox Chase
Coatesville, PA 19320
Contact: Charles P. Bozym, *
Telephone: 610-384-7000
Fax: 610-380-8500
Email: somatcorp@aol.com / URL: http://
www.somatcorp.com
Product Service Description:
Waste Reduction Systems
Dewatering Systems
Food Processing Dewatering Equipment

Sonic Corp.
1 Research Dr
Stratford, CT 06615
Contact: Bill Brakeman, Pres.
Telephone: 203-375-0063
Fax: 203-378-4079
Email: brakemanw@aol.com / URL: http://
www.sonicmixing.com
Product Service Description:
Industrial & standard propeller mixers &
colloid mills
Food products machinery
Ultrasonic Homogenizers
Ultrasonic Dispersers
High Pressure Pumping Systems
In Line Blending Systems
High Pressure Homogenizers
PLC Controlled Mixing & Blending Systems

Sonnenberg & Anderson
200 S. Wacker Drive, 38th Floor
Chicago, IL 60606
Contact: Steven P. Sonnenberg, Partner
Telephone: 312-441-1700
Fax: 312-441-1701
Email: sonnander@aol.com / URL:
Product Service Description:
Legal Services, Customs & International
Trade Law

Sonora Desert Trading Co
PO Box 12308
Scottsdale, AZ 85267-2308
Contact: Michael Hanna, Pres.
Telephone: 602-483-8927
Fax: 602-991-4419
Email: aznatural@aol.com / URL:
arizonanatural.com
Product Service Description:
Mailorder distribution of vitamin supplements

Sonstegard Foods Company
707 E 41st St, Ste 222
Sioux Falls, SD 57105-6050
Contact: Philip Sonstegard, President
Telephone: 605-338-4642
Fax: 605-338-9765
Email: eggs@sdicybernex.net / URL: http://
www.sonstegard.com
Product Service Description:
Egg Products, Dried, Frozen & Liquid

Sooner Trailer Mfg. Co., Inc.
1515 Mccurdy Rd
Duncan, OK 73533-8722
Contact: Jim Callaway, Pres.
Telephone: 580-255-6979
Fax: 580-255-9783
Email: sooner@soonertrailers.com / URL:
http://www.soonertrailers.com
Product Service Description:
Aluminum horse, cattle, hog, cargo, utility &
trailers
Truck trailers

Sorbilite Inc.
1569A Diamond Springs Road
Virginia Beach, VA 23455
Contact: Brigit Pohl, *
Telephone: 757-464-3564
Fax: 757-464-5493
Email: sales@sorbilite.com / URL: http://
www.sorbilite.com
Product Service Description:
Woodworking Machinery, Hi-Pressure
Recyclers
Woodworking Membrane Presses
Plastic Recycling Hi-Pressure Press

Source W Printing
One Stewart Station Drive
Trafford, PA 15085
Contact: Terri L. Marts, President, Ron
Dandrea, VP Marketing & Sales
Telephone: 412-829-6345
Fax: 412-829-6321
Email: martst1@soruce-w.com /
dandrera@source-w.com / URL: http://
www.source-w.com
Product Service Description:
Communications Consultation & Solutions
Interactive Media/Web Application
Development
Visual & Graphic Design / Digital Printing
Commercial Printing / Warehousing &
Distribution Services

South American Dental Exports
1058 E. 33rd St.
Hialeah, FL 33013-3526
Contact: Oscar Lopez, Owner
Telephone: 305-693-8626
Fax: 305-693-8630
Email: rite-dent@ruonline.net / URL:
Product Service Description:
Dental instruments, materials & supplies that
apply to the
Dental sciences, wholesale quantities &
prices

South Beach Fire Services
6619 S Dixie Hwy Ste 182
Miami, FL 33143-7919
Contact: Ali Hosein, Owner
Telephone: 954-435-4485
Fax: 954-441-3330
Email: / URL: http://www.sobefire.com
Product Service Description:
Fire retardant products
Chemical preparations

South Pasadena Publishing Co
PO Box 310
South Pasadena, CA 91031-0310
Contact: William Ericson, Pres.
Telephone: 323-682-1412
Product Service Description:
Publishes and prints weekly newspaper and
quarterly magazine; financial and commercial
printing
Newspapers
Periodicals
Printing_commercial

South Pass Trading/CNL Clothiers
50 E Main St
South Pass City, WY 82520-3404
Contact: Connie N Lindmier, Pres., GM
Telephone: 307-332-6810
Fax: 307-332-5298
Email: info@cnlclothiers.com / URL: http://
www.cnlclothiers.com
Product Service Description:
Manufactures historic 1880s cowboy pommel
slickers and clothing (corporate office)
Waterproof outerwear
Clothing_men's & boys'
Outerwear_women's & misses'

Southco, Inc.
210 N. Brinton Lake Rd.
Concordville, PA 19331
Contact: L.A. Stevens, Tech Writer
Telephone: 610-459-4000
Fax: 610-459-4012
Email: info@southco.com / URL: http://
www.southco.com
Product Service Description:
Fasteners, latches, hinges & rivets

Southern Calif Guide-Westworld
11385 Exposition Blvd # 102
Los Angeles, CA 90064-3014
Contact: Valerie Summers, Pres.
Telephone: 310-391-8255
Fax: 310-391-8255
Email: scgvalerie@aol.com / URL: http://
www.scguIDE.com
Product Service Description:
Publishes monthly magazine including world
wide travel features
Periodicals

Southern Church Envelope Co.
PO Box 1527
Venice, FL 34284-1527
Contact: Phillip King, Sales Mgr.
Telephone: 941-488-3095
Fax: 941-484-0133
Email: / URL: http://
www.envelopeservice.com
Product Service Description:
Church offering, microfiche & commercial
envelopes
Envelopes

Southern Mausoleums, Inc.
PO Box 279
Elberton, GA 30635-0279
Contact: Alan Skelton, GM & Sales Mgr.
Telephone: 706-283-8228
Fax: 706-283-8534
Email: / URL:
Product Service Description:
Granite burial monuments & mausoleums

Southern Truck Equipment Inc
PO Box 21536
Phoenix, AZ 85036-1536
Contact: Darvin Moore, President
Telephone: 602-437-1145
Fax: 602-437-6298
Email: southernTE@aol.com / URL: http://
www.southerntruck.com
Product Service Description:
Manufactures truck bodies and equipment

Southern Turf Nurseries(Mfr)
P.O. Box 230
Brookfield, GA 31727
Contact: Don Roberts, General Manager
Telephone: 912-382-5655
Fax: 912-382-5301
Email: donrobts@ix.netcom.com / URL:
http://www.southernturft.com
Product Service Description:
Turfgrass

Southern Warehouse Corporation
P.O. Box 19160,
Houston, TX 77224-9160
Contact: Dan Verburg, Vice President
Telephone: 713-895-0101
Fax: 713-895-7122
Email: / URL: http://www.southernwhse.com
Product Service Description:
Warehousing & Distribution
Freight & Cargo Transportation

Southland Printing Company, Inc.
213 Airport Drive P.O. Box 7263
Shreveport, LA 71137
Contact: John A. Manno Sr., President
Telephone: 318-221-8662
Fax: 318-221-8738
Email: info@southlandprinting.com / URL:
http://www.southlandprinting.com
Product Service Description:
Parking Tickets (Magnetic, Bar Code, Jumbo
#'s

Southport Machine Inc
PO Box 701
Bonita, CA 91908-0701
Contact: Brian Maloney, Pres.
Telephone: 619-661-5543
Fax: 619-661-5562
Email: southportmachine@funtv.com / URL:
Product Service Description:
Manufactures and repairs metal, steel and
aluminum machine parts for the aerospace
and naval industries

Southwest Metal Fabricators, Inc.
3015 N 114th St
Milwaukee, WI 53222-4208
Contact: John Morin, Pres.
Telephone: 414-771-4877
Fax: 414-771-6062
Email: bigpress@mixcom.com / URL:
Product Service Description:
Metal stampings & fabrication
Metal stampings : Metal products_fabricated
Tooling : Prototyping

Southwest Peterbilt GMC
2600 W Mcdowell Rd
Phoenix, AZ 85009-2973
Contact: John Donahue,
Telephone: 602-272-7611
Fax: 602-352-5729
Email: jdonahue@southwestpeterbilt.com /
URL: http://www.southwestpeterbilt.com
Product Service Description:
Sells new and used trucks; parts and services
for semi trucks
Automobiles & other motor vehicles
Motor vehicle supplies & new parts
General Heavy Duty Repair Shop

Southwest Photovoltaic Systems
212 E Main St
Tomball, TX 77375-6753
Contact: Marshall Blalock Jr., Pres.
Telephone: 281-351-0031
Fax: 281-351-8356
Email: southwestpv.com / URL: http://
www.southwestpv.com
Product Service Description:
Solar electric modules & components
Solar lighting & electric systems &
enclosures : Home power systems
Water pumping systems

Southwest Power Systems, Inc.
P.O. Box 561104
Dallas, TX 75356
Contact: David Muir, *
Telephone: 972-438-5200
Fax: 972-438-5254
Product Service Description:
Circuit Breakers

Southwest Storage
1 N 59th Ave
Phoenix, AZ 85043-3500
Contact: Susan Donahue, V-P., Sales
Telephone: 602-233-3296
Fax: 602-269-1742
Email: swstgdist1@aol.com / URL: http://
www.sw-stg-dist.com
Product Service Description:
Public warehousing; distributes dry, frozen,
and refrigerated foods
Refrigerated warehousing & storage
Line item order selection
Distribution with store door delivery

**Southwestern Automation Systems,
Inc.**
5055 S 33rd St
Phoenix, AZ 85040-2816
Contact: John Philippi, Pres., CEO
Telephone: 602-276-7022
Fax: 602-276-0240
Email: info@sas-controls.com / URL: http://
www.sas-controls.com
Product Service Description:
Distributes PLC's & electrical, pneumatic,
temperature & motion controls, coveyors
Industrial machinery & equipment &
conveyors

Southwestern Process Supply Co.
PO Box 1033
Tulsa, OK 74101-1033
Contact: Claudia C. Hamilton, Pres.
Telephone: 918-582-8211
Fax: 918-582-0066
Email: swprocess@aol.com / URL: http://
www.southwesternprocess.com
Product Service Description:
Screen printing screens, supplies &
equipment

Sozio, Inc., J. E.
19 Progress St
Edison, NJ 08820-1102
Contact: Robert Frantzen, General Mgr.
Telephone: 908-755-7488
Product Service Description:
Fragrances
Toilet preparations

Space Coast General Contractors Inc.
PO Box 3618
Cocoa, FL 32924-3618
Contact: Susan Johnson, Pres.
Telephone: 407-632-9440
Fax: 407-632-9566
Product Service Description:
Aluminum & steel fabrication
Structural metal_fabricated : Steel Sales

Spacelabs Medical Inc
PO Box 97013
Redmond, WA 98073-9713
Contact: Randy Miskimon, VP Intl,
Operations
Telephone: 425-882-3700
Fax: 425-885-4877
Email: / URL: http://www.spacelabs.com
Product Service Description:
Electromedical equipment
Manufactures and services patient monitoring
and clinical information systems
Medical & hospital equipment

Spacewall International
PO Box 659
Stone Mountain, GA 30086
Contact: Gary Mills, President
Telephone: 404-294-9564
Fax: 404-297-7389
Email: / URL: http://www.spacewall-usa.com
Product Service Description:
Store Fixtures & Accessories
Manufactures slot walls store fixtures

Spalding Products
4788 Hwy. 42
Ellenwood, GA 30049
Contact: Gary Thompson, Plt. Mgr.
Telephone: 404-366-8575
Fax: 404-366-8575
Email: / URL:
Product Service Description:
Shuttle buses : Truck & bus bodies
Custom fiberglass & ABS Parts

Spanset, Inc.
PO Box 2828
Sanford, NC 27331-2828
Contact: Robert S. Jasany, Pres.
Telephone: 919-774-6316
Fax: 919-775-5414
Email: Info@spanset-usa.com / URL: http://
www.spanset-usa.com
Product Service Description:
Cargo straps & nets, overhead lifting systems
& woven narrow fabrics : Textile products,
fabricated : Narrow fabric mills

Sparks Industries
PO Box 638, 404 N Columbia Ave
Sheffield, AL 35660-3047
Contact: David L. Haygood, VP Operations
Telephone: 256-381-3524
Fax: 256-381-3525
Email: dhaygood@sparksindustries.com /
URL: http://www.sparksindustries.com
Product Service Description:
Flexible PVC Profiles / T-mold

Speak Easy Languages
757 South Main Street
Plymouth, MI 48170-2046
Contact: Cristina Clark, President
Telephone: 734-459-5556
Fax: 734-459-1460
Email: selanguages@earthlink.net / URL:
Product Service Description:
Translations Services, All Languages

Spec-Temp, Inc.
5406 Us Route 24
Antwerp, OH 45813-9458
Contact: Ray DeLong, Russ Rernhart
Telephone: 419-258-5531
Fax: 419-258-9411
Email: spectemp@bright.net / URL: http://
www.spectemp.com
Product Service Description:
Flat & curved glass tempering & fabrication

Specialty Equipment Co.
1221 Adkins Rd
Houston, TX 77055-6406
Contact: Mike Seiver, Pres,, Robert Love, VP
Telephone: 713-467-1818
Fax: 713-467-9130
Email: info@specialtyequipment.com / URL:
http://www.specialtyequipment.com
Product Service Description:
Conveyors & conveying equipment
Industrial conveyors
Drum filling systems
Liquid filling
Solids filling
Palletizers
Gantry robots

Specialty Extrusion Corp
1580 Kimberly Ave
Fullerton, CA 92831-5213
Contact: George Wright, GM
Telephone: 714-525-4934
Fax: 714-525-5480
Email: n77sd@aol.com / URL:
Product Service Description:
Aluminum extruded products
Manufactures aluminum extruded products

Specified Technologies, Inc.
200 Evans Way
Somerville, NJ 08876-3767
Contact: Charbell Tagher, Pres.
Telephone: 908-526-8000, 800-992-1180
Fax: 908-526-9623
Email: specseal@stifirestop.com / URL: http:/
/www.stifirestop.com
Product Service Description:
Firestopping materials

Spectral Energy Corp.
67 Woodland Ave
Westwood, NJ 07675-3114
Contact: Harry Beck, Pres.
Telephone: 201-664-0876
Fax: 201-664-1214
Email: sales@spectralenergy.com / URL:
http://www.spectralenergy.com
Product Service Description:
Short Arc Lamp Souces
Short Arc Lamp Power Supplies
Monochromators
Solar Simulators
Photomultiplier
High Intensity Monochromatic Illumination
Systems
Deaterium Sources
Fiber Optic Illuminators

Spectrapure Inc
738 S Perry Ln Ste 1
Tempe, AZ 85281-8810
Contact: Charles W Mitsis, Pres.
Telephone: 602-894-5437
Fax: 602-894-6109
Email: / URL:
Product Service Description:
Manufactures water purification equipment
for commercial, household aquariums &
laboratories

Spectrascan International Inc
2812 E Bijou St Ste 102
Colorado Springs, CO 80909-6310
Contact: Jan C Hoigaard, Pres.
Telephone: 719-447-0170
Fax: 719-447-0186
Email: spectrascan@cwix.com / URL: http://
www.spectrascan.net
Product Service Description:
Manufactures manual & automated static
control equipment

Spectrex Corp
3580 Haven Ave
Redwood City, CA 94063-4603
Contact: John M Hoyte, Pres.
Telephone: 650-365-6567
Fax: 650-365-5845
Email: spectrex@spectrex.com / URL: http://
www.spectrex.com
Product Service Description:
Manufactures spectroscopes, electronic gas-
sampling pumps and laser particle counters

Spectro Coating Corp.(Mfr)
Scott Drive, P.O. Box 578
Leominster, MA 01453
Contact: Hemendra K. Shah, President
Telephone: 508/534-1800
Fax: 508-534-4155
Email: flock@spectrocoating.com / URL:
http://www.spectrocoating.com
Product Service Description:
Coated Fabrics, Not Rubberized
Flocked Fabrics
Flocked Suedes & Velvets

Spectrum Aeromed, Inc.
304 4th St. N.
Wheaton, MN 56296
Contact: Shirley Krenz, Ex. V-P.
Telephone: 320-563-4340
Fax: 320-563-8709
Email: aeromed@traversenet.com / URL:
http://www.spectrum-aeromed.com
Product Service Description:
Aircraft quick-change modular life support
systems
Aircraft parts & equipment

Spectrum Naturals Inc
133 Copeland St Ste A
Petaluma, CA 94952-3181
Contact: Jethren Phillips, CEO
Telephone: 707-778-8900
Fax: 707-765-1026
Email: spectrumnaturals@netdex.com / URL:
http://www.spectrumnaturals.com
Product Service Description:
Manufactures organic vegetable oils,
vinegars, condiments and nutritional
supplement oils
Vegetable oil mills
Food preparations
Medicinals & botanicals

Speer Collectibles
5315 S Cobb Dr Se
Smyrna, GA 30080-7416
Contact: John Drucker, Pres., Mktg. & R &
D Mgr.
Telephone: 404-794-4000
Fax: 404-794-4569
Email: speercollectible@mindspring.com /
URL: http://www.speercollectibles.com
Product Service Description:
Lamps, mirrors & decorative accessories
Chandeliers, sconces residential &
commercial
Non electric sconces & wall brackets

Spencer & Reynolds Inc
10156 Sharon Cir
Rancho Cucamonga, CA 91730-5300
Contact: Gerald Reynolds, Pres.
Telephone: 909-466-8070
Fax: 909-466-6998
Email: spencer-reynolds@eee.org / URL:
Product Service Description:
Manufactures store fixtures
Partitions & fixtures_wood

Spira Manufacturing Corp
12721 Saticoy St S Ste B
North Hollywood, CA 91605-3522
Contact: Anthony Bazan, Operations
Manager
Telephone: 818-764-8222
Fax: 818-764-9880
Email: anthony@spira-emi.com / URL: http://
www.spira-emi.com
Product Service Description:
Manufactures EMI/RFI environmental seals
Electronic components
Airvents, shielded
VME Configurations

Spiral-Helix, Inc.
PO Box 6187
Buffalo Grove, IL 60089-6187
Contact: Jan Jorfald, Pres.
Telephone: 847-537-3410
Fax: 847-537-2343
Email: / URL: http://www.spihel.com
Product Service Description:
Spiral Duct Machinery

Split Tee
10620 Lawson River Ave
Fountain Valley, CA 92708-6913
Contact: Brad Butler, Pres.
Telephone: 714-378-3838
Fax: 714-378-3850
Email: splittee@earthlink.net / URL:
Product Service Description:
Clothing_men's & boys'
Mens Gifts

Spradling Originals Inc.
PO Box 96
Trussville, AL 35173-0096
Contact: Chuck Massey, Sales Mgr.
Telephone: 205-655-7404
Fax: 205-655-7406
Email: / URL:
Product Service Description:
Automotive trim & plastic extrusions
Plastic products
Cord welt
Morine zippers

Sprague Controls Inc
1140 NW 3rd Ave
Canby, OR 97013-3441
Contact: Don Gilkison, Fin. Mgr.
Telephone: 503-263-3350
Fax: 503-263-0532
Email: scioregon@canby.com / URL:
Product Service Description:
Designs and manufactures controls and
actuators for the commercial vehicle industry
Fluid power cylinders & actuators
Motor vehicle parts & accessories
Motor vehicle supplies & new parts

Spray Masters Inc.
115 East Linden Street
Rogers, AR 72756-6035
Contact: Robert Sage, Vice President
Telephone: 501-636-5776
Fax: 501-636-3245
Email: bobsage@assembledproducts.com /
Product Service Description:
Ind. High Pressure Cleaning Equipment

Spray Products Corp.
P.O. Box 737
Norristown, PA 19404-0737
Contact: Andrew A. Orr, President
Telephone: 610-277-1010
Fax: 610-277-4390
Email: / URL:
Product Service Description:
Aerosol Paint
Automotive Chemicals

Spring Valley Mfg., Inc.
3107 170th St
New Sharon, IA 50207-8221
Contact: Kevin Flander, Pres.
Telephone: 515-632-8365
Fax: 515-632-8224
Email: / URL:
Product Service Description:
Motor vehicle parts & accessories

Springsoft International Inc.
122 E. Lake Street
Bloomingdale, IL 60108-1127
Contact: Craig Browark, President
Telephone: 708-894-5000
Fax: 708-894-9999
Product Service Description:
Water Treatment Co.
Drinking Water Purification & Water
Softening
Water Filtration
Water Clorination & Disinfection
Ultra Pure De I Water
Reverse Osmosis Systems
Counter Top Water Filters
Portable Water Purification
Global Water Dealers & Service
Product Engineering for Water Treatment

Sprint Rothhammer
PO Box 3840
San Luis Obispo, CA 93403-3840
Contact: Dianne Rothhammer, Chairman
Telephone: 805-541-5330
Fax: 805-541-5339
Email: info@sprintaquatics.com / URL: http://
www.sprintaquatics.com
Product Service Description:
Manufactures, distributes and sells water
sports accessories— goggles, caps, kick
boards & etc.
Aquatic rehabilitation equipment
Aquatic / pool equipment
Aquatic aqua aerobics

Sprint/Rothhammer
PO Box 3840
San Luis Obispo, CA 93403-3840
Contact: Diane Rothhammer,
Telephone: 805-541-5330
Fax: 805-541-5339
Email: info@sprintaquatics.com / URL:
Product Service Description:
Manufactures, distributes & sells water sports
accessories- goggles, water aerobic equipt.
Sporting & athletic goods
Sporting & recreational goods
Aquatic therapy & rehabilitation equipment &
education

St Jon Pet Care Products
1656 240th St
Harbor City, CA 90710-1311
Contact: John Nelson, Pres.
Telephone: 310-326-2720
Fax: 310-626-8026
Email: stjon@stjon.com / URL: http://
www.stjon.com
Product Service Description:
Manufactures animal health care products
Medicinals & botanicals
Companion animal dentistry

Stablewood Inc.
5102 E Fort Lowell Rd
Tucson, AZ 85712-1309
Contact: Marsha J. Willey,
Telephone: 520-325-5008
Fax: 520-318-9630
Email: mjwilley@cwix.com / URL:
Product Service Description:
Conduct private investigations, credit &
criminal histories

Stack-On Products
P.O. Box 489
Wauconda, IL 60084-0489
Contact: Jon Fiscus, *
Telephone: 847-526-1611
Fax: 847-526-6599
Email: jfiscus@stack-on.com / URL: http://
www.stack-on.com
Product Service Description:
Steel Tool Chest & Cabinets
Steel & Plastic Tool Boxes
Small Parts Storage

Stafast Roofing Products
7095 Americana Parkway Dr.
Reynoldsburg, OH 43068-4118
Contact: Sales & Marketing,
Telephone: 614-575-1257
Fax: 614-866-9805
Email: kendausa@computelnet.com / URL:
Product Service Description:
Synthetic rubber and factice derived from
oils, in primary forms or in plates, sheets or
strip
Adhesives based on rubber or plastics
Prepared glues and adhesives

Stallion Technologies Inc
2880 Research Park Dr # 160
Soquel, CA 95073-2000
Contact: Bill Kieley, Pres., CEO
Telephone: 831-477-0440
Fax: 831-477-0444
Email: info@stallion.com / URL: http://
www.stallion.com
Product Service Description:
Manufactures serial I/O and remote access
communication servers for
Intel Based Lans.

Stamped Products, Inc.
PO Box 2773
Gadsden, AL 35903
Contact: Fred Scheidweiler, GM
Telephone: 256-492-8899
Fax: 256-494-3253
Email: stamped.@cybrtyme.com / URL: http:/
/www.stamped.com
Product Service Description:
Metal stampings, automotive & heat & air
conditioning parts
Metal stampings
Metal products_fabricated

Standard Crystal Corp
9940 Baldwin Pl
El Monte, CA 91731-2295
Contact: James Zhang, Pres.
Telephone: 626-443-2121
Fax: 626-443-9049
Email: stdxtl@worldnet.att.net / URL:
Product Service Description:
Manufactures quartz crystals and oscillators
Electronic components

Standard Fusee
P.O. Box 1047
Easton, MD 21619
Contact: John F. Funchion, Sales Manager
Telephone: 410-822-0318
Fax: 410-822-7759
Email: / URL:
Product Service Description:
Safety Flares for Highway, Marine &
Railroad

Standard Pumps Inc.
3230 Industrial Way
Snellville, GA 30039-4927
Contact: Don Murphy, Pres., R & D Mgr.
Telephone: 770-972-9693
Fax: 770-972-9694
Email: standardpump@mindspring.com/ http:/
/www.standardpump.thomasregister.com
Product Service Description:
Pumps & pumping equipment

Standard Steel
500 N Walnut St
Burnham, PA 17009-1698
Contact: Richard C. Rheem, Bus. Dev. Mgr.
Telephone: 717-248-4911
Fax: 717-248-8050
Email: standard@acsworld.net / URL: http://
www.standardsteel.com
Product Service Description:
Railroad Wheels, Axles & Assemblies
Seamless Rings
Open Die Forgings
Ingots, Billets, Press Toll Conversion
Metal Formed Springs
Steel Forgings

Standard Welding Co., Inc.
212 Prospect St
East Hartford, CT 06108-1653
Contact: Richard Ashlaw, Pres.
Telephone: 860-528-9628
Fax: 860-528-9620
Email: / URL:
Product Service Description:
Welding job shop
Industrial machinery

Stanford Glassblowing Labs Inc
4017 Fabian Way
Palo Alto, CA 94303-4608
Contact: Marian Griffin, Pres.
Telephone: 650-494-2255
Fax: 650-494-0458
Email: mas2@prodigy.net / URL:
Product Service Description:
Glass distillation apparatus and custom
laboratory glassware
Glass products from purchased glass

Stanlar Industries
24 Federal Plaza
Bloomfield, NJ 07003-5636
Contact: Sales & Marketing,
Telephone: 201-680-4488
Product Service Description:
Recycled Rubber Interlocking Floor Tiles
Recycled Rubber Door Mats

Stantex
3130 Frederick Ave.
Baltimore, MD 21229-3896
Contact: Ed Grinspan, President
Telephone: 410-233-4400
Fax: 410-233-6317
Email: standardtextile@erols.com / URL:
Product Service Description:
Bed linen of textile materials, not knitted or
crocheted : Bath Towels

Star Enterprises Inc
5763 Arapahoe Ave Ste B
Boulder, CO 80303-1350
Contact: Scott Starsky, Pres.
Telephone: 303-443-0210
Fax: 303-443-0492
Email: sstarsky@aol.com / URL:
Product Service Description:
Network integration & service
Computer repair, sales; upgrades, parts

Star Styled Dancing Supplies
2220 W. 9th Ave.
Hialeah, FL 33010-2091
Contact: Clive Herman, VP
Telephone: 305-885-4135
Fax: 305-885-2384
Email: service@starstyled.com / URL: http://
www.starstyled.com
Product Service Description:
Dance Apparel & Recital Costumes
Flamenco Apparel

Starensier
5 Perkins Way, P.O. Box 408
Newburyport, MA 01950
Contact: Louis Rubenfeld, President
Telephone: 978-462-7311
Fax: 978-465-6223
Email: rubenfeld@starensier.com / URL:
Product Service Description:
Coated Fabrics, Not Rubberized
Footwear: Woven fab of syn fil yn, incl
monofil 67 dec : Woven cotton fabrics

Startel Corporation
17661 Cowan
Irvine, CA 92614-6031
Contact: Debra Roper, Mktg.
Communications Mgr.
Telephone: 949-863-8700
Fax: 949-863-9650
Email: / URL: http://www.startelcorp.com
Product Service Description:
Telecommunications Products

Starwest Botanicals Inc
11253 Trade Center Dr
Rancho Cordova, CA 95742-6223
Contact: Richard Patterson, VP Of Sales
Telephone: 916-638-8100 / 888-273-4372
Fax: 916-638-8293
Email: herbs@starwest-botanicals.com /
URL: http://www.starwest-botanicals.com
Product Service Description:
Manufactures and distributes herbs, spices,
botanical extracts

Stat-Chek Co.(Mfr)
3724 N.E. 145th St.
Seattle, WA 98155
Contact: E.G. Mc Farling, Manager
Telephone: 800/248-6618
Fax: 206-364-5384
Email: / URL:
Product Service Description:
Medical Supplies, I.D. Card Holders
Medical Equip., Inv. Control Signals
Med. Equip., Signal Dev., Chart Holders

State Industrial Supply Corp
7717 N Hartman Ln
Tucson, AZ 85743-9506
Contact: Larry L Larson, Pres.
Telephone: 520-744-0919
Fax: 520-744-6624
Email: / URL:
Product Service Description:
Distributes screws, nuts, bolts, washers,
gaskets, O-rings and seals

Steam Services Inc.
408 S. Teilman Ave.
Fresno, CA 93706
Contact: Robert Astone, President
Telephone: 559-441-1811
Fax: 559-292-0903
Email: cleaning@workmaster.com / URL:
http://www.workmaster.com
Product Service Description:
Carpet Cleaning Preps.
Pet Products
Disinfectants, Carpet & Fabric
Deodorants, Carpet & Fabric

Stearns Product Development
5642 Borwick Ave
South Gate, CA 90280-7404
Contact: Eugene L Raio, Pres.
Telephone: 562-861-0963
Fax: 562-862-2324
Email: / URL:
Product Service Description:
Manufactures pizza machines; heat transfer
machines
Food products machinery
Plate work_fabricated (boiler shops)

Steel Forgings Inc.
PO Box 7365
Shreveport, LA 71137-7365
Contact: Jay Willhoite, General Manager
Telephone: 318-222-3295
Fax: 318-222-3006
Email: sfi@prysm.net / URL: http://
www.steelforging.com
Product Service Description:
Pipe fittings
Pipe & fittings_fabricated

Steel Heddle Mfg. Co. (Mfr)
P.O. Box 1867, 1801 Rutherford Rd.
Greenville, SC 29602
Contact: David Cross, Export Manager
Telephone: 864-244-4110
Fax: 864-292-5846
Email: intl.sales@steelheddle.com / URL:
http://www.steelheddle.com
Product Service Description:
Textile Loom Accessories: Frames,
Hedles,Drop Wires, Reeds
Rolling & Drawing Flat Aluminum Wire
Rolling & Drawing Flat Copper Wire
Flat Rolled Steel Wire

Steel Plant Equipment Corp.
PO Box 130
Eagleville, PA 19408-0130
Contact: Gerard J. Marinari, Pres.
Telephone: 610-539-0980
Fax: 610-539-3711
Email: specgjm@ibm.net / URL: http://
www.specrolls.com
Product Service Description:
Rolling mill machinery & roll coverings
Industrial machinery

Steelbro International
26 Pleasant Lane
Ouster Bay Cove, NY 11771
Contact: Sales & Marketing,
Telephone: 516-746-5512
Fax: 516-746-7930
Email: stlbro@aol.com / URL:
Product Service Description:
Metal Scrap & Primary

Stein Industries Co.
22 Sprague Ave
Amityville, NY 11701-2619
Contact: Stuart Stein, Pres.
Telephone: 516-789-2222
Fax: 516-789-8888
Email: steininc.1@aol.com / URL: http://
Members AOL.Com.Stein Inc.1
Product Service Description:
Theatrical equipment & supplies
Partitions & fixtures, except wood
Popcorn Poppers, Nacho Warmers, Popcorn
Warmers
Concession Stands & any Related Theatre
Lobby Fixtures

Steiner Fabrication Inc
6215 W Van Buren St
Phoenix, AZ 85043-3522
Contact: Melvin Steiner, Sales Mgr.
Telephone: 602-269-8788
Fax: 602-269-0103
Email: / URL: http://
www.steinerfabrication.com
Product Service Description:
Fabricates aluminum, no extruding
Manufacturer of office furniture clone parts

Steinerfilm Inc
987 Simonds Rd
Williamstown, MA 01267-2101
Contact: Else Steiner, Chrm., CEO
Telephone: 413-458-9525
Fax: 413-458-2495
Email: / URL:
Product Service Description:
Metallised Dielectric Film
Dielectric Film for Capacitors

Steinfelds Products
10001 N. Rivergate Blvd.
Portland, OR 97203-6596
Contact: Ray Steinfeld, Chief Executive
Officer
Telephone: 503-286-8241
Fax: 503-289-6854
Email: rayjr@steinfelds.com / URL:
Product Service Description:
Pickles
Cucumbers including gherkins, prepared or
preserved by vinegar or acetic acid
Sauerkraut, prepared or preserved otherwise
than by vinegar or acetic acid, not frozen
Food preparations

Stellram
1 Teledyne Place
La Vergne, TN 37086-3529
Contact: Holly Billik,
Telephone: 800-232-1200
Fax: 615-641-4441
Email: info@stellram.com / URL: http://
www.stellram.com
Product Service Description:
Stellram - a manufacturer of high quality
cutting tools
for metal removal operations: drilling, milling,
threading, turning.

Steltzner Vineyard
5998 Silverado Trl
Napa, CA 94558-9416
Contact: Richard Steltzner, Ptnr.
Telephone: 707-252-7272
Fax: 707-252-2079
Email: wines@steltzner.com / URL: http://
www.steltzner.com
Product Service Description:
Wines, brandy, & brandy spirits
Produces wine

Stemco, Inc.
PO Box 1989
Longview, TX 75606-1989
Contact: Richard Andrews, President
Telephone: 903-758-9981
Fax: 903-232-3508
Email: info@stemco.com / URL: http://
www.stemco.com
Product Service Description:
Truck wheel sealing systems
Motor vehicle parts & accessories

Stemlit Growers
P.O. Box 2779
Wenatchee, WA 98807-2779
Contact: Tom Mathison, Owner
Telephone: 509-662-3602
Fax:
Email: / URL:
Product Service Description:
Fresh Fruits and Vegetables
Apples, fresh
Fruit fresh, pears, cherries
Miscellaneous cargo

StenSource International Inc
18971 Hess Ave
Sonora, CA 95370-9724
Contact: Barbara Wellhausen, Marketing
Telephone: 209-536-1148
Fax: 209-536-1805
Email: marketing@stensource.com / URL:
http://www.stensource.com
Product Service Description:
Manufactures plastic stencils for crafts &
quilting

Stephens Mfg. Co.
P.O. Box 488
Tompkinsville, KY 42167-0488
Contact: Max Stephens, V.P.
Telephone: 502-487-6774
Fax: 502-487-8368
Email: smc@scrte.blue.net / URL: http://
www.stephensmfg.com
Product Service Description:
Concrete batching equipment
Construction Machinery

Sterling Blower Co.
PO Box 219
Forest, VA 24551-0219
Contact: Darrell Childress, Marketing Mgr.
Telephone: 804-525-4030
Fax: 804-525-5740
Email: sterling@sterlingblower.com / URL:
http://www.sterlingblower.com
Product Service Description:
Material handling blowers & conveying &
separation systems
Blowers & fans
Conveyors & conveying equipment
(Pneumatic)

Sterling International Inc
15916 E Sprague Ave
Veradale, WA 99037-8964
Contact: Rod G Schneidmiller, Pres.
Telephone: 509-926-6766
Fax: 509-928-7313
Email: sterling@rescue.com / URL: http://
www.rescue.com
Product Service Description:
Manufactures environmentally safe pest
control products
Plastic products

Stern-Williams Company, Inc.
P.O. BOX 8004
Shawnee Mission, KS 66208-0004
Contact: R.F. Donahue, President
Telephone: 913-362-5635
Fax: 913-362-6689
Email: / URL:
Product Service Description:
Shower Stalls Metal Walls / Terrazzo Rec.
Concrete Prod Terrazzo Shower Floors
Drinking Fountains Metal
Drinking Fountains Stone

Stetco, Inc.
3344 Schierhorn Ct
Franklin Park, IL 60131-2125
Contact: Peter Spiros, Pres.
Telephone: 847-671-4208
Fax: 847-671-5270
Email: sales@stetco.com / URL: http://
www.stetco.com
Product Service Description:
Electronic components
Electrical equipment & supplies

Stevenot Winery
2690 San Domingo Rd
Murphys, CA 95247-9646
Contact: Barden Stevenot, Owner
Telephone: 209-728-3436
Fax: 209-728-3710
Email: info@stevenotwinery.com / URL:
http://www.stevenotwinery.com
Product Service Description:
Wines, brandy, & brandy spirits
Winery and vineyards; produces and sells
wine

Stewart Alexander & Company Inc.
7 Penn Plz.
New York, NY 10001-3900
Contact: Chartering, Ocean Freight,
Telephone: 212-736-2777
Fax: 212-736-3664
Email: stalco@mcimail.com / URL:
Product Service Description:
Freight Transportation Arrangement

Stewart Stamping Corp.
630 Central Park Ave
Yonkers, NY 10704-2018
Contact: John D.Labas, VP
Telephone: 914-965-0816
Fax: 914-965-4431
Email: jlabas@stewartstamping.com / URL:
http://www.stewartstamping.com
Product Service Description:
Metal stampings : Metal stampings, formed
wire products & assemblies : Metal
stamping; Deep Draw

Stewart Surfboards Inc
2102 S El Camino Real
San Clemente, CA 92672-3250
Contact: David Stewart, Ptnr.
Telephone: 949-492-1085 Ext. 3
Fax: 949-492-2009
Email: wwwstewartsrf@aol.com / URL: http:/
/www.stewartsurfboards.com
Product Service Description:
Manufactures Hobie polyurethane foam and
fiberglass surfboards
Sporting & athletic goods
Manufacture Stewart polyurethane / foam &
fiberglass surfboards
Manufacture Munoz polyurethane & foam &
fiberglass surfboards

Stimsonite Corp.
6565 W Howard St
Niles, IL 60714-3303
Contact: Andrea Van Hoosen, Mgr. Export
Operations
Telephone: 847-647-7717
Fax: 847-647-1205
Email: amvanhoose@stimsonite.com / URL:
http://www.stimsonite.com
Product Service Description:
Glass products from purchased glass
Reflective transportation safety devices
Thermoplastic striping material
Thermoplastic application machinery
Preformed pavement markings
Reflective films & signing materials
Truck conspicuity tape
Reflective flexible vinyl

Sto-Chard
953 Newark Ave
Elizabeth, NJ 07208-3516
Contact: Fred Storch, Owner
Telephone: 908-355-1195
Fax: 908-355-1486
Email: / URL:
Product Service Description:
Cookie flavors & canor flavors
Flavoring extracts & syrups

Stock Yards Packing Co. Inc.(Mfr)
340 North Oakley Boulevard
Chicago, IL 60612
Contact: Dan Pollack, President
Telephone: 312/733-6050
Fax: 312-733-0738
Email: / URL: http://www.stockyards.com
Product Service Description:
Meats and Meat Products

Stoel Rives LLP
600 University St., Suite 3600
Seattle, WA 98101-3197
Contact: David Spencer, Partner
Telephone: 206-386-7687
Fax: 206-386-7500
Email: ddspencer@stoel.com / URL: http://
www.stoel.com
Product Service Description:
Legal Services

Stonhard Inc.
One Park Avenue
Maple Shade, NJ 08052
Contact: Sales & Marketing,
Telephone: 609-779-7500
Fax: 609-321-7525
Email: marketing_services@stonhard.com /
URL: http://www.stonhard.com
Product Service Description:
Mfr. & Installer of Polymer Floor, Coatings
& Lining Systems

Storm Products Co Inc
1400 Memorex Dr
Santa Clara, CA 95050-2835
Contact: Raymond L Noble, Pres.
Telephone: 408-565-9800
Fax: 408-565-9820
Email: ray@sc.stormproducts.com / URL:
http://www.stormproducts.com
Product Service Description:
Nonferrous wiredrawing & insulating
Manufactures and distributes wire cables;
custom cable assemblies
Wire products_misc. fabricated
Electronic components
Fiber optic assemblies & components

Straightway Inc.
PO Box 74068
Romulus, MI 48174
Contact: Daniel T. Gregg, President
Telephone: 734-946-0050
Fax: 734-946-1419
Email: straightwy@aol.com / URL:
Product Service Description:
Trucking, all
Export Air Transportation
Ocean Freight Transportation
Packing & Crating
Warehousing & Storage

Strapack, Inc.
30860 San Clemente St.
Hayward, CA 94544-7135
Contact: Jim Hayashi, President
Telephone: 510-475-6000
Fax: 510-475-6090
Email: hayward@strapack.co / URL: http://
www.strapack.com
Product Service Description:
Polypropylene, in primary forms
Packing or wrapping machinery

Strasburg Inc.
3070 Leeman Ferry Rd Sw
Huntsville, AL 35801-5642
Contact: S. Aust, Pres.
Telephone: 205-880-0400
Fax: 205-880-0402
Email: / URL:
Product Service Description:
Children's clothing
Outerwear_girl's & children's
Children's Accessories

Strategic Diagnostics, Inc.
111 Pencader Drive
Newark, DE 19702
Contact: Arthur A. Koch Jr., COO
Phone: 302-456-6789 / Fax: 302-456-6770
Email: sales@sdix.com / http://www.sdix.com
Product Service Description:
Diagnostic substances : Diagnostic reagents
Measuring & controlling devices

Strato, Inc.
50 Ethel Rd. W
Piscataway, NJ 08854-5929
Contact: Marty Kowalski, Director / Mktg.
Telephone: 732-985-3900
Fax: 732-819-8645
URL: http://www.stratomfg.com
Product Service Description:
Air Hose Assemblies for Railroads
Socket Weld Fittings For Railroads
Branch Pipe Tees For Railroads
Brake Cylinder Pressure Taps

Strawberry Patch Publishing
PO Box 52404
Atlanta, GA 30355-0404
Contact: Diane Pfeifer, Owner
Phone: 404-261-2197 / Fax: 404-841-9586
Email: dipfeifer@aol.com / URL: http://
www.strawberrypatch.net
Product Service Description:
Publishing

Strilich Technolgies, Inc.
PO Box 210
Crown Point, IN 46307-0210
Contact: Jeff Strilich, Sales Mgr.
Phone: 219-663-9550 / Fax: 219-663-0158
Email: jefstr@strilich.com / URL: http://
www.strilich.com
Product Service Description:
Coil processing equipment
Metalworking machinery

Stro-Wold International Livestock Svcs. Ltd.
14485 Pike 316
Bowling Green, Missouri, 63334
Contact: R. Marion Strother, President
Phone: 573/324-3373 / Fax: 573-324-3637
Email: strowold@nemonet.com / URL:
Product Service Description:
Livestock & Livestock Products

Stromgren Supports, Inc.
PO Box 1230
Hays, KS 67601-1230
Contact: Joe Flynn, Pres.
Phone: 785-625-4674 / Fax: 785-625-9036
Email: / URL: http://www.stromgren.com
Product Service Description:
Surgical appliances & supplies
Ankle & knee supports

Stronglite Products
P.O. Box 8029
Pine Bluff, AR 71611-8029
Contact: William A. Strong, President
Phone: 870-536-3453 / Fax: 870-536-1033
Email: stronginfo@strong-lite.com / URL:
http://www.strong-lite.com
Product Service Description:
Lightweight insulating concrete
Vermiculite, perlite and chlorites, unexpanded
Absorbents:Pool-Krete Premix for swimming
pool base : Manhole rehabilitation & sewer
lining : Roofing insulation and roof deck
materials : Soil mixes : Refractories
Scented products

Stuewe and Sons, Inc.
2290 S.E. Kiger Island Drive
Corvallis, OR 97333 USA
Contact: Eric Stuewe, President
Telephone: 541-757-7798
Fax: 541-754-6617
Email: info@stuewe.com / URL: http://
www.stuewe.com
Product Service Description:
Plastic Nursery Containers
Plastic Nursery Containers, Wholesale

Stuhr Enterprises, Inc.
PO Box 219
Wilton, IA 52778-0219
Contact: Dawn Stuhr, MIS & Off. Mgr.
Telephone: 319-732-3878
Fax: 319-732-3869
Email: stew@netins.net / URL: http://
www.netins.net/showcase/handles
Product Service Description:
Wood turning
Spinning Wheels

Stylebuilt Accessories, Inc.
99-02 Roosevelt Ave.
Corona, NY 11368-4827
Contact: Jonathan Greenfield, President
Telephone: 718-779-2050
Fax: 718-429-3305
Email: stlblt@aol.com / URL: http://
www.stylebuilt.com
Product Service Description:
Exporting Firms
Table, kitchen or other household articles and
parts thereof, of stainless steel
Decorative Accessories
Household goods
Cosmetic Accessories
Bathroom Accessories
Vanity Trays
Wastebaskets, plated & painted
Giftware

Sub-Con Inc
PO Box 5523
El Monte, CA 91734-1523
Contact: Robert A Loza, Pres.
Telephone: 626-443-9888
Fax: 626-443-2908
Product Service Description:
Packaging, sorting, assembly-line cutting;
cable and mechanical assembly; wire cutting
and harness assembly

Sullins, Inc.
24501 W 111th St
Sapulpa, OK 74066-7435
Contact: James R. Sullins, Pres.
Telephone: 918-224-7370
Fax: 918-224-0064
Email: ndtsales@sullinsndt.com / URL: http://
www.sullinsndt.com
Product Service Description:
Non-destructive testing equipment
Measuring & controlling devices

Sultan & Sons, Inc.
650 Sw 9th Ter
Pompano Beach, FL 33069-4520
Contact: Leon Sultan, CEO
Telephone: 954-782-6600
Fax: 954-786-8650
Email: sammy.sultan@worldnet.att.net / URL:
http://www.sultan-and-sons.com
Product Service Description:
Draperies, bedspreads, vertical & mini blinds
& pleated shades : Curtains & draperies
Commercial & Wholesale Contract Division

Sumitomo Electric Lightwave Corp.
78 Alexander Dr., PO Box 13445
Research Triangle Park, NC 27709-3445
Contact: Fred McDuffee, Vice President
Telephone: 919-541-8100
Fax: 919-541-8265
Email: info@sumitomoelectric.com / URL:
http://www.sumitomoelectric.com
Product Service Description:
Fiber Optic Cable
Fusion Splicing Equipment
Optical Fiber Connectors & Cable
Assemblies
Optical Data Links

Summit Coating Technologies, LLC
25 N 43rd Ave
Phoenix, AZ 85009-4607
Contact: Brian Wojtczak, General Manager
Telephone: 602-455-9365
Fax: 602-455-9370
Email: / URL: http://
www.summitcoating.com
Product Service Description:
Vacuum metalization
EMI/RFI Shielding
Shielding
Conductive Paint

Summit Industries Inc.
PO Box 7329
Marietta, GA 30065-1329
Contact: Phillip M. Meyers, *
Telephone: 404-590-0600
Fax: 404-590-0714
Email: / URL:
Product Service Description:
Auto. Chemical, Leather Upholstery Care

Summit Sales & Marketing
20 View Ln.
Walnut Creek, CA 94596-6719
Contact: Sales & Marketing,
Telephone: 510-934-2301
Fax:
Email: / URL:
Product Service Description:
Lumber / Alder / Aspen
Plywood
Woodenware
Furniture
Edge Olved Panels
Lattice
Doors / Pine

Sun Country Industries Inc.
PO Box 93490
Albuquerque, NM 87199-3490
Contact: J.T. Michelson, Vice President
Telephone: 505-344-1611
Fax: 505-344-1566
Email: suncountry@uswest.net / URL: http://
www.suncountryind.com
Product Service Description:
Precision machining job shop
Jet Engine / Aircraft Parts

Sun Empire Foods
PO Box 376
Kerman, CA 93630-0376
Contact: Sandra K. Dee, Plant Manager
Telephone: 800-252-4786
Fax: 558-846-9488
Email: sunemp@thesocket.com / URL: http://
www.sunempire.com
Product Service Description:
Manufactures candy, chocolate-covered fruits
and nuts : Candy & other confectionery
products : Confectionery

Sun Foundry
297 S Lake St
Burbank, CA 91502-2111
Contact: Kenneth F Kalbfleish Sr, Owner
Telephone: 818-841-7979
Fax: 818-955-9690
Email: sunbronze@pacificnet.net / URL:
http://www.sunbronze.com
Product Service Description:
Non Ferric Foundries
Bronze Art Foundry; Fine art originals &
reproductions-monumental to miniature

Sun Publishing Co.
PO Box 5588
Santa Fe, NM 87502-5588
Contact: Skip Whitson, GM
Telephone: 505-471-5177
Fax: 505-473-4458
Email: sunpub@trail.com / URL: http://
www.sunbooks.com
Product Service Description:
Book Seller

Sunco Powder Systems, Inc.
PO Box 23515
Charlotte, NC 28227-0272
Contact: Victor Bell, Pres.
Telephone: 704-545-3922
Fax: 704-545-8345
Email: suncopowder@juno.com / URL:
Product Service Description:
Rotary airlocks & diverters

Sundance
PO Box 2437
Greeley, CO 80632-2437
Contact: Ralph T O'Donnell, Pres.
Telephone: 970-339-9322
Fax: 970-339-5856
Email: / URL:
Product Service Description:
Manufactures waste and agricultural grinders

Sunkist Growers, Inc., Processed Products Div.
616 E. Sunkist St.
Ontario, CA 91761
Contact: Charles J. Helme, Senior Sales
Manager
Telephone: 909-933-2105
Fax: 909-933-2404
Product Service Description:
Concentrated Juices
Essential Oils

Sunland, Inc.
PO Box 1059
Portales, NM 88130-1059
Contact: Jimmie Shearer, Pres., CEO, GM
Telephone: 505-356-6638
Fax: 505-356-6630
Email: sunlandinc@sunlandinc.com / URL:
http://www.sunlandinc.com
Product Service Description:
Peanut processing
Nuts & seeds_salted & roasted
Peanut Butter

Sunlite Casual Furniture, Inc.
1600 Jones Rd
Paragould, AR 72450-8866
Contact: Shirley Walker, Pers. Mgr.
Telephone: 870-236-8731
Fax: 870-239-6200
Product Service Description:
Wrought iron, tubular & aluminum furniture
Furniture_metal household

Sunnyvale GDI, Inc.
PO Box 1330
Verdi, NV 89439-1330
Contact: Frank Ribelin, Pres.
Telephone: 775-345-8000
Fax: 775-345-8010
Email: gdi@sierra.net / URL: http://
www.sgdi.com
Product Service Description:
Manufactures Outdoor Communication
Modems, Fiber Optic Microwave &
Video Equipment for the Traffic Industry
Modems... FSK to 56kbps & Fiber Optic
Wireless... Microwave & Spread Spectrum
Fiber Optics..SONET, Mux & Modems
Telco...T1 Mux, DSU/CSU & Modems
Video...Cameras, Sysetms & Housings
Training..Schools, Annual & Local Seminars

Sunoco, Inc.
10 Penn Ctr., 1801 Market St.
Philadelphia, PA 19144
Contact: Robert H. Campbell, Chairman &
Chief Executive Officer
Telephone: 215-977-3000
Email: / URL: http://www.sunocoinc.com
Product Service Description:
Petroleum Refining
Antioxidizing preparations and other
compound stabilizers for rubber or plastics
Toluene
Benzene
Xylene
Cyclohexane
Acetone
Phenol
Ethylene
Ethylene oxide

Sunshine Paper Company
12601 E 33rd Ave
Aurora, CO 80011-1839
Contact: Daryl Brady, Pres.
Telephone: 303-341-2990
Fax: 303-341-2995
Email: mgsunpco@aol.com / URL:
Product Service Description:
Press packing papers
Converted paper products

Sunshine Unlimited, Inc.
PO Box 71
Linsborg, KS 67456-0471
Contact: Chester Peterson, President
Telephone: 785-227-3880
Fax: 785-227-3880
Email: / URL:
Product Service Description:
Computer Programming Services
Computer Prepackaged Software
Computer Spreadsheet Towplates

Sunstrand Corporation
4949 Harrison Ave. PO Box 7003
Rockford, IL 61125-7003
Contact: Richard Johann, Mgr./Ex-Im Admin
Telephone: 815-226-6000
Fax: 815-226-2699
Email: / URL:
Product Service Description:
Aircraft & Aerospace Parts
Fluid Pumping Equipment
Ind. Mach. Gears & Speed Reducers
Navigation Equipment Aviation Electronics
Measuring Devices, Accelerometers

Supelco, Inc.(Mfr)
Supelco Park
Bellefonte, PA 16823-0048
Contact: Jose A. Dominicci, Int'l Sales
Telephone: 814-359-5778
Fax: 814-359-4685
Email: jdominic@supelco.sial.com / URL:
Product Service Description:
LC-GC Chromatography Supplies
Gas & Chemical Standards & Reagents
Sample Handling & Extraction & Air Monitor
Devices

Super Precision Design, Inc.
3 Spielman Rd
Fairfield, NJ 07004-3403
Contact: Effat, Pres.
Telephone: 973-227-7330
Fax: 973-227-5223
Email: / URL:
Product Service Description:
Road marking equipment
Traffic control signs

Super Products Corp.
P.O. BOX 27225
Milwaukee, WI 53227-0225
Contact: James C. Wurster, President
Telephone: 414-784-7100
Fax: 414-784-9561
Email: / URL:
Product Service Description:
Industrial Vacuum Loader
Sewer Cleaner Truck Mounted

Super Radiator Coils
P.O. Box 35687
Richmond, VA 23235
Contact: Ray Birk, Export Manager
Telephone: 804/794-2887
Fax: 804-379-2118
Email: ray@rich.srcoils.com / URL: http://
www.srcoils.com
Product Service Description:
Heat Transfer Coils
Cooling Coils
Heating Coils
Evaporator Coils
Condenser Coils

Super Vision International, Inc.
8210 Presidents Dr
Orlando, FL 32809-7623
Contact: Paula Vega, Int. Sales Manager
Telephone: 407-857-9900
Fax: 407-857-0050
Email: pvega@svision.com / URL: http://
www.svision.com
Product Service Description:
Fiberoptic Lighting Products

Super-Sensitive Musical String Co.
1805 Apex Rd
Sarasota, FL 34240-9386
Contact: J. V. Cavanaugh, President
Telephone: 941-371-0016
Fax: 941-378-3617
Email: supersensitive@supersensitive.com /
URL: http://www.supersensitive.com
Product Service Description:
Violin, viola, cello & bass musical strings,
shoulder rests, rosins & polish & sensors

Superb Marine & Industrial Services, Inc.
5730 I 10 Industrial Pkwy N
Theodore, AL 36582-1666
Contact: Gerald Butler, Co-Pres.
Telephone: 334-653-8484
Fax: 334-653-8499
Email: / URL:
Product Service Description:
Rebuilt marine boilers, coolers & industrial machinery : Plate work_fabricated (boiler shops) : Industrial machinery
Machine shop services : Heat exchanger repair: Pump repairs : Valve repairs

Superior Air Freight
1720 S. Military Hwy.
Chesapeake, VA 23320-2612
Contact: Mark Lamb, General Manager
Telephone: 757-855-7772
Fax: 757-855-8300
Email: ops@superiorair.com / URL: http://www.superiorair.com
Product Service Description:
Freight Forwarding, Air

Superior Aluminum Products, Inc.
555 E. Main St., P.O. Box 430
Russia, OH 45363
Contact: Edward L. Borchers, President
Telephone: 937-526-4065
Fax: 937-526-3904
Email: superioralum@wesnet.com / URL:
Product Service Description:
Aluminum Railing & Columns

Superior American Plastics, Inc.
1200 Barclay Blvd
Buffalo Grove, IL 60089-4500
Contact: Mike Lewis, Pres.
Telephone: 847-229-1600
Fax: 847-229-9109
Product Service Description:
Plastic extrusions & compounding
Plastic profile shapes_unsupported

Superior Aqua Enterprises, Inc.
2140 Bispham Rd
Sarasota, FL 34231-5518
Contact: Richard Ganim, Pres.
Telephone: 941-923-2221
Fax: 941-925-4509
Email: superioraq@aol.com. / URL:
Product Service Description:
Water purification equipment

Superior Die Set Corp.
900 W Drexel Ave
Oak Creek, WI 53154-1924
Contact: W.L. Fitzwater, V.P. Sales / Mktg.
Telephone: 414-764-4900
Fax: 414-764-5460
Email: messages@supdio.com / URL: http://www.supdie.com
Product Service Description:
Die sets & mold bases
Dies, tools, jigs & fixtures_special

Superior Furniture
1 Industrial Park Rd
Belton, TX 76513-1922
Contact: D.F. Myers, Pres. & CEO
Telephone: 254-939-3517
Fax: 254-939-1630
Email: fmyers@superiorfurniture.com / URL: http://www.superiorfurniture.com
Product Service Description:
Office furniture_wood : Office chairs
Office furniture, except wood

Superior Grounding Systems
PO Box 2171
Irwindale, CA 91706-1112
Contact: Steven Fan , Owner
Telephone: 626-815-1946
Product Service Description:
Manufactures grounding systems for surge & lighting protection.
Current-carrying wiring devices

Superior Helicopter LLC.
PO Box 250
Glendale, OR 97442-0250
Contact: Gary Jantzer, General Manager
Telephone: 541-832-1167
Fax: 541-832-1139
Email: ken@superiorlumber.com / URL: http://www.superiorlumber.com
Product Service Description:
Helicopter Logging : Fire Fighting
Construction

Superior Honing Equipment Inc.
6691 33rd St E
Sarasota, FL 34243-4124
Contact: Jack Harmount, Pres
Telephone: 941-758-1266
Fax: 941-753-1846
Email: superiorhoning@worldnet.att.net
Product Service Description:
Honing machines & abrasive products

Superior Packing/Superior Farm
1477 Drew Ave Ste 101
Davis, CA 95616-4881
Contact: Dennis Breen, Pres., CEO
Telephone: 530-758-3091
Fax: 530-758-3152
Email: / URL: http://www.superiorfarms.com
Product Service Description:
Meat packing , processing company
Meat packing plants, processing plants
Lamb, American, fresh & frozen
Lamb, Australian, fresh & frozen
Veal, fresh & frozen
Lamb offal, edible
Lamb skins

Superwinch, Inc.
20 Danco Rd.
Putnam, CT 06260
Contact: Eric Pierre,
Telephone: 860-928-7787
Fax: 860-928-1143
Email: eric@superwinch.com / URL:
Product Service Description:
Electrical Hydraulic Winches

Support Products Inc.
PO Box 1185
Effingham, IL 62401-1185
Contact: Sales & Marketing,
Telephone: 217-536-6171
Fax: 217-536-6828
Email: supprod@supportproducts.com / URL: http://www.supportproducts.com
Product Service Description:
Auxiliary Equipment for Printing Web: Ink Leveler: Fountain Solution Controller, Remote Pasting & Softening System
Dot Glue System, Air & Mechanical Bustle
Wheels: Goosenecks, Fountain Dividers, Web Puller, Blanket & Packing Gauge, Powder Dispenser

Supra Products
PO Box 3167
Salem, OR 97302-0167
Contact: Greg Burge, Pres., CEO
Phone: 503-581-9101/ Fax: 503-375-9852
URL: http://www.supra-products.com
Product Service Description:
Hardware : Manufactures lock boxes for the real estate, automotive, consumer and industrial markets

Supreme Chemicals Of Georgia
900 Sun Valley Dr
Roswell, GA 30076-1419
Contact: Peter Dawson, Pres., Pur. Agt.
Telephone: 770-518-7125
Fax: 770-518-4770
Product Service Description:
Cleaning chemicals: Soap & other detergents
Pressure Wash Cleaner : Rust Removers & I nhibitors

Supreme Horse Walker Co.
8061 County Road 61
Florence, AL 35634-5832
Contact: Buddy Smith, Owner
Telephone: 205-766-2343
Fax: 205-766-2343
Product Service Description:
Horse walkers :Farm machinery & equipment

Supreme Perlite Co
4600 N Suttle Rd
Portland, OR 97217-7720
Contact: Frank Petterson, Pres.
Telephone: 503-286-4333
Fax: 503-286-1068
Email: perlite@europa.com / URL: http://www.perlite.com
Product Service Description:
Processes & packages raw & expanded perlite aggregates:horticultural, construction, Ind.

Surf Line Hawaii, Ltd.
1451 Kalani St
Honolulu, HI 96817-4922
Contact: Terence Enriques, V-P.
Telephone: 808-847-5985
Fax: 808-841-5254
Email: jams@jamsworld.com / URL:
Product Service Description:
Clothing_men's & boys'
Outerwear_women's & misses'

Survival Safety Engineering, Inc.
321 Naval Base Rd
Norfolk, VA 23505-3615
Contact: Robert Morse, Pres., Engrg. Mgr.
Telephone: 757-480-5508
Fax: 757-480-5683
Email: sse@norfolk.infi.net / URL: http://www.survivalsafety.com
Product Service Description:
Radar detectors & marine electronics
Search & navigation equipment

Survivor Industries Inc
PO Box 967
Newbury Park, CA 91319-0967
Contact: Howard Wallace, Pres., Robert Stotz, VP
Phone: 805-498-6062/ Fax: 805-499-3708
Email: survivorind@msn.com / URL: http://www.survivorind.com
Product Service Description:
Manufactures emergency preparedness kits and mainstay emergency food and water rations

Suzuki, Myers & Associates, Limited
P.O. Box 852
Novi, MI 48376
Contact: Kayo Yoshimoto, Office Manager
Telephone: 248-344-0909
Fax: 248-344-0092
Email: suzukimyers@mindspring.com / URL: http://www.mindspring.com/~suzukimyers
Product Service Description:
Translation Svcs., Japanese, Technical Interpreting Svcs., Japanese
Mgmt. Consulting Svcs., Japan & Far East
Public Relations Svcs., Japan & Far East
Word Processing Svcs.

Swaim & Sons
34758 Lencioni Ave
Bakersfield, CA 93308-9768
Contact: William Swaim, Pres.
Telephone: 805-392-4151
Fax: 805-392-1525
Email: / URL:
Product Service Description:
General machine shop (job work)
Sucker Rod <oil> pump parts

Swanson Anaheim Corp
4955 E Landon Dr
Anaheim, CA 92807-1972
Contact: Ted Hoberg, Opers. Mgr.
Telephone: 714-970-9005
Fax: 714-970-8709
Email: swanson-anaheim-sales@pacbell.net / URL: http://www.thomasregister.com/swanson
Product Service Description:
Automatic assembly machines, automatic inspection machines, vibratory feeder systems
Machinery_special industry
Process control instruments
Machine tools, metal cutting types
Industrial machinery

Swenson Spreader Co.
PO Box 127
Lindenwood, IL 61049-0127
Contact: Mark Swisher, GM
Telephone: 815-393-4455
Fax: 815-393-4964
Email: swensonsales@swensonspreader.com / URL: http://www.swensonspreader.com
Product Service Description:
Material spreaders & servo controls

Swift & Sons, Inc., M.
PO Box 150
Hartford, CT 06141-0150
Contact: M. A. Swift, Pres.
Telephone: 860-522-1181
Fax: 860-249-5934
Email: / URL:
Product Service Description:
Hot Stamping Foils & Precious Metal Leaf

Sybaritic, Inc.
9220 James Ave S
Minneapolis, MN 55431-2315
Contact: Steven Daffer, Pres.
Telephone: 612-888-8282
Fax: 612-888-8887
Email: alpha33@sybaritic.com / URL: http://www.sybaritic.com
Product Service Description:
Dry & steam heat sauna units
GX-99 massage system
Massage table
Massage & body oils

Sybil's Outrageous Brownies
2647 Ariane Drive
San Diego, CA 92117-3422
Contact: Luann Rein, CEO
Telephone: 619-270-9863
Fax: 619-270-6801
Email: luann@outrageousbrownies.com /
URL: http://www.outrageousbrownies.com
Product Service Description:
Brownies, cookies & related products

Symtron Systems, Inc.
PO Box 950
Fair Lawn, NJ 07410-0950
Contact: John Henning, Pres.
Telephone: 201-794-0200
Fax: 201-794-0561
Email: / URL:
Product Service Description:
Fire training systems
Measuring & controlling devices

**Synalloy Corp., Blackman-Uhler
Chemical Div.**
Croft Industrial Park, P.O. Box 5627
Spartanburg, SC 29304
Contact: Herbert Moore, President
Telephone: 864-585-3661
Fax: 864-596-1501
Email: / URL:
Product Service Description:
Organic Chemicals
Textile Dyestuffs

Syncro Air Lift Corp
1538 E Chestnut Ave Ste A
Santa Ana, CA 92701-6320
Contact: Ray W. Born, CEO
Telephone: 714-569-1275
Fax: 714-569-1278
Email: / URL: http://www.uswinint.com
Product Service Description:
Disign & maintenance, aircraft lifts

Synergistics, Inc.
9 Tech Circle
Natick, MA 01760
Contact: Robert Pogorelc, VP
Telephone: 508/655-1340
Fax: 508-651-2902
Email: syn@tiac.net / URL: http://
www.synergisticsinc.com
Product Service Description:
Access Control Systems For Physical
Security

Synergy International Inc.
W222 North 630 Cheaney Dr.
Waukesha, WI 53186-1697
Contact: David Lanser, International Sales
Manager
Telephone: 414-549-0014
Fax: 414-549-3241
Email: sales @synergyintl.com / URL: http://
www.synergyintl.com
Product Service Description:
Generator sets & control systems

Synnex Information Tech
3797 Spinnaker Ct
Fremont, CA 94538-6537
Contact: Marco Olvera, Int'l Sales
Telephone: 510-668-3630
Fax: 510-668-3769
Email: / URL: http://www.synnex.com
Product Service Description:
Electronic Computers
Parts & accessories for automatic data
processing machines

Syntech Products Corp.
PO Box 370
Toledo, OH 43697-0370
Contact: John Leslie, Pres.
Telephone: 419-241-1215
Fax: 419-241-6943
Email: solutions@syntechproducts.com /
URL: http://www.syntechproducts.com
Product Service Description:
Industrial chemicals
Chemicals_industrial inorganic
Dust Suppression

Synthetic Genetics
3347 Industrial Ct Ste A
San Diego, CA 92121-1031
Contact: Ben Thorton, GM
Telephone: 619-793-2661
Fax: 619-793-2666
Email: nomutants@aol.com / URL: http://
www.syntheticgenetics.com
Product Service Description:
Synthetic DNA for medical research
Drug metabolism bioreagents & services

Syroco Mfr
7528 State Fair Blvd.
Baldwinsville, NY 13027
Contact: Vinny Cannistra, Export Sales Mgr.
Telephone: 315-635-9911 Ext. 2321
Fax: 315-635-5388
Email: cannistra@syroco.com / URL:
Product Service Description:
Resin Household Furniture

Sysdyne Corp.
53 Larkin St
Stamford, CT 06907-2702
Contact: Lyris Hung, President
Telephone: 203-327-3649
Fax: 203-325-3600
Product Service Description:
Computer systems
Electronic computers

System Technology #1
1842 E 3rd St.
Tempe, AZ 85281-2985
Contact: Kathleen Stone, President
Telephone: 602-967-7785
Fax: 602-967-7469
Email: Kathleenstone@msn.com / URL:
Product Service Description:
Refurbished Unisys Computer Hardware,
Wholesale

Systems Management Inc.
10946 Golden West Drive, Suite 100
Hunt Valley, MD 21031
Contact: Ralph F. Petragnani,
Telephone: 410-229-7539
Fax: 410-229-7603
Email: petra@awi-smi.com / URL: http://
www.awi-smi.com
Product Service Description:
Automated Weather Monitoring Devices
Water Pollution Monitoring Devices

Systronics, Inc.
4357 Park Drive, Suite J
Norcross, GA 30093
Contact: Werner F. Goeckel, CEO
Telephone: 770-449-7776
Fax: 770-449-0399
Email: info@systronics-inc.com / URL: http://
www.systronics-inc.com
Product Service Description:
Machine vision inspection & measurement
systems

T & B Structural Systems, Inc.
637 W Hurst Blvd
Hurst, TX 76053-7603
Contact: Tom Taylor, Pres.
Telephone: 817-280-9858
Fax: 817-280-9864
Email: gman0@flash.net / URL: http://
www.tandbstructural.com
Product Service Description:
Retaining wall parts & materials
Steel wire & related products

T & C Mfg. & Operating, Inc.
PO Box 225
Great Bend, KS 67530-0225
Contact: Thomas H. McGlinn, V-P.
Telephone: 316-793-5483
Fax: 316-793-5521
Email: thm_tcmfg@hotmail.com / URL: http:/
/www.tcmfg.com
Product Service Description:
Rubber products_fabricated
Rubber molded products
Irrigation Gaskets

**T & R Concept Inc., DBA: Zigg Zag
Sportswear**
17941 Mitchell S, Suite B
Irvine, CA 92614-6015
Contact: Neil Merrell, Pres.
Telephone: 949-752-6655
Fax: 949-752-6631
Product Service Description:
Manufactures fleece jackets, gloves and hats;
outer clothes and golf apparel

T & R Electric Supply Co., Inc.
PO Box 180
Colman, SD 57017-0180
Contact: James R. Thompson, Pres.
Telephone: 605-534-3555
Fax: 605-534-3861
Email: t-r@t-r.com / URL: http://www.t-r.com
Product Service Description:
Rebuilt transformers
Transformers, except electronic

T Formation Of Tallahassee, Inc.
3463 Garber Dr
Tallahassee, FL 32303-1115
Contact: Alan Gentry, V-P.
Telephone: 850-574-0122
Fax: 850-574-7691
Email: agentry@tformation.com / URL:
Product Service Description:
Screen printing
Embroidery

T L C Precision Wafer Tech, Inc.
1411 W River Rd. North
Minneapolis, MN 55411-3436
Contact: Anju Sohal, Marketing & Sales Mgr.
Telephone: 612-341-2795
Fax: 612-341-2799
Email: tlc@tlcprecision.com / URL: http://
www.tlcprecision.com
Product Service Description:
Semiconductors
Semiconductors & related devices

T M Industries, Inc.
56 State Route 173 Plaza 78
Hampton, NJ 08827-4021
Contact: Gerda Tietje, Pres.
Telephone: 908-730-7674
Fax: 908-730-6501
Email: / URL:
Product Service Description:
Automatic grease lubricators

**T M P Technologies, Inc./Truly
Magic Products**
1200 Northland Ave
Buffalo, NY 14215-3835
Contact: Michael W. Sanok, VP Sales &
Mktg.
Telephone: 716-895-6100
Fax: 716-895-6396
Email: tmpsales@tmptech.com / URL: http://
www.tmptech.com
Product Service Description:
Rubber products_fabricated
Polyurethane foam, molded rubber &
polyesters
Plastic materials & resins

T N T Pizza Crust, Inc.
PO Box 8926
Green Bay, WI 54308-8926
Contact: Larry Kropp, Sales Mgr.
Telephone: 920-431-7240
Fax: 920-431-7249
Email: service@tntcrust.com / URL: http://
www.tntcrust.com
Product Service Description:
Frozen pizza crust
Bakery products_frozen, except bread

T S I Plastics
7705 Central Ave Ne
Minneapolis, MN 55432-2829
Contact: Gary McCready, Pres.
Telephone: 612-784-0240
Fax: 612-784-2259
Product Service Description:
Plastic Fabrication & Molding

T Transportation, Inc.
P.O. Box 410155,
Cambridge, MA 02141-0002
Contact: Paul Janos, Vice President
Telephone: 617-354-0308
Fax: 617-354-0284
Email: / URL:
Product Service Description:
Freight & Cargo Transportation
Trucking

T&S Exports, Div. T&S Brass (Mfr)
P.O. Box 1088 - 2 Saddleback Cove
Travelers Rest, SC 29690
Contact: Nancy Garrett, Export Manager
Telephone: 864-834-4102
Fax: 864-834-3518
Email: tsbrass@tsbrass.com / URL: http://
www.tsbrass.com
Product Service Description:
Faucets & Related Plumbing Fittings

T-Shirts & Graphics
2244 N Grand Ave E
Springfield, IL 62702-4341
Contact: Karla K. Carwile, Pres.
Telephone: 217-544-0881
Fax: 217-544-5816
Email: t-shirtz@t-shirtz.com / URL: http://
www.t-shirtz.com
Product Service Description:
Screen printing, sportswear imprinting &
interior & exterior signs
T-Shirts
Signs & advertising specialties
Sweatshirts
Sports Wear

T-Systems International, Inc.
7545 Carroll Rd.
San Diego, CA 92121-2401
Contact: Sales & Marketing,
Telephone: 619-578-1860
Fax: 619-578-2344
Email: tsysmktg@pacbell.net / URL: http://
www.tsystemsinternational.com
Product Service Description:
Farm and Garden Machinery
Plates, sheets, film, foil and strip of plastics,
not self-adhesive, non-cellular
Polymers of ethylene, in primary forms
Articles of plastics

**T. Miller Popcorn Company
Inc.(Mfr)**
P.O. Box 493
Trenton, MO 64683
Contact: Joe DiGirolamo, President
Telephone: 630-359-6958
Fax: 630-359-6037
Email: buterpop@lyn.net / URL: http://
www.tmillerpopcorn.com
Product Service Description:
Popcorn
Popcorn/Seasoning

T.J. Manufacturing, Inc.
4201 Bell St.
Erie, PA 16511-2859
Contact: Jeff Pasinski, Sales Manager
Telephone: 814-899-3141
Fax: 814-899-9722
Email: tjmfg@ncinter.net / URL: http://
www.ncinter.net/tjmfg
Product Service Description:
Valves
Bronze Valves
Bronze Electrical Connectors
Power Transformer Valves
Distribution Transformer Bushings

T/Mac, Inc.
100 Jersey Ave Bldg D-6
New Brunswick, NJ 08901-3200
Contact: Ted Marks, Pres.
Telephone: 732-247-0022
Fax: 732-247-4622
Email: tmac@tmacinc.com / URL: http://
www.tmacinc.com
Product Service Description:
Radio frequency & microwave power
amplifiers

THF Corp
362 Littlefield Ave
South San Francisco, CA 94080-6103
Contact: Richard Kesler, Pres.
Telephone: 650-588-6570
Fax: 650-588-6678
Email: kessler@thfcorp.net / URL: http://
www.thfcorp.net
Product Service Description:
Manufactures and distributes industrial
fasteners
Bolts, nuts, rivets & washers
Hardware

**TIS Translations & Interpretation
Svc.**
19 Fairway St.
Mount Vernon, NY 10552-1903
Contact: Matilde Deferrari, *
Telephone: 914-664-8061
Fax: 914-699-8077
Product Service Description:
Translations: Written & Spoken, Documents
& Meetings

TNT Tools Inc
4691 W Tufts Ave
Denver, CO 80236-3309
Contact: Mark Trujillo, Pres.
Telephone: 303-794-4741
Fax: 303-795-3338
Email: tnttools@aol.com / URL: http://
www.tnttoolsinc.com
Product Service Description:
Manufactures firefighting equipment
Machinery_general industrial

TP Orthodontics Inc
PO Box 742
Lodi, CA 95241-0742
Contact: Robert E Cunningham, Br. Mgr.
Telephone: 209-368-7545
Fax: 209-368-1233
Email: / URL:
Product Service Description:
Dental equipment & supplies
Orthodontic supplies and services

TP Orthodontics, Inc.
100 Center Plaza
La Porte, IN 46350-9672
Contact: Shirley Stanley, Vice President,
Marketing
Telephone: 219-785-2591
Fax: 219-324-3029
Email: / URL:
Product Service Description:
Orthodontic Products
Barketsbandstubesbonding Adhesives
Instruments Elastic
Arch Wire
Laboratory Services

TPL Communications, Inc.
3370 San Fernando Rd., Unit 206
Los Angeles, CA 90065-1437
Contact: James B. Briggs, President
Telephone: 213-256-3000
Fax: 213-254-3210
Email: electronic@compuserve.com / URL:
http://www.tplcom.com
Product Service Description:
Radio Freq. Power Amplifiers

TRACO
71 Progress Ave
Cranberry Township, PA 16066-3511
Contact: John Kane, Mgr. Tech. Svcs
Telephone: 724-776-7000
Fax: 724-776-7088
Email: john.kane@traco.com / URL: http://
www.traco.com
Product Service Description:
Doors, sash & trim_metal
Replacement windows & doors & aluminum
extruding & finishing

TS-Tek Inc
7727 W 6th Ave Ste E
Lakewood, CO 80215-6078
Contact: Jerry Johnson, Pres.
Telephone: 303-237-5370
Fax: 303-237-5388
Email: ts-tek@ts-tek.com / URL:
Product Service Description:
Computer system integrators; value-added
reseller; develops custom & prepackaged
software
Computer integrated systems design
Prepackaged software
Computer programming services

TST Inc
11601 Etiwanda Ave
Fontana, CA 92337-6929
Contact: Tony Rocha, VP Int'l Sales
Telephone: 909-685-2155
Fax: 909-685-7806
Email: trocha@tst-inc.com / URL: http://
www.tst-inc.com
Product Service Description:
Manufactures secondary aluminum ingots;
Manufactures extrusions & forging billet
Non-ferrous scrap metals; import & export
trading

Taber Industries, Inc.
455 Bryant St
North Tonawanda, NY 14120-7043
Contact: Daniel K. Slawson,
Telephone: 716-694-4000
Fax: 716-694-1450
Email: sales@taberindustries.com / URL:
http://www.taberindustries.com
Product Service Description:
Physical Testing Equipment
Machine Tools Punch Press
Pressure Transducers

Tablecloth Co., Inc.
514 Totowa Ave
Paterson, NJ 07522-1541
Contact: Bernie Cramer, Pres.
Telephone: 973-942-1555
Fax: 800-337-3720
Email: / URL:
Product Service Description:
Tableclotts & napkins. skirting, placmats &
runners

Takaha America Co.
270 Enterprise Dr
Newport News, VA 23603-1300
Contact: Taisuke Okubo, Pres.
Telephone: 757-888-0000
Fax: 757-888-0011
Email: info@takaha.com / URL: http://
www.takaha.com
Product Service Description:
Solenoid

Take Two Sportswear Accessories
1300 N Bristol St Ste 100
Newport Beach, CA 92660-2989
Contact: Becky Brooks, Owner
Telephone: 949-833-1750
Fax: 714-979-1453
Email: / URL:
Product Service Description:
Manufactures sports headwear for women
and men
Hats, caps & millinery

**Talla-Com, Tallahassee
Communications Industries, Inc.**
1720 W Paul Dirac Dr
Tallahassee, FL 32310-3754
Contact: Yehuda Peress, President
Telephone: 850-580-0200
Fax: 850-576-8421
Email: marketing@t-com.com / URL: http://
www.t-com.com
Product Service Description:
Military radios & wireless communications
equipment
Power Amplifiers & Digital Communication
Systems

Tally Printer Corporation
8301 S. 180th St.
Kent, WA 98032
Contact: William Munro, President
Telephone: 425-251-5500
Fax: 425-251-5520
Email: / URL: http://www.tally.com
Product Service Description:
Computer Peripheral Equipment, NEC
Typewriter or similar ribbons, inked or
otherwise prepared
Parts and accessories for automatic data
processing machines and units thereof,
magnetic
Digital automatic data processing machines
containing a central processing unit

Tamer International Ltd
PO Box 65260
Seattle, WA 98155-9260
Contact: Macit Gurol, Pres.
Telephone: 206-364-6761
Fax: 206-364-5369
Email: sales@tamer.com / URL: http://
www.tamer.com
Product Service Description:
Manufactures acid reducers for foods and
beverages
Pharmaceuticals & Antacids
High performance granulation systems

**Tampa Bay International Terminals,
Inc.**
2510 Guy N. Verger Blvd.,
Tampa, FL 33605
Contact: Steven R. Blust, President/Chief
Executive Officer
Telephone: 813-248-6168
Fax: 813-248-6485
Email: / URL: http://www.tbitfl.com
Product Service Description:
Freight & Cargo Transportation
Trucking

Tana Tex Inc.
5009 N Winthrop Ave
Chicago, IL 60640-3123
Contact: Anat Unruh, Pres.
Telephone: 773-561-9270
Fax: 773-561-5469
Email: tanatex@flash.net / URL:
Product Service Description:
Health care fabrics
Textile products_fabricated

Tape Duplicators, Inc.
785 W 83rd St
Hialeah, FL 33014-3613
Contact: Daniel Berrios, Pres.
Telephone: 305-822-7585
Fax: 305-822-7589
Email: danny@tapedup.com / URL:
tape@tapedup.com
Product Service Description:
Audio cassette duplication
Magnetic & optical recording media

Tape-O Corporation
35 Crosby Rd.
Dover, NH 03820-4394
Contact: Staurt Bauder, *
Telephone: 603-743-6636
Fax: 603-743-6645
Email: / URL:
Product Service Description:
Athletic Goods, Adhesive Tape
Fabric, Adhesive Tape
Surgical Supplies, Adhesive Tape

Tapes 'n Tags Mfg.
18 Spencer Tr.
Saint Peters, MO 63376-6021
Contact: Karl Williamson, Ptnr. & Fin. Mgr.
Telephone: 314-936-2700
Fax: 314-922-0364
Email: karl@tapes-n-tags.com / URL: http://www.tapes-n-tags.com
Product Service Description:
Embroidered name tapes & emblems,
engraved nameplates & dog tags

Taratape
250 Canal Rd
Fairless Hills, PA 19030-4306
Contact: Tom Dodd, Pres.
Telephone: 215-736-3644
Fax: 215-428-4510
Email: taratape@aol.com / URL: http://www.taratape.com
Product Service Description:
Industrial packaging tapes
Paper coated & laminated, packaging

Target Materials, Inc.
1145 Chesapeake Ave
Columbus, OH 43212-2284
Contact: Edward R. Funk, Pres., Engrg. Mgr.
Telephone: 614-486-7055
Fax: 614-486-0912
Email: sales@targetmaterials.com / URL:
http://www.targetmaterials.com
Product Service Description:
Superconductive materials, devices &
sputtering targets
Semiconductors & related devices

Tasco Inc
2895 W Oxford Ave Unit 7
Englewood, CO 80110-4370
Contact: Steve McCasland, Pres.
Telephone: 303-762-9952
Fax: 303-762-1205
Email: steve@tasco-usa.com / URL: http://www.tasco-usa.com
Product Service Description:
Manufactures instruments to measure and test
electricity and electric signals
Specialized testers for electrical contractors &
electricians

Tasker Metal Products
PO Box 15368
Los Angeles, CA 90015-0368
Contact: Eugene J Golling, Pres.
Telephone: 213-746-5490
Fax: 213-746-8707
Email: / URL:
Product Service Description:
Crash and restoration body parts for
European
Motor vehicle parts & accessories

Tata, Inc.
101 Park Ave., 26th Fl.
New York, NY 10178-0002
Contact: Ashok Mehta, President
Telephone: 212-557-7979
Fax: 212-557-7987
Email: Tatainc@aol.com / URL: http://www.tata.com/tatainc
Product Service Description:
Hot Rolled Coils
Wire Rods
Wires
Billets, Slabs
Scrap
Pig Iron
Ferro-Chrome, Ferro-Manganese

Tatum Farms International, Inc.
6683 Highway 136 West
Dawsonville, GA 30534-1915
Contact: Sales & Marketing,
Telephone: 706-265-3211
Fax: 706-265-2378
Email: tatum@stc.net / URL:
Product Service Description:
Poultry Hatch :   Poultry Breedin
Frozen Poultry :   Poultry Feeds

Taylor Made Oil Tools, Inc.
PO Box 3404
Houma, LA 70361-3404
Contact: Keith McNeilly, V-P., GM
Telephone: 504-851-5081
Fax: 504-876-4680
Email: taylormade@cajun.net / URL: http://www.taylormadeoiltools.com
Product Service Description:
Oil field tools & coil tubing

Teach-A-Bodies Inc.
7 Dons Dr
Mission, TX 78572-4350
Contact: Nancy Fryer,
Telephone: 956-581-9959
Fax: 956-585-3089
Email: tabdoll@aol.com / URL: http://www.valleyonline.com/tabdolls/
Product Service Description:
Anatomical dolls

Tech Trans International, Inc.
2200 Space Park Drive, Suite 410
Houston, TX 77058
Contact: Beth Williams, *
Telephone: 281-335-8000
Product Service Description:
Translation Services

Tech-Mark Inc
PO Box 1569
Clackamas, OR 97015-1569
Contact: Gil J Martini, Pres., GM
Telephone: 503-655-6117
Fax: 503-655-6368
Email: sales@enviro-pak.com / URL:
Product Service Description:
Manufactures and services food processing
ovens, dryers, steam cabinets and smokers

Techbase International
165 S Union Blvd Ste 510
Denver, CO 80228-2221
Contact: Michael Norred, Pres.
Telephone: 303-980-5300
Fax: 303-969-0022
Email: sales@techbase.com / URL: http://www.techbase.com
Product Service Description:
Develops software for the engineering and
mining fields : Computer programming
services : Prepackaged software

TechnaSeal
4647B Las Positas Road
Livermore, CA 94550-9577
Contact: Joel Fener,
Telephone: 925-455-6380
Fax: 925-455-9404
Email: joel@technaseal.com / URL: http://www.technaseal.com
Product Service Description:
Manufactures impulse heat sealing machinery
used to join flexible thermoplastic films and
laminates : Packaging machinery
Industrial machinery & equipment
Machinery_special industry

Techni Edge Mfg. Corp.
389 Liberty Street
Little Ferry, NJ 07643
Contact: Deborah Williams,
Marketing Director
Telephone: 201-641-7776
Fax: 201-641-0835
Email: info@techniedge.com / URL: http://www.techniedge.com
Product Service Description:
Industrial Blades & Knives

Techni-Chem Inc.
6853 Indy Dr
Belvidere, IL 61008-8769
Contact: John W. Atchison, Pres.
Telephone: 815-547-5900
Fax: 815-544-2824
Email: tci6853@aol.com / URL:
Product Service Description:
Ion exchange equipment, resin & spare parts

Techni-Seal International
P.O. Box 120274
San Antonio, TX 78212
Contact: J.B. Martin, Owner
Telephone: 210/733-9925
Fax: 210/733-0918
Email: tecsea@netxpress.com / URL:
Product Service Description:
Pipe Thread Sealants, Potable Water, Acid

Technical Coating International
150 Backhoe Rd., N.E., Ste. 17
Leland, NC 28451-8506
Contact: David Standbury,
Vice President , Sales
Telephone: 910-371-0860
Fax: 910-371-0929
Email: sales@tciinc.com / URL: http://www.tciinc.com
Product Service Description:
Coating, laminating, print, metallize & slit
plastic film, paper, fabric & foils
Electronic (ESD, anti-stat, barrier &
conductive) (packaging)
Medical (packaging)
Cosmetic (lacquer, lamination)
Window Fashion (metallize, lamination)
Suceptor (metallize, lamination)
Office Supplies (lamination)
Graphic Arts (top coats)
Tape & Label (PSA)

Technical Engineering Sales, Inc.
806 Grand Ave.
Joplin, MO 64801-4902
Contact: Marie Spruk, Pres.
Telephone: 417-781-7360
Fax: 417-781-7361
Email: / URL: http://www.techengsales.com
Product Service Description:
Industrial machinery
General machining job shop

Technical Fabriators, Inc.
205 Dunn Ave.
Piscataway, NJ 08854-2303
Contact: K. Ball, Pres
Telephone: 732-469-7373
Fax: 732-469-9199
Product Service Description:
Industrial Filters

Technical Resource International, Inc.
3202 Tower Oaks Blvd.
Rockville, MD 20852-4200
Contact: Sales & Marketing,
Telephone: 301-231-5250
Fax: 301-231-6377
Email: marketing@tech-res.com / URL: http://www.tech-res-intl.com
Product Service Description:
Miscellaneous Publishing
Motion Picture Production
Research
Information Retrieval
Communications & Outreach

Technical Sales, Inc.
7705 Central Ave.
Minneapolis, MN 55432
Contact: Pat McCready, *
Telephone: 612-784-0240
Fax: 612-784-2259
Product Service Description:
Injection Molded and Machined Plastic Parts

Technology General Corp.
12 Cork Hill Rd
Franklin, NJ 07416-1300
Contact: Charles Fletcher, Pres.
Telephone: 973-827-4143
Fax: 973-827-4613 & 2239
Email: / URL:
Product Service Description:
Spray painting
Ice crushing equipment
Compressors_air & gas
Industrial air & electrical driven mixers
Deep drawn metal products

Technology Research Corporation
5250 140th Avenue North
Clearwater, FL 33760-3728
Contact: Wayne P. Glaser, Vice President,Int'l
Operations
Telephone: 727-535-0572
Fax: 727-530-7375
Email: wglaser@trci.net / URL: http://www.trci.net
Product Service Description:
Portable Ground Fault Circuit Interrupters
Equipment Leakage Current Interrupters
Appliance Leakage Current Interrupters
Fire Safe Extension Cords

Tecnipac Inc
1550 Broadway Ste D
Chula Vista, CA 91911-4059
Contact: Andrew J Taylor, Pres.
Telephone: 619-426-2594
Fax: 619-426-2595
Email: guadalajara@empac.com.mx / URL:
http://www.empac.com.mx
Product Service Description:
Manufactures equipment for bottle packaging,
and labeling
Packaging machinery
Industrial machinery & equipment

Teco
86305 College View Rd
Eugene, OR 97405-9631
Contact: Darin Thompson, Lab Mgr.
Telephone: 541-746-8271
Fax: 541-747-1630
Email: tecotested@worldnet.com / URL:
Product Service Description:
Wood product testing of panel products
(plywood& OSB) & particleboard
Testing laboratories

Tecre Co., Inc.
W 5747 Lost Arrow Rd.
Fond Du Lac, WI 54937
Contact: Ben Braunberger, Pres.
Telephone: 920-922-9168
Fax: 920-922-1429
Email: info@tecre.com / URL: http://www.tecre.com
Product Service Description:
Button assembly machines & die cutting presses : Advertising buttons : Political buttons : Die Cutting Presses / Manual

TeleDirect International, Inc.
17255 North 82nd St.
Scottsdale, AZ 85255
Contact: Lisa Hill,
Telephone: 480-585-6464
Fax: 480-585-3373
Email: ihill@tdirect.com / URL: http://www.tdivect.com
Product Service Description:
Call center software solutions & technology

Teledex Corporation
6311 San Ignacio Avenue
San Jose, CA 95119-1239
Contact:Wei Huang, Int'l Product Mktg. Mgr.
Telephone: 408-574-2646
Fax: 408-574-2645
Email: sales@teledex.com / URL: http://www.teledex.com
Product Service Description:
Telephone Apparatus

Teledyne Water Pik
1730 E Prospect Rd
Fort Collins, CO 80525-1310
Contact: Michael Lambert, Dir. Int'l Mktg.
Telephone: 970-484-1352
Fax: 970-221-8715
Email: / URL: http://www.waterpik.com
Product Service Description:
Dental equipment & supplies : Manufactures oral hygiene products:oral irrigators,electric toothbrushes & plaque removers : Service industry machinery: Shower Heads
Water filters

Teleflex Fluid Systems, Inc.
1 Firestone Dr
Suffield, CT 06078-2611
Contact: Randy Braun,
Telephone: 860-668-1285
Fax: 860-668-2353
Email: / URL: http://www.teleflexhose.com
Product Service Description:
Rubber & Plastic Hose & Belting
Fluoropolymer hose

Teleparts, Inc.
763 C Susquehanna Avenue
Franklin Lakes, NJ 07417
Contact: Doron Miller, *
Telephone: 201/847-9509
Product Service Description:
On/Off Hwy. Eq. Spare Parts, Wholesale

Telesat International Ltd
PO Box 5178
Oregon City, OR 97045-8178
Contact: Dan Berge, CEO
Phone: 503-656-2774/ Fax: 503-657-9945
Email: dan@telesat.net / URL:
Product Service Description:
Manufactures radio and TV broadcasting and communications equipment : Radio & TV communications equipment & global internet bandwidth

Teletrol Systems, Inc.
The Gateway Bldg., 50 Phillippe Cote St.
Manchester, NH 03101
Contact: Joseph H. Klotz, *
Telephone: 603/645-6061
Product Service Description:
Automated Building Control Equipment

Televentas
7500 N.W. 25th St., Unit 7
Miami, FL 33122-1700
Contact: A. Fiallo, President
Telephone: 305-471-8111
Product Service Description:
Electromechanical domestic appliances, with self-contained electric motor
Consumer Electronics
Audio & Video

Tella Tool & Mfg. Co.
1015 N Ridge Ave
Lombard, IL 60148-1210
Contact: Daniel M. Provenzano, Pres.
Telephone: 630-495-0545
Fax: 630-495-3056
Email: lmautone@aol.com / URL: http://www.tellatool.com
Product Service Description:
Metal stampings, sheet metal fabrication, tools, dies, prototypes & precision machining
Dies, tools, jigs & fixtures_special

Tema Isenmann, Inc.
2269 Danforth Dr.
Lexington, KY 40511-1087
Contact: Jay Ford, Pres.
Telephone: 606-252-0613
Fax: 606-254-9877
Email: / URL:
Product Service Description:
Wire products_misc. fabricated
Polyurethane screens

Tempco Electric Heater Corp.
607 N Central Ave
Wood Dale, IL 60191-1452
Contact: Fermin Adames, Pres.
Telephone: 630-350-2252
Fax: 630-350-0232
Email: info@tempco-electric.com / URL: http://www.tempco-electric.com
Product Service Description:
Electric heating elements, thermocouples & aluminum & bronze castings

Templar Food Products
571 Central Ave.
New Providnce, NJ 07974-1546
Contact: Edward D. Reeves, President
Telephone: 908-665-9511
Fax: 908-665-9122
Email: info@icedtea.com / URL: http://www.icedtea.com
Product Service Description:
Groceries and Related Products, NEC
Food preparations

Temple-Inland Forest Products Corp., Building Products Div.
P.o. Drawer N
Diboll, TX 75941
Contact: Carolyn Elmore, Comm. Dir., Corp.
Telephone: 409-829-5511
Fax: 409-829-1329
Email: / URL: http://www.temple.com
Product Service Description:
Sawmills & planing mills, general
Lumber processing

Tempo Lighting
P.O. Box 3297
Hialeah, FL 33013-0297
Contact: Donald E Courtney, Chairman of the Board
Telephone: 305-835-2214
Fax: 305-693-7693
Email: tempolite@aol.com / URL:
Product Service Description:
Lighting Fixtures
Lamps
Lamp Shades

Tenessee Fiberglass Productc, Inc.
PO Box 4364
Oneida, TN 37841-4364
Contact: Lewis A. Casalandra, Executive V.P.
Telephone: 423-569-8460
Fax: 423-569-9831
Email: / URL:
Product Service Description:
Automotive Fiberglass Removable Hardtops
Acrylic / Marble / Gemstone Jetted Tubs
Custom Fiberglass Parts

Tennessee Galvanizing
1535 Industrial Blvd
Jasper, TN 37347-5236
Contact: David Ware, Pres.
Telephone: 423-942-1020
Fax: 423-942-1040
Email: tngalv@worldnet.att.net / URL: http://www.cdc.net/~tngalv/
Product Service Description:
Metal Galvanizing

Tenwood International
5373 3rd St.
Irwindale, CA 91706-2085
Contact: Charles Teng, President
Telephone: 626-338-9831
Fax: 626-338-9209
Email: tenwood@worldnet.att.net / URL:
Product Service Description:
Knock down samll animal & bird cages; wood product in bird nesting cottges, playpens, ladders, rabbit hutch
Saddlery and harness for any animal , of any material
Articles of plastics

Termax Corporation
3950 Industrial Ave
Rolling Meadows, IL 60008-1024
Contact: Joseph Lowry, National Sales Manager
Telephone: 847-253-0640
Fax: 847-253-0679
Email: termax@chicagonet.net / URL:
Product Service Description:
Stamped metal Fasteners
Metal Stampings

Terriss-Consolidated Industries
807 Summerfield Ave., P.O. Box 110
Asbury Park, NJ 07712
Contact: Edward Della Zanna, Sales Manager
Telephone: 732-988-0909
Fax: 732-502-0526
Email: terriss@monmouth.com / URL: http://www.terriss.com
Product Service Description:
Quality Control Laboratory Equipment
Beverage Laboratory Equipment
Beverage Testing Apparatus
Stainless Steel Sanitary Ware
Fabricated Stainless Steel Products
Quality Control Supplies For Soft Drink Industry

Terry Laboratories, Inc.
390 N. Wickham Road, Suite F.
Melbourne, FL 32935
Contact: James Gambino, Executive V.P. / General Manager
Telephone: 407-259-1630
Fax: 407-242-0625
Email: aloe@terrylabs.com / URL: http://www.terrylabs.com
Product Service Description:
Cosmetic Raw Materials, Aloe Vera
Ind. Organic Chemicals, Aloe Vera
Beverages Bases, Aloe Vera

Terry Tools, Inc.
356 S. Elmwood Ave.
Buffalo, NY 14201
Contact: Susan M. Ensign, President
Telephone: 716-854-0633
Fax: 716-847-8830
Email: terrytools@juno.com / URL:
Product Service Description:
Angle Drilling Attachments

Tetra Medical Supply Corp.
6364 W Gross Point Rd
Niles, IL 60714-3916
Contact: Constance A. Shier, Pres., Hum. Res. & Opers. Mgr.
Telephone: 847-647-0590
Fax: 847-647-9034
Email: tetra@tetramed.com / URL: http://www.tetramed.com
Product Service Description:
Hospital supplies, bandages & orthopedic soft goods

Tetra Technologies
25025 Interstate 45
The Woodlands, TX 77380-3034
Contact: Ken Reid, General Manager - Int'l
Telephone: 281-364-2234
Fax: 281-364-4320
Email: kreid@tetratec.com / URL: http://www.tetratec.com
Product Service Description:
Calcium Chloride

Tevco
110 Pomponio Ave.
South Plainfield, NJ 07080-1900
Contact: Eric Wimmer, President
Telephone: 908-754-7306
Fax: 908-756-0934
Email: / URL: http://www.tevco.com
Product Service Description:
Nail polish & nail treatment & allied products

Tex-Ex Export Co., Inc.
P.O. Box 256
Marlboro, NJ 07746-0256
Contact: Sales & Marketing,
Telephone: 732-462-5757
Fax: 732-462-5190
Email: tex-ex@worldnet.att.net / URL:
Product Service Description:
Textiles

Texace Corp.
402 W Nueva
San Antonio, TX 78207-4516
Contact: Bob W. Coleman, Chrm., CEO
Telephone: 210-227-7551
Fax: 210-227-4237
Email: / URL: http://www.texace.tmac.org
Product Service Description:
Hats, caps & straw hats
Golf caps, hats, visors & straw hats

Texas Almet Inc.
2800 E Randol Mill Rd
Arlington, TX 76011-6724
Contact: Norris Stroud, GM, Sales & Mktg.
Phone: 817-640-2345 / Fax: 817-649-3154
Email: texasalmet@msn.com / URL: http://
www.honeycombone.com
Product Service Description:
Honeycomb Core for Aircraft wings, flaps &
engine housings : Aircraft parts & equipment

Texas Composite Inc.
32980 I-10 W.
Boerne, TX 78006
Contact: W. A. McOran-Campbell, Pres.
Telephone: 830-249-3399
Fax: 830-249-3275
Email: acampbell@texascomposite.com /
URL: http://www.texascomposite.com
Product Service Description:
Commercial & military composite aircraft &
aerospace structures
Space Vehicle Structures

Texas Electronics, Inc.
5529 Redfield Street
Dallas, TX 75235
Contact: Jim Young, Operations Manager
Telephone: 214-631-2490 / 800-424-5651
Fax: 214-631-4218
Email: info@texaselectronics.com / URL:
http://www.texaselectronics.com
Product Service Description:
Meteorological instruments, sensors, rain
gauges, weather stations & dataloggers

Texas Greenhouse Co., Inc.
2524 White Settlement Rd
Fort Worth, TX 76107-1453
Contact: Kathy B. Carlile, Pres., CFO
Telephone: 817-335-5447
Fax: 817-334-0818
Email: tgci@airmail.net / URL: http://
www.texasgreenhouse.com
Product Service Description:
Aluminum & glass greenhouses

Texas Jasmine
7520 Harwin Dr.
Houston, TX 77036-2008
Contact: Sales & Marketing,
Telephone: 713-785-2357
Fax: 713-785-2178
Product Service Description:
99 Cent Store Merchandise (Closeouts)
Mostly Domestic Merchandise

Texas Meter & Device Co.
1509 New Dallas Hwy
Waco, TX 76705-2432
Contact: Sam Allison, Pres.
Telephone: 800-247-5116
Fax: 254-799-0266
Email: info@texasmeter.com / URL: http://
www.texasmeter.com
Product Service Description:
Electric watt hour meters, high-voltage
protective equipment & control panels

Texas PMW, Inc.
315 N. Wayside Dr.
Houston, TX 77087
Contact: Gloria Hyman, Cont.
Phone: 713-679-7900 / Fax: 713-679-7920
Email: pennmachine@pdq.net / URL: http://
www.pennusa.com
Product Service Description:
Pipe fittings - forged : Branch Connections
Pipe Nipples

Textron Turf Care and Specialty Products
1721 Packard Ave.
Racine, WI 53403-2561
Contact: Philip J. Tralies, Pres
Telephone: 414-637-6711
Fax: 414-637-4465
Email: / URL: http://www.textron.com
Product Service Description:
Lawn & Garden Equipment
Turf & Commercial Mowing Equipment

The Akro Corporation
1212 7th St. SE
Canton, OH 44707
Contact: Sales & Marketing, *
Telephone: 216-456-4543
Fax: 216-456-0849
Product Service Description:
Consumer, Commerical, Industrial, Food

The Alchemists Inc
PO Box 1660
Green Valley, AZ 85622-1660
Contact: Janice Nagle, Pres.
Telephone: 520-393-7000
Fax: 520-393-0920
Email: / URL:
Product Service Description:
Manufactures brass and sand carved river
rock; copper jewelry

The Barrel Company Inc.
217 So. Washington St.
Winchester, VA 22601
Contact: Nicholas Smart, Owner
Telephone: 540-667-3555
Fax: 540-667-3593
Email: ksmart@visuallink.com / URL: http://
www.distill.com/barrels
Product Service Description:
Casks, barrels, vats, tubs and other coopers'
products and parts thereof, of wood
Wood in chips or particles, nonconiferous

The California Visitors Review
PO Box 92
El Verano, CA 95433-0092
Contact: Douglas Martin, Ptnr.
Telephone: 707-938-3494
Fax: 707-938-3674
Email: / URL:
Product Service Description:
Publishes visitors guide to wine counties
Publishing_miscellaneous

The Capital Controls Group
3000 Advance Ln.
Colmar, PA 18915
Contact: International Sales, *
Telephone: 215-997-4000
Fax: 215-997-4062
Email: marketing@capitalcontrols.com /
URL: http://www.capitalcontrols.com
Product Service Description:
Water Chlorination Equipment

The Catholic Voice
3014 Lakeshore Ave
Oakland, CA 94610-3615
Contact: Monica Clark, Editor
Telephone: 510-893-5339
Fax: 510-893-4734
Email: cathvoice@aol.com / URL:
Product Service Description:
Publishes newspaper and annual directory of
churches and schools
Newspapers
Publishing_miscellaneous

The Chemins Company Inc
1835 East Cheyenne Road
Colorado Springs, CO 80906
Contact: James R Cameron, Pres., CEO
Telephone: 719-579-9650
Fax: 719-579-9651
Email: thecheminsco@msn.com / URL:
Product Service Description:
Manufactures dietary supplements and
nutrients
Vitamins & Minerals, Manufacturing
Sports Nutrition, Manufacturing

The DII Group Inc
6273 Monarch Park Pl.
Longmont, CO 80503-7119
Contact: Ronald R Budacz, Chrm., CEO
Telephone: 303-652-2221
Fax: 303-652-0416
Email: / URL: http://www.diigroup.com
Product Service Description:
Electronic components
Contract electronics manufacturer, electronics
assembly and related services to OEM's; tur
Holding companies
Machinery_special industry

The DU-AL Corp.
1912 Hwy. 142 E.
Covington, GA 30209
Contact: Robert E. Allen Jr., Pres., CFO, R &
D, Sales & Mktg. Mgr.
Telephone: 770-784-9062
Fax: 770-385-7216
Email: aramaic.bible.society@aramaic.org /
URL: http://www.aramaic.org
Product Service Description:
Reusable Cataract Cryoextractor Kits
DU-AL 5' coiled Hose Cryogen Refilling
Systems

The Damron Co Inc
PO Box 422458
San Francisco, CA 94142-2458
Contact: Gina M Gatta, Pres., CEO
Telephone: 415-255-0404
Fax: 415-703-9049
Email: damronco@aol.com / URL: http://
www.damron.com
Product Service Description:
Publishes travel guides targeting the gay and
lesbian clientele
Publishing_miscellaneous

The Glass Table
1876 E Broadway Rd
Tempe, AZ 85282-1641
Contact: Kathie Julian, President
Telephone: 602-966-5289
Fax: 602-966-6753
Email: kathie@theglasstable.com / URL:
http://www.theglasstable.com
Product Service Description:
Manufactures heavy glass tabletops and
wrought iron furniture

The John Wesley Group
800 5th Ave #101-140
Seattle, WA 98104
Contact: Richard Howe, President
Telephone: 206-340-1794
Fax: 206-340-1943
Email: mail@asia-us.com / URL: http://
www.asia-us.com
Product Service Description:
Business Consulting / Product Sourcing
Business Services : Amusement Parks
Cosmetics : Automotive Services
Management Consulting Services

The Language Lab
211 East 43rd Street, #1904
New York, NY 10017
Contact: Ms. Joyce Ferrara,
Telephone: 212-697-2020
Fax: 212-697-2891
Email: langlab@aol.com / URL: http://
www.thelanguagelab.com
Product Service Description:
Translation & Interpreting Services
Type / Desktop , All Languages

The Laser Workshop
710 E Debra Ln
Anaheim, CA 92805-6317
Contact: John Deane, Sr. Ptnr.
Telephone: 714-635-8373
Fax: 714-635-8377
Email: / URL:
Product Service Description:
Industrial laser cutting and engraving
Waterjet cutting

The Lucks Food Equipment Co.
21112 72nd Ave. South
Kent, WA 98032-1339
Contact: Bill Keadle, President
Telephone: 253-872-2180
Fax: 253-872-2013
Email: bkeadle@lucks.com / URL: http://
www.lucks.com
Product Service Description:
Food products machinery
Manufactures bakery and food service
equipment; decorations, flavor
Decorations, flavors, edible image base &
licensed & custom edible images

The Malder Co
1157 Folsom St
San Francisco, CA 94103-3930
Contact: Malcolm R Cressy, Owner
Telephone: 415-626-9492
Fax: 415-626-9693
Email: malcressy@aol.com / URL:
Product Service Description:
Lighting fixture restoration, (custom fixture
manufacturing); sales
Lighting fixtures_residential - commercial

The Martin Company
7704 Clybourn Ave
Sun Valley, CA 91352-4601
Contact: Richard Martin,
Telephone: 818-767-9557
Fax: 818-767-4979
Email: rmsummer@earthlink.net / URL:
Product Service Description:
Manufactures Stainless Steel AN, MS, NAS,
& AS Tube Fittings

The Medical Remarketer
5 Colony Rd
Canton, CT 06019-2403
Contact: Rose Hambley, Publisher
Telephone: 860-693-9055
Fax: 860-693-8115
Email: rosetmr@ad.com / URL: http://
www.medxchange.com/tmr
Product Service Description:
Monthly advertising publication containing all
types of pre-owned medical equipment
Newspapers
Typesetting

The Morning Star Packing Company
13448 Volta Road
Los Bnaos, CA 93635
Contact: Tony Manuel,
Telephone: 209-826-8000
Fax: 209-826-8266
Email: tmanuel@morningstarco.com / URL:
http://www.morningstarco.com
Product Service Description:
Food products manufacturing
Tomato paste, tomatoes diced, tomatoes
whole peel : Tomato sauce, tomato ketchup -
institutional sizes

The Phoenix Company of Chicago, Inc.
555 Pond Dr
Wood Dale, IL 60191-1192
Contact: Terry Rizzo,
Telephone: 630-595-2300
Fax: 630-595-6579
URL: http://www.phoenixofchicago.com
Product Service Description:
Electronic connectors

The Practice Builder Association
18351 Jamboree Rd
Irvine, CA 92612-1011
Contact: Stewart Gandolf, VP Marketing
Telephone: 949-253-7900
Fax: 949-252-1002
Product Service Description:
Publishes newsletter; advertising and
marketing company
Periodicals
Advertising agencies
Management consulting services

The Purolite Company
150 Monument Rd Ste 202
Bala Cynwyd, PA 19004-1725
Contact: Francis Boodoo, Tech, Support
Telephone: 610-668-9090
Fax: 610-668-8139
Email: fboodoo@puroliteusa.com / URL:
http://www.puroliteusa.com
Product Service Description:
Ion Exchange Resin

The Siemon Company
76 Westbury Park Rd.
Watertown, CT 06795 USA
Contact: Robert Carlson, Marketing Director
Telephone: 860-274-2523
Fax: 860-945-8503
Email: info@siemon.com / URL: http://
www.siemon.com
Product Service Description:
Telephone Equipment, Connecting Hardware
Telephone Equipment Fiber Optic Distrib.
Panel / Products
Electrical Work Station Outlets / Work Area
Products
Electrical Instruments, Test Equipment
Cable & Cable Management Products
Structural Cabling Systems

The Skiing Co
929 Pearl St Fl 2
Boulder, CO 80302
Contact: Macy Allatt,
Telephone: 303-448-7679
Fax: 303-448-7638
Email: mallatt@skinet.com / URL: http://
www.skinet.com
Product Service Description:
Publishes monthly downhill skiing magazines
Periodicals

The Western Newspaper
13540 W Camino Del Sol Ste 15
Sun City West, AZ 85375-4436
Contact: Frank Kahler, Pres.
Phone: 602-584-2992 / Fax: 602-584-0950
Product Service Description:
Publishes Sun City West weekly newspaper

The Wolfe Pack
512 Main St # B
Longmont, CO 80501-5537
Contact: Laury Wolfe, Pres.
Telephone: 303-684-0180
Fax: 303-684-0178
Email: wolfepak@frii.com / URL: http://
www.wolfe-pack.com
Product Service Description:
Designs and publishes archival papers with
sports & outdoor : Adventure themes for
scrap books : Publishing_miscellaneous

The Wornick Company
10825 Kenwood Road
Cincinnati, OH 45242
Contact: William F. Quinlan, Pres., CEO
Telephone: 513-794-9800
Fax: 513-794-0107
Email: bquinlan@wornick.com / URL: http://
www.wornick.com
Product Service Description:
Manufactures shelf stable foods
Food preparations

Therm Tech Inc.
PO Box 5318
Kingwood, TX 77325-5318
Contact: William Hedges Jr., Pres.
Telephone: 281-359-7555
Fax: 281-359-7550
Email: brians@thermtech.com / URL:
Product Service Description:
Thermal & Catalytic Oxidizers
Process Heaters
Custom Control Panels - UL Listed

Therma-Fab, Inc.
200 Rich Lex Dr
Lexington, SC 29072-9274
Contact: Bill Watkins, Pres.,
Telephone: 803-794-2543
Fax: 803-796-0999
Email: thermafab@hotmail.com / URL:
Product Service Description:
Sewage lagoon baffles, liners, secondary
containment systems & potable water baffles

Therma-Tron-X Inc.
1155 S Neenah Ave
Sturgeon Bay, WI 54235-1937
Contact: Roger Kinnard, Controller
Telephone: 920-743-6568
Fax: 920-743-5486
Email: ttx@mail.doorcounty-wi.com / URL:
http://www.therma-tron-x.com
Product Service Description:
Industrial Process Furnaces & Ovens
Industrial Washers, Metal
Paint Finishing Machines

Thermafiber L.L.C.
3711 W. Mill St.
Wabash, IN 46992
Contact: Michael Williams, VP. Sales
Phone: 219-563-2111 / Fax: 219-563-8979
Email: mwilliams@thermafiber.com / URL:
http://www.thermafiber.com
Product Service Description:
Mineral wool for thermal, acoustical & fire
protection applications

Thermal Systems America
Madison Blvd.
Canastota, NY 13032
Contact: Dave Quilter, Pres.
Telephone: 315-697-8410
Fax: 315-697-8580
Email: sales@thermalsystemsamerica.com /
URL: http://
www.thermalsystemsamerica.com
Product Service Description:
Refractory systems & shapes for aluminum
applications

Thermal Systems Inc
2757 29th Ave Sw
Tumwater, WA 98512-6104
Contact: Dale Rasmussen, Pres., Fin. & GM
Telephone: 360-352-0539
Fax: 360-943-6442
Email: catheater@mail.tss.net / URL: http://
www.users.tss.net/thermal
Product Service Description:
Heating equipment, except electric
Manufactures infrared catalytic heating
equipment, commercial & industrial;
residential
RV & Boat cabin heaters

Thermatek International Inc.
34065 Homestead Rd.
Gurnee, IL 60031 USA
Contact: Stephen G. Samaras,
Telephone: 847-855-1800
Fax: 847-855-9802
Email: samaras@thermatek.com / URL: http:/
/www.thermatek.com/
Product Service Description:
Industrial & Laboratory Furnaces & Ovens
and
Extrusion Handling Machinery

Thermo Black Clawson Inc.
605 Clark St.
Middletown, OH 45042
Contact: W.J. Fondow, President
Telephone: 513/424-7400
Fax: 513/424-1168
Email: info@blackclawson.com / URL: http://
www.blackclawson.com
Product Service Description:
Pulp & Paper Industry Machinery
Paper Stock Preparation Equip.
Paper Recycling Equip.
Paper Machine Approach Flow Systems

Thermocare, Inc.
PO Box 6069
Incline Village, NV 89450-6069
Contact: Lee Cunningham, President
Telephone: 702-831-1201
Fax: 702-831-1230
Email: thermocare@aol.com / URL: http://
www.thermocare.com
Product Service Description:
Medical Equipment, Portable Intensive Care
Veterinary/Research Equipment: Portable
ICU

Thermodyne Food Service Products
2300 Meyer Rd
Fort Wayne, IN 46803-2910
Contact: Sue Brown, GM & R & D Mgr.
Telephone: 219-422-1941
Fax: 219-426-0427
Email: / URL: http://www.t-dyne.com
Product Service Description:
Ovens
Steamers

Thiel Air Technologies Corp.
1136 S Fort Thomas Ave
Fort Thomas, KY 41075-2465
Contact: Gregory R. Thiel, Technical Director
Telephone: 606-781-4330
Fax: 606-781-2356
Email: thielair@eos.net / URL: http://
www.thielair.com
Product Service Description:
Industrial Air Cleaning Equipment
Air Pollution Control Equipment
Specialists in Collecting Dust, Mist, Smoke,
Fog : Fumes, & Ultra-Fine Liquid & Solid
Contaminants : From Industrial Processes

Thistle Roller Co Inc
209 Van Norman Rd
Montebello, CA 90640-5343
Contact: Lizbeth Karpynec, Pres.
Telephone: 562-948-3705
Fax: 562-942-1042
Email: / URL:
Product Service Description:
Steel and rubber covered rollers for every
industry : Anilox service for printing
machinery : Roller service : Chrome service
Rubber extruding : Paper mill service
Textile service : Corrugated service
Conveyor rolls manufacturing
Machine shop

Thomas Industries, Inc.
1419 Illinois Ave.
Sheboygan, WI 53081-4821
Contact: Export Sales,
Telephone: 920-457-4891
Fax: 920-451-4237
Email: rtaylor@thomasind.com / URL: http://
www.thomaspumps.com
Product Service Description:
Air and Gas Compressors
Air pumps and air or other gas compressors;
Ventilating or recycling hoods incorporating a
fan : Instruments and appliances for medical,
surgical or veterinary sciences and parts and
accessories : Spray guns and similar
appliances

Thomas Industries-Power Air Div.
PO Box 29
Sheboygan, WI 53082-0029
Contact: B. R. Berntson, V-P., GM
Telephone: 920-457-4891
Fax: 920-451-4237
Product Service Description:
Pumps & pumping equipment
OEM air compressors & vacuum pumps

Thomas Pump & Machinery, Inc.
PO Box 2530
Slidell, LA 70459-2530
Contact: Jim Thomas, Pres., Opers. Mgr.
Telephone: 504-649-3000
Fax: 504-649-4300
Email: tpump@thomaspump.com / URL:
http://www.thomaspump.com
Product Service Description:
Pumps & pumping equipment

Thomas Scientific
P.O. Box 99
Swedesboro, NJ 08085-0099
Contact: E. B. Patterson, Jr.,
Chairman of the Board
Telephone: 609-467-2000
Fax: 609-467-3087
Email: value@thomassci.com / URL:
Product Service Description:
Laboratory equip, supplies & reagents

Thor Guard, Inc.
1193 Sawgrass Corporate Pkwy.
Sunrise, FL 33323
Contact: Peter Townsend, Pres.
Telephone: 954-835-0900
Fax: 954-835-0808
Email: sales@thorguard.com / URL: http://
www.thorguard.com
Product Service Description:
Measuring & controlling devices
Lightning warning systems

Thor Tool Corporation
865 Estabrook St
San Leandro, CA 94577-3439
Contact: Mike George, Pres.
Telephone: 510-357-6777
Fax: 510-351-5123
Email: / URL: http://www.thortool.com
Product Service Description:
Manufactures punches, dies and accessories
for turret and single station punch presses
Dies, tools, jigs & fixtures_special
Machine tools, metal forming types

Thunderball Marketing
111 8th Ave., Ste. 212
New York, NY 10011-5201
Contact: Joe Levy, President
Telephone: 212-645-5600
Fax: 212-645-6620
Email: joe@tball.com / URL: http://
www.tball.com
Product Service Description:
Electronic Parts and Equipment
Electrical parts of machinery or apparatus
Electromechanical domestic appliances, with
self-contained electric motor
Miscellaneous cargo

Thunderbird Printing & Screening
417 Gentry Way
Reno, NV 89502-4610
Contact: Walter Huff, Pres.
Telephone: 702-825-3833
Fax: 702-825-3744
Email: / URL: http://www.tbrd.com
Product Service Description:
Commercial printing, lithographic and offset;
silkscreening; hot foil stamping
Lithographic printing_commercial
Printing_commercial

Tideland Signal Corp.
PO Box 52430
Houston, TX 77052-2430
Contact: H. J. Saenger, Pres.
Telephone: 713-681-6101
Fax: 713-681-6233
Email: hg@tidelandsignal.com / URL: http://
www.tidelandsignal.com
Product Service Description:
Marine lanterns, radar beacons, fog signals &
solar electric generators
Buoys, lighted, unlighted

Tigert Co., T. F.
2135 Industrial St
Lancaster, TX 75134-3403
Contact: Gary Radney, Pres.
Telephone: 972-227-5213
Fax: 972-227-9505
Email: / URL:
Product Service Description:
Plate work_fabricated (boiler shops)
Rebuilt boilers & combustion controls
Process control instruments

Tilton Rack & Basket Corp.
66 Passaic Ave
Fairfield, NJ 07004-3510
Contact: Herb Tilton, Pres.
Telephone: 973-226-6010
Fax: 973-227-4155
Email: / URL:
Product Service Description:
Wire products_misc. fabricated
Industrial plating racks
Wire mesh & perforated baskets

Timber Products
P.O. Box 269
Springfield, OR 97477-5404
Contact: Joseph Gonyea, Owner
Telephone: 541-747-4577
Fax: 541-744-5431
Email: rrutan@teamtp.com / URL:
Product Service Description:
Lumber, Plywood, and Millwork
Fiberboard of wood or other ligneous
materials : Plywood, veneered panels &
similar laminated wood

Time Fastener Company Inc
5301 Longley Ln Bldg G
Reno, NV 89511-1842
Contact: John Jukes, Pres.
Telephone: 775-829-1026
Fax: 775-829-1989
Email: / URL: http://www.timesert.com
Product Service Description:
Manufactures industrial thread repair inserts
and tools

Times Leader, Inc.
PO Box 439
Princeton, KY 42445-0439
Contact: Jennifer Beckner, Fin & Off. Mgr.
Telephone: 502-365-5588
Fax: 502-365-7299
Email: timesleader@ziggycom.net / URL:
http://www.wkynet.com/princetonnet/times-
leader/
Product Service Description:
Commercial & Newspaper Printing
Printing, Commercial : Newspapers

Tinby, LLC
5003 North Fwy Ste A
Fort Worth, TX 76106-1836
Contact: Frede H. Heidmann, President
Telephone: 817-740-1166
Fax: 817-740-1170
Email: info@tinbyllc.com / URL: http://
www.tinbyllc.com
Product Service Description:
Polyurethane rollers
Plastic products

Tire & Heavy Equipment, Inc.
1823 E Broadway St
West Memphis, AR 72301-3445
Contact: Terrell B. Smith Jr., Pres.
Telephone: 870-732-1130
Fax: 870-732-5851
Product Service Description:
Tire retreading
Tires & inner tubes

Tire Factory, The
7870 Mexico Rd.
St. Peters, MO 63376
Contact: Ron Smith, *
Telephone: 314-397-6999
Fax: 314-397-5371
Product Service Description:
Tires & Inner Tubes, Auto & Light Truck

Tire Group International Inc
6695 N.W.36 Avenue
Miami, FL 33147
Contact: Antonio R. Gonzalez, CEO. & COO
Telephone: 305-696-0096
Fax: 305-696-5926
Email: tgi@tiregroup.com / URL:
Product Service Description:
Truck Tires : Agricultural / Off-The-Road /
Industrial Tires : Passenger Vehicle / Light
Truck / Specialty Tires : Tubes / Flaps / Tire
Repair Materials / Wheels & Accessories

Tishcon Corporation (Mfr)
30 New York Avenue
Westbury, NY 11590
Contact: Raj Chopra, President
Telephone: 516-333-3050
Fax: 516-997-3660
Email: raj@tishcon.com / URL: http://
www.tishcon.com
Product Service Description:
Vitamins & Health Supplements

Tithe Corp., Skil-aire Div.
1100 Wicomico St
Baltimore, MD 21230-2063
Contact: Lisa Ambrose, Pres., CFO
Telephone: 410-625-7545
Fax: 410-625-6421
Email: email@skil-aire.com / URL: http://
www.skil-aire.com
Product Service Description:
Air conditioners & heat recovery units
Refrigeration & heating equipment

Titon Industries, Inc.
PO Bo x 566848
Atlanta, GA 31156-6848
Contact:Wayne F. Orr, Pres.
Telephone: 770-399-5252
Fax: 770-399-5274
Product Service Description:
Pedestal sinks, marble tops & toilets
Cut stone & stone products

Tm Industries Inc.
Plaza 78, 56 Route 173 West, Suite 1-A
Hampton, NJ 08827
Contact: Arno Tietje, Sales Manager
Telephone: 908-730-7674
Fax: 908-730-6501
Product Service Description:
Automatic Grease Lubricator, Sing. Point

Tocabi America Corp
755 Otay Valley Rd.
Chula Vista, CA 91911-6168
Contact:Katsumi Sayama, Pres.
Telephone: 619-661-6136
Fax: 619-656-8181
Email: sales@tocabi.com / URL: http://
www.tocabi.com
Product Service Description:
Manufactures audio component racks,
television stands & cabinets; kitchen &
bathroom fixture : TV & Radio
cabinets_wood: Furniture_wood household
Furniture_wood office.

Todd Co., A.M.
1717 Douglas Ave., P.O. Box 711
Kalamazoo, MI 49004-0711
Contact: Jeffrey S. Spencer,
Phone: 616-343-2603 / Fax: 616-343-4913
Email: JSS@amtoddks.attmail.com / URL:
Product Service Description:
Spearmint Oil : Peppermint Oil : Lime Oil :
Essential Oils : Mint Flavors

**Todd's Plantation, "Gourmet Coffee
Roasters", Inc.**
115 N 29th St
Billings, MT 59101-2030
Contact: Greg Gustafson, Pres.
Telephone: 406-245-2720
Email: coffee@mcn.net / URL: http://
www.mcn.net/coffee
Product Service Description:
Coffee_roasted
Manufactures roasted coffee
Custom Packaging
Private labeling
Wholesale / Retail

Todds, Ltd.
PO Box 4821
Des Moines, IA 50306-4821
Contact: Alan L. Niedermeier, Pres., Engrg.
& Mktg. Mgr.
Telephone: 515-266-2276
Fax: 515-266-1669
Email: / URL:
Product Service Description:
Food seasonings, sauces & contract
packaging
Food preparations

Toepperweins Of Texas
RR 2 Box 158a
Alleyton, TX 78935-9711
Contact: Hugh Toepperwein, Owner & R &
D Mgr.
Telephone: 409-732-8383
Fax: 409-732-6412
Email: toepper@intertex.net / URL: http://
www.virtualplants.com
Product Service Description:
Manufacturing industries
Silk plants
Preserved plants
Bonsai's
Silk florals
Ceramic fish bowls
Custom designs

Tomahawk Live Trap Co.
1416 East Mohawk Drive
Tomahawk, WI 54487
Contact: Greg Smith, President
Telephone: 715-453-3550
Fax: 715-453-4326
Email: trapem@livetrap.com / URL:
Product Service Description:
Live Animal Traps, Steel Wire

Tomahawk Truck Sales
4382 Moreland Ave.
Conley, GA 30027-2140
Contact: Rea Herring, *
Telephone: 404-362-9052
Fax: 404-362-9460
Product Service Description:
Tractors \ Used

Tomlinson Industries
13700 Broadway Ave.
Cleveland, OH 44125
Contact: Michael E. Figas, President
Telephone: 216-587-3400
Fax: 216-587-0733
Email: jengle@ameritech.net / URL: http://
www.tomlinsonind.com
Product Service Description:
Liquid Food Dispenser Faucets
Coffee Urn & Beverage Dispensing Faucets
Cast Aluminum Platters
Frontier Kettle Soup merchandisers
Concession Foodservice Equipment

Tonex, Inc.
27 Park Row
Wallington, NJ 07057-1629
Contact: Sales & Marketing,
Telephone: 201-773-5135
Fax: (201)916-1091
Email: / URL:
Product Service Description:
Non Dairy Creamers
Instant Coffee

Tools For Bending, Inc.
194 W. Dakota Ave.
Denver, CO 80223
Contact: Ronald Stange, CEO
Telephone: 303-777-7170
Fax: 303-777-4749
Email: tfb@toolsforbending.com / URL:
Product Service Description:
Manufactures Precision Tools for Tube &
Pipe Bending Machines, Hydraulic & Manual
Rotary : Machine Tools, Metal Forming
Types

Top Line Process Equipment Co.
PO Box 264
Bradford, PA 16701-0264
Contact: Vincent J. Monecalvo, Marketing
Manager
Telephone: 814-362-4626
Fax: 814-362-4453
Email: / URL:
Product Service Description:
Centrifugal Pumps, Sanitary
Stainless Steel Fittings Piping Systems
Plumbing Valves Call Butterfly Check,
Diaphragm Valves
Stainless Steel Flanges butt Weld San.

Top-Air Manufacturing, Inc.(Mfr)
317 Savannah Park Rd.
Cedar Falls, IA 50613
Contact: Steven R. Lind, *
Telephone: 319-268-0437
Fax: 319-268-1435
Email: topair@sbtek.net / URL:
Product Service Description:
Farm Machinery & Equipment

**Torner International, Inc. /
Edmundo Torner, CHB**
8025 NW 36th Street, Ste. 319
Miami, FL 33166
Contact: Edmundo Torner, President
Telephone: 305-477-3009
Fax: 305-477-3540
Email: etchb@bridge.net / URL: http://
www.wwdir.com/torner.html
Product Service Description:
Customs Broker
Freight Forwarders
Duty Drawback
Foreign Assembly of U.S. Components

**Torner, Edmundo Customhouse
Brokers**
8025 NW 36th St., Ste. 319,
Miami, FL 33166
Contact: Edmundo Torner, Owner
Telephone: 305-477-3009
Fax: 305-477-3540
Email: etchb@bellsouth.net / URL: http://
www.wwdir.com/torner.html
Product Service Description:
Customs Broker
Freight Forwarder
Freight & Cargo Transportation

**Toshiba America Information
Systems, Inc.**
Telecomunication Systems Div.
PO Box 19724
'Irvine, CA 92623-9724
Contact: Paul Wexler, Senior Vice President
Telephone:949-583-3700
Fax:949-583-3896
URL: http://www.telecom.toshiba.com
Product Service Description:
Manufactures Business phones & voice mail
Telphone & telegraph apparatus
Electronic parts & equipment

Torres Engineering
1630 Palm Ave.
San Mateo, CA 94402-2445
Contact: Dan Torres, Ptnr.
Telephone: 650-571-6887
Fax: 650-571-1507
Email: amps007@aol.com / URL: http://
www.torresengineering.com
Product Service Description:
Manufactures Musical Instruments Parts &
Accessories; Publishes Product Literature
Musical Instruments
Publishing, Miscellaneous
Vacuum Tube Amplifiers
Retail Sales, Musical Instruments

Total Printing Systems
PO Box 375
Newton, IL 62448-0375
Contact: Richard Lindemann, Pres.
Telephone: 618-783-2978
Fax: 618-783-8407
Email: sales@tps1.com / URL: http://
www.tps1.com
Product Service Description:
Government & commercial book printing
Book printing

Touch America Inc.
PO Box 1304
Hillsborough, NC 27278-1304
Contact: Stuart Griffith, Pres., Engrg. Mgr.
Telephone: 919-732-6968
Fax: 919-732-1173
Email: info@touchamerica.com / URL: http://
www.touchamerica.com
Product Service Description:
Surgical appliances & supplies
Massage & spa equipment
Spa therapy products

Tower Stool Company
PO Box 337, 219 Main Street
Faith, SD 57626-0337
Contact: Donna Henschel, Mktg. Mgr.
Telephone: 605-967-2418
Fax: 605-967-2419
Email: towerstoolco@juno.com / URL: http://
www.sdibi.northern.edu/stool/sto_home.htm
Product Service Description:
Folding Wood Stools Compact
Folding Wood Lecterns (Tabletop Models &
Floor Models)
Custom Built Pet Wood Caskets

Toyo Tanso Usa Inc
PO Box 280
Troutdale, OR 97060-0280
Contact: Nao Kondo, Pres.
Telephone: 503-661-7700
Fax: 503-669-9107
Email: / URL: http://www.ttu.com
Product Service Description:
Carbon & graphite products
Manufactures machined graphite parts

Trace Engineering Co
5916 195th St Ne
Arlington, WA 98223-7806
Contact: Sam Vanderhoof, VP Marketing
Phone: 360-435-8826 / Fax: 360-435-2229
Email: inverters@traceengineering.com /
URL: http://www.traceengineering.com
Product Service Description:
Manufactures DC to AC inverters and
inverter/battery charger combinations
Electrical industrial apparatus

Traction International
P.O. Box 13190
Oakland, CA 94661-0190
Contact: Vince Tong, President
Phone: 510-532-6200 / Fax: 510-532-8164
Email: vinceskiii@hotmail.com
Product Service Description:
Farm Machinery and Equipment
Vitrifiable enamels and glazes, engobes and
similar preparations : Paints and varnishes
based on synthetic and other polymers in a
nonaqueous medium : New pneumatic tires,
of rubber, of a kind used on motor cars
Inner tubes, of rubber, of a kind used on
motor cars , buses or trucks : Articles of
asphalt or of similar material : Heavy
Equipment Spare Parts ; Diesel Parts

Trade Metal Inc.
P.O. Box 573
Jericho, NY 11753-2307
Contact: Stanley Straus, President
Telephone: 516-939-0500
Fax: 516-939-0851
Email: trademetal@hotmail.com / URL:
Product Service Description:
Tinplate Waste : Stainless Steel Sheet
Cuttings: Stainless Steel Clad Sheets
Stainless Steel Coils : Secondary Stainless
Steel Circ : T inmill Products
Stainless Steel Plate

Trademark Cosmetics Inc
3263 Trade Center Dr
Riverside, CA 92507-3432
Contact: David Ryngler, Pres.
Telephone: 909-683-2631
Fax: 909-683-2680
Email: tradecos@earthlink.net / URL: http://
www.looking-good.com
Product Service Description:
Manufactures private-label cosmetics
Toilet preparations

Trademark Medical
1053 Headquarters Pk.
Fenton, MO 63026
Contact: Harry O. Tiggard Jr., Pres.
Telephone: 314-349-3270
Fax: 314-349-3294
Email: tradmark@worldnet.att.net / URL:
http://www.medicom.com/trademark
Product Service Description:
Liquid Crystal Temperature Monitors
Custom Medical Apparel / Accessories
Special Oral Hygiene Apparatus

Tradewind Industries, Inc.
7612 Drag Strip Rd
Fairview, TN 37062-8227
Contact: James Chism, Pres.
Phone: 615-799-8300 / Fax: 615-799-8477
Email: tradwnd@aol.com / URL: http://
www.tradewindinc.com/tradewind
Product Service Description:
Acrylic whirlpool bath tubs & shower
Systems

Tradewinds International
P.o. Box 8
Ellendale, TN 38029
Contact: John Augustine, Owner,
Telephone: 901-377-2600
Fax: 901-385-1920
Email: / URL:
Product Service Description:
Wild Rice, Wholesale

**Trading Alliance Division/MTB
Bank**
90 Broad Street
New York, NY 10004
Contact: Peter T. Lipsky, *
Telephone: 212-858-3396
Fax: 212-858-3491
Email: / URL:
Product Service Description:
Back-To-Back Letters of Credit
Transactional Purchase Order & Financing
U.S. Import Financing - Factoring

Traex
P.O. Box 200
Dane, WI 53529-0200
Contact: John W. Parsons, Sales & Marketing
Manager
Telephone: 608-849-2500
Fax: 608-849-2580
Email: 53parjoh@menasha.com / URL: http://
www.menasha.com/traex
Product Service Description:
Plastics Products, NEC
Articles of plastics
Table, kitchen or other household articles and
parts thereof, of stainless steel
Table or kitchen glassware
Table top food service items
Dishracks

Trail Wagons Inc
PO Box 2589
Yakima, WA 98907-2589
Contact: Dan Lukehart, Pres., Joe Holman,
Nat'l Sales Mgr.
Telephone: 509-248-9026
Fax: 509-248-9054
Email: chinook@rv.com / URL: http://
www.chinookrv.com
Product Service Description:
Manufactures custom van and RV
conversions
Motor homes
Specialty Truck & S.U.V. Packages

Trail-Rite Inc
3100 W Central Ave
Santa Ana, CA 92704-5303
Contact: Donald R Williams, Pres.
Telephone: 714-556-4540
Fax: 714-556-5718
Email: / URL:
Product Service Description:
Manufactures boat trailers
Transportation equipment
Boat trailer parts & supplies

Trane Company, The
4833 White Bear Parkway
Saint Paul, MN 55110
Contact: Mark Weldy, General Manager
Telephone: 612-407-4000
Fax: 612-407-4192
Email: / URL:
Product Service Description:
Mechanical Controls, HV/AC
Building Automation Controls
Lighting Controls

Trans Air Manufacturing
P.O. Box 70
Dallastown, PA 17313-0070
Contact: Rick Lehnert, President
Telephone: 717-246-2627
Fax: 717-244-7088
Email: trans-air-lehnert@worldnet.att.net /
URL: http://www.transairmfg.com
Product Service Description:
Air Conditioners

Trans Market Sales & Equipment, Inc.
8915 Maislin Dr
Tampa, FL 33637-6708
Contact: Keith Santi, Pres.
Telephone: 813-988-6146
Fax: 813-988-5547
Product Service Description:
Sanitary food process systems (dairy, juice, pharmaceutical)

Trans-Aqua International, Inc.
PO Box 1029
Kasilof, AK 99610-1029
Contact: Michael J. Morgan, GM
Telephone: 907-283-7322
Fax: 907-283-4404
Email: mjmorgan@hotmail.com / URL:
Product Service Description:
Fish processing
Fish_fresh or frozen prepared

Trans-Border Customs Services Inc.
24100 Southfield Rd. Ste. 335
Southfield, MI 48075
Contact: Renee Nowak, *
Telephone: (810) 557-5100
Product Service Description:
Customhouse Broker

Transcrypt International, Inc.
438 Gateway Boulevard
Burnsville, MN 55337
Contact: Frederick G. Hamer, V.P. Int'L
Telephone: 612-882-5500
Fax: 612-882-5959
Product Service Description:
Two-Way Communications Equipment
Telemetry Products
Electronic Components

Transfer Press Exchange
PO Box 215
Vinemont, AL 35179-0215
Contact: Joe Stallings, GM, Opers
Phone: 256-739-1612 / Fax: 256-739-1642
Email: stalling@airnet.net / URL:
Product Service Description:
Presses (Transfer-Forging, Big Bed Sheet Metal)

Transfer Print Foils, Inc.
9 Cotters Ln
East Brunswick, NJ 08816-2002
Contact: John Duplica, National Sales Mgr.
Telephone: 732-238-1800 / 800-235-3645
Fax: 732-238-7936 / 888-829-3645
Product Service Description:
Metallic foils
Hot stamping foil
Diffraction Foils
Woodgrain foils
Holography
Holograms
Pearl foils
Pigment foils
Special effect foils
Security foils

Transit Sales International
1863 Service Court
Riverside, CA 92507
Contact: Don Prather, VP Sales
phone: 909-682-2557 / Fax: 909-682-2577
Email: tsi@deltanet.com / URL: http://
www.transitsales.com
Product Service Description:
Used Transit Buses

Transmarine Navigation Corporation
301 E. Ocean Blvd. Ste. 570
Long Beach, CA 90802-4828
Contact: Captain Peter Whittington, President
Telephone: 310-432-6941
Fax: 310-590-8470
Product Service Description:
Port Agency

Transoceanic Shipping Company, Inc.
32 East Airline Highway
Kenner, LA 70062
Contact: Paul Wilson, Executive V.P.
Telephone: 504/465-1000
Fax: 504-465-1023
Email: / URL: http://www.transoceanic.com
Product Service Description:
Freight Transportation Arrangement
General Warehousing & Storage
Customs Broker
Packing & Crating
Marine Cargo Handling

Transpo Indsutries, Inc.
20 Jones St.
New Rochelle, NY 10801-6098
Contact: Michael S. Stenko, Pres.
Telephone: 914-636-1000
Fax: 914-636-1282
Email: transpoind@aol.com / URL: http://
www.transpo-industries.com
Product Service Description:
Polymer Concrete & Sealants
Roadway Safety Features

Transtek Associates, Inc.
Lakeside Office Park, Door 9, 599 North Avenue
Wakefield, MA 01880
Contact: Michele Phillips, President
Telephone: 617-245-7980
Fax: 617-245-7993
Email: michele@transtekassociatesinc.com /
URL: http://www.trnastekassociatesinc.com
Product Service Description:
Translation Services

Transtracheal Systems Inc
109 Inverness Dr E Ste J
Englewood, CO 80112-5105
Contact: Les Peterson, Pres., CEO
Telephone: 303-790-4766
Fax: 303-790-4588
Email: cservice@transtracheal.com / URL:
http://www.transtracheal.com
Product Service Description:
Manufactures medical oxygen catheters and apparatus : Surgical & medical instruments
Respiratory assist devices

Transus Container Division
2090 Jonesboro Road, SE.
Atlanta, GA 30315
Contact: Major Wilkerson, *
Telephone: 404-627-1124
Product Service Description:
Trucking, Transportation

Transwood, Inc.
P.O. Box 189,
Omaha, NE 68101-0189
Contact: Sales & Marketing,
Telephone: 402-346-8092
Fax: 402-341-2112
Email: customerservice@transwood.com /
URL: http://www.transwood.com
Product Service Description:
Freight & Cargo Transportation
Trucking

Transworld Plush Toys, Inc.
340 S. San Pedro St., Unit # D
Los Angeles, CA 90013-2263
Contact: Sales & Marketing,
Telephone: 213-620-0173
Fax: 213-626-3763
Email: sales@eplushtory.com / URL: http://
www.eplushtoy.com
Product Service Description:
Plush Toys

Treatment Products Ltd.
4701 W. Augusta Blvd.
Chicago, IL 60651
Contact: Jeff Victor, Vice President
Telephone: 773-626-8888
Fax: 773-626-6200
Email: TREATMENT1@aol.com / URL:
http://www.thetreatment.com
Product Service Description:
Car Waxes & Polishes
Automotive Chemicals
Industrial Chemicals
Chemicals, Car Wash & Detailing
Contract Packaging

Trefilarbed Arkansas, Inc.
PO Box 9450
Pine Bluff, AR 71611-9450
Contact: Jos Jacque', President
Telephone: 870-247-2444
Fax: 870-247-1622
Email: taa.sales@cwixmail.com / URL:
Product Service Description:
Steel cord & wire
Steel wire & related products

Trelleborg YSH, Inc.
400 Aylworth Ave
South Haven, MI 49090-1796
Contact: Mark Brooks, President
Telephone: 616-637-2116
Fax: 616-637-8315
Email: / URL:
Product Service Description:
Mechanical rubber goods
Mechanical rubber goods
Gaskets, packing & sealing devices
Rubber products_fabricated
Mechanical rubber goods

Tres Rios Silver
PO Box 187
Aztec, NM 87410-0187
Contact: Vicki Felder, Ptnr.
Telephone: 505-334-7555
Fax: 505-334-2923
Email: frontierbuckles@acrnet.com / URL:
http://www.frontierbuckles.com
Product Service Description:
Custom Silver-Plated Buckles

Tretina Printing Co., Inc.
1301 Concord Dr.
Hazlet, NJ 07730
Contact: Jan Tretina Sr., Pres.
Telephone: 732-264-2324
Fax: 732-264-0180
Email: tretina@tretinaprinting.com / URL:
http://www.tretinaprinting.com
Product Service Description:
Offset printing & typesetting
Lithographic printing_commercial
Electronic prepress services

Trex Medical, Bennett Division
445 Oak Street
Copiague, NY 11726
Contact: Scott Matovich, V.P. Sales & Marketing
Telephone: 516/691-6100
Fax: 516/691-5713
Email: smatovic@trexmed.com / URL:
Product Service Description:
X-Ray Imaging Apparatus

Tri Tool Inc
3806 Security Park Dr
Rancho Cordova, CA 95742-6916
Contact: Steven Young, Director, Intl Sales
Telephone: 916-351-0144
Fax: 916-351-0372
Email: ttcustserv@aol.com / URL: http://
www.tritool.com
Product Service Description:
Manufactures pipe cutting and welding preparation equipment
Machine tools, metal cutting types

Tri-County Hard Chrome, Inc.
PO Box 157
Edgewater, FL 32132-0157
Contact: Dallas Post, Manager
Telephone: 904-427-9241
Fax: 904-427-4699
Email: jewel@ucnsb.net / URL:
Product Service Description:
Industrial hard chrome plating
Plating & polishing

Tri-Dim Filter Corp.
41416 Christy St.
Fremont, CA 94538-5105
Contact: Linda McDonald, Br. Mgr.
Telephone: 510-490-3556
Fax: 510-490-3593
Email: / URL:
Product Service Description:
Manufactures Commercial & Industrial Air filters for heaters & coolers
Blowers & fans

Tri-Link Technologies Ltd.
205 E 2nd Ave
Pine Bluff, AR 71601-4430
Contact: Gerald C. Thomas, Pres, CEO,
Frank Monroe, VP Sales / Marketing
Telephone: 870-534-7774
Fax: 870-534-7744
Email: fmonroe@trilinktech.com / URL: http:/
/www.trilinktech.com
Product Service Description:
Honeycomb Panels
Composite panels
Fabricated Composite Products

Tri-Rotor, Inc.
36 E. Lawton Street
Torrington, CT 06790-6712
Contact: Henry L. Nikora, President
phone: 860-482-8581 / Fax: 860-482-8435
Product Service Description:
Rotary Pumps, Positive Displacement

Tri-Star International, Inc.
239 West Ave.
Tallmadge, OH 44278-0313
Contact: Issam Farah, President
Telephone: 330-630-2777
Fax: 330-630-2117
Email: shehadi@tristarusa.com / URL: http://
www.tristarusa.com
Product Service Description:
Transmission Parts : Transmission Overhaul
Kits : Filter Kits : Transmissions
Torque Converters : A/C Parts ; Standard
Clutches : Rebuilt hard parts for transmissions

Tri-Went, Inc.
10928 Murdock Dr
Knoxville, TN 37932-3244
Contact: Katherine Turkalo,
Telephone: 423-966-6500
Fax: 423-966-6580
Email: info@tri-went.com / URL: http://
www.tri-went.com
Product Service Description:
Tube bending & fabricating

Tri/Mark Corporation
217 Reliance Road
New Hampton, IA 50659
Contact: Jeff Dolezal, Dir. / Sales & Mktg.
Telephone: 515-394-3488
Fax: 515-394-2392
Email: trimark@sbt.net / URL: http://
www.trimarkhardware.com
Product Service Description:
Vehicle Door Hardware

Triad Machinery Inc
PO Box 301099
Portland, OR 97291-4311
Contact: Michael Hildebrandt, Pres.
Telephone: 503-254-5100
Fax: 503-254-6486
Email: mhildebrandt@triadmachinery.com /
URL: http://www.triadmachinery.com
Product Service Description:
Construction & mining machinery
Distributes construction & mining machinery
& equipment; logging & recycling equipment

Triangle Business Forms, Inc.
26 Beaver St
Ansonia, CT 06401-3250
Contact: Barrington Smith, Pres.
Telephone: 203-735-5920
Fax: 203-732-4630
Email: / URL: http://www.ourprinter.com
Product Service Description:
Business forms & letterhead printing
Manifold business forms : Catalogs,
brochures (thru 5 colors) : Binders

Triangle Metal & Mfg. Co.
PO Box 38271
Houston, TX 77238-8271
Contact: Carolyn Felter Buck, Pres.
phone: 281-445-4251 / Fax: 281-445-4276
Email: triangle@netropolis.net
Product Service Description:
Ventilation Equipment : Blowers & Fans
Waterjet Cutting : Individual / Knockdown B-
BQue Pits

Triangle Package Machinery Co.
6655 W. Diversey Avenue
Chicago, IL 60707-2293
Contact: Samuel Gall, Intl. Accounts Mgr.
Telephone: 773-889-0200
Fax: 773-889-4221
Email: sgall@trianglepackage.com / URL:
http://www.trianglepackage.com
Product Service Description:
Bag Packaging Machinery
Packaging Mach., Vert. Form, Fill, Seal
Weighting Equip., Computer Comb.

Tribometrics Inc.(Mfr)
2475 Fourth Street
Berkeley, CA 94710
Contact: Robert T. Lewis, President
Telephone: 510/540-1247
Fax: 510-527-7247
Email: model56@aol.com / URL:
Product Service Description:
Wear Particle Analyzer

Tricon Colors, LLC
16 Leliarts Ln.
Elmwood Park, NJ 07407
Contact: Joseph S. Aiello, Purchasing
Manager
Telephone: 201-794-3800
Fax: 201-797-4660
Email: triconcolr@aol.com / URL:
Product Service Description:
Dyes : Food Dyes ; Industrial Dyes
Drug Dyes : Cosmetic Dyes

Tridan International, Inc.
P.O. Box 537
Danville, IL 61834-0537
Contact: David Burmeister, Executive VP
Sales
Telephone: 217-443-3592
Fax: 217-443-3894
Email: tridan7@soltec.net / URL: http://
www.tridan.com
Product Service Description:
Metalworking Machinery, NEC
Machinery to produce air conditioning coils
Machinery to produce heat transfer coils
Machinery to produce refrigeration coils
Machinery to produce evaporator &
condenser coils

Tridelta Industries Inc.
7333 Corporate Blvd
Mentor, OH 44060-4865
Contact: William S. Shoup, Export Manager
Telephone: 440-255-1080
Fax: 440-974-2296
Email: bill@tridelta.com / URL: http://
www.tridelta.com
Product Service Description:
Pneumatic/Electric Pressure Switches
Remote Controls, Air Activated
Electronic Controls

Trident Tool, Inc.
PO Box 507
Fornt Royal, VA 22630-0507
Contact: Gary Branchaud, Vice President
Telephone: 540-635-7753
Fax: 540-635-6352
Email: info@tridenttool.com / URL: http://
www.TridentTool.com
Product Service Description:
Bits/Tools/Machines Well Drilling (Cable
Tool) : Bits/Tools/Machines Oil Well Drilling
(Cable Tool) : Wire Rope (Cable)
Bits/Tools/Machines Rock Drilling
Magnetic Retrieving Tools

Tridon
P.O. Box 1600
Nashville, TN 37202-1600
Contact: Mike Reese, Manager
P hone: 615-221-3100 / Fax: 615-223-1526
Email: mreese@acdtridon.com / URL: http://
www.acdtridon.com
Product Service Description:
Clamps : Flashers : Wipers

Trimedica International Inc
PO Box 13837
Scottsdale, AZ 85267-3837
Contact Joseph Christy Pres, Bob Leary,
Phone: 602-998-1041 / Fax: 602-998-1530
Email: sales@trimedica.com / URL: http://
www.trimedica.com
Product Service Description:
Medicinals & botanicals
Manufactures natural health products

Trimline Tool Inc.
4621 Spartan Industrial Dr Sw
Grandville, MI 49418-2511
Contact: Richard F. Sattler, Pres.
Telephone: 616-532-4800
Fax: 616-532-4177
Product Service Description:
Dies, tools, jigs & fixtures_special

Trinity Furniture, Inc.
PO Box 150
Trinity, NC 27370-0150
Contact: Jorge Lagueruela, Pres.
Telephone: 336-472-6660
Fax: 336-475-0037
Email: trifurn@highpoint.com / URL: http://
www.trinityfurniture.com
Product Service Description:
Office seating

Tripac International, Inc.
PO Box 185638
Fort Worth, TX 76181-0638
Contact: Jack O'Brien, Pres.
Telephone: 817-284-1517
Fax: 817-595-4249
Email: enginr@tripacfans.com / URL:
Product Service Description:
Automotive electric cooling fans
Motor vehicle parts & accessories
Heat exchangers, condensers, evaporators,
radiators

Triple S Products
3464 Union Pacific Ave
Los Angeles, CA 90023-3835
Contact: Solomon Motamed, Pres.
Telephone: 323-261-7301
Fax: 323-261-5567
Email: ssschemical@ssschemical.com / URL:
http://www.ssschemical.com
Product Service Description:
Manufactures chemicals for metal colouring
Chemicals for antiquing metals
Patinas & Antiquing

Trism Inc.
PO Box 9000
Kennesaw, GA 30144
Contact: Paul T. Newbourne, V..P. Marketing
Phone: 770-795-4712 / Fax: 770-795-4747
Email: paul.newbourne@trism.com / URL:
http://www.trism.com
Product Service Description:
Overdimensional, Overweight & Heavy Haul
Transportation : Hazardous & Explosive
Materials Transportation
Logistics Services (Project Management)

Triton Equipment Corp.
PO Box 1963 Cathedral Station
New York, NY 10025-1557
Contact: Oscar Dobarro, Mgr. Int'l Sales
Telephone: 212-662-0555
Fax: 212-662-0404
Product Service Description:
Centrifugal Pumps & Parts, Allis Chalmers,
ITT Marlow
Vertical Turbine & Contractor Pumps

Trojan, Inc.
P.O. Box 850, 198 Trojan St.
Mt. Sterling, KY 40353
Contact: Dennis Duzyk, Vice President
Telephone: 606-498-0526
Fax: 606-498-0528
Email: sales@trojaninc.com / URL: http://
www.trojaninc.com
Product Service Description:
Lighting, Shatterproof
Lighting, Energy Efficient
Lighting, Manufacturer

Trophy Glove Co.
122 Washington Ave E
Albia, IA 52531-2027
Contact: Mike Nolan, Sales & Mktg. Mgr.
Telephone: 515-932-2183
Fax: 515-932-7430
Email: / URL:
Product Service Description:
Sporting gloves
Sporting & athletic goods
Gloves & mittens_leather

Trophy Shoppe
429 N Lime Ave
Sarasota, FL 34237-5124
Contact: Harry Stenger, Owner
Telephone: 941-955-2440
Fax: 941-953-3972
Email: trophy@acun.com / URL: http://
www.trophy-shoppe.com
Product Service Description:
Engraved trophies & plaques
Metal products_fabricated
Metal coating & allied services
Crystal
Gavels
Name Tags
Signs
Gifts
Awards
Medals & Ribbons

Tru Lingua Language Systems, Inc.
2081 Business Center Drive, Suite 136
Irvine, CA 92715
Contact: Sandrine Gann,
Telephone: 714-955-1151
Fax: 714-955-1153
Product Service Description:
Translation Services
Interpreting Services

Tru-Fast Corp.
2105 Williams Cty. Rd. 12-c
Bryan, OH 43506
Contact: Duane Spangler, Pres.
Telephone: 419-636-6715
Fax: 419-636-1784
Email: trufast@bright.net / URL: http://
www.tru-fast.com
Product Service Description:
Roof fasteners
Bolts, nuts, rivets & washers
Flexible drain Flashings
Roof Skylight Safety Screws

Tru-Part Manufacturing Co.
232 Lothenbach Ave.
St. Paul, MN 55118-3592
Contact: L.W. Templeton, President
Telephone: 612-455-6681
Fax: 612-455-2111
Email: / URL:
Product Service Description:
Agricultural Tractor & Implement Parts

Tru-Stone Corp.
P.O. Box 430
Wait Park, MN 56387-0430
Contact: Ron Carlson, President
Telephone: 612-251-7171
Fax: 612-259-5073
Email: trustone@cloudnet.com / URL: http://
www.cloudnet.com/~trustone/
Product Service Description:
Precision granite machine bases &
Surface Plates

Truck Equipment Sales, Inc.
PO Box 1987
Dothan, AL 36302-1987
Contact: Mike Byers, Br. Mgr.
Telephone: 334-792-4124
Fax: 334-677-0750
Product Service Description:
Automotive & truck equipment
Motor vehicle parts & accessories

Truck Tracks Inc
5779 4500 N
Rexburg, ID 83440
Contact: Arliss Davies, Pres.
Telephone: 208-356-0662
Fax: 208-356-8392
Email: / URL:
Product Service Description:
Manufactures rubber truck tracks
Rubber products_fabricated

Truck-Lite International Inc.
310 E. Elmwood Avenue
Falconer, NY 14733
Contact: Tim C. Walker, President
Telephone: 716/665-6214
Fax: 716-665-4825
Email: tlcs@netsync.net / URL: http://
www.truck-lite.com
Product Service Description:
Motor Vehicle Lighting

True Pitch, Inc.
PO Box 11
Altoona, IA 50009-0011
Contact: John Goeders, Chrm.
Telephone: 515-967-2303
Fax: 515-967-7619
Email: truepitch@aol.com / URL: http://
www.greengrassusa.com /
pitchingmounds.com
Product Service Description:
Portable baseball mounds & mound materials
Sporting & athletic field materials (Soil)
Grass enhancer (all natural)

Tube Light Co., Inc.
300 E. Park St.
Moonachie, NJ 07074
Contact: Leon H. Jaffe, President
Telephone: 201-641-6660
Fax: 201-641-6413
Email: / URL:
Product Service Description:
Neon Sign Supplies & Equipment
Electric Sign Supplies & Equipment
Screen Printing Supplies & Equipment

Tubetronics
2470 Coral St
Vista, CA 92083-8430
Contact: Troy Steiner, Off. Mgr.
Telephone: 760-598-7979
Fax: 760-598-0809
Email: tubetronics@tubetronics.com / URL:
http://www.tubetronics.com
Product Service Description:
Manufactures metal tube assemblies for
aircraft and aerospace industry

Tubing Seal Cap
601 S Vincent Ave
Azusa, CA 91702-5102
Contact: Michael S Bernath, Pres., CEO
Telephone: 626-334-0361
Fax: 626-334-9270
Email: / URL:
Product Service Description:
Metal stampings
Manufactures deep drawn stampings, door
knobs, brass bed finials, medicine cabinets
and le
Hardware
Furniture_metal household
Fourslide & multislide fabrication
Tubular fabrication

Tubular Textile Machinery
PO Box 2097
Lexington, NC 27293-2097
Contact: Luther F. Page, Sales Dri./ Int'l
Telephone: 336-956-6444
Fax: 336-956-8956
Email: tubetex@infoave.net / URL: http://
www.tubetex.com
Product Service Description:
Knit Goods Shrinkage Control Compactors
Knit Goods Wet Processing Machinery
Knit Goods Dryers

Tucker Millworks, Inc.
PO Box 835
Lithonia, GA 30058-0835
Contact: David E. Lee, Pres.
Telephone: 770-482-8135
Fax: 770-482-4158
Email: / URL:
Product Service Description:
Custom Millwork
Specialty Windows & Doors

Tucson Alternator Exchange Inc
1401 E 20th St
Tucson, AZ 85719-6811
Contact: Daniel Montano, Pres.
Telephone: 520-622-7395
Fax: 520-884-5828
Email: smontano@azstarnet.com / URL:
Product Service Description:
Sells motor vehicle supplies and new parts;
remanufactures alternators and starters
Motor vehicle parts & accessories
Motor vehicle supplies & new parts
Engine electrical equipment

Tucson Container Corporation
PO Box 11561
Tucson, AZ 85734-1561
Contact: John Widera, Pres.
Telephone: 520-746-3171
Fax: 520-741-0962
Email: dzapf@calbox.com / URL: http://
www.calbox.com
Product Service Description:
Manufactures corrugated and solid fiber
boxes
Packaging & Foam Supplier

Tucson Industrial Plastics
PO Box 11038
Tucson, AZ 85734-1038
Contact: Kathy Leetzow, Sales Mgr.
Telephone: 520-746-9286
Fax: 520-746-1697
Email: kathy@tfm-tip.com / URL: http://
206.165.13.201
Product Service Description:
Manufactures billets, flange adapters,
reducers, stub ends & tanks & manholes, in
high density polyethylene
Plastic products

Tufnut Work, The
PO Box 39
Tesuque, NM 87574-0039
Contact: Roland Zinn, Pres.
Telephone: 505-424-1954 / 800-227-0949
Fax: 505-424-1956
Email: tufnut@tufnut.com / URL: http://
www.tufnut.com
Product Service Description:
Theft resistant nuts & computer theft security
cables : Bolts, nuts, rivets & washers (theft
resistant)

Tulox Plastics Corp.
PO Box 984
Marion, IN 46952-0984
Contact: John C. Sciaudone, Pres
Telephone: 765-664-5155
Fax: 765-664-0257
Email: csciaudone@tulox.com / URL: http://
www.tulox.com
Product Service Description:
Clear semi-rigid extruded plastic containers &
injection molded closures
Plastic profile shapes_unsupported

Tumaro's Inc
5300 Santa Monica Blvd Ste 311
Los Angeles, CA 90029-1259
Contact: Herman Jacobs, Pres.
Telephone: 323-464-6317
Fax: 323-464-6299
Email: info@tumaros.com / URL: http://
www.tumaros.com
Product Service Description:
Manufactures gourmet flavored tortillas &
wraps

Turbo Burn Inc
4225 E Joseph Ave
Spokane, WA 99217-6557
Contact: Leonard Hamilton, Pres.
Telephone: 509-487-3609
Fax: 509-483-0148
Email: / URL: http://www.turboburn.com
Product Service Description:
Manufactures water stoves
Mulit Fuel Furnace / Liquid or Solids
Central Heat System / Ind or Res.

Turbo Specialists LLC.
441 Governors Hwy
South Windsor, CT 06074-2510
Contact: Maurice Avery, Pres., GM
Telephone: 860-290-8606
Fax: 860-290-8831
Email: turbo@mail.snet.net / URL:
Product Service Description:
Industrial Turbine Engine Parts
Aircraft engines & engine parts

Turner Envirologic, Inc.
3439 Sw 11th St
Deerfield Beach, FL 33442-8138
Contact: Thomas K. Turner, Pres.
Telephone: 954-422-9787
Fax: 954-422-9723
Email: tenviro@bellsouth.net / URL: http://
www.tenviro.com
Product Service Description:
Air pollution control systems
Blowers & fans
Oxidizers
Scrubbers
Stacks

Tut Systems
2495 Estand Way
Pleasant Hill, CA 94523-3911
Contact: La Monte M. Thompson, Director,
Information Services
Telephone: 925-682-6510
Fax: 925-682-4601
Email: lamonte@tutsys.com / URL: http://
www.tutsys.com
Product Service Description:
Manufactures high-speed networking devices
Communications equipment, nec

Tutuvi
2850 S King St
Honolulu, HI 96826-3540
Contact: Colleen Kimura, Pres., Sales &
Mktg. Mgr.
Telephone: 808-947-5950
Fax: 808-947-5950
Email: / URL:
Product Service Description:
Original Screen prints on fabric / cothing

Twin Marquis, Inc.
328 Johnson Ave
Brooklyn, NY 11206-2802
Contact: Joseph Tang, Pres.
Telephone: 718-386-6868
Fax: 718-417-0049
Email: / URL:
Product Service Description:
Asian noodles, wrappers, dumplings & buns

Twin Technology Inc
317 Brokaw Rd
Santa Clara, CA 95050-4335
Contact: Paul Y. Ko, Pres.
Telephone: 408-970-8806
Fax: 408-970-8809
Email: yongko@aol.com / URL:
Product Service Description:
Manufactures printed circuit boards
(turnkey.consignment)

Tyco Valves & Controls
P.O. Box 40010
Houston, TX 77240-0010
Contact: Gene crouch, VP of Sales &
Marketing
Telephone: 713-466-1176
Fax: 713-937-5417
Email: / URL: http://www.kii.com
Product Service Description:
Butterfly Valves
Knife Gate Valves
Check Valves
Plug Valves
Valve Actuators
Actuators, Electric & Pneumatic
Ball Valves
Sampling Systems

Tyler Camera Systems
14218 Aetna St
Van Nuys, CA 91401-3433
Contact: Nelson Tyler, Pres.
Telephone: 818-989-4420
Fax: 818-989-0423
Email: / URL:
Product Service Description:
Manufacturers and sells stabilized camera &
gun platforms for helicopters, boats and cars

Tyson Seafood Group, Inc.
1900 West Nickerson Street, Suite 200
Seattle, WA 98119
Contact: Alicia Johnson, *
Telephone: 612-361-9451
Fax: 612-361-9452
Email: alicia_johnson@tyson.com / URL:
http://www.tyson.com
Product Service Description:
Surimi Seafood Products: Crab, Lobster,
Shrimp & Scallops : Fillets: Cod, Pollock,
Flounder/Sole, Dover Sole, Pacific Rock Fish
King Crab: Red King Crab Legs & Claws,
Brawn Kings Crab Legs
Blocks

U S Game Systems, Inc.
179 Ludlow St
Stamford, CT 06902-6912
Contact: Granville Gargiulo, Pres.
Telephone: 203-353-8400
Fax: 203-353-8431
Email: usgames@aol.com / URL: http://
www.usgamesinc.com
Product Service Description:
Lithographic printing, custom card decks
Playing cards, tarot decks & games

U S Paper Counters Co.
PO Box 837
Cairo, NY 12413-0837
Contact: Anthony Perzanowski, President
Telephone: 518-622-2600
Fax: 518-622-2695
Email: uspc@wecount.com / URL: http://
www.wecount.com
Product Service Description:
Sheet Counting & Batch-Tabbing Equipment
Security Counters

U-Select-It Corporation
8040 University Blvd.
Des Moines, IA 50325
Contact: Sales & Marketing,
Telephone: 515-274-3641
Fax: 515-274-0390
Email: mceron@wittern.com / URL: http://
www.uselectit.com
Product Service Description:
Vending machines_automatic
Vending machines

U. S. Can Co., Custom & Specialty Division
8901 Yellow Brick Rd.
Baltimore, MD 21237
Contact: Jack Finnell, Sales Mgr.
Telephone: 410-686-6364
Fax: 410-391-9323
Email: specialtysales@uscanco.com / URL:
http://www.uscanco.com
Product Service Description:
Decorative Cans & Tins
Cans, Metal
Cans - Tin : cans - Decorated
Cans - Closures : Cans - Welded
Cans - Hermetic : Seamless Cans

U. S. Cavalry, Inc.
2855 Centennial Ave
Radcliff, KY 40160-9049
Contact: Becky Rogney, Vice President,
Contract Sales
Telephone: 502-351-1164 Ext. 3177
Fax: 502-352-0327
Email: cavpro@uscav.com / URL: http://
www.cavpro.com
Product Service Description:
Men's Milit/Law Enforcement Apparel,
Wholesale
Safety Devices, Body Armor, Wholesale
Optical Night Vision Devices, Wholesale
Holsters, Global Positioning, Wholesale
Rappelling Gear, Commun Dev. Whsle.

U. S. Vanadium Corp.
30 Main Street
Danbury, CT 06810-3004
Contact: Hein Enslin, Pres.
Telephone: 203-790-1555
Fax: 203-790-5750
Email: hein.enslin@hq.stratcor.com / URL:
http://www.stratcor.com
Product Service Description:
Vanadium processing
Chemicals_industrial inorganic

U.S. Airmotive
5439 N.W. 36th St.
Miami Springs, FL 33166
Contact: John Kruse, President
Telephone: 305-885-4991
Fax: 305-887-2405
Email: sales@usairmotive.com / URL: http://
www.usairmotive.com
Product Service Description:
Aircraft Parts & Supplies - including
consumables & ground support
Material handling equipment - forklift export
specials

U.S. Axle, Inc. (Mfr)
275 Shoemaker Road
Pottstown, PA 19464-6433
Contact: David Ice, Vice President, Sales &
Mktg.
Telephone: 610-323-3800
Fax: 610-970-2010
Email: dave.ice@usaxle.com / URL: http://
www.usaxle.com
Product Service Description:
Machined Shafts & Axle Shafts for Constr.
Equip.
Machined Shafts
Machined Shfts & Axle Shafts for Farm
Equipment

U.S. Customs Service
423 Canal St. - Room 245
New Orleans, LA 70130
Contact: Alen H. Paterson, Port Director
Telephone: 504-670-2391
Fax: 504-670-2123
Email: / URL:
Product Service Description:
Government

U.S. Farathane Corp.
38000 Mound Rd.
Sterling Heights, MI 48310
Contact: Andrew J. Greenlee, Executive Vice
President
Telephone: 810-978-2800
Fax: 810-268-6374
Email: agreenle@usfarathane.com / URL:
Product Service Description:
Plastic Products

U.S. Manufacturing Corporation
17717 Masonic Blvd.
Fraser, MI 48026
Contact: B.A. Simon, Senior Vice President
Telephone: 810-293-8744
Fax: 810-293-8908
Email: bsimon@usmfg.com / URL: http://
www.usmfg.com
Product Service Description:
Production Tubular Extrusions; Swaging;
Warm & Hot Forged Products
Automated MIG; Inertia; Friction; Projection
Welding : Full Service Production Machining
& Assembly

U.S. Pet Products
829 Via Alondra
Camarillo, CA 93012
Contact: Peter Brotsis, *
Telephone: 805-383-0041
Product Service Description:
Pet Doors Energy Conserving

U.S. Safety
P.O. Box 15965
Shawne Mission, KS 66285-5965
Contact: Doug Brahl, V.P. Sales & Mktg.
Telephone: 913/599-5555
Fax: 913-599-1703
Email: info@ussafety.com / URL: http://
www.ussafety.com
Product Service Description:
Prescription & Non-Prescription Safety
Glasses, Goggles & Faceshields
Polycarbonate Lenses
Respirators

U.T.C. Tires & Rubber Comp.
6150 N.W. 74th Ave.
Miami, FL 33166-3710
Contact: Jose Zelaya, Owner
Telephone: 305-593-0504
Fax: 305-593-0764
Email: utc9@aol.com / URL:
Product Service Description:
New pneumatic tires, of rubber
Rubber inner tubes

UEI
5500 SW Arctic Dr
Beaverton, OR 97005-4162
Contact: Michael Kane, Pres.
Telephone: 503-644-8723
Fax: 503-643-6322
Email: info@ueitest.com / URL: http://
www.ueitest.com
Product Service Description:
Industrial machinery & equipment
Imports and distributes measuring and test
equipment— electrical, temperature and gas

UGM Inc
1300 Memorex Dr
Santa Clara, CA 95050-2813
Contact: Norihisa Shibukawa, Pres.
Telephone: 408-988-7766
Fax: 408-988-5538
Product Service Description:
Metal stamping

UNI Hosiery Co., Inc.
3829 S. Broadway St.
Los Angeles, CA 90037
Contact: Harry Chung, President
Telephone: 323-846-9900
Fax: 323-846-1755
Email: rubbb@earthlink.com / URL:
Product Service Description:
Coffee : Hosiery : Menswear

US Armor Corp
11843 Smith Ave
Santa Fe Springs, CA 90670-3226
Contact: Stephen E Armellino, Pres.
Telephone: 562-949-1733
Fax: 562-949-1501
Email: / URL: http://www.usarmorcorp.com
Product Service Description:
Manufactures concealable and tactical body
armor (bulletproof vests)

US Battery Manufacturing Co
1675 Sampson Ave
Corona, CA 91719-1889
Contact: Donald E. Wallace, Executive vice
president
Telephone: 909-371-8090
Fax: 909-371-4671
Email: dwallace@usbattery.com / URL: http:/
/www.usbattery.com
Product Service Description:
Manufactures automotive, golf cart, scrubber,
commercial and marine batteries
Batteries_storage

US Dyeing & Finishing Inc
12641 Industry St
Garden Grove, CA 92841-3911
Contact: Charles Kim, Pres.
Telephone: 714-891-8234
Fax: 714-891-6255
Email: info@usdf.com / URL: http://
www.usdf.com
Product Service Description:
Cotton, poly / cotton, synthetic, dyeing &
finishing
Finishing plants, fleecing, sanding,
compacting

US PreFab Inc
6525 W State Ave
Glendale, AZ 85301-1718
Contact: Harry O Woody, Pres.
Telephone: 602-278-1800 / 1800-344-6013
Fax: 623-931-7418
Email: uspi@usprefab.com / URL: http://
www.usprefab.com
Product Service Description:
Manufactures Metal buildings— carports,
carwashes, airplane hangars, storage
warehouses, livestock covers

US Products Inc
10450 N Airport Rd
Hayden Lake, ID 83835-9742
Contact: Josh Gray, Sales Manager
Telephone: 208-772-0573
Fax: 208-772-0577
Email: clean@usproducts.com / URL: http://
www.usproducts.com
Product Service Description:
Manufactures of Carpet, Drapery, &
Upholstery Cleaning Equipment
Manufactures of Hard Floor Polisher &
Ozone Generating Equipment

US Sensor Corp
1832 W Collins Ave
Orange, CA 92867-5425
Contact: Teri Wilfong, VP Sales
Telephone: 714-639-1000
Fax: 714-639-1220
Email: sales@ussensor.com / URL: http://
www.ussensor.com
Product Service Description:
Manufactures thermistors
Temperature sensors

US Tower Corp
1220 N Marcin St
Visalia, CA 93291-9288
Contact: Bruce Kopitar, Pres.
Telephone: 209-733-2438
Fax: 209-733-7194
Email: bruce@ustower.com / URL: http://
www.ustower.com
Product Service Description:
Towers, Steel, Crank-up, Free Standing
Mobile Tower Units, CO.W.S.

USA Magazines Inc
PO Box 39115
Downey, CA 90239-0115
Contact: Carlos Santizo, Pres., CEO
Telephone: 562-903-7788
Fax: 562-903-7857
Email: usamagazines@usa-magazines.com /
URL: http://www.usa-magazines.com
Product Service Description:
High quality steel magazines for most popular
handguns & rifles

UT Technologies, Inc.
11500 West Olympic Blvd.
Los Angeles, CA 90064-1524
Contact: Michael K. Barnoski, President
Telephone: 310-996-0091
Fax: 310-996-0111
Email: mbarnoski@uttechnology.com / URL:
http://www.uttechnology.com
Product Service Description:
Tools & dies & metal stampings

Ultimate International
127 S 8th Ave Ste C
La Puente, CA 91746-3246
Contact: Edward Lee, Pres.
Telephone: 626-369-8096
Fax: 626-961-1288
Email: uintco@aol.com / URL: http://
www.ultimateintl.com
Product Service Description:
Manufactures and sells skinless walnuts
Nuts & seeds_salted & roasted
Seafood, fresh & frozen fish, seacucumber
Commodity broker, soy beans, corn, & oil

Ultimate International
4631 N. Dixie Hwy.
Boca Raton, FL 33431-5030
Contact: Daniel Weckering, Owner
Telephone: 561-347-1531
Product Service Description:
Ethyl alcohol, undenatured
Pharmaceuticals

Ultra Plating Corp.
PO Box 2423
Green Bay, WI 54306-2423
Contact: Gary D. Jensen, V-P., Opers.
Telephone: 920-437-9108 / 1-800-DoUltra
Fax: 920-437-1992
Email: ultra@itol / URL:
Product Service Description:
Industrial hard chrome, cadmium, gold,
electroless nickel & nickel & silver
electroplating : Plating & polishing
Metal coating & allied services

Ultra Seal International
1100 Wilcox Ave.
Los Angeles, CA 90038-1593
Contact: Liz Aguirre, President
Telephone: 323-466-1226
Product Service Description:
Adhesives and Sealants

Ultra Sonic Seal Co.
368 Turner Industrial Way
Aston, PA 19014-3014
Contact: Ron Woolfrey, Sales Manager
Telephone: 610-497-5150
Fax: 610-497-5195
Email: info@ultrasonicseal.com / URL: http://
www.ultrasonicseal.com
Product Service Description:
Ultrasonic, vibration, spin & hot plate plastic
welding equipment

Ultra-Stereo Labs Inc
181 Bonetti Dr
San Luis Obispo, CA 93401-7397
Contact: Jack Cashin, Pres.
Telephone: 805-549-0161
Fax: 805-549-0163
Email: usl@uslinc.com / URL:
Product Service Description:
Manufactures and sells sound equipment and
supplies

Ultrasonic Probs Mfg. Co.
45 Backus Ave
Danbury, CT 06813
Contact: Steven Poyak,
Telephone: 203-792-3212
Fax: 203-792-3212
Email: spoyak@hotmail.com / URL:
Product Service Description:
Ultrasonic replacement probes
Accessories & attachments for
Ultrasonic processors

Ultratape Industries Inc
5675 Fruitland Rd NE
Salem, OR 97301-3336
Contact: Tom Price, Pres.
Telephone: 503-371-6617
Fax: 503-581-3516
Email: ultrtape@open.org / URL: http://
www.cleanroomtape.com
Product Service Description:
Manufactures cleanroom pressure-sensitive
tapes for semiconductor & circuit board
industry : Paper coated & laminated

Uncas MFG. Company (Mfr)
150 Niantic Ave.
Providence, RI 02907
Contact: John M. Corsini, President
Telephone: 401-944-4700
Fax: 401-943-2951
Product Service Description:
Costume & Karat Gold Jewelry

Unexcelled Castings Corp.
663 Old Willets Path
Hauppauge, NY 11788-4105
Contact: Joseph R. Accetta, Pres.
Telephone: 516-234-7270
Fax: 516-234-7290
Email: unexcelled@aol.com / URL:
Product Service Description:
Aluminum & bronze castings : Foundries,
aluminum : Copper foundries

Unico, Inc.
1830 2nd Ave N
Lake Worth, FL 33461-4202
Contact: Christopher Bohlman, Pres.
Telephone: 561-582-3030
Fax: 561-582-8558
Product Service Description:
Oral Electrolyte Solutions : Disposable
Sodium Phosphates Enemas : Disposable
Douches : Liquid Nutritional Supplements
Cough Drops : Nasal Strips

Uniek Inc.
805 Uniek Dr
Waunakee, WI 53597-9585
Contact: Larry Walker, CEO
Telephone: 608-849-9999
Fax: 608-849-9799
Email: uniek@uniekinc.com / URL:
Product Service Description:
Photograph frames & albums
Craft-Plastic Canvas, Yarns, & Cards
Office Products

Unified Machine & Design, Inc.
111 Mountain Ave
Middlesex, NJ 08846-2516
Contact: W. Deininger, President
Telephone: 732-469-7734
Fax: 732-469-2484
Email: wolfgang@unifiedmachine.com /
URL: http://www.unifiedmachine.com
Product Service Description:
Metal & plastic machine parts & prototypes

Unimark Plastics Co.
PO Box 2750
Greenville, SC 29602-2750
Contact: Charles Orth, Pres.
Telephone: 864-879-8100
Fax: 864-877-4976
Email: unimark@alltrista.com / URL:
Product Service Description:
Plastic injection molding
Plastic closures

Union Carbide Corporation
39 Old Ridgebury Rd.
Danbury, CT 06817
Contact: William H. Joyce,
Telephone: 203-794-5300
Fax: 203-794-7130
Email: / URL: http://www.unioncarbide.com
Product Service Description:
Industrial Chemicals
Polyoletins

Union Printing
2321 Pembroke Rd
Hollywood, FL 33020-6253
Contact: Lloyd Stuart, Pres.
Telephone: 954-920-5693
Fax: 954-921-1848
Email: polsign@aol.com / URL:
Product Service Description:
Commercial printing & typesetting
Printing_commercial signs

Uniphase, Laser Division
163 Baypointe Parkway
San Jose, CA 95134
Contact: April Brown, Sales Representative
Telephone: 408-434-1800 Ext. 2060
Fax: 408-954-1177
Email: lasers@uniphase.com / URL: http://
www.uniphase.com
Product Service Description:
Laser Mfr; Helium-Neon, Air cooled Argon,
CW DPSS & UV

Unique Image T-Shirt Co.
306 N. Maryland Ave.
Wilmington, DE 19804-1004
Contact: Robert Gleber, Pres.
Telephone: 302-658-2266
Fax: 302-658-2266
Email: / URL:
Product Service Description:
T-shirt screen printing & embroidery

Unique Laboratories, Inc.
PO Box 4509
Dalton, GA 30719-1509
Contact: Mike Whitaker, Pres.
Telephone: 706-278-7484
Fax: 706-278-7443
Email: / URL: http://www.uniquelabs.com
Product Service Description:
Toiletries
Toilet preparations
Skin protection product
Protects - enhances healing - moisturizes
Won't wash off
All natural ingredients
www.uniquelabs.com

Unique Originals, Inc.
3550 N.W. 58th St.
Miami, FL 33142-2018
Contact: Jay McGrath, VP Sales
Telephone: 305-634-2274
Fax: 305-634-6889
Email: / URL:
Product Service Description:
Furniture
Furniture and parts thereof
Architectural Panels & Moldings Stone

Unique Sports Products, Inc.
840 Mcfarland Rd
Alpharetta, GA 30004-3364
Contact: Gene Niksich, Pres., CFO
Telephone: 770-442-1977
Fax: 770-475-2065
Email: uniquespts@aol.com / URL:
Product Service Description:
Sporting & athletic goods
Sports & athletic equipment
Tennis Accessories
Shoe Repair Products
Head & Wrist Bands

Unique Systems Inc.(Mfr)
1 Saddle Road
Cedar Knolls, NJ 07927-1998
Contact: Kenneth A. Eriksen, *
Telephone: 973-455-0440
Fax: 973-455-7214
Email: sales@uniquesystems.com / URL:
http://www.uniquesystems.com
Product Service Description:
Pumps/Ejectors/Venturi/(Steam-Air-Jet)
Heat Exchangers & Steam Condensers
Replacement Parts for Steam Turbines
Replacement Parts for Compressors

Unique Video Productions
2250 Almond Creek Dr
Reno, NV 89523-1290
Contact: Bill Pearce, Owner
Telephone: 702-747-4236
Fax: 775-747-6799
Email: bpearce@uvp.reno.nv.us / URL:
Product Service Description:
Videotape production
Video production

Unisource
3501 Commerce Pkwy.
Miramar, FL 33025-3918
Contact: John Glaze, Vice President
Telephone: 954-436-0700
Product Service Description:
Printing and Writing Paper
Paper, uncoat, for writing, rolls; Hndmd paper
Articles of paper pulp, paper, paperboard,
cellulose wadding or webs of cellulose fibers
Paper & paperboard, uncoat, rolls or sheets

United Abrasives Inc.
PO Box 75
Willimantic, CT 06226-0075
Contact: Chris Kimball, Export Sales
Manager
Telephone: 860-456-7131
Fax: 860-456-7341
Email: uasait@ad.com / URL:
Product Service Description:
Abrasive Grind/Cut Wheels & Wire Brushes
Coated Abrasives
Tungsten Carbide Burs

United Air Tool, Inc.(Mfr)
P.O. Box 2222
Carson City, NV 89702
Contact: Peggy Pettit, Vice President
Telephone: 775-883-1072
Fax: 775-883-4857
Email: peggy@semp.net / URL:
Product Service Description:
Pneumatic Tools Aerospace Drilling &
Fastening

United Aluminum Corporation
100 United Drive, PO Box 215
North Haven, CT 06473
Contact: Brian L. Gray, Sales Mgr.
Telephone: 203-239-5881
Fax: 203-239-4441
Email: sales@unitedaluminum.com / URL:
http://www.unitedaluminum.com
Product Service Description:
Aluminum Sheet & Strip Coiled
Aluminum Coil
Aluminum Brazing Sheet

United Biotech Inc
110 Pioneer Way
Mountain View, CA 94041-1517
Contact: Wuan Lu, Pres.
Telephone: 650-961-2910
Fax: 650-961-0766
Email: / URL:
Product Service Description:
Manufactures medical diagnostic (ELISA)
test kits & reagents, & Blood Mixer
Raw Materials, Antibodies, Antigens

United Farmers Co-Op
PO Box 4
Lafayette, MN 56054-0004
Contact: Amy Hempstead, GM
Telephone: 507-228-8224
Fax: 507-228-8766
Email: ufcasc@prairie.lakes.com / URL:
Product Service Description:
Fertilizer
Grain
Petroleum
Agronomy
Seed
Feed
Equipment

United General Supply
9320 Harwin Dr.
Houston, TX 77036-1816
Contact: Lawrence Lee, President
Telephone: 713-780-2415
Fax: 713-780-4831
Email: ugs@leetools.com / URL: http://
www.leetools.com
Product Service Description:
Hand Tools, Machinery and Equipment

United Grocers International
800 E. Pescadero Ave.
Tracy, CA 95376
Contact: Mr. Keith Shoemaker, Export Mgr.
Telephone: 209-832-6231
Fax: 209-832-6225
Email: keithshoe@hotmail.com / URL:
Product Service Description:
Dry Cereals
Processed Foods

United Machine Ind. Inc.
4211 SW Mountain Park Way
Redmond, OR 97756-9584
Contact: Vicki Stoltz, Pres.
Telephone: 541-504-1461
Fax: 541-504-1462
Email: unimachine@aol.com / URL:
Product Service Description:
Manufactures sawmill equipment
Woodworking machinery
Metal Fabrication Shop

United Metal Receptacle Inc. (Mfr)
14th & Laurel Streets, P.O. Box 870
Pottsville, PA 17901
Contact: John M. Knaut, Dir./ Sales & Mktg.
Telephone: 570-622-7715
Fax: 570-622-3817
Email: united@unitedrecept.com / URL:
http://www.unitedrecept.com &
www.unitedsafetycontainer.com
Product Service Description:
Trash Containers, Steel : Bomb Containment
Waste Receptacle : Trash Receptacles,
Fiberglass : Explosive Containment &
Storage Receptacle : Smokers Ash Urns,
Steel : Infectious Waste Control Receptacles,
Steel : Trash Receptacles, Aluminum
Drum Tops, Steel

United Pickle Products Corp.
4366 Park Ave
Bronx, NY 10457-2442
Contact: Marvin Weishaus, President
Telephone: 718-933-6060
Fax: 718-362-8522
Email: picklebiz@aol.com / URL: http://
www.unitedpickle.com
Product Service Description:
Pickling & brining pickles, peppers, tomatoes
& relishes : Pickles, sauces & relishes
Fresh cucumbers : Sauerkraut
Brined hot & sweet peppers for coring &
stuffing : Nathans famous pickle products
Carnegie Deli N.Y. Cheesecake

United Roofing Mfg. Co., Inc.
PO Box 30
Eutaw, AL 35462-0030
Contact: Judy Livingston,
V-P., Sales & Mktg.
Telephone: 205-372-3394
Fax: 205-372-2506
Email: united@tusc.net / URL:
Product Service Description:
Saturated roofing felt
Asphalt felts & coatings

United Salt
4800 San Felipe
Houston, TX 77056
Contact: Dan Sutton, President & CEO
Telephone: 713-877-2601
Fax: 713-877-2664
Email: dan_sutton@tum.com
Product Service Description:
Salt, All Types, : Evaporated Salt, (food
grade): Solar Salt, Rock Salt

United States Alumoweld Co.
115 Usac Dr
Duncan, SC 29334-9241
Contact: Jerry Kerns, Sales & Mktg. Mgr.
Telephone: 864-848-1901
Fax: 864-848-1909
Email: sales@alumoweld.com / URL: http://
www.alumoweld.com
Product Service Description:
Aluminum clad steel wire & cable
Overhead Ground Wire-Aluminum-Clad

**United States Can Company,
Custom & Specialty**
8901 Yellow Brick Rd.
Baltimore, MD 21237-2303
Contact: Sales & Marketing,
Telephone: 410-686-6363
Fax: 410-391-9323
Email: specialtysales@uscano.com / URL:
http://www.uscano.com
Product Service Description:
Containers
Steel Tin Cans
Decorated tins
Packaging

United States Energy Corp
1600 N Missile Way
Anaheim, CA 92801-1224
Contact: Brad Newell, VP Sales & Mktg.
Telephone: 714-871-8185
Fax: 714-871-9229
Email: usecorp@msn.com / URL:
Product Service Description:
Manufactures explosion proof alternators and
starters for industrial engines

United States Products Co.
518 Melwood Avenue
Pittsburgh, PA 15213-1194
Contact: L.C. Brown, President
Telephone: 412/621-2130
Fax: 412-621-8740
Email: sales@us-products.com / URL: http://
www.us-products.com
Product Service Description:
Abrasive Lapping Compounds & Slurries
Abrasive Polishing Compounds & Slurries
Abrasive Grinding Compounds & Slurries

**United Technologies Automotive,
Inc.**
1218 Central Indl. Dr.
Saint Louis, MO 63110-2308
Contact: Jim Garcia, GM
Telephone: 314-577-1100
Fax: 314-771-6595
Email: / URL: http://www.utc.com
Product Service Description:
Adhesives & sealants
Sealants, adhesives & rubber
Hose & belting_rubber & plastic
Rubber_synthetic
Rubber products_fabricated

United Textile Machinery Corp.
P.O. Box 4100
Fall River, MA 02723-0401
Contact: Samuel Shapiro,
Telephone: 508-676-8247
Fax: 508-677-4717
Email: utmc@aol.com / URL: http://
www.unitedtextile.com
Product Service Description:
Textile Machinery

United Thread Mills
250 Maple Ave.
Rockville Center, NY 11570
Contact: Ira Henkus, President
Telephone: 516-536-3900
Fax: 516-536-3547
Email: / URL:
Product Service Description:
Sewing thread of manmade filaments, of
synthetic filaments, 100% cotton

Universal Analyzers Inc
1771 S Sutro Ter
Carson City, NV 89706-0364
Contact: Ted Barben, Pres.
Telephone: 775-883-2500
Fax: 775-883-6388
Email: tbarben@powernet.net / URL: http://
www.universalanalyzers.com
Product Service Description:
Manufactures gas sample conditioning
equipment
Process control instruments
Dilution Extractive Sample Systems
Heated Stack Filters

Universal Dairy Equipment
11100 N. Congress Ave.
Kansas City, MO 64153-1222
Contact: Walter Maharay, President
Telephone: 816-891-2430
Fax: 816-891-1690
Email: / URL:
Product Service Description:
Dairy Farm Equipment

Universal Fabric Structures, Inc.
2200 Kumry Rd.
Quakertown, PA 18951-3781
Contact: Tom Garrity, President
Telephone: 215-529-9921
Fax: 215-529-9936
Email: sale@ufsinc.com / URL: http://
www.ufsinc.com
Product Service Description:
Permanent & portable tensioned fabric
structures

**Universal Manufacturing & Const.
Co.**
P.O. Box 2375
Broken Arrow, OK 74013-2375
Contact: Solon D. Young, President
Telephone: 918-455-0430
Fax: 918-451-1730
Email: / URL:
Product Service Description:
Wireline & Well Logging Equipment
Pipe Beveling Equipment & pipe Wrapping

Universal Plastics Color Corp.
114 Beach St
Rockaway, NJ 07866-3512
Contact: Art Valles, Pres.
Telephone: 973-625-9267
Fax: 973-729-3563
Email: / URL:
Product Service Description:
Plastic color concentrates & dry colorants

Universal Tech
PO Box 320
Riverton, KS 66770-0320
Contact: Oldrich Machacek, President
Telephone: 316-783-1361
Fax: 316-783-1360
Email: utecoldm@airmail.net / URL:
Product Service Description:
Comercial Explosives

Universal Tech Corporation
5925 Forest Ln., Suite 500
Dallas, TX 75230-2712
Contact: Oldrich Machacek, President
Telephone: 972-490-9906
Fax: 972-490-9908
Email: utec0idm@airmail.net / URL:
Product Service Description:
Commercial explosives / licensing

Universal Technology Systems
PO Box 7908
Jacksonville, FL 32238-0908
Contact: Tom McEnany, Pres.
Telephone: 904-778-8614
Fax: 904-779-0218
Product Service Description:
Durable medical equipment & electrotherapy
products : Surgical & medical instruments
Wheelchairs & home medical equipment

Universal Tooling Corp.
PO Box 364
Gerry, NY 14740-0364
Contact: Ronald Swanson, Pres., CEO
Telephone: 716-985-4691
Fax: 716-985-4430
Product Service Description:
Dies, tools, jigs & fixtures_special
Plastic & die-cast molds & general machining
job shop : Industrial machinery

Universal Truss, Inc.
320 W Main St
Branford, CT 06405-3414
Contact: Marshall D'Onofrio, Pres.
Telephone: 203-488-7207
Fax: 203-483-1709
Product Service Description:
Structural wood members
Wooden roof & floor trusses

University Games
1633 Adrian Rd
Burlingame, CA 94010-2103
Contact: A Robert Moog, Pres.
Telephone: 650-692-2500
Fax: 650-692-2770
Email: / URL: http://www.ugames.com
Product Service Description:
Games, toys & children's vehicles
Manufactures and wholesales game boards
and toys : Toys & hobby goods & supplies

University Language Center, Inc.
1313 Fifth Street, S.E. Suite 201
Minneapolis, MN 55414
Contact: Therese Shafranski,
Telephone: 612-379-3574
Fax: 612-379-3832
Email: translation@ulanguage.com / URL:
http://www.ulanguage.com
Product Service Description:
Translation Services : Interpreting Services
Accelerated Language Instruction

Univertical Corporation
203 Weatherhead Street
Angola, IN 46703
Contact: Paul H. Walker, Vice President
Telephone: 219-665-1500
Fax: 219-665-1400
Email: phwalker@msn.com / URL:
Product Service Description:
Copper, brass, nickel, lead, tin-lead, tin &
zinc anodes, anode baskets, anode bags &
anode hooks for plating : Copper, nickel & tin
based chemicals for plating : Cyanide based
chemicals for plating

Unlimited Quality Products
710 W Broadway Rd Ste 508
Mesa, AZ 85210-0909
Contact: Philip Stewart, Sales Mgr.
Telephone: 602-461-5235
Fax: 602-461-5238
Email: / URL:
Product Service Description:
Manufactures thermal and acoustical
insulation for the automotive, RV, marine,
aircraft, industrial & construction markets

Up-Time Sports/Nutrition/Medical Ind
P.o. Box 90659
Santa Barbara, CA 93190
Contact: Michael Scigliano, CEO
Telephone: 805-564-3494
Fax: 805-564-4879
Email: mike@up-time.com / URL: http://
www.up-time.com
Product Service Description:
Natural Vitamins
Diet Aids
Energy Supplements

Upsher-Smith Laboratories, Inc.
14905 23rd Ave N
Minneapolis, MN 55447-4708
Contact: Ian Troup, President
Telephone: 612-473-4412
Fax: 612-476-4026
Email: / URL: http://www.upsher-smith.com
Product Service Description:
Pharmaceutical preparations
Pharmaceuticals

Uretek, Inc.
PO Box 326
New Haven, CT 06513-0326
Contact: Brad Kronstat, Cont.
Telephone: 203-468-0342
Fax: 203-469-7385
Email: / URL: http://www.uretek.com
Product Service Description:
Coated fabrics, not rubberized
Textile coating

Usdm Inc
11115 E Montgomery Dr
Spokane, WA 99206-4779
Contact: Kim Fuller, Mgr.
Telephone: 509-891-0558
Fax: 509-891-0559
Email: usdm@foxinternet.net / URL:
Product Service Description:
Manufactures dent removal systems and other
related body shop equipment
Machinery_special industry

Used Equipment Directory
PO Box 823
Hasbrouck Heights, NJ 07604-0823
Contact: Jim Mack / Bob Tannen,
Telephone: 201-393-9558
Fax: 201-393-9553
Email: info@buyused.com / URL: http://
www.buyused.com
Product Service Description:
Used Equipment, Network Database, listing
65,000 machines
Used Equipment Directory / Monthly
Directory of Used
Industrial Equipment for Sales
Secondary Market Guide - Directory of 8000
Used Equipment
Dealers by special categories of equipment.

Ustek, Inc.
4663 Executive Dr
Columbus, OH 43220-3627
Contact: Robert Simon, Pres.
Phone: 614-538-8000/ Fax: 614-538-8002
Email: pcb-sales@ustek.com / URL: http://
www.ustek.com
Product Service Description:
Printed circuit boards

V I P Industries, Inc.
90 Brighton Rd
Clifton, NJ 07012-1606
Contact: John Sonatre, Pres.
Telephone: 973-472-7500
Fax: 973-472-2404
Product Service Description:
Wire harnesses : Electronic components

V M I, Inc.
1125 N Maitlen Dr
Cushing, OK 74023-2920
Contact: Gene Maitlen, Pres.
Telephone: 918-225-7000
Fax: 918-225-0333
Email: vmi@fullnet.net / URL: http://
www.vmi-dredges.com
Product Service Description:
Dredging equipment

V R Systems, Inc.
13310 Up River Rd.
Corpus Christi, TX 78410
Contact: Pete Kourkoubes, Vice President
Telephone: 361-241-5348
Fax: 361-241-5386
Email: petevr@ciris.net / URL: http://
www.vrsystems.net
Product Service Description:
Gas compressor packages : Refrigeration
Skids : Vapor recovery Compressors
Offshore Compressors : Rotary Screw &
Vane Compressors

V T C Inc.
2800 E Old Shakopee Rd
Minneapolis, MN 55425-1350
Contact: Larry Jodsaas, Pres.
Telephone: 612-853-5100
Fax: 612-853-3355
Email: info@vtc.com / URL: http://
www.vtc.com
Product Service Description:
Electronic components & integrated circuits
Electronic components
Semiconductors & related devices

V.T.E., Inc.
PO Box 370
Pellston, MI 49769-0370
Contact: W. R. Van Tielen, Pres.
Telephone: 616-539-8000
Fax: 616-539-0914
Email: sales@vteworld.com / URL: http://
www.vteworld.com
Product Service Description:
Electrical Insulator Caps

VAW Of America Inc
PO Box 6726
Phoenix, AZ 85005-6726
Contact: Bill McCallum, VP West. Reg. Sales
Phone: 602-269-2488 / Fax: 602-272-8208
Email: bmccallum@vawusa.com / URL: http:/
/www.vawusa.com
Product Service Description:
Aluminum extruded products : Manufactures
custom extruded aluminum shapes, electrical
conduit and drawn aluminum tubing

VIE Americas, Inc.
P.O. Box 958
Galstonbury, CT 06033-0972
Contact: Marianne P. Nelson, Manager /
Exports
Telephone: 860-659-1397
Fax: 860-659-9679
Email: vie@worldnet.att.net / URL: http://
www.vieamericas.com
Product Service Description:
All Raw Materials & Parts

Vac-U-Max (Mfr)
37 Rutgers Street
Belleville, NJ 07109
Contact: Ben Samuel, Dir. Int'l Sales
Telephone: 973-759-4400
Fax: 973-759-6449
Email: vacumax37@aol.com / URL: http://
www.vac-u-max.com
Product Service Description:
Conveyors & Conveying Equipment

Vacumetrics, Inc.
4483 McGrath St. 102
Ventura, CA 93003-7737
Contact: John Hoppe, President
Telephone: 805-644-7461
Fax: 805-654-8759
Email: info@vacumed.com / URL: http://
www.vacumed.com
Product Service Description:
Medical Pulmonary Instruments

Val-Fab Inc.
PO Box 877, 944 Apple Blossom La.
Neenah, WI 54957-0877
Contact: Keith J. Picard,
President & CEO
Telephone: 920-722-1009
Fax: 920-722-1685
Email: quality@valfab.com / URL: http://
www.valfab.com
Product Service Description:
Fabricated Structural Metal
Steel fabrication, metal stampings & general
machining job shop

Valley Fixtures Inc
171 Coney Island Dr
Sparks, NV 89431-6317
Contact: Michael Clafton, Dir of Mktg.
Telephone: 702-331-1050
Fax: 702-331-6127
Email: / URL: http://www.valleyfixtures.com
Product Service Description:
Manufactures wood office and store fixtures
Partitions & fixtures_wood
Architectural Millwork

Valley View Industries
13834 Kostner Ave
Crestwood, IL 60445-1913
Contact: David Ignowski,
Ex.ecutive V-P.
Telephone: 708-597-0885
Fax: 708-597-9959
Email: valleyview@valleyviewindustries.com
/ URL: http://www.valleyviewind.com
Product Service Description:
Lawn & garden equipment
Lawn edging products & decorative planters
Plastic products

Valmont Industries Inc.
PO Box 303
West Point, NE 68788-0303
Contact: Joe Langemeier, Plt. Mgr.
Telephone: 402-372-3706
Fax: 402-372-6908
Email: jpl2@valmont.com / URL: http://
www.valmont.com
Product Service Description:
Galvanizing
Metal coating & allied services

Valterra Products
720 Jessie St
San Fernando, CA 91340-2235
Contact: Jeanette Smith, Sales Manager
Telephone: 818-898-1671 X.215
Fax: 818-361-5389
Email: valterra@deltanet.com / URL: http://
www.valterra.com
Product Service Description:
Manufactures plastic gate valves & fittings for
industrial use.
Manufactures component parts & accessories
for recreational vehicles

Valvtron / Tyco Valves & Controls
7230 Empire Central Dr.
Houston, TX 77040
Contact: Rhonda Kalineck, *
Telephone: 713-466-7200
Fax: 713-466-8309
Email: / URL:
Product Service Description:
Ball Valves

Van Hessen & Co., Inc.
110 York St., P.O. Box 44
Taneytown, MD 21787
Contact: G. F. Vigeveno, *
Telephone: 410-751-1032
Fax: 410-876-7798
Email: / URL:
Product Service Description:
Logs

Van Nuys Awning Co Inc
5661 Sepulveda Blvd
Van Nuys, CA 91411-2916
Contact: James W Powell III, Pres.
Telephone: 323-873-3331
Fax: 818-782-6837
Email: / URL:
Product Service Description:
Manufactures canvas and related products,
aluminum awnings

Van Thomas Inc. / Ruggeri Mfg.
35 Industrial Park Cir
Rochester, NY 14624-2403
Contact: Charlie Thomas, Pres.
Telephone: 716-426-1414
Fax: 716-247-0661
Email: stoney33@frontiernet.net / URL:
Product Service Description:
Machining, Sheet Metal, Asseblies
Design & Automation

Van's Delivery Service, Inc.
2400 Turner N.W.
Grand Rapids, MI 49504
Contact: John E. Nieuwenhuis, VP
Operations
Telephone: 616-365-3200
Fax: 616-365-9665
Email: / URL:
Product Service Description:
Contract Carrier
Warehousing & Distribution

Vanco Heavy Lift C.F.S.
711 East Anaheim Street
Wilmington, CA 90744
Contact: Van Hicks, President
Telephone: 310-834-4322 (24 H
Fax: 310-834-7554
Email: vhicks@vanco.net / URL: http://
www.vanco.net
Product Service Description:
Freight & Cargo Transportation
Trucking / Specialized Transport
Crane Handling
Marine Rigging
Bonded Carrier
DOD Certified

Vanguard Research Inc. VRI
10400 Eaton Pl., Suite 450
Fairfax, VA 22030-2201
Contact: Nick Judge, VP/Bus Oper.
Telephone: 703-934-6300
Fax: 703-273-9398
Email: / URL: http://www.vriffx.com
Product Service Description:
Hazardous Waste Processing

Vanguard Tool Corp.
PO Box 128
Fieldale, VA 24089-0128
Contact: Tim Foley, Pres., Hum. Res. Mgr.
Telephone: 540-673-3496
Fax: 540-673-2515
Email: tfoley@neocomm.net / URL: http://
www.vanguardtool.com
Product Service Description:
End mills, router bits & regrinding
Machine tool accessories
Cutting tools

Vanmark Corp.
Industrial Pkwy.
Creston, IA 50801
Contact: Tom Jones, Sales Mgr.
Telephone: 515-782-6575
Fax: 515-782-9209
Email: / URL:
Product Service Description:
Vegetable handling, peeling & frying systems

Vantage Bowling Corporation
870 Parfet St
Lakewood, CO 80215-5521
Contact: Mark Schmidt, Pres.
Telephone: 303-232-7322
Fax: 303-232-8241
Email: info@vantagebowling.com / URL:
http://www.vantagebowling.com
Product Service Description:
Bowling pinsetters, parts, capital equipment

VaporKote Inc
12128 Woodruff Ave
Downey, CA 90241-5642
Contact: Robert T Frazier, Pres.
Telephone: 562-803-3215
Fax: 562-803-1475
Email: vaporkote@aol.com / URL: http://
www.vaporkote.com
Product Service Description:
Provides gas diffusion coating processes on
components for erosion and corrosion
protection
Metal coating & allied services
Mfg. boron hardened bushings for elec.
submersible pump (oil production)
Repair & boron harden refinery FCC pumps
Mfg. aluminized S.S. catalyst reactor screens
for refinery hydrocrackers

Varco Heat Treating Co
PO Box 5500
Garden Grove, CA 92846-0500
Contact: Don A Gay, Pres., CEO
Telephone: 714-895-1155
Fax: 714-891-2755
Email: / URL: http://www.varcoheat.com
Product Service Description:
Heat treating for metal products, controlled
atmosphere, vacuum and open fire;
metallurgical consulting
Heat treating_metal, ISO-9002 compliant
Metal coating & allied services (ie) diamond
& diamond like coatings
Engineering services, metallurgical

Variety Widget Products Inc
1163 Pomona Road, Suite C
Corona, CA 91720-2504
Contact: Eleanor Pravitz, CEO
Telephone: 909-278-3100
Fax: 909-279-5800
Product Service Description:
Sporting & athletic goods

Vaughan Co Inc
364 Monte Elma Rd
Montesano, WA 98563-9723
Contact: Larry D Vaughan, Pres., GM
Telephone: 360-249-4042
Fax: 360-249-6155
Email: sales@chopperpumps.com / URL:
http://www.chopperpumps.com
Product Service Description:
Manufactures Chopper Pumps

Vaupell Industrial Plastics Inc
1144 Nw 53rd St
Seattle, WA 98107-3735
Contact: Syd Darlington, Marketing Director
Telephone: 206-676-8203
Fax: 206-784-9708
Email: syd@vaupell.com / URL: http://
www.vaupell.com
Product Service Description:
Plastic products
Manufactures custom injection molding and
plastic parts

Veka West, Inc.
14250 Lear Blvd.
Reno, NV 89506-2604
Contact: Cory Strawn, Plt. Mgr.
Telephone: 702-972-4090
Fax: 702-972-4099
Email: vwelch@vekainc.com
Product Service Description:
Fabricates extruded vinyl widno & door
systems

Velco Chemicals
101 Executive Blvd.
Elmsford, NY 10523-1316
Contact: Michelle Goldschneider, CEO
Telephone: 914-347-3530
Fax: 914-347-5012
Email: velco@bestweb.net / URL: http://
www.velcochem.com
Product Service Description:
Plastics in general - Thermoplastics, LDPE,
HDPE, PP & PVC
Raw materials for Polyurethane foam - TDI
80/20, MDI, Polyether Polyol
Chemicals for the paint industry -
Penterythritol, Phthalic Anhydride, Titanium
Dioxide Rutile : Anti flammable chemicals -
antimony Trioxide : Industry Chemicals in
general

Velcon Filters Inc
4525 Centennial Blvd
Colorado Springs, CO 80919-3302
Contact: David Taylor, Pres.
Phone: 719-531-5855 / Fax: 719-531-5690
Email: / URL: http://www.velcon.com
Product Service Description:
Machinery_general industrial
Manufactures fuel filters for oil companies,
airlines and related businesses

Vendtronics
2765 Niagara Ln N
Minneapolis, MN 55447-4844
Contact: David O'Brien, Pres.
Telephone: 612-557-2900
Fax: 612-557-7007
Email: info@vendtronics.com / URL: http://
www.vendtronics.com
Product Service Description:
Frozen food vending machines
Vending machines_automatic

Ventana Vineyards Winery Inc
2999 Salinas Hwy # 10
Monterey, CA 93940-5706
Contact: Douglas Meador, Pres.
Telephone: 831-372-7415
Fax: 831-655-1855
Email: info@ventanawines.com / URL: http://
www.ventanawine.com
Product Service Description:
Winery and tasting room

Venture Tape
P.O. Box 384
Rockland, MA 02370-0384
Contact: Lewis S. Cohen, President
Telephone: 781-331-5900
Fax: 781-871-0065
Email: salesinfo@venturetape.com / URL:
http://www.venturetape.com
Product Service Description:
Tapes, Adhesive : Tapes, Double Sided
Tapes, Conductive Foil : Tapes, Foam &
Gasket Laminating : Tapes, Transfer
Adhesives

Verduin Machinery, Inc.
351 10th Ave
Paterson, NJ 07514-2629
Contact: Nicholas Verduin, Pres.
Telephone: 973-742-9789
Fax: 973-742-4215
Email: verduinmch@aol.com / URL:
Product Service Description:
Textile finishing machinery

**Verlo Mattress Factory Stores, Int'l
HQ.,Verlo Mattress Co. Inc.**
W3130 Stae Road 59
Whitewater, WI 53190-0298
Contact: Dave R. Young, V-P.
Telephone: 414-473-8957
Fax: 414-473-4623
Email: dyoung@verlo.com / URL: http://
www.verlo.com
Product Service Description:
Mattresses & bedsprings : Franchisor

Vernon Plastics Corp.
Shelly Road & Ward Hill Ave.
Haverhill, MA 01830
Contact: N. Lee, Ex. VP
Phone: 978-373-1551 / Fax: 978-373-6562
Product Service Description:
Coated Fabrics, not rubberized
Calendered, Printed & Laminated Vinyl
Finishing Plants, Manmade

Versar, Inc.
6850 Versar Center
Springfield, VA 22151-4196
Contact: Sales & Marketing,
Telephone: 703-750-3000
Fax: 703-642-6825
Email: whitelacu@versar.com / URL: http://
www.versar.com
Product Service Description:
Management Services : Engineering Services

Vertical Express
5805 N Wickham Rd
Melbourne, FL 32940-7338
Contact: John Coerse, Owner
Telephone: 407-254-9486
Fax: 407-254-5968
Email: ve@verticalexpress.com / URL: http://
www.verticalexpress.com
Product Service Description:
Custom Window Treatments & Design

Vi-Cas Mfg. Co., Inc.
PO Box 36310
Cincinnati, OH 45236-0310
Contact: James L. Willoughby, Pres.
Telephone: 513-791-7741
Fax: 513-791-6484
Email: vicas@juno.com / URL: http://
www.vi-cas.thomasregister.com
Product Service Description:
Urethane vacuum cups, vacuum cups, suction
cups : Plastic products

Vibco, Inc.
P.O. Box 8
Wyoming, RI 02898-0008
Contact: Ted Wadensten, President
Telephone: 401-539-2392
Fax: 401-539-2584
Email: / URL:
Product Service Description:
Industrial Vibrating Equipment

Vibrac International , LLC
22 Knapp Street
Stamford, CT 06907
Contact: Lawrence A. Siebert, Managing
Director
Telephone: 203-975-2888
Fax: 203-964-1818
Email: / URL: http://www.vibracint.com
Product Service Description:
Carbon Dioxide Measurment in Soft Drinks
Cap Torque Test Equipment

Vicki's Jewelry
2018 Mcculloch Blvd N
Lake Havasu City, AZ 86403-6732
Contact: Vicki Webster, Pres.
Telephone: 520-855-8911
Product Service Description:
Manufactures unassembled jewelry parts;
lapidary work : Jewelers' materials &
lapidary work : Set stones & repair jewelry

Victor Metal Finishing Inc.
PO Box 3703
Hollywood, FL 33083-3703
Contact: Victor Briosi, President
Telephone: 305-981-1969
Fax: 305-964-3995
Email: / URL:
Product Service Description:
Metal Finishing Equipment, Wholesale
Vibratory Deburring Equipment
High Energy Barrel & Disc Finishing
Equipment : Abrasive & Shot Peening
Finishing Equipment

Victory Racing Plate Co. The
1200 Rosedale Ave.
Baltimore, MD 21237-2681
Contact: David Erb, Sales Manager
Telephone: 410-391-6600
Fax: 410-687-4132
Email: plate@erols.com / URL: http://
www.victoryracingplate.com
Product Service Description:
Forged Aluminum Horsehoes/Racing Plates

Vidalia Gold Enterprizes
2305 Georgia Hwy. 56 E.
Uvalda, GA 30473
Contact: Benny Dees,
Telephone: 912-594-8122
Fax: 912-594-6935
Email: / URL:
Product Service Description:
Pickles, sauces, relishes & dressings
Pickles, sauces & salad dressings

Viking Enterprises
4521 Sunbeam Rd
Jacksonville, FL 32257-6111
Contact: Jon Braun, Owner
Telephone: 904-731-5065
Fax:
Email: / URL:
Product Service Description:
Automotive alternators & starters
Engine electrical equipment
Aircondition parts & service

Viking Industries, Inc.
38169 County Road 2
Saint Joseph, MN 56374-8701
Contact: Michael Legatt, Pres., Fin., Opers.
& R & D Mgr.
Telephone: 320-259-0909
Fax: 320-259-4705
Email: / URL:
Product Service Description:
Waterbeds, futons & bedroom furniture

Villa Bella Co.
PO Box 34
Marion, AR 72364-0034
Contact: Mike Briggs, Pres.
Telephone: 870-739-4419
Fax: 870-739-1848
Email: / URL:
Product Service Description:
Metal candle holders, metal pot holders &
decorative accessories
Metal products_fabricated

Vimex CNC Machining
16801 S Broadway St
Gardena, CA 90248-3109
Contact: Carlos Delatorre, Ptnr.
Telephone: 310-329-1192
Fax: 310-329-1198
Email: / URL:
Product Service Description:
CNC machine shop (job work)
Industrial machinery

Vintage Bedding
370 Turnbull Canyon Rd
City Of Industry, CA 91745-1009
Contact: Ron Gallardo, Pres.
Telephone: 626-961-7257
Fax: 626-330-8535
Email: / URL:
Product Service Description:
Manufactures mattresses for beds
Mattresses & bedsprings

Vinylex Corp.
PO Box 7187
Knoxville, TN 37921-0002
Contact: John Shaulis, Pres.
Telephone: 423-690-2211
Fax: 423-691-6273
Email: sales@vinylex.com / URL: http://
www.vinylex.com
Product Service Description:
Plastic extrusions
Plastic products

Viragen, Inc.
865 SW 78th Ave.
Plantation, FL 33324
Contact: Gerald Smith, Pres.
Telephone: 954-233-8746
Fax: 954-233-1414
Email: gsmith@viragen.com / URL: http://
www.viragen.com
Product Service Description:
Interferon
Pharmaceutical preparations

Virginia Iron & Metal Co.
9301 Old Staples Mill Rd
Richmond, VA 23228-2011
Contact: Gene Demestre, Pres., Sales Mgr.
Telephone: 804-266-9638
Fax: 804-266-2937
Email: info@vimco.com / URL: http://
www.vimco.com,
www.cssautomation.com,www.blastshield.com
Product Service Description:
Solar roller shades & insect screens
Drapery hardware & blinds & shades
Security - Blast Protection

Virtual Fund.Com
7090 Shady Oak Road
Eden Prairie, MN 55344-3403
Contact: Lee Newsom, Vice President
Telephone: 612-941-8687
Fax: 612-941-8652
Email: lee.newsom@virtualfund.com / URL:
Product Service Description:
Computer Periph Digital Color Printers
Computer Periph Plain-Paper Typesetter
Comp Periph Chemical-Free Film Printer
Internet Consulting & E-Commerce Tools

Visentech Systems, Inc.
1825 E Plano Pkwy Ste 160
Plano, TX 75074-8570
Contact: H. C. Ham, Pres.
Telephone: 972-423-1677
Fax: 972-423-2717
Email: visentec@ix.netcom.com / URL: http:/
/www.visentech.com
Product Service Description:
LAN Terminals - Unisys, DEC. HP. IBM.
Unix
Thin Client - Unisys, DEC. HP., IBM
Flat Panel Display
Remote Access Server

Visible Productions LLC
116 N College Ave Ste 7
Fort Collins, CO 80524-2459
Contact: J Rowley, Pres.
Telephone: 970-407-7240
Fax: 970-407-7248
Email: / URL:
Product Service Description:
Develops educational multimedia software
Prepackaged software
Custom medical animation
Custom medical illustration
3D human anatomy

Vision Blocks Inc.
1634 Cypress Ave
Melbourne, FL 32935-5931
Contact: George Zabetakis, President
Telephone: 407-254-7478
Fax: 407-255-2359
Email: / URL:
Product Service Description:
Glass Products, Made of Purchased Glass

Vision Pharmaceuticals Inc.
PO Box 400
Mitchell, SD 57301-0400
Contact: Vickie Rengstorff, Vice President
Telephone: 605-996-3356
Fax: 605-996-7072
Email: viva@visionpharm.com / URL: http://
www.visionpharm.com
Product Service Description:
Opthalmic Lubricant
Liquid Skin Cleaners
Toiletries, Skin Enhancers
Lotion Skin Moisturizer

Visual Inspection Technologies
199 Hwy. 206
Flanders, NJ 07836
Contact: Phillip Fass, Asst Mktg. Mgr.
Telephone: 973-448-0077
Fax: 973-448-0044
Email: info@v-i-t.com
URL: http://www.v-i-t.com
Product Service Description:
Fiber optic cameras
Photographic equipment & supplies

Vitec, Inc.
24755 Highpoint Rd.
Cleveland, OH 44122-5961
Contact: R. A. Wynveen, Manager
Telephone: 216-464-4670
Fax: 216-464-5324
Email: vitec@vitec-inc.com / URL: http://
www.vitec-inc.com
Product Service Description:
Bearing Condition Indicator (Baci)
Predictive maintenance data collector (DC+3)
Predictive maintenance software (EP)
Vibration, bearing condition & speed monitor
(SSM) : Vibration, measuring transducers
Vibration meters (M651) : Vibration meter,
analyzer & balancer (M655) : Vibration meter
& bearing tester (M653) : Vibration meter &
mini analyzer (M654) : Vibration monitors (1
to 4 channels) : Vibration monitoring systems
(M2110) (5 to 256 channels) : Vibration
switches (M438) : Vibration transmitters

Vitro Seating Products
PO Box 5440
Saint Louis, MO 63147-0340
Contact: Rick Grove, Mktg & Sales Mgr.
Telephone: 314-241-2265
Fax: 314-241-8723
Email: vitro@l1.net / URL: http://
www.vitroseating.com
Product Service Description:
Furniture & fixtures
Restaurant seating

Viviane Woodard Cosmetics
7712 Densmore Ave
Van Nuys, CA 91406-1919
Contact: Sandy Rohrbacher, President
Phone: 818-989-5818 / Fax: 818-904-3316
Email: viviane@earthlink.net / URL: http://
www.woodard.com
Product Service Description:
Skincare, cosmetics, body, bath & fragrance

Vixen Hill Mfg. Co.
Main St. & R.r. Tracks
Elverson, PA 19520
Contact: Andrea Beringer, Pur., Sales &
Mktg. Mgr.
Telephone: 610-286-0909
Fax: 610-286-2099
Email: vixenhill@voicenet.com / URL: http://
www.vixenhill.com
Product Service Description:
Gazebos : Wood products : Pavilions
Kiosk : Bandstands

Vogel Popcorn
PO Box 69
Hamburg, IA 51640-0069
Contact: Wendy Moran, International Sales
Coordinator
Telephone: 712-382-2634
Fax: 712-382-1357
Email: wmoran@vogelpopcorn.com / URL:
http://www.vogelpopcorn.com
Product Service Description:
Popcorn products

Vogler Equipment
16500 N.W. 7th Ave.
Miami, FL 33169
Contact: Gary Vogler, President
Telephone: 305-653-6000
Fax: 305-653-4614
Email: vogler 555 / URL: http://
www.voglerequipment.com
Product Service Description:
Pallet racks
Material handling equipment
Conveyors
Mezzanines
Used material handling equipment

Volant Sports, LLC
10601 N I-70 Service Rd
Wheat Ridge, CO 80033
Contact: Hank Kashiwa, Pres.
Telephone: 303-420-3900
Fax: 303-456-7810
Email: christap@volantsports.com / URL:
http://www.volantsports.com
Product Service Description:
Manufactures snowboards and skis
Sporting & athletic goods
Sporting & recreational goods

Voltage Multipliers Inc
8711 W Roosevelt Ave
Visalia, CA 93291-9458
Contact: Karen Spano, Sales Admin. Mgr.
Telephone: 559-651-1402
Fax: 559-651-0740
Email: kspano@voltagemultipliers.com /
URL: http://www.voltagemultipliers.com
Product Service Description:
Manufactures surface mount and low and
high-voltage rectifiers and high-voltage
assemblies

Voltronics Corporation
100-10 Ford Road
Denville, NJ 07834
Contact: Ridchard J. Newman, *
Telephone: 973-586-8585
Fax: 973-586-3404
Email: voltron@styx.ios.com / URL:
Product Service Description:
Electronic Trimmer Capacitors
Elec. Microwave Tuners
Variable Capacitors, Non-Magnetic
Trimmer Capacitors, Sealed Surface

Volumatic, Inc.
8219 Industrial Hwy
Macon, GA 31216-7632
Contact: Bob Schmucker, Pres., CFO
Telephone: 912-781-9300
Fax: 912-781-1119
Email: volumatc@hom.net
Product Service Description:
Aircraft components & precision machine
parts : Aircraft parts & equipment

Vortex Engineering
9201 Isaac St Ste A
Santee, CA 92071-5627
Contact: Gene Anderson, Owner
Telephone: 619-258-9660
Fax: 619-258-9770
Email: info@vortexengineering.com / URL:
http://www.vortexengineering.com
Product Service Description:
Designs, develops and builds custom
machinery— membrane filtration, WEB
conversion, recycling, defense laser
Machinery_special industry
Metalworking machinery

Vortex Satcom Systems, Inc.
2211 Lawson Ln
Santa Clara, CA 95054-3311
Contact: Rein Luik, Pres.
Telephone: 408-654-5600
Fax: 408-654-5613
Email: / URL: http://www.tiw.com
Product Service Description:
Satellite Communications Equipment
Dama SCPC Networks
Transcievers & Frequency Converters
Solid State Power Amplifiers & Block
Converters
TDMA Networkers

Vulcan Threaded Products, Inc.
PO Box 509
Pelham, AL 35124-0509
Contact: William Upton, Pres
Telephone:205-664-3733
Fax: 205-620-5150
Product Service Description:
Threaded construction rods
4140 Bars

W & W Mfg.
800 S Broadway
Hicksville, NY 11801-5017
Contact: J. A. Weitzman, Owner
Telephone: 516-942-1933
Fax: 516-942-1944
Product Service Description:
Batteries_primary, dry & wet
Radio batteries

W C E S, Inc.
PO Box 33
Waterbury, CT 06720-0033
Contact: Dominic Perrotti, Pres.
Phone: 203-573-1325 / Fax: 203-574-2943
Product Service Description:
Metal stampings

W O L I C, Inc.
PO Box 380429
Duncanville, TX 75138-0429
Contact: Mr. Charnick,
Telephone: 972-296-0777 / 800-285-8051
Fax: 972-296-7776 / 800-900-9470
Email: wolicusa@msn.com / URL: http://
www.themetro.com/wolic
Product Service Description:
Decorative Lighting

W.A. Charnstrom Co., Inc.
5391 12th Avenue East
Shakopee, MN 55379-1896
Contact: Mike Wagner,
Telephone: 612-403-0303 / 800-328-2962
Fax: 612-403-1113 / 800-916-3215
Email: mail@charnstrom.com / URL: http://
www.charnstrom.com
Product Service Description:
Mail Room Furniture, Sorters, Tables, Carts
Carts, Mail
Sorters, Mail

WD-40 Company
PO Box 80607
San Diego, CA 92138-0607
Contact: Garry Ridge, President
Telephone: 619-275-1400
Fax: 619-275-5823
Email: / URL: http://www.wd40.com
Product Service Description:
Lubricating oils & greases
Manufactures lubricating oil
Surface active agents

WEBB Distributors Inc
299 W 17th St
Yuma, AZ 85364-5638
Contact: Kimball Webb, Br. Mgr.
Telephone: 520-329-6420
Fax: 520-329-0849
Email: / URL:
Product Service Description:
Distributes evaporative coolers, refrigeration,
air conditioning and heating equipment and
supplies
Warm air heating & air conditioning
Refrigeration equipment & supplies

WNA Comet
6 Stuart Rd.
Chelmsford, MA 01824-4186
Contact: Al Medonna, Director of Marketing
Telephone: 978-256-6551
Fax: 978-256-3843
Email: madonnaal@msn.com / URL: http://
www.wna-inc.com
Product Service Description:
Tableware & kitchenware of plastics

WTS of Houston, Inc.
2723 Yale Street
Houston, TX 77008
Contact: Jim Shaw, President/General
Manager
Telephone: 713-861-3658
Fax: 713-865-9100
Email: jim_shaw@wtshouston.com / URL:
http://www.wtshouston.com
Product Service Description:
Customs Broker
Freight Forwarder
Freight & Cargo Transportation
Export Packer
NVOCC

Wabash Alloys, LLC
PO Box 466
Wabash, IN 46992-0466
Contact: E.C. Wingenbach, VP Sales &
Mktg.
Telephone: 219-563-7461
Fax: 219-563-5997
Email: / URL: http://www.wabashalloys.com
Product Service Description:
Secondary Aluminum Alloys (Recycled)

Wabash Instrument Corp.
P.O. Box 707
Wabash, IN 46997
Contact: Shethar Davis, President
Telephone: 219-563-8406
Fax: 219-563-8400
Product Service Description:
Educational Equipment

Wachters Organic Sea Products
360 Shaw Rd
South San Francisco, CA 94080-6606
Contact: Carrie Minucciani, Pres.
Telephone: 650-588-9567
Fax: 650-875-1626
Email: wachterosp@aol.com / URL: http://
www.wachters.com
Product Service Description:
Sea vegetation, vitamins, health nutritional
products, herbs, essences and rare oils
Plant: Soil Conditioners, Cleaning : Laundry
Products : Animal Supplements

Wafer World, Inc.
1100 Technology Pl Ste 104
West Palm Beach, FL 33407-4634
Contact: Sean Quinn, Pres., CFO
Telephone: 561-842-4441
Fax: 561-842-2677
Email: sales@waferworld.com / URL: http://
www.waferworld.com
Product Service Description:
Semiconductors & related devices
Silicon Semiconductor Materials
GaAS semiconductor materials
Germanium semiconductor materials

Waggon Cellers, Inc.
6500 Fm 1541
Amarillo, TX 79118-7817
Contact: Kelley Magee, MIS, Opers., Sales &
Mktg. Mgr.
Telephone: 806-373-1500
Fax: 806-373-1570
Email: / URL: http://www.waggon.com
Product Service Description:
Merchandising carts & kiosks

Wagman Primus Group, LP
10 Runway Rd., Suite I
Levittown, PA 19057
Contact: Richard C. Sheerr, *
Telephone: 215-269-1600
Fax: 215-269-1611
Email: trading@wagprim.com / URL:
Product Service Description:
Trading Co., - Paint / Industrial Applicators
Bristle, Hairs

Wago Corp.
9085 N Deerbrook Trl
Brown Deer, WI 53223-2475
Contact: Michael Lane, Pres.
Telephone: 414-354-5511
Fax: 414-354-1268
Email: / URL: http://www.wago.com
Product Service Description:
Electrical terminal blocks

Wah Yet Inc
28301 Industrial Blvd Ste C
Hayward, CA 94545-4429
Contact: Ying Lau, Owner
Telephone: 510-887-3801
Fax: 510-887-3803
Email: / URL:
Product Service Description:
Manufactures herbal teas & health foods

Wahl Clipper Corp.
2900 Locust St
Sterling, IL 61081-9501
Contact: Greg Wahl, Pres., COO
Telephone: 815-625-6525
Fax: 815-625-6745
Email: admin@wahlclipper.com / URL: http://www.wahlclipper.com
Product Service Description:
Hair clippers & shavers, massagers, cordless soldering irons & personal care appliances
Electric housewares

Wahoo International
2605 Oceanside Blvd Ste D
Oceanside, CA 92054-4585
Contact: Gary Fisher, Pres.
Telephone: 760-967-7873
Fax: 760-967-0146
Email: / URL: http://www.solarez.com
Product Service Description:
Sporting & athletic goods
Manufactures water sporting goods, surfboards and sailboards
UV-Curing resins for construction / repair of composites

Waikiki Aloe
2168 Kalakaua Ave.
Honolulu, HI 96815
Contact: Valerie Lamoureux, President
Telephone: 808-922-7767
Fax: 808-924-8474
Email: info@waikikialoe.com / URL: http://www.waikikialoe.com
Product Service Description:
Skin Care Products & Fragrances

Waikiki Aloe Waikiki Fragrance & Cosmetic Factory
2168 Kalakaua Ave
Honolulu, HI 96815-2319
Contact: Valerie Lamoureux, Owner & R & D Mgr.
Telephone: 808-922-7767
Fax: 808-924-8474
Email: info@waikikialoe.com / URL: http://www.waikikialoe.com
Product Service Description:
Perfumes, colognes & suntan & skin lotions

Waite, R. M. Company
2100 Embarcadero #203
Oakland, CA 94606-5309
Contact: Maureen Russell, Owner
Telephone: 510-535-2585
Fax: 510-535-1798
Email: maureen@rmwaite.com / URL: http://www.rmwaite.com
Product Service Description:
Waterproofing, caulking, lumber
Roofing, roof tiles, BUR roofing
Gypsum board, ceiling tile & accessories
Insulation
Flooring; wood, tile, sheet vinyl

Wakunaga of America Co., Ltd.
23501 Madero
Mission Viejo, CA 92691-2764
Contact: Mitsuru Takiura, President
Telephone: 949-855-2776
Fax: 949-458-2764
Email: mtakiura@msn.com / URL: http://www.kyolic.com
Product Service Description:
Kyolic Aged Garlic Extract Formula
Kyo-Dophilus probiotics formulas
Kyo-Green green food formula
Herbal Formula

Walker Corporation
1555 S. Vintage Ave
Ontario, CA 91761-3655
Contact: J.D. Walker, Jr., Chrm.
Telephone: 909-390-4300
Fax: 909-390-4301
Email: sales@walkercorp.com / URL: http://www.walkercorp.com
Product Service Description:
Design Prototype & Manufacturer of Metal Stamping to 330 Ton,
Slide Forming, In Die Tapping, In Die Assembly. : Constant Force Spring Products,
Spring Reels : Automated Assembly Processes. In Die : Processing

Walker Process Equip., Div. McNish Corporation (Mfr)
840 N. Russell Avenue
Aurora, IL 60506
Contact: Daniel E. Harker, International Sales
Telephone: 630-892-7921
Fax: 630-892-7951
Email: walker.process@walker-process.com / URL: http://www.walker-process.com
Product Service Description:
Water Treatment Equipment
Sewage Treatment Equipment
Waste Water Treatment Equipment

Wallis & Assoc. Cons. Engineers
8031 Broadway
San Antonio, TX 78209
Contact: WM. E. Wallis, President
Telephone: 210/824-7471
Fax: 210/824-7473
Email: / URL:
Product Service Description:
Engineering Svcs., Mechanical & Elec.

Wallsburg Soap Co
1165 Little Hobble Creek Rd
Wallsburg, UT 84082-9735
Contact: Dean House, Owner
Telephone: 435-654-0967
Fax: 435-654-1497
Email: dhouse@shadowlink.net / URL:
Product Service Description:
Manufactures all natural soaps, lotions, creams and ointments (with shea butter)

Waltham Aircraft Clock Corp.
1300 Hwy. 231 S.
Ozark, AL 36360
Contact: Anice C. Camp, Pres.
Telephone: 334-774-3584
Fax: 334-774-7083
Email: waltham@walthamclocks.com / URL: http://www.walthamclocks.com
Product Service Description:
Mechanical aircraft clocks
Overhaul & maintenance of all types of mechanical aircraft clocks

Wamco Corporation
PO Box 19222
Portland, OR 97280-0222
Contact: Waynmon Meuller, General Manager
Telephone: 503-245-5929
Fax: 503-245-8745
Email: wamcocorp@aol.com / URL:
Product Service Description:
Agriculture Irrigation Pumps
Agriculture Pump Parts
Farm Machinery Parts
Construction Machinery Parts
Irrigation Sprinklers & Pivots
Diesel Engine Parts

Wampler Foods, Inc.
PO Box 7275
Broadway, VA 22815-7275
Contact: Jim Hoben, Dir. Intern. Sls.
Phone: 540-896-0715 / Fax: 540-896-5127
Email: rockexport@attmail.com / URL: http://www.wampler.com
Product Service Description:
Poultry slaughtering & processing
Turkey processing & packaging

Ward Rugh, Inc.
P.O. Box 68
Ellensburg, WA 98926-0068
Contact: Rollie Bernth, President
Phone: 509-925-2827 / Fax: 509-962-5536
Product Service Description:
Compressed Oat Hay : Timothy Hay
Alfalfa Hay

Ware Shoals Plastics Inc.
80 Buzhardt Rd.
Ware Shoals, SC 29692
Contact: Bill Sprouse, VP
Telephone: 864-861-2281 / 888-810-0380
Fax: 864-861-9890
Email: wasplastics@backroads.net / URL:
Product Service Description:
Plastic & Metal Machined Parts

Warner Robins Supply Co., Inc.
2756 Watson Blvd
Warner Robins, GA 31093-2948
Contact: Ken Knight, CFO
Phone: 912-953-4100 / Fax: 912-953-7513
Email: wrsc@mindspring.com / URL: http://www.wrsupply.com
Product Service Description:
Roof trusses : Structural wood members
Wall panels

Warner T. Lundahl, Inc.
42-23 Francis Lewis Blvd.
Bayside, NY 11361-2580
Contact: Warner T. Lundahl, President
Phone: 718-279-8586 / Fax: 718-279-9228
Email: lundahlwt@aol.com / URL: http://members.aol.com/lundahlwt//index.html
Product Service Description:
Forestry Equipment & Parts, Export

Warren Communications
PO Box 620219
San Diego, CA 92162-0219
Contact: Sam Warren, Owner
Telephone: 619-236-0984
Fax: (011-526)630-1298
Email: warren@bookwarren / URL: http://www.bookwarren.com
Product Service Description:
Publishes books; laser typesetting; Internet publishing : Book publishing : Typesetting, guest hosue in Playas de Tijuana : Books: "Having Fun in Tijuana", "Baja By Night", "Baja Medical Guide"

Warren Industries, Inc.
6401 Falcon Rd
Rockford, IL 61109-4365
Contact: Jane Durgom-Powers, Pres. & CEO
Phone: 815-874-9555 / Fax: 815-874-4400
Email: jcd-p@worldnet.att.net / URL: http://www.warren-industries.com
Product Service Description:
Machinery_special industry
Slotting, thread rolling, parts washing machinery, special automation equipment, vibratory bowls, Vision Inspection, feeders, conveyors

Wascomat (Mfr)
461 Doughty Blvd.
Inwood, NY 11096
Contact: Marc J. Stern, Chief Operating Officer
Telephone: 516-371-4400
Fax: 516-371-4204
Email: mstern@wascomat.com / URL: http://www.wascomat.com
Product Service Description:
Commercial Washing Machines
Commercial Dryers
Wet Cleaning Machines

Washington Mould Co.
PO Box 518
Washington, PA 15301-0518
Contact: N. A. Greig, Pres.
Telephone: 724-225-7700
Fax: 724-225-0273
Product Service Description:
Foundries_gray & ductile iron
Iron castings, mining machinery replacement parts & general machining job shop

Watco Mfg. Co.
1220 S. Powell Rd.
Independence, MO 64057-2724
Contact: Jim Engard, National Sales Manager
Telephone: 816-796-3900
Fax: 816-796-0875
Product Service Description:
Metal sanitary ware
Bath wastes & overflows

Watec America Corp
3155 E Patrick Ln
Las Vegas, NV 89120-3496
Contact: Kimberly Green, Marketing Mgr.
Telephone: 702-434-6111
Fax: 702-434-3222
Email: / URL: http://www.watec.com
Product Service Description:
Manufactures CCD video cameras & accessories

Water Conditioning/Purification
2800 E Fort Lowell Rd
Tucson, AZ 85716-1568
Contact: Kurt C Peterson, Publisher
Telephone: 520-323-6144
Fax: 520-323-7412
Email: publicom@azstarnet.com / URL: http://www.wcp.net
Product Service Description:
Publishes monthly trade magazine for the water industry : Periodicals

Water Quality Services
3180 Carmine
Carson City, NV 89706
Contact: Vern Achenbach,
Telephone: 775-883-9114 / 800-748-6859
Email: wqs@pyramid.net / URL: http://www.pyramid.net/wqs
Product Service Description:
Water Imporvement Products

Water Resources International
2800 E Chambers St
Phoenix, AZ 85040-3735
Contact: Lowell E Foletta, Pres.
Telephone: 602-268-2580
Fax: 602-268-8080
Email: nadine@water-resources-intl.com / URL: http://www.bestwater.com
Product Service Description:
Manufacturer of Water Treatment Systems: Residential / Commercial / Industrial

Water Services International
PO Box 26897
San Diego, CA 92196-0897
Contact: Barry Safa,
Telephone: 619-689-9512
Fax: 619-530-1594
Email: cyman@ix.netcom.com / URL:
Product Service Description:
Package Sewage Treatment Plants
Package Water Treatment Plants
Desalination Treatment Systems, (Brackish &
Sea Water)
Process Automation & Control Systems

Water Technologies
PO Box 18614
Encino, CA 91416-8614
Contact: Herbert Schindler, V-P.
Telephone: 818-981-2115
Fax: 323-231-7358
Product Service Description:
Manufactures water treatment systems
for treatment of waste water
from process industry, both for legal
discharge and for reuse in same process

Water-Jel Technologies
243 Veterans Blvd
Carlstadt, NJ 07072-2708
Contact: Peter Cohen, Pres.
Telephone: 201-507-8300
Fax: 201-507-8325
Email: info@waterjel.com / URL: http://
www.waterjel.com
Product Service Description:
Manufacturer of First Aid Products
Burn Dressings, Burn Creams, Burn Kits
Hydrocortisone Cream, Triple Antibiotic
Ointment
First Aid Cream, Antiseptic Gel

Waterland Mfg., Inc.
9200 Nw 58th St
Miami, FL 33178-1612
Contact: Egda Salazar, Export Sales Mgr.
Telephone: 305-594-1022
Fax: 305-591-3690
Email: sales@continentaltrailers.com / URL:
http://www.continentaltrailers.com
Product Service Description:
Boat trailers
Transportation equipment
Marine Supplies

Waterloo Industries, Inc.
P.O. Box 2095
Waterloo, IA 50702
Contact: Bill Salyer, Int'l. Sales Manager
Telephone: 319-235-7131
Fax: 319-236-8569
Email: salyer@waterloindustries.com /
URL: http://www.waterloindustries.com
Product Service Description:
Metal Stampings, Tool Storage Products
Plastic Molded Tool Storage Products, Tool
Trolleys : Hospital Carts, Hospital Trolleys
Work Benches

Watersaver International
5870 E. 56th Ave.
Commerce City, CO 80022
Contact: Sales & Marketing,
Telephone: 303-289-1818
Fax: 303-287-3136
Email: info@watersaver.com / URL: http://
www.watersaver.com
Product Service Description:
Plastic Sheet Film : Adhesives
Container Cargo

Waterwise
3608 Parkway Blvd.
Leesburg, FL 34748-9744
Contact: Greg Barber, VP
Telephone: 352-787-5008
Fax: 352-787-8123
Email: waterwise3@aol.com / URL: http://
www.waterwise.com
Product Service Description:
Drinking water, purification systems
Water distillers : Domestic electrical
appliances

Watkins, Watkins & Keenan, CPA's
850 Ridge Lake Blvd., Suite 101
Memphis, TN 38120
Contact: William H. Watkins, Managing
Partner
Telephone: 901-761-2720
Fax: 901-763-3094
Email: wwk@wwkcpas.com / URL: http://
www.wwkcpas.com
Product Service Description:
Tax, Accounting & Auditing Services

Waukesha Cherry-Burrell (Mfr)
611 Sugar Creek Rd.
Delavan, WI 53115
Contact: Patrick Galligan, Dir. of Marketing
Telephone: 414-728-1900
Fax: 414-728-4320
Email: custserv@waukesha-cb.com / URL:
Product Service Description:
Dairy Products Machinery & Equipment
Confectionery Machinery
Food Processing Equipment

**Waukesha Co. Technical College -
International Trade Center**
800 Main St.
Pewaukee, WI 53072-4696
Contact: Barbara Moebius, Assoc.Dean
Telephone: 414-691-5550
Fax: 414-691-5089
Product Service Description:
Video Tape Intl. Trade
International Trade Reference Library

Waverlee Homes Inc.
PO Box 1887
Hamilton, AL 35570-1887
Contact: Phil Fowler, GM, Opers.
Telephone: 205-921-1887
Fax: 205-921-1888
Email: waverlee@sonet.net / URL:
Product Service Description:
Manufactured Housing

Wayne Consultants, Inc.
N16 W22040 Jericho Drive
Waukesha, WI 53186
Contact: Wayne B. Olson, Dir /Marketing,
Telephone: 414-547-5300
Fax: 414-547-5332
Email: chem@execpc.com / URL: http://
www.execpc.com/chem
Product Service Description:
Chemical corrosion preventives for boilers &
cooling towers.

Wayne Engineering Corporation
701 Performance Dr
Cedar Falls, IA 50613
Contact: Linda Worthington, Rita Cyrzan
Phone: 319-266-1721 / Fax: 319-266-8207
Email: info@wayneeng.com / URL: http://
www.wayneeng.com
Product Service Description:
Truck Bodies, Refuse Compactor Collector

We're Organized of No Calif
2501 Mercantile Dr # B
Rancho Cordova, CA 95742-6217
Contact: Joseph Rawlings, Ptnr.
Phone: 916-638-0123 / Fax: 916-638-3067
Product Service Description:
Manufactures modular cabinetry for closets
and garage using high pressure thermofused
laminates : Modular storage cabinets
Garage storage cabinets

Wearbest Sil-Tex Mills Ltd.
PO Box 589
Garfield, NJ 07026-0589
Contact: Irwin Gasner, Pres.
Phone: 973-340-8844 / Fax: 973-340-2900
Product Service Description:
Upholstery fabric
Broadwoven fabric mills, manmade

Weather Tec Corporation
5645 E Clinton Ave
Fresno, CA 93727-1308
Contact: Nick Dvorak, Dir. Sales & Mktg.
Telephone: 209-291-5555
Fax: 209-294-8802
Email: info@weathertec.com / URL: http://
www.weathertec.com
Product Service Description:
Irrigation sprinklers & Micro for Agriculture

Webco Trading
1840 W. 49th St.
Hialeah, FL 33012-2948
Contact: Claudia Ferrera, Manager
Telephone: 305-822-4030
Product Service Description:
Exporting Firms
Acyclic hydrocarbons, saturated

Weben-Jarco, Inc.
PO Box 763460
Dallas, TX 75376-3460
Contact: Gerry Miller, Pres.
Telephone: 214-637-0530
Fax: 214-330-6864
Email: info@weben-jarco.com / URL: http://
www.weben-jarco.com
Product Service Description:
Plate work_fabricated (boiler shops)
Water heaters & storage tanks
High efficiency water heaters & boilers
Mid - efficiency water heaters & boilers
Pre-Packaged hot water systems
Alternative hot water systems
Floor heater systems

Webtech, Inc.
108 N. Gold Dr.
Robbinsville, NJ 08691-1602
Contact: Art Maynard, General Manager
Telephone: 609-259-2800
Fax: 609-259-9311
Email: mayva@ix.netcom.com / URL: http://
www.webtech-hts.com
Product Service Description:
Hot Stamp Labels & decor Pres Sens.

Weigh-Tronix Inc
2320 Airport Blvd
Santa Rosa, CA 95403-8260
Contact: Robert Torre, General Manager
Phone: 707-527-5555 / Fax: 707-579-0180
Email: / URL: http://www.wt-nci.com
Product Service Description:
Measuring & controlling devices : Weighing
and counting devices : Commercial equipment
Scales & balances, except laboratory
Equipment rental & leasing

Weiler And Company Inc.
1116 E. Main Street
Whitewater, WI 53190
Contact: Jim H. Schumacher,
Dir.of Int'l Sales
Telephone: 414-473-5254
Fax: 414-473-5867
Email: sales@weilerinc.com / URL: http://
www.weilerinc.com
Product Service Description:
Food Prod. Mach., Grinders & Mixers
Food Prod. Mach., Grinders / Mixers
Food Prod. Mach., Conveyors, Belt & Screw
Food Prod. Mach., Portioning Equipment
Food Prod. Mach., Dumpers
Complete Ground Meat Processing Systems
Complete Sausage Processing Systems
Complete Meat Separators

Weinschel, Bruno Assocs., Inc.
42 Cessna Ct
Gaithersburg, MD 20879-4145
Contact: Bruno O. Weinschel, Pres.
Telephone: 301-948-8342
Fax: 301-869-9783
Email: sales@weinschelassociates.com /
URL: http://www.weinschelassociates.com
Product Service Description:
RF Microwave components & test equipment

Weldcraft Industries
PO Box 11104
Terra Bella, CA 93270-1104
Contact: Gerald Micke, Pres.
Telephone: 209-784-4322
Fax: 209-784-4620
Email: weldcraft@ocsnet.net / URL:
Product Service Description:
Manufactures farm equipment— harvesters
and pruning towers
Farm machinery & equipment - bulk
harvesting equipment

Welden Steam Generators, Inc.
122 E Rocksylvania Ave
Iowa Falls, IA 50126-2411
Contact: David Welden, Pres.,
Telephone: 515-648-3021
Fax: 515-648-2611
Email: welden@cnsinternet.com / URL: http:/
/www.greenbelt.net/welden
Product Service Description:
Direct fired steam generators

Welding Warehouse
7654 E Slauson Ave
City Of Commerce, CA 90040-3833
Contact: Jim Dohleman, Pres.
Telephone: 323-889-8118
Fax: 323-889-8297
Email: / URL: http://
www.weldingwarehouse.com
Product Service Description:
Welding apparatus
Manufactures welding rods and filler metals
ISO 9002

Wells Aluminum Corp.
809 Glen Eagles Ct Ste 300
Baltimore, MD 21286-2230
Contact: Russell Kupiec, Pres.
Telephone: 410-494-4500
Fax: 410-494-4522
Email: sales@wells-aluminum.com / URL:
http://www.wells-aluminum.com
Product Service Description:
Aluminum extrusions
Aluminum fabrications & other value added
processing

Weltek-Swiss
1500 W Hampden Ave Ste 5k
Englewood, CO 80110-2075
Contact: Douglas Welch, Pres.
Telephone: 303-781-6613
Fax: 303-781-6887
Email: weltek@email.com / URL:
Product Service Description:
Screw machine products (job work); general
machine shop and Swiss style CNC
machining : Screw machine products
Industrial machinery

Wendell's, Inc.
6601 Industry Ave
Ramsey, MN 55303-4552
Contact: Lawerence T. Cody, Pres.
Telephone: 612-576-8200
Fax: 612-576-0995
Email: sales@wendellsinc.com / URL: http://
www.wendellsinc.com
Product Service Description:
Coins, Medallions, Key Tags
Stamps, Engraving, Name Badges

Wenger Manufacturing Inc. (Mfr)
2405 Grand Avenue, Suite 390
Kansas City, MO 64108
Contact: Gary Johnston, *
Telephone: 816-221-5084
Fax: 816-221-5086
Email: / URL:
Product Service Description:
Extrusion Equip., Corn Chips, Cereals, Pasta
Biodegradable Loose-Fill Production Eqp.
Extrusion Equip., Petfoods, Aquatic Feeds

Wescosa Inc
PO Box 66626
Scotts Valley, CA 95067-6626
Contact: T H Ramsey, Pres., GM
Telephone: 408-438-4600
Fax: 408-438-8613
Email: / URL:
Product Service Description:
Manufactures business card trays, files,
fingertip moistening compound, rulers and
signs : Plastic products : Stationery & office
supplies : Signs & advertising specialties
Tools_hand & edge

Wespac Corp.
342 Harriet St.
San Francisco, CA 94103-4716
Contact: M. McCray, Jr., President
Telephone: 415-431-6350
Fax: 415-621-1525
Email: wespaccorp@earthlink.net / URL:
http://www.wespaccorp.com
Product Service Description:
Builders hardware
Window & door hardware
Purchasing agents - construction materials

West Agro, Inc.
11100 N. Congress Ave.
Kansas City, MO 64153-1222
Contact: William Papineau, President
Telephone: 816-891-1600
Fax: 816-891-1595
Email: westagro@swbell.net / URL: http://
www.westagro.com
Product Service Description:
Chemicals & Allied Products, NEC
Iodides & Iodide oxides
Dairy Farm Chemicals
Dairy Farm Processors

West Coast Industries Inc.
14900 Whitman Ave N
Seattle, WA 98133-6532
Contact: Richard Heusser, General Manager
Telephone: 206-365-7513
Fax: 206-365-7483
Email: rheusser@wcoastindustries.com
Product Service Description:
Hardware, Aircraft Tools & Maint. Equip.
Cold Working Tools
Fatigue Enhancement Products

West Tool & Design, Inc.
1220 N Tower Rd
Fergus Falls, MN 56537-1089
Contact: Donald Westra, Pres., R & D Mgr.
Telephone: 218-739-4990
Fax: 218-739-4989
Email: westtool@prairietech.net / URL:
Product Service Description:
Assembly machinery & equipment
Metalworking machinery
Stainless Steel Fabrication -NSF Approved

WestPoint Stevens
1185 Avenue of the Americas,
New York, NY 10036-2601
Contact: Anne Martin, Director of Public
Relations
Telephone: 212-930-2116
Fax: 212-930-3768
Email: martin.anne@westpoint-stevens.com /
URL: http://www.martex.com /
www.westpointstevens.com
Product Service Description:
Blankets
Bed Linens
Towels

WestPro Graphics
4552 Colorado Blvd
Los Angeles, CA 90039-1104
Contact: Douglas D Waldron Jr, Pres.
Telephone: 818-247-7030
Fax: 818-243-4135
Email: / URL: http://
www.westprographics.com
Product Service Description:
Lithographic printing_commercial
Prints color advertising brochures,
informational booklets and marketing
materials
Commercial art & graphic design

Westberg Mfg., Inc.
3400 Westach Way
Sonoma, CA 95476-9709
Contact: R.R. Westberg, Adimin.V.P.
Telephone: 707-938-2121
Fax: 707-938-4968
Email: westach@juno.com / URL: http://
www.westach.com
Product Service Description:
Tachometers, Electric & Industrial
Measuring Dev., Elec. Engine Instruments
Wind Speed & Direction Indicators

Westcon Contact Lens Company Inc
611 Eisenhauer St
Grand Junction, CO 81505-1026
Contact: G Michael Ferris, Pres.
Telephone: 970-245-3845
Fax: 970-245-4516
Email: / URL:
Product Service Description:
Ophthalmic goods
Manufactures contact lenses

Westcott Cove Publishing Co.
PO Box 130
Stamford, CT 06904-0130
Contact: Julius Wilensky, Owner
Telephone: 203-322-0998
Fax: 203-322-1388
Product Service Description:
Nautical Books & Cruising Guides

Western Agricultural Publish
4969 E Clinton Way Ste 119
Fresno, CA 93727-1549
Contact: Paul Baltimore, Pres.
Telephone: 209-252-7000
Fax: 209-252-7387
Product Service Description:
Publishes seven monthly agricultural
magazines : Grape grower magazine & trade
shows : Nut grower magazine & trade shows
Citro Graph Magazine : CA/AZ cotton
magazine : Tree fruit magazine : Agri
business fieldman magazine : Vegetable
magazines

Western Consolidated Foods, Inc.
P.O. Box 255493
Sacramento, CA 95865
Contact: Garry L. Warren, President
Telephone: 916-646-0012
Fax: 916-646-0234
Email: / URL:
Product Service Description:
Tomato Sauces, Puree & Concentrates
Vegetables, Canned
Fruits, Canned

Western Crating Inc.
P.O. Box 60971 AMF
Houston, TX 77205
Contact: Gayla C. Ersler, *
Telephone: 281-590-6916
Fax: 281-590-6229
Email: westpaq / URL: http://
www.westerncrating.com
Product Service Description:
Packing & Crating
Freight Transportation Arrangement
Freight & Cargo: Packing & Crating

Western Farm Service/Cascade
PO Box 269
Tangent, OR 97389-0269
Contact: Robert Long, GM
Telephone: 541-928-3391
Fax: 541-926-8807
Email: bobl@skipnet.com / URL: http://
www.westernfarmservice.com
Product Service Description:
Mixes fertilizers from purchased materials;
sells agricultural and industrial chemicals
Fertilizers, mixing only
Farm supplies

Western Filament Inc
630 Hollingsworth St
Grand Junction, CO 81505-1000
Contact: Wayne Wright, Pres.
Telephone: 970-241-8780
Fax: 970-241-8682
Email: / URL:
Product Service Description:
Manufacturer of Military Spec lacing tapes
Manufacturer of lacing tape for electrical
motors : Manufacturer of expandable sleeving
products : Winders of cops & bobbins
Fabrication of braided & overbraided
products

Western Hybrid Seeds, Inc.
P.O. Box 1169
Hamilton City, CA 95951-1169
Contact: Trevor J. Clarke, President
Telephone: 530-342-3410
Fax: 530-893-5304
Email: WHS@fogcty.com / URL:
Product Service Description:
Contracted Vegetable Production for Seed
Vegetable seeds for sowing & herb seeds for
sowing : Miscellaneous cargo
Seeds, fruit and spores, of a kind used for
sowing

Western Ophthalmics Corporation
19019 36th Avenue West Ste. G.
Lynnwood, WA 98036
Contact: Jack D'Amico, Pres.
Telephone: 800-426-9938
Fax: 800-423-4284
Email: order@westernophthalmics.com /
URL: http://www.western-ophthalmics.com
Product Service Description:
Ophthalmic instruments

Western Polymer Corp
32 Road R Se
Moses Lake, WA 98837-9303
Contact: Michael Townsend, V-P., Opers.
Telephone: 509-765-1803
Fax: 509-765-0327
Email: westpoly@atnet.net / URL: http://
www.westernpolymer.com
Product Service Description:
Manufactures food & cationic industrial
potato starch

Western Roller Corporation
63393 Nels Anderson Rd
Bend, OR 97701-5743
Contact: Doug D Collver, Sales & Mktg.
Mgr.
Telephone: 541-382-5643
Fax: 541-382-0159
Email: / URL: http://www.westernroller.com
Product Service Description:
Printing machinery; web press folder parts
Woodworking machinery; soft feed roller
Polyurethane parts for industry

Western States Mfg. Co.
801-811 Main St., PO Box 3655
Sioux City, IA 51102
Contact: John Lanning, *
Telephone: 712-252-4248
Fax: 712-258-4368
Email: / URL:
Product Service Description:
Tire & Tube Repair Materials

Western Synthetic Fiber
PO Box 6248
Carson, CA 90749-6248
Contact: Mark Bidner, Pres.
Telephone: 310-767-1000
Fax: 310-767-1106
Email: / URL:
Product Service Description:
Manufactures polyester for sofas
Organic fibers, noncellulosic
Cellulosic manmade fibers
Needle punched liquid filtration
High loft HVAC filtration
Paint collection media
Quilting Battings
Geo textiles
Garment fiber fill
Patio Furniture Fiber Fill // Sleeping bag fill

Western Thin Brick & Tile
707 W Buchanan St
Phoenix, AZ 85007-3405
Contact: Don Drew, Mgr.
Telephone: 602-254-7020
Fax: 602-254-7172
Product Service Description:
Manufactures thin brick & veneer pavers
8X8 x 3/4 X 16 Split Face Block

Western Trails Inc
PO Box 460
Bozeman, MT 59771-0460
Contact: Jean Clem, Pres.
Phone: 406-587-5489 / Fax: 406-587-5489
Email: westrn@gomontana.com / URL: http://
www.gomontana.com/cowboysfoods
Product Service Description:
Manufactures grain products: Hulless
NuBarley; bread & pancake mixes, flour

Westheffer Mfg.
PO Box 363, 1235 North 3rd
Lawrence, KS 66044-0363
Contact: Samih Staitieh, Chrm., Pres.
Telephone: 785-843-1633
Fax: 785-843-4486
Email: westheffer@idir.net / URL: http://
www.westheffer.com
Product Service Description:
Agricultural, turf & pest sprayers

Westile
8311 W Carder Ct
Littleton, CO 80125-9705
Contact: A.G. Boros, Ntl. Sales Mgr.
Telephone: 303-791-1700
Fax: 303-791-9906
Email: / URL: http://www.westile.com
Product Service Description:
Concrete products
Manufactures concrete roofing products;
concrete tiles and pavers

Westrex International
25 Denby Rd.
Boston, MA 02134-1605
Contact: Bill Lawson, *
Telephone: 617-254-1200
Fax: 617-254-6848
Email: info@westrex.com / URL: http://
www.westrex.com
Product Service Description:
Cash Registers, Computer Based
P.O.S. / Banking Receipt Printers

Wheelock, Inc.
273 Branchport Ave
Long Branch, NJ 07740-6899
Contact: Gary Shawn, V-P., Fin.
Telephone: 732-222-6880
Fax: 732-222-8707
Email: / URL: http://www.wheelockinc.com
Product Service Description:
Fire alarm signals, audio & visual
Voice systems

Whip-It Products, Inc.
PO Box 30128
Pensacola, FL 32503-1128
Contact: John Watson, Pres.
Telephone: 850-436-2125 / 800-582-0398
Fax: 850-436-2077
Email: jwatsonIII@aol.com / URL:
Product Service Description:
Industrial Strength Cleaning Products
All Purpose Citrus Cleaners
Enviromentally Safe, Degreaser

Whipple International
3292 1/2 N Weber Ave
Fresno, CA 93722-4942
Contact: Art Whipple, Pres.
Telephone: 559-442-1261
Fax: 559-442-4153
Email: / URL:
Product Service Description:
Manufactures Whipple super-chargers, power
boost chargers for automotive, marine racing

Whitehall Lane Winery
1563 Saint Helena Hwy S
Saint Helena, CA 94574-9775
Contact: Michael McLoughlin, GM
Telephone: 707-963-9454
Fax: 707-963-7035
Email: / URL: http://www.whitehall-lane.com
Product Service Description:
Winery and vineyards
Wines, brandy, & brandy spirits

Whiting Corporation
15700 Lathrop Ave
Harvey, IL 60426-5118
Contact: Casey J. Skorpinski, Marketing &
Sales
Telephone: 708-596-6600
Fax: 708-210-5030
Email: / URL:
Product Service Description:
Hoists & Cranes
Railroad Equipment
Transportation Equipment, Nec

Whitlock Instrument
1300 N Texas Ave
Odessa, TX 79761-3899
Contact: Lonnie Heidelbert,
Telephone: 915-337-3412
Fax: 915-335-5926
Email: sales@whitlockinstrument.com / URL:
http://www.whitlockinstrument.com
Product Service Description:
Electrical & electronic test equipment sales &
repair & production machining Mfg.
Lubrication shutdown (DNFT)
Instrumentation Design

Whitmark Inc
PO Box 11750
Tucson, AZ 85734-1750
Contact: Kevin or Syliva, Sales
Telephone: 520-573-7080
Fax: 520-745-8831
Email: sales@whitmark.com / URL: http://
www.whitmark.com
Product Service Description:
Manufactures corrugated boxes, pads and
crates
Boxes_corrugated & solid fiber, foam &
vacuum formed plastics

Wichita Falls Mfg.
PO Box 5326
Wichita Falls, TX 76307-5326
Contact: Richard Jeter, Pres., Opers. Mgr.
Telephone: 940-322-4491
Fax: 940-322-8132
Email: wfmac@wf.net / URL:
Product Service Description:
Oilfield cementing plugs
Oil field float equipment parts
Foundry products, investment castings

Wick Buildings
PO Box 38
Mazomanie, WI 53560-0038
Contact: Tom Wick, V-P., GM
Phone: 608-795-2294 / Fax: 608-795-2534
Email: wickbldg@wickbuildings.com / URL:
http://www.wickbuidings.com
Product Service Description:
Metal clad post frame agricultural &
commercial buildings
Pre-engineered wood buildings

Wieland Precision Machine
570 Central Ave Ste B
Lake Elsinore, CA 92530-2741
Contact: Jim Walsh - VP Sales,
Gary Novak, Sales Mgr.
Telephone: 909-471-1393
Fax: 909-471-1395
Email: wpm@iinet.com / URL: http://
www.wpminc.com
Product Service Description:
Precision machine shop
Heatsinks & other machined parts

Wienk Charolais
44210 205th St.
Lake Preston, SD 57249-9730
Contact: Arnold Wienk, President
Telephone: 605-847-4350
Fax: 605-847-4118
Email: acwienk@dtgnet.com / URL:
Product Service Description:
Charolais Cattle : Charolais Bull Semen

Wiggin Farms
6590 Hillgate Rd
Arbuckle, CA 95912-9712
Contact: Sharon Wiggin, Pres.
Telephone: 530-476-2288
Fax: 530-476-2856
Email: wigginfarms@colusanet.com / URL:
http://www.colusanet.com/wigginfarms
Product Service Description:
California almonds, bulk, consumer, flavored,
diced & sliced

Wiggy's Inc
PO Box 2124
Grand Junction, CO 81502-2124
Contact: Jerry N Wigutow, Pres.
Telephone: 970-241-6465
Fax: 970-241-5921
Email: wiggy@wiggys.com / URL: http://
www.wiggys.com
Product Service Description:
Manufactures sleeping bags and cold weather
garments : Textile products_fabricated
Outerwear_women's & misses'

Wikoff Color Corp.
1886 Merritt Rd.
Fort Mill, SC 29715-7707
Contact: Jim Freid, Director, Export Sales
Telephone: 803-548-2210
Fax: 803-548-5728
Email: cjfreid@cetlink.net / URL: http://
www.wikoff.com
Product Service Description:
Ink Printing : Printing Inks & Coatings

Wilbert Vaults Of Houston, Inc.
10645 Aldine Westfield Rd
Houston, TX 77093-4111
Contact: James Henery, Pres.
Phone: 713-692-6105 / Fax: 713-692-6920
Email: jhenery102.com
Product Service Description:
Concrete products : Concrete burial vaults

Wilcox Natural Products(Mfr)
P.O. Box 391
Boone, NC 28607
Contact: Chuck Wanzer, General Manager
Telephone: 828-264-3615
Fax: 828-264-2831
Email: wilcox@wnp.com / URL: http://
www.goldenseal.com
Product Service Description:
American Ginseng, American Botanicals

Wildcat Mfg. Co., Inc.
P.O. Box 1100
Freeman, SD 57029-1100
Contact: Myron Holzwarth, Sales Manager
Telephone: 605-925-4512
Fax: 605-925-7536
Email: wildcat@sd.cybernex.net / URL: http:/
/www.wildcatinc.com
Product Service Description:
Snowblowers (Farm Equipment)
Pothole Repair Truck, Construction
Equipment : Compost Turners, Farm
Equipment : Trommel Screening Equipment,
Construction Equipment : Snowblowers,
Commercial : Recycling Equipment, Compost
Turners : Recycling Equipment, Trommel
Screens : MSW Sorting Equipment, (MRF)

Wildlife Supply Company /
Trippensee Planetarium Co.
301 Cass Street
Saginaw, MI 48602-2097
Contact: Betty A. Phillips, President
Telephone: 517-799-8100
Fax: 517-799-8115
Email: goto@wildco.com / URL: http://
www.wildco.com
Product Service Description:
Field Sampling Equipment
Astron/Earth Science Models For Schools

Wildwood Farms, Inc.
PO Box 111
Fulton, IL 61252-0111
Contact: Jo A. Aulick, Pres.
Telephone: 815-589-3366
Fax: 815-589-4286
Email: wildwood@sanasys.com / URL: http://
www.wildwoodfarms.com
Product Service Description:
Redwood wildlife feeders, domestic pet
products, garden accessories, deck planters
Feeds_prepared : Containers_wood
Wildlife Feeds-USDA Certified for
International Shipment : Wildlife Feeders &
Housing handcrafted of redwood

Williams Shipping
2513 Tilden Ave.
Brooklyn, NY 11226-5015
Contact: James Williams, Owner
Telephone: 718-826-0070
Product Service Description:
Business Consulting, NEC
Household goods : Passenger motor vehicles
Structures and parts of structures, of iron or
steel

Willis Machine Inc
1445 Donlon St Unit 2-3-4
Ventura, CA 93003-5639
Contact: Harlan Willis, Pres.
Telephone: 805-644-0305
Fax: 805-644-0807
Product Service Description:
Manufactures metal and plastic machine parts
Precision CNC Machinery

Willow Creek Greenhouses Inc
PO Box 1156
Chino Valley, AZ 86323-1156
Contact: Tom Fortner, Pres.
Telephone: 520-636-4441
Fax: 602-252-7313
Email: flowers@goodnet.com / URL:
Product Service Description:
Wholesales nursery supplies and bedding
plants : Flowers & florists' supplies

Wilson & Co., Inc., Thomas C.
2111 44th Ave
Long Island City, NY 11101-5007
Contact: Jane W. Hanley, Chrm.
Telephone: 718-729-3360
Fax: 718-361-2872
Email: tcwilson@tcwilson.com / URL: http://
www.tcwilson.com
Product Service Description:
Tube Cleaners, Air, Water or Electric Driven
Tube Expanders for Boilers, Heat Exchangers
& Condensers : Plate Work, Fabricated
(Boiler Shops) : Torq - Air Matics
Vacuum Leak Detectors : Flo Breakers
Pneumatic Tools :Id, Mikes(ID Measurements
of Boilers, Heat Exchangers & Condensers)

WinTron Inc
250 Runville Road
Bellefonte, PA 16823
Contact: Melissa Hein, *
Telephone: 814-355-1521
Fax: 814-355-1524
Email: / URL:
Product Service Description:
Electronic Coils
Electronic Transformers
High Voltage Power Supplies
Deflection Yokes

Winchester Auburn Mills, Inc
200 Merrimac St
Woburn, MA 01801-1756
Contact: David Steinberg, President
Telephone: 781-935-4110
Fax: 781-935-7349
Email: ropemaker@winaub.com / URL: http:/
/www.winaub.com
Product Service Description:
Cordage & twine
Rope, Twine, Braided Products, Plastic
Extrusions
Thread, Commercial Sewing & Selvage Yarns
Throwster

Windfall Products, Inc.
PO Box 170
Saint Marys, PA 15857-0170
Contact: Eric Wolfe, Chrm., Pres.
Telephone: 814-834-1222
Fax: 814-834-9536
Email: johndi@windfallproducts.com / URL:
http://www.windfallproducts.com
Product Service Description:
Powdered metal parts
Primary metal products

Window Products Inc
10507 E Montgomery Dr
Spokane, WA 99206-4280
Contact: Donald Moyer, Sales Manager
Telephone: 509-922-8128
Fax: 509-924-9473
Email: 102022.1443@compuserve.com /
URL: http://www.windowproducts.com
Product Service Description:
Manufactures vinyl windows and doors
Plastic products

Window Technology, Inc.
611 Mercer Ave
Panama City, FL 32401-2637
Contact: Joe Gorman, Pres.
Telephone: 850-785-9515
Fax: 850-763-0982
Email: / URL:
Product Service Description:
Shutters - Blinds - Draperies

Windsport
PO Box 9425
Austin, TX 78766-9425
Contact: Jane Carlisle, *
Telephone: 512-454-1912
Product Service Description:
Windsocks

Winfield Cabinets
5 Industrial Park
Benton, AR 72015-5074
Contact: Dennis Winfield, Pres.
Telephone: 501-776-1628
Fax: 501-776-3572
Email: / URL:
Product Service Description:
Wooden kitchen cabinets
Kitchen cabinets_wood

Winter, Inc. & Co., F. W.
Delaware Ave. & Elm St.
Camden, NJ 08102
Contact: F. W. Winter, Pres., PR Mgr.
Telephone: 609-963-7490
Fax: 609-963-7463
Email: winterfw@aol.com / URL:
Product Service Description:
Metal & alloy powders

Wiremold Co., The
777 Brook St
Rocky Hill, CT 06067-3403
Contact: Will Rogers, VP, Operations, Ed
Miller, VP, Marketing
Telephone: 860-233-6251
Fax: 860-523-3669
Email: www.wiremold.com / URL: http://
www.wiremold.com
Product Service Description:
Wire & cable management systems
Power quality
Connectivity, structure cabling systems
Specialty lighting distribution systems
Raceways, cable trays, infloor ducts, boxes,
poles

Wireworks Corporation
380 Hillside Ave
Hillside, NJ 07205-1339
Contact: Larry Williams,
Telephone: 908-686-7400
Fax: 908-686-0483
Email: sales@wireworks.com / URL: http://
www.wireworks.com
Product Service Description:
Audio & video cable systems
Radio & TV communications equipment

Wisconsin Oven Corp.
PO Box 873
East Troy, WI 53120-0873
Contact: Henry Kubicki, Pres.
Telephone: 414-642-3938
Fax: 414-363-4018
Email: sales@wisowen.com / URL: http://
www.wisoven.com
Product Service Description:
Furnaces & ovens_industrial
Industrial ovens & furnaces

Witte Co., Inc., The
PO Box 47
Washington, NJ 07882-0047
Contact: Richard Witte, Pres.
Telephone: 908-689-6500
Fax: 908-689-6806
Email: witteco@bellatlantic.net / URL: http://
www.witte.com
Product Service Description:
Vibrating Fluid Bed Dryers & Coolers
Vibrating Screeners
Vibrating Conveyors

Woerner Industries, Inc.
485 Hague St
Rochester, NY 14606-1209
Contact: P. Collins, CEO
Telephone: 716-235-1991
Fax: 716-235-8807
Product Service Description:
Millwork & Church Furniture
Printing Equipment
Check Protection Equipment

Wolf Creek Printing
503 E Frontage Rd
Moville, IA 51039-8220
Contact: Rick Lester, Owner
Telephone: 712-873-5370
Fax: 712-873-5623
Email: wifcrkpr@netins.net / URL:
Product Service Description:
Commercial printing : Printing_commercial
Commercial sheet fed printer
up to 18" X 24". Design work, type &
composition : Letterheads, envelopes,
brochures, multi-part forms, numbering
Scoring & die cutting

Wolohan Lumber
1001 S. Prospect St.
Marion, OH 43302-6298
Contact: David A. Stayner, GM, Opers
Telephone: 740-375-5815
Fax: 740-375-4910
Product Service Description:
Sawmills & planing mills, general
Lumber processing & millwork
Millwork

Wonderly Co., Inc., The
25 Cornell St., P.O. Box 1458
Kingston, NY 12401
Contact: Drew Wonderly, *
Telephone: 914-331-0148
Fax: 914-331-6218
Email: wonderly@ulster.net / URL: http://
www.wonderlys.com
Product Service Description:
Custom Drapes
Custom Bedspreads
Window Treatments

Woodpecker, Inc.
357 Cortlandt St
Belleville, NJ 07109-3201
Contact: Peter Karantonis, President
Telephone: 201-991-1717
Fax: 973-751-4934
Email: woodpeck11 / URL:
Product Service Description:
Laminate furniture
Furniture_household
Furniture, wholesale
Hardware, wholesale : Furniture,
manufactures : Furniture, distributor
Furniture, retail : Components, furniture
Molding : Metal furniture

Woodstock Line Co., The
91 Canal St
Putnam, CT 06260
Contact: Richard Rodensky, President
Telephone: 860-928-6557
Fax: 860-928-1096
Email: info@woodstockline.com / URL:
http://www.woodstockline.com
Product Service Description:
Fishing lines & industrial cordage

Wordnet Inc.
30 Nagog Park, PO Box 2255
Acton, MA 01720-3408
Contact: Lee Chadeayne, *
Telephone: 978-264-0600
Product Service Description:
Translation Services, All Languages

World Commerce Forwarding, Inc.
P.O. Box 60906,
Houston, TX 77205
Contact: Frank Reyes, President
Telephone: 281-209-2697
Fax: 281-209-9356
Email: worldcom@worldcomfwd.com / URL:
http://www.worldcommfwd.com
Product Service Description:
Customs Broker : Freight Forwarder
Freight & Cargo Transportation

**World Equipment & Machine Sales
Company**
29500 Aurora Rd, #15
Solon, OH 44139-1809
Contact: Michael Spiegle, V.P. Export
Telephone: 440-519-1745
Fax: 440-519-1748
Email: msgolf9@aol.com / URL: http://
www.foundry-eqpt.com
Product Service Description:
Metal Working Machinery
Iron & Steel Foundries, Nonferrous Foundries
(Castings) : Iron & Steel Foundries
Nonferrous Foundries

World Journal Inc
231 Adrian Rd
Millbrae, CA 94030-3102
Contact: M Su, Pres.
Telephone: 650-692-9936
Fax: 650-692-8652
Email: minsu@chinesenews.com / URL:
Product Service Description:
Newspapers : Publishes daily newspaper

World Power Technologies, Inc.
19 North Lake Avenue
Duluth, MN 55802
Contact: Elliott Bayly, President
Telephone: 218-722-1492
Fax: 218-722-0791
Email: sales@worldpowertech.com / URL:
http://www.worldpowertech.com
Product Service Description:
Wind Powered Generators
Solar Electricity

World Trade Exporters, Inc.
1801 Cold Springs Road
Liverpool, NY 13090
Contact: Joseph Giancola, Jr., President
Telephone: 315-453-3051
Fax: 315-453-3805
Email: wrldtrdex@aol.com / URL:
Product Service Description:
Electrostatic Scale Control System
Laundry, Drycleaning Coin-op Equipment

World Trading
12999 Executive Drive
Sugar Land, TX 77478
Contact: Gerald Fleishman, Owner
Phone: 281-565-5457 / Fax: 281-565-6636
Email: glenn@surplusparts.com / URL: http://www.surplusparts.com
Product Service Description:
Auto parts: Motor vehicle parts and accessories : Brake Pads, Shoes
Shock Absorbers

World Wide Pet Supply Ass'n
406 South First Avenue
Arcadia, CA 91006-3829
Contact: Doug Poinsexter, Exec. Vice Pres.
Phone: 626-447-2222 / Fax: 626-447-8350
Email: info@wwpsa.com / URL: http://www.wwpsa.com
Product Service Description:
Business Association, Pet Supplies
Misc. Publishing, Pet Ind. Newsletter

World Wide Windows
2116 44th Rd
Long Island City, NY 11101-5023
Contact: Jamie Escobar, Pres., R & D Mgr.
Phone: 718-361-8120 / Fax: 718-786-7429
Email: wwtgould@aol.com
Product Service Description:
Drapery hardware & blinds & shades
Drapery & metal drapery hardware
Brass rods, poles & finials : Glass Finials
Aluminum Track

Worldlink Logistics, Inc.
507 Kresson Rd.
Voorhees, NJ 08043
Contact: Dennis J. Wilkinson, President
Phone: 609-424-4445 / Fax: 609-424-4666
Email: dwilkinson@ibm.net / URL: http://www.worldlinkinternational.com
Product Service Description:
Customs Broker : Freight Forwarder
Freight & Cargo Transportation

Worldwide Filter
PO Box 1758
San Leandro, CA 94577-0175
Contact: Carl W Rhodin, Owner
Telephone: 510-483-5122
Product Service Description:
Manufactures: solvents and penetrants
Lubricating oils & greases

Worswick Industries Inc
7352 Convoy Ct
San Diego, CA 92111-1110
Contact: Regina Black,
Telephone: 619-571-5400
Fax: 619-571-6989
Product Service Description:
Computer cable assemblies— standard, custom and OEM; custom and standard switch boxes : Networking accesories & harnessing

Worthen Industries, Inc., Nylco Div.
71 Amlajack Blvd
Newnan, GA 30265-1009
Contact: Frederic P. Worthen Jr., V-P., Opers.
Telephone: 770-253-7015
Fax: 770-251-0488
Email: nylco@peachcity.com / URL: http://www.worthenind.com
Product Service Description:
Bias binding & coated fabrics
Automotive & apparel trimmings
Coated fabrics, not rubberized

Wyatt West Inc
PO Box 23372
Silverthorne, CO 80498-3372
Contact: Matthew Wyatt, Pres.
Telephone: 970-468-0188
Fax: 970-468-2941
Email: mnwyatt@colorado.net / URL: http://www.wyattwest.com
Product Service Description:
Silk screen printing on clothing
Resort Wear, Casual

Wynnson Enterprises, Inc.
PO Box 440
Meridianville, AL 35759-0440
Contact: Joyce Oberhausen, Pres.
Telephone: 205-828-0752
Fax: 205-828-5668
Product Service Description:
Military spare parts
Machinery_special industry

Wyo-Ben, Inc.
PO Box 1979
Billings, MT 59103
Contact: R.W. Stichman, VP Sales
Telephone: 406-652-6351
Fax: 406-656-0748
Email: email@wyoben.com / URL: http://www.wyoben.com
Product Service Description:
Minerals, ground or treated
Manufactures clay and related minerals
Manufactures Wyoming bentonite products

Wyoming Livestock Roundup
PO Box 170
Worland, WY 82401-0170
Contact: Del Tinsley, Publisher
Telephone: 307-347-3247
Fax: 307-347-3260
Email: tinsley@trib.com / URL: http://www.wyoagcenter.com
Product Service Description:
Publishes Weekly Agriculture Newspaper

Xenia Mfg. Co.
PO Box 237
Xenia, IL 62899-0237
Contact: Andy Knapp, Pres., Engrg. Mgr.
Telephone: 618-678-2218
Fax: 618-678-2311
Product Service Description:
Wire Harnesses

Xico Inc
9737 Eton Ave
Chatsworth, CA 91311-4306
Contact: Joseph J Sheppard, Pres., CEO
Telephone: 818-709-4403
Fax: 818-709-5235
Email: xicoincusa@aol.com / URL: http://www.xico.com
Product Service Description:
Manufactures magnetic strip card readers, encoders and systems

Y K K Ap America, Inc.
100 Firetower Rd.
Dublin, GA 31021
Contact: Akiyoshi Fushie, Ex.VP, Richard Porosky, VP Mfr.
Telephone: 912-277-1955
Fax: 912-277-1950
Email: / URL:
Product Service Description:
Doors, sash & trim, metal
Aluminum doors & window, storefront & curtainwall

Y.M.L.A. Inc
1639 N Main St
Los Angeles, CA 90012-1917
Contact: Larry Block, Pres.
Telephone: 323-222-9932
Fax: 323-222-2716
Email: sam@ymla.com / URL: http://www.ymla.com
Product Service Description:
Manufacturer mens & ladies knit & woven top, pants, shorts, activwear, clubwear
Products include Y.M.L.A. brand names, all categories, Dangerous Willie, Lillie, ladies

Yaley Enterprises, Inc.
7664 Avianca Drive
Redding, CA 96002-9713
Contact: Tom Yaley, Pres.
Telephone: 530-365-5252
Fax: 530-365-6483
Email: yaley@c-zone.net / URL: http://www.yaley.com
Product Service Description:
Manufactures wax; sells candle craft supplies
Manufacturing industries
Toys & hobby goods & supplies
Soap making supplies
Hemp
Natural jute
Ceramic beads
Beeswax

Yarbrough-Timco
9816 Crescent Center Dr # 704
Rancho Cucamonga, CA 91730-5730
Contact: Frank Gowan, V-P., GM
Telephone: 909-948-9955
Fax: 909-948-9593
Email: ytimco.com/ytimco / URL: http://www.ytimco.com/ytimco
Product Service Description:
Manufactures bobbins for transformers

Yargus Mfg., Inc.
PO Box 238
Marshall, IL 62441-0238
Contact: Larry Yargus, Pres.
Telephone: 217-826-6352
Fax: 217-826-8551
Email: / URL: http://www.yargus.com
Product Service Description:
Farm machinery & equipment

Yaz Enterprises
2605 N.W. 75th Ave.
Miami, FL 33122-1431
Contact: David Kronfeld, Owner
Telephone: 305-592-9995
Fax: 305-592-3494
Email: / URL:
Product Service Description:
Toilet Preparations
Perfume

Yeager Sawmill
20803 Highway 160
Durango, CO 81301-6490
Contact: Ronnie Yeager, Owner
Telephone: 970-247-0159
Fax:
Email: / URL:
Product Service Description:
General sawmill (specialy cuts / long & wide)
Sawmills
Logging
Custom log homes

Yeagle Technology, Inc.
140 Nott Hwy
Ashford, CT 06278-1317
Contact: Edward W. Yeagle, Pres., Sales & Mktg. Mgr.
Telephone: 860-429-1908
Fax: 860-429-7176
Email: info@yeagletech.com / URL: http://www.yeagletech.com
Product Service Description:
Vacuum systems
Service industry machinery, Vacuum Equipment

Yenkin-Majestic Paint Corp.(Mfr)
1920 Leonard Ave
Columbus, OH 43236-9004
Contact: Mary-Alice Burrell, *
Telephone: 614-258-3131
Fax: 614-792-5099
Product Service Description:
Paints, Coatings & Finishes

Yergat Packing Co
5451 W Mission Ave
Fresno, CA 93722-5074
Contact: Kirk Yergat, Pres.
Telephone: 209-276-9180
Fax: 209-276-2841
Email: / URL:
Product Service Description:
Picks, processes grapevine leaves
Food preparations

Yergat Packing Co.
5451 W. Mission
Fresno, CA 93722
Contact: Kirk Yergat, President
Telephone: 209-276-9180
Fax: 209-276-2841
Email: / URL:
Product Service Description:
California Grapevine Leaves

York International Corp.
PO Box 1592
York, PA 17405-1592
Contact: Robert N. Pokelwaldt, Chrm.& CEO
Telephone: 717-771-7890
Fax: 717-771-7381
Email: / URL: http://www.york.com
Product Service Description:
Heating, ventilating, air conditioning & refrigeration equipment

Yorktown Precision Technologies
PO Box 218
Yorktown, IN 47396-0218
Contact: Tony Dungan, Dept. Mgr., Die Casting
Telephone: 765-759-7767
Fax: 765-759-4024
Email: yptmold@aol.com / URL:
Product Service Description:
Industrial machinery, tools & die-cast & plastic molds
Dies, tools, jigs & fixtures_special

Young Electric Sign Company Boise
PO Box 4478
Boise, ID 83711-4478
Contact: Bob Williams, Div. Mgr.
Telephone: 208-345-2982
Fax: 208-345-3064
Email: / URL: http://www.yesco.com
Product Service Description:
Signs & advertising specialties
Manufactures, installs and maintains electric and illumination signage and peripheral

Young Farms
950 N. Collier Blvd., Ste. 400
Marco Island, FL 34145-2722
Contact: Alex Young, Owner
Telephone: 941-642-6999
Fax: 941-642-8850
Email: / URL:
Product Service Description:
Hot pepper mash, peppers in brine, sauce

Youngdale Manufacturing Corp
2449 Cades Way
Vista, CA 92083-7831
Contact: Peter Youndale, VP Marketing
Telephone: 1-888-446-4363
Fax: 760-727-8198
Email: mktg@youndale.com / URL:
www.youndale.com
Product Service Description:
Manufacture door hinges
Decorative hardware

Yuasa, Inc.
P.O. Box 14145
Reading, PA 19612-4145
Contact: W.R. Remer, Dir. Export Dept.
Telephone: 610-208-1843
Fax: 610-208-1851
Email: remerw@yuasainc.com / URL:
Product Service Description:
Lift Truck Batteries
Industrial Stationary Batteries

ZAP Power Systems
117 Morris St.
Sebastopol, CA 95472-3825
Contact: Gary Starr,
Telephone: 707-824-4150
Fax: 707-824-4159
Email: zap@zapbikes.com / URL: http://
www.zapbikes.com
Product Service Description:
Electric Bicycles
Electric Scooters
Electric Vehicles
Electric Motorcycles

ZAPWORLD.COM, One Power Drive
117 Morris St
Sebastopol, CA 95472-3858
Contact: Craig Gooch,
Telephone: 707-824-4150
Fax: 707-824-4159
Email: zap@zapword.com / URL: http://
www.zapworld.com
Product Service Description:
Manufactures electric bicycles, scooters,
motorcycles

ZMD International Inc
600 W 15th St
Long Beach, CA 90813-1508
Contact: Yosi Cohen, Pres.
Telephone: 562-628-0071
Fax: 562-628-0080
Email: www.zmdjacob@msn.com / URL:
http://www.zmd.com
Product Service Description:
Manufactures vacuum forming machines
Machinery, thermoforming
Machinery vacuum forming
Plastic forming
Packaging Machines
RF Welding Machines
Heat sealing machines
Roller press die cutter
Temperature controller
Aluminum molds for thermoforming

ZTS, Inc.
6749 Bramble Ave
Cincinnati, OH 45227-3145
Contact: Philip Zimmerman, Pres, CFO, Dave
Zimmerman, General Manager
Telephone: 513-271-2557
Fax: 513-272-1383
Email: testers@ztsinc.com / URL: http://
www.ztsinc.com
Product Service Description:
Camera Testers & Light Meters
Commercial Battery Tester

Zapp USA Inc.
475 International Cir.
Summerville, SC 29483
Contact: George R. Kelly, President
Telephone: 843-851-0700
Fax: 843-851-0010
Email: zappusa.com / URL: http://
www.zappusa.com
Product Service Description:
Wire Products
Stainless steel products & articles , Flat Wire
Stainless steel, carbon steel, nickel alloy,
precision strip

Zecal, Inc.
456 Sanford Rd N
Churchville, NY 14428-9503
Contact: Matt ensenat, Sales Director
Telephone: 716-293-1240 X.105
Fax: 716-293-2558
Email: mensenat@zecal.com / URL:
Product Service Description:
Printed circuit boards
Printed circuit boards
High density packaging
MCM

Zen Noh Grain
P.O. Box 39
Mandeville, LA 70470-0039
Contact: Kevin D. Adams, President
Telephone: 504-867-3500
Fax: 504-867-3506
Email: adamsk@cgb.com / URL:
Product Service Description:
Farm Product Warehousing and Storage
Soybeans, whether or not broken
Corn , other than seed corn
Grain sorghum

Zenith Controls, Inc.
830 W 40th St
Chicago, IL 60609-2501
Contact: Thomas Ferry, Director /Marketing
Telephone: 630-850-6880
Fax: 630-850-6899
Email: sales@zenithcontrols.com / URL:
http://www.zenithcontrols.com
Product Service Description:
Electrical Switchgear

Zenith Screw Products Inc
PO Box 2747
Santa Fe Springs, CA 90670-0747
Contact: Ken Miller, Pres.
Telephone: 562-941-0281
Fax: 562-941-7699
Email: / URL: http://www.zspinc.com
Product Service Description:
Precision machine products
Screw machine products

Zephyr Manufacturing Co. Inc.
201 Hindry Avenue
Inglewood, CA 90301
Contact: Bernard Kersulis, President
Telephone: 310-410-4907
Fax: 310/410-2913
Email: zephyr@zephyrtool.com / URL: http://
www.zephyrtool.com
Product Service Description:
Hand Tools, Screwdriver Bits
Specialty Tools fo Airframe Production &
Maintenance : Air Tools / Accessories
Power Driven Hand Tools, Air

Zero Fastener Co.
PO Box 24146
Houston, TX 77229-4146
Contact: Tom Mullen,
Telephone: 713-675-0123
Fax: 713-675-6066
Email: zerofast@zerofast.com / URL: http://
www.zerofast.com
Product Service Description:
Bolts, nuts, rivets & washers
Nuts & bolts

Zero Zone, Inc.
110 N Oakridge Dr
North Prairie, WI 53153-9792
Contact: Jack Van Der Ploeg, Pres.
Telephone: 414-392-6400
Fax: 414-392-6450
Email: sales@zero-zone.com / URL: http://
www.zero-zone.com
Product Service Description:
Commercial refrigerators & freezers
Refrigeration & heating equipment

Zinsser & Co., Inc., William
173 Belmont Dr
Somerset, NJ 08873-1218
Contact: Rebecca Spencer, Sales Admin.
Mgr.
Telephone: 732-469-8100
Fax: 732-469-4539
Email: rebecca.spencer@zinsser.com / URL:
http://www.zinsser.com
Product Service Description:
Paint primers & sealers
Paints & allied products
Wallcovering removal & prep products
Mildew proof paint

Zoo-Ink Screen Print
707 Cesar Chavez
San Francisco, CA 94124-1211
Contact: Alan Grinberg, Pres.
Telephone: 415-821-6300
Fax: 415-821-6332
Email: / URL: http://www.zoo-ink.com
Product Service Description:
Commercial textile printing : Finishing plants,
cotton : Hand screen printing
Small runs

Zygo Corp.
PO Box 448
Middlefield, CT 06455-0448
Contact: Bruce Robinson, President
Telephone: 860-347-8506
Fax: 860-347-8372
Email: inquire@zygo.com / URL: http://
www.zygo.com
Product Service Description:
Optical instruments & lenses
Precision measuring instruments & optical
components : Electromedical equipment
Automation Systems

U.S. : Product / Service Index

14k Gold Jewelry - **Shine Jewelry**

2-way Radios, Wholesale - **Delta Communications & Electronics**

3d Animation Production - **Graphics plus Printing, Inc.**

3d Human Anatomy - **Visible Productions Llc**

4140 Bars - **Vulcan Threaded Products, Inc.**

99 Cent Store Merchandise (Closeouts) - **Texas Jasmine**

A/C Parts - **Tri-star International, Inc.**

A/C for Telecommunication Facilities - **Compu-aire, Inc.**

A;i,omi, - **Eastern Europe Inc.**

Aa 6063, Aa 6005 - **Gemini Aluminum Corp**

Abbrasive & Shot Peening Finishing Equipment - **Victor Metal Finishing**

Abestos Testing - **Analytica Environmental Lab Inc**

Above Ground Rectangular U.l. Listed Fuel Tanks - **Pritchard Brown**

Abrasion Resistant Coatings for Transparent Materials. - **Sdc Technologies**

Abrasion Resistant Materials, Coatings, Urethanes - **Anti Hydro Internat'l**

Abrasion Wear Testers - **Norman Tool, Inc.**

Abrasive Grind/cut Wheels & Wire Brushes - **United Abrasives Inc.**

Abrasive Grinding Compounds & Slurries - **United States Products Co.**

Abrasive Lapping Compounds & Slurries - **United States Products Co.**

Abrasive Polishing Compounds & Slurries - **United States Products Co.**

Abrasive Prod., Black Silicon Carbide - **Electro Abrasives Corp.**

Abrasive Products - **Composition Materials Co., Inc.**

Abrasive Products - **Gel-tec Co.**

Abrasive Products - **Hess Pumice Products, Inc.**

Abrasive Products - **Jacksonlea**

Abrasive Products - **Realys Inc**

Abrasive Products - **Carter Diamond Tool Corp.**

Abrasive Products, Anti-slip Tapes - **Jessup Manufacturing Co.**

Abrasives (Buffing & Polishing Papers) - **L.a.c. Leather Abrasive Co.**

Abrasives, Bonded, Coated, Grain, Diamond - **Abrasive Distributors**

Abs Resins - **Polymer Trading Services Limited**

Absorbent Media - **Chemco Manufacturing Incorporated**

Absorbents - **Stronglite Products**

Abstract Wall Sculptures (Wood) - **Easley Co., Jeff**

Ac & Dc & Fractional Gear Motors - **E C M Motor Co.**

Ac Delco, Gm, Chrysler, Motorcraft, Ford Auto Parts - **Hi-pro Industries,**

Ac Drives - **Motortronics, Inc.**

Ac Power Distribution and Control Systems for M - **Pulizzi Engineering**

Accelerated Language Instruction - **University Language Center, Inc.**

Accelerator, Clutch Release,-**Automatic Transmission Parts, Inc. A.t.p.**

Accelerometers - **Pace Transducer Co**

Access Control Systems - **Secura Key**

Access Control Systems for Physical Security - **Synergistics, Inc.**

Access Doors - **Flexmaster U S a Inc.**

Accessories - **P T L Equipment Mfg. Co., Inc.**

Accessories - **Arno International, Inc.**

Accessories - **C & M Enterprises**

Accessories & Attachments for - **Ultrasonic Probs Mfg. Co.**

Accessories & Lamps Manufacturer - **Masterpiece Accessories Inc**

Accounting Auditing & Bookkeeping Svcs. - **Mcbride Shopa & Co**

Accumulation Conveyor - **Quantum Conveyor Systems, Llc**

Acetate & Nylon. Over 45 Years of Experience! - **Bezjian Dye-chem, Inc.**

Acetone - **Sunoco, Inc.**

Acid Reducers for Foods and Beverages - **Tamer International Ltd**

Acoustical Ceiling Tile, Export - **Celotex Corporation**

Acoustical Covers - **Remco Technology, Inc.**

Acoustical Materials for Industrial, Auto - **Great Southern Insulation**

Acoustical Metal Ceilings - **Ceilings plus Inc**

Acq Pressure Treated Syp & D.blaze Fire Retardant - **Quality Forest Prod**

Acrylic / Marble / Gemstone Jetted Tubs - **Tenessee Fiberglass Productc,**

Acrylic Based Multipolymer Compounds - **Cyro Industries**

Acrylic Latex Coatings - **Ici Paints International - Export - Licensing**

Acrylic Paint & Elastomeric Coatings - **Bond Paint & Chemicals, Inc.**

Acrylic Polycarbonate Alloys - **Cyro Industries**

Acrylic Sheet & Polycarbonate Sheet Products - **Cyro Industries**

Acrylic Store Display Fixtures for Videos - **Plastic Works Inc**

Acrylic Water Base Ind. Enamel - **Ici Paints International - Licensing**

Acrylic Whirlpool Bath Tubs & Shower Systems - **Tradewind Industries**

Acrylic Whirlpools & Bathware - **Mansfield Plumbing Products, Inc.,**

Acrylic Yarns, Ring-spun - **Cheraw Yarn Mills Inc.**

Activated Carbon & Air & Water Filtering Equipt - **General Carbon Corp.**

Activated Carbon Products - **Calgon Carbon Corporation (Mfr)**

Active Pharmaceutical Ingredients - **Napp Technologies**

Actuators, Electric & Pneumatic - **Tyco Valves & Controls**

Acyclic Hydrocarbons, Saturated - **Webco Trading**

Ada Signage and Specialties - **Best Sign Systems**

Additives for Paint, Latex- **Ashland Chemicals**

Adhesion Testers, Paints & Coatings - **Quad Group**

Adhesive Backs, Decals, Labels & Signs - **Allied Decals Florida, Inc.**

Adhesive Coating & Laminating - **Jessup Manufacturing Co.**

Adhesive Coating Services - **Aetna Felt Corp.**

Adhesive Promoters - **Century Multech**

Adhesives - **A P C M Mfg. Llc**

Adhesives - **Eclectic Products Inc.**

Adhesives - **P.d.i. Inc.**

Adhesives - **Art Institute Glitter**

Adhesives - **Myers Industries, Inc., Myers Tire Supply Div.**

Adhesives - **Watersaver International**

Adhesives & Sealants - **A P C M Mfg. Llc**

Adhesives & Sealants - **Adhesive Systems, Inc.**

Adhesives & Sealants - **Adhesives Research, Inc.**

Adhesives & Sealants - **Dalton Enterprises, Inc.**

Adhesives & Sealants - **Eclectic Products Inc.**

Adhesives & Sealants - **Pro-seal Products Inc**

Adhesives & Sealants - **Sashco Sealants Inc**

Adhesives & Sealants - **Schnee-morehead of California**

Adhesives & Sealants - **United Technologies Automotive, Inc.**

Adhesives & Sealants - **Myro, Inc.**

Adhesives & Sealants & Dispensing Equipment - **Hernon Manufacturing**

Adhesives & Sealants - Uv Cure Epoxies - **Electronic Materials Inc**

Adhesives & Sealants, Joint Fillers - **Crossfield Products Corp**

Adhesives Based on Rubber or Plastics - **Stafast Roofing Products**

Adhesives and Sealants - **Ultra Seal International**

Adhesives and Sealants - **Gti Industries, Inc.**

Adjustable Drop Nipples - **Cold Extrusion Co. Of America, Inc.**

Adjustable Speed Drives, Web Tension Equipt- **Cleveland Motion Control**

Adult & Everyday Greeting Cards - **Comstock Cards Inc**

Adult Novelties - **California Exotic Novelties**

Advanced Medical Collection Products - **Andwin Corporation**

Advanced Technical Ceramics - **Ceradyne, Inc.**

Adventure Themes for Scrap Books - **The Wolfe Pack**

Advertising - **David Adam Promotions Inc**

Advertising Agencies - **The Practice Builder Association**

Advertising Buttons - **Tecre Co., Inc.**

Advertising Medical Cosmetics - **Magnum Group, Inc. Translation**

Advertising Specialties - **National Embroidery Services**

Advertising Specialties - **Gs Sportwear / Golden Squeegee**

Advertising Specialties (Importing) - **Flagman of America**

Advertising Specialties, Promotions, Caps - **David Adam Promotions Inc**

Advertising, Business to Business Marketing - **L.a. Markom De Mexico**

Advertising, Specialty Products and Plastic - **National Pen Corporation**

Aeration & Waste Water Treatment Systems & Equipment - **Aquatec, Inc.**

Aeration Mixers, Wastewater Treatment - **Environmental Dynamics**

Aerial Manlifts - **Pacific Utility Equipment Co**

Aerial Work Platforms: Boomlift, Scissor Lift - **Jlg Industries, Inc.**

Aero Space Mfg. - **Malbert Mitchell Grinding Corp**

Aerodynamic Styling Access Wings - **Donmar Enterprises, Inc.**

Aerosol Container Filling - **Pel Assocs., Inc.**

Aerosol Packaging - **Aero Tech Labs, Inc.**

Aerosol Packaging - **Chemical Packaging Corp.**

Aerosol Paint - **Spray Products Corp.**

Aerosol Paints - **Ici Paints International - Export - Licensing**

Aerosol Tear Gas - **Security Equipment Corp.**
Aerospace - Ice Detectors, Light Controllers - **Dne Technologies Inc.**
Aerospace Cnc & General Machining Job - **Hansen Machine & Tool Co.**
Aerospace Component Manufacturing - **Senga Engineering Inc**
Aerospace Electronics & Medical Components - **Aerospace Manufacturin**
Aerospace Fasteners and Aerospace Bolts - **Hick International Fastener**
Aerospace Hardware - **Aerofast Ltd**
Aerospace Machining - **Lemco**
Aerospace Precision & Cnc Machining - **Austin Continental Industries**
Aerospace Test Stands - **American Design & Mfg.**
Aerospace Tooling & Precision Machine Parts - **Cambridge Specialty Co.**
Aerospace, Military, Commercial Rotary Switches - **Cole Instrument Corp**
Aerospace, Semiconductor & Automotive Industries. - **Fibrotek Industries**
Afff Foam Pumps for Fire Protection Systems - **Edwards Mfg. Inc. (Mfr)**
Agents Worldwide, Air & Ocean - **Moran, J. F. Co., Inc.**
Agglomerators - **Kason Corporation (Mfr)**
Agri Business Fieldman Magazine - **Western Agricultural Publish**
Agricultural / Off-the-road /Industrial Tires - **Tire Group International Inc**
Agricultural Chemicals - **Environmental Soil Systems Inc**
Agricultural Chemicals - **Dr. T's Nature Products Inc.**
Agricultural Chemicals - **Sipcam Agro Usa, Inc.**
Agricultural Chemicals - **Nacco Grow More**
Agricultural Equipment - **Kelley Mfg. Co.**
Agricultural Equipment - **Netafim Irrigation Inc**
Agricultural Farm Tractors - **Agco Corporation**
Agricultural Fertilizers - **Agrimar Corp.**
Agricultural Fungicide - **Agtrol International**
Agricultural Irrigation Equipment Wholesale - **A.g. Equipment, Inc.**
Agricultural Machine - **Laidig Industrial System**
Agricultural Machine - **Johnston Pumps**
Agricultural Machine - **Northern Pump & Irrigation**
Agricultural Tillage & Planting Equipment - **Agco Corporation**
Agricultural Tractor & Implement Parts - **Tru-part Manufacturing Co.**
Agricultural, Horticultural, Forestry- **Pantropic Power Products, Inc.**
Agricultural, Turf & Pest Sprayers - **Westheffer Mfg.**
Agriculture - Fencing Ect. - **Allen Tool Co**
Agriculture Irrigation Pumps - **Wamco Corporation**
Agriculture Pump Parts - **Wamco Corporation**
Agronomy - **United Farmers Co-op**
Air & Hydraulic Centrifugal & Submersible - **Defco, Inc.**
Air & Ocean Freight Forwarding - **Nippon Express Usa, Inc.**
Air & Water Resource & Solid Waste Management - **Marshall Miller & As**
Air Barriers - **Henry Company International**
Air Cargo - **Lufthansa Cargo, Executive Offices Cargo Usa**
Air Cargo Carrier - **Lufthansa Cargo Ag**
Air Cargo Ground Support Equipment / Systems - **Kietek International**
Air Cargo Handling, Weighing & Storing Systems - **Renmark Pacific Corp**
Air Classification , Fine Particle Separation Equip- **Progressive Industries**
Air Cleaners - **Airflow Systems Inc. (Mfr)**
Air Cleaners - **Clean Air Consultants, Inc.**
Air Compressors - **Ciasons Industrial Inc**
Air Compressors - **Jun-air Usa, Inc.**
Air Compressors - **Interdynamics, Inc.**
Air Compressors & Vacuum Pumps - **Quincy Compressor**
Air Cond & Heating Equip., Export - **Rychter Trading Corporation**
Air Conditioner & Refrigeration - **National Compressor Exchange, Inc.**
Air Conditioners - **Trans Air Manufacturing**
Air Conditioners & Heat Recovery Units - **Tithe Corp., Skil-aire Div.**
Air Conditioning & Heating Coils - **Sahar Industries**
Air Conditioning & Refrigeration Compressors - **Aftermarket Specialties**
Air Conditioning Commercial - **Noland**
Air Conditioning Compressor Repair Parts - **Cmp Corporation**
Air Conditioning Condensers - **Sahar Industries**
Air Conditioning Distributor - **Noland**
Air Conditioning Equipment - **Noland**
Air Conditioning Export - **Noland**
Air Conditioning Flushing Equipment - **Robinair, a Div. Of Spx Corp**
Air Conditioning International - **Noland**
Air Conditioning Machines Incorporating a Refrigerating Unit - **Noland**
Air Conditioning Residential - **Noland**
Air Conditioning Units - **Noland**

Air Conditioning Units & Parts - **Innovair Corporation**
Air Conditioning Wholesaler - **Noland**
Air Curtain & Door Systems - **Berner International Corp.**
Air Diffusers & Grilles - **Environmental Technologies, Inc.**
Air Driven, Double Diaphragm Pumps - **All-flo Pump Co.**
Air Duct Cleaning Equipment - **Power Vacuum Trailer Co.**
Air Entangled Polyester Sewing Thread - **American & Efird, Inc.**
Air Filters, Heaters & Coolers, Commerc. & Ind. - **Tri-dim Filter Corp.**
Air Filtration Equipment - **Parts Services International Llc**
Air Filtration Units - **International Enviromental Corp.**
Air Freight Cargo: Transportation & Insurance - **K & K Express**
Air Freight Forwarder - **Lufthansa Cargo, Executive Offices Cargo Usa**
Air Freight Forwarders - **Delgado R. E. Inc.**
Air Freight Forwarders - **Fast Air Carrier S.a.**
Air Freshener, Soap, Hair & Toilet Preps - **Lanman & Kemp-barclay**
Air Handling Units - **Environmental Technologies, Inc.**
Air Hose Assemblies for Railroads - **Strato, Inc.**
Air Intake Filters - **Consler Filtrations Products**
Air Mattresses - **Land and Sky Mfg., Inc.**
Air Operated Hydraulic Pumps - **Az Hydraulic Engineering Inc**
Air Operated Post Drivers - **Rhino Tool Co.**
Air Operated Pumps - **Grover Manufacturing Corp.**
Air Pollution Control Equipment - **Air Chem Systems Inc**
Air Pollution Control Equipment - **Marsulex Environmental Technologies**
Air Pollution Control Equipment - **Thiel Air Technologies Corp.**
Air Pollution Control Equipment - **Moli-tron Company Inc.**
Air Pollution Control Scrubbers - **D R Technology, Inc.**
Air Pollution Control System - **Catalytic Products International, Inc.**
Air Pollution Control Systems - **Turner Envirologic, Inc.**
Air Pollution Monitoring Equipment - **Baldwin Environmental Inc**
Air Preheaters - **Exothermics, Inc.**
Air Pumps and Air or Other Gas Compressors; - **Thomas Industries, Inc.**
Air Sampling Pumps - **Air Dimensions, Inc.**
Air Throttle Valves - **Rhino Tool Co.**
Air Tools / Accessories - **Zephyr Manufacturing Co. Inc.**
Air Transportation Nonscheduled - **Central Air Freight Inc.**
Air Transportation Scheduled - **Central Air Freight Inc.**
Air Valve Replacement Parts (Bendix/midland) - **Pai Industries Inc. (Mfr)**
Air Volume Controls, Gauges, Foot & Check Valves - **Brady Products, Inc.**
Air Washers / Scrubbers / Grease & Particle Extract - **Moli-tron Company**
Air and Gas Compressors - **Thomas Industries, Inc.**
Air to Air Heat Exchangers - **Exothermics, Inc.**
Air-cooled Heat Exchangers - **Hudson Products Corp.**
Air-cooled Steam Condensers - **Hudson Products Corp.**
Aircondition Parts & Service - **Viking Enterprises**
Aircraft - **Micco Aircraft Co.**
Aircraft & Aerospace Parts - **Sunstrand Corporation**
Aircraft & Weapons Components - **A M Precision Machining, Inc.**
Aircraft - Hydraulic Pumps;, Gulfstream, - **National Flight Sales Corp**
Aircraft - Hydraulic Pumps; Citation - **National Flight Sales Corporation**
Aircraft Acrylic Cabin Windows - **Nordam Group Inc., Tranparencies**
Aircraft Cockpit Windows - **Nordam Group Inc., Tranparencies Div. The**
Aircraft Components & Precision Machine Parts - **Volumatic, Inc.**
Aircraft Components & Supplies - **Golden Circle Air, Inc.**
Aircraft Detail Parts Fabrication, Specializing in Forming S - **Hydroform**
Aircraft Engine Bolts - **Morton Manufacturing**
Aircraft Engine Parts, Plastic Seals & Gaskets - **Jonal Laboratories, Inc.**
Aircraft Engine Systems & Flight Safety Parts - **Purdy Corp.**
Aircraft Engines & Aircraft Airframe Parts - **Caravan International**
Aircraft Engines & Engine Parts - **Jonal Laboratories, Inc.**
Aircraft Engines & Engine Parts - **Nelson Aircraft Corp.**
Aircraft Engines & Engine Parts - **Turbo Specialists Llc.**
Aircraft Equipment - **Precise Flight Inc**
Aircraft Ground Service Guide, Aircraft Crash - **Sandpiper Publications**
Aircraft Ground Support Test Equipment - **Aviation Technology, Inc.**
Aircraft Instrument Service - **Aero-mach Labs, Inc.**
Aircraft Kit Manufacturer - **Golden Circle Air, Inc.**
Aircraft Liquid Level Switches- **Aerospace Control Products, Inc.**
Aircraft Parts - **S & S Precision Machine Corp.**
Aircraft Parts & Equipment - **Jonal Laboratories, Inc.**
Aircraft Parts & Equipment - **General Electrodynamics Corp.**

Aircraft Parts & Equipment - **Damar Machine Co**
Aircraft Parts & Equipment - **A M Precision Machining, Inc.**
Aircraft Parts & Equipment - **Aero-mach Labs, Inc.**
Aircraft Parts & Equipment - **Aerospace Control Products, Inc.**
Aircraft Parts & Equipment- **Airborne Technologies, Inc.**
Aircraft Parts & Equipment - **Athens Industries, Inc.**
Aircraft Parts & Equipment - **Britt Metal Processing, Inc.**
Aircraft Parts & Equipment - **Golden Circle Air, Inc.**
Aircraft Parts & Equipment - **Nell Joy Industries, Inc.**
Aircraft Parts & Equipment - **Precise Flight Inc**
Aircraft Parts & Equipment - **Rockwell International Corp.**
Aircraft Parts & Equipment - **Rosen Product Development Inc**
Aircraft Parts & Equipment - **Santa Monica Propeller Inc**
Aircraft Parts & Equipment - **Scotia Technology Div., Lakes Region**
Aircraft Parts & Equipment - **Solo Enterprise Corporation**
Aircraft Parts & Equipment - **Spectrum Aeromed, Inc.**
Aircraft Parts & Equipment - **Texas Almet Inc.**
Aircraft Parts & Equipment - **Volumatic, Inc.**
Aircraft Parts & Supplies - Including Consumables - **U.s. Airmotive**
Aircraft Propellers - **Santa Monica Propeller Inc**
Aircraft Quick-change Modular Life Support Sys-**Spectrum Aeromed, Inc.**
Aircraft Sunvisor Systems - **Rosen Product Development Inc**
Aircraft Turbines & Rebuilt Apu Components - **Britt Metal Processing,**
Aircraft Washers - **Anillo Industries Inc**
Aircraft Wing Tip Lenses - **Nordam Group Inc., Tranparencies Div. The**
Aircraft and Precision Machined Aerospace Parts - **Solo Enterprise Corp**
Aircraft, Aerospace & Distribution - **Mccook Metals, Llc**
Aircraft, Parts. Pistons, Pumps, Etc. - **Austin Continental Industries, Inc.**
Aircraft, Rotor Win, Commercial - **Msi International**
Airline & Ground Support Rubber Products - **Diamond Rubber Products**
Airline Foodservice Equipment - **Brake Funderburk Enterprises, Inc.**
Airline Servicing Equipment - **Charlatte America**
Airline Servicing Equipment, Mobile Gasoline - **Charlatte America**
Airplane Hangar Doors - **Fleming Steel Co.**
Airport - **New Orleans International Airport/ C/o New Orleans Aviation**
Airport Canisters - **Olson Industries, Inc.**
Airport Lighting - **Bifrost**
Airports, Flying Fields, and Services - **Charlatte America**
Airvents, Shielded - **Spira Manufacturing Corp**
Airway Hand Aspirator - **Repro-med Systems, Inc.**
Alarm Clock Quartz - **Equity Industries**
Alarm Control Centers - **Cordell Manufacturing Inc**
Alarm Valves, Dry Valves, Deluge Valves - **Globe Fire Sprinkler Corp.**
Alarms Intrusion Detection Fence Mount - **Perimeter Products, Inc.**
Alarms, Personal Duress - **Perimeter Products, Inc.**
Albums of Paper or Paperboard - **Art Leather Manufacturing Co., Inc.**
Alcohol - **Respond Group of Companies**
Alcohol Oxibase & Alco-level - a Disposable Tes - **Moldowan Lab Inc**
Alcohols - **Petroplast Chemical Corp.**
Alfalfa - **H & H Seed Company Inc**
Alfalfa Hay - **Ward Rugh, Inc.**
Alkyd - Polyurethane Paints & Supply - **Bond Paint & Chemicals, Inc.**
Allegy Relief & Anit-microbial - **Lamb, Inc., J.**
Allergy Free Foods - **Ener-g Foods Inc**
Alligator Clips - **M.m. Electric Products Ltd.**
Alloy Pressure Vessels- **R.C. Technical Welding & Fabricating Co., Inc.**
Alloy Steel - **Professional Services International, Inc.**
Alloys & Plastic in the Form of Strip - **Nasco, Inc.**
Almonds, Fresh or Dried, Shelled - **Pafco Importing Co.**
Almonds, Fresh or Dried, Shelled - **Hilltop Ranch**
Almonds, Fresh or Dried, in Shell - **Pafco Importing Co.**
Aloe Concentrates & Aloe Powders - **Concentrated Aloe Corp.**
Aloha Fashions - Men's & Boys' & Women & Girls - **Silver Needles**
Also Available. Product Mfg to Abma Std. - **Abbott Ball Co. (Mfg)**
Also a Producer of non Kosher Products - **Agri Processors**
Alternate Refrigerant R-414b - **Icor International Inc.**
Alternative Hot Water Systems - **Weben-jarco, Inc.**
Alternators Motor Vehicle - **C.e. Niehoff & Co., Inc.**
Alumina Trihydrate - **Franklin Industrial Minerals**
Alumina, Silica & Zirconia Binder Chemicals - **Remet Corp.**
Aluminized S.s. Catalyst Reactor Screens - **Vaporkote Inc**

Aluminum - **Impol Aluminum**
Aluminum & Steel Siding / Roofing - **Elixir Industries, Inc.**
Aluminum & Bronze Castings - **Unexcelled Castings Corp.**
Aluminum & Fiberglass Flagpoles, Flags - **Heartland Flagpoles, Inc.**
Aluminum & Glass Greenhouses - **Texas Greenhouse Co., Inc.**
Aluminum & Magnesium Die-castings - **Gibbs Die Casting Corp.**
Aluminum & Plywood Decals & Traffic Signs - **P & M Sign, Inc.**
Aluminum & Steel Fabrication - **Space Coast General Contractors Inc.**
Aluminum & Steel Tire Molds - **Quality Mold Inc.**
Aluminum & Wooden Windows - **Clarke's Custom Windows, Inc.**
Aluminum Airboats - **Alaska Airboats**
Aluminum Bars, Rods, & Profiles, alloyed - **Impol Aluminum**
Aluminum Bars, Rods, & Profiles, not alloyed - **Impol Aluminum**
Aluminum Boat Anchors - **Nav-x Corp.**
Aluminum Boats & Yachts - **Peregrine Marine, Inc.**
Aluminum Bottom Dumps - **Beall Corp.**
Aluminum Brazing Sheet - **United Aluminum Corporation**
Aluminum Castings & Machine Patterns - **Baldwin Aluminum Foundry**
Aluminum Castings, Sand & Perminent Mold - **Le Claire Mfg. Co.**
Aluminum Chlorohydrate - **Geo Specialty Chemicals, Inc.**
Aluminum Clad Steel Wire & Cable - **United States Alumoweld Co.**
Aluminum Clad Wood Windows & Patio Drs. - **Hurd Millwork Company,**
Aluminum Coil - **United Aluminum Corporation**
Aluminum Die Castings & Cnc Machining Job Shop - **C & H Die Casting,**
Aluminum Die-castings - **Gibbs Die Casting Corp.**
Aluminum Doors & Window- **Y K K Ap America, Inc.**
Aluminum Doors, Windows and Their Frames - **Efco**
Aluminum Drawn Wire - **Hanover Wire Cloth**
Aluminum Dross Processing - **Marport Smelting Co., Llc**
Aluminum End Dumps - **Beall Corp.**
Aluminum Extruded Products - **E-tec Marine Products Inc.**
Aluminum Extruded Products - **Efco**
Aluminum Extruded Products - **Specialty Extrusion Corp**
Aluminum Extruded Products - **Vaw of America Inc**
Aluminum Extruded Products - **E F C O Corp.**
Aluminum Extrusions - **Gemini Aluminum Corp**
Aluminum Extrusions - **Wells Aluminum Corp.**
Aluminum Extrusions & Castings - **Lewgust Co., Inc.**
Aluminum Fabrications - **Wells Aluminum Corp.**
Aluminum Foil - **Impol Aluminum**
Aluminum Foundry - **Precision Measurement Labs**
Aluminum Generator Enclosures - **Pritchard Brown**
Aluminum Horse, Cattle, Hog, Trailers - **Sooner Trailer Mfg. Co., Inc.**
Aluminum Ladders - **Alaco Ladder Co.**
Aluminum Louvers, Baffles, Reflectors - **A.l.p. Lighting Components, Inc.**
Aluminum Modular T-slot Extrusions - **Items Products Inc.**
Aluminum Molds for Thermoforming - **Zmd International Inc**
Aluminum Nitride Components - **Ceradyne, Inc.**
Aluminum Outdoor Furniture - **Pacific Sun Casual Furniture**
Aluminum Outdoor Furniture, Umbrella- **Carter Grandle Furniture**
Aluminum Pipe & Tubes - **E-tec Marine Products Inc.**
Aluminum Plate & Sheet - **Impol Aluminum**
Aluminum Plate & Sheet - **Mccook Metals, Llc**
Aluminum Plate Bar Pipe Tubing - **Duenner Supply Co. Of Texas**
Aluminum Pump Jack Scaffolding - **Alum-a-pole Corporation**
Aluminum Railing & Columns - **Superior Aluminum Products, Inc.**
Aluminum Rain Handling Systems - **Rainhandler**
Aluminum Sand - **Baja Pacific Light Metals No**
Aluminum Scrap - **Sos Metals, Inc.**
Aluminum Scrap - **Los Angeles Scrap Iron & Metal**
Aluminum Sheet & Strip Coiled - **United Aluminum Corporation**
Aluminum Siding, Residential - **Gentek Building Products**
Aluminum Structural Extrusions. - **M F Automation Inc.**
Aluminum Sulfate - **National Alum Corp.**
Aluminum Sulfate & Alum Polymer Blends - **Russ Chemical Co., Inc.**
Aluminum Tanks, Grills, Picnic Tables - **Dennis Aluminum Products**
Aluminum Track - **World Wide Windows**
Aluminum Wheels for Cars - **Hayes Lemmerz International, Inc.**
Aluminum Wire - **New York Wire Co.**
Aluminum, Stainless, Copper Base Alloy - **Harris-welco Co.**
Aluminum, Vinyl & Wood Windows - **Milgard Manufacturing Co**

Amateur Radio Antennas - **Raibeam**
Ambient Air Sampler-particulates, Gases - **Airmetrics**
Ambulance - **Biomedical International**
American Ginseng, American Botanicals - **Wilcox Natural Products(mfr)**
Amino Acids - L-cysteine, L-cystine - **Accurate Ingredients**
Amino Acids, L-cysteine, L-cystine - **Ingredient Resources, Inc.**
Ammeters - **Faria Corp.**
Amusement Park Bumper Boats - **Bumper Boats, Inc.**
Amusement Parks - **The John Wesley Group**
Analog Panel Meters - **Burton-rogers Co., Calibron Instruments Div.**
Analog Weather Instruments - **Outdoor Environments, Llc.**
Analytical & Assay. Services - **Republic Metals Corp.**
Analytical Devices - **Byk-gardner Usa**
Analytical Environmental Laboratory - **Acz Laboratories Inc**
Analytical Instruments - **General Air Corporation**
Analytical Instruments - **Hach Company**
Analytical Instruments - **Alicat Scientific Inc**
Analytical Instruments - **Epsilon Industrial, Inc.**
Analytical Instruments - **Gilson, Inc.**
Analytical Instruments - **Interface Design Inc.**
Analytical Instruments - **Micromeritics Instrument Corp.**
Analytical Instruments - **Scientific Industries, Inc.**
Analytical Lab Evaporators & Extractors - **Organomation Associates, Inc.**
Analyzer System Packages - **P C & E, Fabcon Div.**
Analyzers, Nox - **Air Instruments & Measurements Inc. (Mfr)**
Analyzers, Process Control - **Air Instruments & Measurements Inc. (Mfr)**
Anatomical Dolls - **Teach-a-bodies Inc.**
Anchor Chambers - **Lindgren R F Enclosures Inc.**
Anchor Rope / Dock Line - **Anchor Buddy**
And Parts and Accessories Thereof - **Mg Electronics**
And Precious Metals. Burnishing Media - **Abbott Ball Co. (Mfg)**
And Products - **Dynamic Sciences Int'l Inc**
Angle Drilling Attachments - **Terry Tools, Inc.**
Anhydrous Disodium Tetraborate, Sodium Borates - **Imc Chemical, Inc.**
Anilox Service for Printing Machinery - **Thistle Roller Co Inc**
Animal Diagnostic Products - **Midland Bioproducts Corp.**
Animal Fats and Oils and Their Fractions - **Original Mink Oil Co.**
Animal Feed - **Fermented Products**
Animal Feed - **Cantrell Hay**
Animal Feed Preparations - **R.j. Commodities**
Animal Feed Preparations , Feed Ingredients - **Biofix Holdings, Inc.**
Animal Health Care Products - **St Jon Pet Care Products**
Animal Health Supplies - **Animal Health Sales, Inc.**
Animal Supplements - **Wachters Organic Sea Products**
Animation - **Communi-creations Inc**
Anitibody Negative (Ibr-bvd) - **Harmon Technological**
Ankle & Knee Supports - **Stromgren Supports, Inc.**
Anodized Aluminum Extrusions & Fittings - **E-tec Marine Products Inc.**
Anodizing - **Electrochem**
Anodizing Systems - **Hbs Equipment Corp**
Antennae - **Caravan International**
Antennas & Power Products - **Centurion International, Inc.**
Anti Flammable Chemicals - Antimony Trioxide - **Velco Chemicals**
Anti-shoplifting Devices - **Se-kure Controls, Inc.**
Anti-static Devices - **Legge Co., Inc., Walter G.**
Antibiotics - **Afassco, Inc.**
Antibody Products - non Specific Antibodies; Specialty Antib - **Nabi**
Antifreeze / Coolant - **Coastal Unilube, Inc.**
Antifreeze Recycling Machinery - **Ecosystem Inc.**
Antioxidizing Preparations and Other Compound Stabilizers- **Sunoco, Inc.**
Antique Car Dealers - **Mustang Auto Sales**
Antiseptic Sprays - **Afassco, Inc.**
Antiseptics, Medicinal - **J Hewitt Inc**
Antiseptics, Wholesale - **J Hewitt Inc**
Aog Handling - **Dan Transport Corporation**
Appalachian Hardwood Lumber, Logs & Veneer - **Jim C. Hamer Co.**
Apparel - **Kowa California Inc.**
Apparel & Accessories - **Best Value Textiles**
Apparel Interlining - **Precision Custom Coatings**
Apparel Used, Wholesale - **General Waste Trading Company**
Apparel, Interlining - **Hollingsworth & Vose Co.**

Apparel: Men Women Children Shoes Sneakers - **Atwood Richards**
Apple Juice, Unfermented - **Ryan Trading**
Apples & Pears, Fresh or Chilled - **Firman Pinkerton**
Apples, Fresh - **Stemlit Growers**
Appliance Leekage Current Interrupters - **Technology Research Corp.**
Appliances - **Maytag International**
Appliances_household - **Advanced Tech Industries, Inc.**
Appliances_household - **American Water Heater Co.**
Appliances_household - **Pennsylvania Sewing Machine Co.**
Applicator of Fusion Bonded - **Cal-coat Corp.**
Aqua Jogger with Fitness Equipment and Women's - **Aqua Jogger**
Aquaculture Equipment & Supplies - **Aquatic Eco-sysyetms Inc.**
Aquaculture Farming Design & Implement - **Msi International**
Aquatic / Pool Equipment - **Sprint Rothhammer**
Aquatic Aqua Aerobics - **Sprint Rothhammer**
Aquatic Rehabilitation Equipment - **Sprint Rothhammer**
Aquatic Therapy & Rehabilitation Equip- **Sprint/Rothhammer**
Aquatic Weed Harvesters, Metal Fabrication - **D & D Products, Inc.**
Arch Wire - **Tp Orthodontics, Inc.**
Archery Equipment - **Accu Rest, Inc.**
Archetechual Wood Working - **All Craft Fabricators, Inc.**
Architectural & Hardwood Plywood Products - **Sieling & Jones, Inc.**
Architectural Metal Work - **Colorado Bridge & Iron Inc**
Architectural Metal Work - **Schuff Steel Company**
Architectural Metal Work - **E F C O Corp.**
Architectural Metal Work - **Big D Metalworks of Texas**
Architectural Metal Work - **Lingo, Inc., Acme Flagpole Div.**
Architectural Metal Work Fabrication - **Big D Metalworks of Texas**
Architectural Millwork - **Construction Design Associates**
Architectural Millwork - **Jim C. Lane Inc.**
Architectural Millwork - **Valley Fixtures Inc**
Architectural Millwork & Wooden Store Fixtures - **Modern Woodcrafts**
Architectural Panels & Moldings Stone - **Unique Originals, Inc.**
Architectural Products for High Quality Buildings- **Intracor-familian Int'l**
Architectural Services - **Burns & Mcdonnell International**
Architectural Services - **Leo A. Daly Company**
Architectural Signs - **Asd, Inc. , Architectural Signage & Design**
Architectural Signs - **Signart, Inc.**
Architectural Treatments, Patching Material - **Anti Hydro International**
Architectural Wall Panels - **Interior Products Inc.**
Architectural Windows, Doors, Storefront - **E F C O Corp.**
Architectural Wood Ceilings - **Interior Products Inc.**
Armatuer Rewinding - **Schulz Electric Co.**
Armet Opaque Armor - **Protection Development International**
Armored Products & Ballistic Law Enforcement - **Alpine Armoring Inc.**
Aroatic Red Cedar - Logs & Lumber - **S.g. International**
Aromatherapy Fragrances - **Montana Essence Company**
Aromatic Jasmin & Basuati Rice - **Sem Chi Rice Products**
Art - **Manic Impressions**
Art Materials - **Hammett Co., Inc., J. L.**
Art Prints & Greeting Cards of Scenic - **Image Maker Enterprises**
Arterial Blood Samplers, Medical Electronic Components - **Radiometer,**
Articles and Equipment for Sports or Outdoor Games - **Gared Sports**
Articles and Equipment for Sports or Outdoor Games - **Lamkin Corp.**
Articles and Equipment for Sports or Outdoor/indoor Games - **Nova Grass**
Articles for the Conveyance or Packing of Goods - **Packaging Center, Inc.**
Articles of Asphalt or of Similar Material - **Traction International**
Articles of Bedding and Similar Furnishings , Fitted or Stuf - **Barkat**
Articles of Copper - **National Copper Products**
Articles of Iron or Steel - **Olympia International, Div. Of Olympic Steel**
Articles of Paper Pulp, Paper, Paperboard - **Maratech International**
Articles of Paper Pulp, Paper, Paperboard - **Cominter Corp.**
Articles of Paper Pulp, Paper, Paperboard - **Unisource**
Articles of Plastics - **Packaging Center, Inc.**
Articles of Plastics - **S.k. Plastics**
Articles of Plastics - **Traex**
Articles of Plastics - **Continental Sprayers / Afa Products,**
Articles of Plastics - **R & D International Inc.**
Articles of Plastics - **T-systems International, Inc.**
Articles of Plastics - **Tenwood International**
Articulated Gate Arms - **National Electric Gate Co.**

Artificial Insemination Equipment - **Action International**
Artificial Limbs - **Garrison's Prosthetic Service**
Asbestos Abatement - **Cardinal Industrial Insulation Co., Inc.**
Ash / Trash Receptacles - **Matel Bank and Desk Accessories**
Ash Handling Replacement Parts - **Power & Industrial Service Corp.**
Ashtrays and Cupholders for Custom Aircraft - **Charles a Starr Company**
Asian Art Prints - **Dharma Publishing**
Asian Noodles, Wrappers, Dumplings & Buns - **Twin Marquis, Inc.**
Asme Fabrication - **Mohawk Mfg. Corp.**
Asphalt & Road Repair Agents - **Golden Bear Oil Specialties**
Asphalt Drum Mixers & Related Equipment - **Almix/asphalt Equipment**
Asphalt Felts & Coatings - **Siplast Inc.**
Asphalt Felts & Coatings - **United Roofing Mfg. Co., Inc.**
Assembles Parts for the Printing Industry; - **Lemco**
Assembles Printed Circuit Boards - **Eagle Star Electronics Llc**
Assembles Propane Trucks - **High Country Proco**
Assembles Three-dimensional Hand Geometry - **Recognition Systems Inc**
Assemblies & Turnkey - **Salco Circuit**
Assembly - **Arc Industries Inc.**
Assembly - **Kurt Manufacturing Co.**
Assembly - **Metal Master Inc**
Assembly Machinery & Equipment - **West Tool & Design, Inc.**
Astron/earth Science Models for Schools - **Wildlife Supply Company**
Ata Accredited - Ba Philosophy - Ma Theology - **Rahoy Coccia Gabriella**
Athletic Field Covers - **M.putterman & Company Inc.**
Athletic Field Maintenance Equipment - **Kromer Co.**
Athletic Foam Pretape Wrap/felt - **Arrowhead Athletics**
Athletic Tape Adhesive/moleskin Adhesive - **Arrowhead Athletics**
Auctioneers,appraisers & Liquidators- **Norman Levy Associates**
Audio & Video - **Televentas**
Audio & Video Accessories - **Allsop, Inc.**
Audio & Video Amplifiers & Electronic Circuits - **Savant Audio & Video**
Audio & Video Cable Systems - **Wireworks Corporation**
Audio & Video Equipment_household - **Ampli-vox Questron**
Audio & Video Equipment_household - **Audioplex Technology, Inc.**
Audio & Video Equipment_household - **Ksc Industries Inc**
Audio & Video Equipment_household - **Savant Audio & Video**
Audio & Video Equipment_household - **Shure Bros. Inc.**
Audio & Video Equipment_household - **Drs Precision Echo**
Audio Cassette Duplication - **Tape Duplicators, Inc.**
Audio Components Racks, TV Stands & Cabinets - **Tocabi America Corp.**
Audio Loudness Meters - **Dorrough Electronics**
Audio Production - **Communi-creations Inc**
Audio, Stereo & Video Cables - **Apature Products, Inc.**
Audio, Video & Compact Disc Labels - **Audico Label Corp.**
Audio, Video, Cd Duplication - **Audico Label Corp.**
Audiometers - **Micro Audiometrics Corp.**
Audiometers and Auditory Trainers - **Eckstein Bros Inc**
Audiometers for Hearing Testing - **Ambco Electronics**
Auto & Home Supply Stores - **Simpson Tool Box Co**
Auto Glass, All Car & Truck - **Sam's Auto Glass & Exports**
Auto Pallet Loaders / Unloaders - **Hk Systems, Inc.**
Auto Parts - **World Trading**
Auto Parts Foreign & Domestic - **J.d. International Used Auto Parts**
Auto Parts Surplus - **Michigan Wholesalers Automotive Supply Co.**
Auto Storage/retrg. - **Hk Systems, Inc.**
Auto Undercoaitngs & Sound Deadeners - **Henry Company International**
Auto. Food Slicing/dicing Mach., Whsle - **Jaccard Corporation**
Auto. Polyurethane Suspension Component - **Energy Suspension**
Auto. Sanitary Liq. Sampling Eq., Whsle. - **Micropure Filtration, Inc.**
Auto. Vending Mach., Amusement/games - **Smart Industries**
Autoclaves & Medical Waste Sterilizers - **Bondtech Corp.**
Autoclovable Bags - **Bondtech Corp.**
Autodesk Reseller and Training Center - **Repro-products & Services**
Automated & Manual I.C. Strip Plating Systems - **Future Automation Inc**
Automated & Manual Wafer Plating Systems - **Future Automation Inc**
Automated Assembly Processes. In Die Processing - **Walker Corporation**
Automated Assembly Services - **Oberg Mfg. Co.**
Automated Mig; Inertia; Friction;- **U.S. Manufacturing Corporation**
Automated Systems - **Service Hydraulics Inc.**
Automated Water Treatment Controllers - **Santa Barbara Control Systems**

Automated Weather Monitoring Devices - **Systems Management Inc.**
Automatic & Semi-automatic Powder - **G E I Mateer-burt Co., Inc.**
Automatic Assembly Machines - **Swanson Anaheim Corp**
Automatic Bagel Production Systems - **Baking Machines**
Automatic Case Packers (Packaging Machinery) - **Sabel Engineering**
Automatic Control Valves & General Machining - **O C V Control Valves**
Automatic Data Processing Machines - **Synnex Information Tech**
Automatic Data Processing Machines - **Tally Printer Corporation**
Automatic Diesel Locomotive Fueling - **Snyder Equipment Co., Inc.**
Automatic Door Mats & Wallswitches - **Larco, Div. Of Acrometal Co**
Automatic Fire Extinguisher Systems - **Fireboy - Xintex**
Automatic Grease Lubricator, Sing. Point - **Tm Industries Inc.**
Automatic Grease Lubricators - **T M Industries, Inc.**
Automatic Recessing Tools - **Cogsdill Tool Products Inc. (Mfr)**
Automatic Regulating Valves - **Cla-val Company**
Automatic Screw Machine Products - **Elge Precision Machining, Inc.**
Automatic Spray Equipment - **Renite Co., Lubrication Engineers**
Automatic Strapping Systems - **Hemisphere Enterprises**
Automatic Tape Systems - **Hemisphere Enterprises**
Automatic Telephone Dialers / Acd - **Noble Systems Corp.**
Automatic Telephone Dialing Equipment - **Immix Telecom Inc.**
Automatic Teller Machine & Equipment Solutions - **Atm Exchange, Inc,**
Automatic Test Equipment - **P E I Electronics Inc.**
Automatic Test Equipment, Printed Circuit Boards - **Loranger Intern'l**
Automatic Transfer & Bypass-isolation Switches - **Lake Shore Electric**
Automatic Transistor Testers - **Fet Test Inc**
Automatic Transmission Parts and Kits - **Automatic Transmission Parts**
Automatic Transmission Ring Gears - **Automatic Transmission Parts**
Automatic Welding Equipment - **Ogden Engineering Corp.**
Automation - **Ap & T Tangent, Inc.**
Automation & Integration - **Industrial Design Fabrication**
Automation Assembly Equipment - **Automated Applications Inc**
Automation Components - **M F Automation Inc.**
Automation Equipment Components - **Robohand, Inc.**
Automation Systems - **Zygo Corp.**
Automobile & Rv Parts, Rv Rentals - **Palm Peterbilt - Gmc Trucks, Inc.**
Automobile Gears - **Midwest Truck & Auto**
Automobile Parts - **Myers Industries, Inc., Myers Tire Supply Div.**
Automobile Parts - **Richard Boas**
Automobile Parts & Accessories, Used - **All Day Used Auto Parts**
Automobile Parts & Supplies- **Justice Brothers, Inc.**
Automobile Related Parts - **Midwest Truck & Auto**
Automobile Seat Covers & Floor Mats - **Sagaz Industries, Inc.**
Automobile Tires - **Lakin Tire East, Inc.**
Automobiles - **Maxport International**
Automobiles - **Nishizawa**
Automobiles & Other Motor Vehicles - **High Country Proco**
Automobiles & Other Motor Vehicles - **Southwest Peterbilt Gmc**
Automobiles Sales & Used Auto Parts & Exporter - **Phillips Motors, Larry**
Automotive & Apparel Trimmings - **Semel's Embroidery & Screen Printi**
Automotive & Apparel Trimmings - **Arrow Creative International, Ltd.**
Automotive & Apparel Trimmings - **Gs Sportwear / Golden Squeegee**
Automotive & Apparel Trimmings - **Print Proz, Inc.**
Automotive & Apparel Trimmings - **Sloan & Assocs. Inc., Leonard**
Automotive & Apparel Trimmings - **Worthen Industries, Inc., Nylco Div.**
Automotive & Apparel Trimmings - **C. M. I. Enterprises**
Automotive & Architectural Glass - **Intraco Corp.**
Automotive & Electronic Components - **Aaron-swiss, Inc.**
Automotive & Heavy Duty Brake Parts - **Hebco Products, Inc.**
Automotive & Heavy Duty Engine Parts - **Intraco Corp.**
Automotive & Jeep Hard Tops - **Fleet Air Industries**
Automotive & Truck Equipment - **Truck Equipment Sales, Inc.**
Automotive Accessories - **Custom Accessories Inc**
Automotive Air Conditioning Condensers & Evaporators - **H P J, Inc.**
Automotive Alternators & Starters - **Viking Enterprises**
Automotive Carburetor Bowls - **Peltier Glass Co., the**
Automotive Chemical Specialties - **Radiator Specialty Co.**
Automotive Chemicals - **Spray Products Corp.**
Automotive Chemicals - **Interdynamics, Inc.**
Automotive Chemicals - **San Juan International, Inc.**
Automotive Chemicals - **Coastal Unilube, Inc.**

Automotive Chemicals - **Treatment Products Ltd.**
Automotive Chemicals - **Berkebile Oil Co.**
Automotive Chemicals & Contract Packaging - **Chemway Systems, Inc.**
Automotive Cleaners - **Justice Brothers, Inc.**
Automotive Cleaners - **K & W Products**
Automotive Cleaners, Waxes, Polishes - **Protect All, Inc.**
Automotive Computer - **Motorola Integrated Electronic Systems Sector**
Automotive Covers - **Budge Industries, Inc.**
Automotive Electric Cooling Fans - **Tripac International, Inc.**
Automotive Exhaust Decoupling Joints - **American Boa, Inc.**
Automotive Fiberglass Hardtops - **Tenessee Fiberglass Productc, Inc.**
Automotive Filter Papers - **Hollingsworth & Vose Co.**
Automotive Floor Mats & Accessories - **Pretty Products, Inc.**
Automotive Fluids & Lubricants - **Intraco Corp.**
Automotive Gasket Composite Materials - **Hollingsworth & Vose Co.**
Automotive Hardware - **Dura Automotive: Stockton Seat Group**
Automotive Hose Reels - **Coxwells, Inc., Dba Coxreels**
Automotive Lenses - **Peltier Glass Co., the**
Automotive Lighting - **Guide Corporation**
Automotive Lighting Equipment, Automotive Components - **Guide Corp**
Automotive Lubricants - **Coastal Unilube, Inc.**
Automotive Machine Shop - **La Machine Shop**
Automotive Machining Job Shop - **D & H Enterprises**
Automotive Parts & General Machining Job Shop - **S T C Machine Shop**
Automotive Parts for Trucks & Special Vehicles - **Intramar, Inc.**
Automotive Screws - **Illinois Tool Works, Inc.**
Automotive Services - **The John Wesley Group**
Automotive Stampings - **M P I International Inc.**
Automotive Stampings - **Quality Mold Inc.**
Automotive Trim & Plastic Extrusions - **Spradling Originals Inc.**
Automotive Vacuum Leak Detection Systems - **Emi-tech Inc.**
Automotive Video Entertainment Systems - **Rosen Product Development**
Automotive Wheel Nuts & Fasteners - **Horizon Technology Group**
Automotive Wire Connectors - **Mize & Co., Inc.**
Automotive and Marine Storage Batteries; Distri - **Exide Corporation**
Automotive, Golf Cart, Scrubber, Commercial and - **Us Battery Mfr. Co**
Automotive, Marine & Aircraft Orbital Polishing Equip - **Gem Industries**
Auxiliary Equipment for Printing Web: Ink Leveler - **Support Products**
Auxiliary Plastics Machinery - **Nutter Machine Inc.**
Auxiliary Printing Equipment - **Nationwide Graphics, Inc.**
Available in Standard U.s. Sizes, Custom - **Milgard Manufacturing Co**
Available in a Variety of Alloys - **Abbott Ball Co. (Mfg)**
Averaging Pitot Tubes - **Mid-west Instrument**
Aviation - Engine Lube/scav Pumps; - **National Flight Sales Corporation**
Aviation - Fuel Nozzles; Tfe331 - **National Flight Sales Corporation**
Aviation - Gas Turbine Engine Overhaul- **National Flight Sales Corp**
Aviation - Turbine Engine Components - **National Flight Sales Corp**
Aviation Products Export - Metals, Parts, Chemicals - **Olympic Aviation**
Avionics Equipment Assembly - **Rockwell International Corp.**
Awards - **Trophy Shoppe**
Awnings - **Cooley Sign & Digital Imaging,**
Awnings, Shades, Medical & Industrial - **Duracote Corp.**
Awnings, Tents and Related Canvas Product**Golden Fleece Designs Inc**
Axial Flow Fans - **Hudson Products Corp.**
Axis Machining - **Brenner Tool & Die, Inc.**
B & S Screw Machine Products - **Cole Screw Machine Products, Inc.**
Babbitt Bearing Repair, Manufacturing - **Mbs Industrial Service Inc**
Baby Bedding - **Marcus Brothers**
Baby Car Seat That Converts into a Stroller - **Safeline Corp**
Baby Care - **Apothecary Products Inc.**
Baby Feeding Accessories - **Pelican Co**
Back Light Display Signs - **Esco International**
Back-up Monitor Systems for Rv's and Buses - **Hoyin Industries**
Backflow Preventers - **Conbraco Industries, Inc.**
Backfilling equipment- **Brown Bear Corp.**
Backflow Prevention Devices - **Conbraco Industries**
Backhoe & Loader Fork Lift Attachments - **Construction Technology, Inc.**
Backhoe Attachments - **Sirex Pulse Hydraulic Systems**
Bacterial Wilt Resistant Tomato Seed - **Seedcraft**
Bag Closures, Twist Ties - **Alcar Industries, Inc.**
Bag Filling Machinery - **Sandbagger Corp.**

Bag Packaging Machinery - **Triangle Package Machinery Co.**
Bag Packers - **Packaging Systems International, Inc.**
Bag Palletizers - **Packaging Systems International, Inc.**
Bagels - **Everybody's Bagel Co Inc**
Bags, Disaster Bag - **Quest & Sons, Inc.**
Bags, Plastic Sterilized for Bioprocessing Fluids - **Newport Biosystems,**
Bags: Plastics, Laminated & Coated - **Caltex Plastics Inc**
Bags: Plastics, Laminated & Coated - **Intertape Polymer**
Bags: Plastics, Laminated, and Coated - **Packaging Center, Inc.**
Bags: Uncoated Paper & Multiwall - **Roses Southwest Papers**
Bags; Plastics, Laminated & Printed up to 8 Colors - **Hershey Industries,**
Bags_textile - **Manic Impressions**
Bakery & Confectionary (Air Brush & Icing Colors) - **Berghausen Corp.**
Bakery Equipment - **Magna Industries, Inc.**
Bakery Flour - **Molinos De Puerto Rico, Inc., a Conagra Company**
Bakery Machinery - **Dutchess Bakers' Machinery Co., Inc.**
Bakery Machinery - **Hurdt & Associates Machinery**
Bakery Mixes, Frozen Bakery Products- **International Multifoods Corp.**
Bakery Products_frozen, Except Bread - **Sara Lee Bakery Co.**
Bakery Products_frozen, Except Bread - **T N T Pizza Crust, Inc.**
Bakery Seasonings - **Old World Spices & Seasonings, Inc.**
Bakery Tables. - **Mapletex**
Bakery and Food Bag Closures - **Alcar Industries, Inc.**
Bakery and Food Service Equipment - **The Lucks Food Equipment Co.**
Baking Ingredients - **Amero Foods Mfg. Corp.**
Balancing Machines - **Balance Specialties Inc. (Mfr)**
Balers - **Alan Ross Machinery Corp**
Balers - Paper Waste - **Balemaster**
Ball Transfers/rollers/casters - **Kietek International, Inc.**
Ball Valves - **Tyco Valves & Controls**
Ball Valves Alloy Steel & Other Metals - **Flo-tork Inc. (Mfr)**
Ball Valves; Threaded, S.w. , B.w., Flanged - **Conbraco Industries**
Ballast Recycling - **Lighting Resources, Inc.**
Ballast, Cd-rom, Nimh Rechargeable Battery Pack - **Delta Products Corp**
Ballcocks & Flushvalves, Plastic & Brass - **Coast Foundry & Mfg Co**
Ballistic Armor - **Ceradyne, Inc.**
Balnton's Single Barrel Bourbon - **Age International**
Bandages - **Afassco, Inc.**
Bandstands - **Vixen Hill Mfg. Co.**
Bank & Cashier Supplies - **Major Metalfab Co.**
Bank Furniture, Checkstands & Accessories - **Matel Bank and Desk Acces**
Bank Vehicles (Vans, Trucks) - Armored - **Alpine Armoring Inc.**
Banknote Destroyers - **Security Engineered Machinery Co.**
Banners - **Bannerville U. S. A. Inc.**
Banners - **Sandy's Trophies**
Banners - **Cooley Sign & Digital Imaging,**
Banners & Signs - **Advanced Graphics & Publishing**
Banquet Tables - **Abco Products**
Bar Code & Scale Label Media, Entertainment Tickets, - **Rittenhouse Co**
Bar Code Printing Machinery - **Imaging Technologies, Inc.**
Bar Coded Labels / Tags - **Lumber Tag Specialties**
Bar Coding & Supplies - **Matrix Imaging Solution**
Bar Coding Equipment & Software - **American Barcode Concepts**
Bar Soap - **Original Bradford Soap Works, Inc.**
Barcode Distribuotr of Printers, Scanners, Software - **Allenwest Inc**
Bare & Electroplated Wire - **Fisk Alloy Wire, Inc.**
Bare & Tinned Copper - **Republic Wire, Inc.**
Bare Wire - **Permaluster Company**
Barium & Radiology Chemicals - **E-z-em, Inc.**
Barketsbandstubesbonding Adhesives - **Tp Orthodontics, Inc.**
Barrels, Drums & Pails_metal - **Evans Cushing, Inc.**
Barricade Signs - **Seton Name Plate Company**
Barrier Bags - **Caltex Plastics Inc**
Base Alloys, Investments, Colloid, Alloy Grinders, Etc. - **Cmp Industries,**
Basic Copper Sulfate - **Silkwood Wholesale, Inc.**
Basket Wholesale, Detail - **Silkwood Wholesale, Inc.**
Basketball Equipment—portable Basketball Sets - **Lifetime Products Inc**
Basswood Veneer for Plywood - **Hamer, Jim C.**
Bath & Body Products - **Alaska Herb Tea Co. (Mfr)**
Bath Salts - **Page Seed Co., Inc.**
Bath Towels - **Stantex**

Bath Wastes & Overflows - **Watco Mfg. Co.**
Bathroom Accessories - **Stylebuilt Accessories, Inc.**
Bathroom Accessories and Bathroom Safety Produc - **Franklin Brass Mfr.**
Batteries - **Bulbtronics, Inc.**
Batteries - **Sanyo Energy (Usa) Corp**
Batteries - **Lighting Resources, Inc.**
Batteries & Battery Packs for Computers - **Fedco Electronics Inc.**
Batteries - Vrla - **Sec Industrial Battery Co., Inc.**
Batteries_primary - **Mathews Assocs, Inc.**
Batteries_primary, Dry & Wet - **W & W Mfg.**
Batteries_storage - **Energy Sales**
Batteries_storage - **Exide Corporation**
Batteries_storage - **Fedco Electronics Inc.**
Batteries_storage - **Mathews Assocs, Inc.**
Batteries_storage - **Pinnacle Research Institute**
Batteries_storage - **Portable Energy Products Inc**
Batteries_storage - **Precious Plate Florida**
Batteries_storage - **Us Battery Manufacturing Co**
Battery Clips, Contacts & Holders - **Keystone Electronics Corp.**
Battery Monitoring Charge Controls, Electronic - **Cruising Equipment Co**
Battery Packs & Batteries - **Fedco Electronics Inc.**
Battery Packs & Batteries - **Mathews Assocs, Inc.**
Battery Separator, Storage Batteries- **Hollingsworth & Vose Co.**
Bearing Condition Indicator (Baci) - **Vitec, Inc.**
Bearings, Gears, Sprockets - **G K N Sinter Metals Emporium**
Bearings, Seals & Speed Reducers - **Minco Sales Corp.**
Bearings, Spherical & Rod End, Aircraft - **Radial Bearing Corp.**
Bearings_ball & Roller - **G K N Sinter Metals Emporium**
Beauty Aid Products, Fragrances and Cosmetics - **Continental Group**
Beauty Disposables - **Barnhardt Manufacturing Co.**
Beauty Products - **Flowery Beauty Products, Inc.**
Beauty Salon Disinfectants - **R. B. R. Productions, Inc.**
Beauty or Make-up Preparations and Preparations - **Hollywood**
Bed Linen of Textile Materials, Not Knitted or Crocheted - **Stantex**
Bed Linens - **Westpoint Stevens**
Bedroom, Dining Room, Ocasional - **Broyhill Furniture Industries, Inc.**
Bedsheets / Towels - **Marcotex International**
Bedspreads & Shower & Window Curtains **Milford Stitching Co., Inc.**
Bedsprings - **Kingsdown, Inc.**
Beef / Poultry - **Agri Processors**
Beef Cattle, Limousin Breeding Stock - **Magness Land & Cattle**
Beef Jerky - **Pacific Sun Industries Inc**
Beef Jerky - **Link Snacks, Inc.**
Beef Jerky, and Turkey Jerkys - **Enjoy Foods International**
Beef Processing - **Colorado Boxed Beef Co., Inc.**
Beef, Veal, Lamb & Poultry - **Agri Processors**
Beeswax - **Yaley Enterprises, Inc.**
Belt Conveyors & Bucket Elevators - **Rbm Manufacturing Co., Inc.**
Belts - **Alamia Inc**
Belts for Disposables Undergarments (Adults) - **Mc Kee Button Co.**
Belts, Leather - **Gould & Goodrich**
Bench Top Furnaces and Ultrasonic Cleaners; Sma - **Ney Dental, Inc.**
Bendable Vinyl Coil & Extruded Profiles - **Alum-a-pole Corporation**
Bent, Laminated & Flat Glass - **Custom Glass Corp.**
Benzene - **Sunoco, Inc.**
Benzoyl Peroxide - **Norac Co., Inc., the**
Bernhardt Furniture & Upholstery - **Designers Resource,**
Beryllium & Copper Die Castings & General Machining Job Shop - **Semco**
Beryllium Alloys - **N G K Metals Corp.**
Beryllium Oxide Ceramics for the Electronics In - **Brush Wellman Inc.**
Beverage Laboratory Equipment - **Terriss-consolidated Industries**
Beverage Testing Apparatus - **Terriss-consolidated Industries**
Beverage Truck Bodies - **Gregory Truck Body & Fire Apparatus, Inc.**
Beverages Bases, Aloe Vera - **Terry Laboratories, Inc.**
Bias Binding & Coated Fabrics - **Worthen Industries, Inc., Nylco Div.**
Bikinis - **Hannah Katherine Fashions Corp.**
Bill Boards - **Cooley Sign & Digital Imaging,**
Billets, Flange Adapters, Reducers, Stub Ends - **Tucson Industrial Plastics**
Billets, Slabs - **Tata, Inc.**
Bimetalic Thermometers - **Helicoid Div., Bristol Babcock Inc.**
Bin Dischargers - **Laidig Industrial System**

Binders - **Triangle Business Forms, Inc.**
Binders, Folders and File Covers, of Paper or Paperboard - **Gti Industries**
Binding Posts - **Eby Co.**
Binding Posts, Etc. - **M.m. Electric Products Ltd.**
Bins - **Laidig Industrial System**
Bio Sludge & Manure Injection Systems - **Hydro Engineering, Inc.**
Biodegradable, Water-based Cleaners - **Soq Environmental Tech Corp**
Biological Products, Bioprocess Containers & Bags - **Newport Biosystems,**
Biological Products, Except Diagnostic - **Genzyme Corp**
Biological Research, Food Supplements - **Biotics Research Corp.**
Biological Safety Equipment, Glove Boxes - **Germfree Laboratories, Inc.**
Biopesticides - **Soil Technologies Corp.**
Bioremediation of Petroleum Contam. - **Bbc International Inc.**
Bird & Rabbit Cages - **Ammermans, the**
Bird & Small Animal Edibles - **Hartz Mountain**
Bird Carvings in Wood - **Painted Bird**
Biscotti Cookies; Distributes Baked Goods - **Bay Area Biscotti Co**
Biscuit & Pancake Mix - **Blackberry Patch, Inc.**
Bits/tools/machines Oil Well Drilling (Cable Tool) - **Trident Tool, Inc.**
Bits/tools/machines Rock Drilling - **Trident Tool, Inc.**
Bits/tools/machines Well Drilling (Cable Tool) - **Trident Tool, Inc.**
Black Granite Surface-plates - **Pyramid Granite & Metals, Inc.**
Black Tahitian Pearl, 18k Gold, 14k Gold Sterling - **Skatell's Jewelers**
Blacksmithing Publication - **Hoffmann Pulications, Blacksmith's Journal**
Blankbooks and Looseleaf Binders - **Art Leather Manufacturing Co.,**
Blanket & Roller Cleaners, Plate - **Burnshine Products**
Blankets - **Westpoint Stevens**
Blankets & Crib Sets - **Owen Mfg. Co., Charles D.**
Blanking Tools - **Diemasters, Inc.**
Blast Doors - **Fleming Steel Co.**
Blast Furnaces & Steel Mills - **Co-steel Raritan**
Blast Furnaces & Steel Mills - **Coilplus-alabama, Inc.**
Blast Furnaces & Steel Mills - **Electralloy**
Blast Furnaces & Steel Mills - **High Steel Structures**
Blast Furnaces & Steel Mills - **Napa Pipe Corporation**
Blast Furnaces & Steel Mills - **Prospect Steel, Inc.**
Blast Resistant Glass - **Custom Glass Corp.**
Blast-resistant Doors, Windows, Walls - **Insulgard Corporation**
Blasting Accessories and Supplies - **D & L Thomas Equipment**
Blasting Equipment - **Abrasive Distributors Corp.**
Bleached Cotton - **Sheftel International**
Bleached Cotton Raw Stock - **Barnhardt Manufacturing Co.**
Bleached Hardwood - **Daiei Papers U.s.a. Corp.**
Blended Food Seasonings - **Legg, Inc., A. C.**
Blenders - **Hamilton Beach/proctor Silex, Inc.**
Blending Systems - **Flexicon Corporation**
Blood Separation and Processing Equipment - **Cobe Bet, Inc.**
Blouses & Shirts_women's & Misses' - **Piccone Apparel Corp**
Blouses & Shirts_women's & Misses' - **Manic Impressions**
Blowers & Fans - **Air Chem Systems Inc**
Blowers & Fans - **Ametek Rotron Tmd - Industrial Products Group**
Blowers & Fans - **Anguil Environmental Systems, Inc.**
Blowers & Fans - **Bruning & Federle Mfg. Co.**
Blowers & Fans - **Clean Air Consultants, Inc.**
Blowers & Fans - **New York Blower Co.**
Blowers & Fans - **Process Equipment, Inc.**
Blowers & Fans - **Roots Division, Dresser Equipment Group Inc**
Blowers & Fans - **Sterling Blower Co.**
Blowers & Fans - **Tri-dim Filter Corp.**
Blowers & Fans - **Triangle Metal & Mfg. Co.**
Blowers & Fans - **Turner Envirologic, Inc.**
Blowers & Fans Systems - **Clean Air Filter Co.**
Blowers & Fans, Mechanical Equipment - **Ship & Shore**
Blowers and Fans - **Lewcott**
Blue Camomile Shampoo - **Aubrey Organics Inc.**
Blue Ribbon Popcorn - **Ellis Popcorn Co., Inc.**
Bms, Flame Scanners & Igniters for All Types of Boilers - **Forney**
Board Level to Total System Electronics. - **Qual-pro Corporation**
Board Stiffeners - **Circuit Components, Inc.**
Boat Building - **Mariah Boats Inc.**
Boat Building & Repairing - **Cable Marine, Inc.**

Boat Building & Repairing - **Alaska Airboats**
Boat Building & Repairing - **Peregrine Marine, Inc.**
Boat Davits / Cradle Lifts / Hoists - **Liftmasters, Inc.**
Boat Horns - **Aqua Signal Corp.**
Boat Lifts - **Quality Boat Lifts, Inc.**
Boat Shoes - **Harken International, Ltd.**
Boat Trailer Parts & Supplies - **Trail-rite Inc**
Boat Trailers - **Trail-rite Inc**
Boat Trailers - **Waterland Mfg., Inc.**
Boat, Snow, Watercraft & Utility Trailers - **Karavan Trailers, Inc.**
Boats & Com., Industrial & Marine Metal Fabrication - **Master Marine,**
Bobbie Burns, Clothing - **Ski Co Inc**
Bobbins - **American & Efird, Inc.**
Bobbins for Transformers - **Yarbrough-timco**
Bodies for Road Tractors for Semi-trailers - **Euclid Hitachi Heavy Eqpt.**
Body Care Products - **Aromaland, Inc.**
Body Posture & Range of Motion Instruments - **Reedco Research**
Boiler & Windbox Access Doors - **Power & Industrial Service Corp.**
Boiler Controls - **Cleaver-brooks**
Boiler, Cooling, Wastewater Treatment - **Pro Chem Tech, International**
Boiler Water Treatment - **Ashland Chemicals**
Boilers - **Cleaver-brooks**
Boilers - **Jerryco Machine & Boilerworks**
Bolted Silos - **Laidig Industrial System**
Bolts - **Portland Bolt & Mfg Company**
Bolts & Nuts - **S P S Technologies, Inc., Automotive Fasteners Group**
Bolts, Nuts & Screws - **Florida Bolt & Nut Co.**
Bolts, Nuts, Rivets & Washers - **Anillo Industries Inc**
Bolts, Nuts, Rivets & Washers - **Diversified Fastener & Tool Co.**
Bolts, Nuts, Rivets & Washers - **Hick International Fastener Div**
Bolts, Nuts, Rivets & Washers - **Illinois Tool Works, Inc.**
Bolts, Nuts, Rivets & Washers - **Liberty Fastener Co.**
Bolts, Nuts, Rivets & Washers - **Portland Bolt & Mfg Company**
Bolts, Nuts, Rivets & Washers - **S P S Technologies, Inc.**
Bolts, Nuts, Rivets & Washers - **Thf Corp**
Bolts, Nuts, Rivets & Washers - **Tru-fast Corp.**
Bolts, Nuts, Rivets & Washers - **Tufnut Work, the**
Bolts, Nuts, Rivets & Washers - **Zero Fastener Co.**
Bolts, Nuts, Screws & Washers - **Earnest Machine Products Co.**
Bolts, Nuts, Studs & Washers - **Northwestern Tools, Inc.**
Bomb Containment Waste Receptacle - **United Metal Receptacle Inc.**
Bonded Carrier - **Euro-american Air Frt. Fwdg Co., Inc.**
Bonded Carrier - **Vanco Heavy Lift C.f.s.**
Bonded Container - **Euro-american Air Frt. Fwdg Co., Inc.**
Bonded Leather - **Empire State Leather Corp.**
Bonded Leather in Sheets & Rolls for Use in Shoe - **Robus Leather**
Bonded Rubber & Metal Aerospace Parts - **Lord Corporation,**
Bonded Storage - **Atlantic Cold Storage Corporation**
Bondstrand / Trackwire - **National Electric Gate Co.**
Bonsai's - **Toepperweins of Texas**
Book Packager - **Rutledge Books, Inc.**
Book Printing - **Total Printing Systems**
Book Printing - **C. S. S. Publishing Co., Inc.**
Book Publisher - **Rutledge Books, Inc.**
Book Publishing - **Harbingers of a New Age**
Book Publishing - **Academic Press**
Book Publishing - **Dharma Publishing**
Book Publishing - **Dragon Enterprises**
Book Publishing - **E M I S, Inc.**
Book Publishing - **Idq Books Worldwide Inc**
Book Publishing - **International Soc for Technology in Education (Iste)**
Book Publishing - **Scott Foresman**
Book Publishing - **Service Quality Institute**
Book Publishing - **Warren Communications**
Book Publishing (Dog Books) - **Doral Publishing Inc**
Book Seller - **Sun Publishing Co.**
Books and Periodicals - **Hispanic Books Distributors Inc**
Books in Meditation, Relaxation, Healing - **Dharma Publishing**
Books, Periodicals - **Hispanic Books Distributors Inc**
Books, Periodicals & Newspapers - **Clear Creek Courant**
Books, Periodicals & Newspapers - **Ranchland News**

Books, Video & Cd's - **Pass Distributing Corporation**
Bore Sizes 50 - 200 Mm - **John Deere Harvester Works, Cylinder Div.**
Boring Bars - Special - **Midwest Ohio Tool Company**
Boring Equipment, Automotive Valve Grinders - **K W Products, Inc.**
Boring or Sinking Machinery - **Centron International Inc.**
Boron Carbide Components - **Ceradyne, Inc.**
Boron Carbide Powder - **Electro Abrasives Corp.**
Boron Hardened Bushings for Elec. Submersible Pump - **Vaporkote Inc**
Boston, Jacksonville, Charleston, New York - **Moran, J. F. Co., Inc.**
Botanical Food Supplements - **Biotics Research Corp.**
Botanicals - Roots, Barks, Herbs - **Herbco International Inc.**
Botanicals, Vegetable Culture Elements - **Biotics Research Corp.**
Bottle Private Label Apple Juice, Cider - **Alljuice Food & Beverage**
Bottled & Bulk Wines - **Delicato Vineyards**
Bottled Pasta Sauces (Non-frozen) - **Amy's Kitchen Inc**
Bottled Salad Dressings, Sauces - **El Toro Food Products Inc**
Bottled Water - **Holmes Ice & Cold Storage Co**
Bottled Water & Sparkling Water - **Grayson Mountain Water Co.**
Bottles - **Pochet of America, Inc.**
Bottles Purified Potable Water - **Erica and Erica International Corp.**
Bottles Wholes - **O. Berk Company**
Bottling Machinery for the Bottled Water Indust - **Mac Company**
Bow Ties & Cummerbunds - **Duron Neckwear Inc**
Bowling Pinsetters, Parts, Capital Equipment - **Vantage Bowling Corp**
Boxes, Corrugated & Solid Fiber - **Forest Packaging Corp.**
Boxes, Corrugated Items, Pads,- **Northwest Paper Box Mfrs Inc**
Boxes, Folding Paperboard - **Boxes.com (a N.j. Corporation)**
Boxes_corrugated & Solid Fiber - **Age Industries, Inc.**
Boxes_corrugated & Solid Fiber - **Northwest Paper Box Mfrs Inc**
Boxes_corrugated & Solid Fiber - **Pacific Western Container**
Boxes_corrugated & solid fiber, foam - **Whitmark Inc**
Boxes_folding Paperboard - **Northwest Paper Box Mfrs Inc**
Boxes_folding Paperboard - **Outlook Graphics**
Boxes_setup Paperboard - **Northwest Paper Box Mfrs Inc**
Braided Cordage & Twisted Rope - **Rocky Mount Cord Co.**
Braided Ropes (Nylon, Polyester, Spectra and Ke - **Pelican Rope Works**
Brail Sign - **Sandy's Trophies**
Brake Cylinder Pressure Taps - **Strato, Inc.**
Brake Fluid - **Coastal Unilube, Inc.**
Brake Lathe Automobile Disc Stabilizer - **Duncan-leigh-schiffer**
Brake Pads, Shoes - **World Trading**
Branch Connections - **Texas Pmw, Inc.**
Branch Pipe Tees for Railroads - **Strato, Inc.**
Brand Names: Kd Waterskis, Kidder Waterskis - **Kd Water Sports**
Branded Cosumer Packages of Macadamia - **Mac Farms of Hawaii, Inc.**
Brass & Laser Cut Polyester Stencils - **American Traditional Stencils**
Brass Engraveable Plates - **Exclusive Findings**
Brass Rods, Poles & Finials - **World Wide Windows**
Brass Scrap - **Los Angeles Scrap Iron & Metal**
Brass Valves - **Conbraco Industries, Inc.**
Brass and Sand Carved River Rock; Copper Jewelr - **The Alchemists Inc**
Brass, Copper, & Plastic Injection Molded Plumbing - **Sioux Chief Mfr. Co**
Brass, Nickel Alloy, Stainless Steel - **Sos Metal San Diego**
Brassiere Underwire - **S & S Industries, Inc.**
Brazing & Soldering Alloys - **Harris-welco Co.**
Bread & Rolls - **Adams Bakery Corp.**
Bread and Bakery Products - **Giuliano-pagano Corp**
Bread and Bakery Products, - **Nabolom Bakery**
Bread, Cake & Related Products - **Adams Bakery Corp.**
Bread, Cake & Related Products - **Bonert's Slice of Pie**
Bread, Cake & Related Products - **Distinctive Foods, Inc.**
Bread, Cake & Related Products - **Everybody's Bagel Co Inc**
Bread, Cake & Related Products - **Giuliano-pagano Corp**
Bread, Cake & Related Products - **J & J Wall Baking Company Inc**
Bread, Cake & Related Products - **Love's Bakery, Inc.**
Bread, Cake & Related Products - **Nabolom Bakery**
Bread, Cake & Related Products - **Neuman Bakery Specialties, Inc.**
Bread, Cake & Related Products - **Sara Lee Bakery Co.**
Bread, Pastry, Cakes, Biscuits - **Catalina Food Ingredients**
Bread, Rolls, Doughnuts & Pies - **Love's Bakery, Inc.**
Breading & Batters - **Catalina Food Ingredients**

Brewer's Grits - **Molinos De Puerto Rico, Inc., a Conagra Company**
Brick - **Sioux City Brick & Tile Co., Sergeant Bluff Plt.**
Brick / Clay Cutting Wires - **Manufacturers Equipment Company-meco**
Brick Stencils & Concrete Color Hardener - **Artcrete, Inc.**
Brick, Stone, and Related Materials - **Lotus Exim International**
Brined Hot & Sweet Peppers - **United Pickle Products Corp.**
Briquettors - **Security Engineered Machinery Co.**
Broadwoven Fabric Mills, Cotton - **Chiquola Industrial Products Group,**
Broadwoven Fabric Mills, Manmade - **Brickle, Hyman & Son, Inc.**
Broadwoven Fabric Mills, Manmade - **Carole Fabrics**
Broadwoven Fabric Mills, Manmade - **Mayfair Mills, Inc.**
Broadwoven Fabric Mills, Manmade - **S-line**
Broadwoven Fabric Mills, Manmade - **Wearbest Sil-tex Mills Ltd.**
Broadwoven Fabric Mills, Wool - **Brickle, Hyman & Son, Inc.**
Broccoli Seeds for Sprouting (Fighting Cancer) - **Seedcraft**
Brochures - **Cps Communications, Inc.**
Broilers, Electric & Gas - **Broaster Co., the**
Bronze Art Foundry; Fine Art Originals & Reproductions - **Sun Foundry**
Bronze Bearings - **Ryder-heil Bronze Inc.**
Bronze Bearings - **American Sleeve Bearing, Llc**
Bronze Boiler Trims - **Conbraco Industries, Inc.**
Bronze Electrical Connectors - **T.j. Manufacturing, Inc.**
Bronze Valves - **Conbraco Industries, Inc.**
Bronze Valves - **T.j. Manufacturing, Inc.**
Bronze and Aluminum Foundry; Bearings - **Advance Aluminum & Brass**
Broom, Brush & Mop Handles, Fibers - **Monahan Co., the Thomas**
Brooms & Brushes - **Groom Industries, Inc.**
Brooms & Brushes - **Abco Products**
Brooms & Brushes - **M & E Mfg. Co.**
Brooms & Brushes - **Monahan Co., the Thomas**
Brooms, Mops & Lumbar Belts - **Abco Products**
Brown Rice, Regular & Parboiled - **Riceland Foods Inc.**
Brownies, Cookies & Related Products - **Sybil's Outrageous Brownies**
Brush Cutting Equipment - **Brown Bear Corp**
Brush Electroplating Equipment - **Brooktronics Engineering Corp**
Brush Plating - **Sifco Selective Plating**
Brushes - Hair, Makeup, Paint, Paint Roller, Fabric, Etc. - **Paul Marsh, Llc**
Brushless Dc Motors - **Bei Sensors & Systems/kimco Magnetics Division**
Buckwheat, Rolled Oats - **R.j. Commodities**
Buddhist Philosphy History, Culture & Art - **Dharma Publishing**
Buffalo, Venison Jerky, Sausages, Canned Prod - **Dale's Wild West Produc**
Builders Hardware - **Wespac Corp.**
Builders Hardware - Forged Iron - **Acorn Manufacturing Co., Inc.**
Builders' Joinery & Carpentry of Wood - **North American Wood Products**
Building Automation Controls - **Trane Company, the**
Building Materials - **Coral Steel Company**
Building Materials - **Bifrost**
Building Supplies - **Horton Homes, Inc.**
Builds Crates; Packaging Service - **Future Packaging Inc**
Builds Custom Power and Sailing Catamarans - **Pedigree Cats Inc**
Builds Related Burners & Cyclonic Systems - **Hudnut Industries Inc**
Builds Scale Models for Architectural Firms - **Global Architectural Mode**
Bulbs, Tubers, Tuberous Roots, Corms - **Golden State Bulb Growers**
Bulk Antiserum - **Midland Bioproducts Corp.**
Bulk Bag Filling Stations - **Flexicon Corporation**
Bulk Bag Unloading Stations - **Flexicon Corporation**
Bulk Materials Handling Equipment - **Intersystems, Inc.**
Bulk Processed Fiberglass Products - **Kasko Enterprises Inc.**
Bulk Supply for Macadamia Grades - **Mac Farms of Hawaii, Inc.**
Bulldozers and Angledozers, Self-propelled - **Nationwide Equipment**
Bullet Resistant Clothing & Soft Body Armor - **Pointblank Body Armor, I**
Bullet Resistant Doors, Windows & Walls - **Insulgard Corporation**
Bullet Resistant Glass - **Custom Glass Corp.**
Bullet Resistant Glass - **Laminated Glass**
Bullet-casting Machinery - **Ballisti-cast Mfg., Inc.**
Bullet-resistant Architectural Armor for Doors, - **Bullet Guard Corp**
Bunk Beds, Bedroom Furniture - **Parris Mfg. Co.**
Buoys, Lighted, Unlighted - **Tideland Signal Corp.**
Burr-Free Cut-Off Metal Parts - **Metal Cutting Corporation**
Burgular Resistant Safes - **Meilink Safe Co., a Fireking International Co.**
Burial Monuments & Granite Processing - **Payton Granite & Monument**

Burn Dressings, Burn Creams, Burn Kits - **Water-jel Technologies**
Burn Treatments & Kits - **Afassco, Inc.**
Burner Systems - **John Zink Company**
Burnishing Tools - **Elliot Tool Technologies, Ltd.**
Bus. Svcs, Manufacturers Agents & Reps - **Pdg Associates, Inc.**
Bus. Svcs., Technology Transfer - **Interdevelopment Inc.**
Buses - Remanufacture & Recondition - **A-z Bus Sales, Inc.**
Buses, Schools, Tourist, All Kind and Sizes. - **Big Abe No.1. Inc.**
Business Association, Pet Supplies - **World Wide Pet Supply Ass'n**
Business Associations - **Americares Foundations**
Business Brokering Services - **Smirnoff Communications Group, Inc.**
Business Card Trays, Files, Fingertip Moistenin - **Wescosa Inc**
Business Check (Both Laser & Continuous) - **New West Business Forms**
Business Consulting - **Leemark, Inc.**
Business Consulting / Product Sourcing - **The John Wesley Group**
Business Consulting Services- **Nevada Automotive Test Center**
Business Consulting Services- **Ets Research & Development Inc**
Business Consulting, Air Research Feas. Imp. - **Century West Engineering**
Business Consulting, Data Communications - **Otm Engineering, Inc.**
Business Consulting, Industrial Recruitment - **Mccord Consulting Group,**
Business Consulting, Nec - **Williams Shipping**
Business Consulting, Site Selection Svcs. - **Mccord Consulting Group,**
Business Consulting, Video - **Otm Engineering, Inc.**
Business Consulting, Voice Communications - **Otm Engineering, Inc.**
Business Enhancements - **R. P. Creations, Inc.**
Business Forms - **Rapid Reproductions Printing**
Business Forms & Letterhead Printing - **Triangle Business Forms, Inc.**
Business Forms Printing - **American Forms, Inc.**
Business Forms Printing - **Colonial Business Forms, Inc.**
Business Forms Printing - **Kenalex Printing Forms, Inc.**
Business Gift Items - **Blue Atlantic, Ltd.**
Business Opportunities - **Shu-re-nu Equipment, Inc.**
Business Research Svcs., Exp. / Imp Asst. - **Interdevelopment Inc.**
Business Services - **Richardson Engineering Svcs Inc**
Business Services - **Medical Gas Services Inc**
Business Services - **The John Wesley Group**
Business Services - **Armstrong Teasdale**
Business Services Nec. - **Platt Electric Supply**
Business Services, Building Products Inspection - **Pfs Corporation**
Business Services, Interior Design - **Leo A. Daly Company**
Business Services, N.e.c. - **Cacheaux, Cavazos, Newton, Martin & Cukja**
Butanols - **Petroplast Chemical Corp.**
Butcher - Block - **Lewgust Co., Inc.**
Butchers & Meatpacking Cutlery - **Cutco Cutlery Corp.**
Butt Weld Pipe Fittings - **Custom Alloy Corporation (Mfr)**
Butterfly Valve Actuators - **Flo-tork Inc. (Mfr)**
Butterfly Valves - **Conbraco Industries**
Butterfly Valves - **Tyco Valves & Controls**
Butterfly Valves, Forged Steel Gate - **Conbraco Industries, Inc.**
Button Assembly Machines & Die Cutting Presses - **Tecre Co., Inc.**
Button Machinery & Supplies, Badge & Button Machines - **Debbeler Co.**
Buy - Sell - Trade Used Trucks - **Export Parts Center**
Buys & Sells Steel, Aluminum, Stainless Steel, Brass - **Interstate Steel Inc.**
Buys and Sells Surplus Technological - **Resource Technology**
Buzzers & Transducers - **Mg Electronics**
By-products for - **Colorado Sweet Gold Llc**
C-dollies and Hitches - **Independent Trailer & Equip Co**
C-meal / Fish Analog - **Darling International Inc.**
Ca/az Cotton Magazine - **Western Agricultural Publish**
Cabinets for Computer Networks - **Chatsworth Products Inc**
Cabinets, Workstations, Tables and Custom - **Metal Master**
Cable - **Respond Group of Companies**
Cable & Cable Management Products - **The Siemon Company**
Cable & Harness Assemblies - **Eby Co.**
Cable Assemblies - **Conectec R F, Inc.**
Cable Management Products - **Chatsworth Products Inc**
Cable Tv Equipment - **Galow Trading**
Cable/harness Assemblies - **Imperial Electronic Assembly**
Cables, T.v. - **Ocalas Corporation**
Cad/cam Machining - **Lemco**
Cadastra L Data Application Developer - **Barclay Maps**

Caffeine, Tolopheroe, Color Extract - **Natra Us Inc.**
Cairox - Potassium Permanganate - **Carus Chemical Co.**
Cajun Dinner Mixes & Specialty Cakes - **Louisiana Gourmet Enterprises**
Cakes, Muffins, Donuts, Danish - **International Multifoods Corp.**
Calcium Chloride - **Tetra Technologies**
Calcium Citrate - **Century Multech**
Calculating & Accounting Equipment - **De La Rue Cash Systems**
Calendered, Printed & Laminated Vinyl - **Vernon Plastics Corp.**
Calibration Equipment - **Arbiter Systems Inc**
Calibrators - **Pierburg Instruments, Inc.**
California Almonds, Bulk, Consumer, Flavored - **Wiggin Farms**
California Grapevine Leaves - **Yergat Packing Co.**
Call Center Software Solutions & Technology - **Teledirect International,**
Camera & Photographic Supply Stores - **Preston Cinema Systems Inc**
Camera Inspection Equipment for Pipelines - **Pearpoint Inc**
Camera Testers & Light Meters - **Zts, Inc.**
Cameras - **Minolta Corporation**
Camete - Calabaza-cocada-alfastor **Las Dos Victorias Candies**
Can Closing Machinery - **Angelus Sanitary Can Machine**
Can Seamers - **Angelus Sanitary Can Machine**
Can Seamers - **Angelus Sanitary Can Machine Co.**
Candies - **Gimbal Brothers Inc**
Candles - **Root Co., Inc., A. I., the**
Candy - **Candy Express**
Candy - **Las Dos Victorias Candies**
Candy & Other Confectionery Products - **Adams & Brooks Inc**
Candy & Other Confectionery Products - **Gimbal Brothers Inc**
Candy & Other Confectionery Products - **Hawaiian Host, Inc.**
Candy & Other Confectionery Products - **Otec, Inc.**
Candy & Other Confectionery Products - **Sun Empire Foods**
Candy and Confectionery Products - **Granlunds Sweet Temptations**
Candy and Other Confectionery Products - **Sconza Candy Co.**
Candy, Chocolate-covered Fruits and Nuts - **Sun Empire Foods**
Cane Sugar Refining - **California & Hawaiian Sugar Co**
Canned & Bottled Salsa, Hot Suaces - **El Toro Food Products Inc**
Canned & Smoke Fish; Smoked Trout - **Hoodsport Winery Inc.**
Canned Food - **Basic Foods International, Inc.**
Canned Fruits & Vegetables - **Chalet Suzanne Foods, Inc.**
Canned Fruits & Vegetables - **Mccain Citrus Inc**
Canned Fruits & Vegetables - **Norpac Foods Inc**
Canned Gourmet Soups & Sauces - **Chalet Suzanne Foods, Inc.**
Canned Macadamia Nuts & Almonds - **Hawaiian Host, Inc.**
Canned Peaches - **California Fruit Packing Company**
Canned Soups - **Chiquita Processing Foods, Llc - Int'l**
Canned Soups (Non-frozen) - **Amy's Kitchen Inc**
Canned Vegetables - **Sew Feiel**
Canned Vegetables (Private Labels) - **Chiquita Processing Foods, Llc**
Cannon Bath Rugs & Scatter Accent Rugs - **Allegra Industries, Inc.**
Canola Specialty Oil - **Intermountain Canola Cargill**
Canopies - **Cover-it Shelters, Inc.**
Cans - Closures - **U. S. Can Co., Custom & Specialty Division**
Cans - Decorated - **U. S. Can Co., Custom & Specialty Division**
Cans - Hermetic - **U. S. Can Co., Custom & Specialty Division**
Cans - Tin - **U. S. Can Co., Custom & Specialty Division**
Cans - Welded - **U. S. Can Co., Custom & Specialty Division**
Cans, Metal - **U. S. Can Co., Custom & Specialty Division**
Cans_metal - **Crown Cork & Seal /Americas Div**
Canvas & Related Products - **Covers Unlimited, Inc.**
Canvas & Related Products - **Floyd's Awning & Canvas Shop**
Canvas & Related Products - **Golden Fleece Designs Inc**
Canvas & Related Products - **Quest & Sons, Inc.**
Canvas & Related Products - **Revere Plastic, Inc.**
Canvas Tarpaulins & Protective Covers - **Revere Plastic, Inc.**
Canvas and Related Products, Aluminum Awnings - **Van Nuys Awning Co**
Cap Torque Test Equipment - **Vibrac International , Llc**
Capacitors - **N W L Capacitors**
Capacitors & Capacitor Switches / Controls - **Cooper Industries**
Capacitors, Resistors - **Hybrid Semiconductors/electronics Inc.**
Cappers (Inline) - **Njm/cli Packaging Systems International**
Capping Equipment - **Filler Specialties, Inc.**
Capsicums - **Gilroy Foods, Inc. (Mfr)**

Capsule Printers - **Ackley Machine Corp.**
Car Amplifiers, Signal Processors and Speakers - **Autotek Corp**
Car Care Chemicals - **Petro Chemical Products Inc.**
Car Dealers, Vans, Suburbans, Ambulances - **Big Abe No.1. Inc.**
Car Seats, Booster Seats & Strollers - **Safeline Corp**
Car Stations - **P T L Equipment Mfg. Co., Inc.**
Car Waxes & Polishes - **Treatment Products Ltd.**
Caramels, Chocolates, & Caramel Apples - **Carousel Candies**
Carbide - Tipped Router Bits, Standard- **Nordic Saw & Tool Mfr.**
Carbide - Tipped Shaper Cutters- **Nordic Saw & Tool Mfr.**
Carbide Cutting Tools - **Micro 100, Inc.**
Carbide Tipped Cutting Tools - **Lexington Cutter, Inc.**
Carbide Tipped Drill Bits - **B & a Mfg. Co.**
Carbide Tool & Die Job Shop - **Eastern Carbide Tool Co. Llc.**
Carbide, Abrasives, Hand Tools & Endmills - **Cutting Edge Tool Supply**
Carbon & Graphite Products - **Carbone of America Corp.**
Carbon & Graphite Products - **Graphite Products Inc**
Carbon & Graphite Products - **Toyo Tanso Usa Inc**
Carbon / Graphite Raw Materials - **Roc Carbon Co.**
Carbon Activation/reactivation Furnaces - **General Carbon Corp.**
Carbon Air Filters - **Calgon Carbon Corporation (Mfr)**
Carbon Brushes - **Carbone of America Corp.**
Carbon Dioxide Blast Cleaning Systems - **Cold Jet, Inc.**
Carbon Dioxide Measurment in Soft Drinks - **Vibrac International , Llc**
Carbon Film Resistors - **Koa Speer Electronics, Inc.**
Carbon Filtering Products, Whsle. - **Calgon Carbon Corporation (Mfr)**
Carbon Monoxide Alarms & Detectors - **Quantum Group, Inc.**
Carbon Paper - **Frye Tech, Inc.**
Carbon Paper & Inked Ribbons - **Paxar Iimak**
Carbon Paper & Inked Ribbons - **Ribbon Division Inc**
Carbon Paper Ink - **Frye Tech, Inc.**
Carbon Water Filters - **Calgon Carbon Corporation (Mfr)**
Carbonated Beverages - **Safeway Stores Inc., Export Sales**
Carboys, Bottles, Flasks and Similar Articles - **All American Containers**
Carburetor Units & Truck Engine Conversion- **Industrial Gastruck, Inc.**
Card Access Security Management Systems- **Cardkey Systems Inc**
Card Cages - **Electronic Packaging Systems**
Cardiopulmonary, Metabolic, Nutritional Assessm - **Sensormedics Corp**
Career Software Products & Services for Career Planning - **Jobquest**
Cargo Control Equipment - **Kinedyne Corp.**
Cargo Insurance - **Global Solutions Insurance Services, Inc.**
Cargo Restraint Systems & Devices - **Cargo Systems, Inc.**
Cargo Straps & Nets, Overhead Lifting Systems - **Spanset, Inc.**
Carnegie Deli N.y. Cheesecake - **United Pickle Products Corp.**
Carnets / Carnet Bonds - **Roanoke Brokerage Services, Inc.**
Carob Powder & Products - **Famarco Ltd. Inc./b & K International**
Carpenters' Hand Tools - **Patterson Avenue Tool Co.**
Carpet Cleaning Machines - **Advance Paper & Maintenance**
Carpet Cleaning Preps. - **Steam Services Inc.**
Carpet Grooming Tools, Chemicals & Brushes - **Groom Industries, Inc.**
Carpet, Drapery, & Upholstery Cleaning - **Us Products Inc**
Carpet, Rugs, Area Rugs & Accessories - **Regal Carpets Inc.**
Carpets - **Mohawk International**
Carpets & Rugs - **Regal Carpets Inc.**
Carpets & Rugs - **Erin's Original Horseplay Rugs**
Carpets and Other Textile Floor Coverings - **Barrett Carpet Mills, Inc.**
Carpets and Other Textile Floor Coverings - **Penichet Carpet**
Carpets and Rugs - **Barrett Carpet Mills, Inc.**
Carrier Rope - **Kenyon & Sons, Inc., William**
Carrier Rope Eqipment - **Kenyon & Sons, Inc., William**
Cars & Trucks - **Sam's Auto Glass & Exports**
Carton Sealing Tape - **Hemisphere Enterprises**
Carton Sortation - **Quantum Conveyor Systems, Llc**
Carts - **Carico Systems**
Carts, Mail - **W.a. Charnstrom Co., Inc.**
Carulite - Air Emission Control Catalysts - **Carus Chemical Co.**
Carusmatic - Potassium Permanganate - **Carus Chemical Co.**
Case & Pallet Conveying Systems & Controls - **Hk Systems, Inc.**
Case Conveyors - **Alvey, Inc.**
Case Good Manufacturer & Exporter - **Incon Overseas Marketing, Inc.**
Casein - **American Casein Co.**

Caseinates - **American Casein Co.**
Cashew Can Openers - **Ashton Food Machinery Co., Inc., Neumunz Div.**
Cashier & Toll Booths, Walkway Covers - **Mardan Fabricators**
Casing, Tubing and Drill Pipe - **Centron International Inc.**
Casino Coins - **Gdc Casino Tokens**
Casino Gaming Equipment; Shufflers & Games - **Shuffle Master, Inc.**
Casio & Sharp Digital Diaries - **Juno International**
Casio Calculators - **Juno International**
Casio Watches - **Juno International**
Casks, Barrels, Vats, Tubs and Other Coopers' Products - **The Barrel Co**
Cast Aluminum Platters - **Tomlinson Industries**
Cast Articles of Iron or Steel - **Aj Weller**
Cast Iron, Ductile, and Steel Castings—municip - **Olympic Foundry Inc**
Cast Polymer Bath Products and - **Six-eleven Ltd Inc**
Cast Table Bases - **Grace Mfg. Co., Inc.**
Caster & Wheels - **Faultless Caster Division**
Casters - **Able Builders Export, Inc.**
Cat Litter - **Hartz Mountain**
Cat Toys - **Purr-fect Growlings**
Catalog & Mail-order Houses - **Just Merino Sheepskin Products**
Catalog Sales Gen Farm Supplies - **Coburn Company, Inc.**
Catalogs, Brochures (Thru 5 Colors) - **Triangle Business Forms, Inc.**
Catalogs, Product Bulletins - **Congdon Printing & Imaging**
Catalyst - **Professional Services International, Inc.**
Catalyst: All-metal, Ceramic - **Catalytic Combustion Corp.**
Catalytic Incinerators - **Catalytic Combustion Corp.**
Cathodic Protection Service - **Energy Economics, Inc.**
Caulks and Sealants for Construction - **Schnee-morehead of California**
Caulks, Sealants, Adhesives - **Ici Paints International - Export - Licensin**
Cautilever Racks - **Andersen Rack Systems Inc**
Ccd Video Cameras & Accessories - **Watec America Corp**
Cd Carrying Cases - **Compu Cover**
Cd Rom Based Character Generators for Cable or Cc Tv - **Magicbox Inc**
Cd, Cd-rom, Dvd Display Fixtuers - **Plastic Works Inc**
Cd-rom Network Servers - **Meridian Data Inc**
Cedar Prefabricated Gazebos, Saunas and Accesso - **Northwest Cedar Inc**
Cedar Storage & Novelty Products- **Cedar & Hardwood Mfg. Company**
Ceiling and Roof Mounted A/c Units - **Compu-aire, Inc.**
Ceilings - **Ceilings plus Inc**
Cellulose Insulation - **Fiber Master Inc./thermocon Inc.**
Cellulose Spray Acoustic Insulation - **Fiber Master Inc./thermocon Inc.**
Cellulosic Manmade Fibers - **Western Synthetic Fiber**
Cellulosic Manmade Fibers - **Durafiber Corp.**
Cement Industry - **Aj Weller**
Cements, Cleaners & Primers for Pvc - **Pacific Plastics**
Cent. Tubes / Snap, Screw, Tethered, Racks - **Quality Scientific Plastics**
Centerless Grinding & Thread Rolling - **A & B Aerospace Inc**
Central Cleaning Systems - **Beam Industries**
Central Heat System / Ind or Res. - **Turbo Burn Inc**
Central Office Alarm Monitoring Servers- **Cordell Manufacturing Inc**
Centrifugal Pumps & Parts, Allis Chalmers - **Triton Equipment Corp.**
Centrifugal Pumps & Pumping Equipment - **Gator Pump, Inc.**
Centrifugal Pumps, Sanitary - **Top Line Process Equipment Co.**
Centrifugal Sifters - **Kason Corporation (Mfr)**
Ceramic Beads - **Yaley Enterprises, Inc.**
Ceramic Capacitors & Dielectric Ceramic Materials - **Radio Materials**
Ceramic Clay & Glaze Additive - **A P T Ii Products Co.**
Ceramic Fish Bowls - **Toepperweins of Texas**
Ceramic Panels for Wear Protection - **Aj Weller**
Ceramic Tableware, Kitchenware - **Lanca Sales, Inc.**
Ceramic Tools - **Seeley's Ceramic Service, Inc.**
Ceramic Wall & Floor Tile - **Ro-tile**
Cereal Breakfast Foods - **Organic Milling Inc**
Certified Appraisals - **Resource Technology**
Certified Destruction of Electronic Scrap - **Ecs Refining**
Certified Organic Fertilizer - **North American Export Company**
Certified Organic Milk & Cheese / Eggs - **Organic Valley / Cropp Cooper**
Certified Supplier for United Defense L.p. - **La Machine Shop Inc.**
Certified Welding & Steel Construction. - **Golten Service**
Certified Welding - High Pressure Systems - **C. H. Hyperbarics, Inc.**
Cgr Has Been in Business since 1963 & Has Plants - **C G R Products Inc.**

Chain Fitting Hardware - **Crosby Group, Inc.**
Chain Tensioner - **Hitachi Maxco, Inc.**
Chains - **Crosby Group, Inc.**
Chains for Conveyors - **Hitachi Maxco, Inc.**
Chainstitch - **Semel's Embroidery & Screen Printing, Inc.**
Chairs for the Handicapped - **Convaid Products Inc**
Chalk Bulletin & Marker Boards - **Aristocrat Industries, Inc.**
Champion Tech Agri Fungicide - **Agtrol International**
Chandeliers, Sconces Residential & Commercial - **Speer Collectibles**
Character Generators and Standard Converters - **Avs Graphics Internation**
Charolais Bull Semen - **Wienk Charolais**
Charolais Cattle - **Wienk Charolais**
Chassis Fitted with Engines for Tractors - **Euclid Hitachi Heavy Equipt**
Check Protection Equipment - **Woerner Industries, Inc.**
Check Signing & Endorsing Machinery- **Cummins-allison Corp.**
Check Valves - **Gulf Valve Company**
Check Valves - **Tyco Valves & Controls**
Check Valves for Flow Control - **Smart Products Inc**
Check-signing Machinery - **Hall-welter Co.**
Check-writing Machinery - **Hall-welter Co.**
Cheese - Imported & Domestic - **Flora Distributors, Inc.**
Cheese Processing Equipment - **International Machinery Exchange**
Cheese Sauce - **Dean Foods (Mfr)**
Cheese Snacks - **Link Snacks, Inc.**
Cheese, Including Cheddar and Colby - **International Custom Products**
Cheese, Natural & Processed - **Berner Cheese Corp.**
Cheese, Natural & Processed - **Galaxy Foods, Inc.**
Cheese, Processed & Natural - **Safeway Stores Inc., Export Sales**
Chelated Liquid Calcium - **C. S. I. Chemical Corp.**
Chem. Paint Additives, Corrosion Inhib. - **Davis Colors**
Chemical Cellulos/dissolving Pulp Dissovling, Fluff & Paper - **Rayonier**
Chemical Corrosion Preventives - **Wayne Consultants, Inc.**
Chemical Engineering Equipment - **Carbone of America Corp.**
Chemical Fasteners - **Polygem**
Chemical Laboratory, Testing - **Humboldt Mfg. Co., Inc.**
Chemical Light Sticks - **Lindgren Pitman**
Chemical Preparations - **Artcrete, Inc.**
Chemical Preparations - **Chemical Distributors, Inc.**
Chemical Preparations - **Dixie Chemical Co., Inc.**
Chemical Preparations - **Driwater Inc**
Chemical Preparations - **Elf Atochem North America Inc.**
Chemical Preparations - **Industrial Specialty Chemicals, Inc.**
Chemical Preparations - **Innovative Organics Inc**
Chemical Preparations - **Jell Chemicals, Inc.**
Chemical Preparations - **Montana Essence Company**
Chemical Preparations - **National Ink**
Chemical Preparations - **Pacific Pac International Inc**
Chemical Preparations - **Pel Assocs., Inc.**
Chemical Preparations - **Petroferm Inc.**
Chemical Preparations - **San Juan International, Inc.**
Chemical Preparations - **Security Equipment Corp.**
Chemical Preparations - **South Beach Fire Services**
Chemical Preparations - **Groom Industries, Inc.**
Chemical Preparations - **Independent Ink Inc**
Chemical Preparations / Engine Wear Protector - **Motorkote Inc**
Chemical Preparations / Fuel Treatment - **Motorkote Inc**
Chemical Preparations, Nec - **Elf**
Chemical Processing - **Dixie Chemical Co., Inc.**
Chemical Processing Equipment- **Pragmatic Environmental Solutions Co**
Chemical Products and Preparations and Residual Products - **Sieflor**
Chemical Reagents - **Neogen Corp.**
Chemical Resistant Epoxies - **Polygem**
Chemical Resistant Materials, Sealers - **Anti Hydro International, Inc.**
Chemical Sealants, Export - **C.r. Laurence Company, Inc.**
Chemical Waxes (Natural) - **Frank B. Ross Co., Inc. (Mfr)**
Chemical Weapons & Training - **J.m.s. Ltd**
Chemicals - **Eastern Europe Inc.**
Chemicals - **Eastern Europe Inc.**
Chemicals & Allied Products - **Hach Company**
Chemicals & Allied Products - **Advance Paper & Maintenance**
Chemicals & Allied Products - **Medical Gas Services Inc**

Chemicals & Allied Products, Export - **Incon Overseas Marketing, Inc.**
Chemicals & Allied Products, Nec - **West Agro, Inc.**
Chemicals - Pharmaceutical, Cosmetic, Paint & Asphalt - **Paul Marsh, Llc**
Chemicals and Allied Products, Nec - **Bush Boake Allen**
Chemicals and Allied Products, Nec - **Imc Chemical, Inc.**
Chemicals for Antiquing Metals - **Triple S Products**
Chemicals for Metal Colouring - **Triple S Products**
Chemicals for the Paint Industry - **Velco Chemicals**
Chemicals for the Semiconductor Industry - **Acsi Inc.**
Chemicals for the Semiconductor Industry - **Svc Labs**
Chemicals, Car Wash & Detailing - **Treatment Products Ltd.**
Chemicals, Cleaners - **National Research & Chemical Co.**
Chemicals, Export - **American Optimum**
Chemicals, Nec., Seafood Testing - **Neogen Corp.**
Chemicals_industrial Inorganic - **Arrow Engineering Inc.**
Chemicals_industrial Inorganic - **Chemway Systems, Inc.**
Chemicals_industrial Inorganic - **Giles Chemical Corp.**
Chemicals_industrial Inorganic - **Houghton International, Inc.**
Chemicals_industrial Inorganic - **Jupiter Chemicals, Inc.**
Chemicals_industrial Inorganic - **National Alum Corp.**
Chemicals_industrial Inorganic - **Ppg Industries Inc.**
Chemicals_industrial Inorganic - **Russ Chemical Co., Inc.**
Chemicals_industrial Inorganic - **Syntech Products Corp.**
Chemicals_industrial Inorganic - **U. S. Vanadium Corp.**
Chemicals_industrial Inorganic - **Norman, Fox & Co**
Chemicals_industrial Organic - **Dragoco Inc.**
Chemicals_industrial Organic - **Innovative Organics Inc**
Chemicals_industrial Organic Solvents - **Svc Labs**
Chemist & Perfumers - **M. C. Marble Co., Inc.**
Chenille - **Semel's Embroidery & Screen Printing, Inc.**
Cherries - **Denice & Filice Packing**
Chew-rite Cushion Dentrue Retainer - **Magnesia Products Inc.**
Chicago Pneumatic Compressor Parts - **Energy Machinery Inc**
Chicken Processing - **Sanderson Farms Inc.**
Child Saftey Device - **Robett Mfg. Co.**
Children's Accessories - **Strasburg Inc.**
Children's Clothing - **Strasburg Inc.**
Children's Furniture - **Children's Furniture Co., the**
China Bristles, Fine Hair, Horse Hair, Synthetics - **Paul Marsh, Llc**
China Paints - **Seeley's Ceramic Service, Inc.**
Chinese Dim-sum & Bakery Products - **Lucky Seven Food Inc**
Chip Screening - **Magnum Machinery Services Inc**
Chlorinated Paraffins - **Dover Chemical Corp., Sub. Of Icc Industries**
Chlorine - **Petroplast Chemical Corp.**
Chlorine- Free Flooring (Non Pvc) - **Amtico International Inc.**
Chloromethyl Naphthalene - **Richard Boas**
Chocolate & Cocoa Products - **Hawaiian Vintage**
Chocolate & Cocoa Products - **Just Truffles**
Chocolate & Cocoa Products - **Kona Paradise Candies Corp.**
Chocolate Angel Mint - **Florida Candy Factory, Inc.**
Chocolate Confectionery, Cheese- **Scott's of Wisconsin / Mille Lacs M. P.**
Chocolate Covered Almonds - **Hawaiian King Candies**
Chocolate Covered Macadamia Nuts - **Hawaiian King Candies**
Chocolate, Truffles - **Hoodsport Winery Inc.**
Chocolate-covered Macadamia Nuts - **Hawaiian Host, Inc.**
Chokes - **Mag-tran Equipment Corp**
Chopper Pumps - **Vaughan Co Inc**
Christmas Wreaths & Other Holiday Balsalm Products - **Flo's Wreaths**
Chrome Service - **Thistle Roller Co Inc**
Chrome, Anodizing & Metal Finishing- **Dixie Electro Plating Co., Inc.**
Chromite - **Refractory Materials International**
Chuck & Machine Tool Parts - **H & R Mfg. & Supply, Inc.**
Church & Institutional Furniture - **Sauder Mfg. Co.**
Church Offering, Microfiche & Commercial- **Southern Church Envelope**
Cigarettes Containing Tobacco - **C & M Enterprises**
Cinematographic Equipment - **General Drapery Services, Inc.**
Circular Cold Saws - **Scotchman Industries, Inc.(Mfr)**
Circular Vibratory Screen Separators - **Kason Corporation (Mfr)**
Cirlex - **Lockwood Industries Inc**
Citro Graph Magazine - **Western Agricultural Publish**
Citrus Juices - **Mccain Citrus Inc**

Citrus Peel - **Gilroy Foods, Inc. (Mfr)**
Civil Engineering, - **Msi International**
Clad Metals Electrical Applications - **Polymetallurgical Corp.**
Clamps - **Tridon**
Clamps, Sign Mountings, Hose Fittings, Applicat - **Band-it-idex Inc**
Classroom and On-site Training - **Methods West Machine Tools**
Clay Roffing Tile - **Sioux City Brick & Tile Co., Sergeant Bluff Plt.**
Clay and Related Minerals - **Wyo-ben, Inc.**
Clean Agent Fire Suppression Systems - **Fire Equipment, Inc**
Clean Room Contaminating Control Products - **Liberty Industries, Inc.**
Clean Room Floor Panels - **Seidelhuber Metal Products Inc**
Clean Room Production Tools - **Excelta Corp**
Clean Room Systems, Heating & Air Conditioning - **Hale Engineering Co**
Clean Room Wiping Cloths - **High-tech Conversions, Inc.**
Clean Rooms Laminar Flow Equipment - **Liberty Industries, Inc.**
Cleaners - **Miller Corp., Harry**
Cleaners & Conditioners: Desensitizers - **Burnshine Products**
Cleaners for the Pulp Paper Industry. - **Eldorado Chemical Co., Inc.**
Cleaners/phosphatizers for Metal Finishing - **Eldorado Chemical Co., Inc.**
Cleaning & Drum Process Systems - **Americlean, Inc.**
Cleaning Chemicals - **Supreme Chemicals of Georgia**
Cleaning Chemicals, Aerosol Paints, Lubricants - **L H B Industries**
Cleaning Compounds, Air Fresheners Deodorizers **Hygienic Products Lab**
Cleaning Compounds, Janitorial - **Jobe Industries Inc.**
Cleaning Compounds, Vehicle (Cars, Buses, Trucks) - **Jobe Industries Inc.**
Cleaning Compounds, for Coffee & Tea Equipment - **Royal Enterprises, I**
Cleaning Fluids & Solutions - **Kyzen Corp.**
Cleaning Products - **Sioux City Brick & Tile Co., Sergeant Bluff Plt.**
Cleaning Solvents - **Petroferm Inc.**
Cleaning Solvents, Paint Strippers, Wax Removers - **Svc Labs**
Cleaning, Polishing, Sanitation Preparations, S - **Dynamic Research Co**
Cleanroom & Esd (Anti-static) Garmetns Includin - **Fibrotek Industries**
Cleanroom Filtration Products - **Purolator Products Air Filtration Co.**
Cleanroom Pressure-sensitive Tapes for Semicond - **Ultratape Industries**
Cleanrooms Meeting Fmrc 4910 Protocol. - **Ats Products**
Cleanser, Natural & Herbal Facial - **Aubrey Organics Inc.**
Clear Plastic Disposable Containersfor Bakery & Food - **Inline Plastics**
Clear Semi-rigid Extruded Plastic Containers - **Tulox Plastics Corp.**
Clicker Dies - **Diemasters, Inc.**
Clinical & Industrial High Pressure Air, Gas - **C. H. Hyperbarics, Inc.**
Clinical Thermometers - **Medical Indicators, L.p.**
Clinical, Diagnostic and Research Use. - **Karlan Research Products Corp**
Close Outs & Regular Line - **Ericyan Ii**
Closed Circuit Television/surveillance - **Diamond Electronics Inc.**
Closed Die Forgings & Stainless & Titanium - **Canton Drop Forge**
Closeout & Obsolete Merchandise - **Lanca Sales, Inc.**
Cloth Baby Carriers - **Cozy Inc**
Clothing - **Noamex**
Clothing & Usedshoes - **General Business International Trade**
Clothing : Contact: Roy Shewitz - **Rowtex**
Clothing Pattern Fabric Cutting, Apparel -**Argus International, Inc.**
Clothing, Men's & Boys' - **Marathon Corp.**
Clothing, Men's & Boys' Work - **J. D American Workwear, Inc.**
Clothing, Mens & Boys - **Alps Sportswear Manufacturing Co , Inc**
Clothing_men's & Boys' - **Robett Mfg. Co.**
Clothing_men's & Boys' - **Apparel Suppliers Ca/pagano W**
Clothing_men's & Boys' - **Canari Cycle Wear**
Clothing_men's & Boys' - **Cattle Kate Inc**
Clothing_men's & Boys' - **La Mar Mfg. Co.**
Clothing_men's & Boys' - **Sauvage Swimwear**
Clothing_men's & Boys' - **Silver Needles**
Clothing_men's & Boys' - **Split Tee**
Clothing_men's & Boys' - **Surf Line Hawaii, Ltd.**
Clothing_men's & Boys' - **South Pass Trading/cnl Clothiers**
Clothing, Mfr. : Ladies, missy, Jrs. & dresses- **B & B Design Collections**
Clutch Forks - **Automatic Transmission Parts, Inc. A.t.p.**
Cnc Cylindricals, Chuckers, Crankshaft, Camshaft - **Aldridge Industries,**
Cnc Laser-cutting, Punching & Aluminum - **Begneaud Mfg. Inc.**
Cnc Machine Shop (Job Work) - **Vimex Cnc Machining**
Cnc Machine Tool Sales, Service - **Methods West Machine Tools**
Cnc Machining - **Rsm Products, Inc.**

Cnc Machining Job Shop - **Doemelt Racing, G. L.**
Cnc Milling - **Metal Master Inc**
Cnc Milling, Tools, Dies, Jigs & Fixtures- **Jd Tool & Machine Co Inc**
Cnc Parts - **Pacific Crest Manufacturing Inc**
Cnc Precision Bar Products - **Cole Screw Machine Products, Inc.**
Cnc Production Machining & Milling - **K & B Machine Works Inc.**
Cnc Turning & Cnc Milling - **A & B Aerospace Inc**
Cnc Wire and Die-sinking Edm - **Methods West Machine Tools**
Coagulant Blends - **Geo Specialty Chemicals, Inc.**
Coagulant Products Nsf Aproved - **Geo Specialty Chemicals, Inc.**
Coal - **Eastern Europe Inc.**
Coal Fired Utility Burner Replacements - **Power & Industrial Service**
Coal Mine Equipment - **Lays Mining Service, Inc.**
Coal Processing - **Lehigh Coal & Navigation Co.**
Coalescing Filters - **Consler Filtrations Products**
Coast Guard & Defence Force Refitting - **Cable Marine, Inc.**
Coated & Laminated Paper , Not Elsewhere Classified - **Forester Rollers**
Coated Abrasives - **United Abrasives Inc.**
Coated Abrasives, Belts, Sheets, Discs, Etc. - **Abrasive Distributors Corp.**
Coated Fabrics, Not Rubberized - **Spectro Coating Corp.(Mfr)**
Coated Fabrics, Not Rubberized - **Starensier**
Coated Fabrics, Not Rubberized - **Uretek, Inc.**
Coated Fabrics, Not Rubberized - **Vernon Plastics Corp.**
Coated Fabrics, Not Rubberized - **Worthen Industries, Inc., Nylco Div.**
Coated Fabrics, Not Rubberized - **Blackburn Mfg. Co.**
Coated Fiberglass Fabric - **Alpha Associates, Inc.**
Coaters on Paper, Film, Plastic, Vinyl, Canvas - **B F Mfg., Inc.**
Coating & Engraving, Nameplates - **Holman Label Company**
Coating & Lining-epoxy - **Apac Products**
Coating & Wrapping Svcs. Steel Pipe - **Current, Inc.**
Coating Plate & Equipment - **Napp Systems Inc**
Coating, Engraving, Enameling, Powder Coating - **Feeley Company, Inc.**
Coating, Laminating, Print, Metallize - **Technical Coating International**
Coatings, Protective - **National Research & Chemical Co.**
Coaxial Rf Vacuum Switches - **Jennings Technology Company**
Cocoa & Cocoa Products - **Garnac Grain**
Cocoa Powder & Cocoa Butter, - **Natra Us Inc.**
Coconut - **Griffin Food Company**
Coding & Marking Devices - **Atomco Corporation**
Coffee - **Uni Hosiery Co., Inc.**
Coffee Brewing and Restaurant Equipment - **Brewmatic Co**
Coffee Flavors - **Flavor Dynamics, Inc.**
Coffee Not Roasted - **Kauai Coffee Company**
Coffee Roasting & Packaging - **Colonial Coffee Roasters, Inc.**
Coffee Urn & Beverage Dispensing Faucets - **Tomlinson Industries**
Coffee, Roasted - **Kauai Coffee Company**
Coffee_roasted - **Colonial Coffee Roasters, Inc.**
Coffee_roasted - **Jbr Inc**
Coffeemakers - **Hamilton Beach/proctor Silex, Inc.**
Coil - **Sahar Industries**
Coil & Ingot Tongs - **Bradley Lifting Corp.**
Coil & Winding - **Permaluster Company**
Coil Processing Equipment - **Strilich Technolgies, Inc.**
Coil Springs - **Duer/carolina Coil Inc.**
Coil Springs - **Curran Coil Spring Inc**
Coil Springs, Four-slide Products, Stampings - **O'hara Metal Products Co**
Coiled Electrical & Air Assemblies - **Phillips Industries**
Coin Jewelry - **Fuller & Son Co., George H.**
Coins, Medallions, Key Tags - **Wendell's, Inc.**
Cold Cathode & Neon - **Bieber Lighting Corp**
Cold Forming Metal Machinery - **Enkotec Co., Inc.**
Cold Glue, Labeling Equipment - **Njm/cli Packaging Systems Int'l**
Cold Rolled Steel Stripmill - **Chicago Steel & Pickling Co.**
Cold Rolled, Hot Rolled, Galvanized & Stainless Steel - **Rolled Steel Prod**
Cold Smoked - Lox - Salmon, Halibut - **Alaskan Dried Foods**
Cold Working Tools - **West Coast Industries Inc.**
Collectable Art Gifts - **Hibel Corp., Edna**
Collection Services - **First Security Bank**
Collector Filters, Spray Booth, Overspray - **Chemco Manufacturing Inc.**
Colloid Milling Machinery - **Chemicolloid Laboratories, Inc.**
Color / Graphics Printing - **Repro-products & Services**

Color Additives for Concrete - **Davis Colors**
Color Changing (Thermochronic) Pigments / Inks - **Davis Liquid Crystals**
Color Changing Toy, Gift & Novelty Items - **Davis Liquid Crystals**
Color Lcd Displays - **Frontline Systems**
Color Separations - **Gonzalez Integrated Marketing**
Color Televisions & Electronic Products - **Five Rivers Electronic Innovati**
Color, Appearance, Physical Test Equipment - **Byk-gardner Usa**
Columbia Gorge Directory - **Hagadone Directories Inc**
Combination End Dump, Bottom Dump Trailers - **Hoss Equipment**
Combine Harvesting Equipment - **Agco Corporation**
Comercial Explosives - **Universal Tech**
Comforters - **Allegra Industries, Inc.**
Comm Equip Not Elsewhere Classified - **Jps Communications Inc**
Comm. Eq. Outdoor Microwave Sensors - **Perimeter Products, Inc.**
Comm. Eq., Emer. Veh. Sirens-speakers - **Code 3, Inc.**
Comm. Equip. Data Communications, Wholesale - **Black Box Corp**
Comm. Research, Feasibility Studies - **Etc De Las Americas, Inc.**
Commercial & Book Printing - **C. S. S. Publishing Co., Inc.**
Commercial & Label Printing - **Matrix Imaging Solution**
Commercial & Military Composite Aircraft - **Texas Composite Inc.**
Commercial & Newspaper Printing - **Times Leader, Inc.**
Commercial & Pad Printing & Pad & Screen Printing Inks - **Prismflex Inc.**
Commercial & Residential Fire Sprinkler - **Globe Fire Sprinkler Corp.**
Commercial & Residential Steel Building Frames - **Hexaport Int'l**
Commercial & Residential Wooden Furniture - **Fine Craft Unlimited**
Commercial & Wholesale Contract Division - **Sultan & Sons, Inc.**
Commercial - Fast Ferry - **Lockheed Martin Launching Systems**
Commercial / Marine Applications - **Outdoor Environments, Llc.**
Commercial Art & Graphic Design - **Westpro Graphics**
Commercial Art & Graphic Design - **Advanced Graphics & Publishing**
Commercial Art & Graphic Design - **Sandy's Trophies**
Commercial Art & Graphic Design - **Neon Fx Sign & Display**
Commercial Art & Graphic Design - **Never Boring Design Associates**
Commercial Baling Systems - **International Baler Corp.**
Commercial Battery Tester - **Zts, Inc.**
Commercial China - **Homer Laughlin China Company, the**
Commercial Cooking & Food Warm Equip. - **Alto-shaam, Inc.**
Commercial Dryers - **Wascomat (Mfr)**
Commercial Energy Recovery- **Des Champs Laboratories Incorporated**
Commercial Equipment - **Aaa Weigh Inc**
Commercial Equipment - **Weigh-tronix Inc**
Commercial Equipment, Access/alarm, W/colour Graphics - **Apollo**
Commercial Equipment, Alarm Systems - **Apollo**
Commercial Equipment, Alarm Systems - **Asti**
Commercial Equipment, Nec - Store Fixtures - **R & D International Inc.**
Commercial Equipment, Security Equipment, W/color Gr. - **Asti**
Commercial Explosives / Licensing - **Universal Tech Corporation**
Commercial Floor Matting - **Pioneer Mat Co., Inc.**
Commercial Food Warming Equipment - **Alto-shaam, Inc.**
Commercial Food Waste Reduction Systems - **Anaheim Marketing Int'l**
Commercial Glass Refrigerator and Freezer Doors - **Anthony International**
Commercial Hi-gay Hid Fixtures - **American Power Products Inc**
Commercial Household Cabinets - **Mod-tech, Inc.**
Commercial Industrial Design- **Enform-aeon Inc**
Commercial Kitchen Hoods - **Gaylord Industries, Inc.**
Commercial Kitchen Ventilation Systems - **Halton Co.**
Commercial Laundry - **Maytag International**
Commercial Laundry Equipment - **Alliance Laundry Systems**
Commercial Laundry Equipment - **Ellis Corporation**
Commercial Laundry Equipment - **Giancola Exports, Inc., D. J.**
Commercial Laundry Machinery - **Pellerin Milnor Corp.**
Commercial Marine Equipment - **Mmc International Corp.**
Commercial Metal Containers - **Dewald Northwest Co**
Commercial Offset & Direct Mail - **Congdon Printing & Imaging**
Commercial Offset Lithography - **Quantum Color Graphics Inc.**
Commercial Ovens, Electrical - **Alto-shaam, Inc.**
Commercial Physical Research - **Signals & Systems Inc.**
Commercial Physical Research - **Pinnacle Research Institute**
Commercial Physical Research - **Creative Science & Technolgoy**
Commercial Physical Research - **Enform-aeon Inc**
Commercial Printing - **Ace Printing Company**

Commercial Printing - **Diego & Son Printing**
Commercial Printing - **El Camino Printers**
Commercial Printing - **Graphic Ways Inc**
Commercial Printing - **Coastal Printing Co.**
Commercial Printing - **Image Printing**
Commercial Printing - **Mitchell Daily Republic**
Commercial Printing - **Roberts Co., the John**
Commercial Printing - **Sandy-alexander, Inc.**
Commercial Printing - **Wolf Creek Printing**
Commercial Printing & Rubber Stamps - **Joplin Printing Co.**
Commercial Printing & Typesetting - **Union Printing**
Commercial Printing / Warehousing - **Source W Printing**
Commercial Printing and Offset - **Giant Horse Printing Inc**
Commercial Printing, Lithographic and Offset - **Alphagraphics Printshops**
Commercial Printing, Lithographic - **Anchor Printing & Graphics**
Commercial Printing, Lithographic - **Thunderbird Printing & Screening**
Commercial Refrigeration Hardware Walk-in - **Premco Machine Co Inc**
Commercial Refrigeration Units - **Nor-lake, Inc. (Mfr)**
Commercial Refrigerators - **Howard-mccray Refrigerator Co. Inc. (Mfr)**
Commercial Refrigerators & Freezers - **Zero Zone, Inc.**
Commercial Research via Minitel - **French Connection, the**
Commercial Scales - **Scientech Inc.**
Commercial Sheet Fed Printer - **Wolf Creek Printing**
Commercial Testing Lab., Environmental - **Etc De Las Americas, Inc.**
Commercial Textile Printing - **Zoo-ink Screen Print**
Commercial Van Conversions - **Crown Divisions of Trans Pro, Inc., the**
Commercial Ventilating Equipment - **Acme Engineering & Mfg. Corp.**
Commercial Washing Machines - **Wascomat (Mfr)**
Commercial Water Heater - **Pvi International**
Commercial Water Purification - **Pure Water, Inc.**
Commercial Web Printing - **Best Litho, Inc.**
Commercial Web Printing, Numbering , Cross Perfs - **L M N Printing Co.**
Commercial and Industrial Light Bulbs - **Agamco Inc**
Commercial and Industrial Steel Bridges - **Colorado Bridge & Iron Inc**
Commercial, Res, Indl. & Automotive Paint - **Hawthorne Paint Co., Inc.**
Commission Weaving, Dyeing, Finishing - **Brickle, Hyman & Son, Inc.**
Commodities - **Molinos De Puerto Rico, Inc., a Conagra Company**
Commodity Broker, Soy Beans, Corn, & Oil - **Ultimate International**
Commodity Contracts Brokers, Dealers - **R.j. Commodities**
Commodity Trading of All Grains - **Noga Commodities**
Common Carrier - **Euro-american Air Frt. Fwdg Co., Inc.**
Common Materials Include Thermoplastics - **Intek Plastics, Inc.**
Communication Antennas - **Raibeam**
Communication Buildings & Shelters - **Craig Indsutries**
Communication Equip., Fiber Optic Cable Systems - **S.i. Tech, Inc.(Mfr)**
Communication Equipment, Nec - **Advantor Corp.**
Communication Equipment, Nec - **Detex International**
Communication Towers, Monopoles - **Gem Engineering Co., Inc.**
Communications & Outreach - **Technical Resource International, Inc.**
Communications Cable Accessories - **A'n D Cable Products Inc**
Communications Consultation & Solutions - **Source W Printing**
Communications Equipment - **E & M Intl.**
Communications Equipment - **Hughes Electron Dynamics**
Communications Equipment - **Micon Telecommunications Inc**
Communications Equipment & Video Distribution - **Multiplex Technology**
Communications Equipment Installation - **Micon Telecommunications Inc**
Communications Equipment, Aei Readers, Radios - **Railroad Signal, Inc.**
Communications Equipment, Nec - **Audioplex Technology, Inc.**
Communications Equipment, Nec - **Ceeco Communications Equipt & En**
Communications Equipment, Nec - **Glenayre Western Multiplex**
Communications Equipment, Nec - **Centurion International, Inc.**
Communications Equipment, Nec - **Ceotronics Inc.**
Communications Equipment, Nec - **Demco Electronics**
Communications Equipment, Nec - **Harmon Industries, Inc.**
Communications Equipment, Nec - **Tut Systems**
Communications Equipment, Nec - **National Electric Gate Co.**
Communications Equipment, Nec - **Litton Industries Inc**
Communications Equipment, Nec - **Kidde Aerospace, Walter**
Communications Equipment, Tone - **B Q Products Inc.**
Communications Systems - **Ceotronics Inc.**
Comp Periph Chemical-free Film Printer - **Virtual Fund.com**

Compact Fluorescent Lamps - **American Power Products Inc**
Companion Animal Dentistry - **St Jon Pet Care Products**
Compaq Reseller - **Repro-products & Services**
Complete Automated Systems Design - **Rbm Manufacturing Co., Inc.**
Complete Cnc Machining & Manufacturing - **Onodi Tool & Engineering**
Complete Electro Mechanical Test System Assembly - **Electronic Mfr. Svc**
Complete Functional Testing of Finished Products - **Electronic Mfr. Svc.**
Complete Ground Meat Processing Systems - **Weiler and Company Inc.**
Complete Line of Restaurant Equipment - **Global Leasing & Sales, Inc.**
Complete Meat Separators - **Weiler and Company Inc.**
Complete Packaging Lines - **Njm/cli Packaging Systems International**
Complete Presslines - **Ap & T Tangent, Inc.**
Complete Sausage Processing Systems - **Weiler and Company Inc.**
Complete Sawmills Re-conditioned - **Hamre Equipment**
Complete Worldwide Logistics Services - **Dynamic Packing & Logistics**
Component Parts & Accessories for Recreational - **Valterra Products**
Component Parts, Electrical Equipment - **Porcelain Products Co.**
Component Parts— Tubing, Fittings, Valves - **Evans Components Inc**
Component Recovery from Electronics - **Ecs Refining**
Components & Helmet Mounts - **Norotos Inc**
Components / Vertical Blinds, Wood Blinds, Mini Blinds - **Arabel**
Components for Analytical Instruments - **Duke Scientific Corporation**
Components for Fluorescent Lighting: - **A.l.p. Lighting Components, Inc.**
Components, Furniture - **Woodpecker, Inc.**
Components, Personal Leather Goods, Belts, Luggage - **Robus Leather**
Components/products, Rf/microwave Components - **Delta Products Co.**
Composite Medical Parts; Aircraft - **Quintus Inc**
Composite Panels - **Tri-link Technologies Ltd.**
Composite Plastic Enclosures for Underground - **Associated Plastics Inc**
Composite Wooden Pallets - **Commercial Pallet Pak Co.**
Composite, Metal & Teflon Hose - **Senior Flexonics Inc., Hose Div.**
Composition Doll Bodies - **Seeley's Ceramic Service, Inc.**
Compost Turners, Farm Equipment - **Wildcat Mfg. Co., Inc.**
Composting Equipment - **Resource Recovery Systems Inc. - Kw**
Compounded Thermoplastic Resins - **Hitech Polymers, Inc.**
Compressed Air Dryers & Filters - **Hankison International**
Compressed Air Filters & Dryers - **Filenco Div.**
Compressed Gas Filters - **Consler Filtrations Products**
Compressed Oat Hay - **Ward Rugh, Inc.**
Compression & Extrusion & Injection Moldings - **Afton Plastics**
Compression: Stationary & Portable - **Minco Sales Corp.**
Compressor Replacement Parts - **Parts Services International Llc**
Compressor Valves - **M & J Valve Services, Inc.**
Compressor Valves - **Parts Services International Llc**
Compressors - **Barber-nichols Incorporated**
Compressors & Vacuum Pumps - **Gardner Denver, Inc. (Mfr)**
Compressors, Air & Gas - **Quincy Compressor**
Compressors_air & Gas - **Bradleys' Hermetics, Inc.**
Compressors_air & Gas - **Ciasons Industrial Inc**
Compressors_air & Gas - **Energy Machinery Inc**
Compressors_air & Gas - **Hermetic Machines Inc.**
Compressors_air & Gas - **Jun-air Usa, Inc.**
Compressors_air & Gas - **Technology General Corp.**
Computer & Keyboard Dust Covers & Accessories - **Compu Cover**
Computer & Software Stores - **Allview Services Inc**
Computer Cable (Lan) - **Essex Group Inc. (Mfr)**
Computer Cable Assemblies— Standard - **Worswick Industries Inc**
Computer Color Graphic Displays - **Geophysical Survey Systems, Inc.**
Computer Disk Liners - **Hollingsworth & Vose Co.**
Computer Equipment, & Supplies, Export - **Alkantec, Inc.**
Computer Equipment, Electronic Parts - **Euro-tech Corporation**
Computer Graphic Design - **Graphics plus Printing, Inc.**
Computer Graphics Boards & Atm / Adsl - **Ixmicro**
Computer Graphics Cards - **Software Integrators**
Computer Hardware, Software & Accessories - **Paul Marsh, Llc**
Computer Integrated Systems Design - **Information Specialist Inc**
Computer Integrated Systems Design - **Capital Information Systems**
Computer Integrated Systems Design - **Ts-tek Inc**
Computer Keyboards (Distribution Office) - **Focus Electronic Corp**
Computer Keyboards Used for Writing- **Intelligent Peripheral Devices**
Computer Maintenance & Repair - **Micon Telecommunications Inc**

Computer Media Backup Products; Computer Tape, - **Peripherals Mfr.Inc**
Computer Networking Hardware - **Myricom Inc**
Computer Periph Digital Color Printers - **Virtual Fund.com**
Computer Periph Plain-paper Typesetter - **Virtual Fund.com**
Computer Periph., Security Devices - **Secure-it Inc. (Mfr)**
Computer Peripheral Equipment - **Digital Interface Systems Inc.**
Computer Peripheral Equipment - **Intelligent Peripheral Devices**
Computer Peripheral Equipment - **Ixmicro**
Computer Peripheral Equipment - **Maxton Security Systems**
Computer Peripheral Equipment - **Myricom Inc**
Computer Peripheral Equipment - **Software Integrators**
Computer Peripheral Equipment - **Aaa Weigh Inc**
Computer Peripheral Equipment, Nec - **Tally Printer Corporation**
Computer Peripherals & Manufacturer Of - **Pdp Systems**
Computer Peripherals - Modems, Multiplixers - **S.i. Tech, Inc.(Mfr)**
Computer Prepackaged Software - **Sunshine Unlimited, Inc.**
Computer Programming Service - **Micon Telecommunications Inc**
Computer Programming Services - **Flir Systems Inc**
Computer Programming Services - **Information Specialist Inc**
Computer Programming Services - **Opendisc Systems Inc**
Computer Programming Services - **Sunshine Unlimited, Inc.**
Computer Programming Services - **Techbase International**
Computer Programming Services - **Ts-tek Inc**
Computer Related Services - **Exergetic Systems Inc**
Computer Repair, Sales; Upgrades, Parts - **Star Enterprises Inc**
Computer Rooms, A/c - **Compu-aire, Inc.**
Computer Servers - **Howard Industries**
Computer Software to Manage an Apparel Manufacturing - **Ag Systems**
Computer Spreadsheet Towplates - **Sunshine Unlimited, Inc.**
Computer Storage Devices - **Allview Services Inc**
Computer Supplies - **Buckley Company**
Computer System Integrators - **Capital Information Systems**
Computer System Integrators; Value-added Reseller; - **Ts-tek Inc**
Computer Systems - **Sysdyne Corp.**
Computer Systems and Components, Servers - **Allview Services Inc**
Computer-aided Repair Work Stations - **Electronic Packaging Co., Inc.**
Computerized Maintenance Managment Systems - **Eagle Technology, Inc.**
Computerized Titration Equipment - **Sanda Corp.**
Computers - **I V Phoenix Group, Inc.**
Computers - **Q E I, Inc.**
Computers & Computer Peripheral Equipment - **C. Hoelzle Associates Inc.**
Computers, Desk Top (Personal) - **Howard Industries**
Computers, Manufacturer - **Computerline International**
Computers, Peripherals & Software - **Allview Services Inc**
Computers, Peripherals & Software - **Pdp Systems**
Computers, Peripherals & Software - **Academic Distributing**
Computers, Peripherals & Software - **Information Specialist Inc**
Computers, Peripherals & Software Hewlett Packard - **Hasp Inc**
Concealable and Tactical Body Armor - **Us Armor Corp**
Concentrate in Plastic & Glass - **Alljuice Food & Beverage**
Concentrated Juices - **Sunkist Growers, Inc., Processed Products Div.**
Concentrates of Essential Oils; - **Bush Boake Allen**
Concession Foodservice Equipment - **Tomlinson Industries**
Concession Stands - **Proctor Companies**
Concession Stands ,Theatre Lobby Fixtures - **Stein Industries Co.**
Concession Trailers - **Chariot Mfg. Co., Inc.**
Concrete & Mortar Fiber Reinforcements - **Durafiber Corp.**
Concrete Batching Equipment - **Stephens Mfg. Co.**
Concrete Block & Brick - **Sioux City Brick & Tile Co., Sergeant Bluff**
Concrete Burial Vaults - **Wilbert Vaults of Houston, Inc.**
Concrete Forming Systems - **Formworks Building Inc**
Concrete Fountians & Statuary - **Henri Studio Inc.**
Concrete Hardener / Sealer - **Curecrete Distribution**
Concrete Molds - **Cleco Manufacturing, Inc.**
Concrete Precast Products, Septic Tanks - **Pocatello Precast Inc**
Concrete Prod Terrazzo Shower Floors - **Stern-williams Company, Inc.**
Concrete Products - **Ro-tile**
Concrete Products - **Advantage Buildings & Exteriors, Inc.**
Concrete Products - **Durafiber Corp.**
Concrete Products - **Heldenfels Enterprises, Inc.**
Concrete Products - **J. J. Precast**

Concrete Products - **Joaquin Manufacturing Corp**
Concrete Products - **Pocatello Precast Inc**
Concrete Products - **Westile**
Concrete Products - **Wilbert Vaults of Houston, Inc.**
Concrete Products; Integrated Portable Shelters - **Joaquin Manufacturing**
Concrete Protection - **Ics Penetron International**
Concrete Protection - **Ics Penetron International Ltd.**
Concrete Pump with Placing Boom - **Schwing America, Inc.**
Concrete Pumps - **Schwing America, Inc.**
Concrete Repair - **Crossfield Products Corp**
Concrete Restoration Epoxies - **Polygem**
Concrete Resurfacing Equipment, Sheet Metal fab- **Equipment Dev.Co.**
Concrete Retaining Wall Products - **Rockwood Retaining Walls, Inc.**
Concrete Roofing Products; Concrete Tiles - **Westile**
Concrete Septic Tanks & Manholes - **J. J. Precast**
Concrete Testing Equipment - **James Instruments, Inc.**
Concrete Texturing Tools and Accessories - **Cobblecrete International Inc**
Concrete Vibrators & Finishing Equipment - **Scheu Products Co.**
Condensed Sweetened Milk - **Pafco Importing Co.**
Condenser Coils - **Super Radiator Coils**
Conduct Private Investigations, Credit & Criminal Histories - **Stablewood**
Conductive Coatings - **Inca Paint & Print**
Conductive Coatings - **Legge Co., Inc., Walter G.**
Conductive Paint - **Summit Coating Technologies, Llc**
Conductivity Monitors and Conductivity Meters - **Myron L Company**
Conduit Underground Piping - **Perma-pipe Ricwil, Industrial**
Cone Penetrometer Testing Equipment - **Art's Manufacturing & Supply**
Confectionery - **Sun Empire Foods**
Confectionery Machinery - **Waukesha Cherry-burrell (Mfr)**
Confectionery Printers - **Ackley Machine Corp.**
Confections - **Candy Express**
Confined Work Space Ventilation - **California Turbo Inc**
Coniferous Wood - **North American Wood Products, Inc.**
Coniferous Wood Sawn or Chipped Lengthwise - **Cascade Empire**
Connectivity, Structure Cabling Systems - **Wiremold Co., the**
Connectors - **Marjan, Inc.**
Connectors - **Hybrid Semiconductors/electronics Inc.**
Connectors - **Eby Co.**
Connectors & Coupling Valves - **Phillips Industries**
Connectors for Your Injection Mold Cooling System - **Jiffy Tite Co., Inc.**
Const. Dredges, New & Used, Wholesale - **A.g. Equipment, Inc.**
Const. Matls., Marble & Granite, Export - **Cma Incorporated**
Constant Force Spring Products, Spring Reels - **Walker Corporation**
Construction - **Superior Helicopter Llc.**
Construction & Agricultural Hydraulic Cylinders - **John Deere Harvester**
Construction & Mining Industry. - **Hendrix Manufacturing Co., Inc.**
Construction & Mining Machinery - **Getz Recycle Inc**
Construction & Mining Machinery - **Sirex Pulse Hydraulic Systems**
Construction & Mining Machinery - **Ani-helser**
Construction & Mining Machinery - **Schwing America, Inc.**
Construction & Mining Machinery - **Michels Machinery Co**
Construction & Mining Machinery - **Triad Machinery Inc**
Construction Bars - **Enderes Tool Company Inc**
Construction Castings - **Barry Pattern & Foundry**
Construction Epoxies - **Polygem**
Construction Equipment - **Construction Technology, Inc.**
Construction Equipment - **Patterson Equipment**
Construction Equipment - **Maxport International**
Construction Equipment & Machinery - **Pacific Cranes & Equipment**
Construction Equipment & Parts - **Sirex, Ltd.**
Construction Equipment, Amphibious - **Quality Industries, Inc.**
Construction Equipment, Used - **Crown Truck Sales**
Construction Equipment, Wholesale - **A.g. Equipment, Inc.**
Construction Machinery - **American Augers Inc.**
Construction Machinery - **Anchor Mfg. Co.**
Construction Machinery - **Equipment Development Co., Inc.**
Construction Machinery - **Euclid Hitachi Heavy Equipment**
Construction Machinery - **Getz Recycle Inc**
Construction Machinery - **Ramsey Winch Co.**
Construction Machinery - **Service International**
Construction Machinery - **Shotcrete Technologies Inc**

Construction Machinery - **Stephens Mfg. Co.**
Construction Machinery & Parts - **Interpax**
Construction Machinery Parts - **Wamco Corporation**
Construction Machinery and Equipment - **Getz Recycle Inc**
Construction Machinery, Counterweights - **Olympic Foundry Inc**
Construction Material, Doors, Windows - **Intramar, Inc.**
Construction Materials - **Border States Electric Supply**
Construction Materials & Equipment - **Border Products Corp**
Construction Services, Utility Lines - **Everett J. Prescott**
Construction Trailers - **S O N Corp.**
Construction Winches - **Maasdam Pow'r-pull Inc.**
Construction and Mining Machinery - **Global Parts & Equipment**
Construction and Mining Machinery - **Hoss Equipment**
Construction and Mining Machinery - **Michels Machinery Co**
Construction and Mining Machinery - **Multiquip**
Construction and Mining Machinery - **Nationwide Equipment**
Construction of Communication Sites - **Gem Engineering Co., Inc.**
Consultant Engineering & Production - **Anderson Seal Co., Inc.**
Consultants: Automation - **Bmi Automation, Inc.**
Consulting - World Shrimp Market - **Shrimp World Inc.**
Consulting Services., Cultural Diversity - **Intercultural Development**
Consulting Svcs., Foreign Trade - **Cacheaux, Cavazos, Newton, Martin**
Consulting for New Products - **Agro-mar Inc of Nevada**
Consulting, Sales, Service and Support - **Omnimark Instrument Corp**
Consumer Electronic Stop Light That Signals Whe - **Metron Solutions Inc**
Consumer Electronics - **Televentas**
Consumer Electronics & Computer Accessories - **Allsop, Inc.**
Consumer Products - **Relaxor / Jb Research Inc**
Consumer Products: All Packaged Consumer Goods - **Atwood Richards**
Contact Lenses - **Benz Research & Development Corp.**
Contact Lenses - **Westcon Contact Lens Company Inc**
Contact Lenses, Export - **Medcorp International**
Contact and Intraocular Lens Lathes, Drills - **Dac International, Inc.**
Container Cargo - **ADRA International**
Container Cargo - **Bandiera Winery**
Container Cargo - **Hardwood Veneer**
Container Cargo - **Nova Grass**
Container Cargo - **Philadelphia Resins**
Container Cargo - **Sheftel International**
Container Cargo - **Watersaver International**
Container Crane Movement - **Bigge Crane & Rigging Co.**
Container Freight Station - **Apollo Warehouse, Inc.**
Container Freight Station - **Bart Trucking**
Container Freight Station - **Penn Terminals Inc.**
Container Handeler Mach. & Forklift - **Pacific Cranes & Equipment Sales**
Container Repairs - **Penn Terminals Inc.**
Containers - **United States Can Company, Custom & Specialty**
Containers Specially Designed and Equipped. - **Packaging Center, Inc.**
Containers Specially Designed and Equipped - **Gilman Brothers**
Containers for Molds - **Quality Mold Inc.**
Containers_wood - **Wildwood Farms, Inc.**
Containers_wood - **Advanced Package Engineering Inc**
Continuous Belt & Industrial Furnace - **Sinterite, Furance Div.**
Continuous Emissions Monitoring Sys. - **Air Instruments & Meas. Inc.**
Contourable Indoor Putting Greens - **Duffy Golf, Inc.**
Contract Assembly - **Conectec R F, Inc.**
Contract Carrier - **Van's Delivery Service, Inc.**
Contract Electronic Assembly - **B Q Products Inc.**
Contract Electronics Manufacturer, Electronics Assembly - **The Dii Group**
Contract Inspection Services Parts, Machines - **Precision Measurement**
Contract Machining - **Senga Engineering Inc**
Contract Manufacturer of Abrasive Specialties; Imprinting - **Realys Inc**
Contract Manufacturing - **Midland Bioproducts Corp.**
Contract Manufacturing - **Lamaur**
Contract Manufacturing - **Mc Clarin Plastics, Inc.**
Contract Manufacturing - **Litec Inc.**
Contract Manufacturing - **Custom Assembly**
Contract Manufacturing - **Mid-south Electronics-alabama, Inc.**
Contract Manufacturing & Sewing - **Covers Unlimited, Inc.**
Contract Manufacturing, Electronics; Plastic - **Five Rivers Electronic Invo**
Contract Packaging - **Treatment Products Ltd.**

Contract Packaging - **Hope Industries**
Contract Packaging - **Dri-rite Co.**
Contract Packaging & Mfr.. Personal Care Products - **Classic Lady Packag**
Contract Packaging for Labor Oriented - **Brooklyn Bow International**
Contract Packaging of Surgical & Medical Instruments - **J-pac Corp.**
Contract Packaging, Plastic Thermoforming - **J-pac Corp.**
Contract Packaging, Private Label Mfr. - **Columbia Cosmetics Mfr., Inc.**
Contract Pharmaceutical Manufacturers - **Sp Pharmaceuticals Llc**
Contract Plastic Sealing Services - **Malo & Weste Corp.**
Contract Upholstery & Panel Fabrics - **Absecon Mills, Inc.**
Contracted Vegetable Production for Seed - **Western Hybrid Seeds, Inc.**
Control Panels & Rebuilt Motors - **Schulz Electric Co.**
Control Systems Integration - **Factory Automation Systems, Inc.**
Controlled Environment, Agriculture - **Aquacare Environment Inc**
Controllers for over 35 Years - **Glentek Inc**
Controllers, Temperature - **Artisan Controls Corporation (Mfr)**
Controls - **Arrowhead Systems Llc**
Controls for Motors - **Precision Motion Controls**
Convention Bureau Construction Equip. - **Conexpo-con Agg Exposition**
Conversion Brakets - Breakaway - **National Electric Gate Co.**
Conversion, Lamination , Tolerance Die Cutting - **Lockwood Industries**
Converted Paper Products - **Book Covers Inc**
Converted Paper Products - **American Scholar Co.**
Converted Paper Products - **Blue Atlantic, Ltd.**
Converted Paper Products - **Roselle Paper Co., Inc.**
Converted Paper Products - **Savage Universal Corporation**
Converted Paper Products - **Sunshine Paper Company**
Converted Paper Products - **Outlook Graphics**
Converted Paper Products - **L H B Industries**
Converted Paper Products - Slitting & Rewinding - **Newark Group, Inc.**
Converted Paper Rools for Pos & Large Format Systems, - **Rittenhouse Co**
Converted Paper, Export - **B&g Export Management Associates**
Convertible Sofas - **Kingsdown, Inc.**
Converts Paper and Paperboard Products - **Savage Universal Corporation**
Conveyor Belt Motion Switch, 2 Channel - **Pyott-boone Electronics**
Conveyor Belt Motion Switch, 3 Channel - **Pyott-boone Electronics**
Conveyor Belting - **Fabreeka International Inc**
Conveyor Belts - **Burrell Leder Beltech, Inc.**
Conveyor Components - **Conveyors Solutions, Inc.**
Conveyor Rollers - **Richard Industries, J.**
Conveyor Rolls Manufacturing - **Thistle Roller Co Inc**
Conveyor Systems - **Quantum Conveyor Systems, Llc**
Conveyorized Spray Washers - **Industrial Process Equipment**
Conveyors - **Arrowhead Systems Llc**
Conveyors - **Busse Inc. (Mfr)**
Conveyors - **Pioneer Conveyors Inc**
Conveyors - **International Baler Corp.**
Conveyors - **Vogler Equipment**
Conveyors & Bucket Elevators - **Nedco Conveyor Technology Corp.**
Conveyors & Conveying , Surge, - **Rbm Manufacturing Co., Inc.**
Conveyors & Conveying Equipment - **Burrell Leder Beltech, Inc.**
Conveyors & Conveying Equipment - **Arrowhead Systems Llc**
Conveyors & Conveying Equipment - **Conveyors Solutions, Inc.**
Conveyors & Conveying Equipment - **Flexicon Corporation**
Conveyors & Conveying Equipment - **Interroll Corp.**
Conveyors & Conveying Equipment - **J D B Dense Flow, Inc.**
Conveyors & Conveying Equipment - **Le Fiell Company**
Conveyors & Conveying Equipment - **Pioneer Conveyors Inc**
Conveyors & Conveying Equipment - **Quantum Conveyor Systems, Llc**
Conveyors & Conveying Equipment - **Renmark-pacific Inc**
Conveyors & Conveying Equipment - **Smoot Co.**
Conveyors & Conveying Equipment - **Specialty Equipment Co.**
Conveyors & Conveying Equipment - **Vac-u-max (Mfr)**
Conveyors & Conveying Equipment - **Chicago Conveyor Corp.**
Conveyors & Conveying Equipment (Pneumatic) - **Sterling Blower Co.**
Conveyors & Equipment - **Northeast Fabricators, L.l.c.**
Conveyors & Other Material Handling Equipment - **Renmark Pacific Corp**
Convyor Blet Motion Switch, 2 Channel - **Pyott-boone Electronics**
Cook-in-bags from -75 Deg. To 490 Deg. - **Hutchison & Co.**
Cooked Shrimp - **Dorado Seafood Inc**
Cookie Flavors & Canor Flavors - **Sto-chard**

Cookies & Crackers - **Bay Area Biscotti Co**
Cookies & Crackers - **Cookies for You, Inc.**
Cookies & Crackers - **Dfp International Inc**
Cooking Equipment, Electric Gas - **Broaster Co., the**
Cooking Equipment, Parts & Accessories - **Alto-shaam, Inc.**
Cooking Products - **Maytag International**
Cooling Coils - **Super Radiator Coils**
Cooling Fans - **Mg Electronics**
Cooling Towers & Heat Exchangers - **Baltimore Aircoil Co., Inc.**
Cooling Water Treatment - **Ashland Chemicals**
Copier Parts & Supplies - **Richard Boas**
Copiers - **Minolta Corporation**
Copiers - **Richard Boas**
Copper & Brass - **Sos Metals, Inc.**
Copper Foundries - **Advance Aluminum & Brass Inc**
Copper Foundries - **Quality Brass & Aluminum Foundry**
Copper Foundries - **Unexcelled Castings Corp.**
Copper Hydroxide - **Agtrol International**
Copper Rod & Wire - **Nippert Co., the**
Copper Rolling & Drawing - Strip, Profiles Shapes - **Nippert Co., the**
Copper Rolling and Drawing - **National Copper Products**
Copper Scrap - **Los Angeles Scrap Iron & Metal**
Copper, Brass, Nickel, Lead, Tin-lead, Tin - **Univertical Corporation**
Copper, Nickel & Tin Based Chemicals for Plating - **Univertical Corp.**
Copper, Tin & Tin Alloys - **Delta Precision Alloys**
Copper/tungsten Heatsinks - **Brush Wellman Inc. Ceramics Div.**
Coputer Peripheral Equipment & Accessories - **Allsop, Inc.**
Cord Sets, Cord Assemblies, Wire Harnesses - **Pacific Electricord Co.**
Cord Welt - **Spradling Originals Inc.**
Cordage & Rope Machinery, Export - **Commision Brokers, Inc.**
Cordage & Twine - **S-line**
Cordage & Twine - **Pelican Rope Works**
Cordage & Twine - **Winchester Auburn Mills, Inc**
Corn - **Delta International**
Corn , Other than Seed Corn - **Zen Noh Grain**
Corn , Other than Seed Corn - **Garnac Grain**
Corn , Other than Seed Corn - **Sew Feiel**
Corn Chips, Cheese Curls, Tortila Chips - **Keystone Food Products Inc.**
Corn Gluten Meal - **Grain Processing Corporation (Mfr)**
Corn Oil - **Basic Foods International, Inc.**
Corn Starch - **Grain Processing Corporation (Mfr)**
Corn Starch and Other Food Ingredients - **Colorado Sweet Gold Llc**
Corn Syrup Solids - **Grain Processing Corporation (Mfr)**
Corn Tortillas & Corn Tortilla Chips - **Fresca Mexican Foods Inc.**
Corn, Blue Yellow & White - Organic - **Henderson Mills Inc.**
Corn-based & Extruded Snack Foods, Popcorn - **Keystone Food Products**
Cornmeal - **Molinos De Puerto Rico, Inc., a Conagra Company**
Corporate Design Neckwear - **Duron Neckwear Inc**
Corporate Identity Packages, Pricelists - **Congdon Printing & Imaging**
Corporate Jet Aircraft - **Gulfstream Aerospace Corp.**
Corrosion Inhibitors - **Miller Corp., Harry**
Corrosion Resist Thermoplastic Valves - **Pacific Plastics**
Corrosion-resistant Coatings - **Columbus Galvanizing Voigt & Schweitz**
Corrosive Resistant Protective Coatings; Dupont Tefzel - **Americoat Corp.**
Corrugated & Chipboard Partitions & Pads - **Innerpac Southwest, Inc.**
Corrugated & Foam Packs - **Future Packaging Inc**
Corrugated Boxes - **Hemisphere Enterprises**
Corrugated Cartons - **Forest Packaging Corp.**
Corrugated Service - **Thistle Roller Co Inc**
Corrugated and Solid Fiber Boxes - **Tucson Container Corporation**
Corrugated boxes, pads and crates - **Whitmark Inc**
Corrugated- Rotary Die Cutter Blankets - **C.u.e., Inc. (Mfr)**
Cosmetic - **Captek Softgel International**
Cosmetic & Medical Brushes, Plastic Injection - **M & E Mfg. Co.**
Cosmetic & Personal Care Products - **Lexard Corporation**
Cosmetic (Lacquer, Lamination) - **Technical Coating International**
Cosmetic Accessories - **Stylebuilt Accessories, Inc.**
Cosmetic Dyes - **Tricon Colors, Llc**
Cosmetic Pencils - **General Pencil Co.**
Cosmetic Raw Materials, Aloe Vera - **Terry Laboratories, Inc.**
Cosmetics - **Classic Cosmetics Inc**

Cosmetics - **Cosmetic Specialty Labs, Inc.**
Cosmetics - **J Hewitt Inc**
Cosmetics - **The John Wesley Group**
Cosmetics & Pharmaceuticals - **Harmony Laboratories, Inc.**
Cosmetics and Hair Care Products - **Sahara Springs Cosmetics**
Cosmetics and Toilet Preparations; Skin Care - **Bioelements Inc**
Cosmetics, Export - **Amos Import/export Management Co.**
Cosmetics, Health & Beauty - **Foreign Trade Marketing**
Cosmetics, Wholesale - **J Hewitt Inc**
Cost Estimating Software - **Richardson Engineering Svcs Inc**
Costume & Karat Gold Jewelry - **Uncas Mfg. Company (Mfr)**
Costume Jewelry, Exc. Prec. Metal or Stones - **J Hewitt Inc**
Costume Jewelry, Novelties and Ornaments - **Future Primitive Designs**
Costumes & Mascots - **Facemakers Inc.**
Cots - **Mahar**
Cotton Batting - **K. G. Fiber, Inc.**
Cotton Candy, Chocolate Items, Snacks - **Otec, Inc.**
Cotton Denims All Weights - **Pride International**
Cotton Fabric - **General Fabrics**
Cotton Gauze Lemon Covers, Foodservice - **Royal Enterprises, Inc.**
Cotton Gin Machinery / Systems - **Continental Eagle**
Cotton Gin, Replace Parts - **Continental Eagle**
Cotton Pharmaceutical Coil, Packaging - **Barnhardt Manufacturing Co.**
Cotton Printed Fabric for the Quilter & Crafter - **General Fabrics**
Cotton Twills - **Pride International**
Cotton Work Gloves - **Mcgough Industries Inc**
Cotton Yarn Nu85%cot No Retail - **Glassmaster**
Cotton Yarns, Open-end - **Cheraw Yarn Mills Inc.**
Cotton, Poly / Cotton, Synthetic - **Us Dyeing & Finishing Inc**
Cottoners - **Njm/cli Packaging Systems International**
Cottonseed Delint / Decorticate - **Continental Eagle**
Cottonseed Delinting - Acid - **Continental Eagle**
Cough Drops - **Unico, Inc.**
Counter Top Water Filters - **Springsoft International Inc.**
Counter Tops - **Kraft Masters Cabinets**
Counter Weight Systems - **General Drapery Services, Inc.**
Countertop Water Filters - **Aqua Power Co.**
Countertop Water Filters - **Aquapower Co.**
Countertops, Furniture & Cabinet Doors - **Moultrie Post Form, Inc.**
Couplers, Compaction Wheels - **Hendrix Manufacturing Co., Inc.**
Couplings - **Foster Co., L. B.**
Coveralls, Lab Coats, Frocks & Hoods - **Fibrotek Industries Inc**
Crab Traps - **Fathoms plus**
Cracked Tube Ice-machines - **Global Leasing & Sales, Inc.**
Craft Supplies - **Art Institute Glitter**
Craft Supplies - **Pressner & Co., Inc., M.**
Craft-plastic Canvas, Yarns, & Cards - **Uniek Inc.**
Crane & Hoist Parts - **Progressive Crane, Inc.**
Crane Handling - **Vanco Heavy Lift C.f.s.**
Crane Rental - **Bigge Crane & Rigging Co.**
Cranes - **Laidig Industrial System**
Cranes - **Progressive Crane, Inc.**
Cranes - **Pacific Cranes & Equipment Sales**
Cranes, Crane Bodies & Air Compressors - **Auto Crane Co.**
Craneway Doors - **Fleming Steel Co.**
Crankshaft Grinding In-situ and in Bench. - **Golten Service**
Crash and Restoration Body Parts for European - **Tasker Metal Products**
Crawler Tractors - **Hoss Equipment**
Cream - **Afassco, Inc.**
Create Your Own Tool Rack On-line; - **Kovil Manufacturing Llc**
Creates and Sells Custom Low Temperature - **A-live Foods**
Crematories - **Simonds Mfg. Corp.**
Crew Agency Representative - **Globe Shipping, Globe Ship Managment**
Critical Care Ventilators - **Sensormedics Corporation**
Critical Medical Compounds - **Foster Corp.**
Crop Preparation Services for Market - **Hilltop Ranch**
Cross Cultural Management Seminar - **Language plus**
Crossborder Marketing Services Company - **L.a. Markom De Mexico, S.A**
Crts Cpus - **Lighting Resources, Inc.**
Crushed Stone - **Franklin Industrial Minerals**
Crushed Stone - **Iron Mountain Trap Rock Co.**

Crushers and Crusher Replacement Parts - **Ani-helser**
Cryogenic Pumps - **Barber-nichols Incorporated**
Crystal - **Trophy Shoppe**
Crystallizers - **Dedert Corp.**
Cucumbers Including Gherkins - **Steinfelds Products**
Cultivates, Dries and Packages Dried Herbs - **Montana Aromatics**
Cummins 855 Replacement Parts - **Pai Industries Inc. (Mfr)**
Cupack Power Rf Packages - **Brush Wellman Inc. Ceramics Div.**
Curcifixes, Church Items, Bibles & Gifts - **Rosary House, Inc.**
Cured in Place Pipelining Kits - **L M K Enterprises, Inc.**
Curing Compounds, Hardeners, Toppingss - **Anti Hydro International**
Curing Tubes - **Myers Industries, Inc., Myers Tire Supply Div.**
Currency & Coin Counting, Wrapping, Sorting - **De La Rue Cash Systems**
Current-carrying Wiring Devices - **Elcon Products International**
Current-carrying Wiring Devices - **Charles E Gillman Company**
Current-carrying Wiring Devices - **Gould Shawmut**
Current-carrying Wiring Devices - **Lyncole Xit Grounding**
Current-carrying Wiring Devices - **National Standard Parts Assocs. Inc.**
Current-carrying Wiring Devices - **Oak Grigsby, Inc.**
Current-carrying Wiring Devices - **Pacific Electricord Company**
Current-carrying Wiring Devices - **Rochester Corp., the**
Current-carrying Wiring Devices - **Superior Grounding Systems**
Curtains & Draperies - **Dezign Sewing Inc.**
Curtains & Draperies - **Kay & L Draperies, Inc.**
Curtains & Draperies - **Sultan & Sons, Inc.**
Curtains & Draperies - **Milford Stitching Co., Inc.**
Curtains; Industrial - **Goff's Curtain Walls/goff's Enterprises Inc.**
Curved Metal & Wood Ceilings - **Ceilings plus Inc**
Custom / Toll Blending - **Petroferm Inc.**
Custom Brokerage - **Euro-american Air Frt. Fwdg Co., Inc.**
Custom Brokerage - **Nippon Express Usa, Inc.**
Custom Built Pet Wood Caskets - **Tower Stool Company**
Custom Canning Available - **Dale's Wild West Products**
Custom Canvas Work, Tarpaulins, Truck Covers, Straps - **Canvas Specialty**
Custom Casework and Store Fixtures - **Benchmark Fixture Corporation**
Custom Cedar Homes, Solid Cedar Homes - **Lindal Cedar Homes**
Custom Components for Medical Device- **Modified Polymer Components**
Custom Compound Purchased Resins - **Foster Corp.**
Custom Compound Thermoplastics - **L N P Engineering Plastics, Inc.**
Custom Computer System Integration; Fuel Pumps - **Gasboy Int'l, Inc.**
Custom Control Panels - **Kirby Risk Service Center**
Custom Control Panels & Buildings - **P C & E, Fabcon Div.**
Custom Control Panels - Ul Listed - **Therm Tech Inc.**
Custom Controls for Electrical Systems - **Pritchard Brown**
Custom Design, Engineering and Fab.of Bulk - **Rbm Manufacturing Co.**
Custom Designed Cedar Home Kits - **Pan Abode Cedar Homes, Inc.**
Custom Designed Industrial Machines - **Industrial Design Fabrication**
Custom Designs - **Toepperweins of Texas**
Custom Die Cutting - **Diemasters, Inc.**
Custom Engineered Seals - **Anderson Seal Co., Inc.**
Custom Extruded Aluminum Shapes, Electrical - **Vaw of America Inc**
Custom Eyelets, Drawn Metal Consulting. - **Progressive Metal Forming**
Custom Fabrication - **Snyder Equipment Co., Inc.**
Custom Fiberglass & Abs Parts - **Spalding Products**
Custom Fiberglass Parts - **Tenessee Fiberglass Productc, Inc.**
Custom Formulation & Mfr. of Phyto-aromatherapy - **Herba Aromatica**
Custom Goldsmith Services - **Gary Stull Goldsmith**
Custom Hand-crafted Buckles - **Frontier Trophy Buckles**
Custom Harness Assemblies - **Electronic Manufacturing Svc**
Custom Homes & Sunrooms - **Greco Homes**
Custom Injection Molding and Plastic Parts - **Vaupell Industrial Plastics**
Custom Jewelry - **House of Fashion Jewelry**
Custom Kitchen Cabinets & Bathroom Vanities - **Fowler Cabinet & Hard**
Custom Labels - **Arrow Creative International, Ltd.**
Custom Log Homes - **Yeager Sawmill**
Custom Manufacturer of Switchgear, Panels - **Electric City Corp.**
Custom Manufacturing - **Accents in Sterling Inc**
Custom Manufacturing of Plastic Products - **J-pac Corp.**
Custom Map Publisher - **Barclay Maps**
Custom Medical Animation - **Visible Productions Llc**
Custom Medical Apparel / Accessories - **Trademark Medical**

Custom Medical Illustration - **Visible Productions Llc**
Custom Microwave Circuit Devices - **Diablo Industries**
Custom Millwork - **Tucker Millworks, Inc.**
Custom Molded, Extruded, Calendared - **Kirkhill Rubber Co**
Custom Neighborhood Electric Vehicles & - **Elmco, Inc.**
Custom Optoelectronic Assemblies - **Silicon Sensors, Llc**
Custom Packaging - **Aero Tech Labs, Inc.**
Custom Plastic Injection Molding - **Hh Ele Corporation**
Custom Printed Pressure Sensitive Labels - **Holman Label Company**
Custom Rubber Molding - **Maloney Technical Product, Inc.**
Custom Rubber & Plastics Mixing - **M. A. Hanna Rubber Compounding**
Custom Sheet Metal Fabrication; Heat Processing - **Ship & Shore a**
Custom Shelters for Electro-mechanical Systems - **Pritchard Brown**
Custom Shims, Stampings and Fillers - **Bolsan West Inc**
Custom Silver-plated Buckles - **Tres Rios Silver**
Custom Sound Shields for Generators - **Great Southern Insulation Corp.**
Custom Trailers - **Pritchard Brown**
Custom Upholstered Furniture for Restaurants - **Denver Seating Inc**
Custom Van and Rv Conversions - **Trail Wagons Inc**
Custom Wedding Invitations; Commercial - **Artco**
Custom Whirlpool Bathing Tubs & Pools - **Six-eleven Ltd Inc**
Custom Window Treatments & Design - **Vertical Express**
Custom Wood Doors - **Executive Door Company**
Custom Wood Frames; Hand Blown Glass; Candles - **Colorado Frame Co.**
Custom, Sundroe, Napkin, Vending Machines - **C & G Manufacturing**
Customer Information Management Specialists - **Cap Gemini America**
Customer Service Training - **Service Quality Institute**
Customhouse Broker - **Cbc International, Inc.**
Customhouse Broker - **Chase Leavitt & Company**
Customhouse Broker - **Delgado R. E. Inc.**
Customized Language Courses - **Language plus**
Customized Scientific High Vacuum Equipt - **Hawe Technical Associates**
Customized Scientific Ultra High Vac. Equipment - **Hta**
Customs Bonds - **Roanoke Brokerage Services, Inc.**
Customs Broker - **Airgroup Express/airgroup Corporation**
Customs Broker - **Argents Express Group**
Customs Broker - **Burlington Air Express Inc.**
Customs Broker - **Campbell & Gardiner, Inc.**
Customs Broker - **Carmenco International**
Customs Broker - **Chantilly Freight Corporation**
Customs Broker - **Commercial International Forwarding Inc.**
Customs Broker - **Corcoran International Corp.**
Customs Broker - **Coughlin Logistics**
Customs Broker - **Dan Transport Corporation**
Customs Broker - **Danzas Corporation**
Customs Broker - **Ferrer Brokers, Inc.**
Customs Broker - **Fpa Customs Brokers, Inc.**
Customs Broker - **Hanlon International**
Customs Broker - **Held & Associates, Inc.**
Customs Broker - **Hendrix, Miles, Hendrix Company**
Customs Broker - **Incare Cargo Services**
Customs Broker - **Inter-jet Systems, Inc.**
Customs Broker - **Inter-world Customs Broker Inc.**
Customs Broker - **Inter-world Customs Broker, Inc.**
Customs Broker - **Interfreight Inc.**
Customs Broker - **Jensen, Norman G., Inc.**
Customs Broker - **Jet Air Service, Inc.**
Customs Broker - **Jet Import Brokers**
Customs Broker - **K & K Express**
Customs Broker - **Keen, R. H. & Co., Inc.**
Customs Broker - **Krieger, Norman, Inc.**
Customs Broker - **L. D. Tonsager & Sons, Inc.**
Customs Broker - **Labelle Rothery Movers, Inc.**
Customs Broker - **Lazer Transportation Services**
Customs Broker - **Mcclary, Swift & Co., Inc.**
Customs Broker - **Norman G. Jensen**
Customs Broker - **Ortiz Villafane, Rene, Inc.**
Customs Broker - **Rapid Air & Ocean**
Customs Broker - **Rausch, Ted L. Co., the**
Customs Broker - **Respond Cargo Services Corp.**
Customs Broker - **Robinson H.w. & Company Inc.**

Customs Broker - **Rogers & Brown Custom Brokers, Inc.**
Customs Broker - **Rosy Services Forwarders Corp.**
Customs Broker - **Schenker International, Inc.**
Customs Broker - **Senderex Cargo Co., Inc.**
Customs Broker - **Torner International, Inc. / Edmundo Torner, Chb**
Customs Broker - **Torner, Edmundo Customhouse Brokers**
Customs Broker - **Transoceanic Shipping Company, Inc.**
Customs Broker - **World Commerce Forwarding, Inc.**
Customs Broker - **Worldlink Logistics, Inc.**
Customs Broker - **Wts of Houston, Inc.**
Customs Broker & Freight Forwarder - **Dartrans, Inc.**
Customs Broker, Freight Forwarder - **Moran, J. F. Co., Inc.**
Customs Broker, Freight Forwarding - **Brown Alcantar & Brown Inc.**
Customs Brokers - **Fritz Companies**
Customshouse Broker - **Seamodal Transport Corp.**
Cut & Installation of Stone Products - **Marbledge, Inc.**
Cut & Stone Products - **Best Sand Corp.**
Cut Stone & Stone Products - **Franklin Industrial Minerals**
Cut Stone & Stone Products - **Iron Mountain Trap Rock Co.**
Cut Stone & Stone Products - **J.r. Mcdade Marble & Granite**
Cut Stone & Stone Products - **Payton Granite & Monument Co.**
Cut Stone & Stone Products - **Penn Big Bed Slate Co., Inc.**
Cut Stone & Stone Products - **Petrified Wood Co**
Cut Stone & Stone Products - **Rowat Cut Stone & Marble Co.**
Cut Stone & Stone Products - **Titon Industries, Inc.**
Cut Stone & Stone Products, Stucco Materials - **Midwest Builders Supply,**
Cuticle Condition for Nails - **Shelton's Sheen Wave Labs Inc**
Cutting Private Label Vitamins, Herbs & Nutr - **Northridge Laboratories**
Cutting Tools - **Pro Tool & Design, Inc.**
Cutting Tools - **Vanguard Tool Corp.**
Cutting Tools - Special - **Midwest Ohio Tool Company**
Cutting Tools Twist Drills Reamers - **Greenfield Industries**
Cutting Tools for the Woodworking Industry - **Lrh Enterprises Inc**
Cutting Tools, Inserts & Safety Equipment - **Cutting Edge Tool Supply**
Cyanide Based Chemicals for Plating - **Univertical Corporation**
Cyclic Crudes & Intermediates - **Nacco Grow More**
Cyclohexane - **Sunoco, Inc.**
Cyclone Collectors - **Marsulex Environmental Technologies Llc**
Cylinder Handling Equipment - **Daetwyler Corp., Max**
Cylinders - **Richard Boas**
Cylinders Rebuilt & Testing - **Service Hydraulics Inc.**
Cypress Lumber - **S.g. International**
Dac Surfacing System for Spectacle Lens - **Dac International, Inc.**
Dairy & Food Processing Equipment - **International Dairy Equipt Assoc.**
Dairy - Related Products - **Galaxy Foods, Inc.**
Dairy Calf Diagnostic Kits - **Midland Bioproducts Corp.**
Dairy Farm Chemicals - **West Agro, Inc.**
Dairy Farm Equipment - **Universal Dairy Equipment**
Dairy Farm Processors - **West Agro, Inc.**
Dairy Milling Equipment - **Coburn Company, Inc.**
Dairy Products - **Galaxy Foods, Inc.**
Dairy Products Machinery & Equipment - **Waukesha Cherry-burrell**
Dairy Products, Except Canned - **International Custom Products**
Dairy Products, Except Dried or Canned - **Marquis Distributing Co**
Dairy Products; Persian Foods - **Shemshad Food Products Inc**
Dairy Seasonings - **Old World Spices & Seasonings, Inc.**
Dairy and Bakery Products - **Marquis Distributing Co**
Dama Scpc Networks - **Vortex Satcom Systems, Inc.**
Dance Apparel & Recital Costumes - **Star Styled Dancing Supplies**
Dance Taps to Specification - **Amc Products, Ltd.**
Dance Wear - **Hannah Katherine Fashions Corp.**
Danskin Cyclewear / Women's Cyclewear - **Canari Cycle Wear**
Data Acquisition Systems & Signal Detectors - **Digital Interface Systems**
Data Collection Systems - **Accu-time Systems**
Data Communication Products for Internet - **Digital Link Corp**
Data Communication Services - **Black Box Corporation**
Data Conversion, Cadastrol Maps (Parcels, Etc) - **Barclay Maps**
Data Gathering & Machine Control Solutions - **Raines Technologies Inc**
Datacomm Equipment - Multiplexers - **Dne Technologies Inc.**
Dates Medjool Variety - **Dulin Date Gardens**
Dc Drives; Wholesales Electronic Parts - **Elmagco Corp**

Dc Power Supplies - **Acme Electric Corp., Power Distribution Products**
Dc to Ac Inverters and Inverter/battery Charger - **Trace Engineering Co**
Dealer / Remarketer Atm's, Banking Equipment - **Atm Exchange, Inc, the**
Dealers by Special Categories of Equipment. - **Used Equipment Directory**
Deaterium Sources - **Spectral Energy Corp.**
Deburring Services - **Barsallo Deburring**
Deburring Tools, One Pass - **Cogsdill Tool Products Inc. (Mfr)**
Decals & Labels - **Sign Connection**
Decals & Lettering - **High Country Proco**
Deck Components, Trellis & Lawn Edging - **Burton Woodworks Inc.**
Decopaper & Vaneer - **International Components Plus, Inc.**
Decorated Tins - **United States Can Company, Custom & Specialty**
Decorations, Flavors, Edible Image Base - **Lucks Food Decorating Co.**
Decorations, Flavors, Edible Image Base - **The Lucks Food Equipment**
Decorative Accessories - **Stylebuilt Accessories, Inc.**
Decorative Cans & Tins - **U. S. Can Co., Custom & Specialty Division**
Decorative Colonial & Southwest Designs - **Acorn Manufacturing Co.,**
Decorative Hand Carved Birds - **Painted Bird**
Decorative Hardware - **Youngdale Manufacturing Corp**
Decorative Hardwood Veneers - **Keystone Veneers, Inc.**
Decorative Laminates ,Industrial Laminates - **Pioneer Plastics Corp.**
Decorative Lighting - **W O L I C, Inc.**
Decorative Polyurethane Wall Mirrors - **Alfred's Pictures Frames Inc**
Decorative Polyurethane Wall Shelves, Corbels - **Alfred's Pictures Frames**
Decorative Soap & Candles - **Lasting Impressions Soaps**
Decoupling Capacitors - **Circuit Components, Inc.**
Deep Cycle Battery Chargers - **Lester Electrical of Nebraska, Inc.**
Deep Draw Stamping Products - **Eastern Carbide Tool Co. Llc.**
Deep Drawn Metal Products - **Technology General Corp.**
Deep Drawn Stampings, Door Knobs, Brass Bed - **Tubing Seal Cap**
Deep Drawn Stampings. - **Progressive Metal Forming Inc.**
Deepwater Floats & Marker Buoys - **Lane-merritt Float Co**
Deer Repellent - **Deer-off, Inc.**
Defatted Wheat Germ - **Research Products Co.**
Defoamers - **Burlington Chemical Co., Inc. (Mfr)**
Defoamers - **Geo Specialty Chemicals, Inc.**
Dehumidifiers - **Oasis Corporation**
Dehumidifiers & Desiccant Wheels - **Advanced Thermal Technologies**
Dehydrated Alfalfa Products - **Ohio Blenders**
Dehydrated Fruits, Vegetables & Soups - **A-live Foods**
Dehydrated Fruits, Vegetables & Soups - **Aunt Rita's, Inc.**
Dehydrated Fruits, Vegetables & Soups - **Frontier Soups**
Dehydrated Garlic, Onion, Parsley - **De Francesco & Sons Inc**
Dehydrated Mexican Food Mixes - **Aunt Rita's, Inc.**
Dehydrated Onion - **Ingredient Resources, Inc.**
Dehydrated Potato Flakes & Flour - **Oregon Potato**
Dehydrated Soups - **Frontier Soups**
Dehydrated Vegetables - **De Francesco & Sons Inc**
Dehydrofrozen Diced Potatoes - **Oregon Potato**
Dehyrdrated Onion & Garlic - **Accurate Ingredients**
Deli Items - Only in Kosher - **Agri Processors**
Delicatessen & Deli Products - **Giuliano-pagano Corp**
Demagnetizers - over 100 Models. - **R.b. Annis Company, Inc.**
Densified Hardwood Pellet Fuel - **Hamer, Jim C.**
Density Measuring Eqpt. - **Cargille Laboratories, Inc.**
Dent Removal Systems and Other Related Body - **Usdm Inc**
Dental & Industrial - **Oryan Industries Inc**
Dental Cabinets - **Royal Dental Manufacturing Co.**
Dental Chairs - **Royal Dental Manufacturing Co.**
Dental Delivery Units - **Royal Dental Manufacturing Co.**
Dental Disposables - **Barnhardt Manufacturing Co.**
Dental Equipment - **Becker-Parkin Dental Supply Co., Inc.**
Dental Equipment & Supplies - **Cuda Products Corp.**
Dental Equipment & Supplies - **Beere Precision Medical Instruments**
Dental Equipment & Supplies - **Dentsply International Inc.**
Dental Equipment & Supplies - **Teledyne Water Pik**
Dental Equipment & Supplies - **Tp Orthodontics Inc**
Dental Instruments, Equipment and Supplies, - **Dentech Corporation**
Dental Instruments, Materials - **South American Dental Exports**
Dental Lab, Scientific Lab & Jewelry Mfg. - **Ney Dental, Inc.**
Dental Laboratory Materials & Eqpt. - **Cmp Industries, Inc.**

Dental Lights - **Royal Dental Manufacturing Co.**
Dental Products, Nitrous Oxide - **Porter Instrument Co.**
Dental Products, Steam Sterilizers - **Porter Instrument Co.**
Dental Prosthetics, Laboratory Products - **Dentsply International Inc.**
Dental Sciences, Wholesale Quantities - **South American Dental Exports**
Dental Stools - **Royal Dental Manufacturing Co.**
Dental Supplies - **Becker-Parkin Dental Supply Co., Inc.**
Denture Cleansers & Adhesives - **Regent Labs Inc.**
Deodorants, Carpet & Fabric - **Steam Services Inc.**
Deodorizing, Disinfecting Cleaner - **Lucas Products Corp.**
Depalletizers - **Alvey, Inc.**
Depilatories and Other Perfumery, Cosmetic - **Hollywood**
Depolymerized Natural, Synthetic - **Elementis Performance Polymers**
Depository Banking, Letters of Credit - **First Security Bank**
Derricks, Cranes - **Service International**
Desalination Treatment Systems - **Water Services International**
Desert Coolers - **Phoenix Manufacturing Inc**
Desiccant & Humidity Indicator Cards - **Caltex Plastics Inc**
Desiccants - **Parts Services International Llc**
Design & Automation - **Van Thomas Inc. / Ruggeri Mfg.**
Design & Bld. Automated Equipment - **Dyer Tool & Die, Inc.**
Design & Manufacture Precision Rotary Switches - **Cole Instrument Corp**
Design & Manufacture Rotary Mechanical - **Cole Instrument Corp**
Design Prototype & Manufacturer of Metal Stamping - **Walker Corp**
Design of All Sign Systems - **Ca Signs**
Design, Dev. & Mfr. of Orthopedic Instruments - **Bioquest Med Prod Dev**
Design, Development & Production of Customized Silicone - **Psi Inc**
Design, Mfr. & Installation of Low & Medium Voltage - **Con-tech Power**
Design, Tool, Build, Produce, Consult. - **Progressive Metal Forming Inc.**
Designing - **Lemco**
Designing and Manufacturing Both Custom and - **Glentek Inc**
Designs & & Distributes Flexible and Multilayer - **Salco Circuit**
Designs & Installs Turn Key, Water Bottling - **Erica and Erica Int'l**
Designs & Men's & Women's Lingerie in Lace - **Pass Distributing Corp**
Designs Interactive Television & Internet Systems - **Gsiglobal , Inc.**
Designs Journals and Stationery Paper Products - **Loose Ends**
Designs Parts & Associated Assemblies for Wafer Probers - **Miller Design**
Designs and Controls and Actuators - **Sprague Controls Inc**
Designs and Heavy Equipment - **Smith Equipment Usa Inc**
Designs and Publishes Archival Papers with Sports - **The Wolfe Pack**
Designs and Thermal Imaging Systems - **Flir Systems Inc**
Designs and Trade Show Exhibits! - **Dieterich & Ball Incorporated**
Designs, & Installation of Interior Decor - **King Design International**
Designs, Develops & Distributes Jobs Exploration Software; - **Jobquest**
Designs, Develops and Builds Custom Machinery - **Vortex Engineering**
Desktop Accessories - **Allsop, Inc.**
Desktop Publishing - **Digital Nation**
Development - **Accurite Development & Mfg**
Develops Clincal Information Systems for Hospitals - **Clinicomp Int'l Inc**
Develops Custom Software for Optical Storage on Cd/rom - **Opendisc Sys**
Develops Educational Multimedia Software - **Visible Productions Llc**
Develops Lpo/lpr, Tcp/ip Network Printing Software - **Brooks Internet**
Develops Markets in the U.s. for Overseas Products - **Ismay International**
Develops Prepackaged Architectural Software - **Art, Inc.**
Develops Prepackaged Family Law Software - **Legal plus Software Group**
Develops Prepackaged Research Software - **Anderson-bell Corp**
Develops Software for the Engineering and Mining Fields - **Techbase Int'l**
Develops Transaction Processing Software for - **American Traffic Systems**
Diabetic Medical Products - **Medicore Inc.**
Diagnostic Enzymes and Biotherapeutic Products - **Genzyme Corp**
Diagnostic Reagents - **Strategic Diagnostics, Inc.**
Diagnostic Substances - **American Laboratories, Inc. (Mfr)**
Diagnostic Substances - **Genzyme Corp**
Diagnostic Substances - **Midland Bioproducts Corp.**
Diagnostic Substances - **Strategic Diagnostics, Inc.**
Diamond & Cbn Wheels & Tools - **Abrasive Distributors Corp.**
Diamond & Platinum Jewelry, Precious Gemstones - **Skatell's Jewelers**
Diamond Bore Sizing Tools - **Accu-cut Diamond Tool Co., Inc.**
Diamond Coated Cutting Tools - Inserts & Round Tools - **Sp3**
Diamond Coating Services - **Sp3**
Diamond Coating Systems - **Sp3**

Diamond Cutting - **Elias Diamond Cutting**
Diamond Cutting (Saw) Blades, Export - **Alkantec, Inc.**
Diamond Grinding Wheels - **I.c.e. (International Carbide & Engineering,**
Diamond Powders & Compounds, Micron - **Industrial Diamond Labs**
Diamond Reclamation - **Industrial Diamond Labs**
Diaphragm Motor Pump Units, Air-driven Pumps - **Flojet Corp**
Diaphragm Seals - **Helicoid Div., Bristol Babcock Inc.**
Dice Cups & Games - **Luckicup Company**
Diced, Sliced, Shredded, Redskin & Mashed Potatoes - **Northern Star Co.,**
Die Cast Dies - **General Precision Tool & Die Inc.**
Die Casting - **Kurt Manufacturing Co.**
Die Cut Paper & Board - **Newark Group, Inc.**
Die Cutting & Laminating of Non-metallic Materials - **C G R Products**
Die Cutting - Decals & Paper Products - **Aggressive Dies & Cutting**
Die Cutting Presses / Manual - **Tecre Co., Inc.**
Die Sets & Mold Bases - **Superior Die Set Corp.**
Die-cut Paper & Board - **Foil Graphics, Inc.**
Die-cut Paper and Board - **Maratech International**
Dielectric Film for Capacitors - **Steinerfilm Inc**
Dies, Carbide Header - **Ford Tool & Machining Inc.**
Dies, Tools, Jigs & Fixtures_special - **Retlaw Tools & Plastics Co., Inc.**
Dies, Tools, Jigs & Fixtures_special - **Rodak Plastics Co., Inc.**
Dies, Tools, Jigs & Fixtures_special - **Chamfer Master Tool Co.**
Dies, Tools, Jigs & Fixtures_special - **Baroli Engineering Inc**
Dies, Tools, Jigs & Fixtures_special - **Owen Tool & Mfg. Co., Inc.**
Dies, Tools, Jigs & Fixtures_special - **Accu-cut Diamond Tool Co., Inc.**
Dies, Tools, Jigs & Fixtures_special - **Brenner Tool & Die, Inc.**
Dies, Tools, Jigs & Fixtures_special - **Concorde Tools, Inc.**
Dies, Tools, Jigs & Fixtures_special - **Fancort Industries, Inc.**
Dies, Tools, Jigs & Fixtures_special - **Genca Corp.**
Dies, Tools, Jigs & Fixtures_special - **General Precision Tool & Die Inc.**
Dies, Tools, Jigs & Fixtures_special - **H & S Tool & Die Co.**
Dies, Tools, Jigs & Fixtures_special - **Heyden Mold & Bench Co.**
Dies, Tools, Jigs & Fixtures_special - **Hoffman Tool & Die Inc.**
Dies, Tools, Jigs & Fixtures_special - **Mc Kee Carbide Tool Co.**
Dies, Tools, Jigs & Fixtures_special - **Pasco Tool & Die**
Dies, Tools, Jigs & Fixtures_special - **Superior Die Set Corp.**
Dies, Tools, Jigs & Fixtures_special - **Tella Tool & Mfg. Co.**
Dies, Tools, Jigs & Fixtures_special - **Thor Tool Corporation**
Dies, Tools, Jigs & Fixtures_special - **Trimline Tool Inc.**
Dies, Tools, Jigs & Fixtures_special - **Universal Tooling Corp.**
Dies, Tools, Jigs & Fixtures_special - **Yorktown Precision Technologies**
Dies, Tools, Jigs & Fixtures_special - **Schulze Manufacturing**
Dies, Tools, Jigs & Fixtures_special - **Pcie Dba; the France Group**
Diesel Engine Cmponents - **Engine Systems**
Diesel Engine Part Overhaul & Reconditioning - **Golten Service**
Diesel Engine Parts - **Diesel Parts of America**
Diesel Engine Parts - **Entrac, Inc.**
Diesel Engine Parts - **Wamco Corporation**
Diesel Engine Service & Spare Parts. - **Golten Service**
Diesel Fuel Injector & Engine Parts - **Diesel Parts of America**
Diesel Motor & Parts - **Export Parts Center**
Diesel Parts - **Traction International**
Diet Aids - **Up-time Sports/nutrition/medical Ind**
Dietary Supplements and Nutrients - **The Chemins Company Inc**
Dietetic Foods, Sports Drinks & Vege Burgers - **Essen Nutrition Corp.**
Differential Pressure Gages - **Mid-west Instrument**
Diffraction Foils - **Transfer Print Foils, Inc.**
Diffraction Patterns, Holograms - **Crown Roll Leaf, Inc.**
Digital Asset Managment - **Iridio**
Digital Audio Telephone & Radio Voice Loggers - **Accurate Sound Corp.**
Digital Automatic Data Processing Machines - **Tally Printer Corporation**
Digital Flow Controllers - **Bristol Babcock Inc.**
Digital Microwave Radios - **Glenayre Western Multiplex**
Digital Panel Meters - **Electro-numerics, Incorporated (Mfr)**
Digital Panel Meters - **Burton-rogers Co., Calibron Instruments Div.**
Digital Pre-press / - **Quantum Color Graphics Inc.**
Digital Prepress and Media Services - **Advanced Graphics & Publishing**
Digital Printing - **Iridio**
Digital Printing - **Cooley Sign & Digital Imaging**
Digital Radio Transmitters - **Continental Electronics Corp.**

Digital Read-out Systems for Scales - **Sargon Digital Inc**
Digital Servo Amplifiers, Servo Motors and Motion - **Glentek Inc**
Digital Television Transmitters - **Continental Electronics Corp.**
Digitizing - **Arrow Creative International, Ltd.**
Digitizing & Reverse Engineering - **Precision Measurement Labs**
Dilution Extractive Sample Systems - **Universal Analyzers Inc**
Dimension - **Maple Valley Hardwoods**
Dimensional Lumber - **Creveling Sawmill**
Dinner Ware Ceramics - **Accent Enterprizes, Inc.**
Direct Current Heaters - **D C Thermal, Inc.**
Direct Fired Steam Generators - **Welden Steam Generators, Inc.**
Direct Foreign Investment - **Definco Ltd.**
Direct Mail Advertising Services - **Anchor Printing & Graphics**
Direct Push Soil Sampling Systems - **Art's Manufacturing & Supply Inc**
Direct Steam Injection Liquid Heaters - **Pick Heaters, Inc.**
Direct Steam Injection Sanitary Heaters - **Pick Heaters, Inc.**
Directories - **Asd, Inc. , Architectural Signage & Design**
Directors - **Masterpiece Prdctns Nevada**
Disabled Drivers Wheelchair Lifts - **Freedom Driving Aids**
Disc Brake Pads - **Rofren Disc Brake, Inc.**
Discharge and for Reuse in Same Process - **Water Technologies**
Discrete Plate - **I P S C O Steel Inc.**
Dishracks - **Traex**
Dishwashers, Household, Export - **Anaheim Marketing International**
Disign & Maintenance, Aircraft Lifts - **Syncro Air Lift Corp**
Disigns & Cd-rom Sound & Music - **Q. up Arts**
Disinfectants, Carpet & Fabric - **Steam Services Inc.**
Disk Packs, Computer Storage Devices - **Peripherals Manufacturing Inc**
Disodium Carbonate - **Imc Chemical, Inc.**
Disperesants - **Geo Specialty Chemicals, Inc.**
Displacement Transducers - **Pace Transducer Co**
Display Fixtures - **Pam International Co., Inc.**
Displays - **Arno International, Inc.**
Disposable Blood Lancets & Splinter Removers - **Medipoint, Inc.**
Disposable Dinnerware - **Lanca Sales, Inc.**
Disposable Douches - **Unico, Inc.**
Disposable Medical Products - **Medicore Inc.**
Disposable Medical Products, Wholesale - **Exelint International, Inc.**
Disposable Medical,veterinary,safety & Coveralls - **General Econopak,**
Disposable Sodium Phosphates Enemas - **Unico, Inc.**
Dist & Trans Line Vibration Controls - **Dulmison Incorporated**
Distibutor of Laboratory Supplies & Equipment - **Service for Science & In**
Distibutor of Siemens & Cutler - Hammer Products - **Electric City Corp.**
Distilled Spirits - **Age International**
Distilled Spirits Flavors - **American Distilling & Manufacturing Co., Inc.**
Distilled Witch Hazel Extracts - **American Distilling & Manufacturing**
Distillers Grains with Solubles - **Grain Processing Corporation (Mfr)**
Distributes Construction & Mining Machinery - **Triad Machinery Inc**
Distribution - **Penn Terminals Inc.**
Distribution - **Apollo Warehouse, Inc.**
Distribution - **Clm, Inc.**
Distribution - **Respond Cargo Services Corp.**
Distribution Services - **Five Rivers Electronic Innovations, Llc**
Docking Lights - **Aqua Signal Corp.**
Document Imaging - **Advanced Graphics & Publishing**
Documentation / Data Waste Disintegrators - **Security Engineered Mach**
Dod Certified - **Vanco Heavy Lift C.f.s.**
Dog & Cat Food - **Natural Life Pet Products**
Dog & Cat Food - **Nutro Products, Inc.**
Dog Biscuits - **Purr-fect Growlings**
Dog Collars & Leashes for pets - **A. Tail We Could Wag**
Dog Treats, Flavored - **Mcgough Industries Inc**
Dog and Cat Food - **Hartz Mountain**
Doggie Bandannas - **Purr-fect Growlings**
Doggie T-shirts - **Purr-fect Growlings**
Doll & Ceramic Molds (Plaster) - **Seeley's Ceramic Service, Inc.**
Doll Accessories - **Bell Ceramics Inc. (Mfr)**
Doll House & Model Railroad Electrical - **Cir-kit Concepts, Inc.**
Domestic & International - **Mark Vii International**
Domestic Electrical Appliances - **Waterwise**
Donut or Doughnut Machines - **Lil Orbits, Inc.**

Door Frames, Framesauer - **Burns, Morris & Stewart, Ltd.**
Door Hardware - **Hollow Metal Specialists, Inc.**
Door Hinges - **Youngdale Manufacturing Corp**
Doors - **Elixir Industries, Inc.**
Doors / Pine - **Summit Sales & Marketing**
Doors, Sash & Trim, Metal - **Y K K Ap America, Inc.**
Doors, Sash & Trim_metal - **Accurate Screening Media, Inc.**
Doors, Sash & Trim_metal - **Clarke's Custom Windows, Inc.**
Doors, Sash & Trim_metal - **E F C O Corp.**
Doors, Sash & Trim_metal - **Traco**
Doors, Windows and Frames and Thresholds for Doors - **Ameri Housing**
Doors—douglas Fir Entry, French Bifold - **Bend Door Co**
Dot Glue System, Air & Mechanical Bustle Wheels - **Support Products**
Dough Dividers, Manually Operated - **Dutchess Bakers' Machinery Co.,**
Dough Dividers, Semi-automatic - **Dutchess Bakers' Machinery Co., Inc.**
Down Hole Electronic Oil Recovery - **Erica and Erica International**
Downhole Oil Field Motors - **B I C O Drilling Tools, Inc.**
Dragline Buckets, Excavator Buckets, Hydraulic - **Hendrix Mfr. Inc.**
Drain Cleaning Tools - **Petersen Products Co.**
Dram / Barre Pumps - **Finish Thompson, Inc.**
Draperies & Bedding - **Dezign Sewing Inc.**
Draperies, Bedspreads & Decorative Fabrics - **Kay & L Draperies, Inc.**
Draperies, Bedspreads & Shades - **Carole Fabrics**
Draperies, Bedspreads, Vertical & Mini Blinds - **Sultan & Sons, Inc.**
Draperies, Curtains, Bedspreads, D - **Gingerich Draperies Inc**
Drapery - **General Drapery Services, Inc.**
Drapery & Metal Drapery Hardware - **World Wide Windows**
Drapery Fabrics - **Carole Fabrics**
Drapery Hardware - **Mcmurray Co**
Drapery Hardware & Blinds & Shades - **Griffith Shade Co.**
Drapery Hardware & Blinds & Shades - **Mcmurray Co**
Drapery Hardware & Blinds & Shades - **Novo Industries Inc.**
Drapery Hardware & Blinds & Shades - **Virginia Iron & Metal Co.**
Drapery Hardware & Blinds & Shades - **World Wide Windows**
Dredge Equipment - **L W T Pit Hog Dredge**
Dredging Equipment - **V M I, Inc.**
Dresses - **Hannah Katherine Fashions Corp.**
Dresses & Blouses_girl's & Children's - **Dorissa of Miami, Inc.**
Dressings - **Griffin Food Company**
Dressings - **Afassco, Inc.**
Dried Florals/evergreens - **Alaska Herb Tea Co. (Mfr)**
Dried Flowers, Pods, Foliages, Cones - **Knud Nielsen Company, Inc.**
Dried Fruit - **Premier Valley Foods, Inc.**
Dried Halibut - **Alaskan Dried Foods**
Dried Onions & Garlic - **Gilroy Foods, Inc. (Mfr)**
Dried Prunes - **Premier Valley Foods, Inc.**
Dried Seasoning Mixes - **Chef Paul Prudhomme's Magic Seasoning Blen**
Drill Bits & Cutters - **Baker Hughes Mining Tools, Inc.**
Drilling Consulting - **Ruen Drilling International**
Drilling Machinery - **Pacific Cranes & Equipment Sales**
Drilling Machines-pipe - **Apac Products**
Drilling Oil & Gas Wells - **Marshall Miller & Associates**
Drilling Steel & Accessories - **Minco Sales Corp.**
Drilling, Tapping, Milling, Spot Welding - **Owen Tool & Mfg. Co., Inc.**
Drink Mixers - **Hamilton Beach/proctor Silex, Inc.**
Drinking Fountains - **Filtrine Manufacturing Company**
Drinking Fountains Metal - **Stern-williams Company, Inc.**
Drinking Fountains Stone - **Stern-williams Company, Inc.**
Drinking Water Filters & 3 Wheel Electric Scooters - **Liberty Mfg., Inc.**
Drinking Water Purification & Water Softening - **Springsoft International**
Drinking Water, Purification Systems - **Waterwise**
Drip Irrigation Equipment - **Salco Products Inc**
Drip and Low-volume Sprinklers for Agriculture - **Bowsmith Inc**
Drive-through Windows & Transaction Drawers - **M C E Systems Corp.**
Driveline Repair Parts - Lift Trucks - **Joseph Industries, Inc.**
Driveway Sealants, Pavement Crack Repair - **Dalton Enterprises, Inc.**
Driving Gloves, Welders Gloves, Leather-cotton Combination - **Edina Mfg.**
Drug Dyes - **Tricon Colors, Llc**
Drug Metabolism Bioreagents & Services - **Synthetic Genetics**
Drugs, Proprietaries & Sundries - **Bioelements Inc**
Drugs, Proprietaries & Sundries - **Shelton's Sheen Wave Labs Inc**

Drugs, Proprietaries, and Sundries - **Hollywood**
Drum & Tote/tank Pumps, Bung Mounting - **Drum-mates, Inc**
Drum Crushers - **Consolidated Baling Machine Co., Inc.(Mfr)**
Drum Dumpers - **Flexicon Corporation**
Drum Filling Systems - **Specialty Equipment Co.**
Drum Mixers Bung Entering & Open Drum - **Drum-mates, Inc**
Drum Scanning - **Digital Nation**
Drum Tops, Steel - **United Metal Receptacle Inc. (Mfr)**
Dry & Steam Heat Sauna Units - **Sybaritic, Inc.**
Dry Bulk Material Conveyors & Systems - **Flexicon Corporation**
Dry Bulk Material Handling Machinery - **Riley Equipment Co., Inc.**
Dry Cereals - **United Grocers International**
Dry Cleaning Equipment - **Giancola Exports, Inc., D. J.**
Dry Cleaning Tunnel Finishing Equip. - **Leonard Automatics, Inc.**
Dry Ice & Propane - **Holmes Ice & Cold Storage Co**
Dry Pet Food - **Safeway Stores Inc., Export Sales**
Dry Products, Housewares, & Toys - **Orgill Inc.**
Dry Spices, Nuts, Oak Barrels, Bottling Machinery - **Paul Marsh, Llc**
Dry Toners - **Coates Electrographics Inc.**
Dry Type Transformers - **Acme Electric Corp.**
Dry, Condensed, Evaporated Products - **Dews Research**
Drying & Cooling Tables - **Ashton Food Machinery Co., Inc., Neumunz**
Drywall - **R a M Products**
Du-al 5' Coiled Hose Cryogen Refilling Systems - **The Du-al Corp.**
Duct Burners - **Forney**
Ductile Iron Compact Fittings 3-48 D - **Griffin Pipe Products Co.**
Ductile Iron Press. Pipe, 3-48 D. - **Griffin Pipe Products Co.**
Ductile Iron Sewer Pipe 4-48 D. - **Griffin Pipe Products Co.**
Ductwork - **Barron Industries, Inc.**
Ductwork - **Lincoln Manufacturing Co.**
Dump Bodies, Truck & Trailer Manuf. - **Penates General Welding**
Dump Truck Bodies - **Rugby Manufacturing Co.**
Dump Truck Bodies - **Paramount Truck Body & Equip**
Dump Trucks Designed for Off-highway Use - **Hoss Equipment**
Dump Trucks, Dirt Hauling Equipment & Trailers - **Crown Truck Sales**
Duplication / Replication- **Peripherals Manufacturing Inc**
Durable Goods - **Petrified Wood Co**
Durable Goods, Nec - **Garnac Grain**
Durable Goods, Nec - **Outdoor Cap**
Durable Goods, Nec - Indian, Pakistani Food - **House of Spices**
Durable Medical Equipment - **Kurt Manufacturing Co.**
Durable Medical Equipment - **Universal Technology Systems**
Dust & Fume Control Systems - **Bruning & Federle Mfg. Co.**
Dust Collecting Equipment - **Airtrol, Inc.**
Dust Collection Equipment - **Airflow Systems Inc. (Mfr)**
Dust Collection Equipment - **Dustvent, Inc.**
Dust Collector Cartridges - **Chemco Manufacturing Incorporated**
Dust Collectors - **Barron Industries, Inc.**
Dust Collectors - **Flexicon Corporation**
Dust Collectors - **Clean Air Consultants, Inc.**
Dust Collectors, Bin Vents - **Midwest International Standard Prod, Inc**
Dust Suppression - **Syntech Products Corp.**
Dust Suppression Chemicals - **Martin Marietta Magnesia Specialties**
Dustair (Clean Smoke Detectors on Site) - **Home Safeguard Industries**
Duty Drawback - **Torner International, Inc. / Edmundo Torner, Chb**
Dye Carriers & Fixatives - **Eastern Color & Chemical Co.**
Dye Sublimation Thermal Transf - **Plasco, Inc.**
Dyed Stretch Nylon, Merino Wool - **Roselon Industries, Inc.**
Dyes - **Tricon Colors, Llc**
Dyes & Dyestuffs - **Organic Dyestuffs Corporation**
Dyestuff Specialist: One of the Largest Independent - **Bezjian Dye-chem,**
Dynamic Merging - **Quantum Conveyor Systems, Llc**
Ear Plugs and Ear Muffs - **Howard Leight Industries**
Ear Surgical Supplies - **Smith & Nephew Inc.**
Early Childhood Ed Materials - **Hammett Co., Inc., J. L.**
Earth-drilling Equipment - **Calweld, Inc**
East Park Tm Cleansing Bar - **East Park Research Inc**
East Park Tm Flu-ban for Relief of Colds or Flu. - **East Park Research Inc**
East Park Tm Olive Leaf Extract - **East Park Research Inc**
East Park Tm Topical Gel - **East Park Research Inc**
Ebonal C, Degreasing - **All Metals Processing Co Inc**

Economic Development Agency - **City of Cincinnati Dept. Econ Dev.**
Edge Grip, Wafer Handler (Silicon Wafers) - **Holbrooks**
Edge Olved Panels - **Summit Sales & Marketing**
Edge-bonded Shims - **Bolsan West Inc**
Edible Fat Preparations - **International Custom Products**
Edible Gelatin - **Nitta Gelatin**
Edible Nuts - **Ferry Roberts Nut**
Edible Oils & Protein Blending - **Perdue Farms Inc. Grain & Oilseed**
Education: Foreign Credentials Evaluations - **International Consultants of**
Educational Equipment - **Wabash Instrument Corp.**
Educational Personal Computer Robots - **General Robotics Corporation**
Educational Publication Printing - **Slosson Educational Publications, Inc.**
Educational Science Kits, Math Manipulatives- **Scott Resources, Inc.**
Educational Services, Business Culture - **Language Masters, Inc.**
Educational Svcs. Corp Language Training - **Language Masters, Inc.**
Egg Products, Dried, Frozen & Liquid - **Sonstegard Foods Company**
Egg-culture Vaccine Machinery - **Rame-hart, Inc.**
Elastic Trim - **Just a Stretch**
Elastomeric Connectors - **Fujipoly America Corp.**
Elastomeric Roof Coatings - **Henry Company International**
Elastomeric Roofing - **Metacrylics**
Elden Country Furniture - **Designers Resource, Dba Country & Casual**
Elec Telecom Equip Refurbishment - **Palco Telecom Service Inc**
Elec Telecom Equipment Repair Shop - **Palco Telecom Service Inc**
Elec Water Heaters Commercial - **Lochinvar Water Heater**
Elec. Appar., Whsle. - **Platt Electric Supply**
Elec. Comp., Microwave Circuits - **Rogers Corporation**
Elec. Equip., Insect Light Traps - **Gilbert Industries Inc.**
Elec. Ind. Coil Winding Machinery - **Armature Coil Equipment Inc.**
Elec. Private Branch Exchange (Pbx) Eq. - **Digital Telephone Sys., Harris**
Elec. Switches - **Platt Electric Supply**
Elec. Water Heaters, Household - **Lochinvar Water Heater**
Elect. Design & Packaging - **Circuit Technology Corp.**
Electric & Hybrid Electric Battery Powered Transit Buses - **Advanced Vehi**
Electric Arc Furnaces - **I P S C O Steel Inc.**
Electric Bicycles - **Zap Power Systems**
Electric Bicycles, Scooters, Motorcycles - **Zapworld.com**
Electric Broilers - **Capitol Products Co., Inc., the**
Electric Cigarette Lighters - **Lectralite Corporation**
Electric Countertop Cooking Range - **Capitol Products Co., Inc., the**
Electric Heating Elements, Thermocouples - **Tempco Electric Heater**
Electric Housewares - **Wahl Clipper Corp.**
Electric Industrial Controls - **Itt Flygt Corp**
Electric Kilns & Furnaces - **Paragon Industries, Inc.**
Electric Knives - **Hamilton Beach/proctor Silex, Inc.**
Electric Lamp Sockets - **Buhl Industries, Inc.**
Electric Lamps (Incandescent), Manufactures - **Decor Guild Mfg., Co.**
Electric Motor Parts & Supplies - **Martindale Electric Company**
Electric Motorcycles - **Zap Power Systems**
Electric Motors - **Kirby Risk Service Center**
Electric Motors - **Emc Technologies**
Electric Motors - **Richard Boas**
Electric Motors Industrial - **Baldor Electric Company**
Electric Motors and Generators - **Cominter Corp.**
Electric Pumps, Submersible - **Itt Flygt Corp**
Electric Sandwich Toaster Grill - **Capitol Products Co., Inc., the**
Electric Scooters - **Zap Power Systems**
Electric Sign Supplies & Equipment - **Tube Light Co., Inc.**
Electric Signs & Aluminum Extrusions - **Sign Products International**
Electric Vehicles - **Zap Power Systems**
Electric Vehicles - **Neighborhood Electric Vehicle Co**
Electric Watt Hour Meters - **Texas Meter & Device Co.**
Electric Welding Contactors - **Jennings Technology Company**
Electric, Hyrdaulic, Pto - Stationary, Floeting, Trailer - **Fisher Pumps Inc**
Electric, Linear Positioning Cylinders - **Hydro-line Inc. Division of Imc,**
Electrical & Electro-optic Connectors for Deepwater - **Ocean Design Inc.**
Electrical & Electronic Test Equipment Sales - **Whitlock Instrument**
Electrical & Fiber Optic Cable - **Rochester Corp., the**
Electrical & Mechanical Components - **M & E Components, Inc.**
Electrical & Optic Penetrators - **Ocean Design Inc.**
Electrical Apparatus & Equipment - **Cummins Sw/power Systems**

Electrical Apparatus & Equipment - **Aaa Weigh Inc**
Electrical Apparatus & Equipment - **Lyncole Xit Grounding**
Electrical Apparatus & Equipment - **Bieber Lighting Corp**
Electrical Apparatus & Equipment - **Salco Circuit**
Electrical Apparatus & Equipment - **Aero-kap Inc**
Electrical Apparatus & Equipment - **Energy Sales**
Electrical Apparatus & Equipment - **Exide Corporation**
Electrical Apparatus & Equipment - **Border States Electric Supply**
Electrical Appliances, Tv & Radios - **Ksc Industries Inc**
Electrical Bus Ducts - **Calvert Co., Inc.**
Electrical Cable Reels - **Ericson Manufacturing, Inc.**
Electrical Cables - **Richard Boas**
Electrical Components - **Allied Dynamics Corp.**
Electrical Connectors - **E F T Systems, Inc.**
Electrical Control Equipment - **Con-tech Power Systems, Inc.**
Electrical Control Panels - **Factory Automation Systems, Inc.**
Electrical Controls, Relays, Solenoids & Valves - **Deltrol Controls**
Electrical Electronic Parts, Aircraft - **Olympic Aviation**
Electrical Equipment - **Bifrost**
Electrical Equipment & Chassis - **Parpro, Inc.**
Electrical Equipment & Motors - **Imperial Electric Co.**
Electrical Equipment & Supplies - **Industrial Fiber Optics**
Electrical Equipment & Supplies - **Autogate**
Electrical Equipment & Supplies - **Calvert Co., Inc.**
Electrical Equipment & Supplies - **Lasag**
Electrical Equipment & Supplies - **Se-kure Controls, Inc.**
Electrical Equipment & Supplies - **Stetco, Inc.**
Electrical Equipment & Supplies, Nec - **Advantor Corp.**
Electrical Equipment, Wiring Supplies- **Border States Electric Supply**
Electrical Grounding Rods; Distributes Ground - **Lyncole Xit Grounding**
Electrical Grounding Systems - **Graphite Sales, Inc.**
Electrical Hydraulic Winches - **Superwinch**
Electrical Industrial Apparatus - **Lake Shore Electric Corp.**
Electrical Industrial Apparatus - **Ross Engineering Corp**
Electrical Industrial Apparatus - **Metrix Instrument Co.**
Electrical Industrial Apparatus - **Exeltech**
Electrical Industrial Apparatus - **Plasmatic Systems, Inc.**
Electrical Industrial Apparatus - **Trace Engineering Co**
Electrical Industrial Apparatus - **Pearson Southwest Marketing**
Electrical Industrial Heaters - **Omega Heater Co., Inc.**
Electrical Instruments, Test Equipment - **The Siemon Company**
Electrical Insulation Materials - **Hollingsworth & Vose Co.**
Electrical Insulator Caps - **V.t.e., Inc.**
Electrical Massage Equipment - **Jb Research Inc**
Electrical Massage Equipment - Oem - **Relaxor / Jb Research Inc**
Electrical Operating System for Gates - **Sergeant at Arms Entry Systems**
Electrical Parts & Lighting Fixture - **Intramar, Inc.**
Electrical Parts of Machinery or Apparatus - **Maratech International**
Electrical Parts of Machinery or Apparatus - **Thunderball Marketing**
Electrical Paste - **Electro-science Labs Inc.**
Electrical Potting Compounds - **Polygem**
Electrical Switches - **Dresser Instrument Div.**
Electrical Switchgear - **Zenith Controls, Inc.**
Electrical Terminal Blocks - **Wago Corp.**
Electrical Terminals - **National Standard Parts Assocs. Inc.**
Electrical Testing Equipment - **Etcon Corp.**
Electrical Work Station Outlets - **The Siemon Company**
Electrical and Electronic Components— Wire - **Aero-kap Inc**
Electrically Conductive Epoxies - **Electronic Materials Inc**
Electricity Measuring Instruments - **Ross Engineering Corp**
Electricity Measuring Instruments - **Betatronix, Inc.**
Electricity Measuring Instruments - **Dorrough Electronics**
Electricity Measuring Instruments - **Fet Test Inc**
Electricity Measuring Instruments - **G D Branch Corp**
Electricity Measuring Instruments - **Global Specialties**
Electricity Measuring Instruments - **Loranger International Corp.**
Electro Fusion Equipment - **Policonductos S.a. De C.v.**
Electro Mechanical Assembly - **Electronic Manufacturing Svc**
Electro-magnetic Locks - **Dynalock Corp.**
Electro-mechanical Assembly - **Litec Inc.**
Electro-mechanical System Integration - **Pritchard Brown**

Electro/mechanical Assembly - **Imperial Electronic Assembly**
Electrodepistied Metal Coatings - **Opti-forms Inc**
Electroformed Reflectors & Products - **Opti-forms Inc**
Electroinc Adhesives & Sealants - **Electronic Materials Inc**
Electrolysis, Skin Care & Medical Equipment - **Clareblend Inc**
Electromagnetic Interference Shields - **Omega Shielding Products Inc.**
Electromechanical Assemblies-harnesses & Cables - **Parpro, Inc.**
Electromechanical Domestic Appliances - **Thunderball Marketing**
Electromechanical Domestic Appliances - **Televentas**
Electromechanical Products & Passive - **Howe & Howe Lexis Sales Corp**
Electromechanical Sensors and Actuators - **Kinetic Ceramics Inc**
Electromedical Equipment - **Zygo Corp.**
Electromedical Equipment - **Noraxon Usa Inc**
Electromedical Equipment - **Coherent Medical Group (Cmg)**
Electromedical Equipment - **Eckstein Bros Inc**
Electromedical Equipment - **Radiometer, Inc.**
Electromedical Equipment - **Spacelabs Medical Inc**
Electromedical Equipment, Fetal Monitors - **Analogic Corporation**
Electromedical Posturography Equipment - **Neurocom International Inc.**
Electron Beam & Laser Beam Systems- **P T R-precision Technologies,**
Electron Tubes Vacuum Capacitors - **Jennings Technology Company**
Electronic & Industrial Chemicals - **Petroferm Inc.**
Electronic & Rf Components - **Delaire U. S. A., Inc.**
Electronic (Esd, Anti-stat, Barrier & Conductive) - **Technical Coating Intl**
Electronic Access Control Devices - **Osi Security Devices**
Electronic Access Control Systems - **Mas-hamilton Group**
Electronic Advertising Displays - **Daktronics, Inc.**
Electronic Assembly - **General Electrodynamics Corp.**
Electronic Assembly - **Havetronix, Inc.**
Electronic Automated Conveyor Controls - **Milwaukee Electronics Corp.**
Electronic Brakes - **Motortronics, Inc.**
Electronic Cable & Wire Harness Assemblies - **Scott Electronics, Inc.**
Electronic Cable - Sheilded & Unsheilded - **Daburn Electronics & Cable**
Electronic Capacitors - **Diablo Industries**
Electronic Capacitors - **N W L Capacitors**
Electronic Capacitors - **Pinnacle Research Institute**
Electronic Capacitors, Ceramic - **Kemet Electronics Corp.**
Electronic Capacitors, Tantalum - **Kemet Electronics Corp.**
Electronic Coils & Transformers - **Cbs (Circuit Board Specialist)**
Electronic Coils, Transformers, Inductors - **M C Davis Company**
Electronic Components - **A. W. Industries Inc.**
Electronic Components - **Aaron-swiss, Inc.**
Electronic Components - **Aero-kap Inc**
Electronic Components - **American Zettler Inc**
Electronic Components - **Artech Industries Inc**
Electronic Components - **Bei Sensors & Systems/Kimco Magnetics**
Electronic Components - **Charles E Gillman Company**
Electronic Components - **Circuit Technology Corp.**
Electronic Components - **Communication Techniques, Inc.**
Electronic Components - **Conectec R F, Inc.**
Electronic Components - **Cory Components Inc**
Electronic Components - **Count on Tools, Inc.**
Electronic Components - **Cui Stack Inc**
Electronic Components - **Eemus Manufacturing Corp**
Electronic Components - **Evans Components Inc**
Electronic Components - **Fujipoly America Corp.**
Electronic Components - **Hartland Sales**
Electronic Components - **Hobi International, Inc.**
Electronic Components - **Interfet Corporation**
Electronic Components - **Inter-technical Export Corporatioin**
Electronic Components - **Keystone Electronics Corp.**
Electronic Components - **Kirby Risk Service Center**
Electronic Components - **Mas-hamilton Group**
Electronic Components - **Mathew Assocs, Inc.**
Electronic Components - **Metrix Instrument Co.**
Electronic Components - **Miteq, Inc.**
Electronic Components - **Litton Industries Inc**
Electronic Components - **Oak Grigsby, Inc.**
Electronic Components - **Omega Shielding Products Inc.**
Electronic Components - **Pacific Consolidated Indus**
Electronic Components - **P E I Electronics Inc.**

Electronic Components - **Permaluster Company**
Electronic Components - **Rochester Corp., the**
Electronic Components - **Ross Engineering Corp**
Electronic Components - **Salco Circuit**
Electronic Components - **Scott Electronics, Inc.**
Electronic Components - **Sentrol Industrial**
Electronic Components - **Signals & Systems Inc.**
Electronic Components - **Spira Manufacturing Corp**
Electronic Components - **Standard Crystal Corp**
Electronic Components - **Storm Products Co Inc**
Electronic Components - **The Dii Group Inc**
Electronic Components - **Transcrypt International, Inc.**
Electronic Components - **V I P Industries, Inc.**
Electronic Components - **V T C Inc.**
Electronic Components - **Se-kure Controls, Inc.**
Electronic Components - **Stetco, Inc.**
Electronic Components & Integrated Circuits - **V T C Inc.**
Electronic Components, Distribution - **Brenneman & Assocs., Inc.**
Electronic Components, Speakers and Connectors; M - **Cui Stack Inc**
Electronic Computers - **Allview Services Inc**
Electronic Computers - **Digital Interface Systems Inc.**
Electronic Computers - **I V Phoenix Group, Inc.**
Electronic Computers - **Synnex Information Tech**
Electronic Computers - **Sysdyne Corp.**
Electronic Computers - **Q E I, Inc.**
Electronic Connectors - **Cory Components Inc**
Electronic Connectors - **Elcon Products International**
Electronic Connectors - **Palco Connector**
Electronic Connectors - **A. W. Industries Inc.**
Electronic Connectors - **The Phoenix Company of Chicago, Inc.**
Electronic Connectors - **Milcon, Inc.**
Electronic Connectors and Cable Harnesses - **Cory Components Inc**
Electronic Controls - **Tridelta Industries Inc.**
Electronic Curcuit Simulation Software - **Global Specialties**
Electronic Design - **Holbrooks**
Electronic Devices - **Maxport International**
Electronic Devices for Injection Molding - **Rjg, Inc**
Electronic Digital Alarm Clock - **Equity Industries**
Electronic Display Nozzles - **Saber Technologies, Llc**
Electronic Enclosures - **American Tool & Engrg Corp**
Electronic Equipment - **Mathers Controls, Inc.**
Electronic Equipment & Parts, Export - **Ocalas Corporation**
Electronic Fluorescent Ballast - **Howard Industries**
Electronic Hardware - **Keystone Electronics Corp.**
Electronic Household Water Heaters - **Advanced Tech Industries, Inc.**
Electronic Integration - **Shock Tech, Inc.**
Electronic Locks - **Meilink Safe Co., a Fireking International Co.**
Electronic Magnifying Instruments for People - **Innoventions Inc**
Electronic Manufacturing Services - **S C I Systems, Inc.**
Electronic Measurement Instruments - **Afab Enterprises**
Electronic Measuring Instruments - **P E I Electronics Inc.**
Electronic Modules - **Motorola Integrated Electronic Systems Sector**
Electronic Moisture Controls for the Concrete Block - **Le Sueur Mfg. Co.**
Electronic Moving Message Signs - **Hi-tech Electronic Displays**
Electronic Parts - **Hartland Sales**
Electronic Parts & Equip. Wholesale - **Advantor Corp.**
Electronic Parts & Equipment - **Cui Stack Inc**
Electronic Parts & Equipment - **Elmagco Corp**
Electronic Parts & Equipment - **Innoventions Inc**
Electronic Parts & Equipment - **Norstan Electronics Inc**
Electronic Parts & Equipment - **Nova Science Inc**
Electronic Parts & Equipment - **Omicron Video**
Electronic Parts & Equipment - **Toshiba America Information Syst. Inc.**
Electronic Parts Organizers, Plastic - **Global Kitting**
Electronic Parts and Equipment - **Norstan Electronics Inc**
Electronic Parts and Equipment - **Thunderball Marketing**
Electronic Parts for the Electronics - **Eemus Manufacturing Corp**
Electronic Pre-press - **Digital Nation**
Electronic Prepress Services - **Tretina Printing Co., Inc.**
Electronic Printed Circuit Boards, Flexible - **Basic Electronics Inc**
Electronic Production Assembly - **Contronic Devices**

Electronic Products - **Emc Technologies**
Electronic Products - **Mathews Assocs, Inc.**
Electronic Programmable Speedometers - **Faria Corp.**
Electronic Prototyping Products - **Global Specialties**
Electronic Repair Svcs - **Delta Communications & Electronics**
Electronic Resistors - **Diablo Industries**
Electronic Rotary Cam & Programmable Limit Switches - **Electro Cam**
Electronic Scales - **Electronic Weighing Systems, Inc.**
Electronic Schematic Archiving - **Digital Interface Systems Inc.**
Electronic Score Boards - **Daktronics, Inc.**
Electronic Scoreboards for Sports Events - **Nevco Scoreboard Co.**
Electronic Sensors - **S C I-agra, Inc.**
Electronic Shielding Strips & Gaskets - **Omega Shielding Products Inc.**
Electronic Sizing and - **Exeter Engineering Inc**
Electronic Switches - **Oak Grigsby, Inc.**
Electronic Switches - **Ancor Communications**
Electronic Tablet Counters for Pharmacies - **Rxcount Corp**
Electronic Terminals, Connectors & Termination Equip- **Amtronics, Inc.**
Electronic Test Equipment - **G D Branch Corp**
Electronic Testing & Measuring Equipment - **Global Specialties**
Electronic Time Switches - **Lumenite Control Technology Inc.**
Electronic Training Products - **Global Specialties**
Electronic Voting Systems - **Daktronics, Inc.**
Electronic Wire Insulated with Pvc - **Daburn Electronics & Cable Corp.**
Electronic Wire & Cable - **National Wire & Cable Corp**
Electronic Wire, Cable and Molded Cables - **Permaluster Company**
Electronic and Electrical Connecto - **Elcon Products International**
Electronic, Appliance & Automotive Stampings - **F & G Multi-slide, Inc.**
Electronics - **Marjan, Inc.**
Electronics - **Mid-south Electronics-alabama, Inc.**
Electronics Plasma Cleaning Equipment - **Plasmatic Systems, Inc.**
Electronics Racks & Enclosures - **Electronic Packaging Systems**
Electronics, Automotive - **L S M Labs, Inc.**
Electronics: Radio Stereo Television Audio- **Atwood Richards**
Electroplating and Plating Equipment - **Hbs Equipment Corp**
Electrostatic Air Filters - **Air Cleaners, Inc.**
Electrostatic Scale Control System - **World Trade Exporters, Inc.**
Electrozone Sensing Particle Size - **Micromeritics Instrument Corp.**
Elevator Panels - **P T L Equipment Mfg. Co., Inc.**
Elevators & Moving Stairways - **P T L Equipment Mfg. Co., Inc.**
Elevators Elec-hydraulic Scissor Type - **Autoquip Corporation**
Elisa Diagnostics; R&d; Initiates - **Creative Science & Technolgoy**
Ellipsometers - **Rudolph Instruments, Inc.**
Ellipsometers for Measuring Thin Film - **Axic Inc**
Embeded Rubber Seals for Concrete Pipe - **Anderson Seal Co., Inc.**
Embellished T's & Fleece - **Marathon Corp.**
Embossers - **Plasco, Inc.**
Embosses, Encodes and Direct Mails - **International Plastic Cards**
Embroidered Name Tapes & Emblems - **Tapes 'N Tags Mfg.**
Embroidered Schiffli Laces & Fabrics - **Hamilton Embroidery Co., Inc.**
Embroideries and Screen Printing on Apparel - **Quality Embroidery**
Embroiders on Fabrics - **Embroidertex West Ltd**
Embroidery - **Gs Sportwear / Golden Squeegee**
Embroidery - **T Formation of Tallahassee, Inc.**
Embroidery - **Jsam**
Embroidery & Screen Printing - **Sloan & Assocs. Inc., Leonard**
Embroidery Yarn , Thread - **Robison-anton Textile Company (Mfr)**
Emc Testing, Ce Marking - **L C R Electronics, Inc.**
Emergency Lighting - **Magnaray International**
Emergency Locator Transmitter for Liferafts - **Artex Aircraft Supplies Inc**
Emergency Locator Transmitters for Aircraft - **Artex Aircraft Supplies Inc**
Emergency Metal Cutters, Hydraulic - **Amkus, Inc.**
Emergency Nickel Cadmium Battery - **A.LP. Lighting Components, Inc.**
Emergency Preparedness Kits and Mainstay - **Survivor Industries Inc**
Emergency Spill Response Ops - **Environmental Services & Technology**
Emergency Vehicle Light Bars - **Code 3, Inc.**
Emg Instruments and Medical Ele - **Noraxon Usa Inc**
Emi / Rfi Shielding - **Omega Shielding Products Inc.**
Emi Filters, Rfi Filters, X & Y Capacitors - **L C R Electronics, Inc.**
Emi/rfi Environmental Seals - **Spira Manufacturing Corp**
Emi/rfi Shielded Enclosures / Shelters - **Joaquin Manufacturing Corp**

Emi/rfi Shielding - **Summit Coating Technologies, Llc**
Emi/rfi Shielding Products - **Alco Technologies Inc**
Emission Control Systems for Air, Soil and - **King Buck Technology**
Emission Control Wet Scrubbers - **Moli-tron Company Inc.**
Emission Spectrometer Service & Parts - **Interface Design Inc.**
Emissions Testing Equipment - **Pierburg Instruments, Inc.**
Emulsifiers (Baking) - **Diehl, Inc.**
Enameling on Porcelain and Gray Iron Castings - **Commercial Enameling**
Encapsulated O-rings, Gaskets, - **Row, Inc.**
Enclosed & Gasketed Assembly Units - **A.l.p. Lighting Components, Inc.**
Encoders - **Plasco, Inc.**
End Mills - **Pine Bluff Cutting Tools, Inc.**
End Mills, Router Bits & Regrinding - **Vanguard Tool Corp.**
Energy Conservation-air Compressors - **Century West Engineering Corp.**
Energy Efficient Flourescent Lighting - **Magnaray International (Mfr)**
Energy Efficient Solar Lighting - **Magnaray International (Mfr)**
Energy Saver: State of the Art Lighting Control Technology - **Electric City**
Energy Supplements - **Up-time Sports/nutrition/medical Ind**
Engine & Drivetrain Manufacturing - **Royal Oak Industries, Inc.**
Engine Block Sealers - **K & W Products**
Engine Coolant Recycling Equipment - **Robinair, a Div. Of Spx Corp**
Engine Dampers - **Cofap of America**
Engine Electrical Equipment - **Lake Shore Electric Corp.**
Engine Electrical Equipment - **Katolight Corp.**
Engine Electrical Equipment - **Viking Enterprises**
Engine Electrical Equipment - **Tucson Alternator Exchange Inc**
Engine Exhaust Spark Arrestors - **Harco Manufacturing Co.**
Engine Gaskets - **Heavy Equipment Parts Co.,**
Engine Generator Sets & Controls - **Katolight Corp.**
Engine Oil Tank Reservoirs & Metal Fabrication - **Fabtron Corp.**
Engine Parts - Lift Truck - **Joseph Industries, Inc.**
Engine Parts, Ie, Fuel - **Scotia Technology Div., Lakes Region Tubular**
Engine_ Diesel Rebuilding - **Cable Marine, Inc.**
Engineer, Design, Systems - **Service Hydraulics Inc.**
Engineering & Assembly Services - **Brake Funderburk Enterprises, Inc.**
Engineering & Design Solutions for Frp - **Mc Clarin Plastics, Inc.**
Engineering & Technical Support - **Quality Mold Inc.**
Engineering Automotive Lighting Optics - **Guide Corporation**
Engineering Consulting, Mechanical & Electrical - **Rocamar Services, Inc.**
Engineering Design & Project Managment - **J.ray Mcdemott, Inc.**
Engineering Instr., Spirit Levels - **Geier & Bluhm, Inc.**
Engineering Resins - **Polymer Trading Services Limited**
Engineering Service - **Railroad Signal, Inc.**
Engineering Services - **Advanced Package Engineering Inc**
Engineering Services - **Le Fiell Company**
Engineering Services - **A H Lundberg Inc**
Engineering Services - **Exergetic Systems Inc**
Engineering Services - **Lyncole Xit Grounding**
Engineering Services - **Gem Engineering Co., Inc.**
Engineering Services - **Basic Electronics Inc**
Engineering Services - **Burns & Mcdonnell International**
Engineering Services - **Itt Flygt Corp**
Engineering Services - **Kbs Exports**
Engineering Services - **Ksa Engineers, Inc.**
Engineering Services - **Leo A. Daly Company**
Engineering Services - **Management Engineering Associates**
Engineering Services - **Otm Engineering, Inc.**
Engineering Services - **Precision Measurement Labs**
Engineering Services - **Versar, Inc.**
Engineering Services and Turnkey Machin - **Methods West Machine Tools**
Engineering Services, Agricultural - **A.g. Equipment, Inc.**
Engineering Services, Automotive - **Nevada Automotive Test Center**
Engineering Services, General - **Marshall Miller & Associates**
Engineering Services, Hazardous Waste - **Century West Engineering**
Engineering Services, Incinerator Plants- **Msi International**
Engineering Services, Metallurgical - **Varco Heat Treating Co**
Engineering Services, Solid Waste - **Century West Engineering Corp.**
Engineering Services, Water Systems - **Century West Engineering Corp.**
Engineering Studies - **Petrotech Inc.**
Engineering Supplies - **Autron Incorporated**
Engineering Svcs, Railroads - **Msi International**

Engineering Svcs., Mechanical & Elec. - **Wallis & Assoc. Cons. Engineers**
Engineering, Laser/cmm Digitizing- **Daco Enterprises Inc**
Engines_internal Combustion - **Cable Marine, Inc.**
Engines_internal Combustion - **Hawthorne Power Systems**
English, Russian - **Sears Steele, Iii**
Engraveable Bookmarks, Keytags, Pet Tags - **Exclusive Findings**
Engraveable Luggage Tags - **Exclusive Findings**
Engraved Molds - **Quality Mold Inc.**
Engraved Stationery - **Brewood Engravers Inc.**
Engraved Trophies & Plaques - **Trophy Shoppe**
Engraves Plaques, Labels and Trophies - **Sandy's Trophies**
Engraving - **Qwikstamp Corporation**
Envelope Printing Machinery - **Halm Industries Company Inc.**
Envelopes - **American Scholar Co.**
Envelopes - **Southern Church Envelope Co.**
Envelopes, Writing Tablets, Construction Paper - **American Scholar Co.**
Enviromental Clean up & Responce Water & Land - **C & B Fosters Inc.**
Enviromental Equipt, composting & Bioremediation - **Brown Bear, Corp**
Enviromental Services - **Aata International Inc.**
Environmentally Safe, Degreaser - **Whip-it Products, Inc.**
Environmental Analytical Laboratory - **Analytica Environmental Lab Inc**
Environmental Chambers, Wet Bench Process - **General Air Corporation**
Environmental Control Gages - **Omni Controls, Inc.**
Environmental Control Systems - **Conserve Engineering Company**
Environmental Doors - **Executive Door Company**
Environmental Systems & Analyzers - **Forney**
Environmentally Friendly Products - **Burnshine Products**
Environmentally Safe Pest Control Products - **Sterling International Inc**
Enzyme - **Dyadic International, Inc.**
Enzyme Cleaners - **Nature Plus, Inc.**
Epitaxial Silicon Wafers - **Reaction Technology Inc**
Epoxide Resins, in Primary Forms - **Philadelphia Resins**
Epoxy & Polyurethane - **Elementis Performance Polymers**
Epoxy Abrasion Resistant Compounds - **Polygem**
Epoxy Floor Coverings - **Corro-shield International, Inc.**
Epoxy Floor Systems - **Polygem**
Epoxy Flooring Systems - **American Hi-tech Flooring Co.**
Epoxy Metering & Dispensing Machines, Adhesive Dispensers - **Glenmarc**
Epoxy Thermoset Prepregs - **A P C M Mfg. Llc**
Equine/vetrinary Instr. & Apparatus - **Neogen Corp.**
Equipment - **United Farmers Co-op**
Equipment - **Lightware Inc**
Equipment & Supply - **Barsallo Deburring**
Equipment Directory - **Used Equipment Directory**
Equipment Leakage Current Interrupters - **Technology Research Corp**
Equipment Rental & Leasing - **Weigh-tronix Inc**
Equipment for Bottle Packaging, and Labeling - **Tecnipac Inc**
Equipment for Processing Fresh Fruits and Veget - **Exeter Engineering Inc**
Equipment for Shotcrete Work; - **Shotcrete Technologies Inc**
Equipment, Network Database - **Used Equipment Directory**
Eraser, Bulk Audio & Vedeo Tape Cassette - **R.b. Annis Company, Inc.**
Erasers - **General Pencil Co.**
Erect in One Day a Self Support Landmark Dart. - **Landmark Tower**
Ergonomic Seating & Work Stations - **Lyon Metal Products Llc**
Esculator Safety Switches - **P T L Equipment Mfg. Co., Inc.**
Esd Bags - **Caltex Plastics Inc**
Esd Static Safe Devices - **Global Kitting**
Espresso - **Great Northern Coffee Co Inc**
Esri Software Var, Business Partner, (Gis Software) - **Barclay Maps**
Essential Oils - **Sunkist Growers, Inc., Processed Products Div.**
Essential Oils - **Todd Co., A.m.**
Essential Oils Products - **Aromaland, Inc.**
Ethnic Foods - **Matador Processors, Inc.**
Ethyl Alcohol - **Grain Processing Corporation (Mfr)**
Ethyl Alcohol, Undenatured - **Ultimate International**
Ethylene - **Sunoco, Inc.**
Ethylene Filters - **Ethylene Control Inc**
Ethylene Oxide - **Sunoco, Inc.**
Ethylene Removal Equipment - **Ethylene Control Inc**
Evaluation of its Applications - **Kld Associates Inc.**
Evaporated Milk - **Diehl, Inc.**

Evaporated Salt, (Food Grade) - **United Salt**
Evaporative Air Cooler Parts and Accessories - **Dial Manufacturing Inc**
Evaporative Air Coolers - **Phoenix Manufacturing Inc**
Evaporative Condensers & Fluid Coolers - **Nauticon, Inc.**
Evaporative Coolers, Refrigeration - **Webb Distributors Inc**
Evaporative Cooling & Ice Thermal Storage Systems - **Baltimore Aircoil**
Evaporator Coils - **Super Radiator Coils**
Evaporators - **Dedert Corp.**
Ew - **Caravan International**
Examination Gloves - **Mexpo International Inc**
Exclusive Cam & Roller Movement Means - **Helicoid Div.,**
Executive Spanish Camp - **Language plus**
Exercise Equipment - **Im & M Exercise Equipment Inc**
Exhaust Emission Analyzers - **Pierburg Instruments, Inc.**
Exhaust Stacks - **Barron Industries, Inc.**
Exhaust Vent & Air Pollution Control Equipment - **Car-mon Products,**
Exhibit Rentals - **Admore Inc.**
Expandable Racks for Bicycles - **Load Llama Products**
Expandable Sleeving Products - **Western Filament Inc**
Expanded Foam Products - **Jsp International**
Expanded Metals for Filtration - **Expanded Technologies Inc.**
Expansion Joints - **Lamons Power Engineering**
Expansion Joints, Removable Pipe Covers - **Pars Manufacturing Co.**
Explosion Proof Alternators and Starters - **United States Energy Corp**
Explosive Containment & Storage Receptacle - **United Metal Receptacle**
Explosive Devices, Cartridges; Initiators, Igniters - **Quantic Industries Inc**
Export Agent and Distributor for Icom, Kenwood - **Nsi Communications**
Export Agent for U.s. Manufacturers - **Paul Marsh, Llc**
Export Air Transportation - **Straightway Inc.**
Export Packer - **Wts of Houston, Inc.**
Exporting Firms - **Biofix Holdings, Inc.**
Exporting Firms - **Cominter Corp.**
Exporting Firms - **Continental Cars, Inc.**
Exporting Firms - **Interpax**
Exporting Firms - **Intramar, Inc.**
Exporting Firms - **Kessler International Corp.**
Exporting Firms - **Lanca Sales, Inc.**
Exporting Firms - **Pexim International**
Exporting Firms - **R.d.d. Enterprises**
Exporting Firms - **Webco Trading**
Exporting Firms - **Stylebuilt Accessories, Inc.**
Exports Disposable Paper Diapers - **Erica and Erica International Corp.**
Exterior & Garage Signage - **Ca Signs**
Exterior Polymer Mouldings - **Marley Mouldings Inc.(Mfr)**
Exterior Rolling & Folding Storm & Security Shutters - **Roll-a-way Inc.**
Exterior Wall Panels - **Advantage Buildings & Exteriors, Inc.**
Extruded & Molded Rubber Products - **Lauren Mfg. Co.**
Extruded Rubber Automotive Products - **Cooper Engineered Products**
Extruded Rubber Products - **Diamond Rubber Products Co., Inc.**
Extruded Sealants - **General Sealants Inc**
Extruders - **Commodore Machine Co.**
Extrudes Aluminum - **Gemini Aluminum Corp**
Extrusion & Injection Molding Equipment - **Flite Technology, Inc.**
Extrusion Handling Machinery - **Thermatek International Inc.**
Extrusion Tooling & Crossheads for Plastics - **Genca Corp.**
Extrusions - **Elixir Industries, Inc.**
Eye & Face Protection, Aosafety - **Aearo Company**
Eye Care Products - **Apothecary Products Inc.**
Eye Glasses Frames, Export - **Arno International, Inc.**
Eyeglass Cases - **L.b.i.**
Eyeglass Frames - **L.b.i.**
Eyeglass Lenses - **L.b.i.**
Eyeglass Spectacle Frames - **L.b.i.**
Eyeglasses - **Economy Optical, Inc.**
Eyeglasses - **Russ Optical, Inc.**
Eyelet Machine Products (Deep Draw) - **Prospect Machine Products, Inc.**
Fabric - **Kowa California Inc.**
Fabric Converting - Specialty Circular Knits - **Sextet Fabrics, Inc.**
Fabric Defect Scanners & Thread Counters - **Matrix Controls Co., Inc.**
Fabric Finishing, Laundry & Bonding - **Geltman Industries**
Fabric Impregnating & Coating - **Current, Inc.**

Fabric Knitting - **Calender Textiles Inc**
Fabric Shower Curtains - **Hospi-tel Manufacturing Co.**
Fabric Welding - **Custom Screens, Inc.**
Fabric Winding Boards & Spools - **Pacific Fabric Reels Inc**
Fabricated Composite Products - **Tri-link Technologies Ltd.**
Fabricated Metal Prod, Cold Headed - **Fortress Mfg. Inc.**
Fabricated Metal Prod., Cold Headed - **Fortress Mfg., Inc. (Mfr)**
Fabricated Metal Products - **Enerfab**
Fabricated Metal Products- **Lighting Metal Specialties**
Fabricated Metal Products, Nec. - **Midwest Art Metal**
Fabricated Plastic Parts - **Harva Co., Inc., the**
Fabricated Plastic Products - **Omega Plastics, Inc.**
Fabricated Rubber Products - **Arlon Silicone Technology Division**
Fabricated Rubber Products - **Colorado Lining International, Inc.**
Fabricated Rubber Products - **Rubber Engineering**
Fabricated Rubber Products Not Elsewhere Classified - **Forester Rollers**
Fabricated Stainless Steel Products - **Terriss-consolidated Industries**
Fabricated Steel Cabinets & Enclosures - **Crown Divisions of Trans Pro,**
Fabricated Structural Metal - **Val-fab Inc.**
Fabricated Structural Steel Frames - **Coronis Building Sytems Inc.**
Fabricated Wire Products - **John Amann Sons Co.**
Fabricated or Sewn, Gasketing, Seals, Blankets - **Mid-mountain Materials**
Fabricates Aluminum, No Extruding - **Steiner Fabrication Inc**
Fabricates Food Service Equipment, Sneeze Guards - **Kevry Corporation**
Fabricates Latex Products - **California Latex Inc**
Fabricates Metal Products - **Metal Master Inc**
Fabricates Pipes and Fittings Cement - **Int'l Fabricators & Engineers**
Fabricates Rubber Linings for Mining Industry - **R Wales & Son Llc**
Fabricates Stainless Steel Tubing; Bends and End Forms - **Accu-tube Corp**
Fabricates Structural Steel Stairs- **Schuff Steel Company**
Fabricates Vinyl Replacement Windows - **Accent Windows Inc**
Fabricates Wire Products, Fan Guards - **Renfro Franklin Co**
Fabricates and Installs Marble - **J.r. Mcdade Marble & Granite**
Fabricating / Welding - **Frazier Industries Inc.**
Fabricating Machinery - **Perfection Machinery**
Fabrication - **Arc Industries Inc.**
Fabrication of Braided & Overbraided Products - **Western Filament Inc**
Fabrics & Textiles - **General Business International Trade**
Fabrics / Vertical Blinds - **Arabel**
Faburaction - **Lemco**
Facial Exercise Equipment - **Facial Concepts Inc.**
Facial Tissues - **Marcal Paper Mills**
Facilities Design - **D W C Assocs., Inc.**
Facility Construction - **Environmental Services & Technology**
Factory Mutual (Fmrc) Approved for Use Without - **Ats Products**
Family Wine Business, Limited Production - **Davis Bynum Winery**
Fan Coil Units - **International Enviromental Corp.**
Faney Stitch Machines, Specialtys - **Richard Sewing Machine**
Fans - **Barron Industries, Inc.**
Fans, Table, Floor, Wall, Window - **Global Electric Products**
Farm & Garden Machinery - **Shindaiwa Inc**
Farm & Garden Machinery, Wholesale - **Orgill Inc.**
Farm Equip., Grain Dryers - **Behlen Mfg. Co.**
Farm Equipment, Field & Brush Mowers - **Country Home Products, Inc.**
Farm Equipment, Power Wagons - **Country Home Products, Inc.**
Farm Equipment, Trimmer / Mower - **Country Home Products, Inc.**
Farm Equipment— Harvesters and Pruning Towers - **Weldcraft Industries**
Farm Irrigation Equipment - **Hydro Engineering, Inc.**
Farm Machinery & Equipment - **Ariens Company**
Farm Machinery & Equipment - **Bowsmith Inc**
Farm Machinery & Equipment - **Conibear Equipment Co., Inc.**
Farm Machinery & Equipment - **D & D Products, Inc.**
Farm Machinery & Equipment - **Kelley Mfg. Co.**
Farm Machinery & Equipment - **Mk Distributors Inc**
Farm Machinery & Equipment - **Nelson Products Co.**
Farm Machinery & Equipment - **Netafim Irrigation Inc**
Farm Machinery & Equipment - **Olson Irrigation Systems**
Farm Machinery & Equipment - **Omaha Standard, Inc.**
Farm Machinery & Equipment - **Supreme Horse Walker Co.**
Farm Machinery & Equipment - **Yargus Mfg., Inc.**
Farm Machinery & Equipment - Bulk Harvesting - **Weldcraft Industries**

Farm Machinery & Equipment, Tractor Canopies - **Perry Co., the**
Farm Machinery Parts - **Wamco Corporation**
Farm Machinery and Equipment - **Mk Distributors Inc**
Farm Machinery and Equipment - **Traction International**
Farm Product Warehousing and Storage - **Zen Noh Grain**
Farm Rototillers - **Country Home Products, Inc.**
Farm Supplies - **Distributors Processing Inc**
Farm Supplies - **Western Farm Service/cascade**
Farm Supplies - **Ag Acid Inc**
Farm Supplies - **H & H Seed Company Inc**
Farm Supplies for Animal Care - **Just Merino Sheepskin Products**
Farm Windmill Heads for Pumping Water - **Dempster Industries, Inc.**
Farm and Garden Machinery - **T-systems International, Inc.**
Farm, Outdoor Power & Right-of-way Maintenance Equipment - **Brown**
Fastener Tooling, Cold Header - **Ford Tool & Machining Inc.**
Fasteners - **Moeller Manufacturing Supply**
Fasteners - **Palnut Co., the**
Fasteners - Latches - **Norse, Inc.**
Fasteners, Latches, Hinges & Rivets - **Southco, Inc.**
Fastening Devices - **Daburn Electronics & Cable Corp.**
Fatigue Enhancement Products - **West Coast Industries Inc.**
Fats & Oils_animal & Marine - **Anamax Corp.**
Fats & Oils_edible - **Intermountain Canola Cargill**
Fats & Oils_edible - **Perdue Farms Inc. Grain & Oilseed Div.**
Faucet Aerators, Check Valves & Flow Controllers - **Neoperl, Inc.**
Faucets & Related Plumbing Fittings - **T&s Exports, Div. T&s Brass**
Faux Stone Table Tops - **Pacific Sun Casual Furniture**
Fcc Cyclones - **Marsulex Environmental Technologies Llc**
Fce Sand - **Refractory Materials International**
Feather Meal - **Darling International Inc.**
Feathers or down - **Culver Duck Farms**
Federal Construction & Development - **Phillips Motors, Larry**
Federal Credit Unions - **Am Castle Employee Federal Credit Union**
Federal Feed & Seed Exporter - **Phillips Motors, Larry**
Feed - **United Farmers Co-op**
Feed Grain - **Penny Newman Milling Llc**
Feed Roll Grinding - **Dalhart R & R Machine Works, Inc.**
Feeds, Prepared - **Animal Health Sales, Inc.**
Feeds, Prepared - **Fermented Products**
Feeds_prepared - **Distributors Processing Inc**
Feeds_prepared - **Free Choice Enterprises**
Feeds_prepared - **Harbingers of a New Age**
Feeds_prepared - **La Crosse Milling Co.**
Feeds_prepared - **Penny Newman Milling Llc**
Feeds_prepared - **Wildwood Farms, Inc.**
Felt Washers, Stripping, Gaskets & Yard Goods - **Aetna Felt Corp.**
Fermentation Alcohol - **Grain Processing Corporation (Mfr)**
Ferrite Cores - **Fair-rite Products Corp.**
Ferro-chrome, Ferro-manganese - **Tata, Inc.**
Ferrous & Non Ferrous Drawing, Stranding- **Delta Precision Alloys**
Ferrous & Non-ferrous Forgings & Elliptical - **Lenape Forge, Inc.**
Fertilizer - **United Farmers Co-op**
Fertilizer Distributors, Drygravity Sprayers - **Dempster Industries, Inc.**
Fertilizer Spreading Equipment - **Conibear Equipment Co., Inc.**
Fertilizer, (Organic), Humicacids, Biological Catalysts. - **Biofix Holdings,**
Fertilizers - **Eastern Europe Inc.**
Fertilizers, Mixing Only - **Agrimar Corp.**
Fertilizers, Mixing Only - **Great Dane Terminal, the**
Fertilizers, Mixing Only - **Western Farm Service/cascade**
Fertilizers, Mixing Only - **Nacco Grow More**
Fetish Accessories & Toys - **Pass Distributing Corporation**
Fiber Cans, Drums & Similar Products - **Northwest Paper Box Mfrs Inc**
Fiber Cans, Drums & Similar Products - **All American Containers, Inc.**
Fiber Glass Reinforced Polyester - **Nvf Company (Mfr)**
Fiber Optic Analog Transmission Systems - **Ross Engineering Corp.**
Fiber Optic Assemblies & Components - **Storm Products Co Inc**
Fiber Optic Cable - **Sumitomo Electric Lightwave Corp.**
Fiber Optic Cable (Side & End Lite) - **Advanced Lighting Systems, Inc.**
Fiber Optic Cable , Hardware - **Dulmison Incorporated**
Fiber Optic Cable Assemblies - **Radiant Communications Corp.**
Fiber Optic Cable Plant Products - **Radiant Communications Corp**

Fiber Optic Cable, Devices - **S.i. Tech, Inc.(Mfr)**
Fiber Optic Cameras - **Visual Inspection Technologies**
Fiber Optic Communication Cable for Video, Rgb, - **Opticomm Corp**
Fiber Optic Components - **Radiant Communications Corp.**
Fiber Optic Illuminators - **Spectral Energy Corp.**
Fiber Optic Lighting Equipment - **Advanced Lighting Systems, Inc.**
Fiber Optic Network Electronics - **Radiant Communications Corp.**
Fiber Optic Patch & Splice - **Radiant Communications Corp.**
Fiber Optic Video Electronics - **Radiant Communications Corp.**
Fiber Optic and Laser Systems for Industry and - **Industrial Fiber Optics**
Fiber Optics Cable - **Industrial Fiber Optics**
Fiber Optics Leds - **Industrial Fiber Optics**
Fiber Optics Photodetectors - **Industrial Fiber Optics**
Fiber Optics..Sonet, Mux & Modems - **Sunnyvale Gdi, Inc.**
Fiber Products for the Book, Game, - **Book Covers Inc**
Fiberboard of Wood or Other Ligneous Materials - **Timber Products**
Fiberglass & Fluoropolymer Insulation Covers - **Remco Technology, Inc.**
Fiberglass Aircraft & Helicopter Skis - **Airglas Engineering Co., Inc.**
Fiberglass Bath Tubs & Shower Units - **American Fiberglass Products,**
Fiberglass Beams, Mfrs.- **Pupi Enterprises LLC**
Fiberglass Boats - **Mariah Boats Inc.**
Fiberglass Columns - **Dixie-pacific Mfg. Co., Inc.**
Fiberglass Fabric - **Alpha Associates, Inc.**
Fiberglass Insulation Mats - **Kasko Enterprises Inc.**
Fiberglass Ladders - **Alaco Ladder Co.**
Fiberglass Pleasure, Patrol & Fishing Boats - **Penn Yan Marine Mfg.**
Fiberglass Reinforced Pipe Systems - **Smith Fiberglass Products Co**
Fiberglass Reinforced Plastic Parts - **D G P Inc.**
Fiberglass Reinoforced Panels - **Kemlite**
Fiberglass Trailers - **Chariot Mfg. Co., Inc.**
Fiberglass Yarn Pvc Coated - **Hanover Wire Cloth**
Fiberoptic Cable - **Fitel Lucent Technologies**
Fiberoptic Lighting Products - **Super Vision International, Inc.**
Fibre Channel Switches - **Ancor Communications**
Fibre Processing Chemicals - **Eastern Color & Chemical Co.**
Fibre Spin Finishes - **Lenox Chemical Company**
Fibre Tubes & Cores - **Newark Group, Inc.**
Ficks Reed Wicker Furniture - **Designers Resource,**
Field Erected Tanks Api-650, Api-620 - **American Tank & Vessel**
Field Erected Vessels Asme - **American Tank & Vessel**
Field Sampling Equipment - **Wildlife Supply Company**
Field Seeds / Forage Seed - **Coffey Seed, Coffey Forage Seeds, Inc.**
Filament Thread - **American & Efird, Inc.**
Filler Paper - **American Scholar Co.**
Film & Digital Photography - **Iridio**
Film and Video Tape Production - **Masterpiece Prdctns Nevada**
Films-to-glass for Glare Heat Shatter - **Plastic-view Atc**
Filter Adhesive - **Elementis Performance Polymers**
Filter Cartridge Elements - **Perry Equipment Corp.**
Filter Cloth, Cotton - **Barnhardt Manufacturing Co.**
Filter Control Valves - **Fleck Controls, Inc.**
Filter Kits - **Tri-star International, Inc.**
Filter Media (Cwth) - **Micronics, Inc.**
Filter Press Plates - **Micronics, Inc.**
Filter Presses - **Micronics, Inc.**
Filterbelts & Filtercloth - **Scapa Filter Media**
Filters - **Quinn Process Equipment Co**
Filters - **Clean Air Filter Co.**
Filters & Filtration Systems - **Process Filtration Div., Parker Hannifin**
Filters, Air - **Perry Equipment Corp.**
Filters, Chemical - **Perry Equipment Corp.**
Filters, Collant - **Perry Equipment Corp.**
Filters, Depth - **Osmonics, Inc.**
Filters, Fuel - **Perry Equipment Corp.**
Filters, Liquid - **Perry Equipment Corp.**
Filters, Paint - **Perry Equipment Corp.**
Filters, Pleated - **Osmonics, Inc.**
Filtration Equipment - Air Filters - **Permatron Corporation**
Filtration Media - **Hollingsworth & Vose Co.**
Filtration for Hazardous Waste, Mining, Water Tre - **Larson & Associates**
Filtration/separation Equipment - **Perry Equipment Corp.**

Finance - **J & B Services: Import / Export**
Financing for Medical Equipment - **Biomedical International**
Find Diamond Sales & Lapidary Work - **Elias Diamond Cutting**
Fine Art Iris Giclee Reproductions - **Omega Graphics, Inc.**
Fine Chemicals - **Norac Co., Inc., the**
Fingernail Files - **Flowery Beauty Products, Inc.**
Fingerprinting Devices (Factory Office) - **Identicator Inc.**
Finished Single Vision Cr-39 Lenses - **L.B.I.**
Finishing Plants, Cotton - **Geltman Industries**
Finishing Plants, Cotton - **Paradise Textiles Co**
Finishing Plants, Cotton - **Zoo-ink Screen Print**
Finishing Plants, Fleecing, Sanding, Compacting - **Us Dyeing & Finishing**
Finishing Plants, Manmade - **Vernon Plastics Corp.**
Fire Alarm Control Systems & Accessories - **Safetech International, Inc.**
Fire Alarm Signals, Audio & Visual - **Wheelock, Inc.**
Fire Dampers - **Environmental Technologies, Inc.**
Fire Detection - **Bifrost**
Fire Detection & Suppression Systems - **E & M Intl.**
Fire Detection & Suppression Systems - **Kidde Aerospace, Walter**
Fire Fighting - **Superior Helicopter Llc.**
Fire Fighting Equipment - **General Safety Equipment**
Fire Fighting Equipment, Pumps, & Apparatus - **Darley & Co., W. S.**
Fire Protection Products - **Central Sprinkler**
Fire Resistant Data Safes - **Meilink Safe Co., a Fireking International**
Fire Resistant Filing Cabinets - **Meilink Safe Co.**
Fire Resistant Safes - **Meilink Safe Co., a Fireking International Co.**
Fire Retardant Coatings - **Nofire Technologies, Inc.**
Fire Retardant Products - **South Beach Fire Services**
Fire Retardent Kitchen Cloths - **Aquapower Co.**
Fire Retardent Kitchen Cloths - **Aqua Power Co.**
Fire Safe Extension Cords - **Technology Research Corporation**
Fire Sprinkler Equipment - **Cold Extrusion Co. Of America, Inc.**
Fire Suppressing & Retarding Agents - **Firefreeze Worldwide, Inc.**
Fire Systems & Detection Equipment - **Chemetron Fire Systems**
Fire Training Systems - **Symtron Systems, Inc.**
Firefighting Equipment - **Tnt Tools Inc**
Firestopping Materials - **Specified Technologies, Inc.**
First Aid & Survival Bandages - **Shawnee Products, Inc.**
First Aid Cream, Antiseptic Gel - **Water-jel Technologies**
First Aid Kits - **Afassco, Inc.**
First Aid Products - **Apothecary Products Inc.**
First Aid Products - **Water-jel Technologies**
Fish - **Maxport International**
Fish & Seafood Processing - **Sahalee of Alaska, Inc.**
Fish Food - **Hartz Mountain**
Fish Processing - **Trans-aqua International, Inc.**
Fish and Seafoods - **Pafco Importing Co.**
Fish, Fresh or Frozen Prepared, Alligator Hides - **Fish Processors Inc**
Fish_fresh or Frozen Prepared - **Alaskan Dried Foods**
Fish_fresh or Frozen Prepared - **Fishery Products International Inc.**
Fish_fresh or Frozen Prepared - **North Atlantic Fish Co , Inc**
Fish_fresh or Frozen Prepared - **P & J Oyster Co., Inc.**
Fish_fresh or Frozen Prepared - **Sahalee of Alaska, Inc.**
Fish_fresh or Frozen Prepared - **Trans-aqua International, Inc.**
Fishing Equipment, Export - **Cma Incorporated**
Fishing Lines & Industrial Cordage - **Woodstock Line Co., the**
Fishing Lures - **Mr. V's, Inc.**
Fishing Rods & Component Parts - **Biscayne Rod Mfg., Inc.**
Fishing Tackle - **Kowa California Inc.**
Fitter Media for Automotive & Industrial Applications - **Fiber Mark Inc.**
Fittings - **D.b.c. Enterprises, Inc.**
Fittings & Valves - **Robinair, a Div. Of Spx Corporation**
Fittings - Plastic - **Policonductos S.a. De C.v.**
Fittings for Water Works and Irrigation - **Apac Products**
Fittings, Carbon Steel, Etc. - **Klm International**
Fixed & Portable Liquid Oxygen Life Support - **Essex Cryogenics of Misso**
Fixed Radio Frequency Inductors - **Koa Speer Electronics, Inc.**
Fixed Wing Scheduled Service - **Era Aviation Inc.**
Fixtures: Free Standing - **Dolphin Mfg. Inc.**
Fixtures; Loose - **Dolphin Mfg. Inc.**
Fixturing - **Accurite Development & Mfg**

Fixturing & Tooling - **Rapid Development Service**
Flag Poles & Lightning Protection Masts - **Lingo, Inc., Acme Flagpole**
Flags & Banners - **Flagman of America**
Flags, Banners & Pennants - **Mainley Flags, Inc.**
Flame Hardening of Iron & Steel Products - **California Surface Hardening**
Flame Retardants - **Dover Chemical Corp., Sub. Of Icc Industries, Inc.**
Flame Retarders - **Eastern Color & Chemical Co.**
Flamenco Apparel - **Star Styled Dancing Supplies**
Flange Insulation Sets - **Houston Mfg. & Specialty Co., Inc.**
Flanges to Awwa Spec. - **Int'l Fabricators & Engineers**
Flannel Plaids - **Laren Industries**
Flare Systems - **John Zink Company**
Flares - **Allied Flare Inc.**
Flashers - **Tridon**
Flat & Curved Glass Tempering & Fabrication - **Spec-temp, Inc.**
Flat Bread - **Distinctive Foods, Inc.**
Flat Glass - **Laminated Glass**
Flat Panel Display - **Visentech Systems, Inc.**
Flat Panel Displays - **Rosen Product Development Inc**
Flat Part, Digitizing Scanner - **Metalsoft, Inc.**
Flat Rolled Steel Wire - **Steel Heddle Mfg. Co. (Mfr)**
Flat Rolled Steel, Sheet and Strip; Steel Slitting, - **Rolled Steel Products**
Flat Wire - **Permaluster Company**
Flat, Cleated & Special Profile - **Fabreeka International Inc**
Flat-rolled Steel - **Pittsburgh Flatroll Co.**
Flatbed Equipment Trailers - **Custom Trailer**
Flatbed Steel Rule Label Dies - **Ashwell Die Corp.**
Flavoring Extracts - **Flavor Dynamics, Inc.**
Flavoring Extracts & Syrups - **Dragoco Inc.**
Flavoring Extracts & Syrups - **Flavor Dynamics, Inc.**
Flavoring Extracts & Syrups - **International Bioflavors Inc.**
Flavoring Extracts & Syrups - **O S F Flavors, Inc.**
Flavoring Extracts & Syrups - **Sto-chard**
Flavoring Extracts & Syrups - **Ptx Food Corp.**
Flavors, Extracts & Syrups (Natural or Artificial) - **Liway International,**
Flea & Tick Powders - **Hartz Mountain**
Fleece Jackets, Gloves and Hats; Outer Clothes - **T & R Concept Inc**
Fleece Sportswear - **Alps Sportswear Manufacturing Co , Inc**
Fleet Management Systems & Equipment - **Gasboy International, Inc.**
Flex & Offset Printing - **Duro Bag Mfg. Co.**
Flexible Air Conditioning Ducts & Fittings - **Flexmaster U S a Inc.**
Flexible Drain Flashings - **Tru-fast Corp.**
Flexible Metal Hose, Assemblies - **American Boa, Inc.**
Flexible Metal Hose, Bellows & Expansion Joint - **Microflex, Inc.**
Flexible Non-metallic Tubing - **Daburn Electronics & Cable Corp.**
Flexible Packaging: Plastics, Laminated & Coated - **Plastic Packaging**
Flexible Power Cords - **Ericson Manufacturing, Inc.**
Flexible Printed Packaging & Bags - **Maine Poly Inc**
Flexible Pvc Profiles / T-mold - **Sparks Industries**
Flexible Shaft Tools - **Jaw Manufacturing Co.**
Flexible Trim & Moulding Manufacturer - **Cobblecrete International Inc**
Flexible Vinyl Extrusions - **Pan American Plastics Co.**
Flexible, Self-skinning Foams for World Wide Markets - **Swd Urethane**
Flo Breakers - **Wilson & Co., Inc., Thomas C.**
Flocked Fabrics - **Spectro Coating Corp.(Mfr)**
Flocked Suedes & Velvets - **Spectro Coating Corp.(Mfr)**
Floor Coatings - **International Paint Inc.**
Floor Covering Stores - **Penichet Carpet**
Floor Coverings - **Bifrost**
Floor Coverings, Hard Surface - **Congoleum Corp.**
Floor Coverings, Hard Surface - **American Hi-tech Flooring Co.**
Floor Coverings_hard Surface, Decorative Finishes, - **Crossfield Products**
Floor Heater Systems - **Weben-jarco, Inc.**
Floor Machines - **Advance Paper & Maintenance**
Floor Tile; Concrete - **Ro-tile**
Floorcare Products - **Maytag International**
Flooring Finishes, Export - **Global Market Partners, Inc.**
Flooring; Wood, Tile, Sheet Vinyl - **Waite, R. M. Company**
Floral Industries - **Knud Nielsen Company, Inc.**
Flotation Machines - **Quinn Process Equipment Co**
Flotation Mattresses - **Land and Sky Mfg., Inc.**

Flour & Other Grain Mill Products - **Heartland Mill, Inc.**
Flour & Other Grain Mill Products - **Penny Newman Milling Llc**
Flour Mixes & Doughs_prepared - **Amero Foods Mfg. Corp.**
Flour Mixes & Doughs_prepared - **Old World Cone**
Flour Tortillas, Homestyle, Die Cut - **Fresca Mexican Foods Inc.**
Flour and Meal of Soybean - **Garnac Grain**
Flourescent Lamps - **Lighting Resources, Inc.**
Flow Control Instruments - **Porter Instrument Co.**
Flow Instruments/industrial Process Type - **Panametrics, Inc**
Flow Measurement Systems - **Perry Equipment Corp.**
Flow Meters - **Pierburg Instruments, Inc.**
Flow Meters & Equipment - **Preso Meters, Corp.**
Flow Switches - **S O R, Inc.**
Flowers & Florists' Supplies - **Willow Creek Greenhouses Inc**
Flowers and Florists' Supplies - **Boyntons Botanicals**
Flowers, Nursery Stock and Florists - **Greenleaf Wholesale Florist Inc**
Fluid Coupling Solutions to Improve Your System Reliability - **Jiffy Tite**
Fluid Couplings & Hose Fittings for Automotive Oem - **Jiffy Tite Co., Inc.**
Fluid Meters & Counting Devices - **Hypro Corp.**
Fluid Meters & Counting Devices - **Lumenite Control Technology Inc.**
Fluid Meters & Counting Devices - **Alicat Scientific Inc**
Fluid Meters & Counting Devices - **Consilium Us, Inc.**
Fluid Meters & Counting Devices - **Matrix Controls Co., Inc.**
Fluid Power Cylinders & Actuators - **Houston Mfg. & Specialty Co., Inc.**
Fluid Power Cylinders & Actuators - **American Cylinder Co., Inc.**
Fluid Power Cylinders & Actuators - **Catching Fluidpower, Inc.**
Fluid Power Cylinders & Actuators - **Defco, Inc.**
Fluid Power Cylinders & Actuators - **Sprague Controls Inc**
Fluid Power Pumps & Motors - **Heavy Duty Hydro Blasting, Inc.**
Fluid Power Pumps & Motors - **Catching Fluidpower, Inc.**
Fluid Power Pumps & Motors - **Defco, Inc.**
Fluid Power Pumps & Motors - **Az Hydraulic Engineering Inc**
Fluid Power Pumps & Motors - **Flojet Corp**
Fluid Power Pumps & Motors - **Rineer Hydraulics**
Fluid Power Pumps & Motors, Cylinders & Valves - **Hydra-tech Systems**
Fluid Power Valves & Hose Fittings - **Bijur Lubricating Corporation**
Fluid Power Valves & Hose Fittings - **American Equipment Sales Co.**
Fluid Power Valves & Hose Fittings - **Faip North America Inc.**
Fluid Power Valves & Hose Fittings - **O C V Control Valves**
Fluid Power Valves & Hose Fittings - **Service Hydraulics Inc.**
Fluid Power Valves Direct Cntl Manual - **Cross Mfg. Inc.**
Fluid Pumping Equipment - **Sunstrand Corporation**
Fluid Transfer Pumps - **American Equipment Sales Co.**
Fluorescent & Halogen Shoplights - **American Power Products Inc**
Fluorescent Lighting Fixtures - **Doane Co., Inc., L. C.**
Fluorescent Night Lights - **American Power Products Inc**
Fluoroelastomer Based Adhesives & Sealants - **Pelseal Technologies, Llc**
Fluoropolymer Hose - **Teleflex Fluid Systems, Inc.**
Flux Recycling Systems - **Ogden Engineering Corp.**
Fly Fishing Tackle - **Jim Teeny, Inc.**
Fly Lines , Leaders, Tippet - **Rio Products International Inc**
Flyswatter / Bugwacker - **Regent Labs Inc.**
Flywheels - **Automatic Transmission Parts, Inc. A.t.p.**
Fm Telemetering Equipment - **Solid State Electronics Corp**
Foam & Fiberglass Surfboards - **Stewart Surfboards Inc**
Foam Felt-compressed Pu - **Crest Foam Industries**
Foam Laminations, Automotive Fabrics Cutting - **C. M. I. Enterprises**
Foam Products - **Swd Urethane**
Foam-fuel Cell - **Crest Foam Industries**
Foam-industrial - Pu Reticulated - **Crest Foam Industries**
Foamed Cushioning, Flame Resistant - **Chestnut Ridge Foam, Inc.**
Foamwood - **Arabel**
Foil Stamping Dies & Materials - **Ikela Co.**
Folded & Roll Towels, Toilet Tissue & Napkins - **Encore Paper Co.**
Folders for Baby Wipes - **Elsner Engineering Works Inc.**
Folding Banquet & Utility Tables & Chairs - **Lifetime Products Inc**
Folding Bottle Carts - **Respond Group of Companies**
Folding Cartons, Contract Packaging Printing - **Outlook Graphics**
Folding Paperboard Boxes & Point-of-purchase Displays - **Boxes.com**
Folding Tables - **Mity Lite**
Folding Trailers - **Fleetwood Enterprises Inc**

Folding Wood Lecterns - **Tower Stool Company**
Folding Wood Stools Compact - **Tower Stool Company**
Food & Cationic Industrial Potato Starch - **Western Polymer Corp**
Food & Vegetable Oil Processing Equipment - **Cantrell International**
Food - Spices & Soup Bases - **Pacific Harvest Products Inc.**
Food Additives, Emulsifiers / Gums- **Liway International, Inc.**
Food All Types: Candy Cookies Cereal Condiments - **Atwood Richards**
Food Bags - **Caltex Plastics Inc**
Food Dyes - **Tricon Colors, Llc**
Food Flavorings - **International Bioflavors Inc.**
Food Flavorings - **O S F Flavors, Inc.**
Food Grade, Epoxy, Nylon and Teflon - **Americoat Corp.**
Food Inspection Equipment - **Par Vision Systems Corporation**
Food Irradiation Processing - **Food Technology Service, Inc.**
Food Manufacturing & Laboratory Equipments - **Liway International, Inc.**
Food Plant Engineering - **Jdc (Hawaii) Inc., Advance Foods**
Food Preparations - **Steinfelds Products**
Food Preparations - **Spectrum Naturals Inc**
Food Preparations - **Alpine Touch Inc**
Food Preparations - **American Miso Co.**
Food Preparations - **Bakemark**
Food Preparations - **Cajun Injector, Inc.**
Food Preparations - **Famarco Ltd. Inc./b & K International**
Food Preparations - **Legg, Inc., A. C.**
Food Preparations - **Peking Noodle Co Inc**
Food Preparations - **Ptx Food Corp.**
Food Preparations - **The Wornick Company**
Food Preparations - **Todds, Ltd.**
Food Preparations - **Yergat Packing Co**
Food Preparations - **Dews Research**
Food Preparations - **Basic Foods International, Inc.**
Food Preparations - **International Custom Products**
Food Preparations - **Templar Food Products**
Food Proc. Mach., Air Filters, Wholesale - **Micropure Filtration, Inc.**
Food Proc. Mach., Gas Filters, Wholesale - **Micropure Filtration, Inc.**
Food Processing Equipment - **Heinzen Manufacturing Inc**
Food Processing Equipment - **Waukesha Cherry-burrell (Mfr)**
Food Processing Machinery - **Extru-tech, Inc.**
Food Processing Machinery, Frozen Block Flakers - **General Machinery**
Food Processing Machinery— Cherry, Olive, Date - **Ashlock Company**
Food Processing Ovens, Dryers, Ste - **Tech-mark Inc**
Food Processors - **Hamilton Beach/proctor Silex, Inc.**
Food Prod. Mach, Conveyors, Belt & Screw - **Weiler and Company Inc.**
Food Prod. Mach., Dumpers - **Weiler and Company Inc.**
Food Prod. Mach., Fresh Meat Dicers - **General Machinery Corporation**
Food Prod. Mach., Grinders & Mixers - **Weiler and Company Inc.**
Food Prod. Mach., Grinders / Mixers - **Weiler and Company Inc.**
Food Prod. Mach., Meat Tenderizers - **General Machinery Corporation**
Food Prod. Mach., Portioning Equipment - **Weiler and Company Inc.**
Food Prod., Mach. Frozen Meat Dicers - **General Machinery Corporation**
Food Prod., Mach. Frozen Meat Grinder - **General Machinery Corp**
Food Products - **Health Valley Foods**
Food Products Machinery - **Bakemark**
Food Products Machinery - **Ashlock Company**
Food Products Machinery - **Bevles Company Inc**
Food Products Machinery - **Cantrell International**
Food Products Machinery - **Delta International**
Food Products Machinery - **Food Technology Service, Inc.**
Food Products Machinery - **Hart Design & Mfg, Inc.**
Food Products Machinery - **Hartel Systems Division,**
Food Products Machinery - **Heinzen Manufacturing Inc**
Food Products Machinery - **Hollymatic Corporation (Mfr)**
Food Products Machinery - **Independent Restaurant & Bakery Equip**
Food Products Machinery - **Magna Industries, Inc.**
Food Products Machinery - **Old World Cone**
Food Products Machinery - **Reading Bakery Systems**
Food Products Machinery - **Solbern Div. Howden Food Eqip.**
Food Products Machinery - **Sonic Corp.**
Food Products Machinery - **Stearns Product Development**
Food Products Machinery - **The Lucks Food Equipment Co.**
Food Products Manufacturing - **California Fruit Packing Co.**

Food Products Manufacturing - **The Morning Star Packing Co.**
Food Seasonings - **Old World Spices & Seasonings, Inc.**
Food Seasonings, Sauces & Contract Packaging - **Todds, Ltd.**
Food Service Cleaning Equipment - **Dipwell Co., Inc., the**
Food Service Kits - **Cambria County Assn. For the Blind & Handicappe**
Food Supplements - **American Laboratories, Inc. (Mfr)**
Food Supplements & Botanicals - **Gnld International**
Food Wholesale - **Lucky Seven Food Inc**
Food, Bakers Equipment and Supplies; Ingredient - **Bakemark**
Food, Dairy, Cosmetic, Chemical & Pharmaceutical - **Hartel Systems**
Foodservice & Retail Packaging Available - **Northern Star Co., Inc.**
Foodservice Disposables - **Lanca Sales, Inc.**
Footwear - **Starensier**
Footwear - **Converse**
Footwear - **Skechers Usa Inc**
Footwear - **Kowa California Inc.**
Footwear, Dance & Gymnastics - **Leo's Dancewear Inc.**
Footwear, Except Rubber - **Red Wing Shoe Co.**
Footwear_men's, Except Athletic - **Poly Masters Industries Inc**
Footwear_women's, Except Athletic - **Poly Masters Industries Inc**
Force Measurement Testing Equipment - **Scalemen of Florida, Inc.**
Force Transducers (Load Cells) - **Pace Transducer Co**
Foreign Assembly of U.s. Components - **Torner International, Inc.**
Foreign Currency Exchange - **First Security Bank**
Foreign Language Voice over - **Magnum Group, Inc. Translation & Relat**
Forestry Equipment - **Netafim Irrigation Inc**
Forestry Equipment & Parts, Export - **Warner T. Lundahl, Inc.**
Forged Aluminum Horsehoes/racing Plates - **Victory Racing Plate Co. The**
Forged Steel Gate, Flobe & Check Valves - **Conbraco Industries**
Forged Steel High Pressure Pipe Fittings - **Pennsylvania Machine Works,**
Forgings, Iron & Steel - **Canton Drop Forge**
Forgings, Nonferrous - **Lenape Forge, Inc.**
Forgings_iron & Steel - **Scot Forge Co.**
Fork-lift Trucks and Other Works Trucks Fitted - **Interpax**
Fork-lift Trucks; Works Trucks with Lifts - **Mustang Industrial Equip**
Form & Trim Tooling - **Fancort Industries, Inc.**
Form-liners Manufacturer - **Cobblecrete International Inc**
Formal Wear - **Duron Neckwear Inc**
Forward - Auger Extruding Heads, Etc. - **Austin Continental Industries**
Foundation Ventilators - **Independent Mfg. Co., Inc.**
Foundries, Aluminum - **Unexcelled Castings Corp.**
Foundries, Gray & Ductile Iron - **Benton Foundry, Inc.**
Foundries, Gray & Ductile Iron - **Deeter Foundry Inc.**
Foundries_aluminum - **Advance Aluminum & Brass Inc**
Foundries_aluminum - **Baja Pacific Light Metals No**
Foundries_aluminum - **Baldwin Aluminum Foundry & Machine Co.**
Foundries_aluminum - **Le Claire Mfg. Co.**
Foundries_aluminum - **Quality Brass & Aluminum Foundry**
Foundries_aluminum - **Coopers & Clarke, Inc**
Foundries_gray & Ductile Iron - **Washington Mould Co.**
Foundries_gray & Ductile Iron - **Olympic Foundry Inc**
Foundries_gray & Ductile Iron & Alum. - **Barry Pattern & Foundry**
Foundries_malleable Iron - **Olympic Foundry Inc**
Foundries_nonferrous - **Advance Aluminum & Brass Inc**
Foundries_nonferrous - **Modern Art Foundry, Inc.**
Foundries_nonferrous - **Oilpure Refiner Co**
Foundries_steel - **Olympic Foundry Inc**
Foundries_steel Investment - **Delvest, Inc.**
Foundry Coke - **A B C Coke**
Foundry Molds & Castings - **Quality Mold Inc.**
Foundry Products, Investment Castings - **Wichita Falls Mfg.**
Fountain Solution Controller, Remote Pasting - **Support Products Inc.**
Four Slide Parts - **Fabor Fourslide, Inc.**
Fourslide & Multislide Fabrication - **Tubing Seal Cap**
Fourslide Metal Stampings - **John Amann Sons Co.**
Fourslide Wire Forms - **John Amann Sons Co.**
Fragrance Items / Potpourri - **Alaska Herb Tea Co. (Mfr)**
Fragrances - **Sozio, Inc., J. E.**
Fragrances & Flavors - **Dragoco Inc.**
Framed Artwork - **Excel Design Inc.**
Frames : Parts & Components for - **Arno International, Inc.**

Franchising of Rockwood Retaining - **Rockwood Retaining Walls, Inc.**
Franchisor - **Verlo Mattress Factory Stores, Int'l Hq.,Verlo Mattress Co.**
Free Access Floor Panels - **Hitachi Maxco, Inc.**
Freeze Dried Fruits, Vegetables, Soups - **Oregon Freeze Dry Inc**
Freeze-dried & Concentrated Vegetable Juices - **Florida Food Products**
Freght Forwarder - **Atlantic Cold Storage Corporation**
Freight & Cargo Transportation - **Airgroup Express/airgroup Corp**
Freight & Cargo Transportation - **Alliance International**
Freight & Cargo Transportation - **Apollo Warehouse, Inc.**
Freight & Cargo Transportation - **Argents Express Group**
Freight & Cargo Transportation - **Atlantic Cold Storage Corporation**
Freight & Cargo Transportation - **Barner, Jerry M. & Sons**
Freight & Cargo Transportation - **Bart Trucking**
Freight & Cargo Transportation - **Bigge Crane & Rigging Co.**
Freight & Cargo Transportation - **Brown Alcantar & Brown Inc.**
Freight & Cargo Transportation - **Burlington Air Express Inc.**
Freight & Cargo Transportation - **Burlington Motor Carriers**
Freight & Cargo Transportation - **Cagema Agencies Inc.**
Freight & Cargo Transportation - **Campbell & Gardiner, Inc.**
Freight & Cargo Transportation - **Carmenco International**
Freight & Cargo Transportation - **Central Transportation Systems**
Freight & Cargo Transportation - **Chantilly Freight Corporation**
Freight & Cargo Transportation - **Chickawaw Container Services**
Freight & Cargo Transportation - **Circle International**
Freight & Cargo Transportation - **Clm, Inc.**
Freight & Cargo Transportation - **Corcoran International Corp.**
Freight & Cargo Transportation - **Dan Transport Corporation**
Freight & Cargo Transportation - **Equipsa, Inc.**
Freight & Cargo Transportation - **Expressway Usa Freightlines Inc.**
Freight & Cargo Transportation - **Foreign Trade Zone 72**
Freight & Cargo Transportation - **Fpa Customs Brokers, Inc.**
Freight & Cargo Transportation - **Fritz Maritime Agencies**
Freight & Cargo Transportation - **Hawks Express Inc.**
Freight & Cargo Transportation - **Held & Associates, Inc.**
Freight & Cargo Transportation - **Hendrix, Miles, Hendrix Company**
Freight & Cargo Transportation - **Ideal Transportation Co. Inc.**
Freight & Cargo Transportation - **Incare Cargo Services**
Freight & Cargo Transportation - **Inter-jet Systems, Inc.**
Freight & Cargo Transportation - **Inter-world Customs Broker, Inc.**
Freight & Cargo Transportation - **J.j. Trucking Services of Jacksonville, .**
Freight & Cargo Transportation - **Jensen, Norman G., Inc.**
Freight & Cargo Transportation - **Jet Air Service, Inc.**
Freight & Cargo Transportation - **Keen, R. H. & Co., Inc.**
Freight & Cargo Transportation - **L. D. Tonsager & Sons, Inc.**
Freight & Cargo Transportation - **Labelle Rothery Movers, Inc.**
Freight & Cargo Transportation - **Landstar Ranger, Inc.**
Freight & Cargo Transportation - **Lazer Transportation Services**
Freight & Cargo Transportation - **Lin Container Freight Station & Distri**
Freight & Cargo Transportation - **Mark Vii International**
Freight & Cargo Transportation - **Match Maker, the**
Freight & Cargo Transportation - **Mcclary, Swift & Co., Inc.**
Freight & Cargo Transportation - **Mediterranean Shipping Company**
Freight & Cargo Transportation - **Nippon Express Usa, Inc.**
Freight & Cargo Transportation - **Ortiz Villafane, Rene, Inc.**
Freight & Cargo Transportation - **Overnite Transportation Co.**
Freight & Cargo Transportation - **R & T Truck Inc.**
Freight & Cargo Transportation - **Rapid Air & Ocean**
Freight & Cargo Transportation - **Respond Cargo Services Corp.**
Freight & Cargo Transportation - **Roadway Express, Inc.**
Freight & Cargo Transportation - **Rogers & Brown Custom Brokers, Inc.**
Freight & Cargo Transportation - **Rosy Services Forwarders Corp.**
Freight & Cargo Transportation - **Schenker International, Inc.**
Freight & Cargo Transportation - **Senderex Cargo Co., Inc.**
Freight & Cargo Transportation - **Southern Warehouse Corporation**
Freight & Cargo Transportation - **T Transportation, Inc.**
Freight & Cargo Transportation - **Tampa Bay International Terminals,**
Freight & Cargo Transportation - **Torner, Edmundo Customhouse Broker**
Freight & Cargo Transportation - **Transwood, Inc.**
Freight & Cargo Transportation - **Vanco Heavy Lift C.f.s.**
Freight & Cargo Transportation - **World Commerce Forwarding, Inc.**
Freight & Cargo Transportation - **Worldlink Logistics, Inc.**

Freight & Cargo Transportation - Wts of Houston, Inc.
Freight & Cargo: Transportation & Insurance - Foreign Trade Zone 42
Freight & Cargo: Transportation & Insurance - Interfreight Inc.
Freight & Cargo: Transportation & Insurance - Robinson H.w. & Co
Freight & Container Transportation - Friendly Public Warehouses Inc.
Freight Consolidation - Atlantic Cold Storage Corporation
Freight Consolidation - Horizon Forwarders Inc.
Freight Forwarder - Airgroup Express/airgroup Corporation
Freight Forwarder - Argents Express Group
Freight Forwarder - Brown Alcantar & Brown Inc.
Freight Forwarder - Burlington Air Express Inc.
Freight Forwarder - Campbell & Gardiner, Inc.
Freight Forwarder - Carmenco International
Freight Forwarder - Chantilly Freight Corporation
Freight Forwarder - Corcoran International Corp.
Freight Forwarder - Dan Transport Corporation
Freight Forwarder - Danzas Corporation
Freight Forwarder - Equipsa, Inc.
Freight Forwarder - Fritz Companies
Freight Forwarder - Held & Associates, Inc.
Freight Forwarder - Hendrix, Miles, Hendrix Company
Freight Forwarder - Incare Cargo Services
Freight Forwarder - Inter-world Customs Broker, Inc.
Freight Forwarder - J. H. World Express, Inc.
Freight Forwarder - Jensen, Norman G., Inc.
Freight Forwarder - Jet Air Service, Inc.
Freight Forwarder - Keen, R. H. & Co., Inc.
Freight Forwarder - Krieger, Norman, Inc.
Freight Forwarder - L. D. Tonsager & Sons, Inc.
Freight Forwarder - Labelle Rothery Movers, Inc.
Freight Forwarder - Lazer Transportation Services
Freight Forwarder - Mcclary, Swift & Co., Inc.
Freight Forwarder - Norman G. Jensen, Inc.
Freight Forwarder - Ortiz Villafane, Rene, Inc.
Freight Forwarder - Rapid Air & Ocean
Freight Forwarder - Rausch, Ted L. Co., the
Freight Forwarder - Respond Cargo Services Corp.
Freight Forwarder - Rogers & Brown Custom Brokers, Inc.
Freight Forwarder - Rosy Services Forwarders Corp.
Freight Forwarder - Schenker International, Inc.
Freight Forwarder - Senderex Cargo Co., Inc.
Freight Forwarder - Torner, Edmundo Customhouse Brokers
Freight Forwarder - World Commerce Forwarding, Inc.
Freight Forwarder - Worldlink Logistics, Inc.
Freight Forwarder - Wts of Houston, Inc.
Freight Forwarder & Chb - Schenker International, Inc.
Freight Forwarder (Nyc, Atl, Mia, Lax, Chi) - Inter-jet Systems, Inc.
Freight Forwarder, Freight & Cargo Transp - Business Aviation Courier
Freight Forwarders - Torner International, Inc. / Edmundo Torner, Chb
Freight Forwarding - Euro-american Air Frt. Fwdg Co., Inc.
Freight Forwarding - Horizon Forwarders Inc.
Freight Forwarding - Interfreight Inc.
Freight Forwarding - K & K Express
Freight Forwarding - Robinson H.w. & Company Inc.
Freight Forwarding - Seamodal Transport Corp.
Freight Forwarding Intl Air/ocean - Migar Enterprises, Inc.
Freight Forwarding Ocean & Air - Schroeder United Van Lines
Freight Forwarding, Air - Superior Air Freight
Freight Forwarding, International - Chase Leavitt & Company
Freight Forwarding, International - Jan Packaging, Inc.
Freight Insurance, International - Roanoke Brokerage Services, Inc.
Freight Transportation Arrangement - Advantagetransportation Inc.
Freight Transportation Arrangement - Central Air Freight Inc.
Freight Transportation Arrangement - Fillette Green Shipping Services
Freight Transportation Arrangement - Stewart Alexander & Company
Freight Transportation Arrangement - Transoceanic Shipping Company,
Freight Transportation Broker, Us/canada - Farmland Transportation Inc.
Freight Transportation, Steamship Agents - Chase Leavitt & Company
Frequency - to - Voltage Converters - Solid State Electronics Corp
Fresh / Frozen Meats - Parts - Farbest Foods, Inc.
Fresh Cov Boxed Beef - Agri Processors

Fresh Cucumbers - United Pickle Products Corp.
Fresh Fruit Equipment - Agri-tech, Inc.
Fresh Fruits & Vegetables - R.b. Packing, Inc
Fresh Fruits and Vegetables - Firman Pinkerton
Fresh Fruits and Vegetables - Stemlit Growers
Fresh Garlic - Denice & Filice Packing
Fresh Greenhouse & Organic Vegetables - Cris-p Produce Co Inc
Fresh Salsa, Sauces and Vegetables - El Toro Food Products Inc
Fresh Tilapia Fish Frozen - Abco Products
Fresh Vegetable Equipment - Agri-tech, Inc.
Fresh and Frozen Packaged Fish - Fishery Products International Inc.
Fresh and Frozen Packaged Fish - North Atlantic Fish Co , Inc
From Industrial Processes - Thiel Air Technologies Corp.
From Process Industry, Both for Legal - Water Technologies
Frontier Kettle Soup Merchandisers - Tomlinson Industries
Frost-proof Yard Hydrants, Well Adapters - Merrill Mfg. Co., Inc.
Frozen & Refrigerated Storage - Atlantic Cold Storage Corporation
Frozen Barbecued Meat Products- Prepared Food Products, Inc.
Frozen Cappuccino & Smoothies - Cappuccino America Corp.
Frozen Chicken - Basic Foods International, Inc.
Frozen Chicken Products - Aspen Foods, a Division of Koch Poultry
Frozen Fish - Basic Foods International, Inc.
Frozen Food Vending Machines - Vendtronics
Frozen Gourmet Desserts - Sam's Homemade Cheesecake Inc
Frozen Kosher Beef - Agri Processors
Frozen Kosher Food - Old Fashioned Kitchen Inc
Frozen Meat - Basic Foods International, Inc.
Frozen Oriental Products - Pacway Food International Corp
Frozen Pastries - Amero Foods Mfg. Corp.
Frozen Pizza Crust - T N T Pizza Crust, Inc.
Frozen Potatoes - Lamb-weston Inc
Frozen Poultry - Tatum Farms International, Inc.
Frozen Poultry - Kosher & non Kosher - Agri Processors
Frozen Seafood - Lins Trading
Frozen Seafood - Arista Industries, Inc.
Frozen Seafood & Seafood Sauces, Clams - Ecrevisse Acadienne (Mfr)
Frozen Seafood Products, Export - Cma Incorporated
Frozen Specialties - Lamb-weston Inc
Frozen Specialties - Amy's Kitchen Inc
Frozen Specialties - Chang Food Company
Frozen Specialties - Matador Processors, Inc.
Frozen Specialties - Old Fashioned Kitchen Inc
Frozen Specialties / Eggrolls - Pacway Food International Corp
Frozen Unbaked Bread, Rolls - J & J Wall Baking Company Inc
Frozen Veal & Lamb Kosher & non Kosher - Agri Processors
Fruit Bars & Chocolate Dipped Fruit Bars - Fruit-a-freeze Inc
Fruit Breads - Neuman Bakery Specialties, Inc.
Fruit Drinks - Mazza Brand - Syrups - House of Spices
Fruit Fresh, Pears, Cherries - Stemlit Growers
Fruit Syrups - Monin, Inc.
Fruits & Vegetables in Glass Jars - Miss Scarlett Inc
Fruits & Vegetables, Frozen - Florida Food Products, Inc.
Fruits & Vegetables, Frozen - Lamb-weston Inc
Fruits & Vegetables, Frozen - Norpac Foods Inc
Fruits & Peppers , Dried or Crushed or Ground - Accurate Ingredients
Fruits, Brandied - Miss Scarlett Inc
Fruits, Canned - Western Consolidated Foods, Inc.
Fruits, Vegetables and Olives - Miss Scarlett Inc
Fryers, Deep Fat Filtration Systems - Pitco Frialator, Inc. (Mfr)
Fuel & Lube Oil Pumping Systems - Snyder Equipment Co., Inc.
Fuel Dispnsing Nozzles - Saber Technologies, Llc
Fuel Emulsions - Petroferm Inc.
Fuel Filters for Oil Companies, Airlines - Velcon Filters Inc
Fuel Management Control Systems - Snyder Equipment Co., Inc.
Fuel Storage Design / Construction - Environmental Services & Technolo
Fuel System Manufacturing - Royal Oak Industries, Inc.
Fuel Treatment - Ashland Chemicals
Fulfillment Services & Storage - Covers Unlimited, Inc.
Full Color Garphics Banners - A Fifty Star Flags, Banners & Flagpoles
Full Color Printing - Sandy's Trophies
Full Line of Deli Items - Agri Processors

Full Service Custom Injection Molding - **Mastercraft Companies**
Full Service Production Machining - **U.s. Manufacturing Corp**
Full Service Transportation Capabilities - **Distribution Services of Americ**
Full Turnkey Manufacturing - **Litec Inc.**
Full Usa Sourcing - **Foreign Trade Marketing**
Fume, Voc, Odor Destruction Systems - **Catalytic Products International,**
Fume-exhaust Duct Work - **Ats Products**
Fumes, Ultra-fine Liquid & Solid Contaminants - **Thiel Air Technologies**
Functionality Testing - **Electronic Manufacturing Svc**
Fund Raising - **Kae Co., Inc.**
Fund Raising - **Marketing Concepts**
Furnaces & Ovens_industrial - **Blasdel Enterprises, Inc.**
Furnaces & Ovens_industrial - **Omega Heater Co., Inc.**
Furnaces & Ovens_industrial - **Paragon Industries, Inc.**
Furnaces & Ovens_industrial - **Wisconsin Oven Corp.**
Furnaces, Ovens, Thermal Processing - **Centorr Vacuum Industries, Inc.**
Furnishings_house - **Best Value Textiles**
Furnishings_house - **Castletech Ltd**
Furnishings_house - **Manic Impressions**
Furnishings_house - **Milford Stitching Co., Inc.**
Furnishings_house - **Owen Mfg. Co., Charles D.**
Furnishings_house - **My Bed, Inc.**
Furniture - **Metal Master**
Furniture - **National Contract Furnishings**
Furniture - **Norco Products**
Furniture - **All American Office Products Inc**
Furniture - **Unique Originals, Inc.**
Furniture - **Summit Sales & Marketing**
Furniture & Fixtures - **Benchmark Fixture Corporation**
Furniture & Fixtures - **Hopeman Brothers Marine Interiors, Llc**
Furniture & Fixtures - **Pacific Crest Manufacturing Inc**
Furniture & Fixtures - **Vitro Seating Products**
Furniture & Fixtures - **Fusion Coatings Inc.**
Furniture & Fixtures, Upholstered Boat & Interiors - **Fine Line Interiors**
Furniture & Sign Industry - **Pacific Crest Manufacturing Inc**
Furniture Finishes - **Lilly Industries, Inc.**
Furniture Hardware, Office Chair Mech. - **Faultless Caster Division**
Furniture and Parts Thereof - **Lane Co., Inc., the**
Furniture and Parts Thereof - **Unique Originals, Inc.**
Furniture, Distributor - **Woodpecker, Inc.**
Furniture, Export - **Incon Overseas Marketing, Inc.**
Furniture, Fetish - **Pass Distributing Corporation**
Furniture, Manufactures - **Woodpecker, Inc.**
Furniture, Retail - **Woodpecker, Inc.**
Furniture, Wholesale - **Woodpecker, Inc.**
Furniture_household - **Pipefine Furniture, Inc.**
Furniture_household - **Woodpecker, Inc.**
Furniture_metal Household - **Sunlite Casual Furniture, Inc.**
Furniture_metal Household - **Tubing Seal Cap**
Furniture_public Building & Related - **Denver Seating Inc**
Furniture_public Building & Related - **Mccammisn Mfg. Co., Inc.**
Furniture_public Building & Related - **Norco Products**
Furniture_public Building & Related - **Precision Booth Mfg.**
Furniture_public Building & Related - **Sauder Mfg. Co.**
Furniture_upholstered Household - **Mc Kinley Leather of Hickory**
Furniture_upholstered Household - **National Contract Furnishings**
Furniture_wood Household - **Bonito Mfg.**
Furniture_wood Household - **Fine Craft Unlimited**
Furniture_wood Household - **Mouldings Unlimited, Inc.**
Furniture_wood Household - **Oakwood Interiors**
Furniture_wood Household - **Tocabi America Corp.**
Furniture _wood Office - **Tocabi America Corp.**
Further Processed Pork & Beef - **Jones Dairy Farm**
Fuseholders, Other Dry Process Electrical Porcelain - **Porcelain Products**
Fuses & Electrical Protection - **Carbone of America Corp.**
Fuses, Fuse and Power Distribution Blocks - **Gould Shawmut**
Fusible Interlining - Polyester, Nylon, Rayon - **Precision Custom Coatings**
Fusion Eqipment - **Policonductos S.a. De C.v.**
Fusion Splicing Equipment - **Sumitomo Electric Lightwave Corp.**
G-shock Watches - **Juno International**
Gaas Semiconductor Materials - **Wafer World, Inc.**

Galvanized Fittings - **Int'l Fabricators & Engineers**
Galvanized Steel Tubing for Structures & Fencing - **Cover-it Shelters, Inc.**
Galvanizing - **Columbus Galvanizing Voigt & Schweitzer, Inc.**
Galvanizing - **Valmont Industries Inc.**
Game Boards and Toys - **University Games**
Games and Specialty Promotional Products -**Interpretive Marketing Prod**
Games and Toys - **John N Hansen Co Inc**
Games, Dolls, Electronic Toys - **Shepher Distribution & Sales**
Games, Toys & Children's Vehicles - **Erin's Original Horseplay Rugs**
Games, Toys & Children's Vehicles - **John N Hansen Co Inc**
Games, Toys & Children's Vehicles - **University Games**
Gang Mowers - **Diamond Turf Equipment Inc.**
Ganite, Marble, Ceramic Tile, Vinyl Tile - **Midwest Builders Supply, Inc.**
Gantry Robots - **Specialty Equipment Co.**
Garage Door Opener Systems, Remote Control Switches - **Genie Co., the**
Garage Storage Cabinets - **We're Organized of No Calif**
Garbage Disposal Units , Household- **Anaheim Marketing International**
Garbage Disposal Units, Commercial - **Anaheim Marketing International**
Garbage Disposers, Commercial - **Garbel Products Company**
Garden Gloves - **Mcgough Industries Inc**
Garden Hose Packaging, Twist Tie Ribbon - **Alcar Industries, Inc.**
Garden Seed Packets - **Page Seed Co., Inc.**
Garden Supplies - **Deer-off, Inc.**
Gardenfrost - **Gilroy Foods, Inc. (Mfr)**
Garment Fiber Fill - **Western Synthetic Fiber**
Garment Manf. Automated Pressing Equip. - **Leonard Automatics, Inc.**
Garment Tunnel Finishing Equip - **Leonard Automatics, Inc.**
Gas & Chemical Standards & Reagents - **Supelco, Inc.(Mfr)**
Gas & Electric Water Heaters - **American Water Heater Co.**
Gas &Liquid Flow Sensors,Meters &Controllers- **Mc Millan Co., Inc., R D**
Gas & Vapor Detectors, MFR- **Gas Tech, Inc.**
Gas Compressor Packages - **V R Systems, Inc.**
Gas Cylinder Trailers - **Evans Mfg. Co., John Evans Trailers**
Gas Filtration Equipment - **International Air Filtration**
Gas Flow Measurement - **Bristol Babcock Inc.**
Gas Insulated Substations - **Mitsubishi Electric Power Products, Inc.**
Gas Meters, Repair & Remanufacturing - **Energy Economics, Inc.**
Gas Powered Recreational Go-karts - **Carter Brothers**
Gas Sample Conditioning Equipment - **Universal Analyzers Inc**
Gas Springs for Trunks & Hoods - **Cofap of America**
Gas Turbine Spare Parts, Hardware & Accessories - **Allied Dynamics**
Gas Water Heaters, Household, to 100 Gal. - **Lochinvar Water Heater**
Gas, Mining, Valves, Piping, Fittings - **Intracor-familian International**
Gaseous Fuels Carburetion Equipment - **Equipment & Systems Engineer**
Gases_industrial - **Scott Specialty Gases**
Gasket, Packing & Sealing Devices - **C G R Products Inc.**
Gaskets & Parts— Cork, Plastic, Rubber, - **Pacific States Felt & Mfg Co**
Gaskets & Sealing Devices - **Sealing Devices, Inc.**
Gaskets, Packing & Sealing Devices - **American High Performance Seals,**
Gaskets, Packing & Sealing Devices - **Embry Engineering & Mfg**
Gaskets, Packing & Sealing Devices - **Houston Mfg. & Specialty Co., Inc.**
Gaskets, Packing & Sealing Devices - **John Crane Inc.**
Gaskets, Packing & Sealing Devices - **Pacific States Felt & Mfg Co**
Gaskets, Packing & Sealing Devices - **R & R Rubber Molding Inc**
Gaskets, Packing & Sealing Devices - **Sealing Devices, Inc.**
Gaskets, Packing & Sealing Devices - **Bentley Manufacturing Co Inc**
Gaskets, Packing & Sealing Devices - **Trelleborg Ysh, Inc.**
Gaskets, Rubber/fiberglass/ceramic - **Pars Manufacturing Co.**
Gaskets Compounds - **K & W Products**
Gasoline Pumps & Dispensers - **Gasboy International, Inc.**
Gasoline Truck Tanks - **Beall Corp.**
Gate & Globe Valve Actuators - **Flo-tork Inc. (Mfr)**
Gate Valves - **Midwest International Standard Prod, Inc**
Gauze Sponges, Bandages & Surgical Dressings - **National Health Care,**
Gavels - **Trophy Shoppe**
Gazebos - **Vixen Hill Mfg. Co.**
Gazebos, Portable Arches, Displays - **B & C Mortensen Wood Prods Inc**
Gdt Var (Street Data for All U.s.a.) - **Barclay Maps**
Gears & Gear Boxes - **Prager Incorporated**
Gears & Gear Boxes, Repair - **Prager Incorporated**
Gel/agm Batteries - **Sec Industrial Battery Co., Inc.**

Gelatin - **Skw Biosystems**
Gelatin and Gelatin Derivatives; Isinglass - **Fici Export**
Gelatine Manufacturer - **Kind & Knox Gelatine, Inc.**
Gen. Ind. Mach., Portable Chillers - **Affinity Industries Inc. (Mfr)**
General Automotive Repair Shops - **Atk North America**
General Contractors; Commercial - **Mcalpine & Salyer Construction**
General Economic Development Programs - **County of Cattaraugus**
General Heavy Duty Repair Shop - **Southwest Peterbilt Gmc**
General Industrial Machine - **Renite Co., Lubrication Engineers**
General Machine Shop (Job Work) - **Ace-tek Manufacturing**
General Machine Shop (Job Work) - **L & M Machining Corporation**
General Machine Shop (Job Work) - **Swaim & Sons**
General Machine Shop (Job Work); Aircraft Parts - **Damar Machine Co**
General Machine Shop (Job Work); - **Malbert Mitchell Grinding Corp**
General Machining & Fabrication - **Field Equipment & Service Co.**
General Machining & Metal Fabrication - **A & B Fabrication & Repair,**
General Machining & Metal Fabrication Job Shop - **Dixie Machine Shop**
General Machining & Tool & Die Job Shop - **H & S Tool & Die Co.**
General Machining Job Shop - **Frazier Industries Inc.**
General Machining Job Shop - **Hedges & Bros., L.p.**
General Machining Job Shop - **K & B Machine Works Inc.**
General Machining Job Shop - **Kemco Tool & Machine Co., Inc.**
General Machining Job Shop - **La Machine Shop Inc.**
General Machining Job Shop - **Miller Machine**
General Machining Job Shop - **Nutter Machine Inc.**
General Machining Job Shop - **R & R Machine Industries, Inc.**
General Machining Job Shop - **Technical Engineering Sales, Inc.**
General Machining Job Shop, Conventional Machining - **A C Products**
General Merchandise - **Foreign Trade Marketing**
General Merchandise - **Nishizawa**
General Purpose Transistors - **Semiconductor Technology, Inc.**
General Sawmill (Specialy Cuts / Long & Wide) - **Yeager Sawmill**
General Sawmill (Wholesale Distribution) - **Hampton Lumber Sales Co**
General Sawmill and Planing Mill - **Avison Forest Products**
General U.s. Made Products, Vehicles - **Paulik International Co.**
General Warehousing - **Jan Packaging, Inc.**
General Warehousing & Storage - **Transoceanic Shipping Company, Inc.**
General Warehousing & Storage - **Simpson Tool Box Co**
General Welding Job Shop - **A C Welding & Engineering**
Generating Sets with Spark-ignition Internal - **Pantropic Power Products,**
Generating Sets, Electric, Parts - **Pantropic Power Products, Inc.**
Generator Power Distribution Equip. - **Con-tech Power Systems, Inc.**
Generator Sets - **J. C. Marine Diesel, Inc.**
Generator Sets & Control Systems - **Synergy International Inc.**
Geno's Ice Cream Mix- **North American Export Company**
Geo Textiles - **Western Synthetic Fiber**
Geo Textiles - **Poly-flex Inc.**
Geocomposites - **Poly-flex Inc.**
Geological Consulting - **Environmental Services & Technology**
Geologists - **Marshall Miller & Associates**
Geometric Die Heads & Chasers - **Greenfield Industries**
Geonet & Geo Composite Product - **Skaps Industries, Inc.**
Geonets - **Poly-flex Inc.**
Geophysical Electronic Equipment - **Geophysical Survey Systems, Inc.**
Geophysical Logging Equipment - **Mount Sopris Instrument Co Inc**
Geophysical Services - **Marshall Miller & Associates**
Geophysicists - **Marshall Miller & Associates**
Geotechnical Drilling Services - **Ruen Drilling International**
Geotechnical Testing Equipment - **Handy Geotechnical Instruments, Inc.**
Geotherm Solar Heat Power Sys - **Barber-nichols Incorporated**
Germanium Semiconductor Materials - **Wafer World, Inc.**
Germicidal Cleaners - **Legge Co., Inc., Walter G.**
Gibberellic Acid - **Agtrol International**
Gift Bags - **Duro Bag Mfg. Co.**
Gift Baskets, Gift Boxes - **Blackberry Patch, Inc.**
Gift Items & Jewelry - **Mistco, Inc.**
Gifts - **Trophy Shoppe**
Giftware - **Stylebuilt Accessories, Inc.**
Ginseng Roots,capsules & Extracts,tea,seeds - **Hsu's Ginseng Enterprises,**
Girls' Dresses - **Dorissa of Miami, Inc.**
Glass & Mirror Cutting & Picture Frames - **City Glass Co.**

Glass Blowing Tools, Equipment - **Glasscraft Inc**
Glass Clad Poly Carbonates - **Laminated Glass**
Glass Coating (Optical Interference) - **Photon Technologies, Inc.**
Glass Containers - **All American Containers, Inc.**
Glass Containers for Conveying, - **All American Containers, Inc.**
Glass Delivery Equipment - **Hansen Machine & Tool Co., N. M.**
Glass Distillation Apparatus - **Stanford Glassblowing Labs Inc**
Glass Engraving - **Sandy's Trophies**
Glass Fibers and Articles Thereof - **Lewcott**
Glass Finials - **World Wide Windows**
Glass Marbles - **Peltier Glass Co., the**
Glass Mold Lubricants - **Renite Co., Lubrication Engineers**
Glass Products from Purchased Glass - **Anthony International**
Glass Products from Purchased Glass - **Baut Studios Inc.**
Glass Products from Purchased Glass - **City Glass Co.**
Glass Products from Purchased Glass - **Coastal Industries, Inc.**
Glass Products from Purchased Glass - **Melotte-Morse-leonatti Stained Gl**
Glass Products from Purchased Glass - **Photon Technologies, Inc.**
Glass Products from Purchased Glass - **Saint George Crystal Ltd.**
Glass Products from Purchased Glass - **Stanford Glassblowing Labs Inc**
Glass Products from Purchased Glass - **Stimsonite Corp.**
Glass Products, Made of Purchased Glass - **Vision Blocks Inc.**
Glass Slivers, Rovings, Yarn and Chopped Strands - **Lewcott**
Glass Washing Equipment, Portable - **Bar Maid Corp.**
Glass to Metal Seals - **Precision Hermetic Technology**
Glass_flat - **Custom Glass Corp.**
Glass_pressed & Blown - **Colorado Frame Company**
Glass_pressed & Blown - **Chemglass Inc.**
Glass_pressed & Blown - **Industrial Fiber Optics**
Glassine & Grease Proof Paper - **Deerfield Specialty Papers, Inc.**
Glassware, Culture Media - **Service for Science & Industries**
Glatt & Regular Kosher Products - **Agri Processors**
Glazes - **Seeley's Ceramic Service, Inc.**
Global Water Dealers & Service - **Springsoft International Inc.**
Globes, Geographical - **George F. Cram Company Inc., the (Mfr)**
Gloves & Mittens, Leather - **Mcgough Industries Inc**
Gloves & Mittens_leather - **Edina Mfg. Co., Inc.**
Gloves & Mittens_leather - **Trophy Glove Co.**
Gloves, Oven Mitts, Aprons, Towels, Chef Clothi - **Best Value Textiles**
Gloves_fabric Dress & Work - **Best Value Textiles**
Glow-in-the-dark- Tapes - **Jessup Manufacturing Co.**
Glu-lam Plant - **Avison Forest Products**
Glue Guns - **Adhesive Technologies, Inc.**
Glue Sticks, Hot Melt - **Adhesive Technologies, Inc.**
Glycols - **Respond Group of Companies**
Gold Jewelry - **Maui Divers of Hawaii, Ltd.**
Gold & Silver - **Dixie Electro Plating Co., Inc.**
Gold, Silver, Tin, Lead Refiners - **Ecs Refining**
Golf Gift Products - **Amerikan Dream Inc.**
Golf & Gift Products - **New American Industries Inc**
Golf & Utility Vehicles - **E-z-go Textron**
Golf Accessories - **Blue Atlantic, Ltd.**
Golf Caps, Hats, Visors & Straw Hats - **Texace Corp.**
Golf Car / Industrial Vehicles / Gas & Electric - **Pro Electric Vehicles, Inc.**
Golf Clubs; Irons Woods - **Diamond Head Golf Club Mfg Co**
Golf Course Maintenance Equipment - **Diamond Turf Equipment Inc.**
Golf Practice Equipment; Hinged Lid Containers- **Shaw-clayton Corp**
Goose & Duck Feathers & down - **Cucker Feather**
Goosenecks, Fountain Dividers, Web Puller, Blanket - **Support Products**
Gourmet - Imported Dry - **Flora Distributors, Inc.**
Gourmet Flavored Tortillas & Wraps - **Tumaro's Inc**
Gourmet Frozen Fruit Bars - **La Perla Ice Cream Co.**
Gourmet Gift Basket Co. - **Bay Area Biscotti Co**
Gourmet Grains - Tabooli, Black Beans - **Enterprising Kitchen**
Government - **U.s. Customs Service**
Government & Commercial Book Printing - **Total Printing Systems**
Government Legal Counsel - **S.k. Ross & Assoc., P.c.**
Government, Maritime & Coast Guard Mattresses - **Hernandez Mattress,**
Gpb Hair Conditioner & Nutrient - **Aubrey Organics Inc.**
Gpib - Modbus Controllers - **Ics Electronics**
Gpib and Vxi Interface Products - **Ics Electronics**

Gps Geodetic Network Rcvr Benchmark - **Allen Osborne Associates Inc**
Gps Reference Receivers Turborogue - **Allen Osborne Associates Inc**
Gps Satellite Controlled Clocks - **Arbiter Systems Inc**
Gps Survey Equipment, Rtk + Postpr. Rascal - **Allen Osborne Associates**
Gps Timing Receivers, E.g. Ttr-6 - **Allen Osborne Associates Inc**
Grading Machines Primarily for Citrus & Potatoes - **Exeter Engineering**
Grain - **United Farmers Co-op**
Grain & Field Beans - **H & H Seed Company Inc**
Grain Abrasives & Fillers - **Composition Materials Co., Inc.**
Grain Products: Hulless Nubarley; - **Western Trails Inc**
Grain Roller / Flaker Mills - **Dalhart R & R Machine Works, Inc.**
Grain Sorghum - **Zen Noh Grain**
Grain Tanks & Accessories - **Behlen Mfg. Co.**
Grains - **Eastern Europe Inc.**
Granite - **Rowat Cut Stone & Marble Co.**
Granite Burial Monuments & Mausoleums - **Southern Mausoleums, Inc.**
Granite Mining - **Marbledge, Inc.**
Granite Surface Plates, Machine Bases - **Mojave Granite Co Inc**
Granite Tile, Slabs, Blocks - **Dakota Granite Company**
Granola and Cereals - **Organic Milling Inc**
Granulators - **Alan Ross Machinery Corp**
Granulators for Recycling Plastics - **Granutec Inc**
Grape Grower Magazine & Trade Shows - **Western Agricultural Publish**
Grapeseed Oil (Special 100 % Natural) Cooking-**Gso: Grapeseed Oil Corp**
Graphic Art Light Bulbs - **Bulbtronics, Inc.**
Graphic Arts (Top Coats) - **Technical Coating International**
Graphic Design - **Gonzalez Integrated Marketing**
Graphic Design & Desktop Publishing - **Congdon Printing & Imaging**
Graphic Designers; Sign Manufacturers - **Never Boring Design Associates**
Graphic Recording Meters - **Geophysical Survey Systems, Inc.**
Graphite Electrodes - **Graphite Sales, Inc.**
Graphite Lubricants - **Dixon Southwestern Graphite Inc.**
Graphite Powder - **Graphite Sales, Inc.**
Graphite Products - **Graphite Products Inc**
Grass Enhancer (All Natural) - **True Pitch, Inc.**
Grating - **Seidelhuber Metal Products Inc**
Gravure Cylinder Engraving Equipment - **Daetwyler Corp., Max**
Gravure Cylinder Plating & Polishing Equipment - **Daetwyler Corp., Max**
Gray & Ductile Iron Castings - **Benton Foundry, Inc.**
Gray Iron Castings - **Deeter Foundry Inc.**
Greases, Oils & Lubricants - **Engineered Lubricants Co.**
Greatest Selection of Disperse Dyes for Polyester - **Bezjian Dye-chem, Inc.**
Green & Kiln Dried, Rough or Planed, Random - **Hamer, Jim C.**
Green, Rough & Sized Heart-centered Cants - **Hamer, Jim C.**
Greenhouse & Nursury Equipment - **Netafim Irrigation Inc**
Greenhouses / Nurseries and Field Flowers. - **Roberts Irrigation Products**
Greens Mowers - **Diamond Turf Equipment Inc.**
Greens Maintenance Systems - **Diamond Turf Equipment Inc.**
Grinders - **Commodore Machine Co.**
Grinding Machine Lubricants - **Miller Corp., Harry**
Grinding Mills - **Quinn Process Equipment Co**
Grinding Wheels, Sticks & Hones - **Abrasive Distributors Corp.**
Grinding; Chrome Plating; Sales of Locomotives - **Chrome Crankshaft Co**
Gripper Elevator / Lowerator - **Arrowhead Systems Llc**
Groceries & Related Products - **A-live Foods**
Groceries & Related Products - **Bay Area Biscotti Co**
Groceries & Related Products - **Alpine Touch Inc**
Groceries & Related Products - **Marquis Distributing Co**
Groceries and Related Products, Nec - **Templar Food Products**
Groceries, Diapers, General Line - **Foreign Trade Marketing**
Groceries, General Line - **Klein Pickle Company**
Groceries, General Line - **Sew Feiel**
Grocery Products - **Basic Foods International, Inc.**
Grocery Stores - **Shurfine**
Ground Effect Flight Cargo Craft - **Commercial Pallet Pak Co.**
Ground Fault Circuit Interrupters - **Ericson Manufacturing, Inc.**
Ground Service Equipment - **Alaco Ladder Co.**
Ground Stations - **Caravan International**
Grounding Systems for Surge Protection - **Superior Grounding Systems**
Groundwater Remediation - **Environmental Services & Technology**
Groundwater Sampling - **Art's Manufacturing & Supply Inc**

Groundwater Sampling, Filtration - **Geotech Environmental Equipment**
Grows Grapes and Produces Wine - **Mayacamas Vineyards**
Grows Organic Vegetables, Melons and Citrus Fruits - **Purepak Inc**
Grows, Packs and Distributes Pickled Products - **Klein Pickle Company**
Growth Stimulants - **Soil Technologies Corp.**
Guidance, Navigation and Control Equipment - **Litton Industries Inc**
Guided Missile & Space Vechicle - **Fay & Quartermaine Machining**
Gulfstream Aircraft Services - **Gulfstream Aerospace Corp.**
Gulfstream Charter Services - **Gulfstream Aerospace Corp.**
Gulfstream Financial Services Corp. - **Gulfstream Aerospace Corp.**
Gulfstream Iv-sp - **Gulfstream Aerospace Corp.**
Gulfstream Lease - **Gulfstream Aerospace Corp.**
Gulfstream Management Services - **Gulfstream Aerospace Corp.**
Gulfstream Shazes - **Gulfstream Aerospace Corp.**
Gulfstream V - **Gulfstream Aerospace Corp.**
Gun Safes - **Meilink Safe Co., a Fireking International Co.**
Gundrilling & Special Machining - **Craftsman Tool & Mold Co.**
Guns - **S T I International, Inc.**
Guy Strain & Spool Insulators - **Porcelain Products Company(mfr)**
Gx-99 Massage System - **Sybaritic, Inc.**
Gym Equipment - **Johnny Gibson Gym Equipment Co**
Gym Equipment, Vinyl Divider Curtains - **M.putterman & Company Inc.**
Gym Floor Covers - **M.putterman & Company Inc.**
Gymnasium Bleacher Seating - **Folding Bleacher Company**
Gymnasium Mats - **Crown Gym Mats, Inc.**
Gypsum Board, Ceiling Tile & Accessories - **Waite, R. M. Company**
Gyro Meat Processing - **Corfu Foods, Inc.**
Gyroscope Stabilizers & Precision Instruments - **Ken-lab, Llc**
Hair Care Products to Distributors - **Beauty plus Beauty Supply**
Hair Clippers & Shavers, Massagers - **Wahl Clipper Corp.**
Hair Lightener , Brightener - **Shelton's Sheen Wave Labs Inc**
Hair Restorers & Hair Loss Tonics - **Rejuvi Cosmetic Laboratory**
Hall Effect Sensors - **Cherry Corporation, the**
Hand & Windmill Pumps, Jacks & Cylindersr - **Dempster Industries, Inc.**
Hand Guns - **Lorcin Engineering**
Hand Hoists - **Maasdam Pow'r-pull Inc.**
Hand Screen Printing - **Zoo-ink Screen Print**
Hand Tools - **Ameritool, Hand Tool Div.**
Hand Tools - **Jaw Manufacturing Co.**
Hand Tools Tube Testing Equipment - **Elliot Tool Technologies, Ltd.**
Hand Tools and Tweezers - **Excelta Corp**
Hand Tools, Machinery and Equipment - **United General Supply**
Hand Tools, Screwdriver Bits - **Zephyr Manufacturing Co. Inc.**
Hand Tools, Wholesale - **Action Tool Co., Inc.**
Hand-carved Woodfaced and Wooden - **Robert Raikes Enterprizes**
Hand-cast Pewter Tableware & Christmas Ornaments - **Hampshire Pewter**
Hand-crafted, Custom Built Golf Clubs - **Artisan Golf**
Hand-held Lawn and Garden Equipment - **Ryobi Outdoor Products Inc**
Handbags, Automotive Interiors, Sports Balls, and - **Robus Leather**
Handmade Chocolate Truffles - **Just Truffles**
Handmade Sterling Silver Rosaries - Our Speciality - **Rosary House, Inc.**
Handtools Levels Plate & Precision - **Geier & Bluhm, Inc.**
Handtools Spirit Level Assemblies - **Geier & Bluhm, Inc.**
Hard Candy - **Simon Candy Co.**
Hard Floor Polisher & Ozone Generating - **Us Products Inc**
Hardens and Grinds Gears, Splines and Shafts - **Phoenix Gear Inc**
Hardfacing Welding Electrodes, Wire - **Rankin Industries Inc**
Hardware - **Band-it-idex Inc**
Hardware - **Coopers & Clarke, Inc.**
Hardware - **Dynalock Corp.**
Hardware - **J R C Web Accessories, Inc.**
Hardware - **Mounting Systems Inc**
Hardware - **Supra Products**
Hardware - **Thf Corp**
Hardware - **Tubing Seal Cap**
Hardware - **Oilpure Refiner Co**
Hardware - **Jensen Tools, Inc.**
Hardware Wholesale - **Orgill Inc.**
Hardware for Emergency & Service Vehicles - **Lewgust Co., Inc.**
Hardware for Full Size Doors & Cabinets - **Acorn Manufacturing Co.,**
Hardware, Aircraft Tools & Maint. Equip. - **West Coast Industries Inc.**

Hardware, Fuses, Connectors & Porcelain - **Cooper Industries**
Hardware, Wholesale - **Woodpecker, Inc.**
Hardware, Wholesale - **Action Tool Co., Inc.**
Hardware: Wall & Floor Coverings - **Atwood Richards**
Hardwood Chips & Unprocessed Bark - **Hamer, Jim C.**
Hardwood Circular Stairs - **Jim C. Lane Inc.**
Hardwood Dimension & Flooring Mills - **Pacific Crest Manufacturing Inc**
Hardwood Dimension and Flooring Mills - **H.a. Stiles**
Hardwood Dowels - **H.a. Stiles**
Hardwood Frame Moldings - **Picture Woods Ltd**
Hardwood Furniture Blanks - **H.a. Stiles**
Hardwood Furniture Panels - **H.a. Stiles**
Hardwood Logs - **Hardwood Veneer**
Hardwood Logs - **Pike Lumber Company, Inc.**
Hardwood Lumber - **Greenmont Lumber Corp. (Mfr)**
Hardwood Lumber - **Pike Lumber Company, Inc.**
Hardwood Lumber - **H.a. Stiles**
Hardwood Lumber & Dimension Mfg. - **Hull Forest Products, Inc.**
Hardwood Lumber, Rough, Sawed - **Hartzell Hardwoods Inc.**
Hardwood Mulch - **Hamer, Jim C.**
Hardwood Sawmill & Chipmill - **Lumlog, Inc.**
Hardwood Squares & Rounds - **H.a. Stiles**
Hardwood Turnings - **H.a. Stiles**
Hardwood Veneer & Plywood - **Sieling & Jones, Inc.**
Hardwood Veneer & Veneer Faces - **Bacon Veneer Co.**
Harvest Seed Processing - **Sims Bros., Inc.**
Has-mat-flamable Material Storage Bldg's - **Joaquin Manufacturing Corp**
Hatchery Ventilation Equiopment- **Chick Master International, Inc.**
Hats, Caps & Millinery - **National Can Manufacturing Inc**
Hats, Caps & Millinery - **Take Two Sportswear Accessories**
Hats, Caps & Straw Hats - **Texace Corp.**
Hats, Caps and Millinery - **National Can Manufacturing Inc**
Hauling & Transportation - **C & B Fosters Inc.**
Haying Equipment - **Agco Corporation**
Hazardous & Explosive Materials Transportation - **Trism Inc.**
Hazardous Material Packing - **Future Packaging Inc**
Hazardous Waste - **Columbian Steel Tank Co.**
Hazardous Waste Management - **Environmental Services & Technology**
Hazardous Waste Management - **A & S Metal Recycling, Inc.**
Hazardous Waste Processing - **Vanguard Research Inc. Vri**
Hazardous Waste Removal - **Cardinal Industrial Insulation Co., Inc.**
Heaby Rigging - **Bigge Crane & Rigging Co.**
Head & Wrist Bands - **Unique Sports Products, Inc.**
Heads, New for Rebuilt Price - **Adhesive Systems, Inc.**
Health & Beauty Products - **Dews Research**
Health Care Fabrics - **Tana Tex Inc.**
Health Care Industries. - **Legge Co., Inc., Walter G.**
Health Consulting - **Jdc (Hawaii) Inc., Advance Foods Div., Oligopower**
Health and Beauty Products - **Bogdana Corporation**
Healthcare Cabinets & Counters, Etc. - **Incon Overseas Marketing, Inc.**
Healthcare Herbal & Vitamins - **Lins Trading**
Hearing Protection, Ear, Peltor - **Aearo Company**
Heat Cure - **Electronic Materials Inc**
Heat Detector Testers - **Home Safeguard Industries Inc.**
Heat Exchanger Repair - **Superb Marine & Industrial Services, Inc.**
Heat Exchangers - **A.c.e. Boiler, Inc.**
Heat Exchangers & Pressure Vessels - **Doyle & Roth Mfg. Co., Inc.**
Heat Exchangers & Steam Condensers - **Affinity Industries Inc. (Mfr)**
Heat Exchangers, Condensers, Evaporators - **Tripac International, Inc.**
Heat Exchangers, Tube & Shell - **R&d Enterprises, Inc.**
Heat Pipe Heat Exchangers - **Hudson Products Corp.**
Heat Processing. - **Hudnut Industries Inc**
Heat Pumps - **Air Energy Heat Pumps**
Heat Reclaiming Units - **Gaylord Industries, Inc.**
Heat Recovery Units - **Professional Services International, Inc.**
Heat Resistant Cabbage Seed - **Seedcraft**
Heat Sealing Machines - **Zmd International Inc**
Heat Shrinkable Tubing - **Reliable Plastics Seals, Inc.**
Heat Transfer Coils - **Super Radiator Coils**
Heat Transfer Coils, Air Conditioning - **Coil Co., Inc.**
Heat Transfer Foils - **Crown Roll Leaf, Inc.**

Heat Treating Furnaces, Electrical - **Holcroft**
Heat Treating for Metal Products - **Varco Heat Treating Co**
Heat Treating_metal - **Advanced Heat Treat Corp.**
Heat Treating_metal - **California Surface Hardening**
Heat Treating_metal - **Deering Fabricators**
Heat Treating_metal, Iso-9002 Compliant - **Varco Heat Treating Co**
Heated & Unheated Air Curtains - **Mars Air Doors**
Heated Stack Filters - **Universal Analyzers Inc**
Heating & Air Conditioning Equipment - **Rheem Air Conditioning Div.**
Heating & Air Conditioning Filters - **Purolator Products Air Filtration**
Heating Boilers Copper Tube - **Lochinvar Water Heater**
Heating Coils - **Super Radiator Coils**
Heating Equip Line & Motor-gen Freq - **Ajax Magnethermic Corp.**
Heating Equipment, Except Electric - **Coil Co., Inc.**
Heating Equipment, Except Electric - **Coil Company Inc.**
Heating Equipment, Except Electric - **Thermal Systems Inc**
Heating Equipment, Portable, Construction, Industrial - **Scheu Products**
Heating, Ventilating, Air Conditioning - **York International Corp.**
Heatsinks & Other Machined Parts - **Wieland Precision Machine**
Heavy Construction Equipment - Reconditioned & New - **Hamre Equip**
Heavy Construction, Nec - **Nova Grass**
Heavy Duty Truck, Industrial - **Ase Supply Inc**
Heavy Equipment - **Pacific Cranes & Equipment Sales**
Heavy Equipment Spare Parts - **Traction International**
Heavy Extrusion Press Tools - **Lake Park Tool & Machine, Inc.**
Heavy Glass Tabletops and Wrought Iron - **The Glass Table**
Heavy Industrial Chrome Plating & Grinding - **Anniston Plating & Metal**
Heavy Lifts - **Penn Terminals Inc.**
Heavy Truck Trailers - **Gem State Manufacturing Inc**
Helical Springs of Iron or Steel - **Century Spring Co., Inc.**
Helicopter & Airplane Transportation Service - **Petroleum Helicopters**
Helicopter - Main Rotor Transmission Pumps - **National Flight Sales Corp**
Helicopter / Fixed Wing Charter Service - **Era Aviation Inc.**
Helicopter / Fixed Wing Contract Service - **Era Aviation Inc.**
Helicopter Logging - **Superior Helicopter Llc.**
Helicopter Logging Consultant - **Sea Forest Enterprises Inc**
Helicopter Parts - **Athens Industries, Inc.**
Helicopter Parts - **S & S Precision Machine Corp.**
Helicopter Parts - **Petroleum Helicopters**
Helicopter Parts & Assemblies - **Sky Mfg. Co.**
Helicopter Transmissions & Rotorhead Components - **Purdy Corp.**
Hemp - **Yaley Enterprises, Inc.**
Herbal Facial Astringent - **Aubrey Organics Inc.**
Herbal Formula - **Wakunaga of America Co., Ltd.**
Herbal Supplements - **International Vitamin Corporation**
Herbal Tea - **Alaska Herb Tea Co. (Mfr)**
Herbal Teas & Health Foods - **Wah Yet Inc**
Herbs, Spices, Botanical Extrac - **Starwest Botanicals Inc**
Hermetic Connectors - **Precision Hermetic Technology**
Hex Rethreader Dies - **Jaw Manufacturing Co.**
Hi End Retouching - **Digital Nation**
Hi-frequency & Sonic Welding - **Quality Embroidery**
Hi-tech Manufacturing Practice - **Cap Gemini America**
Hi-temperature Epoxies - **Polygem**
Hickory Lumber & Dimension - **S.g. International**
Hid Ballast - **Howard Industries**
Hids & Skins - **Anamax Corp.**
High Chair - **Abco Products**
High Density Packaging - **Zecal, Inc.**
High Density Polyethylene - **Geochem International**
High Density Polyethylene - **Respond Group of Companies**
High Efficiency Filter Papers - **Hollingsworth & Vose Co.**
High Efficiency Water Heaters & Boilers - **Weben-jarco, Inc.**
High Energy Barrel & Disc Finishing Equipment - **Victor Metal Finishing**
High Intensity Monochromatic Illumination Systems - **Spectral Energy**
High Loft Hvac Filtration - **Western Synthetic Fiber**
High Performance Engines - **Dvorak Automatic & Machine**
High Performance Granulation Systems - **Tamer International Ltd**
High Performance Parts & Accessories - **Dvorak Automatic & Machine**
High Performance Protective Coatings - **Ameron Intl/protective Coatings**
High Potential Anodes - **Energy Economics, Inc.**

High Pressure Fluid Pumps & Pressure Washers - **Cat Pumps**
High Pressure Homogenizers - **Sonic Corp.**
High Pressure Hose & Air Compressor Hose - **Faip North America Inc.**
High Pressure Laminated Products, Medicine Cabinets - **Double-t Mfg.**
High Pressure Pumping Systems - **Sonic Corp.**
High Quality Mattress Ticking - **Nassau Tape & Webbing Mills, Inc.**
High Quality Steel Magazines - **Usa Magazines Inc**
High Speed Coal Loading System for Trains - **Kanawha Scales & Systems,**
High Speed Sortation Systems - **Hk Systems, Inc.**
High Speed Surface Effect Craft (Marine) - **Commercial Pallet Pak Co.**
High Speed Tapping Machine Attachments - **Procunier Safety Chuck Co.**
High Tech. Circuit Boards in One Day - **Accurate Circuit Engineering**
High Temp & Low Temp Coatings for Bakeware - **Copper Coil Coating**
High Temp Wire & Cable Nonferrouse - **Rockbestos Surprenant Cable**
High Temperature Exhaust Insulation - **Advanced Thermal Products Inc**
High Temperature Metal Working Lubricants - **Dylon Industries, Inc.**
High Vacuum & Uhv Components - **Huntington Mechanical Labs Inc**
High Voltage Capacitors - **N W L Capacitors**
High Voltage Circuit Breakers - **Ross Engineering Corp.**
High Voltage Devices - **Ross Engineering Corp.**
High Voltage Digital Voltmeters - **Ross Engineering Corp.**
High Voltage Low, Med, Hi, Power Transistors - **Semiconductor Technolo**
High Voltage Relays - **Ross Engineering Corp.**
High Voltage Test Instruments - **Jennings Technology Company**
High Voltage Vacuum Contactors - **Ross Engineering Corp.**
High Voltage Wideband Dividers - **Ross Engineering Corp.**
High-end Audio Amplifiers - **Monarchy International**
High-pressure Cleaning Systems - **Aqua Blast Corp.**
High-pressure Gas Containment Systems - **C P Industries, Inc.**
High-speed Audio Tape Duplicators - **Accurate Sound Corporation**
High-speed Machining Systems - **Methods West Machine Tools**
High-speed Networking Devices - **Tut Systems**
High-temp. Refractories - **Pars Manufacturing Co.**
High-temperature-resistant Textiles; Coated - **Mid-mountain Materials Inc**
High-yield Pipeline Fittings - **Dodson Steel Products, Inc.**
Highway Reflectors, Reflective Lenses & Pavement Markers - **Astro Optics**
Highway Testing Equipment - **Dynatest Consulting, Inc.**
Hind Performance Technical Wear - **Saucony, Inc.**
Historic 1880s Cowboy Pommel Slickers - **South Pass Trading/cnl Clothi**
Hobie Polyurethane Foam and Fiberglass Surfboar - **Stewart Surfboards**
Hoists - **Laidig Industrial System**
Hoists & Cranes - **Whiting Corporation**
Hoists - Shawbox & Budgit - **Progressive Crane, Inc.**
Hoists, Cranes & Monorails - **Aurora Systems, Inc.**
Hoists, Cranes & Monorails - **Auto Crane Co.**
Hoists, Cranes & Monorails - **Konecrane Landel Inc**
Hoists, Cranes & Monorails - **Quality Boat Lifts, Inc.**
Hoists, Cranes, Monorail - **Konecrane Landel Inc**
Hoists, Cranes, Monorails & Jibcranes - **Industrial Crane & Equipment**
Holding Companies - **The Dii Group Inc**
Holding Fixtures for Inspecting Machined Parts - **Ica International Inc**
Holding Gates, Livestock - **Priefert Mfg. Co. Inc.(Mfr)**
Hollow Metal Doors & Frames - **Hollow Metal Specialists, Inc.**
Hollow Metal Windows - **Hollow Metal Specialists, Inc.**
Holograms - **Transfer Print Foils, Inc.**
Holography - **Transfer Print Foils, Inc.**
Holsters Leather - **Gould & Goodrich**
Holsters, Global Positioning, Wholesale - **U. S. Cavalry, Inc.**
Holsters, Nylon - **Gould & Goodrich**
Home & Party Casino Tables & Equipment - **Marty Wolf Game Co**
Home Care / Cleaning - **Gnld International**
Home Cleaning Appliances - **Bissell Inc.(Mfr)**
Home Cleaning Chemicals - **Bissell Inc.(Mfr)**
Home Course Audio Cassettes - **Flight Tech, Inc**
Home Decorator Fabric - **General Fabrics**
Home Networking & Internet Sharing Apparatus - **Novaweb Technologies**
Home Power Systems - **Southwest Photovoltaic Systems**
Home Water Purification Equipm - **Pure Water, Inc.**
Homecare & Nursing Home Beds - **Invacare Corporation**
Homefurnishings - **Barth & Dreyfuss of California**
Honey & Hive Products - Pollen, Propolis - **Silver Meadow Honey**

Honeycomb Core for Aircraft Wings, Flaps - **Texas Almet Inc.**
Honeycomb Panels - **Tri-link Technologies Ltd.**
Honing (Sunnen Machines) - **A C Products Co., Inc.**
Honing Machines & Abrasive Products - **Superior Honing Equipment**
Honing Machines and Portable Hones - **Abrasive Service Industries**
Honing from .060 to 18 Inches Id, - **Robert's Honing & Gundrilling Inc.**
Horizontal Earth Boring & Directional Drills, Mud - **American Augers**
Horse & Dog Topical Lotions - **B & S Equine / Cannie Skin Lotion**
Horse & Livestock Trailers, Roof Bows - **Circle S Trailers Inc.**
Horse Equipment & Tack - **Saddle Barn Tack Distributors, Inc.**
Horse Foal Diagnostic Kits - **Midland Bioproducts Corp.**
Horse Radish Oil - **Ingredient Resources, Inc.**
Horse Stalls - **Priefert Mfg. Co. Inc.(Mfr)**
Horse Walkers - **Supreme Horse Walker Co.**
Horse, Stock and Car Carrier Trailers - **Silver Lite Trailers Inc**
Hose & Belting_rubber & Plastic - **United Technologies Automotive, Inc.**
Hose & Belting_rubber & Plastic - **Hydraulic Industrial Resources**
Hose & Belting_rubber & Plastic - **Jason Industrial, Inc.**
Hose & Belting_rubber & Plastic - **Jsj Corp/sparks Belting Div**
Hose & Belting_rubber & Plastic - **Colorado Rubber & Supply Co**
Hose , Military Spec. - **J G B Enterprises, Inc.**
Hose Clamps, Stainless Steel, Worm Drive - **Norton Industries**
Hose Machinery, Export - **Commision Brokers, Inc.**
Hose Reels - **Grover Manufacturing Corp.**
Hose-rubber & Metal - **Lamons Power Engineering**
Hosiery - **Ellis Hosiery Mills, Inc.**
Hosiery - **Uni Hosiery Co., Inc.**
Hospital Carts, Hospital Trolleys - **Waterloo Industries, Inc.**
Hospital Equipments - **Biomedical International**
Hospital Stretchers, Stainless Steel Carts - **Cambridge Manufacturing,**
Hospital Supplies, Bandages & Orthopedic - **Tetra Medical Supply Corp.**
Hospital/clinical Breathing Air & Vacuum Systems - **C. H. Hyperbarics,**
Hot & Cold Adhesive Extrusion & Spray System Parts - **Adhesive Systems,**
Hot Box Detectors - Drag Detectors - **Railroad Signal, Inc.**
Hot Foil Stamping Systems for Label Printing Industry - **Ikela Co.**
Hot Glass Handling Plastic Materials & Resins - **Dura Temp Corp.**
Hot Pepper Mash, Peppers in Brine, Sauce - **Young Farms**
Hot Rolled Coil - **I P S C O Steel Inc.**
Hot Rolled Coils - **Tata, Inc.**
Hot Rolled Heavy Plate - **I P S C O Steel Inc.**
Hot Stamp Iv Solution/blood Bag Printing - **Coding Products**
Hot Stamp Labels & Decor Pres Sens. - **Webtech, Inc.**
Hot Stamp Pipe/fiber Optic Cablewire Marking Ribbon - **Coding Products**
Hot Stamping Dies - **Schwerdtle Stamp Co., Inc.**
Hot Stamping Foil - **Transfer Print Foils, Inc.**
Hot Stamping Foils - **Crown Roll Leaf, Inc.**
Hot Stamping Foils & Precious Metal Leaf - **Swift & Sons, Inc., M.**
Hot Tin Dipping Plating - **Marjan, Inc.**
Hot Water Dispensers, Household- **Anaheim Marketing International**
Hot Water Storage Tanks - **Pvi International**
Hotel & Commercial Furniture - **Intramar, Inc.**
Hotel & Motel Carts, Bellman, Maid Carts - **Cambridge Manufacturing,**
Hotels / Custom Furniture - **Modern Woodcrafts, Inc.**
House Moving Dollies & Pneumatic - **Holland House Moving Inc., Ron**
Household Appliances - **Mid-south Electronics-alabama, Inc.**
Household Articles &Toilet Articles -**Continental Sprayers / Afa Products**
Household Audio & Video Equipment - **Emerson Radio Corp.**
Household Cleaners - **Lexard Corporation**
Household Cleaners / Silver Tarnish Remover - **Regent Labs Inc.**
Household Goods - **Stylebuilt Accessories, Inc.**
Household Goods - **Williams Shipping**
Household Goods, We Are Experienced in Export - **Hunte, Andrew**
Household Laundry Equipment - **Alliance Laundry Systems**
Household Products - **Lamaur**
Housing - **Waverlee Homes Inc.**
Housing - **Fleetwood Enterprises Inc**
Hp Plotters Reseller - **Repro-products & Services**
Hplc, Protein, Chromatography- **Lazar Research Laboratories**
Human Foods, Pet Foods, Aquaculture Foods - **Extru-tech, Inc.**
Human Serum Calibrators - **Midland Bioproducts Corp.**
Humates & Humic Acids - **Live Earth Products**

Humbows, Eggroll, Sliced Roll, Steamed Bun, Etc. - **Lucky Seven Food**
Humidity Instruments - **Cooper Instrument Corporation (Mfr)**
Humidity Instruments/industrial Process - **Panametrics, Inc**
Humphrey Belt Manlifts - **Industrial Crane & Equipment Co., Inc.**
Hunting & Folding Knives - **Cutco Cutlery Corp.**
Hunting, Shooting and Law Enforcement - **Michaels of Oregon Co**
Hv Relays, Vacuum Contactors, Circuit Breakers, - **Ross Engineering**
Hvac Equipment, Electric Heating, - **Environmental Technologies, Inc.**
Hvac Housing & Equipment - **Purolator Products Air Filtration Co.**
Hybrid Pearl Millets - **Coffey Seed, Coffey Forage Seeds, Inc.**
Hybrid Sorghum Sudangrass - **Coffey Seed, Coffey Forage Seeds, Inc.**
Hydraulic & Pneumatic Systems - **Catching Fluidpower, Inc.**
Hydraulic & Traction Elevators - **Mowrey Elevator Company Inc.**
Hydraulic Couplings - **Kurt Manufacturing Co.**
Hydraulic Cylinder Seals - **Heavy Equipment Parts Co.**
Hydraulic Cylinders - **Hydro-line Inc. Division of Imc, Inc.**
Hydraulic Cylinders Tie Rod - **Cross Mfg. Inc.**
Hydraulic Cylinders Welded - **Cross Mfg. Inc.**
Hydraulic Dewatering Pumps - **D & D Machine & Hydraulics**
Hydraulic Extrication Equipment - **Amkus, Inc.**
Hydraulic Filters - **Fairey Arlon Inc.**
Hydraulic Fluid Power Motors - **Cross Mfg. Inc.**
Hydraulic Fluid Pumps - **Cross Mfg. Inc.**
Hydraulic Hose & Fittings - **Catching Fluidpower, Inc.**
Hydraulic Hose Assemblies - **American Equipment Sales Co.**
Hydraulic Hose and Fittings; Army Surplus Equipment An - **Fitting House**
Hydraulic Motors - **Rineer Hydraulics**
Hydraulic Parts, Wholesale - **Hercules Hydraulics Inc.**
Hydraulic Presses - **Ap & T Tangent, Inc.**
Hydraulic Quick Couplers - **Safeway Hydraulics, Inc.**
Hydraulic Torque Wrenches - **Francis Torque Tools**
Hydraulic Trailer & Automotive Hoses - **Hydraulic Industrial Resources**
Hydraulic Transfer Presses - **Ap & T Tangent, Inc.**
Hydraulic Tree-digging Machinery - **Caretree Systems Inc.**
Hydraulics; Welds and Fabricates Parts; C - **American Hydraulics**
Hydro Mix for Tackifier / Water Retention in Hydro Mulch - **Driwater Inc**
Hydroblasting Surface Prep. Equipment - **Heavy Duty Hydro Blasting,**
Hydrocortisone Cream, Triple Antibiotic Ointment - **Water-jel Technologi**
Hydrogeological - **Land & Water Consulting, Inc.**
Hydroloyzed Dairy Proteins - **American Casein Co.**
Hydrolyzed Gelatin - **Skw Biosystems**
Hydrostatic System Testing - **Service Hydraulics Inc.**
Hydroturbines, Submersible - **Itt Flygt Corp**
Hydroxides and Peroxides - **Norac Co., Inc., the**
Hypodermic Syringes / Needles, Wholesale - **Exelint International, Inc.**
I Comp Heat Cure S.m.t. Adhesives - **Electronic Materials Inc**
I.c.u. Equipment - **Biomedical International**
Iata Licenced Agent - **Dan Transport Corporation**
Ibm Authorized Industry Re-marketer, Retailing - **Information Specialist**
Ice / Beverage Dispensers - **Scotsman Industries**
Ice Cream & Frozen Desserts - **Bubbies Homemade Ice Cream & Dessert**
Ice Cream & Frozen Desserts - **Dippin Dots, Inc.**
Ice Cream & Frozen Desserts - **Gise Inc**
Ice Cream & Frozen Desserts - **La Perla Ice Cream Co.**
Ice Cream & Frozen Desserts - **Sam's Homemade Cheesecake Inc**
Ice Cream & Novelties - **Safeway Stores Inc., Export Sales**
Ice Cream Tubs & Ice Cream Mixes - **Luke's Ice Cream**
Ice Cream and Frozen Dessert Powders - **Gise Inc**
Ice Cream, Yogurt & Flavored Ices - **Dippin Dots, Inc.**
Ice Crushing Equipment - **Technology General Corp.**
Ice Dispensers - **Scotsman Industries**
Ice Making Machinery - **Scotsman Industries**
Ice Making Machines - **Proctor Companies**
Ice Merchandising Cabinets - **Biloff Manufacturing Company Inc**
Ice Storage Bins - **Scotsman Industries**
Ice; Public Cold Storage - **Holmes Ice & Cold Storage Co**
Ice_manufactured - **Holmes Ice & Cold Storage Co**
Id Badges & Tags - **Identatronics, Inc.**
Id, Mikes, (Id Measurements of Boilers - **Wilson & Co., Inc., Thomas C.**
Idler Pulleys - **Retlaw Tools & Plastics Co., Inc.**
Illum. Menu Systems - **Mainstreet Menu Systems**

Imaging and Micrographic - **Cmisource.com**
Imaging Supplies - **Rittenhouse Co**
Imc - **Mark Vii International**
Iminodiacetic Acid - **Century Multech**
Imitation Brick - **Kowa California Inc.**
Immunodiagnostic Products - **Midland Bioproducts Corp.**
Impact Drivers - **Jaw Manufacturing Co.**
Import / Export - **Commercial International Forwarding Inc.**
Import / Export Broker - **J & B Services: Import / Export**
Import / Export Services - **Apollo Warehouse, Inc.**
Import/export Hazardous Waste & Scrap Metal - **A & S Metal Recycling**
Importers of High Quality Essential Oils - **Herba Aromatica Inc**
Importing Firms- **Impol Aluminum**
Importing Firms Oriental Food Stuff - **Jianlibao America, Ltd.**
Imports and Distributes Measuring and Test Equipment - **Uei**
Imprinted Promotional Products - **Rolling Hills Progress Center Inc.**
Imprinters - **Plasco, Inc.**
Impulse Heat Sealing Machinery - **Technaseal**
In Line Blending Systems - **Sonic Corp.**
Incense - **Montana Essence Company**
Incinarators - **Biomedical International**
Incineration Equipment - **Soil Purification Inc.**
Incineration Systems - **John Zink Company**
Incinerators - Municipal Waste - **Simonds Mfg. Corp.**
Incinerators - Pathological Waste - **Simonds Mfg. Corp.**
Incinerators Medical Waste - **Simonds Mfg. Corp.**
Incinerators, Air, Solid & Liquid Waste - **Incinerator International Inc.**
Incorporations & Legal Requirments:Product & Service - **L.a. Markom De**
Incubation Systems, plus Software - **Chick Master International, Inc.**
Ind Hydraulic Equipment, Export - **Moos Machine Works**
Ind Instruments, Pressure / Flow Transmitters - **Bec Controls Corp.**
Ind Instruments, Temperature Transmitters - **Bec Controls Corp.**
Ind. Abrasive Products, Export - **C.r. Laurence Company, Inc.**
Ind. Analog to Pneumatic Transducers - **Bec Controls Corp.**
Ind. Batch/cont. Sand Prep. Equip. - **Dependable/redford-carver**
Ind. Braiding Machinery, Export - **Commision Brokers, Inc.**
Ind. Core/mold Blowing Equipment - **Dependable/redford-carver**
Ind. Equip. Tube Cleaners - **Elliot Tool Technologies, Ltd.**
Ind. High Pressure Cleaning Equipment - **Spray Masters Inc.**
Ind. Instruments, Current/voltage Transducers - **Bec Controls Corp.**
Ind. Instruments, Humidity Transmitters - **Bec Controls Corp.**
Ind. Laundry Garment Finishing Equip. - **Leonard Automatics, Inc.**
Ind. Laundry Tunnel Finishing Equip. - **Leonard Automatics, Inc.**
Ind. Mach Pumps Domestic Water Systems - **Shurflo**
Ind. Mach. Automatic Assembly & Testing - **Bodine Assembly & Test Sys**
Ind. Mach. Gears & Speed Reducers - **Sunstrand Corporation**
Ind. Mach. Pumps Marine & Rv - **Shurflo**
Ind. Mach., Pump Spraying Systems - **Shurflo**
Ind. Mach., Pumps, Beverage Dispensing - **Shurflo**
Ind. Mixing, Drying & Reacting Mach. - **Littleford Day., Inc. (Mfr)**
Ind. Oil Skimmers & Decanters - **Douglas Engineering**
Ind. Organic Chemicals, Aloe Vera - **Terry Laboratories, Inc.**
Ind. Pest Rodent Control Equip,- **Public Health Equipment Supply Inc.**
Ind. Sand Reclamation Equip. - **Dependable/redford-carver**
Ind. Trucks, Lugger Skif - **Converto Mfg. Co. Inc. (Mfr)**
Indian Style Pickles, Chutneys, Pastes, & Condiments - **House of Spices**
Indian Style Snack Foods & Sweets - **House of Spices**
Indicating Pressure Switched - **Mid-west Instrument**
Individual / Knockdown B-bque Pits - **Triangle Metal & Mfg. Co.**
Indoor & Outdoor Carpet & Artificial Turf - **Challenger Industries Inc.**
Indoor & Outdoor, Incandescent - **Kichler Lighting Group**
Indoor Tennis Curtains - **M.putterman & Company Inc.**
Induction & Electric Heating - **Inductoheat Inc.**
Induction Furnaces & Heat Equip, Other - **Ajax Magnethermic Corp.**
Induction Furnaces Metal Melting - **Ajax Magnethermic Corp.**
Induction Heating Equipment - **East Coast Induction, Inc.**
Induction Heating and Melting Equipment - **Induction Technology Corp**
Inductors - **Mag-tran Equipment Corp**
Inductors, Coils, Chokes - **L C R Electronics, Inc.**
Industrial - **L S M Labs, Inc.**
Industrial & Aircraft Coatings - **Alpha Coatings Inc.**

Industrial & Commercial High Intensity Lamps - **Eye Lighting Internation**
Industrial & Disposable Medical Gowns - **Poly Conversions Inc.**
Industrial & Institutional Casters & Wheels - **Roll Master Corporation**
Industrial & Laboratory Furnaces & Ovens and - **Thermatek International**
Industrial & Municipal Pumps - **Fairbanks Morse Pump Corp.**
Industrial & Personal Service Paper - **Bakemark**
Industrial & Personal Service Paper - **Savage Universal Corporation**
Industrial & Standard Propeller Mixers & Colloid Mills - **Sonic Corp.**
Industrial Abrasives - **Abrasive Distributors Corp.**
Industrial Adhesive Film - **Dielectric Polymers, Inc.**
Industrial Agricultural & Institutional - **Sentry Chemical Co.**
Industrial Air & Electrical Driven Mixers - **Technology General Corp.**
Industrial Air Cleaning Equipment - **Thiel Air Technologies Corp.**
Industrial Air Filters - **Mart Corporation**
Industrial Applications - **Rockbestos Surprenant Cable Corp.**
Industrial Assembly & Packaging - **Rolling Hills Progress Center Inc.**
Industrial Automation Control Systems - **Facts, Inc.**
Industrial Automation Controls - **Rockwell Automation**
Industrial Automation Systems & Controls - **Alstom Automation Systems**
Industrial Automation Vibration Control Products - **Rodix, Inc.**
Industrial Baling Systems - **International Baler Corp.**
Industrial Battery Chargers - **La Marche Mfg. Company (Mfr)**
Industrial Blades & Knives - **Techni Edge Mfg. Corp.**
Industrial Blowers - **Gardner Denver, Inc. (Mfr)**
Industrial Boot, Shoe & Leather Working Machinery - **Rimoldi of America**
Industrial Buildings & Warehouses - **Mcalpine & Salyer Construction**
Industrial Ceramics - **Coors Ceramics Co-pittsburgh**
Industrial Chemicals - **Houghton International, Inc.**
Industrial Chemicals - **Ppg Industries Inc.**
Industrial Chemicals - **Syntech Products Corp.**
Industrial Chemicals - **Treatment Products Ltd.**
Industrial Chemicals - **Chemical Distributors, Inc.**
Industrial Chemicals - **Union Carbide Corporation**
Industrial Chocks, Blocks & Wedges - **Rucker Lumber Co., Inc.**
Industrial Cloth - **Chiquola Industrial Products Group, Llc**
Industrial Clutches & Brakes - **Dana Corp./wichita Clutch Co.**
Industrial Coatings - **Morton International, Inc.**
Industrial Coatings & Paint - **Kel-glo Corp.**
Industrial Commercial & Institutional High Intensity - **Esco International**
Industrial Commercial, Documentary Videotapes - **Communi-creations Inc**
Industrial Computers - **Hmw Enterprises, Inc.**
Industrial Control Panels - **Con-tech Power Systems, Inc.**
Industrial Controls - **Baldor Electric Company**
Industrial Conveyor Lubrication Equip- **Digilube Systems, Inc.**
Industrial Conveyors - **Specialty Equipment Co.**
Industrial Coolant Recycling Systems - **Richard's Machine Tool Co., Inc.**
Industrial Cutting Tools - **Chamfer Master Tool Co.**
Industrial Degreasers & Cleaners - **Charlie Chemical & Supply, Inc.**
Industrial Dehumidifiers - **Low Humidity Systems, Inc.**
Industrial Detergents; Sells and Repairs Steam - **C & W Enterprises**
Industrial Development Services - **County of Cattaraugus**
Industrial Diamond Tools - **Saber Diamond Tools**
Industrial Diamonds - **Industrial Diamond Labs**
Industrial Dispensing Valves - **Sheepscot Machine Works**
Industrial Drive Gears - **Horsburgh & Scott Co., the**
Industrial Dryers - **Proctor & Schwartz**
Industrial Dryers, Folders, Etc. - **E L X Group, Washex Machinery Co.**
Industrial Dust Collection Equipment - **C.p. Environmental Filters Inc.**
Industrial Dyes - **Tricon Colors, Llc**
Industrial Electric Mixers, Submersible - **Itt Flygt Corp**
Industrial Electronic Control Modules - **Milwaukee Electronics Corp.**
Industrial Energy Recovery Sys - **Des Champs Laboratories Incorporated**
Industrial Equipment - **Professional Services International, Inc.**
Industrial Equipment / Spare Parts - **Respond Group of Companies**
Industrial Equipment Parts & Accessories - **Ralph Tire & Service, Inc.**
Industrial Equipment for Sales - **Used Equipment Directory**
Industrial Equipment— Pulleys - **Alamia Inc**
Industrial Fabrics, Hardware & Trimming Items. - **Astrup Co.**
Industrial Fans - **New York Blower Co.**
Industrial Fans & Blowers - **Acme Engineering & Mfg. Corp.**
Industrial Fans, Material Handling Equipment - **Process Equipment, Inc.**

Industrial Fasteners - **Liberty Fastener Co.**
Industrial Fasteners - **Thf Corp**
Industrial Filter Dust Collectors - **Eco Environmental Filtration, Inc.**
Industrial Filters - **Mott Corp.**
Industrial Filters - **Technical Fabricators**
Industrial Filtration Service - **Micronics, Inc.**
Industrial Finishing, Powder Coating - **Diversified Coatings, Inc.**
Industrial Floor Coverings - **Crossfield Products Corp**
Industrial Flow Meters - **Caldon, Inc.**
Industrial Food Processing - **American European Systems**
Industrial Forklift Trucks - **H & K Equipment Inc.**
Industrial Forklifts - **Mifran Boman Corp**
Industrial Furnaces - **Drever Company**
Industrial Furnaces & Ovens - **Delta H. Systems, Inc.**
Industrial Furnaces & Ovens - **Inductoheat Inc.**
Industrial Gases - **Scott Specialty Gases**
Industrial Grinding Machines & Systems - **Aldridge Industries, Inc.**
Industrial Hard Chrome Plating - **Tri-county Hard Chrome, Inc.**
Industrial Hard Chrome, Cadmium, Gold, Electroless - **Ultra Plating Corp.**
Industrial Heat Cleaning Ovens - **Armature Coil Equipment Inc.**
Industrial Hose & Couplings - **Fitting House Inc**
Industrial Hose & Duct - **Flexmaster U S a Inc.**
Industrial Hose Reels - **Coxwells, Inc., Dba Coxreels**
Industrial Household Caulking - **Sashco Sealants Inc**
Industrial Humidifiers - **Dri Steem Humidifier**
Industrial Hydraulic & Lubrication Systems - **American Design & Mfg.**
Industrial Ice Machines Manufacture - **A & V Refrigeration Corp.**
Industrial Ice Plants - **Semco Manufacturing**
Industrial Instruments & Flow Meters - **Dynasonics**
Industrial Instruments for the Measurement - **Baldwin Environmental Inc**
Industrial Insulation Die-cutting & Processing - **Davis Co., E. J.**
Industrial Laser Cutting and Engraving - **The Laser Workshop**
Industrial Laundry Equipment - **E L X Group, Washex Machinery Co.**
Industrial Lubricants - **Mullen Circle Brand, Inc.**
Industrial Lubricants - **Protect All, Inc.**
Industrial Lubrication Equipment - **Grover Manufacturing Corp.**
Industrial Machinery - **Accurite Development & Mfg**
Industrial Machinery - **Ace-tek Manufacturing**
Industrial Machinery - **American Hydraulics**
Industrial Machinery - **Ani-helser**
Industrial Machinery - **Aurora Custom Machining**
Industrial Machinery - **B. T. M. Inc.**
Industrial Machinery - **Begneaud Mfg. Inc.**
Industrial Machinery - **Best Jig-grinding Service**
Industrial Machinery - **Cannon Industries**
Industrial Machinery - **Cherokee Industries, Inc.**
Industrial Machinery - **Chrome Crankshaft Co**
Industrial Machinery - **Cold Jet, Inc.**
Industrial Machinery - **Damar Machine Co**
Industrial Machinery - **Dahmes Stainless, Inc.**
Industrial Machinery - **Delta Machine & Tool, Inc.**
Industrial Machinery - **Dixie Machine Shop**
Industrial Machinery - **Doerksen Precision Products**
Industrial Machinery - **Elite Mfg. Corp.**
Industrial Machinery - **F S P Machinery**
Industrial Machinery - **F W Tool & Die Works, Inc.**
Industrial Machinery - **Fab-tech Industries of Brevard, Inc.**
Industrial Machinery - **Farrel Corp.**
Industrial Machinery - **Hanson Welding Machines, Inc.**
Industrial Machinery - **Hedges & Bros., L.p.**
Industsial Machinery - **Hoffman Tool & Die Inc.**
Industrial Machinery - **Hughes Compaction Equipment, Inc.**
Industrial Machinery - **Integrity Manufacturing Co**
Industrial Machinery - **Jl Tool & Machine**
Industrial Machinery - **Kemco Tool & Machine Co., Inc.**
Industrial Machinery - **Kovil Manufacturing Llc**
Industrial Machinery - **L & M Machining Corporation**
Industrial Machinery - **La Machine Shop**
Industrial Machinery - **Lasag**
Industrial Machinery - **Lays Mining Service, Inc.**
Industrial Machinery - **Lemco**

Industrial Machinery - **Lockwood Industries Inc**
Industrial Machinery - **M & M Corporation**
Industrial Machinery - **M F Automation Inc.**
Industrial Machinery - **Metal Finishing, Inc.**
Industrial Machinery - **Nilfisk-advance America, Inc.**
Industrial Machinery - **Nutter Machine Inc.**
Industrial Machinery - **O C V Control Valves**
Industrial Machinery - **Plastic Injection Molders Inc.**
Industrial Machinery - **Phoenix Gear Inc**
Industrial Machinery - **Power Vacuum Trailer Co.**
Industrial Machinery - **Professional Services International, Inc.**
Industrial Machinery - **R & R Machine Industries, Inc.**
Industrial Machinery - **Rapid Development Service**
Industrial Machinery - **Robert's Honing & Gundrilling Inc.**
Industrial Machinery - **S T C Machine Shop**
Industrial Machinery - **Standard Welding Co., Inc.**
Industrial Machinery - **Steel Plant Equipment Corp.**
Industrial Machinery - **Swanson Anaheim Corp**
Industrial Machinery - **Superb Marine & Industrial Services, Inc.**
Industrial Machinery - **Technical Engineering Sales, Inc.**
Industrial Machinery - **Universal Tooling Corp.**
Industrial Machinery - **Vimex Cnc Machining**
Industrial Machinery - **Weltek-swiss**
Industrial Machinery & Equipment - **American European Systems**
Industrial Machinery & Equipment - **Bakemark**
Industrial Machinery & Equipment - **Hawthorne Power Systems**
Industrial Machinery & Equipment - **Larson & Associates Inc**
Industrial Machinery & Equipment - **Dial Manufacturing Inc**
Industrial Machinery & Equipment - **Electro Stylus**
Industrial Machinery & Equipment - **Ftc**
Industrial Machinery & Equipment - **Glasscraft Inc**
Industrial Machinery & Equipment - **Hamre Equipment**
Industrial Machinery & Equipment - **James Heavy Equipment Specialist**
Industrial Machinery & Equipment - **M & M Corporation**
Industrial Machinery & Equipment - **Napp Systems Inc**
Industrial Machinery & Equipment - **Omicron Video**
Industrial Machinery & Equipment - **Pacific Utility Equipment Co**
Industrial Machinery & Equipment - **Shindaiwa Inc**
Industrial Machinery & Equipment - **Technaseal**
Industrial Machinery & Equipment - **Tecnipac Inc**
Industrial Machinery & Equipment - **Uei**
Industrial Machinery & Equip, Conveyors - **Southwestern Automation**
Industrial Machinery / Magazine - **Heartland Communications Group Inc**
Industrial Machinery Controls & Safeguards - **Rockford Systems Inc.(Mfr)**
Industrial Machinery and Equipment - **Astechnologies**
Industrial Machinery and Equipment - **Cutting Edge Tool Supply Inc**
Industrial Machinery and Equipment - **Dresser Instrument Div.**
Industrial Machinery and Equipment - **Dynamic Air Inc.**
Industrial Machinery and Equipment - **Morgan Denver Sales Co**
Industrial Machinery and Equipment - Bakery - **Hurdt & Associates Mach**
Industrial Machinery, Movers, Rigging - **Hall Industrial Services**
Industrial Machinery, Tools & Die-cast Molds - **Yorktown Precision Tech**
Industrial Machining - **Semco Inc.**
Industrial Marking / Safety Graphics - **Sign Connection**
Industrial Marking Devices, Inks - **American Marking, Inc.**
Industrial Metal Doors - **Fleming Steel Co.**
Industrial Metal Fabrication - **R O T H B R O S., Inc., a First Energy Co.**
Industrial Mixers & Dispersers - **Myers Engineering Inc. (Mfr)**
Industrial Mixing & Drying Equipment - **Hosokawa Micron Powder Sys**
Industrial Nonwovens - **Precision Custom Coatings**
Industrial Oem & Maintenance Coatings - **Hunting Industrial Coatings**
Industrial Oil & Gas Burner Parts & Boilers, Parts - **Powermaster Pacific**
Industrial Oil, Gas, Marine Coatings & Tank Linings - **International Paint**
Industrial Oils, Chemicals & Metalworking Lubricants - **Chempet Corp.**
Industrial Organic Chemicals, Export - **Chemdesign Corporation, a Bayer**
Industrial Organic Chemicals, N.e.c. - **Burlington Chemical Co., Inc.**
Industrial Organic Chemicals, Nec - **Norac Co., Inc., the**
Industrial Ovens - **Industrial Process Equipment**
Industrial Ovens & Furnaces - **Wisconsin Oven Corp.**
Industrial Packaging Tapes - **Taratape**
Industrial Paint Lines - **F S P Machinery**

Industrial Paint Shop for Metal and Plastic Surfaces - **Inca Paint & Print**
Industrial Pan Washing Machine - **Af Industries, Alvey Washing**
Industrial Paper Folding, Cutting - **Baumfolder Corp.**
Industrial Paper Products, Janitorial Sup - **Advance Paper & Maintenance**
Industrial Phenolic Laminates - **Mapletex**
Industrial Plating Racks - **Tilton Rack & Basket Corp.**
Industrial Process Dryers, Conveyor - **Food Engineering Corporation**
Industrial Process Furnaces & Ovens - **Therma-tron-x Inc.**
Industrial Pumping Systems - **Grover Manufacturing Corp.**
Industrial Pumps - **Finish Thompson Inc.**
Industrial Pumps - **Abel Pumps Corp.**
Industrial Purging Compounds for Plastic Industry Only - **Rapid Purge**
Industrial Refrigeration Equipment - **Refrigeration Resources Co.**
Industrial Rubber Products - **Diamond Rubber Products Co., Inc.**
Industrial Rubber; Hose and Belting - **Colorado Rubber & Supply Co**
Industrial Safety Eye & Head Protection Equipment - **Dalloz Safety, Inc.**
Industrial Safety Mat Systems - **Larco, Div. Of Acrometal Companies,**
Industrial Scales - **Renmark Pacific Corporation**
Industrial Seals & Packings - **American High Performance Seals, Inc.**
Industrial Sewing Machines - **Richard Sewing Machine**
Industrial Sewing Machines & Attachments - **Rimoldi of America**
Industrial Sewing Thread - **American & Efird, Inc.**
Industrial Sewing Thread - **Saunders Thread Co., Inc.**
Industrial Shreding Equipment - **Shred-tech Chicago**
Industrial Soaps, Flake & Powder - **Original Bradford Soap Works, Inc.**
Industrial Soil Sealants and Enzymes - **Seepage Control Inc**
Industrial Specialty Light Bulbs - **Bulbtronics, Inc.**
Industrial Spray Nozzles - **Bete Fog Nozzle Inc. (Mfr)**
Industrial Stackers - **Autoquip Corporation**
Industrial Stationary Batteries - **Yuasa, Inc.**
Industrial Storage Batteries - **Sec Industrial Battery Co., Inc.**
Industrial Strength Cleaning Products - **Whip-it Products, Inc.**
Industrial Structural Steel Coatings - **Environmental Protective Coatings**
Industrial Supplies - **Colorado Rubber & Supply Co**
Industrial Supplies - **American Hydraulics**
Industrial Supplies - **Alamia Inc**
Industrial Supplies - **All American Containers, Inc.**
Industrial Supplies - **Century Spring Co., Inc.**
Industrial Supplies & Hardware - **Advance Paper & Maintenance**
Industrial Supplies, Water, Sewer & Drain, Wholesale - **Everett J. Prescott**
Industrial Thermoforming Machinery - **Maac Machinery Co., Inc.**
Industrial Thread Repair Inserts and Tools - **Time Fastener Company Inc**
Industrial Trailers, Push out - **Converto Mfg. Co. Inc. (Mfr)**
Industrial Trailers, Roll off - **Converto Mfg. Co. Inc. (Mfr)**
Industrial Tub Grinders and Trommel Screens - **Diamond Z Manufacturin**
Industrial Turbine Engine Parts - **Turbo Specialists Llc.**
Industrial Vacuum Cleaners - **Nilfisk-advance America, Inc.**
Industrial Vacuum Cleaners & Loaders- **De Marco Max Vac Corporation**
Industrial Vacuum Loader - **Super Products Corp.**
Industrial Valves - **American Valve & Pump, Inc.**
Industrial Valves, Export - **Moos Machine Works**
Industrial Valves, Manifolds , Cylinders & Systems - **P G I International**
Industrial Vibrating Equipment - **Vibco, Inc.**
Industrial Washers, Metal - **Therma-tron-x Inc.**
Industrial Washing Machinery - **Af Industries, Alvey Washing Equipment**
Industrial Waste Heat Recovery & Heat Exchangers - **Exothermics, Inc.**
Industrial Wastewater Treatment Systems - **Hb Environmental Engineers**
Industrial Waterproofing and Roofing Sealants, - **Pro-seal Products Inc**
Industrial Weighing, Materials Handling Systems - **Renmark-pacific Inc**
Industrial Wiping Cloths - **Sheftel International**
Industrial Wire Rope - **Leschen Wire Rope Co.**
Industrial Wood Products - **Future Packaging Inc**
Industrial Work Gloves - **Shelby Group International**
Industrial Workbenches - **R.w. Hatfield Co., Pro-line Div.**
Industrial Zinc, Rack & Barrel - **Dixie Electro Plating Co., Inc.**
Industry Chemicals in General - **Velco Chemicals**
Industry Including Plastic Cases - **Howe & Howe Lexis Sales Corp**
Infant Bedding & Accessories - **Patchkraft Inc.**
Infection Control Signs; Handwashing Motivation - **Brevis Corp**
Infectious Waste Control Receptacles, Steel - **United Metal Receptacle**
Inflatable Back Support, Rubber - **Ken Mcright Supplies, Inc.**

Inflatable Mattress Overlay, Rubber - **Ken Mcright Supplies, Inc.**
Inflatable Wheel Chair Cushions, Rubber - **Ken Mcright Supplies, Inc.**
Inflatables - **Interpretive Marketing Products**
Info. Retrieval, Used & New Agri. Eq.- **Heartland Communications Grou**
Info. Retrieval, Used & New Const.Eq. - **Heartland Communications Gr**
Info. Retrieval, Used & New Plane/jet Eq. - **Heartland Communications G**
Information Retrieval - **Technical Resource International, Inc.**
Information Technology Consultants; - **Cap Gemini America**
Information: Knowledge Products & Content - **Idq Books Worldwide Inc**
Infra-red Burners, Gas Fired, N.e.c. - **Solaronics, Inc.**
Infra-red Space Heaters, Gas Fired - **Solaronics, Inc.**
Infrared & Convection Ovens, Conveyors - **Blasdel Enterprises, Inc.**
Infrared Catalytic Heating Equipment, - **Thermal Systems Inc**
Infrared Sensing Controls, Timer Modules - **Instrumentation & Control**
Ingots, Billets, PressToll Conversion - **Standard Steel**
Inground Steel Wall Swimming Pool Kits - **Imperial Pools Inc.**
Injection Machinery - **Egla International**
Injection Molded Handlebar Grips, Bicycle Accessories - **Hunt-wilde**
Injection Molded Plastic Parts - **Oberg Mfg. Co.**
Ink Dyes - **Organic Dyestuffs Corporation**
Ink Jet Inks for Printers, Pens, Etc. - **Bezjian Dye-chem, Inc.**
Ink Jet Printers - **Imaging Technologies, Inc.**
Ink Jet Refilling Equipment / Ribbon Production Equipment - **SME**
Ink Printing - **Wikoff Color Corp.**
Ink, Printing - **Prismflex Inc.**
Ink_printing - **A J Daw Printing Ink Co**
Ink_printing - **Inx International Ink Co.**
Ink_printing - **Solar Color Chemical Corp.**
Ink_printing - **Independent Ink Inc**
Inked Surface Testers - **Norman Tool, Inc.**
Inks for Writing and Marking Instruments - **National Ink**
Inner Column - **Foster Co., L. B.**
Inner Tubes, of Rubber - **Traction International**
Innerspring Mattress - **Kingsdown, Inc.**
Innerspring Mattresses - **Land and Sky Mfg., Inc.**
Innovative Foodservice Heating, Holding & - **Bevles Company, Inc.**
Innovative Stamping Corp - **Convention & Trade Show Equipment**
Inorg. Pigments, Concrete Mix-in Color - **Davis Colors**
Inorganic Chemicals & Fluorides - **Advance Research Chemicals, Inc.**
Inorganic Pigments & Dry Colors - **Davis Colors**
Insect & Rodent Control - **Pic Corp.**
Insect Screening-fiberglass - **New York Wire Co.**
Insect Wire Screening, Aluminum - **New York Wire Co.**
Insecticides - **Plato Trading**
Insertable Label Holders - **Aigner Index, Inc.**
Inspection & Quality Control Optical Instruments - **Omex Technologies**
Instant Coffee - **Tonex, Inc.**
Instant Printing - **Instant Copy, Inc.**
Institutional & Contract Mattresses - **Estee Bedding Co., Inc.**
Institutional Silver-plated Holloware - **Grand Silver Co., Inc.**
Instrument & Electrical Services - **Petrotech Inc.**
Instrument Cleaning Brushes - **Sharn, Inc.**
Instrument Valves / Manifolds - **Mid-west Instrument**
Instrumentation Design - **Whitlock Instrument**
Instrumentation for Detection of Ionizing - **Far West Tech Health Physics**
Instruments Elastic - **Tp Orthodontics, Inc.**
Instruments and Appliances for Medical - **Thomas Industries, Inc.**
Instruments and Appliances for Medical - **Americares Foundations**
Instruments to Measure Electricity - **Faria Corp.**
Instruments to Measure and Test Electricity - **Tasco Inc**
Insulated - **Permaluster Company**
Insulated / Non-insulated Rail Joints - **Portec Rail Products Inc.**
Insulated Copper -Thhn & Thw - **Republic Wire, Inc.**
Insulated Glass - **Custom Glass Corp.**
Insulated Hardware Banana Plugs - **Daburn Electronics & Cable Corp.**
Insulated Shipping & Storage Equipment - **H & R Industries, Inc.**
Insulated Spa Covers & Spas - **Blue Water Spa Covers**
Insulated Tools - Osha Approved - **National Electric Gate Co.**
Insulated Wire & Cable - **Brim Electronics Inc.**
Insulated Wire, Cable; Opt Sheath Fib Cables - **Anicom Inc.**
Insulating Glass Units - **Laminated Glass**

Insulating Hardware - **Keystone Electronics Corp.**
Insulation - **Waite, R. M. Company**
Insulation Pins, Hanger & Washers - **Gemco**
Insulation for Metal Buildings - **Mizell Brothers Company**
Insurance / Drawback - **Seamodal Transport Corp.**
Insurance Agent Livestock/animal Insurance - **R & R Insurance Services,**
Insurance Agent, Bull Semen Insurance - **R & R Insurance Services, Inc.**
Insurance Agent, Exim Bank - **Mondics/greenhaw Insurance Agency**
Insurance Agents & Brokers - **R & R Insurance Services, Inc.**
Insurance Broker, Marine & Casualty - **Craig M. Ferguson & Co. Inc.**
Insurance, Property & Casualty - **Kemper International**
Int'l Freight Forwarder - **Quality Customs Broker, Inc.**
Int'l Import-export Forwarder - **Pierce Packaging Company**
Int'l Public Relations - **Smirnoff Communications Group, Inc.**
Integrated Global Logistics - **Commercial International Forwarding Inc.**
Integrated Passive Components - **Koa Speer Electronics, Inc.**
Integrated Process Systems - **Flexicon Corporation**
Integrated Thick-film Circuitry - **Brush Wellman Inc. Ceramics Div.**
Integrator:Satellite ,Wireless Communication - **Satellite Transmission Sys**
Intel Based Lans. - **Stallion Technologies Inc**
Intelligent Motion Controllers - **Oregon Micro Systems**
Interactive Audience,group Reponse Systems - **Ortek Data Systems Inc**
Interactive Cd Rom Design - **Graphics plus Printing, Inc.**
Interactive Media/web Application Development - **Source W Printing**
Interactive, Color Changing Promotional Items - **Davis Liquid Crystals**
Interconnect Hardware & Terminals - **Keystone Electronics Corp.**
Interface Converters, Digital Bridges - **Hull Speed Data Products, Inc.**
Interface Panel, Plc-cntl. & Solid State - **Con-tech Power Systems, Inc.**
Interfacial Tension Apparatus - **Rame-hart, Inc.**
Interferon - **Viragen, Inc.**
Interior & Exterior Signs - **All Neon & Signs**
Interior & Exterior Signs - **Colite International**
Interior & Exterior Signs - **Lynne Signs, Lori**
Interior & Exterior Signs - **Muller Studios**
Interior & Exterior Signs - **Sign Connection**
Interior & Exterior Signs & Fabric Banners - **A B C Sign Design, Llc**
Interior Architectural Signage - **Ca Signs**
Interior Embossed Polymer Moldings- **Marley Mouldings Inc.(Mfr)**
Interior Polymer Moldings, Primed & Prefinished - **Marley Mouldings**
Interlining - Nonwoven & Knit - **Precision Custom Coatings**
Interlining Fabrics - **Facemate Corporation**
Intermodal Transportation - **Apollo Warehouse, Inc.**
Intermodal Transportation & Distribution - **Commercial International For**
Internal Combustion Engines, Generator Sets - **Hawthorne Power Systems**
Internal Fire Suppression Devices. Fmrc Approved - **Ats Products**
International Consulting Svcs. - **Armstrong Teasdale**
International Freight & Cargo Transportation - **All Points International**
International Freight Forwarder - **Cbc International, Inc.**
International Freight Forwarder - **Commercial International Forwarding**
International Freight Forwarder - **Marmara, Inc.**
International Freight Forwarding, Worldwide Service - **Columbia Logistics,**
International Frieght Forwarder - **Coughlin Logistics**
International Logistics & Transportation - **Dartrans, Inc.**
International Mineral Industry Consultants - **Pincock Allen & Holt**
International Sales Base - **Industrial Design Fabrication**
International Trade Reference Library - **Waukesha Co. Technical College -**
Internet Consulting & E-commerce Tools - **Virtual Fund.com**
Internet Media Production - **Communi-creations Inc**
Internet Sales - **Adams & Brooks Inc**
Interpretalk, Over-the-telephone Interpreter Svcs- **Language Services Asso**
Interpreters & Translators - **Language Services Associates**
Interpreting Services - **Tru Lingua Language Systems, Inc.**
Interpreting Services - **University Language Center, Inc.**
Interpreting Services, Major Languages - **Dynamic Language Center, Ltd**
Interpreting Svcs., Japanese - **Suzuki, Myers & Associates, Limited**
Intimate Apparel - **Just a Stretch**
Intraocular Lenses, Viscoelastic Surgical Fluid - **Ocularvision Inc**
Intravenous Infusion Pumps - **Medical Technology Products Inc.**
Inventory Procurement - **Pierce Packaging Company**
Investment Casting Supplies - Expendables & Consumables - **Remet Corp.**
Investment Castings - **Delvest, Inc.**

Iodides & Iodide Oxides - **West Agro, Inc.**
Iol's - **Benz Research & Development Corp.**
Ion Exchange Equipment, Resin & Spare Parts - **Techni-chem Inc.**
Ion Exchange Resin - **The Purolite Company**
Ionized Air & Water Rinsers - **Arrowhead Systems Llc**
Iqf Tunnel & Spiral Freezers - **Freezing System Inc.**
Iron & Steel Foundries - **World Equipment & Machine Sales Company**
Iron & Steel Foundries- **World Equipment & Machine Sales Company**
Iron & Steel Lubricated Tapered Plug Vavles - **Nordstrom Valves, Inc.**
Iron Castings, Gray & Ductile - **Clearfield Machine Company (Mfr)**
Iron Castings, Mining Machinery - **Washington Mould Co.**
Irons - **Hamilton Beach/proctor Silex, Inc.**
Irrigation & Livestock Equipment - **Farm & Ranch Systems South, Llc.**
Irrigation Equipment - **Hector Turf**
Irrigation Equipment - **Northern Pump & Irrigation**
Irrigation Equipment, Wholesale - **Agro Industrial Management**
Irrigation Gaskets - **T & C Mfg. & Operating, Inc.**
Irrigation Injection Pumps - **John Blue Co.**
Irrigation Sprinklers & Micro for Agriculture - **Weather Tec Corporation**
Irrigation Sprinklers & Pivots - **Wamco Corporation**
Irrigation Systems - **Olson Irrigation Systems**
Islands & Back Islands - **Dolphin Mfg. Inc.**
Iso 9002 - **Welding Warehouse**
Iso 9002 Certified - **Litec Inc.**
Iso 9002 Certified Manufacture & Ce Mark - **Axiom Medical Inc**
Italian Pizzelle Cookies - **Dfp International Inc**
Jams, Jellies, Syrups, Vinegar & Honey - **Blackberry Patch, Inc.**
Janitorial Chemicals - **Dr. T's Nature Products Inc.**
Janitorial Cleaning Chemicals - **Midlab, Inc.**
Jaquard Upholstery Fabrics - **Absecon Mills, Inc.**
Jelly / Preserves - **Griffin Food Company**
Jenny Machines, Distributor - **C & W Enterprises**
Jet Engine / Aircraft Parts - **Sun Country Industries Inc.**
Jet Inks - **Coates Electrographics Inc.**
Jewelers' Materials & Lapidary Work - **Fuller & Son Co., George H.**
Jewelers' Materials & Lapidary Work - **Vicki's Jewelry**
Jewelry & Precious Stones - **Accents in Sterling Inc**
Jewelry Boxes (Metal) - **Scotchman Industries, Inc.(Mfr)**
Jewelry Findings - **Fuller & Son Co., George H.**
Jewelry, Precious Metal - **Maui Divers of Hawaii, Ltd**
Jewelry, Precious Metal - **Olympia Gold Inc.**
Jewelry, Precious Metal - **Sardelli & Sons, Inc., T.**
Jewelry, Precious Metal - **Shine Jewelry**
Jewelry, Precious Metal, Manufacturing - **Artistica, Inc.**
Jewelry, Precious Metal. Gem Stones - **Gary Stull Goldsmith**
Jewelry_costume - **Olympia Gold Inc.**
Jewelry_costume - **Future Primitive Designs Ltd**
Jewelry_costume - **House of Fashion Jewelry**
Jewelry_custom - **Entenmann-rovin Company**
Jig Grinding - **Best Jig-grinding Service**
Jigs & Fixtures, Special - **Dyer Tool & Die, Inc.**
Juice of Any Other Single Fruit or Vegetable - **Ryan Trading**
Juicers / Extractors - **Hamilton Beach/proctor Silex, Inc.**
Junction Boxes - **Ocean Design Inc.**
Just in Time Concept - **Dan Transport Corporation**
Juvenile Bedding & Linens - **Allegra Industries, Inc.**
Kapton - **Lockwood Industries Inc**
Kevlar - Spun & Filament - **Saunders Thread Co., Inc.**
Key Chains & Leather Products - **Blackburne, Inc., Perry**
Key Management Systems - **Keyper Systems, Inc.**
Key Pad Testing - **Norman Tool, Inc.**
Key Seaters - **Morrison Co., the D. C.**
Keyboards - **Cherry Corporation, the**
Keyskin Keyboard Protectors - **Compu Cover**
Kf Polymer, Dykor (Kynar) Ryton, Halar - **Americoat Corp.**
Kiln Dried Lumber & Mouldings - **Helsel Lumber Mill, Inc.**
Kiln-dried & Paned Lumber - **Johnson Lumber Co., Llc.**
Kiln-dried Hardwood Lumber - **Hawkeye Forest Products Inc**
Kiosk - **Vixen Hill Mfg. Co.**
Kiosks - **Dolphin Mfg. Inc.**
Kitchen Cabinets & Furniture - **Prada Enterprises, Inc.**

Kitchen Cabinets, Countertops, Bathrooms - **Midwest Builders Supply,**
Kitchen Cabinets_wood - **Fowler Cabinet & Hardware Co**
Kitchen Cabinets_wood - **Kraft Masters Cabinets**
Kitchen Cabinets_wood - **Montgomery Cabinetry Co., Inc.**
Kitchen Cabinets_wood - **Paul's Cabinets Co.**
Kitchen Cabinets_wood - **Winfield Cabinets**
Kitchen Cabinets_wood - **Bonito Mfg.**
Kitchen Cutlery - **Cutco Cutlery Corp.**
Kitchen Exhaust Hoods, (Commercial) - **Moli-tron Company Inc.**
Kitchen Gadgets Assembly, Pad Printing - **Robbins Industries Inc.**
Kits That Convert Standard - **E-z Lift Ltd International**
Kitting Bulk Components - **Parpro, Inc.**
Knife Gate Valves - **Ac Valve Inc.**
Knife Gate Valves - **Tyco Valves & Controls**
Knit & Woven Top, Pants, Shorts, - **Y.m.l.a. Inc**
Knit De Knit, Stuffer Box Crimped, Cilki Ii - **Roselon Industries, Inc.**
Knit Fabric Dyeing & Finishing - **Cleveland Mills**
Knit Goods Dryers - **Tubular Textile Machinery**
Knit Goods Shrinkage Control Compactors - **Tubular Textile Machinery**
Knit Goods Wet Processing Machinery - **Tubular Textile Machinery**
Knit Outerwear Mills - **Alps Sportswear Manufacturing Co , Inc**
Knit Outerwear Mills - **Richland Mills**
Knit Outerwear, Nylon Tricot - **Dorma Mills(mfr)**
Knit Piece Goods - **Richland Mills**
Knitted Bedding Fabrics - **Dorma Mills(mfr)**
Knitted Curtains - **Dorma Mills(mfr)**
Knitted Elastic - **Just a Stretch**
Knock down Samll Animal & Bird Cages- **Tenwood International**
Knurling - **Cole Screw Machine Products, Inc.**
Kolackys - **Neuman Bakery Specialties, Inc.**
Korfe Paper - **Maxport International**
Kraft Paper - **Geochem International**
Kraftliner, Uncoated, Unbleached - **Lotus Exim International**
Kyo-dophilus Probiotics Formulas - **Wakunaga of America Co., Ltd.**
Kyo-green Green Food Formula - **Wakunaga of America Co., Ltd.**
Kyolic Aged Garlic Extract Formula - **Wakunaga of America Co., Ltd.**
Lab Equipment & Apparatus - **F&j Specialty Products, Inc.**
Lab Equipment, Export - **Alkantec, Inc.**
Lab. Glassware & Plasticware, Whsle. - **A. Daigger & Company, Inc.**
Label Printer Applicators - **Imtec Inc.**
Label Printing - **J K Label Co.**
Label Printing Supplies - **Imtec Inc.**
Labeling Equipment - **B & H Manufacturing Co.**
Labeling Machinery for Pressure-sensitive Label - **Apax Corporation**
Labels - **Imtec Inc.**
Labels - **New West Business Forms**
Labels - **First Card Co.**
Labels - **Richard Boas**
Labor & Admin. Service - **Alfa Southwest Maquiladora Svc**
Labor Assister, an Obstetric Device Designed To - **Novatrix Inc**
Laboratory & Industrial Scale - **Pennsylvania Scale Co.**
Laboratory Analytical Devices - **Hosokawa Micron Powder Systems**
Laboratory Analytical Instruments - **Scientech Inc.**
Laboratory Analytical Instruments - **Cypress Systems, Inc.**
Laboratory Apparatus - **Ney Dental, Inc.**
Laboratory Apparatus & - **Dynaoptic-motion Corporation**
Laboratory Apparatus & Furniture - **General Air Corporation**
Laboratory Apparatus & Furniture - **Germfree Laboratories, Inc.**
Laboratory Apparatus & Furniture - **Hamilton Bell Co., Inc.**
Laboratory Apparatus & Furniture - **Brevis Corp**
Laboratory Apparatus & Supp., Whsle. - **A. Daigger & Company, Inc.**
Laboratory Balances & Scales - **Scientech Inc.**
Laboratory Centrifuges - **Hamilton Bell Co., Inc.**
Laboratory Equip, Supplies & Reagents - **Thomas Scientific**
Laboratory Equipment - **Glas-col Apparatus Company (Mfr)**
Laboratory Equipment - **Nor-lake, Inc. (Mfr)**
Laboratory Equipment - **Biomedical International**
Laboratory Equipment, Vortex Mixers, - **Scientific Industries, Inc.**
Laboratory Instruments - **Gilson, Inc.**
Laboratory Plastics, Disposable - **Quality Scientific Plastics**
Laboratory Products & Equipment - **Paul Marsh, Llc**

Laboratory Services - **Tp Orthodontics, Inc.**
Laboratory Testing - **Ctl Engineering, Inc.**
Laboratoryware, Plastics - **Plastinetics, Inc.**
Lace Manufacturer - **Intimate Touch, Inc.**
Lace Trimmings - **Mini-lace, Inc.**
Lacing Tape for Electrical Motors - **Western Filament Inc**
Ladies Sleepwear / Lingerie - **Milco Industries, Inc.**
Ladle Sand - **Refractory Materials International**
Lamb Offal, Edible - **Superior Packing/superior Farm**
Lamb Skins - **Superior Packing/superior Farm**
Lamb, American, Fresh & Frozen - **Superior Packing/superior Farm**
Lamb, Australian, Fresh & Frozen - **Superior Packing/superior Farm**
Laminate Flooring - **Congoleum Corp.**
Laminate Furniture - **Woodpecker, Inc.**
Laminate Rollstock & Tubing - **Caltex Plastics Inc**
Laminated & Wooden Cabinets - **Montgomery Cabinetry Co., Inc.**
Laminated Cabinets, Counters, Store Fixtures - **B & D Custom Cabinets,**
Laminated Fabrics - **Current, Inc.**
Laminated Insulation Materials - **Alpha Associates, Inc.**
Laminated Panels - **Interior Products Inc.**
Laminated Plastics Plate Rods & Tubes - **Current, Inc.**
Laminated Polycarbonates - **Laminated Glass**
Laminated Safety Glass - **Laminated Glass**
Laminates & Architectural Woodwork - **Incon Overseas Marketing, Inc.**
Laminating Adhesives - **Dielectric Polymers, Inc.**
Laminating Machines - **Banner American Products, Inc.**
Laminators, Cameras & Id Supplies - **Fox Laminating Co., Inc.**
Lamp Shades - **Tempo Lighting**
Lamps - **Tempo Lighting**
Lamps & Accessories, Manufacturer - **Masterpiece Accessories Inc**
Lamps, Mirrors & Decorative Accessories - **Speer Collectibles**
Lamps_electric - **Agamco Inc**
Lan Terminals - Unisys, Dec. Hp. Ibm. Unix - **Visentech Systems, Inc.**
Lan/wan Application Products. - **Radiant Communications Corporation**
Landscape Stone - **Rowat Cut Stone & Marble Co.**
Landscaping Equipment - **Netafim Irrigation Inc**
Language Proficiency Testing - **Language plus**
Laparoscopic Surgical Devices - **Mectra Labs, Inc.**
Laptop Accessories - **Allsop, Inc.**
Large Custom Fiberglass and Steel/aluminum Structures - **Guard Lee, Inc.**
Large Diameter, High-pressure Steel Pipes - **Northwest Pipe Company**
Large Inventory on New & Used Machinery - **Richard Sewing Machine**
Large Surface Switches - **Hall Co., the**
Largest Private Label Manufacturer Of - **Realys Inc**
Laser Cutting & Engraving - **Laser Creations Inc.**
Laser Cutting of Flat & Tubular Metals - **G & H Diversified Mfg. Inc.**
Laser Marking & Coating Equipment - **Lasertechnics Marking Corp.**
Laser Metalworking Equip. Chillers - **Affinity Industries Inc. (Mfr)**
Laser Mfr; Helium-neon, Air Cooled Argon - **Uniphase, Laser Division**
Laser Printer Cartridges / fax machines -**Laser Imaging International**
Laser Printing - **Matrix Imaging Solution**
Laser Range Finder - **Litton Systems, Inc. Laser Sys, Inc.**
Laser Toner Cartridges (Rebuilt) - **LRF Business Solutions**
Laser Woodworking Equip. Chillers - **Affinity Industries Inc. (Mfr)**
Laser-welded Stainless Steel Tubing - **Laser Armor Tech Corporation**
Lasers for Ocular and General Surgery - **Coherent Medical Group (Cmg)**
Latan Furniture - **Kowa California Inc.**
Latex & Alkyd. Architectural Finishes - **ICI Paints International**
Latex Glove Dispensers - **Accrafect Products Inc.**
Latin American Business Review - **Haworth Press, Inc., the**
Lattice - **Summit Sales & Marketing**
Laundry Equipment_commercial - **Pellerin Milnor Corp.**
Laundry Machinery - **Maytag International**
Laundry, Drycleaning Coin-op Equipment - **World Trade Exporters, Inc.**
Law / Business / Banking / Astronomy - **Rahoy Coccia Gabriella**
Law Enforcement / Police Products - **Alpine Armoring Inc.**
Law Enforcement Boats - **Penn Yan Marine Mfg. Corp.**
Law Enforcement Equipment - **Darley & Co., W. S.**
Law Enforcement, Survival, Hunting & Camping Gear - **Rothco**
Lawn & Garden Chemicals - **Dr. T's Nature Products Inc.**
Lawn & Garden Equipment - **Nelson Products Co.**

Lawn & Garden Equipment - **Olson Irrigation Systems**
Lawn & Garden Equipment - **Barreto Manufacturing**
Lawn & Garden Equipment - **Doskocil Industries Inc**
Lawn & Garden Equipment - **Textron Turf Care and Specialty Products**
Lawn & Garden Equipment - **Valley View Industries**
Lawn & Garden Equipment - **Alamia Inc**
Lawn & Golf Course Equipment - **Hector Turf**
Lawn Edging Products & Decorative Planters - **Valley View Industries**
Lawn Games Including; Croquet, Bocce - **Ram Sports Inc**
Lawn Mowers - **Carter Brothers**
Lawn-garden Equip, Lawn Aerators - **Broyhill Company, the (Mfr)**
Lbr Logs - **Ellis Enterprises, T. J.**
Lc-gc Chromatography Supplies - **Supelco, Inc.(Mfr)**
Lcd & Transformers - **American Zettler Inc**
Lcd/crt Monitors, Lcd Projectors - **Delta Products Corporation**
Lead Acid 12v 3ah-4000ah - **Sec Industrial Battery Co., Inc.**
Lead Crystal Giftware - **Saint George Crystal Ltd.**
Lead Crystal Lighting Components - **Saint George Crystal Ltd.**
Lead Crystal Stemware, Bar Products - **Saint George Crystal Ltd.**
Lead Forming & Wire Stripping Machines - **Eraser Co., Inc.**
Lead Paint Removal - **Cardinal Industrial Insulation Co., Inc.**
Lead Paint Testing - **Analytica Environmental Lab Inc**
Lead Pencils & Art Goods - **National Pen Corp.**
Lead Pencils & Art Products - **General Pencil Co.**
Leak Detection / Location Equipment - **Perma-pipe Ricwil, Industrial**
Leak Detection, Fuel Oil - **Perma-pipe Ricwil, Industrial**
Leak Detection, Piping - **Perma-pipe Ricwil, Industrial**
Leather - **C. M. I. Enterprises**
Leather & Metal Desk Accessories - **Matel Bank and Desk Accessories**
Leather & Sheep-lined Clothing - **Jh Design Group**
Leather & Sheep-lined Clothing - **Perrone Leathers, Inc.**
Leather & Sheep-lined Clothing - **Pharr Brand Name Apparel, Llc**
Leather & Sheep-lined Clothing - **Sheepskin Coat Factory**
Leather Care Products & Preservatives - **Pecard Leather Care Products**
Leather Furniture - **Mc Kinley Leather of Hickory**
Leather Goods - **Empire State Leather Corp.**
Leather Goods - **Saddle Barn Tack Distributors, Inc.**
Leather Goods - **Blackburne, Inc., Perry**
Leather Goods, Nec - **Robus Leather**
Leather Goods, Nec. - **Gould & Goodrich**
Leather Gun Accessories - **Gould & Goodrich**
Leather Jackets - **Perrone Leathers, Inc.**
Leather Office and Club Chairs, Love Seats - **Monteverdi-young Inc**
Leather Shoes - **Nishizawa**
Leather Tanning & Finishing - **Perrone Leathers, Inc.**
Leather Waterproofer & Conditioners - **Original Mink Oil Co.**
Leather, Nylon & Polyester Computer Carrying Cases - **American Sewing**
Led Lights - **National Electric Gate Co.**
Led Signs - **Action Media Technologies Inc**
Legal Services - **Armstrong Teasdale**
Legal Services - **Cox, Buchanan, Padmore & Shakarchy**
Legal Services - **Parsons Behle & Latimer**
Legal Services - **Stoel Rives Llp**
Legal Services / International - **Cacheaux, Cavazos, Newton, Martin &**
Legal Services International - **Finley & Associates P.a.**
Legal Services, Customs & International Trade Law - **Sonnenberg & Ande**
Legal Services, Immigration & Natural. - **Finley & Associates P.a.**
Legal Services, Import & Export - **Finley & Associates P.a.**
Legal Services, Legislative Consulting - **S.K. Ross & Assoc., P.c.**
Lemon, Cherry, Watermelon Syrup - **Del's Lemonade & Refreshments Inc**
Letterheads, Envelopes, Brochures- **Wolf Creek Printing**
Level Controls - **S O R, Inc.**
Level Controls Instr. Electrical - **Drexelbrook International, Inc.**
Level Gauging Equipment for Liquids and Slurries - **Consilium Us, Inc.**
Level, Density, Weigh Scale - **Kay-ray/sensall, Inc.**
Lexington Furniture & Upholstery - **Designers Resource**
Library & Av Supplies - **Brodart Co.**
Library Furniture - **Brodart Co.**
License Plate & Key Chain Engraving - **Custom Engraving**
License Plate Capture Cameras - **Pearpoint Inc**
Licensed & Custom Edible Images - **Lucks Food Decorating Co.**

Lift Truck Batteries - **Yuasa, Inc.**
Lift Truck Parts - **Master Motor Rebuilders**
Light Bulbs - **Aero-tech Light Bulb Co., Inc.**
Light Dimmers - **Lutron Electronics Co., Inc.**
Light Elec. Displays, Wholesale - **Adaptive Micro Systems, Inc.**
Light Gauge Metal Trusses - **Hexaport International, Ltd.**
Light Industrial R.o. Machines - up to 10,000 Gpd - **Ro Ultratec Usa Inc**
Light Metal Stampings - **Curran Coil Spring Inc**
Light Poles & Brackets & Flagpole Shafts - **Hapco Aluminum Poles**
Light Sources - **Rudolph Instruments, Inc.**
Light Truck and Automobile Four-wheel Drive - **Rancho Suspension**
Lighted Signs - Banners - **Dezion Signs**
Lighting - Sylvania / Osram Distributor, Lamps - **Mia Express Inc.**
Lighting Components - **Paraflex Industries, Inc.**
Lighting Controls - **Trane Company, the**
Lighting Equipment - **Cir-kit Concepts, Inc.**
Lighting Equipment - **Engineered Lighting Products**
Lighting Equipment - **Eye Lighting International of North America, Inc.**
Lighting Equipment - **Made in Maui Neon**
Lighting Equipment - **Paraflex Industries, Inc.**
Lighting Equipment - **R L S Lighting, Inc.**
Lighting Equipment 12v / 24v - **Light Solutions**
Lighting Equipment, Vehicular - **Grote Industries, Inc.**
Lighting Equipment_vehicular - **Guide Corporation**
Lighting Fixture Restoration - **The Malder Co**
Lighting Fixtures - **Tempo Lighting**
Lighting Fixtures - **Engineered Lighting Products**
Lighting Fixtures & Plastic Products - **Paraflex Industries, Inc.**
Lighting Fixtures (50hz) - **Bifrost**
Lighting Fixtures_commercial - **Bieber Lighting Corp**
Lighting Fixtures_commercial - **Doane Co., Inc., L. C.**
Lighting Fixtures_commercial - **Esco International**
Lighting Fixtures_commercial - **Jeb Lighting Co., Llc**
Lighting Fixtures_commercial - **Magnaray International**
Lighting Fixtures_residential - **Kichler Lighting Group**
Lighting Fixtures_residential - Commercial - **The Malder Co**
Lighting Systems - **Garrett Sound & Lighting**
Lighting, Energy Efficient - **Trojan, Inc.**
Lighting, Manufacturer - **Trojan, Inc.**
Lighting, Shatterproof - **Trojan, Inc.**
Lightning Warning Systems - **Thor Guard, Inc.**
Lightweight Insulating Concrete - **Siplast Inc.**
Lightweight Insulating Concrete - **Stronglite Products**
Lightweight, Airline Shippable Cases for - **Lightware Inc**
Lilian Castellani De Fernandez, Counsel - **Armstrong Teasdale**
Lime Oil - **Todd Co., A.m.**
Limestone - **Rowat Cut Stone & Marble Co.**
Limestone All Type of Cuts & Colors - **Jabitex Corporation**
Line Boring of Engine Blocks & In-situ Machining. - **Golten Service**
Line Fishing Tackle, Nets , Decoy Birds - **Fathoms plus**
Line Item Order Selection - **Southwest Storage**
Line Pipe Piling & Structural Steel - **C & R Industries Inc**
Linings, Dress & Bathing Suits - **Dorma Mills(mfr)**
Lip Balm, Cough and Cold Products, Vitamins - **Oralabs Holding Corp**
Liquid Chemical Descalers - **Delta Products Group**
Liquid Copolymers, Erosion - **Environmental Soil Systems Inc**
Liquid Crystal Displays - **Rosen Product Development Inc**
Liquid Crystal Temperature Monitors - **Trademark Medical**
Liquid Crystals & Thermometers & Films - **Davis Liquid Crystals**
Liquid Fertilizer; Tank and Pond Liners - **Liquinox Co**
Liquid Filling - **Specialty Equipment Co.**
Liquid Filling Systems - **Filler Specialties, Inc.**
Liquid Filters - **Consler Filtrations Products**
Liquid Flow Provers, Liquid Density Meters - **Calibron Systems Inc**
Liquid Food Dispenser Faucets - **Tomlinson Industries**
Liquid Level Gauges & Site Flow Indicators - **Jogler, Inc.**
Liquid Level Indicators & Switches - **Madison Co.**
Liquid Level Instruments, Switches & Controls - **Madison Company**
Liquid Level Monitors - **Dynasonics-divison of Racine Federated, Inc.**
Liquid Nutritional Supplements - **Unico, Inc.**
Liquid Skin Cleaners - **Vision Pharmaceuticals Inc.**

Liquid Waste Handling Equipment - **L W T Pit Hog Dredge**
Liquid, Air & Vacuum Diaphragm Pumps - **Smart Products Inc**
Liquox - Sodium Permanganate - **Carus Chemical Co.**
Lithographic Printing Film and Pre-press Services - **Iridio**
Lithographic Printing Plates (Offset) - **Ano-coil Corp.**
Lithographic Printing, Commercial - **Prismflex Inc**
Lithographic Printing, Custom Card Decks - **U S Game Systems, Inc.**
Lithographic Printing_commercial - **Ace Printing Company**
Lithographic Printing_commercial - **Alphagraphics Printshops**
Lithographic Printing_commercial - **Artco**
Lithographic Printing_commercial - **Diego & Son Printing**
Lithographic Printing_commercial - **El Camino Printers**
Lithographic Printing_commercial - **Giant Horse Printing Inc**
Lithographic Printing_commercial - **Gonzalez Integrated Marketing**
Lithographic Printing_commercial - **Graphic Ways Inc**
Lithographic Printing_commercial - **Graphics plus Printing, Inc.**
Lithographic Printing_commercial - **Impulse Wear**
Lithographic Printing_commercial - **Instant Copy, Inc.**
Lithographic Printing_commercial - **Marketing Concepts**
Lithographic Printing_commercial - **National Art Publishing Corp.**
Lithographic Printing_commercial - **Pikes Peak Lithographing Co**
Lithographic Printing_commercial - **Rapid Reproductions Printing**
Lithographic Printing_commercial - **Repro-products & Services**
Lithographic Printing_commercial - **Thunderbird Printing & Screening**
Lithographic Printing_commercial - **Tretina Printing Co., Inc.**
Lithographic Printing_commercial - **Westpro Graphics**
Lithographic Printing_commercial - **Creative Plastics Printing Die**
Lithographic Printing_commercial - **Palone & Associates**
Live Animal Traps, Steel Wire - **Tomahawk Live Trap Co.**
Live Plants , Trees and Shrubs - **Boyntons Botanicals**
Livestock & Grain Handling Equipment - **Hawkeye Steel Products, Inc.**
Livestock & Livestock Products - **Stro-wold International Livestock Svcs.**
Livestock Feed - **Free Choice Enterprises**
Livestock Identification Equipment - **Coburn Company, Inc.**
Livestock Svcs., Swine Breeding - **Forkner Farms / Truline Genetics**
Load Cells - Mechanical, Hydraulic, Electronic - **Scalemen of Florida, Inc.**
Load Cells for Scales - **Artech Industries Inc**
Loading Spouts - **Midwest International Standard Prod, Inc**
Lobster Traps - **Fathoms plus**
Local & Domestic Transportation - **Price Transfer, Inc.**
Local Tax Clearence - **Inter-world Customs Broker, Inc.**
Localization / Translation / Publishing / Globalization - **M2 Limited**
Lock Boxes for the Real Estate, Automotive, - **Supra Products**
Lock out / Tag Out, Emergency Stop & Isolation Equipt - **Esco Services Inc**
Lock-down Devices and Security Products- **Maxton Security Systems**
Locomotive & Transit Cars- **Rockbestos Surprenant Cable Corp.**
Locomotive Engine Turbo Chargers - **Engine Systems**
Locomotive Fueling & Servicing Equipment - **Snyder Equipment Co., Inc.**
Locomotives, Lift Trucks, Die Handlers - **Plymouth Industries, Inc.**
Log Feeder Singulators - **Magnum Machinery Services Inc**
Log Handling Systems - **Magnum Machinery Services Inc**
Log Sunrooms - **Greco Homes**
Loggin Trailers - **Evans Mfg. Co., John Evans Trailers**
Logging - **Sea Forest Enterprises Inc**
Logging - **Algoma Lumber Co.**
Logging - **Yeager Sawmill**
Logging - **Lemhi Post & Poles Inc**
Logging & Sawmill Equipment - **Hamre Equipment**
Logistics - **Mark Vii International**
Logistics - **Respond Cargo Services Corp.**
Logistics / Transporation Services - **Respond Group of Companies**
Logistics Services (Project Management) - **Trism Inc.**
Logo Entrance Way Matting - **Pioneer Mat Co., Inc.**
Logos, Corporate-dimensional - **Asd, Inc. , Architectural Signage & Desi**
Logs - **Hamer, Jim C.**
Logs - **Soliman Brothers**
Long Line Fishing Gear Equipment - **Lindgren Pitman**
Long Shelf Life Tomato Seed - **Seedcraft**
Long Term Food Storage Bags - **Caltex Plastics Inc**
Looseleaf & Printing Industries; Grape Packaging - **Book Covers Inc**
Lord, Atlantic India, 3m, Parco - **C G R Products Inc.**

Los Angeles, Houston, Chicago, Providence - **Moran, J. F. Co., Inc.**
Lotion Skin Moisturizer - **Vision Pharmaceuticals Inc.**
Lottery Tickets - **Marketing Concepts**
Loudspeaker Products (Cem) - **Mg Electronics**
Loudspeaker Products (Commercial Sound) - **Mg Electronics**
Loudspeaker Products (Security) - **Mg Electronics**
Loudspeakers & Enclosures - **Fourjay Industries, Inc.**
Loudspeaking Desk Page Telephone: Model 118 - **Pyott-boone Electronics**
Loudspeaking Page Telephone: Model 112 - **Pyott-boone Electronics**
Loudspeaking Weatherproof Page Telephone: - **Pyott-boone Electronics**
Louvered Doors Solid Woods - **Modern Woodcrafts, Inc.**
Low & Medium Voltage Switchgear - **Pritchard Brown**
Low Fat & Low Salt Cheese & Dairy Products - **Berner Cheese Corp.**
Low Nox Burners - **Forney**
Low Protein, Sodium, Potassium Phophorus Foods - **Ener-g Foods Inc**
Low Temperature Alloys - **Mcp Metalspecialties, Inc.**
Low Voltage Safety Lights - **Ericson Manufacturing, Inc.**
Low Volume Drip and Micro Irrigation Sys - **Olson Irrigation Systems**
Low-voltage Lighting for Spas; Fiber Optic - **Oryan Industries Inc**
Lowest Life Cycle Cost to You - **Helicoid Div., Bristol Babcock Inc.**
Lpg Vaporization Equipment - **Ely Energy, Inc.**
Lpg/air Blending Systems - **Ely Energy, Inc.**
Lube Trucks Fuel Trucks, Firetrucks - **Aresco, Inc.**
Lubricants - **Interdynamics, Inc.**
Lubricants - Compressor - **Parts Services International Llc**
Lubricants for Stamping in the Metal-finishing. - **Eldorado Chemical Co.,**
Lubricating Oil - **Wd-40 Company**
Lubricating Oils & Greases - **L H B Industries**
Lubricating Oils & Greases - **Renite Co., Lubrication Engineers**
Lubricating Oils & Greases - **Elf Atochem North America Inc. Wire Mill**
Lubricating Oils & Greases - **Chempet Corp.**
Lubricating Oils & Greases - **Coastal Unilube, Inc.**
Lubricating Oils & Greases - **Digilube Systems, Inc.**
Lubricating Oils & Greases - **Engineered Lubricants Co.**
Lubricating Oils & Greases - **Lexard Corporation**
Lubricating Oils & Greases - **Monroe Fluid Technology, Inc.**
Lubricating Oils & Greases - **Mullen Circle Brand, Inc.**
Lubricating Oils & Greases - **Petro Chemical Products Inc.**
Lubricating Oils & Greases - **Wd-40 Company**
Lubricating Oils & Greases - **Worldwide Filter**
Lubricating Systems, Centralized - **Bijur Lubricating Corporation**
Lubrication Equipment, Wholesale - **Kent Oil Company Inc.**
Lubrication Shutdown (Dnft) - **Whitlock Instrument**
Luggage - **Lightware Inc**
Luggage - **Pantos Corp**
Luggage Racks Roof & Deck Permanent - **Donmar Enterprises, Inc.**
Luggage Tags, Card Cases & Key Rings - **Blue Atlantic, Ltd.**
Lumber - **Maple Valley Hardwoods**
Lumber - **Hardwood Veneer**
Lumber - **Ellis Enterprises, T. J.**
Lumber - **Soliman Brothers**
Lumber & Plywood - **Quality Forest Products**
Lumber / Alder / Aspen - **Summit Sales & Marketing**
Lumber Exporters - **S.g. International**
Lumber Processing - **Clinton Hardwood Inc.**
Lumber Processing - **Jones Lumber Co., Inc., J. M.**
Lumber Processing - **Krooked Kreek Logging Co.**
Lumber Processing - **New River Building Supply & Lumber Co.**
Lumber Processing - **Temple-inland Forest Products Corp.**
Lumber Processing & Millwork - **Wolohan Lumber**
Lumber Processing & Wooden Products - **Great Northern Lumber, Inc.**
Lumber Processing, Wood Chips & Sawdust - **Algoma Lumber Co.**
Lumber, Plywood & Millwork - **Hampton Lumber Sales Co**
Lumber, Plywood, and Millwork - **Cascade Empire**
Lumber, Plywood, and Millwork - **North American Wood Products, Inc.**
Lumber, Plywood, and Millwork - **Ram Forest Products**
Lumber, Plywood, and Millwork - **Timber Products**
Luminous Ceilings - **Ceilings plus Inc**
Luxury Golf Cars. Cadillacs, Rolls Royce & Others - **Elmco, Inc.**
Luxury Vinyl Flooring - **Amtico International Inc.**
Macadamia Nut Cookies - **Hawaiian King Candies**

Macadamia Nut Products - **Mac Farms of Hawaii, Inc.**
Macadamia Nuts - **Hawaiian King Candies**
Macaroni & Spaghetti - **Carla's Pasta**
Macaroni & Spaghetti - **Ladson Noodle Company**
Macaroni, Spaghetti, Vermicelli and Noodles - **Ladson Noodle Company**
Machine & Sheet Metal Shop - **Litec Inc.**
Machine & Tools (New & Used) - **Paul Marsh, Llc**
Machine Build & Rebuild - **Hansen Machine & Tool Co., N. M.**
Machine Job Shop; Honing Tools - **Desert Laboratories Inc**
Machine Nc & Cnc - **Magnetic Radiation Laboratories Inc.**
Machine Shop - **Jerryco Machine & Boilerworks**
Machine Shop - **Thistle Roller Co Inc**
Machine Shop - **Accurite Development & Mfg**
Machine Shop - **Dvorak Automatic & Machine**
Machine Shop Services - **Superb Marine & Industrial Services, Inc.**
Machine Shop for Custom Plastic and Metal Products - **Price Products Inc**
Machine Shop-manufacturer of Aircraft Comps - **Mac-lyn Industries Inc**
Machine Tool Accessories - **Carter Diamond Tool Corp.**
Machine Tool Accessories - **H & R Mfg. & Supply, Inc.**
Machine Tool Accessories - **Richard's Machine Tool Co., Inc.**
Machine Tool Accessories - **Richmill Usa Inc**
Machine Tool Accessories - **Vanguard Tool Corp.**
Machine Tool Components, Spindles & Slides - **Setco Industries**
Machine Tool Drill Units - **Drillunit**
Machine Tools - **America Excel, Inc.**
Machine Tools - **Burlytic Systems**
Machine Tools - **Luke Tool & Engineering Co.**
Machine Tools - **Premier Machinery**
Machine Tools - **Morrison Co., the D. C.**
Machine Tools - **Richard's Machine Tool Co., Inc.**
Machine Tools Index Tables - **Drillunit**
Machine Tools Metal Cutting Types - **Onsrud Machine Corporation**
Machine Tools Multiple Spindle Heads - **Drillunit**
Machine Tools Punch Press - **Taber Industries, Inc.**
Machine Tools Slides - **Drillunit**
Machine Tools Tap Units - **Drillunit**
Machine Tools, Metal Forming Types - **Tools for Bending, Inc.**
Machine Tools, Cnc & non Cnc - **Perfection Machinery**
Machine Tools, Hydraulic Ironworkers - **Scotchman Industries, Inc.(Mfr)**
Machine Tools, Hydraulic Presses - **Behlen Mfg. Co.**
Machine Tools, Metal Cutting - **Abrasive Service Industries, Century Ho**
Machine Tools, Metal Cutting Types - **America Excel, Inc.**
Machine Tools, Metal Cutting Types - **B & a Mfg. Co.**
Machine Tools, Metal Cutting Types - **Lexington Cutter, Inc.**
Machine Tools, Metal Cutting Types - **Luke Tool & Engineering Co.**
Machine Tools, Metal Cutting Types - **Premier Machinery**
Machine Tools, Metal Cutting Types - **Procunier Safety Chuck Co.**
Machine Tools, Metal Cutting Types - **Republic-lagun Cnc Corp**
Machine Tools, Metal Cutting Types - **Saber Diamond Tools**
Machine Tools, Metal Cutting Types - **Setco Industries**
Machine Tools, Metal Cutting Types - **Carter Diamond Tool Corp.**
Machine Tools, Metal Cutting Types - **Tri Tool Inc**
Machine Tools, Metal Cutting Types - **Swanson Anaheim Corp**
Machine Tools, Metal Cutting Types - **Desert Laboratories Inc**
Machine Tools, Metal Forming Type - **Chambersburg Engineering Co.**
Machine Tools, Metal Forming Types - **Premier Machinery**
Machine Tools, Metal Forming Types - **Hoffman Tool & Die Inc.**
Machine Tools, Metal Forming Types - **Thor Tool Corporation**
Machine Vision Inspection & Measurement Systems - **Systronics, Inc.**
Machined Castings - **Kirby Risk Service Center**
Machined Graphite Parts - **Toyo Tanso Usa Inc**
Machined Graphite Products - **Graphite Sales, Inc.**
Machined Laminated Shims - **Bolsan West Inc**
Machined Parts for the Electronic Connector - **Senga Engineering Inc**
Machined Shafts - **U.s. Axle, Inc. (Mfr)**
Machined Shafts & Axle Shafts for Constr. Equip. - **U.S. Axle, Inc. (Mfr)**
Machined Shfts & Axle Shafts for Farm Equipment - **U.s. Axle, Inc. (Mfr)**
Machiner Tool Accessories - **Onsrud Machine Corporation**
Machinery & Coupling Guards - **Litco, Inc.**
Machinery Consultant - **Chem-tex Machinery, Inc.**
Machinery Parts - **Myers Industries, Inc., Myers Tire Supply Div.**

Machinery Parts, Not Containing Electrical Connectors - **Astechnologies**
Machinery Vacuum Forming - **Zmd International Inc**
Machinery for Filling, Closing, Sealing, Bottles - **Fogg Filler Co.**
Machinery for the Industrial Preparation or Manufacture - **D & S Exports**
Machinery for the Pulp and Paper Industry— Ncg - **A H Lundberg Inc**
Machinery to Produce Air Conditioning Coils - **Tridan International, Inc.**
Machinery to Produce Evaporator Coils - **Tridan International, Inc.**
Machinery to Produce Heat Transfer Coils - **Tridan International, Inc.**
Machinery to Produce Refrigeration Coils - **Tridan International, Inc.**
Machinery, General Industrial - **C. H. Hyperbarics, Inc.**
Machinery, Parts & Supplies for Commercial Laundries - **D & S Exports**
Machinery, Special Industry - **International Shoe Machine Corporation**
Machinery, Special Industry - **Intersystems, Inc.**
Machinery, Special Industry - **James Instruments, Inc.**
Machinery, Special Industry - **H2o, Inc.**
Machinery, Special Industry - Badge & Button Machines - **Debbeler Co.**
Machinery, Thermoforming - **Zmd International Inc**
Machinery_general Industrial - **General Air Corporation**
Machinery_general Industrial - **S E R F I L C O, Ltd.**
Machinery_general Industrial - **Biomarine Inc.**
Machinery_general Industrial - **Ethylene Control Inc**
Machinery_general Industrial - **Flite Technology, Inc.**
Machinery_general Industrial - **General Safety Equipment**
Machinery_general Industrial - **Magnaflux**
Machinery_general Industrial - **Process Filtration Div., Parker Hannifin**
Machinery_general Industrial - **Tnt Tools Inc**
Machinery_general Industrial - **Velcon Filters Inc**
Machinery_special Industry - **Accrafect Products Inc.**
Machinery_special Industry - **Axic Inc**
Machinery_special Industry - **Ballisti-cast Mfg., Inc.**
Machinery_special Industry - **Basic Concepts Inc.**
Machinery_special Industry - **Chemicolloid Laboratories, Inc.**
Machinery_special Industry - **Dac International, Inc.**
Machinery_special Industry - **Eagle Metalizing Coatings Co**
Machinery_special Industry - **General Air Corporation**
Machinery_special Industry - **Glenmarc Mfg. Inc.**
Machinery_special Industry - **M-b Cos., Inc. of Wisconsin**
Machinery_special Industry - **Major Metalfab Co.**
Machinery_special Industry - **Parking Products, Inc.**
Machinery_special Industry - **Proctor & Schwartz**
Machinery_special Industry - **R W C Inc.**
Machinery_special Industry - **Rubber City Machinery Corp.**
Machinery_special Industry - **Saf-tee Siping & Grooving Inc**
Machinery_special Industry - **Swanson Anaheim Corp**
Machinery_special Industry - **Usdm Inc**
Machinery_special Industry - **Vortex Engineering**
Machinery_special Industry - **Warren Industries, Inc.**
Machinery_special Industry - **Wynnson Enterprises, Inc.**
Machinery_special Industry - **Technaseal**
Machinery_special Industry - **Flite Technology, Inc.**
Machinery_special Industry - **The Dii Group Inc**
Machinery_special Industry - **Norman Tool, Inc.**
Machinery_special Industry - **Cambridge Manufacturing, Inc.**
Machinery_special Industry, Mini-trenchers - **Brown Mfg.**
Machines and Equipment - **Aquacare Environment Inc**
Machines and Mechanical Appliances - **Astechnologies**
Machines and Mechanical Appliances - **Pexim International**
Machining Parts for Aircraft and Commercial - **M & M Corporation**
Machining, Sheet Metal, Asseblies - **Van Thomas Inc. / Ruggeri Mfg.**
Machinists Levels - **Geier & Bluhm, Inc.**
Magazine Insert & Business Reply Cards Printing - **Schmidt Printing, Inc.**
Magazine Typesetting - **Elevator World**
Magazines - **Cps Communications, Inc.**
Magnaflux Testing - **Advanced Heat Treat Corp.**
Magnesium Sulfate & Sodium Sulfate - **Giles Chemical Corp.**
Magnetic & Optical Recording Media - **Tape Duplicators, Inc.**
Magnetic Drive Sealless Pumps - **Finish Thompson, Inc.**
Magnetic Field Indicators - **R.b. Annis Company, Inc.**
Magnetic Flexible Label Dies - **Ashwell Die Corp.**
Magnetic Fluorescent Ballast - **Howard Industries**
Magnetic Level Gauges & Controls - **Jogler, Inc.**

Magnetic Palletizers & Depalletizers - **Busse Inc. (Mfr)**
Magnetic Resonance Imaging (Mri) Scanners - **Fonar Corp.**
Magnetic Retrieving Tools - **Trident Tool, Inc.**
Magnetic Separators - **Alan Ross Machinery Corp**
Magnetic Sewing Notions - **Blue Feather Products Inc**
Magnetic Shielding - **Magnetic Radiation Laboratories Inc.**
Magnetic Shields - **Ad-vance Magnetics, Inc.**
Magnetic Strip Card Readers, Encoders - **Xico Inc**
Magnetic Tape Winders / Cleaners / Certifiers - **Bow Industries, Inc.**
Magnets - **Midwest Industries Inc.**
Magnets - **Interpretive Marketing Products**
Mail Order Sortation - **Quantum Conveyor Systems, Llc**
Mail Room Furniture, Sorters, Tables, Carts - **W.a. Charnstrom Co., Inc.**
Mailing - **Matrix Imaging Solution**
Mailorder Distribution of Vitamin Supplements - **Sonora Desert Trading**
Maintenance Equipment & Parts - **Advance Paper & Maintenance**
Major Brands, Bed & Bath Linens - **Ericyan Ii**
Makes Cyclonic Thermoplastic Foam - **Hudnut Industries Inc**
Maltodextrins - **Grain Processing Corporation (Mfr)**
Mammography Paddles & Bushings - **Plastic Works Inc**
Management Consulting Service, Export Ops Sys - **Export Procedures Co.**
Management Consulting Services - **The Practice Builder Association**
Management Consulting Services - **Richardson Engineering Svcs Inc**
Management Consulting Services - **Communication Certification Lab**
Management Consulting Services - **International Relations-advanced Bio**
Management Consulting Services - **The John Wesley Group**
Management Consulting Services, Trade Finance - **Definco Ltd.**
Management Services - **C & M Enterprises**
Management Services - **Versar, Inc.**
Management Services - Export - **D & S Exports**
Manfuacturers of Polyrethane Foam Systems - **Swd Urethane**
Manhole Rehabilitation & Sewer Lining - **Stronglite Products**
Manicure Products - **Flowery Beauty Products, Inc.**
Manifold Business Forms - **Miles Label Company Inc**
Manifold Business Forms - **American Forms, Inc.**
Manifold Business Forms - **Colonial Business Forms, Inc.**
Manifold Business Forms - **Kenalex Printing Forms, Inc.**
Manifold Business Forms - **New West Business Forms**
Manifold Business Forms - **Triangle Business Forms, Inc.**
Manifold Sets - **Robinair, a Div. Of Spx Corporation**
Manual & Automated Static Control Equip- **Spectrascan International**
Manual Cut-off Saws - **Precision Products Co**
Manual Silicon Wafer Probe Stations - **Miller Design & Equipment**
Manual Transmission Ring Gears - **Automatic Transmission Parts, Inc.**
Manufacturing Industries - **Castletech Ltd**
Manufacturing Industries - **Colorado Frame Company**
Manufacturing Industries - **California Wire Products Corp**
Manufacturing Industries - **Root Co., Inc., A. I., the**
Manufacturing Industries - **Entenmann-rovin Company**
Manufacturing Industries - **Michaels of Oregon Co**
Manufacturing Industries - **Future Primitive Designs Ltd**
Manufacturing Industries - **California Exotic Novelties**
Manufacturing Industries - **Dalloz Safety**
Manufacturing Industries - **Flo's Wreaths**
Manufacturing Industries - **Gdc Casino Tokens**
Manufacturing Industries - **Lectralite Corporation**
Manufacturing Industries - **Preserved Treescapes Intl**
Manufacturing Industries - **Silkwood Wholesale, Inc.**
Manufacturing Industries - **Toepperweins of Texas**
Manufacturing Industries - **Yaley Enterprises, Inc.**
Manufacturing Industries to Pet Stores - **Just Merino Sheepskin Products**
Manufacturing Industries, Nec - **Continental Sprayers / Afa Products,**
Manufacturing Industries, Nec - **Marianna Importers**
Manufacturing of Bus Bars & Heatsinks - **Mbs Industrial Service Inc**
Manufacturing. Design — Mold & Tooling Capabilities - **Letro Products**
Map Distributor, California & All U.sa. - **Barclay Maps**
Map Laminating & Wooden Plaques - **First State Map & Globe Co., Inc.**
Marble - **Rowat Cut Stone & Marble Co.**
Marble & Granite - **Marbledge, Inc.**
Marble Composition Books - **American Scholar Co.**
Marinade's & Breading - **Broaster Co., the**

Marinades - **Cajun Injector, Inc.**
Marinades for Meat & Seafood Items - **Catalina Food Ingredients**
Marine / Fish Oils - **Arista Industries, Inc.**
Marine Cable, Wireway & Pipe Hangers & Supports - **Samtan Engineering**
Marine Cargo Handling - **Transoceanic Shipping Company, Inc.**
Marine Coatings— Synthetic Enamels, Paints, - **Kop-coat Inc**
Marine Exhaust Systems, Hardware - **Coopers & Clarke, Inc.**
Marine Hardware - **Harken International, Ltd.**
Marine Interior Products - **Hopeman Brothers Marine Interiors, Llc**
Marine Lanterns, Radar Beacons - **Tideland Signal Corp.**
Marine Propellers - **Michigan Wheel Corporation**
Marine Rigging - **Vanco Heavy Lift C.f.s.**
Marine Roll or Roll off Operations - **Bigge Crane & Rigging Co.**
Marine Supplies - **Waterland Mfg., Inc.**
Marine Vavles & Fittings - **Conbraco Industries**
Marine Waste Water Treatment Plants - **Equipment & Systems Engineer**
Marine and Land Mobile Communications Equip - **Datamarine Int'l**
Marine, Offshore, Agriculture - **Service Hydraulics Inc.**
Markers, Ball Point Pens & Imprinted Pencils - **National Pen Corp.**
Marketing Consulting Services - **Smirnoff Communications Group, Inc.**
Marketing Consulting Services - **Pdg Associates, Inc.**
Marketing Consulting Services - **Interdevelopment Inc.**
Marketing, Financial - **Magnum Group, Inc. Translation & Related Svcs.**
Markets Cds of Traditional and Classical Weddin - **Music Unlimited Inc**
Markets Step Motors & Drivers - **Oregon Micro Systems**
Marking & Decorating Tools & Devices - **Schwerdtle Stamp Co., Inc.**
Marking Devices - **American Traditional Stencils**
Marking Devices - **Electro Stylus**
Marking Devices - **Independent Ink Inc**
Marking Devices - **Joplin Printing Co.**
Marking Devices - **Qwikstamp Corporation**
Marking Devices - **Schwerdtle Stamp Co., Inc.**
Marking Devices - **Shachihata**
Marking Flags & Barricade & Underground Utility Tapes - **Blackburn Mfg**
Marking Inks, Marking Devices, Pads, Ink Stamping - **Independent Ink**
Masking Agents - **O S F Flavors, Inc.**
Masonry Products - **Sioux City Brick & Tile Co., Sergeant Bluff Plt.**
Mass Flow Indicators - **Pierburg Instruments, Inc.**
Mass Metal Finishing— Tumbling, Sand Blasting - **J & H Deburring Inc**
Massage & Body Oils - **Sybaritic, Inc.**
Massage & Spa Equipment - **Touch America Inc.**
Massage Pads, Portable Massage - **Relaxor / Jb Research Inc**
Massage Table - **Sybaritic, Inc.**
Massage, Chiropractic, Salon, Spa Tables; Sells - **Living Earth Crafts**
Master Distributor for the Ilumar Brand of Solar Window Film - **Apd**
Material Handling - **Ogden Engineering Corp.**
Material Handling Blowers & Conveying - **Sterling Blower Co.**
Material Handling Equipment - **Vogler Equipment**
Material Handling Equipment - Forklift Export Specials - **U.S. Airmotive**
Material Handling Equipment, Waste Receptacles - **Hodge Manufacturing**
Material Handling Machinery - **Hurdt & Associates Machinery**
Material Handling Systems - **F S P Machinery**
Material Spreaders & Servo Controls - **Swenson Spreader Co.**
Material Testing Equipment - **Material Testing Technology Co.**
Materials Handling Equipment - **Bradley Lifting Corp.**
Materials Handling Equipment - **Faultless Caster Division**
Materials Handling Systems & Components - **Interroll Corp.**
Materials for Ink Jet Printing Industry - **B F Mfg., Inc.**
Matric Buildings - **S O N Corp.**
Matrix & Data Switching - **Dynetcom, Inc.**
Mats - **Mahar**
Mats - **Home Dynamix**
Mattress Tape - **Nassau Tape & Webbing Mills, Inc.**
Mattresses & Bedsprings - **Custom Bedding Co. & Orange Mattresses**
Mattresses & Bedsprings - **Estee Bedding Co., Inc.**
Mattresses & Bedsprings - **Glideway Bed Carriage Mfg. Co.**
Mattresses & Bedsprings - **Jamison Bedding Co.**
Mattresses & Bedsprings - **My Bed, Inc.**
Mattresses & Bedsprings - **Verlo Mattress Factory Stores**
Mattresses & Bedsprings - **Vintage Bedding**
Mattresses & Box Springs - **Custom Bedding Co. & Orange Mattresses**

Mattresses & Box Springs - **Jamison Bedding Co.**
Mattresses for Beds - **Vintage Bedding**
Mattresses, Boxsprings, Antiques - **Hernandez Mattress, Inc.**
Mattresses, Flame Resistant - **Chestnut Ridge Foam, Inc.**
Mayonnaise, Salsas, Jams & Jellies - **Safeway Stores Inc., Export Sales**
Mcm - **Zecal, Inc.**
Meal Packaging - Cartons & Snacks - **Promotional Resources Group**
Measuring & Controlling Devices - **Strategic Diagnostics, Inc.**
Measuring & Controlling Devices - **Metrix Instrument Co.**
Measuring & Controlling Devices - **King Buck Technology**
Measuring & Controlling Devices - **Alicat Scientific Inc**
Measuring & Controlling Devices - **Cuda Products Corp.**
Measuring & Controlling Devices - **American Design & Mfg.**
Measuring & Controlling Devices - **Byk-gardner Usa**
Measuring & Controlling Devices - **Concord Environmental Equipment**
Measuring & Controlling Devices - **Consilium Us, Inc.**
Measuring & Controlling Devices - **Dalloz Safety, Inc.**
Measuring & Controlling Devices - **Dynatest Consulting, Inc.**
Measuring & Controlling Devices - **Etcon Corp.**
Measuring & Controlling Devices - **Humboldt Mfg. Co., Inc.**
Measuring & Controlling Devices - **Int'l Equipment Distributors**
Measuring & Controlling Devices - **Kidde Aerospace, Walter**
Measuring & Controlling Devices - **Laboratory Testing Supply Inc.**
Measuring & Controlling Devices - **Loranger International Corp.**
Measuring & Controlling Devices - **Matrix Controls Co., Inc.**
Measuring & Controlling Devices - **Medical Indicators, L.p.**
Measuring & Controlling Devices - **Norman Tool, Inc.**
Measuring & Controlling Devices - **Omni Controls, Inc.**
Measuring & Controlling Devices - **Pace Transducer Co**
Measuring & Controlling Devices - **Physical Acoustics**
Measuring & Controlling Devices - **Precision Flow, Inc.**
Measuring & Controlling Devices - **Quantum Group, Inc.**
Measuring & Controlling Devices - **Sullins, Inc.**
Measuring & Controlling Devices - **Symtron Systems, Inc.**
Measuring & Controlling Devices - **Thor Guard, Inc.**
Measuring & Controlling Devices - **Weigh-tronix Inc**
Measuring & Dispensing Pumps - **Fluid Dynamics Inc**
Measuring Dev., Elec. Engine Instruments - **Westberg Mfg., Inc.**
Measuring Devices, Accelerometers - **Sunstrand Corporation**
Measuring Devices, Adhesion & Adherence Testers - **Quad Group**
Measuring Devices, Adhesion Testers - **Quad Group**
Measuring Devices, Diamond Scratch Coat, Tester - **Quad Group**
Measuring Devices, Materials Characterization Tester - **Quad Group**
Measuring Devices, Test Kits - **Neogen Corp.**
Measuring Devices, Universal Materials Testers - **Quad Group**
Measuring Equipment - **First Weigh**
Measuring Instruments Ph, Orp, Temperature, Resistivity - **Myron L Co**
Measuring and Controlling Devices - **Pace Transducer Co**
Measuring and Dispensing Pumps and Polymer - **Fluid Dynamics Inc**
Measuring or Checking Instruments, - **Dresser Instrument Div.**
Meat Chopper Knives and Plates - **Alfa International Corporation**
Meat Cutlet Flattening Device., Whsle - **Jaccard Corporation**
Meat Packing , Processing Company - **Superior Packing/superior Farm**
Meat Packing Plants - **Colorado Boxed Beef Co., Inc.**
Meat Packing Plants - **Hatfield, Inc.**
Meat Packing Plants - **Kirkland's Custom Meats**
Meat Packing Plants, Processing Plants - **Superior Packing/superior Farm**
Meat Processing - **Hatfield, Inc.**
Meat Processing - **Kirkland's Custom Meats**
Meat Processing - **Schmalz European, Inc.**
Meat Processing Equipment - **Linker Machines**
Meat Rub & Marinade Seasonings - **Old World Spices & Seasonings, Inc.**
Meat Slicer Blades and Parts - **Alfa International Corporation**
Meat Snacks - **Link Snacks, Inc.**
Meat by Products / Co-products - **Darling International Inc.**
Meat, Poultry & Fish Soaker Pads - **Paper Pak Products Inc**
Meats and Meat Products - **Stock Yards Packing Co. Inc.(Mfr)**
Mechanical & Electronic Packaging - **Holbrooks**
Mechanical & Electronic Scales - **Pelouze/health-o-meter, Inc.**
Mechanical & Quartz Clocks Movements - **Hermle Black Forest Clocks**
Mechanical Aircraft Clocks - **Waltham Aircraft Clock Corp.**

Mechanical Alarm Clocks - **Equity Industries**
Mechanical Controls, Hv/ac - **Trane Company, the**
Mechanical Design - **Rapid Development Service**
Mechanical Design - **Holbrooks**
Mechanical Equipment - **Bifrost**
Mechanical Meat Tenderizing Machines, Whsle - **Jaccard Corporation**
Mechanical Packaging - **Shock Tech, Inc.**
Mechanical Packing - **Lamons Power Engineering**
Mechanical Pressure Gages - **Faria Corp.**
Mechanical Rubber Goods - **Lamons Power Engineering**
Mechanical Rubber Goods - **Bentley Manufacturing Co Inc**
Mechanical Rubber Goods - **Esco Rubber Products Inc**
Mechanical Rubber Goods - **Kirkhill Rubber Co**
Mechanical Rubber Goods - **Lord Corporation, Mechanical Products,**
Mechanical Rubber Goods - **Rogers Corporation**
Mechanical Rubber Goods - **Trelleborg Ysh, Inc.**
Mechanical Rubber Goods - **R & R Rubber Molding Inc**
Mechanical Seals, Packings & Lapping Machines - **John Crane Inc.**
Mechanical Shovels, Excavators and Shovel Loaders - **Hoss Equipment**
Mechanical Shovels, Excavators and Shovel Loaders - **Nationwide Equip**
Mechanical Shovels, Excavators and Shovel Loaders - **Ameri Housing**
Med. Equip., Signal Dev., Chart Holders - **Stat-chek Co.(mfr)**
Medals & Ribbons - **Trophy Shoppe**
Medical & Electronics Products Packaging - **Alga Plastics Co.**
Medical & Hospital Equipment - **Andwin Corporation**
Medical & Hospital Equipment - **Cobe Bet, Inc.**
Medical & Hospital Equipment - **Ic Medical Inc**
Medical & Hospital Equipment - **J Hewitt Inc**
Medical & Hospital Equipment - **Noraxon Usa Inc**
Medical & Hospital Equipment - **Eckstein Bros Inc**
Medical & Hospital Equipment - **Sensormedics Corporation**
Medical & Hospital Equipment - **Spacelabs Medical Inc**
Medical & Hospital Equipment - **Medical Gas Services Inc**
Medical & Hospital Equipment & Supplies - **National Health Care, Inc.**
Medical & Hospital Equipment Including Kits & Supplies - **Andwin Corp**
Medical & Surgical Supplies & Equip., Wholesale - **Flomed Corporation**
Medical (Packaging) - **Technical Coating International**
Medical Apparatus - **Smith & Nephew Inc.**
Medical Apparatus, Balance Equipment - **Neurocom International Inc.**
Medical Aspirators & Compressor Assembly - **Medical Specifics, Inc.**
Medical Collection Products - **Andwin Corporation**
Medical Diagnostic (Elisa) Test Kits & Reagents - **United Biotech Inc**
Medical Diagnostic Equip., Used, Whsle - **Mass Medical Equipment**
Medical Equip., Inv. Control Signals - **Stat-chek Co.(mfr)**
Medical Equipment - **Medstone International Inc**
Medical Equipment & Supplies - **Caravan International**
Medical Equipment New & Recond, Wholesale - **M.d. International Co.**
Medical Equipment, Portable Intensive Care - **Thermocare, Inc.**
Medical Equipment, Pulmonary Testing - **Multispiro, Inc. / Creative Biom**
Medical Form - **New West Business Forms**
Medical Gases - **Biomedical International**
Medical Id Jewelry - **Apothecary Products Inc.**
Medical Instr. & Supplies, Wholesale - **A.j. Buck & Son**
Medical Instruments - **Cobe Bet, Inc.**
Medical Instruments - **Innovasive Devices Company**
Medical Instruments - **Noraxon Usa Inc**
Medical Instruments & Apparatus - **Cas Medical Systems, Inc. (Mfr)**
Medical Oxygen Catheters and Apparatus - **Transtracheal Systems Inc**
Medical Pulmonary Instruments - **Vacumetrics, Inc.**
Medical Rehabilitation Balance Equipment - **Neurocom International Inc.**
Medical Research Area Detectors and Ccd - **Area Detectors Systems Corp**
Medical Respiratory Instruments - **Hans Rudolph, Inc. (Mfr)**
Medical Rubber Goods, Wholesale - **J Hewitt Inc**
Medical Specialty Light Bulbs - **Bulbtronics, Inc.**
Medical Supplies - **Atwood Richards**
Medical Supplies, I.d. Card Holders - **Stat-chek Co.(mfr)**
Medical Textbook Printing & Typesetting - **E M I S, Inc.**
Medical Ultrasound Equipment - **Atl Ultrasound, Inc.**
Medical Video Couplers for Endoscopes - **Omex Technologies**
Medical Waste Incinerators - **Olivine Corporation**
Medical and Dental Equipment - **Scanrite Systems, Smith Companies**

Medical, Health & Safety - **L S M Labs, Inc.**
Medical, Surgical & Dental Fiber Optic Light Guides - **Cuda Products Cor**
Medicinal Minerals - **Arnet Pharmaceutical Corp.**
Medicinals & Biological Serum Production - **Harmon Technological**
Medicinals & Botanicals - **Spectrum Naturals Inc**
Medicinals & Botanicals - **All American Pharmaceutical & NaturalFood**
Medicinals & Botanicals - **Biomin Industries, Inc.**
Medicinals & Botanicals - **Captek Softgel International**
Medicinals & Botanicals - **Irwin Naturals / 4 Health Inc**
Medicinals & Botanicals - **Madys Company**
Medicinals & Botanicals - **Mallinckrodt Inc.**
Medicinals & Botanicals - **St Jon Pet Care Products**
Medicinals & Botanicals - **Trimedica International Inc**
Medicinals & Botanicals - **Dews Research**
Medicinals & Botanicals - **Oralabs Holding Corp**
Medicines & Pharmaceuticals - **Hobart Laboratories, Inc.**
Medium Voltage Soft Starter - **Motortronics, Inc.**
Melamine Crystal - **Dsm Melamine Americas, Inc.**
Melamine Cyanurate - **Century Multech**
Member, Florida Bar - **Sears Steele, Iii**
Membrane Elements & Housings - **Osmonics, Inc.**
Membrane Switches, Metal & Plastic Panel Fronts, - **Hall Co., the**
Membranes for Reverse Osmosis Water Treatment - **Ro Ultratec Usa Inc**
Memory Modules. - **Pdp Systems**
Men's & Boy's Shirts, Pants & Knit Tops. - **Argus International, Inc.**
Men's & Boys' Clothing - **Canari Cycle Wear**
Men's & Boys' Pants & Jackets - **Robett Mfg. Co.**
Men's & Women's Leather Outerwear - **Pharr Brand Name Apparel, Llc**
Men's & Women's Socks - **Ellis Hosiery Mills, Inc.**
Men's & Women's Tailored Clothing - **La Mar Mfg. Co.**
Men's Activewear and Swimwear - **Sauvage Swimwear**
Men's Clothing - **Marathon Corp.**
Men's Milit/law Enforcement Apparel, Wholesale - **U. S. Cavalry, Inc.**
Men's and Boys' Cyclewear - **Canari Cycle Wear**
Men's and Boys' Neckwear - **Duron Neckwear Inc**
Men's and Women's 1800-style Clothing - **Cattle Kate Inc**
Men's and Women's Clothing - **Apparel Suppliers Ca/pagano W**
Men's and Women's Leather Jackets - **Jh Design Group**
Men's and Women's Lingerie - **9tz Inc**
Men's under Garments - **Nishizawa**
Men's, Ladies, Childrens Shirts, - **California Ranchwear Inc**
Men's, Women's & Children's Socks - **Harriss & Covington Hosiery Mill**
Men's, Women's and Boys' Sweaters- **Alps Sportswear Manufacturing**
Men's, Women's and Children's Leather, Fur - **Sheepskin Coat Factory**
Mens & Boys T-shirts - **Mohnton Knitting Mills, Inc.**
Mens & Boys Thermal Underwear - **Mohnton Knitting Mills, Inc.**
Mens & Womens Military Footwear - **Cove Shoe Co., Matterhorn-corcor**
Mens & Womens Safety Footwear - **Cove Shoe Co., Matterhorn-corcoran**
Mens Gifts - **Split Tee**
Menswear - **Nishizawa**
Menswear - **Uni Hosiery Co., Inc.**
Merchandising Carts & Kiosks - **Waggon Cellers, Inc.**
Merchandising Equipment - **Anthony International**
Merchandising Props & Displays - **Creative Arts**
Merchandising/point-of-sale Pieces & Design. - **L.a. Markom De Mexico,**
Mercury Devices - **Lighting Resources, Inc.**
Mercury Monitors - **Epm Environmental, Inc.**
Merlin, Quintana Roo, Real Bicycles & Components - **Saucony, Inc.**
Merry-go-rounds, Boat-swings, Shooting Galleries - **Howard, Bill**
Mesh for Athletic Wear - **Dorma Mills(mfr)**
Metal Stampings, Tool Storage Products - **Waterloo Industries, Inc.**
Metal & Alloy Powders - **Winter, Inc. & Co., F. W.**
Metal & Plastic First Aid Kits & Cabinets - **Durham Mfg. Co.**
Metal & Plastic Machine Parts & Prototypes - **Unified Machine & Design,**
Metal & Plastic Storage Containers, Fabricated - **Durham Mfg. Co.**
Metal 3-piece Containers - **Crown Cork & Seal /Americas Div**
Metal Access Doors - **Karp Associates, Inc.**
Metal Art Castings & Sculptures - **Modern Art Foundry, Inc.**
Metal Ball Valves - **Nordstrom Valves, Inc.**
Metal Bins, Plastic, Boxes & Storage Cabinets - **Durham Mfg. Co.**
Metal Building Products - **Mason Corp.**

Metal Buildings— Carports, Carwashes, Airplane - Us Prefab Inc
Metal Cabinets, Carts, Benches & Tucks - Hodge Manufacturing Co
Metal Candle Holders, Metal Pot Holders - Villa Bella Co.
Metal Cans, Barrels, Drums & Pails - All American Containers, Inc.
Metal Christmas Ornaments & Gift Items - Desmark Industries, Inc.
Metal Clad Post Frame Buildings - Wick Buildings
Metal Coating & Allied Services - Varco Heat Treating Co
Metal Coating & Allied Services - All Metals Processing of Oc
Metal Coating & Allied Services - Diversified Coatings, Inc.
Metal Coating & Allied Services - Dv Industries Inc
Metal Coating & Allied Services - Metal Finishing Technologies, Inc.
Metal Coating & Allied Services - Sav-on Plating/powder Coating
Metal Coating & Allied Services - Ultra Plating Corp.
Metal Coating & Allied Services - Allen Aircraft Products, Inc.,
Metal Coating & Allied Services - Columbus Galvanizing Voigt & Schwei
Metal Coating & Allied Services - Cooper Coil Coating, Inc.
Metal Coating & Allied Services - Custom Engraving
Metal Coating & Allied Services - Feeley Company, Inc.
Metal Coating & Allied Services - Marjan, Inc.
Metal Coating & Allied Services - Metallic Ceramic Coating Inc.
Metal Coating & Allied Services - Sandy's Trophies
Metal Coating & Allied Services - Valmont Industries Inc.
Metal Coating & Allied Services - Vaporkote Inc
Metal Coating & Allied Services - Trophy Shoppe
Metal Coil Coating, Slitting & Embossing - Cooper Coil Coating, Inc.
Metal Cold Storage Doors, Elec. & Man. - Chase Industries, Inc.
Metal Communication Towers, Non-cable Elevators - Landmark Tower
Metal Cosmetic Boxes - Risdon-ams (Usa) Inc.
Metal Decorating Plate - Napp Systems Inc
Metal Doors, Double Acting, Plastic Clad - Chase Industries, Inc.
Metal Elevators & Escalator Parts - P T L Equipment Mfg. Co., Inc.
Metal Expansion Joints - American Boa, Inc.
Metal Fabrication - C. W. C. Steel Services, Inc.
Metal Fabrication - Litco, Inc.
Metal Fabrication - Mcp Metalspecialties, Inc.
Metal Fabrication - Behlen Mfg. Co.
Metal Fabrication & General Machining Job Shop - Metal Finishing, Inc.
Metal Fabrication & Trusses - Emi-tech Inc.
Metal Fabrication & Welding Job Shop - C & B Fosters Inc.
Metal Fabrication / Engineering - Kietek International, Inc.
Metal Fabrication Shop - United Machine Ind. Inc.
Metal Fabrication, Industrial Steel Ladders- Klose Fabrication, Inc.
Metal Finishing & Buffing Compounds - Jacksonlea
Metal Finishing Equipment - Proceco, Inc.
Metal Finishing Equipment, Wholesale - Victor Metal Finishing Inc.
Metal Finishing, Sulfuric Anodizing, Coating - Allen Aircraft ProductsInc
Metal Finishing; Anodizing, Painting,- Dv Industries Inc
Metal Flag Poles - Pole-tech Co., Inc.
Metal Flexible Hose Products - Omega Flex, Inc.
Metal Foil & Leaf - Foil Graphics, Inc.
Metal Formed Springs - Standard Steel
Metal Forming - R a M Products
Metal Framed Skylights - Metcoe Specialty Co Inc
Metal Furniture - Woodpecker, Inc.
Metal Galvanizing - Tennessee Galvanizing
Metal Honeycomb - Indy Honeycomb
Metal Light Poles - Pole-tech Co., Inc.
Metal Literature Racks - Durham Mfg. Co.
Metal Name Plates & Decals - Nameplates, Inc.
Metal Oxide Resistors - Koa Speer Electronics, Inc.
Metal Perforating - Harrington & King South, Inc.
Metal Plating - Electrochem
Metal Polishing Machinery; Polishes Metal - Rancho Metal Polishing
Metal Powders - Acupowder International, Llc (Mfg)
Metal Processing Chemicals, Soap Powders - Elf Atochem North America
Metal Products - Beall Corp.
Metal Products, Fabricated - Ad-vance Magnetics, Inc.
Metal Products_fabricated - Hutchison & Co.
Metal Products_fabricated - Coopers & Clarke, Inc.
Metal Products_fabricated - Ambox Inc.
Metal Products_fabricated - Bolsan West Inc

Metal Products_fabricated - Southwest Metal Fabricators, Inc.
Metal Products_fabricated - Stamped Products, Inc.
Metal Products_fabricated - Sandy's Trophies
Metal Products_fabricated - Begneaud Mfg. Inc.
Metal Products_fabricated - C & B Fosters Inc.
Metal Products_fabricated - C. W. C. Steel Services, Inc.
Metal Products_fabricated - Contemporary, Inc.
Metal Products_fabricated - Desmark Industries, Inc.
Metal Products_fabricated - Independent Welding Co.
Metal Products_fabricated - Klose Fabrication, Inc.
Metal Products_fabricated - Kurt Manufacturing Co.
Metal Products_fabricated - Magnetic Radiation Laboratories Inc.
Metal Products_fabricated - Mcp Metalspecialties, Inc.
Metal Products_fabricated - Metal Finishing, Inc.
Metal Products_fabricated - Metal Master Inc
Metal Products_fabricated - Microflex, Inc.
Metal Products_fabricated - Panel Built, Inc.
Metal Products_fabricated - Senior Flexonics Inc., Hose Div.
Metal Products_fabricated - Trophy Shoppe
Metal Products_fabricated - Villa Bella Co.
Metal Products_fabricated - Cantrell International
Metal Products_fabricated - Cherokee Industries, Inc.
Metal Products_fabricated - Brake Funderburk Enterprises, Inc.
Metal Products_fabricated - A & B Fabrication & Repair, Inc.
Metal Products_fabricated - B. T. M. Inc.
Metal Products_fabricated - Dixie Machine Shop
Metal Products_fabricated - P & M Sign, Inc.
Metal Residue, Metal Grindings - Sos Metals, Inc.
Metal Roll Forming Equipment - New Tech Machinery Inc
Metal Sanitary Ware - Mansfield Plumbing Products, Inc.
Metal Sanitary Ware - Coast Foundry & Mfg Co
Metal Sanitary Ware - Franklin Brass Manufacturing
Metal Sanitary Ware - Watco Mfg. Co.
Metal Scrap & Primary - Steelbro International
Metal Scrap & Strapping Equipment - Hemisphere Enterprises
Metal Service Centers - Rolled Steel Products Corp
Metal Slitting Warehouse - Guardian Metal Sales, Inc.
Metal Stampings - Ambox Inc.
Metal Stampings - Baroli Engineering Inc
Metal Stampings - Bolsan West Inc
Metal Stampings - Cannon Industries
Metal Stampings - Component Engineers, Inc.
Metal Stampings - Fabor Fourslide, Inc.
Metal Stampings - Harrington & King South, Inc.
Metal Stampings - Hodge Manufacturing Company
Metal Stampings - Magnetic Metals Corp.
Metal Stampings - Moeller Manufacturing Supply
Metal Stampings - Oberg Mfg. Co.
Metal Stampings - O'hara Metal Products Co
Metal Stampings - Owen Tool & Mfg. Co., Inc.
Metal Stampings - Precision Die & Stamping Inc
Metal Stampings - Richards Metal Products, Inc.
Metal Stampings - Risdon-ams (Usa) Inc.
Metal Stampings - S & S Dynamic Mfg. Llc
Metal Stampings - Schulze Manufacturing
Metal Stampings - Southwest Metal Fabricators, Inc.
Metal Stampings - Stamped Products, Inc.
Metal Stampings - Stewart Stamping Corp.
Metal Stampings - Termax Corporation
Metal Stampings - Tubing Seal Cap
Metal Stampings - Ugm Inc
Metal Stampings - W C E S, Inc.
Metal Stamping, Nec Contract - Midwest Art Metal
Metal Stamping; Deep Draw - Stewart Stamping Corp.
Metal Stampings & Deep Drawn Parts - Samtan Engineering Corp
Metal Stampings & Fabrication - Southwest Metal Fabricators, Inc.
Metal Stampings & Fabrication & Laser - Ambox Inc.
Metal Stampings, Fabrication & Machining Innovative Stamping Corp
Metal Stampings & Flat Springs - Excel Spring & Stamping Co.
Metal Stampings & Four Slide & Spot Welding - Animated Mfg. Co.
Metal Stampings & Tank Heads - Commercial Intertech Corp.

Metal Stampings & Tool & Die - **Estad Stamping & Mfg. Co.**
Metal Stampings, Automotive - **Stamped Products, Inc.**
Metal Stampings, Formed Wire Products - **Stewart Stamping Corp.**
Metal Stampings, Sheet Metal Fabrication, Tools, - **Tella Tool & Mfg. Co.**
Metal Stampings; Tool and Die - **Baroli Engineering Inc**
Metal Struts & Accessories - **Phd Manufacturing, Inc.**
Metal Tube Assemblies for Aircraft - **Tubetronics**
Metal Work_miscellaneous - **Flexmaster U S a Inc.**
Metal Work_miscellaneous - **Big D Metalworks of Texas**
Metal Work_miscellaneous - **A C Welding & Engineering**
Metal Work_miscellaneous - **Flite Technology, Inc.**
Metal Work_miscellaneous - **Omega Products, Inc.**
Metal Working Fluids - **Lenox Chemical Company**
Metal Working Fluids - **Protect All, Inc.**
Metal Working Machinery - **World Equipment & Machine Sales Co**
Metal Working Machinery, Used & New - **Machinery Dealers Natl. Assn.**
Metal and Plastic Machine Parts - **Willis Machine Inc**
Metal, Deep Drawn - **Magnetic Radiation Laboratories Inc.**
Metal, Hydroformed - **Magnetic Radiation Laboratories Inc.**
Metal, Leak and Voltage Detectors - **Fisher Research Laboratory**
Metal, Plastic and Steel Machine Parts - **Doerksen Precision Products**
Metal, Steel and Aluminum Machine P - **Southport Machine Inc**
Metal, Wooden & Painted Signs - **Dezion Signs**
Metalfilm Resistors - **Koa Speer Electronics, Inc.**
Metalforming Machinery, Export - **Planet Machinery Company**
Metalizing Equipment & Wire - **Eagle Metalizing Coatings Co**
Metallic / Non-metallic Components - **Litec Inc.**
Metallic Ceramic, Wire Spray - **Metallic Ceramic Coating Inc.**
Metallic Foils - **Transfer Print Foils, Inc.**
Metallic Print Binders - **Eastern Color & Chemical Co.**
Metallic Stearates - **Norac Co., Inc., the**
Metallic Thread - **Robison-anton Textile Company (Mfr)**
Metallised Dielectric Film - **Steinerfilm Inc**
Metallurgical Testing & Failure Analysis - **Advanced Heat Treat Corp.**
Metallurgical Testing Laboratory and Services - **Canyon State Inspection**
Metals & Chemistry Testing - **Analytica Environmental Lab Inc**
Metals Refining - **Republic Metals Corp.**
Metals Service Centers and Offices - **Aj Weller**
Metals Service Centers and Offices - **Olympia International**
Metalworking End Mills - **Greenfield Industries**
Metalworking Fluids of All Types - **Engineered Lubricants Co.**
Metalworking Machine Tool Holders - **Northwestern Tools, Inc.**
Metalworking Machinery - **K W Products, Inc.**
Metalworking Machinery - **Strilich Technolgies, Inc.**
Metalworking Machinery - **West Tool & Design, Inc.**
Metalworking Machinery - **Vortex Engineering**
Metalworking Machinery - **Red Bud Industries**
Metalworking Machinery, Nec - **Tridan International, Inc.**
Metalworking Taps Dies & Gauges - **Greenfield Industries**
Meteorological Instruments, Sensors, Rain Gauges - **Texas Electronics**
Meteorological Radar Equipment - **Enterprise Electronics Corp.**
Meter Mix & Dispensing Equipment - **Sheepscot Machine Works**
Metering Pumps - **Alldos Inc.**
Metering Pumps - **Fluid Metering, Inc.**
Mexican Customs Broker - **Gonzalez T.h. Inc**
Mexico / Canada Dist / Whse - **Pierce Packaging Company**
Mezzanine Systems - Wire / Steel / Fiberglass - **Kietek International, Inc.**
Mezzanines - **Vogler Equipment**
Mgmt Consulting Project Remediation - **Century West Engineering Corp.**
Mgmt. Connsulting - **Leemark, Inc.**
Mgmt. Consulting Svcs., Environ. Eng. - **Etc De Las Americas, Inc.**
Mgmt. Consulting Svcs., Japan & Far East - **Suzuki, Myers & Associates**
Mgmt. Consulting, Remediation Projects - **Etc De Las Americas, Inc.**
Micr Ribbons - **Frye Tech, Inc.**
Micro Positioning Tables for Science Labs - **Dynaoptic-motion Corp**
Microchip Packaging & Opto Products - **Minco Technology Labs, Inc.**
Microelectronic & Liquid Crystal Display Masks, - **Process Technologies**
Microemulsion Fuel Additive - **H2oil Corporation**
Microfiche Envelopes - **National Commercial Envelope Co.**
Microfilm- **Cmisource.com**
Microfilm Equipment - **Connecticut Micrographics, Inc.**

Micromized Sulfur- **Agtrol International**
Microphones & Audio Electronics - **Shure Bros. Inc.**
Microscopes, Micro-projectors- **Ken-A-Vision Mfg. Co., Inc.**
Microwave Communications Equipment - **Glenayre Western Multiplex**
Microwave Electron Tubes - **Hughes Electron Dynamics**
Microwave Instruments - **Resonance Instruments Inc.**
Microwave Ovens - **Emerson Radio Corp.**
Microwave Rotary Couplers - **Kevlin Corporation(mfr)**
Microwave Traveling Wave Tube Amplifiers- **Hughes Electron Dynamics**
Mid - Efficiency Water Heaters & Boilers - **Weben-jarco, Inc.**
Mil - Spec. Connectors - **Precision Hermetic Technology**
Mil/cable Harness Assy. - **Silveron Industries Inc**
Mildew Proof Paint - **Zinsser & Co., Inc., William**
Military & Outdoor Clothing & Accessories - **Rothco**
Military Aircraft - **Airborne Technologies, Inc.**
Military Aircraft Crash Rescue- **Sandpiper Publications**
Military Contractor - **Silveron Industries Inc**
Military Radios & Wireless Equipment - **Talla-com, Tallahassee Comm**
Military Spare Parts - **Wynnson Enterprises, Inc.**
Military Spec Lacing Tapes - **Western Filament Inc**
Military Spec. Pouches - **Caltex Plastics Inc**
Military Tactical Data Systems, Airborne - **Drs Precision Echo**
Military Tents, Clothing, Field Gear, New & Used - **R.d.d. Enterprises**
Military Vehicle Components; Wiring Devices - **Charles E Gillman Co**
Military, Construction - **Service Hydraulics Inc.**
Milk Processing Machinery - **Amtrade International, Inc.**
Milk Products - **Amtrade International, Inc.**
Milk and Cream, Concentrated - **Ps International**
Milk_fluid - **Galaxy Foods, Inc.**
Milled Corn - **Molinos De Puerto Rico, Inc., a Conagra Company**
Milled Rice, Export - **Farmers Rice Cooperative**
Milled Rice, Long, Med., Parboiled - **Riceland Foods Inc.**
Milling Machinery - **Sixnel Sheet Metal**
Milling Machinery - **Morrison Co., the D. C.**
Milling Machines & Turning Equipment - **Republic-lagun Cnc Corp**
Milling Machines, Routers - **Onsrud Machine Corporation**
Millwork - **Wolohan Lumber**
Millwork - **Architectural Windows & Entries, Inc.**
Millwork - **Bend Door Co**
Millwork - **Burns, Morris & Stewart, Ltd.**
Millwork - **Burton Woodworks Inc.**
Millwork - **Construction Design Associates**
Millwork - **Jim C. Lane Inc.**
Millwork - **Sw Sash & Door**
Millwork - **Fagen's Building Center**
Millwork - **Jonathan Virginia, Inc.**
Millwork - **Moultrie Post Form, Inc.**
Millwork - **Clarke's Custom Windows, Inc.**
Millwork & Church Furniture - **Woerner Industries, Inc.**
Milspec Electro/mechanical Components - **Silveron Industries Inc**
Mineral Fillers & Extenders - **Hess Pumice Products, Inc.**
Mineral Jigs - **Quinn Process Equipment Co**
Mineral Oil - **Richard Boas**
Mineral Processing Equipment; Conveyors - **Quinn Process Equipment**
Mineral Products_nonmetallic - **Penn Big Bed Slate Co., Inc.**
Mineral Products_nonmetallic - **American Fiberglass Products, Inc.**
Mineral Wool for Thermal, Acoustical & Fire Protection - **Thermafiber**
Minerals, Ground or Treated - **Dixon Southwestern Graphite Inc.**
Minerals, Ground or Treated - **Hess Pumice Products Inc**
Minerals, Ground or Treated - **Wyo-ben, Inc.**
Mines and Pumice - **Hess Pumice Products Inc**
Mining Antisealants - **Ashland Chemical**
Mini Blinds - **Arabel**
Mini Strip Lights Ul Listed - **Gilbert Mfg. Co.**
Miniature Clutches - **Helander Products, Inc.**
Miniature Hobby Trains - **Athearn Inc**
Mining Crushing & Pulverizing Machinery - **Bradley Pulverizer Co**
Mining Equipment - **Netafim Irrigation Inc**
Mining Machinery - **Shotcrete Technologies Inc**
Mining Machinery - **Ani-helser**
Mining Machinery - **Aresco, Inc.**

Mining Machinery - **Baker Hughes Mining Tools, Inc.**
Mining Machinery - **Smith Equipment Usa Inc**
Mining Truck Parts - **Minco Sales Corp.**
Mining and Industrial Machinery - **Rdo Equipment Co**
Mint Flavors - **Todd Co., A.m.**
Mirror Doors for Closet Openings - **Dunbarton Corp. /Rediframe/slimfol**
Mirror, Safety & Security - **Silver & Co., Inc., Fred**
Mirrors - **Grote Industries, Inc.**
Mirrors, Convex & Dome Safety / Security - **Campus Crafts Inc. (Mfr)**
Mirrors, Parabolic & Elliptical - **Opti-forms Inc**
Misc. Converted Paper Products - **Autron Incorporated**
Misc. Dried Products & Fall Oak Leaves - **Natural Line**
Misc. Metal Fabricators - **Int'l Fabricators & Engineers**
Misc. Publishing, Pet Ind. Newsletter - **World Wide Pet Supply Ass'n**
Misc. Wireformed Products - **Dulmison Incorporated**
Miscellaneous Building Materia - **Karp Associates, Inc.**
Miscellaneous Cargo - **R.d.d. Enterprises**
Miscellaneous Cargo - **Sconza Candy Co.**
Miscellaneous Cargo - **Maratech International**
Miscellaneous Cargo - **Gilman Brothers**
Miscellaneous Cargo - **Lewcott**
Miscellaneous Cargo - **Shachihata**
Miscellaneous Cargo - **Thunderball Marketing**
Miscellaneous Cargo - **Century Spring Co., Inc.**
Miscellaneous Cargo - **Stemlit Growers**
Miscellaneous Cargo - **Western Hybrid Seeds, Inc.**
Miscellaneous Cargo - **Atk North America**
Miscellaneous Cargo - **Americares Foundations**
Miscellaneous Food Stores - **Catalina Food Ingredients**
Miscellaneous Nonmetallic Minerals - **Hess Pumice Products Inc**
Miscellaneous Publishing - **Technical Resource International, Inc.**
Miso & Soy Sauce - **American Miso Co.**
Missile Launching Systems - **Lockheed Martin Launching Systems**
Mist Bottles - **Aquapower Co.**
Mist Collection Equipment - **Airflow Systems Inc. (Mfr)**
Misting & Humidity Equipment - **Corrigan Corp. America**
Mixed Building Material & Hardware - **Global Material Supply**
Mixer Bowls and Accessories - **Alfa International Corporation**
Mixers - **Hamilton Beach/proctor Silex, Inc.**
Mixes Fertilizers - **Western Farm Service/cascade**
Mnaufacturing System Electro - **Motorola Integrated Electronic Systems**
Mobile 120 Volt Ac Inverters & Generators - **Pacific Utility Equipment Co**
Mobile Equipment Seals - **Heavy Equipment Parts Co.**
Mobile Food Bakery Equipment - **Bevles Company Inc**
Mobile Homes - **General Manufactured Housing, Inc.**
Mobile Homes - **Parkwest Industries Inc**
Mobile Tower Units, Co.w.s. - **Us Tower Corp**
Mobile Truck & Bus Washers - **J I M Mfg., Inc.**
Moded Rubber Products - **Diamond Rubber Products Co., Inc.**
Model Railroad Electronic Cont - **Peerless Industries, Inc.**
Modems (Security - Ac or Dc Powered) - **Cordell Manufacturing Inc**
Modems... Fsk to 56kbps & Fiber Optic - **Sunnyvale Gdi, Inc.**
Modern Environmental Maitenance Product for - **Legge Co., Inc., WalterG**
Modular / Manufactured Homes - **Horton Homes, Inc.**
Modular Aluminum Construction Systems - **Items Products Inc.**
Modular Buildings - **Custom Modular Solutions**
Modular Cabinetry for Closets and Garage - **We're Organized of No Calif**
Modular Drawer Cabinets - **Lyon Metal Products Llc**
Modular Storage Cabinets - **We're Organized of No Calif**
Moisture Detectors - **Elliott Bay Industries**
Mold & Die Cast Bases & Frames - **Craftsman Tool & Mold Co.**
Mold & Rot Removal - **Ethylene Control Inc**
Mold Cleaning Systems - **Cold Jet, Inc.**
Mold Release Agents for Rubber - **Axel Plastics Research Laboratories**
Molded & Extruded Parts - **C G R Products Inc.**
Molded Rubber Automotive Products - **Cooper Engineered Products**
Molded Rubber Products & Molded Thermoplastics - **Rahco Rubber, Inc.**
Molded Seals; Injection Molding of Plastics - **Embry Engineering & Mfg**
Molding - **Woodpecker, Inc.**
Molds & Dies - **Pasco Tool & Die**
Molds and Fabricates Plastic Carring Cases - **Melmat Inc**

Molecular Biology Reagents & Selected - **Karlan Research Products Cor**
Molecular Sieves - **Pragmatic Environmental Solutions Company Inc.**
Monitoring & Detection Equipment Concrete Industry - **Le Sueur Mfg. Co.**
Monochromators - **Spectral Energy Corp.**
Monochromators - **Mcpherson Inc.**
Monofilament Fibers - **Glassmaster**
Monofilaments & Chemical Light Sticks - **Lindgren Pitman**
Monofilaments over 1.5mm - **Lindgren Pitman**
Mont Blanc Pens - **Juno International**
Mops - **J W Mfg. Co.**
Morine Zippers - **Spradling Originals Inc.**
Mortar, Plaster, Refractory & Terrazzo Mixing Machinery - **Anchor Mfg. C**
Mosquito & Vector Control Equip - **Public Health Equipment Supply Inc**
Mostly Domestic Merchandise - **Texas Jasmine**
Mot. Veh. Electronic Ignition Systems - **Crane Cams, Inc.**
Mot. Vehicle Engine Controls - **Crane Cams, Inc.**
Motion Control Systems & Plc - **Hmw Enterprises, Inc.**
Motion Picture & Video Production - **Brevis Corp**
Motion Picture & Video Production - **Communi-creations Inc**
Motion Picture & Video Production - **Masterpiece Prdctns Nevada**
Motion Picture Production - **Technical Resource International, Inc.**
Motor Boats, Patrol & Offshore - **Msi International**
Motor Control Center (Mcc) - **Con-tech Power Systems, Inc.**
Motor Homes - **Fleetwood Enterprises Inc**
Motor Homes - **Trail Wagons Inc**
Motor Parts, Marine Propeller Cntl. Comp - **Mathers Controls, Inc.**
Motor Scrapers - **Hoss Equipment**
Motor Vehicle Camshafts - **Crane Cams, Inc.**
Motor Vehicle Lighting - **Truck-lite International Inc.**
Motor Vehicle Parts & Accessories - **Hydraulic Industrial Resources**
Motor Vehicle Parts & Accessories - **Sprague Controls Inc**
Motor Vehicle Parts & Accessories - **S T C Machine Shop**
Motor Vehicle Parts & Accessories - **Aaron-swiss, Inc.**
Motor Vehicle Parts & Accessories - **Autotech Usa**
Motor Vehicle Parts & Accessories - **D & H Enterprises**
Motor Vehicle Parts & Accessories - **Engineered Products Co.**
Motor Vehicle Parts & Accessories - **Excel of Stockton**
Motor Vehicle Parts & Accessories - **Fleet Air Industries**
Motor Vehicle Parts & Accessories - **Foote Axle & Forge Company Llc**
Motor Vehicle Parts & Accessories - **Hebco Products, Inc.**
Motor Vehicle Parts & Accessories - **Horizon Technology Group**
Motor Vehicle Parts & Accessories - **Industrial Gastruck, Inc.**
Motor Vehicle Parts & Accessories - **Mize & Co., Inc.**
Motor Vehicle Parts & Accessories - **Phillips Industries**
Motor Vehicle Parts & Accessories - **Pretty Products, Inc. Rubber Queen**
Motor Vehicle Parts & Accessories - **Rancho Suspension**
Motor Vehicle Parts & Accessories - **Rubber Queen**
Motor Vehicle Parts & Accessories - **Spring Valley Mfg., Inc.**
Motor Vehicle Parts & Accessories - **Stemco, Inc.**
Motor Vehicle Parts & Accessories - **Tasker Metal Products**
Motor Vehicle Parts & Accessories - **Tripac International, Inc.**
Motor Vehicle Parts & Accessories - **Truck Equipment Sales, Inc.**
Motor Vehicle Parts & Accessories - **Tucson Alternator Exchange Inc**
Motor Vehicle Parts and Accessories - **Atk North America**
Motor Vehicle Parts and Accessories - **Continental Cars, Inc.**
Motor Vehicle Parts and Accessories - **Faria Corp.**
Motor Vehicle Parts and Accessories - **Interpax**
Motor Vehicle Parts and Accessories - **Kbs Exports**
Motor Vehicle Parts and Accessories - **Sam's Auto Glass & Exports**
Motor Vehicle Parts and Accessories - **World Trading**
Motor Vehicle Supplies & New Parts - **Exide Corporation**
Motor Vehicle Supplies & New Parts - **Gregory Truck Body & Fire Appa**
Motor Vehicle Supplies & New Parts - **Sprague Controls Inc**
Motor Vehicle Supplies & New Parts - **Southwest Peterbilt Gmc**
Motor Vehicle Supplies & New Parts - **Simpson Tool Box Co**
Motor Vehicle Supplies & New Parts - **Tucson Alternator Exchange Inc**
Motor Vehicle Valve Train Components - **Crane Cams, Inc.**
Motor Vehicles & Car Bodies - **Promotional Trim Components**
Motor Vehicles Parts - **Interdynamics, Inc.**
Motor Vehicles for the Transport of Goods - **Euclid Hitachi Heavy Equip**
Motor Vehicles for the Transport of Goods - **Alpine Armoring Inc.**

Motor Vehicles for the Transport of Goods - **Aresco, Inc.**
Motor Vehicles for the Transport of Goods - **Continental Cars, Inc.**
Motor Vehicles for the Transport of Goods - **Schwing America, Inc.**
Motorcycle Accessories - **Big Bike Parts**
Motorcycle Carrier / Transport Trailers - **Chariot Mfg. Co., Inc.**
Motorcycle Covers - **Big Bike Parts**
Motorcycles Parts and Accessories of - **Harley-davidson, Inc.**
Motorcycles, Bicycles & Parts - **Kendon Industries Inc**
Motorcycles, Bicycles, and Parts - **Harley-davidson, Inc.**
Motorcycles Fitted with an Auxiliary Motors - **Harley-davidson, Inc.**
Motorola Pagers, Accessories & Parts - **Leavitt Communications, Inc.**
Motors & Generators - **Hawthorne Power Systems**
Motors & Generators - **Dial Manufacturing Inc**
Motors & Generators - **E C M Motor Co.**
Motors & Generators - **Electric Motors & Drives, Inc.**
Motors & Generators - **Elmagco Corp**
Motors & Generators - **Imperial Electric Co.**
Motors & Generators - **J. C. Marine Diesel, Inc.**
Motors & Generators - **Schulz Electric Co.**
Motors & Generators - **Bei Sensors & Systems/kimco Magnetics Division**
Moulded & Shaped Wood Products - **H.a. Stiles**
Mounting Hardware & Handles - **Keystone Electronics Corp.**
Mounting Hardware for Speakers and Televisions - **Omnimount Systems**
Moving, Grading, Leveling, Excavating, Extracting Machinery - **Aresco,**
Moving, Grading, Leveling, Excavating - **Kessler International Corp.**
Mri Shielded Enclosures - **Lindgren R F Enclosures Inc.**
Mro, Industrial & Electronic Tools - **General Tool & Supply Co**
Msw Sorting Equipment, (Mrf) - **Wildcat Mfg. Co., Inc.**
Much More. - **Robus Leather**
Mud Logging Instrumentation - **Petron Industries Inc.**
Muffins - **Neuman Bakery Specialties, Inc.**
Mugs - **Sandy's Trophies**
Mulch Processing - **Mat, Inc.**
Mulit Fuel Furnace / Liquid or Solids - **Turbo Burn Inc**
Mulit-chip Module Hybrid Circuits - **Interfet Corporation**
Multi Color Labels, plus Uv Printed Labels up to 7 Colors - **Allenwest Inc**
Multi Purpose - **Carole Fabrics**
Multi-cultural Children's Books - **Dharma Publishing**
Multi-frequency Phase Fluorometers - **Iss Inc.**
Multilatches - **Norse, Inc.**
Multimedia Streaming Engines - **3cx**
Municipal Solid Waste Incinerators - **Olivine Corporation**
Murray & Lanman's Florida Water Cologne - **Lanman & Kemp-barclay &**
Museum & Attraction Exhibits - **Presentation South, Inc.**
Museum Artifact Repair and Space Suit Fabrication - **Guard Lee, Inc.**
Musical Instruments - **Torres Engineering**
Musical Instruments Parts & Accessories; Publis - **Torres Engineering**
Musical Instruments, Accessories - **Shubb Capos**
Musical Magic Show for non Profit Organization - **Jdc (Hawaii) Inc.**
Mustang Auto Sales - **Mustang Auto Sales**
Mustang Parts - New & Used - **Mustang Auto Sales**
Mustang Restoration - **Mustang Auto Sales**
Mustang Service - **Mustang Auto Sales**
Mustard - **Herlocher Foods, Inc.**
Mustard Oil - **Ingredient Resources, Inc.**
Mustards - **Griffin Food Company**
Nail Care Products for Retail Consumers - **International Beauty Design**
Nail Care Products for Salons - **International Beauty Design**
Nail Care Products, Artificial Nails - **Fingers Inc**
Nail Files & Nail Buffers - **Realys Inc**
Nail Polish & Nail Treatment & Allied Products - **Tevco**
Nail Polish, Bear Shape Bottles - **Fingers Inc**
Nail Polish, Cat Shpe Bottles - **Fingers Inc**
Nailed Wood Boxes & Shook - **Future Packaging Inc**
Nailed Wood Boxes & Shook - **Industrial Crating, Inc.**
Name Badges - **Sandy's Trophies**
Name Badges, Awards, & Identification Plates - **Contemporary, Inc.**
Name Tags - **Trophy Shoppe**
Naphtheme Base & Process Oils - **Golden Bear Oil Specialties**
Narrow Fabric Mills - **Just a Stretch**
Narrow Fabric Mills - **Spanset, Inc.**

Nasal Strips - **Unico, Inc.**
Nathans Famous Pickle Products - **United Pickle Products Corp.**
Native American Goods - **Montana Essence Company**
Native Grass Seeds - **Sharp Bros Seed Co.**
Natl Commercial Bank Intl Banking - **First Security Bank**
Natural & Organic Foods - **Health Valley Foods**
Natural & Synthetic Diamond Tools - **Carter Diamond Tool Corp.**
Natural Frequency Vibrating Conveyors. - **Rbm Manufacturing Co., Inc.**
Natural Gas Measuring Instruments & Parts - **Red River Instruments Co.**
Natural Gas Processing Equipment - **Gas Corp. Of America**
Natural Health Products - **Trimedica International Inc**
Natural Herb and Health Products - **Madys Company**
Natural Ingredients - **Unique Laboratories, Inc.**
Natural Jute - **Yaley Enterprises, Inc.**
Natural Mold Inhibitors, Flavor Enhancers - **Ptx Food Corp.**
Natural Stone & Tile Maintenance Products - **Legge Co., Inc., Walter G.**
Natural Vitamins - **Arnet Pharmaceutical Corp.**
Natural Vitamins - **Up-time Sports/nutrition/medical Ind**
Natural Wood Cat Litter & Small Animal Bedding - **Coeur D'alene Fiber...**
Natural and Processed Cheeses - **A & J Cheese Company**
Naturlly Dyred Red Dirt Shirts - **Paradise Sportswear, Inc.**
Nautical Books & Cruising Guides - **Westcott Cove Publishing Co.**
Navigation Equipment Aviation Electronics - **Sunstrand Corporation**
Navigational & Communication Systems - **Caravan International**
Navigational Boat Lights - **Aqua Signal Corp.**
Navigational Marine Electronics - **Advanced Marine Technology Corp.**
Neck Banders - **Njm/cli Packaging Systems International**
Neckwear_men's & Boys' - **Duron Neckwear Inc**
Needle Punched Liquid Filtration - **Western Synthetic Fiber**
Nema - **P T L Equipment Mfg. Co., Inc.**
Neon & Channel Letters Manufacturing - **All Neon & Signs**
Neon Sign Supplies & Equipment - **Tube Light Co., Inc.**
Neon Signs & Gift Items - **Moser & Co. Neon Specialists**
Neon Specializing Sign Company - **Neon Fx Sign & Display**
Neon Technology Eduational Assistance - **All Neon & Signs**
Neon Tubes, Signs, Transformers- **Neon Fx Sign & Display**
Nerve Stimulators Other Medical Devices - **Advantage Development Corp**
Network Analyzers, Lan Cable Tester - **Datacom Textron**
Network Attach Storage Servers - **Meridian Data Inc**
Network Cable Assemblies & Wiring Harnesses - **Custom Cable Industrie**
Network Integration & Service - **Star Enterprises Inc**
Network Managment Software - **Knozall Systems**
Network Monitor & Control Mgmt. Systems - **Satellite Transmission Syst**
Network Resistors - **Koa Speer Electronics, Inc.**
Network Systems Integration - **Digital Interface Systems Inc.**
Networking Accesories & Harnessing - **Worswick Industries Inc**
Neural Network Coal Combustion Optimization - **Net Power Solutions**
New & Used Truck Dealerships - **Simpson Tool Box Co**
New & Used Trucks,trailers and Rv's - **Palm Peterbilt - Gmc Trucks, Inc.**
New Carbide-tipped Cutting Tools - **Nordic Saw & Tool Manufacturer**
New Easy Gate Light Assembly's - **National Electric Gate Co.**
New Gas Meters & Regulators - **Energy Economics, Inc.**
New Gate / Saver Breakaways - **National Electric Gate Co.**
New Pneumatic Tires, of Rubber - **Traction International**
New Pneumatic Tires, of Rubber - **U.t.c. Tires & Rubber Comp.**
New Rubber Injection Equipment - **Hydratecs Injection Equipment, Inc.**
New Scientific High Vacuum Equipment - **Hawe Technical Associates**
New Scientific High Vacuum Equipment - **Hta**
New Scientific Ultra High Vac. Equipment - **Hta**
New Scientific Ultra High Vacuum - **Hawe Technical Associates (Hta)**
Newspaper & Commercial Printing - **Latimer County News-trib**
Newspaper Advertising Representative - **Multimedia, Inc.**
Newspaper Printing - **Glen Ullin Times**
Newspaper Printing & Typesetting - **Birmingham News Co., the**
Newspaper Printing - Public Records Print out - **Blue Sheet Inc., the**
Newspaper Typesetting - **Hill Country Newspapers Inc. / the Boerne Star**
Newspaper Typesetting - **Home with Homeland News & Printing Service**
Newspapers - **Arizona Daily Star**
Newspapers - **Birmingham News Co., the**
Newspapers - **Blue Sheet Inc., the**
Newspapers - **Clear Creek Courant**

Newspapers - El Semanario
Newspapers - Glen Ullin Times
Newspapers - Herburger Publications Inc
Newspapers - Hill Country Newspapers Inc. / the Boerne Star
Newspapers - Lake County Leader
Newspapers - Latimer County News-trib
Newspapers - Partnership Press, Inc.
Newspapers - Seattle Post/intelligencer Div
Newspapers - South Pasadena Publishing Co
Newspapers - The Catholic Voice
Newspapers - The Medical Remarketer
Newspapers - World Journal Inc
Newspapers - Times Leader, Inc.
Ni-cad Batteries - Sec Industrial Battery Co., Inc.
Nickel Alloy Scrap Cobalt Alloys - Sos Metals, Inc.
Nickel Plate, Bar Pipe Tube - Duenner Supply Co. Of Texas
Nickel Silver Engraveable Plates - Exclusive Findings
Nitrogen Generating Equipment - Pacific Consolidated Indus
Nitrous Oxide Gases and Sedation Equipmen - Medical Gas Services Inc
No Rot Polymer Garage Door Trim System - Marley Mouldings Inc.(Mfr)
Nomex-spun & Filament - Saunders Thread Co., Inc.
Non Dairy Creamer - Diehl, Inc.
Non Dairy Creamers - Tonex, Inc.
Non Electric Sconces & Wall Brackets - Speer Collectibles
Non Ferric Foundries - Sun Foundry
Non Ferrous Scrap Metal - Ami Trading
Non Woven Polypropylene Densified Nuggets & Pellets - Bromley Plastics
Non Woven Polypropylene Scrap - Bales / Waste - Bromley Plastics Corp.
Non-alcoholic Beverages - Lins Trading
Non-dairy Creamers - Dean Foods (Mfr)
Non-dairy Milk Substitute: Vanilla, Chocolate - Diehl, Inc.
Non-destructive Testing Equipment - Sullins, Inc.
Non-destructive Testing Materials & Equipment - Magnaflux
Non-destructive Testing Equipment - Physical Acoustics
Non-ferrous Scrap Metals; Import & Export Trading - Tst Inc
Non-gmo Certification Program- Northland Organic Foods / Northland
Non-prescription Drugs - Afassco, Inc.
Non-stick, High Tmperature Teflon Ceramic Reinforced - Americoat Corp.
Non-wovens - Paper Pak Products Inc
Nonconiferous Wood - North American Wood Products, Inc.
Nonconiferous Wood - Ram Forest Products
Nondurable Goods - David Adam Promotions Inc
Nonferrous Die-casting, Except Aluminum - Gibbs Die Casting Corp.
Nonferrous Foundries - Delvest, Inc.
Nonferrous Foundries - World Equipment & Machine Sales Company
Nonferrous Metals_primary - Republic Metals Corp.
Nonferrous Rolling & Drawing - N G K Metals Corp.
Nonferrous Wiredrawing & Insulating - Fitel Lucent Technologies
Nonferrous Wiredrawing & Insulating - Pacific Electricord Company
Nonferrous Wiredrawing & Insulating - Storm Products Co Inc
Nonferrous Wiredrawing & Insulating - Aero-kap Inc
Nonferrous Wiredrawing & Insulating - Permaluster Company
Nonlethal Law Enforcement Weapons - Nova Products
Nonpartisan Political Magazine - California Journal
Nonresidential Construction, Nec - Mcalpine & Salyer Construction
Nonwoven Fabrics - Bba Nonwovens Reemay, Inc.
Nonwoven Polyester & Polypropylene - Reemay, Inc.
Nonwoven Textile Machinery - American Textile Machinery
North Central Washington Directory - Hagadone Directories Inc
Notebook Personal Computers - Howard Industries
Notions - American & Efird, Inc.
Notions, Zippers, Fasteners, Buttons, Needles & Pins - American & Efird,
Novelty Fabric - General Fabrics
Nozzles / Hoses / Filters Replacement - Adhesive Systems, Inc.
Nozzles, Liquid, Hand Dispensing - Drum-mates, Inc
Nuclear Decommissioning - Bigge Crane & Rigging Co.
Nuclear Radiation Detection Instruments - N. Wood Counter Laboratory,
Nuclear Spent Fuel Handling & Transportation - Bigge Crane & Rigging
Nuclear Valves, Turbine Bypass Valves- Control Components, Inc.
Numimed Medication Dispensers - Sharn, Inc.
Nursery Supplies and Bedding Plants - Willow Creek Greenhouses Inc

Nursing & Food Processing Uniforms - Dixon Mfg., Inc.
Nut Grower Magazine & Trade Shows - Western Agricultural Publish
Nut Harvesting Equipment - Bag-a-nut, Inc.
Nutritional & Health Products - International Nutrition, Inc.
Nutritional Beverage Drinks - Dean Foods (Mfr)
Nutritional Supplements - Biomin Industries, Inc.
Nutritional Supplements - International Relations-advanced Bio Institute
Nutro Max & Nutro's Choice Pet Food for Special - Nutro Products, Inc.
Nuts & Bolts - Zero Fastener Co.
Nuts & Seeds, Salted & Roasted - Mac Farms of Hawaii, Inc.
Nuts & Seeds_salted & Roasted - Jade Food Products, Inc.
Nuts & Seeds_salted & Roasted - Sunland, Inc.
Nuts & Seeds_salted & Roasted - Ultimate International
Nuts, Bolts, Screws, & Washers - Earnest Machine Products Co.
Nvocc - Commercial International Forwarding Inc.
Nvocc - Inter-jet Systems, Inc.
Nvocc - Wts of Houston, Inc.
Nvocc / Ocean & Air Consolidators - Equipsa, Inc.
Nvocc Bonded - Dan Transport Corporation
Nylon Building Escape Chutes- Baker Safety Equipment, Inc.
Nylon Cargo Control Straps - S-line
Nylon Tool Bags and Belts for the Construction - Mendoza Textiles Mfr
O.e.m. Food Service Equipment - King Metal Products, Inc.
O.j.c. Drug - Captek Softgel International
Oak (Red & White) Lumber & Logs - S.g. International
Oak Bedroom Furniture - Oakwood Interiors
Oak Home Office - Oakwood Interiors
Oak Wood in the Rough - H.a. Stiles
Oak Wood, Sawn or Chipped Lenghtwise - Ram Forest Products
Oat Processing - La Crosse Milling Co.
Obese Convalescent Supplies - Convaquip Industries, Inc.
Obsolete Mixer Parts for Bakeries - Independent Restaurant & Bakery
Occasional Tables / Benches - Matel Bank and Desk Accessories
Ocean Freight & Cargo Transportation - Columbus Line Usa, Inc.
Ocean Freight Transportation - Straightway Inc.
Ocean Marine Insurance - Roanoke Brokerage Services, Inc.
Ocean Research Vessel - Lockheed Martin Launching Systems
Ocean Shipping & Receiving - Burlington Air Express Inc.
Odor & Pollution Control Equipment - Anguil Environmental Systems,
Odor / Fume Removal Filters Carbon-zeolite - Permatron Corporation
Odor Control Solutions - Nutech Environmental Corp.(Mfr)
Odor Control Systems - Odor Control Co., Inc.
Odor Eliminators - Nature Plus, Inc.
Oem Air Compressors & Vacuum Pumps - Thomas Industries-power Air
Oem Machinery , - Flex-pak Manufacturing Inc
Oem, Private Label & Contract Available - American Sewing Dynamics 1
Office Chairs - Superior Furniture
Office Furniture - Aspects Inc
Office Furniture - Galloway Office Supplies & Equipment
Office Furniture Clone Parts - Steiner Fabrication Inc
Office Furniture and Computer Supplies - All American Office Products
Office Furniture, Except Wood - Metal Master
Office Furniture, Except Wood - Superior Furniture
Office Furniture, Except Wood - Aspects Inc
Office Furniture, Export - Alkantec, Inc.
Office Furniture_wood - Fine Craft Unlimited
Office Furniture_wood - Arcadia Chair Company
Office Furniture_wood - Hale Co., F. E.
Office Furniture_wood - Superior Furniture
Office Intercom & Speaker Systems - Audioplex Technology, Inc.
Office Products - Uniek Inc.
Office Seating - Trinity Furniture, Inc.
Office Supplies & Equipment - Galloway Office Supplies & Equipment
Office Supplies (Lamination) - Technical Coating International
Office/hotel Equip., Stanchions - Matel Bank and Desk Accessories
Offset Printing - Graphics plus Printing, Inc.
Offset Printing & Typesetting - Tretina Printing Co., Inc.
Offset Printing Machinery, Wholesale - Allpress Equipment Inc.
Offshore Compressors - V R Systems, Inc.
Offshore Living Quarters, Any Size or Shape - Hernandez Mattress, Inc.
Oil & Gas Field Exploration - Marshall Miller & Associates

Oil & Gas Field Machinery - **American Augers Inc.**
Oil & Gas Field Machinery - **Gas Corp. Of America**
Oil & Gas Field Machinery - **Goex International, Inc.**
Oil & Gas Field Machinery - **Oilpure Refiner Co**
Oil & Gas Field Machinery - **Republic-lagun Cnc Corp**
Oil & Gas Field Services - **Marshall Miller & Associates**
Oil & Gas Maps for Alaska - **Mapmakers Alaska**
Oil & Gas Safety & Production - **Petrotech Inc.**
Oil & Gas Sales - **Rk Pipe & Supply**
Oil Additives - **K & W Products**
Oil Field Equipment - **Minco Sales Corp.**
Oil Field Equipment - **Cold Extrusion Co. Of America, Inc.**
Oil Field Equipment - **Johnston Pumps**
Oil Field Equipment & Spare Parts - **Intramar, Inc.**
Oil Field Float Equipment Parts - **Wichita Falls Mfg.**
Oil Field Gaskets - **Houston Mfg. & Specialty Co., Inc.**
Oil Field Monitoring Equipment - **Petron Industries Inc.**
Oil Field Tools & Coil Tubing - **Taylor Made Oil Tools, Inc.**
Oil Filtration Systems, Flow Sights & Indicator - **Kaydon Corp.**
Oil Refineries, (Refurbished & Modernized) - **Interdevco & Associates**
Oil Refiners, Diesel Dialyser, Engineering - **Oilpure Refiner Co**
Oil Tight Chain Guards - **Litco, Inc.**
Oil Well Casing and Tubing - **C & R Industries Inc**
Oil Well Perforating & Pipe Recovery Equipment - **Goex International**
Oilfield Cementing Plugs - **Wichita Falls Mfg.**
Oilfield Equipment & Parts - **Sirex, Ltd.**
Oilfield Manufacturing & Repair - **K & B Machine Works Inc.**
Oilpatch Seals, Valve Stem Packing, Wellhead Packoffs - **Gulf Coast Seal,**
Oils, Meals, Other Value Added Products - **Northland Organic Foods**
Oilseed Machinery - **Carver, Inc.**
Oily Water Separators - **Harco Manufacturing Co.**
Ointments - **Afassco, Inc.**
Oleoresins - **Gilroy Foods, Inc. (Mfr)**
Olive Oils & Blended Oils - **Catania Spagna**
Olivine - **Refractory Materials International**
Omni-range Master Locators - **Prospector & Treasure Hunters Hdqters.,**
On-line Particle Size Analysis & Monitoring - **Micromeritics Instrument**
Onan Generators, Natural Gas Engines - **Cummins Sw/power Systems**
One Piece Hydraulic Hose Fittings - **Cold Extrusion Co. Of America, Inc.**
Onion Oil - **Ingredient Resources, Inc.**
Onion Oil - Natural - **Accurate Ingredients**
Onions and Shallots, Fresh or Chilled - **Firman Pinkerton**
Online Communications - **Iridio**
Open Die Forgings - **Standard Steel**
Open Die Forgings & Rolled Rings - **Scot Forge Co.**
Open a Facility on Mexico / Texas Border. - **C G R Products Inc.**
Operating Room - **Biomedical International**
Operator Foreign Trade Zone for Canada - **Pierce Packaging Company**
Operator Foreign Trade Zone for Mexico - **Pierce Packaging Company**
Ophthalmic Goods - **Coastal Vision Center**
Ophthalmic Goods - **Economy Optical, Inc.**
Ophthalmic Goods - **Russ Optical, Inc.**
Ophthalmic Goods - **Westcon Contact Lens Company Inc**
Ophthalmic Instruments - **Western Ophthalmics Corporation**
Ophthalmic Lenses - **L.b.i.**
Opthalmic Lubricant - **Vision Pharmaceuticals Inc.**
Optical Data Links - **Sumitomo Electric Lightwave Corp.**
Optical Equipment - **Kowa California Inc.**
Optical Fiber Connectors- **Sumitomo Electric Lightwave Corp.**
Optical Instrumentation - **Rame-hart, Inc.**
Optical Instruments & Lenses - **Cuda Products Corp.**
Optical Instruments & Lenses - **Innoventions Inc**
Optical Instruments & Lenses - **Ken-lab, Llc**
Optical Instruments & Lenses - **Omex Technologies**
Optical Instruments & Lenses - **Opti-forms Inc**
Optical Instruments & Lenses - **Zygo Corp.**
Optical Instruments & Lenses, Prisms - **Reynard Corp**
Optical Lenses - **L.B.I.**
Optical Night Vision Devices, Wholesale - **U. S. Cavalry, Inc.**
Optical Plastics, Contact Lens Raw Materials - **Benz Research & Dev**
Optical Products and Instruments—lenses - **Reynard Corp**

Optometric Equipment, Export - **Arno International, Inc.**
Or Metric Sizes. - **Milgard Manufacturing Co**
Or Powder for Granitas - **Del's Lemonade & Refreshments, Inc.**
Oral Electrolyte Solutions - **Unico, Inc.**
Oral Hygiene Products:oral Irrigators,electric - **Teledyne Water Pik**
Oranges: Grapefruit - **Roses Southwest Papers**
Orbit (Ball) Lights - **Jeb Lighting Co., Llc**
Organic & Inorganic Fluor Compounds - **Advance Research Chemicals,**
Organic Beans - **Heartland Mill, Inc.**
Organic Chemicals - **Synalloy Corp., Blackman-uhler Chemical Div.**
Organic Chemicals, Non-lethal Weapons - **Aerko International**
Organic Chemicals, Riot Control Weapons - **Aerko International**
Organic Fibers, Noncellulosic - **Western Synthetic Fiber**
Organic Foods, Organic Wine, Coffee - **Lins Trading**
Organic Frozen Foods - **Amy's Kitchen Inc**
Organic Gardening - **Deer-off, Inc.**
Organic Grain & Flour Processing - **Heartland Mill, Inc.**
Organic Oat Products - **Heartland Mill, Inc.**
Organic Peroxides - **Norac Co., Inc., the**
Organic Peroxides, Ether Peroxides, Ketone Peroxides - **Norac Co., Inc.,**
Organic Pigments & Dyes - **Burlington Chemical Co., Inc. (Mfr)**
Organic Rice - **Sem Chi Rice Products**
Organic Sorbets, Soups & Finished Food Products - **Natural Choice Foods**
Organic Sunflower Nutrients - **Heartland Mill, Inc.**
Organic Surface Active Agents - **Lexard Corporation**
Organic Tortilla Chips - **Great Western Tortilla Company, the**
Organic Vegetable Oils, Vinegars, Condiments - **Spectrum Naturals Inc**
Organo Phosphites - **Dover Chemical Corp., Sub. Of Icc Industries, Inc.**
Oriental Flavors / Custom Formulations - **Liway International, Inc.**
Oriental Frozen Food (Eggrools, Wontons, Spring - **Chang Food Company**
Oriental Noodles - **Peking Noodle Co Inc**
Orifice Measurement Equipment - **Precision Flow, Inc.**
Origin & Destination Services, Storage - **Schroeder United Van Lines**
Original Cinnamon Broom & Potpourri - **A Touch of Country Magic**
Original Screen Prints on Fabric / Cothing - **Tutuvi**
Ornamental Nursery Products - **Golden State Bulb Growers**
Orthodontic Products - **Tp Orthodontics, Inc.**
Orthodontic Supplies and Services - **Tp Orthodontics Inc**
Orthopedic & Prosthetic Applicances - **Smith & Nephew United, Inc.**
Orthopedic & Prosthetic Supplies - **Ohio Willow Wood Co.**
Orthopedic Devices - **Restorative Care of America, Inc.**
Orthopedic Instruments - **Smith & Nephew Inc.**
Orthopedic Medical Products - **Beere Precision Medical Instruments**
Orthopedic Prosthetic & Neurosurgical Surgical - **Kinamed**
Orthopedic Supplies - **Smith & Nephew Inc.**
Oscillators & Synthesizers - **Communication Techniques, Inc.**
Ostrim, High-protein, Low-fat Meat Snacks - **Protos Inc.**
Other Mattresses - **Kingsdown, Inc.**
Other Self Service / Retail Industries. - **Kent Corp.**
Other Vegetable Products - **De Francesco & Sons Inc**
Outdoor Communication Modems, Fiber Optic - **Sunnyvale Gdi, Inc.**
Outdoor Fluorescent Lighting Fixtures - **Magnaray International**
Outdoor Lighting and Custom Fixtures - **Bieber Lighting Corp**
Outdoor Power Equipment - **Shindaiwa Inc**
Outerwear_girl's & Children's - **Silver Needles**
Outerwear_girl's & Children's - **Strasburg Inc.**
Outerwear_women's & Misses' - **Apparel Suppliers Ca/pagano W**
Outerwear_women's & Misses' - **Cattle Kate Inc**
Outerwear_women's & Misses' - **La Mar Mfg. Co.**
Outerwear_women's & Misses' - **Sauvage Swimwear**
Outerwear_women's & Misses' - **Silver Needles**
Outerwear_women's & Misses' - **Surf Line Hawaii, Ltd.**
Outerwear_women's & Misses' - **Hannah Katherine Fashions Corp.**
Outerwear_women's & Misses' - **Piccone Apparel Corp**
Outerwear_women's & Misses' - **R & S Sportswear Inc; Dba Filati**
Outerwear_women's & Misses' - **South Pass Trading/cnl Clothiers**
Outerwear_women's & Misses' - **Wiggy's Inc**
Outerwear_women's, Misses', and Men's - **Mary K Active Wear Inc**
Ovens - **Thermodyne Food Service Products**
Ovens - **Heller Industries**
Over Carpet & Padding, Wood Floors - **Schneider Enterprises**

Over the Counter Medications - **Apothecary Products Inc.**
Overdimensional, Overweight & Heavy Haul Transportation - **Trism Inc.**
Overhaul & Maintenance/;Aircraft - **Waltham Aircraft Clock Corp.**
Overhaul & Repair of Aircraft Gas Turbine Engines - **Premier Turbines**
Overhead Conveyor Systems - **Industrial Process Equipment**
Overhead Cranes - **Autoquip Corporation**
Overhead Cranes - **Aurora Systems, Inc.**
Overhead Ground Wire-aluminum-clad - **United States Alumoweld Co.**
Oversize Sheet Printers - **Pikes Peak Lithographing Co**
Oxide Insulated Aluminum Wire - **Pace Transducer Co**
Oxidizers - **Turner Envirologic, Inc.**
Oxygen Generating Equipment - **Pacific Consolidated Indus**
Oxygen Generators - **Ozotech Inc**
Oxygen Permeable Blanks - **Optical Polymer Research, Inc.**
Oyster Processing - **P & J Oyster Co., Inc.**
Ozonation / Equipment - **Mac Company**
Ozone-based water treatment syst. & equip MRF - **Bio Zone**
Ozone Generators - **Envirozone Systems Corp.**
Ozone Generators for Use in Bottled Water - **Ozotech Inc**
Package Sewage Treatment Plants - **Water Services International**
Package Water Treatment Plants - **Water Services International**
Packaged Frozen Foods - **Pacway Food International Corp**
Packaged Make-up Air Systems, Heating, Cooling - **Mars Air Doors**
Packaging - **United States Can Company, Custom & Specialty**
Packaging & Automated Machinery - **F W Tool & Die Works, Inc.**
Packaging & Crating - **Apollo Warehouse, Inc.**
Packaging & Die Cutting Machinery - **Hoover Machine Co., Inc.**
Packaging & Foam Supplier - **Tucson Container Corporation**
Packaging - Shrink, Blister - **Arc Industries Inc.**
Packaging Equipment - **Matrix Imaging Solution**
Packaging Equipment - **Equipment & Systems Engineering**
Packaging Equipment - **Sitma U S A, Inc.**
Packaging Equipment - **Ossid Corp.**
Packaging Mach. Coding & Printing - **Bell-mark Corp.**
Packaging Mach., Vert. Form, Fill, Seal - **Triangle Package Machinery**
Packaging Machinery - **J R C Web Accessories, Inc.**
Packaging Machinery - **All American Containers, Inc.**
Packaging Machinery - **Apax Corporation**
Packaging Machinery - **Flexicell, Inc.**
Packaging Machinery - **G E I Mateer-burt Co., Inc.**
Packaging Machinery - **Greener Corp.**
Packaging Machinery - **Hart Design & Mfg, Inc.**
Packaging Machinery - **Hoover Machine Co., Inc.**
Packaging Machinery - **Hoppmann Corporation**
Packaging Machinery - **Sitma U S A, Inc.**
Packaging Machinery - **Technaseal**
Packaging Machinery - **Tecnipac Inc**
Packaging Machinery - **De La Rue Cash Systems**
Packaging Machinery, L Sealers - **ATW Manufacturing Company**
Packaging Machinery, Secondary - **R.a. Pearson Company**
Packaging Machinery— Shrink-wrapping, Shrink - **Atw Manufacturing**
Packaging Machines - **Zmd International Inc**
Packaging Material - **Future Packaging Inc**
Packaging Material Made of Recycled Paper - **E-tech Products Inc**
Packaging Materials - **Maxport International**
Packaging Subcontractor - **All Metals Processing of Oc**
Packaging, Sorting & Labeling Equipment - **Paul Marsh, Llc**
Packaging, Sorting, Assembly-line Cutting - **Sub-con Inc**
Packing & Crating - **Central Transportation Systems**
Packing & Crating - **Overland Express Company Inc.**
Packing & Crating - **Straightway Inc.**
Packing & Crating - **Transoceanic Shipping Company, Inc.**
Packing & Crating Service - **Future Packaging Inc**
Packing & Crating, Export - **Pierce Packaging Company**
Packing & Crating, Industrial Machinery - **Jan Packaging, Inc.**
Packing & Crating, Military Specs. - **Jan Packaging, Inc.**
Packing Devices - **Pars Manufacturing Co.**
Packing Gauge, Powder Dispenser - **Support Products Inc.**
Packing Materials - **Hemisphere Enterprises**
Packing or Wrapping Machinery - **Strapack, Inc.**
Packing, Crating, Rigging, Container - **Schroeder United Van Lines**

Packing, Crating, Rigging, Shipping - **Dynamic Packing & Logistics**
Pad & Pole Mounted Three-phase Transformers - **Pauwels Transformers**
Pad Printing - **Inca Paint & Print**
Padding & Upholstery Filling, Flame Resistant - **Chestnut Ridge Foam,**
Padlock Management Systems - **Keyper Systems, Inc.**
Pads-single - **Colonial Business Forms, Inc.**
Pain Management Devices - **Microcurrent Research Inc**
Paint & Body Repair - **C & B Fosters Inc.**
Paint Applicators and Related Products - **Quali-tech Manufacturing Co**
Paint Booth Doors - **Fleming Steel Co.**
Paint Collection Media - **Western Synthetic Fiber**
Paint Finishing Machines - **Therma-tron-x Inc.**
Paint Primers & Sealers - **Zinsser & Co., Inc., William**
Paint, Glass - **Cherokee Glass & Mirrors**
Paintings - **Manic Impressions**
Paintless Dent Repair Tools, Body Shop Equipment - **Dent Tools, Inc.**
Paints - **Finishes Unlimited**
Paints & Allied Products - **L H B Industries**
Paints & Allied Products - **Alpha Coatings Inc.**
Paints & Allied Products - **Finishes Unlimited**
Paints & Allied Products - **Graham Paint & Varnish Co., Inc.**
Paints & Allied Products - **Hawthorne Paint Co., Inc.**
Paints & Allied Products - **Hunting Industrial Coatings**
Paints & Allied Products - **Kop-coat Inc**
Paints & Allied Products - **Morton International, Inc.**
Paints & Allied Products - **P R I D E Enterprises, Inc**
Paints & Allied Products - **Zinsser & Co., Inc., William**
Paints & Allied Products - **International Paint Inc.**
Paints & Allied Products; Solvents & Greases - **Products Techniques Inc**
Paints & Moisture Cure Primers - **Environmental Protective Coatings**
Paints & Varnishes - **Graham Paint & Varnish Co., Inc.**
Paints and Allied Products - **Smiland Paint Company**
Paints and Varnishes Based on Synthetic - **Traction International**
Paints, Protective Coatings & Linings - **ICI Paints International**
Paints, Varnishes & Supplies - **Ameron Intl/protective Coatings Group**
Paints, Wholesale - **Ici Paints International - Export - Licensing**
Pallet Conveyors - **Alvey, Inc.**
Pallet Racks - **Vogler Equipment**
Palletizers - **Specialty Equipment Co.**
Palletizers - **Alvey, Inc.**
Palletizers & Depalletizers - **Busse Inc. (Mfr)**
Pallets & Material Handling Containers - **Jeco Plastic Products, Inc.**
Pallets & Skids_wood - **Age Industries, Inc.**
Panelized Metal Building Systems - **Panel Built, Inc.**
Panther Custom Alloy Road Wheels & Accessories - **Prestige Auto**
Papaya (Fruta Maya) - **Roses Southwest Papers**
Paper - **American Fibre Supplies**
Paper & Paperboard, Uncoat, Rolls or Sheets - **Unisource**
Paper & non Woven Wiping Materials - **Disposable Products Company**
Paper Bags & Tissue, Napkins & Towels - **Roses Southwest Papers**
Paper Balers - **Consolidated Baling Machine Co., Inc.(Mfr)**
Paper Baling Equipment - **Harmony Enterprises, Inc. G P I**
Paper Coated & Laminated - **Green Bay Packaging, Inc.**
Paper Coated & Laminated - **Microcosm**
Paper Coated & Laminated - **Miles Label Company Inc**
Paper Coated & Laminated - **Ultratape Industries Inc**
Paper Coated & Laminated, Packaging - **Taratape**
Paper Coated & Laminated, Packaging - **Miles Label Company Inc**
Paper Coating and Laminating; - **Miles Label Company Inc**
Paper Converting Machinery - **Custom Machine Works, Inc.**
Paper Grocery & Sacks - **Duro Bag Mfg. Co.**
Paper Handled Shopping Bag - **Duro Bag Mfg. Co.**
Paper Handling Equipment - **A & B Fabrication & Repair, Inc.**
Paper Industries Machinery - **A H Lundberg Inc**
Paper Industries Machinery - **Hoover Machine Co., Inc.**
Paper Industry Machinery - **Elsner Engineering Works Inc.**
Paper Machine Approach Flow Systems - **Thermo Black Clawson Inc.**
Paper Mill Service - **Thistle Roller Co Inc**
Paper Mills - **Encore Paper Co.**
Paper Mills - **Paper Pak Products Inc**
Paper Napkins - **Marcal Paper Mills**

Paper Products - **Autron Incorporated**
Paper Recycling Equip. - **Thermo Black Clawson Inc.**
Paper Shredders - **Security Engineered Machinery Co.**
Paper Stock Preparation Equip. - **Thermo Black Clawson Inc.**
Paper Towels - **Marcal Paper Mills**
Paper and Paperboard, Coated, Impregnated - **Cominter Corp.**
Paper, Coated & Laminated - **Arlon Engineered Laminates & Coatings**
Paper, Uncoat, for Writing, Rolls; Hndmd Paper - **Unisource**
Paperboard & Pulp Processing - **International Paper Co., Texarkana Mill**
Paperboard Cards - **First Card Co.**
Paperboard Mills - **International Paper Co., Texarkana Mill**
Paperboard Products - **Rock-tenn Company**
Paperless Recorders - **Monarch International Inc. Monarch Instrument**
Parasailing, Diving Custom Boat Bldr. - **Premium Parasail Boats, Inc.**
Parker Seals, O-rings, Polypaks, Rubber Moldings - **Gulf Coast Seal, Inc.**
Parking Gates, Ticket, Coin & Token Machines - **Parking Products, Inc.**
Parking Meters - **Duncan Industries Parking Control Systems**
Parking Tickets - **Southland Printing Company, Inc.**
Particle Size Classification Equipment - **Hosokawa Micron Powder Sys**
Particle Size Reduction Equipment - **Hosokawa Micron Powder Systems**
Particle Size Standards for Calibration - **Duke Scientific Corporation**
Partitions & Fixtures, Except Wood - **Andersen Rack Systems Inc**
Partitions & Fixtures, Except Wood - **California Wire Products Corp**
Partitions & Fixtures, Except Wood - **Plastic Works Inc**
Partitions & Fixtures, Except Wood - **Rapid Rack Industries**
Partitions & Fixtures, Except Wood - **Stein Industries Co.**
Partitions & Fixtures, Wood - **Customcraft Fixtures**
Partitions & Fixtures, Wood - **Mod-tech, Inc.**
Partitions & Fixtures_wood - **Bonito Mfg.**
Partitions & Fixtures_wood - **Fine Craft Unlimited**
Partitions & Fixtures_wood - **Norco Products**
Partitions & Fixtures_wood - **Benchmark Fixture Corporation**
Partitions & Fixtures_wood - **Moultrie Post Form, Inc.**
Partitions & Fixtures_wood - **Newood Display Fixture Mfg Co**
Partitions & Fixtures_wood - **S D Modular Displays, Inc.**
Partitions & Fixtures_wood - **Spencer & Reynolds Inc**
Partitions & Fixtures_wood - **Valley Fixtures Inc**
Partitions & Fixtures_wood - **California Wire Products Corp**
Parts & Service - **Rdo Equipment Co**
Parts for Use with Spark-ignition- **Atk North America**
Parts of Airplanes, Aircrafts and Helicopters - **Kessler International Corp.**
Parts, Milk Processing Machinery - **Amtrade International, Inc.**
Party Favors - **Pressner & Co., Inc., M.**
Passenger Ferries, Conatiner Ships, Yachts - **Interdevco & Associates**
Passenger Motor Vehicles - **Rolls-royce & Bertley Motors Cars Inc.**
Passenger Motor Vehicles - **Alpine Armoring Inc.**
Passenger Motor Vehicles - **Continental Cars, Inc.**
Passenger Motor Vehicles - **Mustang Auto Sales**
Passenger Motor Vehicles - **Williams Shipping**
Passenger Vehicle / Light Truck - **Tire Group International Inc**
Passive Rf Components Dtv, Fm - **Micro Communications, Inc.**
Passives, Linegear, Headed & Cable & Transmission - **Galow Trading**
Pasta - **Carla's Pasta**
Pasta Salad Mixes - **Frontier Soups**
Patches - **Semel's Embroidery & Screen Printing, Inc.**
Patented Ro-drip & Ro-drip Xl Drip - **Roberts Irrigation Products**
Patient Carting Work Stations - **Carstens, Inc.**
Patient Charting Systems - **Carstens, Inc.**
Patient Compliance Aids - **Apothecary Products Inc.**
Patient Monitoring and Clinical In - **Spacelabs Medical Inc**
Patinas & Antiquing - **Triple S Products**
Patinted Baby Plastic Products - **Pelican Co**
Patio Doors & Skylights - **Milgard Manufacturing Co**
Patio Furniture - **Pipefine Furniture, Inc.**
Patio Furniture Fiber Fill // Sleeping Bag Fill - **Western Synthetic Fiber**
Patio Rooms, Garden Rooms and Solariums - **C-thru Industries Inc**
Patterns_industrial - **Precision Measurement Labs**
Pavement Marking Equipment & Power Broom - **M-b Cos., Inc. of W I**
Pavilions - **Vixen Hill Mfg. Co.**
Payphone Related Items - **Independent Welding Co.**
Pc Board Assembly - **Litec Inc.**

Pcb Assembly Fixtures - **Fancort Industries, Inc.**
Pcb Depaneling Machines - **Fancort Industries, Inc.**
Pcb Storage & Transport Racks - **Fancort Industries, Inc.**
Pcr Tubes, Plates, Racks - **Quality Scientific Plastics**
Peanut Blanching Equipment - **Ashton Food Machinery Co., Inc**
Peanut Butter - **Sunland, Inc.**
Peanut Butter Plant Design & Sales - **Ashton Food Machinery Co., Inc.**
Peanut Plant Design & Machinery Sales - **Ashton Food Machinery Co**
Peanut Processing - **Sunland, Inc.**
Peanuts , Not Roasted or Otherwise Cooked, Shelled - **Plato Trading**
Peanuts , Not Roasted or Otherwise Cooked, in Shell - **Plato Trading**
Pearl Foils - **Transfer Print Foils, Inc.**
Peas , Dried Shelled, Dry Beans, Sunflower Seed - **R.J. Commodities**
Peas, Dried Shelled, Including Seed - **Seedcraft**
Pedestal Sinks, marble tops & toilets - **Titon Industries, Inc.**
Peelable Wall Coatings Spray Booth - **Chemco Manufacturing Inc**
Pellet Mill Technology - **Coeur D'alene Fiber... Inc.**
Pelletized Dolomite (Fine-ground) (Bulk or Bagged) - **Ampel Corp.**
Pelletized Gypsum (Bulk or Bagged) - **Ampel Corp.**
Pelletized Limestone (Fine-ground) (Bulk or Bagged) - **Ampel Corp.**
Pendent Tube Alignment Castings - **Power & Industrial Service Corp.**
Pens & Mechanical Pencils - **Autopoint, Inc.**
Pens & Mechanical Pencils - **National Pen Corporation**
People T-shirts - **Purr-fect Growlings**
Pepper Gas - **Aero Tech Labs, Inc.**
Pepper Gas - **Aerko International**
Peppermint Oil - **Todd Co., A.m.**
Peppers - **Mount Olive Pickle Co., Inc.**
Performance Boats & Trailers - **Nordic Boats, Inc.**
Perfume - **Yaz Enterprises**
Perfume Bottle Screen Printing - **Pochet of America, Inc.**
Perfumes - **C & M Enterprises**
Perfumes & Colognes - **Regent Labs Inc.**
Perfumes, Colognes - **Waikiki Aloe Waikiki Fragrance & Cosmetic Fact**
Peridontal Health Brush - **P H B Inc.**
Periodicals - **South Pasadena Publishing Co**
Periodicals - **California Journal**
Periodicals - **Chaos Comics Inc**
Periodicals - **Elevator World**
Periodicals - **Hoffmann Pulications Dba: Blacksmith's Journal**
Periodicals - **Ranchland News**
Periodicals - **Root Co., Inc., A. I., the**
Periodicals - **Southern Calif Guide-westworld**
Periodicals - **The Practice Builder Association**
Periodicals - **The Skiing Co**
Periodicals - **Water Conditioning/purification**
Periodicals - **Academic Press**
Peripheral Control Devices Including Co - **Reliable Communications Inc**
Peripherals; Memory Upgrades - **Pdp Systems**
Permanent & Portable Tensioned - **Universal Fabric Structures, Inc.**
Permanent Magnet Motors - **Imperial Electric Co.**
Personal Care & Toilet Preparations - **Gnld International**
Personal Care Products - **Agro-mar Inc of Nevada**
Personal Care Products-**Shelton's Sheen Wave Labs Inc**
Personal Computer Towers - **Howard Industries**
Personal Grooming Products - **Lamaur**
Personal Security Devices - **Metron Solutions Inc**
Pest Control Chemicals - **Dr. T's Nature Products Inc.**
Pesto Sauces - **Carla's Pasta**
Pet Bottle Preforms - **American Fiber Industries, Llc**
Pet Bottles - **All American Containers, Inc.**
Pet First Aid Kits - **Med-ipet U S A, Inc.**
Pet Food - **Natural Life Pet Products**
Pet Monuments - **Payton Granite & Monument Co.**
Pet Products - **Steam Services Inc.**
Pet Products - **Rover Vinyl Tech Industries**
Pet Products, Pellet Grass Fiber - **Mountain Meadows Pet Products**
Pet Toys - **Hartz Mountain**
Pet and Personal Care Shampoos and Conditioners - **Kaygeeco Inc**
Petrochemicals - **Petroplast Chemical Corp.**
Petroleum - **United Farmers Co-op**

Petroleum & Coal Products - **Lehigh Coal & Navigation Co.**
Petroleum & Liquid, Vapor Conservation, Fire Prevention - **Oceco, Inc.**
Petroleum Crude Export - **Incon Overseas Marketing, Inc.**
Petroleum Hose Reels - **Coxwells, Inc., Dba Coxreels**
Petroleum Products - **Motorkote Inc**
Petroleum Products & Lab Testing - **Engineered Lubricants Co.**
Petroleum Products, Fuel Additives & Lubricants - **Bell Additives, Inc.**
Petroleum Refining - **Sunoco, Inc.**
Ph Electrodes, Meters and Controllers - **Lazar Research Laboratories**
Pharmaceutical - **Norac Co., Inc., the**
Pharmaceutical & Dental Products - **Beutlich, L.p. Pharmaceuticals**
Pharmaceutical Bags - **Caltex Plastics Inc**
Pharmaceutical Gelatin - **Nitta Gelatin**
Pharmaceutical Machinery - **Rame-hart, Inc.**
Pharmaceutical Preparations - **American Laboratories, Inc. (Mfr)**
Pharmaceutical Preparations - **Blansett Pharmacal Co.**
Pharmaceutical Preparations - **Hobart Laboratories, Inc.**
Pharmaceutical Preparations - **Neil Laboratories, Inc.**
Pharmaceutical Preparations - **Upsher-smith Laboratories, Inc.**
Pharmaceutical Preparations - **Viragen, Inc.**
Pharmaceutical Preparations - **Oralabs Holding Corp**
Pharmaceutical Preperations - **Adh Health Products Inc.**
Pharmaceutical Products, Wholesale - **Flomed Corporation**
Pharmaceutical, Edible, Photographic - **Skw Biosystems**
Pharmaceuticals - **Blansett Pharmacal Co.**
Pharmaceuticals - **Neil Laboratories, Inc.**
Pharmaceuticals - **Upsher-smith Laboratories, Inc.**
Pharmaceuticals - **Napp Technologies**
Pharmaceuticals - **Ultimate International**
Pharmaceuticals & Antacids - **Tamer International Ltd**
Pharmaceuticals - Winrho Sdf , Autoplex T, Nabi-hb - **Nabi**
Pharmaceuticals, Health & Beauty - **Arnet Pharmaceutical Corp.**
Phenol - **Sunoco, Inc.**
Pheromone Based Cosmetics - **M. C. Marble Co., Inc.**
Phones, Voice Mail, Business -**Toshiba America Informaton Systems, Inc**
Phonograph Records and Prerecorded Audio Discs - **Reference Recordings**
Phot Equip, Opaque Projectors - **Buhl Industries, Inc.**
Phot Id Sytems - **Plasco, Inc.**
Photo Equip. Overhead Projectors - **Buhl Industries, Inc.**
Photo Id Software - **Plasco, Inc.**
Photo Supplies Emulsions & Chemicals - **Chromaline Corp.**
Photo Supplies Photo Sensitive Films - **Chromaline Corp.**
Photo-radar Equipment - **American Traffic Systems Inc**
Photochemical Etching - **Precision Art Coordinators, Inc.**
Photochemical Machining - **E-fab Inc**
Photocopier Fuser Rollers - **American Custom Coatings, Inc.**
Photocopying & Duplicating Services - **Rapid Reproductions Printing**
Photocopying & Duplicating Services - **Palone & Associates**
Photodiodes - **Silicon Sensors, Llc**
Photograph Frames & Albums - **Uniek Inc.**
Photographic Equipment - **Preston Cinema Systems Inc**
Photographic Equipment & Supplies - **Daetwyler Corp., Max**
Photographic Equipment & Supplies - **Kyle Marine Products Llc**
Photographic Equipment & Supplies - **LRF Business Systems**
Photographic Equipment & Supplies - **Laser Imaging International**
Photographic Equipment & Supplies - **Nacco Grow More**
Photographic Equipment & Supplies - **Preston Cinema Systems Inc**
Photographic Equipment & Supplies - **Visual Inspection Technologies**
Photographic Equipment and Supplies - **National Research & Chemical**
Photographic Equipment, Supplies- **Lightware Inc**
Photographic Gelatin - **Nitta Gelatin**
Photographic Light Bulbs - **Bulbtronics, Inc.**
Photographic Specialties, Foliar Fertilizers - **Nacco Grow More**
Photographic and Micrografhic Equipment - **Houston Fearless 76**
Photomultiplier - **Spectral Energy Corp.**
Photon Counting Spectrofluorometers - **Iss Inc.**
Photopolymer Printing Plates - **Napp Systems Inc**
Physical Medicine - Rehabilitative Instrumentation - **Sense Technology**
Physical Testing Equipment - **Taber Industries, Inc.**
Pick-up Truck Accessories - **Go Industries, Inc.**
Pickles - **Mount Olive Pickle Co., Inc.**

Pickles - **Steinfelds Products**
Pickles & Pickle Relishes, Peppers, Cauliflower, Celery, Car - **Ripon Pickle**
Pickles & Relish & Peppers - **Chipico Pickles**
Pickles, Relish, Olives - **Dean Foods (Mfr)**
Pickles, Sauces & Relishes - **United Pickle Products Corp.**
Pickles, Sauces & Salad Dressings - **Champagne Sauces Inc.**
Pickles, Sauces & Salad Dressings - **Herlocher Foods, Inc.**
Pickles, Sauces & Salad Dressings - **Klein Pickle Company**
Pickles, Sauces & Salad Dressings - **Le Parisien Vinaigrette**
Pickles, Sauces & Salad Dressings - **Vidalia Gold Enterprizes**
Pickles, Sauces, Relishes & Dressings - **Vidalia Gold Enterprizes**
Pickling & Brining Pickles, Peppers- **United Pickle Products Corp.**
Pickling Inhibitors - **Miller Corp., Harry**
Pickling Injector/machines, Whsle - **Jaccard Corporation**
Picks, Processes Grapevine Leaves - **Yergat Packing Co**
Piece Goods & Notions - **Best Value Textiles**
Pies - **Bonert's Slice of Pie**
Piexoceramic Medical Sensors Transducers - **American Piezo Ceramics,**
Piezo Electric Actuators & Power Supplies - **Dynaoptic-motion Corp**
Piezoelectric & Ultrasonic Transducers - **Etalon Inc.**
Pig Iron - **Tata, Inc.**
Pigment Foils - **Transfer Print Foils, Inc.**
Pigments - **Organic Dyestuffs Corporation**
Pigments & Dyes - **Eastern Color & Chemical Co.**
Pillows - **Manic Impressions**
Pillows, Chair Pads, Cushions, Flame Resistant - **Chestnut Ridge Foam,**
Pillows, Golf Cart Seat Covers and Pet Beds - **Castletech Ltd**
Pilot Flush Valves & Strainers - **Hedges & Bros., L.p.**
Pilot Ground Instrument Trainers - **Frasca International, Inc.**
Pilot Plant Equipment - **Quinn Process Equipment Co**
Pinetrator Drum Punch & Sampling Systems - **Americlean, Inc.**
Pints & Cups - **Luke's Ice Cream**
Pintype & Line Post Insulators - **Porcelain Products Company(mfr)**
Pip, Jacketed - **Perma-pipe Ricwil, Industrial**
Pipe & Fittings, Fabricated - **R.c. Technical Welding & Fabricating Co.**
Pipe & Fittings-fabricated - **Sioux Chief Manufacturing Co.,Inc.**
Pipe & Fittings_fabricated - **Foster Co., L. B.**
Pipe & Fittings_fabricated - **Steel Forgings Inc.**
Pipe & Fittings_fabricated - **Klose Fabrication, Inc.**
Pipe & Fittings_fabricated Fusion Epoxy- **Int'l Fabricators & Engineers**
Pipe & Tube Cutoff Machines - **Continental Cutoff Machines**
Pipe Beveling Equipment - **Universal Manufacturing & Const. Co.**
Pipe Cutting Equipment - **Machine Tech, Inc.**
Pipe Cutting and Welding Preparation Equipment - **Tri Tool Inc**
Pipe Fittings - **Steel Forgings Inc.**
Pipe Fittings - Forged - **Texas Pmw, Inc.**
Pipe Hangers & Supports - **Phd Manufacturing, Inc.**
Pipe Hangers Supports & Fittings - **Piping Technology & Products, Inc.**
Pipe Joint Testers & Plugs for Sewers - **Anderson Seal Co., Inc.**
Pipe Markers - **Seton Name Plate Company**
Pipe Nipples - **Texas Pmw, Inc.**
Pipe Palletizing, Skids & Timbers - **Rucker Lumber Co., Inc.**
Pipe Plug - **Petersen Products Co.**
Pipe Supports - **Int'l Fabricators & Engineers**
Pipe Thread Sealants, Potable Water, Acid - **Techni-seal International**
Pipe, Carbon Steel, Fabricated Etc. - **Klm International**
Pipe, Preinsulated - **Perma-pipe Ricwil, Industrial**
Pipe, Steam Traced - **Perma-pipe Ricwil, Industrial**
Pipeline Equipment - **Perry Equipment Corp.**
Pipeline Relining Packers - **Petersen Products Co.**
Pipes - **D.b.c. Enterprises, Inc.**
Piping: Assembly - **Mohawk Mfg. Corp.**
Piping: Pressure - **Mohawk Mfg. Corp.**
Piston Engine & Pt6 Engine Instalations - **Rocky Mountain Propellers Inc**
Pita Bread - **Corfu Foods, Inc.**
Pizza Machines; Heat Transfer Machines - **Stearns Product Development**
Plant Efficiency Studies - **Control Components, Inc.**
Plant: Soil Conditioners, Cleaning - **Wachters Organic Sea Products**
Plant Growth Regulator - **Agtrol International**
Plants - **Greendale Nursery**
Plants and Parts of Plants - **Herbco International Inc.**

Plaques, Signs & Advertising Specialties - **Award Maker**
Plasma Assisted Chemical Vapor Deposition Equipment - **Axic Inc**
Plasma Etch Equipment - **Axic Inc**
Plaster of Paris Molds - **Bell Ceramics Inc. (Mfr)**
Plastering, Drywall & Insulation - **Georgetown Wire Co. K-lath Div**
Plastic & Die-cast Molds - **Universal Tooling Corp.**
Plastic & Metal Machined Parts - **Ware Shoals Plastics Inc.**
Plastic & Rubber Raw Materials - **Artemis Industries Inc.**
Plastic (Pvc) Strip Doors & Curtains - **Chase Industries, Inc.**
Plastic / General Surgery Equip: Aspirators - **Medical Device Resource**
Plastic Bags - **Caltex Plastics Inc**
Plastic Bags - **Plastic Packaging Corp.**
Plastic Bags & Film - **Mega Plastics, Inc.**
Plastic Beakers - **Cargille Laboratories, Inc.**
Plastic Blow Molding - **Promotional Trim Components**
Plastic Bottles - **Nelson Products Co.**
Plastic Bottles - **All American Containers, Inc.**
Plastic Buttons & Button Feeding Equipment - **Mc Kee Button Co.**
Plastic Cards for Access Control, Identification - **Allsafe Co., Inc.**
Plastic Caulking Cartridges & Accessories - **Fischbach U S A, Inc.**
Plastic Centrifugal Pumps - **Finish Thompson, Inc.**
Plastic Clipping - **Hutchison & Co.**
Plastic Closures - **Unimark Plastics Co.**
Plastic Coffee Carafes - **Service Ideas, Inc.**
Plastic Color Concentrates & Dry Colorants - **Universal Plastics Color**
Plastic Colorants - **Carolina Color Corp.**
Plastic Containers - **Russell-stanley Corp.**
Plastic Containers & Blow Molded Products - **Alabama Plastic Container**
Plastic Containers, Blow Molded Parts - **N. E. W. Plastics Corp.**
Plastic Corrugated Returnable Containers - **Advanced Package Engineerin**
Plastic Diffusers, Lenses & Louvers - **A.l.p. Lighting Components, Inc.**
Plastic Equipment Magazine - **Heartland Communications Group Inc.**
Plastic Extruded Tubing & Profiles - **Custom Extrusions & Molding Inc**
Plastic Extrusion Dies - **Akron Tool & Die Co., Inc.**
Plastic Extrusion Equipment & Printers - **Geochem International**
Plastic Extrusion Injection Molding, Pvc - **Available Plastics, Inc.**
Plastic Extrusion Manufacturer - **Intek Plastics, Inc.**
Plastic Extrusions - **Bromley Plastics Corp.**
Plastic Extrusions - **Vinylex Corp.**
Plastic Extrusions & Compounding - **Superior American Plastics, Inc.**
Plastic Fabrication & Molding - **T S I Plastics**
Plastic Film - **Flagship Converters, Inc.**
Plastic Film Converting & Sausage Casing Aluminum Tab - **Hutchison &**
Plastic Foam Products - **Commodore Machine Co.**
Plastic Foam Products - **Creative Arts**
Plastic Foam Products - **Davis Co., E. J.**
Plastic Foam Products - **Hunt-wilde Corp.**
Plastic Foam Products - **I P I International**
Plastic Foam Products - **Mizell Brothers Company**
Plastic Foam Products - **Pantos Corp**
Plastic Foam Products - **Rogers Corporation**
Plastic Foot Valves & Check Valves - **Brady Products Inc.**
Plastic Forming - **Zmd International Inc**
Plastic Garment Hangers - **Batts Inc.**
Plastic Gate Valves & Fittings for Industrial - **Valterra Products**
Plastic Housewares - **Hutzler Mfg. Co., Inc.**
Plastic Injection Molded Products - **Custom Extrusions & Molding Inc**
Plastic Injection Molding - **American Fiber Industries, Llc**
Plastic Injection Molding - **Eclipse Mfg. Co.**
Plastic Injection Molding - **J-mac Plastics Inc.**
Plastic Injection Molding - **Meridian Products Corp.**
Plastic Injection Molding - **Unimark Plastics Co.**
Plastic Injection Molding - **Mid-south Electronics-alabama, Inc.**
Plastic Injection Molding and Mold Making - **Rodak Plastics Co., Inc.**
Plastic Injection Molding, Hot Stamping - **Retlaw Tools & Plastics Co.,**
Plastic Injection Molding, Hot Stamping - **Plastic Injection Molders Inc.**
Plastic Injection Molds - **Omega Plastics, Inc.**
Plastic Injection Products - **Lane-merritt Float Co**
Plastic Insert Molding - **Delta Machine & Tool, Inc.**
Plastic Jewelry Cards - **First Card Co.**
Plastic Laminate Office Furniture - **All Craft Fabricators, Inc.**

Plastic Laminated Countertops & - **Hartson Kennedy Cabinet Top Co.**
Plastic Landfill Lining Materials - **National Seal Co.**
Plastic Liners - **Gse Lining Technology, Inc.**
Plastic Literature Shelves for Floor & Wall - **Gould Plastics, Inc.**
Plastic Macrobins - **Macro Plastics Inc**
Plastic Manhole Forms & Plastic - **Improved Construction Methods**
Plastic Materials - **Rogers Corporation**
Plastic Materials & Basic Shapes - **Apd**
Plastic Materials & Resins - **BJB Enterprises Inc**
Plastic Materials & Resins - **Dura Temp Corp.**
Plastic Materials & Resins - **Environmental Soil Systems Inc**
Plastic Materials & Resins - **Fusion Coatings Inc.**
Plastic Materials & Resins - **T M P Technologies, Inc.**
Plastic Mats & Floor Runners Beverage Containers - **Robbins Corp. E.s.**
Plastic Measuring Canisters - **Robbins Corp. E.s.**
Plastic Molded Tool Storage Products, Tool Trolleys - **Waterloo Industries,**
Plastic Molding Machinery - **F S P Machinery**
Plastic Molds: Injection & Structural Foam - **A-1 Tool**
Plastic Nursery Containers - **Stuewe and Sons, Inc.**
Plastic Nursery Containers, Wholesale - **Stuewe and Sons, Inc.**
Plastic Optical Lenses - **Coastal Vision Center**
Plastic Packaging Products - **Alga Plastics Co.**
Plastic Pipe - **Bowsmith Inc**
Plastic Pipe (Pvc) - **Plastinetics, Inc.**
Plastic Pipe Fittings & Valves - **Plastinetics, Inc.**
Plastic Pipe, Conduit, Pvc - **Available Plastics, Inc.**
Plastic Pipe, Irrigation, Pvc - **Available Plastics, Inc.**
Plastic Pipe, Water Well, Pvc - **Available Plastics, Inc.**
Plastic Printing - **National Plastic Printing, Inc.**
Plastic Products - **Acme Plastic Products Company**
Plastic Products - **Advanced Package Engineering Inc**
Plastic Products - **Afton Plastics**
Plastic Products - **Airglas Engineering Co., Inc.**
Plastic Products - **Ama Plastics**
Plastic Products - **American Fiber Industries, Llc**
Plastic Products - **Andrew M Martin Company Inc**
Plastic Products - **Blackburn Mfg. Co.**
Plastic Products - **Blue Atlantic, Ltd.**
Plastic Products - **Carlisle Foodservice Products**
Plastic Products - **Compu Cover**
Plastic Products - **Creative Plastics Printing Die**
Plastic Products - **D G P Inc.**
Plastic Products - **Delta Machine & Tool, Inc.**
Plastic Products - **East Iowa Plastics, Inc.**
Plastic Products - **Eclipse Mfg. Co.**
Plastic Products - **Embry Engineering & Mfg**
Plastic Products - **First State Map & Globe Co., Inc.**
Plastic Products - **Hh Ele Corporation**
Plastic Products - **Hope Industries**
Plastic Products - **Hunt-wilde Corp.**
Plastic Products - **Hutzler Mfg. Co., Inc.**
Plastic Products - **J-mac Plastics Inc.**
Plastic Products - **John N Hansen Co Inc**
Plastic Products - **Kemlite**
Plastic Products - **Kirkhill Rubber Co**
Plastic Products - **Land and Sky Mfg., Inc.**
Plastic Products - **Lockwood Industries Inc**
Plastic Products - **M & E Mfg. Co.**
Plastic Products - **Macro Plastics Inc**
Plastic Products - **Maine Plastics Inc.**
Plastic Products - **Meridian Products Corp.**
Plastic Products - **N. E. W. Plastics Corp.**
Plastic Products- **National Pen Corporation**
Plastic Products - **Nylacarb Corp.**
Plastic Products - **Pantos Corp**
Plastic Products - **Paraflex Industries, Inc.**
Plastic Products - **Pcie Dba; the France Group**
Plastic Products - **Plastic Injection Molders Inc.**
Plastic Products - **Plastic Works Inc**
Plastic Products - **Plastics Design & Manufacturing**
Plastic Products - **Poly Conversions Inc.**

Plastic Products - **Pupi Enterprises LLC**
Plastic Products - **Quaker Plastic Corp.**
Plastic Products - **R. P. Creations, Inc.**
Plastic Products - **Reflexite Corp.**
Plastic Products - **Reliable Plastics Seals, Inc.**
Plastic Products - **Retlaw Tools & Plastics Co., Inc.**
Plastic Products - **Rhino Linings Usa Inc**
Plastic Products - **Robbins Industries Inc.**
Plastic Products - **Rodak Plastics Co., Inc.**
Plastic Products - **Russell-stanley Corp.**
Plastic Products - **Spradling Originals Inc.**
Plastic Products - **Sterling International Inc**
Plastic Products - **Tinby, Llc**
Plastic Products - **Tucson Industrial Plastics**
Plastic Products - **U.s. Farathane Corp.**
Plastic Products - **Valley View Industries**
Plastic Products - **Vaupell Industrial Plastics Inc**
Plastic Products - **Vi-cas Mfg. Co., Inc.**
Plastic Products - **Vinylex Corp.**
Plastic Products - **Wescosa Inc**
Plastic Products - **Window Products Inc**
Plastic Products (Rings) - **Mc Kee Button Co.**
Plastic Products Fiberoptic Cladding Polymers - **Optical Polymer Researc**
Plastic Products and Plastic Milit - **Mil Bar Plastics Co**
Plastic Products for Cars & Office - **Laser Creations Inc.**
Plastic Products, Insulating Basket Liners- **Plastic Techniques, Inc.**
Plastic Products, Screw Machine Parts, Cold Headed Parts - **Dimco-gray**
Plastic Products, Tool & Die, Metal Stamping - **Mil Bar Plastics Co**
Plastic Products; Plastic Injection Molding - **Acme Plastic Products Co**
Plastic Products; Plastic Injection Molding - **Ama Plastics**
Plastic Profile Shapes, Unsupported - **Bromley Plastics Corp.**
Plastic Profile Shapes_unsupported - **BJB Enterprises Inc**
Plastic Profile Shapes_unsupported - **Superior American Plastics, Inc.**
Plastic Profile Shapes_unsupported - **Tulox Plastics Corp.**
Plastic Profile Shapes_unsupported - **Afton Plastics**
Plastic Profile Shapes_unsupported - **Hunt-wilde Corp.**
Plastic Promotional Products - **Jayline International Corp.**
Plastic Recycling - **Maine Plastics Inc.**
Plastic Sheet Film - **Watersaver International**
Plastic Sheet, Rod & Tube - **Enflo Corp.**
Plastic Sheets & Strips - **Robbins Corp. E.s.**
Plastic Shower Curtains - **Hospi-tel Manufacturing Co.**
Plastic Steel Manhole Steps - **Anderson Seal Co., Inc.**
Plastic Stencils for Crafts & Quilting - **Stensource International Inc**
Plastic Storage Bins - **Gould Plastics, Inc.**
Plastic Thermoforming - **Quaker Plastic Corp.**
Plastic Tubing Coiling Twist Tie Ribbon - **Alcar Industries, Inc.**
Plastic Vacumming - **Promotional Trim Components**
Plastic Weathersealing Products for Windows & Doors - **Intek Plastics, Inc.**
Plastic Window Screen - **Hanover Wire Cloth**
Plasticizers, Synthetic Organic - **C.p. Hall Company, the (Mfr)**
Plastics - **Lamons Power Engineering**
Plastics Injection & Extruder Barrel Insulation - **Insul-vest, Inc.**
Plastics Joining & Precision Cleaning Eqipment - **Branson Ultrasonics**
Plastics Materials and Resins - **Albis**
Plastics Materials and Resins - **Cyro Industries**
Plastics Materials and Resins - **Fici Export**
Plastics Materials and Resins - **Philadelphia Resins**
Plastics Pipe - **Centron International Inc.**
Plastics Products, Nec - **Gilman Brothers**
Plastics Products, Nec - **Glassmaster**
Plastics Products, Nec - **S.k. Plastics**
Plastics Products, Nec - **Traex**
Plastics in General - Thermoplastics, Ldpe, Hdpe, - **Velco Chemicals**
Plastics, Polyethylene Sheet - **Laminations Inc.**
Plastics, Vacuum Forming - **Plastic Development Company(mfr)**
Plate Work Insulated Storage Tanks - **Lochinvar Water Heater**
Plate Work, Fabricated (Boiler Shops) - **Wilson & Co., Inc., Thomas C.**
Plate Work_fabricated (Boiler Shops) - **Schuff Steel Company**
Plate Work_fabricated (Boiler Shops) - **Gas Liquids Recovery Corp.**
Plate Work_fabricated (Boiler Shops) - **Isom Brothers Inc**

Plate Work_fabricated (Boiler Shops) - **Jerryco Machine & Boilerworks**
Plate Work_fabricated (Boiler Shops) - **Superb Marine & Industrial Svcs**
Plate Work_fabricated (Boiler Shops) - **Tigert Co., T. F.**
Plate Work_fabricated (Boiler Shops) - **Weben-jarco, Inc.**
Plate Work_fabricated (Boiler Shops) - **Stearns Product Development**
Plate Work_fabricated (Boiler Shops) Asme - **Ability Engineering Techno**
Platemaking Chemicals - **Ano-coil Corp.**
Platemaking Machinery - **Ano-coil Corp.**
Platemaking Services - **Gonzalez Integrated Marketing**
Platemaking Services - **Iridio**
Platemaking Services - **Napp Systems Inc**
Plates, Sheets, Film, Foil & Strip of Plastic - **Daiei Papers U.SA. Corp.**
Plates, Sheets, Film, Foil and Strip of Plastics - **T-systems International,**
Plates, Sheets, Film, Foil and Strip of Plastics - **Pexim International**
Plates, Sheets, Film, Foil and Strip of Plastics - **Gti Industries, Inc.**
Plates, Sheets, Film, Foil and Strip of Plastics - **Gilman Brothers**
Plates, Sheets, Film, Foil, Tape - **Broward & Johnson**
Plates, Sheets, Film, Foil, Tape and Other Flat Shapes - **Gti Industries, Inc.**
Platform Fabrication & Installation - **J.ray Mcdemott, Inc.**
Plating & Anodizing - **Ara Automated Finishing**
Plating & Polishing - **Coopers & Clarke, Inc.**
Plating & Polishing - **All Metals Processing of Oc**
Plating & Polishing - **Anniston Plating & Metal Finishing, Inc.**
Plating & Polishing - **Barsallo Deburring**
Plating & Polishing - **Chrome Crankshaft Co**
Plating & Polishing - **Diversified Coatings, Inc.**
Plating & Polishing - **Dv Industries Inc**
Plating & Polishing - **Electrochem**
Plating & Polishing - **Metal Finishing Technologies, Inc.**
Plating & Polishing - **Nu-metal Finishing Inc**
Plating & Polishing - **Sav-on Plating/powder Coating**
Plating & Polishing - **Sifco Selective Plating**
Plating & Polishing - **Tri-county Hard Chrome, Inc.**
Plating & Polishing - **Ultra Plating Corp.**
Plating & Polishing Passivate, Zinc Nickel - **All Metals Processing Co Inc**
Plating & Polishing, Grinding I.d. & O.d. - **Dixie Electro Plating Co., Inc.**
Plating Services—black Oxide - **All Metals Processing Co Inc**
Plating of Zinc, Brass, Copper, Bronze - **Sav-on Plating/powder Coating**
Play Rugs for Use with Toy Horses - **Erin's Original Horseplay Rugs**
Playground & Recreational Equipment - **B C I Burke Co., Llc**
Playground Equipment - **Kompan Inc**
Playground Equipment - **Bci Burke Co., Inc.**
Playing Cards - **Hoyle Products**
Playing Cards, Tarot Decks & Games - **U S Game Systems, Inc.**
Plc Controlled Mixing & Blending Systems - **Sonic Corp.**
Plc's & Electrical, Pneumatic - **Southwestern Automation Systems, Inc.**
Pleated Ties - **Duron Neckwear Inc**
Pleating & Stitching - **Embroidertex West Ltd**
Pleating & Stitching - **Scarsdale Quilting Converting Corp., Inc.**
Pleating & Stitching - **Semel's Embroidery & Screen Printing, Inc.**
Pleating & Stitching - **Arrow Creative International, Ltd.**
Pleating & Stitching - **Sloan & Assocs. Inc., Leonard**
Plug Valve Actuators - **Flo-tork Inc. (Mfr)**
Plug Valves - **Tyco Valves & Controls**
Plumbing & Heating Equip. Wholesale - **Orgill Inc.**
Plumbing & Heating Products - **Conbraco Industries, Inc.**
Plumbing & Heating Products - **Conbraco Industries**
Plumbing Chemical Specialties - **Radiator Specialty Co.**
Plumbing Fixture Fittings & Trim - **Franklin Brass Manufacturing**
Plumbing Fixture Fittings & Trim - **Chronomite Labs Inc**
Plumbing Fixture Fittings & Trim - **Interbath, Inc**
Plumbing Fixture Fittings & Trim - **Plumb Shop**
Plumbing Fixture Fittings & Plastic Plumbing -**Frugal Water Corporation**
Plumbing Fixture Fittings and Trim - **Conbraco Industries**
Plumbing Fixture Fittings and Trim - **Delta Faucet**
Plumbing Fixtures, Vitreous - **Mansfield Plumbing Products, Inc.,**
Plumbing Hardware. - **Progressive Metal Forming Inc.**
Plumbing Materials - **Bifrost**
Plumbing Products - **Jay R. Smith Mfg. Co.**
Plumbing Valves Call Butterfly Check - **Top Line Process Equipment Co.**
Plumbing, Heating, Air-conditioning - **Morrison Construction Service**

Plush / Berme Dolls - **Interpretive Marketing Products**
Plush Toys - **Transworld Plush Toys, Inc.**
Plywood - **Summit Sales & Marketing**
Plywood Reels - **Baker Div. Sonoco Products Company**
Plywood, Veneered Panels & Similar Laminated Wood - **Timber Products**
Pneumatic & Electric Actuators - **Conbraco Industries, Inc.**
Pneumatic & Electric Actuators - **Conbraco Industries**
Pneumatic & Mechanical Chucks & Shafts - **J R C Web Accessories, Inc.**
Pneumatic & Roll Markers - **Atomco Corporation ,**
Pneumatic Chisels, Hammer Accessories - **Ajax Tool Works, Inc.**
Pneumatic Conveying Systems - **J D B Dense Flow, Inc.**
Pneumatic Conveyor Systems - **Smoot Co.**
Pneumatic Conveyor Systems & Components - **Chicago Conveyor Corp.**
Pneumatic Cylinders - **Hydro-line Inc. Division of Imc, Inc.**
Pneumatic Demolition Tools:Construction - **American Pneumatic Tool**
Pneumatic Elevators and Conveyors - **Dynamic Air Inc.**
Pneumatic Grain Conveyors - **Neuero Corp.**
Pneumatic Hand Tools - **Muller Studios**
Pneumatic Hose & Fittings - **Catching Fluidpower, Inc.**
Pneumatic Leak Testing Equipment - **Cincinnati Test Systems, Inc.**
Pneumatic Personnel Lifts & Hazardous Location Lighting - **L P I, Inc.**
Pneumatic Tools - **Wilson & Co., Inc., Thomas C.**
Pneumatic Tools Aerospace Drilling & Fastening - **United Air Tool,**
Pneumatic/electric Pressure Switches - **Tridelta Industries Inc.**
Point-of-purchase Displays - **M M I Display Group, Inc.**
Point-of-sale Equipment for the Fast Food - **Frontline Systems**
Polarimeters, Laboratory Instruments - **Rudolph Instruments, Inc.**
Polariscopes - **Rudolph Instruments, Inc.**
Pole Banners, Flags, Flagpoles - **A Fifty Star Flags, Banners & Flagpoles**
Police & Military Equipment - **J.m.s. Ltd**
Polishes & Sanitation Goods - **Dynamic Research Co Inc**
Polishes & Sanitation Goods - **Pecard Leather Care Products**
Polishes & Sanitation Goods - **Soq Environmental Tech Corp**
Polishes & Sanitation Goods - **B-d Chemical Co Inc**
Political Buttons - **Tecre Co., Inc.**
Pollution Control Equipment - **Basic Concepts Inc.**
Pollution Control Equipment - **Oceanside Engineering & Mfg**
Pollution Control Systems - **Ship & Shore a Subsidary of C.d.i.**
Poly-fiber Reels - **Baker Div. Sonoco Products Company**
Polyacetal Synthetic Resins - **Polymer Trading Services Limited**
Polyaluminum Chloride - **Geo Specialty Chemicals, Inc.**
Polyamid Resins - **Polymer Trading Services Limited**
Polycarbonate Lenses - **U.s. Safety**
Polycarbonate Resins - **Polymer Trading Services Limited**
Polyclonal Antibodies - **Midland Bioproducts Corp.**
Polyester - Cotton Yarns, Open-end - **Cheraw Yarn Mills Inc.**
Polyester Core Thread - **American & Efird, Inc.**
Polyester Cubicle Curtains - **Hospi-tel Manufacturing Co.**
Polyester Thread - **American & Efird, Inc.**
Polyester Thread - **Robison-anton Textile Company (Mfr)**
Polyester for Sofas - **Western Synthetic Fiber**
Polyester, Tgic, Polyurethane, Epoxy, Hybrid, Pvc - **Americoat Corp.**
Polyethylene Geomembrane Liners - **Poly-flex Inc.**
Polyethylene Scrap - **Pexim International**
Polyethylne Ball Valves - **Nordstrom Valves, Inc.**
Polyimide Foam - **Davis Co., E. J.**
Polymer Cabinet & Furniture Components - **Marley Mouldings Inc.(Mfr)**
Polymer Concrete & Sealants - **Transpo Indsutries, Inc.**
Polymer Drywall Accessories - **Marley Mouldings Inc.(Mfr)**
Polymer Floor, Coatings & Lining System - **Stonhard Inc.**
Polymer Picture Frame Moldings, Hot Stamped, - **Marley Mouldings**
Polymer Siding & Panel Accessories - **Marley Mouldings Inc.(Mfr)**
Polymer Window & Door Components & Systems - **Marley Mouldings**
Polymer-based Absorbent Products for Source - **Abtech Industries Inc.**
Polymers - **National Alum Corp.**
Polymers of Ethylene, in Primary Forms - **T-systems International, Inc.**
Polyolefin Upholstery Fabrics - **Absecon Mills, Inc.**
Polyoletins - **Union Carbide Corporation**
Polypropylene - **Saunders Thread Co., Inc.**
Polypropylene Compounds - Tale /Caco3 - **Bromley Plastics Corp.**
Polypropylene Retort Divider Sheets - **Remco Products Corp.**

Polypropylene Semi-bulk Bags - **Intertape Polymer**
Polypropylene, in Primary Forms - **Strapack, Inc.**
Polystyrene - **Geochem International**
Polystyrene Foam - **Commodore Machine Co.**
Polysulfides, Polysulfones, and Synthetic Polymers - **Albis**
Polysulfides, Polysulfones, and Synthetic Polymers - **Fici Export**
Polysulfides, Polysulfones, and Synthetic Polymers - **Elf**
Polyurethane Coating Compounds - **Soluol Chemical Co., Inc.**
Polyurethane Foam - **Henry Company International**
Polyurethane Foam, Molded Rubber & Polyesters - **T M P Technologies**
Polyurethane Grouts - **Polygem**
Polyurethane Indoor/outdoor Containers - Natural Line - **Div of Ccc**
Polyurethane Parts for Industry - **Western Roller Corporation**
Polyurethane Picture Frames, Plaques - **Alfred's Pictures Frames Inc**
Polyurethane Products, Cast, Thermoset - **C.u.e., Inc. (Mfr)**
Polyurethane Reproductions of Stone & Wood - **Alfred's Pictures Frames**
Polyurethane Rollers - **Tinby, Llc**
Polyurethane Screens - **Tema Isenmann, Inc.**
Polyurethane Spray Sytems - **Rhino Linings Usa Inc**
Polyurethane Statues, Urns & Pots - **Natural Line**
Polyvinyl Animal Cages and Hammocks - **Rover Vinyl Tech Industries**
Polyvinyl Chloride Resins - **Petroplast Chemical Corp.**
Pond & Water Garden Products - **Henri Studio Inc.**
Pool Chiller - **Air Energy Heat Pumps**
Pool-krete Premix for Swimming Pool Base - **Stronglite Products**
Pools & Spas & Saunas - **Q C a Pools & Spas**
Popcorn - **T. Miller Popcorn Company Inc.(Mfr)**
Popcorn Equipment & Machines - **Proctor Companies**
Popcorn Poppers, Nacho Warmers, Popcorn Warmers - **Stein Industries**
Popcorn Products - **Vogel Popcorn**
Popcorn, Confections & Fudge - **Kornfections & Treasures**
Popcorn, Raw Unpopped, Commercial - **K & W Popcorn Inc. (Mfr)**
Popcorn, Safflower, Organics, Lentils, Flax, Canola - **R.j. Commodities**
Popcorn/seasoning - **T. Miller Popcorn Company Inc.(Mfr)**
Popcorn; Raw, Microwave & Pre-popped - **Noble Popcorn Farms**
Populate Printed Circuit Boards - **Sierra Electronic Assembly**
Porcelain & Stoneware Slips - **Seeley's Ceramic Service, Inc.**
Porcelain Casting Clays & Ceramic Supplies - **Bell Ceramics Inc. (Mfr)**
Porcelain Doll Making Books - **Seeley's Ceramic Service, Inc.**
Porcelain Insulators, High Voltage - **Newell Porcelain Company, Inc.**
Porcelain Monument Portraits - **Dedouch Co. Studios, J. A.**
Porcelain Pin Type Insulator & Line Posts - **Newell Porcelain Company**
Port Agency - **Transmarine Navigation Corporation**
Port, Dry Cell, Rechargable and Disposable Batte - **Energy Sales**
Portable & Modular Displays, Exhibits- **Expo Displays**
Portable A/c Systems - **Compu-aire, Inc.**
Portable Air Separation Equipment - **Pacific Consolidated Indus**
Portable Baseball Mounds & Mound Materials - **True Pitch, Inc.**
Portable Bridges - **Evans Mfg. Co., John Evans Trailers**
Portable Clean Rooms & Components - **Airo Clean, Inc.**
Portable Corrals, Squeeze Chute, Calf Tables, Headgate - **Priefert Mfg. Co.**
Portable Dehumidifiers - **Oasis Corporation**
Portable Generators & Pumps - **Alamia Inc**
Portable Ground Fault Circuit Interrupters - **Technology Research Corp**
Portable Hand Lamps - **Ericson Manufacturing, Inc.**
Portable Inplace Machining - **Field Equipment & Service Co.**
Portable Milking Machines - **Coburn Company, Inc.**
Portable Navigation Lights - **Aqua Signal Corp.**
Portable Parts & Accessories - **Portadrill Corp.**
Portable Pipe Cutting Equip. - **Machine Tech, Inc.**
Portable Soccer Goals - **Goal Oriented Inc**
Portable Truck & Aircraft Weigh Scales - **General Electrodynamics Corp.**
Portable Water Purification - **Springsoft International Inc.**
Portion Control Dairy & Food Packaging Machinery - **Autoprod Inc.**
Posters - **National Art Publishing Corp.**
Potato Products , Refrigerated Potato Products - **Northern Star Co., Inc.**
Potatoes, Avocados, Kiwi, Tree Fruit - **Exeter Engineering Inc**
Potatoes, Dehydrated - **Idaho Frank Association**
Potentionmerters & Electronic Devices - **Betatronix, Inc.**
Pothole Repair Truck, Construction Equipment - **Wildcat Mfg. Co., Inc.**
Potpourri (Scent Filled Packets) - **Page Seed Co., Inc.**

Potting - Sierra Electronic Assembly
Poultry Breedin - Tatum Farms International, Inc.
Poultry By-product Meal - Darling International Inc.
Poultry Feeds - Tatum Farms International, Inc.
Poultry Futher Processor - All-states Quality Foods L.p.
Poultry Hatch - Tatum Farms International, Inc.
Poultry House Clean-out Equipment - Kelley Mfg. Co.
Poultry Incubators - Chick Master International, Inc.
Poultry Slaughtering & Processing - Aspen Foods
Poultry Slaughtering & Processing - Sanderson Farms Inc.
Poultry Slaughtering & Processing - Wampler Foods, Inc.
Poultry Slaughtering and Processing - Culver Duck Farms
Poultry-keeping Machinery - Chick Master International, Inc.
Pound Cake - Neuman Bakery Specialties, Inc.
Powder Coat Painting - Kurt Manufacturing Co.
Powder Coating - All Metals Processing of Oc
Powder Coating & Precision Machining - Pyramid Machine & Tool, Inc.
Powder Coating Ovens - F S P Machinery
Powder Coating Replacement Cartridges - Chemco Manufacturing Inc
Powder Coating Systems - Industrial Process Equipment
Powder Coating for Corrosion Protection - Cal-coat Corp.
Powder Coating: Baked On - Americoat Corp.
Powder Coatings, Electrostatic Fushion Bonded - Mpc International Llc
Powdered Beverage Mixes, Cappuccino - Cocoa - Flavor Dynamics, Inc.
Powdered Cappuccino & Hot Chocolate - Cappuccino America Corp.
Powdered Metal Bearings & Structural Parts - Dynametal Technologies
Powdered Metal Parts - Windfall Products, Inc.
Powdered Vegetable Shortening - Diehl, Inc.
Power & Control Cable Nonferrous - Rockbestos Surprenant Cable Corp.
Power & Hand Tools for Glass - C.r. Laurence Company, Inc.
Power & Signal Card Assemblies - Electronic Manufacturing Svc
Power Actuators, Pneumatic - Flo-tork Inc. (Mfr)
Power Amplifiers - Talla-com, Tallahassee Communications Industries
Power Circuit Breakers- Sf6 - Mitsubishi Electric Power Products, Inc.
Power Conditioning & Distribution Equipment - Liebert Corporation
Power Contrast Injectors for Ct, Angiography & Mr - Liebel-flarsheim
Power Driven Hand Tools, Air - Zephyr Manufacturing Co. Inc.
Power Generating Plants - Msi International
Power Hand Tools - Amkus, Inc.
Power Handtools Retubing Tools - Elliot Tool Technologies, Ltd.
Power Handtools Tube Expanders - Elliot Tool Technologies, Ltd.
Power Inverters - Exeltech
Power Plant Thermal Performance - Exergetic Systems Inc
Power Presses & Related Equipment - Perfection Machinery
Power Protection Equipments - Schweitzer Engineering Labs Inc.
Power Quality - Wiremold Co., the
Power Quality Monitors, Hv. - Ross Engineering Corp.
Power Semiconductors Mosfets, Igbts - Advanced Power Technology Inc
Power Supplies - Mg Electronics
Power Switches & Yard Control Signals - Railroad Signal, Inc.
Power System Analyzers - Arbiter Systems Inc
Power Transformer Valves - T.j. Manufacturing, Inc.
Power Transmission Equipment - Oilpure Refiner Co
Power Transmission Equipment - American Sleeve Bearing, Llc
Power Transmission Equipment - Dana Corp./wichita Clutch Co.
Power-driven Handtools - Platt Electric Supply
Power-driven Handtools - Precision Products Co
Pratt & Whitney Canada Aircraft Engines & Parts - Covington Aircraft
Pratt & Whitney Jet Engine Service Tools - Cambridge Specialty Co., Inc.
Prawn Traps - Fathoms plus
Pre-clinical, Medical Research - Micro-med, Inc.
Pre-engineered Metal Buildings, Wholesale - A.g. Equipment, Inc.
Pre-engineered Steel Buildings - Don Hurst Enterprises
Pre-engineered Wood Buildings - Wick Buildings
Pre-inked Stamps - Qwikstamp Corporation
Pre-packaged Hot Water Systems - Weben-jarco, Inc.
Pre-press - Gonzalez Integrated Marketing
Pre-press Equipment - Daetwyler Corp., Max
Pre-press Equipment Offset Applications - Nu Arc Co., Inc.
Pre-press Equipment Screen Printing Applications - Nu Arc Co., Inc.
Precast Industries - Le Sueur Mfg. Co.

Precious Metal & Costume Jewelry - Olympia Gold Inc.
Precious Metal Consulting - Republic Metals Corp.
Precious Metal Earrings - Sardelli & Sons, Inc., T.
Precious Metal Indicators - Prospector & Treasure Hunters Hdqters
Precious Metal Inlays - Polymetallurgical Corp.
Precious Plating Solutions - Cohler Enterprises
Precision & Production Machining - Cherokee Industries, Inc.
Precision Air Conditioning & Environmental - Liebert Corporation
Precision Carbide & Steel Stamping Dies - Oberg Mfg. Co.
Precision Cleaning - C. H. Hyperbarics, Inc.
Precision Cnc Machine Parts - Bob Lewis Machine Co., Inc.
Precision Cnc Machinery - Willis Machine Inc
Precision Cnc Machining - Brenner Tool & Die, Inc.
Precision Cnc Machining of Aircraft - Fay & Quartermaine Machining
Precision Granite Machine Bases & - Tru-stone Corp.
Precision Instruments, Rotary Transformers, - Himmelstein & Co., S.
Precision Machine Products - Zenith Screw Products Inc
Precision Machine Shop - Wieland Precision Machine
Precision Machine Shop, Rubber Molds - Jd Tool & Machine Co Inc
Precision Machine Tools - Richmill Usa Inc
Precision Machine Turned Parts - A. Berger, Inc.
Precision Machined Night Vision - Norotos Inc
Precision Machined Parts - Luna Defense Systems Inc
Precision Machining - Kurt Manufacturing Co.
Precision Machining - Kovil Manufacturing Llc
Precision Machining & Assembly for Medical - Daco Enterprises Inc
Precision Machining (Job-shop) Prototypes - Finn Tool & Instruments Inc
Precision Machining Job Shop - Elite Mfg. Corp.
Precision Machining Job Shop - A-1 Machining Co.
Precision Machining Job Shop - Aurora Custom Machining
Precision Machining Job Shop - Sun Country Industries Inc.
Precision Machining for the Aerospace - Integrity Manufacturing Co
Precision Measuring Instruments & Optical Components - Zygo Corp.
Precision Metal Fabrication; Slot Machine Manufacture - Aerofab Inc
Precision Metal Reflectors - Opti-forms Inc
Precision Micro-irrigation Produc - Netafim Irrigation Inc
Precision Non-metallic Gaskets and Washers - Bentley Manufacturing Co
Precision Parts - Accurite Development & Mfg
Precision Positioners - Dynaoptic-motion Corporation
Precision Sheet Metal & Enclosures - Fab Industries Inc
Precision Sheet Metal Fabrication - Camcorp Industries
Precision Sheet Metal Fabrications - Pyramid Machine & Tool, Inc.
Precision Sheet Metal, Welding, Metal Stampings - Cannon Industries
Precision Shop Accessories - Finn Tool & Instruments Inc
Precision Stampings & Sheet Metal Assemblies - Schulze Manufacturing
Precision Tool & Die Shop - Pennsylvania Tool & Gages, Inc.
Precision Tooling & Dies - Mc Kee Carbide Tool Co.
Precision Tools for Tube & Pipe Bending Machine - Tools for Bending,
Precision Wire Forms, Leads, Pins- Form Cut Industries, Inc.
Precut Log Home Packages - Appalachian Log Structures Inc.
Predictive Maintenance Data Collector (Dc+3) - Vitec, Inc.
Predictive Maintenance Software (Ep) - Vitec, Inc.
Prefab, Wood Dock Seals & Shelters - Chase Industries, Inc.
Prefabricated Buildings - Porta-Fab Corp.
Prefabricated Greenhouses & Horticultural - Gothic Arch Greenhouses, I
Prefabricated Log Buildings - Oregon Log Home Co Inc
Prefabricated Metal Buildings - Behlen Mfg. Co.
Prefabricated Metal Buildings - C-thru Industries Inc
Prefabricated Metal Buildings - Cover-it Shelters, Inc.
Prefabricated Metal Buildings - Custom Modular Solutions
Prefabricated Metal Buildings - Don Hurst Enterprises
Prefabricated Metal Buildings - Hexaport International, Ltd.
Prefabricated Metal Buildings - Joaquin Manufacturing Corp
Prefabricated Metal Buildings - Mcalpine & Salyer Construction
Prefabricated Portable Shelters, Instant Garages - Cover-it Shelters, Inc.
Prefabricated Wood Buildings - Appalachian Log Structures Inc.
Prefabricated Wood Buildings - Custom Modular Solutions
Prefabricated Wood Buildings - Greco Homes
Prefabricated Wood Buildings - Joaquin Manufacturing Corp
Prefabricated Wood Buildings - Northwest Cedar Inc
Prefabricated Wood Buildings - Oregon Log Home Co Inc

Prefabricated Wood Buildings, Log Homes - **Edgewood Fine Log Structu**
Preformed Pavement Markings - **Stimsonite Corp.**
Premium Cover Materials & Binding Products - **Fiber Mark Inc.**
Premium Quality Micro & Drip Irrigation - **Roberts Irrigation Products**
Premium Soft Packaging - **Jsam**
Prepack Software Design Point of Sale - **Fiscal Systems, Inc.**
Prepack Software, Auto Part Program - **Optimation, Inc.**
Prepack Software, Sheet Metal Fab. - **Optimation, Inc.**
Prepack. Software Design, Risk Analysis Decision Analyis - **Palisade Corp**
Prepackaged Academic & Government Software - **Academic Distributing**
Prepackaged Software - **Idq Books Worldwide Inc**
Prepackaged Software - **Ross Systems Inc.**
Prepackaged Software - **Techbase International**
Prepackaged Software - **Anderson-bell Corporation**
Prepackaged Software - **Jobquest**
Prepackaged Software - **Legal plus Software Group Inc**
Prepackaged Software - **Visible Productions Llc**
Prepackaged Software - **Ts-tek Inc**
Prepackaged Software - Job Shop Custom. - **Information Specialist Inc**
Prepackaged Software Design Financial - **Fiscal Systems, Inc.**
Prepaid Phone Card Vending Equipment - **Imco Inc**
Prepaint Coil Coating of Aluminum & Steel - **Copper Coil Coating**
Preparations for Use on the Hair - **Hollywood**
Prepared Animal Feeds - **Diamond V Mills, Inc.**
Prepared Glues and Adhesives - **Stafast Roofing Products**
Prepared Seafood, Crawfish, Crabmeat, Calamari - **Ecrevisse Acadienne**
Prepares Italian Dry Salami - **P G Molinari & Sons Inc**
Preschool Furniture - **Mahar**
Prescription & Non-prescription Safety Glasses - **U.s. Safety**
Presentation Graphics - **Advanced Graphics & Publishing**
Preserved Plants - **Toepperweins of Texas**
Preserved Trees - **Preserved Treescapes Intl**
Press Packing Papers - **Sunshine Paper Company**
Presses - **Transfer Press Exchange**
Presses; Forming, Deep Drawing & Punching - **Presses, Ltd**
Presses; Hydraulic, Pneumatic, & Manual - **Presses, Ltd**
Pressroom Chemicals Blending - **Jell Chemicals, Inc.**
Pressroom Chemistry: Fountain Solutions - **Burnshine Products**
Pressure & Flow Meas. / Control Instruments - **Mks Instruments, Inc.**
Pressure & Temperature Controls - **S O R, Inc.**
Pressure & Temperature Instruments - **Dresser Instrument Div.**
Pressure & Vacuum Blowers - **Ametek Rotron Tmd - Industrial Products**
Pressure - Sensitive Adhesive Materials - **Adhesives Research, Inc.**
Pressure Controllers / Calibrators - **Mensor Corporation**
Pressure Fryers - **Broaster Co., the**
Pressure Fryers, Display & Holding Cabinets - **Henny Penny Corp.**
Pressure Gauges (Digital) - **Mensor Corporation**
Pressure Gauges - Cam & Roller Design - **Helicoid Div., Bristol Babcock**
Pressure Grouting Equipment - **Chemgrout Inc.**
Pressure Indicating Switches - **Helicoid Div., Bristol Babcock Inc.**
Pressure Instrumentation - **Perma-cal Industries Inc**
Pressure Regulators - **Pierburg Instruments, Inc.**
Pressure Relief Valves - **Smart Products Inc**
Pressure Sensitive Adhesive - **Dielectric Polymers, Inc.**
Pressure Sensitive Coatings - **Microcosm**
Pressure Sensitive Labeling Machinery - **Njm/cli Packaging Systems Intl**
Pressure Sensitive Roll Label Stocks - Paper & Film - **Maratech Intl**
Pressure Temperature Diferential & Vacuum Switches - **Pressure Devices**
Pressure Transducers - **Pace Transducer Co**
Pressure Transducers - **Taber Industries, Inc.**
Pressure Vessels - **Mohawk Mfg. Corp.**
Pressure Vessels— Water Storage Tanks - **Roy E Hanson Jr Manufacturin**
Pressure Wash Cleaner - **Supreme Chemicals of Georgia**
Pressure Washers & Pumps - **Faip North America Inc.**
Pressure Washers , Steam Cleaners - **Allied Industrial Distributors Inc.**
Pressure Washers, Tube Cleaners & Steam Cleaners - **Maxi-vac, Inc.**
Pressure Washing Equipment - **Azure Blue Inc**
Pressure, Vacuum Transducers - **Pressure Devices Inc.**
Pressure-sensitive Roll Labels - **Green Bay Packaging, Inc**
Pressurized Ball Point Pens & Refills - **Fisher Space Pen Co**
Prestressed & Precast Concrete Products - **Heldenfels Enterprises, Inc.**

Pretzel Manufacturer - **Anderson Bakery Company, Inc.**
Pretzels, Potato Chips, Tortilla Chips - **Snyders of Hanover**
Primary & Secondary Unit Substations - **Con-tech Power Systems, Inc.**
Primary Metal Products - **Mott Corp.**
Primary Metal Products - **Windfall Products, Inc.**
Prime Power Generator Sets - **Reagan Equipment Co., Inc.**
Priming, Painting, Plating, Anodizing - **All Metals Processing of Oc**
Print & Apply Labeling Machines - **Apax Corporation**
Printed & Etched Circuit Boards - **Circuit Technology Corp.**
Printed & Solid Textile Piece Goods - **Cranston Apparel Fabrics**
Printed Circuit Bd Assemblies - **Imperial Electronic Assembly**
Printed Circuit Board Assembly - **Eei / Mod-tech Industries**
Printed Circuit Board Assembly - **Electronic Manufacturing Svc**
Printed Circuit Boards - **Accurate Circuit Engineering**
Printed Circuit Boards - **Circuit Manufacturing Technology**
Printed Circuit Boards - **Circuit Technology Corp.**
Printed Circuit Boards - **Eagle Circuits, Inc.**
Printed Circuit Boards - **Empire Electronics Corp.**
Printed Circuit Boards - **Printed Circuit Solutions Mfg.**
Printed Circuit Boards - **Rogers Corporation**
Printed Circuit Boards - **Salco Circuit**
Printed Circuit Boards - **Savant Audio & Video**
Printed Circuit Boards - **Ustek, Inc.**
Printed Circuit Boards - **Zecal, Inc.**
Printed Circuit Boards (Turnkey.consignment) - **Twin Technology Inc**
Printed Circuit Boards, Cable & Harness Manufacture - **Pine Grove Group**
Printed Circuit Boards, Soft Substrates - **Modular Components National,**
Printed Circuit Laminates - **Arlon Materials for Electronics Division**
Printed Circuit and Turnkey Electronic Boards - **Pine Grove Group**
Printed Labels Lithogrphic - **Seton Name Plate Company**
Printed Matter - **Cps Communications, Inc.**
Printed Plastic Cards - **National Plastic Printing, Inc.**
Printed Plastic Cards - **Plasco, Inc.**
Printed Tags, Lithographic - **Seton Name Plate Company**
Printer & Fax Machine Thermal Transfer Ribbons - **Paxar Iimak**
Printer Laminators - **Imtec Inc.**
Printers, Intercoms, Laser Scanners, Cash Drawers - **Esco Services Inc**
Printing - B/c & Coating - **Digital Nation**
Printing Blades, Plating & Washing Equipment - **Daetwyler Corp., Max**
Printing Equipment - **Woerner Industries, Inc.**
Printing Equipment - **Nu Arc Co., Inc.**
Printing Equipment - **Bell-mark Corp.**
Printing Equipment Manufacturer - **Davidson International Inc.**
Printing Inks - **Inx International Ink Co.**
Printing Inks & Coatings - **Wikoff Color Corp.**
Printing Machinery - **Ackley Machine Corp.**
Printing Machinery - **C.m. Graphics**
Printing Machinery Parts, Wholesale - **Allpress Equipment Inc.**
Printing Machinery; Web Press Folder Parts - **Western Roller Corporation**
Printing Press Components, Parts & Equipment - **Printers Repair Parts,**
Printing Press Sheeting & Stacking Equipment - **Evtec Corp.**
Printing Presses - **C.m. Graphics**
Printing Rollers - **Bingham Roller Co.**
Printing Trades Machinery - **J R C Web Accessories, Inc.**
Printing Trades Machinery - **Ackley Machine Corp.**
Printing Trades Machinery - **B & L Machine & Design**
Printing Trades Machinery - **Evtec Corp.**
Printing Trades Machinery - **Lemco**
Printing Trades Machinery - **Nationwide Graphics, Inc.**
Printing Trades Machinery - **Nu Arc Co., Inc.**
Printing Trades Machinery & Equipt. - **Forester Rollers**
Printing and Writing Paper - **Unisource**
Printing on Flexible Packaging Material - **Lithotype Co Inc**
Printing, All Types - **Just a Stretch**
Printing, Commercial - **J K Label Co.**
Printing, Commercial - **Original Impressions, Inc.**
Printing, Commercial - **Prismflex Inc.**
Printing, Commercial - **Times Leader, Inc.**
Printing, Lithographic, Flexographic and Rotogr - **A J Daw Printing Ink**
Printing_commercial - **Brevis Corp**
Printing_commercial - **C. S. S. Publishing Co., Inc.**

Printing_commercial - **Coastal Printing Co.**
Printing_commercial - **Creative Plastics Printing Die**
Printing_commercial - **Davidson International Inc.**
Printing_commercial - **Diversified Coatings, Inc.**
Printing_commercial - **Excel Design Inc.**
Printing_commercial - **Joplin Printing Co.**
Printing_commercial - **Latimer County News-trib**
Printing_commercial - **Lumber Tag Specialties**
Printing_commercial - **Matrix Imaging Solution**
Printing_commercial - **Mitchell Daily Republic**
Printing_commercial - **National Plastic Printing, Inc.**
Printing_commercial - **Outlook Graphics**
Printing_commercial - **Palone & Associates**
Printing_commercial - **Pikes Peak Lithographing Co**
Printing_commercial - **Precision Press**
Printing_commercial - **Process Graphics Corp.**
Printing_commercial - **Psychological Corp., the**
Printing_commercial - **Roberts Co., the John**
Printing_commercial - **Sandy-alexander, Inc.**
Printing_commercial - **Schmidt Printing, Inc.**
Printing_commercial - **South Pasadena Publishing Co**
Printing_commercial - **Thunderbird Printing & Screening**
Printing_commercial - **Wolf Creek Printing**
Printing_commercial Signs - **Union Printing**
Prints Books (Soft & Hard Cover) - **Kni Incorporated**
Prints Business Forms - **New West Business Forms**
Prints Color Advertising Brochures, InformBooklets - **Westpro Graphics**
Prints Membership and Credit Cards- **Creative Plastics Printing Die**
Prints on T-shirts, Sweatshirts and Mugs; Embroidered - **Habitat Softwear**
Prison Transfer Vehicles - Armored - **Alpine Armoring Inc.**
Private Investigations - Worldwide - **Gaslamp Quarter Investigations**
Private Label & Contract Manufacturing - **Health Valley Foods**
Private-label Cosmetics - **Trademark Cosmetics Inc**
Proces Control Instruments - **Hach Company**
Process Aid Additives for Rubber - **Axel Plastics Research Laboratories**
Process Automation & Control Systems - **Water Services International**
Process Control Equipment, Access Control - **Apollo**
Process Control Equipment, Access Control - **Asti**
Process Control Equipment, Card Readers - **Apollo**
Process Control Equipment, Card Readers - **Asti**
Process Control Instruments - **Bei Sensors & Systems/kimco Magnetics**
Process Control Instruments - **Acu-gage Systems**
Process Control Instruments - **American Msi Corp**
Process Control Instruments - **Baldwin Environmental Inc**
Process Control Instruments - **Caldon, Inc.**
Process Control Instruments - **Common Sensing Inc**
Process Control Instruments - **Dynasonics**
Process Control Instruments - **Gas Tech, Inc.**
Process Control Instruments - **Lumenite Control Technology Inc.**
Process Control Instruments - **Madison Co.**
Process Control Instruments - **Mc Millan Co., Inc., R. D.**
Process Control Instruments - **Mks Instruments, Inc.**
Process Control Instruments - **Myron L Company**
Process Control Instruments - **N-con Systems Co., Inc.**
Process Control Instruments - **Paragon Water Systems**
Process Control Instruments - **Petrotech Inc.**
Process Control Instruments - **Porter Instrument Co.**
Process Control Instruments - **Preso Meters, Corp.**
Process Control Instruments - **Tigert Co., T. F.**
Process Control Instruments - **Sargon Digital Inc**
Process Control Instruments - **Solid State Electronics Corp**
Process Control Instruments - **Swanson Anaheim Corp**
Process Control Instruments - **Universal Analyzers Inc**
Process Control Systems for Rubber & Plastics Industries - **Fet Test Inc**
Process Control, Elec. Transmitters - **Bristol Babcock Inc.**
Process Heaters - **Therm Tech Inc.**
Process Level, Flow, Pressure, Liquid Analysis - **Endress & Hauser, Inc.**
Process Lines - Steel - **Fata Hunter, Inc.**
Process Liquid Chillers - **Affinity Industries Inc. (Mfr)**
Process Liquid Chillers - **Filtrine Manufacturing Company**
Processed Foods - **United Grocers International**

Processed Peanut Products - **Damascus Peanut Co.**
Processes & Smokes Meats; Wholesale Neutural- **Bar-s Foods Co.**
Producers - **Masterpiece Prdctns Nevada**
Product Engineering for Water Treatment - **Springsoft International Inc.**
Product Orienting Systems - **Ackley Machine Corp.**
Product Stackers - **Quantum Conveyor Systems, Llc**
Production - **Accurite Development & Mfg**
Production & Prototype Machining Job Shop - **A. I. M. Inc.**
Production Stairs - **Jim C. Lane Inc.**
Production Tubular Extrusions - **U.S. Manufacturing Corporation**
Production in Oil Wells - **Erica and Erica International Corp.**
Products / Merchandise with Earth Flag Logo - **Apollo Energy**
Products Include Y.m.l.a. Brand Names, - **Y.m.l.a. Inc**
Products Which Are Pc Compatible - **Novaweb Technologies Inc**
Products for Aircraft, Marine, Automotive, Tents, - **Duracote Corp.**
Products for Automotive & Construction Glass - **C.r. Laurence Company,**
Products for Commercial Fisherman - **Dennis Aluminum Products**
Products for Plumbing, Industrial - **Intracor-familian International**
Professional Equipment, Nec - **Service for Science & Industries**
Professional Lawn Mowers Ride-on - **Excel Industries, Inc.**
Professional Treatment for Problem Skin - **Rejuvi Cosmetic Laboratory**
Profilers - **International Cybernetics Corp.**
Profilographs - **International Cybernetics Corp.**
Project Cargo Handling - **Dan Transport Corporation**
Promotional Toys - Retailer - **Promotional Resources Group**
Propane Tanks & Gas Plant Equipment - **Gas Liquids Recovery Corp.**
Proportional Control Valves - **Alicat Scientific Inc**
Props and Similar Equipment - **Able Builders Export, Inc.**
Protective Bedding; Waterproof, - **Lamb, Inc., J.**
Protective Coatings - **Ameron Intl/protective Coatings Group**
Protective Coatings, Industrial and Maintenance - **Products Techniques**
Protective Knee Pads, Export - **Global Market Partners, Inc.**
Protective Padding for Skiing Area's - **Idaho Sewing for Sports**
Protects - Enhances Healing - Moisturizes - **Unique Laboratories, Inc.**
Protein Feeds - **Anamax Corp.**
Proto Types Tru Production - **Accurate Circuit Engineering**
Prototype - **Accurite Development & Mfg**
Prototype Equipment - **D W C Assocs., Inc.**
Prototyping - **Southwest Metal Fabricators, Inc.**
Provides Gas Diffusion Coating Processes on Components - **Vaporkote Inc**
Provides Plating, Electronic Component Plating - **Nu-metal Finishing Inc**
Provides Smt, Tht Printed Board Assembly - **Reliable Communications**
Proximity Access Control Products - **Keri Systems Inc**
Ptfe Coated Fiberglass - **Saunders Thread Co., Inc.**
Public Relations Svcs.,Japan & Far East -**Suzuki, Myers & Associates, Ltd**
Public Warehouse - **Euro-american Air Frt. Fwdg Co., Inc.**
Public Warehousing; Distributes Dry, Frozen - **Southwest Storage**
Public-transport Type Passenger Motor Vehicles- **Rivers Bus & Rv Sales**
Publisher - **Haworth Press, Inc., the**
Publisher , Diversity at Work :Trainers Guide - **Intercultural Development**
Publishers, Industrial Trade Magazines - **Cahners Business Information**
Publishes Newspaper & Directory of Churches - **The Catholic Voice**
Publishes Apparel Manufacturers' and Contractors' - **Jasa Publications**
Publishes Books on Eastern Philosophy - **Dharma Publishing**
Publishes Books, Lithographic and Poster Reproduction - **Coast Publishing**
Publishes Books; Laser Typesetting - **Warren Communications**
Publishes Daily Newspaper - **Seattle Post/intelligencer Div**
Publishes Daily Newspaper - **World Journal Inc**
Publishes Daily Newspaper (Editorial Department) - **Arizona Daily Star**
Publishes Educational Books - **International Soc for Technology in Educ**
Publishes History Coloring Books - **Dragon Enterprises**
Publishes Legal & Judicial Direcotories - **Forster-long Inc.**
Publishes Monthly Comic Books - **Chaos Comics Inc**
Publishes Monthly Downhill Skiing Magazines - **The Skiing Co**
Publishes Monthly Magazine - **Southern Calif Guide-westworld**
Publishes Monthly Trade Magazine:Water Industry - **Water Conditioning**
Publishes Music Books & Software - **Alfred Publishing Co Inc**
Publishes Newsletter; Advertising - **The Practice Builder Association**
Publishes Newspapers and Other Publications - **Herburger Publications**
Publishes Periodicals - **Ranchland News**
Publishes Relocation Guides - **Metropolitan Graphics**

Publishes Road Maps for the Bay Area & Maps - **Barclay Maps**
Publishes Scientific Books in the Biological - **Annual Reviews Inc**
Publishes Scientific, Technological, Medical Books - **Academic Press**
Publishes Seven Monthly Agricultural - **Western Agricultural Publish**
Publishes Shrimp Market Analysis - **Shrimp World Inc.**
Publishes Sun City West Weekly Newspaper - **The Western Newspaper**
Publishes Technical Estimating Manuals; - **Richardson Engineering Svcs**
Publishes Telephone Directories- **Hagadone Directories Inc**
Publishes Travel Guides :Gay and Lesbian Client - **The Damron Co Inc**
Publishes Visitors Guide to Wine Counties - **The California Visitors**
Publishes Weekly Agriculture Newspaper - **Wyoming Livestock Roundup**
Publishes Weekly Hispanic Bilingual Newspaper - **El Hispanic News**
Publishes Weekly Newspaper - **Clear Creek Courant**
Publishes Weekly Newspaper - **El Semanario**
Publishes Weekly Newspaper - **Philippine News Inc**
Publishes Weekly Newspaper and Shopper - **Lake County Leader**
Publishes Yearly Metropolitan Relocation - **Metropolitan Graphics**
Publishes and Prints Weekly Newspaper - **South Pasadena Publishing Co**
Publishing - **Strawberry Patch Publishing**
Publishing , Miscellaneous - **Barclay Maps**
Publishing, Miscellaneous - **Health Impact Inc**
Publishing, Miscellaneous - **Torres Engineering**
Publishing_miscellaneous - **Lake County Leader**
Publishing_miscellaneous - **The Catholic Voice**
Publishing_miscellaneous - **The Wolfe Pack**
Publishing_miscellaneous - **International Soc for Technology in Educ**
Publishing_miscellaneous - **Coast Publishing**
Publishing_miscellaneous - **East-west Publishing Company**
Publishing_miscellaneous - **Jasa Publications**
Publishing_miscellaneous - **Metropolitan Graphics**
Publishing_miscellaneous - **Richardson Engineering Svcs Inc**
Publishing_miscellaneous - **The California Visitors Review**
Publishing_miscellaneous - **The Damron Co Inc**
Publsihing Miscellaneous - **Gonzalez Integrated Marketing**
Puddings - **Dean Foods (Mfr)**
Puff Stickers - **Interpretive Marketing Products**
Pulp & Paper Industry Machinery - **Thermo Black Clawson Inc.**
Pulp Mills - **International Paper Co., Texarkana Mill**
Pulse Signal Translators - **Alicat Scientific Inc**
Pulsed Laser Sources & Laser Cutting, Welding - **Lasag**
Pulses, All Types - **Ps International**
Pulverizing Machinery - **Bradley Pulverizer Company (Mfr)**
Pumice Stones - **Flowery Beauty Products, Inc.**
Pumice, Other than Crude or in Irregular - **Hess Pumice Products, Inc.**
Pump & Motors Rebuilt - **Service Hydraulics Inc.**
Pump & Pump System Controls - **Pritchard Brown**
Pump Columns - **Foster Co., L. B.**
Pump Repairs - **Superb Marine & Industrial Services, Inc.**
Pump Skids; Sncr/scr - **Oceanside Engineering & Mfg**
Pump and Compression Parts - **Minco Sales Corp.**
Pumping Systems for Pools and Spa's - **Premier Spring Water Inc**
Pumps - **Barber-nichols Incorporated**
Pumps - **Gardner Denver, Inc. (Mfr)**
Pumps - **Kraissl Co., Inc., the**
Pumps - **Hotsy Corporation, the**
Pumps - **Johnston Pumps**
Pumps & Filters - **S E R F I L C O, Ltd.**
Pumps & Pumping - **Columbian Steel Tank Co.**
Pumps - Pumping Equipment - **Quinn Process Equipment Co**
Pumps & Pumping Equipment - **A B S Pumps, Inc.**
Pumps & Pumping Equipment - **Abel Pumps Corp.**
Pumps & Pumping Equipment - **Air Dimensions, Inc.**
Pumps & Pumping Equipment - **Alldos Inc.**
Pumps & Pumping Equipment - **Cat Pumps**
Pumps & Pumping Equipment - **Defco, Inc.**
Pumps & Pumping Equipment - **Fairbanks Morse Pump Corp.**
Pumps & Pumping Equipment - **Gator Pump, Inc.**
Pumps & Pumping Equipment - **Hale Products, Inc.**
Pumps & Pumping Equipment - **Heavy Duty Hydro Blasting, Inc.**
Pumps & Pumping Equipment - **Hypro Corp.**
Pumps & Pumping Equipment - **Mth Tool Co. Inc.**

Pumps & Pumping Equipment - **Pacer Pumps**
Pumps & Pumping Equipment - **Premier Spring Water Inc**
Pumps & Pumping Equipment - **S E R F I L C O, Ltd.**
Pumps & Pumping Equipment - **Saber Technologies, Llc**
Pumps & Pumping Equipment - **Standard Pumps Inc.**
Pumps & Pumping Equipment - **Thomas Industries-power Air Div.**
Pumps & Pumping Equipment - **Thomas Pump & Machinery, Inc.**
Pumps & Related Pump Systems - **Gorman Rupp Co., the**
Pumps & Rescue Tools - **Hale Products, Inc.**
Pumps and Pumping Equipment - **Pantropic Power Products, Inc.**
Pumps for Drainage & Irrigation - **Quality Industries, Inc.**
Pumps for Liquids - **Continental Sprayers / Afa Products**
Pumps, Bailers, Filters, Meters, - **Geotech Environmental Equipment**
Pumps, Cylinders, Valves, Wholesale - **Hercules Hydraulics Inc.**
Pumps, Meters - **John Blue Co.**
Pumps, Mining & Oilfeild - **Minco Sales Corp.**
Pumps, Rotary Displacement - **Granco Pump, Div. Challenge Mfg.**
Pumps-irrigation, Oilfield, Flood, Dewater, Industrial - **Fisher Pumps Inc**
Punches, Chisels, Pry Bars - **Mayhew Tools**
Punches, Dies and Accessories for Turret - **Thor Tool Corporation**
Puple Table Onions - **Denice & Filice Packing**
Purchasing Agent & Consolidations - **Paul Marsh, Llc**
Purchasing Agents - Construction Materials - **Wespac Corp.**
Pure Vanilla Extract - **Nielsen-massey Vanillas(mfr)**
Purpose Citrus Cleaners - **Whip-it Products, Inc.**
Putty Knives, Paint Scrappers & Joint Knives - **Hyde Manufacturing Co.**
Puzzles - **Hoyle Products**
Pvc & Cpvc Plastic Fittings, Unions, Flanges, Etc. - **Pacific Plastics**
Pvc & Cpvc Plastic Pipes - **Pacific Plastics**
Pvc / Vertical Blinds - **Arabel**
Pvc Coated Electrical Products - **Mpc International Llc**
Pvc Coated Metal Outdoor Residential - **Fusion Coatings Inc.**
Pvc Coating & Epoxy Coating for Electrical Supplies - **Mpc International**
Pvc Pipe & Well Screens - **Brady Products Inc.**
Pvc Windows & Patio Doors - **Hurd Millwork Company, Inc.**
Pvm Ps, Centrifugal - **Osmonics, Inc.**
Quality Brooms and Wet Mops- **California Mop Manufacturing**
Quality Control Laboratory Equipment - **Terriss-consolidated Industries**
Quality Control Supplies for Soft Drink Ind- **Terriss-consolidated Ind**
Quartz Crystals and Oscillators - **Standard Crystal Corp**
Quartz Wall Clocks - **Equity Industries**
Quick Connect Coupling for Cooling Systems - **Jiffy Tite Co., Inc.**
Quick Disconnect Fluid Coupling for High Flow Industrial App - **Jiffy Tite**
Quick Printing and Copying - **Rapid Reproductions Printing**
Quillaia Extract & Powder - **Berghausen Corp.**
Quilted Fabrics & Bedspreads - **Scarsdale Quilting Converting Corp.,**
Quilting & Other Machines: Mattress Industry - **Gribetz International**
Quilting Battings - **Western Synthetic Fiber**
Quilting Machines - **American Professional Quilting Systems**
R & D, Volume Filling - **Columbia Cosmetics Manufacturing, Inc.**
R&d for Various Related Energy Products; Low Em - **Br Laboratories Inc**
R&d of Batteries and Capacitors - **Pinnacle Research Institute**
R.f. Sealing Equipment - **Cosmos Electronic Machine Corp. (Mfr)**
Race Track Equipment - **Larcom & Mitchell**
Raceways, Cable Trays, Infloor Ducts, Boxes, Poles - **Wiremold Co., the**
Racing & Athletic Padding - **Idaho Sewing for Sports**
Rack Mounted Batteries - **Sec Industrial Battery Co., Inc.**
Racking for Pallets - **Andersen Rack Systems Inc**
Racks and Shelving for Computer Networks - **Chatsworth Products Inc**
Racquetball Court Wall & Ceiling Panels - **Fiberesin Industries, Inc.**
Radar Detectors & Marine Electronics - **Survival Safety Engineering, Inc.**
Radar Equipment, Ground Penetrating - **Geophysical Survey Systems, Inc.**
Radar Fm Discriminators - **Solid State Electronics Corp**
Radiator Block Sealers - **K & W Products**
Radio & TC Communications Equipment - **Micon Telecommunications**
Radio & Tv Broadcasting Comm Equip - **Jps Communications Inc**
Radio & Tv Communications - **Telesat International Ltd**
Radio & Tv Communications Equipment - **B a F Communications Corp.**
Radio & Tv Communications Equipment - **Accurate Sound Corporation**
Radio & Tv Communications Equipment - **Apature Products, Inc.**
Radio & Tv Communications Equipment - **Continental Electronics Corp.**

Radio & Tv Communications Equipment - **D H Satellite**
Radio & Tv Communications Equipment - **Dwin Electronics Inc**
Radio & Tv Communications Equipment - **Kintronic Laboratories, Inc.**
Radio & Tv Communications Equipment - **Miteq, Inc.**
Radio & Tv Communications Equipment - **Omicron Video**
Radio & Tv Communications Equipment - **Prodelin Corp.**
Radio & Tv Communications Equipment - **R. F. Technology, Inc.**
Radio & Tv Communications Equipment - **Solid State Electronics Corp**
Radio & Tv Communications Equipment - **Wireworks Corporation**
Radio Antenna & Broadcasting Equipment - **Kintronic Laboratories, Inc.**
Radio Batteries - **W & W Mfg.**
Radio Freq. Power Amplifiers - **Tpl Communications, Inc.**
Radio Frequency & Microwave Power Amplifiers - **T/mac, Inc.**
Radio Frequency Interference Shielded Enclosures - **Lindgren R F Enclos**
Radio Frequency Transmitters - **Continental Electronics Corp.**
Radio Station Automation Equipment - **Smarts Broadcast Systems**
Radio and Tv Broadcasting and Communications - **Telesat International**
Radioactive Diagnostic Pharmaceuticals - **Mallinckrodt Inc.**
Radius Furniture Components - **Interior Products Inc.**
Radius Store Fixtures - **Interior Products Inc.**
Radon & Radiation Monitoring Instruments - **Rad-elec Inc.**
Radon Fans & Supplies - **Professional Discount Supply**
Raffle & Coupon Book & Ticket Printing & Typesetting - **L M N Printing**
Rags - **Consolidated Trading**
Rags - **Sheftel International**
Rail Grinding & Rail Flaw Detection Services - **Pandrol Jackson Inc.**
Rail Lubrication Systems - **Portec Rail Products Inc.**
Rail Operation Control Centers - **Railroad Signal, Inc.**
Rail or Rubber Tired Haulage Equipment - **Brookville Mining Equipment**
Railroad Crossing Gate Arms - **National Electric Gate Co.**
Railroad Crossing Signal & Communication Equip- **Harmon Industries,**
Railroad Crossing Signals - **Railroad Signal, Inc.**
Railroad Equipment - **National Electric Gate Co.**
Railroad Equipment - **Portec Rail Products Inc.**
Railroad Equipment - **Whiting Corporation**
Railroad Equipment Rail Cars & Kits - **Msi International**
Railroad Equipment, Including Loco- **Brookville Mining Equipment**
Railroad Maintenance Equipment, Manufacturer - **Pandrol Jackson Inc.**
Railroad Maintenance Materials - **Portec Rail Products Inc.**
Railroad Wheels, Axles & Assemblies - **Standard Steel**
Railway & Bridge Maintenance - **Osmose Wood Preserving, Inc.**
Railway & Industrial Cleaning Equipment - **Proceco, Inc.**
Railway or Tramway Locomotives - **Hatch & Kirk**
Railway or Tramway Locomotives - **Kessler International Corp.**
Rainbow Trout, Channel Catfish, Tilapia, Sturgeon - **Fish Processors Inc**
Rainhandler Rain Dispersal System - Better than Gutters - **Rainhandler**
Rapid Prototypes to Volume Mfg. - **Litec Inc.**
Rappelling Gear, Commun Dev. Whsle. - **U. S. Cavalry, Inc.**
Raschel Lace Allover, Nylon /Lycra - **Mini-lace, Inc.**
Raw & Blanched Shelled & Inshell Peanuts - **Damascus Peanut Co.**
Raw & Expanded Perlite Aggregates - **Supreme Perlite Co**
Raw Aloe Vera into Liquid Form - **Agro-mar Inc of Nevada**
Raw Cane Sugar - **California & Hawaiian Sugar Co**
Raw Cotton Fabric - **Consolidated Trading**
Raw Materials & Machinery for the Textile Industry - **Paul Marsh, Llc**
Raw Materials & Parts - **Vie Americas, Inc.**
Raw Materials for Polyurethane Foam - **Velco Chemicals**
Raw Materials, Antibodies, Antigens - **United Biotech Inc**
Rawhide Bones & Natural Treats - **Hartz Mountain**
Rayon Thread - **Robison-anton Textile Company (Mfr)**
Reactivation Services - **Calgon Carbon Corporation (Mfr)**
Reactive Ion Etch Equipment - **Axic Inc**
Reactors - **Mag-tran Equipment Corp**
Reactors - **R.e. Uptegraff Mfg. Company**
Reading Glasses, Export - **Arno International, Inc.**
Real Estate Agents - **Segrest International Realtors**
Real-estate - **J & B Services: Import / Export**
Rebuilding Service & Vacuum Pumps- **Evey Engineering Co., Inc.**
Rebuilt Air Cond & Refrigeration Compressors - **Hermetic Machines Inc.**
Rebuilt Boats & Boat Engines - **Cable Marine, Inc.**
Rebuilt Boilers - **Jerryco Machine & Boilerworks**

Rebuilt Boilers & Combustion Controls - **Tigert Co., T. F.**
Rebuilt Electric Motors - **Electric Motors & Drives, Inc.**
Rebuilt Forklift Motors - **Master Motor Rebuilders**
Rebuilt Hard Parts for Transmissions - **Tri-star International, Inc.**
Rebuilt Hydraulic Machinery & Parts - **Service Hydraulics Inc**
Rebuilt Industrial Machinery - **Hall Industrial Services**
Rebuilt Laser Printer Toner Cartridges - **Pendl Co., Inc.**
Rebuilt Marine Boilers, Coolers - **Superb Marine & Industrial Services,**
Rebuilt Plastic Injection Molds - **Heyden Mold & Bench Co.**
Rebuilt Printing Equipment & Machined Parts - **B & L Machine & Design**
Rebuilt Rubber Processing Machinery - **Rubber City Machinery Corp.**
Rebuilt Transformers - **T & R Electric Supply Co., Inc.**
Rebuilt Transmission Components Lift Trk. - **Joseph Industries, Inc.**
Recanon and Sharp Copiers - **Recycled Business Systems Llc**
Rechargeable Batteries - **Power-sonic Corp**
Rechargeable Battery Electrode Substrate - **Precious Plate Florida**
Rechargeable Sealed-lead Cells and Batteries - **Portable Energy Products**
Reciprocating Natural Gas Compressors - **Ariel Corp.**
Reclosers & Distribution Switchgear - **Cooper Industries**
Recomputer Printer Ribbons and Toner Cartridges - **Ribbon Division Inc**
Record & Prerecorded Tape Stores - **Health Impact Inc**
Records & Tapes, Prerecorded - **Q. up Arts**
Records & Tapes_prerecorded - **Flight Tech, Inc**
Recreational Vehicle Dealers - **Rivers Bus & Rv Sales**
Rectifiers - **Dynapower Corporation**
Rectifiers and Dc Power Supplies - **Hbs Equipment Corp**
Recycle Crushers for Asphalt - **Getz Recycle Inc**
Recycle Crushers for Concrete - **Getz Recycle Inc**
Recycle Crushers for Wood - **Getz Recycle Inc**
Recycled Computer Supplies - **Greendisk Inc**
Recycled Magnetic Diskettes - **Greendisk Inc**
Recycled Plastic Lumber - **Polywood, Inc.**
Recycled Rubber Door Mats - **Stanlar Industries**
Recycled Rubber Interlocking Floor Tiles - **Stanlar Industries**
Recycles Tires into Rubber Granules - **Bas Recycling Inc**
Recycling & Solid Waste Trucks - **Kann Mfg. Corp.**
Recycling & Waste Handling Equipment - **Harmony Enterprises, Inc. G P**
Recycling Electronic Equipment - **Hobi International, Inc.**
Recycling Equipment, Compost Turners - **Wildcat Mfg. Co., Inc.**
Recycling Equipment, Trommel Screens - **Wildcat Mfg. Co., Inc.**
Recycling Machinery - **Ecosystem Inc.**
Recycling Machinery - Used - **Alan Ross Machinery Corp**
Recycling Old Asphalt Roadbase Material. - **C S S Technology Inc.**
Recycling of Hazardous Tin & Tin/lead Material - **Ecs Refining**
Red & White Wines - **Columbia Winery**
Red Light Cameras - **American Traffic Systems Inc**
Red, Cedar, Oak & Cherry Wood Wall Coverings - **American Cedarworks,**
Redox, Dissolved Oxygen, Conductivity - **Lazar Research Laboratories**
Reducing Lighting Costs 20-50% - **Electric City Corp.**
Redwood Wildlife Feeders, Domestic Pet Products, - **Wildwood Farms**
Reefer Service Worldwide - **Horizon Forwarders Inc.**
Reel Sharpening Compounds - **Gel-tec Co.**
Reel to Reel Continuous Plating of Gold,- **Delta Precision Alloys**
Refined Cane Sugar- **California & Hawaiian Sugar Co**
Refinery & Chemical Plant Equipment & Spare Parts - **Intramar, Inc.**
Refines & Smelts Prescious Metals - **Eastern Smelting & Refining**
Refines and Smelts Precious Metals - **Aaa Precious Metals Inc**
Reflective Devices - **Grote Industries, Inc.**
Reflective Films & Signing Materials - **Stimsonite Corp.**
Reflective Flexible Vinyl - **Stimsonite Corp.**
Reflective Transportation Safety Devices - **Stimsonite Corp.**
Reformer Tubes - **Professional Services International, Inc.**
Refrac. Grains/powder, Silicon Carbide - **Electro Abrasives Corp.**
Refractive Index Matching Liquids - **Cargille Laboratories, Inc.**
Refractometers (Inline) - **Afab Enterprises**
Refractories - **Stronglite Products**
Refractory Bonding Mortars - **Respond Group of Companies**
Refractory Materials - **Refractory Materials International**
Refractory Systems & Shape - **Thermal Systems America**
Refrig. Compressor Crankshafts - **Cmp Corporation**
Refrigerant - Automotive - **Interdynamics, Inc.**

Refrigerant Charging Equipment - **Robinair, a Div. Of Spx Corporation**
Refrigerant Identification - **Robinair, a Div. Of Spx Corporation**
Refrigerant Leak Detection Instruments - **Robinair, a Div. Of Spx Corp**
Refrigerant Recovery & Recycling Equipment -**Robinair, a Div. Of Spx**
Refrigerant Recovery Equipment Assembly - **Icor International Inc.**
Refrigerant Recovery Recycling / Recharging Machines - **Liberty Mfg.,**
Refrigerated Deli Products - **Old Fashioned Kitchen Inc**
Refrigerated Hawaiian Food, Salads - **Hawaiian Eateries, Inc.**
Refrigerated Salad Dressings, Seafood Sauces - **Fisherman's Wharf Food**
Refrigerated Warehousing & Storage - **Holmes Ice & Cold Storage Co**
Refrigerated Warehousing & Storage - **Southwest Storage**
Refrigeration & Heating Equipment - **Coil Co., Inc.**
Refrigeration & Heating Equipment - **Bradleys' Hermetics, Inc.**
Refrigeration & Heating Equipment - **Advanced Thermal Technologies**
Refrigeration & Heating Equipment - **Air Energy Heat Pumps**
Refrigeration & Heating Equipment - **Baltimore Aircoil Co., Inc.**
Refrigeration & Heating Equipment - **Dial Manufacturing Inc**
Refrigeration & Heating Equipment - **Dri Steem Humidifier**
Refrigeration & Heating Equipment - **Flojet Corp**
Refrigeration & Heating Equipment - **Freezing System Inc.**
Refrigeration & Heating Equipment - **Kool Star**
Refrigeration & Heating Equipment - **Low Humidity Systems, Inc.**
Refrigeration & Heating Equipment - **Nor-lake, Inc. (Mfr)**
Refrigeration & Heating Equipment - **Phoenix Manufacturing Inc**
Refrigeration & Heating Equipment - **Premco Machine Co Inc**
Refrigeration & Heating Equipment - **Refrigeration Resources Co.**
Refrigeration & Heating Equipment - **Rheem Air Conditioning Div.**
Refrigeration & Heating Equipment - **Sahar Industries**
Refrigeration & Heating Equipment - **Tithe Corp., Skil-aire Div.**
Refrigeration & Heating Equipment - **Zero Zone, Inc.**
Refrigeration Compressor Parts - **Bradleys' Hermetics, Inc.**
Refrigeration Compressor Repair Parts - **Cmp Corporation**
Refrigeration Condensers - **Indiana Tube**
Refrigeration Equipment - **Semco Manufacturing**
Refrigeration Equipment - **Maytag International**
Refrigeration Equipment - **Nauticon, Inc.**
Refrigeration Equipment & Supplies - **Premco Machine Co Inc**
Refrigeration Equipment & Supplies - **Webb Distributors Inc**
Refrigeration Skids - **V R Systems, Inc.**
Refrigeration or Freezing Equipment - **National Copper Products**
Refurbished Semiconductor Manufacturing Equipment - **Axic Inc**
Refurbished Unisys Computer Hardware, Wholesale - **System Technology**
Refurbishes & Overstock Telephones - **Kalman Electronics of Arizona**
Refurbishing of Used Industrial Laundry Equipment - **Pagotto Industries**
Refuse & Storage Containers - Mfg. - **Consolidated Fabricators Corp.**
Refuse Trucks (Parks & Beaches) - **Broyhill Company, the (Mfr)**
Relaxers - Color Rinsers - **Shelton's Sheen Wave Labs Inc**
Relays & Ind. Controls - **Platt Electric Supply**
Relays & Industrial Controls - **Alstom Automation Systems Corp.**
Relays & Industrial Controls - **Anaheim Automation**
Relays & Industrial Controls - **Cleveland Motion Controls, Inc.**
Relays & Industrial Controls - **Deltrol Controls**
Relays & Industrial Controls - **Facts, Inc.**
Relays & Industrial Controls - **Genie Co., the**
Relays & Industrial Controls - **Kay-ray/sensall, Inc.**
Relays & Industrial Controls - **Lutron Electronics Co., Inc.**
Relays & Industrial Controls - **Metrix Instrument Co.**
Relays & Industrial Controls - **Precision Motion Controls**
Relays & Industrial Controls - **Rockwell Automation**
Relays & Industrial Controls - **Omicron Video**
Relays & Substation Automation - **Cooper Industries**
Relief Blankets & Military Blankets - **Brickle, Hyman & Son, Inc.**
Relish - **Mount Olive Pickle Co., Inc.**
Remanufactured Natural Gas Engines - **Reagan Equipment Co., Inc.**
Remanufactured Scientific High Vacuum Equipment - **Hta**
Remanufactured Scientific Ultra High Vac. Equipment - **Hta**
Remanufactured Scientific Ultra High Vacuum - **Hawe Technical Ass(Hta)**
Remanufactured Supermarket Equipment - **E B I/r J Trausch Industries**
Remote Access Server - **Visentech Systems, Inc.**
Remote Controls, Air Activated - **Tridelta Industries Inc.**
Remote Video Surveillance for the Security - **Alpha Systems Lab Inc**

Remotely Operated Latches - **Norse, Inc.**
Removable & Reusable Blankets - **Remco Technology, Inc.**
Removable Floor Coverings Spray Booth - **Chemco Manufacturing Inc**
Removable Insulation Blankets - **Cardinal Industrial Insulation Co., Inc.**
Removals - **Micon Telecommunications Inc**
Rendered Chicken Fat, Chicken Broth-**All-states Quality Foods L.p.**
Rendering & Vegetable Oil Equipment & Parts - **Picard Inc., C. A.**
Rendering , Feed Mill & Heavy - **Gainsville Welding &Rendering Equip.**
Rent Boilers - **Jerryco Machine & Boilerworks**
Repair & Boron Harden Refinery Fcc Pumps - **Vaporkote Inc**
Repair & Reconditioning of Reduction Gears Clutches - **Golten Service**
Repair & Reconditioning of Thrusters, Stabilizer Fins, - **Golten Service**
Repair / Overhaul Propellers; Hartzell- **Rocky Mountain Propellers Inc**
Repair / Overhaul, Govenors - **Rocky Mountain Propellers Inc**
Repair Boilers - **Jerryco Machine & Boilerworks**
Repair Services - **C & W Enterprises**
Repair Services - **Ani-helser**
Repair Services - **Azure Blue Inc**
Repair Services - **American Hydraulics**
Repair Services - **Allied Dynamics Corp.**
Repair Services - **James Heavy Equipment Specialist**
Repair Services - Spindles & Slides - **Setco Industries**
Repair Services for Bar Code Equipment - **American Barcode Concepts**
Repair of Deck Equipment, Winches & Cranes - **Golten Service**
Repairs & Resilicon Wafer Probers- **Miller Design & Equipment**
Replacement Axle Shafts - **Foote Axle & Forge Company Llc**
Replacement Filter Cartridges - **Consler Filtrations Products**
Replacement Parts for All Major Twisters - **Pritchett Technology, Inc.**
Replacement Parts for Gas Welding - **Seal-seat Company**
Replacement Windows & Doors & Aluminum Extruding - **Traco**
Rescue & Fire Fighting Equipment - **Glas-master / Wehr Engineering**
Rescue Equipment - **Gibbs Products Inc**
Research - **Accurite Development & Mfg**
Research - **Technical Resource International, Inc.**
Researches, Develops & Diagnostic Test Kits - **Dade Behring Inc.**
Resemiconductor Equipment - **Alpha Technology**
Resid / Comm, Building, Pre-cut Cedar - **International Homes of Cedar**
Resident Light Fixtures; Table, Floor & Wall Lamps - **Decor Guild Mfg.,**
Residential & Commercial Fluorescent Lighting Fixtures - **Lampi, Llc**
Residential & Commercial - **Carter Grandle Furniture**
Residential & Commercial Insulation, Export - **Celotex Corporation**
Residential & Commercial Roofing, Export - **Celotex Corporation**
Residential & Light Commercial: - **Milgard Manufacturing Co**
Residential Elevators - **Mowrey Elevator Company Inc.**
Residential Lighting - **Bw Lighting Corp**
Residential Lighting Fixtures - **Global Electric Products**
Residential Oak Accessories - **Bw Lighting Corp**
Residential and Com. Fluorescent Lights - **American Power Products Inc**
Residential, Commercial, Industrial - **Scalewatcher North America Inc.**
Resin Binders - **Eastern Color & Chemical Co.**
Resin Fountains & Garden Gift Products - **Henri Studio Inc.**
Resin Household Furniture - **Syroco Mfr**
Resin Impregnated Paper Products - **Mapletex**
Resins, Polyols, and Coatings - **Swd Urethane**
Resistance Welding Electrodes - **Nippert Co., the**
Resistance Welding Equipment - **Morrow Tech Industries**
Resistivity Monitors - **Myron L Company**
Resistor, Resostro Capacitors, Resistor - **Koa Speer Electronics, Inc.**
Resort Wear for Men, Women and Children - **Guava Beach**
Resort Wear, Casual - **Wyatt West Inc**
Resorts / Hotels / Small Municipalities - **Lifesource Engineering Inc.**
Respirator Filter Systems - **Clean Air Filter Co.**
Respirators - **U.s. Safety**
Respiratory Assist Devices - **Transtracheal Systems Inc**
Respiratory Care Devices for Oxygen Delivery - **Chad Therapeutics Inc**
Respiratory Protection, Aosafety - **Aearo Company**
Responding - **Permaluster Company**
Restaurant Booths - **Precision Booth Mfg.**
Restaurant Equipment— Sinks, Tables, Shelves - **Fab Industries Inc**
Restaurant Form - **New West Business Forms**
Restaurant Furniture, Table Tops, Signage - **Pacific Crest Manufacturing**

Restaurant Interiors / Fixtures - **Modern Woodcrafts, Inc.**
Restaurant Seating - **Vitro Seating Products**
Restaurant Support - **Lanca Sales, Inc.**
Retail Franchise - **Candy Express**
Retail Packaging - **Lanca Sales, Inc.**
Retail Sales, Musical Instruments - **Torres Engineering**
Retail, Wholesail, Commercial - **Silkwood Wholesale, Inc.**
Retails Educational Video and Audio Tapes; Educ - **Health Impact Inc**
Retaining Wall Parts & Materials - **T & B Structural Systems, Inc.**
Retort Crate Loaders & Unloaders - **Busse Inc. (Mfr)**
Reusable Bio-medical Waste Containers - **Bondtech Corp.**
Reusable Cataract Cryoextractor Kits - **The Du-al Corp.**
Revenue Meter Standards - **Arbiter Systems Inc**
Reverse Osmosis Equipment - **H2o, Inc.**
Reverse Osmosis Systems - **Springsoft International Inc.**
Reverse Osmosis Water Desalination Systems - **Aquamatch Inc**
Revolving Doors - Manufacturer - **Boon Edam, Inc.**
Rewinders for Consumer Products - **Elsner Engineering Works Inc.**
Rf Cable Assemblies - **Delaire U. S. A., Inc.**
Rf Coaxial Cables - **B Q Products Inc.**
Rf Contract Manufacturer - **Delaire U. S. A., Inc.**
Rf Emission Measuring & Control Systems- **Dynamic Sciences Int'l Inc**
Rf Microwave Components & Test Equip - **Weinschel, Bruno Assocs., Inc.**
Rf Welding Machines - **Zmd International Inc**
Ribbon & Transmission Cable Asemblies - **Electronic Manufacturing Svc**
Ribbons & Bows for Apparel & Retail - **Brooklyn Bow International**
Ribbons, Bowls, Desk Accessories - **Classic Medallics, Inc. (Mfr)**
Rice - **Brahmandeva Federation**
Rice - **Garnac Grain**
Rice - **Parisi-virana Co., Inc.**
Rice Byproducts, Export - **Farmers Rice Cooperative**
Rice Milling - **Sem Chi Rice Products**
Rice, Long Grain Polished or Brown Rice - **Sem Chi Rice Products**
Rice, Semi-milled or - **Ps International**
Rigid Vinyl Extrusions - **Pan American Plastics Co., Div. Of Hunt-wilde**
Risers - Gas - **Policonductos S.a. De C.v.**
Road Base Stabilizer - **C S S Technology Inc.**
Road Building - **Krooked Kreek Logging Co.**
Road Construction & Asphalt Mixing Equipment - **Midland Machinery**
Road Marking Equipment - **Super Precision Design, Inc.**
Road Tractors for Semi-trailers - **Aresco, Inc.**
Road Tractors for Semi-trailers - **Schwing America, Inc.**
Road Tractors for Semi-trailers - **Crown Truck Sales**
Road Tractors for Semi-trailers - **Ameri Housing**
Road Wheels and Parts - **Harley-davidson, Inc.**
Roadway Safety Features - **Transpo Indsutries, Inc.**
Roasted Coffee - **Great Northern Coffee Co Inc**
Roasted Coffee - **Jbr Inc**
Robotic Arm & Nozzle Assemblies- **Shotcrete Technologies Inc**
Robotic Packaging Equipment - **Flexicell, Inc.**
Robotic System, Integrtor - **Rapid Development Service**
Robotic Systems & Materials Handling Systems - **Bmi Automation, Inc.**
Robotic Welding Equipment - **Morrow Tech Industries**
Robots and Electro/mechanical Exhibits - **Guard Lee, Inc.**
Rock Drilling Equipment for Mining Construction - **D & L Thomas Equip**
Rodeo Gear - **Saddle Barn Tack Distributors, Inc.**
Roll Forming - **R a M Products**
Roll-off Containers - Steel & Poly - **Bucks Fabricating**
Roll-out Awnings - **Cover-it Shelters, Inc.**
Roller Burnishing Tools - **Cogsdill Tool Products Inc. (Mfr)**
Roller Press Die Cutter - **Zmd International Inc**
Roller Service - **Thistle Roller Co Inc**
Roller, Centrifugal, Diaphragm, Pistons, Plunger, - **Hypro Corp.**
Rolling & Drawing Flat Aluminum Wire - **Steel Heddle Mfg. Co. (Mfr)**
Rolling & Drawing Flat Copper Wire - **Steel Heddle Mfg. Co. (Mfr)**
Rolling & Drawing, Copper Alloy - **Fisk Alloy Wire, Inc.**
Rolling Magnetic Gasketing System - **Smoke Guard Corporation**
Rolling Mill Machinery - **Hoffman Tool & Die Inc.**
Rolling Mill Machinery - **Enkotec Co., Inc.**
Rolling Mill Machinery & Roll Coverings - **Steel Plant Equipment Corp.**
Rollout Programs - **Dolphin Mfg. Inc.**

Roof Algae, Mold & Fungas Inhibitors - **Rainhandler**
Roof Coating Protective Insulating - **Spm Thermo-shield, Inc.**
Roof Coatings & Cements - **Henry Company International**
Roof Fasteners - **Tru-fast Corp.**
Roof Panel Machine, Mfg. - **New Tech Machinery Inc**
Roof Skylight Safety Screws - **Tru-fast Corp.**
Roof Trusses - **Warner Robins Supply Co., Inc.**
Roof Underlayments - **Henry Company International**
Roofing & Waterproofing Materials - **Siplast Inc.**
Roofing Hatchets & Equipment - **A. J. C. Hatchet Co.**
Roofing Insulation and Roof Deck Materials - **Stronglite Products**
Roofing Slate, Structural Slate, Floor- **Penn Big Bed Slate Co., Inc.**
Roofing, Roof Tiles, Bur Roofing - **Waite, R. M. Company**
Rooftop Exhaust Packages - **Gaylord Industries, Inc.**
Roots Organic Biostimulant - **North American Export Company**
Rope, Twine, Braided Products - **Winchester Auburn Mills, Inc**
Rosa Mosqueta Rose Hip Moistuurizing Cream - **Aubrey Organics Inc.**
Rotary & Percussion Rebuilt Drill Bits. - **Hutchens Bit Service, Inc.**
Rotary Airlocks & Diverters - **Sunco Powder Systems, Inc.**
Rotary Blowers, Vacuum Pumps & Centrifugal Compressors - **Roots**
Rotary Cutting Dies - **American Die Technology Inc.**
Rotary Furnace Manufacturer Design & Installation - **Marport Smelting**
Rotary Gear Pumps / for All Processing Industries - **Edwards Mfg. Inc.**
Rotary Joints, Swivels & Couplings - **Rotary Systems Inc.**
Rotary Pumps, Positive Displacement - **Tri-rotor, Inc.**
Rotary Screw & Vane Compressors - **V R Systems, Inc.**
Rotary Swaging - **Richard Industries, J.**
Rotating Equipment Carbon /Ptfe Replacement Parts - **Roc Carbon Co.**
Rotational - Molded Poly Planters - **Henri Studio Inc.**
Rotational Molding, Injection Molding, R.v. Tanks - **Inca Plastics Molding**
Rotational, Agricultural Plastic Water Tanks - **High Country Plastics Inc**
Rotationally Molded Plastic Products - **Jeco Plastic Products, Inc.**
Rotisseries - **Broaster Co., the**
Rotogravure Printing, Autoclavable Indicating Inks - **Alcar Industries, Inc.**
Rototillers and Trenchers - **Barreto Manufacturing**
Rough Cut Lumber - **Lemhi Post & Poles Inc**
Rough and Finished Petrified Wood Products - **Petrified Wood Co**
Round & Shaped & Electroplated Wire - **Delta Precision Alloys**
Routers (Ac or Dc Powered) - **Cordell Manufacturing Inc**
Rubber & Metal Coupled Hoses - **J G B Enterprises, Inc.**
Rubber & Plastic Compounds - **M. A. Hanna Rubber Compounding**
Rubber & Plastic Hose & Belting - **Teleflex Fluid Systems, Inc.**
Rubber & Plastic Pipeline Products - **Maloney Technical Product, Inc.**
Rubber & Plastics Compounding Equipment, - **Farrel Corp.**
Rubber Extruding - **Thistle Roller Co Inc**
Rubber Hose - **Fitting House Inc**
Rubber Injection Equipment - **Hydratecs Injection Equipment, Inc.**
Rubber Inner Tubes - **U.t.c. Tires & Rubber Comp.**
Rubber Lined Pipe - **Rubber Engineering**
Rubber Liners for Ball & Sag Mill Grinding - **Rubber Engineering**
Rubber Molded Products - **T & C Mfg. & Operating, Inc.**
Rubber Molding & Extrusions - **Pelmor Labs, Inc.**
Rubber Plumbing Items - **Esco Rubber Products Inc**
Rubber Processing Chemicals - **C.p. Hall Company, the (Mfr)**
Rubber Products - **Radiator Specialty Co.**
Rubber Products - **Lakin Tire East, Inc.**
Rubber Products_fabricated - **United Technologies Automotive, Inc.**
Rubber Products_fabricated - **Trelleborg Ysh, Inc.**
Rubber Products_fabricated - **Bas Recycling Inc**
Rubber Products_fabricated - **Bingham Roller Co.**
Rubber Products_fabricated - **California Latex Inc**
Rubber Products_fabricated - **Colorado Rubber & Supply Co**
Rubber Products_fabricated - **Cooper Engineered Products**
Rubber Products_fabricated - **Jsp International**
Rubber Products_fabricated - **Lauren Mfg. Co.**
Rubber Products_fabricated - **Lockwood Industries Inc**
Rubber Products_fabricated - **Metal Rubber Corporation**
Rubber Products_fabricated - **R Wales & Son Llc**
Rubber Products_fabricated - **Rahco Rubber, Inc.**
Rubber Products_fabricated - **T & C Mfg. & Operating, Inc.**
Rubber Products_fabricated - **T M P Technologies, Inc**

Rubber Products_fabricated - **Truck Tracks Inc**
Rubber Rollers; Bonds Rubber to Metal - **Diamond Rubber Products Co.,**
Rubber Rollers; Bonds Rubber to Metal - **Metal Rubber Corporation**
Rubber Sealing Devices (Job Shop) - **R & R Rubber Molding Inc**
Rubber Timing Belts - **Jason Industrial, Inc.**
Rubber Truck Tracks - **Truck Tracks Inc**
Rubber and Plastics Footwear - **Converse**
Rubber and Thermoplastic Conveyor Belting - **Jsj Corp/sparks Belting**
Rubber, Plastic, Pvc, & Urethane - **Fabreeka International Inc**
Rubber, Synthetic - **L S M Labs, Inc.**
Rubber_synthetic - **Psi Inc**
Rubber_synthetic - **United Technologies Automotive, Inc.**
Rubberstamps - **Qwikstamp Corporation**
Rugelach - **Neuman Bakery Specialties, Inc.**
Rugged Enclosures, Cabinets, Racks, Cases - **Shock Tech, Inc.**
Rugs - **Home Dynamix**
Rupture Discs, Holders, Alarm Systems, Vent Panels - **Continental Disc**
Rust Removers & Inhibitors - **Supreme Chemicals of Georgia**
Rv & Boat Cabin Heaters - **Thermal Systems Inc**
Rvvd Air Conditioning Equipment - **Noland**
Rx Ultra Suave, Chemo Therapy Brushes - **P H B Inc.**
S/s Storage & Process Tanks - **International Machinery Exchange**
Saccharimeters, Laboratory Instruments - **Rudolph Instruments, Inc.**
Saccharimeters, Nir - **Rudolph Instruments, Inc.**
Saddlery and Consumer Products - **Just Merino Sheepskin Products**
Saddlery and Harness for Any Animal - **Hartz Mountain**
Saddlery and Harness for Any Animal - **Tenwood International**
Safe Deposit Boxes - **Allied Security Equipment**
Safe Replacement Solvents for Acetone, Xylene, I,i,i-tca - **Svc Labs**
Safe-arm Devices, Arm-fire Devices - **Quantic Industries Inc**
Safes, Iron & Steel - **Allied Security Equipment**
Safety & Detection Mirrors, Loss Prevention - **Protex International Corp.**
Safety Devices, Body Armor, Wholesale - **U. S. Cavalry, Inc.**
Safety Equpment & Gear - **Alamia Inc**
Safety Flares for Highway, Marine & Railroad - **Standard Fusee**
Safety Interlocks and Sensors for Oems - **Sentrol Industrial**
Safety Personal Protection Equipment - Eye, Face - **Dalloz Safety**
Safety Work Clothing - **J. D American Workwear, Inc.**
Sailboat Equipment - **Harken International, Ltd.**
Sailing Watches - **Harken International, Ltd.**
Saints Medals, Religiuos Art & Jewelry, Holy Cards - **Rosary House, Inc.**
Salad Dressings & Lime Juice & Lemon Juice - **Nellie & Joe's, Inc.**
Salads, Savorys, Spreads - **Miss Scarlett Inc**
Sales / Service / O&m - **Lifesource Engineering Inc.**
Sales, Service and Parts for Engines- **James Heavy Equipment Specialist**
Salmon Jerky & Seafood Snack Products - **Alaskan Dried Foods**
Salmon, Prepared or Preserved, Whole or in Pieces, - **Pafco Importing Co.**
Salt Tablets, Season Tablets - **Cargill Salt Co/dispensing Sys**
Salt, All Types, - **United Salt**
Salty Snacks - **Link Snacks, Inc.**
Salvaging - **Arc Industries Inc.**
Sample Handling & Extraction & Air Monitor Devices - **Supelco, Inc.**
Sample Storage Systems - **Cargille Laboratories, Inc.**
Sample and Single Use Sized Plastic Packages - **Andrew M Martin Co.**
Sampling Equipment for Smoke Stacks - **Epm Environmental, Inc.**
Sampling Equipment for Soil, Soil - **Art's Manufacturing & Supply Inc**
Sampling Systems - **Tyco Valves & Controls**
Sanblasting - **C & B Fosters Inc.**
Sand Bag Filling Machinery - **Sandbagger Corp.**
Sand-casts Brass and Aluminum - **Quality Brass & Aluminum Foundry**
Sandblasting; Pretreatment - **Americoat Corp.**
Sands, Natural, Except Metal Bearing or - **Philadelphia Resins**
Sanitary Basket Washing Machine - **Af Industries, Alvey Washing Equip**
Sanitary Food Process Systems - **Trans Market Sales & Equipment, Inc.**
Sanitary Pan Washing Machinery - **Af Industries, Alvey Washing**
Sanitary Paper Products - **Paper Pak Products Inc**
Sanitary Paper Products - **Roses Southwest Papers**
Sanitary Wall Coverings & Ceiling Panels - **Kemlite**
Sanitary Ware, Water Control Valves - **Coast Foundry & Mfg Co**
Sanitation & Disinfection Products for Poultry, - **Sentry Chemical Co.**
Sap, Baan, Oracle, Enterprise - **Cap Gemini America**

Satellite Communication Trucks - **B a F Communications Corp.**
Satellite Communications Equipment - **Vortex Satcom Systems, Inc.**
Satellite Earth Station Antennas - **Prodelin Corp.**
Satellite Systems & Payloads - **Caravan International**
Saturated & Coated Substrates for Tape Applications - **Fiber Mark Inc.**
Saturated Roofing Felt - **United Roofing Mfg. Co., Inc.**
Sauces, Salad Dressings and Pickled Vegetables - **Champagne Sauces Inc.**
Saucony Running & Biking Performance Apparel - **Saucony, Inc.**
Sauerkraut - **United Pickle Products Corp.**
Sauerkraut, Prepared or Preserved - **Steinfelds Products**
Sausage Linking & Peeling, Machinery - **Linker Machines**
Sausages & Other Prepared Meat Products - **Bar-s Foods Co.**
Sausages & Other Prepared Meat Products - **Corfu Foods, Inc.**
Sausages & Other Prepared Meat Products - **P G Molinari & Sons Inc**
Sausages & Other Prepared Meat Products - **Sara's Sausage**
Sausages and Prepared Meat Products; Processes - **Sara's Sausage**
Saves 50% of Payroll - **Alfa Southwest Maquiladora Svc**
Saw Blades - **Chamfer Master Tool Co.**
Saw Sharpening Supplies - **I.c.e. (International Carbide & Engineering**
Sawmill & Dry Kiln Operations - **Big Timber Inc. (Mfr)**
Sawmill Equipment - **United Machine Ind. Inc.**
Sawmills - **Yeager Sawmill**
Sawmills & Planing Mills, General - **Algoma Lumber Co.**
Sawmills & Planing Mills, General - **Avison Forest Products**
Sawmills & Planing Mills, General - **Clinton Hardwood Inc.**
Sawmills & Planing Mills, General - **Creveling Sawmill**
Sawmills & Planing Mills, General - **Great Northern Lumber, Inc.**
Sawmills & Planing Mills, General - **Hampton Lumber Sales Co**
Sawmills & Planing Mills, General - **Helsel Lumber Mill, Inc.**
Sawmills & Planing Mills, General - **Johnson Lumber Co., Llc.**
Sawmills & Planing Mills, General - **Jones Lumber Co., Inc., J. M.**
Sawmills & Planing Mills, General - **Krooked Kreek Logging Co.**
Sawmills & Planing Mills, General - **New River Building Supply & Lumb**
Sawmills & Planing Mills, General - **Temple-inland Forest Products Corp**
Sawmills & Planing Mills, General - **Wolohan Lumber**
Sawmills; Timberlands; Kiln Drying Facilities; Veneer Mill- **Hamer, Jim C.**
Saws, Circular, High Speed, Steel & Carbide - **Martindale Electric Co.**
Sbs Membranes - **Henry Company International**
Scaffold, Steel - **Able Builders Export, Inc.**
Scales - **Scalemen of Florida, Inc.**
Scales & Balances - **King J.a. & Company**
Scales & Balances - **Scalemen of Florida, Inc.**
Scales & Balances, Except Laboratory - **Aaa Weigh Inc**
Scales & Balances, Except Laboratory - **Electronic Weighing Systems,**
Scales & Balances, Except Laboratory - **General Electrodynamics Corp.**
Scales & Balances, Except Laboratory - **Pelouze/health-o-meter, Inc.**
Scales & Balances, Except Laboratory - **Pennsylvania Scale Co.**
Scales & Balances, Except Laboratory - **Polyproducts Corp.**
Scales & Balances, Except Laboratory - **Weigh-tronix Inc**
Scales Uld Air Cargo - **Kietek International, Inc.**
Scales and Bar Code Inventory Control Systems; - **Aaa Weigh Inc**
Scanners: Fiche / Jackets & 16/35mm Roll Film - **Houston Fearless 76**
Scented Products - **Stronglite Products**
Schiffli Yarn - **Robison-anton Textile Company (Mfr)**
School Buses - **ADRA International**
School Buses - **Mastin Motors**
School Furniture & Equipment - **Hammett Co., Inc., J. L.**
School Furniture & Equipment; Institutional - **Norco Products**
School Supplies Instructional Materials - **Hammett Co., Inc., J. L.**
Schools & Educational Services - **Bioelements Inc**
Scientific Glassware - **Chemglass Inc.**
Scientific High Vacuum Equipment - **Hawe Technical Associates (Hta)**
Scientific High Vacuum Equipment - **Hta**
Scientific Instruments - **Mcpherson Inc.**
Scientific Instruments, Radiation Shielding, - **Gamma Products, Inc.**
Scientific Instruments, Whsle. - **A. Daigger & Company, Inc.**
Scientific Instruments; Flow Meters, Controller - **Alicat Scientific Inc**
Scientific Specialty Light Bulbs - **Bulbtronics, Inc.**
Scientific Spectrometer Instrumentation - **Interface Design Inc.**
Scientific Ultra High Vacuum Equipment - **Hta**
Scientific Underwater sensor anti-fouling devices- **Oceanogarphic Ind. Inc**

Scoring & Die Cutting - **Wolf Creek Printing**
Scr Power Controllers - **Motortronics, Inc.**
Scrap - **Tata, Inc.**
Scrap & Waste Materials - **Bas Recycling Inc**
Scrap Copper & Aluminum, Export - **Cma Incorporated**
Scrap Metal - **Sos Metals, Inc.**
Scrap Metal Including Aluminum, Copper - **Sos Metal San Diego**
Scrap Metal Recycler - **A & S Metal Recycling, Inc.**
Scrapping Tools - **Diemasters, Inc.**
Scratch-off Tickets & Promotional Items - **Marketing Concepts**
Screen Frame & Accessories - **Mason Corp.**
Screen Printing - **Bannerville U. S. A. Inc.**
Screen Printing - **Custom Screens, Inc.**
Screen Printing - **T Formation of Tallahassee, Inc.**
Screen Printing - **Chromaline Corp.**
Screen Printing - **Schofield Printing, Inc.**
Screen Printing & Point-of-purchase Displays - **Process Graphics Corp.**
Screen Printing Ink - **Solar Color Chemical Corp.**
Screen Printing Screens, Supplies - **Southwestern Process Supply Co.**
Screen Printing Supplies & Equipment - **Tube Light Co., Inc.**
Screen Printing, Flexographic, Offset, Letterpress - **Palone & Associates**
Screen Printing, Sportswear Imprinting - **T-shirts & Graphics**
Screens - Hammers (Agricultural Replacement Parts) - **Fabtron Corp.**
Screw Conveyors - **Flexicon Corporation**
Screw Drivers,punches,chisels - **Enderes Tool Company Inc**
Screw Extractors - **Jaw Manufacturing Co.**
Screw Machine CNC- **American Precision Machine Products, Inc.**
Screw Machine Products - **Afton Plastics**
Screw Machine Products - **American Precision Machine Products, Inc.**
Screw Machine Products - **Chester Precision Co.**
Screw Machine Products - **Cole Screw Machine Products, Inc.**
Screw Machine Products - **Delo Screw Products, a Park-ohio Co.**
Screw Machine Products - **Fortress Mfg., Inc. (Mfr)**
Screw Machine Products - **Prime Screw Machine Products Inc.**
Screw Machine Products - **Weltek-swiss**
Screw Machine Products - **Zenith Screw Products Inc**
Screw Machine Products - **Owen Tool & Mfg. Co., Inc.**
Screw Machine Products - **Fortress Mfg. Inc.**
Screw Machine Products (Job Work); - **Weltek-swiss**
Screw Machine Products, Air Precision Parts - **A & B Aerospace Inc**
Screw Machine Products, Shafts, Dowels- **Dowels, Pins & Shafts, Inc.**
Screw Machine Products, Single & Multi Spindle - **Rsm Products, Inc.**
Screw Machining - **Kurt Manufacturing Co.**
Screw Thread Inserts and Related Tooling - **Helical Wire Inc**
Screws, Nuts, Bolts, Washers, Gaskets, O-rings - **State Industrial Supply**
Scrubbers - **Turner Envirologic, Inc.**
Sculpturing Epoxies - **Polygem**
Sea & Air Freight - **Dartrans, Inc.**
Sea Vegetation, Vitamins, Health Nutritional -**Wachters Organic Sea**
Sea Water Converters - **Culligan Wate Conditioning, Inc.**
Seafood Appetizers, Boneless Stuffed Chickens - **Ecrevisse Acadienne**
Seafood Extracts - All Natural, Powder & Pastes - **Accurate Ingredients**
Seafood, Fresh & Frozen Fish, Seacucumber - **Ultimate International**
Sealants for Ships - **Henry Company International**
Sealants, Adhesives & Rubber - **United Technologies Automotive, Inc.**
Sealed Latches - **Norse, Inc.**
Seals & Seal Kits, Industrial, Wholesale - **Hercules Hydraulics Inc.**
Seals & Seal Kits, Mob. Hydraul. - **Hercules Hydraulics Inc.**
Seam Weld Gantries - **Ogden Engineering Corp.**
Seamless Cans - **U. S. Can Co., Custom & Specialty Division**
Seamless Gutter Machine, Mfg. - **New Tech Machinery Inc**
Seamless Rings - **Standard Steel**
Search & Navigation Equipment - **Aqua Signal Corp.**
Search & Navigation Equipment - **Drs Precision Echo**
Search & Navigation Equipment - **Enterprise Electronics Corp.**
Search & Navigation Equipment - **Flir Systems Inc**
Search & Navigation Equipment - **Litton Industries Inc**
Search & Navigation Equipment - **Oceanographic Industries, Inc.**
Search & Navigation Equipment - **Survival Safety Engineering, Inc.**
Searches / Partnering, Developing Sales - **L.a. Markom De Mexico, S.a.**
Seasonal Decorations, Theatrical & Floral Supplies - **Consolidated Display**

Seasonings Pizza & Pasta - **Chef Paul Prudhomme's Magic Seasoning**
Seat Belts & Safety Straps - **Safe Strap Co., Inc.**
Seat Recliner Mechanisms - **Excel of Stockton**
Seat Systems Hardware - **Excel of Stockton**
Seat Track Mechanisms - **Excel of Stockton**
Second Hand Clothing - **Noamex**
Secondary Aluminum - **Fata Hunter, Inc.**
Secondary Aluminum Alloys (Recycled) - **Wabash Alloys, Llc**
Secondary Aluminum Ingots; Extrusi - **Tst Inc**
Secondary Market Guide - **Used Equipment Directory**
Secondary Nonferrous Metals - **Lockwood Industries Inc**
Secondary Nonferrous Metals - **Co-steel Raritan**
Secondary Nonferrous Metals - **Aaa Precious Metals Inc**
Secondary Nonferrous Metals - **Marport Smelting Co., Llc**
Secondary Stainless Steel Circ - **Trade Metal Inc.**
Secretarial & Legal Secretarial - **Pc Services**
Security & Alarm Systems & Equipment - **Detex International**
Security - Blast Protection - **Virginia Iron & Metal Co.**
Security Concerns, Library Services, Membership - **Allsafe Co., Inc.**
Security Counters - **U S Paper Counters Co.**
Security Doors, Windows, Walls - **Insulgard Corporation**
Security Foils - **Transfer Print Foils, Inc.**
Security Glass - **Custom Glass Corp.**
Security Glass - **Laminated Glass**
Security Lighting - **Magnaray International**
Security Pen Sets - **Matel Bank and Desk Accessories**
Security Products for the Self-storage Industry - **Demco Electronics**
Security Revolving Doors, Manufacturer - **Boon Edam, Inc.**
Security Screens - **Accurate Screening Media, Inc.**
Security System Services - **Advantor Corp.**
Security Systems - **Protex International Corp.**
Security, Sports, Landscape, Decorative - **R L S Lighting, Inc.**
See Our Www.a1machining.com Web Page. - **A-1 Machining Co.**
Seed - **United Farmers Co-op**
Seed Processing Machinery - **Carver, Inc.**
Seed Production - **H & H Seed Company Inc**
Seed Sales - **Sims Bros., Inc.**
Seed and Grain - **H & H Seed Company Inc**
Seedless Watermelon Seed - **Seedcraft**
Seeds of Coriander - **Seedcraft**
Seeds, Fruit and Spores - **Western Hybrid Seeds, Inc.**
Seersuckers - **Laren Industries**
Seismic Equipment for the Oil Field Ind- **Int'l Equipment Distributors**
Self-contained Breathing Apparatus - **Biomarine Inc.**
Self-priming Centrifugal Pumps & Hand Pumps - **Pacer Pumps**
Self-vulcanizing Repairs - **Par Products**
Semen, Embryos - **Maplehurst Genetics Intl. Inc.**
Semi - Trailers - **Flow Boy Manufacturing Co.**
Semi Precision Steel Balls - **Abbott Ball Co. (Mfg)**
Semi-permanent Release Coating - **Axel Plastics Research Laboratories**
Semi-trailer Tanks - **Beall Corp.**
Semiconductor Equipment, New & Used - **Alpha Technology**
Semiconductor Etching Equipment An - **Raines Technologies Inc**
Semiconductor Processing Equipment - **Axic Inc**
Semiconductors - **New Jersey Semicondutor Products, Inc.**
Semiconductors - **T L C Precision Wafer Tech, Inc.**
Semiconductors & Drams, Wholesale - **Advanced Circuit Enterprises**
Semiconductors & Related Devices - **Diablo Industries**
Semiconductors & Related Devices - **Flip Chip Technologies Llc**
Semiconductors & Related Devices - **Interfet Corporation**
Semiconductors & Related Devices - **Kinetic Ceramics Inc**
Semiconductors & Related Devices - **New Jersey Semicondutor Products,**
Semiconductors & Related Devices - **Pdp Systems**
Semiconductors & Related Devices - **Solarex**
Semiconductors & Related Devices - **T L C Precision Wafer Tech, Inc.**
Semiconductors & Related Devices - **Target Materials, Inc.**
Semiconductors & Related Devices - **Wafer World, Inc.**
Semiconductors & Related Devices - **V T C Inc.**
Semiconductors & Related Devices for Video - **Pmc Electronics**
Semifinished Metal Products, Export - **Incon Overseas Marketing, Inc.**
Semivitreous Table & Kitchenware - **Accent Enterprizes, Inc.**

Sensors to Measure Rotary or Linear Position - **Midori America Corp**
Serial I/o and Remote Access Communication - **Stallion Technologies Inc**
Service & Mechanics Trucks for Mining & Construction - **Aresco, Inc.**
Service & Repair of Waste Handling Equipment. - **Golten Service**
Service Bodies & Ladder Racks - **Pacific Utility Equipment Co**
Service Establishment Equipment - **C & W Enterprises**
Service Establishment Equipment - **Brewmatic Co**
Service Establishment Equipment - **Howard, Bill**
Service Industry Equipment, Liquor Control Systems - **Berg Co., Div. Dc**
Service Industry Machinery - **Aqua Blast Corp.**
Service Industry Machinery - **Aquatec, Inc.**
Service Industry Machinery - **Azure Blue Inc**
Service Industry Machinery - **Bondtech Corp.**
Service Industry Machinery - **Brewmatic Co**
Service Industry Machinery - **Enting Water Conditioning Inc.**
Service Industry Machinery - **Ftc**
Service Industry Machinery - **Henny Penny Corp.**
Service Industry Machinery - **Osmonics, Inc.**
Service Industry Machinery - **Teledyne Water Pik**
Service Industry Machinery, Vacuum Equipment - **Yeagle Technology, Inc.**
Service Pin Jewelry, Official Police and Fire - **Entenmann-rovin Company**
Service Repair Parts - Backhoe Loaders - **Joseph Industries, Inc.**
Service Station Equipment Repair, Electronic Compoenet Parts - **Esco Svc**
Service Wireholders,cleats,knobs,tubes - **Porcelain Products Co.**
Servicing Retail, Food Service & Industrial - **Catania Spagna**
Servo Systems - **Bei Sensors & Systems/kimco Magnetics Division**
Sesame Oil - **Arista Industries, Inc.**
Set Stones & Repair Jewelry - **Vicki's Jewelry**
Setup & Dismantle of Exhibits - **Admore Inc.**
Severe Service Control Valves - **Control Components, Inc.**
Sewage Lagoon Baffles, Liners, Secondary Containment Sys - **Therma-fab,**
Sewage Treatment Equipment - **Walker Process Equip.**
Sewer & Drain Cleaning Equipment - **Municipal Equipment Exports**
Sewer & Sink Cleaning Machines - **My-tana Mfg. Co., Inc.**
Sewer Cleaner Truck Mounted - **Super Products Corp.**
Sewer Cleaning Tools - **Petersen Products Co.**
Sewing Machine Parts - **Richard Sewing Machine**
Sewing Machines - **Pennsylvania Sewing Machine Co.**
Sewing Machines - **Astechnologies**
Sewing Manufacturer, by Contract - **New American Industries Inc**
Sewing Thread of Manmade Filaments - **United Thread Mills**
Sewing Threads - **American & Efird, Inc.**
Sewn Products - **Jg Creations Inc**
Sexy Lingerie & Hosiery & Stockings - **Pass Distributing Corporation**
Shackles - **Crosby Group, Inc.**
Shafts & Keyways to 2 Inches O.d. (5cm) - **A C Products Co., Inc.**
Shampoo for Hair - **Marianna Importers, Exporters & Manufacturers,**
Shampoos, Conditioners & Relaxers - **Biocare Labs**
Sharp Calculators - **Juno International**
Sheaves - **Crosby Group, Inc.**
Sheepskins - **Just Merino Sheepskin Products**
Sheet Counting & Batch-tabbing Equipment - **U S Paper Counters Co.**
Sheet Metal Fabrication - **Messina Metal Mfg**
Sheet Metal Fabrication - **R O T H B R O S., Inc., a First Energy Co.**
Sheet Metal Fabrication - **Sixnel Sheet Metal**
Sheet Metal Fabrication & Precision Mach - **Fab-tech Industries of Breva**
Sheet Metal Fabrication & Ultra Seam Metal Roofing - **Shurtleff-g aH A R**
Sheet Metal Fabrication, Metal Fabrication - **Lewgust Co., Inc.**
Sheet Metal Mfg., Carbon Steel, Stainless Steel, Aluminum - **Liberty Mfg.,**
Sheet Metal Roofing Materials - **Architectural Building Components**
Sheet Metal Work - **Metal Master**
Sheet Metal Work - **American Tool & Engrg Corp**
Sheet Metal Work - **Cannon Industries**
Sheet Metal Work - **Fab-tech Industries of Brevard, Inc.**
Sheet Metal Work - **Flexmaster U S a Inc.**
Sheet Metal Work - **Messina Metal Mfg**
Sheet Metal Work - **Northeast Fabricators, L.l.c.**
Sheet Metal Work - **Sixnel Sheet Metal**
Sheet Metal Work - **Metal Master Inc**
Sheet Metal Work - **Nelson Products Co.**
Sheet Metal Work - **Essex Cryogenics of Missouri, Inc.**

Sheet Metal Work (Food Service Equipment) - **Broadway Sheet Metal**
Sheet Metal Work, Hvac Caps and Flashings, - **Artis Metals Company Inc**
Sheet Metal Work, Truck & Trailer Parts - **Lewgust Co., Inc.**
Sheet Vinyl Flooring - **Congoleum Corp.**
Sheetmetal Fabrication Software - **Metalsoft, Inc.**
Sheets & Pillow Cases Poly/cotton Blend - **Allegra Industries, Inc.**
Shelf & Rack Label Holders - **Aigner Index, Inc.**
Shelf Stable Foods - **The Wornick Company**
Shelled Pecans - **Green Valley Pecan Company**
Shellfish Frozen, Prepared - **Fishery Products International Inc.**
Shellfish Traps, Lobster, Shrimp, Crab, Prawns - **Fathoms plus**
Shielded Gaskets & Vents - **Alco Technologies Inc**
Shielding - **Summit Coating Technologies, Llc**
Ship & Boat Models Sales, Repairs & Appraisals - **Ship Chandler**
Ship Brokers & Agents - **Shinwa (Usa) Inc.**
Ship Loaders - **Neuero Corp.**
Ship Management - **Globe Shipping, Globe Ship Managment, Inc.**
Ship Owners Representative - **Globe Shipping, Globe Ship Managment,**
Ship Unloaders - **Neuero Corp.**
Ship Worldwide - **Silkwood Wholesale, Inc.**
Shipboard Electronics & Communications Equip. - **Litton Data Systems,**
Shipboard Racks, Cabinets, Enclosures - **Shock Tech, Inc.**
Shipping Documents Preparation - **Schroeder United Van Lines**
Shirting Fabrics - **Pride International**
Shirts_men's & Boys' - **Manic Impressions**
Shock & Vibration Mounts, Shock & Vibration Analysis - **Shock Tech, Inc.**
Shock Absorbers - **World Trading**
Shoe Lace Machinery, Export - **Commision Brokers, Inc.**
Shoe Machinery - **International Shoe Machine Corporation**
Shoe Repair Equipment & Supplies - **Shu-re-nu Equipment, Inc.**
Shoe Repair Products - **Unique Sports Products, Inc.**
Shoe Trees / Shoe Care - **Rochester Shoe Tree Company**
Shooting Sports Equipment - **Action International**
Shop Fabricated Tanks & Vessels - **American Tank & Vessel**
Shoring - **Able Builders Export, Inc.**
Short Arc Lamp Power Supplies - **Spectral Energy Corp.**
Short Arc Lamp Souces - **Spectral Energy Corp.**
Short Range Video Transmitters & Receivers - **Pmc Electronics**
Short to Medium Run Book Printer - **Giant Horse Printing Inc**
Shot End Components - **Semco Inc.**
Shotcrete Accelerators, Chemicals - **Shotcrete Technologies Inc**
Shovels Polypropylene Food Grade - **Remco Products Corp.**
Show Services & Warehousing - **Dieterich & Ball Incorporated**
Showcases - **Dolphin Mfg. Inc.**
Showcases / Cashwraps / Gondolas - **Modern Woodcrafts, Inc.**
Shower Door Hardware - **C.r. Laurence Company, Inc.**
Shower Heads - **Teledyne Water Pik**
Shower Organization - **Interbath, Inc**
Shower Stalls Metal Walls / Terrazzo Rec. - **Stern-williams Company, Inc.**
Showerheads, Handheld Showers and Accessories - **Interbath, Inc**
Shredders - **Alan Ross Machinery Corp**
Shredders - Paper Waste - **Balemaster**
Shrimp Frozen, Prepared - **Fishery Products International Inc.**
Shrimp Traps - **Fathoms plus**
Shrink Packaging Machinery - **Shanklin Corporation**
Shrink Systems & Supplies - **Hemisphere Enterprises**
Shutters - Blinds - Draperies - **Window Technology, Inc.**
Shuttle Buses - **Spalding Products**
Sign Frames - **Asd, Inc. , Architectural Signage & Design**
Signage, Displays & Graphic Design - **Alpha 1 Studio, Inc.**
Signs - **Adaptive Micro Systems, Inc.**
Signs - **Grande Ronde Sign Co**
Signs - **Seton Name Plate Company**
Signs - **Signs & Signs, Inc.**
Signs - **Trophy Shoppe**
Signs & Advertising Specialties - **A B C Sign Design, Llc**
Signs & Advertising Specialties - **Action Media Technologies Inc**
Signs & Advertising Specialties - **Admore Inc.**
Signs & Advertising Specialties - **All Neon & Signs**
Signs & Advertising Specialties - **American Sign Company**
Signs & Advertising Specialties - **Brevis Corp**

Signs & Advertising Specialties - **Ca Signs**
Signs & Advertising Specialties - **Colite International**
Signs & Advertising Specialties - **Consolidated Display Co., Inc.**
Signs & Advertising Specialties - **Cooley Sign & Digital Imaging**
Signs & Advertising Specialties - **Couch & Philippi Inc**
Signs & Advertising Specialties - **Design Display, Inc.**
Signs & Advertising Specialties - **Dezion Signs**
Signs & Advertising Specialties - **Grande Ronde Sign Co**
Signs & Advertising Specialties - **Hi-tech Electronic Displays**
Signs & Advertising Specialties - **Lynne Signs, Lori**
Signs & Advertising Specialties - **M M I Display Group, Inc.**
Signs & Advertising Specialties - **Made in Maui Neon**
Signs & Advertising Specialties - **Moser & Co. Neon Specialists**
Signs & Advertising Specialties - **Muller Studios**
Signs & Advertising Specialties - **Nameplates, Inc.**
Signs & Advertising Specialties - **National Pen Corporation**
Signs & Advertising Specialties - **Neon Fx Sign & Display**
Signs & Advertising Specialties - **Never Boring Design Associates**
Signs & Advertising Specialties - **P & D Polygraphics, Inc.**
Signs & Advertising Specialties - **P & M Sign, Inc.**
Signs & Advertising Specialties - **Pacific Crest Manufacturing Inc**
Signs & Advertising Specialties - **Presentation South, Inc.**
Signs & Advertising Specialties - **Process Graphics Corp.**
Signs & Advertising Specialties - **Signart, Inc.**
Signs & Advertising Specialties - **T-shirts & Graphics**
Signs & Advertising Specialties - **Wescosa Inc**
Signs & Advertising Specialties - **Young Electric Sign Company Boise**
Signs Exterior - **Asd, Inc. , Architectural Signage & Design**
Signs and Advertising Displays for Grocery - **King Design International**
Signs and Banners - **American Sign Company**
Signs, Botanical Garden - **Asd, Inc. , Architectural Signage & Design**
Signs, Braille - **Asd, Inc. , Architectural Signage & Design**
Signs, Displays & Architectural Scale Models - **P & D Polygraphics, Inc.**
Signs, Displays and Fascia - **Couch & Philippi Inc**
Signs, Tenant - **Asd, Inc. , Architectural Signage & Design**
Sikorsky Helicopter Parts & Tools - **Cambridge Specialty Co., Inc.**
Silica Sand & Gravel Processing - **Best Sand Corp.**
Silicne Release Papers & Film - **Maratech International**
Silicon Carbide Components - **Ceradyne, Inc.**
Silicon Nitride Components - **Ceradyne, Inc.**
Silicon Semiconductor Materials - **Wafer World, Inc.**
Silicone & Pvc Extrusion, Silicone Molding, Oem/custom - **Axiom Medical**
Silicone Rubber Electronic Components - **Fujipoly America Corp.**
Silicone Rubber Hot Stamps - **Schwerdtle Stamp Co., Inc.**
Silicone Rubber Products - **L S M Labs, Inc.**
Silicone Specialties - **Petroferm Inc.**
Silk Florals - **Toepperweins of Texas**
Silk Flower Distributor - **Silkwood Wholesale, Inc.**
Silk Folage Assembly, Distributor - **Silkwood Wholesale, Inc.**
Silk Plants - **Toepperweins of Texas**
Silk Press - Creme Press , Scalp Conditioner - **Shelton's Sheen Wave Labs**
Silk Screen Printing on Clothing - **Wyatt West Inc**
Silo Bottom Unloaders - **Laidig Industrial System**
Silos - **Laidig Industrial System**
Silver Recovery Equipment - **Environmental Solutions, Inc.**
Silver Recovery Equipment - **Environmental Compliance Systems, Inc.**
Silver, Brass & Copper Inlayed Wooden Bowls - **Alaska Gift & Gallery**
Silverware - **Haber Co., D. W.**
Silverware & Plated Ware - **Haber Co., D. W.**
Simulated Cast Metal Signs & Plaques - **P & D Polygraphics, Inc.**
Simulation, Animation & Visualization of Traffic Flow - **Kld Associates**
Singl Filer - **Arrowhead Systems Llc**
Single Sheets - **Colonial Business Forms, Inc.**
Single-blade Precision Reaming & Boring Systems - **Cogsdill Tool Products Inc. (Mfr)**
Single-family Housing Construction - **Oregon Log Home Co Inc**
Single-phase Power Systems, All Sizes - **Liebert Corporation**
Singlefilers - **Busse Inc. (Mfr)**
Site Acquisition - Zoning - **Gem Engineering Co., Inc.**
Site Development - **Pierce Packaging Company**
Siwng Doors - **Fleming Steel Co.**

Sized Infant to 4xl - **Paradise Sportswear, Inc.**
Ski Area Supplies - **Idaho Sewing for Sports**
Ski Equipment - **Master Line U S A**
Skid Mounted Process & Control Equipment - **P C & E, Fabcon Div.**
Skid Mounted Steam Turbine Generator Modules - **Geothermal Power Co.**
Skid Steer Loaders & Hay Moving Equipment - **Hecla Industries, Llp**
Skid Steer Pallet Forks - **Construction Technology, Inc.**
Skin Bleaching Gel - **Rejuvi Cosmetic Laboratory**
Skin Care Products - **Gabrielle, Inc.**
Skin Care Products - **Lily of Colorado**
Skin Care Products & Fragrances - **Waikiki Aloe**
Skin Care and Hair Care Products, Lotions - **Lois Yee Cosmetics Inc**
Skin Lotions Creams & Gels - **Rejuvi Cosmetic Laboratory**
Skin Protection Product - **Unique Laboratories, Inc.**
Skincare, Cosmetics, Body, Bath - **Viviane Woodard Cosmetics**
Skis the Ski - **Ski Co Inc**
Skylights - **Major Industries, Inc.**
Slatless Bed Firming Rails, Frames - **Glideway Bed Carriage Mfg. Co.**
Slatwall, Knockdown Store Fixtures - **Nationwide Retail Interiors Inc**
Sleep Diagnostic Instrumentation - **Sensormedics Corporation**
Sleeping Bags and Cold Weather Garments - **Wiggy's Inc**
Slide Forming, in Die Tapping, in Die Assembly. - **Walker Corporation**
Slide Imaging - **Advanced Graphics & Publishing**
Sliding Closet Door Guides - **Schneider Enterprises**
Sligh Home Office Furniture - **Designers Resource**
Slip Rings - **Kevlin Corporation(mfr)**
Slot Walls Store Fixtures - **Spacewall International**
Slotting, Thread Rolling, Parts Washing Machinery - **Warren Industries,**
Sludge Pumps - **Schwing America, Inc.**
Slurry Saw Blades & X-ray Diffraction Machines - **Alvord Systems, Inc.**
Small Air-cooled Engines & Parts - **Ase Supply Inc**
Small Arms - **Lorcin Engineering**
Small Arms - **S T I International, Inc.**
Small Casters - **Respond Group of Companies**
Small Community Systems - **Culligan Wate Conditioning, Inc.**
Small Diameter Low Carbon Steel Tubing - **Indiana Tube**
Small Metal / Wood Packaged - **Advantage Buildings & Exteriors, Inc.**
Small Parcel Sortation - **Quantum Conveyor Systems, Llc**
Small Product Feeding Systems - **Ackley Machine Corp.**
Small Runs - **Zoo-ink Screen Print**
Small to Large Lots, Precision Machining - **A C Products Co., Inc.**
Smoke Detector Tester & Accessories - **Home Safeguard Industries Inc**
Smoked & Jarred Alaskan Oysters - **Alaskan Dried Foods**
Smoked & Jarred Halibut - **Alaskan Dried Foods**
Smoked Salmon-kipperd - **Alaskan Dried Foods**
Smoked and Jarred Salmon - **Alaskan Dried Foods**
Smokers Ash Urns, Steel - **United Metal Receptacle Inc. (Mfr)**
Smokestack Emission Monitoring Equipment - **Apex Instruments**
Snack Foods - **Link Snacks, Inc.**
Snack Grits - **Molinos De Puerto Rico, Inc., a Conagra Company**
Snacks - **Delyse Inc**
Snaptight, Containment and Utility Boxes - **Cni Manufacturing**
Snow Body Insert - **Fair Manufacturings, Inc.(Mfr)**
Snow Throwers, Riding Mowers, Tillers, Garden Tractors - **Ariens Co**
Snowblowers (Farm Equipment) - **Wildcat Mfg. Co., Inc.**
Snowblowers, Commercial - **Fair Manufacturings, Inc.(Mfr)**
Snowblowers, Commercial - **Wildcat Mfg. Co., Inc.**
Snowboards and Skis - **Volant Sports, Llc**
Snowboards, Wakeboards, Skateboards - **Pcie Dba; the France Group**
Soap & Other Detergents - **Burlington Chemical Co., Inc. (Mfr)**
Soap & Other Detergents - **C & W Enterprises**
Soap & Other Detergents - **Hotsy Corporation, the**
Soap & Other Detergents - **L H B Industries**
Soap & Other Detergents - **Norman, Fox & Co**
Soap & Other Detergents - **Supreme Chemicals of Georgia**
Soap & Other Detergents - **B-d Chemical Co Inc**
Soap - Natural / No Animal Products - **Enterprising Kitchen**
Soap Active Products - **Lexard Corporation**
Soap Base, Milled, Translucent - **Original Bradford Soap Works, Inc.**
Soap Making Supplies - **Yaley Enterprises, Inc.**
Soaps, Detergents, Amides and Esters; Custom - **Norman, Fox & Co**

Soaps, Lotions, Creams and Ointment - **Wallsburg Soap Co**
Social Housing - **Hexaport International, Ltd.**
Socket Weld Fittings for Railroads - **Strato, Inc.**
Sockets - **Bulbtronics, Inc.**
Sockets - **Eby Co.**
Sodium Citrate - **Century Multech**
Sodium Ferrocyanide - **Century Multech**
Sodium Hypochlorite - **Equipment & Systems Engineering**
Sodium Sulfates - **Imc Chemical, Inc.**
Sodium Sulfide - **Jupiter Chemicals, Inc.**
Soft Gels - **International Vitamin Corporation**
Soft Plastic Fishing Lures: Worms, Lizards, Shads, & Etc. - **Sims Bait Mfg.**
Soft Side Luggage, Sporting Goods, Coolers - **Pantos Corp**
Software Design, Access / Alarm - Windows 95 - **Apollo**
Software Design, Access/alarm -Windows 95 - **Asti**
Software Development & Integration - **Factory Automation Systems, Inc.**
Software Localization - **Language Interface, Ltd.**
Soil Amendments for Farming - **Ag Acid Inc**
Soil Conditioners - **Live Earth Products**
Soil Mixes - **Stronglite Products**
Soil Moisture Measuring & Sampling Instrumentation - **Irrometer Co. Inc.**
Soil Sampling Equipment & Drilling Rigs - **Concord Environmental Equi**
Soil Stabilization - **Nature Plus, Inc.**
Soil Stabilization Equipment - **Soil Purification Inc.**
Soil, Concrete & Asphalt Testing Equipment - **Laboratory Testing Supply**
Solar Chargers for Portable Devices - **Powerline Solar Products, Inc.**
Solar Cookers / Dryers- **Friendly Appropriate Solar Technologies**
Solar Electric Modules & Components - **Southwest Photovoltaic Systems**
Solar Electricity - **World Power Technologies, Inc.**
Solar Energy Collectors - **Heliodyne, Inc. (Mfr)**
Solar Hot Water - **Heliodyne, Inc. (Mfr)**
Solar Lighting - **Magnaray International**
Solar Lighting & Electric Systems - **Southwest Photovoltaic Systems**
Solar Panels - **Solarex**
Solar Protection Screening - **New York Wire Co.**
Solar Roller Shades & Insect Screens - **Virginia Iron & Metal Co.**
Solar Salt, Rock Salt - **United Salt**
Solar Simulators - **Spectral Energy Corp.**
Solder Recovery System - **Fancort Industries, Inc.**
Soldering Equipment - **Esico-triton**
Soldering Paste, Chemicals, Solder Bar - **Qualitek International, Inc.**
Solenoid - **Takaha America Co.**
Solenoid and Motor Housing. - **Progressive Metal Forming Inc.**
Solenoids - **Oak Grigsby, Inc.**
Solid & Envelope Density - **Micromeritics Instrument Corp.**
Solid Carbide & Pcd Tipped Rotary Cutting Tools - **Micro Carbide Corp**
Solid Carbide Router Bits - **Hayes Tool Inc.(Mfr)**
Solid State & Electromechanical Choppers - **Solid State Electronics Corp**
Solid State Microwave Components - **Miteq, Inc.**
Solid State Motor Starters - **Motortronics, Inc.**
Solid State Motor Starters - **Benshaw, Inc.**
Solid State Power Amplifiers - **Vortex Satcom Systems, Inc.**
Solid State Relays - **Solid State Electronics Corp**
Solid State Timing Devices - **Artisan Controls Corporation (Mfr)**
Solid Surface Countertops & Products - **Hartson Kennedy Cabinet Top**
Solid Wire for Mig & Tig Welding - **Eureka Welding Alloys**
Solids Filling - **Specialty Equipment Co.**
Solvent & Coolant Distillation Equipment - **Finish Thompson Inc.**
Solvent & Oil Recovery Equipment - **Pragmatic Environmental Solutions**
Solvent Extraction Mixer-settlers - **Quinn Process Equipment Co**
Solvent Recovery Equipment - **Finish Thompson, Inc.**
Solvents and Penetrants - **Worldwide Filter**
Sonic Nozzle Provers for Gas Meters - **Energy Economics, Inc.**
Sortation Systems - **Quantum Conveyor Systems, Llc**
Sorters, Mail - **W.a. Charnstrom Co., Inc.**
Sound & Heat Insulation Blankets & Covers - **Great Southern Insulation**
Sound Damping for Automotive - **Elementis Performance Polymers**
Sound Deapening Carpet Underlayment - **Great Southern Insulation**
Sound Equipment and Supplies - **Ultra-stereo Labs Inc**
Sound Proof Upholstered Walls - **General Drapery Services, Inc.**
Sound Systems - **Garrett Sound & Lighting**

Sound Systems & Amplifiers - **Ampli-vox Questron**
Soup & Pasta Seasonings - **Old World Spices & Seasonings, Inc.**
Soup Base Mixes - **International Custom Products**
Soups, Frozen - **Norpac Foods Inc**
Southern Yellow Pine Lumber - **S.g. International**
Soybean Processing & Refining - **Cenex Harvest States Cooperatives**
Soybeans - **Delta International**
Soybeans, Whether or Not Broken - **Zen Noh Grain**
Soybeans, Whether or Not Broken - **Garnac Grain**
Spa Heating - **Air Energy Heat Pumps**
Spa Therapy Products - **Touch America Inc.**
Space Theme Park Design and Construction - **Guard Lee, Inc.**
Space Vehicle Components - **Aerospace Manufacturing Inc**
Space Vehicle Structures - **Texas Composite Inc.**
Space Vehicle and Aircraft Replicas (Full Scale) - **Guard Lee, Inc.**
Spalding Massagers - **Equity Industries**
Spanish & From/into Most Languages - **Magnum Group, Inc.**
Spanish Course on Video - **Language plus**
Spare Parts, Consumables & Tools - **Intramar, Inc.**
Spare Tire Covers for Sport Utility Vehicles - **Autotech Usa**
Spark Wheels - **Elge Precision Machining, Inc.**
Sparking Files & Spark Lighters - **Elge Precision Machining, Inc.**
Spary, Pour & Froth, Rigid Flotation - **Swd Urethane**
Spas - **Plastic Development Company(mfr)**
Spas, Acrylic - **Imperial Pools Inc.**
Spc Gaging Systems - **Kurt Manufacturing Co.**
Speaker Baffles & Mounting Dev., Metal - **Fourjay Industries, Inc.**
Speaker Enclosures - **Fourjay Industries, Inc.**
Speakers - **Ksc Industries Inc**
Spearmint Oil - **Todd Co., A.m.**
Spec. Machinery, Environ. Disposal - **Consolidated Baling Machine Co.,**
Spec. Machinery, Recycling Equipment - **Consolidated Baling Machine**
Special 24 Outlet Heads / Slot Heads - **Adhesive Systems, Inc.**
Special Design Equipment - **Alaco Ladder Co.**
Special Effect Foils - **Transfer Print Foils, Inc.**
Special Hot / Cold Adhesive Systems - **Adhesive Systems, Inc.**
Special Industrial Machinery - **Hess Machine International**
Special Machinery - **Rapid Development Service**
Special Oral Hygiene Apparatus - **Trademark Medical**
Special Precision Metal Cutting Tools - **Midwest Ohio Tool Company**
Special Projects - **Arc Industries Inc.**
Special Trade Contractors, Nec - **Mustang Industrial Equipment**
Specialists in Collecting Dust, Mist, Smoke, Fog - **Thiel Air Technologies**
Specialized Cleaning Compounds - **Eldorado Chemical Co., Inc.**
Specialized Heavy Transportation - **Bigge Crane & Rigging Co.**
Specialized Testers for Electrical Contractors & Electrician - **Tasco Inc**
Specializing in All Rubber Compounds - **C G R Products Inc.**
Specializing in Prime & Waste Paper Worldwide - **Horizon Forwarders**
Specializing in Welding & Diamond Finishing - **Heyden Mold & Bench**
Specialty Alloy Fabrication Services - **Sinterite, Furance Div.**
Specialty Cheeses - Refrigerated - **Sfi Anco Fine Cheese**
Specialty Chemicals for the Computer Disk Drive - **Innovative Organics**
Specialty Components - **Elizabeth Carbide Components**
Specialty Confectionery - **Adams & Brooks Inc**
Specialty Dairy , Powders - **Diehl, Inc.**
Specialty Eyelets to Blueprint - **Prospect Machine Products, Inc.**
Specialty Fluorescent Lamps - **Light Sources, Inc.**
Specialty Inks, Epoxy, Flexo, Indel, Jet - **Ranger Industries**
Specialty Lighting Distribution Systems - **Wiremold Co., the**
Specialty Lubricating Oils, Treatments & Greases - **Kent Oil Company**
Specialty Name Brand Construction Materials - **Border Products Corp**
Specialty Papers - **Pepperell Paper Co., Inc.**
Specialty Papers - **Deerfield Specialty Papers, Inc.**
Specialty Products Abs Systems - **M & E Components, Inc.**
Specialty Sauces - **Dean Foods (Mfr)**
Specialty Tapes, Pressure Sensitive - **Jessup Manufacturing Co.**
Specialty Textured Yarns: Nylon, Poly, Olefin - **Roselon Industries, Inc.**
Specialty Tools Fo Airframe Production & Maintenance - **Zephyr MFR.**
Specialty Truck & S.u.v. Packages - **Trail Wagons Inc**
Specialty Windows & Doors - **Tucker Millworks, Inc.**
Specialty Wire & Cable Compounds - **Foster Corp.**

264

Specialty Wires - **Permaluster Company**
Spectrometers - **Epsilon Industrial, Inc.**
Spectrometers - **Mcpherson Inc.**
Spectroscopes, Electronic Gas-sampling Pumps - **Spectrex Corp**
Speed Changers, Drives & Gears - **G K N Sinter Metals Emporium**
Speed Changers, Drives & Gears - **Horsburgh & Scott Co., the**
Speed Changers, Drives & Gears - **Phoenix Gear Inc**
Speed Lathes - **Morrison Co., the D. C.**
Speed Measurement, Tachometer - **Scalemen of Florida, Inc.**
Speed, Temperature & Motion Sensors - **Smith Systems, Inc.**
Speedometer Cables & Gears - **Automatic Transmission Parts, Inc. A.t.p.**
Spice and Seasoning Products - **Alpine Touch Inc**
Spiceblends for Meat, Poultry, Processed Meats - **Catalina Food Ingredien**
Spices - **House of Spices**
Spices - **Catalina Food Ingredients**
Spices & Botanicals - **Famarco Ltd. Inc./b & K International**
Spinal Support Systems - **Bremer Group, Co.**
Spinning Wheels - **Stuhr Enterprises, Inc.**
Spiral Bevel, Spur & Helical Gears, Curvic Couplings - **Purdy Corp.**
Spiral Duct Machinery - **Spiral-helix, Inc.**
Spiral Tubes; Small Convolute Tubes - **Pacific Fabric Reels Inc**
Spiral Weldseam Pipe Making Equipment - **Pacific Roller Die Co., Inc.**
Spirometers & Related Access- **Multispiro, Inc. / Creative Biomedics**
Split Face Block - **Western Thin Brick & Tile**
Spoilers & Running Boards - **Promotional Trim Components**
Sponge, Foam & Felt - **Pacific States Felt & Mfg Co**
Sport & Leisure Shoes & Work Boots - **Red Wing Shoe Co.**
Sport Balls from Composite Leather - **Ram Sports Inc**
Sport Truck Accessories - **Donmar Enterprises, Inc.**
Sporting & Amusement Fiberglass Fabrication - **R. P. Creations, Inc.**
Sporting & Athletic Field Materials (Soil) - **True Pitch, Inc.**
Sporting & Athletic Goods - **Accu Rest, Inc.**
Sporting & Athletic Goods - **Artisan Golf**
Sporting & Athletic Goods - **Aqua Jogger**
Sporting & Athletic Goods - **B C I Burke Co., Llc**
Sporting & Athletic Goods - **Biscayne Rod Mfg., Inc.**
Sporting & Athletic Goods - **Castletech Ltd**
Sporting & Athletic Goods - **Centerline Sports Inc**
Sporting & Athletic Goods - **Diamond Head Golf Club Mfg Co**
Sporting & Athletic Goods - **Duffy Golf, Inc.**
Sporting & Athletic Goods - **Goal Oriented Inc**
Sporting & Athletic Goods - **Johnny Gibson Gym Equipment Co**
Sporting & Athletic Goods - **Kd Water Sports**
Sporting & Athletic Goods - **Load Llama Products**
Sporting & Athletic Goods - **Master Line U S A**
Sporting & Athletic Goods - **Michaels of Oregon Co**
Sporting & Athletic Goods - **O'brien International**
Sporting & Athletic Goods - **Pantos Corp**
Sporting & Athletic Goods - **Pcie Dba; the France Group**
Sporting & Athletic Goods - **Q C a Pools & Spas**
Sporting & Athletic Goods - **Ram Sports Inc**
Sporting & Athletic Goods - **Solo Enterprise Corporation**
Sporting & Athletic Goods - **Sprint/rothhammer**
Sporting & Athletic Goods - **Stewart Surfboards Inc**
Sporting & Athletic Goods - **Trophy Glove Co.**
Sporting & Athletic Goods - **Unique Sports Products, Inc.**
Sporting & Athletic Goods - **Variety Widget Products Inc**
Sporting & Athletic Goods - **Volant Sports, Llc**
Sporting & Athletic Goods - **Wahoo International**
Sporting & Athletic Goods & Outdoor Furniture - **Lifetime Products Inc**
Sporting & Athletic Padding - **Idaho Sewing for Sports**
Sporting & Hunting Knives - **Ka-bar Knives, Inc.**
Sporting & Recreational Goods - **Sprint/rothhammer**
Sporting & Recreational Goods - **Volant Sports, Llc**
Sporting Gloves - **Trophy Glove Co.**
Sporting Goods - **Jaypro Corporation**
Sporting Goods: Exercise Equipment - **Atwood Richards**
Sporting Shoes - **Maxport International**
Sporting and Recreational Goods - **Gared Sports**
Sporting and Recreational Goods - **Lamkin Corp.**
Sports & Athletic Equipment - **Unique Sports Products, Inc.**

Sports & Religious Jewelry - **Classic Medallics, Inc. (Mfr)**
Sports Field Finishing - **Diamond Turf Equipment Inc.**
Sports Field Mowing - **Diamond Turf Equipment Inc.**
Sports Headwear- **Take Two Sportswear Accessories**
Sports Nutrition Food Products - **Protos Inc.**
Sports Nutrition, Manufacturing - **The Chemins Company Inc**
Sports Products: Tennis, Running Tracks- **Intracor-familian International**
Sports Wear - **T-shirts & Graphics**
Sportwear, Embroidery - **National Embroidery Services**
Spot-spitter , the Original Mini-sprayer, - **Roberts Irrigation Products**
Spouts - **Interbath, Inc**
Spray Glitter 3 - Colors - **Shelton's Sheen Wave Labs Inc**
Spray Guns and Similar Appliances - **Thomas Industries, Inc.**
Spray Painting - **Technology General Corp.**
Sprayers - **Diamond Turf Equipment Inc.**
Sprayers (All Types) - **Broyhill Company, the (Mfr)**
Spread - Spectrum Radiomodems - **Solid State Electronics Corp**
Springs, Stampings, Wire Forms- **Connor Formed Metal Products**
Springs_steel, Except Wire - **Duer/carolina Coil Inc.**
Springs_steel, Except Wire - **O'hara Metal Products Co**
Spun Polyester Sewing Thread - **American & Efird, Inc.**
Spurgears - **Lemco**
Squash Court Wall Panels - **Fiberesin Industries, Inc.**
Stabilized Camera & Gun Platforms - **Tyler Camera Systems**
Stabilizers for Ice Crea - **National Stabilizers Inc**
Stabilizing Base Material. - **C S S Technology Inc.**
Stabilizing Sub-base Material. - **C S S Technology Inc.**
Stabilur / Cult-ur Urinary Stabilizers - **Cargille Laboratories, Inc.**
Stacker Cranes - **Aurora Systems, Inc.**
Stacks - **Turner Envirologic, Inc.**
Stacks - **Lincoln Manufacturing Co.**
Stadium Cushions - **Kae Co., Inc.**
Stage & Studio Specialty Bulbs - **Bulbtronics, Inc.**
Staging - **Garrett Sound & Lighting**
Stained & Etched Glass, Aluminum Sash & Doors - **Baut Studios Inc.**
Stained Glass- **Melotte-Morse-Leonatti Stained Glass, Inc.**
Stainless Steel & Alloy Ingots, Bars & Billets - **Electralloy**
Stainless Steel An, Ms, Nas, & as Tube Fittings - **The Martin Company**
Stainless Steel Centrifugal Pumps - **Finish Thompson, Inc.**
Stainless Steel Clad Sheets - **Trade Metal Inc.**
Stainless Steel Coils - **Trade Metal Inc.**
Stainless Steel Dryers, Food Processing Equipment - **Dahmes Stainless**
Stainless Steel Fabrication -Nsf Approved - **West Tool & Design, Inc.**
Stainless Steel Fabrication : Design, - **Huntington Mechanical Labs Inc**
Stainless Steel Fittings Piping Systems - **Top Line Process Equipment Co.**
Stainless Steel Flanges Butt Weld San. - **Top Line Process Equipment Co.**
Stainless Steel Food Equipment Legs - **Deering Fabricators**
Stainless Steel Pipe & Tubing - **Avesta Sheffield Pipe Co.**
Stainless Steel Plaste Rod Pipe Grating - **Duenner Supply Co. Of Texas**
Stainless Steel Plate - **Trade Metal Inc.**
Stainless Steel Plate & Tubular Exchangers - **Exothermics, Inc.**
Stainless Steel Products & Articles , Flat Wire - **Zapp Usa Inc.**
Stainless Steel Products for Industry, Medical - **Metal Master**
Stainless Steel Sanitary Ware - **Terriss-consolidated Industries**
Stainless Steel Scrap - **Sos Metals, Inc.**
Stainless Steel Scrap - **Los Angeles Scrap Iron & Metal**
Stainless Steel Sheet Cuttings - **Trade Metal Inc.**
Stainless Steel Valves - **Conbraco Industries, Inc.**
Stainless Steel, Carbon Steel, Nickel Alloy - **Zapp Usa Inc.**
Stainless Steel, Import - **American Optimum**
Stainless Steel, Showers & Boat Doors - **Omega Products, Inc.**
Stainless, Carbon, Brass, Aluminum - **Abbott Ball Co. (Mfg)**
Stains & Coatings - **Osmose Wood Preserving, Inc.**
Stair Nosings & Treads - **Barry Pattern & Foundry**
Stair Parts - **Jim C. Lane Inc.**
Stake, Grain & Livestock Bodies & Hydraulic Hoists - **Omaha Standard,**
Stamp Cancelling Machines, Post Office - **International Peripheral Sys.**
Stamp Pads, Commercial, Decorative - **Ranger Industries**
Stamped Metal Fasteners - **Termax Corporation**
Stamping Dies - **Anchor Tool & Die Company**
Stamps, Engraving, Name Badges - **Wendell's, Inc.**

Stamship Line / Agent - **Cagema Agencies Inc.**
Stand-alone Battery-powered Security Gate Systems - **Autogate**
Stand-up Trailers to Haul Motorcycles - **Kendon Industries Inc**
Standard & Industrial Fasteners - **Diversified Fastener & Tool Co.**
Standard Clutches - **Tri-star International, Inc.**
Standard and Non-standard Size Balls - **Acra-ball & Manufacturing Co**
Standard, Brushless, High Performance, Analog - **Glentek Inc**
Standard/custom Computer Power Supplies, Power - **Delta Products Corp**
Standby Diesel Generator Sets - **Reagan Equipment Co., Inc.**
Standing Seam Metal Roofing Contractor - **Shurtleff-g a H a R a N, Inc.**
Stapling Systems - **Hemisphere Enterprises**
Static Dewatering Sleeves - **Kason Corporation (Mfr)**
Stationary & Office Supplies - **Hammett Co., Inc., J. L.**
Stationary & Office Supplies, Export - **B&g Export Management Assoc.**
Stationary Diesel Engines and Components - **Energy Machinery Inc**
Stationery & Office Supplies - **Wescosa Inc**
Stationery & Office Supplies - **All American Office Products Inc**
Stationery Products - **American Scholar Co.**
Stationery Products - **Autron Incorporated**
Stationery Products - **Brewood Engravers Inc.**
Stationery, Technical & Security Paper - **Gilbert Paper**
Steam Boilers - **A.c.e. Boiler, Inc.**
Steam Cleaning Equipment - **Hotsy Corporation, the**
Steam Hot Water Boilers - **Pvi International**
Steam Tube Dryers - **Dedert Corp.**
Steamers - **Thermodyne Food Service Products**
Steamers for Cleaning and Degreasing Small Part - **Ftc**
Steamship Agent - **Fritz Maritime Agencies**
Steamship Agents - **Ayala Luis A. Colon Sucrs. Inc.**
Steamship Agents - **Interbulk Shipping, Inc.**
Steamship Companies - **Shinwa (Usa) Inc.**
Steel - **Eastern Europe Inc.**
Steel & Aluminum Precision Coil Processing - **Coilplus-Alabama, Inc.**
Steel Articles - **Richard Boas**
Steel Bifold Doors - **Dunbarton Corp. /Rediframe/slimfold**
Steel Boiler Trims - **Conbraco Industries, Inc.**
Steel Bottom Dumps - **Beall Corp.**
Steel Building Trusses & Rafters - **Adams Truss, Inc.**
Steel Castings - **Buckeye Steel Castings Company**
Steel Chests, Boxes, Work Benches, Cabinets, - **Knaack Mfg. Co.**
Steel Coil Handling Equipment - **Red Bud Industries**
Steel Component Parts - **Saegertown Mfg. Corp.**
Steel Cord & Wire - **Trefilarbed Arkansas, Inc.**
Steel Distributors & Warehouses - **Cragin Metals, L.l.c.**
Steel Door Frames (Prefinished) - **Dunbarton Corp. /Rediframe/slimfold**
Steel Drums - **Evans Cushing, Inc.**
Steel End Dumps - **Beall Corp.**
Steel Fabrication - **High Steel Structures**
Steel Fabrication - **Prospect Steel, Inc.**
Steel Fabrication - **R a M Products**
Steel Fabrication, Augers & Machine Parts - **Auger Fabrication**
Steel Fabrication, Metal Stampings - **Val-fab Inc.**
Steel Forgings - **Standard Steel**
Steel Forms for Concrete - **Avon Mfg., Inc.**
Steel Generator Enclosures - **Pritchard Brown**
Steel Gondola Display Shelving for - **Kent Corp.**
Steel Grating - **Quirin Machine Shop Inc., E. A.**
Steel Hatches - **Avon Mfg., Inc.**
Steel Mills - **I P S C O Steel Inc.**
Steel Pickling, Slitting & Cold Rolling - **Chicago Steel & Pickling Co.**
Steel Pipe & Fittings, Wholesale - **American Piping Products, Inc.**
Steel Pipe & Tubes - **Napa Pipe Corporation**
Steel Pipe & Tubes - **Avesta Sheffield Pipe Co.**
Steel Pipe & Tubes - **Metal-matic Inc.**
Steel Pipe & Tubes - **Northwest Pipe Company**
Steel Pipe , Wholesale - **Ohio Pipe & Steel Corp.**
Steel Pipe Cement Lined, Tape Coated - **Int'l Fabricators & Engineers**
Steel Pipe Fittings - **Dodson Steel Products, Inc.**
Steel Plate, Channels & Bars - **Minco Sales Corp.**
Steel Post Pullers - **Allen Tool Co**
Steel Products - **D.b.c. Enterprises, Inc.**

Steel Profiles - **R a M Products**
Steel Racks, Bins, Shelves - **Crown Divisions of Trans Pro, Inc., the**
Steel Racks, Lockers & Tool Storage - **Lyon Metal Products Llc**
Steel Rebar & Fabrication - **Coral Steel Company**
Steel Reheating Furnaces, Fuel Fired - **Holcroft**
Steel Rods - **Baker Div. Sonoco Products Company**
Steel Roll Forming - **Ohio Moulding Corp., the**
Steel Rule Cutting Dies - **Diemasters, Inc.**
Steel Sales - **Space Coast General Contractors Inc.**
Steel Service Center - Tin Mill Products - **Arbon Steel & Service, Inc.**
Steel Shearing - **Cragin Metals, L.l.c.**
Steel Shop Equipment & Shelving - **Lyon Metal Products Llc**
Steel Siding, Residential - **Gentek Building Products**
Steel Stairs / Steel Railings & Fencing - **Lance Metal Arts**
Steel Storage Cabinets— Flammable, Modular - **Norren Manufacturing**
Steel Storage Tanks - **Safe T-tank Corp.**
Steel Structures, Prefabricated- **Intracor-familian International**
Steel Tanks - **Isom Brothers Inc**
Steel Tin Cans - **United States Can Company, Custom & Specialty**
Steel Truck Parts - **Midwest Truck & Auto**
Steel Tube & Bar Cutting - **Richard Industries, J.**
Steel Tube & Bar Fabrication - **Richard Industries, J.**
Steel Tubing - **Metal-matic Inc.**
Steel Tv and Security Camera Mounts - **Mounting Systems Inc**
Steel Valves - **Conbraco Industries, Inc.**
Steel Wire - **Atlantic Wire Co., the**
Steel Wire & Related Products - **Co-steel Raritan**
Steel Wire & Related Products - **Atlantic Wire Co., the**
Steel Wire & Related Products - **T & B Structural Systems, Inc.**
Steel Wire & Related Products - **Trefilarbed Arkansas, Inc.**
Steel Wire & Related Products - **Cambria County Assn. For the Blind**
Steel Wire Rods, Metal Recycling & Rolling - **Co-steel Raritan**
Steel Wire and Related Products - **Florida Wire & Cable Inc.**
Steel Wire, Cold Heading Quality - **Atlantic Wire Co., the**
Steel Wire, Copper & Liquor Coated - **Atlantic Wire Co., the**
Steel Wire, Rivet Quality - **Atlantic Wire Co., the**
Steel and Rubber Covered Rollers for Every Industry - **Thistle Roller Co**
Steer Rye Dies - **Aggressive Dies & Cutting**
Steering Dampers - **Cofap of America**
Stellram - a Manufacturer of High Quality Cutting Tools - **Stellram**
Step Motor Drivers and Controllers - **Anaheim Automation**
Stereo Speakers - **Maxport International**
Sterile Pharmaceutical Products - **Sp Pharmaceuticals Llc**
Sterilization - **Biomedical International**
Sterilized Plastic Bags for Biotech Fluids - **Newport Biosystems, Inc.**
Sterling Silver Jewelry - **Morning Sun**
Sterling Silver with Semi-precious Stones - **Accents in Sterling Inc**
Stevedores - **Ayala Luis A. Colon Sucrs. Inc.**
Stiffener Fitting Gantries - **Ogden Engineering Corp.**
Stocking Distr. For Carbon Blocks & Kdf Cartridges - **Ro Ultratec Usa Inc**
Stocking Distr. For Filter Hsg's & Cartridges - **Ro Ultratec Usa Inc**
Stocking Distr. For Hi-pressure Pumps - **Ro Ultratec Usa Inc**
Stollen - **Neuman Bakery Specialties, Inc.**
Stoppers, Caps, Lids s - **All American Containers, Inc.**
Storage - **Labelle Rothery Movers, Inc.**
Storage Area Networks - **Ancor Communications**
Storage Racks and Material Handling Equipment - **Rapid Rack Industries**
Storage Tanks - **A.c.e. Boiler, Inc.**
Store & Office Interiors Decor - **Modern Woodcrafts, Inc.**
Store Fixtures - **Customcraft Fixtures**
Store Fixtures - **Spencer & Reynolds Inc**
Store Fixtures & Accessories - **Spacewall International**
Straight Truck Roll off Hoists - **Converto Mfg. Co. Inc. (Mfr)**
Strainers and Filters - **Kraissl Co., Inc., the**
Stranded Wire, Ropes and Cables - **Florida Wire & Cable Inc.**
Stranded Wire, Ropes and Cables - **Anicom Inc.**
Streaming Media Solutions - **3cx**
Strech Systems & Supplies - **Hemisphere Enterprises**
Strip - **Permaluster Company**
Stripping; Burn off Old Powder Coat - **Americoat Corp.**
Stroboscopes - **Monarch International Inc. Monarch Instrument Div.**

Structural Adhesive - **Elementis Performance Polymers**
Structural Cabling Systems - **The Siemon Company**
Structural Glazed Tile - **Sioux City Brick & Tile Co., Sergeant Bluff Plt.**
Structural Insulated Building Panels - **Enercept, Inc.**
Structural Metal_fabricated - **Joaquin Manufacturing Corp**
Structural Metal_fabricated - **Adams Truss, Inc.**
Structural Metal_fabricated - **Colorado Bridge & Iron Inc**
Structural Metal_fabricated - **Schuff Steel Company**
Structural Metal_fabricated - **Space Coast General Contractors Inc.**
Structural Metal_fabricated - **Big D Metalworks of Texas**
Structural Metal_fabricated - **Klose Fabrication, Inc.**
Structural Steel & Color Metal Fabrication - **Midwest Builders Supply,**
Structural Steel Plates - **Professional Services International, Inc.**
Structural Systems for Earth Sheltered Storage - **Formworks Building Inc**
Structural Systems for Shelters - **Formworks Building Inc**
Structural Wood Members - **Fagen's Building Center**
Structural Wood Members - **Le Truss Co., Tien**
Structural Wood Members - **Now Structures, Inc.**
Structural Wood Members - **Universal Truss, Inc.**
Structural Wood Members - **Warner Robins Supply Co., Inc.**
Structures and Parts of Structures- **Morrison Construction Service**
Structures and Parts of Structures, of Iron or Steel - **Williams Shipping**
Stuctural Clay Products - **Geo Specialty Chemicals, Inc.**
Studs & Tracks - **R a M Products**
Stump Grinders and Chippers, Root Cutters, Tren - **Doskocil Industries Inc**
Subcontractor for Printed Circuit Boards - **Sierra Electronic Assembly**
Subdividers and Developers, Nec - **Ameri Housing**
Submersible Industrial Pumps, Mixers & Aerators - **A B S Pumps, Inc.**
Submersible Pumps, Iohp & under for Water Wells - **Dempster Industries,**
Subminiature Incandescent Lamps - **Lumitron Corp.**
Subsea Connection Systems - **Ocean Design Inc.**
Subsea System Design & Pipelay - **J.ray Mcdemott, Inc.**
Subsidy Book Publisher - **Rutledge Books, Inc.**
Subtrates Including Laminated - **Duro Bag Mfg. Co.**
Suceptor (Metallize, Lamination) - **Technical Coating International**
Sucker Rod <Oil> Pump Parts - **Swaim & Sons**
Sucker Rod Couplings - **Cold Extrusion Co. Of America, Inc.**
Sudan - **H & H Seed Company Inc**
Sugar - **Parisi-virana Co., Inc.**
Sugar Confectionary , Not Containing Cocoa - **Sconza Candy Co.**
Sugar Confectionary , Not Containing Cocoa - **Americares Foundations**
Sugar, All Grades - **Ps International**
Sun Protective Active Wear-men, Women - **Mary K Active Wear Inc**
Sun Shades - **General Drapery Services, Inc.**
Sun-dried Tomato Products, Sun-dried Tomatoes - **Mooney Farms**
Sunglass Cases - **L.b.i.**
Sunglass Frames - **L.b.i.**
Sunglasses - **Harken International, Ltd.**
Sunglasses - **L.b.i.**
Sunglasses, Export - **Arno International, Inc.**
Sunroof Wind Deflectors - **Donmar Enterprises, Inc.**
Sunroofs Pop-up Sliding & Electric - **Donmar Enterprises, Inc.**
Sunscreen Spf5-spf20 - **Rejuvi Cosmetic Laboratory**
Sunviser Systems - **Rosen Product Development Inc**
Super Alloy Plate & Sheet - **Pittsburgh Flatroll Co.**
Superconductive Materials- **Target Materials, Inc.**
Supermarkets, Drug, Discount, Autoparts & - **Kent Corp.**
Supersweet (Sh2) Sweet Corn Seed - **Seedcraft**
Supervisory Controls, Data Acquisition - **Bristol Babcock Inc.**
Supplements in Tablet - **Northridge Laboratories Inc**
Supplier of Software Products & Services to the Telecommunic - **Probita**
Suppliers of Equipment Services, & Ingredients - **Ernest F Mariani Co.**
Suppliers of Top Quality Dyes Made in the U.s.a. - **Bezjian Dye-chem, Inc.**
Supply Chain Managment / Logistics - **Distribution Services of America**
Suppression Filters, Surge Suppression - **L C R Electronics, Inc.**
Surety Bonds - **Roanoke Brokerage Services, Inc.**
Surface Active Agents - **Ashland Chemical**
Surface Active Agents - **Burlington Chemical Co., Inc. (Mfr)**
Surface Active Agents - **Norman, Fox & Co**
Surface Active Agents - **Wd-40 Company**
Surface Analysis Instruments & Equipment - **Micromeritics Instrument**

Surface Coatings, Pvd Etc. - **Advanced Heat Treat Corp.**
Surface Mount and Low and High-voltage - **Voltage Multipliers Inc**
Surface Plates - **Tru-stone Corp.**
Surface Tension Apparatus - **Rame-hart, Inc.**
Surfact Mount Components - **Hall Co., the**
Surfactants - **Petroferm Inc.**
Surfboard - **Stewart Surfboards Inc**
Surge Protection Devices - **Circuit Components, Inc.**
Surge Protectors: Telephone & Telegraph Apptus - **Pacific Electricord Co**
Surgical & Medical Instruments - **Cuda Products Corp.**
Surgical & Medical Instruments - **Advantage Development Corp**
Surgical & Medical Instruments - **Area Detectors Systems Corp**
Surgical & Medical Instruments - **Creative Science & Technolgoy**
Surgical & Medical Instruments - **Essex Cryogenics of Missouri, Inc.**
Surgical & Medical Instruments - **Ic Medical Inc**
Surgical & Medical Instruments - **Innovasive Devices Company**
Surgical & Medical Instruments - **J Hewitt Inc**
Surgical & Medical Instruments - **Ken-a-vision Mfg. Co., Inc.**
Surgical & Medical Instruments - **Mectra Labs, Inc.**
Surgical & Medical Instruments - **Medical Specifics, Inc.**
Surgical & Medical Instruments - **Medicore Inc.**
Surgical & Medical Instruments - **Modified Polymer Components**
Surgical & Medical Instruments - **Transtracheal Systems Inc**
Surgical & Medical Instruments - **Universal Technology Systems**
Surgical Apparatus - **Smith & Nephew Inc.**
Surgical Appliances & Supplies - **Cambridge Manufacturing, Inc.**
Surgical Appliances & Supplies - **Carstens, Inc.**
Surgical Appliances & Supplies - **Garrison's Prosthetic Service**
Surgical Appliances & Supplies - **Gunnell Inc.**
Surgical Appliances & Supplies - **Kinamed**
Surgical Appliances & Supplies - **Ohio Willow Wood Co.**
Surgical Appliances & Supplies - **Pointblank Body Armor, Inc.**
Surgical Appliances & Supplies - **Porex Surgical, Inc.**
Surgical Appliances & Supplies - **Repro-med Systems, Inc.**
Surgical Appliances & Supplies - **Shawnee Products, Inc.**
Surgical Appliances & Supplies - **Smith & Nephew United, Inc.**
Surgical Appliances & Supplies - **Stromgren Supports, Inc.**
Surgical Appliances & Supplies - **Touch America Inc.**
Surgical Instruments - **Scanlan International Inc.**
Surgical Instruments, Cardiovascular & Vascular - **Scanlan International**
Surgical Instruments, Disposable Single Use - **Scanlan International Inc.**
Surgical Smoke Evacuation - **Ic Medical Inc**
Surgical Supplies - **Porex Surgical, Inc.**
Surgical Wound Drains, Catheters, Cannulas - **Axiom Medical Inc**
Surgical and Medical Equipment - **Ic Medical Inc**
Surgical and Medical Instruments - **J Hewitt Inc**
Surveying Services - **Ksa Engineers, Inc.**
Surveying Services - **Leo A. Daly Company**
Surveying Services - **Marshall Miller & Associates**
Suspenders, Contract Sewing - **Industrial Opportunities**
Suspension Insulators- **Porcelain Products Company(mfr)**
Suspension Shock Absorbers for Motor Vehicles - **Cofap of America**
Suspension Struts for Motor - **Cofap of America**
Svc. Ind. Equip., Sprayers/foggers- **Public Health Equipment Supply Inc.**
Swaging Sleaves - **Crosby Group, Inc.**
Sweatshirts - **T-shirts & Graphics**
Sweeper Vacuums - **Diamond Turf Equipment Inc.**
Sweepers - **Advance Paper & Maintenance**
Sweet Corn, Prepared or Preserved, Not Frozen - **Sew Feiel**
Swimming Pool Accessories - **S.k. Plastics**
Swimming Pool Chillers - **Air Energy Heat Pumps**
Swimming Pool Cooling - **Air Energy Heat Pumps**
Swimming Pool Covers - **S.k. Plastics**
Swimming Pool Heat Pumps - **Air Energy Heat Pumps**
Swimming Pool Heaters - **Air Energy Heat Pumps**
Swimming Pool Heating - **Air Energy Heat Pumps**
Swimming Pool Heating & Cooling - **Air Energy Heat Pumps**
Swimming Pool Liners - **S.k. Plastics**
Swimming Pool Steps, One-piece - **Imperial Pools Inc.**
Swimwear - **Nishizawa**
Swimwear - Men's & Boys' & Women & Girls - **Silver Needles**

Swiss Precision Products - **Cole Screw Machine Products, Inc.**
Switch & Bus Insulators - **Porcelain Products Company(mfr)**
Switch & Bus Insulators Cap Pin & Post - **Newell Porcelain Company,**
Switches - **Mid-west Instrument**
Switches - **Mg Electronics**
Switches, Snap Action, Elec. Circuitry - **Cherry Corporation, the**
Switches; Current Loop Conversion Devices - **Reliable Communications**
Switchgear & Switchboard Apparatus - **Factory Automation Systems, Inc.**
Switchgear & Switchboard Apparatus - **Gould Shawmut**
Switchgear & Switchboard Apparatus - **Kanawha Scales & Systems, Inc.**
Switchgear & Switchboard Apparatus - **Lake Shore Electric Corp.**
Switchgear & Switchboard Apparatus - **Park Metal Products Co.**
Switchgear & Switchboard Apparatus - **Ross Engineering Corp**
Switchgear & Switchgear Apparatus - **Hawaii Pacific Associates**
Switchgear Shelters - **Pritchard Brown**
Switchgear Vacuum Interrupters - **Jennings Technology Company**
Swords & Medieval Armor - **Grace Mfg. Co., Inc.**
Synthetic Coatings for Eifs, Glitter Coatings - **Pleko Southwest Inc**
Synthetic Dna for Medical Research - **Synthetic Genetics**
Synthetic Polymers in Primary Forms - **Pexim International**
Synthetic Resins - **Polymer Trading Services Limited**
Synthetic Resins - **Egla International**
Synthetic Rubber and Factice - **Stafast Roofing Products**
Synthetic Staple Fibers, Carded - **Fici Export**
Synthetic resins and plastics materials - **BJB Enterprises Inc**
Syringe Filling Machinery - **Rame-hart, Inc.**
Syrup - **Dean Foods (Mfr)**
Syrups - **Griffin Food Company**
System Integrators, Satellite Earth Stations - **Applied Telecommunications**
Systems Engineering Analysis & Training - **Cooper Industries**
Systems Integration - **Petrotech Inc.**
T-shirt Screen Printing - **Print Proz, Inc.**
T-shirt Screen Printing & Embroidery - **Unique Image T-shirt Co.**
T-shirt, Sweatshirt, & Tote Bag Heat Transfers - **Impulse Wear**
T-shirts - **T-shirts & Graphics**
TP T H Fungicide - **Agtrol International**
Table Skirting, Linens, Place Mats; Pipe & Drap - **Drapes 4 Show Inc.**
Table Top Food Service Items - **Traex**
Table or Kitchen Glassware - **Traex**
Table, Kitchen or Other Household Articles - **Traex**
Table, Kitchen or Other Household Articles - **Delta Faucet**
Table, Kitchen or Other Household Articles - **Stylebuilt Accessories, Inc.**
Tablecloths & Napkins. Skirting, Placmats & Runners - **Tablecloth Co.,**
Tablet Counters - **Njm/cli Packaging Systems International**
Tablet Dispensing Machines, Brine Makers - **Cargill Salt Co/dispensing**
Tablet Printers - **Ackley Machine Corp.**
Tableware & Kitchenware of Plastics - **Wna Comet**
Tableware and Kitchenware of Plastics - **Lanca Sales, Inc.**
Tach/hourmeters - **Faria Corp.**
Tachmoteters - **Faria Corp.**
Tachometers - **Monarch International Inc. Monarch Instrument Div.**
Tachometers, Electric & Industrial - **Westberg Mfg., Inc.**
Tackle Blocks - **Crosby Group, Inc.**
Tactical Training Aids - **Crown Gym Mats, Inc.**
Tallow - **Darling International Inc.**
Tambour Panels - **Interior Products Inc.**
Tank Lining - **Enerfab**
Tank Parts - **Caravan International**
Tank Trailer Parts - **Heil Trading Co. Inc.**
Tank Trailers - **Beall Corp.**
Tank Welders - **Ogden Engineering Corp.**
Tanks & Tank Components - **Charles E Gillman Company**
Tanks, Ast, Custom, Fuel - **Joaquin Manufacturing Corp**
Tanks, New for Rebuilt for Noldson - **Adhesive Systems, Inc.**
Tape & Label (Psa) - **Technical Coating International**
Tapes, Adhesive - **Venture Tape**
Tapes, Conductive Foil - **Venture Tape**
Tapes, Double Sided - **Venture Tape**
Tapes, Foam & Gasket Laminating - **Venture Tape**
Tapes, Transfer Adhesives - **Venture Tape**
Tappets, Mechanical - **A C Products Co., Inc.**

Taps, Cocks, Valves - **Conbraco Industries**
Taps, Cocks, Valves and Similar Appliances for Pipes - **Delta Faucet**
Target Designators - **Litton Systems, Inc. Laser Sys, Inc.**
Tarps, Gym Mats, Boat, Pool & Truck Covers - **Quest & Sons, Inc.**
Tax, Accounting & Auditing Services **Watkins, Watkins & Keenan, Cpa's**
Td Relays - **Instrumentation & Control Systems, Inc.**
Tdma Networkers - **Vortex Satcom Systems, Inc.**
Tea & Beverages - **Jianlibao America, Ltd.**
Tea Blending & Potpourri - **Alaska Herb & Tea Co.**
Tea Concentrates - **Monin, Inc.**
Tear Gas - **Aero Tech Labs, Inc.**
Tear Gas - **Aerko International**
Technical Translations - **Sears Steele, Iii**
Technical Translations, Typesetting - **Magnum Group, Inc**
Technical, Legal, Medical - **International Translating Br., Inc.**
Tees, Polos, Sweatshirts - **Paradise Sportswear, Inc.**
Teflon Gaskets & Packing - **Houston Mfg. & Specialty Co., Inc.**
Teflon, Peek, Ryton (Pps), Nylon Machining - **Gulf Coast Seal, Inc.**
Tektronix Color Printers - **Pendl Co., Inc.**
Telco...T1 Mux, Dsu/csu & Modems - **Sunnyvale Gdi, Inc.**
Telecom, Pcs & Cable Service Provider - **Barclay Maps**
Telecomm Equipment, Digital Announcers - **Electronic Tele-communicati**
Telecommunication & Data Systems - **Dynetcom, Inc.**
Telecommunication Equipment, Voice Response - **Electronic Tele-commu**
Telecommunication Equipments - **Electronic Tele-communications, Inc**
Telecommunication Modems & Multiplexers - **S.i. Tech, Inc.(Mfr)**
Telecommunications Billing & Customer Care Practice - **Cap Gemini Ame**
Telecommunications Products - **Startel Corporation**
Telecommunications, Data Communications - **Dcr / Diversified Communi**
Teleconferencing Peripherals - **Forum Communications Systems, Inc.**
Telemetry Products - **Transcrypt International, Inc.**
Telephone & Telegraph Apparatus - **Ceeco Communications Equipment**
Telephone & Telegraph Apparatus - **Dynetcom, Inc.**
Telephone & Telegraph Apparatus - **Forum Communications Systems,**
Telephone & Telephone Apparatus - **Jps Communications Inc**
Telephone & Telegraph Apparatus - **Micon Telecommunications Inc**
Telephone & Telegraph Apparatus - **Pacific Phoinix Inc.**
Telephone & Telegraph Apparatus - **Solid State Electronics Corp**
Telephone & Telephone Apparatus - **Toshiba America Information Sys. In**
Telephone Answering Machine / Digital Audio Type - **Racom Products**
Telephone Apparatus - **Teledex Corporation**
Telephone Communication- Except Radio - **Otm Engineering, Inc.**
Telephone Communications Exc. Radio - **Micon Telecommunications Inc**
Telephone Enclosures - **Independent Welding Co.**
Telephone Equipment & Systems - **Ceeco Communications Equipment &**
Telephone Equipment Fiber Optic Distrib. Panel / Products - **The Siemon**
Telephone Equipment, Connecting Hardware - **The Siemon Company**
Telephone Inside Wiring Cable - **Essex Group Inc. (Mfr)**
Telephone Wire & Cable - **Essex Group Inc. (Mfr)**
Telephone, Telegraph and Interface Equipment - **Micon Telecommunicatio**
Telephones, Coinless Stainless Steel - **Ceeco**
Telephony Servers / Cti - **Noble Systems Corp.**
Teleprinter - **Racom Products Inc.**
Telescopic Platform Seating - **Folding Bleacher Company**
Television & Satellite Equipment - **R. F. Technology, Inc.**
Television Antennas - **D H Satellite**
Television Broadcast Studio Equipment; Custom - **Omicron Video**
Television Lift Cabinets - **Auton Company**
Television Lifts - **Auton Company**
Television Projectors and Line Doublers - **Dwin Electronics Inc**
Television Service - **Masterpiece Prdctns Nevada**
Television and Radio - **Mg Electronics**
Telphonic Intercom Systems - **Racom Products Inc.**
Temperature Controller - **Zmd International Inc**
Temperature Controls - **Omega Heater Co., Inc.**
Temperature Controls for Plastics Industry - **American Msi Corp**
Temperature Gages - **Faria Corp.**
Temperature Sensors - **Us Sensor Corp**
Temperature Sensors - **Smart Sensors Inc.**
Tempest Security / Surveillance Mil Std - **Dynamic Sciences Int'l Inc**
Temporary Bank & Office Buildings - **S O N Corp.**

Temporary Lighting - **Ericson Manufacturing, Inc.**
Tennis Accessories - **Unique Sports Products, Inc.**
Tennis Court Lighting - **Magnaray International**
Tents & Canapys - **Floyd's Awning & Canvas Shop**
Tents, Canopies, Fabric Tension Structures - **Canvas Specialty**
Terminal Operators - **Penn Terminals Inc.**
Terminal Servers (Ac or Dc Powered) - **Cordell Manufacturing Inc**
Terminal Units - **Environmental Technologies, Inc.**
Terpineols - **Bush Boake Allen**
Terrazzo, Tile, Marble, Mosaic Work - **Georgetown Wire Co. K-lath Div**
Terry & Velour Towels - **Allegra Industries, Inc.**
Terry Towelling - **Barth & Dreyfuss of California**
Test & Measuring Instruments, Export - **Alkantec, Inc.**
Test Burn-in Sockets for Semiconductors - **Nova Science Inc**
Test Equipment - **Sirex Pulse Hydraulic Systems**
Test Equipment & Power Supplies - **Milwaukee Electronics Corp.**
Test Fixtures and Test Probes for Testing - **Alphatest Corporation**
Test Jacks - **Eby Co.**
Test Printing - **Psychological Corp., the**
Tester, Abrasion - **Norman Tool, Inc.**
Testers, Key Pad - **Norman Tool, Inc.**
Testing Equipment - **Rapid Development Service**
Testing Equipment - **Material Testing Technology Co.**
Testing Lab & Services - **Oregon Analytical Laboratory**
Testing Laboratories - **All Metals Processing of Oc**
Testing Laboratories - **Canyon State Inspection**
Testing Laboratories - **Oregon Analytical Laboratory**
Testing Laboratories - **Teco**
Testing Laboratories, Automotive - **Nevada Automotive Test Center**
Testing Laboratory - **Communication Certification Lab**
Testing Laboratory and Services for Agriculture - **North West Labs Inc**
Textbook & Multimedia Educational Materials, K-6 - **Scott Foresman**
Textile Auxiliaries - **Organic Dyestuffs Corporation**
Textile Balers - **Consolidated Baling Machine Co., Inc.(Mfr)**
Textile Chemicals - **Arrow Engineering Inc.**
Textile Coating - **Uretek, Inc.**
Textile Curing Ovens, Dryers, Laminators, - **Lessco**
Textile Dye & Print Auxiliaries - **Eastern Color & Chemical Co.**
Textile Dyestuffs - **Synalloy Corp., Blackman-uhler Chemical Div.**
Textile Embroidery & Screen Printing - **Semel's Embroidery & Screen Pri**
Textile Finishing Machinery - **Verduin Machinery, Inc.**
Textile Goods - **K. G. Fiber, Inc.**
Textile Goods - **Paschall Export-import Co., Inc.**
Textile Goods - **Nishizawa**
Textile Goods, Erosion Control Blanket - **North American Green**
Textile Heat Seal Mending Products & Plastic Eyeshields - **Lucas Products**
Textile Loom Accessories: Frames, Hedles, - **Steel Heddle Mfg. Co. (Mfr)**
Textile Machinery - **Allstates Textile Machinery**
Textile Machinery - **Atkins Machinery Inc.**
Textile Machinery - **Babcock Textile Machinery, Inc.**
Textile Machinery - **Bellwether Inc.**
Textile Machinery - **Chem-tex Machinery, Inc.**
Textile Machinery - **Gribetz International, Inc.**
Textile Machinery - **Shaffer & Max**
Textile Machinery - **United Textile Machinery Corp.**
Textile Machinery - Air Filters - **Mart Corporation**
Textile Machinery / Ovens / Dryers - **King International Inc.**
Textile Machinery Loom Beams - **Briggs-shaffner Co.**
Textile Machinery Section Beams - **Briggs-shaffner Co.**
Textile Machinery Tricot Beams - **Briggs-shaffner Co.**
Textile Machinery: Air Entanglers & Rewinders - **Pritchett Technology,**
Textile Manufacturer, Weave, Finish, Diecut, - **Facemate Corporation**
Textile Piece Goods & Remnants - **Sheftel International**
Textile Products - **Parisi-virana Co., Inc.**
Textile Products & Articles - **Barth & Dreyfuss of California**
Textile Products, Fabricated - **Spanset, Inc.**
Textile Products_fabricated - **A B C Sign Design, Llc**
Textile Products_fabricated - **Blackburn Mfg. Co.**
Textile Products_fabricated - **Cozy Inc**
Textile Products_fabricated - **Flagman of America**
Textile Products_fabricated - **Jg Creations Inc**

Textile Products_fabricated - **Safe Strap Co., Inc.**
Textile Products_fabricated - **Sagaz Industries, Inc.**
Textile Products_fabricated - **Sextet Fabrics, Inc.**
Textile Products_fabricated - **Tana Tex Inc.**
Textile Products_fabricated - **Wiggy's Inc**
Textile Products_fabricated - **Cambria County Assn. For the Blind**
Textile Screen Printers - **Gs Sportwear / Golden Squeegee**
Textile Screen Printing & Embroidery - **Arrow Creative International**
Textile Screen Printing & Embroidery - **Original Design Silkscreen Co.**
Textile Seconds - **Marcotex International**
Textile Service - **Thistle Roller Co Inc**
Textile Softeners - **Burlington Chemical Co., Inc. (Mfr)**
Textile Waste Processing - **Paschall Export-import Co., Inc.**
Textile Waste, Wholesale - **General Waste Trading Company**
Textile Wiping Cloths - **Kamen Wiping Materials Co., Inc.**
Textile Yarn Lubricants - **Eastern Color & Chemical Co.**
Textile Yarn Lubricants, Antistats & Cohesive Agents - **Lenox Chemical**
Textiles - **Tex-ex Export Co., Inc.**
Textiles - **Manrob Sales**
Textiles, Wholesale & Converting - **Medal Textiles, Inc.**
Textured & Twisted Synthetic Fiber Yarns - **Jefferson Mills, Inc.**
Textured Nylon & Polyester Yarns - **Jefferson Mills, Inc.**
Texturized Sewing Thread - **American & Efird, Inc.**
The American Bar - Canadian Bar - Mexican Bar - Int'l Bar - **Forster-long**
The American Bench , Judges of the Nation - **Forster-long Inc.**
The Duration of Second Stage Labor - **Novatrix Inc**
The Earth Flag - **Apollo Energy**
The Worlds Leading Supplier of Quality Puppies - **Hunte, Andrew**
Theater & Television Studio Rigging Equipment - **Albrecht Co, Inc., Peter**
Theatrical Equipment & Supplies - **Stein Industries Co.**
Theatrical Hardware - **General Drapery Services, Inc.**
Theft Deterrent Products - **Protex International Corp.**
Theft Resistant Nuts & Computer Theft Security Cables - **Tufnut Work,**
Themed Fixtures - **Creative Arts**
Theming Specialist - **R. P. Creations, Inc.**
Therapeutic Support Surfaces / Low Air Loss Systems - **Invacare Corp.**
Thermal & Acoustical Insulation - **Fabrication Specialties**
Thermal & Catalytic Oxidizers - **Therm Tech Inc.**
Thermal Incinerators - **Catalytic Combustion Corp.**
Thermal Insulation Systems- **Advanced Thermal Products Inc**
Thermal Insulators - **Fujipoly America Corp.**
Thermal Processing Furnaces - **Sinterite, Furance Div.**
Thermal Transfer Ribbons & Blank Labels - **Allenwest Inc**
Thermal Treatment Equipment - **Soil Purification Inc.**
Thermal and Acoustical Insulation - **Unlimited Quality Products**
Thermally Conductive Epoxies - **Electronic Materials Inc**
Thermistors - **Us Sensor Corp**
Thermo-sensitive Labeling Equipment - **Njm/cli Packaging Systems Intl**
Thermoformed Plastic Products - **American Fiberglass Products, Inc.**
Thermoformers - **Commodore Machine Co.**
Thermoforming - **Alga Plastics Co.**
Thermoforming & Fiber Reinforced Composites - **Mc Clarin Plastics, Inc.**
Thermometer Tubes (Glass Liquid Filled) - **Hartley Gove Sons**
Thermometers - **Cooper Instrument Corporation (Mfr)**
Thermoplastic Application Machinery - **Stimsonite Corp.**
Thermoplastic Resin Compounding - **Foster Corp.**
Thermoplastic Resins - **Geochem International**
Thermoplastic Striping Material - **Stimsonite Corp.**
Thermoplastics Injection Molding - **Nylacarb Corp.**
Thermoset Composite Laminates - **Nvf Company (Mfr)**
Thermoset Knobs & Handles, Electromechanical - **Dimco-gray Co.**
Thermoset Plastic Products to Help People Breath - **Hartlee System Inc**
Thick Film Flat Chip Resistors - **Koa Speer Electronics, Inc.**
Thickeners - **Quinn Process Equipment Co**
Thin Brick & Veneer Pavers - **Western Thin Brick & Tile**
Thin Client - Unisys, Dec. Hp., Ibm - **Visentech Systems, Inc.**
Thin Film Deposition Equipment - **Maxtek Inc**
Thin Film Deposition Equipment, Proce- **Materials Research Group, Inc.**
Thin Film Flat Chip Resistors - **Koa Speer Electronics, Inc.**
Thin Film Microwave Integrated Circuits, Chip - **Diablo Industries**
Thin Film Optical Coatings - **Opti-forms Inc**

Thin Film Thickness Measurement Equipment - **Axic Inc**
Thin-layer Chromatography Plates - **Analtech, Inc.**
Thread - **Robison-anton Textile Company (Mfr)**
Thread Restoring Files - **Jaw Manufacturing Co.**
Thread Rolling - **Cole Screw Machine Products, Inc.**
Thread, Commercial Sewing & Selvage Yarns - **Winchester Auburn Mills,**
Threaded Construction Rods- **Vulcan Threaded Products, Inc.**
Three Axis Modules - **Setco Industries**
Three-phase Uninterruptible Power Systems - **Liebert Corporation**
Through - Hole & Surface Mount Printed Circuit Board - **Electronic Mfr.**
Through Hole - Mixed or Smt Tec. - **Sierra Electronic Assembly**
Throughout the World - **International Nutrition, Inc.**
Throwster - **Winchester Auburn Mills, Inc**
Thru-hole Pcb's - **Parpro, Inc.**
Tight Fitting Smoke - and Draft-control - **Smoke Guard Corporation**
Timber Harvesting - **Krooked Kreek Logging Co.**
Timber Marking - **Krooked Kreek Logging Co.**
Time-released Gel for Watering Plants - **Driwater Inc**
Timers - **Cooper Instrument Corporation (Mfr)**
Timers for Industrial Use - **Artisan Controls Corporation (Mfr)**
Timothy Hay - **Ward Rugh, Inc.**
Tin, 90/10 and 60/40 Tin Lead Coatings - **Marjan, Inc.**
Tinmill Products - **Trade Metal Inc.**
Tinplate Waste - **Trade Metal Inc.**
Tips / Stnd, Filtered, Robotic, Conductive - **Quality Scientific Plastics**
Tire Making Machinery Parts - **Myers Industries, Inc.**
Tire Repair Materials - **Myers Industries, Inc., Myers Tire Supply Div.**
Tire Repair Plugs - **Par Products**
Tire Retreading - **Tire & Heavy Equipment, Inc.**
Tire Siping and Grooving Machines - **Saf-tee Siping & Grooving Inc**
Tire Vulcanizers - **Lincoln Manufacturing Co.**
Tires & Inner Tubes - **Tire & Heavy Equipment, Inc.**
Tires & Tubes - **Alamia Inc**
Tires - Used / New - **Ebm Imports**
Tires Sealant for Sealing Tires - **Airseal Products Company**
Tires and Tubes - **Ralph Tire & Service, Inc.**
Tires, Tubes, Batteries - **American Omni Trading**
Tissue Culture Incubator & Hot Box Systems - **Billups-rothenberg, Inc.**
Tissue Paper, Hospital Underpads, Ob Pads - **Paper Pak Products Inc**
Titanium - **Sos Metals, Inc.**
Titanium Diboride Components - **Ceradyne, Inc.**
Titanium, Metal Residue, Also Plastic - **Sos Metal San Diego**
To Replace All Other Types. Install in 4-5 Munites - **Schneider Enterprises**
Toaster Ovens - **Hamilton Beach/proctor Silex, Inc.**
Toasters - **Hamilton Beach/proctor Silex, Inc.**
Tobacco, Not Stemmed/stripped - **Lane Co., Inc., the**
Tofu and Soy Milk Equipment; Consulting Service - **Bean Machines Inc**
Toilet Paper - **Marcal Paper Mills**
Toilet Preparations - **Original Bradford Soap Works, Inc.**
Toilet Preparations - **Biocare Labs**
Toilet Preparations - **Bioelements Inc**
Toilet Preparations - **Classic Cosmetics Inc**
Toilet Preparations - **Cosmetic Specialty Labs, Inc.**
Toilet Preparations - **Dews Research**
Toilet Preparations - **Gabrielle, Inc.**
Toilet Preparations - **Lamaur**
Toilet Preparations - **Lily of Colorado**
Toilet Preparations - **Magnesia Products Inc.**
Toilet Preparations - **Oralabs Holding Corp**
Toilet Preparations - **Shelton's Sheen Wave Labs Inc**
Toilet Preparations - **Sozio, Inc., J. E.**
Toilet Preparations - **Trademark Cosmetics Inc**
Toilet Preparations - **Unique Laboratories, Inc.**
Toilet Preparations - **Yaz Enterprises**
Toilet Preparations, Oils, Hand Cream, Soaps - **Alaska Herb & Tea Co.**
Toilet Seats, Plastic - **Magnolia, Div. Sanderson Plmbg.**
Toilet Seats, Soft Vinyl - **Magnolia, Div. Sanderson Plmbg.**
Toilet Seats, Wood - **Magnolia, Div. Sanderson Plmbg.**
Toiletries - **Unique Laboratories, Inc.**
Toiletries, Skin Enhancers - **Vision Pharmaceuticals Inc**
Toilets, Portable - **Able Builders Export, Inc.**

Toll Plaza Simulation & Evaluation - **Kld Associates Inc.**
Toll Slitting Services - **Nasco, Inc.**
Toll Transmission - **Micon Telecommunications Inc**
Toluene - **Sunoco, Inc.**
Tomato Juice - **Sew Feiel**
Tomato Paste - **The Morning Star Packing Company**
Tomato Sauces - **The Morning Star Packing Company**
Tomato Sauces, Puree & Concentrates - **Western Consolidated Foods, Inc.**
Toner Cartridge Remanufacturing - **Cannon Industries**
Toners & Ribbons - **Galloway Office Supplies & Equipment**
Tontalum Capacitors - **Koa Speer Electronics, Inc.**
Tool & Cutter Grinders, Manual- **Morgan Denver Sales Co**
Tool & Die & Metal Stampings Job Shop - **Owen Tool & Mfg. Co., Inc.**
Tool & Die Job Shop - **Brenner Tool & Die, Inc.**
Tool & Die Job Shop - **Hoffman Tool & Die Inc.**
Tool & Die Maintenance Welding Electrodes - **Eureka Welding Alloys**
Tool Design & Production - **S & S Dynamic Mfg. Llc**
Tool Racks for End Mills & Collets - **Jl Tool & Machine**
Tool, Sample, Circuit Board & Industrial Cases - **Platt Luggage, Inc.**
Tooling - **Southwest Metal Fabricators, Inc.**
Tooling - **Accurite Development & Mfg**
Tooling & Jig Fixture Work - **Lemco**
Tooling Rework Programs - **Hansen Machine & Tool Co., N. M.**
Tooling for Plastic Products - **Commodore Machine Co.**
Tools - **Myers Industries, Inc., Myers Tire Supply Div.**
Tools & Dies & Metal Stampings - **Ut Technologies, Inc.**
Tools - Special Cutting - **Midwest Ohio Tool Company**
Tools, Hardware, Mcmaster Care, Grainger - **Minco Sales Corp.**
Tools_hand & Edge - **Wescosa Inc**
Tools_hand & Edge - **A. J. C. Hatchet Co.**
Tools_hand & Edge - **Ameritool, Hand Tool Div.**
Tools_hand & Edge - **Cobblecrete International Inc**
Tools_hand & Edge - **Daiber Co., Inc., E. J.**
Tools_hand & Edge - **Embee Corp.**
Tools_hand & Edge - **Groom Industries, Inc.**
Tools_hand & Edge - **Patterson Avenue Tool Co.**
Tooth Brushes, Floss, Probes, Pediatric - **P H B Inc.**
Top Entry Ball Vavles - **Conbraco Industries**
Top Weight & Bottom Weight - **Laren Industries**
Topographic 3d Surveys - **Msi International**
Torq - Air Matics - **Wilson & Co., Inc., Thomas C.**
Torque Converters - **Tri-star International, Inc.**
Torque Tools - **Daiber Co., Inc., E. J.**
Tortilla Chips, Baked, Reduced Fat & Fried - **Great Western Tortilla Co.**
Tote Bags - **Manic Impressions**
Towels - **Westpoint Stevens**
Towers, Steel, Crank-up, Free Standing - **Us Tower Corp**
Toys - **Pressner & Co., Inc., M.**
Toys & Hobby Goods & Supplies - **John N Hansen Co Inc**
Toys & Hobby Goods & Supplies - **University Games**
Toys & Hobby Goods & Supplies - **Yaley Enterprises, Inc.**
Toys, Books, Games & Software - **Discovery Toys**
Toys, Sheepskin Stuffed, Export - **Cma Incorporated**
Track & Base Automatic Transmission Parts Reman. - **Roberson Products**
Track & Roller Hardware - **Goff's Curtain Walls/goff's Enterprises Inc.**
Track & Trace - **Dan Transport Corporation**
Tracky Mats - **Liberty Industries, Inc.**
Tractor Cab Air Pressurizers - **Harco Manufacturing Co.**
Tractor Parts - **Heavy Equipment Parts Co.**
Tractor Welders - **Ogden Engineering Corp.**
Trade Association, Machinery Dealers - **Machinery Dealers Natl. Assn.**
Trade Association: International Sandler, Travis & Rosenberg, P.a.
Trade Financing - **Definco Ltd.**
Trade Show & Point-of-purchase Displays - **A B F Industries Inc.**
Trade Show Displays - **S D Modular Displays, Inc.**
Trade Show Displays - **Design Display, Inc.**
Trade Show Exhibits - **Process Graphics Corp.**
Trade Show Exhibits & Advertising Displays - **Presentation South, Inc.**
Trade Show Exhibits, Show Rooms, Museums - **Admore Inc.**
Traffic Control Signs - **Super Precision Design, Inc.**
Traffic Enforcement - **American Traffic Systems Inc**

Traffic Engineering Products - **Egla International**
Traffic Engineering Studies & Visualization - **Kld Associates Inc.**
Traffic Paint - **P R I D E Enterprises, Inc., Baker Paint Industry**
Traffic Safety Products - **Radiator Specialty Co.**
Trailer Mounted Concrete Pumps - **Schwing America, Inc.**
Trailer Wire Harness - **Phillips Industries**
Trailers & Wagons for Sugarcane - **Quality Industries, Inc.**
Trailers for Collecting,sorting - **Dempster Industries, Inc.**
Train Control - Wayside Signals - **Railroad Signal, Inc.**
Training Devices, Military and Aerospace - **Guard Lee, Inc.**
Training Seminars Communications - **Otm Engineering, Inc.**
Training Seminars Cultural- **Intercultural Development**
Training..Schools, Annual & Local Seminars - **Sunnyvale Gdi, Inc.**
Trans. Svcs, Truck/rig. Oversized Units - **Jan Packaging, Inc.**
Transaction Hardware for Money Handling - **C.r. Laurence Company, Inc.**
Transcievers & Frequency Converters - **Vortex Satcom Systems, Inc.**
Transducers / Transmitters - **Dresser Instrument Div.**
Transfer and Progressive - **Progressive Metal Forming Inc.**
Transformer Bushings - **T.j. Manufacturing, Inc.**
Transformer Cooling Fans, 950-8600 Cfm, - **California Turbo Inc**
Transformers - **Dynapower Corporation**
Transformers - **Mag-tran Equipment Corp**
Transformers - **Powertronix Corporation**
Transformers - **R.e. Uptegraff Mfg. Company**
Transformers - **Snc Manufacturing Co., Inc.**
Transformers - **Kirby Risk Service Center**
Transformers - **Cooper Industries**
Transformers & Magnetic Products - **Jackson Transformer Co.**
Transformers: Electronic Circuit Boards - **Cbs (Circuit Board Specialist)**
Transformers, Except Electronic - **Acme Electric Corp.,**
Transformers, Except Electronic - **Jackson Transformer Co.**
Transformers, Except Electronic - **T & R Electric Supply Co., Inc.**
Transformers, Except Electronic up to 500 Mva - **Pauwels Transformers**
Transformers, Induction Neutralizing - **Snc Manufacturing Co., Inc.**
Transformers, Pole Pds, U/g - **Howard Industries**
Transistor Semiconductors- **Interfet Corporation**
Transistors & Diodes - **Hybrid Semiconductors/electronics Inc.**
Transit Buses - **Transit Sales International**
Transit Priority Simulation & Evaluation - **Kld Associates Inc.**
Transit Sanitary Water Cabinets - **Snyder Equipment Co., Inc.**
Transit, Tour & Shuttle Buses - **El Dorado National Co.**
Transl Svcs Tech, Legal, Finance, Software Locali- **Echo International**
Transl. Svcs, Computer Science Specialty - **Margaret Cullen Expert Tran**
Transl. Svcs., Medical, Business Spec. - **Margaret Cullen Expert Translat**
Translation & Interpreting Services - **The Language Lab**
Translation & Interpreting Services- **International Translating Br., Inc.**
Translation & Interpreting Services, Travel - **Genevieve Tournebize - Iliev**
Translation & Localization Services - **Lingo Systems**
Translation / Interpreting : English / Italian - **Rahoy Coccia Gabriella**
Translation Services - **Language Interface, Ltd.**
Translation Services - **Linguistic Systems**
Translation Services - **Sears Steele, Iii**
Translation Services - **Transtek Associates, Inc**
Translation Services - **Tru Lingua Language Systems, Inc.**
Translation Services - **University Language Center, Inc.**
Translation Services French <—> English - **French Connection, the**
Translation Services, All Languages - **Dynamic Language Center, Ltd**
Translation Services, Sp / Eng Transl - **Language Express**
Translation Services, Technical, Legal, Medical - **Language Masters, Inc.**
Translation Services: English>spanish - **Dr. Saul Cano**
Translation Svcs., English, Spanish - **A.s. Contin Inc.**
Translation Svcs., French to English - **Margaret Cullen Expert Translatio**
Translation Svcs., French, German, Spanish - **Hunter, Anne M.**
Translation Svcs., French, Portuguese - **A.s. Contin Inc.**
Translation Svcs., Japanese, Technical - **Suzuki, Myers & Associates, Ltd**
Translation Svcs., Spanish to English - **Margaret Cullen Expert Translat**
Translation Svcs.english into Italian & Italian into English - **Russ Paladino**
Translations Services, All Languages - **Speak Easy Languages**
Transmission Apparatus Incorporating Reception Apparatus - **Anicom Inc.**
Transmission Overhaul Kits - **Tri-star International, Inc.**
Transmission Parts - **Tri-star International, Inc.**

Transmission Replacement Parts (Fuller) - **Pai Industries Inc. (Mfr)**
Transmissions - **Tri-star International, Inc.**
Transp Engine - **Ctl Engineering, Inc.**
Transpiration Conveyor - **Quantum Conveyor Systems, Llc**
Transporation for Cargo - **Falconroc Management Services, Inc.**
Transportation - **Amser Logistics, Inc.**
Transportation Equipment - **Circle S Trailers Inc.**
Transportation Equipment - **E-z-go Textron**
Transportation Equipment - **Evans Mfg. Co., John Evans Trailers**
Transportation Equipment - **Hyundai Precision & Industry**
Transportation Equipment - **Independent Trailer & Equip Co**
Transportation Equipment - **Karavan Trailers, Inc.**
Transportation Equipment - **Midland Steel Products Co.**
Transportation Equipment - **Neighborhood Electric Vehicle Co**
Transportation Equipment - **Silver Lite Trailers Inc**
Transportation Equipment - **Trail-rite Inc**
Transportation Equipment - **Waterland Mfg., Inc.**
Transportation Equipment & Supplies - **Aerofast Ltd**
Transportation Equipment, Nec - **Whiting Corporation**
Transportation Safety Analyses - **Kld Associates Inc.**
Transportation Services, Nec - **Central Air Freight Inc.**
Transporting Equipment - **Bevles Company, Inc.**
Trap Rakes - **Diamond Turf Equipment Inc.**
Trash Compactors, Household - **Anaheim Marketing International**
Trash Containers, Steel - **United Metal Receptacle Inc. (Mfr)**
Trash Receptacles, Aluminum - **United Metal Receptacle Inc. (Mfr)**
Trash Receptacles, Fiberglass - **United Metal Receptacle Inc. (Mfr)**
Trasnsistors, Diodes, Semiconductors - **Solid State Electronics Corp**
Travel Agencies - Trade & Business - **Ets Research & Development Inc**
Travel Trailers & Campers - **Parkwest Industries Inc**
Travel Trailers & Campers - **Silver Lite Trailers Inc**
Travel Trailers & Slide-in Truck Campers - **Fleetwood Enterprises Inc**
Tray Stand - **Abco Products**
Trays, Dishes, Plates, Cups - **Lanca Sales, Inc.**
Tree Fruit Magazine - **Western Agricultural Publish**
Tree Transplanters - **Big John Tree Transplanter Mfg., Inc.**
Trench Boxes - **Int'l Fabricators & Engineers**
Trench Grates & Frames - **Barry Pattern & Foundry**
Trim - **American & Efird, Inc.**
Trolley Mine Hardware - **Minco Sales Corp.**
Trolleys & Kill Floor Equipment for Red Meat - **Le Fiell Company**
Trommel Screening Equipment - **Wildcat Mfg. Co., Inc.**
Trophies, Medals, Medallions, Plaques, Cups - **Classic Medallics, Inc.**
Trophies, Plaques & Awards - **Emblem & Badge Inc.**
Tropical Artificial Palms - **Silkwood Wholesale, Inc.**
Tropical Silk Flower Arrangements - **Silkwood Wholesale, Inc.**
Trousers & Slacks_men's & Boys' - **Platoon Uniform & Sportswear**
Trousers & Slacks_men's & Boys' - **Robett Mfg. Co.**
Truck & Bus Bodies - **El Dorado National Co.**
Truck & Bus Bodies -**Gregory Truck Body & Fire Apparatus, Inc.**
Truck & Bus Bodies - **High Country Proco**
Truck & Bus Bodies - **Rancho Suspension**
Truck & Bus Bodies - **Spalding Products**
Truck & Bus Chassis Frames & Components - **Midland Steel Products Co.**
Truck & Trailer Tarps - **Shur - Co., Inc.**
Truck Axle Replacement Parts (Rockwell / Eaton) - **Pai Industries Inc.**
Truck Bodies - **Rugby Manufacturing Co.**
Truck Bodies and Equipment - **Southern Truck Equipment Inc**
Truck Bodies, Refuse Compactor Collector - **Wayne Engineering Corp**
Truck Conspicuity Tape - **Stimsonite Corp.**
Truck Hoists - **Rugby Manufacturing Co.**
Truck Parts - **Phillips Industries**
Truck Platforms - **Rugby Manufacturing Co.**
Truck Replacement Parts (Mack) - **Pai Industries Inc. (Mfr)**
Truck Safety Equipment - **Grote Industries, Inc.**
Truck Scale Data Collection Systems - **Kanawha Scales & Systems, Inc.**
Truck Tanker Trailers, Wholesale - **Heil Trading Co. Inc.**
Truck Tarps, Canvas - **Improved Construction Methods**
Truck Tires - **Lakin Tire East, Inc.**
Truck Tires - **Tire Group International Inc**
Truck Trailer Airline Components - **M & E Components, Inc.**

Truck Trailers - **Chariot Mfg. Co., Inc.**
Truck Trailers - **Circle S Trailers Inc.**
Truck Trailers - **Gem State Manufacturing Inc**
Truck Trailers - **Kendon Industries Inc**
Truck Trailers - **Sooner Trailer Mfg. Co., Inc.**
Truck Trailers, Wholesale - **Heil Trading Co. Inc.**
Truck Wheel Sealing Systems - **Stemco, Inc.**
Trucking - **Alliance International**
Trucking - **Apollo Warehouse, Inc.**
Trucking - **Barner, Jerry M. & Sons**
Trucking - **Bart Trucking**
Trucking - **Bigge Crane & Rigging Co.**
Trucking - **Burlington Motor Carriers**
Trucking - **Central Transportation Systems**
Trucking - **Chickawaw Container Services**
Trucking - **Circle International**
Trucking - **Hawks Express Inc.**
Trucking - **Ideal Transportation Co. Inc.**
Trucking - **Landstar Ranger, Inc.**
Trucking - **Lin Container Freight Station & Distribution Center**
Trucking - **Mark Vii International**
Trucking - **Match Maker, the**
Trucking - **Mediterranean Shipping Company (Usa) Inc.**
Trucking - **Nippon Express Usa, Inc.**
Trucking - **Overnite Transportation Co.**
Trucking - **Port Elizabeth Terminal & Warehouse**
Trucking - **R & T Truck Inc.**
Trucking - **Roadway Express, Inc.**
Trucking - **T Transportation, Inc.**
Trucking - **Tampa Bay International Terminals, Inc.**
Trucking - **Transwood, Inc.**
Trucking & Warehousing - **Expressway Usa Freightlines Inc.**
Trucking / Specialized Transport - **Vanco Heavy Lift C.f.s.**
Trucking Except Local - **Advantagetransportation Inc.**
Trucking Except Local - **Central Air Freight Inc.**
Trucking Statewide - **Friendly Public Warehouses Inc.**
Trucking, All - **Straightway Inc.**
Trucking, Except Local - **Everett J. Prescott**
Trucking, Transportation - **Canal Cartage Company**
Trucking, Transportation - **Houston Transfer & Storage Co.**
Trucking, Transportation - **Overland Express Company Inc.**
Trucking, Transportation - **Pace Motor Lines Inc.**
Trucking, Transportation, Warehousing - **Mawson & Mawson Inc.**
Trucking, Warehousing & Distribution - **Dartrans, Inc.**
Trucks & Parts - **Parisi-virana Co., Inc.**
Trucks & Parts - **Murray, Thomas W.**
Trucks & Tractors_industrial - **B a F Communications Corp.**
Trucks & Tractors_industrial - **H & K Equipment Inc.**
Trucks & Tractors_industrial - **Holland House Moving Inc., Ron**
Trucks & Tractors_industrial - **Mifran Boman Corp**
Trucks & Tractors_industrial - **Rapid Rack Industries**
Trucks & Tractors_industrial - **Smith Equipment Usa Inc**
Trucks & Trailers, Wholesale - **Arrow Truck Saels Inc.**
Trucks Sales & Exports - **Phillips Motors, Larry**
Trucks, Tractors, Used & New - **Crown Truck Sales**
Trucks; Parts and Services for Semi Truck - **Southwest Peterbilt Gmc**
Tub & Shower Enclosures & Shower Doors - **Coastal Industries, Inc.**
Tub Grinders, Livestock Feeding Equipment - **Burrows Enterprises Inc**
Tube Bending & Fabricating - **Tri-went, Inc.**
Tube Bending Machinery - **Nutter Machine Inc.**
Tube Cleaners, Air, Water or Electric Driven - **Wilson & Co., Inc., Thomas**
Tube Expanders for Boilers - **Wilson & Co., Inc., Thomas C.**
Tube Manufacturing Equip., Export - **Planet Machinery Company**
Tube/pipe Bending Machines - **Mckee - Addison Tube Forming**
Tube/pipe Bending Tools - **Mckee - Addison Tube Forming**
Tube/pipe Sizing & Endforming - **Mckee - Addison Tube Forming**
Tube/pipe Sizing & Endforming Tools - **Mckee - Addison Tube Forming**
Tubes / Flaps / Tire Repair Materials - **Tire Group International Inc**
Tubes and Pipes of Refined Copper - **National Copper Products**
Tubes, Pipes & Hollow Profiles, Iron & Steel - **Aj Weller**
Tubes, Pipes & Hollow Profiles, Iron & Steel - **Roberts Industries**

Tubes, Pipes and Hoses, Rigid, of Plastics - **Centron International Inc.**
Tubing Hill Supplies - **Idaho Sewing for Sports**
Tubing, Mylar & Plastic Films - **Hutchison & Co.**
Tubs Polyethylene Food Grade - **Remco Products Corp.**
Tubular Aircraft Components - **Scotia Technology Div., Lakes Region**
Tubular Fabrication - **Tubing Seal Cap**
Tubulars & Drilling Equipment - **Rk Pipe & Supply**
Tungsten Carbide Burs - **United Abrasives Inc.**
Tungsten Carbide, Tool Steel & Ceramic- **Elizabeth Carbide Components**
Turbine Engine Components - **International Turbine Systems**
Turbine Engine Components - **Aerospace Manufacturing Inc**
Turbine Pumps, J Line Submersible - **J. Line Pump Company**
Turbine Water Pumps, J Line Vertical - **J. Line Pump Company**
Turbines & Turbine Generator Sets - **Engine Systems**
Turbines Steam Hydro Organic Vapors - **Barber-nichols Incorporated**
Turbo Charger Service & Spare Parts - **Golten Service**
Turbulence - **Roberts Irrigation Products**
Turf & Commercial Mowing - **Textron Turf Care and Specialty Products**
Turfgrass - **Southern Turf Nurseries(mfr)**
Turfgrass & Forage Seed , Contract Production - **Ampac Seed Company**
Turkey & Eggs - **Delta International**
Turkey Processing & Packaging - **Wampler Foods, Inc.**
Turkey Slaughtering & Processing - **Farbest Foods, Inc.**
Turnbuckles - **Crosby Group, Inc.**
Turnkey - **Sierra Electronic Assembly**
Turnkey Hospitals - **Biomedical International**
Turnkey and Consignment Electronic Mfrg - **Qual-pro Corporation**
Turnstyles, Manufacturer - **Boon Edam, Inc.**
Twill Nasear Uniform Jackets - **Jh Design Group**
Twine Machinery, Export - **Commision Brokers, Inc.**
Twine, Cordage, Rope and Cable, - **Glassmaster**
Twist Tie Ribbon on Spools Machine Application - **Alcar Industries, Inc.**
Two Car Carrier Beds - **Dual-tech, Inc.**
Two-way Communications Equipment - **Transcrypt International, Inc.**
Type / Desktop , All Languages - **The Language Lab**
Type of Fabrics, Seconds & Close-out - **Jabitex Corporation**
Types of Coating Applied, Functional - **Americoat Corp.**
Types of Coating Applied: Decorative - **Americoat Corp.**
Types of Truck Bodies - **Omaha Standard, Inc.**
Typesetting - **Home with Homeland News & Printing Services**
Typesetting - **Hill Country Newspapers Inc. / the Boerne Star**
Typesetting - **The Medical Remarketer**
Typesetting - **Elevator World**
Typesetting - **E M I S, Inc.**
Typesetting - **Service Quality Institute**
Typesetting - **Advanced Graphics & Publishing**
Typesetting - **Digital Nation**
Typesetting - **Iridio**
Typesetting & Voice Overs - **International Translating Br., Inc.**
Typesetting, Guest Hosue in Playas De Tijuana - **Warren Communications**
Typewriter or Similar Ribbons, Inked - **Tally Printer Corporation**
U-joints (Spicer-type) - **Pai Industries Inc. (Mfr)**
U.s. & International Taxes - **Mcbride Shopa & Co**
U.s. Customs Bonds - **Global Solutions Insurance Services, Inc.**
U.s. Customs Broker - **Quality Customs Broker, Inc.**
U.s. Customs Broker, Freight Forwarding - **Gonzalez T.h. Inc**
U.s. Customs Central Exam Site - **Lin Container Freight Station & Distr**
U.s. Customs Centralized Examination Station - **Price Transfer, Inc.**
U.s. Customs Control Exam Site - **Expressway Usa Freightlines Inc.**
Ul Listed - **Electric City Corp.**
Ultra Pure De I Water - **Springsoft International Inc.**
Ultra Violet Lights - **Culligan Wate Conditioning, Inc.**
Ultra-violet Water Treatment Systems - **Clean Water Systems Intl**
Ultraground Fan Filter Modules - **Airo Clean, Inc.**
Ultralight Plane Kits, Manufacturer - **Golden Circle Air, Inc.**
Ultrasonic Cleaners, Cleaning Chemistry - **Daetwyler Corp., Max**
Ultrasonic Dispersers - **Sonic Corp.**
Ultrasonic Homogenizers - **Sonic Corp.**
Ultrasonic Processors - **Ultrasonic Probs Mfg. Co.**
Ultrasonic Replacement Probes - **Ultrasonic Probs Mfg. Co.**
Ultrasonic, Vibration, Spin & Hot Welding Equi - **Ultra Sonic Seal Co.**

Ultraviolet Germicidal Lamps - **Light Sources, Inc.**
Ultraviolet Tanning Lamps - **Light Sources, Inc.**
Ultraviolet Water Sterilizers - **Filtrine Manufacturing Company**
Umbrellas - **Cover-it Shelters, Inc.**
Unassembled Jewelry Parts; Lapidary Work - **Vicki's Jewelry**
Under Cabinet Lights - **American Power Products Inc**
Under-the-counter Water Filter - **Aquapower Co.**
Underground Protective Lining - **Colorado Lining International, Inc.**
Underground Storage Tank Design - **Environmental Services & Technolo**
Underground Storage Tanks - **Containment Solutions, Inc.**
Underwater Television Cameras - **Kyle Marine Products Llc**
Underwater Vehicles, Manufacturer - **Deep Ocean Engineering Inc**
Underwear & Nightwear_men's & Boys' - **9tz Inc**
Underwear_women's & Children's - **9tz Inc**
Unitary Air Conditioners - **Nordyne Inc.**
Unsaturated Acyclic Terpene Alcohols - **Bush Boake Allen**
Unscramblers - **Njm/cli Packaging Systems International**
Unsupported Plastics Film & Sheet - **Flagship Converters, Inc.**
Unsupported Plastics Film & Sheet - **Hutchison & Co.**
Unsupported Plastics Film & Sheet - **Afton Plastics**
Unsupported Plastics Film & Sheet - **Enflo Corp.**
Unsupported Plastics Film and Sheet - **Broward & Johnson**
Upholstered Aircraft Furniture & Wing Covers - **Fine Line Interiors**
Upholstered Household Furniture - **Broyhill Furniture Industries, Inc.**
Upholstered Parson Chairs - **Moultrie Post Form, Inc.**
Upholstered Wood Furniture - **National Contract Furnishings**
Upholstery Fabric - **Wearbest Sil-tex Mills Ltd.**
Upholstery Fabric Made with Both Cotton - **Dicey Fabrics**
Upholstery Fabrics - **Carole Fabrics**
Ups/telecom Batteries - **Sec Industrial Battery Co., Inc.**
Urea Resins - **Petroplast Chemical Corp.**
Urethane Foam Chemicals & Dispensing Equipment - **I P I International**
Urethane Foam Chemicals, Dispensing Equipment - **Foam Supplies, Inc.**
Urethane Vacuum Cups, Vacuum Cups, Suction Cups - **Vi-cas Mfg. Co.,**
Urethanes, Felts, Foams, Velcro - **C G R Products Inc.**
Urinal Screens & Bowl Cleaners - **Hygienic Products Laboratories**
Urological Imaging & Procedural Systems - **Liebel-flarsheim**
Urology Equipment - **Medstone International Inc**
Used Clothing - **ADRA International**
Used Material Handling Equipment - **Vogler Equipment**
Utilities Trading / Deregulation Practice - **Cap Gemini America**
Utility Pole Maintenance - **Osmose Wood Preserving, Inc.**
Utility Trailers & Lowbeds - **Evans Mfg. Co., John Evans Trailers**
Utility Trailers Open & Enclosed - **Chariot Mfg. Co., Inc.**
Utilizes Water Purification - **Erica and Erica International Corp.**
Uv And/or Heat Cure Epoxy B.g.a. Underfills - **Electronic Materials Inc**
Uv And/or Heat Cure Epoxy Chip Glop Tops - **Electronic Materials Inc**
Uv And/or Heat Cured Optical Epoxies - **Electronic Materials Inc**
Uv Cure Encapsulants - **Electronic Materials Inc**
Uv-cured Adhesives & Coatings - **Northwest Coatings Corp.**
Uv-curing Resins for Construction - **Wahoo International**
Vacuum & Controlled Atmosphere Furnaces - **Centorr Vacuum Industries,**
Vacuum Cleaners - **Eco Vacuum Mfg. Corp.**
Vacuum Cleaners - **Advance Paper & Maintenance**
Vacuum Cleaners, Household - **Beam Industries**
Vacuum Cleaners, Household - **Eco Vacuum Mfg. Corp.**
Vacuum Cleaners_household - **Genie Co., the**
Vacuum Coating Equipment - **Boc Coating Technology**
Vacuum Formed / Injection Molded Plastics - **Elixir Industries, Inc.**
Vacuum Forming Machines - **Zmd International Inc**
Vacuum Forming; Pressure Forming - **Plastics Design & Manufacturing**
Vacuum Ion Nitriding & Induction Hardening - **Advanced Heat Treat**
Vacuum Leak Detectors - **Wilson & Co., Inc., Thomas C.**
Vacuum Metalization - **Summit Coating Technologies, Llc**
Vacuum Metalizers, New & Rebuilt - **Evey Engineering Co., Inc.**
Vacuum Ovens - **Morrow Tech Industries**
Vacuum Packaging Machines, Whsle - **Jaccard Corporation**
Vacuum Packed Vegetables, Shredded Cabbage - **Hawaiian Eateries, Inc.**
Vacuum Pumps - **Robinair, a Div. Of Spx Corporation**
Vacuum Pumps New & Rebuilt - **Evey Engineering Co., Inc.**
Vacuum Relays - **Jennings Technology Company**

Vacuum Systems - **Yeagle Technology, Inc.**
Vacuum Tube Amplifiers - **Torres Engineering**
Vacuum Valves, Motion Feed Throughs - **Huntington Mechanical Labs**
Vacuum, Cryogenic, & Scientific Equipment - **Ability Engineering Te.**
Valve Actuators - **Tyco Valves & Controls**
Valve Remanufacture - **Nordstrom Valves, Inc.**
Valve Repairs - **Superb Marine & Industrial Services, Inc.**
Valves - **Interbath, Inc**
Valves - **D.b.c. Enterprises, Inc.**
Valves - **T.j. Manufacturing, Inc.**
Valves - **K F Industries, Inc.**
Valves - **Kraissl Co., Inc., the**
Valves - **Professional Services International, Inc.**
Valves & Pipe Fittings - **Continental Disc Corp.**
Valves & Pipe Fittings - **Dodson Steel Products, Inc.**
Valves & Pipe Fittings - **Evans Components Inc**
Valves & Pipe Fittings - **Fleck Controls, Inc.**
Valves & Pipe Fittings - **Leonard Valve Co.**
Valves & Pipe Fittings - **Pennsylvania Machine Works, Inc.**
Valves - Plastic - **Policonductos S.a. De C.v.**
Valves, Crane, Balon, Cooper & Kinka, Etc. - **Klm International**
Valves-alarm-for Fire Protection Service - **Central Sprinkler**
Valves_industrial - **American Valve & Pump, Inc.,**
Valves_industrial - **M & J Valve Services, Inc.**
Valves_industrial - **P G I International**
Van Interiors - Sales & Installation - **Pacific Utility Equipment Co**
Van, Pick-up, Automobile Parts - **G M M Van Dock Distributors**
Vanadium Processing - **U. S. Vanadium Corp.**
Vanilla Extracts - **O S F Flavors, Inc.**
Vanilla Extracts - **American Distilling & Manufacturing Co., Inc.**
Vanities - **Kraft Masters Cabinets**
Vanity Trays - **Stylebuilt Accessories, Inc.**
Vapor / Liquid Equipment Packages - **Calgon Carbon Corporation (Mfr)**
Vapor Detection Equipment - Gasoline, Co, Propane - **Fireboy - Xintex**
Vapor Recovery Compressors - **V R Systems, Inc.**
Vapor Recovery Nozzles - **Saber Technologies, Llc**
Vapor Recovery Pumps - **Saber Technologies, Llc**
Variable Frequency Drives - **Benshaw, Inc.**
Various Chemical Preparations, Detergents - **B-d Chemical Co Inc**
Vavle Lifters, Mechanical - **A C Products Co., Inc.**
Vbm, Hbm, Gantry Mills - **Mc Neil & N R M, Inc.**
Veal, Fresh & Frozen - **Superior Packing/superior Farm**
Vectran - **Saunders Thread Co., Inc.**
Vegatable Oils - **Petroferm Inc.**
Vegetable / Nut Oils - **Arista Industries, Inc.**
Vegetable Handling, Peeling & Frying Systems - **Vanmark Corp.**
Vegetable Harvesting Equipment - **Semco Manufacturing**
Vegetable Juice - **Sew Feiel**
Vegetable Magazines - **Western Agricultural Publish**
Vegetable Oil Mills - **Spectrum Naturals Inc**
Vegetable Oils & Shortenings - **Catania Spagna**
Vegetable Seed - **H & H Seed Company Inc**
Vegetable Seeds - **Harris Moran Seed Co.**
Vegetable Seeds for Planting - **Seedcraft**
Vegetable Seeds for Sowing - **Western Hybrid Seeds, Inc.**
Vegetable Washing, Grading & Packing Equipt - **Semco Manufacturing**
Vegetables, Canned - **Western Consolidated Foods, Inc.**
Vegetables, Dried and Vegetable Mixtures, Dried - **Herbco International**
Vegetarian Pet Food Supplements- **Harbingers of a New Age**
Vegetation Stud - **Land & Water Consulting, Inc.**
Vehical Signage - **Dezion Signs**
Vehicle Door Hardware - **Tri/mark Corporation**
Vehicle Lubrication Equipment - **Grover Manufacturing Corp.**
Vehicle Scales - **Scalemen of Florida, Inc.**
Vehicle Sensor Systems - **Mfm Sensors Inc**
Vehiclesused in Factories, Distribution Centers - **Charlatte America**
Vending Machines - **U-select-it Corporation**
Vending Machines (Skill Crane) Amusement Games - **Rainbow Crane**
Vending Machines_automatic - **De La Rue Cash Systems**
Vending Machines_automatic - **U-select-it Corporation**
Vending Machines_automatic - **Vendtronics**

Veneer - **Ellis Enterprises, T. J.**
Veneer - **Soliman Brothers**
Veneer Board - **Franklin Hardwoods, Inc.**
Veneer Clippers - **Elliott Bay Industries**
Veneer Logs - **Ellis Enterprises, T. J.**
Veneer Stone - **Rowat Cut Stone & Marble Co.**
Ventilating Equipment, Agricultural - **Acme Engineering & Mfg. Corp.**
Ventilation & Emissions Control Eng. - **Conserve Engineering Company**
Ventilation Equipment - **Triangle Metal & Mfg. Co.**
Ventilation Fans - **Professional Discount Supply**
Vermiculite, Perlite and Chlorites, Unexpanded - **Stronglite Products**
Vertical Blinds - **Novo Industries Inc.**
Vertical Blinds - **Arabel**
Vertical Blinds & Shades - **Griffith Shade Co.**
Vertical Lift Doors - **Fleming Steel Co.**
Vertical Turbine & Contractor Pumps - **Triton Equipment Corp.**
Vertical Turbine Pumps, Linshaft & Submersible - **Dempster Industries,**
Vertical Turbine, Lineshaft & Submersible Pumps - **National Pump**
Verticutters - **Diamond Turf Equipment Inc.**
Vessels: Stainless Steel - **Mohawk Mfg. Corp.**
Veterinary Biological Products - **American Laboratories, Inc. (Mfr)**
Veterinary Consulting, Food Animals - **Schnepper-international, Inc.**
Veterinary Diagnostic Substances - **Maplehurst Genetics Intl. Inc.**
Veterinary Drugs, Wholesale - **A.j. Buck & Son**
Veterinary Equip. & Supp., Wholesale - **A.j. Buck & Son**
Veterinary Medicines & Supp., Wholesale - **Schnepper-international, Inc.**
Veterinary Supplies - **Coburn Company, Inc.**
Veterinary/research Equipment: Portable Icu - **Thermocare, Inc.**
Vibrating, Marking & Etching Instruments- **Electro Stylus**
Vibrating Conveyors - **Witte Co., Inc., the**
Vibrating Fluid Bed Dryers & Coolers - **Witte Co., Inc., the**
Vibrating Fluid Bed Dryers / Coolers - **Kason Corporation (Mfr)**
Vibrating Screeners - **Witte Co., Inc., the**
Vibration Analyzers, Switches, Monitors - **Metrix Instrument Co.**
Vibration Machinery Mounting Pads - **Kellett Enterprises Inc.(Mfr)**
Vibration Meter & Bearing Tester (M653) - **Vitec, Inc.**
Vibration Meter & Mini Analyzer (M654) - **Vitec, Inc.**
Vibration Meter, Analyzer & Balancer (M655) - **Vitec, Inc.**
Vibration Meters - **Monarch International Inc. Monarch Instrument Div.**
Vibration Meters (M651) - **Vitec, Inc.**
Vibration Monitoring Systems (M2110) (5 to 256 Channels) - **Vitec, Inc.**
Vibration Monitors (1 to 4 Channels) - **Vitec, Inc.**
Vibration Switches (M438) - **Vitec, Inc.**
Vibration Transmitters - **Vitec, Inc.**
Vibration, Bearing Condition & Speed Monitor (Ssm) - **Vitec, Inc.**
Vibration, Measuring Transducers - **Vitec, Inc.**
Vibratory Bowls, Vision Inspection, Feeders - **Warren Industries, Inc.**
Vibratory Conveyors, Screeners, Distrib. - **Food Engineering Corporation**
Vibratory Deburring Equipment - **Victor Metal Finishing Inc.**
Video Based Measuring Instruments - **Acu-gage Systems**
Video Electronics - **Rosen Product Development Inc**
Video Entertainment Systems - **Rosen Product Development Inc**
Video Equipment for the Traffic Industry - **Sunnyvale Gdi, Inc.**
Video Games Sales - **Miracles Amusement**
Video Imaging Systems & Supplies - **Identatronics, Inc.**
Video Inspection Cameras for Engines - **Hoyin Industries**
Video Inspection Equipment Design - **Rs Technical Services Inc**
Video Inspection Systems for Pipe - Sewers - Tanks - **Hoyin Industries**
Video Phones and Integrated Circuits - **Pmc Electronics**
Video Production - **Garrett Sound & Lighting**
Video Production - **Unique Video Productions**
Video Tape Intl. Trade - **Waukesha Co. Technical College**
Video-based, Live-facilitated Management, - **Crestcom International Ltd**
Video...Cameras, Sysetms & Housings - **Sunnyvale Gdi, Inc.**
Videos for Children - **Facemakers Inc.**
Videotape Production - **Unique Video Productions**
Vigor / Grobet Tools - **Arno International, Inc.**
Vinaigrette Salad Dressings and Dressing Bases - **Le Parisien Vinaigrette**
Vintage Men & Ladies Pocket Watches - **Gary Stull Goldsmith**
Viny Looseleaf Binders - **Allied Decals Florida, Inc.**
Vinyl - **C. M. I. Enterprises**

Vinyl & Polyester Reflective Tape - **Reflexite Corp.**
Vinyl Laminated & Coated Non-textile - **Duracote Corp.**
Vinyl Letters & Graphics to Order - **Dezion Signs**
Vinyl Liners, Swimming Pools - **Imperial Pools Inc.**
Vinyl Siding - **Elixir Industries, Inc.**
Vinyl Siding, Residential - **Gentek Building Products**
Vinyl Signs - **Cooley Sign & Digital Imaging,**
Vinyl Signs & Graphics - **Dezion Signs**
Vinyl Tile - **Home Dynamix**
Vinyl Tile Flooring - **Congoleum Corp.**
Vinyl Windows - **Northern Windows Corp.**
Vinyl Windows and Doors - **Window Products Inc**
Violin, Viola, Cello & Bass Musical Strings - **Super-sensitive Musical Stri**
Vip Protection Vehicles - Armored - **Alpine Armoring Inc.**
Visual & Graphic Design / Digital Printing - **Source W Printing**
Vitamin / Mineral Premixes - **Research Products Co.**
Vitamin Powders, Liquids- **All American Pharmaceutical & Natural**
Vitamin/mineral Pharmaceutical Preps. - **Biotics Research Corp.**
Vitamins - **Captek Softgel International**
Vitamins - **International Vitamin Corporation**
Vitamins & Health Supplements - **Tishcon Corporation (Mfr)**
Vitamins & Minerals, Manufacturing - **The Chemins Company Inc**
Vitamins Minerals & Herbs - **Adh Health Products Inc.**
Vitamins and Health Food Supplements; Beauty - **Highland Laboratories**
Vitamins, Herbs & All High Quality Nutritional - **Irwin Naturals**
Vitamins, Immune Response / Arthritis - **Food Science Laboratories**
Vitreous China s - **Mansfield Plumbing Products, Inc**
Vitrifiable Enamels and Glazes, Engobes - **Traction International**
Vme Configurations - **Spira Manufacturing Corp**
Voc, Air Toxicity and Odor Control Systems - **Smith Eng & Environment**
Voice Processing Equipment - **Electronic Tele-communications, Inc**
Voice Systems - **Wheelock, Inc.**
Volatile & Semi-volatile Organic Testing - **Analytica Environmental Lab**
Volatile Oil of Horseradish - Natural - **Accurate Ingredients**
Volatile Oil of Mustard - Natural - **Accurate Ingredients**
Volleyball Equipment - **Centerline Sports Inc**
Voltmeters - **Faria Corp.**
Volumetric Fillers - **Ashton Food Machinery Co., Inc., Neumunz Div.**
Votive Candle Holders - **Peltier Glass Co., the**
Vulcanized Fibre Sheets & Rods - **Nvf Company (Mfr)**
Wafer Bumping Services - **Flip Chip Technologies Llc**
Wafer Prober Controller Hardware & Software - **Miller Design & Equipt**
Waffle Cone and Belgian Waffle Equipment - **Old World Cone**
Walk Behind Industrial Commercial Vacuum Sweepers - **Elgee Mfg. Co.**
Walk-in & Cooler & Freezers - **Craig Indsutries**
Walk-in Coolers and Freezers - **Kool Star**
Wall & Mantle Clocks - **Hermle Black Forest Clocks**
Wall Coatings Protective Insulating - **Spm Thermo-shield, Inc.**
Wall Covering Tools & Hand Knives - **Hyde Manufacturing Co.**
Wall Framing - **R a M Products**
Wall Hung A/c Systems - **Compu-aire, Inc.**
Wall Panels - **Warner Robins Supply Co., Inc.**
Wallcovering Removal & Prep Products - **Zinsser & Co., Inc., William**
Wallets & Accessories - **National Can Manufacturing Inc**
Walnut Lumber & Logs - **S.g. International**
Walnuts - **Ultimate International**
Wardrobe Hanger Bars, Metal Products - **Estad Stamping & Mfg. Co.**
Warehouse & Distribution - **Nippon Express Usa, Inc.**
Warehouse Barcode Systems - **Allenwest Inc**
Warehouse Equipment - **Hemisphere Enterprises**
Warehouse Services - **Penn Terminals Inc.**
Warehouse Storage - **Friendly Public Warehouses Inc.**
Warehouses and Distributes Pickup Truck Accessories - **Simpson Tool Box**
Warehousing - **Amser Logistics, Inc.**
Warehousing - **Bart Trucking**
Warehousing - **Brown Alcantar & Brown Inc.**
Warehousing - **Clm, Inc.**
Warehousing - **Keen, R. H. & Co., Inc.**
Warehousing - **Port Elizabeth Terminal & Warehouse**
Warehousing - **Pierce Packaging Company**
Warehousing & Distribution - **Canal Cartage Company**

Warehousing & Distribution - **Houston Transfer & Storage Co.**
Warehousing & Distribution - **Overland Express Company Inc.**
Warehousing & Distribution - **Pace Motor Lines Inc.**
Warehousing & Distribution - **Southern Warehouse Corporation**
Warehousing & Distribution - **Van's Delivery Service, Inc.**
Warehousing & Distribution - **Distribution Services of America**
Warehousing & Distribution - **Hawks Express Inc.**
Warehousing & Distribution - **Jet Air Service, Inc.**
Warehousing & Distribution - **Price Transfer, Inc.**
Warehousing & Storage - **Straightway Inc.**
Warehousing Packaging & Distribution - **Coughlin Logistics**
Warehousing, Fulfillment - **Congdon Printing & Imaging**
Warm Air Furnaces - **Nordyne Inc.**
Warm Air Heating & Air Conditioning - **Cummins Sw/power Systems**
Warm Air Heating & Air Conditioning - **Dial Manufacturing Inc**
Warm Air Heating & Air Conditioning - **Phoenix Manufacturing Inc**
Warm Air Heating & Air Conditioning - **Webb Distributors Inc**
Warmers, Food - **Broaster Co., the**
Warning Light Clusters - **Faria Corp.**
Warp Knit Textile Products - **Milco Industries, Inc.**
Warp Knit Textiles, Nylon Tricots - **Dorma Mills(mfr)**
Washer Pressure - **Hotsy Corporation, the**
Washers - Shims - Spacers - **Moeller Manufacturing Supply**
Washing, Bleaching or Dyeing Machines - **Pagotto Industries**
Waste - Water Treatment Systems - **Sirex Pulse Hydraulic Systems**
Waste Recycling Equipment - **Consolidated Baling Machine Co.,**
Waste Reduction . - **Resource Recovery Systems Inc. - Kw**
Waste Reduction Equipment - **Consolidated Baling Machine Co.,**
Waste Water Treatment - **Ashland Chemical**
Waste Water Treatment Equipment - **Walker Process Equip., Div. Mcnish**
Waste and Agricultural Grinders - **Sundance**
Waste and Scrap of Paper or Paperboard - **Lotus Exim International**
Waste and Scrap of Paper or Paperboard - **Noga Commodities**
Waste and Scrap of Unbleached Kraft Paper - **Lotus Exim International**
Waste to Energy Systems - **Simonds Mfg. Corp.**
Waste, Parings and Scrap, of Plastics - **Broward & Johnson**
Wastebaskets, Plated & Painted - **Stylebuilt Accessories, Inc.**
Wastewater Equip/systems - **Martin Marietta Magnesia Specialties**
Wastewater Equipment - **Netafim Irrigation Inc**
Wastewater Treatment - **Environmental Services & Technology**
Wastewater Treatment Equipment - **Chief Industries, Inc.**
Wastewater Treatment Equipment - **Ellis Corporation**
Wastewater Treatment Equipment - **Jet, Inc.**
Watches Customized - **Europawatch.com**
Watches, Clocks, Calculators, Electronics & Novelties - **Aaa International**
Water & Wastewater Treatment Equipment - **Smith & Loveless, Inc.**
Water / Wastewater Treatment Systems - **Pro Chem Tech, Internatinal,**
Water Analysis Test Kits & Equipment - **Chemetrics, Inc.**
Water Based Adhesives, Pressure Sensitive - **Dyna-tech Adhesives, Inc.**
Water Based Die Release Agents - **Renite Co., Lubrication Engineers**
Water Boilers - **A.c.e. Boiler, Inc.**
Water Bottling - **Erica and Erica International Corp.**
Water Chillers - **Affinity Industries Inc. (Mfr)**
Water Clorination & Disinfection - **Springsoft International Inc.**
Water Conditioning Equip., Wholesale - **Premier Manufactured Systems,**
Water Conditioning Equipment - **Culligan Wate Conditioning, Inc.**
Water Conservation Products, Omni Flow Control - **Chronomite Labs Inc**
Water Cooled Capacitors - **N W L Capacitors**
Water Coolers - **Oasis Corporation**
Water Distillers - **Waterwise**
Water Districts Applications Developer - **Barclay Maps**
Water Filters - **Culligan Wate Conditioning, Inc.**
Water Filters - **Teledyne Water Pik**
Water Filtration - **Springsoft International Inc.**
Water Filtration & Purification - **Aquion Partners, L.p.**
Water Filtration (Com & Residential) - **Anaheim Marketing International**
Water Filtration Equipment - **Paragon Water Systems**
Water Filtration Units - **Gnld International**
Water Hammer Arresters - **Sioux Chief Manufacturing Co.,Inc.**
Water Heaters - **A.c.e. Boiler, Inc.**
Water Heaters & Storage Tanks - **Weben-jarco, Inc.**

Water Imporvement Products - **Water Quality Services**
Water Pollution Monitoring Devices - **Systems Management Inc.**
Water Pumping Systems - **Southwest Photovoltaic Systems**
Water Purification & Filtration Equipment - **Hotsy Corporation, the**
Water Purification & Wastewater Treat - **Lifesource Engineering Inc.**
Water Purification / Treatment - **Bifrost**
Water Purification Equip - **Premier Manufactured Systems, Inc.**
Water Purification Equipment - **Culligan Wate Conditioning, Inc.**
Water Purification Equipment - **Filtrine Manufacturing Company**
Water Purification Equipment - **Lifestream Watersystems Inc**
Water Purification Equipment - **Osmonics, Inc.**
Water Purification Equipment - **Superior Aqua Enterprises, Inc.**
Water Purification Equipment for Commercial - **Spectrapure Inc**
Water Quality Dissolved Gas Sensor - **Common Sensing Inc**
Water Quality Monitoring & Control Systems - **N-con Systems Co., Inc.**
Water Resistant Products. - **B F Mfg., Inc.**
Water Skis, Kneeboards and Wakeboards - **O'brien International**
Water Skis, Wakeboards and Accessories - **Kd Water Sports**
Water Softener Control Valves - **Fleck Controls, Inc.**
Water Softeners, Deionizers - **Enting Water Conditioning Inc.**
Water Sporting Goods, Surfboards and Sailboards - **Wahoo International**
Water Sports Accessories - **Sprint Rothhammer**
Water Sports Accessories-- **Sprint/Rothhammer**
Water Stoves - **Turbo Burn Inc**
Water Supply - **Environmental Services & Technology**
Water Tank Manufacturing Equipment - **Morgan Denver Sales Co**
Water Temperature Control Valves - **Leonard Valve Co.**
Water Treatment - **Eldorado Chemical Co., Inc.**
Water Treatment - **Columbian Steel Tank Co.**
Water Treatment & Air Purification Equipment - **Aqua-flo, Inc.**
Water Treatment & Sewage Treatment Plants - **Msi International**
Water Treatment Chemicals - **Ashland Chemicals**
Water Treatment Chemicals - **Ques Industries, Inc.**
Water Treatment Co. - **Springsoft International Inc.**
Water Treatment Compounds - **Industrial Specialty Chemicals, Inc.**
Water Treatment Electronic Descaling - **Scalewatcher North America Inc.**
Water Treatment Equipment - **Walker Process Equip.**
Water Treatment Plants - **Equipment & Systems Engineering**
Water Treatment Pulp & Paper Chemicals - **Geo Specialty Chemicals, Inc.**
Water Treatment Purification Commercial - **Hawaii Pacific Associates**
Water Treatment Systems - **Water Technologies**
Water Treatment Systems, Manufacturer of Rainsoft - **Aquion Partners,**
Water Treatment Systems: Residential - **Water Resources International**
Water Treatment Units - **Miox Corp.**
Water Trucks & Tanks - **Hoss Equipment**
Water Walls / Columns Made into Store Fixtures - **Fiero Enterprises, Inc.**
Water Walls, Bubbling Palm Trees & Lamps - **Cole Enterprises**
Water Well & Pump Accessories - **Brady Products Inc.**
Water Well Drilling - **Ruen Drilling International**
Water Well Location & Design - **Environmental Services & Technology**
Water-soluble Metal Working Fluids- **Monroe Fluid Technology, Inc.**
Waterbeds, Futons & Bedroom Furniture - **Viking Industries, Inc.**
Waterblasting Services - **Heavy Duty Hydro Blasting, Inc.**
Waterjet Cutting - **The Laser Workshop**
Waterjet Cutting - **Triangle Metal & Mfg. Co.**
Waterjet Cutting - **Signart, Inc.**
Waterproffing Materials, Concrete Admixt- **Anti Hydro International, Inc.**
Waterproof Outerwear - **South Pass Trading/cnl Clothiers**
Waterproofing - **Henry Company International**
Waterproofing - **Crossfield Products Corp**
Waterproofing Compounds - **Ics Penetron International**
Waterproofing Compounds - **Ics Penetron International Ltd.**
Waterproofing, Caulking, Lumber - **Waite, R. M. Company**
Waterwell Drilling Equipment & Supplies - **D & L Thomas Equipment**
Wax Emulsions for Gypsum Industry - **Henry Company International**
Wax; Sells Candle Craft Supplies - **Yaley Enterprises, Inc.**
Waxed Paper - **Marcal Paper Mills**
Waxes - **Remet Corp.**
Waxes - **Petroferm Inc.**
Wear Particle Analyzer - **Tribometrics Inc.(Mfr)**
Wear Resistant Steel Plate - **Aj Weller**

Wear Technology - **Aj Weller**
Wear Testers - **Norman Tool, Inc.**
Wearing Apparel (Used) - **Mexxon International**
Weatherproof Field Books - **J.l. Darling Corporation**
Weatherproof Writing & Copier Paper - **J.l. Darling Corporation**
Weaving & Finishing Mills - **Absecon Mills, Inc.**
Weaving Machinery Parts - **Bellwether Inc.**
Weaving Mills, Manmade Fiber - **Absecon Mills, Inc.**
Website Development - **Iridio**
Weft Knit Fabric Mills - **Calender Textiles Inc**
Weft Knit Fabric Mills - **Cleveland Mills**
Weigh Batching Systems - **Flexicon Corporation**
Weighing and Counting Devices - **Weigh-tronix Inc**
Weighing, Control & Data Collection Sys- **Kanawha Scales & Systems,**
Weighting Equip., Computer Comb. - **Triangle Package Machinery Co.**
Weld Gantries - **Ogden Engineering Corp.**
Welded / Bolted Steel Storage Tanks - **Pittsburg Tank & Tower Co., Inc.**
Welded Silos - **Laidig Industrial System**
Welded Steel Tubes - **Midwest Art Metal**
Welded and Woven Wire Products - **Georgetown Wire Co. K-lath Div**
Welding - **Field Equipment & Service Co.**
Welding & Hard-facing & Thermal Spraywire - **Polymet Corp.**
Welding Accessories - **Harris-welco Co.**
Welding Accessories - **Inweld Corp.**
Welding Alloys - **Inweld Corp.**
Welding Apparatus - **Ogden Engineering Corp.**
Welding Apparatus - **Welding Warehouse**
Welding Equipment Chillers - **Affinity Industries Inc. (Mfr)**
Welding Job Shop - **Standard Welding Co., Inc.**
Welding Machinery - **Hanson Welding Machines, Inc.**
Welding Machines, High Frequency - **Cosmos Electronic Machine Corp.**
Welding Repair - **Lemco**
Welding Repair - **American Hydraulics**
Welding Rods and Filler Metals - **Welding Warehouse**
Welding, General Machining, Metal Fabrication - **B. T. M. Inc.**
Wet Cleaning Machines - **Wascomat (Mfr)**
Wet Corn Milling - **Colorado Sweet Gold Llc**
Wheat - **Delta International**
Wheat Free & Gluten Free Foods - **Ener-g Foods Inc**
Wheat Germ Oil - **Research Products Co.**
Wheat Milling - **Cenex Harvest States Cooperatives**
Wheel Chocks - **Diamond Rubber Products Co., Inc.**
Wheel Loaders - **Hoss Equipment**
Wheel Polishing Machines - **Rancho Metal Polishing**
Wheelchair Lifts, Chair Stair Climbs - **Flinchbaugh Co., Inc.**
Wheelchairs - **Gunnell Inc.**
Wheelchairs & Home Medical Equipt - **Universal Technology Systems**
Whey - **International Custom Products**
Whip Toppings - **Diehl, Inc.**
Whipple Super-chargers, Power Boost Chargers - **Whipple International**
Whirlpool Baths - **Jason International, Inc.**
Whirlpool Baths - **Plastic Development Company(mfr)**
White Ash Lumber - **S.g. International**
Wholesale Closeouts - **Cwc Inventories, Inc.**
Wholesale, Export & Domestic - **Ericyan Ii**
Wild Bird Food - **Audubon Park Co**
Wild Flower Seeds - **Sharp Bros Seed Co.**
Wild Rice, Wholesale - **Tradewinds International**
Wildflower Seed & Grass Seed Harvester - **Miller Ag-renewal, Inc.**
Wildlife Feeders & Housing Handcrafted of Redwood - **Wildwood Farms,**
Wildlife Feeds-USDA Certified - **Wildwood Farms, Inc.**
Wildlife Lithographic Prints, Stamps- **National Art Publishing Corp.**
Winches - **Ramsey Winch Co.**
Winches Rebuilt & Testing - **Service Hydraulics Inc.**
Wind Powered Generators - **World Power Technologies, Inc.**
Wind Speed & Direction Indicators - **Westberg Mfg., Inc.**
Wind Tunnel Modeling - **Cermak Peterka Petersen, Inc.**
Winders of Cops & Bobbins - **Western Filament Inc**
Window & Door Hardware - **Wespac Corp.**
Window & Door Systems, Fabricates Extruded- **Veka West, Inc.**
Window Fashion - **Technical Coating International**

Window Shades for Airport Control Towers - **Plastic-view Atc**
Window Treatment Polymer Components - **Marley Mouldings Inc.(Mfr)**
Window-based Terminals & Motherboard. - **Delta Products Corporation**
Windows & Patio Doors - **Hurd Millwork Company, Inc.**
Windows, BlocksNoise Reduction Windows - **Midwest Builders Supply**
Wine - **Beringer Wine Estates**
Wine - **Louis M Martini Winery**
Wine - **Steltzner Vineyard**
Wine & Distilled Beverages - **Bargetto's Santa Cruz Winery**
Wine & Distilled Beverages - **Davis Bynum Winery**
Wine, Brandy, & Brandy Spirits - **Hoodsport Winery Inc.**
Wine, from Grapes & Grape must with Alcohol - **Bandiera Winery**
Winery - **Asv Wines Inc**
Winery - **Round Hill Winery**
Winery and Tasting Room - **Ventana Vineyards Winery Inc**
Winery and Vineyards - **Orfila Vineyards Inc**
Winery and Vineyards - **Whitehall Lane Winery**
Winery and Vineyards- **Bargetto's Santa Cruz Winery**
Winery and Vineyards; Produces and Sells Wine - **Stevenot Winery**
Wines - **Elk Run Vineyards Inc.**
Wines - **Mayacamas Vineyards**
Wines - **Robert Pepi Winery**
Wines & Juice - **Asv Wines Inc**
Wines, Brandy, & Brandy Spirits - **Bargetto's Santa Cruz Winery**
Wines, Brandy, & Brandy Spirits - **Beringer Wine Estates**
Wines, Brandy, & Brandy Spirits - **Davis Bynum Winery**
Wines, Brandy, & Brandy Spirits - **Louis M Martini Winery**
Wines, Brandy, & Brandy Spirits - **Orfila Vineyards Inc**
Wines, Brandy, & Brandy Spirits - **Round Hill Winery**
Wines, Brandy, & Brandy Spirits - **Steltzner Vineyard**
Wines, Brandy, & Brandy Spirits - **Stevenot Winery**
Wines, Brandy, & Brandy Spirits - **Whitehall Lane Winery**
Wines; Crushing and Producing Services - **Pedrizzetti Winery**
Winter Ski Gloves - **Mcgough Industries Inc**
Wipers - **Tridon**
Wipes & Swabs - **Afassco, Inc.**
Wiping Cloths, Wholesale - **General Waste Trading Company**
Wiping Rags: George Cotter - **Rowtex**
Wire & Cable Machinery, Export - **Commision Brokers, Inc.**
Wire & Cable Management Systems - **Wiremold Co., the**
Wire & Cable, Tubing, Wholesale - **Alpha Wire Company**
Wire & Stitching Wire - **Ideal Stitcher Company(mfr)**
Wire / Cable - **Bifrost**
Wire Cables; Custom Cable Assem - **Storm Products Co Inc**
Wire Containers - **Carico Systems**
Wire Crimping Tools - **Mpi Products Div. Of Miro Precision**
Wire Formed Products - **Fortress Mfg. Inc.**
Wire Formed Products - **Fortress Mfg., Inc. (Mfr)**
Wire Forming - **Fabor Fourslide, Inc.**
Wire Forms - **Curran Coil Spring Inc**
Wire Harness - **Kirby Risk Service Center**
Wire Harnesses - **Gilbert Mfg. Co.**
Wire Harnesses - **V I P Industries, Inc.**
Wire Harnesses - **Xenia Mfg. Co.**
Wire Harnesses & Electronic Sub-assemblies - **Brenneman & Assocs., Inc.**
Wire Lubricants & Drawing Oils - **Lenox Chemical Company**
Wire Markers - **Plastic Extruded Parts Inc.(Mfr)**
Wire Mesh & Perforated Baskets - **Tilton Rack & Basket Corp.**
Wire Mesh Partitions and In-plant Office Partit - **California Wire Products**
Wire Mesh Products - **Behlen Mfg. Co.**
Wire Products - **Zapp Usa Inc.**
Wire Products - Misc. Fabricated - **Acme Wire Products Co., Inc.**
Wire Products, Fine Diameter - **Molecu Wire Corporation**
Wire Products, Misc. Fabricated - **Leschen Wire Rope Co.**
Wire Products, Wire Forming - **Rsm Products, Inc.**
Wire Products_misc. Fabricated - **California Wire Products Corp**
Wire Products_misc. Fabricated - **Storm Products Co Inc**
Wire Products_misc. Fabricated - **Alloy Wire Belt**
Wire Products_misc. Fabricated - **Ammermans, the**
Wire Products_misc. Fabricated - **Cambria County Assn. For the Blind**
Wire Products_misc. Fabricated - **Carico Systems**

Wire Products_misc. Fabricated - **Georgetown Wire Co. K-lath Div**
Wire Products_misc. Fabricated - **Gilbert Mfg. Co.**
Wire Products_misc. Fabricated - **Piggott Wire & Cable Company**
Wire Products_misc. Fabricated - **Renfro Franklin Company**
Wire Products_misc. Fabricated - **Rochester Corp., the**
Wire Products_misc. Fabricated - **S & S Industries, Inc.**
Wire Products_misc. Fabricated - **Tema Isenmann, Inc.**
Wire Products_misc. Fabricated - **Tilton Rack & Basket Corp.**
Wire Reinforced Plastic Fencing - **Robbins Corp. E.s.**
Wire Rods - **Tata, Inc.**
Wire Rope (Cable) - **Trident Tool, Inc.**
Wire Rope Cutters - **Morse Starrett Products Company**
Wire Rope Fitting Hook Hardwar - **Crosby Group, Inc.**
Wire Rope Fittings - **Crosby Group, Inc.**
Wire Springs & Forms, Precision - **Excel Spring & Stamping Co.**
Wire Strippers & Cable Preparation Tools - **Ripley Co., Inc.**
Wire Stitchers & Staplers, Industrial - **Ideal Stitcher Company(mfr)**
Wire Wheels & Power Brushes - **Abrasive Distributors Corp.**
Wire Wrapping - **Electronic Manufacturing Svc**
Wire and Cable - **Piggott Wire & Cable Company**
Wire, Cable & Tubing Cutters - **Eraser Co., Inc.**
Wireless Communications Equipment - **Glenayre Western Multiplex**
Wireless Data Communications Equipment - **Glenayre Western Multiplex**
Wireless Drive-thru Intercoms - **H.m. Electronics, Inc.**
Wireless Ethernet Bridges - **Glenayre Western Multiplex**
Wireless Portable Public Address Systems - **Portatalk Electronics Inc**
Wireless... Microwave & Spread Spectrum - **Sunnyvale Gdi, Inc.**
Wireline & Well Logging Equipment - **Universal Manufacturing & Const.**
Wires - **Tata, Inc.**
Wiring Devices: Plugs & Connectors - **Ericson Manufacturing, Inc.**
Wiring Hanesses - **Grote Industries, Inc.**
Wms/mis - **Pierce Packaging Company**
Women's & Children's Clothing - **R & S Sportswear Inc; Dba Filati**
Women's & Children's Clothing - **Jh Design Group**
Women's & Misses Clothing - **Mary K Active Wear Inc**
Women's Athletic Wear - **Leo's Dancewear Inc.**
Women's Dance Apparel - **Leo's Dancewear Inc.**
Women's, Misses' and Juniors' Outerwear— Pants - **Piccone Apparel**
Women's, Misses' and Juniors' Sportswear - **R & S Sportswear Inc**
Won't Wash off - **Unique Laboratories, Inc.**
Wood & Plastic Bleacher Seating - **Folding Bleacher Company**
Wood Blinds - **Arabel**
Wood Carts, Dollies, Platform Trucks - **Cambridge Manufacturing, Inc.**
Wood Ceilings - **Ceilings plus Inc**
Wood Chips - **American Wood Fibre, Inc.**
Wood Doors - **Hollow Metal Specialists, Inc.**
Wood Fiber Blankets - **Mat, Inc.**
Wood Fillers - **Eclectic Products Inc.**
Wood Finishing - **G-wood Finishing Co. Inc.**
Wood Flooring, Export - **Global Market Partners, Inc.**
Wood Household Furniture - **Lane Co., Inc., the**
Wood Household Furniture - **Broyhill Furniture Industries, Inc.**
Wood Ladders - **Alaco Ladder Co.**
Wood Library Furniture - Tbl, Shlv, Seating - **Buckstaff Company**
Wood Lockers Plastic Laminate - **Fiberesin Industries, Inc.**
Wood Mouldings - **Picture Woods Ltd**
Wood Mulch Products (Soil Guard, Mat-fiber) - **Mat, Inc.**
Wood Office Furniture - **All Craft Fabricators, Inc.**
Wood Office Furniture - **Arcadia Chair Company**
Wood Office and Store Fixtures - **Valley Fixtures Inc**
Wood Paneling, Wholesale - **Pdg Associates, Inc.**
Wood Preservatives - **Osmose Wood Preserving, Inc.**
Wood Preserving - **B & M Wood Products**
Wood Preserving - **Fontana Wholesale Lumber**
Wood Product Flooring - **Premier Hardwood Products Inc.**
Wood Product Testing of Panel Products - **Teco**
Wood Products - **Alaska Gift & Gallery**
Wood Products - **American Wood Fibre, Inc.**
Wood Products - **City Glass Co.**
Wood Products - **Colorado Frame Company**
Wood Products - **Excel Design Inc.**

Wood Products - **First State Map & Globe Co., Inc.**
Wood Products - **Franklin Hardwoods, Inc.**
Wood Products - **Great Northern Lumber, Inc.**
Wood Products - **Lemhi Post & Poles Inc**
Wood Products - **Northwest Cedar Inc**
Wood Products - **P & M Sign, Inc.**
Wood Products - **Vixen Hill Mfg. Co.**
Wood Products (Home Use) - **Purnell Co., R. C.**
Wood Products, Stone Products, Marble Products - **Jonathan Virginia, Inc.**
Wood Shelving and Store Fixtures - **Newood Display Fixture Mfg Co**
Wood Stakes Lath Wedges & Cedar Planters - **Cor Enterprises**
Wood Stove & Fireplace Temperature Control Devices - **Condar Co.**
Wood Turning - **Stuhr Enterprises, Inc.**
Wood Waste Incinerators - **Olivine Corporation**
Wood Windows and Doors - **Sw Sash & Door**
Wood Working - **Arc Industries Inc.**
Wood in Chips or Particles, Nonconiferous - **The Barrel Company Inc.**
Wood, Clad and Aluminum Doors; Vinyl- **Integra Window & Door Inc**
Wooden & Plastic Clocks & Banners - **Hanover Clocks & Banners**
Wooden & Plastic Motel & Hotel Furniture - **Mccammisn Mfg. Co., Inc.**
Wooden & Steel Toy Guns & Archery Sets - **Parris Mfg. Co.**
Wooden Bookcases - **Hale Co., F. E.**
Wooden Cabinets - **Kraft Masters Cabinets**
Wooden Cabinets - **Paul's Cabinets Co.**
Wooden Clock Frames, Cabinets, Countertops & Millwork - **Bonito Mfg.**
Wooden Columns, Posts - **Dixie-pacific Mfg. Co., Inc.**
Wooden Crates - **Industrial Crating, Inc.**
Wooden Crutches - **Geo E. Alexander & Son, Inc.**
Wooden Disk Boxes - **Compu Cover**
Wooden Display Cases, Humidifiers, Funeral Urns - **Jonathan Virginia**
Wooden Fence Posts and Poles - **Lemhi Post & Poles Inc**
Wooden Fence Posts, Poles, Gates - **B & M Wood Products**
Wooden Folding Chairs - **Royal Sales Corp.**
Wooden Furniture, Infant, Juvenile & Teen - **Child Craft Industries, Inc.**
Wooden Garment Hangers - **Batts Inc.**
Wooden Handles - **H.a. Stiles**
Wooden House & Garden Planters - **Rucker Lumber Co., Inc.**
Wooden Household Furniture Mouldings - **Mouldings Unlimited, Inc.**
Wooden Kitchen Cabinets - **Winfield Cabinets**
Wooden Literature Shelves for Floor & Wall - **Gould Plastics, Inc.**
Wooden Pallets - **Atco Pallet Co.**
Wooden Pallets & Corrugated Boxes - **Age Industries, Inc.**
Wooden Pallets, Hardwood Grade Lumber, Kd & Green - **B & B Lumber**
Wooden Plaques - **Master Craft Plaque Co.**
Wooden Products - **Cor Enterprises**
Wooden Reels - Wire & Cable - **Baker Div. Sonoco Products Company**
Wooden Roof & Floor Trusses - **Now Structures, Inc.**
Wooden Roof & Floor Trusses - **Universal Truss, Inc.**
Wooden Sign Carving Equipment - **Kimball Sign & Woodcarving Co.**
Wooden Storage Products - **Purnell Co., R. C.**
Wooden Store Fixtures - **Dolphin Mfg. Inc.**
Wooden Store Fixtures - **Huck Store Fixture Co.**
Wooden Trusses - **Le Truss Co., Tien**
Wooden Trusses & Doors - **Fagen's Building Center**
Wooden Windows, Entry Ways - **Architectural Windows & Entries, Inc.**
Wooden-cased Lead Pencils - **General Pencil Co.**
Woodenware - **Summit Sales & Marketing**
Woodgrain Foils - **Transfer Print Foils, Inc.**
Woodvneer, Melamine, Polyester - **International Components Plus, Inc.**
Woodworking Machine - **Lobo Machinery Corp.**
Woodworking Machinery - **Lrh Enterprises Inc**
Woodworking Machinery - **Magnum Machinery Services Inc**
Woodworking Machinery - **Onsrud Machine Corporation**
Woodworking Machinery - **Precision Products Co**
Woodworking Machinery - **United Machine Ind. Inc.**
Woodworking Machinery & Designer - **Magnum Machinery Services Inc**
Woodworking Machinery for Cabinetmaking - **Castle Inc**
Woodworking Machinery; Soft Feed Roller - **Western Roller Corporation**
Wool & Leather Outerwear Jackets - **Jh Design Group**
Wool & Synthetic Fiber - **Brickle, Hyman & Son, Inc.**
Word Processing Svcs. - **Suzuki, Myers & Associates, Limited**

Word Processing; Typesetting Service - **Pc Services**
Work Benches - **Waterloo Industries, Inc.**
Workholdings - **Kurt Manufacturing Co.**
Worldwide Distribution - **Pierce Packaging Company**
Worldwide Neon Service - **Made in Maui Neon**
Worldwide Network - **Dan Transport Corporation**
Worldwide Offshore Oil & Gas Construction - **J.ray Mcdemott, Inc.**
Woven Cotton Fabrics - **Mayfair Mills, Inc.**
Woven Cotton Fabrics - **Starensier**
Woven Cotton Fabrics - **Glassmaster**
Woven Cotton Fabrics - **Outdoor Cap**
Woven Cotton Fabrics & Knits - **Jsam**
Woven Elastic - **Just a Stretch**
Woven Fab of Syn Fil Yn, Incl Monofil 67 Dec - **R.d.d. Enterprises**
Woven Fab of Syn Fil Yn, Incl Monofil 67 Dec - **Starensier**
Woven Fabrics - Cottons & Blends - **Laren Industries**
Woven Wire Conveyor Belts, Round and Flat Wire; - **Alloy Wire Belt**
Woven Wire Products, Insect Screening - **Hanover Wire Cloth**
Wrap Around Cover Books - **Colonial Business Forms, Inc.**
Writers - **Masterpiece Prdctns Nevada**
Writing Instruments - **Autopoint, Inc.**
Wrought Iron Furniture - **Grace Mfg. Co., Inc.**
Wrought Iron, Tubular & Aluminum Furniture - **Sunlite Casual Furniture,**
Www.uniquelabs.com - **Unique Laboratories, Inc.**
Wyoming Bentonite Products - **Wyo-ben, Inc.**
X-ray Accessories - **Pulse Medical Products, Inc.**
X-ray Apparatus & Tubes - **Area Detectors Systems Corp**
X-ray Apparatus & Tubes - **Fonar Corp.**
X-ray Fluorescence Equipment - **Axic Inc**
X-ray Food Inspection Equipment - **Par Vision Systems Corporation**
X-ray Imaging Apparatus - **Trex Medical, Bennett Division**
Xerox Wide Format Reseller - **Repro-products & Services**
Xylene - **Sunoco, Inc.**
Yarn Dyed Fabrics & Printed Fabrics - **Laren Industries**
Yarn in Seconds & Close-out - **Jabitex Corporation**
Yellow Grease - **Darling International Inc.**
Yellow Onions - **Denice & Filice Packing**
Yogurt - **Brown Cow West Corporation**
Yogurt & Sugar Free Tubs & Mixes - **Luke's Ice Cream**
Yucca Juice Feed Additives - **Distributors Processing Inc**
Zeolite Molecular Sieve Materi - **Respond Group of Companies**
Zinc, Nickel, Electroless Nickel, Copper, - Metal Finishing Technologies,
Zircon - **Refractory Materials International**
Zoological Signs - **Asd, Inc. , Architectural Signage & Design**

Mexico: Company Listings Of Products & Services

A. C. Mexicana, S. A. de C.
Carr. Central 57, Km. 420
San Luis Potosi, S.L.P 78090
Contact: Lic. Oscar Guzman
Dibene, Marketing Director
PHONE: 525/358-7423
Product/Service Description:
Fork-lift and works trucks, nesoi

A. G. Electronica, S. A. de C. V.
Republica de Uruguay No. 14
Mexico, D. F. 06000
Contact: Ing. Juan Antonio Garcia
Maldonado, Director General
PHONE: 525/512-0962, 521-1017
Product/Service Description:
Electric storage batteries, incl
separators, parts

AIQUIFAR, S.A. de C.V.
Carretera Vecinal San Pablo
Topilej
MEXICO, D.F.
Contact: MR. Angel Gonzalez,
Director General
PHONE: 525/639-6064 536-4551
Product/Service Description:
Food preparations, nesoi, canned

AMP de Mexico, S. A. de C. V.
Alfredo Nobel No. 28
Tlalnepantla, MEX 54060
Contact: Ing. Alvaro Alcocer
Brizuela, Marketing Director
PHONE: 525/398-7611, 729-0400
Product/Service Description:
Cable, etc nesoi of cu nt ins nt md
into artcls

Abast. y Rep. Hospitalarias, S.A.
Calzada de Tlalpan No. 4456-109
Mexico, D.F. 14050
Contact: Lic. Jose Guadalupe
Lopez Vitolas, General Manager
PHONE: 525/655-0252, 573-2343
Product/Service Description:
Medical, surgical, dental or vet
inst, no elec, pt

Abastecedora de Sobres, S.A. DE C.V
Dr. Martinez Del Rio No. 102
Mexico, D.F. 06720
Contact: Mr. Antonio Sanchez,
PHONE: 525/578-1564
Product/Service Description:
Envelopes of paper/paperboard, for
correspondence

Abastecedores Lumon, S.A. de C.V.
Halcon #37
Izcali, EDM 54760
Contact: Ing. Gabriel Mondragon,
Director
PHONE: 525/877-0164
Product/Service Description:
Electromagnets, permanent
magnets etc & parts

Abasto Basico, S.A. de C.V.
Central de Abasto, Bodega F-8A
Mexico, D.F. 09040
Contact: Arq. Jose Fco. Mendoza
E., Purchasing director
PHONE: 525/694-2329
Product/Service Description:
Soap; organic surf-act prep for
soap use, bars etc

Abrasivos y Servicios Industriales,
Ave. Cuitlahuac No. 141
Mexico, D. F. 02600
Contact: Sr. Hernan Calleja,
Director General
PHONE: (525) 556-2277, 556-2135
Product/Service Description:
Abrasives on a base material oth
thn fabrc o paper

Accesorios para Laboratorio, S.A.
Victor Hugo No. 74
Mexico, D.F. 11590
Contact: Mr. Rene Wolf
Leitenberg, Director General
PHONE: 525/525-0596
Product/Service Description
Laboratory ware

Accesorios y Autopartes Sport,
Peralvillo No. 71
Mexico, D.F. 06200
Contact: Mr. Julio Torres Aguilera,
Director General
PHONE: 525/529-7642,529-7673
Product/Service Description:
Automotive Parts & Supplies

Aceites y Grasas Lubricantes, S.A
Damasco No. 28 Col. Romero
Rubio
Mexico, D.F. 14500
Contact: Ing. Jose de Jesus Palacio
Villalobos, General Manager
PHONE: 525/789-0949
Product/Service Description:
Additives for lubricating oils,

Aceites, Aislantes Y Lubricantes
Viveros de la Colina No. 318
Tlalnepantla, EDM 54080
Contact: Ing. Alejandro Funes C.,
Director
PHONE: 525/398-8886,398-8831
Product/Service Description:
Oil (not crude) from petrol &
bitum mineral etc.

Acondicionamiento Quimico Para
Av. Taxquena No.1818 - D39
Mexico, D.F. 04280
Contact: Mr. Francisco Ardura,
Director General
PHONE: 525/549-5207,689-9716
Product/Service Description:
Water filtering or purifying
machinery & apparatus

Aerodinamica, S.A. de C.V.
Anil No. 831
Mexico, D.F. 08400
Contact: Lic. Rafael Guizar,
Director
PHONE: 525/681-5736
Product/Service Description:
Hydrometers,
thermometers,pyrometers etc

Aerotecnica, S.A. de C.V.
Uxmal No. 380
Mexico, D.F. 03020
Contact: Mr. Markus Giger,
Director
PHONE: 525/536-7429, 536-7208
Product/Service Description:
Hydrometers, thermometers,
pyrometers etc; pts etc

Agricultura Nacional, S.A. DE C.V.
Blvd Adolfo Ruiz Cortinez No. 7
Atizapan, EDM 54500
Contact: Ing. Luis Y. Quijano,
Director General
PHONE: 525/824-3622,824-3623
Product/Service Description:
Fertilizers

Agropecuaria Valmo, S.A. de C.V.
Blvd. Kino y Periferico Ote.
Hermosillo, SON 83160
Contact: Mr. Pedro Mario
Valenzuela, Administrator
PHONE: 52-62/14-4343, 14-4298
Product/Service Description:
Agricultural Services

Agropecuaria e Industrial del
Leocadio Salcedo 207
Hermosillo, SON 83140
Contact: Mr. Jorge Luis Moreno
Garcia, General Director
PHONE: 52-62/15-4310
Product/Service Description:
Food industry residues & waste;
prep animal feed

Agua del Rey
Cedro 9
Poza Rica, VER 93240
Contact: Mr. Hector Raul Marquez
Ruiz, General Manager
PHONE: 52-782/200-02, 309-02
Product/Service Description:
Waters, natural etc, not sweetened
etc; ice & snow

Aguirre, R.M.F.Sistemas y Recubr.
Av.Juarez # 136,
Cananea, SON
Contact: Mr. Martin Aguirre,
Owner
PHONE: 52-633/2-5627
Product/Service Description:
Paint & varnish from synth etc
polymers aqueous md

Ahome Acuicola, S.A. de C.V.
Blvd. Lopez Mateos No. 2213,
Edif.
Los Mochis, SIN 81200
Contact: Mr. Luis Miguel Hurtado
F., Director General
PHONE: 52-681/5-0903
Product/Service Description:
Shrimps and prawns, prepared or
preserved, nesoi

Aireco, S.A.
Convento de San Jeronimo No. 2
Tlalnepantla, MEX 54050
Contact: Ing. Heriberto Rodriguez,
Director General
PHONE: 525/361-9431
Product/Service Description:
Tools for working in the hand,
pneumatic etc, pts

Aislantes, Climas y Controles,
Lima No. 931-217
Mexico, D.F. 07300
Contact: Mr. Fernando Padilla,
Director
PHONE: 525/760-3630, 752-7319
Product/Service Description:
Air conditioning machines etc not
incl refrig unit

Albany International, S.A. de C.V.
Km. 17.5 Carretera Tlanepantla
Tlanepantla, EMEX 54800
Contact: Ing. Enrique Garcia,
General Manager
PHONE: 525/625-1600, 873-3522
Product/Service Description:
Filters & parts & accessories for
instr & appratus

Albatros Textil, S.A. de C.V.
Av. Industria Textil, No. 8 - B
Naucalpan, E.M. 53370
Contact: Lic. Jaime Sitt, Director
PHONE: 525/300-7840,
300-8940
Product/Service Description:
Textile fabric nesoi, coated etc
nesoi, cotton

Alcampo Caza y Pesca, S.A. de C.V.
Av. Revolucion No. 134
Mexico, D.F. 11800
Contact: Mr. Augusto Acevedo,
Director General
PHONE: 525/515-2218
Product/Service Description:
Camping goods nesoi, of textile
materials nesoi

Aleaciones Y Soldaduras, S.A.
Calle 2, No. 3 - A, locales D Y E
Naucalpan, EDM 53370
Contact: Mr. Jose Luis Sedano,
Director General
PHONE: 525/358-1731, 358-7674
Product/Service Description:
Wire, rods etc for soldering etc &
met spray, bmpt

Alexander Batteries de Mexico,
Av. Nuevo Leon No. 253 - 202
Mexico, D. F. 11800
Contact: Mr. Armando Toral
Navarrete, General Director
PHONE: 525/277-8623, 277-8619
Product/Service Description:
Primary cells & batteries, parts

Alimentos Cientificos del Nayart,
Inustriales Nayaritas No. 129
Tepic, NAY 63000
Contact: Mr. Ignacio Luna
Langarica, General Director
PHONE: 52-321/3-3477, 3-2086
Product/Service Description:
Food industry residues & waste;
prep animal feed

Alta Mecanica Industrial,
Av. Industria No. 55
Tlalnepantla, EDM 54170
Contact: Ing. Enrique
Ibarguengoitia, Director General
PHONE: 525/3923111,0135,
Product/Service Description:
Air brakes & parts for veh of
heading 8605 or 8606

Alta Resistencia, S.A.
Rio Tiber No. 70
Mexico, D.F. 06500
Contact: Mr. Luis Emilio Jimenez
Cacho, Director General Owner
PHONE: 525/525-1645 to 54
Product/Service Description:
Wire of alloy steel nesoi

Aludec, S.A. de C.V.
Playa Pie de la Cuesta No. 215
09440, D.F MEXICO
Contact: Mr. Daniel Estrada
Camacho, General Administrator
PHONE: 525/672-7526/609-0436
Product/Service Description:
Aluminum alloy profiles nesoi

Alumarq, S.A. de C.V.
Matagalpa No. 1122
Mexico, D.F 07360
Contact: Arq. Jose Carlos Estrada
Cardenas, Director
PHONE: 525/752-2066
Product/Service Description:
Aluminum alloy profiles nesoi

Aluminio Azteca, S.A.
Poniente 126 No. 318
Mexico, D.F. 07750
Contact: Ing. Victor Perez,
Director
PHONE: 525/755-2341
Product/Service Description:
Aluminum and articles thereof

Aluminio Gutsa, S.A. de C.V.
Xicontencalt No. 327
Mexico, D.F. 04000
Contact: Mr. Antonio Gutierrez,
Director
PHONE: 525/604-7306, 658-1051
Product/Service Description:
Aluminum alloy profiles nesoi

Aminotec, S.A. de C.V.
Londres 105 - 309
Mexico, D.F. 04100
Contact: Lic. Corina Teran
Espinoza, Director General
PHONE: 525/554-9045, 658-7893
Product/Service Description:
Food preparations nesoi

Ammex Asociados, S.A. de C.V.
Logo Silverio No. 224
Mexico, D.F. 11320
Contact: MR. ROGELIO PEREZ,
GENERAL MANAGER
PHONE: 525/260-4508 AND
260-3008
Product/Service Description:
Advertising Printing
(Lithographic)

Anahuac Formados y Plasticos, S.A.
Av. Azcapotzalco No. 96
Mexico, D.F. 11410
Contact: Mr. Gabriel Cardenas,
Director
PHONE: 525/527-2656, 527-2636
Product/Service Description:
Plastics and articles thereof

Andromeda Internacional S.A.de C.V.
Toronjil No. 109-5
Mexico, D.F. 02810
Contact: Mr. Saul Fuentes, General
Manager
PHONE: 905/4082221 celular
Product/Service Description:
Apparel & Accessory Stores

Angasa, S.A. DE C.V.
Anaxagoras No. 736-1
Mexico, D.F. 03100
Contact: Mr. Jose Anton G.,
PHONE: 525/543-5410, 523-3104
Product/Service Description:
Chemical & residual prod,

Arctic Circle International,
Calzada San Bartolo No. 264
Mexico, D.F.
Contact: Mr. Alejandro Lozano
PHONE: 525/396-0903, 552-8900
Product/Service Description:
Air conditioning machines

Arie, S. A. de C. V.
Bahia Del Espiritu Santo No. 21
Mexico, D. F. 11300
Contact: Lic. Josef Derzavich G.,
General Manager
PHONE: 525/260-1502, 260-2371
Product/Service Description:
Screws, bolts, nuts, washers etc,
iron or steel

Armani, S.A. de C.V.
Arroz No. 17
Mexico, D.F. 09820
Contact: Ing. Ernesto Ruiz,
General Director
PHONE: 525-582-1755,
581-8944
Product/Service Description:
Buckles and buckle clasps a parts,
base metal

Arquitectos Metalicos, S.A de C. V.
Oriente 107 No. 3605
Mexico, D.F. 07850
Contact: Mr. Raul Gonzalez,
General Manager
PHONE: 525/751-8895,551-4088
Product/Service Description:
Metals products; machinery &
transport equipment

Arsa y Compania, S.A. de C.V.
Instituto Tecnico Industrial No.192
Mexico, D.F. 11340
Contact: Mr. Ricardo Sanchez
Gonzalez, Director General
PHONE: 525/341-4715
Product/Service Description:
Mufflers and exhaust pipes for
motor vehicles

Articulos Decorativos, S.A. de C.V.
Mier y Pesado No. 317-Locales 11
Mexico, D.F. 03100
Contact: Ms Alejandra Ramirez,
Sales Executive
PHONE: (525) 687-2409/
1867/2333
Product/Service Description:
Advertising

Articulos Ortopedicos Alfa
Dr. Vertiz No. 1039
Mexico, D.F. 03020
Contact: Mr. Manuel Alvarez
Carrillo, Director
PHONE: 525/543-1281
Product/Service Description:
Invalid carriages, nesoi

Articulos de Limpieza Santa Cruz
Fco. Javier Mina No. 106
Mexico, D.F. 09700
Contact: Mr. Dario Sanchez,
Director General
PHONE: 525/693-6612
Product/Service Description:
Cleaning preparations

Asesores en Teleinformatica Astel,
Jose Maria Rico No. 121 - desp
204
Mexico, D.F. 03230
Contact: Ing. Laurencio Hurtado,
Director
PHONE: 525/524-1911
Product/Service Description:
Electric, laser or oth light or
photon beam etc

Asiste, S.A. de C.V. (Asesoria en
Av. Mexico No. 47-3
Mexico, D.F. 06100
Contact: Ing. Moises Polishuk,
Director General
PHONE: 525/211-5759 211-8107
Product/Service Description:
Automatic data process machines;
magn reader etc

Auto Refacciones Especializadas,
Av. Cuauhtemoc 1338
Mexico, D.F., 03310
Contact: Mr. Mario Doniz, ,
PHONE: 525/559-5422
Product/Service Description:
Articles of or clad with precious
metal nesoi

Autocristales Jelussem, S.A. de
Presidentes No. 19
Mexico, D.F. 03570
Contact: Mr. Jesus Cerralde,
Director
PHONE: 525/672-5586, 672-4481
Product/Service Description:
Windshields of laminated safety
glass

Automatizacion Y Lubricacion
Calle 3 Norte No. 42
Ecatepec, EDM 55080
Contact: C.P. Anastacio Ramirez,
Director
PHONE: 525/787-2343, 787-0081
Product/Service Description:
Lubricating preps, antirust &
treating texiles etc

Autoplas, S. A. de C. V.
Ave. C.F.E. Esq. Joya de San Elias
San Luis Potosi, S.L.P 78090
Contact: Ing. Carlos De la Hoz,
Commercial Manager
PHONE: 525/596-3588, 726-9011
Product/Service Description:
Acrylic polymers nesoi, in primary
forms

B&B Iluminacion
Insurgentes Sur No. 51-B
Mexico, D.F. 06700
Contact: Lic. Miguel Angel Bravo,
General Manager
PHONE: 525/564-5507
Product/Service Description:
Electric lamps and lighting fittings,
nesoi

Baleros Nacionales E Importados
Calle 3 NO. 526
Mexico, D.F. 11480
Contact: Mr. Raymundo
Delgadillo, Gerente
PHONE: 525/395-5644, 395-4883
Product/Service Description:
Machine tools for working metal,

Barhnos de Mexico, S.A. de C.V.
Lorenzo Bouturini No. 14 Esq.
Dia-
Mexico, D.F. 06800
Contact: Mr. Jaime Barba Ramirez,
Director
PHONE: 525/578-0530, 578-3190
Product/Service Description:
Beauty & skin care preparation,

Bayard International Mexicana,
Tlaxcala No. 193 - B
Mexico, D.F. 06100
Contact: Mr. Alejandro Williams,
General Manager
PHONE: 525/264-1868, -7362
Product/Service Description:
Air conditioning mach etc incl
refrig unit etc

Berne Hermanos, S.A. de
Brea No. 181
Mexico, D.F. 08400
Contact: Mr. Manuel Bernechea,
Director (Owner)
PHONE: 525/657-1874
Product/Service Description:
Articles of jewelry & pts, of prec
metal or clad

Beta Refrigeracion
Rinconada Del Sur Edificio 64
Mexico, D.F 16050
Contact: Ing. Gabriel Farias Reyes,
Director (Owner)
PHONE: 525/653-3752
Product/Service Description:
Air conditioning mach etc incl
refrig unit etc

Bibermex, S. A. de C. V.
Kramer No. 60
Mexico, D.F. 04030
Contact: Ms. Laura Castillo
Vallejo, Director
PHONE: 525/549-4248, 689-3912
Product/Service Description:
Personal toilet etc prep nesoi,
shaving, bath etc.

Bio-Fer Internacional, S.A.
Carr. Mexico-Laredo K.m. 116.5
Actopan, HG. 42500
Contact: Ing. Luis Vazquez
Noriega, General Manager
Product/Service Description:
Fertilizers, nesoi

Biomundo Sun Chlorella de Mexico
Av. Cuauhtemoc No. 220, Piso 2
Mexico, D.F. 06720
PHONE: 525/578-0618
Product/Service Description:
Food preparations

Biotecnologia y Nutricion, S.A. de
Pino Suarez No. 53
Mexico, D.F. 14205
Contact: Mr. Miguel Rico
Ramirez, President
PHONE: 525/631-4232
Product/Service Description:
Vitamins, natural or synthetic,
dosage etc form

Bobimex, S.S. de C.V.
Ayuntamiento No. 93 Desp. 108
Mexico, D.F. 06500
Contact: Pedro Escobar, ,
PHONE: 525/512-4276 518-2899
Product/Service Description:
Transformers nesoi, power
handling cap nov 1 kva

Bolsas Finas San Luis, S.A. de C.V.
Fray S. Teresa de Mier No. 422-B
Mexico, D.F. 15810
Contact: Mr. Luis Jacobo Salume,
Director
PHONE: 525/768-3115, 552-3006
Product/Service Description:
Plastics and articles thereof

Bombas y Control de Fluidos,
Av. Articulo 27 Constitucional .
Mexico, D.F. 07730
Contact: Mr. Victor Cruz Cuellar,
General Director
PHONE: 525/587-5075,587-2664
Product/Service Description:
Pumps for liquids, nesoi

Bomhere, S.A. de C.V.
Chihuahua No. 136-3
Mexico, D.F. 06700
Contact: Mr. Jose Alvarez,
Director
PHONE: 525/564-9366,
564-9344
Product/Service Description:
Headgear nesoi, whether or not
lined or trimmed

Bostik Mexicana, S.A.
Col. Alce Blanco
Naucalpan, EDM 53370
Contact: Lic. Carlos Gavaldon E.,
General Director
PHONE: 525/576-4055/576-7644
Product/Service Description:
Prepared glues & adhesives nesoi;
glue retail pack

Botones Cel, S.A. de C.V.
Calle 13 No. 58
Nezahualcoyotl, EDM 057460
Contact: Mr. Jorge Espinoza
Munoz, Director
PHONE: 525/758-2203, 700-0669
Product/Service Description:
Buttons, nesoi

Braley Marmoles y Granitos, S.A.
Calle 7 No. 2
Naucalpan, EDM 53340
Contact: Mr. Hesiquio Bravo
Leyva, Director
PHONE: 525/363-1083, 363-3905
Product/Service Description:
Marble and travertine cut in blocks
or slabs

Bufete de Construcciones Asesoria
Calz. Echegaray No. 22-300
Naucalpan, EDM 53100
Contact: Arq. Juan Lopez Perez,
Director
PHONE: 525/363-3120, 373-2273
Product/Service Description:
Aluminum alloy profiles nesoi

Bufete de Tecnologia Solar, S.A.
Parque Real No. 2
Mexico, D.F. 04890
Contact: Mr. Roldolfo Martinez,
General Director
PHONE: 525/677-6957
Product/Service Description:
Pumps for liquids, nesoi

Bujias Champion de Mexico, S.A.
150 Poniente No. 956
Mexico, D.F. 02300
Contact: Mr. Manuel Torres,
Gerente
PHONE: 525/567-0052, 567-7200
Product/Service Description:
Automotive Parts & Supplies

Bur-Flo, S.A. de C.V.
Puebla 260 - 401
Mexico, D.F. 06700
Contact: Sra. Ma. del Carmen
Gonzalez Gregg, Admin. Manager
PHONE: 525/511-7221, 533-4371
Product/Service Description:
Water filtering or purifying
machinery & apparatus

Cad-Cam, S.A. de C.V.
Blvd. Manuel A. Camacho 700-101
Mexico, D.F. 11200
Contact: Ing. Morris Behar,
General Manager
PHONE: 525/395-0670 557-6262
Product/Service Description:
Automatic data process machines;
magn reader etc

Cadena Automotriz, S.A. de C.V.
Santos Degollado No. 588
San Luis Potosi, SLP 78250
Contact: Sales & Marketing, ,
PHONE: 52-48/13-8080
Product/Service Description:
Suspension shock absorbers for
motor vehicles

Cafe El Marino, S.A. de C.V.
Carr. Internacional Km. 1192 al
Sur
Mazatlan, SIN 82180
Contact: C.P. Javier Lizarraga
Mercado, General Director
PHONE: 52-69/80-1878
Product/Service Description:
Coffee, tea, mate & spices

Cafeteras Internacionales, SA CV
Av. Chimalhuacan S N Esq.Mte.
Alto
Mexico, MEX 57810
Contact: Mr. Carlos Heras V.,
Administrative Manager
PHONE: 525/855-0799,855-0799
Product/Service Description:
Aluminum cooking and
kitchenware, cast

Cajas de Carton Murguia, S.A. de
Periferico Sur No. 4225 4to. piso
Mexico, D.F. 14210
Contact: Lic. Gilberto Mendez,
Purchasing Manager
PHONE: 525/644-5028,644-0582
Product/Service Description:
Containers (boxes, bags etc)

Calefaccion y Ventilacion S.A. de
Prolongacion Calle 18 No. 246
Mexico, D.F. 01180
Contact: Mr. Sergio Armella
PHONE: 525/515-5180 al 85
Product/Service Description:
Air conditioning mach etc incl

Calmecac Consultores, S.A. de C.V.
Tehuantepec No. 125
Mexico, D.F. 06760
Contact: Ing. Roberto Cruz,
PHONE: 525/564-9475
Product/Service Description:
Records, tapes & other recorded
sound media etc

Campos Herrera Rafael - La Casa del
Ave. Pablo Rivera No. 1174
Mexicali, B.C.N 21290
Contact: Mr. Rafael Campos
Herrera, Owner and Director
PHONE: 52-65/65-4050
Product/Service Description:
Densified wd blocks/plates/strips/
profile shapes

Cap. Francisco A. Sundfeld
Petrarca 223-904
Mexico, D.F. 11570
Contact: Mr. Francisco Sundfeld,
Director and Owner
PHONE: 525/250-6030, 254-5475
Product/Service Description:
Food industry residues & waste;
prep animal feed

Capaco, S.A. de C.V.
Leon Tolstoi No. 25-5
Mexico, D.F. 11590
Contact: Mr. Alain Giberstein,
PHONE: 525/208-6526
Product/Service Description:
Advertising Printing

Capello Interiores, S.A. de
Rio Mixcoac No. 19 esq. Murcia
Mexico, D.F. 03920
Contact: Dr. Rafael Escalona
PHONE: 525/598-4493, 611-2577
Product/Service Description:
Frames or mounts for photographic
slides

Carbat, S.A. de C.V.
Via Gustavo Baz No. 243-16
Mexico, D.F. 53310
Contact: Mr. Carlos Balsa, General
Manager
PHONE: 525-363-3826
Product/Service Description:
Heat exchangers

Carre, S.A. de C.V.
Hidalgo #3-A
Naucalpan, E.M. 53560
Contact: Lic. Luis Raul Gonzalez,
Director General
PHONE: 525/358-1388
Product/Service Description:
Bells etc (nonelec), ornaments, ph
frames etc bmpt

Carrocerias Cea, S.A. de C.V.
Floresta No. 179
Mexico, D.F. 02080
Contact: Mr. Roberto Merino S.,
Director
PHONE: 525/561-3053
Product/Service Description:
Automotive Parts & Supplies

Carton Fenix, S.A. de C.V.
Catarroja No. 871, esq. Canal de
Mexico, D.F. 09860
Contact: Mr. Rafael Anaya,
Director
PHONE: 525/656-0786/0846
Product/Service Description:
Cartons etc paper; office box files
etc, paper etc

Carvel Print, S.A. de C.V.
Adolfo Prieto No. 815 - A
Mexico, D.F. 03100
Contact: Ing. Rafael Cardenas,
Director
PHONE: 525/682-9352, 682-8978
Product/Service Description:
Automotive Parts & Supplies

Casa Autrey, S.A. de C.V.
Fray Servando T. de Mier No. 100
Mexico, D.F. 06080
Contact: Lic. Agustin Bonilla
Lopez, Executive Director
PHONE: 525/227-4500
Product/Service Description:
Pharmaceutical products

Casa Barba, S.A. de C.V.
Lorenzo Boturini No. 14
Mexico, D.F. 06800
Contact: Mr. Jaime Barba, Director
General
PHONE: 525/578-3190,578-0530
Product/Service Description:
Essential oils etc; perfumery,
cosmetic etc preps

Casa Distex, S.A. de C.V.
Calle 3 No. 40
Estado de Mexico, MEX 53560
Contact: Lic. Luis Felipe Gonzalez
Z., General Director
PHONE: 525/576-3023/7288/2994
Product/Service Description:
Pipe, reinforced combine w
textiles, w o fittings

Casa Marzam, S.A. de C.V.
Norte 20 No. 5031
Mexico, D.F. 07370
Contact: Mr. Roberto Hernandez,
PHONE: 525/605-1967, ext. 2713
Product/Service Description:
Pharmaceutical products

Casa Monroy, S.A. de C.V.
Victoria No. 77
Mexico, D.F. 06050
Contact: Mr. Hector Monroy,
General Director
PHONE: 525/512-3896,521-5454
Product/Service Description:
Hydraulic fluid power pumps,

Casa Pena-Venta y Reparacion de
Georgia No. 42
Mexico, D.F. 03810
Contact: Mr. Guillermo Orozco,
General Manager
PHONE: 525/687-5896, 543-0312
Product/Service Description:
Invalid carriages, mechanically
propelled or not

Casa Rocas, S.A. de C.V.
Av. San Antonio No. 341
Mexico, D.F. 03810
Contact: Ms. Carmen Ymay
Casabal, Administrative Manager
PHONE: 525/598-6254, 611-9989
Product/Service Description:
Laboratory ware

Casa Sommer, S.A. de C.V.
Blvd. Toluca No. 13
Estado de Mexico, MEX 53568
Contact: Daniel Manjarres,
Purchasing Manager
PHONE: 525/576-7511
Product/Service Description:
Ball bearings

Caseer,S.A.
Convento de Acolman No. 2-C,
Estado de Mexico, MEX 54050
Contact: Mr. Enrique Revilla,
General Manager
PHONE: 525/362-1097
Product/Service Description:
Derricks; cranes; mobile lifting

Catarinas Universales
Insurgentes Norte No. 1681
Mexico, D. F. 07800
Contact: Mr. Roberto Espinoza,
General Manager
PHONE: 525/781-5688
Product/Service Description:
Articles of plastics, nesoi

Central De Instrumentacion Y
Revolucion No. 23 - Desp 2
Tlalnepantla, E.MEX 54000
Contact: Ing. Javier Garcia Avila,
PHONE: 525/390-0135
Product/Service Description:
Automatic regulating or control
instruments; parts

Central Mexicana de Joyeria Fina
Madero No. 67 - f
Mexico, D.F. 06000
Contact: Mr. Leon Maya, Director
PHONE: 525/521-3322
Product/Service Description:
Jewelry and parts thereof, of oth
precious metal

Central de Autopartes
Dr. Morones Prieto No. 123
Mexico, D.F. 06720
Contact: C.P. Roberto Castro
Meneses, General Manager
PHONE: 525/538-1362
Product/Service Description:
Automotive Parts & Supplies

Central de Hidraulica Y Sistemas,
Obxidiana No. 125
Mexico, D.F. 97819
Contact: Mr. Daniel Sanchez,
PHONE: 525/781-8232
Product/Service Description:
Pumps for liquids; liquid

Central de Profiles Y Tubos
Vicente Guerrero No. 59
Mexico, D.F. 09300
Contact: Lic. Lic. Alejandro
Guajardo, General Manager
PHONE: 525/694-7400, 694-8060
Product/Service Description:
Rods & profile shape vulcanized
rub, cellular rub

Central del Software, S.A. de C.V.
Av. Revolucion No. 1134 Piso 2
Mexico, D.F. 03900
Contact: Ing. Efrain Pardo,
Director General
PHONE: 525/664-4980
Product/Service Description:
Recorded media for sound
including master prod rcd

Centro Ecologico Mexicano S.A C.V.
Mision de San Ignacio #10613
Tijuana, B.C
Contact: Mr. Guillermo Ruiz
Hernandez, Administrator
PHONE: 52-66/34-2155 or 34-2158
Product/Service Description:
Chemical & residual prod,

Centro de Calentadores
Av. Jose Marti No. 211
Mexico, D.F. 11800
Contact: Mr. Jose Manuel Cedrun,
Director General
PHONE: 525/518-6880
Product/Service Description:
Elec water, space & soil heaters;
hair etc dry, pt

Centro de Validaciones y
Mozart No. 5119
Zapopan, JAL. 46737
Contact: Mr. Felipe Cuevas Ruiz,
General Director
PHONE: 525/671-8431, 673-1522
Product/Service Description:
Inst & apprts, measuring checking
pressure

Cepillos y Productos de Aseo,
Calz. San Lorenzo No. 279-32A
Mexico, D.F. 09850
Contact: Lic. Roberto Michelsen,
General Manager
PHONE: 525/6126400, 612-3044
Product/Service Description:
Cleaning preparations

Chinamex, S.A. de C.V.
Puente de Xoco No. 39 Col. Xoco
Mexico, D.F. 03330
Contact: Mr. Lauro Ortega,
General Director
PHONE: 525/688-285, 604-7732
Product/Service Description:
Chemical & residual prod,
chemical etc ind nesoi

Chocolates Turin, S.A. de C.V.
Calz. de Guadalupe No. 402
Mexico, D.F. 07800
Contact: Mr. Octavio Penaloza
Sandoval, General Director
PHONE: 525/537-6273
Product/Service Description:
Chocolate & other food products
containing cocoa

Cia. Manufacturera de Ropa El Angel
Privada de Galeana No. 900
Tulancingo, HGO. 43630
Contact: Mr. Angel Lases Fadel,
President
PHONE: 52-775/3-2419, 3-0673
Product/Service Description:
Nar wov fab nesoi >5%
elastomeric yrn rubber thrd

Cia. Proveedora de Ind. S.A. de C.
Cordova 142 Col. Roma
Mexico, D.F. 6700
Contact: Mr. Luis Delgado Vega,
General Manager
PHONE: 525/574-7103 -7769 -7658
Product/Service Description:
Oscilloscopes, spectrum analyzers
etc, parts etc

Cia. Proveedora de Industrias, S.A.
Cordoba No. 142
Mexico, D. F. 06700
Contact: Ing. Luis Delgado Vega,
General Manager
PHONE: 525/574-7103
Product/Service Description:
Scales fr continuous weighing of
goods on conveyor

Cia. de Cosmeticos Summer, S.A. de
Cardenas No. 5, esq. Constitucion
Tlalnepantla, EDM 54055
Contact: Lic. Alberto Romero P.,
Director General
PHONE: 525/361-8549, 398-0518
Product/Service Description:
Beauty, make-up & skin-care prep;
manicure etc prp

Cientifica Vela Quin, S.A. de C.V.
Clzda. Jose Vanconcelos No. 202
Mexico, D.F. 06140
Contact: Mr. Mario Vela Salas,
General Manager
PHONE: 525/286-2410, 553-1303
Product/Service Description:
Laboratory ware

Cima Computacion e Informatica,
Cali # 534
Mexico, D.F. 07300
Contact: Sales & Marketing, ,
PHONE: 525/577-7830, 577-3524
Product/Service Description:
Electric, laser or oth light or
photon beam etc

Cimentaciones Tecnicas, S.A. de C.V
Blvd. M. Avila Camacho No. 1994-602
Tlalnepantla, EDM 54055
Contact: Mr. Agustin Galindo
Moran, General Manager
PHONE: 525/398-7162 -6851, -7743
Product/Service Description:
Pile-drivers and pile-extractors

Cimentaciones Y Puertos, S.A.
Homero No. 526-702
Mexico, D.F., D.F. 11560
Contact: Mr. Rolando Ugalde,
General Manager
PHONE: 525/360-3563
Product/Service Description:
Pile-drivers and pile-extractors

Climas y Refacciones, S.A. de C.V.
Real Del Monte No. 260
Mexico, D.F. 07870
Contact: Mr. Vicente Hernandez,
General Director
PHONE: 525/781-3899, 781-3389
Product/Service Description:
Air conditioning machines (temp
& hum change), pts

Cobra Electronica, S. A. de C.V.
Calle Navarra No. 210-301
Mexico, D.F. 03400
Contact: Sales & Marketing, ,
PHONE: 525/579-2297 579-0483
Product/Service Description:
Electrical apparatus for switching
etc, ov 1000 v

Cocinas de Acero Inoxidable,
Anahuac No. 49
Mexico, D.F. 04950
Contact: Ing. Marco Olea, Director
General
PHONE: 525/594-9021, 594-5720
Product/Service Description:
Hospital furniture

Coloide Mexicana S.A. de C.V.
48 Sur Centenario No. 205
Jiutepec, MOR 62500
Contact: Mr. Juan Cintron
Patterson, President
PHONE: 52-73/191105/191103
Product/Service Description:
Chemical & residual prod,
chemical etc ind nesoi

Comercial Autoindustrial, S.A. de
Versalles No. 57 - 601
Mexico, D.F. 06600
Contact: Mr. Gabriel Llano
Medina, Director General
PHONE: 525/703-3610,3498,3885
Product/Service Description:
Automotive maintenance machines

Comercial Cavisa, S.A. de C.V.
Izcoatl No. 62
Mexico, D.F. 11370
Contact: Mr. Roberto Camacho Villa, Adminsitrative Director
PHONE: 525/566-6904
Product/Service Description:
Automotive Parts & Supplies

Comercial Despa, S.A.
Insurgentes Sur 686-303
Mexico, D.F. 03100
PHONE: 525/536-6686, 536-8774
Product/Service Description:
Medical, surgical, dental or vet inst, no elec, pt

Comercial Gricom, S.A. de
Buen Tono # 184
Mexico, D.F. 07800
PHONE: 525/537-7380
Product/Service Description:
Valves f oleohydraulic pneumatic

Comercial Jermosam, S.A.
Lago Xochimilco No. 135 E-3
Mexico, D.F. 11320
Contact: Mr. Moises Harari R.,
PHONE: 525/341-9277, 341-1016
Product/Service Description:
Containers nesoi w outer surface

Comercial LLantera Sullivan
Heliopolis No. 210
Mexico, D.F. 02080
Contact: Mr. Jose Buenrostro A., Director General
PHONE: 525/396-8502, 396-8837
Product/Service Description:
Automotive Parts & Supplies

Comercial Maderera Diana, S.A.
Antigua Calzada de Guadalupe No. 53
Mexico, D.F. 02020
Contact: Mr. Rafael Ortiz, Director General
PHONE: 525/394-0374
Product/Service Description:
Wood and articles of wood; wood charcoal

Comercializadora Industrial Omega
La Corona 217
Mexico, D.F. 07800
Contact: Mr. Guillermo Vela, General Manager
PHONE: 525/517-1783
Product/Service Description:
Plates, sheets, film, foil & strip nesoi, plastics

Comercializadora Lugol-Mex, S.A.
Ajusco No. 28
Mexico, D.F. 01010
Contact: Ing. Eduardo Saenz, Director General
PHONE: 525/593-6579
Product/Service Description:
Lubricating preps, antirust & treating texiles etc

Comercializadora Y Distribuidora
Moras No. 318
Mexico, D.F. 03100
Contact: Mr. Carlos Carreno, General Manager
PHONE: 525/559-6147
Product/Service Description:
Orthopedic appl; artif body pts; hear aid; pts etc

Comintra
Tenayuca No. 196
Mexico, D.F. 03650
Contact: Mr. Jose Palomares, General Manager
PHONE: 525/604-6303
Product/Service Description:
Filter/purify machine & apparatus for liquid nesoi

Compania Toronto, S.A. de C.V.
Calz. San Esteban No. 55 Pte.
Naucalpan, E.M. 53560
Contact: Mr. Moises Espinosa Rodriguez, General Manager
PHONE: 525/576-6564, 576-6560
Product/Service Description:
Automotive Parts & Supplies

Compucentro de Servicios
Calz. Camarones No. 275, piso 1 "C"
Mexico, D.F. 02800
Contact: Ing. Mario Rodriguez, Sole Administrator
PHONE: 525/556-1891 556-4481
Product/Service Description:
Automatic data process machines; magn reader etc

Comunicaciones e Informatica, S.A.
Periferico Sur No. 5472
Mexico, D.F. 04700
Contact: Ing. Carlos Alcazar, Director General
PHONE: 525/665-7807
Product/Service Description:
Records, tapes & other recorded sound media etc

Conductores Latincasa, S.A. de C.V.
Antonio Caso No. 205-Piso 4
Mexico, D. F. 06470
Contact: Ing. Leobardo Garcia Mendez, Commercial Director
PHONE: (525) 729-3300, 566-8955
Product/Service Description:
Cable, etc nesoi of cu nt ins nt md into artcls

Conelec, S. A.
Apartado Postal No. 392
Puebla, PUE. 72000
Contact: Ing. Carlos Santamaria, Manufacture Plant Director
PHONE: 52-22/43-2255
Product/Service Description:
Conveyors, pneumatic

Consorcio Industrial Serrano
Boyaca No. 599
Mexico, D.F. 07740
Contact: Mr Carlos Serrano,
PHONE: 525/368-5938 567-0492
Product/Service Description:
Plastics and articles thereof

Consorcio Industrial de Rines
H. Galeana No. 4
Mexico, D.F. 09000
Contact: Mr. Dionisio Garrido Oro, General Manager
PHONE: 525/694-5752
Product/Service Description:
Automotive Parts & Supplies

Consorcio en Ecologia Aplicada,
Torreon No. 16
Mexico, D.F. 06760
Contact: Mr. Mauricio Jessurun S., President
PHONE: 525/564-9612, 564-9590
Product/Service Description:
Air & Water Resource & Solid Waste Management

Constru-Centro, S.A. de C.V.
Av. Mateo Aleman No. 40
Mexico, D.F. 11520
Contact: Mr. Eliot Balanza, Internacional Purchansing Manager
PHONE: 525/255-5070, -4950,5136
Product/Service Description:
Insulating fittings for machines nesoi

Construcciones Electricas mas
Calz. tulyehualco No. 3491
Mexico', D.F. 09840
Contact: Sales & Marketing, ,
PHONE: 525/582-8788
Product/Service Description:
Elect switches f voltage not over

Consupharma, S.A. de C.V.
Av. Insurgentes Sur No. 4120
Mexico, D.F. 14090
Contact: Lic. Claudia Torelli, Cosmetics
PHONE: 525/626-7631 to 7640
Product/Service Description:
Beauty & skin care preparation

Coprosa Consultores Y Provedores
Av. Rio San Joaquin No. 102
Mexico, D.F. 11520
Contact: Mr. Mario Buendia, Sales Manager
PHONE: 525/250-1011,545-3652
Product/Service Description:
Pumps for liquids; liquid elevators; parts thereof

Coreteme, S.A. de C.V.
Serapio Rendon No. 95
Mexico, D.F. 06770
Contact: Mr. Rafael Valdez, Marketing Manager
PHONE: 525/566-1050
Product/Service Description:
Medical, surgical, dental or veterinary furn etc

Cornejo Cornejo Ma. Elena
Czada. Adolfo Lopez Mateos No. 2410
Tehuacan, PUE. 75760
Contact: Mrs. Ma. Elena Cornejo Cornejo, Owner
PHONE: 52-238/2-2348
Product/Service Description:
Food industry residues & waste

Corpisa, S.A. DE C.V.
Av. Del Rosal No. 139
Mexico, D.F. 01470
Contact: ING. Gonzalo Martinez,
PHONE: 525/593-0524
Product/Service Description:
Relays for voltage

Corporacion Coral, S.A. de
Calle E N0. 20
Mexico, D.F. 53020
Contact: Mr. Leon Passy
PHONE: 525/ 560-0100
Product/Service Description:
Plastics and articles

Corporacion Impresora, S.A. de C.V
Emiliano Zapata No. 201-A
Tlalnepantla, EDMEX 54090
Contact: Jaime Lopez, Mr.
PHONE: 525/398-8922,
Product/Service Description:
Packing containers nesoi of paper, pprbrd, etc

Corporacion Integral Diesel, S.A.
Calz. Vallejo No. 1110, A-302
Tlalnepantla, EDM 54170
Contact: Mr. Luis Antonio Vargas, Director General
PHONE: 525/389-0423, -3423
Product/Service Description:
Pumps for liquids, nesoi

Corporacion Logistica, S.A. de C.V.
Dr. Jimenez No. 162
Mexico, D.F. 06720
Contact: Mr. Victor Alvarez Palacios, Director General
PHONE: 525/761-6379, 761-8309
Product/Service Description:
Medical, surgical, dental or vet inst, no elec, pt

Corporativo Lumen, S.A. de C.V.
Azafran # 581-C
Mexico, D.F. 08400
Contact: Mr. Luis Quesada, General Director
PHONE: 525/657-1251, 657-1247
Product/Service Description:
Apparel, Piece Goods and Notions

Criser, S.A. de C.V.
Malaga No. 107
Mexico, N.L. 67130
Contact: Ing. Ing. Sergio N. Rovira Adame, Director
PHONE: 52/83/7908-20
Product/Service Description:
Plastics and articles thereof

Cristales de Cuarzo,S.A. de C.V.
Araucarias No. 11
Mexico, D.F. 16038
Contact: Ing. Marco Antonio Parisi, President
PHONE: 525/653-3231/4259
Product/Service Description:
Quartz (other than natural sands)

Cromos Y Novedades de Mexico, S.A.
Martin Carrera no. 287
07070 Mexico, D.F. MEXICO
Contact: Mr. Eduardo Canal
PHONE: 525/577-2625, 553-3061
Product/Service Description:
Articles of jewelry & pts, of prec metal or clad

Cuidados Basicos, S.A. de C.V.
Aguascalientes # 179
Mexico, D.F. 06100
Contact: Mr. Gerson Santa Cruz, Director General
PHONE: 525/264-4383, 574-2770
Product/Service Description:
Inst & appliances for medical,surgical, etc,nesoi

Curacreto, S.A. de C.V.
Calz. de Minas No. 31
Mexico, D.F. 01280
Contact: Mr. Jorge Robles Ramos,
PHONE: 525/563-3327, 563-3339
Product/Service Description:
Prepared additives for cements, mortars concretes

DIMASA, S.A. DE C.V.
Ferrocarril de Cuernavaca No. 163
Mexico, D.F. 11320
Contact: LIC. ERNESTO BARRERA PEREZ, N A
PHONE: 525/399-3217,3426
Product/Service Description:
Aluminum alloy profiles nesoi

DIPSA Distribuidora Meny,
Central de Abasto Pasillo 5,
Mexico, D.F. 09000
Contact: Mr. Daniel Samra,
PHONE: 525/694-7129, 4041
Product/Service Description:
Plastics and articles thereof

Decoraciones y Novedades,
Norte Sur No. 8
Naucalpan, E.M. 53370
Contact: Mr. Francisco Rivera
PHONE: 525/358-9722
Product/Service Description:
Floor cover (rolls & tiles) & wall cover, plastics

Decovitrales
Lirios No. 102
Naucalpan, 53160 EDO DE MEX
Contact: Mr. Erico Wetzel
PHONE: 525/560-5419
Product/Service Description:
Glass and glassware

Decsa,
Prol. 5 de Mayo No. 24
Naucalpan, MEX 53300
Contact: Mr. Adolfo Ibanez, Sales
PHONE: 525/360-0873/360-6316
Product/Service Description:
Cleaning preparations

Degussa Mexico, S.A. de C.V.
Calz. Mexico-Xochmilco No. 5149
Mexico, D. F. 14610
Contact: Mr. Gunter Deck Haas, Director General
PHONE: 525/673-1391
Product/Service Description:
Dental cements and other dental fillings etc

Delta Aluminio y Vidrio, S.A. de
Prolongacion 5 de Febrero
Mexico, D.F 03660
Contact: Ing. Eleazar Davial, General Manager
PHONE: 525/672-0036/672-0287
Product/Service Description:
Aluminum alloy hollow profiles

Dentaurum de Mexico, S.A. DE C.V.
Av. de las Palmas 735-105
Mexico, D.F. 11000
Contact: Mr. Carlos A. Bolio A.,
PHONE: 525/520-2421, 520-2802
Product/Service Description:
Dental cements and other dental fillings etc

Deportes Marti, S.A. de C.V.
Francisco I. Madero No. 12
Mexico, D.F. 14420
Contact: Mr. Julio Gutierrez
PHONE: 525/628-2800
Product/Service Description:
Articles & equip for sports etc

Desarrollo Ecologico Industrial,
Cienfuegos No. 868
Mexico, D.F., 01 07300
Contact: Mr. Ignacio Sarmiento, General Director
PHONE: 525/752-4635,-7783
Product/Service Description:
Administration of Environmental Quality Programs

Diagnosticos Administrativos por
Jose Vasconcelos No. 83
Mexico, D.F. 06140
Contact: Ing. Miguel Angel Joachin, Director General
PHONE: 525/286-5477 286-0052
Product/Service Description:
Records, tapes & other recorded sound media etc

Dicamex, S.A. de C.V.
Londres No. 188 - 302
Mexico, D.F. 06600
PHONE: 525/533-4131, 208-9812
Product/Service Description:
Water filtering or purifying machinery & apparatus

Diesel Jupiter S.A. de C.V.
Bizet 47
Mexico, D.F. 07870
Contact: Mr. Raul Urban Duran
PHONE: 525/537-36-58
Product/Service Description:
Automotive Parts & Supplies

Dieselar Industrial, S.A.
Calz. S.J. de Aragon 322
Mexico, D.F. 07460
Contact: Mr. Raul Caballero, Manager
PHONE: 525/781-5558, 781-5559
Product/Service Description:
Engines and motors nesoi, and parts thereof

Dina Diesel de Cuautitlan
Lateral Autopista Mexico
Cuautitlan Iz, E.M. 54730
Contact: Mr. Armando Vega
PHONE: 525/872-0887/4979/0888
Product/Service Description:
Trucks, nesoi

Diseno Hidraulico y Tecnologia
Jose Maria Rico No. 212, 8th floor
Mexico, D.F. 03100
Contact: Dr. Ernesto Espino de la O, General Director
PHONE: 525/524-3795,-8194,-3815
Product/Service Description:
Air & Water Resource & Solid Waste Management

Diseno Integral Tecnico de
Gustavo Baz No. 252-2-25
Tlalnepantla, EDO 54060
Contact: Mr. Armando Romero Mariscal Renstrom, General Director
PHONE: 525/361-2247, 361-2354
Product/Service Description:
Meas & checkng instrument, appliances & mach nesoi

Diseno en Cadena, S.A. de C.V.
Madero No. 55-305
Mexico, D.F. 06000
Contact: Mr. Javier Villapando Cherem, Administrative Director
PHONE: 525/393-3991, 393-3593
Product/Service Description:
Jewelry and parts thereof, of oth precious metal

Diseno y Display, S.A.
Arizona No. 97 - P.B.
Mexico, D.F. MEXICO
Contact: Mr. Jesus Gonzalez O., Director General
PHONE: 525/543-0099
Product/Service Description:
Display units w/color cathode ray tube

Diseno y Metalmecanica, S. A. de
Tezozomoc No. 246-3
Mexico, D. F. 02729
Contact: Ing. Felipe Nieto Sanchez, General Manager
PHONE: 525/561-9936/9986/352-
Product/Service Description:
Dies drw o extr mtl a pts thrf

Dispositivos Electronicos y de
Rep. del Salvador No. 20-D
Mexico, D.F. 06000
Contact: Mr. Elias Schnadower, Purchasing Director
PHONE: 525/521-0185, 512-6565
Product/Service Description:
Hand input devices, transmit data to computer

Dist. de Jabones Decorativos
Amores 1415, Local 8
Mexico, D.F. 03100
Contact: Ms. Leonor Marinez, General Manager
PHONE: 525/688-4592
Product/Service Description:
Soap & oth organic surf act prod, toilet use, bars

Dist. de Quimicos y Farmaceuticos,
Hortensia No. 122
Mexico, D.F. 06400
Contact: Ing. Jesus Sosa, International Business Director
PHONE: 525/547-5570, 547-7028
Product/Service Description:
Medical, surgical, dental or vet inst, no elec, pt

Distribuciones Industriales CPC,
Av. Tercer Anillo de Circ. 27
Mexico, D.F. 11200
Contact: Mr. Jorge Omar Mujaes, General Manager
PHONE: 525/557-0528, 2297
Product/Service Description:
Apparel articles and accessories, not knit etc.

Distribuciones Lema, S.A. de C.V.
Nueva No. 102-A
Naucalpan, E.M. 53340
Contact: Ing. Manuel Esparza Farias, Director General
PHONE: 525/373-6677/6301/3568
Product/Service Description:
Chromium and articles thereof, inc waste and scrap

Distribuidor Restaurantero,
Until 12/94 Dolores 4-Local A
Mexico, D. F. 06050
Contact: Lic. Victor Perez G., General Administrator
PHONE: 525/532-7911, 609-1972
Product/Service Description:
Ceramic tableware & kitchenware, porcelain & china

Distribuidora Altamar, S.A. de C.V.
Juan Diego No. 11
Mexico, D.F. 07020
Contact: Mr. Jesus Almarza, Director General
PHONE: 525/754-4580, 4535
Product/Service Description:
Salmon, nesoi, fresh or chilled

Distribuidora Automotriz
Patriotismo No. 69
Mexico, D.F. 11800
Contact: Mr. Angel Diaz San Juan, Sales Manager
PHONE: 525/516-0425, 0427
Product/Service Description:
Engine and motor parts, nesoi
Automotive parts

Distribuidora Automotriz Xochimilco
Prolong.Division del Norte No. 5251
Mexico, D.F. 16030
Contact: Mr. Antonio Pedraza Rodriguez, General Director
PHONE: 525/676-9310, 4111
Product/Service Description:
Automotive Dealers, N.e.c.
Automotive supplies

Distribuidora Dimex, S.A. DE C.V.
Trigo No. 83
09810 Mexico, D.F. MEXICO
Contact: Ing. Jose Quintana, Administrative Manager
PHONE: 525/582-6246, 582-7353
Product/Service Description:
Conegar & substitutes for vinegar from acetic acid

Distribuidora Echegaray,
Prolongacion 5 de Mayo No 24
Naucalpan, MEX. 53300
Contact: Mr. Adolfo Ibanes,
PHONE: 525/360-0873, 6316
Product/Service Description:
Cleaning preparations

Distribuidora Fiberglass
Jalapa No. 102
Mexico, D.F. 06700
Contact: Mr. Jaime Echeverria
PHONE: 525/533-6653, 6654
Product/Service Description:
Glaziers putty, resin cements,
caulking comps etc

**Distribuidora Internacional
Tame,**
Av. Ejercito Nacional No. 253-A
Mexico, D.F. 11320
Contact: Lic. Oscar Tame Yapur,
Director General
PHONE: 525/203-9910/
5927,5451238
Product/Service Description:
Motorcycles (incl mopeds) &
cycles with aux motor

Distribuidora Internacional
Ave. Ninos Heroes No. 1001
Mexicali, B.C.N 21220
Contact: Mr. Manuel Aguilar
Barajas, Owner
PHONE: 52-65/61-9141
Product/Service Description:
Quicklime, slaked lime

Distribuidora Nacional de
Avenida Revolucion No. 344
Mexico, D.F. 11800
Contact: Lic. Eduardo Enrique
Ayala, Director General
PHONE: 525/516-6617, 516-6869
Product/Service Description:
Automotive Parts & Supplies

**Distribuidora Naturista
Hadad**
Mina 201-2
Mexico, D.F. 06350
Contact: Mr. Arturo Ojeda,
PHONE: 525/535-3242
Product/Service Description:
Vitamins, natural or synthetic

**Distribuidora R.O.M., S.A.
de C.V.**
Dr. Martinez del Rio No. 55
Mexico, D.F. 01895
Contact: Mr. Pablo Ortiz-
Monasterio, General Manager
PHONE: 525/578-8379
Product/Service Description:
Cigar cheroot cigarillo cigs of tob
substits nesoi

**Distribuidora Tecnica
Industrial**
Monrovia 1021 Local B
Mexico, D.F. 03300
Contact: Mr. Marco Mendoza,
General Manager
PHONE: 525/605-2993, 0295
Product/Service Description:
Air conditioning machines (temp
& hum change), pts

Distribuidora de Cintas
Carrillo Puerto No. 245
Mexico, D.F. 11400
Contact: Mr. Rogelio Vargas
Palacios, Commercial Manager
PHONE: 525/527-6762, 527-9587
Product/Service Description:
Self-adhesive plates, sheets, film
etc of plastics

**Distribuidora de Envases de
Mexico**
Av. Div. Del Norte No. 1020
Mexico, D.F. 03100
Contact: Mr. Ruben Lopez Santos,
PHONE: 525/559-0719, 2867
Product/Service Description:
Plastics and articles thereof

**Distribuidora de Maderas
Finas,**
Blvd. Lazaro Cardenas No. 1152
Mexicali, B.C.N 21110
Contact: Mr. Sergio Ricardo Parra
Ponce, President
PHONE: 52-65/66-8373, 66-8374
Product/Service Description:
Veneer sheets etc, not over 6 mm
thick

Distribuidora de Productos
Agustin Gutierrez No. 40
Mexico, D.F. 03340
Contact: Mr. Alejandro Ezquerro
Alcocer, Director General
PHONE: 525/604-9010, 604-8471
Product/Service Description:
Blinds

**Distribuidora de Resortes
Diaz,**
Michoacan No. 86
Tlalnepantla, E.M. 54190
Contact: Mr. Pascual Diaz
Guzman, Director General
PHONE: 525/569-4906
Product/Service Description:
Filters & parts & accessories for
instr & appratus

Distribuidora de Uniformes
Division Del Norte # 2943
Mexico, D.F. 04330
Contact: Mr. Alejandro Pavon,
PHONE: 525/549-0948
Product/Service Description:
T-shirts, singlets etc, knit etc,
textiles nesoi

Drogueros, S.A. de C.V.
Obrero Mundial No. 358
Mexico, D.F. 03020
Contact: Mr. Santiago Ros Gubern,
Director General
PHONE: 525/639-2810/639-7325
Product/Service Description:
Pharmaceutical products

Duroplast, S.A. de C.V.
Esfuerzo No. 4-F
Naucalpan, MEX 53560
Contact: Mr. Thomas Egerstrom,
Director General
PHONE: 525/358-2988
Product/Service Description:
Activated carbon

**ELF Lubricantes Mexico,
S.A. de**
Morelos No. 9
Tlalnepantla, MEX 54090
Contact: Ing. Francisco J. Palma,
Marketing Director
PHONE: 525/361-5326/4591
Product/Service Description:
Lubricating prep for text etc

Ejecutivos en Proveeduria,
Bolivar No. 1215
Mexico, D.F. 03630
Contact: Guillermina Berzunza,
PHONE: 525/532-0427
Product/Service Description:
Apparel articles

Ekco, S.A. de C.V.
16 de septiembre No. 31
Mexico, D.F. 02160
Contact: Lic. Luis Slim, Director
General
PHONE: 525/328-2711
Product/Service Description:
Stainless steel cooking and
kitchenware

El Ancla de Paz y Noriega
Vidal Alcocer No. 108,
Mexico, D.F. 06020
Contact: Mr. Jose Luis Noriega,
Director General
PHONE: 525/795-1920, 2831
Product/Service Description:
Pipe tools and parts thereof, base
metal

**Elastomeros Falcon, S.A.
de C.V.**
Heliotropo No. 145
Mexico, D.F. 06450
Contact: Ing. Juan Ventosa,
Administrative Manager
PHONE: 525/547-7529, 547-7532
Product/Service Description:
Automotive Parts & Supplies

Elastonsa, S.A.
Ponciano Diaz No. 200
Sgo.Tianguist., MEX 52600
Contact: Ing. Carlos Yanaculis
PHONE: 52-723-36260
Product/Service Description:
Rubber, unvulcanized, in plates,
sheets, and strip

Electro Puertas, S.A.
Diego Becerra No. 51-A
Mexico, D.F. 03900
Contact: Ing. Manuel Zamudio,
PHONE: 525/593-2108, 593-7333
Product/Service Description:
Doors and their frames and
thresholds, of wood

Electro Spider International
Circuito Educadores No. 11
Mexico, EDM 53100
Contact: Mr. Marco Perea Maya, Director General
PHONE: 525/393-6967
Product/Service Description:
Doors and their frames, thresholds, of wood, nesoi

Electromecanica Ingenieria
Tomillo No. 63
Mexico, D.F. 02800
Contact: Ing. Jose Luis Rodriguez J., Director General
PHONE: 525/556-8791
Product/Service Description:
Air cond mach incorporating a refrig unit, nesoi

Electronica Administrativa, S.A.
Amores No. 334
Mexico, D.F. 03100
Contact: Lic. Egmont Eccius, General Director
PHONE: 525/682-4087 536-4444
Product/Service Description:

Electronica, Ingenieria y
Calle 13 No. 74
Mexico, D.F. 03800
Contact: Mr. Jose Guadalupe Fajardo Rodriguez, General Director
PHONE: 525/273-2895 273-2207
Product/Service Description:
Trans appar for radiotelephony etc; tv cameras

Emilio Carmona Cortez y Asociados,
Juan Cousin No. 151
Mexico, D.F. 01460
Contact: Mr. Emilio Carmona Cortez, General Director
PHONE: 525/611-6828,2372
Product/Service Description:
Safety(incl sports)hdgr,whether not lined trimmed

Empaques Casablanca, S.A. de C.V.
Alce Blanco No. 24
Naucalpan, E.M. 53370
Contact: Mr. Rogelio Santiago, Sales Manager
PHONE: 525/373-2133, 370-3133
Product/Service Description:
Corrugated ppr/pbrd, w/n perforated nesoi roll/sht

Empaques Plasticos de Mexico
Calle Pastor s n
Los Reyes,Texcoco, EDM 56500
Contact: Mr. Carlos Jimenez, General Manager
PHONE: 525/855-3500. 855-1051
Product/Service Description:
Plastics and articles thereof

Empaques y Especialidades del
Santa Lucia No. 135 - Fracc.
Mexico, D.F. 02760
Contact: Mr. Manuel Morodo Garcia, General Manager
PHONE: 525/561-5011,5296,5227
Product/Service Description:
Corrugated ppr/pbrd, w/n perforated nesoi roll/sht

Empresas Ca-Le de Tlaxcala, S.A.
Manzana 2 Seccion C
Tetla, TLAX
Contact: Lic. Alejandro Rodriguez Cantu, Marketing and planning director
PHONE: 52-241/27-072, al 74
Product/Service Description:
Electric storage batteries, incl separators, parts

Empresas Marien, S.A. de C.V.
Blvd. M. Avila Camacho 937-20
Echegaray, EDM 53310
Contact: Mr. Enrique Suarez, General Director (owner)
PHONE: 525/360-6011, 360-5930
Product/Service Description:
Wire of alloy steel nesoi

Encargos Y Comisiones, S.A. de C.V.
Matanzas # 1036
Mexico, D.F. 07360
Contact: Mr. Salvador Razo Blanco, General Manager
PHONE: 525/586-3684, 9968
Product/Service Description:
Automobiles & Other Motor Vehicles

Engranes de Mexico, S.A. de C.V.
M. Othon de Mendizabal Ote. 480
Mexico, D.F. 07710
Contact: Mr. Jose Rivera, General Manager
PHONE: 525/586-1900, 1905
Product/Service Description:
Gear boxes,parts,subhd8701.20,hdg8702 or 8704

Equipo de Medicion S.A.
Obrero Mundial No. 891
Mexico, D.F. 03400
Contact: Mr. Jose Hernandez, General Manager
PHONE: 525/538-0130,538-0307
Product/Service Description:
Compressors, ref & a/c,exc ammonia,exc 3 n/exc10hp

Equipo para Hospitales, S.A.
Miguel Angel de Quevedo No. 1024
Mexico, D.F. 04040
Contact: Mr. Rodolfo de la Torre Pacheco, General Manager
PHONE: 525/689-0800
Product/Service Description:
Electrocardiographs

Equipomex, S.A. DE C.V.
Adolfo Prieto 1149
Mexico City, D.F. 03100
Contact: Ing. Alejandro Flores Acuna, Director General
PHONE: 525/559-0206/575-4332
Product/Service Description:
Trucks, nesoi

Equipos Especializados Delta,
Adolfo Prieto No. 1649, Office 902
Mexico, D.F. 03100
Contact: Ing. Francisco Velazquez, Director
PHONE: (525) 534-4930/524-0474
Product/Service Description:
Tanks

Equipos Y Compresores de Aire, S.A.
Via Dr. Gustavo Baz No. 203
Mexico, D.F. 54070
Contact: Lic. Maricela Da Silva Lopez, General Manager
PHONE: 525/361-9411
Product/Service Description:
Compressors used in refrigerating equipment

Especialidades Quimicas Monterrey,
Agricultura No. 11
Mexico, D.F. 11800
Contact: Ing. Edmundo Gil Garcia, Director General
PHONE: 525/215-0103, 515-0186
Product/Service Description:
Oil (not crude) from petrol & bitum mineral etc.

Etica Ensenada, S. A. de C. V.
Ave. Hidalgo No. 885
Ensenada, B.C.N 22830
Contact: Ing. Alvaro Petanic Novoa, General Manager
PHONE: 52-667/6-02-05
Product/Service Description:
Transformers, nesoi, unrated

Exclusivas Jessica, S.A. de C.V.
Insurgentes Sur No. 339, 1st floor
Mexico, D.F. 06170
Contact: Mr. Alejandro Ruiz Villagran, Director General
PHONE: 525/564-8860/9079
Product/Service Description:
Apparel & Accessory Stores

Exclusivas Michel, S.A. de
Venustiano Carranza 71, PB
Mexico, D.F. 06000
Contact: Mr. Mauricio Cohen,
General Director
PHONE: 525/518-4004/2888
Product/Service Description:
Textile card clothing and similar
fabrics

Exicsa, Explotacion e
Ave. Lomas Verdes No. 20
Naucalpan, MEX 53120
Contact: Ing. Francisco Avendano,
Marketing Director
PHONE: 525/572-0940
Product/Service Description:
Suspension shock absorbers for
motor vehicles

Fabrelab, S.A. de C.V.
Lago Caneguin No. 143-A
Mexico, D.F. 11270
Contact: Mr. Crescencio Sanchez,
General Manager
PHONE: 525/399-7283
Product/Service Description:
Glass and glassware

Fabrica de Bicicletas
Calle 8 No. 5
Naucalpan, MEX 53370
Contact: Mr. Moises Pasol W,
Sales Manager
PHONE: 525/358-8577 / 358-
8484
Product/Service Description:
Bicycles & oth cycles (inc del
tricycle) no motor

Fabricaciones Industriales
Rio TIber No. 78
Mexico, D.F. 06500
Contact: Ing. Isaac Franklin
Unkind, General Director
PHONE: 525/229-8500
Product/Service Description:
Tubes, pipes & hoses, nesoi

**Fabricantes de Iluminacion
Nacional**
Calle 1910 No. 637-A
Mexico, D.F. 07330
Contact: Inr. Juvencio Villar
PHONE: 525/586-7960
Product/Service Description:
Electric lamps and lighting

Fanal, S.A.
Plutarco Elias Calles No. 119
Mexico, D.F. 08500
Contact: Lic. Anselmo Trevino G.,
General Manager
PHONE: 525/657-0088
Product/Service Description:
Locks except motor vehicle or
furniture, base metl

Farias Process, S.A.
Av. Patriotismo No. 570
Mexico, D.F. 03910
Contact: Mr. Enrique Farias
Castaneda, Director General
PHONE: 525/563-3152
Product/Service Description:
Labels of paper or paperboard

Federico Ruiz Vasconcelos
Uruguay No. 100
Mexico, D.F. 06060
Contact: Mr. Ramon Ruiz,
PHONE: 525/510-0326
Product/Service Description:
Buckles and buckle clasps a parts

**Ferreteria y Madereria
Popular S.A.**
Carr.San Luis Km. 13.5
Mexicali, B.C.N MEXICO
Contact: Mr. Roberto Villalobos,
PHONE: 52/65/61-6970, 65/61-
Product/Service Description:
Wood, tongued, grooved, molded

Fetasa Tijuana, S. A. de C.
Ave. 20 de Noviembre No. 185
Tijuana, B.C. 22430
Contact: Eng. Rosalina Murillo
Rogers, President
PHONE: 52/66/81-4881
Product/Service Description:
Rods,sticks & profile shapes,of
polymr vin chlorid

**Filtro Especialidades
Omega**
Norte 15 No. 4809
Mexico, D.F. 07760
Contact: Ing. Antonio Medina,
General Mamager
PHONE: 525/368-5066
Product/Service Description:
Filters & parts & accessories for
instr & appratus

**Filtros Baldwin de Mexico,
S.A. de**
Calle 10 No. 137
Iztapalapa, D.F. 09070
Contact: Lic. Reynaldo Rojas,
Director General
PHONE: 525/582-3322, 670-1625
Product/Service Description:
Oil or fuel filters for internal
combustion engine

**Filtros Y Equipo Industrial,
S.A.**
Morelos No. 199
Mexico, D.F. 09880
Contact: Mr. Jorge Silva Cazares,
General Manager
PHONE: 525/656-4687, 656-2730
Product/Service Description:
Filters & parts & accessories for
instr & appratus

Filtros y Medios Filtrantes
Prolongacion Cerro de las Cruces
Tlalnepantla, MEX 54040
Contact: Ing. Leopoldo Rosas,
General Director
PHONE: 525/379-8792
Product/Service Description:
Filter/purify machine & apparatus
for liquid nesoi

Firesa
Revillagigedo No. 84-A
Mexico, D.F. 06000
Contact: Mr. Jorge Davalos, Sales
Manager
PHONE: 525/512-8539
Product/Service Description:
Electric apparatus for line
telephony etc, parts

**Flagasa-Fab Lab. de
Alimentos para**
Poniente 146 No. 900
Mexico, D.F. 02300
Contact: Mr. Luis Miguel Hernaiz
Vigil, Commercial Director
PHONE: 525/567-3811
Product/Service Description:
Food industry residues & waste;
prep animal feed

**Fleetguard de Mexico, S.A.
de C.V.**
Adolfo Lopez Mateos No. 8
Atizapan, Edo. de Mex., MEX
52966
Contact: Ing. Jose Luis Casado, ,
PHONE: 525/824-7254, 7255,
7256
Product/Service Description:
Antifreezing prep & prepared
deicing fluids

**Formas Continuas Para
Negocios**
Recreo No. 26.
Mexico, D.F. 08300
Contact: Sales & Marketing, ,
PHONE: 525/538-0515
Product/Service Description:
Registers, notebooks, binders, bus
forms etc, papr

**Fortraco Mexicana, S.A. de
C.V.**
Viena No. 249
Mexico, D.F. 04100
Contact: Mr. Francisco Martin del
Campo, President and Director
General
PHONE: 525/554-1542
Product/Service Description:
Aircraft,nesoi

**Frenos Hidraulicos
Automotrices,**
Av. La Presa No. 6, 3a Secc
Tlalnepantla, MEX 54180
Contact: Sales & Marketing, ,
PHONE: 525/586-6766, 586-
2063,
Product/Service Description:
Hydraulic brake fluids liq for
hydraulic trans etc

**G.B.W. de Mexico S.A. de
C.V.**
Poniente 116 No. 576
Mexico, D.F. 02300
Contact: Ing. Rafael Del Rio H.,
President and General Director
PHONE: 525/567-9011
Product/Service Description:
Ink, printing, writing, drawing etc,
concen or not

Garo Filtros de Aire, S.A. de C.V.
Union No. 148
Mexico, D.F. 08100
Contact: Mr. Gabriel Rojas, General Manager
PHONE: 525/763-4722
Product/Service Description:
Filter or purify mach & apparatus for liquid,nesoi

Gimbel Mexicana, S. A. de
Sonora No. 189
Mexico, D. F. 06100
Contact: Mr. Carlos Gimbel, President and Director General
PHONE: 525/584-3800, 574-0768
Product/Service Description:
Handsaws & met pts; saw blades; base mtl saw parts

Graco Mexicana, S.A. de
Arquimides No. 3 Piso 4
Mexico, D.F. 11560
Contact: Mr. Jose Mendoza,
PHONE: 525/280-2024
Product/Service Description:
Heat exchangers

Grupo Agromora, S.A. de
Central de Abasto, 1a. Peatonal
Mexico, D.F. 09040
Contact: Ms. Concepcion Hernandez, General Manager
PHONE: 525/694-4559, 694-1512
Product/Service Description:
Seeders

Grupo Aluvisa, S.A. de C.V.
Col. La Cruz
Mexico, D.F. 08310
Contact: Arq. Jose Carlos Lombana, General Manager
PHONE: 525/657-1344
Product/Service Description:
Aluminum alloy profiles nesoi

Grupo Avicola del Centro, S.P.R. de
5 de Mayo No. 23000
San Luis Potosi, SLP 78350
Contact: Mr. Jaime Oliva, Director
PHONE: 52-48/15-0101
Product/Service Description:
Chickens, ducks, geese, turkeys, and guineas, live

Grupo Bambu S.A. de C.V.
Negrete No. 110
San Luis Potosi, SLP 78849
Contact: Mr. Juan Francisco Ibarra, General Director
PHONE: 52-48/18-1883,18-1889
Product/Service Description:
Textile fabrics nesoi coated etc with pvc, cotton

Grupo Cerro
Calzada Guadalupe no. 20
Mexico, D.F. 11410
Contact: Ing. Ing. Mario Flores, Comercial Director
PHONE: 525/399-4569,399-4569
Product/Service Description:
Pumps for liquids, nesoi

Grupo Cibernetica Gerencial,
Av. Coyoacan No. 320
Mexico, D.F. 03100
Contact: C.P. Jose Luis Martinez, General Manager
PHONE: 525/669-0844, 682-1467
Product/Service Description:
Automatic data process machines

Grupo Comercial Cap, S.A. DE C.V.
Miguel Angel No. 49 Bis
Mexico, D.F. 03700
Contact: Mr. Pablo Suarez de Miguel, Director General
PHONE: 525/598-5542, 598-5548
Product/Service Description:
Beauty, make-up & skin-care prep; manicure etc prp

Grupo Condumex - Division de
Dr. Gustavo Baz No. 340
Tlalnepantla, MEX. 54040
Contact: Ing. Enrique Hill Bochelel, Director General
PHONE: (525) 310-6577, 310-1179
Product/Service Description:
Solar cells in modules or panels

Grupo Echlin Automotriz, S.A. de
Av. Ano de Juarez No. 223
Mexico, D.F. 09070
Contact: Mr. Guillermo Vela Reyna, Director General
PHONE: 525/582-6199
Product/Service Description:
Parts & access for motor vehicles (head 8701-8705)

Grupo Elmex
San Borja No. 103, 162-A
Mexico, D.F. 03100
Contact: Mr. Ignacio Ashby, General Director
PHONE: 525/575-3230
Product/Service Description:
Electric lamps and lighting fittings, nesoi

Grupo Empresarial Arva S.A. de C.V.
Rembrandt No. 87
Mexico, D.F. 03700
Contact: Mr Arturo Vazquez Caballero, General Director
PHONE: 525/598 5858/563 2304
Product/Service Description:
Iron and steel

Grupo Gace, S.A. de C.V.
Calle 2a. No. 206
Gomez Palacio, DGO 35078
Contact: Mr. Patricio Ceniceros Lopez, General Manager
PHONE: 52/17/19-0306
Product/Service Description:
Packing or wrapping machinery

Grupo Industrial Bimbo, S.
Aristoteles No. 131
Mexico, D. F. 11560
Contact: Sales & Marketing, ,
PHONE: 525/229-6600
Product/Service Description:
Sugar confectionery

Grupo Industrial Marathon, S.A.
Amsterdam No. 248-5
Mexico, D.F. 06170
Contact: Ing. Oscar Pliego
PHONE: 525/264-0850
Product/Service Description:
Rubber, unvulcanized, in plates,

Grupo Industrial Toluca, S.A. de
APARTADO POSTAL 109
TOLUCA, EDOMX 50070
Contact: Sales & Marketing, ,
PHONE: 52-72/14-9066
Product/Service Description:
Footwear lea upper nesoi with a metal toe-cap

Grupo Industrial y Comercial Medico
Av. Cuauhtemoc No. 1146
Mexico, D.F. 03650
Contact: Sales & Marketing, ,
PHONE: 525/605-3107, 604-7483
Product/Service Description:
Dental fittings and parts and accessories

Grupo Ingenieria Servicios
San Marcos No. 130
Mexico, D.F. 14000
Contact: Mr. Dulce Pena, Director General
PHONE: 525/655-5200, 655-7323
Product/Service Description:
Air & Water Resource & Solid Waste Management

Grupo Joman Telecomunicaciones, S.A
Sur 109-A No. 437
Mexico, D.F. 09090
Contact: Ing. Jorge Ramirez, General Director
PHONE: 525/581-0388 670-3230
Product/Service Description:
Electric apparatus for line telephony etc, parts

Grupo M.M., S.A. de C.V.
Cda. Mayorazgo de Luyando No. 50
Mexico, D.F. 03330
Contact: Mr. Alberto Urueta, Marketing Manager
PHONE: 525/604-8263, 604-8175
Product/Service Description:
Medical surgical dental veternary furniture, nesoi

Grupo Quimico Industrial de Toluca
Camino Viejo a San Lorenzo
Toluca, MEX 50010
Contact: Mr. Carlos L. Corzo
Rodriguez, Director
PHONE: 52/72/72-44-38
Product/Service Description:
Chemical & residual prod,
chemical etc ind nesoi

Grupo Tea, S.A. de C.V.
Patriotismo No. 767
Mexico, D.F. 03910
Contact: Lic. Mr. Juan Pablo
PHONE: 525/626-0123/626-0161
Product/Service Description:
Automatic data process machines;
magn reader etc

Grupo Textil La Marina, S.A.
Centeotl No. 289
Atzcapotzalco, D.F. 02760
Contact: Lic. Rafael Vazquez
Quezada, General Director
PHONE: 525/561-1900
Product/Service Description:
Fishing rods & tackle; nets; decoys
etc; parts etc

Grupo Valsa, S.A. de C.V.
Calle Union No. 25
Mexico, D.F. 08100
Contact: Lic. Mario Garza,
PHONE: 525/763-9388/558-5267
Product/ServiceDescription:
Aluminum alloy profiles nesoi

Gutierrez Ayala Juan Jose
Roldan No. 121, Acc. A - C
Mexico, D.F. 06090
Contact: Mr. Juan Jose Gutierrez
Ayala, General Manager
PHONE: 525/522-0170
Product/Service Description:
Cleaning preparations

Harry Mazal, S.A. de C.V.
Laguna Tamiahua No. 204
Mexico, D.F. 11320
Contact: Prof. Hector Tello
PHONE: 525/396-1133/4049
Product/Service Description:
Process control inst&apprts for
complete systems

Hercules, S. A. de C. V.
Antiguo Camino a Culhuacan
Mexico, D. F. 09820
Contact: Ing. Ignacio Rubio,
Commercial Director
PHONE: 525/670-2802
Product/Service Description:
Jacks and hoists,hydraulic,exc blt-
in jack systems

Hermanos Ugartechea, S.A. de C.V.
Portal de las Flores No. 10-A
Oaxaca, OAX. 68000
Contact: Mr. Francisco
Ugartechea, Director
PHONE: 52/51-697-19
Product/Service Description:
Food preparations nesoi

Herrajes, Dados y Moldes, S.A De
Dr. Alberto Swain No.250
Torreon, COAH 27019
Contact: Mr. J. Guillermo Beick,
PHONE: 52/17/50-6444
Product/Service Description:
Machine tools for working metal,

Herramientas Exclusivas y
Mariano Azuela No. 194
Mexico, D. F. 06400
Contact: Mr. German Nuno
Fernandez, General Manager
PHONE: 525/547-0448
Product/Service Description:
Machine tools for drilling, boring,
milling etc

Herramientas Vallejo, S.A.
Poniente 122 No. 340
Mexico, D.F. 07750
Contact: Ms. Margarita Tellez de
Rivas, Purchases Director
PHONE: 525/587-6111, 587-7204
Product/Service Description:
Handsaws & met pts; saw blades;
base mtl saw parts

Hertel de Mexico, S. A.
Matias Romero No. 1359
Mexico, D. F. 03600
Contact: Ing. Gerardo Cortes
PHONE: 525/605-8277
Product/Service Description:
Powder-actuated handtools

Hidro Industrial, S. A.
Estenografos No. 38
Mexico, D.F. 09400
Contact: Mr. Rafael Mujica B.,
General Director
PHONE: 525/633-4086
Product/Service Description:
Fluorine, chlorine, bromine &
iodine

Holzer y Cia., S.A de C.V.
Campos Eliseos No. 345, piso 10
Mexico, D.F. 11570
Contact: Mr. Andres Holzer,
Director General
PHONE: 525/327-1010
Product/Service Description:
Clock or watch jewels

Homemart De Mexico, S.A.
Av. Lomas Verdes No. 904
Naucalpan, MEX 54500
Contact: Mr. Michael Wolk,
Manager merchandising
PHONE: 525/360-4948
Product/Service Description:
Mowers for lawn, parks or sports
grounds, nesoi

I.A.S.I., S.A. de C.V.
Cerrada de Altata No. 14
Mexico, D.F. 06100
Contact: Ing. Ricardo Ricardez,
General Director
PHONE: 525/516-1477
Product/Service Description:
Records, tapes & other recorded
sound media etc

I.T.M. Representaciones de Baja
Ave. de las Americas No. 1010-4
Tijuana, B. C. 22440
PHONE: 52-66/81-4108, 81-9226
Product/Service Description:
Transformers, nesoi, unrated

Iberoamerican Cultural Exchange
Calle 49 No. 282
Merida, YUC 97119
Contact: Mr. Arturo Esquivel
PHONE: 52/99/44-1839
Product/Service Description:
Telephonic apparatus, carrier-
current line system

Idar De Mexico, S.A. De C.V.
Republica de Uruguay No. 83 - E
Mexico, D.F. 06000
Contact: Mr Rafael Arditti,
Director Sales
PHONE: 525\521-5310
Product/Service Description:
Jewelry and parts thereof, of oth
precious metal

Idea, Forma y Color, S.A. de C.V.
Enrique Rebsamen No. 322
Mexico, D.F. 03020
Contact: Mr. Jose Pastor I.,
Exports Director
PHONE: 525/639-4121
Product/Service Description:
Cards, printed, nesoi

Idelco, S.A. de C.V.
Dr. Lucio No. 102, Locales 2,3 y 4
Mexico, D.F. 06720
Contact: Mr. Isaac Ilitzky, General
Manager
PHONE: 525/588-6777
Product/Service Description:
Textile wall coverings

Importaciones Exportaciones y
La Llanura No. 106
Naucalpan, MEX 53340
Contact: Mr. Edgar Ramirez Mac
Naught, Director General
PHONE: 525/560-2525
Product/Service Description:
Advertising N.e.c.

Importaciones y Exportaciones Fe-
Avenida 1 No. 20 bajos
Mexico, D.F. 03800
Contact: Mr. Jorge Ferreiro, Owner
PHONE: 525/273-1076, 273-1842
Product/Service Description:
Air & Water Resource & Solid
Waste Management

Importaciones y Exportaciones Mursa
Aldama No. 172B-1
Morelia, MICH 58000
Contact: Mr. Jesus Arturo Murillo,
General Manager
PHONE: 52/43/13-7281
Product/Service Description:
Automotive Parts & Supplies

Importadora Electronica Alta
Cumbres de Maltrata No. 359-201
Mexico, D.F. 03020
Contact: Dra. Maria Jesus Franco
PHONE: 525/696-3918
Product/Service Description:
Light-sensing tubes

Importadora Electronica
Rep. del Salvador 17-C
Mexico, MEX. 06080
PHONE: 525/512-3792 512-3872
Product/Service Description:
Microphones; loudspeakers;

Importadora Electronica, S.A. de
Republica del Salvador No. 17-C
Mexico, D.F. 06080
Contact: Ing. Bernardo
Finkeastein, Director General
PHONE: 525/512-3792
Product/Service Description:
Microphones; loudspeakers; sound
amplifier etc, pt

Impulsora Diesel, S.A. DE C.V.
Calz. Vallejo No. 1030
Mexico, D.F. 02300
Contact: LIC. Julio Javier
Manzano Alba, General Manager
PHONE: 525/587-7733,587-8955
Product/Service Description:
Automotive Parts & Supplies

Impulsora Mexicana de Productos
Gustavo Baz No. 262 Int. 2-2
Tlalnepantla, E.M. 54060
Contact: Mr. Miguel Rivero
Legarreta, President
PHONE: 525/397-8538 397-7415
Product/Service Description:
Plastics and articles thereof

Impulsora de Filtros Para Equipo
Via A. Lopez Mateos No. 73
Tlalnepantla, E.M. 54050
Contact: Mr. Jose Galvan Davila,
Sole Administrator
PHONE: 525/397-1890, 361-6416
Product/Service Description:
Filters & parts & accessories for
instr & appratus

Inarco, S.A. De C.V. (Ingenier
Felix Berenguer No. 126
Mexico, D.F. 11000
Contact: Ing. Francisco Cervantes,
Executive Vice President
PHONE: 525/540-6360
Product/Service Description:
Architectural and ornamental
work, iron or steel

Incopi-Industrializadora y Comercia
Manuel Carpio No. 224
Mexico, D.F. 06400
Contact: Mr. Rodolfo Shrader
Macias, Director General
PHONE: 525/541-0953, 541-0711
Product/Service Description:
Parts of truck assemblies, nesoi

Ind. Hospitalaria Internacional,
Manuel Acuna No. 60
Mexico, D.F. 09280
Contact: Sales & Marketing, ,
PHONE: 525/ 693-6783
Product/Service Description:
Inst & appliances for
medical,surgical, etc,nesoi

Ind. Hospitalaria Internacional, S.
Manuel Acuna No. 60
Mexico, D.F. 09280
Contact: Mr. Hector Morales
Zaragoza, Director General
PHONE: 525/693-6783, 691-6271
Product/Service Description:
Orthopedic appl; artif body pts;
hear aid; pts etc

Industria Electrica Automotriz S.A.
Autopista Mexico Queretaro No.
3000
Tlalnepantla, MEX 54040
Contact: Sr. Miguel Angel Ruelas,
Gerente de Ventas
PHONE: 525/379-5075, 379-9377
Product/Service Description:
Automotive Parts & Supplies

Industria Mexicana de Equipo
Xola No. 1152, esq. Pitagoras
Mexico, D.F. 03100
Contact: Mr. Luis Martinez G.,
General Manager
PHONE: 525/639-6580
Product/Service Description:
Outboard engines for marine
propulsion

Industrial Tornillera Figueroa,
Nicolas Bravo No. 41
Mexico, D.F. 09210
Contact: Mr. Andres Flores
Figueroa, Director General
PHONE: 525/763-2377
Product/Service Description:
Bolts w wo their nuts o wshrs, of
iron or steel

Industrial de Rueda y Rodajas
Via Gustavo Baz No. 393
Naucalpan, EDOME 54060
Contact: Ing. Carlos Monterrubio,
General Manager
PHONE: 525/374-0001
Product/Service Description:
Fork-lift and works trucks, nesoi

Industrias Ahedo, S.A. de C.V.
Pino No. 440
Mexico, D.F. 06760
Contact: Ing. Justo Dieguez,
General Director
PHONE: 525/547-5705 to 09
Product/Service Description:
Buckles and buckle clasps a parts,
base metal

Industrias Alpha, S.A. de C.V.
Niza No. 76
Mexico, D.F. 06600
Contact: Mr. Francisco Briseno,
General Manager
PHONE: 525/533-1417, 533-2385
Product/Service Description:
Bakery mach & mach f manuf
macaroni,spaghetti,etc

Industrias Conelec, S. A. de C. V.
Jose Vasconcelos No. 184
Mexico, D. F. 06140
Contact: Mr. Miguel Angel
Riquelme, Director General
PHONE: 525/211-6000, 553-0633
Product/Service Description:
Dc motors & generators w output
> 750w; n ov 75 kw

Industrias Continental, S.A. de C.V
Azafran No. 341-A
Mexico, D.F. 08400
Contact: Mr. Octavio Alvarez
Cano, General Manager
PHONE: 525/648-0121, 680-7812
Product/Service Description:
Stoves, ranges etc, nonel domest &
pts, ir & steel

Industrias Cormetal, S.A. de C.V.
Jose Vasconcelos No. 218-101
Mexico, D. F. 06140
Contact: Ing. Rodolfo Payan
Renteria, Director General
PHONE: 525/286-1413, 256-3447
Product/Service Description:
Lathes for remov mtl, n/c, mulit
spin, new, nesoi

Industrias Figursa S.A.
Primer retorno de Zempoala No. 8
Cuautitlan, MX 547750
Contact: Mr. Emilio Figueroa,
General Manager
PHONE: 525/871-5405
Product/Service Description:
Laboratory ware

Industrias Man de Mexico, S.A.
Avenida 5 No. 103
Mexico, D.F. 09070
Contact: Mr. Luis Perez
PHONE: 525/581-8011
Product/Service Description:
Fans, nesoi

Industrias Marino, S.A.
Carr. Internacional km. 1193.5
Mazatlan, SIN. 82180
Contact: Mr. Arturo Lizarraga
Mercado, General Manager
PHONE: 52/69/84-9311, 84-9398
Product/Service Description:
Coffee, tea, mate & spices

Industrias Marro, S.A.
Ave. San Lorenzo No. 279-16-A
Mexico, D.F.
Contact: Ing. Rafael Martinez,
Sales Manager
PHONE: 525/612-7721
Product/Service Description:
Pneumatic elevators and conveyors

Industrias Meza, S.A.
1a. Privada Dr. Duran No. 21
Mexico, D.F. 06720
Contact: Mr. Salvador Meza
PHONE: 525/519-0362
Product/Service Description:
Dust collection and air purification
equipment

Industrias Monterrubio, S.A. de
Economia No. 31
Mexico, D.F. 15700
Contact: Mr. Eduardo
Monterrubio, Director General
PHONE: 525/571-7973/571-3324
Product/Service Description:
Wood and articles of wood; wood
charcoal

Industrias Plasticas
Calle 6 No. 12
Xalostoc, EDOME 55340
Contact: Mr. Alberto Hinojosa,
PHONE: 525/755-3555
Product/Service Description:
Polyvinyl chloride,not mixed with
any oth substanc

Industrias Quetzal, S.A. DE C.V.
Paseo de la Reforma No. 2976
Mexico, D. F. 05100
Contact: Mr. Carlos Madrazo,
Director General
PHONE: 525/259-2522, 259-9620
Product/Service Description:
Stoves, ranges etc, nonel domest &
pts, ir & steel

Industrias Therme, S.A. de
Bosques de Alison No. 47-A 5to
piso
Mexico, D.F. 05120
Contact: Mr. Ricardo Hojel,
General Director
PHONE: 525/259-3359
Product/Service Description:
Reaction initiators & acceler &
catalyt prep nesoi

Industrias de Precision,
Av. San Nicolas No. 2
Tlalnepantla, EDOME 54030
Contact: Mr. Carlos Madrazo
Shopferer, Director General
PHONE: 525/310-4370
Product/Service Description:
Parts & accessories for adp
machines & units

Iner, S.A. DE C.V.
Av. Del Parque No. 10
Mexico, D.F. 01040
Contact: Ing. Justino Reyes,
General Manager
PHONE: 525/662-1788, 662-2999
Product/Service Description:
Soda fountain,beer dispensing
equip, refrigerated

Info-Sistemas, Computacion Y Comu-
Kepler No. 105 Esq. Rosseau
Mexico, D.F. 11590
Contact: MAT. GUADALUPE DE
SEGOVIA, DIR. COMERCIAL
PHONE: 525/203-7126
Product/Service Description:
Records, tapes & other recorded
sound media etc

Inforamet, S.A. de C.V.
Blvd. Aeropuerto No. 324, altos 1
Mexico, D.F. 15500
Contact: Ing. Hector Axel Vargas,
General Manager
PHONE: 525/ 785-4760, 785-8858
Product/Service Description:
Navigational instruments and
appliances, nesoi

Infra, S.A. de C.V.
Felix Guzman # 16
Naucalpan, EDM
Contact: Mr. Edgar Arturo Arteaga
Luna, Manager
PHONE: 525/557-5040, 557-6200
Product/Service Description:
Medical, surgical, dental or
veterinary furn etc

Ing. Carlos Gutierrez P.
Victoria No. 68
Mexico, D.F. 07810
Contact: Ing. Carlos Gutierrez P.,
General Director
PHONE: 525/781-8740
Product/Service Description:
Greases, lubricating, with or w out
additives

Ingenieria Peruel, S.A. de C.V.
Ayuntamiento No. 162-A
Mexico, D.F. 06040
Contact: Mr. Salvador Castilla,
Manager
PHONE: 525-5182631
Product/Service Description:
Air conditioning mach etc incl
refrig unit etc

Ingenieria en Automatizacion
Plaza Rotherdam No. 9
Cuautitlan, EDOME 54700
Contact: Ing. Juan Jose Munoz
Navarro, General Director
PHONE: 525/871-1511, 871-1512
Product/Service Description:
Machine tools for forging,
bending, stamping etc

Ingenieria en Moldes y Troqueles,
Calzada de Guadalupe No. 147-B
Naucalpan, EDOME 53460
Contact: Ing. Veremundo Valencia,
Director General
PHONE: 525/300-4416
Product/Service Description:
Die casting machines

Ingenieria y Control de Instrumen-
Laguna Del Carmen No. 132
Mexico, D.F. 11320
Contact: Ing. Jesus Meneses Mata,
PHONE: 525/396-3560,396-0266
Product/Service Description:
Parts for steam and other vapor
turbines

Ingenieria y Procesamiento
San Lorenzo No.153
Mexico, D.F. 03100
Contact: Ing. Luis Ramos L.
PHONE: 525/575-4077,575-2092
Product/Service Description:
Process control inst&appts,
flow&liq level control

Ingenieria y Procesos Industriales,
Eulalia Guzman No. 232
Mexico, D.F. 06450
Contact: Ing. Ulpiano Flores
PHONE: 525/541-3197
Product/Service Description:
Automotive gear oils

Inman, S. A.
Av. Hermilo Mena No. 10
Tlalnepantla, MEX. 54180
Contact: Ing. Oscar Calderon
Garcia, General Manager
PHONE: 525/718-3036
Product/Service Description:
Conveyor or transmiss belts of
vulcanized rubber

Inmobiliaria y Comercializadora
Blvd.La Herradura local W5 Inter-
Mexico, D.F.
Contact: Mr. Eduardo Zarate,
PHONE: 525/251-0480/251-8414
Product/Service Description:
Perfumes and toilet waters

Insertos, Pastillas y Herramientas,
Proyectistas No. 27
Mexico, D.F. 09400
Contact: Lic. Luis Alberto
Gutierrez, Director General
PHONE: 525/633-8330, 633-0714
Product/Service Description:
Tools for boring or broaching, and
base metal pts

Instalaciones Especializadas de
Malagon No. 63
Mexico City, D.F. 09860
Contact: Angel Romero, Projects
Manager
PHONE: 525/656-3841/3901
Product/Service Description:
Air cond mach incorporating a
refrig unit, nesoi

Instalaciones y Servicios Especia-
Trojes No. 49-PB
Mexico, D.F. 09810
Contact: Ing. Enrique Arellano,
PHONE: 525/582-5176, 670-5786
Product/Service Description:
Electrical apparatus for switching

Instituto Nacional de Ecologia
Rio Elba No. 20 1er. piso
Mexico, D.F. 06500
Contact: Sales & Marketing, ,
PHONE: 525/553-9406
Product/Service Description:
Electroplating, electrophoresis and
electrolysis m

Instrumedico, S. A. de C. V.
Av. Torres de Ixtapatongo No. 346
Mexico, D. F. 01780
Contact: Ing. Arturo Meza,
General Manager
PHONE: 525/683-2852, 683-5778
Product/Service Description:
Medical, surgical, dental or vet
inst, no elec, pt

Instrumentos Optoelectronicos, S.A.
Calzada de la Viga No. 1595
Mexico, D.F. 09470
Contact: Ing. Carlos Segovia,
Marketing Director
PHONE: 525/581-6311
Product/Service Description:
Liquid crystal devices nesoi;
lasers; opt appl; pt

Instrumentos de Medicion
Alfredo Chavero No. 71
Mexico, D.F. 06800
Contact: Mr. Mario Merino,
Production Manager
PHONE: 525/761-3160
Product/Service Description:
Inst etc measure or check flow,
level etc, pts etc

Integracion Decorativa, S.A.
Av. Veracruz No. 20
Mexico, D.F. 06700
Contact: Mr. Edgar Villason, Sales
Manager
PHONE: 525/553-2943, 211-9965
Product/Service Description:
Carpets & oth textile floor
coverings, tufted

Intelmex, S.A. de C.V.
Gertrudis Sanchez No. 77
Mexico, D.F. 15450
Contact: Ing. Pedro Samano,
Manager
PHONE: 525/393-2806
Product/Service Description:
Records, tapes & other recorded
sound media etc

Inter Export, S.A. de C.V.
Insurgentes Sur 300-121
Mexico, D.F. 06700
Contact: Mr. Jose Manuel Pedrero,
Director General
PHONE: 525/574-4760, 584-5184
Product/Service Description:
Organic chemicals

Interaccion en Informatica, S.A. de
Insugentes Sur No. 1032 - 303
Mexico, D.F. 03100
Contact: Ing. Ramon Millan
Gamez, General Director
PHONE: 525/575-6091/575-6098
Product/Service Description:
Recorded media for sound
including master prod rcd

Inyectora de Plasticos Y Metales, .
Calle 3 No. 45
Estado de Mexico, 53370
MEXICO
Contact: Mr. Rogelio Gonzalez,
Director General
PHONE: 525/576-6988
Product/Service Description:
Injection-molding mach for work
rubber or plastic

J.J. Herramientas, S.A. de C.V.
Norte 24-A No. 2-Accesoria B
Mexico, D.F. 07800
Contact: Mr. Jose Luis Ortiz,
General Manager
PHONE: 525/537-9421, 517-3443
Product/Service Description:
Tools for boring or broaching, and
base metal pts

J.J. Plas, S.A. de C.V.
Av. Coyoacan 1426
Mexico, D.F. 03100
Contact: Mr. Julio Takeda Iwadare,
Director
PHONE: 525/534-4001, 660-1549
Product/Service Description:
Plastics and articles thereof

JT Baker S.A. de C.V.
Plomo No. 2 Fraccionamiento
Ind.
Mexico, MX. 55320
Contact: Mrs. Silvia Escobedo
Solic, Sales Manager
PHONE: 525/569-1100
Product/Service Description:
Chemicals and related products, us
goods returned

Jardineria 2000, S.A.
Av. San Jeronimo 1010
Mexico, D.F. 01200
Contact: Mr. Enrique Haro,
General Manager.
PHONE: 525/595-2298, 683-1781
Product/Service Description:
Fertilizers

Jardines Proyectos y Construcciones
Victoria No. 50
Mexico, D.F. 017800
Contact: Mr. Guillermo Flores
Garcia, Director General
PHONE: 525/595-6444, 681-0285
Product/Service Description:
Live plants (including their roots)
etc, nesoi

Jony-Zip, S.A. de C.V.
Uruguay No. 73-B, Desp. 501
Mexico, D.F. 06000
Contact: Mr. Jonathan Brauner,
Director
PHONE: 525/510-1549
Product/Service Description:
Sewing thread artificial filaments
for retail sale

Jose de la Torre, S.A. de
Patriotismo No. 399 Piso 3
Mexico, D.F. 03800
Contact: Ing. Carlos De la Torre
Leslie, Director General
PHONE: 525/273-2664, 273-2724
Product/Service Description:
Compression-ignition internal
comb piston engines

Joyeria La Princesa, S.A. De C.V.
Tacuba No. 92
Mexico, D.F. 06000
Contact: Mr. Gabriel Galvez,
Director General
PHONE: 525/521-2128
Product/Service Description:
Jewelry and parts thereof, of oth
precious metal

Joyma Industrial, S. A.
Biologo Maximino Martinez
Mexico, D.F. 02870
Contact: Ing. Joaquin Avila
PHONE: 525/341-0520
Product/Service Description:
Castors, and parts thereof, of base metal

Juntas de Expansion de Mexico,
San Lorenzo No. 141
Mexico, D.F. 03100
Contact: Mr. Juan Vilchis, Director General
PHONE: 525/575-2350
Product/Service Description:
Rubber and articles thereof

Kardel de Mexico, S.A.
Apdo. Postal 576
Garza Garcia, N.L. 66250
Contact: David Cardenas-Rudderow, General Director
PHONE: 52/3/35-6322 / 35-6382
Product/Service Description:
Central heating boilers

Kinfil, S.A. De C.V.
Ave. San Lorenzo No. 279 - 34
Mexico, D.F. 09850
Contact: Mr. Jose Antonio Borja Vazquez, General Manager
PHONE: 525/612-1066
Product/Service Description:
Filters & parts & accessories for instr & appratus

Krupper Internacional,
Progreso No. 185-104
Mexico, D.F. 08200
Contact: Mr. Francisco G. Ross, General Manager
PHONE: 525/516-5785
Product/Service Description:
Machine tools for material

L.G. Seguridad, S.A. DE C.V.
Calle 3, No. 355
Mexico, D.F. 02930
Contact: Ms. Maria Garcia Castillo, Director General
PHONE: 525/355-1550, 355-1133
Product/Service Description:
M/b trousers overalls shorts etc cotton, knit

L.J. Iluminacion, S.A.
Marcelino Davalos No. 13
Mexico, D.F. 06880
Contact: Ing. Manuel Martinez Ojeda, Commercial Director
PHONE: 525/530-4520
Product/Service Description:
Electric lamps and lighting fittings, nesoi

La Hacienda S.A. DE C.V.
Lauro Villar No.68
Mexico, D.F. 02440
Contact: Mr. Alejandro Benito, Director of food supply
PHONE: 525/382-0446,382-3012
Product/Service Description:
Food industry residues & waste; prep animal feed

Labatt Mexico, S.A.
esquina Lerdo
Mexico, D.F. 06920
Contact: Lic. Noel Trainor, Director General
PHONE: 525/583-3522
Product/Service Description:
Wov fabric, synth staple fib nu 85% synth st fiber

Laboratorios Sanfer, S.A.
General J. Cano No. 35
Mexico, D.F. 11850
Contact: Dr. Ernesto Amtmann Obregon, President and CEO
PHONE: 525/277-7000
Product/Service Description:
Pharmaceutical products

Lazer, S.A. De C.V.
Insurgentes Sur No. 216 - 207
Mexico, D.F. 06700
Contact: Ing. Arturo Campero, General Manager
PHONE: 525/207-4665
Product/Service Description:
Cast articles of iron or steel nesoi

Leon Weill, S.A.
Av. Coyoacan No. 1153
Mexico, D.F. 03210
Contact: Mr. Fernando Tellez, Sales Manager
PHONE: 525/559-4311
Product/Service Description:
Machine tools for drilling, boring, milling etc

Leyva Mendez Construccion,
Salvador Alvarado No. 65-1
Mexico, D.F. 11800
Contact: Ing. Alejandro Gutierrez Baez, President
PHONE: 525/515-2537
Product/Service Description:
Air & Water Resource & Solid Waste Management

Libreria Guadalupana, S.A.
Isabel la Catolica No. 1 - C
06000 Mexico, D.F. MEXICO
Contact: Ms Clara Centeno de Fuentes, Administrator
PHONE: 525/521-7515
Product/Service Description:
Books, brochures & similar printed matter

Limpieza Gapi, S.A. de C.V.
Cascada No.708
Mexico, D.F. 09450
Contact: Dra Concepcion Braniff,
PHONE: 525/536-2164,
Product/Service Description:
Cleaning preparations

Limpieza Industrial Co. S.A. de C..
Ave. de la Piedra # 16
Atizapan, EDM 54600
Contact: Mrs. Ma. Eugenia Ortega
PHONE: 525/398-8928
Product/Service Description:
Cleaning preparations

Linde de Mexico, S.A.
Blvd. M. Avila Camacho No. 32
Mexico, D.F. 11000
Contact: Mr. Thomas Von Krannichfeldt, Director General
PHONE: 525/627-9500
Product/Service Description:
Gas-operate mch f solderg, brazng,weldg, hand-dir

Litoquim S.A.
Soja No. 153
Mexico, D.F. 09810
Contact: Mr. Guillermo Vega,
PHONE: 525/582-0190,581-6017
Product/Service Description:
Ink, printing, writing, drawing etc,

Lopez Mercantil Distribuidora,
Lopez No. 24 1er. piso
Mexico, D.F. 06050
Contact: Mr. Joel Munoz y Ricardi, General Manager
PHONE: 525/521-2994
Product/Service Description:
Sunglasses

Lubricantes y Derivados,S.A. C.V.
Homero No. 109-703
Mexico, D.F. 11560
Contact: Ing. Jose Mendez, General Director
PHONE: 525/255-3695, 250-7108
Product/Service Description:
White mineral oil, not medicinal grade

Lugo Castro y Cia., S.A. de C.V.
Ave. Instituto Politecnico No. 2033
Mexico, D.F. 07300
Contact: Mr. Gabriel Lugo, General Manager
PHONE: 525/762-3931
Product/Service Description:
Interchange tools for hand- or machine-tools, bmpt

Lukas, S. A.
Ave. Parque Lira No. 79
Mexico, D.F. 11850
Contact: Ing. Lutz Kauffmann, Director General
PHONE: 525/516-0500, 516-0507
Product/Service Description:
Dies drw o extr mtl a pts thrf

M.P.S. Mayorista, S.A. de C.V.
Xola No. 621
Mexico, D.F. 03100
Contact: Ing. Mejia Martin, General Manager
PHONE: 525/325-0993
Product/Service Description:
Automatic data process machines; magn reader etc

MHO Especialidades Electromecanicas
Juan Sebastian Bach No. 220
Mexico, D.F. 07870
Contact: Armando Velazquez, Ing
PHONE: 525/759-02-99
Product/Service Description:
Antennas and antenna reflectors and parts

Macro Electrica de Baja California,
Ave. Ferrocarril No. 320
Tijuana, B.C. 22430
Contact: Ing. Alfonso Cuentas Ochoa, Director General
PHONE: 52/66/22-0177
Product/Service Description:
Tubes, pipes & hoses, of polymer of vinyl chlordie

Madepla, S.A.
Col. Leyes de la Reforma
Mexico, D.F. 09310
Contact: Ing. Juan Carlos Hernandez, General Manager
PHONE: 525/694-4355
Product/Service Description:
Tubes, pipes & hoses, of polymer of vinyl chlordie

Maderas Industrializadas Campar,
Republicas No. 241-A
Mexico, D.F. 03310
Contact: Mr. Gerardo Campuzano,
PHONE: 525/604-0448, 688-4939
Product/Service Description:
Pallets, box pallets and other load

Maderas Selvamex, S.A. de C.V.
Calzada Vallejo No. 1043 y 1049
Mexico, D.F. 07700
Contact: Mr. Bruno Sanchez, General Manager
PHONE: 525/368-0146, 368-4075
Product/Service Description:
Wood in the rough, stripped or not of sapwood etc

Maderas del Norte y o

Sergio Alfon-
Prolong. H. Colegio Militar S N
Mexicali, B.C.N 21220
Contact: Ing. Sergio Alfonso Pozo Campillo, Owner
PHONE: 52/65/67-1458
Product/Service Description:
Veneer sheets etc, not over 6 mm thick

Madereria San Antonio, S.A. de C.V.
Blvd. Benito Juarez No. 4330
Mexicali, B.C. 21060
Contact: Sr. Ignacio Rene Vazquez Gudino, General Director
PHONE: 52/65/61-7502
Product/Service Description:
Wood marquetry, etc; wood caskets and cases, etc.

Madereria la Rancherita, S.A de C.V
Av. Anahuac No. 785
Mexicali, BCN 21060
Contact: Mr. Javier Orozco Languren, President
PHONE: 52/65/57-3070, 57-0590
Product/Service Description:
Cement clinkers

Madererias Toluca, S. A. de C. V.
Euler No. 152-401
Mexico, D.F. 11570
Contact: Mr. Jose Luis Vargas, Administrative Manager
PHONE: 525/255-0810
Product/Service Description:
Wood sawn or chipped length, sliced etc, ov6mm th

Madererias y Ferreterias Las
Blvd. Diaz Ordaz No. 189
Tijuana, B.C.N 22610
Contact: Mr. Florentino Hernandez Ramos, Director General
PHONE: 52/66/86-8615
Product/Service Description:
Coniferous wood in the rough, not treated

Mak Electronics, S.A. de C.V.
Republica del Salvador No. 26 A
Mexico, D.F. 06070
Contact: Mr. Miguel Moscona Yossifova, Director General
PHONE: 525/512-2152, 510-3322
Product/Service Description:
Electrical apparatus for switching etc, nov 1000 v

Manuel E. Delgado B. y Corp.
Calle 68 No. 450-A x 49 y 51
Merida, YUC
Contact: Mr. Manuel Delgado Barbosa, Director
PHONE: 52/28-83-80 or 14-67-65
Product/Service Description:
Office and desk equip a prts, of base metal

Manufacturera Burst, S.A. de C. V.
Periferico Sur No. 5474
Mexico, D.F. 04710
Contact: Mr. Jaime Barajas Oliver, General Director
PHONE: 525/606-3224 606-6434
Product/Service Description:
Video discs, recorded

Manufacturera Century, S.A. de C.V.
Felix Parra No. 20
Mexico, D.F. 03900
Contact: Mr. Francisco Briseno R., General Director
PHONE: 525/563-2611/2616
Product/Service Description:
Air compressors,rotary,stationary,exceeding 74.6k

Manufacturera Waco, S.A. de C.V.
Diaz Miron No. 623
Leon, GTO 37000
Contact: Mr. Juan Antonio Rios Cardona, Purchasing Director
PHONE: 52/47/13-6424
Product/Service Description:
Boots rub plast no stitch ov ankle nov knee nesoi

Maquiladora de Resortes Industria-
Sur 133 No. 2514
Mexico, D.F. 08730
Contact: Mr. Isaac Sanchez, General Director
PHONE: 525/657-2454
Product/Service Description:
Springs & leaves for springs, iron or steel

Maquinaria Electrica Pisa
Av. Rio Consulado No. 205
Mexico, D.F. 02980
Contact: Ing. Armando Avila Garcia, General Manager
PHONE: 525/715-4093
Product/Service Description:
Transformers, nesoi, unrated

Maquinaria Industrial para la
Xavier Sorondo No. 60-Interior 3
Mexico, D.F. 03530
Contact: Mr. Donat Jud Schudel, General Manager
PHONE: 525/271-5882/277-0270
Product/Service Description:
Grinding balls a sim artic for mills, cst, ios nes

Maquinaria Panamericana,
Autopista Mexico-Queretaro No. 3065
Tlanepantla, MEX. 54040
Contact: ING. HUGO PEREZ GONZALEZ, GENERAL DIRECTOR
PHONE: 525/390-6900
Product/Service Description:
Cab chassis, dumpers designed for off-highway use

Maquinaria para Moliendas y
Plutarco Elias Calles No. 290
Mexico, D.F. 08620
Contact: Mr. Carlos Bejem, Director General
PHONE: 525/657-9133
Product/Service Description:
Grinding balls a sim artic for mills, cst, ios nes

Maquinaria y Caminos
Lazaro Cardenas Sur No. 580
Mexico, D.F 03400
Contact: Sales & Marketing, ,
PHONE: 525/590-8411,590-9522
Product/Service Description:
Stoves, ranges etc, nonel domest &
pts, ir & steel

**Maquinas, Accesorios y
Herramientas**
Cacamatzin No. 64-B y C
Mexico, D.F. 11320
Contact: Ing. Ramon Herrera,
General Manager
PHONE: 525/396-2242, 396-1843
Product/Service Description:
Electro-discharge machine tools
for removing matl

**Marlo Y Asociados, S.A. de
C.V.**
Havre No. 67-405
Mexico, D.F. 06600
Contact: Ing. Jose Bernardo Lopez,
Director
PHONE: 525/511-9204
Product/Service Description:
Tanks

Marve Industrial, S. A. de
Prado de Pirules No. 3, Manzana
Mexico, D. F. 57179
Contact: Ing. Arturo Velasco,
PHONE: 525/766-7068
Product/Service Description:
Belting & belts for
machinery,nesoi

McGean Roco de Mexico,
Bolivar No. 752
Mexico, D.F. 03400
Contact: Mrs. Andrea Pastrana,
PHONE: 525/590-6225
Product/Service Description:
Electroplating, electrophoresis

Medi-Lab, S.A. DE C.V.
Alvaro Obregon No. 190
Mexico, D.F. 06700
Contact: Mr. Salvador Escamilla,
PHONE: 525/584-5800, 584-2089
Product/Service Description:
Medical, surgical, dental or vet

Mel de Mexico, S.A. de C.V.
Lago Texcoco No. 189
Mexico, D.F. 11320
Contact: Mr Victor Cortez, General
Manager
PHONE: 525/260-2310
Product/Service Description:
Laboratory ware

Mereco Internacional, S.A.
Puebla No. 260, Piso 5
Mexico, D.F. 06700
Contact: Lic. Rene Enriques
Valenzuela, Director General
PHONE: 525/514-6053
Product/Service Description:
Cleaning preparations

**Metales, Materiales y
Servicios**
Av. San Jeronimo No. 630-Local
13-C
Mexico, D. F. 10110
Contact: Sr. Luis Pellat Reynaud,
General Manager
PHONE: 525/683-8612
Product/Service Description:
Aluminum and articles thereof

Metalmaq, S.A. de C.V.
Miguel de Mendoza No. 35
Mexico, D.F. 01600
Contact: Mr. Werner Klamroth,
General Manager
PHONE: 525/593-5122
Product/Service Description:
Dies drw o extr mtl a pts thrf

**Metrologia Mexicana, S.A.
de C.V.**
Roberto Gayol No. 21
Mexico, D.F. 031000
Contact: Ing. Pedro Ramirez
Jurado, General Manager
PHONE: 525/575-6133, 575-0764
Product/Service Description:
Instruments for measuring length,

Mex, S.A. de C. V.
Avila Camacho No. 2292
Guadalajara, JAL. 44210
Contact: Mr. Sergio Malo, Gerente
PHONE: 52/623-6602
Product/Service Description:
Communications satellites

**Mexican Printing Supply,
S.A.**
Calz. de Tlalpan No. 393
Mexico, D.F. 03400
Contact: Mr. Roberto Garcia,
General Manager
PHONE: 525/519-0760
Product/Service Description:
Stainless steel in ingots or other
primary forms

**Mexicana de Climas, S.A.
de C.V.**
Calle 60 No. 280
Merida, YUC 97127
Contact: Mr. Juan Habib Abimeri,
General Director
PHONE: 52/99/20-0500, 20-0505
Product/Service Description:
Air conditioning mach etc incl
refrig unit etc

**Mexicana de
Electromecanicos, S.A.**
Washington No. 55
Guadalajara, JAL 44440
Contact: Mr. Jacobo Shemaria,
Director General
PHONE: 523/663-7777
Product/Service Description:
Games, coin-or token-operated,
nesoi

**Mexico Limpio, S.A. de
C.V.**
Circuito Cientificos No. 21
Naucalpan, MEX 53100
Contact: Lic. Arturo Carrillo
Vergara, Director General
PHONE: 525/562-4923, 572-5049
Product/Service Description:
Parts & access for motor vehicles
(head 8701-8705)

**Mezquite Maderas
Procesadas, S. A.**
Czada. Luis Echeverria No. 916
Mexicali, B.C.N 21250
Contact: Ing. Alejandro Trevino
Garza, General Director
PHONE: 52/65/65-0713
Product/Service Description:
Packing cases etc of wood; pallets
etc of wood

**Micor de Mexico, S.A. de
C.V.**
Ave. Revolucion No. 1606
Chihuahua, CHIH. 31170
Contact: Lic. Jorge Abraham
Ramos, Administrative Manager
PHONE: 52/14/16-6677
Product/Service Description:
Bandsaw blades exc mtl ctting,
parts, base metal

**Micro Abrasivos, S.A. de
C.V.**
Calle 4 No. 23
Ecatepec, EDMEX 55340
Contact: Lic. Guillermo Bolanos
Animas, General Manager
PHONE: 525/755-4895
Product/Service Description:
Mac tools fr finish mtl using
abrasives,nesoi,used

Micro Azteca, S.A. de C.V.
Viaducto Rio Piedad No. 256-4
Mexico, D.F. 06850
Contact: Mr. Andres Gonzalez,
Sales Manager
PHONE: 525/519-0727, 530-4896
Product/Service Description:
Automatic data process machines;
magn reader etc

**Microfilmacion y
Comunicaciones,**
San Pedro No. 109 Norte
Garza Garcia, N.L. 66220
Contact: Ing. Fernando Vazquez,
Director Purchasing
PHONE: 52/83/35-4832
Product/Service Description:
Microfilm readers not capable of
producing copies

**Minco Mexicana, S.A. de
C. V.**
Homero No. 1425-1005
Mexico, D.F. 11510
Contact: Mr. Patricio Mc Grath,
Sales Director
PHONE: 525/395-5555
Product/Service Description:
Pumps for liquids, nesoi

Moldeados Plasticos, S.A. de C.V.
Javier Rojo Gomez No. 278
Mexico, D.F. 09300
Contact: Mr. Jorge Senkel,
Director General
PHONE: 525/686-2022, 686-1998
Product/Service Description:
Molds for rbr/plast, injection/
compression type

Molduras y Marcos Pedroza,
Km. 16.5 Carr. a Tecate No. 102-B
Tijuana, B.C.
Contact: Mr. Jorge Ignacio Gallego
Salas, President
PHONE: 52/66/89-4353, 89-4106
Product/Service Description:
Wooden frames paintings,
photographs, mirrors, etc

Motores McMillan, S.A. de C.V.
Apartado Postal No. 298
Naucalpan, MEX. 54500
Contact: Ing. Enrique Merikanskas
B., Gerente General
PHONE: 525/572-4030, 572-4122
Product/Service Description:
Household art & pts, ir & st; ir or
steel wool etc

Motores Y Refacciones Piramide
Calzada de Guadalupe No. 4
Cuautitlan Izcalli, MEX 54700
Contact: Mr. Hugo Velez, Director
General
PHONE: 525/872-4480, 872-2545
Product/Service Description:
Engines and motors nesoi, and
parts thereof

Multiform, S.A.
Calle Sta. Cruz No. 5
Zapotitlan, EDMEX 13210
Contact: Ing. Oscar Braunstein,
General Director
PHONE: 525/845-0244
Product/Service Description:
Lubricating preps, antirust treating

Multiservicio de Mantenimiento
Sur 79 No. 4226
Mexico, D.F. 06850
Contact: Mr. Arturo Alvarez,
PHONE: 525/530-1893/5386246
Product/Service Description:
Electromechanical hand tool parts

Murad Asesores, S.A.
Jose Marti No. 296
Mexico, D.F. 11800
Contact: Mr. Manuel Murad
Robles, General Director
PHONE: 525/272-8866,272-8739
Product/Service Description:
Administration of Environmental
Quality & Housing Programs

Muz-Her, S.A. de C.V.
Planicie No. 25
Mexico, D.F. 14010
Contact: Mr. Rodolfo Muzquiz,
General Manager
PHONE: 525/665-0235
Product/Service Description:
Machine tools for drilling, boring,
milling etc

Navarifrut, S.A. de C.V.
Navafrut, S.A. de C.V.
Mexico, D.F. 09040
Contact: Ms. Claudia P. Nava
Ricano, General Manager
PHONE: 52/65/526-100
Product/Service Description:
Bananas and plantains, fresh or
dried

Negociaciones Internacionales
Lago Rasna No. 25 4o
Mexico, D.F. 11320
PHONE: 525/207-9860 208-2355
Product/Service Description:
Air conditioning machines (temp
& hum change), pts

Neko Technologies, S.A.
Gaviotas No. 54
Mexico, D.F. 07460
Contact: Mr. Jose Cervera,
PHONE: 525/577-6518
Product/Service Description:
Air conditioning machines (temp
& hum change), pts

Neo-Tech International, S.A. de C.V
B. Simonin Esq. J. Alvarez
Coatzacoalcos, VER. 96518
Contact: Ing. Mario Machaen
Zamora, General Manager
PHONE: 52/921/5-06-23
Product/Service Description:
Tubes, pipes etc, seamless nesoi, ir
nesoi & steel

Nicro, S.A. de C.V.
Pirul No. 33
Tlalnepantla, MEX 54080
Contact: Mr. Pablo Pages Lopez
PHONE: 525/361-1188, 361-0514
Product/Service Description:
Wire of iron & nonalloy steel

Nitro Mex, S. A. de C. V.
Manuel Villalongin No. 74
Mexico, D.F. 06500
Contact: Ing. Julian Fernandez
Castello, General Manager
PHONE: 525/566-04-26
Product/Service Description:
Fertilizers contain nitrates and
phosphates

Novias Tete, S.A.
Insurgentes Sur No. 428-Local A
Mexico, D.F. 06760
Contact: Mrs. Esther Santiago de
D., General Manager and Owner
PHONE: 525/564-4513
Product/Service Description:
Apparel & Accessory Stores

Novidea Sistemas Computacionales,
Rio Ebro No. 80
Mexico, D.F. 06500
Contact: Ing. Raul Ochoa
PHONE: 525/514-0204
Product/Service Description:
Records, tapes & other recorded
sound media etc

Nueva Editorial Interamericana
Cedro No. 512
Mexico, D.F. 06450
Contact: Mr. Rafael Sainz,
PHONE: 525/541-3155
Product/Service Description:
Textbooks

Nueva Papelera Famer Plus, S.A. de
Independencia No. 940
San Luis Potosi, SLP 78000
Contact: Mr. Jose Luis Martinez
Delgado, General Manager
PHONE: 52/48/12-2429, 14-0483
Product/Service Description:
Paper & paperboard & articles (inc
papr pulp artl)

Nuremex, S.A. de C.V.
Pastores No.3 - G
Mexico, D.F. 09820
Contact: Mr. Maximino Ruiz,
General Manager
PHONE: 525/670-0106
Product/Service Description:
Pipes etc nesoi, riveted etc, of iron
or steel

Nutrimentos del Sureste, S.A de C.V
Av. Jose Ma. Castro Tejero 417
Merida, YUC 97288
Contact: Mr. Adolfo Peniche
Lopez, General Director
PHONE: 52/99/46-0791
Product/Service Description:
Food industry residues & waste;
prep animal feed

Nutrisa, S.A. De C.V.
Periferico Sur No. 5482
Mexico, D.F. 04700
Contact: Ms. Ma. Lourdes Renero
Alvarez, Commercial Director
PHONE: 525/665-5802
Product/Service Description:
Natural sponges of animal origin

Ofinobel, S.A. de C.V.
Citlaltepetl No. 66 esq. Nvo. Leon
Mexico, D.F. 06170
Contact: C.P. Rolando Rodriguez
PHONE: 525/286-5412
Product/Service Description:
Wooden furniture

Olaris, S.A. de C.V.
Av. Patriotismo No. 371
Mexico, D.F. 03800
Contact: MR. Roland Zobrist,
PHONE: 525/271-6917
Product/Service Description:
Printing

Omci, S.A de C. V.
Valladolid No. 19 Col. Roma
Mexico, D.F. 06700
Contact: Mr. Ricardo Villalobos,
Marketing Manager
PHONE: 525/207-3721
Product/Service Description:
Tv cam tube,image convert &
intensifiers

Opecsa, S.A.
Cerrada de Altata No. 14
Mexico, D.F. 06100
Contact: Lic. Rafael Ricardez,
General Manager
PHONE: 525/516-1477
Product/Service Description:
Electronic key telephone systems

Organizacion Agor, S.A.
Av. Insurgentes Sur No. 1748-502
Mexico, D.F. 01030
Contact: Mr. Eduardo Oropeza
Suarez, Director
PHONE: 525/663-5232
Product/Service Description:
Prep or pres fish; caviar & caviar
substitutes

**Organizacion Contable
Mexicana S.A.**
Barras No. 30
Mexico, D.F. 07300
Contact: C.P. Juan Jose Irezabal,
PHONE: 525/754-7815
Product/Service Description:
Records, tapes & other recorded

**Organizacion de Ventas
Industriales**
Local 12, Lote 1, Distrito C-44 a
Cuautitlan Izcalli, EDOME 54700
Contact: Mr. Jorge Garcia Corral
PHONE: 525/881-1357
Product/Service Description:
Winches and capstans powered by
electric motors

Oxigeno de Veracruz
Esteban Morales No. 1770-A
Veracruz, VER 91700
Contact: Mr. Domingo Montalvo
Zarrabal, Director and Owner
PHONE: 52/29/34-5524
Product/Service Description:
Oxygen

PEMEX Refinacion
Marina Nacional No. 329 Edif. B-
2
Mexico, D.F. 11311
Contact: Ing. Jaime Azuara, Chief
Industrial Refinery Unit
PHONE: 525/250-5677
Product/Service Description:
Greases, lubricating, with or w out
additives

**Panamericana Abarrotera,
S.A. de**
Lago Athabaska No. 64-C
Mexico, D.F. 11290
Contact: Mr. Carmona Edmundo,
Sales Manager
PHONE: 525/399-6769
Product/Service Description:
Food preparations flour, starch,
dairy etc, nesoi

**Partes de Colision
Automotriz**
Ave. Sur 12 No. 428
Mexico, D.F. 08500
Contact: Mr. Roberto Velazquez
Rivera, Production Manager
PHONE: 525/763-5480
Product/Service Description:
Parts & access for motor vehicles
(head 8701-8705)

**Partes para Moldes DME,
S.A. de C.V**
Ave. Uno - Lote 10-A
Tultitlan, EDOME 54900
Contact: Lic. Pablo Rico, Sales
Manager
PHONE: 525/872-4791, 872-0332
Product/Service Description:
Molds for rbr/plast, injection/
compression type

**Patrones de Calibracion,
S.A.**
Jose Ma. Rico 212-604, B
Mexico, D.F. 03100
Contact: Ing. Javier Martinez
Ocampo, General Manager
PHONE: 52/73/16-0199, 13-
3659
Product/Service Description:
Ind prep,manuf food,drink exc
ext,prep anim,veg ol

Pavel de Mexico, S.A. de
Sierra Mojada No. 415
Mexico, D.F. 11000
Contact: Lic. Federico Velez
Alvarez, Director General
PHONE: 525/540-5442, 282-4593
Product/Service Description:
Perfume oil blends, prod use
finished perfume base

**Peleteria Continental, S.A.
de C.V.**
Av. Pino Suarez No. 17
Mexico, D.F. 06060
Contact: Mr. Juan Bernardi,
General Manager
PHONE: 525/510-0749, 510-3569
Product/Service Description:
Buckles and buckle clasps a parts,
base metal

**Petroleo Quimica, S.A. de
C.V.**
America No. 100
Mexico, D.F. 04040
Contact: Ing. Ismael Palomares,
General Director
PHONE: 525/544-7846
Product/Service Description:
Supported catalysts, nesoi

Pixart, S.A. de C.V.
Lamartine No. 160-1
Mexico, D.F. 11570
Contact: Lic. Jaime Varon,
Director General
PHONE: 525/531-1901
Product/Service Description:
Video recording or playing
equip,exc tape

**Plasticos Automotrices
Dina,**
Margaritas No. 433, Piso No. 1
Mexico, D.F. 01050
Contact: Ing. Jose Maria Gonzalez,
Marketing Sales Manager
PHONE: 525/325-0927
Product/Service Description:
Plastics and articles thereof

**Plasticos Geminis, S.A. de
C.V.**
Calle seis No. 194
Mexico, D.F. 08100
Contact: Mr. Antonio Rodriguez
Hernandez, Director General
PHONE: 525/758-5358
Product/Service Description:
Polyethylene having a spec gravity
of 0.94 or more

**Plasticos Laminados
Joremi**
Benito Juarez No. 4
Tlalnepantla, EDMEX 54040
Contact: Mr. Jorge Reyes Milan,
General Manager
PHONE: 525/361-6168,397-5431
Product/Service Description:
Automotive Parts & Supplies

**Plasticos Riomar, S. A. de
C. V.**
Primavera No. 25
Mexico, D. F. 53070
Contact: Ing. Raul del Rio,
Director General
PHONE: 525/576-7768 373-8646
Product/Service Description:
Molds for rbr/plast, injection/
compression type

Plasticos Romay, S.A.
San Lorenzo No. 262
Mexico, D.F. 03200
Contact: Mr. Rodolfo May,
Director General
PHONE: 525/575-4711
Product/Service Description:
Molds f rubber or plastics exc
inject or compressn

**Polisulfuros de Mexico,
S.A. de C.V**
Montes Urales No. 355-B
Mexico, D.F. 11000
Contact: Ing. Jorge Diaz Rivera,
PHONE: 525/202-2506
Product/Service Description:
Fertilizers, nesoi

Potosina de Bronces, S.A. de C.V.
Juan del Jarro No. 105-A
San Luis Potosi, SLP 78020
Contact: Mr. Alfonso Tellez Gallardo, Director
PHONE: 52/48/14-76-11
Product/Service Description:
Casting mach used in metallurgy or metal foundries

Precimaq, S.A. de C.V.
Av. de los Maestros No. 430
Mexico, D.F. 02800
Contact: MR ERIC GABBERT,
PHONE: 525/355-6946
Product/Service Description:
Mach, nesoi, f moldg or formg rubber or plastics

Precision Control de Mexico, S.A.
Plan de San Luis No. 400-398
Mexico, D.F. 02800
Contact: Mr. Alejandro Pardo,
PHONE: 525/556-4616/4515
Product/Service Description:
Air compressors,rotary, stationary,exceeding 74.6k

Prefabricados E Ingenieria
Chilapa 93
Mexico, D.F. 014000
Contact: Mr. Francisco Reyes,
PHONE: 525/655-3124
Product/Service Description:
Prefabricated buildings

Prendas Tejidas de Puebla,
5 de Mayo No. 207
Puebla, PUE. 72000
Contact: Sr. Raul Maldonado Rossano, General Manager
PHONE: 52/22/32-9322, 32-9326
Product/Service Description:
Women's or girls' blouses, shirts

Prevision Y Planeacion Multiple,
Blvd. A. L. Mateos No. 307 Ote.
Leon, GTO. 37000
Contact: Lic. Genaro Escobar V
PHONE: 52/47/145728
Product/Service Description:
Administration of Environmental Quality Programs

Procesa Ingenieria y Ecologia,
Rancho Seco No. 127
Mexico, D.F. 04930
Contact: Lic. Arturo Davila Villareal, General Director
PHONE: 525/671-6813
Product/Service Description:
Air & Water Resource & Solid Waste Management

Procesadora y Comercializadora,
Calle 36 C No. 3
Cd. del Carmen, CAMP 24139
Contact: Mr. Manuel Rivera Zamora, General Manager
PHONE: 52/938/218-75
Product/Service Description:
Crabmeat, prepared or preserved, nesoi

Produccion Mecanica, S. A.
Calle San Francisco #10-Bis Local 1
Naucalpan, MEX. 53560
Contact: Mr. Mario Lizarraga Peon, General Manager
PHONE: 525/358-2979, 576-4636
Product/Service Description:
Metals products; machinery & transport equipment

Productos Deshidratados de Mexico,
Lopez Rayon y 10 de Mayo, Edif.
Los Mochis, SIN. 81220
Contact: Mr. Idelfonso Salido, Director General
PHONE: 52/681/2-4080, 2-4049
Product/Service Description:
Dried vegetables, whole, cut etc., no added prep

Productos Donelli S.A de C.V.
Escape No. 3
Mexico, MX 53370
Contact: Mr. Eduardo Kleyff, Director General
PHONE: 525/576-5899/358-8797
Product/Service Description:
Pantyhose, socks & other hosiery, knit or crochet

Productos Especializados de Acero,
Poniente 134 No. 854
Mexico, D.F. 02300
Contact: Ing. Alejandro Reyes, Purchasing Manager
PHONE: 525/567-6011/7022
Product/Service Description:
Cast articles nesoi, of iron or steel

Productos Floraphil, S.A. de C.V
Fco I. Madero No.7
Tlanepantla, EDOME 54090
Contact: Mr. Moises Hernandez Olguin, Owner
PHONE: 525/565-4055
Product/Service Description:
Fertilizers

Productos Fragante, S.A. de C.V.
Calle 6, No. 72
Mexico, D.F. 08100
Contact: Mr. Carlos Lopez Suarez, Director General
PHONE: 525/758-2379/2499
Product/Service Description:
Wov fabric, synth staple fib nu 85% synth st fiber

Productos Industriales de
Oriente 237 C No. 25-A
Mexico, D.F. 08500
Contact: Ing. Luis Ramirez, General Manager
PHONE: 525/558-9880, 758-8253
Product/Service Description:
Injection type molds for rubber or plastics, nesoi

Productos Industrializados del
Canal Lateral 18Km. 911.6 Via FFCC
Los Mochis, SIN 81200
Contact: Mr. Eduardo Correra Quintero, General Director
PHONE: 52/681/20-664, 52-626
Product/Service Description:
Tomato paste

Productos Internacionales Tanaka
Av. Cuauhtemoc No. 740
Mexico, D.F. 03020
Contact: Mr. Jorge Terrazas, Purchasing Manager
PHONE: 525/523-3058
Product/Service Description:
Automotive Parts & Supplies

Productos Medicos en General,
Guillermo Barroso No. 11
Tlalnepantla, EDM 54080
Contact: Ing. Albert Pla Andreu, General Manager
PHONE: 525/394-2854, 394-5411
Product/Service Description:
Pharmaceutical products

Productos Nacobre, S.A.
Via Gustavo Baz No. 4874
Tlalnepantla, MEX 54110
Contact: Mr. Patricio Slim, Director
PHONE: 525/310-0706, 311-1745
Product/Service Description:
Alum plt sht strp rec o sqr aly nt cl ov 6.3mm thk

Productos Neumaticos, S.A.
Calz. La Naranja No. 129
Mexico, D.F. 53370
Contact: Mr. Jorge Rojas, General
PHONE: 525/358-2199
Product/Service Description:
Filters & parts & accessories for instr & appratus

Productos Quimicos Industriales
Carretera Central Km. 422.6
S.L.P., SLP 78090
Contact: Mr. Armando De la Parra, Director General
Product/Service Description:
Starches; inulin

Productos Quimicos Servis,
Guillermo Prieto No. 106
Mexico, D.F. 13300
Contact: Lic. Roberto Camino G.,
PHONE: 525/841-4154,
Product/Service Description:
Adhesives based on rubber or plastics nesoi

Productos Texaco, S.A. de C.V. y o
Insurgentes Sur No. 1822
Mexico, D.F. 01030
Contact: Mr. Thomas Hauk,
Director General
PHONE: 525/227-5300
Product/Service Description:
Greases, lubricating, with or w out additives

Productos Valery, S.A. de C.V.
Diego de Osorio No. 155 - P.H.
Mexico, D.F. 11000
Contact: Mr. Peter Kuntz, Director General
PHONE: 525/520-5993
Product/Service Description:
Fruit nesoi, fresh

Productos del Convento, S.A. de
Avenida 5 No. 253
Mexico, D.F. 09070
Contact: Lic. Juan Rodriguez Escamilla, General Manager
PHONE: 525/581-2433/581-0477
Product/Service Description:
Chocolate & other food products containing cocoa

Productps de Marmol Puente, S.A.
Uxmal No. 759
Mexico, D.F. 03650
Contact: Ing. Ramon Puente,
Production Manager
PHONE: 525/605-7307,601-0191
Product/Service Description:
Suspension shock absorbers for motor vehicles

Profesionales en Energia Enpro,
Tehuantepec No. 475-P.B.
Mexico, D.F. 11500
Contact: Ing. Manuel de Diego M.,
Technical Director
PHONE: 525/574-7982, 574-7905
Product/Service Description:
Electrical apparatus for switching etc, nov 1000 v

Promani, S.A. de C.V.
Viveros del Rocio No. 1-C
Tlalnepantla, EDOME 54080
Contact: C.P. Ramon Jurado,
General Manager
PHONE: 525//98-5868
Product/Service Description:
Waterproof footwear rubber/plastic covers the knee

Promocion Y Servicios Deportivos
Insurgentes Sur No. 3756
Mexico, D.F. 14060
Contact: Arq. Halim Matouk,
General Manager
PHONE: 525/606-6016
Product/Service Description:
Camping goods nesoi, of textile materials nesoi

Promociones y Construcciones
Washington Ote. 1410
Monterrey, NL 64000
Contact: Lic. Jorge de la Garza,
Director General
PHONE: 52/83/43-8900, 59-8100
Product/Service Description:
Clays, other

Promotora Comercial Acuario, S. A.
Rio Culiacan No. 980 y Czada.
Inde-
Mexicali, B.C.N 21270
Contact: Mr. Jose Luis Monge Amezcua, General Director
PHONE: 52/65/66-8600
Product/Service Description:
Railway, tramway sleepers, wood, not impregnated

Promotora Nacional de Eventos
Gabriel Mancera No. 728-A
Mexico, D.F. 03100
Contact: Lic. Salvador Jimenez,
Director General
PHONE: 525/682-7359/7968/8764
Product/Service Description:
Advertising

Promotora de Equipos y Soldaduras,
Totomoxco No. 3, esq. Camarones
Mexico, D.F. 02050
Contact: Ing. Joaquin Soto,
General Manager
PHONE: 525/352-8715/352-2535
Product/Service Description:
Western red alder sawn lengthwise over 6mm, rough

Protecciones Electricas, S.A. de CV
Blvd. Avila Camacho No. 92-2
Naucalpan, EDOME 53500
Contact: Ing. Wilfrido Gonzalez B., General Manager
PHONE: 525/358-4847, 358-1871
Product/Service Description:
Primary cells & batteries, parts

Protexa, S.A. DE C.V.
Electron No. 16
Naucalpan, EDM 53370
Contact: Mr. Enrique Gonzalez Del Valle, Marketing Manager
PHONE: 525/300-0652, 300-6880
Product/Service Description:
Silicones, in primary forms

Proveacero y Servicio, S. A.
25 de Febrero de 1861 Esq. Paso de
Mexico, D. F. 09310
Contact: C.P. Gilberto Nares Rodriguez, General Manager
PHONE: 525/694-0167, 600-5823
Product/Service Description:
Angles, shapes & sections of iron & nonalloy steel

Proveedora Agricola e Industrial
General Cano 140 y 142
Mexico, D. F. 11850
Contact: Ing. Emilio Chavez Guzman, Director General
PHONE: 525/515-0813, 516-3168
Product/Service Description:
Seeds, fruits and spores used for sowing,

Proveedora Azucarera, S.A. de C.V.
Uxmal No. 403
Mexico, D.F. 03020
Contact: Ing. Manuel Zulbaran,
Manager
PHONE: 525/687-5473687-5044
Product/Service Description:
Engines and motors nesoi, and parts thereof

Proveedora Industrial Marvill
Gral. F. Murguia No. 38
Mexico, D.F. 02400
Contact: Mr. Marcos Villeda S.,
Purchasing Manager
PHONE: 525/352-0670, 352-2282
Product/Service Description:
Adhesive tape not over 20 cm wide

Proveedora Solfer, S.A. de C.V.
Poniente 116 No. 243
Mexico, D.F. 07370
Contact: Mr Robertino Ferrara,
General Manager
PHONE: 525/537-5159
Product/Service Description:
Cleaning preparations

Proveedora de Alimentos Avepecuario
Calle 49 No. 488-A
Merida, YUC. 97000
Contact: Mr. Luis Medina Duarte,
President
PHONE: 52/99/28-2471, 28-2523
Product/Service Description:
Preparations used in animal feeding

Proveedora de Papel, S.A. de C. V.
Dr. Andrade No. 84
Mexico, D.F. 06720
Contact: Lic. Jose Sanchez Lizardi,
Director General
PHONE: 525/761-6010, 761-6005
Product/Service Description:
Paper & paperbd coated, etc

Proveedora del Hogar, S.A. de C.V.
Cerro de la Silla 815
Monterrey, N.L.
Contact: Mr. Fernando Jacobo Gomez, Commercial Manager
PHONE: 52/65/61-7305
Product/Service Description:
Tableware & other household articles etc, plastics

Proveg, S.A. de C.V.
Blvd Lopez Mateos No. 160
Mexico, D.F. 01180
Contact: Lic. Juan Antonio Vega Perez, General Manager
PHONE: 525/516-0863, 516-0864
Product/Service Description:
Stoves, ranges etc, nonel domest

Proyectos Luminicos y
Via Adolfo Lopez Mateos No. 72
Naucalpan, MEX. 53240
Contact: Ing. Sergio Garcia Anaya, Director General
PHONE: 525/360-5247, 560-9136
Product/Service Description:
Electric lamps and lighting fittings, nesoi

Puerta Segura, S.A. de C.V.
Parque Lira No. 79-100
Mexico, D.F. 11750
Contact: Ing. Ing. Carlos Martinez
PHONE: 525/516-1073,272-4590
Product/Service Description:
Doors and their frames and thresholds, of wood

Purificaciones Tecnologicas, S.A.
Calle Estrella No. 4, Desp 201-B
Mexico, D.F. 09000
PHONE: 525/685-3914, 685-5283
Product/Service Description:
Filter/purify machine & apparatus for liquid nesoi

Purina S.A. DE C.V.
Paseo de la Reforma No. 295 P
Mexico, D.F. 06500
Contact: Mr. Ward Polk Warren,
Product/Service Description:
Food industry residues & waste

Pyrolac S.A. de C.V.
Vainilla No. 186
Mexico, D.F. 08400
Contact: Ing. Enrique Matin Soto, Director General
PHONE: 525/650-5089, 650-2513
Product/Service Description:
Ink, printing, writing, drawing etc, concen or not

Quimica Omega S.A. de C.V.
Jose Ma. Morelos No. 70-B
Naucalapan, EMEX 53489
Contact: Mr. Javier Guerra, SHAREOWNER
PHONE: 525/300-7363
Product/Service Description:
Air & Water Resource & Solid Waste Management

R.R. Refrigeracion, S. A. de C. V.
Via Gustavo Baz 393
Naucalpan, EMEX 53160
Contact: Ing. Arturo Ruiz C., President
PHONE: 525/393-3422, 393-9065
Product/Service Description:
Refrigerators, freezers etc; heat pumps nesoi, pts

Radio Surtidora, S.A.
Av. Uruguay No. 25
Mexico, D.F. 06000
Contact: Ing. Alejandro Margules, General Manager
PHONE: 525/521-3954 525/521-7166
Product/Service Description:
Oscilloscopes, spectrum analyzers etc, parts etc

Ramso Comercial, S.A. de C.V.
Insurgentes Norte No. 300
Mexico, D.F. 06400
Contact: Mr. Ramon Sobero San Martin, Director
PHONE: 525/541-0911, 547-4301
Product/Service Description:
Digital elec scales, wght cap

Reactores Electronicos Mexicanos
Santo Domingo No. 42
Mexico, D.F. 02460
Contact: Mr. Guido Arena, Sole Administrator
PHONE: 525/561-8823
Product/Service Description:
Electronic integrated circuits & microassembl, pts

Rebin, S. A. de C. V.
Ave. Chapultepec No. 246-103-B
Mexico, D. F. 06700
Contact: Ing. Guillermo Catalan Garcia, Sole Administrator
PHONE: 525/207-3964
Product/Service Description:
Electric motors, dc > 74.6 w but < 746 w

Recubrimientos Electroliticos
Albeniz No. 170
Mexico, D.F. 07870
Contact: Lic. Augusto Muriel de la R., General Manager
PHONE: 525/355-5782
Product/Service Description:
Electroplating, electrophoresis and electrolysis m

Recubrimientos Metalicos de Mexico,
Pelicano No. 229
Mexico, D.F. 07460
Contact: Ing. Carlos Cielak, Plant Manager
PHONE: 525/577-0811, 577-0001
Product/Service Description:
Electroplating, electrophoresis and

Recursos de Alta Calidad S.A. de
Homero No. 425 "A" Piso 2 - 202
Mexico, D.F., MEX 11560
Contact: Arq. Ricardo Saslavsky, Director General
PHONE: 525/255-2454
Product/Service Description:
Newspapers, journals & periodicals

Redes Via Satelite, S.A. de C.V.
Av. Mexico No. 516
Mexico, D.F. 10400
Contact: Ing. Dionisio Arras, President
PHONE: 525/568-7765
Product/Service Description:
Television antennas, nesoi

Refaccionaria Diesel Cuautitlan,
Andre Ma. Ampere No. 10
Cuautitlan Izc, EDOME 54730
Contact: Mr. Carlos Gomez Flores V, Manager Purchasing
PHONE: 525/872-35-16
Product/Service Description:
Automobiles & Other Motor Vehicles

Refaccionaria Jacobo, S.A. DE C.V.
Lago Chalco No. 107
Mexico, D.F. 11320
Contact: Ing. Abraham Gonzalez Zaragoza, Director General
PHONE: 525/396-0666, 396-4377
Product/Service Description:
Engines and motors nesoi, and parts thereof

Refacciones Carbu-Servicio, S.A. de
Dr. Jose Maria Vertiz No. 454
Mexico, D.F. 06780
Contact: Ing. Alfredo Sanchez Suarez, Director General
PHONE: 525/538-7745, 538-7045
Product/Service Description:
Fuel-injection pumps for compression-ignition engs

Refacciones Textiles Canet
Centenario No. 99
Mexico, D.F. 04100
Contact: Mr. Rafael Canet Rubi,
PHONE: 525/554-5856,554-5834
Product/Service Description:
Textile products etc for technical uses nesoi

Refacciones Y Motores, S.A.
Calle 21 No. 49
Mexico, D.F. 02600
Contact: Mr. Carlos Aviles
Iglesias, Director General
PHONE: 525/587-8355, 5874515
Product/Service Description:
Automotive Parts & Supplies

Refacciones y Servicios Latinos,
Sur 20 No. 335
Mexico, D.F. 08500
Contact: Mr. Rosendo Lima
Rodriguez, General Manager
PHONE: 525/763-5706
Product/Service Description:
Oil or fuel filters for internal combustion engine

Remosa de Mexico, S. A.
Ave. San Jose S N Esq. San Juan
Tlalnepantla, EDOME 54180
Contact: Lic. Jorge Solis Alvarez,
Director General
PHONE: 525/754-5698
Product/Service Description:
Bodies for vehicles of heading 8704

Remsa Electric Motors, S.A
Holanda No. 3
Mexico, D.F. 04210
Contact: Mr. Mario H. Gottfried
PHONE: 525/688-2059
Product/Service Description:
Other motor fuels nesoi

Reparacion de Partes Automotriz
Lago Superior No. 18
Mexico, D.F. 11410
Contact: Mr. Rafael Cruz Cortes,
PHONE: 525/399-03792
Product/Service Description:
Drive axles with differential for motor vehicles

Representaciones Agro Industriales
Ninos Heroes No. 255-Sur
Los Mochis, SIN. 81200
Contact: Ing. Jose Luis Yamini,
General Manager
PHONE: 52/681/2-70-15
Product/Service Description:
Ammonia in aqueous solution

Representaciones Comerciales de
SM6.M2 Agrupamiento 27, Depto.
1
Iztapalapa, D.F. 09200
Contact: Mr. Felipe de Jesus Lopez
Estrada, General Manager
PHONE: 525/691-5243
Product/Service Description:
Machine tools for working metal, nesoi

Representaciones Kagima, S.A.
Canela No. 189
Mexico, D.F. 08400
Contact: Mr. Carlos Garcia,
General Manager
PHONE: 525/654-3677/657-1780
Product/Service Description:
hesive tape not over 20 cm wide

Representaciones y Productos de
Republica de Panama 128
Toluca, EDOME 53130
Contact: Mr. Jose Ricardo Maccise
Yitani, General Director
PHONE: 52/72/12-8500, 12-1184
Product/Service Description:
Miscellaneous edible preparations

Repromex Ingenieros, S. A. de C.V.
Clavelinas No. 195-2
Mexico, D.F. 02800
Contact: Ing. Jose Yapur R.,
Director General
PHONE: 525/556-1749, 556-9027
Product/Service Description:
Electrical apparatus for switching etc, ov 1000 v

Reps. e Invest. medicas, S.A. de C.
Calzada de Tlalpan No. 2548
Mexico, D.F. 04460
Contact: LIC. FERNANDO
ESPINOZA ABDALA,
PRESIDENTE Y DIRECTOR
GENERAL
PHONE: 525/662-9444/0662/8718
Product/Service Description:
Medicinal & pharmaceutical products, donated

Requena, S.A. de C.V.
Orizaba No. 92
Mexico, D.F. 06700
Contact: Mr. Rolando Requena,
PHONE: 525/525-6077/207-4175
Product/Service Description:
Medical, surgical, dental or vet

Retenes y Refacciones
6 de Octubre 54-3
Mexico, D.F. 07730
Contact: Mr. Jaime Mauro Sixto,
PHONE: 525/754-0503
Product/Service Description:
Monofil, cr-sect ovimm, rods, sticks etc, plastics

Rhacor, S.A. de C.V.
Dr. Arteaga No. 39-301
Mexico, D.F. 01000
Contact: Mr. Roberto Hernandez
A., Director General
PHONE: 525/644-4782/5651
Product/Service Description:
Pressure-reducing control valves, taps, cocks, et

Rime Control Systems, S.A. de C.V.
Virginia Fabregas No. 66-A
Mexico, D.F. 06470
Contact: Ing. Armando Castaneda
Vargas, Director General
PHONE: 525/705-1430,705-2377
Product/Service Description:
Process control inst&apprts for complete systems

Rines Deportivos Luna
Rio Viaducto Piedad No. 1927
Mexico, D.F. 08420
Contact: Mr. Juan Luna Ortiz,
PHONE: 525/758-4650
Product/Service Description:
Automotive Parts & Supplies

Rines Hazama, S.A. de C.V.
Antonio Solis No. 4, c Eje Central
Mexico, D.F. 06800
Contact: Mr. Ismael Hazama Ogei,
Director General Purchases
PHONE: 525/530-1449
Product/Service Description:
Automotive Parts & Supplies

Rines R.N, S.A.
General Prim No. 71
Mexico, D.F. 03600
Contact: Mr. Jose Ramos Neri,
General Manager
PHONE: 525/382-0311
Product/Service Description:
Automotive Parts & Supplies

Rines Y Servicio Figueroa, S.A. de
Av. Ing. Eduardo Molina No. 4411
Mexico, D.F. 07890
Contact: Mr. Jaime Figueroa,
Director Purchasing
PHONE: 525/760-1682
Product/Service Description:
Automotive Parts & Supplies

Rines de Acero Kelsey Hayes, S.A.
Hidalgo, esq. Plano Regulador No.
8: Tlalnepantla, Edo de Mex, MEX
54080
Contact: Ing. Alberto de Icaza,
Commercial Director
PHONE: 525/562-4933
Product/Service Description:
Automotive Parts & Supplies

Ripett, S.A. de C.V.
Reforma No. 59
Mexico, D.F. 09880
Contact: Mr. Fernando Escobar,
Director General
PHONE: 525/695-2199,
Product/Service Description:
Floor cover & wall cover, plastics

Rocha Licea Y Compania, S.A.
San Simon No. 256
06450 Mexico, D.F. MEXICO
Contact: Lic. Carlos Licea, General
PHONE: 525/583-1136, 583-2127
Product/Service Description:
Bendng foldng etc mach for work met n nmcal contrl

Rochester Mexico, S.A.
Motolinia No. 8, Locales A, B y C
Mexico, D.F. 06000
Contact: Mr. Eliseo Espina
PHONE: 525/521-7531
Product/Service Description:
Orthopedic appl; artif body pts;

Roda Hule, S.A.
Cadaques No. 51
Mexico, D.F. 09860
Contact: Mr. Arturo Garcia Ramos,
General Manager
PHONE: 525/656-1592
Product/Service Description:
Fork-lift and works trucks, nesoi

Rodymueble S.A. de C.V.
Av. Cuauhtemoc No. 130
Mexico, D.F. 06720
Contact: Mr. Ruben Chavez,
Director General
PHONE: 525/578-6778, 578-4725
Product/Service Description:
Wooden furniture of a kind used in
offices

Rolcar, S.A. de C.V.
Fulton No. 17
Tlalnepantla, E.M.
Contact: Mr. Victor Manuel Lopez
Lopez, General Manager
PHONE: 52/49/14-1155, 11-6511
Product/Service Description:
Automotive Parts & Supplies

Romaq, S.A. de C.V.
Bosque del Castillo No. 2
Mexico, D.F. 52760
Contact: Mrs. Gloria Schultz
Contreras, General Director
PHONE: 525/589-4092 294-6752
Product/Service Description:
Air conditioning machines etc not
incl refrig unit

Roosin de Mexico, S. A.
Circuito Actores No. 141
Naucalpan, EDOME 53100
Contact: Ing. Andres Robles Pena,
General Manager
PHONE: 525/572-9315
Product/Service Description:
Chromatographs and
electrophoresis instruments

**Rotork Servo Controles de
Mexico,**
Adolfo Prieto 1149
D.F., MEX. 03100
Contact: Mr. Ing. Alejandro Flores
PHONE: 525/575-0272, 559-2959
Product/Service Description:
Lifting, handling, loading

Rouitex, S.A. de C.V.
Reforma No. 4905
Puebla, PUE 72160
Contact: Mr. Rodolfo Zeyenny,
Director
PHONE: 52/22-488156
Product/Service Description:
Automotive Parts & Supplies

Ruben Barrios Frenos, S.A.
Manuel Ma. Contreras No. 61
Mexico, D.F. 06470
Contact: Mr. Mauricio Quijano,
Service Manager
PHONE: 525/ 535-3840
Product/Service Description:
Brakes & parts,nesoi,f veh of
headng 8605 or 8606

Ruedas Y Carretillas, S.A.
Fray Servando Teresa De Mier
Esq.
Mexico, D.F. 15810
Contact: MR. Froilan Gaston
Balderabano, General Manager
PHONE: 525/768-3183
Product/Service Description:
Fork-lift and works trucks, nesoi

**Saft Nife Mexico, S.A. de
C.V.**
San Luis Tlatilco No. 25
Naucalpan, EDOME 53470
Contact: Lic. Roberto Troop
Pliego, General Director
PHONE: 525/576-2611
Product/Service Description:
Primary cells & batteries, parts

Saltex, S. A.
Lazaro Cardenas No. 12-A
Mexico, D. F. 06800
Contact: Sr. Jacques Taransaud
Zertuche, Administrator
PHONE: 525/588-3811, 588-8777
Product/Service Description:
Textile printing machinery

San Gerardo Textil, S.A.
Carr. Panamericana Km. 519
Aguascalientes, AGS 20340
Contact: Mr. Jose Ma. Barba
Gonzalez, Director General
PHONE: 52/49/16-710949
Product/Service Description:
Yarn & fine an hair, retail pk, not
un 85% wl or h

**Sanborn Hermanos, S.A. de
C.V.**
Viaducto M. Aleman No. 705
Mexico, D.F. 15850
Contact: Serafin Gonzalez C.
PHONE: 525/650-2795
Product/Service Description:
Newspapers, journals &
periodicals

**Sanford de Mexico, S.A. de
C.V.**
Norte 59 No. 834, Col.
Azcapotzalco
Mexico, D.F. 02300
Contact: Mr. Edgar Santoyo
PHONE: 525/567-0518,587-3955
Product/Service Description:
Office or school supplies of plastic

Satena, S.A. de C.V.
Avena No. 445
Mexico, D.F. 08400
Contact: Ing. Faustino Barra
Garcia, Sales Manager
PHONE: 525/657-0063/657-0174
Product/Service Description:
Tanks

Saunamex, S.A.
Poniente 122 No. 551-A
Mexico, D.F. 02300
Contact: C.P. Antonia De La Rosa,
Sales Director
PHONE: 525/567-0283
Product/Service Description:
Drying machines, nesoi

**Schrader Bellows Parker,
S.A. de**
Calle 9 No. 6
Naucalpan, E.M. 53370
Contact: Lic. Alejandro Peralta,
PHONE: 525/358-1823, 576-2411
Product/Service Description:
Valves f oleohydraulic or
pneumatic transmissions

**Secretaria De Desarrollo
Social**
Rio Elba No. 20 3er. piso
Mexico, D.F. 06500
Contact: Ing. Fulgencio Aguilar,
PHONE: 525/553-3377
Product/Service Description:
Polymers of vinyl acetate,

Sederia La Nueva, S. A.
Regina No. 32-A Piso 2
Mexico, D.F. 06080
Contact: Mr. Jaime, Cohen C.,
PHONE: 525/709-2426/2528
Product/Service Description:
Apparel, Piece Goods and Notions

Sedin, S.A. de C.V.
Oyamel MZ 2 Lote 1
Mexico, D.F. 14108
Contact: Mr. Mario Guevara,
General Director
PHONE: 525/645-9919/631-7421
Product/Service Description:
Stainless steel ingots and other
primary forms

Segall Publicidad S.R.L.
Camino a Sta. Teresa No. 13,-19
Mexico, D.F. 06500
Contact: Arq. Sergio Gallardo
Ramos, General Director
PHONE: 525/652-5569, 652-1703
Product/Service Description:
Date sealing or numbering
stamps,etc for hand oper

Selbach y Asociados, S.A.
Irapuato No. 12
Mexico, D.F. 06170
Contact: Mr. Eduardo Selbach,
PHONE: 525/515-4036,-7557,
Product/Service Description:
Administration of Environmental
Quality & Housing Programs

Servi Aluminio, S.A.
Av. Revolucion No. 610
Mexico, D.F. 03800
Contact: Lic. Ricardo Bravo,
PHONE: 525/598-8244,598-8563
Product/Service Description:
Architectural and ornamental
work, iron or steel

Servicam, S.A.
Zacatecas No. 174
Mexico, D.F. 06700
Contact: Mr. Adolfo Hidalgo
PHONE: 525/564-0341, 584-1661
Product/Service Description:
Orthopedic appl; artif body pts;

Servicio Automotriz Roque
Donizetti No. 204
Mexico, D.F. 07870
Contact: Mr. Roque Hernandez
Castro, Director General
PHONE: 525/537-5757
Product/Service Description:
Automotive Parts & Supplies

Servicio Polimodal de Audio Video y
Martires Irlandeses No. 136-1 y 2
Mexico, D.F. 04120
Contact: Mr. Ezequiel Escartin
Morales, General Manager
PHONE: 525/689-0059/689-4427
Product/Service Description:
Advertising

Servicio de Medicion y Control,
Revillagigedo No. 34-2 Piso
Mexico, D. F. 06050
Contact: Mrs. Maria Elena de
Lopez Gamez, Purchasing
Product/Service Description:
Instruments for measuring length,

Servicios Industriales y Proyectos,
Blvd. Santa Cruz No. 155
Naucalpan de Juarez, MEX 53140
Contact: Mr. Salvador Aburto
Gonzalez, General Manager
PHONE: 525/560-14-43
Product/Service Description:
Process control inst&apprts for
complete systems

Servicios Topograficos para
Romero # 54
Mexico, D.F. 03610
Contact: Ing. Aurelio Nez
PHONE: 525/579-74-48
Product/Service Description:
Photogrammetrical surveying
instruments & applnces

Servicios Y Refacciones
Prol. Emperadores No. 235
Mexico, D.F. 03310
Contact: Mr. Abel Clemente
PHONE: 525/605-93-66
Product/Service Description:
Water filtering or purifying

Servicios de Ingenieria, S.A.
Zempoala No. 492-Int. 2
Mexico, D.F. 03600
Contact: Ing. Victor Vargas Varela,
Director
PHONE: 525/654-3560, 674-0965
Product/Service Description:
Switches, nesoi

Servicios de Materiales Electricos,
Revillagigedo No. 34-C.P.
Mexico, D.F. 06050
Contact: C.P. Alberto de la Serna
Aguilar, Director General
PHONE: 525/510-4024 / 512-1957
Product/Service Description:
Electric signal, safety or traffic
control equip

Servicos Integrales de Telefonia
Av. Nuevo Leon No. 253 piso 4
Mexico, D.F. 11800
Contact: LIC. VERGARA
FERNANDO, GERENTE
GENERAL
PHONE: 525/277-60-04 272-00-76
Product/Service Description:
Electric, laser or oth light or
photon beam etc

Serviempaques Marba, S.A. de C.V.
Poniente 122 No. 485
Mexico, D.F. 02300
Contact: Ing. Raul Martinez
Barron, General Director Secretary
PHONE: 525/587-2277, 587-2366
Product/Service Description:
Plastics and articles thereof

Servifiestas Bemoyo
Av. Canada 233
Queretaro, QRO 131559
Contact: Mr. Benjamin Mondragon
Mendoza, Owner
PHONE: 524/2-13-1391,13-1573
Product/Service Description:
Table, kitchen etc articles & pts,
stainless steel

Serving, S.A. de C.V.
PROVIDENCIA NO.179
Mexico, D.F. 13210
Contact: Mr. Jorge Centeno
Membrilla, General Director
PHONE: 525/696-3130, 696-5476
Product/Service Description:
Oven,cooking stove &
plate,range,roaster, nesoi

Serviteck, S.A. de C.V.
Alamo No. 91
Tlalnepantla, EDM. 54040
Contact: Lic. Fernando Matan,
Director General
PHONE: 525/398-3380/9591
Product/Service Description:
Speedometers and tachometers;
stroboscopes

Set-Cap
Santa Anita No. 737 A 101
Mexico, D.F. 03570
Contact: Ing. Roberto Leon
Garibay, Manager
PHONE: 525/538-1733
Product/Service Description:
Central heating boilers

Silos y Camiones, S. A. de C. V.
Blvd. Felipe Angeles No. 1606
Pachuga, HGO. 42080
Contact: Ing. Romualdo Telleria
Beltran, General Manager
PHONE: 52/771/3-3600-02, 3-4322
Product/Service Description:
Pneumatic elevators and conveyors

Singer Mexicana, S.A. de C.V.
Av. Nuevo Leon 250-Pisos 9, 10 y 11
Mexico, D. F. 06100
Contact: Mr. Mark McGuiness
Capwell, General Director
PHONE: 525/272-0107
Product/Service Description:
Stoves, ranges etc, nonel domest &
pts, ir & steel

Sistemas Admin. de Informacion
Av. Coyoacan No. 912
Mexico, D.F. 03100
Contact: Ms. Georgina Jimenez
Rodriguez, Assistant
PHONE: 525/559-1339
Product/Service Description:
Typewriter etc ribbons, inked or
prep; ink pads

Sistemas Comerciales Dicotel,
Prol. Calle 16 No. 230-A
Mexico, D.F. 01180
Contact: Mr. Oscar Morales,
Administrative Director
PHONE: 525/273-0018
Product/Service Description:
Hybrid integrated circuits

Sistemas Hormiga, S.A. de C.V.
Victor Hugo No. 10
Mexico, D. F. 03440
Contact: Mr. Berndt Wilmanns,
General Manager
PHONE: 525/696-6268, 696-6253
Product/Service Description:
Jacks and hoists,hydraulic,exc blt-
in jack systems

Sistemas Protectores, S.A. de C.V.
Zarco No. 203
Mexico, D.F. 06300
Contact: Mr. Antonio Mera M.,
General Director
PHONE: 525/597-1787 / 1483
Product/Service Description:
Safes, cash or deed boxes etc a
prts, base metal

Sistemas y Manufacturas
Calle Dos No. 118
Mexico, D. F. 09070
Contact: Lic. Lic. Arturo
Merikanskas Halpern, General
Manager
PHONE: 525/581-5862, 525-6664
Product/Service Description:
Metals products; machinery &
transport equipment

Slim Royal, S.A. de C.V.
Cadiz No. 67
Mexico, D.F. 03400
Contact: Mr. Koichi Meguro Sato,
Director General
PHONE: 525/519-2500, 519-4107
Product/Service Description:
Electrocardiographs

Sodi Asociados, S.A.
Moscu No. 105
Tlalnepantla, EDOME 54020
Contact: I.Q.I. Alejandro Diaz Q.,
Plant Manager
PHONE: 525/379-5010, 379-1084
Product/Service Description:
Rubber and articles thereof

Soland and Piers, S. A. de C. V.
Alamo Plateado No. 1-PH-1, 6 y 7
Naucalpan, EDOME 53320
Contact: Ing. Roberto Sanchez,
Chairman of the Board
PHONE: 525/343-6331
Product/Service Description:
Electric transform, static Electric
transform, static

Soldaduras Y Accesorios
Victoria Ote 3808-B
Mexico, D.F. 07820
Contact: Mr. Guillermo Vallejo,
Sales Manager
PHONE: 525/577-00-77
Product/Service Description:
Wire, rods etc for soldering etc &
met spray, bmpt

Soporte Tecnologico, S. A. de C. V.
Ave. Sonora No. 123-301
Mexico, D. F. 06140
Contact: Ing. Victor Manuel del
Castillo, Director General
PHONE: 525/211-0621, 211-0397
Product/Service Description:
Screws, bolts, nuts, washers etc,
iron or steel

Square D' Company Mexico, S.A. de
Czada. Javier Rojo Gomez No. 1121
Mexico, D. F. 09300
Contact: Mr. Gregg Brown,
Director General
PHONE: 525/686-3000
Product/Service Description:
Electrical apparatus for switching
etc, ov 1000 v

Suburbia S.A. de C.V.
Av. Avila Camacho No.487 P.A.
Mexico, D.F. 11220
Contact: Mr. Cesareo Fernandez,
Director General
PHONE: 525/395-1088
Product/Service Description:
Perfumes and toilet waters

Suministro De Especialidades, S.A.
Pirineos No. 148
Mexico, D.F. 03300
Contact: Mr. Gerardo Toussaint,
General Director
PHONE: 525/602-1870
Product/Service Description:
Rubber, unvulcanized, in plates,
sheets, and strip

Suministros de Equipos Industriales
Rafael Buelna y Articulo 27 No.4015
Tijuana, B.C. 22100
Contact: Mr. Ramiro Gomez Meza,
Sole Administrator
PHONE: 52/66/80-5729
Product/Service Description:
Air cond mach incorporating a
refrig unit, nesoi

Suministros y Proyectos
Cruz Galvez No. 184
Mexico, D. F. 02800
Contact: Lic. Javier Garza
Gutierrez, General Director
PHONE: 525/355-4937, 355-7990
Product/Service Description:
Micrometers, calipers and gauges

Surtidora Industrial del Sureste,
Heriberto Jara No. 401
Coatzacoalcos, VER. 96529
Contact: Ing. Ricardo Gomez,
General Director
PHONE: 52/921-41391
Product/Service Description:
Pumps fitted with measuring
device, nesoi

Surtidora Mexico, S. A. de C. V.
Dr. Gustavo Baz No. 193
Tlalnepantla, EDOME 54080
Contact: Sr. Jorge Nunez, Gerente
PHONE: 525/361-6807, 361-6557
Product/Service Description:
Rubber, unvulcanized, in plates,
sheets, and strip

Surtidora de Joyeria, S.A. de C.V.
Madero No. 55-111, primer piso
Mexico, D.F. 06000
Contact: Mr. Jacobo Hanono A.,
Director General
PHONE: 525/512-1455
Product/Service Description:
Jewelry and parts thereof, of oth
precious metal

Surtidores de Equipo Para Cocinas
Via Gustavo Baz No. 333
Naucalpan, E.M. 53310
Contact: Ing. Jorge Arturo Perez,
General Manager
PHONE: 525/393-81-83 393-81-
Product/Service Description:
Furniture of plastics

Tableros y Controles, S.A.
San Francisco No. 765
Mexico, D.F. 03100
Contact: Ing. Roberto Garcia,
General Director
PHONE: 525/543-9476
Product/Service Description:
Electrical apparatus for switching
etc, nov 1000 v

Talabarteria Hipodromo, S.A. DE
Fernandez de Lizardi No. 2
Mexico, D.F. 11220
Contact: Mr. Aristeo Garcia,
General Manager
PHONE: 525/557-6884, 557-3153
Product/Service Description:
Buckles and buckle clasps a parts,
base metal

Talabarteria La Herradura, S.A.
Musset No. 357-B
Mexico, D.F. 11550
Contact: Mr. Efrain Yudovich,
General Director
PHONE: 525/531-9164
Product/Service Description:
Buckles and buckle clasps a parts,
base metal

Tandem Computers de Mexico,
Moras No. 313
Mexico, D.F. 03100
Contact: Ing. Jean Marie Gabbai,
Marketing Manager
PHONE: 525/559-9177 228-8500
Product/Service Description:
Automatic data process machines;
magn reader etc

Tau Omega Ingenieria, S. A. de C.V.
Atlixco No. 66-3
Mexico, D. F. 06140
Contact: Mr. Eduardo Nino de
Rivera, Director General
PHONE: 525/286-4623
Product/Service Description:
Gears, exc transmission elements,

Tecnica en Materiales Electricos
Ernesto Pugiber No. 58
Mexico, D.F. 06070
Contact: Ing. Alonso Tenorio, ING
PHONE: 525/521-29-06 y 512-91-80
Product/Service Description:
Electric motors and generators (no
sets)

Tecnica en Soporteria, S.A. DE C.V.
Ave. Presidente Juarez No. 27
54050 Estado, DE MEXICO
Contact: Mr. James Fox, Director General
PHONE: 525/390-27-09
Product/Service Description:
Clamps and similar handtools, not vises, and parts

Tecnicos en Comunic-acion e
Av. Juan Terrazas No. 314 Norte
Torreon, COAH 27140
Contact: Mr. Guillermo Navarrete C., General Manager
PHONE: 52/17/16-2864
Product/Service Description:
Electric apparatus for line telephony etc, parts

Tecnicos en Iluminacion de Mexico,
Sonora No. 68
Mexico, D.F. 06760
Contact: Mr. Jorge Lopez Mora, General Manager
PHONE: 525/286-9669
Product/Service Description:
Electric lamps and lighting fittings, nesoi

Tecnicos en Refacciones para
Norte 85 No. 480
Mexico, D. F. 02060
Contact: Lic. Jose Ricardo Gonzalez Calderon, Manager
PHONE: 525/352-0788
Product/Service Description:
Gloves, mittens and mitts of cotton, knitted

Tecnipuerta, S. de R.L. de C.V.
Cipres No. 72
Ecatepec de Mor, EDM 55340
Contact: Mr. Fernando Gonzalez, General Manager
PHONE: 525/569-72-28
Product/Service Description:
Automatic regulating or control instruments; parts

Tecnolite, S.A. de C.V.
Calzada de las Armas No. 697
Mexico, D.F. 02710
Contact: Ing. Mario Enriquez Enriquez, General Manager
PHONE: 525/359-2519
Product/Service Description:
Electric lamps and lighting fittings, nesoi

Tecnologia Y Control de
Minerva No. 72
Mexico, D.F. 03940
Contact: C.P. Carlos Lara Osorno, General Manager
PHONE: 525/663-5309,661-8971
Product/Service Description:
Air & Water Resource & Solid Waste Management

Tecnologia de Vibraciones y
Cordoba No. 42-804
Mexico, D.F. 06700
Contact: Ing. Jose Maria Sainz H., General Manager
PHONE: 525/533-45-47, 533-45-08
Product/Service Description:
Instr & appl f medical surgical dental vet, nesoi

Tecnologia en Lubricantes
Abasolo No. 2
Mexico, D.F. 04100
Contact: Ing. Jose Pequeno H., General Manager
PHONE: 525/554-5041
Product/Service Description:
Greases, lubricating, with or w out additives

Telas, No Tejidos, S.A. DE C.V
Yacatas No.80
Mexico, D.F. 03020
Contact: Mr. Miguel Rico Ramirez, President
PHONE: 525/538-56-12 ,530-34-04
Product/Service Description:
Wov fabric, synth staple fib nu 85% synth st fiber

Tele Productos Mexicanos, S. A. de
Via Gustavo Baz No. 47-B
Tlalnepantla, MEX. 54080
Contact: Sr. David Azcarraga Rhodas, Gerente General
PHONE: 525/572-1522, 562-0926
Product/Service Description:
Electric apparatus for line telephony etc, parts

Telecomunicaciones de Mexico
Eje Central Lazaro Cardenas No. 567
Mexico, D.F. 03020
Contact: Lic. Carlos Mier y Teran, Director General
PHONE: 525/629-1170
Product/Service Description:
Communications satellites

Termometros Mexicanos, S.A. de C.V.
Sierra Santa Rosa No. 47
Mexico, D.F.
Contact: Ing. Alfonso Montes, Director General
PHONE: 525/355-12-59 355-45-26
Product/Service Description:
Thermometers liquid-filled, direct reading, nesoi

Terrazos Esmon, S.A. de C.V.
Prol. San Antonio No. 13
Mexico, D.F. 01180
Contact: Lic. Jesus Sanchez, Marketing Director
PHONE: 525/277-35-22
Product/Service Description:
Floor cover (rolls & tiles) & wall cover, plastics

Tessman y Cia., S.A.
Playa Pie de la Cuesta No. 238
Mexico, D.F. 08840
Contact: Mr. Conrado Wacuz Caballero, General Manager
PHONE: 525/672-89-99 672-80-
Product/Service Description:
Air conditioning mach etc incl refrig unit etc

Tiempo, S. A.
Monte Caucaso 915, 1st floor
Mexico, D.F. 11000
Contact: Mr. Armando Toledo, Director
PHONE: 525/272-5651,
Product/Service Description:
Clocks and watches and parts thereof

Tizacril, S.A. de C.V.
Km. 49.5 Carretera Mexico-Pachuca
Tizayuca, HGO. 43820
Contact: Mr. Ricardo Gutierrez, Director General
PHONE: 52/779/6-2334 6-2274
Product/Service Description:
Articles of plastics, nesoi

Tonormex
Calle 5 de Febrero No. 110
Mexico, D.F.
Contact: Mrs. Amelia Movellan, Director General
PHONE: 525/846-08-11
Product/Service Description:
Articles & equip for sports etc nesoi; pools; pts

Tornillos y Candados, S. A. de C.V.
Salonica No. 212 Esq. Ave. Granjas
Mexico, D. F. 02060
Contact: Mr. Nicolas Torreblanca Ruiz, Director General
PHONE: 525/396-0627, 396-6426
Product/Service Description:
Bolts w wo their nuts o wshrs, of iron or steel

Tractocamiones Kenworth
Norte 45 No. 601
Mexico, D.F. 02300
Contact: Lic. Francisco Mantecon Cazares, Director General
PHONE: 525/368-3351, 567-3144
Product/Service Description:
Trucks, nesoi
Truck parts, nesoi

Transformadores Y Equipos

Casma No. 520
07300 Mexico, D.F. MEXICO
Contact: Ing. David Villa,
Purchasing Manager
PHONE: 525/754-53-26
Product/Service Description:
Electric transform, static converters & induct, pt

Transformadores Y Maquinaria,

Salvador Diaz Miron No. 239
06400 Mexico, D.F. MEXICO
Contact: Ing. Jorge Rangel Luna,
Sales
PHONE: 525/541-33-45
Product/Service Description:
Electric transform, static converters & induct, pt

Transformadores y Control, S. A. de

Norte 45 No. 940-D
Mexico, D. F. 02300
Contact: Ing. Leonardo Barbosa
Bonilla, General Director
PHONE: 525/567-4543, 567-4598
Product/Service Description:
Electric motors and generators (no sets)

Translimite S.A. de C.V.

Heroes de Churubusco No. 7
Mexico, D.F. 11870
Contact: Lic. Carlos Armella,
General Director
PHONE: 525/271-8381/272-1762
Product/Service Description:
Metals products; machinery & transport equipment

Transmisiones TSP, S.A. de C.V.

Km.181.5 Autopista Mexico
Queretaro
Cd.Pedro Domecq, QRO.
MEXICO
Contact: Ing. Rodolfo Rodriguez
Mendoza, General Manager
PHONE: 467/5-0222/5-0289
Product/Service Description:
Automotive Parts & Supplies and Assessories

Transmisiones y Repuestos de

Calle Norte 80-A No. 6205
Mexico, D.F. 06839
Contact: Mr. Roberto Angeles,
Sales Manager
PHONE: 525/751-3432,766-8501
Product/Service Description:
Power supplies

Transparent Products of Mexico

Norte 1-C No. 4923
Mexico, D.F. 07770
Contact: Mr. Juan Archundia,
General Manager
PHONE: 525/368-03-93
Product/Service Description:
Cast & rolled glass, in sheets or profiles etc

Traxit Comunicaciones, S.A. de C.V.

Av. del Bosque No. 6144-A
Puebla, PUE MEXICO
Contact: Mr. Maldonado Eduardo,
President
PHONE: 52/22/44-51-93 44-59-91
Product/Service Description:
Reception apparatus for radiotelephony etc

Trinity Industries de Mexico,

Prol. Francisco I. Madero s n
Frontera, COAH 25650
Contact: Javier Valdivieso, ,
PHONE: 52/86/36-03-12/36-06-12
Product/Service Description:
Tanks

Tro-Grim, S.A. de C.V.

Eje Central L. Cardenas Nte. # 619
Mexico, D.F. 07700
Contact: Mr. Manuel Grimaldo
Manzano, Director General
Purchases Manager
PHONE: 525/754-5544, 754-3381
Product/Service Description:
Elect lighting visual signlng eq ex for bicycles

Tropic Pizza, S. A. de C. V.

Costera Miguel Aleman No. 54-1
Acapulco, GRO. 39850
Contact: Mr. Tomas Biedul
Sonovsky, Administrator
PHONE: 52/74/81-0076, 81-0052
Product/Service Description:
Coffee, roasted, not decaffeinated

Troquel-Mex, S. A.

Ave. Risco No. 51
Ecatepec, MEX. 55340
Contact: Ing. Ernesto Morales,
PHONE: 525/755-0090
Product/Service Description:
Stampings of bodies of 8701 to 8705

Tuberias PVC, S.A.

Ayuntamiento No. 60-E
Mexico, D.F. 06470
Contact: Mrs. Isabel Jimenez,
PHONE: 525/518-4333
Product/Service Description:
Tubes, pipes & hoses & their fittings, of plastics

Tubesa, S.A. de C.V.

Culiacan No. 123 - 707
Mexico, D.F. 06170
Contact: Ing. Jose Luis Sanchez L.,
General Director
PHONE: 525/271-9311/9130
Product/Service Description:
Tubes, pipes etc, seamless, iron nesoi & steel

U.S. Sanitary de Mexico,

Av. Centenario No. 412
Mexico, D.F. 02770
Contact: Lic. Arturo Villegas,
Director General
PHONE: 525/561-09-00
Product/Service Description:
Cleaning preparations

UHDE de Mexico Ingenieria, Construc

Blvd. M.A. Camacho No. 6-A
12vo pis
Naucalpan, EDMEX 53900
Contact: Ing. Francisco Guerrero
PHONE: 525/557-6389
Product/Service Description:
Air & Water Resource & Solid Waste Management

Ultravision 2001, S.A. DE C.V.

Circuito Medicos No. 22
53100 Estado, DE MEXICO
Contact: Mr. Alejandro Goebel,
Director General
PHONE: 525/572-97-33 572-21-55
Product/Service Description:
Optical elements, mounted; parts & accessories

Union de Productores Agropecuarios

3 Norte No. 11
Tecamachalco, PUE. 75480
Contact: Lic. Florentino Alonso
Hidalgo, General Director
PHONE: 52/242/2-0060
Product/Service Description:
Bovine animals, live, nesoi

Universal de Resinas Y Fibras,S.A.

Av. Observatorio No. 525
Mexico, D.F. 01110
Contact: Mr. Miguel Angel
Gutierrez, General Manager
PHONE: 525/272-08-92 272-29-38
Product/Service Description:
Glaziers putty, resin cements, caulking comps etc

Univex, S. A. de C. V.

Ave. de las Palmas No. 751-Piso 2
Mexico, D. F. 11010
Contact: Ing. Eduardo Piccolo
Calvera, Marketing Manager
PHONE: 525/520-9048, 520-9049
Product/Service Description:
Fertilizers, nesoi

Urresko, S. A. de C. V.

KM. 42.5 Autopista Mexico-Queretaro
Tepotzotlan, MEX 54600
Contact: Santiago Aguirre Alberdi,
Director General
PHONE: 525/876-0675, 876-0685
Product/Service Description:
Tools, cutlery etc. of base metal & parts thereof

Vamsa Ingenieria, S.A. de C.V.
Torres Adalid No. 1856
Mexico, D.F. 03020
Contact: Ing. Jorge Baltazar,
General Manager
PHONE: 525/669-1883
Product/Service Description:
Filters & parts & accessories for
instr & appratus

Vare, S. A. de C. V.
Alfonso Ceballos No. 20
Mexico, D. F. 15500
Contact: Mr. Marcos Sepulveda,
Imports Manager
PHONE: 525/786-0320
Product/Service Description:
Tools, cutlery etc. of base metal &
parts thereof

Veco, S.A. de C.V.
Pirineos No. 263
Mexico, D.F. 03340
Contact: Mr. Angel Luis De
Vechhi Armella, General Director
PHONE: 525/688-3566/3977
Product/Service Description:
Air or vac pumps, compr & fans;
hoods & fans; pts

Velcon, S.A. de C.V.
Carretera Panamericana Km 284
Celaya, GTO 38000
Contact: Mrs. Martha Moreno
Valdes, Marketing Director
PHONE: 52/4/611-0277
Product/Service Description:
Automotive Parts & Supplies

Vendematic, S.A. de C.V.
Poniente 134 No. 580 Bis
Mexico, D.F.
Contact: Lic. Xavier De Irezabal,
PHONE: 525/567-2212
Product/Service Description:
Automatic goods-vending
machines, parts

Vendor, S.A. de C.V.
Calz. Mexico Coyoacan No. 340
Mexico, D.F. 03340
Contact: Mr. Sergio Athie,
PHONE: 525/688-92-22
Product/Service Description:
Lamps & lighting fittings & parts

Via med, S.A. de C.V.
Sinaloa No. 147
Mexico, D.F. 06700
Contact: Mr. Jack Dorotinsky G.,
Director General
PHONE: 525/208-2370, 208-7022
Product/Service Description:
Medical, surgical, dental or vet
inst, no elec, pt

Vicente Suarez Garcia
Gral. Salvador Alvarado No. 60
Mexico, D.F. 11800
Contact: Ing. Vicente Suarez G.,
General Manager
PHONE: 525/271-3976
Product/Service Description:
Automotive Parts & Supplies

Videoproceso, S.A. de C.V.
Lago Yojoa No. 158
Mexico, D.F. 11470
Contact: Mr. Tomas Zarate,
Director General
PHONE: 525/250-3192 250-6480
Product/Service Description:
Automatic data process machines;
magn reader etc

Vidrieria Oviedo, S.A.
Nogal No. 40
Mexico, D.F. 06400
Contact: Mr. Jose Luis Sanchez,
General Manager
PHONE: 525/535-09-12
Product/Service Description:
Door clsrs (exc atmtc) a pts, bs
mtl, for building

Vidrieria y Aluminio, S.A.
Blvd. 4 Poniente No. 2111
Puebla, PUE 72100
Contact: Mr. Jaime Gutierrez,
General Manager
PHONE: 52/22/30-3633
Product/Service Description:
Door clsrs (exc atmtc) a pts, bs
mtl, for building

Vidrios Laresgoiti, S.A.
Cuauhtemoc No. 156
Mexico, D.F. 06720
Contact: Jonas Laresgoiti,
PHONE: 525/578-3211
Product/Service Description:
Cast & rolled glass, in sheets

Vidrios Universo, S.A.
Municipio Libre No. 183
Mexico, D.F. 03300
Contact: Mrs. Marisela Soria,
Director General
PHONE: 525/605-24=43
Product/Service Description:
Glass and glassware

Vigilancia, Guardias y Alarmas, S.A
Benjamin Franklin No. 222
Mexico, D.F. 11800
Contact: Ing. Rudi Salazar,
General Director
PHONE: 525/516-1618/6446
Product/Service Description:
Electric sound or visual signaling
apparatus, pts

Vitrocrisa Cubiertos, S. A. de C.V.
Calle Uno No. 60
Xalostoc, EDOME 53340
Contact: Ing. Javier Escobedo,
Plant Manager
PHONE: 525/227-6510
Product/Service Description:
Tableware etc of base metal, &
base metal parts

Vulcanus de Mexico, S.A. de C.V.
Lago Chapala No. 63
Mexico, D.F. 11320
Contact: Mr. Oscar Haggerman,
Administrative Manager
PHONE: 525/396-3064, 396-3084
Product/Service Description:
Drilling mach for remove met, n
numerical controld

Vycisa, S.A.
Avena No. 138
Mexico, D.F. 09810
Contact: Mr. David Hernandez,
General Manager
PHONE: 525/581-88-32
Product/Service Description:
Door clsrs (exc atmtc) a pts, bs
mtl, for building

Watson Phillips y Cia. Sucs. S. A.
Sn.Francisco Cuautlalpan 101-103
Naucalpan, MEX. 53370
Contact: L.A.E. Clyde Louis
Young Grose, General Director
PHONE: 525/576-2833
Product/Service Description:
Pharmaceutical products

William Young & Co., S.A. de C.V.
Cuauhtemoc No. 146
D.F., MEX. 07000
Contact: Mr. Lic. Rodolfo Nagel,
Director General
PHONE: 525/577-32-15
Product/Service Description:
Otanulated slag fr iron or steel
manufacture

Mexico : Product / Service Index

Abrasives on a base material oth thn fab paper- *Abrasivos y Servicios Industr*

Acrylic polymers nesoi, in primary forms - *Autoplas, S. A. de C. V.*

Activated carbon - *Duroplast, S.A. de C.V.*

Additives for lubricating oils, nesoi - *Aceites y Grasas Lubricantes, S.A*

Adhesive tape not over 20 cm wide - *Representaciones Kagima, S.A.*

Adhesive tape not over 20 cm wide - *Proveedora Industrial Marvill*

Adhesives based on rubber or plastics nesoi - *Productos Quimicos Servis,*

Administration of Environmental Quality - *Murad Asesores*

Administration of Environmental Quality Programs - *Selbach y Asociados,*

Administration of Environmental Quality Programs - *Desarrollo Ecologico*

Administration of Environmental Quality Programs - *Prevision Y Planeacion*

Advertising - *Articulos Decorativos, S.A. de C.V.*

Advertising - *Promotora Nacional de Eventos*

Advertising - *Servicio Polimodal de Audio Video y*

Advertising N.e.c. - *Importaciones Exportaciones y*

Advertising Printing (Lithographic) - *Ammex Asociados, S.A. de C.V.*

Advertising Printing (Lithographic) - *Capaco, S.A. de C.V.*

Advertising Printing (Lithographic) - *Olaris, S.A. de C.V.*

Agricultural Services - *Agropecuaria Valmo, S.A. de C.V.*

Air & Water Resource & Solid Waste Management - *Consorcio en Ecologia*

Air & Water Resource & Solid Waste Management - *Diseno Hidraulico y*

Air & Water Resource & Solid Waste Management - *Grupo Ingenieria*

Air & Water Resource & Solid Waste Management - *Importaciones y*

Air & Water Resource & Solid Waste Management - *Leyva Mendez*

Air & Water Resource & Solid Waste Management - *Procesa Ingenieria y*

Air & Water Resource & Solid Waste Management - *Quimica Omega S.A.*

Air & Water Resource & Solid Waste Management - *Tecnologia Y Control*

Air & Water Resource & Solid Waste Management - *UHDE de Mexico*

Air brakes & parts for veh of heading 8605 or 8606 - *Alta Mecanica I*

Air compressors,rotary,stationary,exceeding 74.6k - *Manufacturera Century,*

Air compressors,rotary,stationary,exceeding 74.6k - *Precision Control de*

Air cond mach incorporating a refrig unit, nesoi - *Electromecanica*

Air cond mach incorporating a refrig unit, nesoi - *Instalaciones*

Air cond mach incorporating a refrig unit, nesoi - *Suministros de Equipos*

Air conditioning mach etc incl refrig unit etc - *Bayard International*

Air conditioning mach etc incl refrig unit etc - *Beta Refrigeracion*

Air conditioning mach etc incl refrig unit etc - *Calefaccion y Ventilacion S.A. de*

Air conditioning mach etc incl refrig unit etc - *Ingenieria Peruel, S.A. de C.V.*

Air conditioning mach etc incl refrig unit etc - *Mexicana de Climas, S.A. de C.V.*

Air conditioning mach etc incl refrig unit etc - *Tessman y Cia., S.A.*

Air conditioning mach etc incl refrig unit - *Ventas, Instalaciones y Servicios,*

Air conditioning machines (temp & hum change), pts - *Arctic Circle*

Air conditioning machines (temp & hum change), pts - *Climas y*

Air conditioning machines (temp & hum change), pts - *Distribuidora Tecnica*

Air conditioning machines (temp & hum change), pts - *Negociaciones*

Air conditioning machines (temp & hum change), pts - *Neko Technologies,*

Air conditioning machines etc not incl refrig unit - *Aislantes, Climas y*

Air conditioning machines etc not incl refrig unit - *Romaq, S.A. de C.V.*

Air or vac pumps, compr & fans; hoods & fans; pts - *Veco, S.A. de C.V.*

Aircraft,nesoi - *Fortraco Mexicana, S.A. de C.V.*

Alum plt sht strp rec o sqr aly nt cl ov 6.3mm - *Productos Nacobre, S.A.*

Aluminum alloy hollow profiles - *Delta Aluminio y Vidrio, S.A. de*

Aluminum alloy profiles nesoi - *Aludec, S.A. de C.V.*

Aluminum alloy profiles nesoi - *Alumarq, S.A. de C.V.*

Aluminum alloy profiles nesoi - *Aluminio Gutsa, S.A. de C.V.*

Aluminum alloy profiles nesoi - *Bufete de Construcciones Asesoria*

Aluminum alloy profiles nesoi - *DIMASA, S.A. DE C.V.*

Aluminum alloy profiles nesoi - *Grupo Aluvisa, S.A. de C.V.*

Aluminum alloy profiles nesoi - *Grupo Valsa, S.A. de C.V.*

Aluminum and articles thereof - *Aluminio Azteca, S.A. de C.V.*

Aluminum and articles thereof - *Metales, Materiales y Servicios*

Aluminum cooking and kitchenware, cast - *Cafeteras Internacionales, SA*

Ammonia in aqueous solution - *Representaciones Agro Industriales*

Angles, shapes & sections of iron & nonalloy steel - *Proveacero y Servicio,*

Antennas and antenna reflectors and parts - *MHO Especialidades*

Antifreezing prep & prepared deicing fluids - *Fleetguard de Mexico, S.A. de*

Apparel & Accessory Stores - *Andromeda Internacional S.A.de C.V.*

Apparel & Accessory Stores - *Exclusivas Jessica, S.A. de C.V.*

Apparel & Accessory Stores - *Novias Tete, S.A.*

Apparel articles and accessories, not knit etc. - *Distribuciones Industriales*

Apparel articles and accessories, not knit etc. - *Ejecutivos en Proveeduria,*

Apparel, Piece Goods and Notions - *Corporativo Lumen, S.A. de C.V.*

Apparel, Piece Goods and Notions - *Sederia La Nueva, S. A. de C.V.*

Architectural and ornamental work, iron or steel - *Inarco, S.A. De C.V.*

Architectural and ornamental work, iron or steel - *Servi Aluminio, S.A. de*

Articles & equip for sports etc nesoi; pools; pts - *Deportes Marti, S.A. de*

Articles & equip for sports etc nesoi; pools; pts - *Tonormex*

Articles of jewelry & pts, of prec metal or clad - *Berne Hermanos, S.A. de C.V.*

Articles of jewelry & pts, of prec metal or clad - *Cromos Y Novedades de*

Articles of or clad with precious metal nesoi - *Auto Refacciones*

Articles of plastics, nesoi - *Catarinas Universales, S. A.*

Articles of plastics, nesoi - *Tizacril, S.A. de C.V.*

Automatic data process machines; magn reader etc - *Asiste, S.A. de C.V.*

Automatic data process machines; magn reader etc - *Cad-Cam, S.A. de C.V.*

Automatic data process machines; magn reader etc-*Compucentro de Servicio*

Automatic data process machines; magn reader-*Grupo Cibernetica Gerencial,*

Automatic data process machines; magn reader etc - *Grupo Tea, S.A. de C.V.*

Automatic data process machines; magn reader etc - *M.P.S. Mayorista, S.A.*

Automatic data process machines; magn reader etc - *Micro Azteca, S.A. de*

Automatic data process machines; magn reader etc - *Tandem Computers*

Automatic data process machines; magn reader etc - *Videoproceso, S.A. de*

Automatic goods-vending machines, parts - *Vendematic, S.A. de C.V.*

Automatic regulating or control instruments parts-*Central De Instrumentacion*

Automatic regulating or control instruments; parts - *Tecnipuerta, S. de R.L*

Automobiles & Other Motor Vehicles - *Encargos Y Comisiones, S.A. de C.V.*

Automobiles & Other Motor Vehicles - *Refaccionaria Diesel Cuautitlan,*

Automotive Dealers, N.e.c. - *Distribuidora Automotriz Xochimilco*

Automotive Parts & Supplies - *Accesorios y Autopartes Sport,*

Automotive Parts & Supplies - *Bujias Champion de Mexico, S.A.*

Automotive Parts & Supplies - *Carrocerias Cea, S.A. de C.V.*

Automotive Parts & Supplies - *Carvel Print, S.A. de C.V.*

Automotive Parts & Supplies - *Central de Autopartes, S.A. de C.V*

Automotive Parts & Supplies - *Comercial Cavisa, S.A. de C.V.*

Automotive Parts & Supplies - *Comercial LLantera Sullivan*

Automotive Parts & Supplies - *Compania Toronto, S.A. de C.V.*

Automotive Parts & Supplies - *Consorcio Industrial de Rines*

Automotive Parts & Supplies - *Diesel Jupiter S.A. de C.V.*

Automotive Parts & Supplies - *Distribuidora Nacional de*

Automotive Parts & Supplies - *Elastomeros Falcon, S.A. de C.V.*

Automotive Parts & Supplies - *Importaciones y Exportaciones Mursa*

Automotive Parts & Supplies - *Impulsora Diesel, S.A. DE C.V.*

Automotive Parts & Supplies - *Industria Electrica Automotriz S.A.*

Automotive Parts & Supplies - *Plasticos Laminados Joremi*

Automotive Parts & Supplies - *Productos Internacionales Tanaka*

Automotive Parts & Supplies - *Refacciones Y Motores, S.A. de C.V.*

Automotive Parts & Supplies - *Rines Deportivos Luna*

Automotive Parts & Supplies - *Rines Hazama, S.A. de C.V.*

Automotive Parts & Supplies - *Rines R.N, S.A.*

Automotive Parts & Supplies - *Rines Y Servicio Figueroa, S.A. de*

Automotive Parts & Supplies - *Rines de Acero Kelsey Hayes, S.A.*

Automotive Parts & Supplies - *Rolcar, S.A. de C.V.*

Automotive Parts & Supplies - *Rouitex, S.A. de C.V.*

Automotive Parts & Supplies - *Servicio Automotriz Roque, S.A.*

Automotive Parts & Supplies - *Transmisiones TSP, S.A. de C.V.*

Automotive Parts & Supplies - *Velcon, S.A. de C.V.*

Automotive Parts & Supplies - *Vicente Suarez Garcia*

Automotive gear oils - *Ingenieria y Procesos Industriales,*

Automotive maintenance machines - *Comercial Autoindustrial, S.A. de*

Bakery mach & mach f manuf macaroni,spaghetti,etc - *Industrias Alpha,*

Ball bearings - *Casa Sommer, S.A. de C.V.*

Bananas and plantains, fresh or dried - *Navarifrut, S.A. de C.V.*

Bandsaw blades exc mtl ctting, parts, base metal - *Micor de Mexico, S.A*

Beauty & skin care preparation, nesoi - *Barhnos de Mexico, S.A. de C.V.*

Beauty & skin care preparation, nesoi - *Consupharma, S.A. de C.V.*

Beauty, make-up & skin-care prep; manicure etc prp - *Cia. de Cosmeticos*

Beauty, make-up & skin-care prep; manicure etc prp - *Grupo Comercial*

Bells etc (nonelec), ornaments, ph frames etc bmpt - *Carre, S.A. de C.V.*

Belting & belts for machinery,nesoi - *Marve Industrial, S. A. de C. V.*

Bendng foldng etc mach for work met - *Rocha Licea Y Compania,*

Bicycles & oth cycles (inc del tricycle) no motor - *Fabrica de Bicicletas*

Blinds(including venetian blinds)of plastic - *Distribuidora de Productos*

Bodies for vehicles of heading 8704 - *Remosa de Mexico, S. A.*

Bolts w wo their nuts o wshrs, of iron or steel - *Industrial Tornillera Figueroa,*

Bolts w wo their nuts o wshrs, of iron or steel - *Tornillos y Candados, S. A. de*

Books, brochures & similar printed matter - *Libreria Guadalupana,*

Boots rub plast no stitch ov ankle nov knee nesoi - *Manufacturera Waco,*

Bovine animals, live, nesoi - *Union de Productores Agropecuarios*

Brakes & parts,nesoi,f veh of headng 8605 or 8606 - *Ruben Barrios Frenos*

Buckles and buckle clasps a parts, base metal - *Armani, S.A. de C.V.*

Buckles and buckle clasps a parts, base metal - *Federico Ruiz Vasconcelos*

Buckles and buckle clasps a parts, base metal - *Industrias Ahedo, S.A. de C.*

Buckles and buckle clasps a parts, base metal - *Peleteria Continental, S.A.*
Buckles and buckle clasps a parts, base metal - *Talabarteria Hipodromo,*
Buckles and buckle clasps a parts, base metal - *Talabarteria La Herradura,*
Buttons, nesoi - *Botones Cel, S.A. de C.V.*
Cab chassis, dumpers - *Maquinaria Panamericana,*
Cable, etc nesoi of cu nt ins nt md into artcls - *AMP de Mexico, S. A. de C.V.*
Cable, etc nesoi of cu nt ins nt md into artcls - *Conductores Latincasa, S.A*
Camping goods nesoi, of textile materials nesoi - *Alcampo Caza y Pesca,*
Camping goods nesoi, of textile materials nesoi - *Promocion Y Servicios*
Cards, printed, nesoi - *Idea, Forma y Color, S.A. de C.V.*
Carpets & oth textile floor coverings, tufted - *Integracion Decorativa, S.A.*
Cartons etc paper; office box files etc, paper etc - *Carton Fenix, S.A. de C.V.*
Cast & rolled glass, in sheets or profiles etc - *Transparent Products of Mexico*
Cast & rolled glass, in sheets or profiles etc - *Vidrios Laresgoiti, S.A. de C.V.*
Cast articles nesoi, of iron or steel - *Productos Especializados de Acero,*
Cast articles of iron or steel nesoi - *Lazer, S.A. De C.V.*
Casting mach used in metallurgy or metal foundries - *Potosina de Bronces,*
Castors, and parts thereof, of base metal - *Joyma Industrial, S. A. de C. V.*
Cement clinkers - *Madereria la Rancherita, S.A de C.V*
Central heating boilers - *Kardel de Mexico, S.A.*
Central heating boilers - *Set-Cap*
Ceramic tableware & kitchenware, porcelain & china - *Distribuidor*
Chemical & residual prod, chemical etc ind nesoi - *Angasa, S.A. DE C.V.*
Chemical & residual prod, chemical etc ind nesoi - *Centro Ecologico*
Chemical & residual prod, chemical etc ind nesoi - *Chinamex, S.A. de C.V.*
Chemical & residual prod, chemical etc ind nesoi - *Coloide Mexicana S.A.*
Chemical & residual prod, chemical etc ind nesoi - *Grupo Quimico I*
Chemicals and related products, us goods returned - *JT Baker S.A. de C.V.*
Chickens, ducks, geese, turkeys, and guineas, live - *Grupo Avicola del*
Chocolate & other food products containing cocoa - *Chocolates Turin, S.A.*
Chocolate & other food products containing cocoa - *Productos del*
Chromatographs and electrophoresis instruments - *Roosin de Mexico, S. A.*
Chromium and articles thereof, inc waste and scrap - *Distribuciones Lema,*
Cigar cheroot cigarillo cigs of tob substits nesoi - *Distribuidora R.O.M., S.A.*
Clamps and similar handtools, not vises, and parts - *Tecnica en Soporteria,*
Clays, other - *Promociones y Construcciones*
Cleaning preparations - *Articulos de Limpieza Santa Cruz*
Cleaning preparations - *Cepillos y Productos de Aseo,*
Cleaning preparations - *Decsa,*
Cleaning preparations - *Distribuidora Echegaray,*
Cleaning preparations - *Gutierrez Ayala Juan Jose*
Cleaning preparations - *Limpieza Gapi, S.A. de C.V.*
Cleaning preparations - *Limpieza Industrial Co. S.A. de C..*
Cleaning preparations - *Mereco Internacional, S.A. de C.V.*
Cleaning preparations - *Proveedora Solfer, S.A. de C.V.*
Cleaning preparations - *U.S. Sanitary de Mexico,*
Clock or watch jewels - *Holzer y Cia., S.A de C.V.*
Clocks and watches and parts thereof - *Tiempo, S. A.*
Coffee, roasted, not decaffeinated - *Tropic Pizza, S. A. de C. V.*
Coffee, tea, mate & spices - *Cafe El Marino, S.A. de C.V.*
Coffee, tea, mate & spices - *Industrias Marino, S.A. de C.V.*
Communications satellites - *Mex, S.A. de C. V.*
Communications satellites - *Telecomunicaciones de Mexico*
Compression-ignition internal comb piston engines - *Jose de la Torre, S.A.*
Compressors used in refrigerating equipment - *Equipos Y Compresores de*
Compressors, ref & a/c,exc ammonia,exc 3 n/exc10hp - *Equipo de Medicion*
Conegar & substitutes for vinegar from acetic acid - *Distribuidora Dimex,*
Coniferous wood in the rough, not treated - *Madererias y Ferreterias Las*
Containers (boxes, bags etc), closurers etc, plast - *Cajas de Carton*
Containers nesoi w outer surface plstc text mtrls - *Comercial Jermosam,*
Conveyor or transmiss belts of vulcanized rubber - *Inman, S. A.*
Conveyors, pneumatic - *Conelec, S. A.*
Corrugated ppr/pbrd, w/n perforated nesoi roll/sht - *Empaques Casablanca,*
Corrugated ppr/pbrd, w/n perforated nesoi roll/sht - *Empaques y*
Crabmeat, prepared or preserved, nesoi - *Procesadora y*
Date sealing or numbering stamps,etc for hand oper - *Segall Publicidad*
Dc motors & generators w output > 750w; n ov 75 kw - *Industrias Conelec,*
Densified wd blocks/plates/strips/profile shapes - *Campos Herrera Rafael -*
Dental cements and other dental fillings etc - *Degussa Mexico, S.A. de C.V.*
Dental cements and other dental fillings etc - *Dentaurum de Mexico, S.A.*
Dental fittings and parts and accessories - *Grupo Industrial y Comercial*
Derricks; cranes; mobile lifting frames etc - *Caseer,S.A.*
Die casting machines - *Ingenieria en Moldes y Troqueles,*
Dies drw o extr mtl a pts thrf - *Diseno y Metalmecanica, S. A. de*
Dies drw o extr mtl a pts thrf - *Lukas, S. A.*
Dies drw o extr mtl a pts thrf - *Metalmaq, S.A. de C.V.*
Digital elec scales, wght cap not exc 30 kg, nesoi - *Ramso Comercial, S.A.*
Display units w/color cathode ray tube - *Diseno y Display, S.A.*
Door clsrs (exc atmtc) a pts, bs mtl, for building - *Vidrieria Oviedo, S.A.*
Door clsrs (exc atmtc) a pts, bs mtl, for building - *Vidrieria y Aluminio, S.A.*
Door clsrs (exc atmtc) a pts, bs mtl, for building - *Vycisa, S.A.*

Doors and their frames and thresholds, of wood - *Electro Puertas, S.A. de*
Doors and their frames and thresholds, of wood - *Puerta Segura, S.A. de*
Doors and their frames, thresholds, of wood, nesoi - *Electro Spider*
Dried vegetables, whole, cut etc., no added prep - *Productos*
Drilling mach for remove met, n numerical controld - *Vulcanus de Mexico,*
Drive axles with differential for motor vehicles - *Reparacion de Partes*
Drying machines, nesoi - *Saunamex, S.A.*
Dust collection and air purification equipment - *Industrias Meza, S.A. de C.V.*
Elec water, space & soil heaters; hair etc dry, pt - *Centro de Calentadores*
Elect lighting visual signlng eq ex for bicycles - *Tro-Grim, S.A. de C.V.*
Elect switches f voltage not over 1000 v - *Construcciones Electricas mas*
Electric apparatus for line telephony etc, parts - *Firesa*
Electric apparatus for line telephony etc, parts - *Grupo Joman*
Electric apparatus for line telephony etc, parts - *Tecnicos en Comunicacion*
Electric apparatus for line telephony etc, parts - *Tele Productos Mexicanos,*
Electric lamps and lighting fittings, nesoi - *B&B Iluminacion*
Electric lamps and lighting fittings - *Fabricantes de Iluminacion Nacional*
Electric lamps and lighting fittings, nesoi - *Grupo Elmex*
Electric lamps and lighting fittings, nesoi - *L.J. Iluminacion, S.A. De C.V.*
Electric lamps and lighting fittings, nesoi - *Proyectos Luminicos y*
Electric lamps and lighting fittings, nesoi - *Tecnicos en Iluminacion de Mexico,*
Electric lamps and lighting fittings, nesoi - *Tecnolite, S.A. de C.V.*
Electric motors and generators (no sets) - *Tecnica en Materiales Electricos*
Electric motors and generators (no sets) - *Transformadores y Control, S. A.*
Electric motors, dc > 74.6 w but < 746 w - *Rebin, S. A. de C. V.*
Electric signal, safety or traffic control - *Servicios de Materiales Electricos,*
Electric sound or visual signaling apparatus, pts - *Vigilancia, Guardias y*
Electric storage batteries, incl separators, parts - *A. G. Electronica, S. A. de*
Electric storage batteries, incl separators, parts - *Empresas Ca-Le de*
Electric transform, static converters & induct, pt - *Soland and Piers, S. A. de*
Electric transform, static converters & induct, pt - *Transformadores Y*
Electric transform, static converters & induct, pt - *Transformadores Y*
Electric, laser or oth light or photon beam etc - *Asesores en Teleinformatica*
Electric, laser or oth light or photon beam etc - *Cima Computacion e*
Electric, laser or oth light or photon beam etc - *Servicos Integrales de*
Electrical apparatus for switching etc, nov 1000 v - *Mak Electronics, S.A. de*
Electrical apparatus for switching etc, nov 1000 v - *Profesionales en*
Electrical apparatus for switching etc, nov 1000 v - *Tableros y Controles,*
Electrical apparatus for switching etc, ov 1000 v - *Cobra Electronica, S. A.*
Electrical apparatus for switching etc, ov 1000 v - *Instalaciones y Servicios*
Electrical apparatus for switching etc, ov 1000 v - *Repromex Ingenieros, S.*
Electrical apparatus for switching etc, ov 1000 v - *Square D' Company*
Electro-discharge machine tools for removing matl - *Maquinas, Accesorios*
Electrocardiographs - *Equipo para Hospitales, S.A.*
Electrocardiographs - *Slim Royal, S.A. de C.V.*
Electromagnets, permanent magnets etc & parts - *Abastecedores Lumon,*
Electromechanical hand tool parts - *Multiservicio de Mantenimiento*
Electronic integrated circuits & microassembl, pts - *Reactores Electronicos*
Electronic key telephone systems - *Opecsa, S.A.*
Electroplating, electrophoresis and electrolysis m - *Instituto Nacional de*
Electroplating, electrophoresis and electrolysis m - *McGean Roco de*
Electroplating, electrophoresis and electrolysis m - *Recubrimientos*
Electroplating, electrophoresis and electrolysis m - *Recubrimientos*
Engine and motor parts, nesoi - *Distribuidora Automotriz*
Engines and motors nesoi, and parts thereof - *Dieselar Industrial, S.A. de*
Engines and motors nesoi, and parts thereof - *Motores Y Refacciones*
Engines and motors nesoi, and parts thereof - *Proveedora Azucarera, S.A.*
Engines and motors nesoi, and parts thereof - *Refaccionaria Jacobo, S.A.*
Envelopes of paper/paperboard, for correspondence - *Abastecedora de*
Essential oils etc; perfumery, cosmetic etc preps - *Casa Barba, S.A. de C.V.*
Fans, nesoi - *Industrias Man de Mexico, S.A.*
Fertilizers - *Agricultura Nacional, S.A. DE C.V.*
Fertilizers - *Jardineria 2000, S.A.*
Fertilizers - *Productos Floraphil, S.A. de C.V*
Fertilizers contain nitrates and phosphates - *Nitro Mex, S. A. de C. V.*
Fertilizers, nesoi - *Bio-Fer Internacional, S.A. de C.V*
Fertilizers, nesoi - *Polisulfuros de Mexico, S.A. de C.V*
Fertilizers, nesoi - *Univex, S. A. de C. V.*
Filter or purify mach & apparatus for liquid,nesoi - *Garo Filtros de Aire, S.A.*
Filter/purify machine & apparatus for liquid nesoi - *Comintra*
Filter/purify machine & apparatus for liquid nesoi - *Filtros y Medios*
Filter/purify machine & apparatus for liquid nesoi - *Purificaciones*
Filters & parts & accessories for instr & appratus - *Albany International,*
Filters & parts & accessories for instr & appratus - *Distribuidora de*
Filters & parts & accessories for instr & appratus - *Filtro Especialidades*
Filters & parts & accessories for instr & appratus - *Filtros Y Equipo I*
Filters & parts & accessories for instr & appratus - *Impulsora de Filtros*
Filters & parts & accessories for instr & appratus - *Kinfil, S.A. De C.V.*
Filters & parts & accessories for instr & appratus - *Productos Neumaticos,*
Filters & parts & accessories for instr & appratus - *Vamsa Ingenieria, S.A.*
Fishing rods & tackle; nets; decoys etc; parts etc - *Grupo Textil La Marina,*

Floor cover (rolls & tiles) & wall cover, plastics - *Decoraciones y*
Floor cover (rolls & tiles) & wall cover, plastics - *Ripett, S.A. de C.V.*
Floor cover (rolls & tiles) & wall cover, plastics - *Terrazos Esmon, S.A. de C.V.*
Fluorine, chlorine, bromine & iodine - *Hidro Industrial, S. A.*
Food industry residues & waste; prep animal feed - *Agropecuaria e Industrial*
Food industry residues & waste; prep animal feed - *Alimentos Cientificos*
Food industry residues & waste; prep animal feed - *Cap. Francisco A.*
Food industry residues & waste; prep animal feed - *Cornejo Cornejo Ma.*
Food industry residues & waste; prep animal feed - *Flagasa-Fab Lab. de*
Food industry residues & waste; prep animal feed - *La Hacienda S.A. DE C*
Food industry residues & waste; prep animal feed - *Nutrimentos del*
Food industry residues & waste; prep animal feed - *Purina S.A. DE C.V.*
Food preparations flour, starch, dairy etc, nesoi - *Panamericana Abarrotera,*
Food preparations nesoi - *Aminotec, S.A. de C.V.*
Food preparations nesoi - *Biomundo Sun Chlorella de Mexico*
Food preparations nesoi - *Hermanos Ugartechea, S.A. de C.V.*
Food preparations, nesoi, canned - *AIQUIFAR, S.A. de C.V.*
Footwear lea upper nesoi with a metal toe-cap - *Grupo Industrial Toluca, S.A.*
Fork-lift and works trucks, nesoi - *A. C. Mexicana, S. A. de C. V.*
Fork-lift and works trucks, nesoi - *Industrial de Rueda y Rodajas*
Fork-lift and works trucks, nesoi - *Roda Hule, S.A.*
Fork-lift and works trucks, nesoi - *Ruedas Y Carretillas, S.A.*
Frames or mounts for photographic slides - *Capello Interiores, S.A. de C.V.*
Fruit nesoi, fresh - *Productos Valery, S.A. de C.V.*
Fuel-injection pumps for compression-ignition engs - *Refacciones Carbu-*
Furniture of plastics - *Surtidores de Equipo Para Cocinas*
Games, coin-or token-operated, nesoi - *Mexicana de Electromecanicos, S.A.*
Gas-operate mch f solderg, brazng, weldg, hand-dir - *Linde de Mexico, S.A.*
Gear boxes, parts, subhd8701.20, hdg8702 or 8704 - *Engranes de Mexico*
Gears, exc transmission elements, entered separate - *Tau Omega*
Glass and glassware - *Decovitrales*
Glass and glassware - *Fabrelab, S.A. de C.V.*
Glass and glassware - *Vidrios Universo, S.A.*
Glaziers putty, resin cements, caulking comps etc - *Distribuidora Fiberglass*
Glaziers putty, resin cements, caulking comps etc - *Universal de Resinas Y*
Gloves, mittens and mitts of cotton, knitted or cr - *Tecnicos en Refacciones*
Greases, lubricating, with or w out additives - *Ing. Carlos Gutierrez P.*
Greases, lubricating, with or w out additives - *PEMEX Refinacion*
Greases, lubricating, with or w out additives - *Productos Texaco, S.A. de*
Greases, lubricating, with or w out additives - *Tecnologia en Lubricantes*
Grinding balls a sim artic for mills, cst, ios nes - *Maquinaria Industrial para*
Grinding balls a sim artic for mills, cst, ios nes - *Maquinaria para Moliendas*
Hand input devices, transmit data to computer - *Dispositivos Electronicos y*
Handsaws & met pts; saw blades; base mtl saw parts - *Gimbel Mexicana, S.*
Handsaws & met pts; saw blades; base mtl saw parts - *Herramientas*
Headgear nesoi, whether or not lined or trimmed - *Bomhere, S.A. de C.V.*
Heat exchangers - *Carbat, S.A. de C.V.*
Heat exchangers - *Graco Mexicana, S.A. de C.V.*
Hospital furniture - *Cocinas de Acero Inoxidable,*
Household art & pts, ir & st; ir or steel wool etc - *Motores McMillan, S.A. de*
Hybrid integrated circuits - *Sistemas Comerciales Dicotel,*
Hydraulic brake fluids liq for hydraulic trans etc - *Frenos Hidraulicos*
Hydraulic fluid power pumps, nesoi - *Casa Monroy, S.A. de C.V.*
Hydrometers, thermometers, pyrometers etc; pts etc - *Aerodinamica, S.A.*
Hydrometers, thermometers, pyrometers etc; pts etc - *Aerotecnica, S.A. de*
Ind prep, manuf food, drink exc ext, prep anim, veg ol - *Patrones de*
Injection type molds for rubber or plastics, nesoi - *Productos Industriales de*
Injection-molding mach for work rubber or plastic - *Inyectora de Plasticos Y*
Ink, printing, writing, drawing etc, concen or not - *G.B.W. de Mexico S.A. de*
Ink, printing, writing, drawing etc, concen or not - *Litoquim S.A.*
Ink, printing, writing, drawing etc, concen or not - *Pyrolac S.A. de C.V.*
Inst & appliances for medical, surgical, etc, nesoi - *Cuidados Basicos, S.A.*
Inst & appliances for medical, surgical, etc, nesoi - *Ind. Hospitalaria*
Inst & apprts, measuring checking pressure - *Centro de Validaciones y*
Inst etc measure or check flow, level etc, pts etc - *Instrumentos de*
Instr & appl f medical surgical dental vet, nesoi - *Tecnologia de Vibraciones*
Instruments for measuring length, nesoi - *Metrologia Mexicana, S.A. de C.V.*
Instruments for measuring length, nesoi - *Servicio de Medicion y Control,*
Insulating fittings for machines nesoi - *Constru-Centro, S.A. de*
Interchange tools for hand- or machine-tools, bmpt - *Lugo Castro y Cia.,*
Invalid carriages, mechanically propelled or not - *Casa Pena-Venta y*
Invalid carriages, nesoi - *Articulos Ortopedicos Alfa*
Iron and steel - *Grupo Empresarial Arva S.A. de C.V.*
Jacks and hoists, hydraulic, exc blt-in jack systems - *Hercules, S. A. de C. V.*
Jacks and hoists, hydraulic, exc blt-in jack systems - *Sistemas Hormiga, S.A.*
Jewelry and parts thereof, of oth precious metal - *Central Mexicana de*
Jewelry and parts thereof, of oth precious metal - *Diseno en Cadena, S.A.*
Jewelry and parts thereof, of oth precious metal - *Idar De Mexico, S.A. De*
Jewelry and parts thereof, of oth precious metal - *Joyeria La Princesa, S.A.*
Jewelry and parts thereof, of oth precious metal - *Surtidora de Joyeria, S.A.*
Labels of paper or paperboard, printed or not - *Farias Process, S.A.*

Laboratory ware - *Accesorios para Laboratorio, S.A.*
Laboratory ware - *Casa Rocas, S.A. de C.V.*
Laboratory ware - *Cientifica Vela Quin, S.A. de C.V.*
Laboratory ware - *Industrias Figursa S.A.*
Laboratory ware - *Mel de Mexico, S.A. de C.V.*
Lamps & lighting fittings & parts etc nesoi - *Vendor, S.A. de C.V.*
Lathes for remov mtl, n/c, mulit spin, new, nesoi - *Industrias Cormetal, S.A.*
Lifting, handling, loading & unload machines nesoi - *Rotork Servo Controles*
Light-sensing tubes - *Importadora Electronica Alta*
Liquid crystal devices nesoi; lasers; opt appl; pt - *Instrumentos*
Live plants (including their roots) etc, nesoi - *Jardines Proyectos y*
Locks except motor vehicle or furniture, base metl - *Fanal, S.A.*
Lubricating prep for text etc, no petr etc oil - *ELF Lubricantes Mexico, S.A.*
Lubricating preps, antirust & treating texiles etc - *Automatizacion Y*
Lubricating preps, antirust & treating texiles etc - *Comercializadora Lugol-*
Lubricating preps, antirust & treating texiles etc - *Multiform, S.A.*
M/b trousers overalls shorts etc cotton, knit - *L.G. Seguridad, S.A. DE C.V.*
Mac tools fr finish mtl using abrasives, nesoi, used - *Micro Abrasivos, S.A. de*
Mach, nesoi, f moldg or formg rubber or plastics - *Precimaq, S.A. de C.V.*
Machine tools for drilling, boring, milling etc - *Herramientas Exclusivas y*
Machine tools for drilling, boring, milling etc - *Leon Weill, S.A.*
Machine tools for drilling, boring, milling etc - *Muz-Her, S.A. de C.V.*
Machine tools for forging, bending, stamping etc - *Ingenieria en*
Machine tools for material removal by laser etc - *Krupper Internacional,*
Machine tools for working metal, nesoi - *Baleros Nacionales E Importados*
Machine tools for working metal, nesoi - *Herrajes, Dados y Moldes, S.A De*
Machine tools for working metal, nesoi - *Representaciones Comerciales de*
Marble and travertine cut in blocks or slabs - *Braley Marmoles y Granitos,*
Meas & checkng instrument, appliances & mach nesoi - *Diseno Integral*
Medical surgical dental veterinary furniture, nesoi - *Grupo M.M., S.A. de C.V.*
Medical, surgical, dental or vet inst, no elec, pt - *Abast. y Rep.*
Medical, surgical, dental or vet inst, no elec, pt - *Comercial Despa, S.A.*
Medical, surgical, dental or vet inst, no elec, pt - *Corporacion Logistica,*
Medical, surgical, dental or vet inst, no elec, pt - *Dist. de Quimicos y*
Medical, surgical, dental or vet inst, no elec, pt - *Instrumedico, S. A. de C.*
Medical, surgical, dental or vet inst, no elec, pt - *Medi-Lab, S.A. DE C.V.*
Medical, surgical, dental or vet inst, no elec, pt - *Requena, S.A. de C.V.*
Medical, surgical, dental or vet inst, no elec, pt - *Via med, S.A. de C.V.*
Medical, surgical, dental or veterinary furn etc - *Coreteme, S.A. de C.V.*
Medical, surgical, dental or veterinary furn etc - *Infra, S.A. de C.V.*
Medicinal & pharmaceutical products, donated - *Reps. e Invest. medicas,*
Metals products; machinery & transport equipment - *Arquitectos Metalicos,*
Metals products; machinery & transport equipment - *Produccion Mecanica,*
Metals products; machinery & transport equipment - *Sistemas y*
Metals products; machinery & transport equipment - *Translimite S.A. de C.V.*
Microfilm readers not capable of producing copies - *Microfilmacion y*
Micrometers, calipers and gauges - *Suministros y Proyectos*
Microphones; loudspeakers; sound amplifier etc, pt - *Importadora*
Microphones; loudspeakers; sound amplifier etc, pt - *Importadora*
Miscellaneous edible preparations - *Representaciones y Productos de*
Molds f rubber or plastics exc inject or compressn - *Plasticos Romay, S.A.*
Molds for rbr/plast, injection/compression type - *Moldeados Plasticos, S.A.*
Molds for rbr/plast, injection/compression type - *Partes para Moldes DME,*
Molds for rbr/plast, injection/compression type - *Plasticos Riomar, S. A. de*
Monofil, cr-sect ovimm, rods, sticks etc, plastics - *Retenes y Refacciones*
Motorcycles (incl mopeds) & cycles with aux motor - *Distribuidora*
Mowers for lawn, parks or sports grounds, nesoi - *Homemart De Mexico,*
Mufflers and exhaust pipes for motor vehicles - *Arsa y Compania, S.A. de*
Nar wov fab nesoi >5% elastomeric yrn rubber thrd - *Cia. Manufacturera de*
Natural sponges of animal origin - *Nutrisa, S.A. De C.V.*
Navigational instruments and appliances, nesoi - *Inforamet, S.A. de C.V.*
Newspapers, journals & periodicals - *Recursos de Alta Calidad S.A. de*
Newspapers, journals & periodicals - *Sanborn Hermanos, S.A. de C.V.*
Office and desk equip a prts, of base metal - *Manuel E. Delgado B. y Corp.*
Office or school supplies of plastic - *Sanford de Mexico, S.A. de C.V.*
Oil (not crude) from petrol & bitum mineral etc. - *Aceites, Aislantes Y*
Oil (not crude) from petrol & bitum mineral etc. - *Especialidades Quimicas*
Oil or fuel filters for internal combustion engine - *Filtros Baldwin de Mexico,*
Oil or fuel filters for internal combustion engine - *Refacciones y Servicios*
Optical elements, mounted; parts & accessories - *Ultravision 2001, S.A. DE*
Organic chemicals - *Inter Export, S.A. de C.V.*
Orthopedic appl; artif body pts; hear aid; pts etc - *Comercializadora Y*
Orthopedic appl; artif body pts; hear aid; pts etc - *Ind. Hospitalaria*
Orthopedic appl; artif body pts; hear aid; pts etc - *Rochester Mexico, S.A.*
Orthopedic appl; artif body pts; hear aid; pts etc - *Servicam, S.A.*
Oscilloscopes, spectrum analyzers etc, parts etc - *Cia. Proveedora de Ind.*
Oscilloscopes, spectrum analyzers etc, parts etc - *Radio Surtidora, S.A.*
Otanulated slag fr iron or steel manufacture - *William Young & Co., S.A. de*
Other motor fuels nesoi - *Remsa Electric Motors, S.A.*
Outboard engines for marine propulsion - *Industria Mexicana de Equipo*
Oven, cooking stove & plate, range, roaster, nesoi - *Serving, S.A. de C.V.*

Oxygen - *Oxigeno de Veracruz*
Packing cases etc of wood; pallets etc of wood - *Mezquite Maderas*
Packing containers nesoi of paper, pprbrd, etc - *Corporacion Impresora,*
Packing or wrapping machinery, nesoi - *Grupo Gace, S.A. de C.V.*
Paint & varnish from synth etc polymers aqueous md - *Aguirre,*
Pallets, box pallets and other load boards of wood - *Maderas I*
Pantyhose, socks & other hosiery, knit or crochet - *Productos Donelli S.A*
Paper & paperbd coated, etc, with plastics nesoi - *Proveedora de Papel,*
Paper & paperboard & articles (inc papr pulp artl) - *Nueva Papelera Famer*
Parts & access for motor vehicles (head 8701-8705) - *Grupo Echlin*
Parts & access for motor vehicles (head 8701-8705) - *Mexico Limpio, S.A.*
Parts & access for motor vehicles (head 8701-8705) - *Partes de Colision*
Parts & accessories for adp machines & units - *Industrias de Precision,*
Parts for steam and other vapor turbines - *Ingenieria y Control de*
Parts of truck assemblies, nesoi - *Incopi-Industrializadora y Comercia*
Perfume oil blends, prod use finished perfume base - *Pavel de Mexico, S.A.*
Perfumes and toilet waters - *Inmobiliaria y Comercializadora*
Perfumes and toilet waters - *Suburbia S.A. de C.V.*
Personal toilet etc prep nesoi, shaving, bath etc. - *Bibermex, S. A. de C. V.*
Pharmaceutical products - *Casa Autrey, S.A. de C.V.*
Pharmaceutical products - *Casa Marzam, S.A. de C.V.*
Pharmaceutical products - *Drogueros, S.A. de C.V.*
Pharmaceutical products - *Laboratorios Sanfer, S.A. de C.V.*
Pharmaceutical products - *Productos Medicos en General,*
Pharmaceutical products - *Watson Phillips y Cia. Sucs. S. A.*
Photogrammetrical surveying instruments & applnces - *Servicios*
Pile-drivers and pile-extractors - *Cimentaciones Tecnicas, S.A. de C.V*
Pile-drivers and pile-extractors - *Cimentaciones Y Puertos, S.A.*
Pipe tools and parts thereof, base metal - *El Ancla de Paz y Noriega, S.A.*
Pipe, reinforced combine w textiles, w o fittings - *Casa Distex, S.A. de C.V.*
Pipes etc nesoi, riveted etc, of iron or steel - *Nuremex, S.A. de C.V.*
Plastics and articles thereof - *Anahuac Formados y Plasticos, S.A.*
Plastics and articles thereof - *Bolsas Finas San Luis, S.A. de C.V.*
Plastics and articles thereof - *Consorcio Industrial Serrano*
Plastics and articles thereof - *Corporacion Coral, S.A. de C.V.*
Plastics and articles thereof - *Criser, S.A. de C.V.*
Plastics and articles thereof - *DIPSA Distribuidora Meny,*
Plastics and articles thereof - *Distribuidora de Envases de Mexico*
Plastics and articles thereof - *Empaques Plasticos de Mexico*
Plastics and articles thereof - *Impulsora Mexicana de Productos*
Plastics and articles thereof - *J.J. Plas, S.A. de C.V.*
Plastics and articles thereof - *Plasticos Automotrices Dina,*
Plastics and articles thereof - *Serviempaques Marba, S.A. de C.V.*
Plates, sheets, film, foil & strip nesoi, plastics - *Comercializadora Industrial*
Pneumatic elevators and conveyors - *Industrias Marro, S.A. De C.V.*
Pneumatic elevators and conveyors - *Silos y Camiones, S. A. de C. V.*
Polyethylene having a spec gravity of 0.94 or more - *Plasticos Geminis,*
Polymers of vinyl acetate, in aqueous dispersion - *Secretaria De Desarrollo*
Polyvinyl chloride,not mixed with any oth substanc - *Industrias Plasticas*
Powder-actuated handtools and parts, base metal - *Hertel de Mexico, S. A.*
Power supplies - *Transmisiones y Repuestos de*
Prefabricated buildings - *Prefabricados E Ingenieria Civil*
Prep or pres fish; caviar & caviar substitutes - *Organizacion Agor, S.A. de C.V.*
Preparations used in animal feeding - *Proveedora de Alimentos Avepecuario*
Prepared additives for cements, mortars concretes - *Curacreto, S.A. de C.V.*
Prepared glues & adhesives nesoi; glue retail pack - *Bostik Mexicana, S.A.*
Pressure-reducing control valves, taps, cocks, et - *Rhacor, S.A. de C.V.*
Primary cells & batteries, parts - *Alexander Batteries de Mexico,*
Primary cells & batteries, parts - *Protecciones Electricas, S.A. de CV*
Primary cells & batteries, parts - *Saft Nife Mexico, S.A. de C.V.*
Process control inst&apprts for complete systems - *Harry Mazal, S.A. de C.V.*
Process control inst&apprts for complete systems - *Rime Control Systems,*
Process control inst&apprts for complete systems - *Servicios Industriales y*
Process control inst&appts,flow&liq level control - *Ingenieria y*
Pumps fitted with measuring device, nesoi - *Surtidora Industrial del*
Pumps for liquids, nesoi - *Bombas y Control de Fluidos,*
Pumps for liquids, nesoi - *Bufete de Tecnologia Solar, S.A.*
Pumps for liquids, nesoi - *Corporacion Integral Diesel, S.A.*
Pumps for liquids, nesoi - *Grupo Cerro*
Pumps for liquids, nesoi - *Minco Mexicana, S.A. de C. V.*
Pumps for liquids; liquid elevators; parts thereof - *Central de Hidraulica Y*
Pumps for liquids; liquid elevators; parts thereof - *Coprosa Consultores Y*
Quartz (other than natural sands) - *Cristales de Cuarzo,S.A. de C.V.*
Quicklime, slaked lime and hydraulic lime - *Distribuidora Internacional de*
Railway, tramway sleepers, wood, not impregnated - *Promotora Comercial*
Reaction initiators & acceler & catalyt prep nesoi - *Industrias Therme, S.A.*
Reception apparatus for radiotelephony etc - *Traxit Comunicaciones, S.A.*
Recorded media for sound including master prod rcd - *Central del Software,*
Recorded media for sound including master prod rcd - *Interaccion en*
Records, tapes & other recorded sound media etc - *Calmecac Consultores,*
Records, tapes & other recorded sound media etc - *Comunicaciones e*
Records, tapes & other recorded sound media etc - *Diagnosticos*
Records, tapes & other recorded sound media etc - *Electronica*
Records, tapes & other recorded sound media etc - *I.A.S.I., S.A. de C.V.*
Records, tapes & other recorded sound media etc - *Info-Sistemas,*
Records, tapes & other recorded sound media etc - *Intelmex, S.A. de C.V.*
Records, tapes & other recorded sound media etc - *Novidea Sistemas*
Records, tapes & other recorded sound media etc - *Organizacion Contable*
Refrigerators, freezers etc; heat pumps nesoi, pts - *R.R. Refrigeracion, S. A.*
Registers, notebooks, binders, bus forms etc, papr - *Formas Continuas*
Relays for voltage 60 v or more but nt over 1000v - *Corpisa, S.A. DE C.V.*
Rods & profile shape vulcanized rub, cellular rub - *Central de Profiles Y Tubos*
Rods,sticks & profile shapes,of polymr vin chlorid - *Fetasa Tijuana, S. A.*
Rubber and articles thereof - *Juntas de Expansion de Mexico,*
Rubber and articles thereof - *Sodi Asociados, S.A.*
Rubber, unvulcanized, in plates, sheets, and strip - *Elastonsa, S.A.*
Rubber, unvulcanized, in plates, sheets, and strip - *Grupo Industrial*
Rubber, unvulcanized, in plates, sheets, and strip - *Suministro De*
Rubber, unvulcanized, in plates, sheets, and strip - *Surtidora Mexico, S. A.*
Safes, cash or deed boxes etc a prts, base metal - *Sistemas Protectores,*
Safety(incl sports)hdgr,whether not lined trimmed - *Emilio Carmona Cortez*
Salmon, nesoi, fresh or chilled - *Distribuidora Altamar, S.A. de C.V.*
Scales fr continuous weighing of goods on conveyor - *Cia. Proveedora de I*
Screws, bolts, nuts, washers etc, iron or steel - *Arie, S. A. de C. V.*
Screws, bolts, nuts, washers etc, iron or steel - *Soporte Tecnologico, S. A.*
Seeders - *Grupo Agromora, S.A. de C.V.*
Seeds, fruits and spores used for sowing - *Proveedora Agricola e Industrial*
Self-adhesive plates, sheets, film etc of plastics - *Distribuidora de Cintas*
Sewing thread artificial filaments for retail sale - *Jony-Zip, S.A. de C.V.*
Shrimps and prawns, prepared or preserved, nesoi - *Ahome Acuicola, S.A.*
Silicones, in primary forms - *Protexa, S.A. DE C.V.*
Soap & oth organic surf act prod - *Dist. de Jabones Decorativos*
Soap; organic surf-act prep for soap use, bars etc - *Abasto Basico, S.A*
Soda fountain,beer dispensing equip, refrigerated - *Iner, S.A. DE C.V.*
Solar cells in modules or panels - *Grupo Condumex - Division de*
Speedometers and tachometers; stroboscopes - *Serviteck, S.A. de C.V.*
Springs & leaves for springs - *Maquiladora de Resortes Industria-*
Stainless steel cooking and kitchenware - *Ekco, S.A. de C.V.*
Stainless steel in ingots or other primary forms - *Mexican Printing Supply, S.A.*
Stainless steel ingots and other primary forms - *Sedin, S.A. de C.V.*
Stampings of bodies of 8701 to 8705 - *Troquel-Mex, S. A.*
Starches; inulin - *Productos Quimicos Industriales*
Stoves, ranges etc, nonel domest & pts, ir & steel - *Industrias Continental,*
Stoves, ranges etc, nonel domest & pts, ir & steel - *Industrias Quetzal, S.A.*
Stoves, ranges etc, nonel domest & pts, ir & steel - *Maquinaria y Caminos,*
Stoves, ranges etc, nonel domest & pts, ir & steel - *Proveg, S.A. de C.V.*
Stoves, ranges etc, nonel domest & pts, ir & steel - *Singer Mexicana, S.A.*
Sugar confectionery, without cocoa, nesoi - *Grupo Industrial Bimbo, S. A.*
Sunglasses - *Lopez Mercantil Distribuidora,*
Supported catalysts, nesoi - *Petroleo Quimica, S.A. de C.V.*
Suspension shock absorbers for motor vehicles - *Cadena Automotriz, S.A.*
Suspension shock absorbers for motor vehicles - *Exicsa, Explotacion e*
Suspension shock absorbers for motor vehicles - *Productps de Marmol*
Switches, nesoi - *Servicios de Ingenieria, S.A.*
T-shirts, singlets etc, knit etc, textiles nesoi - *Distribuidora de Uniformes*
Table, kitchen etc articles & pts, stainless steel - *Servifiestas Bemoyo*
Tableware & other household articles etc, plastics - *Proveedora del Hogar,*
Tableware etc of base metal, & base metal parts - *Vitrocrisa Cubiertos, S.*
Tanks - *Equipos Especializados Delta,*
Tanks - *Marlo Y Asociados, S.A. de C.V.*
Tanks - *Satena, S.A. de C.V.*
Tanks - *Trinity Industries de Mexico,*
Telephonic apparatus, carrier-current line system - *Iberoamerican Cultural*
Television antennas, nesoi - *Redes Via Satelite, S.A. de C.V.*
Textbooks - *Nueva Editorial Interamericana*
Textile card clothing and similar fabrics - *Exclusivas Michel, S.A. de C.V.*
Textile fabric nesoi, coated etc nesoi, cotton - *Albatros Textil, S.A. de C.V.*
Textile fabrics nesoi coated etc with pvc, cotton - *Grupo Bambu S.A. de C.V.*
Textile printing machinery - *Saltex, S. A.*
Textile products etc for technical uses nesoi - *Refacciones Textiles Canet,*
Textile wall coverings - *Idelco, S.A. de C.V.*
Thermometers liquid-filled, direct reading, nesoi - *Termometros Mexicanos,*
Tomato paste - *Productos Industrializados del*
Tools for boring or broaching, and base metal pts - *Insertos, Pastillas y*
Tools for boring or broaching, and base metal pts - *J.J. Herramientas, S.A.*
Tools for working in the hand, pneumatic etc, pts - *Aireco, S.A.*
Tools, cutlery etc. of base metal & parts thereof - *Urresko, S. A. de C. V.*
Tools, cutlery etc. of base metal & parts thereof - *Vare, S. A. de C. V.*
Trans appar for radiotelephony etc; tv cameras - *Electronica, Ingenieria y*
Transformers nesoi, power handling cap nov 1 kva - *Bobimex, S.S. de C.V.*
Transformers, nesoi, unrated - *Etica Ensenada, S. A. de C.V.*
Transformers, nesoi, unrated - *I.T.M. Representaciones de Baja*

Transformers, nesoi, unrated - *Maquinaria Electrica Pisa*
Trucks, nesoi - *Dina Diesel de Cuautitlan*
Trucks, nesoi - *Equipomex, S.A. DE C.V.*
Trucks, nesoi - *Tractocamiones Kenworth*
Tubes, pipes & hoses & their fittings, of plastics - *Tuberias PVC, S.A.*
Tubes, pipes & hoses, nesoi - *Fabricaciones Industriales TUMEX,*
Tubes, pipes & hoses, of polymer of vinyl chlordie - *Macro Electrica de Baja*
Tubes, pipes & hoses, of polymer of vinyl chlordie - *Madepla, S.A.*
Tubes, pipes etc, seamless nesoi, ir nesoi & steel - *Neo-Tech International,*
Tubes, pipes etc, seamless, iron nesoi & steel - *Tubesa, S.A. de C.V.*
Tv cam tube,image convert & intensifiers - *Omci, S.A de C. V.*
Typewriter etc ribbons, inked or prep; ink pads - *Sistemas Admin. de l*
Valves f oleohydraulic or pneumatic transmissions - *Comercial Gricom, S.A.*
Valves f oleohydraulic or pneumatic transmissions - *Schrader Bellows*
Veneer sheets etc, not over 6 mm thick - *Distribuidora de Maderas Finas,*
Veneer sheets etc, not over 6 mm thick - *Maderas del Norte y o Sergio Alfon-*
Video discs, recorded - *Manufacturera Burst, S.A. de C. V.*
Video recording or playing equip,exc tape - *Pixart, S.A. de C.V.*
Vitamins, natural or synthetic, dosage etc form - *Biotecnologia y Nutricion,*
Vitamins, natural or synthetic, dosage etc form - *Distribuidora Naturista Hadad*
Water filtering or purifying machinery & apparatus - *Acondicionamiento*
Water filtering or purifying machinery & apparatus - *Bur-Flo, S.A. de C.V.*
Water filtering or purifying machinery & apparatus - *Dicamex, S.A. de C.V.*
Water filtering or purifying machinery & apparatus - *Servicios Y Refacciones,*
Waterproof footwear rubber/plastic covers the knee - *Promani, S.A. de C.V.*
Waters, natural etc, not sweetened etc; ice & snow - *Agua del Rey*
Western red alder sawn lengthwise over 6mm, rough - *Promotora de*
White mineral oil, not medicinal grade - *Lubricantes y Derivados,S.A. C.V.*
Winches and capstans powered by electric motors - *Organizacion de*
Windshields of laminated safety glass - *Autocristales Jelussem, S.A. de*
Wire of alloy steel nesoi - *Alta Resistencia, S.A.*
Wire of alloy steel nesoi - *Empresas Marien, S.A. de C.V.*
Wire of iron & nonalloy steel - *Nicro, S.A. de C.V.*
Wire, rods etc for soldering etc & met spray, bmpt - *Aleaciones Y*
Wire, rods etc for soldering etc & met spray, bmpt - *Soldaduras Y*
Women's or girls' blouses and shirts cotton, knit - *Prendas Tejidas de*
Wood and articles of wood; wood charcoal - *Comercial Maderera Diana,*
Wood and articles of wood; wood charcoal - *Industrias Monterrubio, S.A.*
Wood in the rough, stripped or not of sapwood etc - *Maderas Selvamex,*
Wood marquetry, etc; wood caskets and cases, etc. - *Madereria San*
Wood sawn or chipped length, sliced etc, ov6mm th - *Madererias Toluca, S.*
Wood, tongued, grooved, molded etc, coniferous - *Ferreteria y Madereria*
Wooden frames paintings, photographs, mirrors, etc - *Molduras y Marcos*
Wooden furniture of a kind used in offices - *Ofinobel, S.A. de C.V.*
Wooden furniture of a kind used in offices - *Rodymueble S.A. de C.V.*
Wov fabric, synth staple fib nu 85% synth st fiber - *Labatt Mexico, S.A. DE*
Wov fabric, synth staple fib nu 85% synth st fiber - *Productos Fragante,*
Wov fabric, synth staple fib nu 85% synth st fiber - *Telas, No Tejidos, S.A.*
Yarn & fine an hair, retail pk, not un 85% wl or h - *San Gerardo Textil, S.A.*

Canada: Company Listings Of Products & Services

264362 Alberta Ltd.
422, 10120 Brookpark Blvd. S.W.
Calgary, AB T2W 3G3
Contact: Vern Reiling, President
PHONE: 403/238-3613
Product/Service Description:
Oil (not crude) from petrol &
bitum mineral etc.

Airobec international
5665 des Epinettes
Montreal, QC H1T 2S5
Contact: Mr. Jean Paul Bourdages,
President
PHONE: 514/254-8055
Product/Service Description:
Roofing tiles, chimney pots, cowls,
ch liners etc

Alpha Eagle Group Ltd.
1795 Meyerside Drive, Unite 5
Mississauga, ON L5T 1E3
Contact: Mr. Jim Tomson, Vice
President
PHONE: (905) 564-1540
Product/Service Description:
Cleaning preparations

Arjay Engineering Ltd.
2495 Haines Road
Mississauga, ON L4Y 1Y7
Contact: Mr. Greg Reeves,
President
PHONE: 416/277-4541
Product/Service Description:
Chickens, young, not cut in pieces,
frozen

Audiospec Inc.
7123 Fir Tree Drive, Unit 5
Mississauga, ON L5S 1G4
Contact: Ms. Sally Coulter, Office
Manager
PHONE: 905/673-6463
Product/Service Description:
Audio frequency electric
amplifiers, nesoi

Award Buying Group
1595 Bedford Hwy. #501
Bedford, NS B4A 3ZP
Contact: Mr. John Macdougall,
President
PHONE: 902-835-7242
Product/Service Description:
Hardware Stores

B.B. GLAZER
60 Sheraton Drive suite 12
Montreal Qest, QC H4X 1N4
Contact: B. Glazer, President
PHONE: 514/488-2262
Product/Service Description:
Railway etc track construct
material, iron & steel , steel iron
products

B.N. Marketing Services
411 Flett Drive
Airdrie, AB T4B 2G4
Contact: Bob Nelles, Sales
Marketing & PR Specialist
PHONE: 403/948-3515
Product/Service Description:
Nuts nesoi, fresh or dried

Bandages Universels Inc.
2125 boul. Industriel
Chambly, QC J3L 4C5
Contact: Mme. Martine Girard,
Presidente
PHONE: 514/658-8663
Product/Service Description:
Bandages etc coated etc or in retail
medic etc fm

Behar Marketing Ltd.
4850 Cote des Neiges Suite 2009
Montreal, QC H3V 1G5
Contact: Mr. Robin Behar,
President
PHONE: 514/739-8157
Product/Service Description:
Hospital furniture

Blay-Trem
2025 D'Arviva
St Bruno, QC J3U 3R7
Contact: Mrs. Micheline Sullivan,
PHONE: 514/441-2928
Product/Service Description:
Articles of leather, nesoi

Bouchard & Freres, Inc.
553 Couture
Roberval, QC G8H 2W2
Contact: Ms. Jacqueline Bouchard,
President
PHONE: 418/275-1888
Product/Service Description:
Miscellaneous Durable Goods

Bow River Iron Works Ltd
4137 16 Street S.E.
Calgary, AB T2G 3T7
Contact: Ludy Maric, Manager
PHONE: 403/269-6944
Product/Service Description:
Semifinished products of iron or
nonalloy steel

Canica
234 Picard
St-Eustache, QC J7R 5A1
Contact: Mr. Rejean Du Cap,
Consultant
PHONE: 514/472-0067
Product/Service Description:
Articles of iron or steel, nesoi

Cantech Corporation
1916-27 Ave. N.E.
Calgary, AB T2E 7A5
Contact: Steve Schmeeckle,
Marketing Manager
Sales International
PHONE: 403/250-9888
Product/Service Description:
Automatic regulating or control
instruments; parts ; Insturments ,
regulating control.

Choreo Systems Inc.
203-47 Colborne St.
Toronto, ON M5E 1P8
Contact: Mr. John Lugsdin,
President
PHONE: 416/360-0516
Product/Service Description:
Computer & Data Processing
Service

Chummy Canada Inc.
160 East Beaver Creek Rd., Unit
Richmond Hill, ON L4B 3L4
Contact: Catherine Chum,
PHONE: 905/882-1657
Product/Service Description:
Woven fabrics of combed wool or
fah >=85% wl fah o

Comai
4855 Ch. Cote St. Luc
Montreal, QC H3W 2H5
Contact: Mr. Richard Sachs,
Owner
PHONE: 514/483-0509
Product/Service Description:
Video recording or playing
equip,exc tape

**Commonwealth Sales
Group**
32 Meadowlane Drive
Kitchener, ON N2N 1E9
Contact: Mr. Horold Smith,
President
PHONE: 519/571-0934
Product/Service Description:
Lawn & Garden Services

Creation Imagine
220 Cure Boivin
Boisbriand, QC J7G 2K8
Contact: Mr. Gerard Valiquette,
Owner
PHONE: 514/430-5063
Product/Service Description:
Wov cot fab, unbl pl wv nun 85%
cot nov 100 g m2

Datrem Wholesalers
131 Denault
Kirkland, QC H9J 3X4
Contact: Mr. Darrin Tremblay,
PHONE: 514/695-5321
Product/Service Description:
Food preparations nesoi

Davco Tooling Inc.
52 McIntyre Place, Unite E
Kitchener, ON N2R 1H9
Contact: Mr. Dave Elford, President
PHONE: 519/895-113030
Product/Service Description:
Clamps and similar handtools, not
vises, and parts

**Dept Economic Development
& Tourism**
P.O. Box 6000
Fredericton, NB E3B 5H1
Contact: Mr. Jim McKay, Manager,
Trade
PHONE: 506/453-2875
Product/Service Description:
Administration of General
Economic Programs

**Distribution
perimaitre(perimaster)**
4403 des Industries
Laval, QC
Contact: Mr. Yvon Lauzon,
President
PHONE: 514/661-5560
Product/Service Description:
Metal furniture nesoi

Eagle Enterprises
241 9790 Bonaventure Dr. S.E.
Calgary, AB T2J 0E6
Contact: Jerry Presiloski, Owner
PHONE: 403/252-2719
Product/Service Description:
Stoves, ranges etc, nonel domest &
pts, ir & steel

**Enershare Technology
Corporation**
87 Bakersfield Street
North York, ON M3J 1Z4
Contact: Mr. Rajan Balchandani,
Vice President
PHONE: 416/638-9317
Product/Service Description:
Super-heated water boilers

**Equipment sport metro
Inc.**
8278 St- Laurent #100
Montreal, QC H2P 2L8
Contact: Mr. G. Levert, President
PHONE: 514/687-8495
Product/Service Description:
Parts of garments and clothing

**Espace de l'UMA
Intercom**
1 rue Ozias Leduc
Blainville, QC J7C 4E7
Contact: Mr. Said Loukil,
President
PHONE: 514/979-6821
Product/Service Description:
Hand input devices, transmit data
to computer

Euredan
2304 Blvd. Keller
Ville St. Laurent, QC H4K 2P8
Contact: Mr. Alex Bechlian,
PHONE: 514/331-7442
Product/Service Description:
Building Construction, General
Contractors & Operative Builders

Factory Direct Marketing
9161 21 Street S.E.
Calgary, AB T2C 3Z4
Contact: Patrick Williams,
President
PHONE: 403/236-2218
Product/Service Description:
Electric sound or visual signaling
apparatus, pts

Ferreri M
63 Athlone
Montreal, QC H5A 1B5
Contact: Mr. Franco Ferreri,
PHONE: 514/874-1551
Product/Service Description:
Articles for pocket or
handbag,comp/patent leather

Frank Stein Sales Ltd.
39 Beaver Valley Rd.
Downsview, ON M3H 4S2
Contact: Mr. Frank Stein
PHONE: 416/635-7365
Product/Service Description:
Stationery Supplies

Future Ware Inc.
1992 Yonge Street
Toronto, ON M4S 1Z7
Contact: Edgar Ware, President
PHONE: 416/483-9563
Product/Service Description:
Injection type molds for rubber or
plastics, nesoi

**G.B Distributrices services
enr.**
2220 rue Robertine Barry
Montreal, QC H4N 3G1
Contact: Mr. Gerald Boudreau,
President
PHONE: 514/856-3432
Product/Service Description:
Automatic vending mach with
heating or refrig unit

G.B. Enterprises
1203 145 Point Dr. N.W.
Calgary, AB T3B 4W1
Contact: Gary Boyko, President
PHONE: 403/283-7720
Product/Service Description:
Articles of nat or cult pearls, prec
semprc stones

**G.B. Strachan Investments
Ltd.**
4489 Shane Court
Burlington, ON L7L 5M6
Contact: Mr. George Strachan,
President
PHONE: 905/632-9625
Product/Service Description:
Golf clubs, complete

G.L. Ward Inc.
108 Oakes Road
Fall River, NS B2T 1J5
Contact: Mr. Greg Ward, President
PHONE: 902-861-3320
Product/Service Description:
Water filtering or purifying
machinery & apparatus

G.O. Gauthier Inc.
69, de l'Erabliere
Mont Shefford, QC J0E 2N0
Contact: Mr. Gaston Gauthier,
President
PHONE: 514/539-3771
Product/Service Description:
Fruit nesoi, fresh

Galvacor Inc.
790 Boul St. Joseph
Quebec City, PQ G2K 1W6
Contact: Mr. Andre Simard, Vice
President, Development
PHONE: 418-648-0858
Product/Service Description:
Metal Services, Coating and Allied
Services

General Realty Ltd.
5556 Sullivan
Halifax, NS B3K 1X7
Contact: Mr. John Renouf,
President
PHONE: 902-454-7424
Product/Service Description:
Chocolate & other food products
containing cocoa

Geomet Instruments
1014 Birch Street
New Minas, NS B4N 4H4
Contact: Mr. Phill Mosher, Sales &
Marketing
PHONE: 902-681-4347
Product/Service Description:
Meas & checkng instrument,
appliances & mach nesoi

Gestion Gerald Diotte Inc.
354 Larochelle Street
Repentigny, QC J6A 5W1
Contact: Mr. Gerald Diotte,
PHONE: 514/654-5663
Product/Service Description:
Portland cement, aluminous
cement, slag cement etc

Global Medichem (Canada)
D274 1600 90 Ave S.W.
Calgary, AB T2V 5A8
Contact: Alfred Dei-Baning,
Managing Director
PHONE: 403/255-5944
Product/Service Description:
Medical, surgical, dental or vet
inst, no elec, pt

Grand Saddlery
108 8 Ave S.E.
Calgary, AB T2G 0K6
Contact: Bert Strandberg,
PHONE: 403/269-3293
Product/Service Description:
Saddlery & harness for any animal,
of any material

Guss Associates

5 Robindale Rd.
Winnipeg, MAN R3R 1G6
Contact: Dave Guss, Sales &
Marketing
PHONE: 204/8880497
Product/Service Description:
Parts for engines

Guy Tetreult Agencies Ltd.

6152 Boul. Robert
St. Leonard, QC H1P 1N1
Contact: Mr. Guy Tetreault,
President
PHONE: 514/326-3453
Product/Service Description:
Fishing rods & tackle; nets; decoys
etc; parts etc

H.D. Super Sport

84 Chateaugauy
Huntingdon, QC J0S 1H0
Contact: Mr. Harvey Davignon,
PHONE: 514/264-6173
Product/Service Description:
Automotive Parts & Supplies

HTRC Automation Inc.

285, rue Laval, C.P. 990
Bromptonville, QC J0B 1H0
Contact: Benoit Laplante,
Presidnet
PHONE: 819-846-6577
Product/Service Description:
Rolls for rolling mills, cast steel

Ho Fung Trading (Canada) Co. Ltd.

55 West Beaver Creek Road, Unit
25
Richmond Hill, ON L4B 1K5
Contact: Maria G. Wong, Ho Fund
Trading (Canada) Company Ltd.
PHONE: 905/881-6823
Product/Service Description:
Wood, tongued, grooved, molded
etc, nonconiferous

Hodgson Agencies Inc.

148 Young Cres. P.O. Box 188
Stavely, AB ???
Contact: Lea Hodgson, Manager
PHONE: 403/549-3969
Product/Service Description:
Made-up clothing access nesoi,
parts etc, knit etc

Horizon Industries

5200 St-Francois
St-Laurent, QC H4S 1J8
Contact: Mr. Ross Anderson, Vice
President
PHONE: 514/633-1016
Product/Service Description:
Floor covering coated etc on a
nonwoven base nesoi

Independant Elevator Inc.

8405 Rsnard
Brossard, QC J4X 1R6
Contact: Mr. Bernard Lennon,
President
PHONE: 514/845-4129
Product/Service Description:
Elevators, pneumatic

Industrial sales services

1336 Deval D'Espoir
Laval, QC H7Y 1X6
Contact: Mr. Bernard Richard,
President
PHONE: 514/689-3197
Product/Service Description:
Tools for pressing, stamping or
punching, b m pts

Inforev Ltd.

9365 Roussel
Brossard, Quebec, QC J4X 2R3
Contact: Mr. B. Greenly, President
PHONE: 514/659-6207
Product/Service Description:
Computer Related Services N.e.c.

International business Co

1460 Dr Penfield ave Suite 703
Montreal, QC
Contact: Mr. R. Sawhney, Sales &
Marketing
PHONE: 514/849-6434
Product/Service Description:
Hard rubber in all forms; articles
of hard rubber

Intersphere International Ltd.

3, 1725 30 Ave N.E.
Calgary, AB T2E 7P6
Contact: Alvin Kang, President
PHONE: 403/250-8868
Product/Service Description:
Mach nesoi, moving, grad etc;
pile-dr; snoplow etc

Investors Research Service

5773 Glenarden
Cote St. Luc, QC H4W 2A5
Contact: Mr. Leonard Rosen,
Owner
PHONE: 514/482-3609
Product/Service Description:
Durable Goods, N.e.c.

Jack Atkinson & Assoc.

P.O. Box 22
Amherst, NS B4H 3Y6
Contact: Mr. John Atkinson,
President
PHONE: 902-667-9985
Product/Service Description:
Agric hort forest machy & lawn
ground roller parts

Kahnawake Building

P.O. Box 280
Kahnawake, QC J0L 1B0
Contact: Ms. Sandra McKernan,
PHONE: 514/632-7028
Product/Service Description:
Construction Materials, N.e.c.

Kalmoni Establishments

20 Venture Dr., Unit 1
Scarborough, ON M1B 3R7
Contact: J. Kalmoni, Kalmoni
PHONE: 416/283-4278
Product/Service Description:
New pneumatic tires of rubber, for
buses or trucks

L.S. Marketing

2816 26 St. S.W.
Calgary, AB T3E 2B2
Contact: Larry Slemchuck, Partner
PHONE: 403/246-7280
Product/Service Description:
Books, brochures & similar printed
matter

Lem & Walters Ltd.

Bench Point
Bench Point, PEI C0A 1N0
Contact: Mr. Alan Baker, Sales &
Marketing
PHONE: 902/962-3069
Product/Service Description:
Monofil, cr-sect ovimm, rods,
sticks etc, plastics

Les Agences Roger Boutin

333L chemin du Tremblay
Boucherville, QC J4B 7M1
Contact: Mr. Jean Boutin,
President
PHONE: 514/449-3080
Product/Service Description:
Tools for working in the hand,
pneumatic etc, pts

Les immeubles Univest ltee

980 rue St Antoine Ouest # 980
Montreal, QC H3C 1A8
Contact: Mr. Maurice Fefer,
President
PHONE: 514/878-1797
Product/Service Description:
Medical, surgical, dental or
veterinary furn etc

Lise Filion

30 Hazalwood.
Dollard des Ormeaux., QC H9A
2N6
Contact: Ms. Lise Filion,
Representant
PHONE: 514/684-2945
Product/Service Description:
Tableware & other household
articles etc, plastics

Lorne Shields Intertrade Corp.

555 Oakdale
Downsview, ON M3N 1V7
Contact: Mr. Lorne Shields,
President
PHONE: 416/749-7860
Product/Service Description:
Headgear nesoi, whether or not
lined or trimmed

MMCT International

4144 Dorchester
Westmount, QC H3Z 1V1
Contact: Mr. A. Vez,
President
PHONE: 514/933-3042
Product/Service Description:
Optic, photo etc, medic or surgical
instrments etc

Maintenance Jordan.
1330 Des Champs
Lac St Calaules, QC G0A 2H0
Contact: Mr. G. Claes,
Representant
PHONE: 418/849-8723
Product/Service Description:
Electric apparatus for line
telephony etc, parts

**Maniago Sport Distributor
Ltd.**
4455 Alaska Street
Burnaby, B.C. V5C 5T3
Contact: Mr. Dennis Ferrey,
Sales Manager
PHONE: 604/294-3414
Product/Service Description:
Footwear nesoi
Shoes
Sneakers

**Modular Plastic Systems,
Inc.**
P.O. Box 63, TD Bank Tower, TD
Ctr.
Toronto, ON M5K 1E7
Contact: Stuart Gordon, Modular
Plastic Systems, Inc.
PHONE: 416/601-9841
Product/Service Description:
Glass slivers, rovings, yarn and
chopped strands

Motiva Inc.
1193 Tecumseh
Dollard des Ormeaux, QC H9B
2Y9
Contact: Mr. Guy Beauchamp,
President
PHONE: 514/683-5446
Product/Service Description:
Computer Programming and Other
Software Services

Nestev Supplies
1324 Sunvista Way S.E.
Calgary, AB T2X 3G3
Contact: Christine Peterson,
President
PHONE: 403/256-3231
Product/Service Description:
Articles of jewelry & pts, of prec
metal or clad

New World
106, 9930 - 86 Avenue
Edmonton, AB T6E 2L7
Contact: Sales & Marketing, Sales
& Marketing
PHONE: 403/433-0903
Product/Service Description:
Articles & equip for sports etc
nesoi; pools; pts

Noraic Marketing
3524 49 St. S.W.
Calgary, AB T3E 6N8
Contact: Einar Slitten, President
PHONE: 403/830-3093
Product/Service Description:
Records, tapes & other recorded
sound media etc

**Norman H. Collin and
Associates**
6 - 4620 Manilla Road SE
Calgary, AB T2G 4B7
Contact: Dean Collin, General
Manager
PHONE: 403/243-3422
Product/Service Description:
Ceramic sinks, washbasins, water
closet bowls etc

Olsen Well Services Ltd.
642 Prospect Dr. S.W.
Calgary, AB T1A 4C1
Contact: Lloyd Olsen, President
PHONE: 403/527-5680
Product/Service Description:
Automatic data process machines;
magn reader etc

Orchard International
5915 Airport Road., Suite 605
Mississauga, ON L4V 1T1
Contact: Christine Peters, Orchard
International
PHONE: 905/677-8882
Product/Service Description:
Perfumery, cosmetic or toilet
preparations, nesoi

Oxyval Inc.
1970 rue Michelin
Chomeday, Laval, QC H7L 5C2
Contact: Mr. Yvon Locas,
President
PHONE: 514/687-7046
Product/Service Description:
Air or vac pumps, compr & fans;
hoods & fans; pts

Paquet enr.
7202 Roi-Rene
Anjou, QC H1K 3G6
Contact: Mr. Robert Paquet
PHONE: 514/351-7098
Product/Service Description:
Pantyhose, socks & other hosiery,
knit or crochet

Parval Equipment Ltd
9208 - 27 Avenue
Edmonton, AB T6N 1B2
Contact: Ralph Parsons, President
PHONE: 403/437-2334
Product/Service Description:
Taps, cocks, valves etc for pipes,
tanks etc, pts

Piercey's Supplies Ltd.
PO Box 816
Dartmouth, NS B2Y 3Z3
Contact: Mr. Dwight Fitzmorris,
PHONE: 902/468-2828
Product/Service Description:
Builders' ware of plastics, nesoi

Polar Bear Water Distiller
4824 Macleod Trail S.
Calgary, AB T2G 0A8
Contact: Charlie Blackmore, Sales
Rep.
PHONE: 403/245-2965
Product/Service Description:
Centrifuges; filter etc mach for liq
or gases; pts

**Polymer International
(N.S.) Inc.**
Abbey Avenue
Truro, NS B2N 5G6
Contact: Dale McSween, Sales &
Marketing
PHONE: 902/895-1686
Product/Service Description:
Plastics and articles thereof

**Prostitch Sportswear &
Embroidery**
#1 3424 26 St. N.E.
Calgary, AB T1Y 4T7
Contact: Jerry Jackman, Sales Rep.
PHONE: 403/291-4913
Product/Service Description:
Men's or boys' shirts, knitted or
crocheted

Quivala, Inc.
4541 Harris
Laval, PQ H7T 2P1
Contact: Mr. Earl Olshansky,
President
PHONE: 514/687-2495
Product/Service Description:
Lubricating prep for text etc, no
petr etc oil

RMC Sales
27 Sunmount Court S.E.
Calgary, AB T2X 2X8
Contact: Skip Cummins, Owner
PHONE: 403/256-0038
Product/Service Description:
Screws, bolts, nuts, washers etc,
iron or steel

Ramtech Enterprises Ltd.
50 Glenwood Place
Cochrane, AB T0L 0W3
Contact: Edward Thrush, Sales &
Marketing
PHONE: 403/932-4773
Product/Service Description:
Chemical & residual prod,
chemical etc ind nesoi

Remix Inc.
4450 Promenade Paton #1115
Montreal, QC H7W 5J7
Contact: Mr. Vincent Remilliard,
Representant
PHONE: 514/686-8169
Product/Service Description:
Beauty & skin care preparation,
nesoi

Rimar Enterprises
P.O. Box 6134 STN. A
Calgary, AB T2H 2L4
Contact: Richard Otte, Manager
PHONE: 403/251-5600
Product/Service Description:
Articles of asphalt or of similar
material

Robco Imex Inc.
4150 St. Catherine St. West
Montreal, QC H3Z 2Y5
Contact: Mr. Willi Jaeggi, Director
Export Marketing
PHONE: 514/939-2252
Product/Service Description:
Polymers of ethylene, in primary
forms

Sandra Meilleur
180 Mckenzie Lake Cove S.E.
Calgary, AB T2Z 1L1
Contact: Sandra Meilleur, Account
Exec.
PHONE: 403/257-1967
Product/Service Description:
Wooden frames paintings,
photographs, mirrors, etc

Schelling Marketing &
2156 Sherbrooke West Suit 17
Montreal, QC H3H 1G7
Contact: Mr. R.F. Schelling,
President
PHONE: 514/932-8444
Product/Service Description:
Management, Consulting & Public
Relations Services

Science Is...
7715 Hunterburn Hill N.W.
Calgary, AB T2K 4S5
Contact: George Pasterik,
PHONE: 403/274-7878
Product/Service Description:
Compound optical microscopes;
parts & accessories

Secru-Pack Services Inc.
204 3804 Macleod Tr. S.W.
Calgary, AB T2G 2P2
Contact: Dale Scully, Owner
PHONE: 403/287-9235
Product/Service Description:
Labels of paper or paperboard,
printed or not

Sefor Inc.
8134 Blvd. Levesque Est
Laval, QC H7S 267
Contact: Mr. Claude Chenier,
President
PHONE: 514/326-6000
Product/Service Description:
Motor Vehicles & Automotive
Parts & Supplies

Sico Incorporated
2505 rue de la Metropole
Longeuiel, QC G4G 1E5
Contact: Ms. Manon Beauchemin,
General Counsel & Secretary
PHONE: 514/527-5111
Product/Service Description:
Paint & varnish from synth etc
polymers nonaq, etc

Strome Sales Ltd.
3333 Chaucer Avenue
North Vancouver, B.C. V7K 2C2
Contact: Mr. Sandy Strome,
President
PHONE: 604/986-4339
Product/Service Description:
Paints & varnishes,aqueus, acrylic
or vinyl polymr

Summit Watch Company
6565 Kildare Road #303
Montreal, QC H4W 1B6
Contact: Mr. Bram Aron, President
PHONE: 514/488-5089
Product/Service Description:
Jewelry of precious or
semiprecious stones

Sunrise Sales
25 Marshall St. # 602
Richmond Hill, ON L4C 0A3
Contact: Mr. Les Goldford,
PHONE: 905/770-3058
Product/Service Description:
Soap & oth organic surf act prod,
toilet use, bars

Suntec Products Inc.
35 Deercrest Cl. S.E.
Calgary, AB T2T 5S2
Contact: Tom Hamers, General M.
PHONE: 403/278-0155
Product/Service Description:
Textile book cov fab; trac cl; paint
canvas etc

Sure - Foot Distributing
P.O. Box 76
Acme, AB T0M 0A0
Contact: Roy McCord, President
PHONE: 403/546-4419
Product/Service Description:
Articles nesoi of unharded
vulcanized rubber

Sure Products Sales
P.O. Box 1201
Brandon, MB R7A 6A4
Contact: Bill Iwasiuk, Owner
PHONE: 204/725-0376
Product/Service Description:
Hardware, fixtures, castors etc &
parts, base metl

Teletheque Inc.
445 Jean Talon ouest # 105
Montreal, QC H3N 1R1
Contact: Mr. Walter Zcobro,
President
PHONE: 514/336-6959
Product/Service Description:
Trade advertising material,
commercial catalog etc

**The Electric Colourfast
Printing**
1515 B2 Matheson Blvd. E.,
Mississauga, ON L4W 2P5
Contact: Andrew Mimnagh, The
Electric Colourfast Printing Corp.
PHONE: 905/238-0307
Product/Service Description:
Polyvinyl chloride, not mixed with
other substance

The Steeves Agency
9 Bayview Drive
Amherst, NS B4H 4E6
Contact: Verne Steeves, Partner
PHONE: 902/667-5703
Product/Service Description:
Baths, washbasins, lavatory seats
etc of plastics

Thermofort Inc
740 Industriel Blvd., Locale 223
Blainville, QC J7C 3V4
Contact: Mr. Andre Potvin,
General Manager
PHONE: 514-437-1986
Product/Service Description:
Blankets and traveling rugs

**Transcontinental Coatings
Inc.**
220 Coral Sands Pl. N.E.
Calgary, AB T3O 3O2
Contact: George Matyus, President
PHONE: 403/228-8091
Product/Service Description:
Polyester Coaatings

Transworld Imports Inc.
#115 - 11960 Hammersmith Way,
Richmond, B.C. V7A 5C9
Contact: Mr. Michael Somers,
Manager
PHONE: 604-272-3432
Product/Service Description:
Jewelry and parts thereof, of silver

**Vendormatic Equipment
Inc.**
5210 Finch Ave. E., Unit 24
Scarborough, ON M1S 4Z8
Contact: Mr. Nick Mantonakis,
PHONE: 416/69-8778
Product/Service Description:
Automatic goods-vending
machines, parts

**Westburne Industrial Ent.
Ltd.**
P.O. Box 8840, Stn. A
Halifax, NS B3K 5M5
Contact: Mr. Duncan Harvey
PHONE: 902/455-1571
Product/Service Description:
Telegraphic apparatus

Wicker Emporium Ltd.
8778
Halifax, NS B3K 5M4
Contact: Mr. David Yorke, VP
PHONE: 902/492-3250
Product/Service Description:
Casein, caseinates and other casein
derivatives

**Wilson Public Relations
Inc.**
Suite 400, 475 Howe Street,
Vancouver, B.C. V6C 2B3
Contact: Ms. Jan Bofenkamp,
PHONE: 604/681-7189
Product/Service Description:
Management Consulting

Wishbone Enterprises
P.O. Box 54
Tantallon, NS B0J 3J0
Contact: Mr. Dave Smith,
President
PHONE: 902/823-2382
Product/Service Description:
Machinery etc for temp chang treat
mat; w heat, pt

Canada : Product / Service Index

Agric hort forest machy & lawn ground roller parts - *Jack Atkinson*
Air or vac pumps, compr & fans; hoods & fans; pts - *Oxyval Inc.*
Articles & equip for sports etc nesoi; pools; pts - *New World*
Articles for pocket or handbag,comp/patent leather - *Ferreri M*
Articles nesoi of unharded vulcanized rubber - *Sure - Foot Distributi*
Articles of asphalt or of similar material - *Rimar Enterprises*
Articles of iron or steel, nesoi - *Canica*
Articles of jewelry & pts, of prec metal or clad - *Nestev Supplies*
Articles of leather, nesoi - *Blay-Trem*
Articles of nat or cult pearls, prec semprc stones - *G.B. Enterprises*
Audio frequency electric amplifiers, nesoi - *Audiospec Inc.*
Automatic data process machines; - *Olsen Well Services Ltd.*
Automatic goods-vending machines - *Vendormatic Equipment Inc.*
Automatic regulating or control instruments - *Cantech Corporation*
Automatic vending mach - *G.B Distributrices services enr.*
Automotive Parts & Supplies - *H.D. Super Sport*
Bandages etc coated - *Bandages Universels Inc.*
Baths, washbasins, lavatory seats - *The Steeves Agency*
Beauty & skin care preparation, nesoi - *Remix Inc.*
Blankets and traveling rugs - *Thermofort Inc*
Books, brochures & similar printed matter - *L.S. Marketing*
Builders' ware of plastics, nesoi - *Piercey's Supplies Ltd.*
Building Construction, General Contractors - *Euredan*
Casein, caseinates and other casein derivatives - *Wicker Emporium*
Centrifuges; filter etc mach for liq-*Polar Bear Water Distiller*
Ceramic sinks, washbasins *Norman H. Collin and Associates*
Chemical & residual prod - *Ramtech Enterprises Ltd.*
Chickens, young, not cut in pieces, frozen - *Arjay Engineering Ltd.*
Chocolate & other food products - *General Realty Ltd.*
Clamps and similar handtools, not vises - *Davco Tooling Inc.*
Cleaning preparations - *Alpha Eagle Group Ltd.*
Compound optical microscopes; parts & accessories - *Science Is...*
Computer & Data Processing Service - *Choreo Systems Inc.*
Computer Programming and Other Software Services - *Motiva Inc.*
Computer Related Services N.e.c. - *Inforev Ltd.*
Construction Materials, N.e.c. - *Kahnawake Building*
Durable Goods, N.e.c. - *Investors Research Service*
Electric apparatus for line telephony etc - *Maintenance Jordan.*
Electric sound visual signaling apparatus- *Factory Direct Marketing*
Elevators, pneumatic - *Independant Elevator Inc.*
Fishing rods & tackle; nets; decoys - *Guy Tetreult Agencies Ltd.*
Floor covering coated etc on a nonwoven base - *Horizon Industries*
Food preparations nesoi - *Datrem Wholesalers*
Footwear nesoi - *Maniago Sport Distributor Ltd.*
Fruit nesoi, fresh - *G.O. Gauthier Inc.*
Glass slivers, rovings, yarn - *Modular Plastic Systems, Inc.*
Golf clubs, complete - *G.B. Strachan Investments Ltd.*
Hand input devices, transmit data to computer - *Espace de l'UMA*
Hard rubber in all forms - *International business Co*
Hardware Stores - *Award Buying Group*
Hardware, fixtures, castors etc & parts, - *Sure Products Sales*
Headgear - *Lorne Shields Intertrade Corp.*
Hospital furniture - *Behar Marketing Ltd.*
Injection type molds for rubber or plastics, nesoi - *Future Ware Inc.*
Jewelry and parts thereof- *Zurich Gold Distributors Ltd.*
Jewelry and parts thereof, of silver - *Transworld Imports Inc.*
Jewelry of precious or semiprecious stones - *Summit Watch Co.*
Labels of paper or paperboard - *Secru-Pack Services Inc.*
Lawn & Garden Services - *Commonwealth Sales Group*
Lubricating prep for text etc, no petr etc oil - *Quivala, Inc.*
Mach nesoi, moving, grad etc; pile-dr - *Intersphere International*
Machinery etc for temp chang treat mat - *Wishbone Enterprises*
Made-up clothing access - *Hodgson Agencies Inc.*
Management Consulting - *Wilson Public Relations Inc.*
Management, Consulting & Public Relations - *Schelling Marketing*
Meas & checkng instrument - *Geomet Instruments*

Medical, surgical, dental or vet instt - *Global Medichem (Canada)*
Medical, surgical, dental or veterinary - *Les immeubles Univest ltee*
Men's or boys' shirts - *Prostitch Sportswear & Embroidery*
Metal Services, Coating and Allied Services - *Galvacor Inc.*
Metal furniture nesoi - *Distribution perimaitre(perimaster)*
Miscellaneous Durable Goods - *Bouchard & Freres, Inc.*
Monofil, cr-sect ovimm, rods, sticks , plastics - *Lem & Walters Ltd*
Motor Vehicles & Automotive Parts & Supplies - *Sefor Inc.*
New pneumatic tires of rubber - *Kalmoni Establishments Inc.*
Nuts nesoi, fresh or dried - *B.N. Marketing Services*
Oil (not crude) from petrol & bitum mineral etc - *264362 Alberta Ltd.*
Optic, photo etc, or surgical instrments etc - *MMCT International*
Paint & varnish from synth etc polymers - *Sico Incorporated*
Paints & varnishes,aqueus, acrylic - *Strome Sales Ltd.*
Pantyhose, socks & other hosiery, knit or crochet - *Paquet enr.*
Parts for engines - *Guss Associates*
Parts of garments/clothing accessories-*Equipment sport metro Inc.*
Perfumery, cosmetic or toilet preparations - *Orchard International*
Plastics and articles thereof - *Polymer International (N.S.) Inc.*
Polyethers,expoxides & polyesters- *Transcontinental Coatings Inc.*
Polymers of ethylene, in primary forms - *Robco Imex Inc.*
Polyvinyl chloride - *The Electric Colourfast Printing*
Portland cement, aluminous cement - *Gestion Gerald Diotte Inc.*
Railway etc track construct material, iron & steel - *B.B. GLAZER*
Records, tapes & other recorded sound media - *Noraic Marketing*
Rolls for rolling mills, cast steel - *HTRC Automation Inc.*
Roofing tiles, chimney pots, cowls- *Airobec international*
Saddlery & harness for any animal,of any material - *Grand Saddlery*
Screws, bolts, nuts, washers etc, iron or steel - *RMC Sales*
Semifinished products of iron - *Bow River Iron Works Ltd*
Soap & oth organic surf act prod, toilet use, bars - *Sunrise Sales*
Stationery Supplies - *Frank Stein Sales Ltd.*
Stoves, ranges etc, nonel domest & pts - *Eagle Enterprises*
Super-heated water boilers - *Enershare Technology Corporation*
Tableware & other household articles etc, plastics - *Lise Filion*
Taps, cocks, valves etc for pipes, tanks - *Parval Equipment Ltd*
Telegraphic apparatus - *Westburne Industrial Ent. Ltd.*
Textile book cov fab; trac cl; paint canvas - *Suntec Products Inc.*
Tools for pressing, stamping or punching - *Industrial sales services*
Tools for working in the hand - *Les Agences Roger Boutin*
Trade advertising material, commercial catalog etc - *Teletheque Inc.*
Video recording or playing equip,exc tape - *Comai*
Water filtering or purifying machinery & apparatus - *G.L. Ward Inc.*
Women's or girls' suits, not knit, textiles nesoi - *YFI Inc.*
Wood, tongued, grooved, molded - *Ho Fung Trading (Canada) Co.*
Wooden frames paintings, photographs - *Sandra Meilleur*
Wov cot fab, unbl pl wv nun 85% - *Creation Imagine*
Woven fabrics of combed wool - *Chummy Canada Inc.*

SIC Code Description

Abrasive Products - 3291
Accident and Health Insurance - 6321
Accounting, Auditing, and Bookkeeping - 8721
Adhesives and Sealants - 2891
Adjustment and Collection Services - 7322
Administration of Educational Programs - 9411
Administration of General Economic Prgrams - 9611
Administration of Public Health Programs - 9431
Administration of Social & Manpower Progr - 9441
Administration of Veterans' Affairs - 9451
Advertising Agencies - 7311
Advertising, Nec - 7319
Agricultural Chemicals, Nec - 2879
Air Courier Services - 4513
Air Transportation, Nonscheduled - 4522
Air Transportation, Scheduled - 4512
Air and Gas Compressors - 3563
Air, Water, and Solid Waste Management - 9511
Aircraft - 3721
Aircraft Engines and Engine Parts - 3724
Aircraft Parts and Equipment, Nec - 3728
Airports, Flying Fields, and Services - 4581
Alkalies and Chlorine - 2812
Aluminum Die-castings - 3363
Aluminum Extruded Products - 3354
Aluminum Foundries - 3365
Aluminum Rolling and Drawing, Nec - 3355
Aluminum Sheet, Plate, and Foil - 3353
Ammunition, Except For Small Arms, Nec - 3483
Amusement Parks - 7996
Amusement and Recreation, Nec - 7999
Analytical Instruments - 3826
Animal Aquaculture - 0273
Animal Specialties, Nec - 0279
Animal Specialty Services - 0752
Animal and Marine Fats and Oils - 2077
Anthracite Mining - 1231
Apartment Building Operators - 6513
Apparel Belts - 2387
Apparel and Accessories, Nec - 2389
Architectural Metalwork - 3446
Architectural Services - 8712
Armature Rewinding Shops - 7694
Asbestos Products - 3292
Asphalt Felts and Coatings - 2952
Asphalt Paving Mixtures and Blocks - 2951
Auto Exhaust System Repair Shops - 7533
Auto and Home Supply Stores - 5531
Automatic Vending Machines - 3581
Automobile Parking - 7521
Automobiles and Other Motor Vehicles - 5012
Automotive Dealers, Nec - 5599
Automotive Glass Replacement Shops - 7536
Automotive Repair Shops, Nec - 7539
Automotive Services, Nec - 7549
Automotive Stampings - 3465
Automotive Transmission Repair Shops - 7537
Automotive and Apparel Trimmings - 2396
Bags: Plastic, Laminated, and Coated - 2673
Bags: Uncoated Paper and Multiwall - 2674
Ball and Roller Bearings - 3562
Bank Holding Companies - 6712
Barber Shops - 7241
Beauty Shops - 7231
Beef Cattle Feedlots - 0211
Beef Cattle, Except Feedlots - 0212
Beer and Ale - 5181

Beet Sugar - 2063
Berry Crops - 0171
Biological Products, Except Diagnostic - 2836
Bituminous Coal and Lignite-surface Mining - 1221
Bituminous Coal-underground Mining - 1222
Blankbooks and Looseleaf Binders - 2782
Blast Furnaces and Steel Mills - 3312
Blowers and Fans - 3564
Boat Dealers - 5551
Boatbuilding and Repairing - 3732
Bolts, Nuts, Rivets, and Washers - 3452
Book Printing - 2732
Book Publishing - 2731
Book Stores - 5942
Bookbinding and Related Work - 2789
Books, Periodicals, and Newspapers - 5192
Botanical and Zoological Gardens - 8422
Bottled and Canned Soft Drinks - 2086
Bowling Centers - 7933
Bras, Girdles, and Allied Garments - 2342
Bread, Cake, and Related Products - 2051
Brick and Structural Clay Tile - 3251
Brick, Stone, and Related Material - 5032
Bridge, Tunnel, and Elevated Highway - 1622
Broadwoven Fabric Mills, Cotton - 2211
Broadwoven Fabric Mills, Manmade - 2221
Broadwoven Fabric Mills, Wool - 2231
Broiler, Fryer, and Roaster Chickens - 0251
Brooms and Brushes - 3991
Building Maintenance Services, Nec - 7349
Burial Caskets - 3995
Bus Charter Service, Except Local - 4142
Bus Terminal and Service Facilities - 4173
Business Associations - 8611
Business Consulting, Nec - 8748
Business Services, Nec - 7389
Business and Secretarial Schools - 8244
Cable and Other Pay Television Services - 4841
Calculating and Accounting Equipment - 3578
Camera and Photographic Supply Stores - 5946
Candy and Other Confectionery Products - 2064
Candy, Nut, and Confectionery Stores - 5441
Cane Sugar Refining - 2062
Canned Fruits and Specialties - 2033
Canned Specialties - 2032
Canned and Cured Fish and Seafoods - 2091
Canvas and Related Products - 2394
Carbon Black - 2895
Carbon Paper and Inked Ribbons - 3955
Carbon and Graphite Products - 3624
Carburetors, Pistons, Rings, Valves - 3592
Carpentry Work - 1751
Carpet and Upholstery Cleaning - 7217
Carpets and Rugs - 2273
Carwashes - 7542
Cash Grains, Nec - 0119
Catalog and Mail-order Houses - 5961
Cellulosic Manmade Fibers - 2823
Cement, Hydraulic - 3241
Cemetery Subdividers and Developers - 6553
Central Reserve Depository, Nec - 6019
Ceramic Wall and Floor Tile - 3253
Cereal Breakfast Foods - 2043
Cheese; Natural and Processed - 2022
Chemical Preparations, Nec - 2899
Chemical and Fertilizer Mining - 1479
Chemicals and Allied Products, Nec - 5169

Chewing Gum - 2067
Chewing and Smoking Tobacco - 2131
Chicken Eggs - 0252
Child Day Care Services - 8351
Children's and Infants' Wear Stores - 5641
Chocolate and Cocoa Products - 2066
Cigarettes - 2111
Cigars - 2121
Citrus Fruits - 0174
Civic and Social Associations - 8641
Clay Refractories - 3255
Clay and Related Minerals, Nec - 1459
Coal Mining Services - 1241
Coal and Other Minerals and Ores - 5052
Coated Fabrics, Not Rubberized - 2295
Coin-operated Amusement Devices - 7993
Coin-operated Laundries and Cleaning - 7215
Cold Finishing of Steel Shapes - 3316
Colleges and Universities - 8221
Combination Utilities, Nec - 4939
Commercial Art and Graphic Design - 7336
Commercial Banks, Nec - 6029
Commercial Equipment, Nec - 5046
Commercial Laundry Equipment - 3582
Commercial Lighting Fixtures - 3646
Commercial Nonphysical Research - 8732
Commercial Photography - 7335
Commercial Physical Research - 8731
Commercial Printing, Gravure - 2754
Commercial Printing, Lithographic - 2752
Commercial Printing, Nec - 2759
Commodity Contracts Brokers, Dealers - 6221
Communication Services, Nec - 4899
Communications Equipment, Nec - 3669
Computer Facilities Management - 7376
Computer Integrated Systems Design - 7373
Computer Maintenance and Repair - 7378
Computer Peripheral Equipment, Nec - 3577
Computer Related Services, Nec - 7379
Computer Rental and Leasing - 7377
Computer Storage Devices - 3572
Computer Terminals - 3575
Computer and Software Stores - 5734
Computers, Peripherals, and Software - 5045
Concrete Block and Brick - 3271
Concrete Products, Nec - 3272
Concrete Work - 1771
Confectionery - 5145
Construction Machinery - 3531
Construction Materials, Nec - 5039
Construction Sand and Gravel - 1442
Construction and Mining Machinery - 5082
Converted Paper Products, Nec - 2679
Conveyors and Conveying Equipment - 3535
Cookies and Crackers - 2052
Copper Foundries - 3366
Copper Ores - 1021
Copper Rolling and Drawing - 3351
Cordage and Twine - 2298
Corn - 0115
Correctional Institutions - 9223
Corrugated and Solid Fiber Boxes - 2653
Costume Jewelry - 3961
Cotton - 0131
Cotton Ginning - 0724
Cottonseed Oil Mills - 2074
Courier Services, Except By Air - 4215

Hosiery, Nec - 2252
Hospital and Medical Service Plans - 6324
Hotels and Motels - 7011
House Slippers - 3142
Household Appliance Stores - 5722
Household Appliances, Nec - 3639
Household Audio and Video Equipment - 3651
Household Cooking Equipment - 3631
Household Furnishings, Nec - 2392
Household Furniture, Nec - 2519
Household Laundry Equipment - 3633
Household Refrigerators and Freezers - 3632
Household Vacuum Cleaners - 3635
Housing Programs - 9531
Hunting, Trapping, Game Propagation - 0971
Ice Cream and Frozen Deserts - 2024
Individual and Family Services - 8322
Industrial Buildings and Warehouses - 1541
Industrial Furnaces and Ovens - 3567
Industrial Gases - 2813
Industrial Inorganic Chemicals, Nec - 2819
Industrial Launderers - 7218
Industrial Machinery and Equipment - 5084
Industrial Machinery, Nec - 3599
Industrial Organic Chemicals, Nec - 2869
Industrial Patterns - 3543
Industrial Sand - 1446
Industrial Supplies - 5085
Industrial Trucks and Tractors - 3537
Industrial Valves - 3491
Industrial and Personal Service Paper - 5113
Information Retrieval Services - 7375
Inorganic Pigments - 2816
Inspection and Fixed Facilities - 4785
Installing Building Equipment - 1796
Instruments To Measure Electricity - 3825
Insurance Agents, Brokers, and Service - 6411
Insurance Carriers, Nec - 6399
Intercity and Rural Bus Transportation - 4131
Intermediate Care Facilities - 8052
Internal Combustion Engines, Nec - 3519
International Affairs - 9721
Investment Advice - 6282
Investment Offices, Nec - 6726
Investors, Nec - 6799
Irish Potatoes - 0134
Iron Ores - 1011
Iron and Steel Forgings - 3462
Irrigation Systems - 4971
Jewelers' Materials and Lapidary Work - 3915
Jewelry Stores - 5944
Jewelry and Precious Stones - 5094
Jewelry, Precious Metal - 3911
Job Training and Related Services - 8331
Junior Colleges - 8222
Kaolin and Ball Clay - 1455
Kidney Dialysis Centers - 8092
Knit Outerwear Mills - 2253
Knit Underwear Mills - 2254
Knitting Mills, Nec - 2259
Labor Organizations - 8631
Laboratory Apparatus and Furniture - 3821
Lace and Warp Knit Fabric Mills - 2258
Laminated Plastics Plate and Sheet - 3083
Land, Mineral, and Wildlife Conservation - 9512
Landscape Counseling and Planning - 0781
Laundry and Garment Services, Nec - 7219
Lawn and Garden Equipment - 3524
Lawn and Garden Services - 0782
Lead Pencils and Art Goods - 3952
Lead and Zinc Ores - 1031
Leather Gloves and Mittens - 3151
Leather Goods, Nec - 3199

Leather Tanning and Finishing - 3111
Leather and Sheep-lined Clothing - 2386
Legal Counsel and Prosecution - 9222
Legal Services - 8111
Legislative Bodies - 9121
Libraries - 8231
Life Insurance - 6311
Lighting Equipment, Nec - 3648
Lime - 3274
Linen Supply - 7213
Liquefied Petroleum Gas Dealers - 5984
Liquor Stores - 5921
Livestock - 5154
Livestock Services, Except Veterinary - 0751
Loan Brokers - 6163
Local Bus Charter Service - 4141
Local Passenger Transportation, Nec - 4119
Local Trucking With Storage - 4214
Local Trucking, Without Storage - 4212
Local and Suburban Transit - 4111
Logging - 2411
Lubricating Oils and Greases - 2992
Luggage - 3161
Luggage and Leather Goods Stores - 5948
Lumber and Other Building Materials - 5211
Lumber, Plywood, and Millwork - 5031
Macaroni and Spaghetti - 2098
Machine Tool Accessories - 3545
Machine Tools, Metal Cutting Type - 3541
Machine Tools, Metal Forming Type - 3542
Magnetic and Optical Recording Media - 3695
Malleable Iron Foundries - 3322
Malt - 2083
Malt Beverages - 2082
Management Consulting Services - 8742
Management Investment, Open-ended - 6722
Management Services - 8741
Manifold Business Forms - 2761
Manufactured Ice - 2097
Manufacturing Industries, Nec - 3999
Marinas - 4493
Marine Cargo Handling - 4491
Marking Devices - 3953
Masonry and Other Stonework - 1741
Mattresses and Bedsprings - 2515
Measuring and Controlling Devices, Nec - 3829
Measuring and Dispensing Pumps - 3586
Meat Packing Plants - 2011
Meat and Fish Markets - 5421
Meats and Meat Products - 5147
Mechanical Rubber Goods - 3061
Medical Equipment Rental - 7352
Medical Laboratories - 8071
Medical and Hospital Equipment - 5047
Medicinals and Botanicals - 2833
Membership Organizations, Nec - 8699
Membership Sports and Recreation Clubs - 7997
Membership-basis Organization Hotels - 7041
Men's Footwear, Except athletic - 3143
Men's and Boy's Clothing - 5136
Men's and Boy's Clothing, Nec - 2329
Men's and Boy's Furnishings - 2321
Men's and Boy's Neckwear - 2323
Men's and Boy's Suits and Coats - 2311
Men's and Boy's Trousers and Slacks - 2325
Men's and Boy's Underwear and Nightwear - 2322
Men's and Boy's Work Clothing - 2326
Men's and Boys' Clothing Stores - 5611
Merchandising Machine Operators - 5962
Metal Barrels, Drums, and Pails - 3412
Metal Cans - 3411
Metal Coating and Allied Services - 3479
Metal Doors, Sash, and Trim - 3442

Metal Foil and Leaf - 3497
Metal Heat Treating - 3398
Metal Household Furniture - 2514
Metal Mining Services - 1081
Metal Ores, Nec - 1099
Metal Sanitary Ware - 3431
Metal Stampings, Nec - 3469
Metals Service Centers and Offices - 5051
Metalworking Machinery, Nec - 3549
Millwork - 2431
Mineral Wool - 3296
Minerals, Ground or Treated - 3295
Mining Machinery - 3532
Miscellaneous Apparel and Accessories - 5699
Miscellaneous Business Credit - 6159
Miscellaneous Fabricated Wire Products - 3496
Miscellaneous Food Stores - 5499
Miscellaneous General Merchandise - 5399
Miscellaneous Homefurnishings - 5719
Miscellaneous Marine Products - 0919
Miscellaneous Metalwork - 3449
Miscellaneous Nonmetallic Mining - 1499
Miscellaneous Personal Services - 7299
Miscellaneous Publishing - 2741
Miscellaneous Retail Stores, Nec - 5999
Mobile Home Dealers - 5271
Mobile Home Site Operators - 6515
Mobile Homes - 2451
Mortgage Bankers and Correspondents - 6162
Motion Picture Distribution Services - 7829
Motion Picture Theaters, Except Drive-in - 7832
Motion Picture and Tape Distribution - 7822
Motion Picture and Video Production - 7812
Motor Homes - 3716
Motor Vehicle Parts and Accessories - 3714
Motor Vehicle Parts, Used - 5015
Motor Vehicle Supplies and New Parts - 5013
Motor Vehicles and Car Bodies - 3711
Motorcycle Dealers - 5571
Motorcycles, Bicycles, and Parts - 3751
Motors and Generators - 3621
Museums and Art Galleries - 8412
Musical Instrument Stores - 5736
Musical Instruments - 3931
Nailed Wood Boxes and Shook - 2441
Narrow Fabric Mills - 2241
National Commercial Banks - 6021
National Security - 9711
Natural Gas Distribution - 4924
Natural Gas Liquids - 1321
Natural Gas Transmission - 4922
New and Used Car Dealers - 5511
News Dealers and Newsstands - 5994
News Syndicates - 7383
Newspapers - 2711
Nitrogenous Fertilizers - 2873
Nonclassifiable Establishments - 9999
Nonclay Refractories - 3297
Noncommercial Research Organizations - 8733
Noncurrent-carrying Wiring Devices - 3644
Nondeposit Trust Facilities - 6091
Nondurable Goods, Nec - 5199
Nonferrous Die-castings Except Aluminum - 3364
Nonferrous Forgings - 3463
Nonferrous Foundries, Nec - 3369
Nonferrous Rolling and Drawing, Nec - 3356
Nonferrous Wiredrawing and Insulating - 3357
Nonmetallic Mineral Products, - 3299
Nonmetallic Mineral Services - 1481
Nonresidential Building Operators - 6512
Nonresidential Construction, Nec - 1542
Nonwoven Fabrics - 2297
Nursing and Personal Care, Nec - 8059

Office Equipment - 5044
Office Furniture, Except Wood - 2522
Office Machines, Nec - 3579
Offices and Clinics of Chiropractors - 8041
Offices and Clinics of Dentists - 8021
Offices and Clinics of Medical Doctors - 8011
Offices and Clinics of Optometrists - 8042
Offices and Clinics of Osteopathic Physicians - 8031
Offices and Clinics of Podiatrists - 8043
Offices of Health Practitioner - 8049
Oil Royalty Traders - 6792
Oil and Gas Exploration Services - 1382
Oil and Gas Field Machinery - 3533
Oil and Gas Field Services, Nec - 1389
Operative Builders - 1531
Ophthalmic Goods - 3851
Optical Goods Stores - 5995
Optical Instruments and Lenses - 3827
Ordnance and Accessories, Nec - 3489
Organic Fibers, Noncellulosic - 2824
Ornamental Nursery Products - 0181
Ornamental Shrub and Tree Services - 0783
Outdoor Advertising Services - 7312
Packaged Frozen Goods - 5142
Packaging Machinery - 3565
Packing and Crating - 4783
Paint, Glass, and Wallpaper Stores - 5231
Painting and Paper Hanging - 1721
Paints and Allied Products - 2851
Paints, Varnishes, and Supplies - 5198
Paper Industries Machinery - 3554
Paper Mills - 2621
Paper; Coated and Laminated Packaging - 2671
Paper; Coated and Laminated, Nec - 2672
Paperboard Mills - 2631
Partitions and Fixtures, Except Wood - 2542
Passenger Car Leasing - 7515
Passenger Car Rental - 7514
Passenger Transportation Arrangement - 4729
Patent Owners and Lessors - 6794
Pens and Mechanical Pencils - 3951
Pension, Health, and Welfare Funds - 6371
Periodicals - 2721
Personal Credit Institutions - 6141
Personal Leather Goods, Nec - 3172
Petroleum Bulk Stations and Terminals - 5171
Petroleum Products, Nec - 5172
Petroleum Refining - 2911
Petroleum and Coal Products, Nec - 2999
Pharmaceutical Preparations - 2834
Phosphate Rock - 1475
Phosphatic Fertilizers - 2874
Photocopying and Duplicating Services - 7334
Photofinish Laboratories - 7384
Photographic Equipment and Supplies - 3861
Photographic Studios, Portrait - 7221
Physical Fitness Facilities - 7991
Pickles, Sauces, and Salad Dressings - 2035
Piece Goods and Notions - 5131
Pipelines, Nec - 4619
Plastering, Drywall, and Insulation - 1742
Plastics Bottles - 3085
Plastics Foam Products - 3086
Plastics Materials and Basic Shapes - 5162
Plastics Materials and Resins - 2821
Plastics Pipe - 3084
Plastics Plumbing Fixtures - 3088
Plastics Products, Nec - 3089
Platemaking Services - 2796
Plating and Polishing - 3471
Pleating and Stitching - 2395
Plumbing Fixture Fittings and Trim - 3432
Plumbing and Hydronic Heating Supplies - 5074

Plumbing, Heating, Air-conditioning - 1711
Police Protection - 9221
Polishes and Sanitation Goods - 2842
Political Organizations - 8651
Porcelain Electrical Supplies - 3264
Potash, Soda, and Borate Minerals - 1474
Potato Chips and Similar Snacks - 2096
Pottery Products, Nec - 3269
Poultry Hatcheries - 0254
Poultry Slaughtering and Processing - 2015
Poultry and Eggs, Nec - 0259
Poultry and Poultry Products - 5144
Power Laundries, Family and Commercial - 7211
Power Transmission Equipment, Nec - 3568
Power-driven Handtools - 3546
Prefabricated Metal Buildings - 3448
Prefabricated Wood Buildings - 2452
Prepackaged Software - 7372
Prepared Feeds, Nec - 2048
Prepared Flour Mixes and Doughs - 2045
Prerecorded Records and Tapes - 3652
Pressed and Blown Glass, Nec - 3229
Primary Aluminum - 3334
Primary Batteries, Dry and Wet - 3692
Primary Copper - 3331
Primary Metal Products - 3399
Primary Nonferrous Metals, Nec - 3339
Printed Circuit Boards - 3672
Printing Ink - 2893
Printing Trades Machinery - 3555
Printing and Writing Paper - 5111
Private Households - 8811
Process Control Instruments - 3823
Products of Purchased Glass - 3231
Professional Equipment, Nec - 5049
Professional Organizations - 8621
Psychiatric Hospitals - 8063
Public Building and Related Furniture - 2531
Public Golf Courses - 7992
Public Order and Safety, Nec - 9229
Public Relations Services - 8743
Pulp Mills - 2611
Pumps and Pumping Equipment - 3561
Racing, Including Track Operation - 7948
Radio Broadcasting Stations - 4832
Radio and T.v. Communications Equipment - 3663
Radio and Television Repair - 7622
Radio, Television, Publisher Representatives - 7313
Radio, Television, and Electronic Stores - 5731
Radiotelephone Communication - 4812
Railroad Equipment - 3743
Railroad Property Lessors - 6517
Railroads, Line-haul Operating - 4011
Raw Cane Sugar - 2061
Ready-mixed Concrete - 3273
Real Estate Agents and Managers - 6531
Real Estate Investment Trusts - 6798
Real Property Lessors, Nec - 6519
Reconstituted Wood Products - 2493
Record and Prerecorded Tape Stores - 5735
Recreational Vehicle Dealers - 5561
Refined Petroleum Pipelines - 4613
Refrigerated Warehousing and Storage - 4222
Refrigeration Equipment and Supplies - 5078
Refrigeration Service and Repair - 7623
Refrigeration and Heating Equipment - 3585
Refuse Systems - 4953
Regulation of Agricultural Marketing - 9641
Regulation, Administration of Transportation - 9621
Regulation, Administration of Utilities - 9631
Relays and Industrial Controls - 3625
Religious Organizations - 8661
Rental of Railroad Cars - 4741

Repair Services, Nec - 7699
Residential Care - 8361
Residential Construction, Nec - 1522
Residential Lighting Fixtures - 3645
Retail Bakeries - 5461
Retail Nurseries and Garden Stores - 5261
Reupholstery and Furniture Repair - 7641
Rice - 0112
Rice Milling - 2044
Roasted Coffee - 2095
Robes and Dressing Gowns - 2384
Rolling Mill Machinery - 3547
Roofing, Siding, and Insulation - 5033
Roofing, Siding, and Sheetmetal Work - 1761
Rooming and Boarding Houses - 7021
Rubber and Plastics Footwear - 3021
Rubber and Plastics Hose and Beltings - 3052
Salted and Roasted Nuts and Seeds - 2068
Sanitary Food Containers - 2656
Sanitary Paper Products - 2676
Sanitary Services, Nec - 4959
Sausages and Other Prepared Meats - 2013
Savings Institutions, Except Federal - 6036
Saw Blades and Handsaws - 3425
Sawmills and Planing Mills, General - 2421
Scales and Balances, Except Laboratory - 3596
Schiffli Machine Embroideries - 2397
School Buses - 4151
Schools and Educational Services - 8299
Scrap and Waste Materials - 5093
Screw Machine Products - 3451
Search and Navigation Equipment - 3812
Secondary Nonferrous Metals - 3341
Secretarial and Court Reporting - 7338
Security Brokers and Dealers - 6211
Security Systems Services - 7382
Security and Commodity Exchanges - 6231
Security and Commodity Service - 6289
Semiconductors and Related Devices - 3674
Semivitreous Table and Kitchenware - 3263
Service Establishment Equipment - 5087
Service Industry Machinery, Nec - 3589
Services Allied To Motion Pictures - 7819
Services, Nec - 8999
Setup Paperboard Boxes - 2652
Sewerage Systems - 4952
Sewing, Needlework, and Piece Goods - 5949
Sheep and Goats - 0214
Sheet Metalwork - 3444
Shellfish - 0913
Shipbuilding and Repairing - 3731
Shoe Repair and Shoeshine Parlors - 7251
Shoe Stores - 5661
Short-term Business Credit - 6153
Signs and Advertising Specialties - 3993
Silver Ores - 1044
Silverware and Plated Ware - 3914
Single-family Housing Construction - 1521
Skilled Nursing Care Facilities - 8051
Small Arms - 3484
Small Arms Ammunition - 3482
Soap and Other Detergents - 2841
Social Services, Nec - 8399
Softwood Veneer and Plywood - 2436
Soil Preparation Services - 0711
Soybean Oil Mills - 2075
Soybeans - 0116
Space Propulsion Units and Parts - 3764
Space Research and Technology - 9661
Space Vehicle Equipment, Nec - 3769
Special Dies, Tools, Jigs, and Fixtures - 3544
Special Industry Machinery, Nec - 3559
Special Product Sawmills, Nec - 2429

Special Trade Contractors, Nec - 1799
Special Warehousing and Storage, Nec - 4226
Specialty Hospitals, Except Psychiatric - 8069
Specialty Outpatient Clinics, Nec - 8093
Speed Changers, Drives, and Gears - 3566
Sporting Goods and Bicycle Shops - 5941
Sporting and Recreation Goods - 5091
Sporting and Recreational Camps - 7032
Sporting and athletic Goods, Nec - 3949
Sports Clubs, Managers, and Promoters - 7941
State Commercial Banks - 6022
State Credit Unions - 6062
Stationery Products - 2678
Stationery Stores - 5943
Stationery and Office Supplies - 5112
Steam and Air-conditioning Supply - 4961
Steel Foundries, Nec - 3325
Steel Investment Foundries - 3324
Steel Pipe and Tubes - 3317
Steel Springs, Except Wire - 3493
Steel Wire and Related Products - 3315
Storage Batteries - 3691
Structural Clay Products, Nec - 3259
Structural Steel Erection - 1791
Structural Wood Members, Nec - 2439
Subdividers and Developers, Nec - 6552
Sugarcane and Sugar Beets - 0133
Surety Insurance - 6351
Surface Active Agents - 2843
Surgical Appliances and Supplies - 3842
Surgical and Medical Instruments - 3841
Surveying Services - 8713
Switchgear and Switchboard Apparatus - 3613
Switching and Terminal Services - 4013
Synthetic Rubber - 2822
Tanks and Tank Components - 3795
Tax Return Preparation Services - 7291
Taxicabs - 4121
Telegraph and Other Communications - 4822
Telephone Communication, Except Radio - 4813
Telephone and Telegraph Apparatus - 3661
Television Broadcasting Stations - 4833
Terrazzo, Tile, Marble, Mosaic Work - 1743
Testing Laboratories - 8734
Textile Bags - 2393
Textile Goods, Nec - 2299
Textile Machinery - 3552
Theatrical Producers and Services - 7922
Thread Mills - 2284
Throwing and Winding Mills - 2282
Timber Tracts - 0811
Tire Cord and Fabrics - 2296
Tire Retreading and Repair Shops - 7534
Tires and Inner Tubes - 3011
Tires and Tubes - 5014
Title Insurance - 6361
Title abstract Offices - 6541
Tobacco - 0132
Tobacco Stemming and Redrying - 2141
Tobacco Stores and Stands - 5993
Tobacco and Tobacco Products - 5194
Toilet Preparations - 2844
Top and Body Repair and Paint Shops - 7532
Tour Operators - 4725
Towing and Tugboat Service - 4492
Toys and Hobby Goods and Supplies - 5092
Trailer Parks and Campsites - 7033
Transformers, Except Electric - 3612
Transportation Equipment and Supplies - 5088
Transportation Equipment, Nec - 3799
Transportation Services, Nec - 4789
Travel Agencies - 4724
Travel Trailers and Campers - 3792

Tree Nuts - 0173
Truck Rental and Leasing, Without Drivers - 7513
Truck Trailers - 3715
Truck and Bus Bodies - 3713
Trucking Terminal Facilities - 4231
Trucking, Except Local - 4213
Trusts, Nec - 6733
Trusts: Educational, Religious, Etc. - 6732
Turbines and Turbine Generator Sets - 3511
Turkeys and Turkey Eggs - 0253
Typesetting - 2791
U.S. Postal Service - 4311
Unsupported Plastics Film and Sheet - 3081
Unsupported Plastics Profile Shapes - 3082
Upholstered Household Furniture - 2512
Uranium-radium-vanadium Ores - 1094
Urban and Community Development - 9532
Used Car Dealers - 5521
Used Merchandise Stores - 5932
Utility Trailer Rental - 7519
Valves and Pipe Fittings, Nec - 3494
Variety Stores - 5331
Vegetable Oil Mills, Nec - 2076
Vegetables and Melons - 0161
Vehicular Lighting Equipment - 3647
Veterinary Services For Livestock - 0741
Veterinary Services, Specialties - 0742
Video Tape Rental - 7841
Vitreous China Table and Kitchenware - 3262
Vitreous Plumbing Fixtures - 3261
Vocational Schools, Nec - 8249
Warm Air Heating and Air Conditioning - 5075
Watch, Clock, and Jewelry Repair - 7631
Watches, Clocks, Watchcases, and Parts - 3873
Water Passenger Transportation - 4489
Water Supply - 4941
Water Transportation Services, Nec - 4499
Water Transportation of Freight - 4449
Water Well Drilling - 1781
Water, Sewer, and Utility Lines - 1623
Waterproof Outerwear - 2385
Weft Knit Fabric Mills - 2257
Welding Apparatus - 3548
Welding Repair - 7692
Wet Corn Milling - 2046
Wheat - 0111
Wine and Distilled Beverages - 5182
Wines, Brandy, and Brandy Spirits - 2084
Wire Springs - 3495
Women's Accessory and Specialty Stores - 5632
Women's Clothing Stores - 5621
Women's Footwear, Except athletic - 3144
Women's Handbags and Purses - 3171
Women's Hosiery, Except Socks - 2251
Women's and Children's Clothing - 5137
Women's and Children's Underwear - 2341
Women's and Misses' Blouses and Shirts - 2331
Women's and Misses' Outerwear, Nec - 2339
Women's and Misses' Suits and Coats - 2337
Women's, Junior's, and Misses' Dresses - 2335
Wood Containers, Nec - 2449
Wood Household Furniture - 2511
Wood Kitchen Cabinets - 2434
Wood Office Furniture - 2521
Wood Pallets and Skids - 2448
Wood Partitions and Fixtures - 2541
Wood Preserving - 2491
Wood Products, Nec - 2499
Wood Television and Radio Cabinets - 2517
Woodworking Machinery - 3553
Wrecking and Demolition Work - 1795
X-ray Apparatus and Tubes - 3844
Yarn Spinning Mills - 2281

Spanish SIC Code Descriptions

0111 Trigo
0115 Maíz
0112 Arroz
0116 Soja
0119 Granos de Valor en Efectivo
0131 Algodón
0132 Tabaco
0133 Caña de Azúcar & Azúcar de Remolacha
0134 Patatas Irlandesas
0139 Cosechas de Campo ex. Valor en Efectivo
0161 Verduras & Melones
0170 Arboles de Frutas & Nueces
0171 Cultivo de Bayas
0172 Uvas
0173 Arboles de Nueces
0174 Frutas Cítricas
0175 Árboles Deciduos de Frutas
0179 Arboles de Frutas & Nueces
0181 Productos Ornamentales de Jardín
0182 Alimentos Cultivados en el Cubierto
0191 Cultivo General, Especialmente Cosechas
0211 Ganado de Carne, Lote Alimentador
0212 Ganado de la Carne, Exc. Lote Alim.
0213 Cerdos
0214 Ovejas & Cabras
0219 Ganado General
0241 Granjas de Lechería
0251 Pollo de Asar & Freír
0252 Huevos de Pollo
0253 Pavos & Huevos de Pavo
0254 Criaderos de Pollería
0259 Pollería & Huevos
0271 Conejos & Animales de Pelo
0272 Caballos & Otros Equinos
0273 Cultura Acuática Animal
0279 Especialidades de Animales
0291 Granjas en General, Principalmente Anim
0711 Servício de Preparación de la Tierra
0721 Cosecha, Plantación & Protección
0722 Cultivo, Cosecha
0723 Cosechas,Servício de Preparación para el
0724 Algodón, Despepitar
0741 Servicios Veterinarios, Ganado
0742 Servicios Veterinarios, Especialidades
0751 Servicios al Ganado, Exc. Veterinario
0752 Servicios de Especialidad Animal
0761 Contratistas del Labor de la Granja
0762 Servício de Gerencia de Granjas
0781 Paisajes, Consejo & Diseño
0782 Servício de Césped & Jardín
0783 Svcos. de Arbusto Ornamental & Arbol
0811 Zonas de Madera
0831 Productos de Bosque
0851 Servícios de Silvicultura
0912 Peces de Aletas/Pescados
0913 Mariscos
0919 Productos Marinos Misceláneos
0921 Criaderos del Pez & Reservas
0971 Caza, Entrampa, Juego Sostiene
1000 Minería de Metal
1011 Menas de Hierro
1021 Menas de Cobre
1031 Menas de Plomo & Zinco
1041 Menas de Oro
1044 Menas de Plata
1061 Menas de Liga de Hierro, Exc. Vanádio
1081 Servícios de Minería de Metal

1094 Menas de Uranio- Radio-Vanádio
1099 Menas de Metales
1222 Carbón Bituminoso - Subsuelo
1231 Minería de Antracita
1241 Servícios de Minería de Carbón
1311 Petróleo Crudo & Gas Natural
1321 Gas Líquido Natural
1381 Taladra de Aceite & Pozos de Gas
1382 Servicios de Exploración de Aceite & Gas
1389 Servícios de Campo, Aceite & Gas
1411 Roca de Dimensión
1422 Grava de Caliza
1423 Grava de Granito
1429 Grava de Piedra
1442 Arena de Construcción & Gruesa
1446 Arena Industrial
1455 Caolín & Arcilla de Bola
1459 Arcilla & Minerales Relacionados
1474 Potasa, Soda, & Minerales de Borato
1475 Fosfato en Roca
1479 Minería de Químicos & Fertilizantes
1481 Servícios de Minerales No-metálicos
1499 Minerales No-metálicos, Miscel.
1522 Construcción Residencial
1531 Constructores Operativos
1541 Edifícios Industriales & Almacenes
1542 Construcción No-Residential
1611 Construcción de Calles & Carreteras
1622 Puente, Túnel, & Carretera Elevada
1623 Conductos de Agua, Cloaca, & Utilidad
1629 Construcción Pesada
1711 Plomería, Calefacción, AireAcondicionado
1721 Pintura & Papel de Pared
1731 Trabajos Eléctricos
1741 Albañilería & Otras Obras de Sillería
1742 Enyeso, Drywall, & Aislamiento
1743 Terrazzo, Azulejo, Mármol & Mosaico
1751 Trabajos de Carpintería
1752 Instalación de Pisos y servícios
1761 Tejados, Revestimientos yChapa de Metal
1771 Trabajos de Concreto
1781 Taladradores de Pozo de Agua
1791 Erección de Acero Estructural
1793 Vidrio & Servícios
1794 Trabajo de Excavación
1795 Servícios de Demolición
1796 Edificio, Instalación de Equipos
1799 Contratistas Especiales del Comercio
2011 Plantas de Empaque de Carne
2013 Salchichas & Otras Carnes Preparadas
2015 Pollería, Matanza & Proceso
2021 Mantequilla Cremosa
2022 Queso, Natural & Procesado
2023 Prods. Secos, Condensados, Evaporados
2024 Helados & Postres Congelados
2026 Leche, Líquido
2032 Especialidades Enlatadas
2033 Frutas en Conserva & Verduras
2034 Frutas Deshidratadas, Vegs, Sopas
2035 Encurtidos, Salsas,& Mojos de Ensalada
2037 Frutas & Verduras Congeladas
2038 Especialidades Congeladas
2041 Harina & Otros Prods. de Molino de Grano
2043 Cereal, Comidas del Desayuno
2044 Molienda de Arroz
2045 Mezclas Preparadas de Harina & Masas
2046 Molienda Mojada de Maíz

2047 Comida de Gato & Perro
2048 Comida Preparada
2051 Pan, Torta, y Prods. Relacionados
2052 Galletas & Crackers
2061 Azúcar de Caña Crudo
2062 Azúcar de Caña Refinado
2063 Azúcar de Remolacha
2064 Dulces & Otros Prods. de Confección
2066 Chocolate & Productos de Cacao
2067 Chicle
2068 Nueces & Semillas, Saladas, Tostadas
2074 Molinos de Aceite de Semilla de Algodón
2075 Molinos de Aceite de Soja
2076 Molinos de Aceite Vegetal
2077 Aceites & Gorduras Marinas & Animales
2079 Aceites & Gorduras Comestibles
2082 Bebidas de Malta
2083 Malta
2084 Vino, Coñac, & Derivativos del Coñac
2085 Licores Mezclados & Destilados
2087 Condimentos, Sabores, Extratos & Jarabe
2092 Pescado Preparado, Fresco o Congelado
2095 Café Tostado
2096 Patatas Fritas & Bocadillos Similares
2097 Hielo Fabricado
2098 Macarrones & Fideo
2099 Preparaciones de Comida
2111 Cigarrillos
2121 Cigarros
2131 Tabaco, Masticar & Fumar
2141 Tabaco, Despalillar & Resecar
2211 Molinos de Tejido Velarte, Algodón
2221 Molinos de Tejido Velarte, Artificial
2231 Molinos de Tejido Velarte, Lana
2241 Molinos, Tejido Estrecho
2251 Calcetería de Mujeres, Excepto Calcetines
2252 Calcetería
2253 Molinos de Tejidos de Ropa Exterior
2254 Molinos de Tejidos de Ropa Interior
2257 Molinos de Tejidos de Trama
2258 Molinos de Tejidos de Encajes
2259 Molinos de Tejidos
2261 Plantas de Acabamiento, Algodón
2262 Plantas de Acabamiento, Artificial
2269 Plantas de Acabamiento
2273 Alfombras
2281 Molinos de Hilado de Estambre
2282 Molinos de Tirado & Enrollo
2284 Molinos de Hilo
2295 Tejidos Cubiertos, No Encauchados
2296 Cordón de Neumático & Tejidos
2297 Tejidos sin Trama
2298 Cordaje & Bramante
2299 Géneros de Textil
2321 Hombres & Muchachos, Camisas
2325 Hombres & Muchachos, Pantaloneses
2326 Hombres & Muchachos, Ropa de Trabajo
2329 Hombres & Muchachos, Ropa
2331 Señoras & Señoritas, Blusas & Camisas
2335 Vestidos de Mujeres, Jrs' & Señoritas
2337 Señoras & Señoritas, Trajes & Chaquetas
2339 Señoras & Señoritas, Ropa Exterior
2341 Mujeres & Niños, Ropa Interior
2342 Sostenes, Cintos, & Géneros Aliados
2361 Vestidos& Blusas de Muchachas & Niñas,
2369 Muchachas & Niñas, Ropa Exterior
2371 Géneros de Piel

2381 Vestidos de Tejido & Guantes de Trabajo
2384 Enaguas, Batas
2385 Ropa Exterior, Impermeable
2386 Ropa de Cuero & Forro de Oveja
2387 Cinturones, de Ropa
2389 Ropa & Accesorios
2391 Cortinas & Pañerías
2392 Artículos del Hogar
2393 Bolsas de Textil
2394 Lona & Productos Relacionados
2395 Pliega & Sutura
2396 Automotriz & Adornoses de la Ropa
2397 Máquinas de Bordados Schiffli
2399 Prods. Fabricados de Textil
2411 Madereros
2426 Madera Dura & Molinos de Pisos
2429 Aserraderos de Productos Especiales
2431 Trabajos en Madera
2434 Armarios de Cocina de Madera
2435 Madera dura, Chapas & Contrachapado
2436 Madera Suave, Chapas & Contrachapado
2439 Miembros Estructurales de Madera
2441 Cajas de Madera Clavadas & Talas
2448 Tarimas de Madera & Rodillos
2449 Recipientes de Madera
2451 Hogares Móviles
2452 Edificios de Madera Prefabricados
2491 Preservativos de la Madera
2493 Productos de Madera Reconstituida
2499 Productos de Madera
2511 Muebles del Hogar, Madera
2512 Muebles del Hogar, Tapizados
2514 Muebles del Hogar, Metal
2515 Colchones & Colchones de Muelles
2517 Armarios de Radio& Televisión de Madera
2519 Mueble de Casa,
2521 Mueble de Oficina de Madera
2522 Mueble de Oficina, Excepto Madera
2531 Edificio Público & Muebles Relacionados
2541 Particiones de Madera & Adornos
2542 Particiones & Adornos, Exc. de Madera
2591 Pañería de Cortinas, Equipos
2599 Muebles & Adornos
2611 Molinos de Pulpa
2621 Molinos de Papel
2631 Molinos de Cartón
2652 Cajas de Cartón de Montaje
2653 Cajas Arrugadas & de Fibra Sólida
2656 Recipientes de Comida Sanitarios
2657 Cajas de Cartón, Plegas
2672 Papel Revestido & Laminado
2673 Bolsas: Plástico Laminado & Revestido
2675 Papel & Cartón, Die-cut
2676 Productos Sanitarios de Papel
2677 Sobres
2678 Productos de Papelería
2679 Conversión de Productos del Papel
2711 Periódicos
2721 Publicación de periódicos
2731 Publicación de Libros
2732 Impresión de Libros
2741 Publicación Miscelánea
2752 Impresión Comercial, Litogravura
2754 Impresión Comercial, Gravura
2759 Impresión Comercial
2761 Formulários Múltiples de Negocios
2771 Tarjetas de Saludo
2789 Encuadernación & Trabajo Relacionado
2791 Tipografía
2796 Servício de Clisé
2812 Álcalis & Cloro
2813 Gases Industriales

2816 Pigmentos Inorgánicos
2819 Químicos, Industrial Inorgánico
2821 Materiales de Plásticos & Resinas
2822 Caucho Sintético
2823 Celulose, Fibras Artificiales
2824 Fibras Orgánicas, No-Celulose
2833 Medicinas & Botánicas
2834 Preparaciones Farmacéuticas
2835 Substancias de Diagnóstico
2836 Prods. Biológicos Exc. Diagnóstico
2841 Jabón & Otros Detergentes
2842 Pulidores & Géneros de Higienización
2843 Agentes Activos de Superficie
2844 Preparaciones de Retrete
2851 Pintura & Productos Aliados
2861 Cola & Químicos de Madera
2865 Crudos Cíclicos & Intermedios
2869 Químicos, Industrial Orgánico
2873 Fertilizantes, Nitrogénio
2874 Fertilizantes, Fosfatos
2875 Fertilizantes, Solo Mexcla
2879 Químicos Agrícolas
2891 Adesivos & Sellantes
2892 Explosives
2893 Tinta de Impresión
2895 Carbono Negro
2899 Preparados Químicos
2911 Petróleo, Refinación
2951 Asfalto, Mezcla de Pavimento & Bloques
2952 Asfalto, Fieltro & Capas
2992 Lubrificantes, Aceite & Grasas
2999 Petróleo & Productos de Carbón
3011 Llantas & Tubos de Aire
3021 Calzados de Caucho & Plásticos
3052 Mangueras & Tiras de Caucho & Plásticos
3053 Juntas, Equipo de Embalaje & Sellaje
3061 Géneros de Caucho, Mecánico
3069 Productos Fabricados de Caucho
3081 Plásticos, Membrana & Hoja
3082 Plásticos, Formas de contorno
3083 Laminados Plásticos, Chapa & Hoja
3084 Plásticos, Tuberías
3085 Plásticos Botellas
3086 Plásticos, Productos de Espuma
3087 Compuesto Especiales, Comprado
3088 Plásticos, Adornos de Plomería
3089 Productos de Plásticos
3111 Cuero Curtido & Acabamiento
3131 Calzado, Material Cortado
3142 Zapatillas de Casa
3143 Calzados de Hombres, Excepto Atléticos
3144 Calzados de Mujeres, Exc. Atlético
3149 Calzados, Excepto Caucho
3151 Cuero, Guantes & Mitones
3161 Maletínes de Equipaje
3171 Bolsas de Mano, Mujeres
3172 Géneros de Cuero Personales
3199 Géneros de Cuero
3211 Vidrio plano
3221 Recipientes de Vidrio
3229 Vidrio, Aplastado & Soplado
3231 Productos de Vidrio Comprado
3241 Cemento, Hidráulico
3251 Ladrillo & Azulejo de Arcilla Estructural
3253 Pared & Piso, Cerámica & Azulejo
3255 Arcilla Refractária
3259 Productos Estructurales de Arcilla
3261 Adornos de Plomería Vítreos
3262 Porcelana Vítrea,
3263 Arts. de Mesa & Cocina Semi Vítreos
3264 Porcelana, Suministros Eléctricos de
3269 Productos de Alfarería

3271 Bloques de Concreto & Ladrillo
3272 Productos de Concreto
3273 Concreto Listo para Uso
3274 Cal
3275 Productos de Yeso
3281 Piedra Cortada & Productos de Piedra
3291 Productos abrasivos
3292 Productos de Asbesto
3295 Minerales, Molidos o Preparados
3296 Lana Mineral
3297 Refractários, no de Arcilla
3299 Prods Minerales, no de Metal
3312 Hornos de Explosión & Molinos de Acero
3313 Productos Electrometalúrgicos
3316 Acabamiento al Frío de Formas de Acero
3317 Cañería de Acero & Tubos
3321 Fundiciones de Hierro Dúctil & Gris
3322 Fundiciones de Hierro Maleable
3324 Fundiciones de Acero, Inversión
3325 Fundiciones de Acero
3331 Cobre Primario
3334 Aluminio Primario
3339 Metales Primarios No Ferrosos
3341 Metales Secundarios No Ferrosos
3351 Cobre, Laminación & Estiramiento
3353 Hoja de Aluminio, Chapa & Lamina
3354 Aluminio, Productos de Eyección
3355 Aluminio, Laminación & Estiramiento
3356 Laminación & Estiramiento, No-ferroso
3363 Aluminio, Fundición de Molde
3365 Fundiciones de Aluminio
3366 Fundiciones de Cobre
3369 Fundiciones No-ferrosas
3398 Tratamiento de Metales al calor
3399 Productos Primarios del Metal
3411 Metal , Latas
3412 Metal, Barriles, Tambores, & Cubos
3421 Cuchillería
3423 Herramientas de Mano & Tiracantos
3425 Hojas de Sierras & Serruchos
3429 Ferretería
3431 Mercancías de Metal Sanitario
3432 Adornos de Plomería Ajustes & Encajes
3433 Equipo de Calefacción, Exc. Eléctrico
3441 Metal Fabricado, Estructural
3442 Puertas de Metal, Fajas, & Ajustes
3444 Trabajo de Metal en Plancha
3446 Trabajo de Metal Arquitectónico
3448 Edificios de Metal Prefabricados
3449 Trabajos de Metal, Misceláneo
3451 Productos de Máquinas de Tornillo
3452 Pernos,Tuercas, Remaches & Arandelas
3463 Artículos de Fundiciones No Ferrosos
3465 Timbrados, Automotriz
3466 Coronas & Cierres
3469 Timbrados de Metal
3471 Chapeado & Pulido
3479 Capa de Metal & Svcs Aliados
3482 Munición de Armas Pequeñas
3483 Munición, Exc. Armas Pequeñas
3484 Armas Pequeñas
3489 Artillería & Accesorios
3491 Válvulas Industriales
3493 Muelles de Acero, Excepto Alambre
3494 Válvulas & Ajustes de Cañería
3495 Muelles de Alambre
3496 Productos de Alambre Fabricados, Misc.
3497 Metal, Laminilla & Hoja
3498 Cañería & Ajustes Fabricados
3499 Productos de Metal Fabricado
3511 Turbinas & Generadores de Turbina
3523 Maquinaria de Granja & Equipos

3519 Motores de Combustión Interior & Equipos
3524 Equipo de Jardín & Césped
3531 Maquinaria de Construcción
3532 Maquinaria de Minería
3533 Maquinaria de Campo a Gas & Aceite
3534 Ascensores & Escaleras Móviles
3535 Esteras Portadoras
3536 Alzadoras, Grúas & Monocarriles
3537 Camiones Industriales & Tractores
3543 Dibujos Industriales
3545 Accesorios de Herramientas Mecánicas
3546 Herramientas de Mano, fuerza
3547 Maquinaria de Molino de Laminación,
3548 Aparato de Soldadura
3549 Maquinaria de Trabajos de Metal
3552 Maquinaria de Textil
3553 Maquinaria de Trabajos de Madera
3554 Maquinaria de Industrias de Papel
3555 Maquinaria, Impresión Comercial
3556 Maquinaria de los Productos Alimentários
3559 Maquinaria Especial de Industria
3561 Bombas & Equipo de Bombas
3562 Rodamientos de Bola & Rollos
3563 Compresores de Aire & Gas
3564 Sopladores & Ventiladores
3565 Maquinaria de Empaquetamiento
3567 Estufas Industriales & Hornos
3568 Equipo de Fuerza, Transm.
3569 Maquinaria Industrial Gnrl.
3571 Computadoras Electrónicas
3575 Pantallas de Computadora
3577 Equipo de Computadora, Periféricos
3578 Equipo de Intervención & Contabilidad
3579 Máquinas de Oficina
3581 Máquinas, Vendas Automáticas
3585 Refrigeración & Calefacción
3582 Equipo de Lavandería Comercial
3586 Bombas de Medida & Distribuición
3589 Maquinaria de Industria de Servicio
3592 Carburadores, Pistones, Anillos, Válvulas
3593 Fuerza de Flúido, Cilindros & Activadores
3594 Fuerza de Flúido, Bombas & Motores
3596 Balanzas & Escalas, Exc. Laborats
3599 Maquinaria Industrial
3612 Transformadores, Excepto electrónicos
3621 Motores & Generadores
3624 Carbono & Productos del Grafito
3625 Relés & Controles Industriales
3629 Aparatos Indust. Eléctricos
3631 Equipo de Cocina Doméstico
3632 Refrigs & Congeladores, Doméstico
3633 Equipo de Lavandería, Doméstico
3634 Equipo Eléctrico Doméstico, Ventiladores
3635 Aspiradoras, Domésticos
3639 Aparatos Domésticos
3641 Lámparas Eléctricas
3643 Aparatos Eléctricos, Con Corriente
3644 Aparatos Eléctricos, Sin Corriente
3645 Adornos de Iluminación, Residenciales
3646 Adornos de Iluminación, Comerciales
3647 Equipo de Iluminación, Auto
3651 Equipo de Audio & Video, Residencial
3648 Equipo de Iluminación
3652 Discos & Cintas Pregrabados
3661 Teléfono & Aparato de Telégrafo
3663 Comunicaciones de Radio & Televisión
3671 Válvulas de Electrón
3669 Equipo de Comunicaciones
3672 Tableros, Circuito Impreso
3674 Semiconductores & Relacionados Aparato
3675 Condensadores electrónicos
3676 Resistencias electrónicas

3677 Espirales Electrónicos & Transformadores
3678 Conectores electrónicos
3679 Componentes Electrónicos
3691 Baterías de Almacenamiento
3692 Baterías Primarias, Seco & Mojado
3694 Motores, Equipo Eléctrico
3699 Equipo Eléctrico, Suministros
3711 Vehículos de Motor & Carrocerías de Carr
3713 Camión & Carrocerías de Autobús
3714 Vehículo de motor Partes & Aceso.
3715 Remolques de Camión
3716 Hogares Motorizados
3721 Aeronaves
3724 Motores de Avión & Partes de Motores
3728 Avión, Partes & Equipo
3731 Construcción & Reparo de Navios
3732 Construcción & Reparo de Buques
3751 Motocicletas, Bicicletas, & Partes
3743 Equipo de Ferrocarril
3761 Proyectiles Guiados & Vehículo de Espaci
3764 Unidades de Propulsión Espacial & Partes
3769 Equipo de Vehículos Espaciales
3792 Trailers de Viaje
3795 Tanques & Componentes de Tanque
3799 Equipo de Transportación
3812 Equipo de Navegación & Busca
3821 Aparato de Laboratorio & Muebles
3822 Controles de Ambientes
3823 Instrumentos de Control de Proceso
3824 Aparatos, Medida & Cuenta de Flúidos
3825 Electricidad, Instrumentos de Medida
3826 Instrumentos Analíticos
3827 Instrumentos Opticos & Lentes
3829 Aparatos de Medida & Control
3841 Instrumentos Médicos & Quirúrgicos
3842 Aparatos Quirúrgicos & Suministros
3843 Equipo dental & Suministros
3844 Aparato de Radiografía & Tubos
3845 Equipo Electromédico
3851 Géneros Oftálmicos
3861 Equipo Fotográfico & Suministros
3873 Relojes, Cajas & Pts
3911 Joya, Metal Precioso
3914 Plata Labrada & Artículos Chapeados
3915 Joyeros & Trabajos de Lapidária
3931 Instrumentos Musicales
3942 Muñecas & Animales Rellenos
3944 Juegos, Juguetes & Autos de Niños
3949 Géneros, Deportivo & Atlético
3951 Plumas & Lápices Mecánicos
3952 Lápices de Grafito & Arte, Géneros
3953 Aparatos Marcadores
3955 Papel Carbono & Cintas Entintadas
3961 Joyas de Fantasía
3965 Broche, Botón, Agujas & Alfiler
3991 Escobas & Cepillos
3993 Especialidades de Publicidad
3995 Arquetas de Entierro
3996 Revestimientos de Pisos, Superficie Dura
3999 Fábricas Industriales
4013 Servicios de Terminal & Cambio
4111 Tránsito Local & Suburbano
4119 Transporte Local de Pasajeros
4121 Taxies
4141 Autobús, Servicio Local de Flete
4142 Autobús Servicio de Flete , Exc. Local
4151 Autobúses Escolares
4173 Términal de Autobús & Servicios
4213 Transporte en camión, Excepto Local
4215 Servs. de Mensajero , Excepto por Aire
4222 Depósito & Almacenamiento Refrigerado
4225 Depósito, General & Almacenamiento

4226 Depósito, Especial & Almacenamiento
4311 E.E.U.U.,Servício Postal
4412 Alto Mar, Transp. de Carga Extrangero
4424 Alto Mar, Trans de Carga Doméstico
4432 Transporte de Carga- Grandes Lagos
4449 Transporte Marítimo de Carga
4482 Barcas de Transbordo
4489 Transporte Marítimo, Pasajeros
4491 Manejos de Carga Marítima
4492 Servício de Remolque
4493 Marinas
4499 Servicios de Transporte Marítimo
4512 Transportación Aérea, Hora Fija
4499 Servicios de TransporteMarítimo
4512 Transportación Aérea, Hora Fija
4513 Servício de Mensajero Aéreo
4522 Transportación Aérea, Sin Hora Fija
4581 Aeropuertos, Campos de Vuelo & Servs
4600 Oleoducto, Excepto Gas Natural
4612 Oleoductos de Petróleo Crudo
4613 Oleoductos de Petróleo Refinado
4619 Oleoductos
4724 Agencias de Viaje
4725 Operadores de Turismo
4729 Servício deTransp. de Pasajeros
4731 Servício de Transporte de Carga
4741 Arriendo de Carros de Ferrocarril
4783 Embalaje & Empaque
4785 Inspección & Medioses Fijos
4789 Servício de Transportación
4812 Radio/teléfono, Comunicaciones
4813 Teléfono, Communicaciones Ex
4822 Telégrafo & Otras Comunicaciones
4832 Estaciones de radiodifusión
4833 Emisora de Televisión
4899 Servícios de Comunicaciones
4911 Servicios Eléctricos
4922 Transmisión de Gas Natural
4923 Transmisión de Gas & Distribución
4924 Distribución de Gas Natural
4925 Producción de Gas y / o Distrib
4931 Eléctrico& Otros Serv. Combinados
4932 Gas & Otro Servicios Combinados
4939 Utilidades de Combinación
4941 Suministro de Agua
4952 Servicio de Desagüe de Cloacas
4953 Sistemas de Desecho
4959 Servicios Sanitarios
4971 Sistemas de Irrigación
5012 Automóviles & Otros Vehículo de motor
5013 Vehículos de Motor,Suminis. Partes ueva
5014 Llantas & Tubos
5015 Piezas de Vehículos de Motor, Usadas
5023 Artículos para el Hogar
5021 Muebles
5032 Ladrillo, Piedra & Material Relacionado
5033 Tejados, Revestimientos & Aislamiento
5039 Materiales de Construcción
5043 Equipo Fotográfico & Suministros
5044 Equipo de Oficina
5045 Computadoras, Periféricos, & Software
5046 Equipo Comercial
5047 Equipo Médico & de Clínica
5048 Géneros Oftálmicos
5049 Equipo Profesional
5051 Servicio de Metal, Centros & Oficinas
5052 Carbón & Otros Minerales & Menas
5063 Aparato Eléctrico & Equipamnt
5064 Aparatos Eléctricos, Televisión & Radio
5065 Partes electrónicas & Equipo
5072 Ferretería
5074 Suministro de Plomería & Calor Hidrónico

5078 Refrigeración, Equipo & Sumin.
5082 Construcción & Maquinaria de Minería
5083 Maquinaria de Granja & Jardín
5084 Maquinaria Industrial & Equipos
5085 Suministros Industriales
5087 Equipo de Establecimientos de Servicio
5088 Equipo de Transportación & Sumin.
5091 Géneros Deportivos & Recreationales
5092 Juegos & Géneros de Hobby & Suministros
5093 Trozos & Materiales Desechados
5094 Joyas & Piedras Preciosas
5099 Géneros Durables
5111 Papel, Impresión & Escritura
5112 Suministros de Papelería & Oficina
5113 Papel Industrial & de Servicio Personal
5122 Drogas, Proprietarias & Artículos diversos
5131 Géneros de Piezas & Nociones
5136 Ropas de Hombres & Muchachos
5137 Ropas de Mujeres & Niños
5139 Calzados
5141 Comestibleses, Línea General
5142 Comidas Heladas, Empaquetadas
5144 Pollería & Productos de Pollería
5145 Confitería
5146 Pez & Mariscoses
5147 Carnes & Productos de la Carne
5148 Frutas Frescas & Verduras
5149 Comestibleses & Prods Relacionados
5153 Granos & Frijoles del Campo
5154 Ganado
5159 Materiales Crudos, Productos de Granja
5162 Material de Plásticos & Forma Básica
5169 Químicos & Productos Aliados
5172 Productos del Petróleo
5181 Cerveza & Cerveza Inglesa
5182 Vino & Bebidas Destiladas
5191 Suministros de la Granja
5192 Libros, Publicación Periódica & Periódicos
5193 Suministros de Flores & Floricultores
5194 Tabaco & Productos del Tabaco
5198 Pintura, Barnices, & Suministros
5199 Géneros No-durable
5211 Madera & Otros Materiales de Construc.
5251 Casas de Ferretería
5261 Tiendas de Césped & Jardín
5271 Distribuidores de Casas Motorizadas
5311 Tiendas Mayores
5331 Tiendas de Variedad
5399 Tiendas Comerciales, Misc
5411 Tiendas de Comestibles
5421 Mercados de Carne & Pez
5431 Comércio de Frutas & Verduras
5441 Tiendas de Dulce, Nuez & Confección
5451 Tiendas de Productos de Lechería
5461 Panaderías de Menudeo
5499 Tiendas de Comida Miscelánea
5511 Distribuidores de Carros Nuevos & Usado
5521 Distribuidores de Carro Usados
5541 Estaciones de Servicio de Gasolina
5551 Distribuidores de Barcos
5561 Distribuidores de Vehículo Recreational
5571 Distribuidores de Motocicleta
5599 Distribuidores, Automotriz
5611 Tiendas de Ropa, Hombres & Muchachos
5621 Tiendas de Mujeres
5632 Tiendas de Mujeres, Accesorios & Detalle
5641 Tiendas de Ropas, Uso Niño & Infante
5651 Tiendas de Ropa Familiar
5661 Tiendas de Zapatos
5699 Misc. Ropas & Accesorios
5712 Tiendas de Mueble

5713 Almacenes de Cubiertos de Pisos
5714 Pañería & Tapicería
5719 Tiendas de Artículos Domésticos, Misc.
5722 Tiendas de Electrodomésticos de la Casa
5731 Tiendas de Electrónicas, Radio, Televisión
5734 Computadora & Software
5735 Tienda de Discos & Cintas Pregrabadas
5736 Tiendas de Instrumentos Musicales
5812 Restaurantes
5813 Barras & Lugares de Bebida
5912 Farmácias & Tiendas Propietárias
5921 Tiendas de Licores
5932 Tiendas de Mercancía Usada
5942 Librerías
5943 Tiendas de Papelería
5944 Tiendas de Joya
5945 Tiendas de Hobby, Juguete, & Juegos
5946 Cámara & Fotografía, Suministros
5948 Tiendas de Equipaje & Géneros de Cuero
5949 Tiendas de Costura & Artículos por Pieza
5961 Catálogo & Ventas por Correo
5963 Establecimientos de Venta Directa
5983 Distribuidores de Aceite Combustible
5984 Distribuidores de Gas de Petróleo Líquido
5989 Distribuidores de Combustibles
5992 Floricultores
5993 Tiendas & quioscos de Tabaco
5994 Distribuidores & Quioscos de Periódicos
5995 Tiendas de Opticos
5999 Negocios Misc.
6011 Bancos de Reserva Federal
6019 Depositario Central de Reserva
6021 Bancos Nacionales Comerciales
6022 Bancos Comerciales deEstado
6029 Bancos Comerciales
6035 Instituciones Federales de Ahorro
6036 Instituciones del Ahorro Exc. Federal
6061 Uniones de Crédito Federales
6062 Uniones de Crédito del Estado
6081 Banco Extranjero, Sucursales & Agencias
6091 Banco, Trust, No Depositario
6111 Crédito Federal & Patrocinado Federal
6141 Instituciones Personales de Crédito
6153 Crédito de Negocios a Corto plazo
6159 Misc., Instituciones de Crédito de Negocio
6163 Agentes de Préstamo
6211 Agentes de Garantía & Negociantes
6221 Negociantes & Agentes de Valores
6231 Intercambio de Seguridad & Valores
6282 Consejo de Inversiones
6289 Servícios de Seguridad & Valores
6311 Seguro de Vida
6321 Seguro de Salud & Accidentes
6324 Planos de Servício de Clínica & Médico
6331 Seguro de Fuego, Marino & Accidente
6351 Garantía de Seguro
6361 Seguro de Títulos
6371 Fundos de Jubilación, Salud & Bienestar
6399 Agentes de Seguro
6411 Agentes de Seguro, Servício & Corredoría
6512 Operadores de Edificios No-residenciales
6513 Operadores de Edificios de Apartamentos
6515 Operadores de Areas de Casas Móviles
6519 Arrendadores de Bienes Raíces
6531 Agentes & Gerentes de Bienes Raíces
6541 Oficinas de Abstractos de Títulos
6552 Subdivisores & Diseñadores
6553 Cementerio, Subdivisión & Desarrollo
6719 Compañías de Participación Accionaria
6722 Inversión, Gerencia
6726 Oficinas de Inversión
6732 Bancos de Depósito, Educativo, Religioso

6733 Banco de Depósitos
6792 Comerciantes de Derechos de Aceite
6794 Dueños & Arrendadores de Patentes
6798 Inversión de Depósitos de Bienes Raíces
6799 Inversores
7011 Hoteles & Moteles
7021 Pensiones & Moradas
7032 Campos, Deportivo & Recreational
7041 Organiz. de Hotel Basado en Miembros
7211 Lavanderías, Familia & Comercial
7212 Limpiadores & Planchadores a Seco
7213 Suministro de Lienzo
7217 Limpieza de Alfombra & Tapicería
7218 Lavanderías, Industrial
7219 Svcs. de Lavanderías & Vestiduras
7221 Estudios Fotográficos, Retrato
7231 Salones de Belleza
7241 Barbería
7251 Zapato, Reparo & Betunada
7261 Servicios de Entierro & Hornos Crematorio
7299 Servicios Personales, Variados
7311 Agencias de Publicidad
7312 Publicidad al Aire Libre
7313 Radio, Televisión, Representaciones
7319 Publicidade
7322 Servícios de Ajuste & Colección
7323 Servícios de Información de Crédito
7331 Servícios de Publicidad, Correo Directo
7334 Servícios de Fotocopia & Reproducción
7335 Fotografía Comercial
7336 Arte Comercial & Dibujo Gráfico
7349 Servícios de Mantenimiento de Edificios
7352 Arriendo de Equipo Médico
7353 Arriendo de Equipo Pesado, Construcción
7359 Arriendo de Equipo & Arrendamiento
7361 Agencias de Empleo
7363 Servícios de Suministro de la Ayuda
7372 Software, Lista, Comercial
7373 Computadora
7374 Proceso & Preparación de Datos
7375 Servícios de Recuperación de Información
7377 Arriendo & Arrendamiento de Computador
7378 Mantenimiento de Computadora
7379 Computadora, Servicios relacionados
7381 Servícios de Detective & Carro Armado
7382 Servícios de Sistemas de Seguridad
7383 Sindicatos de Noticias
7384 Laboratorios de Fotografías
7389 Servícios de Negocios
7513 Arriendo de Camión, Sin Chófer
7514 Arriendo de Carros de Pasajeros
7515 Arrendamiento de Carros de Pasajero
7519 Arriendo de Remolque de Utilidad
7521 Estacionamiento de Automóvil
7536 Vidrio Automatriz, Taller de Reparos
7539 Reparación, Taller de Reparos
7542 Lavadoras de Carros
7549 Servicios automotores
7622 Servicios de Reparación, Radio, Televisor
7623 Servicios de Reparación, Refrigeración
7629 Servicios de Reparación Eléctrica
7631 Servicios de Reparación, Reloj & Joya
7641 Tapizaría & Reparación de Muebles
7692 Servicios de Reparación, Soldadura
7699 Servicios de Reparación
7812 Productos de Video & Película
7819 Svcs. Relacion. Películas
7822 Servicios de Distrib. de Cintas & Películas
7829 Servicios de Distrib. de Películas
7832 Teatros de Cine, Exc.Drive-In
7833 Drive-In Teatros de Cine
7841 Arriendo de Cintas de Video

7911 Estudios de Baile, Escuelas& Instituciones
7922 Productores de Svco. Teatral
7929 Entretenedores & Grupos
7933 Centros de Boliche
7948 Hipódromos, Incl.Operaciones
7991 Establecimientos Deportivos de Salud
7992 Cursos de Golf Públicos
7996 Parques de Diversión
7999 Entretenimiento & Recreación
8011 Oficinas & Clínicas, Médicos
8021 Oficinas & Clínicas, Dentistas
8031 Oficinas, Médico Osteopático
8041 Oficinas de Clínicas, Quiropráticos
8042 Oficinas de Clínicas, Optometristas
8043 Oficinas de Clínicas, Podiatria
8049 Oficinas, Prácticos de Salud
8052 Establecimientos de Cuidado Intermediári
8059 Establecimientos de Cuidado Personal
8062 Hospital Quirúrgico & Médico Gnrl.
8063 Clínicas de Psiquiatría
8069 Clínicas Especializadas, Exc. Psiquiatría
8071 Laboratorios Médicos
8072 Laboratorios Dentales
8092 Centros de Diálisis de Riñón
8099 Salud & Svcs. Aliados
8111 Servicios Légales
8211 Escuelas Elementarias & Secundarias
8221 Universidades
8222 Universidades Ménores
8231 Bibliotecas
8243 Enseñanza de Proceso de Datos
8244 Escuelas de Secretaria & Negocios
8249 Escuelas de la Vocación
8299 Svcs. Educativos & Escuelas
8322 Servicios de la Familia & Individuales
8351 Servicios de Guardería, Niños
8361 Cuidado Residencial
8399 Servicios Sociales
8412 Museos de Arte, Galerías
8422 Jardines Zoológicos & Botánicos
8611 Asociaciones de Negocio
8621 Organizaciones Profesionales
8631 Organizaciones de Labor
8641 Asociaciones Civicas y Sociales
8651 Organizaciones Politicas
8661 Organizaciones Religiosas
8699 Organizaciones de Miembros
8711 Servicios de Ingenieria
8712 Servicios de Arquitectura
8713 Servicios de Agrimensura
8731 Pesquisa Comercial, Física
8732 Pesquisa Comercial, No Física
8733 Organización de Pesquisa, No Comercial
8734 Laboratories de Prueba
8741 Servicios de Gerencias
8742 Servicios de Gerencia Consultante
8743 Servicios de Relaciones Publicas
8744 Establecimientos de Apoyo de Servícios
8748 Consultorio de Negocios
8999 Servicios
9111 Oficinas Ejecutivas
9121 Entidades de Legislatura
9131 Executivo & Legislativo, Combinación
9199 Gobierno General
9211 Corte el 9222 Consejo Legal, Cortes
9221 Protección Policíaca & Prosecución
9223 Instituciones Correccionales
9224 Protección del Fuego
9229 Orden Público & Seguridad
9311 Finanzas, Impuestos & Política Monetaria
9411 Admin. de Programas Educativos
9431 Admin. de Programas de la Salud Pública

9441 Admin. de Progs. Sociales & del Labor
9451 Admin de Asuntos de Veteranos
9531 Programa de Habitación
9532 Desarrollo Urbano & de la Comunidad
9611 Admin. de Progs Económicos en General
9621 Regulación, Admin de Transporte
9631 Regulación, Admin de Utilidades
9641 Regulación, Marketing, Agrícola
9651 Regulación, Sectores Comerciales Misc.
9661 Pesquisas del Espacio & Tecnología
9711 Seguridad Nacional
9721 Asuntos Internacionales

SIC Code Company Index

111 - Consolidated Trading
111 - Lins Trading
111 - Northland Organic Foods / Northland
179 - Dulin Date Gardens
181 - Golden State Bulb Growers
711 - GSO: Grapeseed Oil Corporation
723 - Hilltop Ranch
751 - National Research & Chemical Co.
752 - Hunte, Andrew
111 - Delta International
112 - Brahmandeva Federation
112 - Parisi-Virana Co., Inc.
115 - Colorado Cereal, Inc. (Mfr)
115 - Delta International
115 - Henderson Mills Inc.
116 - Delta International
119 - Eastern Europe Inc.
1081 - Marshall Miller & Associates
1381 - Marshall Miller & Associates
1389 - Marshall Miller & Associates
1389 - Minco Sales Corp.
1389 - RK Pipe & Supply
1389 - Tetra Technologies
139 - Arista Industries, Inc.
1479 - United Salt
1541 - Morrison Construction Service
1542 - Mini Golf, Inc.
1542 - Morrison Construction Service
1623 - Everett J. Prescott
1629 - Environmental Services & Technology
1629 - Geothermal Power Company Inc.
1629 - Nova Grass
1711 - H2oil Corporation
1711 - Morrison Construction Service
173 - Green Valley Pecan Company
173 - Santa Cruz Valley Pecan Company
1731 - Applied Telecommunications Inc.
1731 - Micon Telecommunications Inc
1737 - Micon Telecommunications Inc
1742 - Morrison Construction Service
1752 - Stonhard Inc.
1761 - Morrison Construction Service
1781 - Ruen Drilling International
1796 - Simonds Mfg. Corp.
1799 - Able Builders Export, Inc.
1799 - Colorado Lining International, Inc.
1799 - Fire Equipment, Inc
1799 - ICS Penetron International
1799 - ICS Penetron International Ltd.
1799 - Mustang Industrial Equipment
1799 - Thermal Science, Inc.
181 - Condor Seed Production Inc. (Mfr)
181 - Golden State Bulb Growers
181 - Sharp Bros Seed Co.
2011 - Agri Processors
2011 - Colorado Boxed Beef Co., Inc.
2011 - Hatfield, Inc.
2011 - Jones Dairy Farm
2011 - Kirkland's Custom Meats
2011 - Schmalz European, Inc.
2011 - Superior Packing/Superior Farm
2013 - Bar-S Foods Co.
2013 - Burke Corporation
2013 - Corfu Foods, Inc.
2013 - Enjoy Foods International
2013 - L & E International Service
2013 - P G Molinari & Sons Inc
2013 - Pacific Sun Industries Inc
2013 - SARA's Sausage
2015 - AJC International Inc.
2015 - All-States Quality Foods L.P.
2015 - Aspen Foods, a division of Koch
2015 - Culver Duck Farms
2015 - Ecrevisse Acadienne (Mfr)
2015 - Ecrevisse Acadienne (Mfr), West
2015 - Farbest Foods, Inc.
2015 - Greene Poultry, Don

2015 - International Dehydrated Foods Inc.
2015 - Sanderson Farms Inc.
2015 - Sonstegard Foods Company
2015 - Tyson Seafood Group, Inc.
2015 - Wampler Foods, Inc.
2021 - Darigold Inc.
2021 - Organic Valley / Cropp Cooperative
2022 - A & J Cheese Company
2022 - Berner Cheese Corp.
2022 - Darigold Inc.
2022 - Galaxy Foods, Inc.
2022 - SFI Anco Fine Cheese
2022 - Safeway Stores Inc., Export Sales
2022 - Scott's Of Wisconsin / Mille Lacs M.
2023 - American Casein Co.
2023 - Darigold Inc.
2023 - Dean Foods (Mfr)
2023 - Diehl, Inc.
2023 - Safeway Stores Inc., Export Sales
2024 - Arista Industries, Inc.
2024 - Bubbies Homemade Ice Cream
2024 - Dippin Dots, Inc.
2024 - Fruit-A-Freeze Inc
2024 - Gise Inc
2024 - Greene Poultry, Don
2024 - JDC (Hawaii) Inc., Advance Foods
2024 - La Perla Ice Cream Co.
2024 - Luke's Ice Cream
2024 - Safeway Stores Inc., Export Sales
2024 - Sam's Homemade Cheesecake Inc
2026 - Brown Cow West Corporation
2032 - Dale's Wild West Products
2033 - Blackberry Patch, Inc.
2033 - Borden Foods Corp.
2033 - Chalet Suzanne Foods, Inc.
2033 - Chiquita Processing Foods, LLC -
2033 - Diehl, Inc.
2033 - El Toro Food Products Inc
2033 - Griffin Food Company
2033 - L & E International Service
2033 - McCain Citrus Inc
2033 - Miss Scarlett Inc
2033 - Mooney Farms
2033 - Nellie & Joe's,
2033 - Sunkist Growers, Inc., Processed
2033 - Western Consolidated Foods, Inc.
2033 - Yergat Packing Co.
2034 - A-Live Foods
2034 - Aunt Rita's, Inc.
2034 - California Prune Board
2034 - De Francesco & Sons Inc
2034 - Ferry Roberts Nut
2034 - Frontier Soups
2034 - Gilroy Foods, Inc. (Mfr)
2034 - Griffin Food Company
2034 - Idaho Frank Association
2034 - Oregon Freeze Dry Inc
2035 - Champagne Sauces Inc.
2035 - Chipico Pickles
2035 - Essen Nutrition Corp.
2035 - Fisherman's Wharf Food Product
2035 - Griffin Food Company
2035 - Herlocher Foods, Inc.
2035 - Klein Pickle Company
2035 - Le Parisien Vinaigrette
2035 - Mount Olive Pickle Co., Inc.
2035 - Pacific Poultry Co. Ltd.
2035 - Ripon Pickle Co., Inc.
2035 - Steinfelds Products
2035 - United Pickle Products Corp.
2035 - Vidalia Gold Enterprizes
2037 - Del's Lemonade & Refreshments, Inc.
2037 - Florida Food Products, Inc.
2037 - Lamb-Weston Inc
2037 - Norpac Foods Inc
2037 - Western Consolidated Foods, Inc.
2038 - Amy's Kitchen Inc

2038 - Chang Food Company
2038 - Matador Processors, Inc.
2038 - Natural Choice Foods
2038 - Northern Star Co., Inc.
2038 - Old Fashioned Kitchen Inc
2038 - Pacway Food International Corp
2038 - Prepared Food Products, Inc.
2038 - Purepak Inc
2038 - Shemshad Food Products Inc
2038 - Tumaro's Inc
2041 - Heartland Mill, Inc.
2041 - Molinos de Puerto Rico, Inc.
2041 - Western Trails Inc
2043 - L & E International Service
2043 - Organic Milling Inc
2044 - Riceland Foods Inc.
2044 - Sem Chi Rice Products
2045 - Amero Foods Mfg. Corp.
2045 - Diehl, Inc.
2046 - Colorado Sweet Gold LLC
2046 - Grain Processing Corporation (Mfr)
2046 - Western Polymer Corp
2047 - Hartz Mountain
2047 - Natural Life Pet Products
2047 - Nutro Products, Inc.
2047 - Purr-Fect Growlings
2048 - Animal Health Sales, Inc.
2048 - Audubon Park Co
2048 - Diamond V Mills, Inc.
2048 - Distributors Processing Inc
2048 - Fermented Products
2048 - Free Choice Enterprises
2048 - Harbingers Of a New Age
2048 - International Nutrition, Inc.
2048 - La Crosse Milling Co.
2048 - Penny Newman Milling LLC
2048 - Wildwood Farms, Inc.
2051 - Adams Bakery Corp.
2051 - Bonert's Slice Of Pie
2051 - Casey Sales Company Incorporated
2051 - Distinctive Foods, Inc.
2051 - Everybody's Bagel Co Inc
2051 - Fresca Mexican Foods Inc.
2051 - Giuliano-Pagano Corp
2051 - J & J Wall Baking Company Inc
2051 - Love's Bakery, Inc.
2051 - Mrs. Cubbison's Foods
2051 - Nabolom Bakery
2051 - Neuman Bakery Specialties, Inc.
2051 - Sybil's Outrageous Brownies
2052 - Bay Area Biscotti Co
2052 - Cookies For You, Inc.
2052 - DFP International Inc
2052 - Hawaiian King Candies
2053 - Sara Lee Bakery Co.
2053 - T N T Pizza Crust, Inc.
2060 - Carousel Candies
2062 - California & Hawaiian Sugar Co
2062 - Monin, Inc.
2064 - Adams & Brooks Inc
2064 - Candy Express
2064 - Delyse Inc
2064 - Florida Candy Factory, Inc.
2064 - Gimbal Brothers Inc
2064 - Granlunds Sweet Temptations
2064 - Hawaiian Host, Inc.
2064 - Las Dos Victorias Candies
2064 - Otec, Inc.
2064 - Sconza Candy Co.
2064 - Simon Candy Co.
2064 - Sun Empire Foods
2066 - Hawaiian King Candies
2066 - Hawaiian Vintage
2066 - Just Truffles
2066 - Kona Paradise Candies Corp.
2067 - Gum Tech International(Mfr)
2068 - AJC International Inc.

2068 - Damascus Peanut Co.
2068 - Hawaiian King Candies
2068 - Jade Food Products, Inc.
2068 - Keystone Food Products Inc.
2068 - Mac Farms of Hawaii, Inc.
2068 - Sunland, Inc.
2068 - Ultimate International
2068 - Wiggin Farms
2071 - Reliable Plastics Seals, Inc.
2076 - Spectrum Naturals Inc
2077 - Anamax Corp.
2077 - Arista Industries, Inc.
2077 - Cucker Feather
2079 - Diehl, Inc.
2079 - Intermountain Canola Cargill
2079 - Perdue Farms Inc. Grain & Oilseed
2084 - ASV Wines Inc
2084 - Bandiera Winery
2084 - Bargetto's Santa Cruz Winery
2084 - Beringer Wine Estates
2084 - Columbia Winery
2084 - Davis Bynum Winery
2084 - Delicato Vineyards
2084 - Elk Run Vineyards Inc.
2084 - Hoodsport Winery Inc.
2084 - Louis M Martini Winery
2084 - Mayacamas Vineyards
2084 - Orfila Vineyards Inc
2084 - Pedrizzetti Winery
2084 - Robert Pepi Winery
2084 - Round Hill Winery
2084 - Steltzner Vineyard
2084 - Stevenot Winery
2084 - Ventana Vineyards Winery Inc
2084 - Whitehall Lane Winery
2085 - AGE International
2086 - Grayson Mountain Water Co.
2086 - Safeway Stores Inc., Export Sales
2087 - Berghausen Corp.
2087 - Cappuccino America Corp.
2087 - Dragoco Inc.
2087 - Flavor Dynamics, Inc.
2087 - Griffin Food Company
2087 - International Bioflavors Inc.
2087 - Liway International, Inc.
2087 - Nielsen-Massey Vanillas(Mfr)
2087 - O S F Flavors, Inc.
2087 - Sto-Chard
2087 - Tamer International Ltd
2087 - Terry Laboratories, Inc.
2089 - Alljuice Food & Beverage
2090 - Omega Products, Inc.
2091 - Hoodsport Winery Inc.
2092 - Alaskan Dried Foods
2092 - Dorado Seafood Inc
2092 - Ecrevisse Acadienne (Mfr)
2092 - Ecrevisse Acadienne (Mfr), West
2092 - Fish Processors Inc
2092 - Fishery Products International Inc.
2092 - North Atlantic Fish Co , Inc
2092 - P & J Oyster Co., Inc.
2092 - Sahalee Of Alaska, Inc.
2092 - Trans-Aqua International, Inc.
2095 - Alaska Herb Tea Co. (Mfr)
2095 - Colonial Coffee Roasters, Inc.
2095 - Great Northern Coffee Co Inc
2095 - JBR Inc
2095 - Kauai Coffee Company
2095 - L & E International Service
2095 - Todd's Plantation, "Gourmet Coffee
2096 - Borden Foods Corp.
2096 - Kornfections & Treasures
2096 - Noble Popcorn Farms
2096 - Snyders of Hanover
2096 - Vogel Popcorn
2097 - Holmes Ice & Cold Storage Co
2098 - Borden Foods Corp.

2098 - Carla's Pasta
2098 - Ladson Noodle Company
2099 - Alaska Herb & Tea Co.
2099 - Alpine Touch Inc
2099 - American Miso Co.
2099 - BakeMark
2099 - Batchmaster
2099 - Cajun Injector, Inc.
2099 - Chef Paul Prudhomme's Magic
2099 - Colorado Cereal, Inc. (Mfr)
2099 - Ellis Popcorn Co., Inc.
2099 - Ener-G Foods Inc
2099 - Famarco Ltd. Inc./B & K International
2099 - Fresca Mexican Foods Inc.
2099 - Gilroy Foods, Inc. (Mfr)
2099 - Great Western Tortilla Company, The
2099 - Hawaiian Eateries, Inc.
2099 - Health Valley Foods
2099 - K & W Popcorn Inc. (Mfr)
2099 - L & E International Service
2099 - Legg, Inc., A. C.
2099 - Link Snacks, Inc.
2099 - Louisiana Gourmet Enterprises
2099 - Lucky Seven Food Inc
2099 - National Stabilizers Inc
2099 - Old World Spices & Seasonings, Inc.
2099 - PTX Food Corp.
2099 - Pacific Harvest Products Inc.
2099 - Peking Noodle Co Inc
2099 - Protos Inc.
2099 - Sims Bros., Inc.
2099 - T. Miller Popcorn Company Inc.(Mfr)
2099 - The Wornick Company
2099 - Todds, Ltd.
2099 - Twin Marquis, Inc.
2099 - Wah Yet Inc
2099 - Wakunaga of America Co., Ltd.
2099 - Yergat Packing Co
212 - Magness Land & Cattle
212 - Wienk Charolais
2189 - National Research & Chemical Co.
2200 - Scapa Filter Media
2211 - Barnhardt Manufacturing Co.
2211 - Chiquola Industrial Products Group,
2211 - Public Health Equipment Supply Inc.
2221 - Absecon Mills, Inc.
2221 - American & Efird, Inc.
2221 - Brickle, Hyman & Son, Inc.
2221 - Carole Fabrics
2221 - Dicey Fabrics
2221 - Mayfair Mills, Inc.
2221 - S-Line
2221 - Wearbest Sil-Tex Mills Ltd.
2231 - Absecon Mills, Inc.
2241 - Alpha Associates, Inc.
2241 - C.M. Offray & Son Inc./Lion Ribbon
2241 - Just A Stretch
2241 - Tape-O Corporation
2241 - U.S. Label Corporation (Mfr)
2252 - Ellis Hosiery Mills, Inc.
2252 - Harriss & Covington Hosiery Mills,
2253 - Alps Sportswear Manufacturing Co ,
2253 - Dorma Mills(Mfr)
2253 - Richland Mills
2257 - Calender Textiles Inc
2257 - Cleveland Mills
2259 - Dorma Mills(Mfr)
2261 - Geltham Industries
2261 - Paradise Textiles Co
2261 - US Dyeing & Finishing Inc
2261 - Zoo-Ink Screen Print
2269 - Ericyan II
2269 - Pioneer Mat Co., Inc.
2273 - Barrett Carpet Mills, Inc.
2273 - Challenger Industries Inc.
2273 - Mohawk International
2273 - Regal Carpets Inc.
2281 - Cheraw Yarn Mills Inc.
2281 - Jones Companies LTD. (Mfr)
2281 - Robison-Anton Textile Company
2281 - Roselon Industries, Inc.
2282 - American & Efird, Inc.
2282 - Intimate Touch, Inc.

2282 - Jefferson Mills, Inc.
2284 - American & Efird, Inc.
2284 - Robison-Anton Textile Company
2284 - Saunders Thread Co., Inc.
2295 - Current, Inc.
2295 - Duracote Corp.
2295 - Duracote Corporation
2295 - Jessup Manufacturing Co.
2295 - Lewcott
2295 - Mid-Mountain Materials Inc
2295 - Spectro Coating Corp.(Mfr)
2295 - Starensier
2295 - Uretek, Inc.
2295 - Vernon Plastics Corp.
2297 - BBA Nonwovens Reemay, Inc.
2297 - Hollingsworth & Vose Co.
2297 - Mid-Mountain Materials Inc
2297 - Reemay, Inc.
2298 - Anchor Buddy
2298 - Kenyon & Sons, Inc., William
2298 - Mid-Mountain Materials Inc
2298 - Pelican Rope Works
2298 - Rocky Mount Cord Co.
2298 - Winchester Auburn Mills, Inc
2298 - Woodstock Line Co., The
2299 - Aetna Felt Corp.
2299 - Chestnut Ridge Foam, Inc.
2299 - Drapes 4 Show Inc.
2299 - Facemate Corporation
2299 - K. G. Fiber, Inc.
2299 - Kamen Wiping Materials Co., Inc.
2299 - Keating Fibre Inc
2299 - Mid-Mountain Materials Inc
2299 - North American Green
2299 - Paschall Export-Import Co., Inc.
2299 - Spectro Coating Corp.(Mfr)
2299 - Tex-Ex Export Co., Inc.
2311 - California Ranchwear Inc
2321 - Paradise Sportswear, Inc.
2322 - 9TZ Inc
2322 - Mohnton Knitting Mills, Inc.
2323 - Duron Neckwear Inc
2325 - Platoon Uniform & Sportswear
2325 - Robett Mfg. Co.
2326 - Dixon Mfg., Inc.
2326 - Insul-Vest, Inc.
2326 - J. D American Workwear, Inc.
2329 - Apparel Suppliers CA/Pagano W
2329 - Canari Cycle Wear
2329 - Cattle Kate Inc
2329 - Guava Beach
2329 - La Mar Mfg. Co.
2329 - Marathon Corp.
2329 - Sauvage Swimwear
2329 - Silver Needles
2329 - Split Tee
2329 - Surf Line Hawaii, Ltd.
2329 - T & R Concept Inc.,
2329 - Y.M.L.A. Inc
2331 - Argus International, Inc.
2331 - Precision Custom Coatings
2335 - B & B Design Collections
2339 - Hannah Katherine Fashions Corp.
2339 - Leo's Dancewear Inc.
2339 - Mary K Active Wear Inc
2339 - Piccone Apparel Corp
2339 - R & S Sportswear Inc; dba FILATI
2339 - Star Styled Dancing Supplies
2341 - Milco Industries, Inc.
2353 - National Can Manufacturing Inc
2353 - New Era Cap Co., Inc.
2353 - Take Two Sportswear Accessories
2353 - Texace Corp.
2361 - Dorissa Of Miami, Inc.
2369 - Rowtex
2369 - Strasburg Inc.
2369 - United Textile
2381 - Best Value Textiles
2385 - South Pass Trading/CNL Clothiers
2386 - JH Design Group
2386 - Pass Distributing Corporation
2386 - Perrone Leathers, Inc.
2386 - Pharr Brand Name Apparel, LLC

2386 - Sheepskin Coat Factory
2387 - Authentic Mexican Imports
2389 - Facemakers Inc.
2389 - Fibrotek Industries Inc
2389 - Industrial Opportunities, Inc., Elastic
2391 - Chase Industries, Inc.
2391 - Dezign Sewing Inc.
2391 - General Drapery Services, Inc.
2391 - Gingerich Draperies Inc
2391 - Goff's Curtain Walls/Goff's
2391 - Hospi-Tel Manufacturing Co.
2391 - Kay & L Draperies, Inc.
2391 - Sol-R-Veil
2391 - Sultan & Sons, Inc.
2392 - Castletech Ltd
2392 - Chestnut Ridge Foam, Inc.
2392 - J W Mfg. Co.
2392 - Kae Co., Inc.
2392 - Lamb, Inc., J.
2392 - Manic Impressions
2392 - Milford Stitching Co., Inc.
2392 - Owen Mfg. Co., Charles D.
2392 - Patchkraft Inc.
2392 - Tablecloth Co., Inc.
2392 - WestPoint Stevens
2392 - Wonderly Co., Inc., The
2393 - Keeper Thermal Bag Co. Inc.
2393 - Mendoza Textiles Manufacturing
2394 - Canvas Specialty
2394 - Covers Unlimited, Inc.
2394 - Floyd's Awning & Canvas Shop
2394 - Golden Fleece Designs Inc
2394 - M.Putterman & Company Inc.
2394 - New American Industries Inc
2394 - Quest & Sons, Inc.
2394 - Revere Plastic, Inc.
2394 - Rothco
2394 - Shur - Co., Inc.
2394 - Universal Fabric Structures, Inc.
2394 - Van Nuys Awning Co Inc
2395 - Embroidertex West Ltd
2395 - National Embroidery Services
2395 - Quality Embroidery
2395 - Scarsdale Quilting Converting Corp.,
2395 - Semel's Embroidery & Screen
2396 - Arrow Creative International, Ltd.
2396 - Bannerville U. S. A. Inc.
2396 - Custom Screens, Inc.
2396 - GS Sportwear / Golden Squeegee
2396 - Geka Brush Manufacturing
2396 - Habitat Softwear
2396 - Mini-Lace, Inc.
2396 - Original Design Silkscreen Co.
2396 - Print Proz, Inc.
2396 - Sloan & Assocs. Inc., Leonard
2396 - T Formation Of Tallahassee, Inc.
2396 - T-Shirts & Graphics
2396 - Tutuvi
2396 - Unique Image T-Shirt Co.
2396 - Worthen Industries, Inc., Nylco Div.
2396 - Wyatt West Inc
2397 - Hamilton Embroidery Co., Inc.
2397 - Robison-Anton Textile Company
2399 - A B C Sign Design, LLC
2399 - A Fifty Star Flags, Banners &
2399 - AMC Products, Ltd.
2399 - Baker Safety Equipment, Inc.
2399 - Blackburn Mfg. Co.
2399 - Blue Water Spa Covers
2399 - Brooklyn Bow International
2399 - Burrell Leder Beltech, Inc.
2399 - Cozy Inc
2399 - Dixie Yarns, Inc.
2399 - Flagman Of America
2399 - Gould & Goodrich
2399 - Jg Creations Inc
2399 - Mainley Flags, Inc.
2399 - Safe Strap Co., Inc.
2399 - Sagaz Industries, Inc.
2399 - Sextet Fabrics, Inc.
2399 - Spanset, Inc.
2399 - Tana Tex Inc.
2399 - Wiggy's Inc

2399 - Windsport
2411 - Maple Valley Hardwoods
2411 - Sea Forest Enterprises Inc
2411 - Superior Helicopter LLC.
2411 - Van Hessen & Co., Inc.
2421 - Algoma Lumber Co.
2421 - Avison Forest Products
2421 - Bacon Veneer Co.
2421 - Big Timber Inc. (Mfr)
2421 - Clinton Hardwood Inc.
2421 - Creveling Sawmill
2421 - Great Northern Lumber, Inc.
2421 - Greenmont Lumber Corp. (Mfr)
2421 - Hampton Lumber Sales Co
2421 - Hardwood Veneer
2421 - Hartzell Hardwoods
2421 - Helsel Lumber Mill, Inc.
2421 - Jim C. Hamer Co.
2421 - Johnson Lumber Co., Llc.
2421 - Jones Lumber Co., Inc., J. M.
2421 - Krooked Kreek Logging Co.
2421 - Lumlog, Inc.
2421 - Miller Mill Co., Inc., T.R.
2421 - New River Building Supply & Lumber
2421 - North American Wood Products, Inc.
2421 - Pike Lumber Company, Inc.
2421 - Rucker Lumber Co., Inc.
2421 - Temple-Inland Forest Products Corp.,
2421 - Wolohan Lumber
2421 - Yeager Sawmill
2426 - Amtico International Inc.
2426 - Challinor Wood Products
2426 - H.A. Stiles
2426 - Hamer, Jim C.
2426 - Hawkeye Forest Products Inc
2426 - Hull Forest Products, Inc.
2426 - North American Wood Products, Inc.
2429 - North American Wood Products, Inc.
2431 - Architectural Windows & Entries, Inc.
2431 - B & C Mortensen Wood Prods Inc
2431 - Bend Door Co
2431 - Burns, Morris & Stewart, Ltd.
2431 - Burton Woodworks Inc.
2431 - Construction Design Associates
2431 - Elixir Industries, Inc.
2431 - Executive Door Company
2431 - Hurd Millwork Company, Inc.
2431 - Jim C. Lane Inc.
2431 - Marley Mouldings Inc.(Mfr)
2431 - Modern Woodcrafts, Inc.
2431 - SW Sash & Door
2431 - Stuhr Enterprises, Inc.
2431 - Tucker Millworks, Inc.
2431 - Woerner Industries, Inc.
2434 - B & D Custom Cabinets, Inc.
2434 - Fowler Cabinet & Hardware Co
2434 - Kraft Masters Cabinets
2434 - Montgomery Cabinetry Co., Inc.
2434 - Paul's Cabinets Co.
2434 - Prada Enterprises, Inc.
2434 - We're Organized of No Calif
2434 - Winfield Cabinets
2435 - Interior Products Inc.
2435 - International Components Plus, Inc.
2435 - Keystone Veneers, Inc.
2435 - Sieling & Jones, Inc.
2436 - Baker Div. Sonoco Products Company
2439 - Fagen's Building Center
2439 - Le Truss Co., Tien
2439 - Now Structures, Inc.
2439 - Universal Truss, Inc.
2439 - Warner Robins Supply Co., Inc.
2440 - Acorn Industries Inc. (Mfr)
2441 - Dynamic Packing & Logistics
2441 - Future Packaging Inc
2441 - Industrial Crating, Inc.
2442 - Ellis Enterprises, T. J.
2448 - Acorn Industries Inc. (Mfr)
2448 - Age Industries, Inc.
2448 - Atco Pallet Co.
2448 - B & B Lumber Co., Inc.
2448 - Commercial Pallet Pak Co.
2449 - Master Craft Plaque Co.

2451 - General Manufactured Housing, Inc.
2451 - Parkwest Industries Inc
2451 - Waverlee Homes Inc.
2452 - Appalachian Log Structures Inc.
2452 - Chase Industries, Inc.
2452 - Edgewood Fine Log Structures Ltd
2452 - Greco Homes
2452 - Horton Homes, Inc.
2452 - Industrial Acoustics Co. Inc.
2452 - International Homes Of Cedar (Mfr)
2452 - Joaquin Manufacturing Corp
2452 - Lindal Cedar Homes
2452 - Northwest Cedar Inc
2452 - Oregon Log Home Co Inc
2452 - Pan Abode Cedar Homes, Inc.
2452 - Sol-R-Veil
2452 - Sybaritic, Inc.
2452 - Wick Buildings
2491 - B & M Wood Products
2491 - Dixie-Pacific Mfg. Co., Inc.
2491 - Fontana Wholesale Lumber
2491 - Miller Mill Co., Inc., T.R.
2499 - ARC Industries Inc.
2499 - Alaska Gift & Gallery
2499 - American Wood Fibre, Inc.
2499 - Amerikan Dream Inc.
2499 - Aristocrat Industries, Inc.
2499 - Baker Div. Sonoco Products Company
2499 - Batts Inc.
2499 - Coeur d'alene Fiber... Inc.
2499 - Colorado Frame Company
2499 - Cor Enterprises
2499 - Dolphin Mfg. Inc.
2499 - Emblem & Badge Inc.
2499 - Excel Design Inc.
2499 - Franklin Hardwoods, Inc.
2499 - Jonathan Virginia, Inc.
2499 - Lemhi Post & Poles Inc
2499 - Magnolia, Div. Sanderson Plmbg.
2499 - Mat, Inc.
2499 - North American Wood Products, Inc.
2499 - Painted Bird
2499 - Picture Woods Ltd
2499 - Premier Hardwood Products Inc.
2499 - Purnell Co., R. C.
2499 - Robert Raikes Enterprizes
2499 - Rochester Shoe Tree Company
2499 - Vixen Hill Mfg. Co.
2499 - Werner Ladder Co.
2511 - All Craft Fabricators, Inc.
2511 - Bonito Mfg.
2511 - Cedar & Hardwood Mfg. Company
2511 - Children's Furniture Co., The
2511 - Easley Co., Jeff
2511 - Fine Craft Unlimited
2511 - Lane Co., Inc., The
2511 - Mouldings Unlimited, Inc.
2511 - Oakwood Interiors
2511 - Royal Sales Corp.
2511 - Tower Stool Company
2512 - Broyhill Furniture Industries, Inc.
2512 - Child Craft Industries, Inc.
2512 - Duraform
2512 - Mc Kinley Leather Of Hickory
2512 - Monteverdi-Young Inc
2512 - National Contract Furnishings
2514 - Carter Grandle Furniture
2514 - Mahar
2514 - Pacific Sun Casual Furniture
2514 - Sunlite Casual Furniture, Inc.
2515 - Chestnut Ridge Foam, Inc.
2515 - Custom Bedding Co. & Orange
2515 - Estee Bedding Co., Inc.
2515 - Glideway Bed Carriage Mfg. Co.
2515 - Hernandez Mattress, Inc.
2515 - Invacare Corporation
2515 - Jamison Bedding Co.
2515 - Kingsdown, Inc.
2515 - My Bed, Inc.
2515 - Verlo Mattress Factory Stores, Int'l
2515 - Viking Industries, Inc.
2515 - Vintage Bedding
2517 - Tocabi America Corp

2519 - Auton Company
2519 - Duraform
2519 - Pipefine Furniture, Inc.
2519 - Syroco Mfr
2519 - Woodpecker, Inc.
2520 - Brodart Co.
2521 - Arcadia Chair Company
2521 - Double-T Mfg. Corp.
2521 - Hale Co., F. E.
2521 - Stablewood Inc.
2521 - Superior Furniture
2521 - Trinity Furniture, Inc.
2522 - Aspects Inc
2522 - Lyon Metal Products LLC
2522 - Matel Bank and Desk Accessories
253 - Delta International
2531 - Buckstaff Company
2531 - Denver Seating Inc
2531 - Folding Bleacher Company
2531 - Jonti-Craft, Inc.
2531 - McCammisn Mfg. Co., Inc.
2531 - Norco Products
2531 - Precision Booth Mfg.
2531 - Sauder Mfg. Co.
2536 - Autoquip Corporation
254 - Tatum Farms International, Inc.
2541 - A B F Industries Inc.
2541 - Admore Inc.
2541 - Benchmark Fixture Corporation
2541 - Customcraft Fixtures
2541 - Enercept, Inc.
2541 - Expo Displays
2541 - Fiberesin Industries, Inc.
2541 - Innerpac Southwest, Inc.
2541 - Keyper Systems, Inc.
2541 - Mod-Tech, Inc.
2541 - Moultrie Post Form, Inc.
2541 - Nationwide Retail Interiors Inc
2541 - Newood Display Fixture Mfg Co
2541 - PAM International Co., Inc.
2541 - S D Modular Displays, Inc.
2541 - Spacewall International
2541 - Spencer & Reynolds Inc
2541 - Valley Fixtures Inc
2541 - Waggon Cellers, Inc.
2542 - Andersen Rack Systems Inc
2542 - Auton Company
2542 - California Wire Products Corp
2542 - Chatsworth Products Inc
2542 - E B I/R J Trausch Industries
2542 - Fiero Enterprises, Inc.
2542 - Fourjay Industries, Inc.
2542 - Hartson Kennedy Cabinet Top Co.
2542 - Huck Store Fixture Co.
2542 - Kent Corp.
2542 - Norren Manufacturing Inc
2542 - Plastic Works Inc
2542 - Rapid Rack Industries
2542 - Stein Industries Inc
2542 - Tri-Link Technologies Ltd.
2591 - Griffith Shade Co.
2591 - McMurray Co
2591 - Novo Industries Inc.
2591 - Plastic-View ATC
2591 - Vertical Express
2591 - Virginia Iron & Metal Co.
2591 - Window Technology, Inc.
2591 - World Wide Windows
2599 - Ashton Food Machinery Co., Inc.,
2599 - Duraform
2599 - Essential Products Co., Inc.
2599 - Fine Line Interiors
2599 - Hopeman Brothers Marine Interiors,
2599 - Living Earth Crafts
2599 - Mity Lite
2599 - Pacific Crest Manufacturing Inc
2599 - R.W. Hatfield Co., Pro-Line Div.
2599 - Vitro Seating Products
2611 - Autron Incorporated
2611 - Custom Machine Works, Inc.
2611 - IRA Levy & Associates
2611 - Keating Fibre Inc
2621 - Ahern International Sales Corp.

2621 - Book Covers Inc
2621 - Daiei Papers U.S.A. Corp.
2621 - Encore Paper Co.
2621 - Gilbert Paper
2621 - Hollingsworth & Vose Co.
2621 - Keating Fibre Inc
2621 - Marcal Paper Mills
2621 - Paper Pak Products Inc
2621 - Pepperell Paper Co., Inc.
2631 - Chemco Manufacturing Incorporated
2631 - Fiber Mark Inc.
2631 - International Paper Co., Texarkana
2631 - Rock-Tenn Company
2641 - Contronic Devices
2641 - Dielectric Polymers, Inc.
2653 - Forest Packaging Corp.
2653 - Northwest Paper Box Mfrs Inc
2653 - Pacific Western Container
2653 - Tucson Container Corporation
2653 - Whitmark Inc
2655 - All American Containers, Inc.
2655 - Conitex (USA) Inc. (MFR)
2655 - Duraform
2655 - Newark Group, Inc.
2657 - Boxes.Com (A N.J. Corporation)
2657 - Promotional Resources Group
2671 - Deerfield Specialty Papers, Inc.
2671 - E-Tech Products Inc
2671 - Mapletex
2671 - Taratape
2672 - Aigner Index, Inc.
2672 - Allenwest Inc
2672 - Allied Decals Florida, Inc.
2672 - Forester Rollers
2672 - Green Bay Packaging, Inc./ Coated
Products Operations
2672 - Holman Label Company
2672 - J.L. Darling Corporation
2672 - Jessup Manufacturing Co.
2672 - Microcosm
2672 - Miles Label Company Inc
2672 - Ultratape Industries Inc
2672 - Webtech, Inc.
2673 - Caltex Plastics Inc
2673 - Hershey Industries, Inc.
2673 - Intertape Polymer
2673 - Packaging Center, Inc.
2673 - Packaging Supply Corp.
2674 - Duro Bag Mfg. Co.
2674 - Roses Southwest Papers
2675 - Maratech International
2675 - Pressner & Co., Inc., M.
2676 - Disposable Products Company Inc.
2677 - American Scholar Co.
2677 - Southern Church Envelope Co.
2678 - Autron Incorporated
2678 - Brewood Engravers Inc.
2678 - Loose Ends
2679 - American Cedarworks, Inc.
2679 - Blue Atlantic, Ltd.
2679 - Pacific Fabric Reels Inc
2679 - Roselle Paper Co., Inc.
2679 - Savage Universal Corporation
2679 - Sunshine Paper Company
2711 - Arizona Daily Star
2711 - Birmingham News Co., The
2711 - Blue Sheet Inc., The
2711 - Clear Creek Courant
2711 - El Hispanic News
2711 - El Semanario
2711 - Glen Ullin Times
2711 - Herburger Publications Inc
2711 - Hill Country Newspapers Inc. / The
2711 - Home With Homeland News &
2711 - Lake County Leader
2711 - Latimer County News-Trib
2711 - Partnership Press, Inc.
2711 - Philippine News Inc
2711 - Seattle Post/Intelligencer Div
2711 - South Pasadena Publishing Co
2711 - The Catholic Voice
2711 - The Medical Remarketer
2711 - The Western Newspaper

2711 - The Wolfe Pack
2711 - World Journal Inc
2711 - Wyoming Livestock Roundup
2721 - CPS Communications, Inc.
2721 - Cahners business Information
2721 - California Journal
2721 - Chaos Comics Inc
2721 - Chilton Company
2721 - Elevator World
2721 - Hoffmann Pulications DBA:
2721 - Ranchland News
2721 - Root Co., Inc., A. I., The
2721 - Southern Calif Guide-Westworld
2721 - The Practice Builder Association
2721 - The Skiing Co
2721 - Used Equipment Directory
2721 - Water Conditioning/Purification
2721 - Western Agricultural Publish
2731 - Academic Press
2731 - Alfred Publishing Co Inc
2731 - Annual Reviews Inc
2731 - Dharma Publishing
2731 - Doral Publishing Inc
2731 - Dragon Enterprises
2731 - E M I S, Inc.
2731 - IDQ Books Worldwide Inc
2731 - International Soc For Technology In
2731 - Malibu Publishing
2731 - Sandpiper Publications
2731 - Scott Foresman
2731 - Service Quality Institute
2731 - Warren Communications
2732 - KNI Incorporated
2732 - Total Printing Systems
2741 - Barclay Maps
2741 - Coast Publishing
2741 - ETS Research & Development Inc
2741 - East-west Publishing Company
2741 - Forster-Long Inc.
2741 - Hagadone Directories Inc
2741 - Health Impact Inc
2741 - Image Maker Enterprises
2741 - Intercultural Development
2741 - JASA Publications
2741 - Metropolitan Graphics
2741 - Richardson Engineering Svcs Inc
2741 - Scott Resources, Inc.
2741 - Slosson Educational Publications, Inc.
2741 - Technical Resource International, Inc.
2741 - The California Visitors Review
2741 - The Damron Co Inc
2741 - Westcott Cove Publishing Co.
2741 - World Wide Pet Supply Ass'n
2752 - ACE Printing Company
2752 - AlphaGraphics Printshops
2752 - Anchor Printing & Graphics
2752 - Artco
2752 - Best Litho, Inc.
2752 - Congdon Printing & Imaging
2752 - Diego & Son Printing
2752 - El Camino Printers
2752 - Giant Horse Printing Inc
2752 - Gonzalez Integrated Marketing
2752 - Graphic Ways Inc
2752 - Graphics Plus Printing, Inc.
2752 - Hoyle Products
2752 - Impulse Wear
2752 - Imtec Inc.
2752 - Instant Copy, Inc.
2752 - Marketing Concepts
2752 - National Art Publishing Corp.
2752 - Pikes Peak Lithographing Co
2752 - Quantum Color Graphics Inc.
2752 - Rapid Reproductions Printing
2752 - Repro-Products & Services
2752 - Seton Name Plate Company
2752 - Tapes 'n Tags Mfg.
2752 - Thunderbird Printing & Screening
2752 - Tretina Printing Co., Inc.
2752 - U S Game Systems, Inc.
2752 - U.S. Label Corporation (Mfr)
2752 - WestPro Graphics
2759 - C. S. S. Publishing Co., Inc.

2759 - Chromaline Corp.
2759 - Coastal Printing Co.
2759 - Creative Plastics Printing Die
2759 - Image Printing
2759 - J K Label Co.
2759 - Joplin Printing Co.
2759 - L M N Printing Co., Inc.
2759 - Lithotype Co Inc
2759 - Lumber Tag Specialties
2759 - Mapmakers Alaska
2759 - Matrix Imaging Solution
2759 - Mitchell Daily Republic
2759 - Nameplates, Inc.
2759 - National Plastic Printing, Inc.
2759 - Original Impressions, Inc.
2759 - Outlook Graphics
2759 - Palone & Associates
2759 - Pochet Of America, Inc.
2759 - Precision Press
2759 - Prismflex Inc.
2759 - Process Graphics Corp.
2759 - Psychological Corp., The
2759 - Roberts Co., The John
2759 - Sandy-Alexander, Inc.
2759 - Schmidt Printing, Inc.
2759 - Schofield Printing, Inc.
2759 - Shrimp World Inc.
2759 - Source W Printing
2759 - Southland Printing Company, Inc.
2759 - Times Leader, Inc.
2759 - Union Printing
2759 - Wolf Creek Printing
2761 - American Forms, Inc.
2761 - Colonial Business Forms, Inc.
2761 - Kenalex Printing Forms, Inc., Kenalex
2761 - New West Business Forms
2761 - Triangle Business Forms, Inc.
2771 - Comstock Cards Inc
2771 - The Wolfe Pack
2782 - Art Leather Manufacturing Co., Inc.
2789 - Haworth Press, Inc., The
2791 - Advanced Graphics & Publishing
2791 - Digital Nation
2791 - HeyMac Publishing, Inc.
2791 - PC Services
2791 - Rutledge Books, Inc.
2791 - Strawberry Patch Publishing
2791 - Sun Publishing Co.
2796 - Ano-Coil Corp.
2796 - Iridio
2796 - NAPP Systems Inc
2796 - Tube Light Co., Inc.
2800 - Hach Company
2811 - Lexard Corporation
2813 - Aero Tech Labs, Inc.
2813 - Icor International Inc.
2813 - Scott Specialty Gases
2816 - Davis Colors
2816 - Elementis Specialties, Colorants &
2819 - ACSI Inc.
2819 - Advance Research Chemicals, Inc.
2819 - Arrow Engineering Inc.
2819 - Calgon Carbon Corporation (Mfr)
2819 - Catalytic Products International, Inc.
2819 - Chemway Systems, Inc.
2819 - Dover Chemical Corp., Sub. of ICC
2819 - E-Z-Em, Inc.
2819 - Exclusive Findings
2819 - General Carbon Corp.
2819 - Giles Chemical Corp.
2819 - Houghton International, Inc.
2819 - Jupiter Chemicals, Inc.
2819 - Martin Marietta Magnesia Specialties
2819 - McCann's Engineering & Mfr. Co.
2819 - National Alum Corp.
2819 - PPG Industries Inc.
2819 - Permatron Corporation
2819 - Radio Materials Corp.
2819 - Remet Corp.
2819 - Research Products Co.
2819 - Respond Group of Companies
2819 - Russ Chemical Co., Inc.
2819 - SVC Labs

2819 - Syntech Products Corp.
2819 - U. S. Vanadium Corp.
2821 - Albis
2821 - Artemis Industries Inc.
2821 - BJB Enterprises Inc
2821 - CYRO Industries
2821 - DSM Melamine Americas, Inc.
2821 - Dielectric Polymers, Inc.
2821 - Dura Temp Corp.
2821 - Eastern Color & Chemical Co.
2821 - Environmental Soil Systems Inc
2821 - FICI Export
2821 - Fusion Coatings Inc.
2821 - Hitech Polymers, Inc.
2821 - Lewcott
2821 - NVF Company (Mfr)
2821 - Philadelphia Resins
2821 - Pleko Southwest Inc
2821 - Polymer Trading Services Limited
2821 - Rayonier
2821 - Rogers Corporation
2821 - The Purolite Company
2822 - L S M Labs, Inc.
2822 - PSI Inc
2823 - Fiber Master Inc./Thermocon Inc.
2824 - Western Synthetic Fiber
2831 - American Laboratories, Inc. (Mfr)
2833 - All American Pharmaceutical &
2833 - American Laboratories, Inc. (Mfr)
2833 - Arnet Pharmaceutical Corp.
2833 - Biomin Industries, Inc.
2833 - Biotics Research Corp.
2833 - Captek Softgel International
2833 - Casey Sales Company Incorporated
2833 - Concentrated Aloe Corp.
2833 - East Park Research Inc
2833 - Food Science Laboratories
2833 - GNLD International
2833 - Harmon Technological
2833 - International Vitamin Corporation
2833 - Irwin Naturals / 4 Health Inc
2833 - Kind & Knox Gelatine, Inc.
2833 - Madys Company
2833 - Mallinckrodt Inc.
2833 - Montana Aromatics
2833 - SKW Biosystems
2833 - St Jon Pet Care Products
2833 - Starwest Botanicals Inc
2833 - The Chemins Company Inc
2833 - Tishcon Corporation (Mfr)
2833 - Trimedica International Inc
2833 - Up-Time Sports/Nutrition/Medical Ind
2833 - Wachters Organic Sea Products
2834 - ADH Health Products Inc.
2834 - Algon
2834 - American Distilling & Manufacturing
2834 - American Laboratories, Inc. (Mfr)
2834 - Apothecary Products Inc.
2834 - Arnet Pharmaceutical Corp.
2834 - B & S Equine / Cannie Skin Lotion
2834 - Beutlich, L.P. Pharmaceuticals
2834 - Biotics Research Corp.
2834 - Blansett Pharmacal Co.
2834 - E. Fougera & Co.
2834 - Flomed Corporation
2834 - Grand Laboratories, Inc.
2834 - Herbco International Inc.
2834 - Highland Laboratories
2834 - Hobart Laboratories, Inc.
2834 - J Hewitt Inc
2834 - Neil Laboratories, Inc.
2834 - Northridge Laboratories Inc
2834 - SP Pharmaceuticals LLC
2834 - Unico, Inc.
2834 - Upsher-Smith Laboratories, Inc.
2834 - Viragen, Inc.
2835 - Andwin Corporation
2835 - Dade Behring Inc.
2835 - Genzyme Corp
2835 - Maplehurst Genetics Intl. Inc.
2835 - Midland Bioproducts Corp.
2835 - Strategic Diagnostics, Inc.
2836 - Moldowan Lab Inc

2836 - Newport Biosystems, Inc.
2836 - Synthetic Genetics
2841 - Bissell Inc.(Mfr)
2841 - Burlington Chemical Co., Inc. (Mfr)
2841 - C & W Enterprises
2841 - Elementis Specialties, Colorants &
2841 - Hotsy Corporation, The
2841 - Jobe Industries Inc.
2841 - Justice Brothers, Inc.
2841 - Kaygeeco Inc
2841 - L H B Industries
2841 - Lasting Impressions Soaps
2841 - Lexard Corporation
2841 - Miller Corp., Harry
2841 - Norman, Fox & Co
2841 - Original Bradford Soap Works, Inc.
2841 - Royal Enterprises, Inc. (Mfr), Urnex
2841 - SOQ Environmental Tech Corp
2841 - Star Brite
2841 - Supreme Chemicals Of Georgia
2841 - Vision Pharmaceuticals Inc.
2842 - AbTech Industries Inc.
2842 - Alkota Cleaning Systems
2842 - American & Efird, Inc.
2842 - Charlie Chemical & Supply, Inc.
2842 - Dynamic Research Co Inc
2842 - High-Tech Conversions, Inc.
2842 - Hygienic Products Laboratories
2842 - Jacksonlea
2842 - Kyzen Corp.
2842 - Lilly Industries, Inc.
2842 - Midlab, Inc.
2842 - National Research & Chemical Co.
2842 - Nature Plus, Inc.
2842 - Nutech Environmental Corp.(Mfr)
2842 - Pecard Leather Care Products
2842 - Penray Companies Inc.(Mfr)
2842 - Rapid Purge Corp.
2842 - SOQ Environmental Tech Corp
2842 - Sentry Chemical Co.
2842 - Star Brite
2842 - Steam Services Inc.
2842 - Treatment Products Ltd.
2842 - Whip-It Products, Inc.
2843 - Burlington Chemical Co., Inc. (Mfr)
2843 - Eastern Color & Chemical Co.
2843 - Elementis Specialties, Colorants
2843 - Lenox Chemical Company
2843 - Lexard Corporation
2843 - Miller Corp., Harry
2843 - Renite Co., Lubrication Engineers
2844 - A Touch Of Country Magic
2844 - Agro-Mar Inc Of Nevada
2844 - Ahern International Sales Corp.
2844 - Ashland Chemical
2844 - Aubrey Organics Inc.
2844 - Biocare Labs
2844 - Bioelements Inc
2844 - Bogdana Corporation
2844 - Classic Cosmetics Inc
2844 - Columbia Cosmetics Manufacturing,
2844 - Cosmetic Specialty Labs, Inc.
2844 - Creations Aromatiques, Inc.
2844 - Dews Research
2844 - Eldorado Chemical Co., Inc.
2844 - Enterprising Kitchen
2844 - Essential Products Co., Inc.
2844 - Fingers Inc
2844 - Foreign Trade Marketing
2844 - Fort Pitt Acquisition
2844 - Gabrielle, Inc.
2844 - Geka Brush Manufacturing
2844 - Harmony Laboratories, Inc.
2844 - Herba Aromatica Inc
2844 - International Beauty Design
2844 - J Hewitt Inc
2844 - Lamaur
2844 - Lanman & Kemp-Barclay & Co.
2844 - Lexard Corporation
2844 - Lily Of Colorado
2844 - Lois Yee Cosmetics Inc
2844 - M. Brown & Sons, Inc.
2844 - Magnesia Products Inc.

2844 - OraLabs Holding Corp
2844 - Original Bradford Soap Works, Inc.
2844 - Para Laboratories, Inc., / Queen
2844 - R. B. R. Productions, Inc.
2844 - Rejuvi Cosmetic Laboratory
2844 - Sahara Springs Cosmetics
2844 - Shelton's Sheen Wave Labs Inc
2844 - Sozio, Inc., J. E.
2844 - Terry Laboratories, Inc.
2844 - The John Wesley Group
2844 - Trademark Cosmetics Inc
2844 - Unique Laboratories, Inc.
2844 - Vision Pharmaceuticals Inc.
2844 - Viviane Woodard Cosmetics
2844 - Waikiki Aloe
2844 - Waikiki Aloe Waikiki Fragrance &
2844 - Wallsburg Soap Co
2844 - Yaz Enterprises
2851 - Alpha Coatings Inc.
2851 - Ameron Intl/Protective Coatings
2851 - Bond Paint & Chemicals, Inc.
2851 - Chemco Manufacturing Incorporated
2851 - E/M Corporation (Mfr)
2851 - Elementis Specialties, Colorants &
2851 - Environmental Protective Coatings,
2851 - Finishes Unlimited
2851 - G-Wood Finishing Co. Inc.
2851 - GE Vallecitos Nuclear Center
2851 - Graham Paint & Varnish Co., Inc.
2851 - Hawthorne Paint Co., Inc.
2851 - Hunting Industrial Coatings
2851 - ICI Paints International - Export -
2851 - Kel-Glo Corp.
2851 - Kop-Coat Inc
2851 - Morton International, Inc.
2851 - P R I D E Enterprises, Inc., Baker
2851 - Penray Companies Inc.(Mfr)
2851 - Pettit Paint Co., Inc.
2851 - Products Techniques Inc
2851 - SPM Thermo-Shield, Inc.
2851 - Smiland Paint Company
2851 - Spray Products Corp.
2851 - Star Brite
2851 - Tevco
2851 - Wagman Primus Group, LP
2851 - Yenkin-Majestic Paint Corp.(Mfr)
2851 - Zinsser & Co., Inc., William
2859 - Prismflex Inc.
2861 - Electro-Science Labs Inc.
2861 - Osmose Wood Preserving, Inc.
2865 - Bezjian Dye-Chem, Inc.
2865 - Burlington Chemical Co., Inc. (Mfr)
2865 - Eastern Color & Chemical Co.
2865 - Elementis Specialties, Colorants &
2865 - Renite Co., Lubrication Engineers
2865 - Synalloy Corp., Blackman-Uhler
2865 - Tricon Colors, LLC
2865 - Universal Plastics Color Corp.
2869 - Aerko International
2869 - Burlington Chemical Co., Inc. (Mfr)
2869 - C.P. Hall Company, The (Mfr)
2869 - Diehl, Inc.
2869 - Dyadic International, Inc.
2869 - Live Earth Products
2869 - Norac Co., Inc., The
2869 - Supelco, Inc.(Mfr)
2869 - Terry Laboratories, Inc.
2873 - Live Earth Products
2873 - North American Export Company
2874 - Carus Chemical Co.
2875 - Agrimar Corp.
2875 - C. S. I. Chemical Corp.
2875 - Great Dane Terminal, The
2875 - Liquinox Co
2875 - Resource Recovery Systems Inc. -
2875 - United Farmers Co-Op
2875 - Western Farm Service/Cascade
2879 - Atlas Chemical Corporation (MFR)
2879 - Deer-Off, Inc.
2879 - Dr. T's Nature Products Inc.
2879 - Pic Corp.
2879 - Public Health Equipment Supply Inc.
2879 - Sipcam Agro USA, Inc.

2879 - Soil Technologies Corp.
2890 - Contronic Devices
2891 - A P C M Mfg. Llc
2891 - Adhesive Systems, Inc.
2891 - Adhesive Technologies, Inc.
2891 - Adhesives Research, Inc.
2891 - Arlon Engineered Laminates &
2891 - Convenience Products (Mfr)
2891 - Dalton Enterprises, Inc.
2891 - Dielectric Polymers, Inc.
2891 - Dyna-Tech Adhesives, Inc.
2891 - Eclectic Products Inc.
2891 - Electronic Materials Inc
2891 - Elementis Performance Polymers
2891 - General Sealants Inc
2891 - Hernon Manufacturing Inc.
2891 - Northwest Coatings Corp.
2891 - P.D.I. INC.
2891 - Pelseal Technologies, LLC
2891 - Polygem
2891 - Pro-Seal Products Inc
2891 - Sashco Sealants Inc
2891 - Schnee-Morehead of California
2891 - Seepage Control Inc
2891 - Star Brite
2891 - Techni-Seal International
2891 - Ultra Seal International
2891 - United Technologies Automotive, Inc.
2892 - Abrasive Distributors Corp.
2892 - Quantic Industries Inc
2893 - A J Daw Printing Ink Co
2893 - Inx International Ink Co.
2893 - Solar Color Chemical Corp.
2893 - Wikoff Color Corp.
2899 - Agtrol International
2899 - Allied Flare Inc.
2899 - Anti Hydro International, Inc.
2899 - Aromaland, Inc.
2899 - Atlantic Pacific Automotive
2899 - B-D Chemical Co Inc
2899 - Bijur Lubricating Corporation
2899 - Chemetrics, Inc.
2899 - Chemical Distributors, Inc.
2899 - Cohler Enterprises
2899 - Daburn Electronics & Cable Corp.
2899 - Dixie Chemical Co., Inc.
2899 - DriWater Inc
2899 - E/M Corporation (Mfr)
2899 - ELF
2899 - Eastern Color & Chemical Co.
2899 - Eastern Europe Inc.
2899 - Elf Atochem North America Inc. Wire
2899 - Ewald Instrument Group
2899 - Firefreeze Worldwide, Inc.
2899 - Frank B. Ross Co., Inc. (Mfr)
2899 - Geo Specialty Chemicals, Inc.
2899 - Geochem International
2899 - Industrial Specialty Chemicals, Inc.
2899 - Innovative Organics Inc
2899 - Interdynamics, Inc.
2899 - International Lubricants, Inc.
2899 - Intraco Corp.
2899 - Jell Chemicals, Inc.
2899 - John Zink Company
2899 - K & W Products
2899 - Keystone Electronics Corp.
2899 - Montana Essence Company
2899 - Motorkote Inc
2899 - National Ink
2899 - National Research & Chemical Co.
2899 - Nofire Technologies Inc.
2899 - Odor Control Co., Inc.
2899 - Pacific Pac International Inc
2899 - Pel Assocs., Inc.
2899 - Penray Companies Inc.(Mfr)
2899 - Petroferm Inc.
2899 - Pro Chem Tech, Internatinal, Inc.
2899 - Prosoco Inc.
2899 - Qualitek International, Inc.
2899 - Ques Industries, Inc.
2899 - Radiator Specialty Co.
2899 - Ranger Industries
2899 - San Juan International, Inc.

2899 - Security Equipment Corp.
2899 - South Beach Fire Services
2899 - Specified Technologies, Inc.
2899 - Standard Fusee
2899 - State Insulation Corp.
2899 - Steam Services Inc.
2899 - Summit Industries Inc.
2899 - Tata, Inc.
2899 - Treatment Products Ltd.
2899 - Triple S Products
2899 - Velco Chemicals
2899 - Wayne Consultants, Inc.
2900 - INTERDEVCO & Associates
2911 - Bell Additives, Inc.
2911 - Golden Bear Oil Specialties
2911 - Interdynamics, Inc.
2911 - Sunoco, Inc.
2935 - Embroidertex West Ltd
2951 - C S S Technology Inc.
2952 - Henry Company International
2952 - Metacrylics
2952 - Siplast Inc.
2952 - United Roofing Mfg. Co., Inc.
299 - Stro-Wold International Livestock Svcs.
2992 - Astro Enterprises Int'l., Inc. (Mfr) /
2992 - Chempet Corp.
2992 - Coastal Unilube, Inc.
2992 - Digilube Systems, Inc.
2992 - Engineered Lubricants Co.
2992 - International Lubricants, Inc.
2992 - Lexard Corporation
2992 - Monroe Fluid Technology, Inc.
2992 - Mullen Circle Brand, Inc.
2992 - Petro Chemical Products Inc.
2992 - Protect All, Inc.
2992 - WD-40 Company
2999 - A B C Coke
2999 - Lehigh Coal & Navigation Co.
3011 - Airseal Products Company
3011 - EBM Imports
3011 - FCI Marketing Inc. (Mfr)
3011 - Lakin Tire East, Inc.
3011 - Reynolds Tire & Rubber
3011 - Tire & Heavy Equipment, Inc.
3011 - Tire Factory, The
3011 - Tire Group International Inc
3021 - Converse
3021 - Skechers USA Inc
3041 - Norton Industries
3052 - Daburn Electronics & Cable Corp.
3052 - FCI Marketing Inc. (Mfr)
3052 - Fabreeka International Inc
3052 - Goodyear International Corporation
3052 - Goodyear Rubber Products Corp.
3052 - Hydraulic Industrial Resources
3052 - J G B Enterprises, Inc.
3052 - JSJ Corp/Sparks Belting Div
3052 - Jason Industrial, Inc.
3052 - Mid-West Instrument
3052 - Teleflex Fluid Systems, Inc.
3053 - American High Performance Seals,
3053 - Anderson Seal Co., Inc.
3053 - C G R Products Inc.
3053 - Embry Engineering & Mfg
3053 - Gulf Coast Seal, Inc.
3053 - Houston Mfg. & Specialty Co., Inc.
3053 - John Crane Inc.
3053 - Lamons Power Engineering
3053 - Malo & Weste Corp.
3053 - Mid-Mountain Materials Inc
3053 - Pacific States Felt & Mfg Co
3053 - Pars Manufacturing Co.
3053 - R & R Rubber Molding Inc
3053 - ROW, Inc.
3053 - Seal-Seat Company
3053 - Sealing Devices, Inc.
3053 - Sepco (Mfr)
3061 - Bentley Manufacturing Co Inc
3061 - Esco Rubber Products Inc
3061 - Kirkhill Rubber Co
3061 - Lord Corporation, Mechanical
Products, Division
3061 - Pelmor Labs, Inc.

3061 - Rogers Corporation
3061 - Trelleborg YSH, Inc.
3069 - Arlon Silicone Technology Division
3069 - Axel Plastics Research Laboratories
3069 - BAS Recycling Inc
3069 - Bingham Roller Co.
3069 - California Latex Inc
3069 - Colorado Lining International, Inc.
3069 - Colorado Rubber & Supply Co
3069 - Continental Disc Corp.
3069 - Cooper Engineered Products, Div. Of
3069 - Diamond Rubber Products Co., Inc.
3069 - Forester Rollers
3069 - JSP International
3069 - Jonal Laboratories, Inc.
3069 - Kerotest Manufacturing Corp. (Mfr)
3069 - Lauren Mfg. Co.
3069 - Lockwood Industries Inc
3069 - M. A. Hanna Rubber Compounding
3069 - Maloney Technical Product, Inc.
3069 - Metal Rubber Corporation
3069 - Mexpo International Inc
3069 - Par Products
3069 - R & R Rubber Molding Inc
3069 - R Wales & Son LLC
3069 - Rahco Rubber, Inc.
3069 - Rubber Engineering
3069 - T & C Mfg. & Operating, Inc.
3069 - T M P Technologies, Inc./Truly Magic
3069 - The Akro Corporation
3069 - Truck Tracks Inc
3069 - Western Filament Inc
3069 - Western States Mfg. Co.
3070 - Stanlar Industries
3081 - Broward & Johnson
3081 - Flagship Converters, Inc.
3081 - GSE Lining Technology, Inc.
3081 - Hutchison & Co.
3081 - Imperial Pools Inc.
3081 - Laminations Inc.
3081 - Mega Plastics, Inc.
3081 - Plastic-View ATC
3081 - Remco Products Corp.
3082 - Bromley Plastics Corp.
3082 - Quaker Plastic Corp.
3082 - Superior American Plastics, Inc.
3082 - Tulox Plastics Corp.
3083 - Current, Inc.
3083 - Major Industries, Inc.
3083 - Pioneer Plastics Corporation
3083 - Smoke Guard Corporation
3084 - Available Plastics, Inc.
3084 - Centron International Inc.
3084 - Pacific Plastics
3084 - Plastinetics, Inc.
3084 - Policonductos S.A. de C.V.
3085 - All American Containers, Inc.
3086 - Advanced Thermal Products Inc
3086 - C. M. I. Enterprises
3086 - Chestnut Ridge Foam, Inc.
3086 - Commodore Machine Co.
3086 - Creative Arts
3086 - Crest Foam Industries
3086 - Davis Co., E. J.
3086 - I P I International
3086 - Mizell Brothers Company
3086 - Rogers Corporation
3086 - SWD Urethane
3087 - Carolina Color Corp.
3087 - Foam Supplies, Inc.
3087 - Foster Corp.
3087 - L N P Engineering Plastics, Inc.
3087 - Longwood Products / Plastic
3088 - Imperial Pools Inc.
3088 - Jason International, Inc.
3088 - Plastic Development Company(MFR)
3088 - Tradewind Industries, Inc.
3089 - AMA Plastics
3089 - ARC Industries Inc.
3089 - ATS Products
3089 - Acme Plastic Products Company
3089 - Advanced Package Engineering Inc
3089 - Afton Plastics

3089 - Airglas Engineering Co., Inc.
3089 - Alabama Plastic Container
3089 - Alcar Industries, Inc.
3089 - Alfred's Pictures Frames Inc
3089 - Alga Plastics Co.
3089 - Allsafe Co., Inc.
3089 - American Fiber Industries, Llc
3089 - Andrew M Martin Company Inc
3089 - Associated Plastics Inc
3089 - Available Plastics, Inc.
3089 - Batts Inc.
3089 - Benz Research & Development Corp.
3089 - Berner International Corp.
3089 - C.U.E., Inc. (Mfr)
3089 - CMO Enterprises Inc.
3089 - Cargo Systems, Inc.
3089 - Carlisle FoodService Products
3089 - Classic Lady Packaging, Inc.
3089 - Compu Cover
3089 - Congoleum Corp.
3089 - Corro-Shield International, Inc.
3089 - Custom Extrusions & Molding Inc
3089 - D G P Inc.
3089 - Daco Enterprises Inc
3089 - Dasco Pro Inc (Mfr)
3089 - Dimco-Gray Co.
3089 - East Iowa Plastics, Inc.
3089 - Eclipse Mfg. Co.
3089 - Enflo Corp.
3089 - First Card Co.
3089 - First State Map & Globe Co., Inc.
3089 - Geka Brush Manufacturing
3089 - Gentek Building Products
3089 - Gilman Brothers
3089 - Glassmaster
3089 - Global Kitting
3089 - H & R Industries, Inc.
3089 - HH ele Corporation
3089 - Hanover Wire Cloth
3089 - Harva Co., Inc., The
3089 - Hope Industries
3089 - Hubbell / The Ohio Brass Co. (Mfr)
3089 - Hunt-Wilde Corp.
3089 - Hutzler Mfg. Co., Inc.
3089 - Improved Construction Methods
3089 - Inca Plastics Molding Co Inc
3089 - Inline Plastics Corp.
3089 - Insulgard Corporation
3089 - Intek Plastics, Inc.
3089 - International Plastic Cards
3089 - J-Mac Plastics Inc.
3089 - J-Pac Corp.
3089 - Jayline International Corp.
3089 - Jeco Plastic Products, Inc.
3089 - Kasko Enterprises Inc.
3089 - Kemlite
3089 - Land And Sky Mfg., Inc.
3089 - Lane-Merritt Float Co
3089 - Laser Creations Inc
3089 - Lucas Products Corp.
3089 - M. A. Hanna Rubber Compounding
3089 - M.M. Electric Products Ltd.
3089 - Macro Plastics Inc
3089 - Maine Plastics Inc.
3089 - Maine Poly Inc
3089 - Marley Mouldings Inc.(Mfr)
3089 - Mc Clarin Plastics, Inc.
3089 - Mc Kee Button Co.
3089 - Melmat Inc
3089 - Meridian Products Corp.
3089 - Mil Bar Plastics Co
3089 - Minco Technology Labs, Inc.
3089 - Myro, Inc.
3089 - N. E. W. Plastics Corp.
3089 - NVF Company (Mfr)
3089 - National Seal Co.
3089 - Northerm Windows Corp.
3089 - Nylacarb Corp.
3089 - Omega Plastics, Inc.
3089 - Optical Polymer Research, Inc.
3089 - Pan American Plastics Co., Div. of.
3089 - Plano International
3089 - Plastic Injection Molders Inc.

342

3089 - Plastic Techniques, Inc.
3089 - Plastics Design & Manufacturing
3089 - Plastinetics, Inc.
3089 - Poly Conversions Inc.
3089 - Poly-Flex Inc.
3089 - Polywood, Inc.
3089 - Porta-Fab Corp.
3089 - Pupi Enterprises LLC
3089 - Quaker Plastic Corp.
3089 - R. P. Creations, Inc.
3089 - Reflexite Corp.
3089 - Reliable Plastics Seals, Inc.
3089 - Remco Products Corp.
3089 - Remco Technology, Inc.
3089 - Retlaw Tools & Plastics Co., Inc.
3089 - Robbins Corp. E.S.
3089 - Robbins Industries Inc.
3089 - Rodak Plastics Co., Inc.
3089 - Rover Vinyl Tech Industries
3089 - Russell-Stanley Corp.
3089 - S.K. Plastics
3089 - Service Ideas, Inc.
3089 - Shaw-Clayton Corporation
3089 - Six-Eleven Ltd Inc
3089 - Skaps Industries, Inc.
3089 - Smith Fiberglass Products Company
3089 - Sparks Industries
3089 - Spradling Originals Inc.
3089 - Sterling International Inc
3089 - Stuewe and Sons, Inc.
3089 - T S I Plastics
3089 - Technical Coating International
3089 - Tinby, LLC
3089 - Trademark Medical
3089 - Traex
3089 - Tucson Industrial Plastics
3089 - U.S. Farathane Corp.
3089 - US Products Inc
3089 - Uniek Inc.
3089 - Unimark Plastics Co.
3089 - United Metal Receptacle Inc. (Mfr)
3089 - Vaupell Industrial Plastics Inc
3089 - Veka West Inc
3089 - Vi-Cas Mfg. Co., Inc.
3089 - Vinylex Corp.
3089 - Ware Shoals Plastics Inc.
3089 - Waterloo Industries, Inc.
3089 - Werner Ladder Co.
3089 - Wescosa Inc
3089 - Western Roller Corporation
3089 - Window Products Inc
3089 - Wiremold Co., The
3099 - Pace Manufacturing, Inc.
3111 - Smuckers Harness Shop Inc.
3134 - Sioux Chief Manufacturing Co.,Inc.
3143 - Cove Shoe Co., Matterhorn-Corcoran
3144 - Poly Masters Industries Inc
3149 - Leo's Dancewear Inc.
3149 - Red Wing Shoe Co.
3149 - Saucony, Inc.
3151 - Edina Mfg. Co., Inc.
3151 - McGough Industries Inc
3151 - Shelby Group International
3161 - Lightware Inc
3161 - Pantos Corp
3161 - Platt Luggage, Inc.
3199 - American Sewing Dynamics 1
3199 - Empire State Leather Corp.
3199 - Gould & Goodrich
3199 - Just Merino Sheepskin Products
3199 - Matel Bank and Desk Accessories
3199 - Robus Leather
3199 - Saddle Barn Tack Distributors, Inc.
3199 - Smuckers Harness Shop Inc.
3211 - Custom Glass Corp.
3211 - Laminated Glass
3211 - Naugatuck Glass Company, The
3221 - All American Containers, Inc.
3229 - Chemglass Inc.
3229 - Hanover Wire Cloth
3229 - Industrial Fiber Optics
3229 - Peltier Glass Co., The
3229 - Precision Art Coordinators, Inc.

3229 - Radiant Communications Corp.
3231 - ARC Industries Inc.
3231 - Allied Products Int'l, Inc.
3231 - Analtech, Inc.
3231 - Anthony International
3231 - Apollo Energy
3231 - Astro Optics Corp.
3231 - Authentic Mexican Imports
3231 - Baut Studios Inc.
3231 - Campus Crafts Inc. (Mfr)
3231 - City Glass Co.
3231 - Coastal Industries Inc.
3231 - Cole Enterprises
3231 - Melotte-Morse-Leonatti Stained
3231 - Milgard Manufacturing Co
3231 - Naugatuck Glass Company, The
3231 - Photon Technologies, Inc.
3231 - Saint George Crystal Ltd.
3231 - Silver & Co., Inc., Fred
3231 - Spec-Temp, Inc.
3231 - Stanford Glassblowing Labs Inc
3231 - Stimsonite Corp.
3231 - Supelco, Inc.(Mfr)
3231 - The Glass Table
3231 - Vision Blocks Inc.
3231 - Washington Mould Co.
3251 - Western Thin Brick & Tile
3253 - Hitachi Maxco, Inc.
3253 - Ro-Tile
3255 - Dylon Industries, Inc.
3255 - Thermal Systems America
3259 - A P T II Products Co.
3261 - Mansfield Plumbing Products, Inc.,
3262 - Homer Laughlin China Company, The
3263 - M&C Enterprises, div of Accent
3263 - Transpo Indsutries, Inc.
3264 - Brush Wellman Inc. Ceramics Div.
3264 - Ceradyne, Inc.
3264 - Fair-Rite Products Corp.
3264 - Midwest Industries Inc.
3264 - Newell Porcelain Company, Inc.
3264 - Porcelain Products Company(Mfr)
3269 - Authentic Mexican Imports
3269 - Bell Ceramics Inc. (Mfr)
3269 - Dedouch Co. Studios, J. A.
3269 - Heany Industries Inc.
3269 - Natural Line
3269 - Natural Line - Div of CCC
3269 - Seeley's Ceramic Service, Inc.
3271 - Sioux City Brick & Tile Co., Sergeant
3272 - Advantage Buildings & Exteriors, Inc.
3272 - Anti Hydro International, Inc.
3272 - Cleco Manufacturing, Inc.
3272 - Columbia Machine, Inc.
3272 - Custom Building Products
3272 - Durafiber Corp.
3272 - Flow Boy Manufacturing Co.
3272 - Heldenfels Enterprises, Inc.
3272 - J. J. Precast
3272 - Joaquin Manufacturing Corp
3272 - Pocatello Precast Inc
3272 - Rockwood Retaining Walls, Inc.
3272 - Simonds Mfg. Corp.
3272 - Stern-Williams Company, Inc.
3272 - Westile
3272 - Wilbert Vaults Of Houston, Inc.
3275 - Bell Ceramics Inc. (Mfr)
3281 - Ampel Corp.
3281 - Best Sand Corp.
3281 - Dakota Granite Company
3281 - Franklin Industrial Minerals
3281 - Iron Mountain Trap Rock Co.
3281 - J.R. McDade Marble & Granite
3281 - M. C. Marble Co., Inc.
3281 - Marbledge, Inc.
3281 - Mojave Granite Co Inc
3281 - Payton Granite & Monument Co.
3281 - Penn Big Bed Slate Co., Inc.
3281 - Petrified Wood Co
3281 - Pyramid Granite & Metals, Inc.
3281 - Rowat Cut Stone & Marble Co.
3281 - Stern-Williams Company, Inc.
3281 - Titon Industries, Inc.

3281 - United Metal Receptacle Inc. (Mfr)
3291 - Abrasive Distributors Corp.
3291 - Anti Hydro International, Inc.
3291 - Composition Materials Co., Inc.
3291 - Divine Brothers Company (Mfr)
3291 - Electro Abrasives Corp.
3291 - Gel-Tec Co.
3291 - Hess Pumice Products, Inc.
3291 - I.C.E. (International Carbide &
3291 - Industrial Diamond Labs
3291 - Jessup Manufacturing Co.
3291 - Realys Inc
3291 - Superior Honing Equipment Inc.
3291 - United Abrasives Inc.
3291 - United States Products Co.
3292 - Cardinal Industrial Insulation Co., Inc.
3292 - Fabrication Specialties
3292 - Great Southern Insulation Corp.
3293 - Hot Cell Services Corporation
3295 - Dixon Southwestern Graphite Inc.
3295 - Graphite Sales, Inc.
3295 - Hess Pumice Products Inc
3295 - Industrial Diamond Labs
3295 - RDM Multi-Enterprises Inc.
3295 - Stronglite Products
3295 - Supreme Perlite Co
3295 - Victor Metal Finishing Inc.
3295 - Wyo-Ben, Inc.
3296 - Alpha Associates, Inc.
3296 - Tenessee Fiberglass Productc, Inc.
3296 - Thermafiber L.L.C.
3297 - Coors Ceramics Co-Pittburgh
3297 - Pars Manufacturing Co
3297 - Refractory Materials International
3299 - 3M IBD/Export.
3299 - American Fiberglass Products, Inc.
3299 - Burlington Chemical Co., Inc. (Mfr)
3299 - Elementis Specialties, Colorants &
3299 - Henri Studio Inc.
3299 - Keating Fibre Inc
3299 - Marshall Thomas Co. Inc.
3299 - Miller Corp., Harry
3299 - Soluol Chemical Co., Inc.
3299 - Synalloy Corp., Blackman-Uhler
3299 - Wonderly Co., Inc., The
3312 - Arbon Steel & Service, Inc.
3312 - Auger Fabrication
3312 - Chicago Steel & Pickling Co.
3312 - Co-Steel Raritan
3312 - Coilplus-Alabama, Inc.
3312 - Consolidated Fabricators Corp.
3312 - Cragin Metals, L.L.C.
3312 - Electralloy
3312 - High Steel Structures
3312 - I P S C O Steel Inc.
3312 - Indiana Tube
3312 - NAPA Pipe Corporation
3312 - Ohio Moulding Corp., The
3312 - Pittsburgh Flatroll Co.
3312 - Prospect Steel, Inc.
3312 - Quirin Machine Shop Inc., E. A.
3312 - R A M Products
3312 - Standard Steel
3312 - Tennessee Galvanizing
3315 - Atlantic Wire Co., The
3315 - Florida Wire & Cable Inc.
3315 - T & B Structural Systems, Inc.
3315 - Trefilarbed Arkansas, Inc.
3315 - Trident Tool, Inc.
3315 - Zapp USA Inc.
3316 - Rolled Steel Products Corp
3317 - Avesta Sheffield Pipe Co.
3317 - L M H Enterprises, Inc.
3317 - Laser Armor Tech Corporation
3317 - Metal-Matic Inc.
3317 - Midwest Art Metal
3317 - Northwest Pipe Company
3317 - Richard Industries, J.
3321 - Benton Foundry, Inc.
3321 - Clearfield Machine Company (Mfr)
3321 - Crosby Group, Inc.
3321 - Deeter Foundry Inc.
3321 - Griffin Pipe Products Co.

3321 - Washington Mould Co.
3321 - World Equipment & Machine Sales
3322 - Olympic Foundry Inc
3324 - Buckeye Steel Castings Company
3324 - Delvest, Inc.
3334 - Duenner Supply Co. Of Texas
3334 - Fata Hunter, Inc.
3334 - TST Inc
3339 - Duenner Supply Co. Of Texas
3339 - ECS Refining
3339 - Environmental Dynamics, Inc.(Mfr)
3339 - Republic Metals Corp.
3339 - SOS Metal San Diego
3341 - AAA Precious Metals Inc
3341 - Eastern Smelting & Refining
3341 - Marport Smelting Co., Llc
3341 - Polymetallurgical Corp.
3341 - Wabash Alloys, LLC
3345 - Duke Scientific Corporation
3351 - Fisk Alloy Wire, Inc.
3351 - Harris-Welco Co.
3351 - Mueller Industries Inc.(Mfr)
3351 - National Copper Products
3351 - Republic Wire, Inc.
3351 - Steel Heddle Mfg. Co. (Mfr)
3353 - Items Products Inc.
3353 - McCook Metals, LLC
3353 - United Aluminum Corporation
3354 - E-Tec Marine Products Inc.
3354 - EFCO
3354 - Gemini Aluminum Corp
3354 - Specialty Extrusion Corp
3354 - VAW Of America Inc
3354 - Wells Aluminum Corp.
3354 - Werner Ladder Co.
3355 - Hanover Wire Cloth
3355 - Steel Heddle Mfg. Co. (Mfr)
3356 - Kester Solder, Div. Litton Industries
3356 - N G K Metals Corp.
3356 - Nippert Co., The
3357 - Brim Electronics Inc.
3357 - Delta Precision Alloys
3357 - Dulmison Incorporated
3357 - Essex Group Inc. (Mfr)
3357 - Fitel Lucent Technologies
3357 - Opticomm Corp
3357 - Pacific Electricord Company
3357 - Permaluster Company
3357 - Rockbestos Surprenant Cable Corp.
3357 - S.I. Tech, Inc.(Mfr)
3357 - Storm Products Co Inc
3357 - Sumitomo Electric Lightwave Corp.
3357 - Super Vision International, Inc.
3363 - C & H Die Casting, Inc.
3363 - Gibbs Die Casting Corp.
3363 - Nav-X Corp.
3364 - Mueller Industries Inc.(Mfr)
3365 - Advance Aluminum & Brass Inc
3365 - Baja Pacific Light Metals No
3365 - Baldwin Aluminum Foundry &
3365 - Le Claire Mfg. Co.
3365 - Precision Measurement Labs
3365 - Quality Brass & Aluminum Foundry
3365 - Superior Aluminum Products, Inc.
3365 - Unexcelled Castings Corp.
3366 - Sun Foundry
3369 - Conbraco Industries, Inc.
3369 - Delvest, Inc.
3369 - Modern Art Foundry, Inc.
3369 - Ryder-Heil Bronze Inc.
3398 - Advanced Heat Treat Corp.
3398 - California Surface Hardening
3398 - Deering Fabricators
3398 - Diamond Head Golf Club Mfg Co
3398 - Varco Heat Treating Co
3399 - Harris-Welco Co.
3399 - Mott Corp.
3399 - Windfall Products, Inc.
3399 - Winter, Inc. & Co., F. W.
3411 - All American Containers, Inc.
3411 - CMO Enterprises Inc.
3411 - Crown Cork & Seal /Americas Div
3411 - Dewald Northwest Co

3411 - Mason Corp.
3411 - Progressive Metal Forming Inc.
3411 - U. S. Can Co., Custom & Specialty
3411 - United Metal Receptacle Inc. (Mfr)
3412 - All American Containers, Inc.
3412 - Evans Cushing, Inc.
3421 - Cutco Cutlery Corp.
3421 - Ka-Bar Knives, Inc.
3421 - Micro 100, Inc.
3421 - Techni Edge Mfg. Corp.
3421 - Zephyr Manufacturing Co. Inc.
3423 - A. J. C. Hatchet Co.
3423 - Ameritool, Hand Tool Div.
3423 - Cobblecrete International Inc
3423 - Daiber Co., Inc., E. J.
3423 - Dasco Pro Inc (Mfr)
3423 - Elliot Tool Technologies, LTD.
3423 - Embee Corp.
3423 - Enderes Tool Company Inc
3423 - Esico-Triton
3423 - Excelta Corp
3423 - Fischbach U S A, Inc.
3423 - Francis Torque Tools
3423 - Geier & Bluhm, Inc.
3423 - Groom Industries, Inc.
3423 - Hyde Manufacturing Co.
3423 - Laidig Industrial System
3423 - MPI Products Div. of Miro Precision
3423 - Mayhew Tools
3423 - Morse Starrett Products Company
3423 - Patterson Avenue Tool Co.
3423 - Ripley Co., Inc.
3423 - Zephyr Manufacturing Co. Inc.
3425 - Alvord Systems, Inc.
3425 - Chamfer Master Tool Co.
3429 - Able Builders Export, Inc.
3429 - Acorn Manufacturing Co., Inc.
3429 - BAND-IT-IDEX Inc
3429 - Coopers & Clarke, Inc.
3429 - Daburn Electronics & Cable Corp.
3429 - Divine Brothers Company (Mfr)
3429 - Donlee Technologies, Inc.
3429 - Dynalock Corp.
3429 - Faultless Caster Division
3429 - Intool Inc., Industrial Energy Products
3429 - J R C Web Accessories, Inc.
3429 - Keystone Electronics Corp.
3429 - Mounting Systems Inc
3429 - Omnimount Systems
3429 - Pace Manufacturing, Inc.
3429 - Schlage Lock Company (Mfr)
3429 - Schneider Enterprises
3429 - Supra Products
3429 - Tri/Mark Corporation
3429 - Werner Ladder Co.
3429 - Wespac Corp.
3429 - West Coast Industries Inc.
3429 - Youngdale Manufacturing Corp
3431 - Coast Foundry & Mfg Co
3431 - Fab Industries Inc
3431 - Franklin Brass Manufacturing
3431 - Stern-Williams Company, Inc.
3431 - Terriss-Consolidated Industries
3431 - Watco Mfg. Co.
3432 - Chronomite Labs Inc
3432 - Conbraco Industries
3432 - Delta Faucet
3432 - Frugal Water Corporation
3432 - Interbath, Inc
3432 - Jay R. Smith Mfg. Co.
3432 - Mueller Steam Specialty Co.,
3432 - Neoperl, Inc.
3432 - Plumb Shop
3432 - Stern-Williams Company, Inc.
3432 - Valterra Products
3433 - BR Laboratories Inc
3433 - Cleaver-Brooks
3433 - Coil Co., Inc.
3433 - Coil Company Inc.
3433 - Friendly Appropriate Solar
3433 - Heliodyne, Inc. (Mfr)
3433 - John Zink Company
3433 - Lochinvar Water Heater

3433 - North American Export Company
3433 - PVI International
3433 - Power & Industrial Service Corp.
3433 - Scheu Products Co.
3433 - Solaronics, Inc.
3433 - Therm Tech Inc.
3433 - Thermal Systems Inc
3434 - Joaquin Manufacturing Corp
3440 - Wells Aluminum Corp.
3441 - Adams Truss, Inc.
3441 - American Towers and Structures Inc.
3441 - Colorado Bridge & Iron Inc
3441 - Coral Steel Company
3441 - Coronis Building Sytems Inc.
3441 - Intool Inc., Industrial Energy Products
3441 - Kevry Corporation
3441 - Mason Corp.
3441 - Midwest Builders Supply, Inc.
3441 - Pritchard Brown
3441 - Schuff Steel Company
3441 - Space Coast General Contractors Inc.
3441 - US Tower Corp
3441 - Val-Fab Inc.
3442 - Accent Windows Inc
3442 - Accurate Screening Media, Inc.
3442 - Chase Industries, Inc.
3442 - Clarke's Custom Windows, Inc.
3442 - Dunbarton Corp. /Rediframe/Slimfold
3442 - E F C O Corp.
3442 - Fleming Steel Co.
3442 - Hollow Metal Specialists, Inc.
3442 - Hot Cell Services Corporation
3442 - M C E Systems Corp.
3442 - Roll-a-Way Inc.
3442 - TRACO
3442 - Y K K Ap America, Inc.
3443 - A.C.E. Boiler, Inc.
3443 - Ability Engineering Technology, Inc.
3443 - Affinity Industries Inc. (Mfr)
3443 - Barron Industries, Inc.
3443 - Behlen MFG. Co.
3443 - C P Industries, Inc., Christy Park Plt.
3443 - CAE Screenplates Inc. (Mfr)
3443 - CNI Manufacturing
3443 - Columbian Steel Tank Co.
3443 - Containment Solutions, Inc.
3443 - Dennis Aluminum Products
3443 - Donlee Technologies, Inc.
3443 - Doyle & Roth Mfg. Co., Inc.
3443 - Ely Energy, Inc.
3443 - Enerfab
3443 - Exothermics, Inc.
3443 - Fabtron Inc
3443 - Gas Liquids Recovery Corp.
3443 - Gaylord Industries, Inc.
3443 - Hudson Products Corp.
3443 - Isom Brothers Inc
3443 - Jerryco Machine & Boilerworks
3443 - Lochinvar Water Heater
3443 - Luxfer Gas Cylinders
3443 - Mohawk Mfg. Corp.
3443 - PVI International
3443 - Pittsburg Tank & Tower Co., Inc.
3443 - R&D Enterprises, Inc.
3443 - Roy E Hanson Jr Manufacturing
3443 - Safe T-Tank Corp.
3443 - Scheu Products Co.
3443 - Sheepscot Machine Works
3443 - Standard Steel
3443 - Structural North America
3443 - Superb Marine & Industrial Services,
3443 - Therma-Fab, Inc.
3443 - Tigert Co., T. F.
3443 - Unique Systems Inc.(Mfr)
3443 - United Metal Receptacle Inc. (Mfr)
3443 - Weben-Jarco, Inc.
3444 - Aerofab Inc
3444 - Alco Technologies Inc
3444 - American Tool & Engrg Corp
3444 - Architectural Building Components
3444 - Artis Metals Company Inc
3444 - Begneaud Mfg. Inc.
3444 - Broadway Sheet Metal

3444 - Camcorp Industries
3444 - Cannon Industries
3444 - Ceilings Plus Inc
3444 - Elixir Industries, Inc.
3444 - Fab-Tech Industries Of Brevard, Inc.
3444 - Flexmaster U S A Inc.
3444 - Formworks Building Inc
3444 - Gentek Building Products
3444 - Lewgust Co., Inc.
3444 - Lighting Metal Specialties
3444 - Mardan Fabricators
3444 - Messina Metal Mfg
3444 - Metcoe Specialty Co Inc
3444 - Nasco, Inc.
3444 - Northeast Fabricators, L.L.C.
3444 - R O T H B R O S., Inc., A First
3444 - Rainhandler
3444 - Ship & Shore a Subsidary of C.D.I.
3444 - Shurtleff-G A H A R A N, Inc.
3444 - Sixnel Sheet Metal
3444 - Steiner Fabrication Inc
3446 - Alum-a-pole Corporation
3446 - Big D Metalworks Of Texas
3446 - Exclusive Findings
3446 - Grace Mfg. Co., Inc.
3446 - Heartland Flagpoles, Inc.
3446 - Lance Metal Arts
3446 - Lingo, Inc., Acme Flagpole Div.
3446 - Pole-Tech Co., Inc.
3446 - Seidelhuber Metal Products Inc
3446 - Werner Ladder Co.
3448 - Airo Clean, Inc.
3448 - Behlen MFG. Co.
3448 - C-Thru Industries Inc
3448 - Cover-It Shelters, Inc.
3448 - Custom Modular Solutions
3448 - Don Hurst Enterprises
3448 - Gothic Arch Greenhouses, Inc.
3448 - Hexaport International, Ltd.
3448 - Imperial Pools Inc.
3448 - Industrial Acoustics Co. Inc.
3448 - Joaquin Manufacturing Corp
3448 - McAlpine & Salyer Construction
3448 - Nor-Lake, Inc. (Mfr)
3448 - Texas Greenhouse Co., Inc.
3448 - US PreFab Inc
3449 - A C Welding & Engineering
3451 - A & B Aerospace Inc
3451 - American Precision Machine Products,
3451 - Automatics & Machinery Co., Inc.
3451 - Chester Precision Co.
3451 - Cole Screw Machine Products, Inc.
3451 - Delo Screw Products, A Park-Ohio
3451 - Dowels, Pins & Shafts, Inc.
3451 - Elge Precision Machining, Inc.
3451 - Form Cut Industries, Inc.
3451 - Fortress Mfg., Inc. (Mfr)
3451 - Prime Screw Machine Products Inc
3451 - RSM Products, Inc.
3451 - Vulcan Threaded Products, Inc.
3451 - Weltek-Swiss
3451 - Zenith Screw Products Inc
3452 - Anillo Industries Inc
3452 - Atlas Bolt & Screw Company (Mfr)
3452 - Diversified Fastener & Tool Co.
3452 - Earnest Machine Products Co.
3452 - Florida Bolt & Nut Co.
3452 - Helical Wire Inc
3452 - Hick International Fastener Div
3452 - Illinois Tool Works, Inc.
3452 - Liberty Fastener Co.
3452 - Moeller Manufacturing Supply
3452 - Morton Manufacturing
3452 - Norse, Inc.
3452 - Northwestern Tools, Inc.
3452 - Palnut Co., The
3452 - Portland Bolt & Mfg Company
3452 - S P S Technologies, Inc., Automotive
3452 - Southco, Inc.
3452 - THF Corp
3452 - Termax Corporation
3452 - Therma-Tron-X Inc.
3452 - Time Fastener Company Inc

3452 - Tru-Fast Corp.
3452 - Tufnut Work, The
3452 - Zero Fastener Co.
3458 - Daburn Electronics & Cable Corp.
3462 - Canton Drop Forge
3462 - Kop-Flex, Inc., Emerson Power
3462 - Scot Forge Co.
3462 - Standard Steel
3463 - Lenape Forge, Inc.
3463 - Victory Racing Plate Co. The
3465 - M P I International Inc.
3465 - Quality Mold Inc.
3467 - Dixie Seal & Stamp Co., Inc. (Mfr)
3469 - Accushim Inc. (Mfr)
3469 - Ambox Inc.
3469 - Animated Mfg. Co.
3469 - Baroli Engineering Inc
3469 - Bolsan West Inc
3469 - Charles A Starr Company Inc
3469 - Commercial Intertech Corp.
3469 - Component Engineers, Inc.
3469 - Dixie Seal & Stamp Co., Inc. (Mfr)
3469 - EBway Corporation
3469 - Eaton Corp., Engineered Fasteners
3469 - Estad Stamping & Mfg. Co.
3469 - Expanded Technologies Inc.
3469 - F & G Multi-Slide, Inc.
3469 - Fabor Fourslide, Inc.
3469 - G & H Diversified Mfg. Inc.
3469 - Geka Brush Manufacturing
3469 - Harrington & King South, Inc.
3469 - Indy Honeycomb
3469 - Innovative Stamping Corp
3469 - John Amann Sons Co.
3469 - Lindgren R F Enclosures Inc.
3469 - Magnetic Metals Corp.
3469 - Midwest Art Metal
3469 - Oberg Mfg. Co.
3469 - Owen Tool & Mfg. Co., Inc.
3469 - Precision Die & Stamping Inc
3469 - Richards Metal Products, Inc.
3469 - Risdon-AMS (USA) Inc.
3469 - S & S Dynamic Mfg. Llc
3469 - Saegertown Mfg. Corp.
3469 - Schulze Manufacturing
3469 - Southwest Metal Fabricators, Inc.
3469 - Stamped Products, Inc.
3469 - Stewart Stamping Corp.
3469 - Termax Corporation
3469 - Tubing Seal Cap
3469 - UGM Inc
3469 - W C E S, Inc.
3469 - Walker Corporation
3469 - Waterloo Industries, Inc.
3471 - ARA Automated Finishing
3471 - All Metals Processing Co Inc
3471 - All Metals Processing of OC
3471 - Anniston Plating & Metal Finishing,
3471 - Barsallo Deburring
3471 - CAE Screenplates Inc. (Mfr)
3471 - Chrome Crankshaft Co
3471 - DV Industries Inc
3471 - Diversified Coatings, Inc.
3471 - Dixie Electro Plating Co., Inc.
3471 - Electrochem
3471 - J & H Deburring Inc
3471 - Metal Finishing Technologies, Inc.
3471 - National Research & Chemical Co.
3471 - Nu-Metal Finishing Inc
3471 - Polymetallurgical Corp.
3471 - Sav-On Plating/Powder Coating
3471 - Sifco Selective Plating
3471 - Tri-County Hard Chrome, Inc.
3471 - Ultra Plating Corp.
3479 - Allen Aircraft Products, Inc., Metal
3479 - American Custom Coatings, Inc.
3479 - Americoat Corp.
3479 - Cal-Coat Corp.
3479 - Columbus Galvanizing Voigt &
3479 - Commercial Enameling Co
3479 - Cooper Coil Coating, Inc.
3479 - Copper Coil Coating
3479 - Current, Inc.

3479 - Custom Engraving
3479 - E-FAB Inc
3479 - E/M Corporation (Mfr)
3479 - Feeley Company, Inc.
3479 - Heany Industries Inc.
3479 - Holman Label Company
3479 - Inca Paint & Print
3479 - MPC International LLC
3479 - Marjan, Inc.
3479 - Metallic Ceramic Coating Inc.
3479 - Pyramid Machine & Tool, Inc.
3479 - SDC Technologies Inc
3479 - SP3
3479 - Sandy's Trophies
3479 - Summit Coating Technologies, LLC
3479 - The Laser Workshop
3479 - Valmont Industries Inc.
3479 - VaporKote Inc
3483 - Universal Tech
3484 - Lorcin Engineering
3484 - Nova Products
3484 - S T I International, Inc.
3484 - USA Magazines Inc
3491 - A.Y. McDonald Mfg. Co.
3491 - AC Valve Inc.
3491 - American Valve & Pump, Inc.
3491 - Bijur Lubricating Corporation
3491 - Brady Products Inc.
3491 - Cla-val Company
3491 - D.B.C. Enterprises, Inc.
3491 - Flo-Tork Inc. (Mfr)
3491 - Gulf Valve Company
3491 - Hercules Hydraulics Inc.
3491 - Kerotest Manufacturing Corp. (Mfr)
3491 - Keystone Biffi Actuators, & Controls
3491 - Keystone Vanessa, Inc.
3491 - M & J Valve Services, Inc.
3491 - Merrill Mfg. Co., Inc.
3491 - Mid-West Instrument
3491 - Mueller Steam Specialty Co.
3491 - P G I International
3491 - Park Corporation
3491 - Parts Services International LLC
3491 - Sheepscot Machine Works
3491 - Smart Products Inc
3491 - T.J. Manufacturing, Inc.
3491 - Tyco Valves & Controls
3491 - Valvtron / Tyco Valves & Controls
3492 - American Boa, Inc.
3492 - American Equipment Sales Co.
3492 - Cross Mfg. Inc.
3492 - Faip North America Inc.
3492 - Hydra-Tech Systems Inc.
3492 - Jiffy Tite Co., Inc.
3492 - O C V Control Valves
3492 - SafeWay Hydraulics, Inc.
3492 - Service Hydraulics Inc.
3493 - Connor Formed Metal Products
3493 - Cross Mfg. Inc.
3493 - Duer/Carolina Coil Inc.
3493 - O'Hara Metal Products Co
3493 - Standard Steel
3494 - A.Y. McDonald Mfg. Co.
3494 - APAC Products
3494 - Control Components, Inc.
3494 - Custom Alloy Corporation (Mfr)
3494 - Dodson Steel Products, Inc.
3494 - Evans Components Inc
3494 - Fleck Controls, Inc.
3494 - K F Industries, Inc.
3494 - Kraissl Co., Inc., The
3494 - Leonard Valve Co.
3494 - Nordstrom Valves, Inc.
3494 - PHD Manufacturing, Inc.
3494 - Pennsylvania Machine Works, Inc.
3494 - Piping Technology & Products, Inc.
3494 - Sebewaing Tool & Engineering
3494 - The Martin Company
3494 - Top Line Process Equipment Co.
3495 - Behlen MFG. Co.
3495 - Curran Coil Spring Inc
3495 - Excel Spring & Stamping Co.
3496 - Acme Wire Products Co., Inc.

3496 - Alloy Wire Belt
3496 - Ammermans, The
3496 - Blackburne, Inc., Perry
3496 - Cambria County Assn. For The Blind
3496 - Carico Systems
3496 - Dulmison Incorporated
3496 - Electronic Packaging Systems
3496 - Form Cut Industries, Inc.
3496 - Fortress Mfg. Inc.
3496 - Fortress Mfg., Inc. (Mfr)
3496 - Gemco
3496 - Georgetown Wire Co. K-Lath Div
3496 - Gilbert Mfg. Co.
3496 - Hanover Wire Cloth
3496 - John Amann Sons Co.
3496 - Leschen Wire Rope Co.
3496 - Manufacturers Equipment Company-
3496 - Molecu Wire Corporation
3496 - New York Wire Co.
3496 - Piggott Wire & Cable Company
3496 - Polymet Corp.
3496 - Renfro Franklin Company
3496 - Rochester Corp., The
3496 - S & S Industries, Inc.
3496 - Steel Heddle Mfg. Co. (Mfr)
3496 - Tema Isenmann, Inc.
3496 - Tilton Rack & Basket Corp.
3496 - Tomahawk Live Trap Co.
3496 - United States Alumoweld Co.
3497 - Crown Roll Leaf, Inc.
3497 - Foil Graphics, Inc.
3497 - Swift & Sons, Inc., M.
3497 - Transfer Print Foils, Inc.
3498 - D.B.C. Enterprises, Inc.
3498 - Foster Co., L. B.
3498 - Int'l Fabricators & Engineers
3498 - R.C. Technical Welding & Fabricating
3498 - Steel Forgings Inc.
3498 - Texas PMW, Inc.
3498 - Tri-Went, Inc.
3498 - Tubetronics
3499 - ACuPowder International, LLC (Mfg)
3499 - Accu-Tube Corporation
3499 - Allied Security Equipment
3499 - Artcrete, Inc.
3499 - Award Maker
3499 - Baker Div. Sonoco Products Company
3499 - Begneaud Mfg. Inc.
3499 - Bete Fog Nozzle Inc. (Mfr)
3499 - Bucks Fabricating
3499 - Bullet Guard Corp
3499 - C & B Fosters Inc.
3499 - C. W. C. Steel Services, Inc.
3499 - Contemporary, Inc.
3499 - Coxwells, Inc., dba CoxReels
3499 - Desmark Industries, Inc.
3499 - Durham Mfg. Co.
3499 - Enerfab
3499 - Fortress Mfg. Inc.
3499 - Fortress Mfg., Inc. (Mfr)
3499 - Independent Welding Co.
3499 - Innovative Stamping Corp
3499 - John Amann Sons Co.
3499 - Klose Fabrication, Inc.
3499 - Knaack Mfg. Co.
3499 - Kurt Manufacturing Co.
3499 - Landmark Tower Corp.
3499 - Larco, Div. Of Acrometal Companies,
3499 - Litco, Inc.
3499 - MCP Metalspecialties, Inc.
3499 - Magnetic Radiation Laboratories Inc.
3499 - Metal Cutting Corporation (Mfr)
3499 - Metal Finishing, Inc.
3499 - Metal Master
3499 - Metal Master Inc
3499 - Microflex, Inc.
3499 - Midwest Art Metal
3499 - Panel Built, Inc.
3499 - Precision Machine Products
3499 - Senior Flexonics Inc., Hose Div.
3499 - Terriss-Consolidated Industries
3499 - Trident Tool, Inc.
3499 - Tridon

3499 - Trophy Shoppe
3499 - Villa Bella Co.
3499 - Werner Ladder Co.
3511 - Barber-Nichols Incorporated
3511 - Engine Systems
3511 - ITT Flygt Corp
3511 - International Turbine Systems
3511 - Standard Steel
3511 - Unique Systems Inc.(Mfr)
3511 - Welden Steam Generators, Inc.
3511 - World Power Technologies, Inc.
3514 - Diesel Parts of America
3515 - Entrac, Inc.
3519 - Cable Marine, Inc.
3519 - Hawthorne Power Systems
3523 - AGCO Corporation
3523 - Ariens Company
3523 - Ashton Food Machinery Co., Inc.,
3523 - Bag-A-Nut, Inc.
3523 - Behlen MFG. Co.
3523 - Bowsmith Inc
3523 - Broyhill Company, The (Mfr)
3523 - Burrows Enterprises Inc
3523 - Carver, Inc.
3523 - Coburn Company, Inc.
3523 - Conibear Equipment Co., Inc.
3523 - Country Home Products, Inc.
3523 - D & D Products, Inc.
3523 - Dalhart R & R Machine Works, Inc.
3523 - Dempster Industries, Inc.
3523 - Farm & Ranch Systems South, Llc.
3523 - Hawkeye Steel Products, Inc.
3523 - Hecla Industries, LLP
3523 - Hydro Engineering, Inc.
3523 - J-Star Industries Inc.
3523 - John Blue Co.
3523 - Kelley Mfg. Co.
3523 - Kromer Co.
3523 - Lindsay International Sales Corp.
3523 - MK Distributors Inc
3523 - Maxijet, Inc.
3523 - Miller Ag-Renewal, Inc.
3523 - Mister Landscaper, Inc
3523 - Nelson Products Co.
3523 - Netafim Irrigation Inc
3523 - Olson Irrigation Systems
3523 - Omaha Standard, Inc.
3523 - Pierce Corporation
3523 - Priefert Mfg. Co. Inc.(Mfr)
3523 - Renite Co., Lubrication Engineers
3523 - Riley Equipment Co., Inc.
3523 - Roberts Irrigation Products
3523 - Salco Products Inc
3523 - Semco Manufacturing
3523 - Sundance
3523 - Supreme Horse Walker Co.
3523 - Top-Air Manufacturing, Inc.(Mfr)
3523 - Traction International
3523 - Wamco Corporation
3523 - Weather Tec Corporation
3523 - Weldcraft Industries
3523 - Westheffer Mfg.
3523 - Wildcat Mfg. Co., Inc.
3523 - Yargus Mfg., Inc.
3524 - Barreto Manufacturing
3524 - Big John Tree Transplanter Mfg., Inc.
3524 - Broyhill Company, The (Mfr)
3524 - Caretree Systems Inc.
3524 - Carter Brothers
3524 - Diamond Turf Equipment Inc.
3524 - Doskocil Industries Inc
3524 - Excel Industries, Inc.
3524 - Fair Manufacturing, Inc.(Mfr)
3524 - Ryobi Outdoor Products Inc
3524 - Textron Turf Care and Specialty
3524 - Valley View Industries
3531 - Allen Tool Co
3531 - Almix/Asphalt Equipment Co., Inc.
3531 - American Augers Inc.
3531 - Anchor Mfg. Co.
3531 - Brown Bear Corp.
3531 - Chemgrout Inc.
3531 - Consolidated Baling Machine Co.,

3531 - Construction Technology, Inc. (DBA,
3531 - Eastern Europe Inc.
3531 - Equipment Development Co., Inc.
3531 - Euclid Hitachi Heavy Equipment
3531 - Getz Recycle Inc
3531 - Hendrix Manufacturing Co., Inc.
3531 - Le Sueur Mfg. Co.
3531 - Midland Machinery Co., Inc.
3531 - Mount Sopris Instrument Co Inc
3531 - Patterson Equipment
3531 - Quality Industries, Inc.
3531 - Ramsey Winch Co.
3531 - Service International
3531 - Shotcrete Technologies Inc
3531 - Sirex Pulse Hydraulic Systems
3531 - Stephens Mfg. Co.
3531 - Super Precision Design, Inc.
3531 - Swenson Spreader Co.
3531 - Tomahawk Truck Sales
3531 - Tru-Part Manufacturing Co.
3531 - V M I, Inc.
3531 - Wildcat Mfg. Co., Inc.
3532 - Ani-Helser
3532 - Aresco, Inc.
3532 - Baker Hughes Mining Tools, Inc.
3532 - Bradley Pulverizer Company (Mfr)
3532 - Brookville Mining Equipment Corp.
3532 - Calweld, Inc
3532 - Goodtrade Corporation
3532 - Park Corporation
3532 - Prospector & Treasure Hunters
3532 - Quinn Process Equipment Co
3532 - Schramm, Inc.(Mfr)
3532 - Smith Equipment USA Inc
3532 - Trident Tool, Inc.
3533 - Cold Extrusion Co. Of America, Inc.
3533 - Degen Pipe & Supply Co.
3533 - Gas Corp. Of America
3533 - Goex International, Inc.
3533 - J.Ray McDemott, Inc.
3533 - Oilpure Refiner Co
3533 - Portadrill Corp.
3533 - Schramm, Inc.(Mfr)
3533 - Taylor Made Oil Tools, Inc.
3533 - Trident Tool, Inc.
3533 - Universal Manufacturing & Const. Co.
3533 - Wichita Falls Mfg.
3534 - Autoquip Corporation
3534 - Elevator Industries Inc.
3534 - Mowrey Elevator Company Inc.
3534 - P T L Equipment Mfg. Co., Inc.
3535 - Alvey, Inc.
3535 - Arrowhead Systems LLC
3535 - Busse Inc. (Mfr)
3535 - Chicago Conveyor Corp.
3535 - Continental Conveyor & Equip.
3535 - Conveyors Solutions, Inc.
3535 - Flexicon Corporation
3535 - Food Engineering Corporation
3535 - Forenta, L.P.
3535 - H.K. Systems, Von Gal Palletizers
3535 - HK Systems, Inc.
3535 - Hodge Manufacturing Company
3535 - Interroll Corp.
3535 - J D B Dense Flow, Inc.
3535 - Jeco Plastic Products, Inc.
3535 - KieTek International, Inc.
3535 - Le Fiell Company
3535 - MAC Equipment, Inc.
3535 - Nedco Conveyor Technology Corp.
3535 - Neuero Corp.
3535 - Northeast Fabricators, L.L.C.
3535 - Pioneer Conveyors Inc
3535 - Quantum Conveyor Systems, LLC
3535 - RBM Manufacturing Co., Inc.
3535 - Renmark Pacific Corporation
3535 - Renmark-Pacific Inc
3535 - Screw Conveyor Corp. (Mfr)
3535 - Smoot Co.
3535 - Specialty Equipment Co.
3535 - Vac-U-Max (Mfr)
3536 - Aurora Systems, Inc.
3536 - Auto Crane Co.

3536 - Bradley Lifting Corp.
3536 - Crosby Group, Inc.
3536 - Industrial Crane & Equipment Co.,
3536 - Konecrane Landel Inc
3536 - Liftmasters, Inc.
3536 - Little Lift Inc.
3536 - Maasdam Pow'r-Pull Inc.
3536 - Quality Boat Lifts, Inc.
3536 - Superwinch, Inc.
3536 - Whiting Corporation
3537 - Alvey, Inc.
3537 - Autoquip Corporation
3537 - B A F Communications Corp.
3537 - Broyhill Company, The (Mfr)
3537 - Busse Inc. (Mfr)
3537 - Converto Mfg. Co. Inc. (Mfr)
3537 - Faultless Caster Division
3537 - H & K Equipment Inc.
3537 - H.K. Systems, Von Gal Palletizers
3537 - HK Systems, Inc.
3537 - Holland House Moving Inc., Ron
3537 - JLG Industries, Inc.
3537 - L P I, Inc.
3537 - Mifran Boman Corp
3541 - Abrasive Service Industries, Century
3541 - America Excel, Inc.
3541 - Amkus, Inc.
3541 - Automatics & Machinery Co., Inc.
3541 - B & A Mfg. Co.
3541 - Burlytic Systems
3541 - Continental Cutoff Machines
3541 - Gem Industries, Inc.
3541 - Lexington Cutter, Inc.
3541 - Luke Tool & Engineering Co.
3541 - Machine Tech, Inc.
3541 - Midwest Ohio Tool Company
3541 - National Acme (Mfr)
3541 - Original Saw Company, The (Mfr)
3541 - Park Corporation
3541 - Pine Bluff Cutting Tools, Inc.
3541 - Premier Machinery
3541 - Procunier Safety Chuck Co.
3541 - Rancho Metal Polishing
3541 - Republic-Lagun CNC Corp
3541 - Saber Diamond Tools
3541 - Scotchman Industries, Inc.(Mfr)
3541 - Setco Industries
3541 - Universal Manufacturing & Const. Co.
3541 - Victor Metal Finishing Inc.
3542 - AP & T Tangent, Inc.
3542 - Angelus Sanitary Can Machine
3542 - Behlen MFG. Co.
3542 - Chambersburg Engineering Co.
3542 - McKee - Addison Tube Forming
3542 - Morgan Denver Sales Co
3542 - Morrison Co., The D. C.
3542 - Presses, LTD
3542 - Scotchman Industries, Inc.(Mfr)
3542 - Taber Industries, Inc.
3542 - Tools For Bending, Inc.
3543 - Barry Pattern & Foundry
3543 - D W C Assocs., Inc.
3543 - Precision Measurement Labs
3544 - A-1 Tool
3544 - Accu-Cut Diamond Tool Co., Inc
3544 - Aggressive Dies & Cutting
3544 - Ajax Tool Works, Inc.
3544 - American Die Technology Inc.
3544 - Anchor Tool & Die Company
3544 - Ashwell Die Corp.
3544 - Avon Mfg., Inc.
3544 - Brenner Tool & Die, Inc.
3544 - Concorde Tools, Inc.
3544 - Craftsman Tool & Mold Co.
3544 - Dent Tools, Inc.
3544 - Diemasters, Inc.
3544 - Dyer Tool & Die, Inc.
3544 - Eastern Carbide Tool Co. Llc.
3544 - Elixir Industries, Inc.
3544 - Fancort Industries, Inc.
3544 - Finish Thompson, Inc.
3544 - Ford Tool & Machining Inc.
3544 - Geka Brush Manufacturing

3544 - Genca Corp.
3544 - General Precision Tool & Die Inc.
3544 - H & S Tool & Die Co.
3544 - Heyden Mold & Bench Co.
3544 - Hoffman Tool & Die Inc.
3544 - JD Tool & Machine Co Inc
3544 - JL Tool & Machine
3544 - Lake Park Tool & Machine, Inc.
3544 - Mastercraft Companies
3544 - Mc Kee Carbide Tool Co.
3544 - McKee - Addison Tube Forming
3544 - Oberg Mfg. Co.
3544 - Organic Dyestuffs Corporation
3544 - Pace Manufacturing, Inc.
3544 - Pasco Tool & Die
3544 - Samtan Engineering Corp
3544 - Sebewaing Tool & Engineering
3544 - Superior Die Set Corp.
3544 - Technical Sales, Inc.
3544 - Tella Tool & Mfg. Co.
3544 - The Steinlite Corp.(Mfr)
3544 - Thor Tool Corporation
3544 - Trimline Tool Inc.
3544 - UT Technologies, Inc.
3544 - Universal Tooling Corp.
3544 - Van Thomas Inc. / Ruggeri Mfg.
3544 - Yorktown Precision Technologies
3545 - Carter Diamond Tool Corp.
3545 - Cogsdill Tool Products Inc. (Mfr)
3545 - Command Corporation Intl. (Mfr)
3545 - Drillunit
3545 - Elliot Tool Technologies, LTD.
3545 - Eraser Co., Inc.
3545 - Giddings & Lewis Drill Unit
3545 - Greenfield Industries
3545 - H & R Mfg. & Supply, Inc.
3545 - Hayes Tool Inc.(Mfr)
3545 - Hutchens Bit Service, Inc.
3545 - ICA International Inc
3545 - Martindale Electric Company
3545 - Metalsoft, Inc.
3545 - Micro Carbide Corp
3545 - Mid-West Instrument
3545 - Midwest Ohio Tool Company
3545 - Mount Hope Machinery Co.
3545 - Northwestern Tools, Inc.
3545 - Oberg Mfg. Co.
3545 - Precision/Triumph Twist Drill
3545 - Pro Tool & Design, Inc.
3545 - Richard's Machine Tool Co., Inc.
3545 - Richmill USA Inc
3545 - Robinair, A Div. of SPX Corporation
3545 - Sunco Powder Systems, Inc.
3545 - Vanguard Tool Corp.
3546 - American Pneumatic Tool
3546 - Amkus, Inc.
3546 - Cambridge Specialty Co., Inc.
3546 - Elliot Tool Technologies, LTD.
3546 - Nordic Saw & Tool Manufacturer
3546 - Platt Electric Supply
3546 - Terry Tools, Inc.
3546 - United Air Tool, Inc.(Mfr)
3546 - Wilson & Co., Inc., Thomas C.
3546 - Zephyr Manufacturing Co. Inc.
3547 - Enkotec Co., Inc.
3547 - Mount Hope Machinery Co.
3547 - New Tech Machinery Inc
3547 - Steel Plant Equipment Corp.
3548 - Affinity Industries Inc. (Mfr)
3548 - Atlantic Research Corp., Unit of
3548 - Cosmos Electronic Machine Corp.
3548 - Daburn Electronics & Cable Corp.
3548 - Eureka Welding Alloys
3548 - Inweld Corp.
3548 - Jennings Technology Company
3548 - Morrow Tech Industries
3548 - Ogden Industries Inc
3548 - Rankin Industries Inc
3548 - Tri Tool Inc
3548 - Ultra Sonic Seal Co.
3548 - Welding Warehouse
3549 - 3M IBD/Export.
3549 - Affinity Industries Inc. (Mfr)

3549 - K W Products, Inc.
3549 - Spiral-Helix, Inc.
3549 - Strilich Technolgies, Inc.
3549 - Tridan International, Inc.
3549 - West Tool & Design, Inc.
355 - Chicago Conveyor Corp.
3551 - Vanmark Corp.
3552 - Allstates Textile Machinery
3552 - American & Efird, Inc.
3552 - American Textile Machinery
3552 - Atkins Machinery Inc.
3552 - Babcock Textile Machinery, Inc.
3552 - Bellwether Inc.
3552 - Briggs-Shaffner Co.
3552 - Chem-Tex Machinery, Inc.
3552 - Dietrich & Son, Inc.
3552 - Gribetz International, Inc.
3552 - Kellett Enterprises Inc.(Mfr)
3552 - King International Inc.
3552 - Mart Corporation
3552 - Mount Hope Machinery Co.
3552 - Pritchett Technology, Inc.
3552 - Reed Chatwood Inc.
3552 - Shaffer & Max
3552 - Steel Heddle Mfg. Co. (Mfr)
3552 - Tubular Textile Machinery
3552 - United Textile Machinery Corp.
3552 - Verduin Machinery, Inc.
3553 - Affinity Industries Inc. (Mfr)
3553 - Castle Inc.
3553 - Kimball Sign & Woodcarving Co.
3553 - LRH Enterprises Inc
3553 - Magnum Machinery Services Inc
3553 - Onsrud Machine Corporation
3553 - Original Saw Company, The (Mfr)
3553 - Precision Products Co
3553 - Ross & White Co.
3553 - Sorbilite Inc.
3553 - United Machine Ind. Inc.
3554 - A H Lundberg Inc
3554 - A. Daigger & Company, Inc.
3554 - Ahern International Sales Corp.
3554 - B & H Manufacturing Co.
3554 - Beloit Corp., Fiber Systems Div.
3554 - Dec-E-Tech
3554 - Electro-Steam Generator Corp.
3554 - Elsner Engineering Works Inc.
3554 - Lynare Scientific, Inc.
3554 - McCann's Engineering &
3554 - Reliance Glass Works, Inc.
3554 - Scientech Inc.
3554 - Terriss-Consolidated Industries
3554 - Thermo Black Clawson Inc.
3555 - Ackley Machine Corp.
3555 - B & L Machine & Design
3555 - Baumfolder Corp.
3555 - Burnshine Products
3555 - Davidson International Inc.
3555 - Evtec Corp.
3555 - Forester Rollers
3555 - Halm Industries Company Inc.
3555 - Idea Engineering Company (Mfr)
3555 - Ikela Co.
3555 - Imaging Technologies, Inc.
3555 - Imtec Inc.
3555 - LEMCO
3555 - Nationwide Graphics, Inc.
3555 - Nu Arc Co., Inc.
3555 - Printers Repair Parts, Inc.
3555 - Service Tectonics, Inc.
3555 - Southwestern Process Supply Co.
3555 - Thistle Roller Co Inc
3555 - Transfer Press Exchange
3556 - Agri-Tech, Inc.
3556 - Alfa International Corporation
3556 - Ashlock Company
3556 - Baking Machines
3556 - Bean Machines Inc
3556 - Berg Co., Div. DC Int'l
3556 - Bevles Company Inc
3556 - Bevles Company Inc
3556 - CAE Screenplates Inc. (Mfr)
3556 - Cantrell International

3556 - Carver, Inc.
3556 - Dedert Corp.
3556 - Delta International
3556 - Dutchess Bakers' Machinery Co., Inc.
3556 - Engineered Plastics, Inc.
3556 - Exeter Engineering Inc
3556 - Food Technology Service, Inc.
3556 - General Machinery Corporation (Mfr)
3556 - Hart Design & Mfg, Inc.
3556 - Hartel Systems Division, Advanced
3556 - Heinzen Manufacturing Inc
3556 - Hollymatic Corporation (Mfr)
3556 - Independent Restaurant & Bakery
3556 - International Dairy Equipment
3556 - International Machinery Exchange
3556 - Lil Orbits, Inc.
3556 - Linker Machines
3556 - Lucks Food Decorating Co.
3556 - Magna Industries, Inc.
3556 - McCann's Engineering &
3556 - Motoman, Inc (Mfr)
3556 - Old World Cone
3556 - Par Vision Systems Corporation
3556 - Picard Inc., C. A.
3556 - Reading Bakery Systems
3556 - Ross & White Co.
3556 - Solbern Div. Howden Food Eqip.
3556 - Sonic Corp.
3556 - Stearns Product Development
3556 - Tech-Mark Inc
3556 - The Lucks Food Equipment Co.
3556 - Thermodyne Food Service Products
3556 - Tomlinson Industries
3556 - Trans Market Sales & Equipment, Inc.
3556 - Waukesha Cherry-Burrell (Mfr)
3556 - Weiler And Company Inc.
3556 - Wenger Manufacturing Inc. (Mfr)
3559 - Accrafect Products Inc.
3559 - Albrecht Co, Inc., Peter
3559 - Americlean, Inc.
3559 - Aqua-Flo, Inc.
3559 - Autoprod Inc.
3559 - Axic Inc
3559 - Ballisti-Cast Mfg., Inc.
3559 - Basic Concepts Inc.
3559 - Basic Electronics Inc
3559 - Bodine Assembly & Test Systems
3559 - Brooktronics Engineering Corp
3559 - Brown Mfg.
3559 - Chemicolloid Laboratories, Inc.
3559 - Cherokee Industries, Inc.
3559 - Columbia Machine, Inc.
3559 - Consolidated Baling Machine Co.,
3559 - Continental Eagle
3559 - D R Technology, Inc.
3559 - DAC International, Inc.
3559 - Debbeler Co.
3559 - Dependable/Redford-Carver
3559 - Divine Brothers Company (Mfr)
3559 - Douglas Engineering
3559 - Duncan-Leigh-Schiffer
3559 - Eagle Metalizing Coatings Co
3559 - Elizabeth Carbide Components
3559 - Environmental Compliance Systems,
3559 - Environmental Solutions, Inc.
3559 - Ewald Instrument Corp.
3559 - Finish Thompson Inc.
3559 - Flex-Pak Manufacturing Inc
3559 - Future Automation Inc - A Technic
3559 - Gainesville Welding & Rendering
3559 - General Air Corporation
3559 - Glas-Master / Wehr Engineering
3559 - Glenmarc Mfg. Inc.
3559 - H2O, Inc.
3559 - HBS Equipment Corp
3559 - Heavy Duty Hydro Blasting, Inc.
3559 - Hess Machine International
3559 - Hudnut Industries Inc
3559 - Huntington Mechanical Labs Inc
3559 - Hydratecs Injection Equipment, Inc.
3559 - Idea Engineering Company (Mfr)
3559 - Industrial Design Fabrication
3559 - International Shoe Machine

3559 - Intersystems, Inc.
3559 - J I M Mfg., Inc.
3559 - James Instruments, Inc.
3559 - Kaydon Corp.
3559 - Littleford Day., Inc. (Mfr)
3559 - M-B Cos., Inc. Of Wisconsin
3559 - Maac Machinery Co., Inc.
3559 - Major Metalfab Co.
3559 - Materials Research Group, Inc.
3559 - Mc Neil & N R M, Inc.
3559 - Motoman, Inc (Mfr)
3559 - Myers Engineering Inc. (Mfr)
3559 - Newark Caplan Sewing Machine,inc
3559 - Pacific Roller Die Co., Inc.
3559 - Parking Products, Inc.
3559 - Perry Equipment Corp.
3559 - Proceco, Inc.
3559 - Proctor & Schwartz
3559 - R W C Inc.
3559 - Raines Technologies Inc
3559 - Reaction Technology Inc
3559 - Rimoldi of America
3559 - Rubber City Machinery Corp.
3559 - RxCount Corp
3559 - SME, a division of FAES USA, Inc.
3559 - Saf-Tee Siping & Grooving Inc
3559 - Sebewaing Tool & Engineering
3559 - Service Tectonics, Inc.
3559 - Shred-Tech Chicago
3559 - Spray Masters Inc.
3559 - Swanson Anaheim Corp
3559 - Tecre Co., Inc.
3559 - Usdm Inc
3559 - Victor Metal Finishing Inc.
3559 - Vortex Engineering
3559 - Warren Industries, Inc.
3559 - Wenger Manufacturing Inc. (Mfr)
3559 - Witte Co., Inc., The
3559 - Wynnson Enterprises, Inc.
3559 - ZMD International Inc
3561 - A B S Pumps, Inc.
3561 - A.Y. McDonald Mfg. Co.
3561 - ABEL Pumps Corp.
3561 - Air Dimensions, Inc.
3561 - All-Flo Pump Co.
3561 - Alldos Inc.
3561 - Atlantic Trading Company Ltd.
3561 - Barber-Nichols Incorporated
3561 - Brady Products Inc.
3561 - CAT PUMPS
3561 - Columbian Steel Tank Co.
3561 - Dempster Industries, Inc.
3561 - Edwards Mfg. Inc. (Mfr)
3561 - Fairbanks Morse Pump Corp.
3561 - Fisher Pumps Inc
3561 - Fluid Metering, Inc.
3561 - GNY Equipment LLC
3561 - Gardner Denver, Inc. (Mfr)
3561 - Gator Pump, Inc.
3561 - Gorman Rupp Co., The
3561 - Granco Pump, Div. Challenge Mfg.
3561 - Great Plains Industries, Inc.
3561 - Hale Products, Inc.
3561 - Harco Manufacturing Co.
3561 - Hypro Corp.
3561 - ITT Flygt Corp
3561 - J. Line Pump Company
3561 - Kason Corporation (Mfr)
3561 - Kiteguild International Inc.
3561 - Kraissl Co., Inc., The
3561 - MTH Tool Co. Inc.
3561 - Minco Sales Corp.
3561 - Pacer Pumps
3561 - Pantropic Power Products, Inc.
3561 - Park Corporation
3561 - Penray Companies Inc.(Mfr)
3561 - Premier Spring Water Inc
3561 - Rotor Tech Inc.
3561 - S E R F I L C O, Ltd.
3561 - Saber Technologies, LLC
3561 - Schwing America, Inc.
3561 - Shurflo
3561 - Standard Pumps Inc.

3561 - Sunstrand Corporation
3561 - Thomas Industries-Power Air Div.
3561 - Thomas Pump & Machinery, Inc.
3561 - Top Line Process Equipment Co.
3561 - Tri-Rotor, Inc.
3561 - Unique Systems Inc.(Mfr)
3561 - Vaughan Co Inc
3561 - Wamco Corporation
3562 - Abbott Ball Co. (Mfg)
3562 - Acra-Ball & Manufacturing Co
3562 - G K N Sinter Metals Emporium
3562 - MBS Industrial Service Inc
3563 - Ariel Corp.
3563 - Barber-Nichols Incorporated
3563 - Bradleys' Hermetics, Inc.
3563 - Ciasons Industrial Inc
3563 - D & L Thomas Equipment
3563 - Energy Machinery Inc
3563 - Evey Engineering Co., Inc.
3563 - Filpro Corporation
3563 - Gardner Denver, Inc. (Mfr)
3563 - Goodtrade Corporation
3563 - Hermetic Machines Inc.
3563 - Jun-Air USA, Inc.
3563 - Minco Sales Corp.
3563 - Quincy Compressor
3563 - Robinair, A Div. of SPX Corporation
3563 - Thomas Industries, Inc.
3563 - Unique Systems Inc.(Mfr)
3563 - V R Systems, Inc.
3564 - Acme Engineering & Mfg. Corp.
3564 - Air Chem Systems Inc
3564 - Airflow Systems Inc (Mfr)
3564 - Airtrol, Inc.
3564 - Ametek Rotron TMD - Industrial
3564 - Anguil Environmental Systems, Inc.
3564 - Barron Industries, Inc.
3564 - Bruning & Federle Mfg. Co.
3564 - Calgon Carbon Corporation (Mfr)
3564 - California Turbo Inc
3564 - Car-Mon Products, Inc.
3564 - Clean Air Consultants, Inc.
3564 - Clean Air Filter Co.
3564 - Dustvent, Inc.
3564 - Eco Environmental Filtration, Inc.
3564 - Environmental Technologies, Inc.
3564 - Filenco Div.
3564 - Gardner Denver, Inc. (Mfr)
3564 - Gaylord Industries, Inc.
3564 - Hankison International
3564 - Independent Mfg. Co., Inc.
3564 - L C R Electronics, Inc.
3564 - Lewcott
3564 - Liberty Industries, Inc.
3564 - Marsulex Environmental Technologies
3564 - Mart Corporation
3564 - Midwest International Standard Prod,
3564 - New York Blower Co.
3564 - Permatron Corporation
3564 - Perry Equipment Corp.
3564 - Process Equipment, Inc.
3564 - Roots Division, Dresser Equipment
3564 - Smith Eng & Environmental Corp
3564 - Sterling Blower Co.
3564 - Thiel Air Technologies Corp.
3564 - Tri-Dim Filter Corp.
3564 - Triangle Metal & Mfg. Co.
3564 - Turner Envirologic, Inc.
3565 - ATW Manufacturing Company
3565 - All American Containers, Inc.
3565 - Angelus Sanitary Can Machine Co.
3565 - Apax Corporation
3565 - Ashton Food Machinery Co., Inc.,
3565 - Bell-Mark Corp.
3565 - ERICA and ERICA
3565 - Elsner Engineering Works Inc.
3565 - Equipment & Systems Engineering
3565 - Filler Specialties, Inc.
3565 - Flexicell, Inc.
3565 - Flower Products Company
3565 - Fogg Filler Co.
3565 - G E I Mateer-Burt Co., Inc.
3565 - Gafco-Worldwide, Inc.

3565 - Greener Corp.
3565 - Hart Design & Mfg, Inc.
3565 - Hoover Machine Co., Inc.
3565 - Hoppmann Corporation
3565 - Lasertechnics Marking Corp.
3565 - Mac Company
3565 - Motoman, Inc (Mfr)
3565 - NJM/CLI Packaging Systems
3565 - Packaging Systems International, Inc.
3565 - Prototype Equipment Corporations
3565 - R.A. Pearson Company
3565 - Sandbagger Corp.
3565 - Shanklin Corporation
3565 - Shrinkfast Marketing (Mfr)
3565 - Sitma U S A, Inc.
3565 - TechnaSeal
3565 - Tecnipac Inc
3565 - Triangle Package Machinery Co.
3566 - Horsburgh & Scott Co., The
3566 - Phoenix Gear Inc
3566 - Prager Incorporated
3566 - Sunstrand Corporation
3567 - Ajax Magnethermic Corp.
3567 - Alkota Cleaning Systems
3567 - Armature Coil Equipment Inc.
3567 - Blasdel Enterprises, Inc.
3567 - Catalytic Combustion Corp.
3567 - Centorr Vacuum Industries, Inc.
3567 - D C Thermal, Inc.
3567 - DELTA H. SYSTEMS, INC.
3567 - Drever Company
3567 - East Coast Induction, Inc.
3567 - Food Engineering Corporation
3567 - Holcroft
3567 - Incinerator International Inc.
3567 - Induction Technology Corp
3567 - Inductoheat Inc.
3567 - Industrial Process Equipment
3567 - Lessco
3567 - Lochinvar Water Heater
3567 - Lydon Brothers Corporation
3567 - Olivine Corporation
3567 - Omega Heater Co., Inc.
3567 - Paragon Industries, Inc.
3567 - Powermaster Pacific
3567 - Simonds Mfg. Corp.
3567 - Sinterite, Furance Div.
3567 - Soil Purification Inc.
3567 - Tempco Electric Heater Corp.
3567 - Therma-Tron-X Inc.
3567 - Thermatek International Inc.
3567 - Turbo Burn Inc
3567 - Wisconsin Oven Corp.
3568 - American Sleeve Bearing, Llc
3568 - Dana Corp./Wichita Clutch Co.
3568 - Dynametal Technologies
3568 - Helander Products, Inc.
3568 - Kop-Flex, Inc., Emerson Power
3568 - Radial Bearing Corp.
3568 - Rotary Systems Inc.
3569 - Adhesive Technologies, Inc.
3569 - Affinity Industries Inc. (Mfr)
3569 - Alpha Wire Company
3569 - Amkus, Inc.
3569 - Aqua Power Co.
3569 - Aquapower Co.
3569 - Automated Applications Inc
3569 - Automatics & Machinery Co., Inc.
3569 - BMI Automation, Inc.
3569 - BOC Coating Technology
3569 - Biomarine Inc.
3569 - CAE Screenplates Inc. (Mfr)
3569 - CMO Enterprises Inc.
3569 - Central Sprinkler
3569 - Chemco Manufacturing Incorporated
3569 - Commision Brokers, Inc.
3569 - Consler Filtrations Products
3569 - Cox Recorders
3569 - Diamond Z Manufacturing
3569 - Drum-Mates, Inc, Drum Mixer &
3569 - Ethylene Control Inc
3569 - Fairey Arlon Inc.
3569 - Filpro Corporation

3569 - Flite Technology, Inc.
3569 - General Safety Equipment
3569 - Globe Fire Sprinkler Corp.
3569 - Grover Manufacturing Corp.
3569 - Harco Manufacturing Co.
3569 - Harmony Enterprises, Inc. G P I
3569 - Hosokawa Micron Powder Systems
3569 - Ideal Stitcher Company(Mfr)
3569 - International Baler Corp.
3569 - International Reserve Equip.
3569 - Jaffrey Fire Protection Co., Inc.
3569 - Kason Corporation (Mfr)
3569 - Kent Oil Company Inc.
3569 - Larson & Associates Inc
3569 - Liberty Mfg., Inc.
3569 - MAC Equipment, Inc.
3569 - Magnaflux
3569 - Mars Air Doors
3569 - Micronics, Inc.
3569 - Miller Design & Equipment
3569 - Moli-Tron Company Inc.
3569 - Motoman, Inc (Mfr)
3569 - Ossid Corp.
3569 - P C & E, Fabcon Div.
3569 - Parts Services International LLC
3569 - Perry Equipment Corp.
3569 - Pick Heaters, Inc.
3569 - Process Filtration Div., Parker
3569 - Robohand, Inc.
3569 - Rockford Systems Inc.(Mfr)
3569 - T M Industries, Inc.
3569 - TNT Tools Inc
3569 - Technical Fabricators, Inc.
3569 - The Capital Controls Group
3569 - Tm Industries Inc.
3569 - Velcon Filters Inc
3569 - Wildcat Mfg. Co., Inc.
3571 - Allview Services Inc
3571 - CliniComp International Inc
3571 - Computerline International
3571 - Digital Interface Systems Inc.
3571 - Exergetic Systems Inc
3571 - Hollingsworth & Vose Co.
3571 - I V Phoenix Group, Inc.
3571 - Stallion Technologies Inc
3571 - Synnex Information Tech
3571 - Sysdyne Corp.
3572 - International Cybernetics Corp.
3572 - Peripherals Manufacturing Inc
3573 - Geophysical Survey Systems, Inc.
3575 - Visentech Systems, Inc.
3577 - Cherry Corporation, The
3577 - Focus Electronic Corporation
3577 - IXMICRO
3577 - Intelligent Peripheral Devices
3577 - Maxton Security Systems
3577 - Meridian Data Inc
3577 - Myricom Inc
3577 - Ortek Data Systems Inc
3577 - Powerline Solar Products, Inc.
3577 - S C I Systems, Inc.
3577 - S.I. Tech, Inc.(Mfr)
3577 - Secure-IT Inc. (Mfr)
3577 - Software Integrators
3577 - Tally Printer Corporation
3577 - Virtual Fund.Com
3577 - Xico Inc
3578 - De La Rue Cash Systems
3578 - Frontline Systems
3578 - Westrex International
3579 - Accu-Time Systems
3579 - Banner American Products, Inc.
3579 - Cummins-Allison Corp.
3579 - Hatzlachh Supply Inc.
3579 - International Peripheral Systems
3581 - C & G Manufacturing
3581 - Imco Inc
3581 - Rainbow Crane Corp
3581 - Smart Industries
3581 - U-Select-It Corporation
3581 - Vendtronics
3581 - Vision Pharmaceuticals Inc.
3582 - Alliance Laundry Systems

3582 - E L X Group, Washex Machinery Co.
3582 - Ellis Corporation
3582 - Forenta, L.P.
3582 - Giancola Exports, Inc., D. J.
3582 - Leonard Automatics, Inc.
3582 - Maxi-Vac, Inc.
3582 - Pellerin Milnor Corp.
3582 - Wascomat (Mfr)
3582 - World Trade Exporters, Inc.
3583 - Water Services International
3584 - Maytag International
3585 - A & V Refrigeration Corp.
3585 - Advanced Thermal Technologies
3585 - Affinity Industries Inc. (Mfr)
3585 - Aftermarket Specialties, Inc.
3585 - Air Energy Heat Pumps
3585 - Baltimore Aircoil Co., Inc.
3585 - Biloff Manufacturing Company Inc
3585 - Cmp Corporation
3585 - Compu-Aire, Inc.
3585 - Consolidated Baling Machine Co.,
3585 - Continental Enterprises
3585 - Cooper Instrument Corporation (Mfr)
3585 - Craig Indsutries
3585 - Des Champs Laboratories
3585 - Dial Manufacturing Inc
3585 - Donlee Technologies, Inc.
3585 - Dri Steem Humidifier
3585 - Filtrine Manufacturing Company
3585 - Freezing System Inc.
3585 - Hastings Industries
3585 - Hawe Technical Associates (HTA)
3585 - Hosokawa Micron Powder Systems
3585 - Howard-McCray Refrigerator Co. Inc.
3585 - Indiana Tube
3585 - International Baler Corp.
3585 - Kool Star
3585 - Low Humidity Systems, Inc.
3585 - McCann's Engineering &
3585 - Mueller Industries Inc.(Mfr)
3585 - National Compressor Exchange, Inc.
3585 - Nauticon, Inc.
3585 - Nor-Lake, Inc. (Mfr)
3585 - Nordyne Inc.
3585 - Oasis Corporation
3585 - Phoenix Manufacturing Inc
3585 - Premco Machine Co Inc
3585 - Proctor Companies
3585 - Purolator Products Air Filtration Co.
3585 - Refrigeration Resources Co.
3585 - Rheem Air Conditioning Div.
3585 - Robinair, A Div. of SPX Corporation
3585 - Sahar Industries
3585 - Scotsman Industries
3585 - State Insulation Corp.
3585 - Super Radiator Coils
3585 - Technology General Corp.
3585 - Tithe Corp., Skil-aire Div.
3585 - York International Corp.
3585 - Zero Zone, Inc.
3586 - Cargill Salt Co/Dispensing Sys
3586 - Fluid Dynamics Inc
3586 - GNY Equipment LLC
3586 - Great Plains Industries, Inc.
3586 - Mueller Steam Specialty Co., A
United Dominion Co., Fluid Central Div.
3589 - Alkota Cleaning Systems
3589 - Allied Industrial Distributors Inc.
3589 - Alto-Shaam, Inc.
3589 - Aqua Blast Corp.
3589 - AquaTec, Inc.
3589 - Aquacare Environment Inc
3589 - Aquamatch Inc
3589 - Azure Blue Inc
3589 - Balemaster
3589 - Bar Maid Corp.
3589 - Bio Zone
3589 - Bondtech Corp.
3589 - Brake Funderburk Enterprises, Inc.
3589 - Brewmatic Co
3589 - Broaster Co., The
3589 - Calgon Carbon Corporation (Mfr)
3589 - Chief Industries, Inc.

3589 - Chlorine & Chemical Supply Co.
3589 - Clean Water Systems Intl
3589 - Corrigan Corp. America
3589 - Culligan Wate Conditioning, Inc.
3589 - De Marco MAX VAC Corporation
3589 - Delta Products Group
3589 - Dipwell Co., Inc., The
3589 - Elgee Mfg. Co.
3589 - Elite Mfg. Corp.
3589 - Ellis Corporation
3589 - Enting Water Conditioning Inc.
3589 - Environmental Dynamics, Inc.(Mfr)
3589 - Equipment & Systems Engineering
3589 - FTC
3589 - Filtrine Manufacturing Company
3589 - Gafco-Worldwide, Inc.
3589 - Garbel Products Company
3589 - General Ecology, Inc.
3589 - HB Environmental Engineers Inc
3589 - Hawaii Pacific Associates
3589 - Henny Penny Corp.
3589 - Horner Discus International
3589 - Hotsy Corporation, The
3589 - Hydrolab Corporation
3589 - J-Star Industries Inc.
3589 - Jet, Inc.
3589 - King Metal Products, Inc.
3589 - LifeSource Engineering Inc.
3589 - Lifestream Watersystems Inc
3589 - MIOX Corp.
3589 - Martin Marietta Magnesia Specialties
3589 - My-Tana Mfg. Co., Inc.
3589 - Omnifilter
3589 - Osmonics, Inc.
3589 - Ozotech Inc
3589 - Pitco Frialator, Inc. (Mfr)
3589 - Premier Manufactured Systems, Inc.
3589 - Pure Water, Inc.
3589 - RO Ultratec USA Inc
3589 - Ross & White Co.
3589 - Santa Barbara Control Systems
3589 - Scalewatcher North America Inc.
3589 - Smith & Loveless, Inc.
3589 - Solaronics, Inc.
3589 - Somat Company (Mfr)
3589 - Spectrapure Inc
3589 - Springsoft International Inc.
3589 - Super Products Corp.
3589 - Superior Aqua Enterprises, Inc.
3589 - Walker Process Equip., Div. McNish
3589 - Water Resources International
3589 - Water Technologies
3589 - Yeagle Technology, Inc.
3591 - SEC Industrial Battery Co., Inc.
3593 - American Cylinder Co., Inc.
3593 - Catching Fluidpower, Inc.
3593 - Cross Mfg. Inc.
3593 - Defco, Inc.
3593 - Hercules Hydraulics Inc.
3593 - Hydro-Line Inc. Division of IMC, Inc.
3593 - Sprague Controls Inc
3594 - AZ Hydraulic Engineering Inc
3594 - Cross Mfg. Inc.
3594 - D & D Machine & Hydraulics
3594 - Flojet Corp
3594 - Hotsy Corporation, The
3594 - Rineer Hydraulics
3596 - AAA Weigh Inc
3596 - Balance Specialties Inc. (Mfr)
3596 - Electronic Weighing Systems, Inc.
3596 - First Weigh
3596 - General Electrodynamics Corp.
3596 - Hydro-Line Inc. Division of IMC, Inc.
3596 - J-Star Industries Inc.
3596 - King J.A. & Company
3596 - Pelouze/Health-O-Meter, Inc.
3596 - Pennsylvania Scale Co.
3596 - Polyproducts Corp.
3596 - Scalemen Of Florida, Inc.
3596 - Scientech Inc.
3596 - Triangle Package Machinery Co.
3599 - A & B Fabrication & Repair, Inc.
3599 - A C Products Co., Inc.

3599 - A-1 Machining Co.
3599 - A. I. M. Inc.
3599 - Accurite Development & Mfg
3599 - Ace-Tek Manufacturing
3599 - Aerospace Manufacturing Inc
3599 - Air Cleaners, Inc.
3599 - Akron Tool & Die Co., Inc.
3599 - Aldridge Industries, Inc.
3599 - Alexeff-Synder Enterprises
3599 - American Hydraulics
3599 - Atlantic Machine Tools Inc.
3599 - Atomco Corporation , Tru-Mark
3599 - Aurora Custom Machining
3599 - Automatics & Machinery Co., Inc.
3599 - B. T. M. Inc.
3599 - Basic Electronics Inc
3599 - Best Jig-Grinding Service
3599 - Bob Lewis Machine Co., Inc.
3599 - CAE Screenplates Inc. (Mfr)
3599 - Cherokee Industries, Inc.
3599 - Cold Jet, Inc.
3599 - Daco Enterprises Inc
3599 - Damar Machine Co
3599 - Delta Machine & Tool, Inc.
3599 - Desert Laboratories Inc
3599 - Dixie Machine Shop
3599 - Doemelt Racing, G. L.
3599 - Doerksen Precision Products
3599 - Ecosystem Inc.
3599 - Elizabeth Carbide Components
3599 - Elliot Tool Technologies, LTD.
3599 - Envirozone Systems Corp.
3599 - Equipment & Systems Engineering
3599 - Eraser Co., Inc.
3599 - F S P Machinery
3599 - F W Tool & Die Works, Inc.
3599 - Farrel Corp.
3599 - Field Equipment & Service Co.
3599 - Finn Tool & Instruments Inc
3599 - Frazier Industries Inc.
3599 - H2O, Inc.
3599 - Hall Industrial Services
3599 - Hansen Machine & Tool Co., N. M.
3599 - Hanson Welding Machines, Inc.
3599 - Hedges & Bros., L.P.
3599 - Horner Discus International
3599 - Hughes Compaction Equipment, Inc.
3599 - ITT Flygt Corp
3599 - Integrity Manufacturing Co
3599 - John Deere Harvester Works, Cylinder
3599 - K & B Machine Works Inc.
3599 - Kemco Tool & Machine Co., Inc.
3599 - Kovil Manufacturing LLC
3599 - L & M Machining Corporation
3599 - LA Machine Shop
3599 - La Machine Shop Inc.
3599 - Larcom & Mitchell
3599 - Lays Mining Service, Inc.
3599 - Litec Inc.
3599 - M & M Corporation
3599 - M F Automation Inc.
3599 - Mac-Lyn Industries Inc
3599 - Malbert Mitchell Grinding Corp
3599 - Michigan Wheel Corporation
3599 - Miller Machine
3599 - Nilfisk-Advance America, Inc.
3599 - Nutter Machine Inc.
3599 - Oceanside Engineering & Mfg
3599 - Olson Industries, Inc.
3599 - Omega Flex, Inc.
3599 - Onodi Tool & Engineering Co.
3599 - Pennsylvania Tool & Gages, Inc.
3599 - Perma-Pipe Ricwil, Industrial
3599 - Power Vacuum Trailer Co.
3599 - Prager Incorporated
3599 - Pragmatic Environmental Solutions
3599 - Price Products Inc
3599 - R & R Machine Industries, Inc.
3599 - Rame-Hart, Inc.
3599 - Rapid Development Service
3599 - Roberson Products
3599 - Robert's Honing & Gundrilling Inc.
3599 - Rolling Hills Progress Center Inc.

3599 - Royal Oak Industries, Inc.
3599 - S T C Machine Shop
3599 - Semco Inc.
3599 - Senga Engineering Inc
3599 - Shu-Re-Nu Equipment, Inc.
3599 - Soil Purification Inc.
3599 - Southport Machine Inc
3599 - Standard Welding Co., Inc.
3599 - Sun Country Industries Inc.
3599 - Swaim & Sons
3599 - Techni-Chem Inc.
3599 - Technical Engineering Sales, Inc.
3599 - U.S. Manufacturing Corporation
3599 - Ultrasonic Probs Mfg. Co.
3599 - Unified Machine & Design, Inc.
3599 - Vimex CNC Machining
3599 - Water Quality Services
3599 - West Coast Industries Inc.
3599 - Wieland Precision Machine
3599 - Willis Machine Inc
3610 - Support Products Inc.
3612 - Acme Electric Corp., Power
3612 - Basic Electronics Inc
3612 - Con-Tech Power Systems, Inc.
3612 - Dulmison Incorporated
3612 - Dynapower Corporation
3612 - Howard Industries
3612 - Jackson Transformer Co.
3612 - Liebert Corporation
3612 - Mag-Tran Equipment Corp
3612 - Park Corporation
3612 - Pauwels Transformers Inc.
3612 - Powertronix Corporation
3612 - Pulizzi Engineering Inc
3612 - R.E. Uptegraff Mfg. Company
3612 - SNC Manufacturing Co., Inc.
3612 - T & R Electric Supply Co., Inc.
3612 - Technology Research Corporation
3612 - Yarbrough-Timco
3613 - Cole Instrument Corp
3613 - Electric City Corp.
3613 - Electro Cam Corp.
3613 - Factory Automation Systems, Inc.
3613 - Gould Shawmut
3613 - Hall Co., The
3613 - Hawaii Pacific Associates
3613 - Jennings Technology Company
3613 - Kanawha Scales & Systems, Inc.
3613 - Lake Shore Electric Corp.
3613 - Mid-West Instrument
3613 - Mitsubishi Electric Power Products,
3613 - Park Corporation
3613 - Park Metal Products Co.
3613 - Platt Electric Supply
3613 - Ross Engineering Corp
3613 - Ross Engineering Corp.
3613 - Shallbetter, Inc.
3613 - Southwest Power Systems, Inc.
3613 - Technology Research Corporation
3613 - Transcrypt International, Inc.
3613 - Wago Corp.
3613 - Zenith Controls, Inc.
3621 - Avs Graphics International
3621 - B I C O Drilling Tools, Inc.
3621 - Baldor Electric Company
3621 - E C M Motor Co.
3621 - Electric Motors & Drives, Inc.
3621 - Elmagco Corp
3621 - Glentek Inc
3621 - Hatzlachh Supply Inc.
3621 - Imperial Electric Co.
3621 - International Enviromental Corp.
3621 - J. C. Marine Diesel, Inc.
3621 - Kevlin Corporation(Mfr)
3621 - Martindale Electric Company
3621 - Master Motor Rebuilders
3621 - Pass & Seymour/Legrand(Mfr)
3621 - WinTron Inc
3623 - Cosmos Electronic Machine Corp.
3623 - Ewald Instrument Corp.
3624 - Carbone Of America Corp.
3624 - Graphite Products Inc
3624 - Roc Carbon Co.

3624 - Toyo Tanso Usa Inc
3625 - Alstom Automation Systems Corp.
3625 - Anaheim Automation
3625 - Artisan Controls Corporation (Mfr)
3625 - Baldor Electric Company
3625 - Basic Electronics Inc
3625 - Brady Products, Inc.
3625 - Cleveland Motion Controls, Inc.
3625 - Con-Tech Power Systems, Inc.
3625 - Cruising Equipment Company
3625 - Deltrol Controls
3625 - Facts, Inc.
3625 - Genie Co., The
3625 - Hale Engineering Co.
3625 - ITT Flygt Corp
3625 - Jennings Technology Company
3625 - Kay-Ray/Sensall, Inc.
3625 - Kinedyne Corp.
3625 - Lutron Electronics Co., Inc.
3625 - Mathers Controls, Inc.
3625 - Metrix Instrument Co.
3625 - Motortronics, Inc.
3625 - Pass & Seymour/Legrand(Mfr)
3625 - Platt Electric Supply
3625 - Precision Motion Controls
3625 - Rjg, Inc
3625 - Rockwell Automation
3625 - Rodix, Inc.
3625 - Schulz Electric Co.
3629 - Dynapower Corporation
3629 - Exeltech
3629 - Hull Speed Data Products, Inc.
3629 - P C & E, Fabcon Div.
3629 - Plasmatic Systems, Inc.
3629 - Scalemen Of Florida, Inc.
3629 - Trace Engineering Co
3629 - Whitlock Instrument
3631 - Capitol Products Co., Inc., The
3631 - Emerson Radio Corp.
3633 - Alliance Laundry Systems
3634 - Fostoria Industries Inc. (Mfr)
3634 - Halton Co.
3634 - JB Research Inc
3634 - Oasis Corporation
3634 - Proctor Companies
3634 - Professional Discount Supply
3634 - Relaxor / JB Research Inc
3634 - Wahl Clipper Corp.
3635 - Beam Industries
3635 - Eco Vacuum Mfg. Corp.
3639 - Advanced Tech Industries, Inc.
3639 - American Water Heater Co.
3639 - Dahmes Stainless, Inc.
3639 - Hamilton Beach/Proctor Silex, Inc.
3639 - Lochinvar Water Heater
3639 - Mid-South Electronics-Alabama, Inc.
3639 - Pennsylvania Sewing Machine Co.
3641 - Aero-Tech Light Bulb Co., Inc.
3641 - Agamco Inc
3641 - Light Sources, Inc.
3641 - Lumitron Corp.
3643 - Amtronics, Inc./Teriminal Div.
3643 - Basic Electronics Inc
3643 - Buhl Industries, Inc.
3643 - Daniel Woodhead Company
3643 - E F T Systems, Inc.
3643 - Hubbell / The Ohio Brass Co. (Mfr)
3643 - Linemaster Switch Corp.
3643 - Lyncole XIT Grounding
3643 - Mid-West Instrument
3643 - National Standard Parts Assocs. Inc.
3643 - Oak Grigsby, Inc.
3643 - Pass & Seymour/Legrand(Mfr)
3643 - Pressure Devices Inc.
3643 - Superior Grounding Systems
3643 - The Phoenix Company of Chicago,
3643 - The Siemon Company
3643 - Voltage Multipliers Inc
3644 - Daniel Woodhead Company
3644 - Instrumentation & Control Systems,
3644 - Pass & Seymour/Legrand(Mfr)
3645 - American Power Products Inc
3645 - BW Lighting Corp

3645 - Global Electric Products
3645 - Kichler Lighting Group
3645 - Lampi, LLC
3645 - Speer Collectibles
3645 - Tempo Lighting
3645 - The Malder Co
3645 - W O L I C, Inc.
3646 - Bieber Lighting Corp
3646 - Cherry Corporation, The
3646 - Decor Guild Mfg., Co.
3646 - Doane Co., Inc., L. C.
3646 - Esco International
3646 - Fostoria Industries Inc. (Mfr)
3646 - Hapco Aluminum Poles
3646 - Jeb Lighting Co., Llc
3646 - Magnaray International
3646 - Masterpiece Accessories Inc
3646 - Oryan Industries Inc
3647 - Code 3, Inc. Div of Public Safety
3647 - Grote Industries, Inc.
3647 - Guide Corporation
3647 - K-D Lamp Company (Mfr)
3647 - Tridon
3647 - Truck-Lite International Inc.
3648 - A.L.P. Lighting Components, Inc.
3648 - Advanced Lighting Systems, Inc.
3648 - Bulbtronics, Inc.
3648 - Cir-Kit Concepts, Inc.
3648 - Daniel Woodhead Company
3648 - Engineered Lighting Products
3648 - Eye Lighting International Of North
3648 - Fostoria Industries Inc. (Mfr)
3648 - Light Solutions
3648 - Made In Maui Neon
3648 - Paraflex Industries, Inc.
3648 - R L S Lighting, Inc.
3648 - Southwest Photovoltaic Systems
3648 - Tideland Signal Corp.
3648 - Trojan, Inc.
3649 - Schulze Manufacturing
3651 - Allsop, Inc.
3651 - Ampli-Vox Questron
3651 - Atlas/Soundolier, Atapco Security
3651 - Audico Label Corp.
3651 - Audioplex Technology, Inc.
3651 - Emerson Radio Corp.
3651 - Five Rivers Electronic Innovations,
3651 - Fourjay Industries, Inc.
3651 - Hatzlachh Supply Inc.
3651 - Himmelstein & Co., S.
3651 - KSC Industries Inc
3651 - Micro Audiometrics Corp.
3651 - Portatalk Electronics Inc
3651 - Savant Audio & Video
3651 - Shure Bros. Inc.
3651 - Ultra-Stereo Labs Inc
3652 - Flight Tech, Inc
3652 - Music Unlimited Inc
3652 - Q. Up Arts
3652 - Reference Recordings
3653 - Jun-Air USA, Inc.
3661 - CEECO Communications Equipment
3661 - Ceeco
3661 - Cordell Manufacturing Inc
3661 - DCR / Diversified Communications
3661 - DNE Technologies Inc.
3661 - Digital Link Corp
3661 - Digital Telephone Sys., Harris Corp.
3661 - Dynetcom, Inc.
3661 - Electronic Tele-Communications, Inc
3661 - Forum Communications Systems, Inc.
3661 - JPS Communications Inc
3661 - Micon Telecommunications Inc
3661 - Noble Systems Corp.
3661 - NovaWeb Technologies Inc
3661 - PMC Electronics
3661 - Pacific Phoinix Inc.
3661 - S.I. Tech, Inc.(Mfr)
3661 - Startel Corporation
3661 - Teledex Corporation
3661 - The Siemon Company
3661 - Toshiba America Information Systems,
3662 - Geophysical Survey Systems, Inc.

3663 - Accurate Sound Corporation
3663 - Alpha Systems Lab Inc
3663 - Apature Products, Inc.
3663 - Artex Aircraft Supplies Inc
3663 - Atlantic Research Corp., Unit of
3663 - Continental Electronics Corp.
3663 - D H Satellite
3663 - DWIN Electronics Inc
3663 - Datamarine International Inc
3663 - Diamond Electronics Inc.
3663 - Emx Inc.
3663 - GSIGLOBAL , INC.
3663 - Gem Engineering Co., Inc.
3663 - Glenayre Western Multiplex
3663 - Hoyin Industries
3663 - JPS Communications Inc
3663 - Kintronic Laboratories, Inc.
3663 - MagicBox Inc
3663 - Micon Telecommunications Inc
3663 - Micro Communications, Inc.
3663 - Omicron Video
3663 - Perimeter Products, Inc.
3663 - Prodelin Corp.
3663 - R. F. Technology, Inc.
3663 - Raibeam
3663 - Satellite Transmission Systems
3663 - Scala Electronic Corporation
3663 - Smarts Broadcast Systems
3663 - Solid State Electronics Corp
3663 - Sunnyvale GDI, Inc.
3663 - Talla-Com, Tallahassee
3663 - Telesat International Ltd
3663 - Vortex Satcom Systems, Inc.
3663 - Wireworks Corporation
3669 - ASTI
3669 - Advantor Corp.
3669 - Apollo
3669 - B Q Products Inc.
3669 - Basic Electronics Inc
3669 - Centurion International, Inc.
3669 - Ceotronics Inc.
3669 - Chemetron Fire Systems
3669 - Code 3, Inc. Div of Public Safety
3669 - Demco Electronics
3669 - Detex International
3669 - Dynamic Sciences Int'l Inc
3669 - E & M Intl.
3669 - H.M. Electronics, Inc.
3669 - Harmon Industries, Inc.
3669 - Home Safeguard Industries Inc.
3669 - Hughes Electron Dynamics
3669 - Immix Telecom Inc.
3669 - JPS Communications Inc
3669 - Metron Solutions Inc
3669 - Micon Telecommunications Inc
3669 - Multiplex Technology Inc
3669 - Performahome (Mfr)
3669 - Perimeter Products, Inc.
3669 - Protex International Corp.
3669 - Pyott-Boone Electronics
3669 - Railroad Signal, Inc.
3669 - Recognition Systems Inc
3669 - S.I. Tech, Inc.(Mfr)
3669 - Safetech International, Inc.
3669 - Sumitomo Electric Lightwave Corp.
3669 - Synergistics, Inc.
3669 - Tut Systems
3669 - Wheelock, Inc.
3671 - Jennings Technology Company
3671 - Teltron Technologies, Inc.
3672 - Accurate Circuit Engineering
3672 - Arlon Materials for Electronics
3672 - Basic Electronics Inc
3672 - Circuit Manufacturing Technology
3672 - Circuit Technology Corp.
3672 - EEI / Mod-Tech Industries
3672 - Eagle Circuits, Inc.
3672 - Eagle Star Electronics LLC
3672 - Electronic Manufacturing Svc
3672 - Empire Electronics Corp.
3672 - Modular Components National, Inc.
3672 - Pine Grove Group
3672 - Printed Circuit Solutions Mfg.

3672 - Reliable Communications Inc
3672 - Rogers Corporation
3672 - Salco Circuit
3672 - Sense Technology Inc.
3672 - Sierra Electronic Assembly
3672 - Star Enterprises Inc
3672 - Twin Technology Inc
3672 - Ustek, Inc.
3672 - Zecal, Inc.
3674 - Advanced Power Technology Inc
3674 - Affinity Industries Inc. (Mfr)
3674 - Alpha Technology
3674 - Cherry Corporation, The
3674 - Diablo Industries
3674 - Flip Chip Technologies LLC
3674 - Forenta, L.P.
3674 - Hybrid Semiconductors/Electronics
3674 - InterFET Corporation
3674 - Kinetic Ceramics Inc
3674 - Monarchy International
3674 - New Jersey Semicondutor Products,
3674 - PDP Systems
3674 - Semiconductor Technology, Inc.
3674 - Silicon Sensors, LLC
3674 - Smith Systems, Inc.
3674 - Solarex
3674 - T L C Precision Wafer Tech, Inc.
3674 - Target Materials, Inc.
3674 - TeleDirect International, Inc.
3674 - Wafer World, Inc.
3675 - Circuit Components, Inc.
3675 - Kemet Electronics Corp.
3675 - N W L Capacitors
3675 - Steinerfilm Inc
3675 - Voltronics Corporation
3676 - KOA Speer Electronics, Inc.
3676 - US Sensor Corp
3677 - CBS (Circuit Board Specialist)
3677 - KOA Speer Electronics, Inc.
3677 - M C Davis Company
3677 - WinTron Inc
3678 - Autosplice, Inc.
3678 - Cory Components Inc
3678 - Custom Assembly
3678 - Daniel Woodhead Company
3678 - Eby Co.
3678 - Elcon Products International
3678 - IEH Corp.
3678 - Ocean Design Inc.
3678 - Palco Connector
3678 - Sumitomo Electric Lightwave Corp.
3679 - 3M IBD/Export.
3679 - A. W. Industries Inc.
3679 - Aaron-Swiss, Inc.
3679 - Aero-KAP Inc
3679 - American Piezo Ceramics, Inc.
3679 - American Zettler Inc
3679 - Ancor Communications
3679 - Artech Industries Inc
3679 - B Q Products Inc.
3679 - BEI Sensors & Systems/Kimco
3679 - Basic Electronics Inc
3679 - Brenneman & Assocs., Inc.
3679 - Communication Techniques, Inc.
3679 - Conectec R F, Inc.
3679 - Count On Tools, Inc.
3679 - Cui Stack Inc
3679 - Custom Cable Industries Inc.
3679 - Delaire U. S. A., Inc.
3679 - Delta Products Corporation
3679 - Eemus Manufacturing Corp
3679 - Etalon Inc.
3679 - Fujipoly America Corp.
3679 - Havetronix, Inc.
3679 - Hobi International, Inc.
3679 - Holbrooks
3679 - Imperial Electronic Assembly
3679 - Kevlin Corporation(Mfr)
3679 - Keystone Electronics Corp.
3679 - Kirby Risk Service Center
3679 - Luna Defense Systems Inc
3679 - MITEQ, Inc.
3679 - Mas-Hamilton Group

3679 - Mathews Assocs, Inc.
3679 - Mensor Corporation
3679 - Mid-South Electronics-Alabama, Inc.
3679 - Milwaukee Electronics Corp.
3679 - Motorola Integrated Electronic
3679 - National Wire & Cable Corp
3679 - Omega Shielding Products Inc.
3679 - Pacific Consolidated Indus
3679 - Parpro, Inc.
3679 - Petron Industries Inc.
3679 - Plastic Extruded Parts Inc.(Mfr)
3679 - Precision Hermetic Technology
3679 - Qual-Pro Corporation
3679 - R.B. Annis Company, Inc.
3679 - Rhino Linings USA Inc
3679 - Rogers Corporation
3679 - S C I-Agra, Inc.
3679 - Scott Electronics, Inc.
3679 - Sentrol Industrial
3679 - Signals & Systems Inc.
3679 - Silveron Industries Inc
3679 - Spira Manufacturing Corp
3679 - Standard Crystal Corp
3679 - Sub-Con Inc
3679 - Sumitomo Electric Lightwave Corp.
3679 - T/Mac, Inc.
3679 - Takaha America Co.
3679 - The DII Group Inc
3679 - V I P Industries, Inc.
3679 - V T C Inc.
3679 - V.T.E., Inc.
3679 - Voltronics Corporation
3679 - Weinschel, Bruno Assocs., Inc.
3679 - Worswick Industries Inc
3691 - A.L.P. Lighting Components, Inc.
3691 - Energy Sales
3691 - Entenmann-Rovin Company
3691 - Exide Corporation
3691 - Fedco Electronics Inc.
3691 - Hollingsworth & Vose Co.
3691 - Keystone Electronics Corp.
3691 - Mathews Assocs, Inc.
3691 - Pinnacle Research Institute
3691 - Portable Energy Products Inc
3691 - Power-Sonic Corp
3691 - Precious Plate Florida
3691 - SANYO Energy (USA) Corp
3691 - SEC Industrial Battery Co., Inc.
3691 - US Battery Manufacturing Co
3692 - La Marche Mfg. Company (Mfr)
3692 - Mathews Assocs, Inc.
3692 - W & W Mfg.
3692 - Yuasa, Inc.
3694 - Benshaw, Inc.
3694 - C.E. Niehoff & Co., Inc.
3694 - Harco Manufacturing Co.
3694 - Katolight Corp.
3694 - Reagan Equipment Co., Inc.
3694 - United States Energy Corp
3694 - Viking Enterprises
3694 - Xenia Mfg. Co.
3695 - GreenDisk Inc
3695 - Prospect Machine Products, Inc.
3695 - R.B. Annis Company, Inc.
3695 - Tape Duplicators, Inc.
3698 - B Q Products Inc.
3698 - Bow Industries, Inc.
3698 - Security Engineered Machinery Co.
3699 - Advantor Corp.
3699 - Autogate
3699 - Autosplice, Inc.
3699 - Boon Edam, Inc.
3699 - Branson Ultrasonics Corp.
3699 - Calvert Co., Inc.
3699 - Cardkey Systems Inc
3699 - Con-Tech Power Systems, Inc.
3699 - Cooper Industries
3699 - Electronic Packaging Co., Inc.
3699 - Fisher Research Laboratory
3699 - Gilbert Industries Inc.
3699 - Keri Systems Inc
3699 - Lasag
3699 - Lester Electrical Of Nebraska, Inc.

3699 - M & E Components, Inc.
3699 - OSI Security Devices
3699 - P T R-Precision Technologies, Inc.
3699 - Se-Kure Controls, Inc.
3699 - Secura Key
3699 - Sergeant At Arms Entry Systems
3699 - Shock Tech, Inc.
3699 - Stetco, Inc.
3699 - Tube Light Co., Inc.
3699 - Uniphase, Laser Division
3711 - Darley & Co., W. S.
3711 - G M M Van Dock Distributors
3711 - Promotional Trim Components
3711 - Quality Industries, Inc.
3711 - Rolls-Royce & Bertley Motors Cars
3711 - ZAP Power Systems
3713 - Advanced Vehicle Systems, Inc.
3713 - CEI "Pacer"
3713 - E-Z Lift Ltd International
3713 - El Dorado National Co.
3713 - Gregory Truck Body & Fire
3713 - Grote Industries, Inc.
3713 - High Country Proco
3713 - Paramount Truck Body & Equip
3713 - Penates General Welding
3713 - Southern Truck Equipment Inc
3713 - Spalding Products
3713 - Transit Sales International
3713 - Wayne Engineering Corporation
3714 - A. Berger, Inc.
3714 - Autotech USA
3714 - Autotek Corp.
3714 - Budge Industries, Inc.
3714 - Crane Cams, Inc.
3714 - Crown Divisions Of Trans Pro, Inc.,
3714 - D & H Enterprises
3714 - Donmar Enterprises, Inc.
3714 - Dura Automotive: Stockton Seat
3714 - Dvorak Automatic & Machine
3714 - Energy Suspension
3714 - Engineered Products Co.
3714 - Excel Of Stockton
3714 - Fleet Air Industries
3714 - Foote Axle & Forge Company LLC
3714 - Freedom Driving Aids
3714 - Gasboy International, Inc.
3714 - Go Industries, Inc.
3714 - H P J, Inc.
3714 - Hayes Lemmerz International, Inc.
3714 - Hebco Products, Inc.
3714 - Horizon Technology Group
3714 - Industrial Gastruck, Inc.
3714 - Interdynamics, Inc.
3714 - K-D Lamp Company (Mfr)
3714 - Malvern Racing
3714 - Mathers Controls, Inc.
3714 - Mfm Sensors Inc
3714 - Mize & Co., Inc.
3714 - Perry Equipment Corp.
3714 - Phillips Industries
3714 - Pretty Products, Inc. / Rubber Queen
3714 - Rancho Suspension
3714 - Rofren Disc Brake, Inc.
3714 - Roll Master Corporation
3714 - Rubber Queen
3714 - Screw Conveyor Corp. (Mfr)
3714 - Spring Valley Mfg., Inc.
3714 - Stemco, Inc.
3714 - Synergy International Inc.
3714 - Tasker Metal Products
3714 - Tripac International, Inc.
3714 - Truck Equipment Sales, Inc.
3714 - Tucson Alternator Exchange Inc
3714 - U.S. Axle, Inc. (Mfr)
3714 - United Textile
3714 - Unlimited Quality Products
3714 - Whipple International
3715 - Borco Equipment Co.
3715 - Chariot Mfg. Co., Inc.
3715 - Circle S Trailers Inc.
3715 - Dual-Tech, Inc.
3715 - Gem State Manufacturing Inc
3715 - Kann Mfg. Corp.

3715 - Kendon Industries Inc
3715 - Sooner Trailer Mfg. Co., Inc.
3716 - Fleetwood Enterprises Inc
3716 - Trail Wagons Inc
3721 - Gulfstream Aerospace Corp.
3721 - MSI International
3721 - Micco Aircraft Co.
3724 - Austin Continental Industries, Inc.
3724 - Covington Aircraft Engine
3724 - Nelson Aircraft Corp.
3724 - Premier Turbines
3724 - Purdy Corp.
3724 - Turbo Specialists LLC.
3728 - A M Precision Machining, Inc.
3728 - Aero-Mach Labs, Inc.
3728 - Aerospace Control Products, Inc.
3728 - Airborne Technologies, Inc.
3728 - Athens Industries, Inc.
3728 - Britt Metal Processing, Inc.
3728 - Caravan International
3728 - GNY Equipment LLC
3728 - Golden Circle Air, Inc.
3728 - Hydroform USA Inc
3728 - Nell Joy Industries, Inc.
3728 - Nordam Group Inc., Tranparencies
3728 - Precise Flight Inc
3728 - Rockwell International Corp., Collins
3728 - Rosen Product Development Inc
3728 - S & S Precision Machine Corp.
3728 - Santa Monica Propeller Inc
3728 - Scotia Technology Div., Lakes Region
3728 - Sky Mfg. Co.
3728 - Solo Enterprise Corporation
3728 - Spectrum Aeromed, Inc.
3728 - Sunstrand Corporation
3728 - Syncro Air Lift Corp
3728 - Texas Almet Inc.
3728 - Texas Composite Inc.
3728 - Volumatic, Inc.
3728 - Worldwide Filter
3730 - Penn Yan Marine Mfg. Corp.
3731 - Deep Ocean Engineering Inc
3731 - El Dorado National Co.
3731 - INTERDEVCO & Associates
3731 - Penn Yan Marine Mfg. Corp.
3731 - Phoenix Barge Corporation
3732 - Alaska Airboats
3732 - Bass Hunter Boats Inc.
3732 - Bumper Boats, Inc.
3732 - Harken International, Ltd.
3732 - MSI International
3732 - Mariah Boats Inc.
3732 - Master Marine, Inc.
3732 - Nordic Boats, Inc.
3732 - Pedigree Cats Inc
3732 - Peregrine Marine, Inc.
3732 - Premium Parasail Boats, Inc.
3732 - Ship Chandler
3732 - Star Brite
3743 - Brookville Mining Equipment Corp.
3743 - Filpro Corporation
3743 - MSI International
3743 - National Electric Gate Co.
3743 - Pandrol Jackson Inc.
3743 - Plymouth Industries, Inc.
3743 - Portec Rail Products Inc.
3743 - Snyder Equipment Co., Inc.
3743 - Strato, Inc.
3743 - Whiting Corporation
3751 - Big Bike Parts
3751 - Harley-Davidson, Inc.
3751 - ZAPWORLD.COM, One Power
3761 - Lockheed Martin Launching Systems
3764 - Atlantic Research Corp., Unit of
3769 - DNE Technologies Inc.
3769 - Fay & Quartermaine Machining
3769 - Guard Lee, Inc.
3792 - S O N Corp.
3795 - Charles E Gillman Company
3799 - Custom Trailer
3799 - E-Z-Go Textron
3799 - Elmco, Inc.
3799 - Evans Mfg. Co., John Evans Trailers

3799 - Hyundai Precision & Industry
3799 - Independent Trailer & Equip Co
3799 - Karavan Trailers, Inc.
3799 - Midland Steel Products Co.
3799 - Neighborhood Electric Vehicle Co
3799 - Powertech! Marine Propellers
3799 - Protection Development International
3799 - Silver Lite Trailers Inc
3799 - Trail-Rite Inc
3799 - Waterland Mfg., Inc.
3799 - Whiting Corporation
3811 - Omnimark Instrument Corp
3811 - The Steinlite Corp.(Mfr)
3812 - AZUR Enviromental
3812 - Advanced Marine Technology Corp.
3812 - Allen Osborne Associates Inc
3812 - American Traffic Systems Inc
3812 - Aqua Signal Corp.
3812 - Basic Electronics Inc
3812 - DRS Precision Echo
3812 - Enterprise Electronics Corp.
3812 - Flir Systems Inc
3812 - Frasca International, Inc.
3812 - Garrett Metal Detectors
3812 - Geophysical Survey Systems, Inc.
3812 - Litton Data Systems, Division
3812 - Litton Industries Inc
3812 - Litton Systems, Inc. Laser Sys, Inc.
3812 - Oceanographic Industries, Inc.
3812 - Sunstrand Corporation
3812 - Survival Safety Engineering, Inc.
3812 - Texas Electronics, Inc.
3816 - Chromaline Corp.
3821 - Ad-Vance Magnetics, Inc.
3821 - Billups-Rothenberg, Inc.
3821 - Cargille Laboratories, Inc.
3821 - Dynaoptic-Motion Corporation
3821 - F&J Specialty Products, Inc.
3821 - Germfree Laboratories, Inc.
3821 - Glas-Col Apparatus Company (Mfr)
3821 - Granutec Inc
3821 - Hamilton Bell Co., Inc.
3821 - Nor-Lake, Inc. (Mfr)
3821 - Organomation Associates, Inc.
3821 - Progressive Industries, Inc.
3821 - Sanda Corp.
3821 - Spectral Energy Corp.
3821 - The Steinlite Corp.(Mfr)
3822 - Condar Co.
3822 - King Buck Technology
3822 - Mensor Corporation
3822 - Pass & Seymour/Legrand(Mfr)
3822 - S O R, Inc.
3822 - Simonds Mfg. Corp.
3822 - Smart Sensors Inc.
3822 - Teletrol Systems, Inc.
3822 - Trane Company, The
3822 - Tridelta Industries, Inc.
3823 - ASTI
3823 - Acu-Gage Systems
3823 - Air Instruments & Measurements Inc.
3823 - American MSI Corp
3823 - Apollo
3823 - Artisan Controls Corporation (Mfr)
3823 - Baldwin Environmental Inc
3823 - Bec Controls Corp.
3823 - Bristol Babbock Inc.
3823 - Caldon, Inc.
3823 - Calibron Systems Inc
3823 - Chemtrac Systems, Inc.
3823 - Cincinnati Test Systems, Inc.
3823 - Cleaver-Brooks
3823 - Common Sensing Inc
3823 - Dynasonics
3823 - Dynasonics-Divison of Racine
3823 - Endress & Hauser, Inc.
3823 - Engineered Inspection Systems
3823 - Environmental Dynamics, Inc.(Mfr)
3823 - Gas Tech Inc
3823 - Geotech Environmental Equipment
3823 - Hach Company
3823 - Helicoid Div., Bristol Babbock Inc.
3823 - Innovative Sensors, Incorporated

3911 - Gary Stull Goldsmith
3911 - Maui Divers Of Hawaii, Ltd.
3911 - Morning Sun
3911 - Olympia Gold Inc.
3911 - Sardelli & Sons, Inc., T.
3911 - Shine Jewelry
3911 - Skatell's Jewelers
3911 - Tres Rios Silver
3914 - Grand Silver Co., Inc.
3914 - Haber Co., D. W.
3914 - Hampshire Pewter Co.
3914 - Rosary House, Inc.
3915 - Elias Diamond Cutting
3915 - Fuller & Son Co., George H.
3915 - Vicki's Jewelry
3931 - Shubb Capos
3931 - Super-Sensitive Musical String Co.
3931 - Torres Engineering
3942 - Bell Ceramics Inc. (Mfr)
3944 - Athearn Inc
3944 - Carter Brothers
3944 - Discovery Toys
3944 - Erin's Original Horseplay Rugs
3944 - International Hobbycraft Co., Inc.
3944 - Interpretive Marketing Products
3944 - John N Hansen Co Inc
3944 - Jonti-Craft, Inc.
3944 - Luckicup Company
3944 - Parris Mfg. Co.
3944 - Pelican Co
3944 - Pressner & Co., Inc., M.
3944 - Safeline Corp
3944 - Shuffle Master, Inc.
3944 - University Games
3949 - Accu Rest, Inc.
3949 - Alfa Southwest Maquiladora Svc
3949 - Aqua Jogger
3949 - Arrowhead Athletics
3949 - Artisan Golf
3949 - Astrup Co. (Distributor)
3949 - B C I Burke Co., LLC
3949 - Biscayne Rod Mfg., Inc.
3949 - Centerline Sports Inc
3949 - Crown Gym Mats, Inc.
3949 - Diamond Head Golf Club Mfg Co
3949 - Duffy Golf, Inc.
3949 - Gibbs Products Inc
3949 - Goal Oriented Inc
3949 - Horner Discus International
3949 - IM & M Exercise Equipment Inc
3949 - Idaho Sewing For Sports
3949 - Imperial Pools Inc.
3949 - Jaypro Corporation
3949 - Jim Teeny, Inc.
3949 - Johnny Gibson Gym Equipment Co
3949 - Jonti-Craft, Inc.
3949 - KD Water Sports
3949 - Kompan Inc
3949 - Lifetime Products Inc
3949 - Load Llama Products
3949 - M.Putterman & Company Inc.
3949 - Master Line U S A
3949 - Michaels Of Oregon Co
3949 - Mr. V's, Inc.
3949 - O'Brien International
3949 - PCIE DBA; The France Group
3949 - Porter Athletic Equipment (Mfr)
3949 - Q C A Pools & Spas
3949 - RAM Sports Inc
3949 - Rio Products International Inc
3949 - Sims Bait Mfg. Co.
3949 - Ski Co Inc
3949 - Sprint Rothhammer
3949 - Sprint/Rothhammer
3949 - Stewart Surfboards Inc
3949 - Tape-O Corporation
3949 - Trophy Glove Co.
3949 - True Pitch, Inc.
3949 - Turbo 2-N-1 Grips Inc. (Mfr)
3949 - Unique Sports Products, Inc.
3949 - Vantage Bowling Corporation
3949 - Variety Widget Products Inc
3949 - Volant Sports, LLC

3949 - Wahoo International
3951 - Autopoint, Inc.
3951 - Fisher Space Pen Co
3951 - Matel Bank and Desk Accessories
3952 - Art Institute Glitter
3952 - C2F, Inc.
3952 - General Pencil Co.
3952 - National Pen Corp.
3953 - American Marking, Inc.
3953 - American Traditional Stencils
3953 - Electro Stylus
3953 - Independent Ink Inc
3953 - Qwikstamp Corporation
3953 - Schwerdtle Stamp Co., Inc.
3953 - Shachihata
3953 - StenSource International Inc
3953 - Wendell's, Inc.
3955 - Coding Products
3955 - Frye Tech, Inc.
3955 - Paxar Iimak
3955 - Ribbon Division Inc
3955 - Rittenhouse Co
3961 - Entenmann-Rovin Company
3961 - Future Primitive Designs Ltd
3961 - House Of Fashion Jewelry
3961 - Inch of Gold Inc(Mfr)
3961 - J Hewitt Inc
3961 - The Alchemists Inc
3961 - Uncas MFG. Company (Mfr)
3965 - American & Efird, Inc.
3965 - Eaton Corp., Engineered Fasteners
3965 - JHB International, Inc.
3991 - 3M IBD/Export.
3991 - Abco Products
3991 - California Mop Manufacturing
3991 - International Hobbycraft Co., Inc.
3991 - M & E Mfg. Co.
3991 - Monahan Co., The Thomas
3991 - P H B Inc.
3991 - Quali-Tech Manufacturing Co
3993 - 3M IBD/Export.
3993 - ASD, Inc. , Architectural Signage
3993 - Action Media Technologies Inc
3993 - Adaptive Micro Systems, Inc.
3993 - All Neon & Signs
3993 - Alpha 1 Studio, Inc.
3993 - American Sign Company
3993 - Best Sign Systems
3993 - Brevis Corp
3993 - CA Signs
3993 - Colite International
3993 - Consolidated Display Co., Inc.
3993 - Cooley Sign & Digital Imaging, A
3993 - Couch & Philippi Inc
3993 - Daktronics, Inc.
3993 - Design Display, Inc.
3993 - Dezion Signs
3993 - Dieterich & Ball Incorporated
3993 - Fox Laminating Co., Inc.
3993 - Grande Ronde Sign Co
3993 - Hi-Tech Electronic Displays
3993 - King Design International
3993 - Lynne Signs, Lori
3993 - M M I Display Group, Inc.
3993 - Mainstreet Menu Systems
3993 - Moser & Co. Neon Specialists
3993 - Muller Studios
3993 - Nameplates, Inc.
3993 - National Pen Corporation
3993 - Neon Fx Sign & Display
3993 - Never Boring Design Associates
3993 - P & D Polygraphics, Inc.
3993 - P & M Sign, Inc.
3993 - Presentation South, Inc.
3993 - Seton Name Plate Company
3993 - Sign Connection
3993 - Sign Products International
3993 - Signart, Inc.
3993 - Signs & Signs, Inc.
3993 - Young Electric Sign Company Boise
3995 - Southern Mausoleums, Inc.
3996 - American Hi-Tech Flooring Co.
3996 - Congoleum Corp.

3996 - Crossfield Products Corp
3996 - International Paint Inc.
3999 - A Tail We Could Wag
3999 - ARC Industries Inc.
3999 - Alaska Herb Tea Co. (Mfr)
3999 - Allied Dynamics Corp.
3999 - Authentic Mexican Imports
3999 - Blue Feather Products Inc
3999 - California Exotic Novelties
3999 - California Fruit Packing Company
3999 - Chemical Packaging Corp.
3999 - Continental Sprayers / AFA Products,
3999 - Dalloz Safety
3999 - Elge Precision Machining, Inc.
3999 - Elliott Bay Industries
3999 - Flo's Wreaths
3999 - Flowery Beauty Products, Inc.
3999 - Frigid Fluid Co.
3999 - GDC Casino Tokens
3999 - General Robotics Corporation
3999 - George F. Cram Company Inc., The
3999 - Global Architectural Models
3999 - Identicator Inc.
3999 - J.M.S. Ltd
3999 - Knud Nielsen Company, Inc.
3999 - Lectralite Corporation
3999 - MMC International Corp.
3999 - Marianna Importers, Exporters &
3999 - Marty Wolf Game Co
3999 - Meilink Safe Co., A Fireking
3999 - Mistco, Inc.
3999 - Mountain Meadows Pet Products
3999 - New Pig Corporation (Mfr)
3999 - Original Mink Oil Co.
3999 - Preserved Treescapes Intl
3999 - Pressner & Co., Inc., M.
3999 - Purr-Fect Growlings
3999 - Royal Dental Manufacturing Co.
3999 - Seton Name Plate Company
3999 - Silkwood Wholesale, Inc.
3999 - Stack-On Products
3999 - TPL Communications, Inc.
3999 - The Morning Star Packing Company
3999 - Toepperweins Of Texas
3999 - Trans Air Manufacturing
3999 - U.S. Pet Products
3999 - Vitec, Inc.
3999 - Wildlife Supply Company / Trippensee
3999 - Yaley Enterprises, Inc.
4213 - AdvantageTransportation Inc.
4213 - Central Air Freight Inc.
4213 - Desmoines Truck Brokers Inc.
4213 - Everett J. Prescott
4213 - Straightway Inc.
4214 - A.N. Deringer, Inc.-Hdqrs.
4214 - Big Soo Terminal
4214 - Boasso America Corporation
4214 - Canal Cartage Company
4214 - Circle International
4214 - Houston Transfer & Storage Co.
4214 - Jan Packaging, Inc.
4214 - Mawson & Mawson Inc.
4214 - McGovern G. T. Trucking &
4214 - Overland Express Company Inc.
4214 - Pace Motor Lines Inc.
4214 - Penn Terminals Inc.
4214 - Southern Warehouse Corporation
4214 - Transoceanic Shipping Company, Inc.
4214 - Van's Delivery Service, Inc.
4221 - Zen Noh Grain
4222 - Southwest Storage
4226 - Schroeder United Van Lines
4491 - Georgia Ports Authority
4491 - Transoceanic Shipping Company, Inc.
4510 - Omega Products, Inc.
4512 - Central Air Freight Inc.
4512 - Era Aviation Inc.
4512 - Lufthansa Cargo, Executive Offices
4522 - Central Air Freight Inc.
4522 - Petroleum Helicopters
4522 - Straightway Inc.
4581 - Arinc Incorporated
4581 - Charlatte America

4581 - New Orleans International Airport/
4731 - "K" Line America, Inc.
4731 - A.N. Deringer, Inc.-Hdqrs.
4731 - AMSER Logistics, Inc.
4731 - AdvantageTransportation Inc.
4731 - Airgroup Express/Airgroup
4731 - All Points International Inc.
4731 - Alliance International
4731 - Apollo Warehouse, Inc.
4731 - Argents Express Group
4731 - Atlantic Cold Storage Corporation
4731 - Ayala Luis A. Colon Sucrs. Inc.
4731 - Barner, Jerry M. & Sons
4731 - Bart Trucking
4731 - Big Soo Terminal
4731 - Bigge Crane & Rigging Co.
4731 - Brown Alcantar & Brown Inc.
4731 - Burlington Air Express Inc.
4731 - Burlington Motor Carriers
4731 - Business Aviation Courier
4731 - C & L Transportation Inc.
4731 - CBC International, Inc.
4731 - CLM, Inc.
4731 - Cagema Agencies Inc.
4731 - Cambell & Gardiner
4731 - Campbell & Gardiner, Inc.
4731 - Canal Cartage Company
4731 - Carmenco International
4731 - Central Air Freight Inc.
4731 - Central Transportation Systems
4731 - Chantilly Freight Corporation
4731 - Chase Leavitt & Company
4731 - Chickawaw Container Services
4731 - Circle International
4731 - Columbus Line USA, Inc.
4731 - Commercial International Forwarding
4731 - Corcoran International Corp.
4731 - Coughlin Logistics
4731 - DANZAS Corporation
4731 - Dan Transport Corporation
4731 - Dartrans, Inc.
4731 - Delgado R. E. Inc.
4731 - Distribution Services of America
4731 - Equipsa, Inc.
4731 - Euro-American Air Frt. Fwdg Co.,
4731 - Expressway USA Freightlines Inc.
4731 - FPA Customs Brokers, Inc.
4731 - FalconRoc Management Services, Inc.
4731 - Farmland Transportation Inc.
4731 - Fast Air Carrier S.A.
4731 - Ferrer Brokers, Inc.
4731 - Fillette Green Shipping Services
4731 - Foreign Trade Zone 42
4731 - Foreign Trade Zone 72
4731 - Friendly Public Warehouses Inc.
4731 - Fritz Companies
4731 - Fritz Maritime Agencies
4731 - Gonzalez T.H. Inc
4731 - Gonzalez T.H. Inc.
4731 - Hanjin Shipping Co. Ltd.
4731 - Hanlon International
4731 - Hawks Express Inc.
4731 - Held & Associates, Inc.
4731 - Hendrix, Miles, Hendrix Company
4731 - Horizon Forwarders Inc.
4731 - Houston Transfer & Storage Co.
4731 - Hydra Management Inc.
4731 - Ideal Transportation Co. Inc.
4731 - Incare Cargo Services
4731 - Inter-Jet Systems, Inc.
4731 - Inter-World Customs Broker Inc.
4731 - Inter-World Customs Broker, Inc.
4731 - Interbulk Shipping, Inc.
4731 - Interfreight Inc.
4731 - J. H. World Express, Inc.
4731 - J.J. Trucking Services of Jacksonville,
4731 - Jan Packaging, Inc.
4731 - Jensen, Norman G., Inc.
4731 - Jet Air Service, Inc.
4731 - Jet Import Brokers
4731 - K & K Express
4731 - Keen, R. H. & Co., Inc.
4731 - Kirkpatrick Shipping Inc.

4731 - Krieger, Norman, Inc.
4731 - L. D. Tonsager & Sons, Inc.
4731 - LaBelle Rothery Movers, Inc.
4731 - Landstar Ranger, Inc.
4731 - Lazer Transportation Services
4731 - Lin Container Freight Station &
4731 - Lufthansa Cargo AG
4731 - Lufthansa Cargo, Executive Offices
4731 - Mark VII International
4731 - Marmara, Inc.
4731 - Match Maker, The
4731 - McClary, Swift & Co., Inc.
4731 - Mediterranean Shipping Company
4731 - Migar Enterprises, Inc.
4731 - Moran, J. F. Co., Inc.
4731 - Movement Control, Inc.
4731 - National Customs Brokers &
4731 - Nippon Express USA, Inc.
4731 - Norman G. Jensen, Inc.
4731 - Ortiz Villafane, Rene, Inc.
4731 - Overland Express Company Inc.
4731 - Overnite Transportation Co.
4731 - Pace Motor Lines Inc.
4731 - Penn Terminals Inc.
4731 - Port Elizabeth Terminal & Warehouse
4731 - Price Transfer, Inc.
4731 - Quality Customs Broker, Inc.
4731 - R & T Truck Inc.
4731 - Rapid Air & Ocean
4731 - Rausch, Ted L. Co., The
4731 - Respond Cargo Services Corp.
4731 - Roadway Express, Inc.
4731 - Robinson H.W. & Company Inc.
4731 - Rogers & Brown Custom Brokers,
4731 - Rosy Services Forwarders Corp.
4731 - Schenker International, Inc.
4731 - Schroeder United Van Lines
4731 - Seamodal Transport Corp.
4731 - Senderex Cargo Co., Inc.
4731 - Shinwa (USA) Inc.
4731 - Southern Warehouse Corporation
4731 - St. John Bros. Inc.
4731 - Stewart Alexander & Company Inc.
4731 - Straightway Inc.
4731 - Superior Air Freight
4731 - T Transportation, Inc.
4731 - Tampa Bay International Terminals,
4731 - Torner International, Inc. / Edmundo
4731 - Torner, Edmundo Customhouse
4731 - Trans-Border Customs Services Inc.
4731 - Transmarine Navigation Corporation
4731 - Transoceanic Shipping Company, Inc.
4731 - Transus Container Division
4731 - Transwood, Inc.
4731 - Trism Inc.
4731 - Vanco Heavy Lift C.F.S.
4731 - WTS of Houston, Inc.
4731 - Western Crating Inc.
4731 - World Commerce Forwarding, Inc.
4731 - World Freight Audit Co.
4731 - Worldlink Logistics, Inc.
4783 - ARC Industries Inc.
4783 - Jan Packaging, Inc.
4783 - Pierce Packaging Company
4783 - Schroeder United Van Lines
4783 - Straightway Inc.
4783 - Transoceanic Shipping Company, Inc.
4783 - Western Crating Inc.
4789 - Boasso America Corporation
4789 - Central Air Freight Inc.
4789 - Jan Packaging, Inc.
4813 - Micon Telecommunications Inc
4813 - OTM Engineering, Inc.
4899 - Black Box Corporation
4941 - Morgan Denver Sales Co
4953 - BBC International Inc.
4953 - Simonds Mfg. Corp.
4953 - Vanguard Research Inc. VRI
4959 - Larson & Associates Inc
4971 - Hector Turf
5011 - 3CX
5011 - ATM Exchange, Inc, The
5011 - EMC Technologies

5011 - Maxport International
5011 - Radiant Communications Corporation
5011 - Tru-Stone Corp.
5012 - A-Z Bus Sales, Inc.
5012 - Alkantec, Inc.
5012 - Arrow Truck Saels Inc.
5012 - Beall Corp.
5012 - Heil Trading Co. Inc.
5012 - Maple Valley Hardwoods
5012 - Mastin Motors
5012 - Murray, Thomas W.
5012 - Phillips Motors, Larry
5012 - Southwest Peterbilt GMC
5013 - American Optimum
5013 - Aquion Partners, L.P.
5013 - Ase Supply Inc
5013 - Atlantic Pacific Automotive
5013 - Atlantic Research Corp., Unit of
5013 - Automatic Transmission Parts, Inc.
5013 - Cofap of America
5013 - Custom Accessories Inc
5013 - Hi-Pro Industries, Inc.
5013 - Hollingsworth & Vose Co.
5013 - Intraco Corp.
5013 - Justice Brothers, Inc.
5013 - K & W Products
5013 - Magna Interior Systems
5013 - Michigan Wholesalers Automotive
5013 - Midwest Truck & Auto
5013 - Minco Sales Corp.
5013 - PAI Industries Inc. (Mfr)
5013 - Palm Peterbilt - GMC Trucks, Inc.
5013 - Parts Services International LLC
5013 - Paulik International Co.
5013 - Perry Co., The
5013 - Petersen Products Co.
5013 - Prestige Auto
5013 - Rugby Manufacturing Co.
5013 - Simpson Tool Box Co
5013 - Star Brite
5013 - Treatment Products Ltd.
5014 - Hawker Pacific, Inc.
5014 - Myers Industries, Inc., Myers Tire
5014 - Ralph Tire & Service, Inc.
5014 - Tyson Seafood Group, Inc.
5015 - All Day Used Auto Parts
5015 - Export Parts Center
5015 - J.D. International Used Auto Parts
5015 - Tri-Star International, Inc.
5021 - All American Office Products Inc
5021 - Designers Resource, DBA Country &
5021 - Flaghouse, Inc.
5021 - Incon Overseas Marketing, Inc.
5021 - Marcus Brothers
5021 - Unique Originals, Inc.
5023 - Allegra Industries, Inc.
5023 - Arabel
5023 - Authentic Mexican Imports
5023 - Barth & Dreyfuss of California
5023 - Central Lock & Hardware Supply Co.
5031 - Cascade Empire
5031 - Fiberesin Industries, Inc.
5031 - Global Market Partners, Inc.
5031 - Integra Window & Door Inc
5031 - Interdynamics, Inc.
5031 - North American Wood Products, Inc.
5031 - PDG Associates, Inc.
5031 - Quality Forest Products
5031 - Ram Forest Products
5031 - S.G. International
5031 - Timber Products
5032 - Lotus Exim International
5032 - State Insulation Corp.
5033 - Celotex Corporation
5039 - A.G. Equipment, Inc.
5039 - Acorn Industries Inc. (Mfr)
5039 - Border Products Corp
5039 - CMA Incorporated
5043 - National Research & Chemical Co.
5044 - Minolta Corporation
5044 - W.A. Charnstrom Co., Inc.
5045 - A'n D Cable Products Inc
5045 - Academic Distributing

5045 - Alkantec, Inc.
5045 - American Barcode Concepts
5045 - C. Hoelzle Associates Inc.
5045 - Euro-Tech Corporation
5045 - Information Specialist Inc
5045 - System Technology #1
5046 - AF Industries, Alvey Washing
5046 - Adaptive Micro Systems, Inc.
5046 - Alfa International Corporation
5046 - Extru-Tech, Inc.
5046 - Global Leasing & Sales, Inc.
5046 - Nevco Scoreboard Co.
5046 - R & D International Inc.
5047 - A.J. Buck & Son
5047 - Alkantec, Inc.
5047 - Becker-Parkin Dental Supply Co., Inc.
5047 - Biomedical International
5047 - Exelint International, Inc.
5047 - Flaghouse, Inc.
5047 - M.D. International Co.
5047 - Mass Medical Equipment
5047 - Microcurrent Research Inc
5047 - National Health Care, Inc.
5047 - Schnepper-International, Inc.
5047 - Smith & Nephew Inc.
5047 - South American Dental Exports
5047 - Trademark Medical
5048 - Arno International, Inc.
5048 - Cargille Laboratories, Inc.
5048 - Global Material Supply
5048 - Johnston Pumps
5048 - L.A.C. Leather Abrasive Co.
5048 - Maxport International
5048 - Optical Polymer Research, Inc.
5048 - Stellram
5049 - A. Daigger & Company, Inc.
5049 - Autron Incorporated
5049 - Quality Scientific Plastics
5049 - Service For Science & Industries
5049 - Thomas Scientific
5051 - AJ Weller
5051 - American Piping Products, Inc.
5051 - Eastern Europe Inc.
5051 - Guardian Metal Sales, Inc.
5051 - Incon Overseas Marketing, Inc.
5051 - Interstate Steel Inc.
5051 - Ohio Pipe & Steel Corp.
5051 - Olympia International, Div. of
5051 - Roberts Industries
5051 - SOS Metals, Inc.
5051 - Trade Metal Inc.
5051 - Univertical Corporation
5051 - World Equipment & Machine Sales
5052 - Eastern Europe Inc.
5063 - Alkantec, Inc.
5063 - Border States Electric Supply
5063 - Cummins SW/Power Systems
5063 - Ericson Manufacturing, Inc.
5063 - Forney
5063 - Garrett Sound & Lighting
5063 - Howe & Howe Lexis Sales Corp
5063 - Mitronic Trading Corp
5063 - Pearson Southwest Marketing
5063 - Platt Electric Supply
5064 - Anaheim Marketing International
5064 - MG Electronics
5065 - Advanced Circuit Enterprises
5065 - Advantor Corp.
5065 - Atlas/Soundolier, Atapco Security &
5065 - Delta Communications & Electronics
5065 - Eastern Europe Inc.
5065 - Eby Co.
5065 - HMW Enterprises, Inc.
5065 - Hartland Sales
5065 - Heller Industries
5065 - Inter-Technical Export Corporatioin
5065 - Kalman Electronics Of Arizona
5065 - Keystone Electronics Corp.
5065 - Leavitt Communications, Inc.
5065 - Mitronic Trading Corp
5065 - Norstan Electronics Inc
5065 - Ocalas Corporation
5065 - SEOCAL, Incorporated

5065 - The Phoenix Company of Chicago,
5065 - Thunderball Marketing
5072 - Action Tool Co., Inc.
5072 - C.R. Laurence Company, Inc.
5072 - Central Lock & Hardware Supply Co.
5072 - Jensen Tools, Inc.
5072 - Mitronic Trading Corp
5072 - Orgill Inc.
5072 - State Industrial Supply Corp
5074 - C.P. Environmental Filters Inc.
5074 - Chlorine & Chemical Supply Co.
5074 - Orgill Inc.
5074 - Pacific Plastics
5074 - Premier Manufactured Systems, Inc.
5074 - Radiator Specialty Co.
5074 - T&S Exports, Div. T&S Brass (Mfr)
5074 - Waterwise
5075 - Calgon Carbon Corporation (Mfr)
5075 - Moli-Tron Company Inc.
5075 - Noland
5075 - Rychter Trading Corporation
5075 - WEBB Distributors Inc
5081 - Black Box Corporation
5082 - A.G. Equipment, Inc.
5082 - Able Builders Export, Inc.
5082 - Aftermarket Parts Inc.
5082 - C & R Industries Inc
5082 - Global Parts & Equipment
5082 - Heavy Equipment Parts Co., Div. of
5082 - Hoss Equipment
5082 - Michels Machinery Co
5082 - Multiquip
5082 - Nationwide Equipment
5082 - RDO Equipment Co
5082 - Schwing America, Inc.
5082 - Teleparts, Inc.
5082 - Triad Machinery Inc
5083 - A.G. Equipment, Inc.
5083 - Agro Industrial Management
5083 - Chick Master International, Inc.
5083 - High Country Plastics Inc
5083 - Northern Pump & Irrigation
5083 - Orgill Inc.
5083 - T-Systems International, Inc.
5083 - Universal Dairy Equipment
5084 - Ahern International Sales Corp.
5084 - Alaco Ladder Co.
5084 - Alan Ross Machinery Corp
5084 - Allpress Equipment Inc.
5084 - American European Systems
5084 - Astechnologies
5084 - Atlantic Machine Tools Inc.
5084 - Automatics & Machinery Co., Inc.
5084 - Barber-Nichols Incorporated
5084 - C.M. Graphics
5084 - Carolina Medical, Inc.
5084 - Commision Brokers, Inc.
5084 - Cranston Apparel Fabrics
5084 - Crown Hollander Inc.
5084 - Cutting Edge Tool Supply Inc
5084 - Dec-E-Tech
5084 - Dresser Instrument Div.
5084 - Dynamic Air Inc.
5084 - Ernest F Mariani Co.
5084 - Gafco-Worldwide, Inc.
5084 - General Tool & Supply Co
5084 - Glasscraft Inc
5084 - Hall-Welter Co.
5084 - Hamre Equipment
5084 - Harris-Welco Co.
5084 - Hatch & Kirk
5084 - Hurdt & Associates Machinery
5084 - Jaccard Corporation
5084 - James Heavy Equipment Specialist
5084 - Joseph Industries, Inc.
5084 - Lobo Machinery Corp.
5084 - MAC Equipment, Inc.
5084 - Machinery Dealers Natl. Assn.
5084 - Methods West Machine Tools
5084 - Micropure Filtration, Inc.
5084 - Miller Corp., Harry
5084 - Minco Sales Corp.
5084 - Moos Machine Works

5084 - Morgan Denver Sales Co
5084 - Motoman, Inc (Mfr)
5084 - Norman Levy Associates
5084 - Omni Trade International
5084 - Pacific Utility Equipment Co
5084 - Parts Services International LLC
5084 - Parts Tires Imports
5084 - Perfection Machinery Sales, Inc.
5084 - Planet Machinery Company
5084 - Progressive Crane, Inc.
5084 - Resource Technology
5084 - Richard Sewing Machine
5084 - Sabel Engineering Corp.
5084 - Shindaiwa Inc
5084 - Sirex, Ltd.
5084 - Smart Products Inc
5084 - Southwestern Automation Systems,
5084 - Trident Tool, Inc.
5084 - Triton Equipment Corp.
5084 - UEI
5084 - United General Supply
5084 - Vibco, Inc.
5084 - Victor Metal Finishing Inc.
5084 - Vogler Equipment
5084 - Warner T. Lundahl, Inc.
5084 - World Equipment & Machine Sales
5085 - Abrasive Distributors Corp.
5085 - Alamia Inc
5085 - All American Containers, Inc.
5085 - C.R. Laurence Company, Inc.
5085 - CMO Enterprises Inc.
5085 - Century Spring Co., Inc.
5085 - Consolidated Purchasing Overseas
5085 - Cutting Edge Tool Supply Inc
5085 - D.B.C. Enterprises, Inc.
5085 - EPM Environmental, Inc.
5085 - Everett J. Prescott
5085 - Fitting House Inc
5085 - Goodyear Rubber Products Corp.
5085 - Helicoid Div., Bristol Babcock Inc.
5085 - Hercules Hydraulics Inc.
5085 - Hitachi Maxco, Inc.
5085 - International Air Filtration
5085 - International Tool Boxes
5085 - K & W Products
5085 - KLM International
5085 - Minco Sales Corp.
5085 - Moos Machine Works
5085 - O. Berk Company
5085 - Pierburg Instruments, Inc.
5085 - Plano International
5085 - Sepco (Mfr)
5085 - United States Can Company, Custom
5087 - HTA
5087 - Howard, Bill
5087 - Pagotto Industries
5087 - World Trade Exporters, Inc.
5088 - 3M IBD/Export.
5088 - Aerofast Ltd
5088 - American Tank & Vessel
5088 - Avjet Corporation
5088 - Boasso America Corporation
5088 - Hawker Pacific, Inc.
5088 - National Flight Sales Corporation
5088 - Olympic Aviation
5088 - Petroplast Chemical Corp.
5088 - Rhino Tool Co.
5091 - CMA Incorporated
5091 - Fathoms Plus
5091 - Flaghouse, Inc.
5091 - Gared Sports
5091 - Lamkin Corp.
5091 - Letro Products
5091 - Lindgren Pitman
5092 - CMA Incorporated
5092 - Shepher Distribution & Sales
5092 - Transworld Plush Toys, Inc.
5093 - A & S Metal Recycling, Inc.
5093 - AMI Trading
5093 - CMA Incorporated
5093 - General Waste Trading Company
5093 - Los Angeles Scrap Iron & Metal
5093 - Sheftel International

5094 - Accents In Sterling Inc
5094 - Classic Medallics, Inc. (Mfr)
5097 - Alpine Armoring Inc.
5097 - Biofix Holdings, Inc.
5097 - Cominter Corp.
5097 - Continental Cars, Inc.
5097 - Interpax
5097 - Intramar, Inc.
5097 - Kessler International Corp.
5097 - Lanca Sales, Inc.
5097 - MIA Express Inc.
5097 - Municipal Equipment Exports
5097 - Perfection Machinery
5097 - Pexim International
5097 - R.D.D. Enterprises
5097 - Sieflor
5097 - Waite, R. M. Company
5097 - Webco Trading
5098 - Action International
5098 - American Omni Trading
5098 - Amtrade International, Inc.
5098 - Bifrost
5098 - Century Multech
5098 - Egla International
5098 - Equity Industries
5098 - General Business International Trade
5098 - Hibel Corp., Edna
5098 - Home Dynamix
5098 - Impol Aluminum
5098 - Jianlibao America, Ltd.
5098 - Kowa California Inc.
5098 - Marcotex International
5098 - Nassau Tape & Webbing Mills, Inc.
5098 - National Pump
5098 - Nishizawa
5098 - Page Seed Co., Inc.
5098 - Paul Marsh, LLC
5098 - Peerless Industries, Inc.
5098 - Plasco, Inc.
5098 - Pride International
5098 - Professional Services International,
5098 - Richard Boas
5098 - Stylebuilt Accessories, Inc.
5098 - Summit Sales & Marketing
5098 - Watersaver International
5099 - Galow Trading
5099 - Garnac Grain
5099 - Global Market Partners, Inc.
5099 - Globe Shipping, Globe Ship
5099 - House of Spices
5099 - Innovair Corporation
5099 - Intracor-Familian International
5099 - JSAM
5099 - Jabitex Corporation
5099 - Noamex
5099 - Nuclear Security Services Corp.
5099 - Outdoor Cap
5099 - Pacific Cranes & Equipment Sales
5099 - Strapack, Inc.
5099 - Televentas
5099 - Texas Jasmine
5111 - Autron Incorporated
5111 - Unisource
5112 - B&G Export Management Associates
5112 - Hammett Co., Inc., J. L.
5113 - Advance Paper & Maintenance
5113 - American Fibre Supplies
5113 - B&G Export Management Associates
5113 - GTI Industries, Inc.
5113 - Hemisphere Enterprises
5122 - 3M IBD/Export.
5122 - A.J. Buck & Son
5122 - Amos Import/Export Management Co.
5122 - Beauty Plus Beauty Supply
5122 - Continental Group
5122 - Hollywood
5122 - J Hewitt Inc
5122 - Nabi
5122 - Napp Technologies
5122 - Scenario International Co.
5122 - Sonora Desert Trading Co
5131 - Absecon Mills, Inc.
5131 - Classic Medallics, Inc. (Mfr)

5131 - General Fabrics
5131 - General Waste Trading Company
5131 - Laren Industries
5131 - Manrob Sales
5131 - Medal Textiles, Inc.
5131 - Stantex
5131 - United Thread Mills
5136 - T-Shirts & Graphics
5136 - U. S. Cavalry, Inc.
5136 - UNI Hosiery Co., Inc.
5137 - North American Export Company
5137 - Tonex, Inc.
5141 - Accurate Ingredients
5141 - Atwood Richards
5141 - Basic Foods International, Inc.
5141 - Flora Distributors, Inc.
5141 - Foreign Trade Marketing
5141 - Ingredient Resources, Inc.
5141 - L & E International Service
5141 - PS International
5141 - Sew Feiel
5141 - United Grocers International
5142 - CMA Incorporated
5143 - International Custom Products
5143 - Marquis Distributing Co
5146 - Pafco Importing Co.
5146 - Tyson Seafood Group, Inc.
5147 - AJC International Inc.
5147 - Darling International Inc.
5147 - Stock Yards Packing Co. Inc.(Mfr)
5148 - AJC International Inc.
5148 - Cris-P Produce Co Inc
5148 - Denice & Filice Packing
5148 - Firman Pinkerton
5148 - Ohio Blenders
5148 - Oregon Potato
5148 - Premier Valley Foods, Inc.
5148 - R.B. Packing, Inc
5148 - Stemlit Growers
5149 - Catania Spagna
5149 - Cenex Harvest States Cooperatives
5149 - Hsu's Ginseng Enterprises, Inc.
5149 - International Multifoods Corp.
5149 - Natra US Inc.
5149 - Omni Trade International
5149 - Progenix Corporation(Mfr)
5149 - Silver Meadow Honey
5149 - Templar Food Products
5149 - Wilcox Natural Products(Mfr)
5153 - Farmers Rice Cooperative
5153 - Tradewinds International
5162 - APD
5162 - Gould Plastics, Inc.
5162 - VIE Americas, Inc.
5162 - WNA Comet
5169 - American Optimum
5169 - Bush Boake Allen
5169 - C.R. Laurence Company, Inc.
5169 - Chemdesign Corporation, A Bayer
5169 - Curecrete Distribution
5169 - IMC Chemical, Inc.
5169 - Incon Overseas Marketing, Inc.
5169 - Legge Co., Inc., Walter G.
5169 - M. Brown & Sons, Inc.
5169 - Medical Gas Services Inc
5169 - Nitta Gelatin
5169 - Organic Dyestuffs Corporation
5169 - Sunkist Growers, Inc., Processed
5169 - Todd Co., A.M.
5169 - Tonex, Inc.
5169 - Union Carbide Corporation
5169 - Universal Tech Corporation
5169 - West Agro, Inc.
5171 - Incon Overseas Marketing, Inc.
5172 - Astro Enterprises Int'l., Inc. (Mfr) /
5172 - Berkebile Oil Co.
5172 - Central Illinois Manufacturing Co
5172 - Kent Oil Company Inc.
5191 - AG Acid Inc
5191 - AMPAC Seed Company
5191 - Cantrell Hay
5191 - H & H Seed Company Inc
5191 - Harris Moran Seed Co.

5191 - Seedcraft
5191 - Ward Rugh, Inc.
5191 - Western Hybrid Seeds, Inc.
5191 - Young Farms
5192 - Hispanic Books Distributors Inc
5193 - Boyntons Botanicals
5193 - Greendale Nursery
5193 - Greenleaf Wholesale Florist Inc
5193 - Roland's Floral Supply
5193 - Stuewe and Sons, Inc.
5193 - Willow Creek Greenhouses Inc
5198 - Global Market Partners, Inc.
5198 - Organic Dyestuffs Corporation
5199 - David Adam Promotions Inc
5199 - GTI Industries, Inc.
5199 - General Waste Trading Company
5199 - Lighting Resources, Inc.
5199 - Pace Manufacturing, Inc.
5199 - Scotchman Industries, Inc.(Mfr)
5199 - Sol-R-Veil
5199 - Tenwood International
5211 - Karp Associates, Inc.
5211 - Marley Mouldings Inc.(Mfr)
5211 - Soliman Brothers
5211 - Stafast Roofing Products
5231 - Cherokee Glass & Mirrors
5231 - Sam's Auto Glass & Exports
5251 - Jaw Manufacturing Co.
5261 - Coffey Seed, Coffey Forage Seeds,
5411 - Shurfine
5461 - Anderson Bakery Company, Inc.
5499 - Catalina Food Ingredients
5511 - Big Abe No.1. Inc. Auto Sales,
5511 - Cars & Custom Inc.
5521 - Crown Truck Sales
5521 - Mustang Auto Sales
5531 - U.T.C. Tires & Rubber Comp.
5531 - World Trading
5561 - Rivers Bus & RV Sales
5571 - Pro Electric Vehicles, Inc.
5599 - U.S. Airmotive
5651 - T-Shirts & Graphics
5699 - T-Shirts & Graphics
5712 - Atlas/Soundolier, Atapco Security &
5712 - Ochman Systems, Edward
5713 - Penichet Carpet
5731 - Juno International
5734 - Ochman Systems, Edward
5812 - Afassco, Inc.
5812 - Proctor Companies
5855 - Norotos Inc
5912 - Afassco, Inc.
5941 - BCI Burke Co., Inc.
5943 - Galloway Office Supplies &
5943 - Ochman Systems, Edward
5945 - Promotional Resources Group
5949 - American Professional Quilting
5961 - Coburn Company, Inc.
5963 - Milcon, Inc.
5963 - Ultimate International
5973 - Ochman Systems, Edward
5999 - Anicom Inc.
5999 - Classic Medallics, Inc. (Mfr)
6021 - First Security Bank
6061 - AM Castle Employee Federal Credit
6099 - First Security Bank
6099 - Trading Alliance Division/MTB Bank
6221 - Net Power Solutions
6221 - Noga Commodities
6221 - R.J. Commodities
6331 - A.N. Deringer, Inc.-Hdqrs.
6331 - Global Solutions Insurance Services,
6331 - Kemper International
6331 - Roanoke Brokerage Services, Inc.
6351 - Global Solutions Insurance Services,
6351 - Roanoke Brokerage Services, Inc.
6411 - American International Marine Agency
6411 - Craig M. Ferguson & Co. Inc.
6411 - Mondics/Greenhaw Insurance Agency
6411 - R & R Insurance Services, Inc.
6411 - Redding Rhodes & Associates
6411 - Richard T. Opie & Company, Inc.
6531 - Segrest International Realtors

6531 - The Barrel Company Inc.
6552 - Ameri Housing
6794 - Envirobate Inc.
711 - Land & Water Consulting, Inc.
723 - Hilltop Ranch
7311 - Global Vision
7313 - Multimedia, Inc.
7322 - First Security Bank
7342 - Hickory Specialties
7349 - ARC Industries Inc.
7359 - Able Builders Export, Inc.
7359 - Avjet Corporation
7361 - ARC Industries Inc.
7371 - Brooks Internet Software Inc
7371 - Container Machinery Corp.
7371 - Eagle Technology, Inc.
7371 - HASP Inc
7371 - Micon Telecommunications Inc
7371 - OpenDisc Systems Inc
7371 - Probita Inc
7371 - Ross Systems Inc.
7371 - Sunshine Unlimited, Inc.
7371 - Techbase International
7372 - ASTI
7372 - Anderson-Bell Corporation
7372 - Apollo
7372 - Art, Inc.
7372 - Eskra Inc. (Mfr)
7372 - Fiscal Systems, Inc.
7372 - Jobquest
7372 - Knozall Systems
7372 - Legal Plus Software Group Inc
7372 - Optimation, Inc.
7372 - Palisade Corporation
7372 - Visible Productions LLC
7373 - Capital Information Systems
7373 - Eskra Inc. (Mfr)
7373 - International Systems
7373 - TS-Tek Inc
7375 - Heartland Communications Group Inc.
7375 - Technical Resource International, Inc.
7375 - Used Equipment Directory
7378 - Micon Telecommunications Inc
7379 - Cap Gemini America
7379 - GEO. S. Olive & Co., LLC
7379 - International Systems
7381 - Gaslamp Quarter Investigations /
7382 - 3M IBD/Export.
7382 - Advantor Corp.
7389 - A.S. Contin Inc.
7389 - ALPNET. INC.
7389 - Ann Edgar
7389 - Babel Ltd.
7389 - Cacheaux, Cavazos, Newton, Martin
7389 - Conexpo-Con Agg Exposition
7389 - Container Machinery Corp.
7389 - Crown Hollander Inc.
7389 - Cybertec, Inc.
7389 - Doris Schraft
7389 - Dr. Saul Cano
7389 - Dri-Rite Co.
7389 - Dvorak International Linguistics
7389 - Dynamic Language Center, Ltd
7389 - Echo International
7389 - Export FSC International LTD
7389 - French Connection, The
7389 - GEO. S. Olive & Co., LLC
7389 - Genevieve Tournebize - Iliev
7389 - Giovanna Cavagna
7389 - Hunter, Anne M.
7389 - International Translating Br., Inc.
7389 - International Word Factory
7389 - Ismay International L.L.C.
7389 - Julia P. Poger Associates
7389 - Keiko Hirokawa
7389 - Language Express
7389 - Language Interface, Ltd.
7389 - Language Masters, Inc.
7389 - Language Plus
7389 - Language Services Associates
7389 - Leo A. Daly Company
7389 - Lingo Systems
7389 - Linguistic Solutions

7389 - Linguistic Systems
7389 - M2 Limited
7389 - Magnum Group, Inc. Translation
7389 - Margaret Cullen Expert Translations
7389 - Neil Langdon Inglis
7389 - PDG Associates, Inc.
7389 - PFS Corporation
7389 - Platt Electric Supply
7389 - Radlex
7389 - Rahoy Coccia Gabriella
7389 - Russ Paladino
7389 - Ryan Trading
7389 - Sears Steele, III
7389 - Smirnoff Communications Group, Inc.
7389 - Spanish Language Services
7389 - Speak Easy Languages
7389 - Suzuki, Myers & Associates, Limited
7389 - TIS Translations & Interpretation Svc.
7389 - Tech Trans International, Inc.
7389 - The John Wesley Group
7389 - The Language Lab
7389 - Translation Company of America, Inc.
7389 - Tru Lingua Language Systems, Inc.
7389 - University Language Center, Inc.
7389 - Wordnet Inc.
751 - Forkner Farms / Truline Genetics
751 - Maplehurst Genetics Intl. Inc.
751 - Wienk Charolais
752 - Hunte, Andrew
7534 - Lincoln Manufacturing Co.
7538 - ATK North America
7538 - Golten Service
7549 - The John Wesley Group
7623 - Morrison Construction Service
7629 - Delta Communications & Electronics
7629 - Mexxon International
7629 - Miller Design & Equipment
7629 - Palco Telecom Service Inc
7699 - CWC Inventories, Inc.
7699 - ESCO Services Inc
7699 - Hot Cell Services Corporation
7699 - Precision Machine Products
7699 - Rocky Mountain Propellers Inc
7812 - Communi-Creations Inc
7812 - Communication Concepts Unlimited
7812 - Masterpiece Prdctns Nevada
7812 - Technical Resource International, Inc.
7812 - Unique Video Productions
782 - Southern Turf Nurseries(Mfr)
7832 - Plato Trading
7841 - Waukesha Co. Technical College -
7993 - Miracles Amusement
7996 - The John Wesley Group
7999 - Texas Shooters Range Inc.
8111 - Armstrong Teasdale
8111 - Cacheaux, Cavazos, Newton, Martin
8111 - Cox, Buchanan, Padmore & Shakarchy
8111 - Finley & Associates P.A.
8111 - Jaeckle Fleischmann & Mugel, LLP
8111 - Parsons Behle & Latimer
8111 - S.K. Ross & Assoc., P.C.
8111 - Sonnenberg & Anderson
8111 - Stoel Rives LLP
8221 - Hawthorne University
8231 - Waukesha Co. Technical College -
8244 - Hawthorne University
8299 - Crestcom International Ltd
8299 - ELS Language Centers
8299 - Global Protocol
8299 - Hawthorne University
8299 - Jim O'Neil Environmental Consultant
8299 - Language Masters, Inc.
8299 - OTM Engineering, Inc.
8499 - Omega Graphics, Inc.
8517 - Racom Products Inc.
8520 - Racom Products Inc.
8611 - AmeriCares Foundations
8611 - Machinery Dealers Natl. Assn.
8611 - Sandler, Travis & Rosenberg, P.A.
8611 - World Wide Pet Supply Ass'n
8699 - ADRA International
8700 - Smirnoff Communications Group, Inc.

8711 - A.G. Equipment, Inc.
8711 - Anderson Seal Co., Inc.
8711 - Burns & McDonnell International
8711 - CTL Engineering, Inc.
8711 - Century West Engineering Corp.
8711 - Cermak Peterka Petersen, Inc.
8711 - Conserve Engineering Company
8711 - ETC de Las Americas, Inc.
8711 - GE Vallecitos Nuclear Center
8711 - ITT Flygt Corp
8711 - KBS Exports
8711 - KLD Associates Inc.
8711 - KSA Engineers, Inc.
8711 - Land & Water Consulting, Inc.
8711 - Leo A. Daly Company
8711 - Management Engineering Associates
8711 - Marshall Miller & Associates
8711 - Nevada Automotive Test Center
8711 - OTM Engineering, Inc.
8711 - Pincock Allen & Holt
8711 - Precision Measurement Labs
8711 - Texas Shooters Range Inc.
8711 - Versar, Inc.
8711 - Wallis & Assoc. Cons. Engineers
8712 - Burns & McDonnell International
8712 - Leo A. Daly Company
8713 - Leo A. Daly Company
8713 - Marshall Miller & Associates
8713 - McLarens Toplis North America, Inc.
8721 - Berg, DeMarco, Lewis, Sawatski &
8721 - GEO. S. Olive & Co., LLC
8721 - McBride Shopa & Co
8721 - Schmeltzer: Master Group
8721 - Watkins, Watkins & Keenan, CPA's
8731 - ACZ Laboratories Inc
8731 - Biotics Research Corp.
8731 - Enform-Aeon Inc
8731 - National Research & Chemical Co.
8731 - Technical Resource International, Inc.
8731 - Tecre Co., Inc.
8731 - Wildlife Supply Company / Trippensee
8734 - Analytica Environmental Lab Inc
8734 - CTL Engineering, Inc.
8734 - Canyon State Inspection
8734 - Communication Certification Lab
8734 - EMS Laboratories
8734 - ETC de Las Americas, Inc.
8734 - Nevada Automotive Test Center
8734 - North West Labs Inc
8734 - Oregon Analytical Laboratory
8734 - Teco
8734 - West Coast Industries Inc.
8741 - C & M Enterprises
8741 - D & S Exports
8741 - Versar, Inc.
8742 - Armstrong Teasdale
8742 - Century West Engineering Corp.
8742 - Communication Certification Lab
8742 - DeFinco Ltd.
8742 - Export Procedures Co.
8742 - GEO. S. Olive & Co., LLC
8742 - International Consultants of Del.
8742 - International Relations-Advanced Bio
8742 - Jim O'Neil Environmental Consultant
8742 - Leemark, Inc.
8742 - NSI Communications Inc.
8742 - PDG Associates, Inc.
8742 - The John Wesley Group
8748 - AG Systems
8748 - Armstrong Teasdale
8748 - Berg, DeMarco, Lewis, Sawatski &
8748 - Cacheaux, Cavazos, Newton, Martin
8748 - Century West Engineering Corp.
8748 - Columbia Logistics, Inc.
8748 - Communication Concepts Unlimited
8748 - ETC de Las Americas, Inc.
8748 - Global Associates, LLC
8748 - Interdevelopment Inc.
8748 - J & B Services: Import / Export
8748 - L.A. MarKom de Mexico, S.A. de
8748 - Leemark, Inc.
8748 - McCord Consulting Group, Inc.
8748 - Nevada Automotive Test Center

8748 - OTM Engineering, Inc.
8748 - Rocamar Services, Inc.
8748 - Schnepper-International, Inc.
8748 - Sea Forest Enterprises Inc
8748 - Suzuki, Myers & Associates, Limited
8748 - The John Wesley Group
8748 - Williams Shipping
8748 - cmiSource.com
8749 - Performahome (Mfr)
8911 - MSI International
8999 - AATA International Inc.
8999 - Crown Hollander Inc.
8999 - Marshall Miller & Associates
8999 - Technical Resource International, Inc.
901 - Aquatic Eco-Sysytems Inc.
9100 - Aqua Power Co.
9100 - SOS Metal San Diego
9100 - Steelbro International
919 - Diehl, Inc.
9224 - Fireboy - Xintex
9311 - U.S. Customs Service
9511 - Marshall Miller & Associates
9611 - City of Cincinnati Dept. Econ Dev.
9611 - County of Cattaraugus
9621 - Georgia Ports Authority
9621 - Port of Palm Beach District
9641 - South Dakota Dept. Of Agriculture
9999 - Barkat

Harmonized System-SIC Code Cross-Reference

HS-010111= SIC-0272
HS-010119= SIC-0272
HS-010120= SIC-0272
HS-010210= SIC-0241
HS-010290= SIC-0211
HS-010310= SIC-0213
HS-010391= SIC-0213
HS-010392= SIC-0213
HS-010410= SIC-0214
HS-010420= SIC-0214
HS-010511= SIC-0259
HS-010519= SIC-0259
HS-010591= SIC-0259
HS-010599= SIC-0259
HS-010600= SIC-0279
HS-020110= SIC-2011
HS-020120= SIC-2011
HS-020130= SIC-2011
HS-020210= SIC-2011
HS-020220= SIC-2011
HS-020230= SIC-2011
HS-020311= SIC-2011
HS-020312= SIC-2011
HS-020312= SIC-2011
HS-020319= SIC-2011
HS-020321= SIC-2011
HS-020322= SIC-2011
HS-020329= SIC-2011
HS-020410= SIC-2011
HS-020421= SIC-2011
HS-020422= SIC-2011
HS-020423= SIC-2011
HS-020430= SIC-2011
HS-020441= SIC-2011
HS-020442= SIC-2011
HS-020443= SIC-2011
HS-020450= SIC-2011
HS-020500= SIC-2011
HS-020610= SIC-2011
HS-020621= SIC-2011
HS-020622= SIC-2011
HS-020629= SIC-2011
HS-020630= SIC-2011
HS-020641= SIC-2011
HS-020649= SIC-2011
HS-020680= SIC-2011
HS-020690= SIC-2011
HS-020710= SIC-2015
HS-020721= SIC-2015
HS-020722= SIC-2015
HS-020723= SIC-2015
HS-020731= SIC-2015
HS-020739= SIC-2015
HS-020741= SIC-2015
HS-020742= SIC-2015
HS-020743= SIC-2015
HS-020750= SIC-2015
HS-020810= SIC-2015
HS-020820= SIC-2015
HS-020890= SIC-2015
HS-020900= SIC-2011
HS-021011= SIC-2011
HS-021012= SIC-2011
HS-021019= SIC-2011

HS-021020= SIC-2011
HS-021090= SIC-2011
HS-030110= SIC-0273
HS-030191= SIC-0273
HS-030192= SIC-0273
HS-030193= SIC-0273
HS-030199= SIC-0273
HS-030211= SIC-0912
HS-030212= SIC-0912
HS-030212= SIC-0273
HS-030219= SIC-0912
HS-030221= SIC-0912
HS-030222= SIC-0912
HS-030223= SIC-0912
HS-030229= SIC-0912
HS-030231= SIC-0912
HS-030232= SIC-0912
HS-030233= SIC-0912
HS-030239= SIC-0912
HS-030240= SIC-0912
HS-030250= SIC-0912
HS-030261= SIC-0912
HS-030262= SIC-0912
HS-030263= SIC-0912
HS-030264= SIC-0912
HS-030265= SIC-0912
HS-030266= SIC-0912
HS-030269= SIC-0912
HS-030269= SIC-0912
HS-030270= SIC-0912
HS-030310= SIC-0912
HS-030321= SIC-0912
HS-030322= SIC-0912
HS-030329= SIC-0912
HS-030331= SIC-0912
HS-030332= SIC-0912
HS-030333= SIC-0912
HS-030339= SIC-0912
HS-030341= SIC-0912
HS-030342= SIC-0912
HS-030343= SIC-0912
HS-030349= SIC-0912
HS-030350= SIC-0912
HS-030360= SIC-0912
HS-030371= SIC-0912
HS-030372= SIC-0912
HS-030373= SIC-0912
HS-030374= SIC-0912
HS-030375= SIC-0912
HS-030376= SIC-0912
HS-030377= SIC-0912
HS-030378= SIC-0912
HS-030379= SIC-0912
HS-030379= SIC-0912
HS-030380= SIC-0912
HS-030410= SIC-0912
HS-030420= SIC-0912
HS-030490= SIC-0912
HS-030510= SIC-2091
HS-030520= SIC-2091
HS-030530= SIC-2091
HS-030541= SIC-2091
HS-030542= SIC-2091
HS-030549= SIC-2091

HS-030551= SIC-2091
HS-030559= SIC-2091
HS-030561= SIC-2091
HS-030562= SIC-2091
HS-030563= SIC-2091
HS-030569= SIC-2091
HS-030611= SIC-0913
HS-030612= SIC-0913
HS-030613= SIC-0913
HS-030614= SIC-0913
HS-030619= SIC-0913
HS-030619= SIC-0913
HS-030621= SIC-0913
HS-030622= SIC-0913
HS-030623= SIC-0913
HS-030624= SIC-0913
HS-030624= SIC-0913
HS-030629= SIC-0913
HS-030710= SIC-0913
HS-030721= SIC-0913
HS-030729= SIC-0913
HS-030731= SIC-0913
HS-030739= SIC-0913
HS-030741= SIC-0913
HS-030749= SIC-0913
HS-030751= SIC-0913
HS-030759= SIC-0913
HS-030760= SIC-0913
HS-030791= SIC-0913
HS-030799= SIC-0913
HS-040110= SIC-2026
HS-040120= SIC-2026
HS-040130= SIC-2026
HS-040210= SIC-2023
HS-040221= SIC-2023
HS-040229= SIC-2023
HS-040291= SIC-2023
HS-040299= SIC-2023
HS-040310= SIC-2026
HS-040390= SIC-2026
HS-040410= SIC-2023
HS-040490= SIC-2023
HS-040500= SIC-2021
HS-040610= SIC-2022
HS-040620= SIC-2022
HS-040630= SIC-2022
HS-040640= SIC-2022
HS-040690= SIC-2022
HS-040700= SIC-0259
HS-040811= SIC-2015
HS-040819= SIC-2015
HS-040891= SIC-2015
HS-040899= SIC-2015
HS-040900= SIC-0279
HS-041000= SIC-0919
HS-050100= SIC-9900
HS-050210= SIC-2011
HS-050290= SIC-0279
HS-050300= SIC-9900
HS-050400= SIC-2011
HS-050510= SIC-9900
HS-050590= SIC-2077
HS-050610= SIC-2011
HS-050690= SIC-2011

HS-050710= SIC-9900
HS-050790= SIC-9900
HS-050800= SIC-0919
HS-050900= SIC-0919
HS-051000= SIC-2011
HS-051110= SIC-0211
HS-051191= SIC-2077
HS-051199= SIC-0211
HS-060110= SIC-0181
HS-060120= SIC-0181
HS-060210= SIC-0181
HS-060220= SIC-0181
HS-060230= SIC-0181
HS-060240= SIC-0181
HS-060291= SIC-0182
HS-060299= SIC-0181
HS-060310= SIC-0181
HS-060390= SIC-0181
HS-060410= SIC-0831
HS-060491= SIC-0811
HS-060499= SIC-0811
HS-070110= SIC-0134
HS-070190= SIC-0134
HS-070200= SIC-0161
HS-070310= SIC-0161
HS-070320= SIC-0161
HS-070390= SIC-0161
HS-070410= SIC-0161
HS-070420= SIC-0161
HS-070490= SIC-0161
HS-070511= SIC-0161
HS-070519= SIC-0161
HS-070521= SIC-0161
HS-070529= SIC-0161
HS-070610= SIC-0161
HS-070690= SIC-0161
HS-070700= SIC-0161
HS-070810= SIC-0161
HS-070820= SIC-0161
HS-070890= SIC-0119
HS-070910= SIC-0161
HS-070920= SIC-0161
HS-070930= SIC-0161
HS-070940= SIC-0161
HS-070951= SIC-0182
HS-070952= SIC-0182
HS-070960= SIC-0161
HS-070970= SIC-0161
HS-070990= SIC-0161
HS-071010= SIC-2037
HS-071021= SIC-2037
HS-071022= SIC-2037
HS-071029= SIC-2037
HS-071030= SIC-2037
HS-071040= SIC-2037
HS-071080= SIC-2037
HS-071090= SIC-2037
HS-071110= SIC-2035
HS-071120= SIC-2035
HS-071130= SIC-2035
HS-071140= SIC-2035
HS-071190= SIC-2035
HS-071210= SIC-2034
HS-071220= SIC-2034

HS-071230= SIC-2034
HS-071290= SIC-2034
HS-071310= SIC-0119
HS-071310= SIC-0119
HS-071320= SIC-0119
HS-071331= SIC-0119
HS-071332= SIC-0119
HS-071333= SIC-0119
HS-071339= SIC-0119
HS-071340= SIC-0119
HS-071350= SIC-0119
HS-071390= SIC-0119
HS-071410= SIC-0139
HS-071420= SIC-0139
HS-071490= SIC-0139
HS-080110= SIC-2068
HS-080120= SIC-2068
HS-080130= SIC-2068
HS-080211= SIC-0173
HS-080212= SIC-2068
HS-080221= SIC-0173
HS-080222= SIC-2068
HS-080231= SIC-0173
HS-080232= SIC-2068
HS-080240= SIC-2068
HS-080250= SIC-0173
HS-080290= SIC-0173
HS-080290= SIC-2068
HS-080300= SIC-0179
HS-080410= SIC-2034
HS-080420= SIC-2034
HS-080430= SIC-0179
HS-080440= SIC-0179
HS-080450= SIC-0179
HS-080510= SIC-0174
HS-080520= SIC-0174
HS-080530= SIC-0174
HS-080540= SIC-0174
HS-080590= SIC-0174
HS-080610= SIC-0172
HS-080620= SIC-2034
HS-080710= SIC-0161
HS-080720= SIC-0179
HS-080810= SIC-0175
HS-080820= SIC-0175
HS-080910= SIC-0175
HS-080920= SIC-0175
HS-080920= SIC-0175
HS-080930= SIC-0175
HS-080940= SIC-0175
HS-081010= SIC-0171
HS-081020= SIC-0171
HS-081030= SIC-0171
HS-081040= SIC-0171
HS-081090= SIC-0179
HS-081110= SIC-2037
HS-081120= SIC-2037
HS-081190= SIC-2037
HS-081210= SIC-2035
HS-081220= SIC-2035
HS-081290= SIC-2035
HS-081310= SIC-2034
HS-081320= SIC-2034
HS-081330= SIC-2034

HS-081340= SIC-2034
HS-081350= SIC-2034
HS-081400= SIC-2034
HS-090111= SIC-0179
HS-090112= SIC-0179
HS-090121= SIC-2095
HS-090122= SIC-2095
HS-090130= SIC-9100
HS-090140= SIC-2095
HS-090210= SIC-2099
HS-090220= SIC-2099
HS-090230= SIC-2099
HS-090240= SIC-2099
HS-090300= SIC-2099
HS-090411= SIC-2099
HS-090412= SIC-2099
HS-090420= SIC-2099
HS-090500= SIC-0179
HS-090610= SIC-0181
HS-090620= SIC-2099
HS-090700= SIC-2099
HS-090810= SIC-2099
HS-090820= SIC-2099
HS-090830= SIC-2099
HS-090910= SIC-2099
HS-090920= SIC-2099
HS-090930= SIC-2099
HS-090940= SIC-2099
HS-090950= SIC-2099
HS-091010= SIC-2099
HS-091020= SIC-2099
HS-091030= SIC-2099
HS-091040= SIC-2099
HS-091050= SIC-2099
HS-091091= SIC-2099
HS-091099= SIC-2099
HS-100110= SIC-0111
HS-100110= SIC-0111
HS-100110= SIC-0111
HS-100190= SIC-0111
HS-100200= SIC-0119
HS-100300= SIC-0119
HS-100400= SIC-0119
HS-100510= SIC-0115
HS-100590= SIC-0115
HS-100610= SIC-0112
HS-100620= SIC-2044
HS-100630= SIC-2044
HS-100640= SIC-2044
HS-100700= SIC-0119
HS-100810= SIC-0119
HS-100820= SIC-0119
HS-100830= SIC-0119
HS-100890= SIC-0119
HS-110100= SIC-2041
HS-110210= SIC-2041
HS-110220= SIC-2041
HS-110230= SIC-2044
HS-110290= SIC-2041
HS-110311= SIC-2041
HS-110312= SIC-2041
HS-110313= SIC-2041
HS-110314= SIC-2044
HS-110319= SIC-2041

HS-110321= SIC-2041	HS-130213= SIC-2087	HS-152190= SIC-2899	HS-190540= SIC-2051	HS-220590= SIC-2084	HS-251329= SIC-1499
HS-110329= SIC-2041	HS-130214= SIC-0831	HS-152200= SIC-2843	HS-190590= SIC-2051	HS-220600= SIC-2084	HS-251400= SIC-1411
HS-110411= SIC-2043	HS-130219= SIC-0831	HS-160100= SIC-2011	HS-200110= SIC-2035	HS-220710= SIC-2085	HS-251511= SIC-1411
HS-110412= SIC-2043	HS-130220= SIC-2099	HS-160210= SIC-2032	HS-200120= SIC-2035	HS-220720= SIC-2869	HS-251512= SIC-1411
HS-110419= SIC-2043	HS-130231= SIC-2833	HS-160220= SIC-2015	HS-200190= SIC-2035	HS-220810= SIC-2085	HS-251520= SIC-1411
HS-110421= SIC-2043	HS-130232= SIC-2099	HS-160231= SIC-2015	HS-200210= SIC-2033	HS-220820= SIC-2084	HS-251611= SIC-1411
HS-110422= SIC-2043	HS-130239= SIC-2099	HS-160231= SIC-2015	HS-200290= SIC-2033	HS-220830= SIC-2085	HS-251612= SIC-1411
HS-110423= SIC-2043	HS-140110= SIC-0831	HS-160239= SIC-2015	HS-200310= SIC-2033	HS-220840= SIC-2085	HS-251621= SIC-1411
HS-110429= SIC-2043	HS-140120= SIC-0831	HS-160239= SIC-2015	HS-200320= SIC-2033	HS-220850= SIC-2085	HS-251622= SIC-1411
HS-110430= SIC-2043	HS-140190= SIC-0831	HS-160241= SIC-2011	HS-200410= SIC-2037	HS-220890= SIC-2085	HS-251690= SIC-1411
HS-110510= SIC-2034	HS-140210= SIC-0831	HS-160242= SIC-2011	HS-200490= SIC-2037	HS-220900= SIC-2099	HS-251710= SIC-1422
HS-110520= SIC-2034	HS-140291= SIC-0831	HS-160249= SIC-2011	HS-200510= SIC-2032	HS-230110= SIC-2077	HS-251720= SIC-1499
HS-110610= SIC-2034	HS-140299= SIC-0831	HS-160250= SIC-2011	HS-200520= SIC-2096	HS-230120= SIC-2077	HS-251730= SIC-1499
HS-110620= SIC-2034	HS-140310= SIC-0139	HS-160290= SIC-2011	HS-200530= SIC-2033	HS-230210= SIC-2041	HS-251741= SIC-1429
HS-110630= SIC-2034	HS-140390= SIC-0831	HS-160300= SIC-2011	HS-200540= SIC-2033	HS-230220= SIC-2044	HS-251749= SIC-1429
HS-110710= SIC-2083	HS-140410= SIC-0139	HS-160411= SIC-2091	HS-200551= SIC-2032	HS-230230= SIC-2041	HS-251810= SIC-1429
HS-110720= SIC-2083	HS-140420= SIC-2074	HS-160411= SIC-2091	HS-200559= SIC-2033	HS-230240= SIC-2041	HS-251820= SIC-3274
HS-110811= SIC-2046	HS-140490= SIC-0139	HS-160412= SIC-2091	HS-200560= SIC-2033	HS-230250= SIC-2041	HS-251830= SIC-3295
HS-110812= SIC-2046	HS-150100= SIC-2011	HS-160413= SIC-2091	HS-200570= SIC-2033	HS-230310= SIC-2046	HS-251910= SIC-1459
HS-110813= SIC-2046	HS-150200= SIC-2011	HS-160414= SIC-2091	HS-200580= SIC-2033	HS-230320= SIC-2062	HS-251990= SIC-3295
HS-110814= SIC-2046	HS-150200= SIC-2077	HS-160415= SIC-2091	HS-200590= SIC-2033	HS-230330= SIC-2082	HS-252010= SIC-1499
HS-110819= SIC-2046	HS-150300= SIC-2077	HS-160416= SIC-2091	HS-200600= SIC-2064	HS-230400= SIC-2075	HS-252020= SIC-3275
HS-110820= SIC-2834	HS-150410= SIC-2077	HS-160419= SIC-0912	HS-200710= SIC-2032	HS-230500= SIC-2076	HS-252100= SIC-1429
HS-110900= SIC-2046	HS-150420= SIC-2077	HS-160419= SIC-2091	HS-200791= SIC-2033	HS-230610= SIC-2074	HS-252210= SIC-3274
HS-120100= SIC-0116	HS-150420= SIC-2077	HS-160420= SIC-2091	HS-200791= SIC-2033	HS-230620= SIC-2076	HS-252220= SIC-3274
HS-120210= SIC-0139	HS-150430= SIC-2077	HS-160430= SIC-2091	HS-200799= SIC-2033	HS-230630= SIC-2076	HS-252230= SIC-3241
HS-120220= SIC-0139	HS-150510= SIC-2299	HS-160510= SIC-2091	HS-200811= SIC-2099	HS-230640= SIC-2076	HS-252310= SIC-3241
HS-120300= SIC-0173	HS-150590= SIC-2869	HS-160520= SIC-2091	HS-200819= SIC-2068	HS-230650= SIC-2076	HS-252321= SIC-3241
HS-120400= SIC-0119	HS-150600= SIC-2077	HS-160530= SIC-2091	HS-200820= SIC-2033	HS-230660= SIC-2076	HS-252329= SIC-3241
HS-120500= SIC-0139	HS-150710= SIC-2075	HS-160540= SIC-2091	HS-200830= SIC-2033	HS-230690= SIC-2046	HS-252330= SIC-3241
HS-120600= SIC-0119	HS-150790= SIC-2075	HS-160590= SIC-2091	HS-200840= SIC-2033	HS-230700= SIC-2084	HS-252390= SIC-3241
HS-120710= SIC-0139	HS-150810= SIC-2076	HS-170111= SIC-2062	HS-200850= SIC-2033	HS-230810= SIC-0831	HS-252400= SIC-1499
HS-120720= SIC-0131	HS-150890= SIC-2076	HS-170112= SIC-2062	HS-200860= SIC-2033	HS-230890= SIC-2033	HS-252510= SIC-1499
HS-120730= SIC-0139	HS-150910= SIC-2076	HS-170191= SIC-2062	HS-200870= SIC-2033	HS-230910= SIC-2047	HS-252520= SIC-1499
HS-120740= SIC-0139	HS-150990= SIC-2076	HS-170199= SIC-2062	HS-200880= SIC-2033	HS-230990= SIC-2048	HS-252530= SIC-9100
HS-120750= SIC-0119	HS-151000= SIC-2076	HS-170210= SIC-2023	HS-200891= SIC-2033	HS-230990= SIC-2048	HS-252610= SIC-1499
HS-120760= SIC-0119	HS-151110= SIC-2076	HS-170220= SIC-2099	HS-200892= SIC-2033	HS-240110= SIC-0132	HS-252620= SIC-1499
HS-120791= SIC-0139	HS-151190= SIC-2076	HS-170230= SIC-2046	HS-200899= SIC-2033	HS-240120= SIC-0132	HS-252700= SIC-1499
HS-120792= SIC-0173	HS-151211= SIC-2076	HS-170240= SIC-2046	HS-200911= SIC-2037	HS-240130= SIC-0132	HS-252810= SIC-1474
HS-120799= SIC-0173	HS-151219= SIC-2076	HS-170250= SIC-2046	HS-200919= SIC-2037	HS-240210= SIC-2121	HS-252890= SIC-1474
HS-120810= SIC-2075	HS-151221= SIC-2074	HS-170260= SIC-2046	HS-200920= SIC-2037	HS-240220= SIC-2111	HS-252910= SIC-1459
HS-120890= SIC-2076	HS-151229= SIC-2074	HS-170290= SIC-2062	HS-200930= SIC-2037	HS-240290= SIC-2111	HS-252921= SIC-1479
HS-120911= SIC-0133	HS-151311= SIC-2076	HS-170310= SIC-2062	HS-200940= SIC-2037	HS-240310= SIC-2131	HS-252922= SIC-1479
HS-120919= SIC-0181	HS-151319= SIC-2076	HS-170390= SIC-2062	HS-200950= SIC-2033	HS-240391= SIC-2141	HS-252930= SIC-1459
HS-120921= SIC-0139	HS-151321= SIC-2076	HS-170410= SIC-2067	HS-200960= SIC-2037	HS-240399= SIC-2131	HS-253010= SIC-1499
HS-120922= SIC-0139	HS-151329= SIC-2076	HS-170490= SIC-2064	HS-200970= SIC-2037	HS-250100= SIC-1479	HS-253020= SIC-1499
HS-120923= SIC-0139	HS-151410= SIC-2076	HS-180100= SIC-0173	HS-200980= SIC-2033	HS-250200= SIC-1479	HS-253030= SIC-1479
HS-120924= SIC-0139	HS-151490= SIC-2076	HS-180200= SIC-0173	HS-200990= SIC-2033	HS-250310= SIC-1479	HS-253040= SIC-1479
HS-120925= SIC-0139	HS-151511= SIC-2076	HS-180310= SIC-2066	HS-210110= SIC-2095	HS-250390= SIC-2819	HS-253090= SIC-1499
HS-120926= SIC-0139	HS-151519= SIC-2076	HS-180320= SIC-2066	HS-210120= SIC-2099	HS-250410= SIC-3295	HS-260111= SIC-1011
HS-120929= SIC-0139	HS-151521= SIC-2046	HS-180400= SIC-2066	HS-210130= SIC-2095	HS-250490= SIC-3295	HS-260112= SIC-1011
HS-120930= SIC-0181	HS-151529= SIC-2046	HS-180500= SIC-2066	HS-210210= SIC-2099	HS-250510= SIC-1446	HS-260120= SIC-3295
HS-120991= SIC-0181	HS-151529= SIC-2046	HS-180610= SIC-2066	HS-210220= SIC-2099	HS-250590= SIC-1446	HS-260200= SIC-1061
HS-120999= SIC-0181	HS-151530= SIC-2076	HS-180620= SIC-2066	HS-210230= SIC-2099	HS-250610= SIC-1411	HS-260300= SIC-1021
HS-121010= SIC-0139	HS-151540= SIC-2076	HS-180620= SIC-2066	HS-210310= SIC-2035	HS-250621= SIC-1411	HS-260400= SIC-1061
HS-121020= SIC-0139	HS-151550= SIC-2076	HS-180631= SIC-2066	HS-210320= SIC-2033	HS-250629= SIC-1411	HS-260500= SIC-1061
HS-121110= SIC-0831	HS-151560= SIC-2076	HS-180632= SIC-2066	HS-210330= SIC-2035	HS-250700= SIC-1455	HS-260600= SIC-1099
HS-121120= SIC-0831	HS-151590= SIC-2076	HS-180690= SIC-2066	HS-210390= SIC-2035	HS-250810= SIC-1459	HS-260700= SIC-1031
HS-121190= SIC-0139	HS-151610= SIC-2079	HS-190110= SIC-2023	HS-210410= SIC-2034	HS-250820= SIC-1459	HS-260800= SIC-1031
HS-121210= SIC-0831	HS-151620= SIC-2079	HS-190120= SIC-2045	HS-210420= SIC-2032	HS-250830= SIC-1459	HS-260900= SIC-1099
HS-121220= SIC-0919	HS-151710= SIC-2079	HS-190190= SIC-2082	HS-210500= SIC-2024	HS-250840= SIC-1459	HS-261000= SIC-1061
HS-121230= SIC-0175	HS-151790= SIC-2079	HS-190211= SIC-2098	HS-210610= SIC-2075	HS-250850= SIC-1459	HS-261100= SIC-1061
HS-121291= SIC-0133	HS-151800= SIC-2076	HS-190219= SIC-2098	HS-210690= SIC-2033	HS-250860= SIC-1459	HS-261210= SIC-1094
HS-121292= SIC-0133	HS-151911= SIC-2899	HS-190219= SIC-2099	HS-220110= SIC-2086	HS-250870= SIC-1459	HS-261220= SIC-1099
HS-121299= SIC-0139	HS-151912= SIC-2899	HS-190220= SIC-2099	HS-220190= SIC-2097	HS-250900= SIC-1429	HS-261310= SIC-1061
HS-121300= SIC-0139	HS-151913= SIC-2899	HS-190230= SIC-2099	HS-220210= SIC-2086	HS-251010= SIC-1475	HS-261390= SIC-1061
HS-121410= SIC-2048	HS-151913= SIC-2899	HS-190240= SIC-2099	HS-220290= SIC-2026	HS-251020= SIC-1475	HS-261400= SIC-1099
HS-121490= SIC-0139	HS-151919= SIC-2899	HS-190300= SIC-2099	HS-220300= SIC-2082	HS-251110= SIC-1479	HS-261510= SIC-1099
HS-130110= SIC-0831	HS-151920= SIC-2869	HS-190410= SIC-2043	HS-220410= SIC-2084	HS-251120= SIC-1479	HS-261590= SIC-1061
HS-130120= SIC-0831	HS-151930= SIC-2869	HS-190490= SIC-2099	HS-220421= SIC-2084	HS-251200= SIC-1499	HS-261610= SIC-1044
HS-130190= SIC-0831	HS-152010= SIC-2841	HS-190510= SIC-2051	HS-220429= SIC-2084	HS-251311= SIC-1499	HS-261690= SIC-1041
HS-130211= SIC-0831	HS-152090= SIC-2841	HS-190520= SIC-2051	HS-220430= SIC-2084	HS-251319= SIC-1499	HS-261710= SIC-1099
HS-130212= SIC-0831	HS-152110= SIC-2899	HS-190530= SIC-2051	HS-220510= SIC-2084	HS-251321= SIC-1499	HS-261790= SIC-1099

HS-261800= SIC-3312	HS-280540= SIC-2819	HS-282810= SIC-2819	HS-284290= SIC-2819	HS-290522= SIC-2869	HS-291450= SIC-2869
HS-261900= SIC-3312	HS-280610= SIC-2819	HS-282890= SIC-2819	HS-284310= SIC-2819	HS-290529= SIC-2869	HS-291461= SIC-2869
HS-262011= SIC-3339	HS-280620= SIC-2819	HS-282911= SIC-2819	HS-284321= SIC-2819	HS-290531= SIC-2869	HS-291469= SIC-2869
HS-262019= SIC-3339	HS-280700= SIC-2819	HS-282919= SIC-2819	HS-284329= SIC-2819	HS-290532= SIC-2869	HS-291470= SIC-2869
HS-262020= SIC-3339	HS-280800= SIC-2873	HS-282990= SIC-2819	HS-284330= SIC-2819	HS-290539= SIC-2869	HS-291511= SIC-2869
HS-262030= SIC-3331	HS-280910= SIC-2819	HS-283010= SIC-2819	HS-284390= SIC-2819	HS-290541= SIC-2869	HS-291512= SIC-2869
HS-262040= SIC-3334	HS-280920= SIC-2874	HS-283020= SIC-2819	HS-284410= SIC-2819	HS-290542= SIC-2869	HS-291513= SIC-2869
HS-262050= SIC-3339	HS-281000= SIC-2819	HS-283030= SIC-2819	HS-284420= SIC-2819	HS-290543= SIC-2869	HS-291521= SIC-2869
HS-262090= SIC-3339	HS-281111= SIC-2819	HS-283090= SIC-2819	HS-284430= SIC-2819	HS-290544= SIC-2869	HS-291522= SIC-2869
HS-262100= SIC-9100	HS-281119= SIC-2819	HS-283110= SIC-2819	HS-284440= SIC-2819	HS-290549= SIC-2869	HS-291523= SIC-2869
HS-270111= SIC-1231	HS-281121= SIC-2813	HS-283190= SIC-2819	HS-284450= SIC-2819	HS-290550= SIC-2869	HS-291524= SIC-2869
HS-270112= SIC-1221	HS-281122= SIC-2819	HS-283210= SIC-2819	HS-284510= SIC-2819	HS-290611= SIC-2869	HS-291529= SIC-2869
HS-270119= SIC-1221	HS-281123= SIC-2819	HS-283220= SIC-2819	HS-284590= SIC-2819	HS-290612= SIC-2869	HS-291531= SIC-2869
HS-270120= SIC-2999	HS-281129= SIC-2819	HS-283230= SIC-2819	HS-284610= SIC-2819	HS-290613= SIC-2869	HS-291532= SIC-2869
HS-270210= SIC-1221	HS-281210= SIC-2819	HS-283311= SIC-2819	HS-284690= SIC-2819	HS-290614= SIC-2869	HS-291533= SIC-2869
HS-270220= SIC-1221	HS-281290= SIC-2819	HS-283319= SIC-2819	HS-284700= SIC-2819	HS-290619= SIC-2869	HS-291534= SIC-2869
HS-270300= SIC-1499	HS-281310= SIC-2819	HS-283321= SIC-2819	HS-284810= SIC-2819	HS-290621= SIC-2869	HS-291535= SIC-2869
HS-270400= SIC-3312	HS-281390= SIC-2819	HS-283322= SIC-2819	HS-284890= SIC-2819	HS-290629= SIC-2869	HS-291539= SIC-2869
HS-270500= SIC-3312	HS-281410= SIC-2819	HS-283323= SIC-2819	HS-284910= SIC-2819	HS-290711= SIC-2869	HS-291540= SIC-2869
HS-270600= SIC-3312	HS-281420= SIC-2819	HS-283324= SIC-2819	HS-284920= SIC-3291	HS-290712= SIC-2865	HS-291550= SIC-2869
HS-270710= SIC-2865	HS-281511= SIC-2812	HS-283325= SIC-2819	HS-284920= SIC-3291	HS-290713= SIC-2865	HS-291560= SIC-2869
HS-270720= SIC-2865	HS-281512= SIC-2812	HS-283326= SIC-2819	HS-284990= SIC-3291	HS-290714= SIC-2865	HS-291570= SIC-2899
HS-270730= SIC-2865	HS-281520= SIC-2812	HS-283327= SIC-2819	HS-285000= SIC-2819	HS-290715= SIC-2865	HS-291590= SIC-2899
HS-270740= SIC-2865	HS-281530= SIC-2812	HS-283329= SIC-2819	HS-285100= SIC-2819	HS-290719= SIC-2865	HS-291611= SIC-2869
HS-270750= SIC-2865	HS-281610= SIC-2819	HS-283330= SIC-2819	HS-290110= SIC-2911	HS-290721= SIC-2865	HS-291612= SIC-2869
HS-270760= SIC-2865	HS-281620= SIC-2819	HS-283340= SIC-2819	HS-290110= SIC-2911	HS-290722= SIC-2865	HS-291613= SIC-2869
HS-270791= SIC-2865	HS-281630= SIC-2819	HS-283410= SIC-2819	HS-290121= SIC-2911	HS-290723= SIC-2865	HS-291614= SIC-2869
HS-270799= SIC-2865	HS-281700= SIC-2819	HS-283421= SIC-2819	HS-290122= SIC-2911	HS-290729= SIC-2865	HS-291615= SIC-2899
HS-270810= SIC-2865	HS-281810= SIC-3291	HS-283422= SIC-2819	HS-290123= SIC-2911	HS-290730= SIC-2869	HS-291619= SIC-2869
HS-270820= SIC-2865	HS-281820= SIC-2819	HS-283429= SIC-2819	HS-290124= SIC-2911	HS-290810= SIC-2869	HS-291620= SIC-2869
HS-270900= SIC-1311	HS-281830= SIC-2819	HS-283510= SIC-2819	HS-290129= SIC-2911	HS-290820= SIC-2869	HS-291631= SIC-2869
HS-271000= SIC-2911	HS-281910= SIC-2819	HS-283521= SIC-2874	HS-290211= SIC-2865	HS-290890= SIC-2869	HS-291632= SIC-2869
HS-271111= SIC-1321	HS-281990= SIC-2819	HS-283522= SIC-2819	HS-290219= SIC-2865	HS-290911= SIC-2869	HS-291633= SIC-2869
HS-271112= SIC-1321	HS-282010= SIC-2819	HS-283523= SIC-2819	HS-290220= SIC-2911	HS-290919= SIC-2869	HS-291639= SIC-2869
HS-271113= SIC-1321	HS-282090= SIC-2819	HS-283524= SIC-2819	HS-290230= SIC-2865	HS-290920= SIC-2869	HS-291711= SIC-2869
HS-271114= SIC-2911	HS-282110= SIC-2816	HS-283525= SIC-2819	HS-290241= SIC-2865	HS-290930= SIC-2869	HS-291712= SIC-2869
HS-271119= SIC-1321	HS-282120= SIC-2816	HS-283526= SIC-2819	HS-290242= SIC-2865	HS-290941= SIC-2869	HS-291713= SIC-2869
HS-271121= SIC-1311	HS-282200= SIC-2819	HS-283529= SIC-2819	HS-290243= SIC-2865	HS-290942= SIC-2869	HS-291714= SIC-2869
HS-271129= SIC-1321	HS-282300= SIC-2816	HS-283531= SIC-2819	HS-290244= SIC-2865	HS-290943= SIC-2869	HS-291719= SIC-2869
HS-271210= SIC-2911	HS-282410= SIC-2816	HS-283539= SIC-2819	HS-290250= SIC-2865	HS-290944= SIC-2869	HS-291720= SIC-2869
HS-271220= SIC-2999	HS-282420= SIC-2816	HS-283610= SIC-2873	HS-290260= SIC-2865	HS-290949= SIC-2869	HS-291731= SIC-2869
HS-271290= SIC-2999	HS-282490= SIC-2816	HS-283620= SIC-2812	HS-290270= SIC-2865	HS-290950= SIC-2869	HS-291732= SIC-2869
HS-271311= SIC-2911	HS-282510= SIC-2819	HS-283630= SIC-2812	HS-290290= SIC-2865	HS-290960= SIC-2869	HS-291733= SIC-2869
HS-271312= SIC-2999	HS-282520= SIC-2819	HS-283640= SIC-2812	HS-290311= SIC-2869	HS-291010= SIC-2869	HS-291734= SIC-2869
HS-271320= SIC-2911	HS-282530= SIC-2819	HS-283650= SIC-2819	HS-290312= SIC-2869	HS-291020= SIC-2869	HS-291735= SIC-2869
HS-271390= SIC-2911	HS-282540= SIC-2819	HS-283660= SIC-2819	HS-290313= SIC-2869	HS-291030= SIC-2869	HS-291736= SIC-2869
HS-271410= SIC-1499	HS-282550= SIC-2819	HS-283670= SIC-2819	HS-290314= SIC-2869	HS-291090= SIC-2869	HS-291737= SIC-2869
HS-271490= SIC-1499	HS-282560= SIC-2819	HS-283691= SIC-2819	HS-290315= SIC-2869	HS-291100= SIC-2869	HS-291739= SIC-2869
HS-271500= SIC-2951	HS-282570= SIC-2819	HS-283692= SIC-2819	HS-290316= SIC-2869	HS-291211= SIC-2869	HS-291811= SIC-2869
HS-271600= SIC-9900	HS-282580= SIC-2816	HS-283693= SIC-2819	HS-290319= SIC-2869	HS-291212= SIC-2869	HS-291812= SIC-2869
HS-280110= SIC-2812	HS-282590= SIC-2819	HS-283699= SIC-2819	HS-290321= SIC-2869	HS-291213= SIC-2869	HS-291813= SIC-2869
HS-280120= SIC-2819	HS-282611= SIC-2819	HS-283711= SIC-2819	HS-290322= SIC-2869	HS-291219= SIC-2869	HS-291814= SIC-2869
HS-280130= SIC-2819	HS-282612= SIC-2819	HS-283719= SIC-2819	HS-290323= SIC-2869	HS-291221= SIC-2869	HS-291815= SIC-2869
HS-280130= SIC-2819	HS-282619= SIC-2819	HS-283720= SIC-2819	HS-290329= SIC-2869	HS-291229= SIC-2869	HS-291816= SIC-2869
HS-280200= SIC-2819	HS-282620= SIC-2819	HS-283800= SIC-2819	HS-290330= SIC-2869	HS-291230= SIC-2869	HS-291817= SIC-2869
HS-280300= SIC-2895	HS-282630= SIC-2819	HS-283911= SIC-2819	HS-290340= SIC-2869	HS-291241= SIC-2869	HS-291819= SIC-2869
HS-280410= SIC-2813	HS-282690= SIC-2819	HS-283919= SIC-2819	HS-290351= SIC-2869	HS-291242= SIC-2869	HS-291821= SIC-2865
HS-280421= SIC-2813	HS-282710= SIC-2819	HS-283920= SIC-2819	HS-290359= SIC-2869	HS-291249= SIC-2869	HS-291822= SIC-2833
HS-280429= SIC-2813	HS-282720= SIC-2819	HS-283990= SIC-2819	HS-290361= SIC-2869	HS-291250= SIC-2869	HS-291823= SIC-2865
HS-280429= SIC-2813	HS-282731= SIC-2819	HS-284011= SIC-2819	HS-290362= SIC-2869	HS-291260= SIC-2869	HS-291829= SIC-2869
HS-280430= SIC-2813	HS-282732= SIC-2819	HS-284019= SIC-2819	HS-290369= SIC-2869	HS-291300= SIC-2869	HS-291830= SIC-2869
HS-280440= SIC-2813	HS-282733= SIC-2819	HS-284020= SIC-2819	HS-290410= SIC-2869	HS-291411= SIC-2869	HS-291900= SIC-2869
HS-280450= SIC-2813	HS-282734= SIC-2819	HS-284030= SIC-2819	HS-290420= SIC-2869	HS-291412= SIC-2869	HS-292010= SIC-2869
HS-280461= SIC-3339	HS-282735= SIC-2819	HS-284110= SIC-2819	HS-290490= SIC-2869	HS-291413= SIC-2869	HS-292090= SIC-2869
HS-280469= SIC-3339	HS-282736= SIC-2819	HS-284120= SIC-2816	HS-290511= SIC-2869	HS-291419= SIC-2869	HS-292111= SIC-2869
HS-280470= SIC-2819	HS-282737= SIC-2819	HS-284130= SIC-2819	HS-290512= SIC-2869	HS-291421= SIC-2833	HS-292112= SIC-2869
HS-280480= SIC-2819	HS-282738= SIC-2819	HS-284140= SIC-2819	HS-290513= SIC-2869	HS-291422= SIC-2869	HS-292119= SIC-2869
HS-280490= SIC-3339	HS-282739= SIC-2819	HS-284150= SIC-2819	HS-290514= SIC-2869	HS-291423= SIC-2869	HS-292121= SIC-2869
HS-280511= SIC-2819	HS-282741= SIC-2819	HS-284160= SIC-2819	HS-290515= SIC-2869	HS-291429= SIC-2869	HS-292122= SIC-2869
HS-280519= SIC-2819	HS-282749= SIC-2819	HS-284170= SIC-2819	HS-290516= SIC-2869	HS-291430= SIC-2869	HS-292129= SIC-2869
HS-280521= SIC-2819	HS-282751= SIC-2819	HS-284180= SIC-2819	HS-290517= SIC-2869	HS-291441= SIC-2869	HS-292130= SIC-2869
HS-280522= SIC-2819	HS-282759= SIC-2819	HS-284190= SIC-2819	HS-290519= SIC-2869	HS-291449= SIC-2869	HS-292141= SIC-2865
HS-280530= SIC-2819	HS-282760= SIC-2819	HS-284210= SIC-2819	HS-290521= SIC-2869		HS-292142= SIC-2865

HS-292143= SIC-2865	HS-293621= SIC-2833	HS-310240= SIC-2873	HS-330119= SIC-2899	HS-360300= SIC-2892	HS-381190= SIC-2899
HS-292144= SIC-2865	HS-293622= SIC-2833	HS-310250= SIC-2873	HS-330121= SIC-2899	HS-360410= SIC-2899	HS-381210= SIC-2899
HS-292145= SIC-2865	HS-293623= SIC-2833	HS-310260= SIC-2873	HS-330122= SIC-2899	HS-360490= SIC-2899	HS-381220= SIC-2899
HS-292149= SIC-2865	HS-293624= SIC-2833	HS-310270= SIC-2873	HS-330123= SIC-2899	HS-360500= SIC-3999	HS-381230= SIC-2899
HS-292151= SIC-2865	HS-293625= SIC-2833	HS-310280= SIC-2873	HS-330124= SIC-2899	HS-360610= SIC-2899	HS-381300= SIC-2899
HS-292159= SIC-2865	HS-293626= SIC-2833	HS-310290= SIC-2873	HS-330125= SIC-2899	HS-360690= SIC-2899	HS-381400= SIC-2851
HS-292211= SIC-2869	HS-293627= SIC-2833	HS-310310= SIC-2874	HS-330126= SIC-2899	HS-370110= SIC-3861	HS-381511= SIC-2819
HS-292212= SIC-2869	HS-293628= SIC-2833	HS-310320= SIC-3312	HS-330129= SIC-2899	HS-370120= SIC-3861	HS-381512= SIC-2819
HS-292213= SIC-2869	HS-293629= SIC-2833	HS-310390= SIC-2874	HS-330130= SIC-2899	HS-370130= SIC-3861	HS-381519= SIC-2819
HS-292219= SIC-2833	HS-293690= SIC-2833	HS-310410= SIC-1474	HS-330190= SIC-2899	HS-370191= SIC-3861	HS-381590= SIC-2819
HS-292219= SIC-2869	HS-293710= SIC-2833	HS-310420= SIC-2874	HS-330210= SIC-2869	HS-370199= SIC-3861	HS-381600= SIC-3255
HS-292221= SIC-2865	HS-293721= SIC-2833	HS-310430= SIC-2874	HS-330290= SIC-2844	HS-370210= SIC-3861	HS-381710= SIC-2865
HS-292222= SIC-2865	HS-293722= SIC-2833	HS-310490= SIC-2874	HS-330300= SIC-2844	HS-370220= SIC-3861	HS-381720= SIC-2865
HS-292229= SIC-2865	HS-293729= SIC-2833	HS-310510= SIC-2874	HS-330410= SIC-2844	HS-370231= SIC-3861	HS-381800= SIC-3674
HS-292230= SIC-2865	HS-293791= SIC-2833	HS-310520= SIC-2874	HS-330420= SIC-2844	HS-370232= SIC-3861	HS-381900= SIC-2911
HS-292241= SIC-2833	HS-293792= SIC-2833	HS-310530= SIC-2874	HS-330430= SIC-2844	HS-370239= SIC-3861	HS-382000= SIC-2899
HS-292242= SIC-2869	HS-293799= SIC-2833	HS-310540= SIC-2874	HS-330491= SIC-2844	HS-370241= SIC-3861	HS-382100= SIC-2835
HS-292249= SIC-2869	HS-293810= SIC-2833	HS-310551= SIC-2874	HS-330499= SIC-2844	HS-370242= SIC-3861	HS-382200= SIC-2835
HS-292249= SIC-2833	HS-293890= SIC-2833	HS-310559= SIC-2874	HS-330510= SIC-2844	HS-370243= SIC-3861	HS-382310= SIC-2899
HS-292249= SIC-2869	HS-293910= SIC-2833	HS-310560= SIC-2874	HS-330520= SIC-2844	HS-370244= SIC-3861	HS-382320= SIC-2869
HS-292249= SIC-2869	HS-293921= SIC-2833	HS-310590= SIC-2874	HS-330530= SIC-2844	HS-370251= SIC-3861	HS-382330= SIC-3291
HS-292250= SIC-2869	HS-293929= SIC-2833	HS-320110= SIC-2861	HS-330590= SIC-2844	HS-370252= SIC-3861	HS-382340= SIC-2899
HS-292250= SIC-2869	HS-293930= SIC-2833	HS-320120= SIC-2861	HS-330610= SIC-2844	HS-370253= SIC-3861	HS-382350= SIC-3273
HS-292310= SIC-2869	HS-293940= SIC-2833	HS-320130= SIC-2861	HS-330690= SIC-2844	HS-370254= SIC-3861	HS-382350= SIC-3272
HS-292320= SIC-2869	HS-293950= SIC-2833	HS-320190= SIC-2861	HS-330710= SIC-2844	HS-370255= SIC-3861	HS-382390= SIC-3299
HS-292390= SIC-2869	HS-293960= SIC-2833	HS-320210= SIC-2843	HS-330720= SIC-2844	HS-370256= SIC-3861	HS-390110= SIC-2821
HS-292410= SIC-2869	HS-293970= SIC-2833	HS-320290= SIC-2843	HS-330730= SIC-2844	HS-370291= SIC-3861	HS-390120= SIC-2821
HS-292421= SIC-2879	HS-293990= SIC-2833	HS-320300= SIC-2861	HS-330741= SIC-2899	HS-370292= SIC-3861	HS-390130= SIC-2821
HS-292429= SIC-2869	HS-294000= SIC-2869	HS-320411= SIC-2865	HS-330749= SIC-2841	HS-370293= SIC-3861	HS-390190= SIC-2821
HS-292511= SIC-2869	HS-294110= SIC-2833	HS-320412= SIC-2865	HS-330790= SIC-2844	HS-370294= SIC-3861	HS-390210= SIC-2821
HS-292519= SIC-2869	HS-294120= SIC-2833	HS-320413= SIC-2865	HS-340111= SIC-2841	HS-370295= SIC-3861	HS-390220= SIC-2821
HS-292520= SIC-2869	HS-294130= SIC-2833	HS-320414= SIC-2865	HS-340119= SIC-2841	HS-370310= SIC-3861	HS-390230= SIC-2821
HS-292610= SIC-2869	HS-294140= SIC-2833	HS-320415= SIC-2865	HS-340120= SIC-2841	HS-370320= SIC-3861	HS-390290= SIC-2821
HS-292620= SIC-2869	HS-294150= SIC-2833	HS-320416= SIC-2865	HS-340211= SIC-2843	HS-370390= SIC-3861	HS-390311= SIC-2821
HS-292690= SIC-2879	HS-294190= SIC-2833	HS-320417= SIC-2865	HS-340212= SIC-2843	HS-370400= SIC-9900	HS-390319= SIC-2821
HS-292700= SIC-2869	HS-294200= SIC-2869	HS-320419= SIC-2865	HS-340213= SIC-2843	HS-370510= SIC-9900	HS-390320= SIC-2821
HS-292800= SIC-2869	HS-300120= SIC-2833	HS-320419= SIC-2865	HS-340219= SIC-2843	HS-370520= SIC-9900	HS-390330= SIC-2821
HS-292910= SIC-2869	HS-300190= SIC-2833	HS-320420= SIC-2865	HS-340219= SIC-2843	HS-370590= SIC-9900	HS-390390= SIC-2821
HS-292990= SIC-2869	HS-300210= SIC-2836	HS-320490= SIC-2865	HS-340220= SIC-2841	HS-370610= SIC-9900	HS-390410= SIC-2821
HS-293010= SIC-2869	HS-300220= SIC-2836	HS-320500= SIC-2865	HS-340290= SIC-2841	HS-370690= SIC-9900	HS-390421= SIC-2821
HS-293020= SIC-2879	HS-300231= SIC-2836	HS-320610= SIC-2816	HS-340311= SIC-2843	HS-370710= SIC-3861	HS-390422= SIC-2821
HS-293030= SIC-2869	HS-300239= SIC-2836	HS-320620= SIC-2816	HS-340319= SIC-2843	HS-370790= SIC-3861	HS-390430= SIC-2821
HS-293040= SIC-2869	HS-300290= SIC-2836	HS-320630= SIC-2816	HS-340391= SIC-2843	HS-380110= SIC-3299	HS-390440= SIC-2821
HS-293090= SIC-2879	HS-300310= SIC-2834	HS-320641= SIC-2816	HS-340399= SIC-2843	HS-380120= SIC-3624	HS-390450= SIC-2821
HS-293100= SIC-2869	HS-300320= SIC-2834	HS-320642= SIC-2816	HS-340410= SIC-2842	HS-380130= SIC-3624	HS-390461= SIC-2821
HS-293211= SIC-2869	HS-300331= SIC-2834	HS-320643= SIC-2816	HS-340420= SIC-2842	HS-380190= SIC-3624	HS-390469= SIC-2821
HS-293212= SIC-2869	HS-300339= SIC-2834	HS-320649= SIC-2816	HS-340490= SIC-2842	HS-380210= SIC-2819	HS-390490= SIC-2821
HS-293213= SIC-2869	HS-300340= SIC-2834	HS-320650= SIC-2816	HS-340510= SIC-2842	HS-380290= SIC-2816	HS-390511= SIC-2821
HS-293219= SIC-2869	HS-300390= SIC-2834	HS-320710= SIC-2816	HS-340520= SIC-2842	HS-380300= SIC-2861	HS-390519= SIC-2821
HS-293221= SIC-2869	HS-300410= SIC-2834	HS-320720= SIC-2899	HS-340530= SIC-2842	HS-380400= SIC-2611	HS-390520= SIC-2821
HS-293229= SIC-2879	HS-300420= SIC-2834	HS-320730= SIC-2899	HS-340540= SIC-2841	HS-380510= SIC-2861	HS-390590= SIC-2821
HS-293290= SIC-2879	HS-300431= SIC-2834	HS-320740= SIC-2899	HS-340590= SIC-2842	HS-380520= SIC-2861	HS-390610= SIC-2821
HS-293311= SIC-2869	HS-300432= SIC-2834	HS-320810= SIC-2851	HS-340600= SIC-3999	HS-380590= SIC-2861	HS-390690= SIC-2821
HS-293319= SIC-2869	HS-300439= SIC-2834	HS-320820= SIC-2851	HS-340700= SIC-3843	HS-380610= SIC-2861	HS-390710= SIC-2821
HS-293319= SIC-2869	HS-300439= SIC-2834	HS-320890= SIC-2851	HS-340700= SIC-3952	HS-380620= SIC-2861	HS-390720= SIC-2821
HS-293321= SIC-2869	HS-300440= SIC-2834	HS-320910= SIC-2851	HS-340700= SIC-3843	HS-380630= SIC-2861	HS-390730= SIC-2821
HS-293329= SIC-2869	HS-300450= SIC-2834	HS-320990= SIC-2851	HS-350110= SIC-2023	HS-380690= SIC-2861	HS-390740= SIC-2821
HS-293331= SIC-2869	HS-300490= SIC-2834	HS-321000= SIC-2851	HS-350190= SIC-2891	HS-380700= SIC-2861	HS-390750= SIC-2821
HS-293339= SIC-2879	HS-300490= SIC-2834	HS-321100= SIC-2851	HS-350190= SIC-2869	HS-380810= SIC-2879	HS-390760= SIC-2821
HS-293340= SIC-2869	HS-300510= SIC-3842	HS-321210= SIC-3497	HS-350210= SIC-2015	HS-380820= SIC-2879	HS-390791= SIC-2821
HS-293351= SIC-2869	HS-300590= SIC-3842	HS-321290= SIC-2816	HS-350210= SIC-2015	HS-380830= SIC-2879	HS-390799= SIC-2821
HS-293359= SIC-2869	HS-300610= SIC-3842	HS-321290= SIC-2851	HS-350290= SIC-2869	HS-380840= SIC-2879	HS-390810= SIC-2821
HS-293361= SIC-2869	HS-300620= SIC-2835	HS-321310= SIC-3952	HS-350300= SIC-2899	HS-380890= SIC-2879	HS-390890= SIC-2821
HS-293369= SIC-2869	HS-300630= SIC-2835	HS-321390= SIC-3952	HS-350400= SIC-2075	HS-380910= SIC-2843	HS-390910= SIC-2821
HS-293371= SIC-2869	HS-300640= SIC-3843	HS-321410= SIC-2851	HS-350510= SIC-2046	HS-380991= SIC-2843	HS-390920= SIC-2821
HS-293379= SIC-2869	HS-300650= SIC-3842	HS-321490= SIC-2851	HS-350520= SIC-2891	HS-380992= SIC-2899	HS-390930= SIC-2821
HS-293390= SIC-2869	HS-300660= SIC-2834	HS-321511= SIC-2893	HS-350610= SIC-2891	HS-380999= SIC-2843	HS-390940= SIC-2821
HS-293410= SIC-2869	HS-310000= SIC-2873	HS-321519= SIC-2893	HS-350691= SIC-2891	HS-381010= SIC-2899	HS-390950= SIC-2821
HS-293420= SIC-2869	HS-310100= SIC-2873	HS-321590= SIC-3952	HS-350699= SIC-2891	HS-381090= SIC-2899	HS-390950= SIC-2821
HS-293430= SIC-2869	HS-310210= SIC-2873	HS-330111= SIC-2899	HS-350710= SIC-2869	HS-381111= SIC-2899	HS-391000= SIC-2821
HS-293490= SIC-2869	HS-310221= SIC-2873	HS-330112= SIC-2899	HS-350790= SIC-2869	HS-381119= SIC-2899	HS-391110= SIC-2821
HS-293500= SIC-2833	HS-310229= SIC-2873	HS-330113= SIC-2899	HS-360100= SIC-2892	HS-381121= SIC-2899	HS-391190= SIC-2821
HS-293610= SIC-2833	HS-310230= SIC-2873	HS-330114= SIC-2899	HS-360200= SIC-2892	HS-381129= SIC-2899	HS-391211= SIC-2821

HS-391212= SIC-2821	HS-392610= SIC-3089	HS-410110= SIC-2011	HS-430310= SIC-2371	HS-450310= SIC-2499	HS-480910= SIC-3955
HS-391220= SIC-2821	HS-392620= SIC-3089	HS-410121= SIC-2011	HS-430390= SIC-2371	HS-450390= SIC-2499	HS-480920= SIC-3955
HS-391231= SIC-2821	HS-392630= SIC-3089	HS-410122= SIC-2011	HS-430400= SIC-2371	HS-450410= SIC-2499	HS-480990= SIC-3955
HS-391239= SIC-2821	HS-392640= SIC-3089	HS-410129= SIC-2011	HS-440110= SIC-2411	HS-450490= SIC-2499	HS-481011= SIC-2621
HS-391290= SIC-2821	HS-392690= SIC-3089	HS-410130= SIC-2011	HS-440121= SIC-2411	HS-460110= SIC-2499	HS-481012= SIC-2621
HS-391310= SIC-2869	HS-400110= SIC-0831	HS-410140= SIC-2011	HS-440122= SIC-2411	HS-460120= SIC-2499	HS-481021= SIC-2621
HS-391390= SIC-2822	HS-400121= SIC-0831	HS-410210= SIC-2011	HS-440130= SIC-2499	HS-460191= SIC-2499	HS-481029= SIC-2621
HS-391390= SIC-2822	HS-400122= SIC-0831	HS-410221= SIC-2011	HS-440200= SIC-2861	HS-460199= SIC-2499	HS-481031= SIC-2621
HS-391400= SIC-2821	HS-400129= SIC-0831	HS-410229= SIC-2011	HS-440310= SIC-2491	HS-460210= SIC-2499	HS-481032= SIC-2621
HS-391510= SIC-9100	HS-400130= SIC-0831	HS-410310= SIC-2011	HS-440310= SIC-2491	HS-460290= SIC-2499	HS-481039= SIC-2621
HS-391520= SIC-9100	HS-400211= SIC-2822	HS-410320= SIC-2011	HS-440320= SIC-2411	HS-470100= SIC-2611	HS-481091= SIC-2621
HS-391530= SIC-9100	HS-400219= SIC-2822	HS-410390= SIC-2011	HS-440331= SIC-2411	HS-470200= SIC-2611	HS-481099= SIC-2621
HS-391590= SIC-9100	HS-400220= SIC-2822	HS-410410= SIC-3111	HS-440332= SIC-2411	HS-470311= SIC-2611	HS-481110= SIC-2621
HS-391610= SIC-3082	HS-400231= SIC-2822	HS-410421= SIC-3111	HS-440333= SIC-2411	HS-470319= SIC-2611	HS-481121= SIC-2672
HS-391620= SIC-3082	HS-400239= SIC-2822	HS-410422= SIC-3111	HS-440334= SIC-2411	HS-470321= SIC-2611	HS-481129= SIC-2672
HS-391690= SIC-3082	HS-400241= SIC-2822	HS-410429= SIC-3111	HS-440335= SIC-2411	HS-470321= SIC-2611	HS-481131= SIC-2621
HS-391710= SIC-2011	HS-400249= SIC-2822	HS-410429= SIC-3111	HS-440391= SIC-2411	HS-470329= SIC-2611	HS-481139= SIC-2621
HS-391721= SIC-3052	HS-400251= SIC-2822	HS-410431= SIC-3111	HS-440392= SIC-2411	HS-470411= SIC-2611	HS-481140= SIC-2621
HS-391722= SIC-3052	HS-400259= SIC-2822	HS-410439= SIC-3111	HS-440399= SIC-2411	HS-470419= SIC-2611	HS-481190= SIC-2621
HS-391723= SIC-3052	HS-400260= SIC-2822	HS-410511= SIC-3111	HS-440410= SIC-2411	HS-470421= SIC-2611	HS-481200= SIC-2621
HS-391729= SIC-3052	HS-400270= SIC-2822	HS-410512= SIC-3111	HS-440410= SIC-2411	HS-470429= SIC-2611	HS-481310= SIC-2675
HS-391731= SIC-3052	HS-400280= SIC-2822	HS-410519= SIC-3111	HS-440420= SIC-2411	HS-470500= SIC-2611	HS-481320= SIC-2621
HS-391732= SIC-3052	HS-400291= SIC-2822	HS-410520= SIC-3111	HS-440500= SIC-2499	HS-470610= SIC-2611	HS-481390= SIC-2621
HS-391733= SIC-3052	HS-400299= SIC-2822	HS-410611= SIC-3111	HS-440610= SIC-2411	HS-470691= SIC-2611	HS-481410= SIC-2679
HS-391739= SIC-3052	HS-400300= SIC-3069	HS-410612= SIC-3111	HS-440690= SIC-2411	HS-470710= SIC-9100	HS-481420= SIC-2679
HS-391740= SIC-3089	HS-400400= SIC-9100	HS-410619= SIC-3111	HS-440710= SIC-2491	HS-470720= SIC-9100	HS-481430= SIC-2679
HS-391810= SIC-3996	HS-400510= SIC-3069	HS-410620= SIC-3111	HS-440721= SIC-2421	HS-470730= SIC-9100	HS-481490= SIC-2679
HS-391890= SIC-3089	HS-400520= SIC-3069	HS-410710= SIC-3111	HS-440722= SIC-2421	HS-470790= SIC-9100	HS-481500= SIC-3996
HS-391910= SIC-2672	HS-400591= SIC-3069	HS-410721= SIC-3111	HS-440723= SIC-2421	HS-480100= SIC-2621	HS-481610= SIC-3955
HS-391990= SIC-2672	HS-400599= SIC-3069	HS-410729= SIC-3111	HS-440791= SIC-2421	HS-480210= SIC-9900	HS-481620= SIC-3955
HS-392010= SIC-3081	HS-400610= SIC-3011	HS-410790= SIC-3111	HS-440792= SIC-2421	HS-480220= SIC-2621	HS-481630= SIC-3955
HS-392020= SIC-3081	HS-400690= SIC-3069	HS-410800= SIC-3111	HS-440799= SIC-2421	HS-480230= SIC-2621	HS-481690= SIC-3955
HS-392030= SIC-3081	HS-400700= SIC-3069	HS-410900= SIC-3111	HS-440810= SIC-2436	HS-480240= SIC-2621	HS-481710= SIC-2677
HS-392041= SIC-3081	HS-400811= SIC-3069	HS-411000= SIC-9100	HS-440810= SIC-2436	HS-480251= SIC-2621	HS-481720= SIC-2678
HS-392042= SIC-3081	HS-400819= SIC-3069	HS-411100= SIC-3111	HS-440820= SIC-2435	HS-480252= SIC-2621	HS-481730= SIC-2678
HS-392051= SIC-3081	HS-400821= SIC-3069	HS-420100= SIC-3199	HS-440890= SIC-2435	HS-480253= SIC-2621	HS-481810= SIC-2676
HS-392059= SIC-3081	HS-400829= SIC-3069	HS-420211= SIC-3161	HS-440910= SIC-2411	HS-480260= SIC-2621	HS-481820= SIC-2676
HS-392061= SIC-3081	HS-400910= SIC-3052	HS-420212= SIC-3161	HS-440920= SIC-2411	HS-480300= SIC-2621	HS-481830= SIC-2676
HS-392062= SIC-3081	HS-400920= SIC-3052	HS-420219= SIC-3161	HS-441010= SIC-2493	HS-480411= SIC-2621	HS-481840= SIC-2676
HS-392063= SIC-3081	HS-400930= SIC-3052	HS-420221= SIC-3171	HS-441090= SIC-2493	HS-480419= SIC-2621	HS-481850= SIC-2676
HS-392069= SIC-3081	HS-400940= SIC-3052	HS-420222= SIC-3171	HS-441111= SIC-2493	HS-480421= SIC-2621	HS-481890= SIC-2676
HS-392071= SIC-3081	HS-400950= SIC-3052	HS-420229= SIC-3171	HS-441119= SIC-2493	HS-480429= SIC-2621	HS-481910= SIC-2656
HS-392072= SIC-3081	HS-400950= SIC-3714	HS-420231= SIC-3172	HS-441121= SIC-2493	HS-480431= SIC-2621	HS-481920= SIC-2657
HS-392073= SIC-3081	HS-401010= SIC-3052	HS-420232= SIC-3172	HS-441129= SIC-2493	HS-480439= SIC-2621	HS-481930= SIC-2674
HS-392079= SIC-3081	HS-401091= SIC-3052	HS-420239= SIC-3172	HS-441131= SIC-2493	HS-480441= SIC-2621	HS-481940= SIC-2674
HS-392091= SIC-3081	HS-401099= SIC-3052	HS-420291= SIC-3949	HS-441139= SIC-2493	HS-480442= SIC-2621	HS-481950= SIC-2656
HS-392092= SIC-3081	HS-401110= SIC-3011	HS-420292= SIC-3161	HS-441191= SIC-2493	HS-480449= SIC-2621	HS-481960= SIC-2652
HS-392093= SIC-3081	HS-401120= SIC-3011	HS-420292= SIC-3161	HS-441199= SIC-2493	HS-480451= SIC-2621	HS-482010= SIC-2782
HS-392094= SIC-3081	HS-401130= SIC-3011	HS-420299= SIC-3161	HS-441211= SIC-2435	HS-480452= SIC-2621	HS-482020= SIC-2782
HS-392099= SIC-3081	HS-401140= SIC-3011	HS-420310= SIC-2386	HS-441212= SIC-2435	HS-480459= SIC-2621	HS-482030= SIC-2782
HS-392111= SIC-3089	HS-401150= SIC-3011	HS-420321= SIC-3949	HS-441219= SIC-2436	HS-480510= SIC-2621	HS-482040= SIC-2761
HS-392112= SIC-3089	HS-401191= SIC-3011	HS-420329= SIC-3151	HS-441221= SIC-2435	HS-480521= SIC-2621	HS-482050= SIC-2782
HS-392113= SIC-3089	HS-401199= SIC-3011	HS-420330= SIC-2389	HS-441229= SIC-2435	HS-480522= SIC-2621	HS-482090= SIC-2782
HS-392114= SIC-3089	HS-401210= SIC-9200	HS-420340= SIC-2389	HS-441291= SIC-2436	HS-480523= SIC-2621	HS-482110= SIC-2752
HS-392119= SIC-3089	HS-401220= SIC-9200	HS-420400= SIC-3199	HS-441299= SIC-2436	HS-480529= SIC-2621	HS-482190= SIC-2672
HS-392190= SIC-3089	HS-401290= SIC-3011	HS-420500= SIC-3199	HS-441300= SIC-2426	HS-480529= SIC-2621	HS-482210= SIC-2655
HS-392210= SIC-3088	HS-401310= SIC-3011	HS-420610= SIC-3999	HS-441400= SIC-2499	HS-480530= SIC-2621	HS-482290= SIC-2655
HS-392220= SIC-3089	HS-401310= SIC-3011	HS-420690= SIC-3999	HS-441510= SIC-2449	HS-480540= SIC-2621	HS-482311= SIC-2672
HS-392290= SIC-3088	HS-401320= SIC-3011	HS-430110= SIC-0271	HS-441520= SIC-2448	HS-480550= SIC-2621	HS-482319= SIC-2672
HS-392310= SIC-3089	HS-401390= SIC-3011	HS-430120= SIC-0271	HS-441600= SIC-2449	HS-480560= SIC-2621	HS-482320= SIC-2675
HS-392321= SIC-2673	HS-401410= SIC-3069	HS-430130= SIC-0271	HS-441700= SIC-2499	HS-480570= SIC-2621	HS-482320= SIC-2675
HS-392329= SIC-2673	HS-401490= SIC-3069	HS-430140= SIC-0271	HS-441810= SIC-2431	HS-480580= SIC-2631	HS-482330= SIC-2675
HS-392330= SIC-3085	HS-401511= SIC-3069	HS-430150= SIC-0271	HS-441820= SIC-2431	HS-480610= SIC-2621	HS-482340= SIC-2752
HS-392340= SIC-3089	HS-401519= SIC-3069	HS-430160= SIC-0271	HS-441830= SIC-2426	HS-480620= SIC-2621	HS-482351= SIC-2675
HS-392350= SIC-3089	HS-401590= SIC-3069	HS-430170= SIC-0271	HS-441840= SIC-2439	HS-480630= SIC-2621	HS-482359= SIC-2621
HS-392390= SIC-3089	HS-401610= SIC-3069	HS-430180= SIC-0271	HS-441850= SIC-2429	HS-480640= SIC-2621	HS-482359= SIC-2678
HS-392410= SIC-3089	HS-401691= SIC-3069	HS-430190= SIC-0271	HS-441890= SIC-2439	HS-480710= SIC-2621	HS-482360= SIC-2656
HS-392490= SIC-2392	HS-401692= SIC-3053	HS-430211= SIC-3999	HS-441900= SIC-2499	HS-480791= SIC-2621	HS-482370= SIC-2679
HS-392510= SIC-3089	HS-401693= SIC-3053	HS-430212= SIC-3999	HS-442010= SIC-2499	HS-480799= SIC-2621	HS-482390= SIC-2675
HS-392520= SIC-3089	HS-401694= SIC-3069	HS-430213= SIC-3999	HS-442090= SIC-2499	HS-480810= SIC-2653	HS-490110= SIC-2752
HS-392530= SIC-2591	HS-401695= SIC-3069	HS-430219= SIC-3999	HS-442110= SIC-2499	HS-480820= SIC-2621	HS-490191= SIC-2731
HS-392530= SIC-3089	HS-401699= SIC-3069	HS-430220= SIC-3999	HS-442190= SIC-2431	HS-480830= SIC-2621	HS-490199= SIC-2731
HS-392590= SIC-3089	HS-401700= SIC-3069	HS-430230= SIC-3999	HS-450200= SIC-2499	HS-480890= SIC-2621	HS-490210= SIC-2711

HS-490290= SIC-2711	HS-520515= SIC-2281	HS-520951== SIC-2211	HS-531010== SIC-2299	HS-550310== SIC-2824	HS-551432== SIC-2221
HS-490300= SIC-3944	HS-520521= SIC-2281	HS-520952== SIC-2211	HS-531090== SIC-2299	HS-550320== SIC-2824	HS-551433== SIC-2221
HS-490400= SIC-2752	HS-520522= SIC-2281	HS-520959== SIC-2211	HS-531100== SIC-2299	HS-550330== SIC-2824	HS-551439== SIC-2221
HS-490510= SIC-2752	HS-520523= SIC-2281	HS-521011== SIC-2211	HS-540110== SIC-2284	HS-550340== SIC-2824	HS-551441== SIC-2221
HS-490591= SIC-2752	HS-520524= SIC-2281	HS-521012== SIC-2211	HS-540120== SIC-2284	HS-550390== SIC-2824	HS-551442== SIC-2221
HS-490599= SIC-2752	HS-520525= SIC-2281	HS-521019== SIC-2211	HS-540210== SIC-2824	HS-550410== SIC-2823	HS-551443== SIC-2221
HS-490600= SIC-9900	HS-520531= SIC-2281	HS-521021== SIC-2211	HS-540220== SIC-2824	HS-550490== SIC-2823	HS-551449== SIC-2221
HS-490700= SIC-2752	HS-520532= SIC-2281	HS-521022== SIC-2211	HS-540231== SIC-2824	HS-550510== SIC-2824	HS-551511== SIC-2221
HS-490810= SIC-2752	HS-520533= SIC-2281	HS-521029== SIC-2211	HS-540232== SIC-2824	HS-550520== SIC-2823	HS-551512== SIC-2221
HS-490890= SIC-2752	HS-520534= SIC-2281	HS-521031== SIC-2211	HS-540233== SIC-2824	HS-550610== SIC-2824	HS-551513== SIC-2221
HS-490900= SIC-2752	HS-520535= SIC-2281	HS-521032== SIC-2211	HS-540239== SIC-2824	HS-550620== SIC-2824	HS-551519== SIC-2221
HS-491000= SIC-2752	HS-520541= SIC-2281	HS-521039== SIC-2211	HS-540241== SIC-2824	HS-550630== SIC-2824	HS-551521== SIC-2221
HS-491110= SIC-2741	HS-520542= SIC-2281	HS-521041== SIC-2211	HS-540242== SIC-2824	HS-550690== SIC-2824	HS-551522== SIC-2221
HS-491191= SIC-2752	HS-520543= SIC-2281	HS-521042== SIC-2211	HS-540243== SIC-2824	HS-550700== SIC-2823	HS-551529== SIC-2221
HS-491199= SIC-2752	HS-520544= SIC-2281	HS-521049== SIC-2211	HS-540249== SIC-2824	HS-550810== SIC-2284	HS-551591== SIC-2221
HS-500100= SIC-0279	HS-520545= SIC-2281	HS-521051== SIC-2211	HS-540251== SIC-2824	HS-550820== SIC-2284	HS-551592== SIC-2221
HS-500200= SIC-0279	HS-520611= SIC-2281	HS-521052== SIC-2211	HS-540252== SIC-2824	HS-550911== SIC-2281	HS-551599== SIC-2221
HS-500310= SIC-0279	HS-520612= SIC-2281	HS-521059== SIC-2211	HS-540259== SIC-2824	HS-550912== SIC-2281	HS-551611== SIC-2221
HS-500390= SIC-0279	HS-520613= SIC-2281	HS-521111== SIC-2211	HS-540261== SIC-2824	HS-550921== SIC-2281	HS-551612== SIC-2221
HS-500400= SIC-2281	HS-520614= SIC-2281	HS-521112== SIC-2211	HS-540262== SIC-2824	HS-550922== SIC-2281	HS-551613== SIC-2221
HS-500500= SIC-2281	HS-520615= SIC-2281	HS-521119== SIC-2211	HS-540269== SIC-2824	HS-550931== SIC-2281	HS-551614== SIC-2221
HS-500600= SIC-2281	HS-520621= SIC-2281	HS-521121== SIC-2211	HS-540310== SIC-2823	HS-550932== SIC-2281	HS-551621== SIC-2221
HS-500710= SIC-2221	HS-520622= SIC-2281	HS-521122== SIC-2211	HS-540320== SIC-2823	HS-550941== SIC-2281	HS-551622== SIC-2221
HS-500720= SIC-2221	HS-520623= SIC-2281	HS-521129== SIC-2211	HS-540331== SIC-2823	HS-550942== SIC-2281	HS-551623== SIC-2221
HS-500790= SIC-2221	HS-520624= SIC-2281	HS-521131== SIC-2211	HS-540332== SIC-2823	HS-550951== SIC-2281	HS-551624== SIC-2221
HS-510111= SIC-0214	HS-520625= SIC-2281	HS-521132== SIC-2211	HS-540333== SIC-2823	HS-550952== SIC-2281	HS-551631== SIC-2221
HS-510119= SIC-0214	HS-520631= SIC-2281	HS-521139== SIC-2211	HS-540339== SIC-2823	HS-550953== SIC-2281	HS-551632== SIC-2221
HS-510121= SIC-2299	HS-520632= SIC-2281	HS-521139== SIC-2211	HS-540341== SIC-2823	HS-550959== SIC-2281	HS-551633== SIC-2221
HS-510129= SIC-2299	HS-520633= SIC-2281	HS-521141== SIC-2211	HS-540342== SIC-2823	HS-550961== SIC-2281	HS-551634== SIC-2221
HS-510130= SIC-2299	HS-520634= SIC-2281	HS-521142== SIC-2211	HS-540349== SIC-2823	HS-550962== SIC-2281	HS-551641== SIC-2221
HS-510210= SIC-0214	HS-520635= SIC-2281	HS-521143== SIC-2211	HS-540410== SIC-3949	HS-550969== SIC-2281	HS-551642== SIC-2221
HS-510220= SIC-0272	HS-520641= SIC-2281	HS-521149== SIC-2211	HS-540490== SIC-2824	HS-550991== SIC-2281	HS-551643== SIC-2221
HS-510310= SIC-2299	HS-520642= SIC-2281	HS-521151== SIC-2211	HS-540500== SIC-2823	HS-550992== SIC-2281	HS-551644== SIC-2221
HS-510320= SIC-2299	HS-520643= SIC-2281	HS-521152== SIC-2211	HS-540610== SIC-2824	HS-550999== SIC-2281	HS-551691== SIC-2221
HS-510330= SIC-2299	HS-520644= SIC-2281	HS-521159== SIC-2211	HS-540620== SIC-2823	HS-551011== SIC-2281	HS-551692== SIC-2221
HS-510400= SIC-2299	HS-520645= SIC-2281	HS-521211== SIC-2211	HS-540710== SIC-2221	HS-551012== SIC-2281	HS-551693== SIC-2221
HS-510510= SIC-2299	HS-520710= SIC-2281	HS-521212== SIC-2211	HS-540720== SIC-2221	HS-551020== SIC-2281	HS-551694== SIC-2221
HS-510521= SIC-2299	HS-520790= SIC-2281	HS-521213== SIC-2211	HS-540730== SIC-2221	HS-551030== SIC-2281	HS-560110== SIC-2399
HS-510529= SIC-2299	HS-520811= SIC-2211	HS-521214== SIC-2211	HS-540741== SIC-2221	HS-551090== SIC-2281	HS-560121== SIC-2299
HS-510530= SIC-2299	HS-520812= SIC-2211	HS-521215== SIC-2211	HS-540742== SIC-2221	HS-551110== SIC-2281	HS-560122== SIC-2299
HS-510540= SIC-2299	HS-520813= SIC-2211	HS-521221== SIC-2211	HS-540743== SIC-2221	HS-551120== SIC-2281	HS-560129== SIC-2299
HS-510610= SIC-2231	HS-520819= SIC-2211	HS-521222== SIC-2211	HS-540744== SIC-2221	HS-551130== SIC-2281	HS-560130== SIC-2299
HS-510620= SIC-2281	HS-520821= SIC-2211	HS-521223== SIC-2211	HS-540751== SIC-2221	HS-551211== SIC-2221	HS-560210== SIC-2299
HS-510710= SIC-2281	HS-520822= SIC-2211	HS-521224== SIC-2211	HS-540752== SIC-2221	HS-551219== SIC-2221	HS-560221== SIC-2299
HS-510720= SIC-2281	HS-520823= SIC-2211	HS-521225== SIC-2211	HS-540753== SIC-2221	HS-551221== SIC-2221	HS-560229== SIC-2299
HS-510810= SIC-2281	HS-520829= SIC-2211	HS-530110== SIC-0139	HS-540754== SIC-2221	HS-551229== SIC-2221	HS-560290== SIC-2299
HS-510820= SIC-2281	HS-520831= SIC-2211	HS-530121== SIC-0139	HS-540760== SIC-2221	HS-551291== SIC-2221	HS-560290== SIC-2299
HS-510910= SIC-2281	HS-520832= SIC-2211	HS-530129== SIC-0139	HS-540771== SIC-2221	HS-551299== SIC-2221	HS-560290== SIC-2299
HS-510990= SIC-2281	HS-520833= SIC-2211	HS-530130== SIC-2299	HS-540772== SIC-2221	HS-551311== SIC-2221	HS-560300== SIC-2297
HS-511000= SIC-2281	HS-520839= SIC-2211	HS-530210== SIC-0139	HS-540773== SIC-2221	HS-551312== SIC-2221	HS-560410== SIC-2241
HS-511111= SIC-2231	HS-520839= SIC-2211	HS-530290== SIC-2299	HS-540774== SIC-2221	HS-551313== SIC-2221	HS-560420== SIC-2295
HS-511119= SIC-2231	HS-520841= SIC-2211	HS-530310== SIC-0139	HS-540781== SIC-2221	HS-551319== SIC-2221	HS-560490== SIC-2295
HS-511120= SIC-2231	HS-520842= SIC-2211	HS-530390== SIC-2299	HS-540782== SIC-2221	HS-551321== SIC-2221	HS-560500== SIC-2295
HS-511130= SIC-2231	HS-520842= SIC-2211	HS-530410== SIC-0139	HS-540783== SIC-2221	HS-551322== SIC-2221	HS-560600== SIC-2299
HS-511190= SIC-2231	HS-520843= SIC-2211	HS-530490== SIC-2299	HS-540784== SIC-2221	HS-551323== SIC-2221	HS-560710== SIC-2298
HS-511211= SIC-2231	HS-520849= SIC-2211	HS-530511== SIC-0173	HS-540791== SIC-2221	HS-551329== SIC-2221	HS-560721== SIC-2298
HS-511219= SIC-2231	HS-520851= SIC-2211	HS-530519== SIC-2299	HS-540792== SIC-2221	HS-551331== SIC-2221	HS-560729== SIC-2298
HS-511220= SIC-2231	HS-520852= SIC-2211	HS-530521== SIC-0139	HS-540793== SIC-2221	HS-551332== SIC-2221	HS-560730== SIC-2298
HS-511230= SIC-2231	HS-520853= SIC-2211	HS-530529== SIC-2299	HS-540794== SIC-2221	HS-551333== SIC-2221	HS-560741== SIC-2298
HS-511290= SIC-2231	HS-520859= SIC-2211	HS-530591== SIC-0139	HS-540810== SIC-2221	HS-551339== SIC-2221	HS-560749== SIC-2298
HS-511300= SIC-2231	HS-520911= SIC-2211	HS-530599== SIC-2299	HS-540821== SIC-2221	HS-551341== SIC-2221	HS-560750== SIC-2298
HS-520100= SIC-0131	HS-520912= SIC-2211	HS-530610== SIC-2299	HS-540822== SIC-2221	HS-551342== SIC-2221	HS-560790== SIC-2298
HS-520210= SIC-2299	HS-520919= SIC-2211	HS-530620== SIC-2299	HS-540823== SIC-2221	HS-551343== SIC-2221	HS-560811== SIC-2298
HS-520291= SIC-2299	HS-520921= SIC-2211	HS-530710== SIC-2299	HS-540824== SIC-2221	HS-551349== SIC-2221	HS-560819== SIC-2298
HS-520299= SIC-2299	HS-520922= SIC-2211	HS-530720== SIC-2299	HS-540831== SIC-2221	HS-551411== SIC-2221	HS-560890== SIC-2298
HS-520300= SIC-2299	HS-520929== SIC-2211	HS-530810== SIC-2299	HS-540832== SIC-2221	HS-551412== SIC-2221	HS-560900== SIC-2298
HS-520411= SIC-2284	HS-520931== SIC-2211	HS-530820== SIC-2299	HS-540833== SIC-2221	HS-551413== SIC-2221	HS-570110== SIC-2273
HS-520419= SIC-2284	HS-520932== SIC-2211	HS-530830== SIC-2299	HS-540834== SIC-2221	HS-551419== SIC-2221	HS-570190== SIC-2273
HS-520420= SIC-2284	HS-520939== SIC-2211	HS-530890== SIC-2299	HS-550110== SIC-2824	HS-551421== SIC-2221	HS-570210== SIC-2273
HS-520511= SIC-2281	HS-520941== SIC-2211	HS-530911== SIC-2299	HS-550120== SIC-2824	HS-551422== SIC-2221	HS-570220== SIC-2273
HS-520512= SIC-2281	HS-520942== SIC-2211	HS-530919== SIC-2299	HS-550130== SIC-2824	HS-551423== SIC-2221	HS-570231== SIC-2273
HS-520513= SIC-2281	HS-520943== SIC-2211	HS-530921== SIC-2299	HS-550190== SIC-2824	HS-551429== SIC-2221	HS-570232== SIC-2273
HS-520514= SIC-2281	HS-520949== SIC-2211	HS-530929== SIC-2299	HS-550200== SIC-2823	HS-551431== SIC-2221	HS-570239== SIC-2273

HS-570241== SIC-2273	HS-590691== SIC-3069	HS-610459=== SIC-2337	HS-620112== SIC-2311	HS-620799== SIC-2384	HS-630311== SIC-2391
HS-570242== SIC-2273	HS-590699== SIC-3069	HS-610461=== SIC-2369	HS-620113== SIC-2385	HS-620811== SIC-2341	HS-630312== SIC-2391
HS-570249== SIC-2273	HS-590700== SIC-2295	HS-610462=== SIC-2369	HS-620119== SIC-2311	HS-620819== SIC-2341	HS-630319== SIC-2391
HS-570251== SIC-2273	HS-590800== SIC-2241	HS-610463=== SIC-2369	HS-620191== SIC-2311	HS-620821== SIC-2341	HS-630391== SIC-2391
HS-570252== SIC-2273	HS-590900== SIC-2241	HS-610469=== SIC-2369	HS-620192== SIC-2311	HS-620822== SIC-2341	HS-630392== SIC-2391
HS-570259== SIC-2273	HS-591000== SIC-2241	HS-610510== SIC-2321	HS-620193== SIC-2311	HS-620829== SIC-2341	HS-630399== SIC-2391
HS-570291== SIC-2273	HS-591110== SIC-3069	HS-610520== SIC-2321	HS-620199== SIC-2311	HS-620891== SIC-2384	HS-630411== SIC-2392
HS-570292== SIC-2273	HS-591110== SIC-3069	HS-610590== SIC-2321	HS-620211== SIC-2337	HS-620891== SIC-2341	HS-630419== SIC-2392
HS-570299== SIC-2273	HS-591120== SIC-2241	HS-610610== SIC-2331	HS-620212== SIC-2385	HS-620892== SIC-2384	HS-630491== SIC-2392
HS-570310== SIC-2273	HS-591131== SIC-2231	HS-610620== SIC-2331	HS-620213== SIC-2385	HS-620892== SIC-2341	HS-630492== SIC-2392
HS-570320== SIC-2273	HS-591132== SIC-2231	HS-610690== SIC-2331	HS-620219== SIC-2337	HS-620899== SIC-2384	HS-630493== SIC-2392
HS-570330== SIC-2273	HS-591140== SIC-2241	HS-610711== SIC-2322	HS-620291== SIC-2337	HS-620899== SIC-2341	HS-630499== SIC-2392
HS-570390== SIC-2273	HS-591190== SIC-2241	HS-610712== SIC-2322	HS-620292== SIC-2337	HS-620910== SIC-2369	HS-630510== SIC-2393
HS-570410== SIC-2299	HS 600121== SIC-2257	HS-610719== SIC-2322	HS-620293== SIC-2337	HS-620920== SIC-2369	HS-630520== SIC-2393
HS-570490== SIC-2299	HS-600122== SIC-2257	HS-610721== SIC-2322	HS-620299== SIC-2337	HS-620930== SIC-2369	HS-630531== SIC-2393
HS-570500== SIC-2273	HS-600129== SIC-2257	HS-610722== SIC-2322	HS-620311== SIC-2311	HS-620990== SIC-2369	HS-630539== SIC-2393
HS-580110== SIC-2231	HS-600191== SIC-2257	HS-610729== SIC-2322	HS-620312== SIC-2311	HS-621010== SIC-2389	HS-630590== SIC-2393
HS-580121== SIC-2211	HS-600192== SIC-2257	HS-610791== SIC-2322	HS-620319== SIC-2311	HS-621020== SIC-2385	HS-630611== SIC-2394
HS-580122== SIC-2211	HS-600199== SIC-2257	HS-610792== SIC-2322	HS-620321== SIC-2311	HS-621030== SIC-2385	HS-630612== SIC-2394
HS-580123== SIC-2211	HS-600210== SIC-2257	HS-610799== SIC-2322	HS-620322== SIC-2329	HS-621040== SIC-2385	HS-630619== SIC-2394
HS-580124== SIC-2211	HS-600220== SIC-2257	HS-610811== SIC-2341	HS-620323== SIC-2311	HS-621040== SIC-2385	HS-630621== SIC-2394
HS-580125== SIC-2211	HS-600230== SIC-2257	HS-610819== SIC-2341	HS-620329== SIC-2311	HS-621050== SIC-2385	HS-630622== SIC-2394
HS-580126== SIC-2211	HS-600241== SIC-2257	HS-610821== SIC-2341	HS-620331== SIC-2311	HS-621111== SIC-2329	HS-630622== SIC-2394
HS-580131== SIC-2221	HS-600242== SIC-2257	HS-610822== SIC-2341	HS-620332== SIC-2311	HS-621112== SIC-2339	HS-630629== SIC-2394
HS-580132== SIC-2221	HS-600243== SIC-2257	HS-610829== SIC-2341	HS-620333== SIC-2311	HS-621120== SIC-2329	HS-630631== SIC-2394
HS-580133== SIC-2221	HS-600249== SIC-2257	HS-610831== SIC-2341	HS-620339== SIC-2311	HS-621131== SIC-2329	HS-630639== SIC-2394
HS-580134== SIC-2221	HS-600291== SIC-2257	HS-610832== SIC-2341	HS-620341== SIC-2325	HS-621132== SIC-2329	HS-630641== SIC-2394
HS-580135== SIC-2221	HS-600292== SIC-2257	HS-610839== SIC-2341	HS-620342== SIC-2325	HS-621133== SIC-2329	HS-630649== SIC-2394
HS-580136== SIC-2221	HS-600293== SIC-2257	HS-610891== SIC-2341	HS-620343== SIC-2325	HS-621139== SIC-2329	HS-630691== SIC-2394
HS-580190== SIC-2221	HS-600299== SIC-2257	HS-610892== SIC-2341	HS-620349== SIC-2325	HS-621141== SIC-2369	HS-630699== SIC-2394
HS-580211== SIC-2211	HS-610110== SIC-2311	HS-610899== SIC-2341	HS-620411== SIC-2337	HS-621142== SIC-2369	HS-630710== SIC-2392
HS-580219== SIC-2211	HS-610120== SIC-2311	HS-610910== SIC-2322	HS-620412== SIC-2337	HS-621143== SIC-2369	HS-630720== SIC-3842
HS-580220== SIC-2221	HS-610130== SIC-2311	HS-610990== SIC-2321	HS-620413== SIC-2337	HS-621149== SIC-2369	HS-630790== SIC-2241
HS-580230== SIC-2221	HS-610190== SIC-2311	HS-611010== SIC-2329	HS-620419== SIC-2337	HS-621210== SIC-2342	HS-630800== SIC-3999
HS-580310== SIC-2211	HS-610210== SIC-2337	HS-611020== SIC-2329	HS-620421== SIC-2337	HS-621220== SIC-2342	HS-630900== SIC-9200
HS-580390== SIC-2221	HS-610220== SIC-2337	HS-611030== SIC-2329	HS-620422== SIC-2337	HS-621230== SIC-2342	HS-631010== SIC-9100
HS-580390== SIC-2221	HS-610230== SIC-2337	HS-611090== SIC-2329	HS-620423== SIC-2337	HS-621290== SIC-2389	HS-631090== SIC-9100
HS-580410== SIC-2258	HS-610290== SIC-2337	HS-611110== SIC-2369	HS-620429== SIC-2337	HS-621310== SIC-2389	HS-640110== SIC-3021
HS-580421== SIC-2258	HS-610311== SIC-2311	HS-611120== SIC-2369	HS-620431== SIC-2337	HS-621320== SIC-2389	HS-640191== SIC-3021
HS-580429== SIC-2258	HS-610312== SIC-2311	HS-611130== SIC-2369	HS-620432== SIC-2337	HS-621390== SIC-2389	HS-640192== SIC-3021
HS-580430== SIC-2258	HS-610319== SIC-2311	HS-611190== SIC-2369	HS-620433== SIC-2337	HS-621410== SIC-2369	HS-640192== SIC-3021
HS-580500== SIC-9900	HS-610321== SIC-2311	HS-611211== SIC-2329	HS-620439== SIC-2337	HS-621420== SIC-2369	HS-640199== SIC-3021
HS-580610== SIC-2241	HS-610322== SIC-2311	HS-611212== SIC-2329	HS-620441== SIC-2335	HS-621430== SIC-2369	HS-640211== SIC-3021
HS-580620== SIC-2241	HS-610323== SIC-2311	HS-611219== SIC-2369	HS-620442== SIC-2335	HS-621440== SIC-2369	HS-640219== SIC-3021
HS-580631== SIC-2241	HS-610329== SIC-2311	HS-611220== SIC-2369	HS-620443== SIC-2335	HS-621490== SIC-2369	HS-640220== SIC-3021
HS-580632== SIC-2241	HS-610331== SIC-2311	HS-611231== SIC-2329	HS-620444== SIC-2335	HS-621510== SIC-2323	HS-640230== SIC-3021
HS-580639== SIC-2241	HS-610332== SIC-2311	HS-611239== SIC-2329	HS-620449== SIC-2335	HS-621520== SIC-2323	HS-640291== SIC-3021
HS-580640== SIC-2241	HS-610333== SIC-2311	HS-611241== SIC-2339	HS-620451== SIC-2337	HS-621590== SIC-2323	HS-640299== SIC-3021
HS-580710== SIC-2241	HS-610339== SIC-2311	HS-611249== SIC-2339	HS-620452== SIC-2337	HS-621600== SIC-2381	HS-640311== SIC-3149
HS-580790== SIC-2399	HS-610341== SIC-2325	HS-611300== SIC-2385	HS-620453== SIC-2337	HS-621710== SIC-2389	HS-640319== SIC-3149
HS-580810== SIC-2241	HS-610342== SIC-2325	HS-611410== SIC-2369	HS-620459== SIC-2337	HS-621790== SIC-2369	HS-640320== SIC-3149
HS-580890== SIC-2396	HS-610343== SIC-2325	HS-611420== SIC-2369	HS-620461== SIC-2369	HS-630110== SIC-3634	HS-640330== SIC-3144
HS-580900== SIC-2299	HS-610349== SIC-2325	HS-611430== SIC-2369	HS-620462== SIC-2369	HS-630120== SIC-2392	HS-640340== SIC-3143
HS-581010== SIC-2395	HS-610411== SIC-2337	HS-611490== SIC-2369	HS-620463== SIC-2369	HS-630130== SIC-2392	HS-640351== SIC-3143
HS-581091== SIC-2395	HS-610412== SIC-2337	HS-611511== SIC-2252	HS-620469== SIC-2369	HS-630140== SIC-2392	HS-640359== SIC-3143
HS-581092== SIC-2395	HS-610413== SIC-2337	HS-611512== SIC-2252	HS-620510== SIC-2321	HS-630190== SIC-2392	HS-640391== SIC-3143
HS-581099== SIC-2395	HS-610419== SIC-2337	HS-611519== SIC-2252	HS-620520== SIC-2321	HS-630210== SIC-2392	HS-640399== SIC-3142
HS-581100== SIC-2395	HS-610421== SIC-2337	HS-611520== SIC-2252	HS-620530== SIC-2321	HS-630221== SIC-2392	HS-640411== SIC-3021
HS-590110== SIC-2295	HS-610422== SIC-2337	HS-611591== SIC-2252	HS-620590== SIC-2321	HS-630222== SIC-2392	HS-640419== SIC-3143
HS-590190== SIC-2295	HS-610423== SIC-2337	HS-611592== SIC-2252	HS-620610== SIC-2331	HS-630229== SIC-2392	HS-640420== SIC-3143
HS-590210== SIC-2296	HS-610429== SIC-2337	HS-611593== SIC-2252	HS-620620== SIC-2331	HS-630231== SIC-2392	HS-640510== SIC-3143
HS-590220== SIC-2296	HS-610431== SIC-2337	HS-611599== SIC-2252	HS-620630== SIC-2331	HS-630232== SIC-2392	HS-640520== SIC-3142
HS-590290== SIC-2296	HS-610432== SIC-2337	HS-611610== SIC-3069	HS-620640== SIC-2331	HS-630239== SIC-2392	HS-640590== SIC-3149
HS-590310== SIC-2295	HS-610433== SIC-2337	HS-611691== SIC-2381	HS-620690== SIC-2331	HS-630240== SIC-2392	HS-640610== SIC-3131
HS-590310== SIC-2295	HS-610439== SIC-2337	HS-611692== SIC-2381	HS-620711== SIC-2322	HS-630251== SIC-2392	HS-640620== SIC-3069
HS-590310== SIC-2295	HS-610441== SIC-2335	HS-611693== SIC-2381	HS-620719== SIC-2322	HS-630252== SIC-2392	HS-640691== SIC-3131
HS-590320== SIC-2295	HS-610442== SIC-2335	HS-611699== SIC-2381	HS-620721== SIC-2322	HS-630253== SIC-2392	HS-640699== SIC-2252
HS-590390== SIC-2295	HS-610443== SIC-2335	HS-611710== SIC-2369	HS-620722== SIC-2322	HS-630259== SIC-2392	HS-650100== SIC-2353
HS-590410== SIC-3996	HS-610444== SIC-2335	HS-611720== SIC-2323	HS-620729== SIC-2322	HS-630260== SIC-2392	HS-650200== SIC-2353
HS-590491== SIC-3996	HS-610449== SIC-2335	HS-611780== SIC-2389	HS-620791== SIC-2384	HS-630291== SIC-2392	HS-650300== SIC-2353
HS-590492== SIC-3996	HS-610451== SIC-2337	HS-611790== SIC-2369	HS-620791== SIC-2322	HS-630292== SIC-2392	HS-650400== SIC-2353
HS-590500== SIC-2679	HS-610452== SIC-2337	HS-620111== SIC-2311	HS-620792== SIC-2384	HS-630293== SIC-2392	HS-650510== SIC-3999
HS-590610== SIC-3069	HS-610453=== SIC-2337	HS-620112== SIC-2385	HS-620792== SIC-2322	HS-630299== SIC-2392	HS-650590== SIC-2353

HS-650610== SIC-3842	HS-681520== SIC-3299	HS-701590== SIC-3231	HS-720140= SIC-3313	HS-721031= SIC-3312	HS-721923= SIC-3312
HS-650691= SIC-3069	HS-681591= SIC-3295	HS-701610== SIC-3231	HS-720211= SIC-3313	HS-721039= SIC-3312	HS-721924= SIC-3312
HS-650692= SIC-2371	HS-681599= SIC-3295	HS-701690== SIC-3231	HS-720219= SIC-3313	HS-721041= SIC-3312	HS-721931= SIC-3312
HS-650699= SIC-2353	HS-690100== SIC-3297	HS-701710== SIC-3229	HS-720221= SIC-3313	HS-721049= SIC-3312	HS-721932= SIC-3312
HS-650700= SIC-2396	HS-690210== SIC-3297	HS-701720= SIC-3229	HS-720229= SIC-3313	HS-721050= SIC-3312	HS-721933= SIC-3312
HS-660110== SIC-3999	HS-690210== SIC-3297	HS-701790= SIC-3229	HS-720230= SIC-3313	HS-721060= SIC-3312	HS-721934= SIC-3312
HS-660191== SIC-3999	HS-690220== SIC-3255	HS-701790= SIC-3229	HS-720241= SIC-3313	HS-721070= SIC-3312	HS-721935= SIC-3312
HS-660199== SIC-3999	HS-690290== SIC-3255	HS-701810= SIC-3961	HS-720249= SIC-3313	HS-721090= SIC-3312	HS-721990= SIC-3312
HS-660200== SIC-3999	HS-690310== SIC-3297	HS-701820= SIC-3231	HS-720250= SIC-3313	HS-721111= SIC-3312	HS-722011= SIC-3312
HS-660310== SIC-3999	HS-690320== SIC-3255	HS-701890= SIC-3231	HS-720260= SIC-3313	HS-721112= SIC-3312	HS-722012= SIC-3312
HS-660320== SIC-3999	HS-690390== SIC-3255	HS-701910= SIC-3229	HS-720270= SIC-3313	HS-721119= SIC-3312	HS-722020= SIC-3312
HS-660390== SIC-3999	HS-690410== SIC-3251	HS-701920= SIC-2241	HS-720280= SIC-3313	HS-721121= SIC-3312	HS-722090= SIC-3312
HS-670100== SIC-3999	HS-690490== SIC-3251	HS-701931= SIC-3229	HS-720291= SIC-3313	HS-721122= SIC-3312	HS-722100= SIC-3312
HS-670210== SIC-3999	HS-690510== SIC-3259	HS-701932= SIC-3229	HS-720292= SIC-3313	HS-721129= SIC-3312	HS-722210= SIC-3312
HS-670290== SIC-3999	HS-690590== SIC-3259	HS-701939= SIC-3296	HS-720293= SIC-3313	HS-721130= SIC-3312	HS-722220= SIC-3312
HS-670300== SIC-3999	HS-690600== SIC-3259	HS-701990= SIC-3296	HS-720299= SIC-3313	HS-721141= SIC-3312	HS-722230= SIC-3312
HS-670411== SIC-3999	HS-690710== SIC-3253	HS-702000= SIC-3229	HS-720310= SIC-3313	HS-721149= SIC-3312	HS-722240= SIC-3312
HS-670419== SIC-3999	HS-690790== SIC-3253	HS-710110= SIC-3915	HS-720390= SIC-3313	HS-721190= SIC-3312	HS-722300= SIC-3315
HS-670420== SIC-3999	HS-690810== SIC-3253	HS-710121= SIC-0919	HS-720410= SIC-9100	HS-721210= SIC-3312	HS-722410= SIC-3312
HS-670490== SIC-3999	HS-690890== SIC-3253	HS-710122= SIC-3915	HS-720421= SIC-9100	HS-721221= SIC-3312	HS-722490= SIC-3312
HS-680100== SIC-3281	HS-690911== SIC-3269	HS-710210= SIC-3915	HS-720429= SIC-9100	HS-721229= SIC-3312	HS-722510= SIC-3312
HS-680210== SIC-3281	HS-690919== SIC-3269	HS-710221= SIC-3915	HS-720430= SIC-9100	HS-721230= SIC-3312	HS-722520= SIC-3312
HS-680221== SIC-3281	HS-690919== SIC-3269	HS-710229= SIC-3915	HS-720441= SIC-9100	HS-721240= SIC-3312	HS-722530= SIC-3312
HS-680222== SIC-3281	HS-690990== SIC-3269	HS-710231= SIC-3915	HS-720449= SIC-9100	HS-721250= SIC-3312	HS-722540= SIC-3312
HS-680223== SIC-3281	HS-691010== SIC-3261	HS-710239= SIC-3915	HS-720450= SIC-9100	HS-721260= SIC-3312	HS-722550= SIC-3312
HS-680229== SIC-3281	HS-691190== SIC-3269	HS-710239= SIC-3915	HS-720510= SIC-3399	HS-721310= SIC-3312	HS-722590= SIC-3312
HS-680291== SIC-3281	HS-691200== SIC-3269	HS-710310= SIC-3915	HS-720521= SIC-3399	HS-721320= SIC-3312	HS-722610= SIC-3312
HS-680292== SIC-3281	HS-691310== SIC-3269	HS-710391= SIC-3915	HS-720529= SIC-3399	HS-721331= SIC-3312	HS-722620= SIC-3312
HS-680293== SIC-3281	HS-691390== SIC-3269	HS-710399= SIC-3915	HS-720610= SIC-3312	HS-721339= SIC-3312	HS-722691= SIC-3312
HS-680299== SIC-3281	HS-691410== SIC-3269	HS-710399= SIC-3915	HS-720690= SIC-3312	HS-721341= SIC-3312	HS-722692= SIC-3312
HS-680300== SIC-3281	HS-691490== SIC-3269	HS-710410= SIC-3915	HS-720711= SIC-3312	HS-721349= SIC-3312	HS-722692= SIC-3312
HS-680410== SIC-3291	HS-700100== SIC-3229	HS-710420= SIC-3915	HS-720712= SIC-3312	HS-721350= SIC-3312	HS-722699= SIC-3312
HS-680421== SIC-3291	HS-700210== SIC-3229	HS-710490= SIC-3915	HS-720719= SIC-3312	HS-721410= SIC-3312	HS-722710= SIC-3312
HS-680422== SIC-3291	HS-700220== SIC-3229	HS-710510= SIC-3291	HS-720720= SIC-3312	HS-721420= SIC-3312	HS-722720= SIC-3312
HS-680423== SIC-3291	HS-700231== SIC-3229	HS-710590= SIC-3291	HS-720811= SIC-3312	HS-721430= SIC-3312	HS-722790= SIC-3312
HS-680430== SIC-3291	HS-700232== SIC-3229	HS-710610= SIC-3399	HS-720812= SIC-3312	HS-721440= SIC-3312	HS-722810= SIC-3312
HS-680510== SIC-3291	HS-700239== SIC-3229	HS-710691= SIC-3339	HS-720813= SIC-3312	HS-721450= SIC-3312	HS-722820= SIC-3312
HS-680520== SIC-3291	HS-700311== SIC-3211	HS-710692= SIC-3356	HS-720814= SIC-3312	HS-721460= SIC-3312	HS-722830= SIC-3312
HS-680530== SIC-3291	HS-700319== SIC-3211	HS-710700= SIC-3356	HS-720821= SIC-3312	HS-721510= SIC-3312	HS-722830= SIC-3312
HS-680610== SIC-3296	HS-700320== SIC-3231	HS-710811= SIC-3399	HS-720822= SIC-3312	HS-721520= SIC-3312	HS-722840= SIC-3312
HS-680620== SIC-3295	HS-700330== SIC-3231	HS-710812= SIC-3339	HS-720823= SIC-3312	HS-721530= SIC-3312	HS-722850= SIC-3312
HS-680690== SIC-3296	HS-700410== SIC-3211	HS-710813= SIC-3356	HS-720824= SIC-3312	HS-721540= SIC-3312	HS-722850= SIC-3312
HS-680710== SIC-2952	HS-700490== SIC-3211	HS-710900= SIC-3356	HS-720831= SIC-3312	HS-721590= SIC-3312	HS-722860= SIC-3312
HS-680790== SIC-2952	HS-700510== SIC-3211	HS-711011= SIC-3339	HS-720832= SIC-3312	HS-721610= SIC-3312	HS-722860= SIC-3312
HS-680800== SIC-3272	HS-700521== SIC-3211	HS-711019= SIC-3356	HS-720833= SIC-3312	HS-721621= SIC-3312	HS-722870= SIC-3312
HS-680911== SIC-3275	HS-700529== SIC-3211	HS-711021= SIC-3339	HS-720834= SIC-3312	HS-721622= SIC-3312	HS-722880= SIC-3312
HS-680919== SIC-3275	HS-700530== SIC-3231	HS-711029= SIC-3356	HS-720835= SIC-3312	HS-721631= SIC-3312	HS-722910= SIC-3315
HS-680990== SIC-3299	HS-700600== SIC-3231	HS-711031= SIC-3339	HS-720841= SIC-3312	HS-721632= SIC-3312	HS-722920= SIC-3315
HS-681011== SIC-3271	HS-700711== SIC-3231	HS-711039= SIC-3356	HS-720842= SIC-3312	HS-721633= SIC-3312	HS-722990= SIC-3315
HS-681019== SIC-3272	HS-700719== SIC-3231	HS-711041= SIC-3339	HS-720843= SIC-3312	HS-721640= SIC-3312	HS-730110= SIC-3312
HS-681019== SIC-3272	HS-700721== SIC-3211	HS-711049= SIC-3356	HS-720844= SIC-3312	HS-721650= SIC-3312	HS-730120= SIC-3312
HS-681020== SIC-3272	HS-700721== SIC-3211	HS-711100= SIC-3356	HS-720845= SIC-3312	HS-721660= SIC-3312	HS-730120= SIC-3312
HS-681091== SIC-3272	HS-700729== SIC-3211	HS-711210= SIC-9100	HS-720890= SIC-3312	HS-721690= SIC-3312	HS-730210= SIC-3312
HS-681099== SIC-3272	HS-700800== SIC-3231	HS-711220= SIC-9100	HS-720911= SIC-3312	HS-721711= SIC-3315	HS-730210= SIC-3312
HS-681110== SIC-3292	HS-700910== SIC-3231	HS-711290= SIC-9100	HS-720912= SIC-3312	HS-721712= SIC-3315	HS-730210= SIC-3312
HS-681120== SIC-3292	HS-700991== SIC-3231	HS-711311= SIC-3911	HS-720913= SIC-3312	HS-721713= SIC-3315	HS-730210= SIC-3312
HS-681130== SIC-3292	HS-700992== SIC-3231	HS-711319= SIC-3911	HS-720914= SIC-3312	HS-721719= SIC-3315	HS-730220= SIC-3312
HS-681190== SIC-3292	HS-701010== SIC-3221	HS-711320= SIC-3911	HS-720921= SIC-3312	HS-721721= SIC-3315	HS-730230= SIC-3499
HS-681210== SIC-3292	HS-701090== SIC-3221	HS-711411= SIC-3914	HS-720922= SIC-3312	HS-721722= SIC-3315	HS-730240= SIC-3499
HS-681220== SIC-3292	HS-701110== SIC-3229	HS-711419= SIC-3914	HS-720923= SIC-3312	HS-721723= SIC-3315	HS-730290= SIC-3499
HS-681230== SIC-3292	HS-701120== SIC-3229	HS-711420= SIC-3914	HS-720924= SIC-3312	HS-721729= SIC-3315	HS-730300= SIC-3321
HS-681240== SIC-3292	HS-701190== SIC-3229	HS-711510= SIC-3496	HS-720931= SIC-3312	HS-721731= SIC-3315	HS-730410= SIC-3312
HS-681250== SIC-3842	HS-701200== SIC-3229	HS-711590= SIC-3356	HS-720932= SIC-3312	HS-721732= SIC-3315	HS-730420= SIC-3312
HS-681260== SIC-3292	HS-701310== SIC-3229	HS-711610= SIC-3911	HS-720933= SIC-3312	HS-721733= SIC-3315	HS-730431= SIC-3312
HS-681270== SIC-3292	HS-701321== SIC-3229	HS-711620= SIC-3911	HS-720934= SIC-3312	HS-721739= SIC-3315	HS-730439= SIC-3312
HS-681290== SIC-3292	HS-701329== SIC-3229	HS-711711= SIC-3961	HS-720941= SIC-3312	HS-721810= SIC-3312	HS-730441= SIC-3312
HS-681290== SIC-3053	HS-701331== SIC-3229	HS-711719= SIC-3961	HS-720942= SIC-3312	HS-721890= SIC-3312	HS-730449= SIC-3312
HS-681290== SIC-3292	HS-701332== SIC-3229	HS-711790= SIC-3961	HS-720943= SIC-3312	HS-721911= SIC-3312	HS-730451= SIC-3312
HS-681310== SIC-3292	HS-701339== SIC-3229	HS-711810= SIC-3499	HS-720944= SIC-3312	HS-721912= SIC-3312	HS-730459= SIC-3312
HS-681390== SIC-3292	HS-701391== SIC-3229	HS-711890= SIC-3499	HS-720990= SIC-3312	HS-721913= SIC-3312	HS-730490= SIC-3312
HS-681410== SIC-3299	HS-701399== SIC-3229	HS-720110= SIC-3312	HS-721011= SIC-3312	HS-721914= SIC-3312	HS-730511= SIC-3312
HS-681490== SIC-3299	HS-701400== SIC-3229	HS-720120= SIC-3312	HS-721012= SIC-3312	HS-721921= SIC-3312	HS-730512= SIC-3312
HS-681510== SIC-3624	HS-701510== SIC-3229	HS-720130= SIC-3312	HS-721020= SIC-3312	HS-721922= SIC-3312	HS-730519= SIC-3312

HS-730520= SIC-3312	HS-732010= SIC-3493	HS-741220= SIC-3494	HS-780300= SIC-3356	HS-820220= SIC-3425	HS-830260= SIC-3699
HS-730531= SIC-3648	HS-732020= SIC-3493	HS-741300= SIC-3357	HS-780411= SIC-3356	HS-820220= SIC-3425	HS-830300= SIC-3499
HS-730539= SIC-3312	HS-732090= SIC-3493	HS-741410= SIC-3496	HS-780419= SIC-3356	HS-820231= SIC-3425	HS-830400= SIC-2522
HS-730590= SIC-3312	HS-732111= SIC-3631	HS-741490= SIC-3496	HS-780420= SIC-3399	HS-820232= SIC-3425	HS-830510= SIC-2782
HS-730610= SIC-3312	HS-732112= SIC-3631	HS-741510= SIC-3399	HS-780500= SIC-3356	HS-820240= SIC-3425	HS-830520= SIC-3315
HS-730620= SIC-3312	HS-732113= SIC-3631	HS-741521= SIC-3452	HS-780600= SIC-3499	HS-820291= SIC-3425	HS-830590= SIC-3496
HS-730630= SIC-3312	HS-732181= SIC-3433	HS-741529= SIC-3452	HS-790111= SIC-3341	HS-820299= SIC-3425	HS-830610= SIC-3931
HS-730640= SIC-3312	HS-732182= SIC-3631	HS-741531= SIC-3452	HS-790112= SIC-3341	HS-820310= SIC-3423	HS-830621= SIC-3914
HS-730650= SIC-3312	HS-732183= SIC-3433	HS-741532= SIC-3452	HS-790120= SIC-3341	HS-820320= SIC-3421	HS-830629= SIC-3914
HS-730660= SIC-3312	HS-732190= SIC-3631	HS-741539= SIC-3452	HS-790200= SIC-9100	HS-820330= SIC-3421	HS-830630= SIC-3499
HS-730690= SIC-3312	HS-732211= SIC-3433	HS-741600= SIC-3493	HS-790310= SIC-3339	HS-820340= SIC-3423	HS-830710= SIC-3599
HS-730711= SIC-3321	HS-732219= SIC-3433	HS-741700= SIC-3631	HS-790390= SIC-3399	HS-820411= SIC-3423	HS-830790= SIC-3599
HS-730719= SIC-3321	HS-732290= SIC-3585	HS-741810= SIC-3499	HS-790400= SIC-3356	HS-820412= SIC-3423	HS-830810= SIC-3965
HS-730721= SIC-3494	HS-732310= SIC-3291	HS-741820= SIC-3431	HS-790500= SIC-3356	HS-820420= SIC-3423	HS-830820= SIC-3965
HS-730722= SIC-3494	HS-732391= SIC-3499	HS-741910= SIC-3496	HS-790600= SIC-3356	HS-820510= SIC-3423	HS-830890= SIC-3965
HS-730723= SIC-3494	HS-732392= SIC-3499	HS-741991= SIC-3432	HS-790710= SIC-3444	HS-820520= SIC-3423	HS-830890= SIC-3965
HS-730729= SIC-3494	HS-732393= SIC-3499	HS-741991= SIC-3499	HS-790790= SIC-3499	HS-820530= SIC-3423	HS-830910= SIC-3466
HS-730791= SIC-3494	HS-732393= SIC-3499	HS-741999= SIC-3499	HS-790790= SIC-3499	HS-820540= SIC-3423	HS-830990= SIC-3466
HS-730792= SIC-3494	HS-732394= SIC-3499	HS-750110= SIC-3339	HS-800110= SIC-3339	HS-820551= SIC-3423	HS-831000= SIC-3993
HS-730792= SIC-3494	HS-732399= SIC-3499	HS-750120= SIC-3339	HS-800120= SIC-3339	HS-820559= SIC-3423	HS-831110= SIC-3548
HS-730792= SIC-3494	HS-732410= SIC-3431	HS-750210= SIC-3339	HS-800200= SIC-9100	HS-820560= SIC-3548	HS-831120= SIC-3548
HS-730793= SIC-3494	HS-732421= SIC-3431	HS-750220= SIC-3339	HS-800300= SIC-3356	HS-820570= SIC-3423	HS-831130= SIC-3548
HS-730793= SIC-3494	HS-732429= SIC-3431	HS-750300= SIC-9100	HS-800400= SIC-3356	HS-820580= SIC-3423	HS-831190= SIC-3548
HS-730799= SIC-3494	HS-732490= SIC-3431	HS-750400= SIC-3399	HS-800510= SIC-3497	HS-820590= SIC-3423	HS-840110= SIC-3443
HS-730799= SIC-3494	HS-732510= SIC-3321	HS-750511= SIC-3356	HS-800520= SIC-3399	HS-820600= SIC-3423	HS-840120= SIC-3569
HS-730810= SIC-3441	HS-732591= SIC-3321	HS-750512= SIC-3356	HS-800600= SIC-3356	HS-820711= SIC-3532	HS-840130= SIC-3569
HS-730820= SIC-3441	HS-732599= SIC-3321	HS-750521= SIC-3356	HS-800700= SIC-3499	HS-820712= SIC-3532	HS-840140= SIC-3443
HS-730830= SIC-3442	HS-732611= SIC-3499	HS-750522= SIC-3356	HS-810110= SIC-3399	HS-820720= SIC-3544	HS-840211= SIC-3443
HS-730840= SIC-3446	HS-732619= SIC-3499	HS-750610= SIC-3356	HS-810191= SIC-3356	HS-820730= SIC-3544	HS-840212= SIC-3443
HS-730890= SIC-3441	HS-732620= SIC-3496	HS-750620= SIC-3356	HS-810192= SIC-3356	HS-820740= SIC-3544	HS-840219= SIC-3443
HS-730900= SIC-3443	HS-732690= SIC-3499	HS-750711= SIC-3356	HS-810193= SIC-3356	HS-820750= SIC-3544	HS-840220= SIC-3443
HS-731010= SIC-3412	HS-740110= SIC-3331	HS-750712= SIC-3356	HS-810199= SIC-3356	HS-820760= SIC-3544	HS-840290= SIC-3443
HS-731010= SIC-3412	HS-740120= SIC-3331	HS-750720= SIC-3494	HS-810210= SIC-3399	HS-820770= SIC-3544	HS-840310= SIC-3433
HS-731021= SIC-3412	HS-740200= SIC-3331	HS-750800= SIC-3499	HS-810291= SIC-3339	HS-820780= SIC-3544	HS-840390= SIC-3433
HS-731029= SIC-3412	HS-740311= SIC-3331	HS-760110= SIC-3334	HS-810292= SIC-3356	HS-820790= SIC-3544	HS-840410= SIC-3443
HS-731100= SIC-3443	HS-740312= SIC-3331	HS-760120= SIC-3334	HS-810293= SIC-3356	HS-820790= SIC-3544	HS-840420= SIC-3443
HS-731210= SIC-3496	HS-740313= SIC-3331	HS-760200= SIC-9100	HS-810299= SIC-3356	HS-820810= SIC-3544	HS-840490= SIC-3443
HS-731290= SIC-3496	HS-740319= SIC-3331	HS-760310= SIC-3399	HS-810310= SIC-9100	HS-820820= SIC-3423	HS-840510= SIC-3569
HS-731300= SIC-3496	HS-740321= SIC-3331	HS-760320= SIC-3399	HS-810310= SIC-3399	HS-820830= SIC-3423	HS-840590= SIC-3569
HS-731411= SIC-3496	HS-740322= SIC-3331	HS-760410= SIC-3354	HS-810310= SIC-3356	HS-820840= SIC-3423	HS-840611= SIC-3511
HS-731419= SIC-3496	HS-740323= SIC-3331	HS-760421= SIC-3354	HS-810390= SIC-3356	HS-820890= SIC-3423	HS-840619= SIC-3511
HS-731420= SIC-3496	HS-740329= SIC-3331	HS-760429= SIC-3354	HS-810411= SIC-3339	HS-820900= SIC-3544	HS-840690= SIC-3511
HS-731430= SIC-3496	HS-740400= SIC-9100	HS-760511= SIC-3357	HS-810419= SIC-3339	HS-821000= SIC-3423	HS-840710= SIC-3724
HS-731441= SIC-3496	HS-740500= SIC-3331	HS-760519= SIC-3357	HS-810420= SIC-9100	HS-821110= SIC-3421	HS-840721= SIC-3519
HS-731442= SIC-3496	HS-740610= SIC-3399	HS-760521= SIC-3357	HS-810430= SIC-3399	HS-821191= SIC-3914	HS-840729= SIC-3519
HS-731449= SIC-3496	HS-740620= SIC-3399	HS-760521= SIC-3357	HS-810490= SIC-3356	HS-821192= SIC-3421	HS-840731= SIC-3714
HS-731450= SIC-3449	HS-740710= SIC-3351	HS-760529= SIC-3357	HS-810510= SIC-3356	HS-821193= SIC-3421	HS-840732= SIC-3714
HS-731511= SIC-3496	HS-740721= SIC-3351	HS-760611= SIC-3353	HS-810590= SIC-3356	HS-821194= SIC-3421	HS-840733= SIC-3714
HS-731512= SIC-3496	HS-740722= SIC-3351	HS-760612= SIC-3353	HS-810600= SIC-3356	HS-821210= SIC-3421	HS-840734= SIC-3714
HS-731519= SIC-3496	HS-740729= SIC-3351	HS-760691= SIC-3353	HS-810710= SIC-3356	HS-821220= SIC-3421	HS-840790= SIC-3519
HS-731520= SIC-3496	HS-740811= SIC-3357	HS-760692= SIC-3353	HS-810790= SIC-3356	HS-821290= SIC-3421	HS-840790= SIC-3519
HS-731581= SIC-3496	HS-740819= SIC-3357	HS-760711= SIC-3353	HS-810810= SIC-9100	HS-821300= SIC-3421	HS-840810= SIC-3519
HS-731582= SIC-3496	HS-740821= SIC-3357	HS-760719= SIC-3497	HS-810890= SIC-3356	HS-821410= SIC-3421	HS-840820= SIC-3519
HS-731589= SIC-3496	HS-740822= SIC-3357	HS-760720= SIC-3497	HS-810910= SIC-3339	HS-821420= SIC-3421	HS-840890= SIC-3519
HS-731590= SIC-3496	HS-740829= SIC-3357	HS-760810= SIC-3354	HS-810990= SIC-3356	HS-821490= SIC-3421	HS-840910= SIC-3724
HS-731600= SIC-3499	HS-740911= SIC-3351	HS-760820= SIC-3354	HS-811000= SIC-3339	HS-821510= SIC-3914	HS-840910= SIC-3724
HS-731700= SIC-3315	HS-740919= SIC-3351	HS-760900= SIC-3494	HS-811100= SIC-3339	HS-821520= SIC-3421	HS-840991= SIC-3714
HS-731811= SIC-3452	HS-740921= SIC-3351	HS-761010= SIC-3442	HS-811211= SIC-9100	HS-821591= SIC-3914	HS-840999= SIC-3519
HS-731812= SIC-3452	HS-740929= SIC-3351	HS-761090= SIC-3444	HS-811219= SIC-3339	HS-821599= SIC-3914	HS-841011= SIC-3511
HS-731813= SIC-3452	HS-740931= SIC-3351	HS-761100= SIC-3443	HS-811220= SIC-3339	HS-830110= SIC-3429	HS-841012= SIC-3511
HS-731814= SIC-3452	HS-740939= SIC-3351	HS-761210= SIC-3499	HS-811230= SIC-3339	HS-830120= SIC-3429	HS-841013= SIC-3511
HS-731815= SIC-3452	HS-740940= SIC-3351	HS-761290= SIC-3411	HS-811240= SIC-3339	HS-830130= SIC-3429	HS-841090= SIC-3511
HS-731816= SIC-3452	HS-740990= SIC-3351	HS-761300= SIC-3443	HS-811291= SIC-3339	HS-830140= SIC-3429	HS-841111= SIC-3724
HS-731819= SIC-3452	HS-741011= SIC-3351	HS-761410= SIC-3357	HS-811299= SIC-3356	HS-830150= SIC-3429	HS-841112= SIC-3724
HS-731821= SIC-3452	HS-741012= SIC-3351	HS-761490= SIC-3357	HS-811300= SIC-3499	HS-830160= SIC-3429	HS-841121= SIC-3724
HS-731822= SIC-3452	HS-741021= SIC-3497	HS-761510= SIC-3365	HS-820110= SIC-3423	HS-830170= SIC-3429	HS-841122= SIC-3724
HS-731823= SIC-3452	HS-741021= SIC-3497	HS-761520= SIC-3431	HS-820120= SIC-3423	HS-830210= SIC-3429	HS-841181= SIC-3724
HS-731824= SIC-3452	HS-741022= SIC-3497	HS-761610= SIC-3399	HS-820130= SIC-3423	HS-830220= SIC-3429	HS-841182= SIC-3724
HS-731829= SIC-3452	HS-741110= SIC-3351	HS-761690= SIC-3499	HS-820140= SIC-3423	HS-830230= SIC-3429	HS-841191= SIC-3511
HS-731910= SIC-3965	HS-741121= SIC-3351	HS-780110= SIC-3339	HS-820150= SIC-3421	HS-830241= SIC-3429	HS-841199= SIC-3511
HS-731920= SIC-3965	HS-741122= SIC-3351	HS-780191= SIC-3339	HS-820160= SIC-3421	HS-830242= SIC-3429	HS-841210= SIC-3764
HS-731930= SIC-3965	HS-741129= SIC-3351	HS-780199= SIC-3339	HS-820190= SIC-3423	HS-830249= SIC-2591	HS-841221= SIC-3593
HS-731990= SIC-3965	HS-741210= SIC-3494	HS-780200= SIC-9100	HS-820210= SIC-3425	HS-830250= SIC-2599	HS-841229= SIC-3561

HS-841231= SIC-3593	HS-842131= SIC-3714	HS-843131= SIC-3536	HS-844340= SIC-3555	HS-845730= SIC-3541	HS-846921= SIC-3579
HS-841239= SIC-3594	HS-842139= SIC-3564	HS-843139= SIC-3533	HS-844350= SIC-3552	HS-845811= SIC-3541	HS-846929= SIC-3579
HS-841280= SIC-3599	HS-842191= SIC-3633	HS-843141= SIC-3531	HS-844360= SIC-3555	HS-845819= SIC-3541	HS-846931= SIC-3579
HS-841290= SIC-3561	HS-842199= SIC-3569	HS-843142= SIC-3531	HS-844390= SIC-3552	HS-845891= SIC-3541	HS-846939= SIC-3579
HS-841311= SIC-3586	HS-842211= SIC-3639	HS-843143= SIC-3533	HS-844400= SIC-3552	HS-845899= SIC-3541	HS-847010= SIC-3578
HS-841319= SIC-3586	HS-842219= SIC-3639	HS-843149= SIC-3531	HS-844511= SIC-3552	HS-845910= SIC-3541	HS-847021= SIC-3578
HS-841320= SIC-3561	HS-842220= SIC-3565	HS-843210= SIC-3523	HS-844512= SIC-3552	HS-845921= SIC-3541	HS-847029= SIC-3578
HS-841330= SIC-3714	HS-842230= SIC-3565	HS-843221= SIC-3523	HS-844513= SIC-3552	HS-845929= SIC-3541	HS-847030= SIC-3578
HS-841340= SIC-3531	HS-842240= SIC-3565	HS-843229= SIC-3523	HS-844519= SIC-3569	HS-845931= SIC-3541	HS-847040= SIC-3578
HS-841350= SIC-3561	HS-842290= SIC-3639	HS-843230= SIC-3523	HS-844520= SIC-3552	HS-845939= SIC-3541	HS-847050= SIC-3578
HS-841360= SIC-3594	HS-842310= SIC-3596	HS-843240= SIC-3523	HS-844530= SIC-3552	HS-845940= SIC-3541	HS-847090= SIC-3579
HS-841370= SIC-3561	HS-842320= SIC-3596	HS-843280= SIC-3523	HS-844540= SIC-3552	HS-845951= SIC-3541	HS-847110= SIC-3571
HS-841381= SIC-3561	HS-842330= SIC-3596	HS-843290= SIC-3523	HS-844590= SIC-3552	HS-845959= SIC-3541	HS-847120= SIC-3571
HS-841382= SIC-3561	HS-842381= SIC-3596	HS-843311= SIC-3524	HS-844610= SIC-3552	HS-845961= SIC-3541	HS-847191= SIC-3571
HS-841391= SIC-3714	HS-842382= SIC-3596	HS-843319= SIC-3524	HS-844621= SIC-3552	HS-845969= SIC-3541	HS-847192= SIC-3577
HS-841392= SIC-3561	HS-842389= SIC-3596	HS-843320= SIC-3523	HS-844629= SIC-3552	HS-845970= SIC-3541	HS-847193= SIC-3572
HS-841410= SIC-3563	HS-842390= SIC-3596	HS-843330= SIC-3523	HS-844630= SIC-3552	HS-846011= SIC-3541	HS-847199= SIC-3571
HS-841420= SIC-3563	HS-842410= SIC-3999	HS-843340= SIC-3523	HS-844711= SIC-3552	HS-846019= SIC-3541	HS-847210= SIC-3579
HS-841430= SIC-3585	HS-842420= SIC-3563	HS-843351= SIC-3523	HS-844712= SIC-3552	HS-846021= SIC-3541	HS-847220= SIC-3579
HS-841440= SIC-3563	HS-842430= SIC-3559	HS-843352= SIC-3523	HS-844720= SIC-3552	HS-846029= SIC-3541	HS-847230= SIC-3579
HS-841451= SIC-3564	HS-842481= SIC-3523	HS-843353= SIC-3523	HS-844790= SIC-3552	HS-846031= SIC-3541	HS-847290= SIC-3578
HS-841459= SIC-3714	HS-842489= SIC-3569	HS-843359= SIC-3523	HS-844811= SIC-3552	HS-846039= SIC-3541	HS-847310= SIC-3579
HS-841460= SIC-3564	HS-842490= SIC-3559	HS-843360= SIC-3556	HS-844819= SIC-3552	HS-846040= SIC-3541	HS-847321= SIC-3579
HS-841480= SIC-3563	HS-842511= SIC-3536	HS-843390= SIC-3524	HS-844820= SIC-3552	HS-846090= SIC-3541	HS-847329= SIC-3579
HS-841490= SIC-3634	HS-842519= SIC-3536	HS-843410= SIC-3523	HS-844831= SIC-3552	HS-846110= SIC-3541	HS-847330= SIC-3571
HS-841510= SIC-3585	HS-842520= SIC-3531	HS-843420= SIC-3556	HS-844832= SIC-3569	HS-846120= SIC-3541	HS-847340= SIC-3579
HS-841581= SIC-3585	HS-842531= SIC-3531	HS-843490= SIC-3523	HS-844833= SIC-3552	HS-846130= SIC-3541	HS-847410= SIC-3531
HS-841582= SIC-3585	HS-842539= SIC-3531	HS-843510= SIC-3556	HS-844839= SIC-3552	HS-846140= SIC-3541	HS-847420= SIC-3531
HS-841583= SIC-3585	HS-842541= SIC-3534	HS-843590= SIC-3556	HS-844841= SIC-3552	HS-846150= SIC-3541	HS-847431= SIC-3531
HS-841590= SIC-3585	HS-842542= SIC-3569	HS-843610= SIC-3523	HS-844842= SIC-3552	HS-846190= SIC-3541	HS-847432= SIC-3531
HS-841610= SIC-3433	HS-842549= SIC-3569	HS-843621= SIC-3523	HS-844849= SIC-3552	HS-846210= SIC-3542	HS-847439= SIC-3531
HS-841620= SIC-3433	HS-842611= SIC-3536	HS-843629= SIC-3523	HS-844851= SIC-3552	HS-846221= SIC-3542	HS-847480= SIC-3569
HS-841630= SIC-3433	HS-842612= SIC-3537	HS-843680= SIC-3531	HS-844859= SIC-3552	HS-846229= SIC-3542	HS-847490= SIC-3532
HS-841690= SIC-3433	HS-842619= SIC-3536	HS-843691= SIC-3523	HS-844900= SIC-3552	HS-846231= SIC-3542	HS-847510= SIC-3569
HS-841710= SIC-3569	HS-842620= SIC-3531	HS-843699= SIC-3531	HS-845011= SIC-3633	HS-846239= SIC-3542	HS-847520= SIC-3569
HS-841720= SIC-3556	HS-842630= SIC-3531	HS-843710= SIC-3556	HS-845012= SIC-3633	HS-846241= SIC-3542	HS-847590= SIC-3569
HS-841780= SIC-3569	HS-842641= SIC-3531	HS-843780= SIC-3556	HS-845019= SIC-3633	HS-846249= SIC-3542	HS-847611= SIC-3581
HS-841790= SIC-3567	HS-842649= SIC-3531	HS-843790= SIC-3556	HS-845020= SIC-3633	HS-846291= SIC-3542	HS-847619= SIC-3581
HS-841810= SIC-3632	HS-842691= SIC-3531	HS-843810= SIC-3556	HS-845090= SIC-3633	HS-846299= SIC-3542	HS-847690= SIC-3581
HS-841821= SIC-3632	HS-842699= SIC-3531	HS-843820= SIC-3556	HS-845110= SIC-3633	HS-846310= SIC-3542	HS-847710= SIC-3559
HS-841822= SIC-3632	HS-842710= SIC-3537	HS-843830= SIC-3556	HS-845121= SIC-3633	HS-846320= SIC-3542	HS-847720= SIC-3559
HS-841829= SIC-3632	HS-842720= SIC-3537	HS-843840= SIC-3556	HS-845129= SIC-3633	HS-846330= SIC-3542	HS-847730= SIC-3559
HS-841830= SIC-3632	HS-842790= SIC-3537	HS-843850= SIC-3556	HS-845130= SIC-3633	HS-846390= SIC-3542	HS-847740= SIC-3559
HS-841840= SIC-3632	HS-842810= SIC-3534	HS-843850= SIC-3556	HS-845140= SIC-3552	HS-846410= SIC-3569	HS-847751= SIC-3559
HS-841850= SIC-3585	HS-842820= SIC-3535	HS-843860= SIC-3556	HS-845150= SIC-3552	HS-846420= SIC-3569	HS-847759= SIC-3559
HS-841850= SIC-3585	HS-842831= SIC-3535	HS-843880= SIC-3556	HS-845180= SIC-3633	HS-846490= SIC-3569	HS-847780= SIC-3559
HS-841861= SIC-3585	HS-842832= SIC-3535	HS-843890= SIC-3556	HS-845190= SIC-3633	HS-846510= SIC-3553	HS-847790= SIC-3559
HS-841869= SIC-3585	HS-842833= SIC-3535	HS-843910= SIC-3554	HS-845210= SIC-3639	HS-846591= SIC-3553	HS-847810= SIC-3569
HS-841869= SIC-3585	HS-842839= SIC-3535	HS-843920= SIC-3554	HS-845221= SIC-3569	HS-846592= SIC-3553	HS-847890= SIC-3569
HS-841891= SIC-3585	HS-842840= SIC-3534	HS-843930= SIC-3554	HS-845229= SIC-3569	HS-846593= SIC-3553	HS-847910= SIC-3531
HS-841899= SIC-3585	HS-842850= SIC-3532	HS-843991= SIC-3554	HS-845230= SIC-3965	HS-846594= SIC-3553	HS-847920= SIC-3556
HS-841911= SIC-3639	HS-842860= SIC-3534	HS-843999= SIC-3554	HS-845240= SIC-2517	HS-846595= SIC-3553	HS-847930= SIC-3553
HS-841919= SIC-3639	HS-842890= SIC-3537	HS-844010= SIC-3555	HS-845290= SIC-3639	HS-846596= SIC-3553	HS-847940= SIC-3542
HS-841920= SIC-3842	HS-842911= SIC-3531	HS-844090= SIC-3555	HS-845310= SIC-3569	HS-846599= SIC-3554	HS-847981= SIC-3569
HS-841931= SIC-3523	HS-842919= SIC-3531	HS-844110= SIC-3554	HS-845320= SIC-3569	HS-846610= SIC-3544	HS-847982= SIC-3569
HS-841932= SIC-3569	HS-842920= SIC-3531	HS-844120= SIC-3554	HS-845380= SIC-3569	HS-846620= SIC-3544	HS-847982= SIC-3569
HS-841939= SIC-3556	HS-842930= SIC-3531	HS-844130= SIC-3554	HS-845390= SIC-3569	HS-846630= SIC-3544	HS-847989= SIC-3585
HS-841940= SIC-3556	HS-842940= SIC-3531	HS-844140= SIC-3554	HS-845410= SIC-3559	HS-846691= SIC-3569	HS-847990= SIC-3549
HS-841950= SIC-3443	HS-842951= SIC-3531	HS-844180= SIC-3554	HS-845420= SIC-3321	HS-846692= SIC-3553	HS-848010= SIC-3544
HS-841960= SIC-3569	HS-842952= SIC-3531	HS-844190= SIC-3554	HS-845420= SIC-3559	HS-846693= SIC-3541	HS-848020= SIC-3544
HS-841981= SIC-3589	HS-842959= SIC-3531	HS-844210= SIC-3555	HS-845430= SIC-3542	HS-846694= SIC-3542	HS-848030= SIC-3543
HS-841989= SIC-3554	HS-843010= SIC-3531	HS-844220= SIC-3555	HS-845490= SIC-3542	HS-846711= SIC-3546	HS-848041= SIC-3544
HS-841990= SIC-3554	HS-843020= SIC-3524	HS-844230= SIC-3555	HS-845510= SIC-3547	HS-846719= SIC-3546	HS-848049= SIC-3544
HS-842010= SIC-3552	HS-843031= SIC-3532	HS-844240= SIC-3555	HS-845521= SIC-3547	HS-846781= SIC-3546	HS-848050= SIC-3544
HS-842091= SIC-3552	HS-843039= SIC-3532	HS-844250= SIC-2796	HS-845522= SIC-3547	HS-846789= SIC-3546	HS-848060= SIC-3544
HS-842099= SIC-3559	HS-843041= SIC-3532	HS-844250= SIC-2796	HS-845530= SIC-3321	HS-846791= SIC-3546	HS-848071= SIC-3544
HS-842111= SIC-3523	HS-843049= SIC-3533	HS-844311= SIC-3555	HS-845590= SIC-3547	HS-846792= SIC-3546	HS-848079= SIC-3544
HS-842112= SIC-3633	HS-843050= SIC-3531	HS-844312= SIC-3579	HS-845610= SIC-3699	HS-846799= SIC-3546	HS-848110= SIC-3494
HS-842119= SIC-3569	HS-843061= SIC-3531	HS-844319= SIC-3555	HS-845620= SIC-3541	HS-846810= SIC-3548	HS-848120= SIC-3492
HS-842121= SIC-3569	HS-843062= SIC-3531	HS-844321= SIC-3555	HS-845630= SIC-3541	HS-846820= SIC-3548	HS-848130= SIC-3494
HS-842122= SIC-3569	HS-843069= SIC-3531	HS-844329= SIC-3555	HS-845690= SIC-3541	HS-846880= SIC-3548	HS-848140= SIC-3494
HS-842123= SIC-3714	HS-843110= SIC-3536	HS-844330= SIC-3555	HS-845710= SIC-3541	HS-846890= SIC-3548	HS-848180= SIC-3432
HS-842129= SIC-3569	HS-843120= SIC-3537		HS-845720= SIC-3541	HS-846910= SIC-3579	HS-848190= SIC-3494

HS-848210= SIC-3562	HS-850910= SIC-3635	HS-852010= SIC-3579	HS-853649= SIC-3625	HS-860400= SIC-3743	HS-871200= SIC-3751
HS-848220= SIC-3562	HS-850920= SIC-3639	HS-852020= SIC-3661	HS-853650= SIC-3625	HS-860500= SIC-3743	HS-871310= SIC-3842
HS-848230= SIC-3562	HS-850930= SIC-3639	HS-852031= SIC-3651	HS-853661= SIC-3643	HS-860610= SIC-3743	HS-871390= SIC-3842
HS-848240= SIC-3562	HS-850940= SIC-3634	HS-852039= SIC-3651	HS-853669= SIC-3678	HS-860620= SIC-3743	HS-871411= SIC-3751
HS-848250= SIC-3562	HS-850980= SIC-3634	HS-852090= SIC-3579	HS-853690= SIC-3613	HS-860630= SIC-3743	HS-871419= SIC-3751
HS-848280= SIC-3562	HS-850990= SIC-3635	HS-852110= SIC-3651	HS-853710= SIC-3643	HS-860691= SIC-3743	HS-871420= SIC-3842
HS-848291= SIC-3562	HS-851010= SIC-3634	HS-852190= SIC-3651	HS-853720= SIC-3643	HS-860692= SIC-3743	HS-871491= SIC-3751
HS-848299= SIC-3562	HS-851020= SIC-3999	HS-852210= SIC-3679	HS-853810= SIC-3643	HS-860699= SIC-3743	HS-871492= SIC-3751
HS-848310= SIC-3714	HS-851090= SIC-3634	HS-852290= SIC-3679	HS-853890= SIC-3613	HS-860711= SIC-3743	HS-871493= SIC-3751
HS-848320= SIC-3562	HS-851110= SIC-3694	HS-852290= SIC-3679	HS-853910= SIC-3641	HS-860712= SIC-3743	HS-871494= SIC-3751
HS-848330= SIC-3562	HS-851120= SIC-3694	HS-852311= SIC-3695	HS-853921= SIC-3641	HS-860719= SIC-3321	HS-871495= SIC-3751
HS-848340= SIC-3566	HS-851130= SIC-3694	HS-852312= SIC-3695	HS-853922= SIC-3641	HS-860721= SIC-3743	HS-871496= SIC-3751
HS-848350= SIC-3714	HS-851130= SIC-3694	HS-852313= SIC-3695	HS-853929= SIC-3641	HS-860729= SIC-3743	HS-871499= SIC-3751
HS-848360= SIC-3568	HS-851140= SIC-3694	HS-852320= SIC-3695	HS-853931= SIC-3641	HS-860730= SIC-3743	HS-871500= SIC-3944
HS-848390= SIC-3568	HS-851150= SIC-3694	HS-852390= SIC-3695	HS-853939= SIC-3641	HS-860791= SIC-3743	HS-871610= SIC-3792
HS-848410= SIC-3053	HS-851180= SIC-3694	HS-852410= SIC-3652	HS-853940= SIC-3641	HS-860799= SIC-3743	HS-871620= SIC-3715
HS-848490= SIC-3053	HS-851190= SIC-3694	HS-852421= SIC-3652	HS-853990= SIC-3641	HS-860800= SIC-3669	HS-871631= SIC-3715
HS-848510= SIC-3599	HS-851210= SIC-3647	HS-852422= SIC-9900	HS-854011= SIC-3671	HS-860900= SIC-3443	HS-871639= SIC-3715
HS-848590= SIC-3599	HS-851220= SIC-3647	HS-852423= SIC-9900	HS-854012= SIC-3671	HS-870110= SIC-3524	HS-871640= SIC-3799
HS-850110= SIC-3621	HS-851230= SIC-3699	HS-852490= SIC-9900	HS-854020= SIC-3671	HS-870120= SIC-3711	HS-871680= SIC-3523
HS-850120= SIC-3621	HS-851240= SIC-3714	HS-852510= SIC-3663	HS-854030= SIC-3671	HS-870130= SIC-3531	HS-871690= SIC-3715
HS-850131= SIC-3621	HS-851290= SIC-3647	HS-852520= SIC-3663	HS-854041= SIC-3671	HS-870190= SIC-3531	HS-880110= SIC-3721
HS-850132= SIC-3621	HS-851310= SIC-3648	HS-852530= SIC-3663	HS-854042= SIC-3671	HS-870210= SIC-3711	HS-880190= SIC-3721
HS-850133= SIC-3621	HS-851390= SIC-3648	HS-852530= SIC-3663	HS-854049= SIC-3671	HS-870290= SIC-3711	HS-880211= SIC-3721
HS-850134= SIC-3621	HS-851410= SIC-3567	HS-852610= SIC-3812	HS-854081= SIC-3671	HS-870310= SIC-3799	HS-880212= SIC-3721
HS-850140= SIC-3566	HS-851420= SIC-3567	HS-852691= SIC-3812	HS-854089= SIC-3671	HS-870321= SIC-3711	HS-880220= SIC-3721
HS-850151= SIC-3566	HS-851430= SIC-3567	HS-852692= SIC-3812	HS-854091= SIC-3671	HS-870322= SIC-3711	HS-880230= SIC-3721
HS-850152= SIC-3621	HS-851440= SIC-3567	HS-852711= SIC-3651	HS-854099= SIC-3671	HS-870323= SIC-3711	HS-880240= SIC-3721
HS-850153= SIC-3621	HS-851490= SIC-3567	HS-852719= SIC-3651	HS-854110= SIC-3674	HS-870324= SIC-3711	HS-880250= SIC-3663
HS-850161= SIC-3621	HS-851511= SIC-3423	HS-852721= SIC-3651	HS-854121= SIC-3674	HS-870331= SIC-3711	HS-880310= SIC-3728
HS-850162= SIC-3621	HS-851519= SIC-3423	HS-852729= SIC-3651	HS-854129= SIC-3674	HS-870332= SIC-3711	HS-880320= SIC-3728
HS-850163= SIC-3621	HS-851521= SIC-3548	HS-852731= SIC-3651	HS-854130= SIC-3674	HS-870333= SIC-3711	HS-880330= SIC-3728
HS-850164= SIC-3621	HS-851529= SIC-3548	HS-852732= SIC-3651	HS-854140= SIC-3674	HS-870390= SIC-3711	HS-880390= SIC-3663
HS-850211= SIC-3621	HS-851531= SIC-3548	HS-852739= SIC-3651	HS-854150= SIC-3674	HS-870410= SIC-3531	HS-880400= SIC-2399
HS-850212= SIC-3621	HS-851539= SIC-3548	HS-852790= SIC-3663	HS-854160= SIC-3679	HS-870421= SIC-3711	HS-880510= SIC-3728
HS-850213= SIC-3621	HS-851580= SIC-3699	HS-852810= SIC-3651	HS-854190= SIC-3674	HS-870422= SIC-3711	HS-880520= SIC-3699
HS-850213= SIC-3621	HS-851590= SIC-3548	HS-852820= SIC-3651	HS-854211= SIC-3674	HS-870423= SIC-3531	HS-890110= SIC-3731
HS-850220= SIC-3621	HS-851610= SIC-3639	HS-852910= SIC-3679	HS-854219= SIC-3674	HS-870431= SIC-3711	HS-890120= SIC-3731
HS-850230= SIC-3511	HS-851621= SIC-3634	HS-852990= SIC-3651	HS-854220= SIC-3674	HS-870432= SIC-3711	HS-890130= SIC-3731
HS-850240= SIC-3621	HS-851629= SIC-3634	HS-853010= SIC-3669	HS-854280= SIC-3679	HS-870490= SIC-3711	HS-890190= SIC-3731
HS-850300= SIC-3621	HS-851631= SIC-3634	HS-853080= SIC-3669	HS-854290= SIC-3674	HS-870510= SIC-3537	HS-890200= SIC-3731
HS-850410= SIC-3612	HS-851632= SIC-3634	HS-853090= SIC-3669	HS-854310= SIC-3699	HS-870520= SIC-3533	HS-890310= SIC-3069
HS-850421= SIC-3612	HS-851633= SIC-3634	HS-853110= SIC-3669	HS-854320= SIC-3825	HS-870530= SIC-3711	HS-890391= SIC-3732
HS-850422= SIC-3612	HS-851640= SIC-3634	HS-853120= SIC-3679	HS-854330= SIC-3569	HS-870540= SIC-3711	HS-890392= SIC-3732
HS-850423= SIC-3612	HS-851650= SIC-3631	HS-853180= SIC-3679	HS-854380= SIC-3676	HS-870590= SIC-3711	HS-890399= SIC-3732
HS-850431= SIC-3677	HS-851660= SIC-3631	HS-853190= SIC-3669	HS-854390= SIC-3699	HS-870600= SIC-3711	HS-890400= SIC-3731
HS-850432= SIC-3677	HS-851671= SIC-3634	HS-853210= SIC-3629	HS-854411= SIC-3357	HS-870710= SIC-3711	HS-890510= SIC-3731
HS-850433= SIC-3612	HS-851672= SIC-3634	HS-853221= SIC-3675	HS-854419= SIC-3357	HS-870790= SIC-3713	HS-890520= SIC-3731
HS-850434= SIC-3612	HS-851679= SIC-3634	HS-853222= SIC-3675	HS-854420= SIC-3357	HS-870810= SIC-3465	HS-890590= SIC-3731
HS-850440= SIC-3679	HS-851680= SIC-3699	HS-853223= SIC-3675	HS-854430= SIC-3694	HS-870821= SIC-2399	HS-890600= SIC-3731
HS-850450= SIC-3677	HS-851710= SIC-3661	HS-853224= SIC-3675	HS-854441= SIC-3357	HS-870829= SIC-3465	HS-890710= SIC-3069
HS-850490= SIC-3612	HS-851720= SIC-3577	HS-853225= SIC-3675	HS-854449= SIC-3357	HS-870831= SIC-3714	HS-890790= SIC-3443
HS-850511= SIC-3499	HS-851730= SIC-3661	HS-853229= SIC-3675	HS-854451= SIC-3357	HS-870839= SIC-3714	HS-890800= SIC-9100
HS-850519= SIC-3264	HS-851740= SIC-3661	HS-853230= SIC-3675	HS-854459= SIC-3357	HS-870840= SIC-3714	HS-900110= SIC-3357
HS-850520= SIC-3625	HS-851781= SIC-3669	HS-853290= SIC-3675	HS-854460= SIC-3357	HS-870850= SIC-3531	HS-900120= SIC-3851
HS-850530= SIC-3699	HS-851782= SIC-3661	HS-853310= SIC-3676	HS-854470= SIC-3357	HS-870860= SIC-3531	HS-900130= SIC-3851
HS-850590= SIC-3699	HS-851790= SIC-3661	HS-853321= SIC-3676	HS-854511= SIC-3624	HS-870870= SIC-3531	HS-900140= SIC-3851
HS-850611= SIC-3692	HS-851810= SIC-3651	HS-853329= SIC-3676	HS-854519= SIC-3624	HS-870880= SIC-3714	HS-900150= SIC-3851
HS-850612= SIC-3692	HS-851821= SIC-3651	HS-853331= SIC-3676	HS-854520= SIC-3624	HS-870891= SIC-3523	HS-900190= SIC-3827
HS-850613= SIC-3692	HS-851822= SIC-3651	HS-853339= SIC-3643	HS-854590= SIC-3624	HS-870892= SIC-3523	HS-900190= SIC-3827
HS-850619= SIC-3692	HS-851829= SIC-3651	HS-853340= SIC-3625	HS-854610= SIC-3229	HS-870893= SIC-3523	HS-900211= SIC-3827
HS-850620= SIC-3692	HS-851830= SIC-3661	HS-853390= SIC-3676	HS-854620= SIC-3264	HS-870894= SIC-3523	HS-900211= SIC-3827
HS-850690= SIC-3692	HS-851840= SIC-3661	HS-853400= SIC-3672	HS-854690= SIC-3644	HS-870899= SIC-3523	HS-900219= SIC-3827
HS-850710= SIC-9100	HS-851850= SIC-3651	HS-853510= SIC-3643	HS-854710= SIC-3264	HS-870911= SIC-3537	HS-900220= SIC-3827
HS-850720= SIC-9100	HS-851890= SIC-3661	HS-853521= SIC-3613	HS-854720= SIC-3644	HS-870919= SIC-3537	HS-900220= SIC-3827
HS-850730= SIC-3691	HS-851910= SIC-3651	HS-853529= SIC-3613	HS-854790= SIC-3644	HS-870990= SIC-3537	HS-900290= SIC-3827
HS-850740= SIC-3691	HS-851921= SIC-3651	HS-853530= SIC-3643	HS-854800= SIC-3699	HS-871000= SIC-3795	HS-900311= SIC-3851
HS-850780= SIC-3691	HS-851929= SIC-3651	HS-853540= SIC-3678	HS-860110= SIC-3743	HS-871110= SIC-3751	HS-900319= SIC-3851
HS-850790= SIC-3691	HS-851931= SIC-3651	HS-853590= SIC-3678	HS-860120= SIC-3743	HS-871120= SIC-3751	HS-900390= SIC-3851
HS-850810= SIC-3546	HS-851939= SIC-3651	HS-853610= SIC-3613	HS-860210= SIC-3743	HS-871130= SIC-3751	HS-900410= SIC-3851
HS-850820= SIC-3546	HS-851940= SIC-3579	HS-853620= SIC-3613	HS-860290= SIC-3743	HS-871140= SIC-3751	HS-900490= SIC-3851
HS-850880= SIC-3546	HS-851991= SIC-3651	HS-853630= SIC-3643	HS-860310= SIC-3743	HS-871150= SIC-3751	HS-900510= SIC-3827
HS-850890= SIC-3546	HS-851999= SIC-3651	HS-853641= SIC-3625	HS-860390= SIC-3743	HS-871190= SIC-3751	HS-900580= SIC-3827

HS-900590= SIC-3827	HS-901850= SIC-3841	HS-910211= SIC-3873	HS-930100= SIC-3484	HS-950510= SIC-3229	HS-961610= SIC-3999
HS-900610= SIC-3861	HS-901890= SIC-3841	HS-910212= SIC-3873	HS-930200= SIC-3484	HS-950590= SIC-2675	HS-961620= SIC-2399
HS-900620= SIC-3861	HS-901910= SIC-3841	HS-910219= SIC-3873	HS-930310= SIC-3484	HS-950611= SIC-3949	HS-961700= SIC-3429
HS-900630= SIC-3861	HS-901920= SIC-3842	HS-910221= SIC-3873	HS-930320= SIC-3484	HS-950612= SIC-3949	HS-961700= SIC-3429
HS-900640= SIC-3861	HS-902000= SIC-3949	HS-910229= SIC-3873	HS-930330= SIC-3484	HS-950619= SIC-3949	HS-961800= SIC-3999
HS-900651= SIC-3861	HS-902111= SIC-3842	HS-910291= SIC-3873	HS-930390= SIC-3484	HS-950621= SIC-3949	HS-970110= SIC-9200
HS-900652= SIC-3861	HS-902119= SIC-3842	HS-910299= SIC-3873	HS-930400= SIC-3484	HS-950629= SIC-3949	HS-970190= SIC-9200
HS-900653= SIC-3861	HS-902121= SIC-3843	HS-910310= SIC-3873	HS-930510= SIC-3484	HS-950631= SIC-3949	HS-970200= SIC-9200
HS-900659= SIC-3861	HS-902129= SIC-3843	HS-910390= SIC-3873	HS-930521= SIC-3484	HS-950632= SIC-3949	HS-970300= SIC-9200
HS-900661= SIC-3861	HS-902130= SIC-3842	HS-910400= SIC-3873	HS-930529= SIC-3484	HS-950639= SIC-3949	HS-970400= SIC-9200
HS-900662= SIC-3641	HS-902140= SIC-3842	HS-910511= SIC-3873	HS-930590= SIC-3484	HS-950640= SIC-3949	HS-970500= SIC-9200
HS-900669= SIC-3861	HS-902150= SIC-3845	HS-910519= SIC-3873	HS-930610= SIC-3482	HS-950651= SIC-3949	HS-970500= SIC-9200
HS-900691= SIC-3861	HS-902190= SIC-3842	HS-910521= SIC-3873	HS-930621= SIC-3482	HS-950659= SIC-3949	HS-970600= SIC-9200
HS-900699= SIC-3861	HS-902211= SIC-3844	HS-910529= SIC-3873	HS-930629= SIC-3482	HS-950661= SIC-3949	
HS-900711= SIC-3861	HS-902219= SIC-3844	HS-910591= SIC-3873	HS-930630= SIC-3482	HS-950662= SIC-3949	
HS-900719= SIC-3861	HS-902221= SIC-3844	HS-910599= SIC-3873	HS-930690= SIC-3482	HS-950669= SIC-3949	
HS-900719= SIC-3861	HS-902229= SIC-3669	HS-910610= SIC-3579	HS-930700= SIC-3421	HS-950670= SIC-3949	
HS-900721= SIC-3861	HS-902230= SIC-3844	HS-910620= SIC-3824	HS-940110= SIC-2599	HS-950691= SIC-3949	
HS-900729= SIC-3861	HS-902290= SIC-3844	HS-910690= SIC-3873	HS-940120= SIC-2599	HS-950699= SIC-3949	
HS-900791= SIC-3861	HS-902300= SIC-3999	HS-910700= SIC-3625	HS-940130= SIC-2599	HS-950710= SIC-3949	
HS-900792= SIC-3861	HS-902410= SIC-3829	HS-910811= SIC-3873	HS-940140= SIC-2515	HS-950720= SIC-3949	
HS-900810= SIC-3861	HS-902480= SIC-3829	HS-910812= SIC-3873	HS-940150= SIC-2599	HS-950730= SIC-3949	
HS-900820= SIC-3861	HS-902490= SIC-3829	HS-910819= SIC-3873	HS-940161= SIC-2599	HS-950790= SIC-3949	
HS-900820= SIC-3861	HS-902511= SIC-3829	HS-910820= SIC-3873	HS-940169= SIC-2599	HS-950800= SIC-3599	
HS-900830= SIC-3861	HS-902519= SIC-3829	HS-910891= SIC-3873	HS-940171= SIC-2599	HS-960110= SIC-3999	
HS-900840= SIC-3861	HS-902520= SIC-3829	HS-910899= SIC-3873	HS-940179= SIC-2599	HS-960190= SIC-3999	
HS-900890= SIC-3861	HS-902580= SIC-3829	HS-910911= SIC-3873	HS-940180= SIC-2599	HS-960200= SIC-2899	
HS-900911= SIC-3861	HS-902590= SIC-3829	HS-910919= SIC-3873	HS-940190= SIC-2599	HS-960310= SIC-3991	
HS-900912= SIC-3861	HS-902610= SIC-3823	HS-910990= SIC-3873	HS-940210= SIC-3843	HS-960321= SIC-3991	
HS-900921= SIC-3861	HS-902620= SIC-3823	HS-911011= SIC-3873	HS-940290= SIC-2599	HS-960329= SIC-3991	
HS-900922= SIC-3861	HS-902680= SIC-3823	HS-911012= SIC-3873	HS-940310= SIC-2599	HS-960330= SIC-3991	
HS-900930= SIC-3861	HS-902690= SIC-3823	HS-911019= SIC-3873	HS-940320= SIC-2514	HS-960340= SIC-3991	
HS-900990= SIC-3861	HS-902710= SIC-3826	HS-911090= SIC-3873	HS-940330= SIC-2599	HS-960350= SIC-3991	
HS-901010= SIC-3861	HS-902720= SIC-3826	HS-911110= SIC-3873	HS-940340= SIC-2434	HS-960390= SIC-3991	
HS-901020= SIC-3861	HS-902730= SIC-3826	HS-911120= SIC-3873	HS-940350= SIC-2599	HS-960400= SIC-3999	
HS-901030= SIC-3861	HS-902740= SIC-3861	HS-911180= SIC-3873	HS-940360= SIC-2599	HS-960500= SIC-3172	
HS-901090= SIC-3861	HS-902750= SIC-3823	HS-911190= SIC-3873	HS-940370= SIC-2599	HS-960610= SIC-3965	
HS-901110= SIC-3827	HS-902780= SIC-3826	HS-911210= SIC-3873	HS-940380= SIC-2599	HS-960621= SIC-3965	
HS-901120= SIC-3827	HS-902790= SIC-3823	HS-911280= SIC-3873	HS-940390= SIC-2599	HS-960622= SIC-3965	
HS-901180= SIC-3827	HS-902810= SIC-3824	HS-911290= SIC-3873	HS-940410= SIC-2515	HS-960629= SIC-3965	
HS-901190= SIC-3827	HS-902820= SIC-3824	HS-911310= SIC-3911	HS-940421= SIC-2515	HS-960630= SIC-3965	
HS-901210= SIC-3826	HS-902830= SIC-3825	HS-911320= SIC-3911	HS-940429= SIC-2515	HS-960711= SIC-3965	
HS-901290= SIC-3826	HS-902890= SIC-3825	HS-911390= SIC-3172	HS-940430= SIC-2399	HS-960719= SIC-3965	
HS-901310= SIC-3827	HS-902910= SIC-3824	HS-911410= SIC-3873	HS-940490= SIC-2392	HS-960720= SIC-3965	
HS-901310= SIC-3827	HS-902920= SIC-3824	HS-911420= SIC-3915	HS-940510= SIC-3648	HS-960810= SIC-3951	
HS-901320= SIC-3699	HS-902990= SIC-3824	HS-911430= SIC-3873	HS-940520= SIC-3648	HS-960820= SIC-3951	
HS-901380= SIC-3827	HS-903010= SIC-3829	HS-911440= SIC-3873	HS-940530= SIC-3699	HS-960831= SIC-3951	
HS-901390= SIC-3827	HS-903020= SIC-3825	HS-911490= SIC-3873	HS-940540= SIC-3648	HS-960839= SIC-3951	
HS-901410= SIC-3812	HS-903031= SIC-3825	HS-920110= SIC-3931	HS-940550= SIC-3648	HS-960840= SIC-3951	
HS-901420= SIC-3812	HS-903039= SIC-3825	HS-920120= SIC-3931	HS-940560= SIC-3993	HS-960840= SIC-3951	
HS-901480= SIC-3812	HS-903040= SIC-3825	HS-920190= SIC-3931	HS-940591= SIC-3229	HS-960850= SIC-3951	
HS-901490= SIC-3812	HS-903081= SIC-3825	HS-920210= SIC-3931	HS-940592= SIC-3648	HS-960860= SIC-3951	
HS-901510= SIC-3829	HS-903089= SIC-3825	HS-920290= SIC-3931	HS-940599= SIC-3648	HS-960891= SIC-3951	
HS-901520= SIC-3829	HS-903090= SIC-3829	HS-920290= SIC-3931	HS-940600= SIC-2452	HS-960899= SIC-3951	
HS-901530= SIC-3829	HS-903110= SIC-3569	HS-920300= SIC-3931	HS-950100= SIC-3944	HS-960910= SIC-3952	
HS-901540= SIC-3829	HS-903120= SIC-3825	HS-920410= SIC-3931	HS-950210= SIC-3942	HS-960920= SIC-3952	
HS-901580= SIC-3829	HS-903130= SIC-3827	HS-920420= SIC-3931	HS-950291= SIC-3942	HS-960990= SIC-3952	
HS-901590= SIC-3829	HS-903140= SIC-3827	HS-920510= SIC-3931	HS-950299= SIC-3942	HS-961000= SIC-2599	
HS-901600= SIC-3596	HS-903180= SIC-3825	HS-920590= SIC-3931	HS-950310= SIC-3944	HS-961100= SIC-3953	
HS-901710= SiC-3829	HS-903190= SIC-3827	HS-920600= SIC-3931	HS-950320= SIC-3944	HS-961210= SIC-3955	
HS-901720= SIC-3829	HS-903210= SIC-3822	HS-920710= SIC-3931	HS-950330= SIC-3944	HS-961220= SIC-3953	
HS-901730= SIC-3545	HS-903220= SIC-3822	HS-920790= SIC-3931	HS-950341= SIC-3942	HS-961310= SIC-3999	
HS-901780= SIC-3545	HS-903281= SIC-3823	HS-920810= SIC-3999	HS-950349= SIC-3942	HS-961320= SIC-3999	
HS-901790= SIC-3829	HS-903289= SIC-3694	HS-920890= SIC-3931	HS-950350= SIC-3944	HS-961330= SIC-3999	
HS-901790= SIC-3829	HS-903290= SIC-3823	HS-920890= SIC-3999	HS-950360= SIC-3944	HS-961380= SIC-3999	
HS-901811= SIC-3845	HS-903300= SIC-3823	HS-920910= SIC-3999	HS-950370= SIC-3944	HS-961390= SIC-3999	
HS-901819= SIC-3845	HS-910111= SIC-3873	HS-920920= SIC-3999	HS-950380= SIC-3944	HS-961410= SIC-2499	
HS-901820= SIC-3845	HS-910112= SIC-3873	HS-920930= SIC-3931	HS-950390= SIC-3944	HS-961420= SIC-3999	
HS-901831= SIC-3841	HS-910119= SIC-3873	HS-920991= SIC-3931	HS-950410= SIC-3944	HS-961490= SIC-3999	
HS-901832= SIC-3841	HS-910121= SIC-3873	HS-920992= SIC-3931	HS-950420= SIC-3949	HS-961511= SIC-3089	
HS-901839= SIC-3841	HS-910129= SIC-3873	HS-920993= SIC-3931	HS-950430= SIC-3999	HS-961519= SIC-3999	
HS-901841= SIC-3843	HS-910191= SIC-3873	HS-920994= SIC-3931	HS-950440= SIC-2752	HS-961590= SIC-3965	
HS-901849= SIC-3843	HS-910199= SIC-3873	HS-920999= SIC-3931	HS-950490= SIC-3944	HS-961590= SIC-3999	